PENGUIN BOOKS

TOTAL TELEVISION

Alex McNeil was born in Washington, D.C., in 1948. Having earned his bachelor's degree in history at Yale, he graduated cum laude from the Boston College Law School in 1973. Since then he has been employed by the Massachusetts Appeals Court—first as law clerk, then as administrative assistant—to Chief Justice Allan M. Hale. His lifes-long hobbies record collecting and, of course, television watching, for which he long ago developed the interest that led him to write *Total Television*.

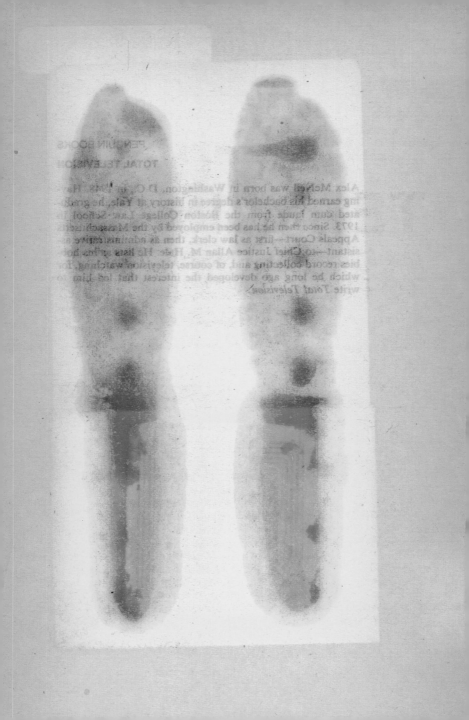

*** TOTAL TELEVISION

A COMPREHENSIVE GUIDE TO PROGRAMMING FROM 1948 TO 1980

by Alex McNeil

PENGUIN BOOKS

Penguin Books Ltd, Harmondsworth,
Middlesex, England
Penguin Books, 625 Madison Avenue,
New York, New York 10022, U.S.A.
Penguin Books Australia Ltd, Ringwood,
Victoria, Australia
Penguin Books Canada Limited, 2801 John Street,
Markham, Ontario, Canada L3R 1B4
Penguin Books (N.Z.) Ltd, 182–190 Wairau Road,
Auckland 10, New Zealand

First published 1980

ISBN 0 14 00.4911 8

Printed in the United States of America by
Offset Paperback Mfrs., Inc., Dallas, Pennsylvania
Set in CRT Times Roman

CONTENTS

INTRODUCTION

This is a book for the TV fan—particularly for the person who, like me, is fascinated by the parade of television series that passes each year and who enjoys watching the shows come and go as much as watching the shows themselves. More than half of the population alive today have never known life without television. We've woken up with Dave Garroway and Captain Kangaroo and gone to bed with Jack Paar and Johnny Carson. In between we've laughed at Lucy and Archie and Uncle Miltie, wept with Kunta Kinte, and screamed at Elvis and the Beatles. We've seen a young President buried, a war in living color, and an Eagle land on the moon. We've seen a lot.

For the past twelve years I have collected information on more than 3,400 series, network and syndicated, prime time and daytime. The series are listed alphabetically in Part I, which takes up most of this book. More detailed information on the scope of that part may be found in the explanatory notes preceding Part I.

To give a fuller picture of television programming, other material is also included:

Part II is a chronological list of special programs and broadcasts (the list is entirely subjective).

Part III is a set of charts showing the prime-time fall schedules for the three major commercial networks.

Part IV is a list of Emmy and Peabody Award winners.

Part V is a list of the top-rated series for each season.

Information has been gathered from many sources: from watching the series themselves, from the networks, and from a number of periodicals and books. Among the most useful periodicals were: *TV Guide*, which assumed its present format in April 1953; *Variety*, which covers the television industry and reviews almost every new series; *The New York Times*; and the *New York Herald Tribune*, which ceased publication in 1966. Among the most helpful books were: Vincent Terrace's *The Complete Encyclopedia of Television Programs 1947–1976* (A. S. Barnes & Co., 1976), an important first step in chronicling the vast array of television series; *The New York Times Encyclopedia of Television* (Times Books, 1977), by Les Brown, a wide-ranging compendium of information about the entire medium; and the several editions of Nina David's *TV Season* (Oryx Press), a comprehensive annual compilation of programming, beginning with the 1974–1975 season. The reader may also be interested in a recently published book, *The Complete Directory to Prime Time Network Television 1946–Present*, by Tim Brooks and Earle Marsh (Ballantine, 1979).

Though I have tried to insure that the information included here is accurate and up to date, I am sure that I have not been completely successful and I would appreciate any additions, corrections, comments, or suggestions.

Finally, I offer my very special thanks to several people who have helped me a lot: David and Jane Otte, Kathryn Court and Pat Mulcahy at Penguin Books, Tim Rupp (researcher extraordinaire), Gary Grossman, Ronna Levinsohn of ABC, Joan Quick of CBS, Doris Katz of NBC, Bill Behanna of the A. C. Nielsen Company, and Jill McNeil.

★★★ PART I

ON AND OFF

Explanatory notes: It is difficult, if not impossible, to define a "series." Included here are open-ended, regularly scheduled programs, regardless of their duration; thus, *Turn-On,* a 1969 show which was canceled after only one showing, is included, while *Project 20,* the overall title for a large number of irregularly scheduled news and cultural documentaries on NBC, is not included (significant *Project 20* specials are noted in Part II of this book, however). A show like *Hallmark Hall of Fame* falls somewhere in between—it was regularly scheduled during its first seasons and is now seen a few times a year on an irregular basis; such a show is included in this part.

Also included are closed-end, multiple-episode programs, commonly known as "miniseries," such as *Roots, America,* and *The Six Wives of Henry VIII.* These programs have been included if the program contained four or more episodes or segments and if the episodes or segments were scheduled at regular intervals.

Shows which were broadcast during or after the fall of 1948 are included. Though network broadcasting existed prior to that time, the fall of 1948 was chosen as a starting date for several reasons: there was a tremendous growth in the number of broadcasting stations and the number of television sets during that year; television's first big stars—Milton Berle, Ed Sullivan, and Arthur Godfrey—all came to the medium during the 1948–1949 season; seven-days-a-week, four-network broadcasting began in New York in August 1948; and broadcasting took on a true national character during the 1948–1949 season, as coaxial cables linking the East with the Midwest in January 1949 made simultaneous broadcasting to different areas of the country a reality.

Series are listed alphabetically, by the titles by which they were most commonly known rather than by their exact titles. Thus, *The Adventures of Ozzie and Harriet* is listed under *Ozzie and Harriet,* and *The Many Loves of Dobie Gillis* is listed under *Dobie Gillis.*

Following the title appears the network affiliation (if any). The networks are:

> ABC—the American Broadcasting Company, which numbered only fourteen affiliates in 1953, when its present corporate structure was established, but which has become TV's most successful network
>
> CBS—the Columbia Broadcasting System (now simply CBS, Inc.), founded in 1927, and which (with

NBC) was one of the two major networks during television's early years

DUMONT—a small network established by Allen B. DuMont Laboratories in 1946; with few primary affiliates, the network never made money and perished in 1955

NBC—the National Broadcasting Company, a subsidiary of RCA; founded in 1926, it became the first network to begin regular television broadcasting (April 1939), and together with CBS was a major network from the outset

NET—National Educational Television; in a sense, NET was less a true network than a distributor of programs to individual educational stations throughout the country; it was not until late 1966 that simultaneous broadcasting began on educational outlets

PBS—Public Broadcasting Service, the successor to NET; established in 1969, it distributes programs (both by simultaneous transmission and by physical delivery) to educational stations

Not all series are carried by a network, however. Many are offered directly to individual stations or jointly owned groups of stations; that method of distribution is known as syndication, and the word "syndicated" appears following the title of series so distributed.

The network or syndication affiliation applies only to first-run episodes or segments of a series. If a series was rerun on another network, or if its reruns were offered in syndication, no such affiliation is indicated. It should be noted that virtually all successful network programs are eventually offered in syndication (as reruns) following the completion of their original network runs.

Following the network or syndication affiliation, the running dates are listed. For network series, the dates are those of the original network run. If a series returned to a network in reruns (as did *I Love Lucy,* both in prime time and in daytime), or if a series ran simultaneously in first runs and in reruns (as did *Gunsmoke,* reruns of which were shown under the title *Marshal Dillon* for several seasons on CBS), the dates of the reruns are not included. Dates listed are those for the New York City affiliates of the networks, unless otherwise indicated (generally speaking, most CBS and NBC series were carried at the same time by all affiliates, as have been most ABC series since the early 1960s; several ABC series of the 1940s and 1950s, and most DuMont series, were not broadcast simultaneously by most network affiliates). Exact dates for some NET series are not included, as most NET programs were distributed by mail or messenger, at least until late 1966. Similarly, exact dates for syndicated series are not given, for individual stations which broadcast a syndicated series may air it whenever they choose; unless otherwise noted, the dates listed for a syndicated series are the dates when it was in production. A few syndicated series, notably *Fernwood 2-Night* and *America 2Night,* were offered to most stations for broadcast on the same dates; in those instances, exact dates are indicated.

Following the dates is a description of the series and a list of its cast. The cast includes players who were "regulars"; that is, those who appeared often enough to be considered regular performers. The list is intended to be reasonably complete, but for certain series (especially serials) it is impossible to include every performer who appeared on more than one episode. If a cast member left a series while it was still in production, the dates of his or her participation (where known) are noted. Notable guest appearances are also included where appropriate.

Series that premiered early in 1980 are included in the Appendix. Obviously information on some series will have changed after this book has gone to press; therefore, changes which occurred after March 1980 have not been included.

Certain kinds of shows are not contained here: series which consist entirely of motion pictures (such as NBC's *Saturday Night at the Movies* or *The ABC Tuesday Movie of the Week*); motion picture shorts or serials subsequently distributed to television stations (such as the *Our Gang* or *Little Rascals* comedies, *The Three Stooges* or *Renfrew of the Mounted*); shows which consisted entirely of reruns of other series (such as *Royal Playhouse,* which consisted of *Fireside Theatre* reruns); shows which consisted entirely of unsold pilot films (such shows occasionally surfaced on network TV during the summer, under a title such as *Comedy Spot*); irregularly scheduled sports broadcasts; nonnetwork shows of less than ten minutes' length; and regionally and locally televised programs.

Lastly, it should be noted that series are listed alphabetically by the *first* word; thus, for example, *All in the Family* precedes *Allen Ludden's Gallery.* A series whose title begins with a single letter will be found at the beginning of that letter; thus, *M*A*S*H, The M & M Candy Carnival, M-G-M Parade, M Squad* and *M.V.P.* all appear at the beginning of the "M" listings. Series beginning with *Dr.* or *Mr.* are listed as though the first words were spelled out in full, and hyphenated words are deemed to be one word for purposes of alphabetizing.

ABC AFTERNOON PLAYBREAK ABC

31 OCTOBER 1973–14 AUGUST 1975   Irregularly scheduled ninety-minute dramatic specials for the afternoon-viewing audience. Presentations included: "The Things I Never Said," with Diana Hyland and Joseph Campanella (31 October 1973); "The Last Bride of Salem," with Bradford Dillman (who won an Emmy for his performance) and Lois Nettleton (8 May 1974); "Heart in Hiding," with Kay Lenz (Emmy) and Clu Gulagher (14 November 1974); "Oh! Baby, Baby, Baby . . ." with Bert Convy and Judy Carne (5 December 1974); and "The Girl Who Couldn't Lose," with Julie Kavner and Jack Carter (13 February 1975; Emmys for outstanding daytime drama and for director Mort Lachman).

ABC AFTERSCHOOL SPECIALS ABC

4 OCTOBER 1972–   Sixty-minute specials, both dramatic and documentary, for young people. Broadcast on occasional Wednesday afternoons. Presentations included: "Last of the Curlews," an ecology-oriented cartoon from Hanna-Barbera studios (4 October 1972); "Rookie of the Year," an Emmy award winner starring Jodie Foster (3 October 1973); "Cyrano," a Hanna-Barbera cartoon with the voices of José Ferrer (recreating his 1950 film role), Joan Van Ark, and Kurt Kasznar (6 March 1974); "Winning and Losing," a documentary about the 1974 South Dakota Senate race (6 November 1974); "Santiago's America," with Ruben Figueroa, filmed in Spanish Harlem (19 February 1975); "The Secret Life of T. K. Dearing," with Jodie Foster (23 April 1975); and "Me & Dad's New Wife," with Kristy McNichol (18 February 1976). "Mighty Moose and the Quarterback Kid," with Brandon Cruz and Dave Madden (1 December 1976); "My Mom's Having a Baby," with Dr. Lendon Smith and Shane Sinutko (16 February 1977).

ABC ALBUM (PLYMOUTH PLAYHOUSE) ABC

12 APRIL 1953–5 JULY 1953   Thirteen-week half-hour dramatic anthology series, seen on Sunday evenings. Presentations included: "Justice," with Paul Douglas and Lee Grant (12 April, the pilot for the series of the same title); "Jamie," with Brandon DeWilde and Ernest Truex (26 April, the pilot for that series); Charles Dickens' "A Tale of Two Cities," with Wendell Corey, Wanda Hendrix, and Judith Evelyn (3 May and 10 May); and Daphne du Maurier's "The Split Second," with Geraldine Fitzgerald (7 June).

THE ABC COMEDY HOUR

12 JANUARY 1972–5 APRIL 1972   Seven segments of this thirteen-week
comedy-variety series brought together a group of highly talented impressionists calling themselves The Kopykats: Rich Little, Frank Gorshin,
George Kirby, Marilyn Michaels, Charlie Callas, Joe Baker, and Fred
Travalena (last four segments). Those segments were later syndicated under the title *The Kopykats.* Guest hosts included Steve Lawrence (19 January), Orson Welles with Ron Moody (26 January), Ed Sullivan with
Will Jordan (9 February), Raymond Burr (23 February), Robert Young
(8 March), Debbie Reynolds (22 March), and Tony Curtis (5 April). The
other six segments of the series included two Alan King specials, a Friars
Club toast of Sammy Davis, Jr., and a revival of "Hellzapoppin" with
Jack Cassidy and Ronnie Schell.

ABC NEWS
ABC

12 OCTOBER 1953–   For many years ABC ran a distant
third to CBS and NBC in news and public affairs programming. Although the network offered an evening newscast as early as 1948, few
affiliates chose to carry it. In the fall of 1952 a new, more ambitious effort
was attempted (see *All-Star News*), but by January of 1953 that series was
seen only once a week. It was not until the fall of 1953 that Monday-
through-Friday newscasts were resumed, with John Daly as the anchorman (except on Tuesdays during the 1953-1954 season, when Taylor
Grant filled in). Daly, who had been a CBS radio correspondent from
1937 to 1949, had been with ABC for four years before being named vice
president in charge of news, special events, and public affairs. For the remainder of the 1950s Daly was the virtual personification of ABC News.
The network scrapped the evening broadcasts during the 1957–1958 season, but returned in the fall of 1958 with a new idea—early-evening and
late-evening newscasts. Don Goddard handled the early broadcast, while
John Daly anchored the late one, which, though unsuccessful, is significant in that it was network television's first regularly scheduled late-
night newscast.

Daly left ABC News late in 1960 (his last broadcast was on 16 December; he would continue to host *What's My Line?* on CBS for another six
years), and was succeeded as head of ABC News by James C. Hagerty,
who had been President Eisenhower's press secretary. Following Daly's
departure the parade of anchormen and women, most of them refugees
from other networks, got underway; from 1961 to 1978 ABC has put at
least ten people behind its anchor desks, while CBS has relied on just two
and NBC three. ABC first employed John Cameron Swayze, who had anchored NBC's *Camel News Caravan* from 1948 to 1956, then Bill Shadel.
On 26 March 1962, Ron Cochran, formerly of CBS, came aboard and remained until 29 January 1965. On 1 February 1965, Peter Jennings, a
thirty-year-old Canadian, took over. It was during Jennings's tenure that

ABC's evening newscasts expanded to thirty minutes nightly; again, ABC was the third network to lengthen its early-evening newscast. Jennings departed on 29 December 1967, and, as 1968 began, Bob Young was at the anchor desk.

Young lasted only until 24 May; Frank Reynolds succeeded him on 27 May. Reynolds, who had previously worked at ABC's Chicago affiliate, was the lone anchorman for a year, until he was joined by Howard K. Smith on 26 May 1969. Smith, a former CBS Washington correspondent, had been with ABC for seven years. ABC now seemed committed to the dual anchor concept popularized by Chet Huntley and David Brinkley at NBC. After Reynolds departed on 4 December 1970, he was succeeded the following Monday by Harry Reasoner, another CBS alumnus. The Smith-Reasoner team stayed together until 12 September 1975, after which Reasoner remained behind the desk while Smith did commentary and analysis.

In a bold move consummated in the spring of 1976, ABC lured NBC's Barbara Walters away from the *Today* show. A multiyear, multimillion dollar contract, the opportunity to produce several specials, and the distinction of being television's first anchorwoman were offers that Walters could not refuse. She joined Reasoner at ABC's anchor desk on 4 October 1976; though the ratings for ABC's evening newscast rose slightly, the network remained third in the news race. When ABC Sports chief Roone Arledge became head of ABC News and Sports in 1977, Reasoner's future was rumored to be in doubt.

Under Arledge's aegis major changes were made in the summer of 1978. Reasoner was released from his contract and returned to CBS News. ABC elected to deemphasize the anchor concept, at least temporarily, and in July of 1978 *ABC World News Tonight* was introduced. The new format featured not one desk, but four, staffed by Frank Reynolds in Washington, Peter Jennings in London, Max Robinson in Chicago, and Barbara Walters in New York; Howard K. Smith continued to provide commentary.

In February 1980 ABC announced plans to inaugurate a twenty-minute late-night newscast, to be aired four nights a week at 11:30 p.m.

ABC SCOPE ABC

11 NOVEMBER 1964–27 JANUARY 1968   A news analysis program hosted by Howard K. Smith. The series focused mainly on the war in Vietnam.

ABC SPORTS REVIEW ABC

21 AUGUST 1948–26 APRIL 1949   One of the network's first sports programs, *ABC Sports Review* was a fifteen-minute roundup of the week's sports news, hosted by Joe Hasel.

ABC STAGE 67 ABC

14 SEPTEMBER 1966–11 MAY 1967 Among the few high points of this sixty-minute dramatic anthology series were appearances by John Gielgud in "The Love Song of Barney Kempinski" (14 September); Olivia DeHavilland in "Noon Wine" (23 November, her first TV dramatic appearance); and Ingrid Bergman in "The Human Voice" (4 May, her last TV appearance to date). Hubbell Robinson was the executive producer of the series.

THE ABC WEEKEND SPECIAL ABC

10 SEPTEMBER 1977– Weekend daytime series for children which presented some first-run dramas and some reruns of shows originally aired on *The ABC Afterschool Specials.*

ABC'S WIDE WORLD OF ENTERTAINMENT ABC

1 JANUARY 1973–5 SEPTEMBER 1975 The umbrella title for ABC's late night programming after it became clear that *The Dick Cavett Show* would never overtake NBC's *Tonight* show. During 1973 *The Dick Cavett Show,* which had been shown nightly for three years, was cut back to one week per month. Jack Paar was lured back to network television, and thus *Jack Paar Tonite* occupied another week each month. The remaining evenings consisted of made-for-TV movies, variety programs, and a rock-music series produced by Dick Clark called *In Concert* (usually broadcast Fridays).

ABC'S WIDE WORLD OF SPORTS ABC

29 APRIL 1961– This durable "athletic anthology" series has captured the thrill of victory and the agony of defeat in virtually every known sporting event from every corner of the globe. Host Jim McKay (formerly host of *The Verdict Is Yours)* has been with the series from the beginning. Principal commentators over the years have included Howard Cosell, Frank Gifford, Bill Flemming, Chris Schenkel, Keith Jackson, Bud Palmer, Bob Beattie, and Warner Wolf. Executive producer: Roone Arledge. The premiere telecast presented the Drake Relays from Des Moines and the Penn Relays from Philadelphia.

A.E.S. HUDSON STREET ABC

23 MARCH 1978–20 APRIL 1978 Created by the crew responsible for *Barney Miller, A.E.S. Hudson Street* was a half-hour hospital sitcom which bore more than a superficial resemblance to *Barney Miller.* Set in the Emergency Service section of a large New York hospital, it starred Gregory Sierra (a *Barney Miller* alumnus) as Dr. Tony Menzies, chief resident. Also featured were Stefan Gierasch as Mr. Karbo, the administrator; Rosana Soto as Rosa, a nurse pregnant with her eighth child; Allan Miller as Dr. Glick, a psychiatrist; Susan Peretz as Foshko, a

paramedic; Ralph Manza as Stanky, an ambulance driver; Ray Stewart as Newton, a gay nurse; and Bill Cort as Dr. Jerry Mackler, an intern. Danny Arnold, Tony Sheehan, and Chris Hayward created the series.

AG-U.S.A. SYNDICATED
1974– Half-hour documentary series on agricultural topics, hosted by John Stearns.

A.M. AMERICA ABC
6 JANUARY 1975–31 OCTOBER 1975 ABC's entry into early-morning programming. Bill Beutel was the host of the two-hour Monday-to-Friday show which, like NBC's *Today*, combined news, interviews, and features. Stephanie Edwards served as cohost until May. Peter Jennings read the news. Semiregular contributors included columnist Jack Anderson, naturalist Roger Caras, former senator Sam Ervin, former mayor John Lindsay, Boston physician Dr. Timothy Johnson, civil rights activist Rev. Jesse Jackson, and Ralph Story (who also served as West Coast cohost). The show failed to catch on and was replaced by *Good Morning, America*.

THE ABBOTT AND COSTELLO SHOW SYNDICATED
1952 One of America's most popular comedy teams, Bud Abbott (the irascible straight man) and Lou Costello (the fat funny man) made fifty-two half-hour films for television. The shows incorporated many of their best burlesque routines. Their supporting cast included Sid Fields (as their cigar-chomping landlord), Hillary Brooke (as Lou's girlfriend, who lived across the hall in the rooming house), Bill Barber (as Lou's pal Hercules), Joe Besser (as Lou's pal Stinky), Gordon Jones, Joe Kirk, and Joan Shawlee. Lou's brother, Pat Costello, succeeded Jean Yasbrough as producer of the series. After the TV series Abbott and Costello made two or three more motion pictures before splitting up. Costello died in 1959.

THE ABBOTT AND COSTELLO SHOW SYNDICATED
1966 Hanna-Barbera Productions produced an animated cartoon series based on the characters of Bud Abbott and Lou Costello; it was one of the first cartoon series based on real people. Abbott supplied his own voice, and Stan Irwin provided Costello's.

ABE BURROWS' ALMANAC CBS
4 JANUARY 1950–29 MARCH 1950 A half hour of comedy and conversation on Wednesday nights, hosted by humorist Abe Burrows. Abe's guests on the premiere included songwriters Adolph Green and Betty Comden.

ABOUT FACES   ABC

4 JANUARY 1960–30 JUNE 1961   A daytime game show hosted by Ben Alexander which, like *Place the Face,* featured pairs of contestants whose paths had crossed previously; the first contestant to recall their association won a prize.

ACADEMY THEATER   NBC

25 JULY 1949–12 SEPTEMBER 1949   A summer replacement for *Tele-Theatre, Academy Theater* was a Monday-night dramatic anthology series.

ACAPULCO   NBC

27 FEBRUARY 1961–24 APRIL 1961   An attempt to salvage the *Klondike* series by moving its stars down the Pacific Coast and ahead a century. The two *Klondike* costars, Ralph Taeger (now Patrick Malone) and James Coburn (now Gregg Miles), were cast as adventurer beach bums. Also featured were Allison Hayes as Chloe, a nightclub entertainer, and Telly Savalas as Carver, a lawyer. Like most midseason format changes (e.g., *Headmaster/The New Andy Griffith Show; The John Forsythe Show*), this one was unsuccessful.

ACCENT   ABC

26 FEBRUARY 1961–9 SEPTEMBER 1962   This wide-ranging documentary and cultural series was seen on Sundays for most of its run. John Ciardi was the principal host, though James Fleming, Ray Stewart, and Alexander Kendrick also participated. The premiere telecast, a tribute to poet Robert Frost, featured an appearance by President John F. Kennedy.

ACCIDENTAL FAMILY   NBC

15 SEPTEMBER 1967–5 JANUARY 1968   Situation comedy about a Las Vegas comic, recently widowed, who owned a farm in California where dwelt a divorcée and her young daughter, who agreed to care for the comic's young son while he was on the job. With Jerry Van Dyke as comic Jerry Webster; Lois Nettleton as divorcée Susannah Kramer; Ben Blue as Susannah's uncle, Ben McGrath, the handyman; Teddy Quinn as Jerry's son Sandy; Susan Benjamin as Susannah's daughter Tracy; and Larry D. Mann as Jerry's manager, Marty.

ACCUSED   ABC

3 DECEMBER 1958–30 SEPTEMBER 1959   A midseason replacement consisting of half-hour courtroom dramas, broadcast on Wednesdays. With Edgar Allan Jones, Jr. (a law professor in real life) as the presiding judge.

ACROBAT RANCH ABC

19 AUGUST 1950–12 MAY 1951 One of the first network children's shows to be aired on Saturday mornings, *Acrobat Ranch* was an audience participation show in which kids competed in games and stunts. Broadcast live from Chicago, the half-hour show was hosted by Jack Stillwell and featured Billy and Valerie Alberts.

ACROSS THE BOARD ABC

1 JUNE 1959–9 OCTOBER 1959 A crossword game show, hosted daily by Ted Brown.

ACROSS THE SEVEN SEAS SYNDICATED

1962 Travelogue, hosted by Jack Douglas.

ACT IT OUT NBC

20 FEBRUARY 1949–7 AUGUST 1949 Bill Cullen hosted this early game show on which a group of actors acted out a scene; a telephone call was then placed to a home viewer, who could win a prize if he or she could describe, in a single word, the nature of the scene performed.

ACTION AUTOGRAPHS ABC

24 APRIL 1949–8 JANUARY 1950 This series of interviews with celebrities and human interest films was hosted first by Jack Brand, later by Ed Prentiss.

ACTION IN THE AFTERNOON CBS

2 FEBRUARY 1953–29 JANUARY 1954 Television's only live western was broadcast on weekday afternoons from suburban Philadelphia, though the action was set in the town of Huberle, Montana. Jack Valentine starred in the half-hour show which also featured Mary Elaine Watts and Barry Cassell. Blake Ritter was the narrator.

ACTORS HOTEL ABC

25 SEPTEMBER 1951–13 MAY 1952 A situation comedy set at a boardinghouse, with William Edmunds as Carlo Corelli and Alan Dale as Uncle Antonio.

ACTORS' STUDIO ABC/CBS

26 SEPTEMBER 1948–26 OCTOBER 1949 (ABC); 1 NOVEMBER 1949–31 JANUARY 1950 (CBS) One of television's earliest dramatic anthology series, *Actors' Studio* was broadcast live from New York. Twenty-four-year-old Marlon Brandon made an extremely rare TV appearance on 9 January 1949, when he starred in "I'm No Hero." Other notable guest appearances on the half-hour show included those by Jessica Tandy ("Portrait of a Madonna," 26 September 1948); Jocelyn Brando (Mar-

lon's sister, who starred in "The Thousand Dollar Bill" on 17 October 1948, and "A Day in Town" on 2 January 1949); Kim Hunter ("Ropes," 7 November 1948; "The Return to Kansas City," 1 November 1949); Tom Ewell ("Ropes" and "A Reputation," 7 April 1949); and Henry Jones ("The Timid Guy," 24 January 1950). See also *The Play's the Thing.*

THE ADAMS CHRONICLES   PBS
20 JANUARY 1976–13 APRIL 1976   Thirteen-part hour-long dramatic series depicting the lives of the Massachusetts Adams family from 1750 to 1900; the Adams Papers—journals and other writings of the principals—were the primary source for the screenplays, which were written by nine veteran playwrights. The cast included George Grizzard as John Adams; Kathryn Walker and Leora Dana as Abigail Adams; W. B. Brydon as Samuel Adams; David Birney and William Daniels as John Quincy Adams; David Hooks as George Washington; Robert Symonds as Ben Franklin; Curt Dawson as John Hancock; John Houseman as Jeremiah Gridley; Peter Brandon as Henry Adams; John Beal as Charles Francis Adams; Nicholas Pryor as John Quincy Adams II; Charles Siebert as Charles Francis Adams II; and Charles Tenney as Brooks Adams. Executive producer: Jac Venza for WNET, New York.

ADAM'S RIB   ABC
14 SEPTEMBER 1973–28 DECEMBER 1973   A short-lived version of the 1949 Spencer Tracy–Katharine Hepburn movie comedy about two newlyweds, both lawyers. With Ken Howard as Adam Bonner, an assistant district attorney; Blythe Danner as Amanda Bonner, an associate at Kipple, Kipple & Smith; Ron Rifkin as Roy Mendelsohn, another assistant D.A.; Edward Winter as lawyer Kip Kipple; Dena Dietrich as Amanda's secretary, Grace Peterson. Most of the episodes dealt with women's rights; one hour-long special episode, adapted directly from the movie, pitted Adam and Amanda against each other in the courtroom: he prosecuting a woman who shot her wayward husband, she defending her.

ADAM-12   NBC
21 SEPTEMBER 1968–26 AUGUST 1975   Jack Webb developed this successful series about two Los Angeles police officers; their patrol car identification was Adam-12. Like Webb's own *Dragnet* series, this one stressed authenticity, even in such details as police radio broadcasts. Typically, the officers responded to several calls during each half-hour episode, rather than dealing with just one crime (that technique would later be used to advantage in Webb's *Emergency!*). Starring television veteran Martin Milner as veteran officer Pete Malloy and Kent McCord (né Kent McWhirter when he was featured as one of Rick Nelson's frat pals on *Ozzie and Harriet*) as his rookie partner, Jim Reed. With William

Boyett as Sergeant MacDonald, their commanding officer; Gary Crosby as Officer Wells; and Fred Stromsoe as Officer Woods. Created by Jack Webb and Robert A. Cinader; produced by Tom Williams.

THE ADDAMS FAMILY ABC
18 SEPTEMBER 1964–2 SEPTEMBER 1966 A situation comedy based on the bizarre cartoon characters created by Charles Addams. For television, Addams provided his motley characters with names (they'd never had any in his cartoons), and the producers made it clear that they were basically a nuclear family. With Carolyn Jones as Morticia Addams, the macabre matriarch; John Astin as her husband, lawyer Gomez Addams; Ken Weatherwax as son Pugsley; Lisa Loring as daughter Wednesday; Jackie Coogan (sans hair and eyebrows) as Morticia's kindly Uncle Fester; six-foot-nine Ted Cassidy as the laconic Lurch, their butler; Blossom Rock as Grandmama, Gomez's mom; Felix Silla as the amorphous Cousin Itt. Produced by David Levy and Nat Perrin. In retrospect ABC's *The Addams Family* seems a bit better than CBS's *The Munsters,* another 1964 sitcom about a family of eccentrics, although both shows lasted only two seasons. Excessive gimmickry probably helped kill them both off.

THE ADDAMS FAMILY NBC
8 SEPTEMBER 1973–30 AUGUST 1975 An animated version of the 1964 series, shown on Saturday mornings. The voices of Ted Cassidy and Jackie Coogan from the original cast were used. Produced by Hanna-Barbera studios, the animation was actually done in England. The second season consisted entirely of reruns.

ADLAI STEVENSON REPORTS ABC
1 OCTOBER 1961–26 MAY 1963 One of the few television programs "starring" a top government official (*Meet the Veep* was another), this Sunday-afternoon series focused on international issues and on the United Nations in particular; Stevenson was the United States representative to the UN at the time. Arnold Michaelis, who coproduced the Peabody award winning series with Stanley A. Frankel, served as host.

THE AD-LIBBERS CBS
3 AUGUST 1951–1 SEPTEMBER 1951 A five-week summer replacement for *Mama,* on which a celebrity panel ad-libbed to suggestions supplied by home viewers. Hosted by Peter Donald, the celebrity panel included Jack Lemmon and Cynthia Stone, who would later star together in *Heavens to Betsy.*

THE ADMIRAL BROADWAY REVUE NBC and DUMONT
28 JANUARY 1949–3 JUNE 1949 A Friday-night variety hour, *The Admiral Broadway Revue* held the exceedingly rare distinction of having

been broadcast on two networks simultaneously. More importantly, it was the start of the television career of a twenty-seven-year-old comedian named Sid Caesar. The show was produced by Max Liebman, who had previously worked with Caesar and who would later produce Caesar's *Your Show of Shows*. Other regulars on *The Admiral Broadway Revue* included Imogene Coca, Mary McCarty, Marge and Gower Champion, Bobby Van, and Tom Avera. Charles Sanford conducted the orchestra. The format of the show was similar to that of *Your Show of Shows*, relying heavily on monologues and satires of movies and plays. Its sponsor, Admiral, was a major manufacturer of television sets. See also *Your Show of Shows*.

ADVENTURE   CBS
10 MAY 1953–8 JULY 1956   An educational series for children produced by CBS in conjunction with the American Museum of Natural History in New York. It was hosted first by Mike Wallace, later by Charles Collingwood. Produced by Perry Wolff.

ADVENTURE AT SCOTT ISLAND
See HARBOURMASTER

ADVENTURE CALLS   SYNDICATED
1966   Richard Simmons (Sergeant Preston) hosted this nonfiction series about modern-day adventurers.

ADVENTURE THEATRE   NBC
16 JUNE 1956–1 SEPTEMBER 1956   A summer replacement for *Your Hit Parade,* it consisted of half-hour dramas filmed in England. Hosted by Paul Douglas the series was rerun the following summer.

THE ADVENTURER   SYNDICATED
1972   In this half-hour series filmed in Europe, Gene Barry starred as Steve Bradley, an international movie star who moonlights as a spy. With Barry Morse as Parminter, Bradley's contact man.

THE ADVENTURERS   SYNDICATED
1966   European import about two journalists, with Edward Meeks and Yves Renier.

ADVENTURES IN JAZZ   CBS
22 JANUARY 1949–24 JUNE 1949   Prime-time jazz music program, hosted by Fred Robbins. Robert L. Bach was the producer, Ralph Levy the director.

ADVENTURES IN PARADISE ABC

5 OCTOBER 1959–1 APRIL 1962   Handsome Gardner McKay, a virtual unknown (he'd done the syndicated *Boots and Saddles*), sailed to stardom as Adam Troy in this 20th Century-Fox adventure hour set in the South Pacific and based very loosely on James Michener's book. Troy was captain of the *Tiki*, an 85-foot schooner which plied the warm waters of the South Pacific. Assisting him from time to time were James Holden as Clay Baker, Troy's first mate for the first two seasons (Baker got a job at the Bali Maki Hotel as the third season began); Guy Stockwell (1961–1962) as Chris Parker, the new first mate; Linda Lawson (1959–1960) as Renée, owner of Renée's Bar in Tahiti; Weaver Levy (1959–1960) as Oliver Kee; Henry Slate (1959–1960) as Bulldog Lovey; George Tobias (1959–1961) as Penrose; Sondi Sodsai, Miss Thailand of 1960 (1960–1961), as Sondi; Marcel Hillaire (1960–1962) as Inspector Bouchard; and Lani Kai (1960–1962) as Kelly. Barbara Steele, who starred in several European horror films during the 1960s, made her only American TV appearance on one episode, "Daughter of Illusion," broadcast 12 December 1960. The first network show set in the South Pacific, *Adventures in Paradise* was one of the few successful series set outside the United States. Its success seems to have done little for Gardner McKay, however, whose television appearances since 1962 have been infrequent; McKay has since turned his talents to writing.

THE ADVENTURES OF BLACK BEAUTY SYNDICATED

1972   Anna Sewell's classic book about a girl and her horse was made into a limited series of half-hour programs, produced in Great Britain. With Judi Bowker as Vicky Gordon; Roderick Shaw as her brother Kevin; William Lucas as their father James Gordon; and Tom Maidea as Albert.

THE ADVENTURES OF CHAMPION CBS

30 SEPTEMBER 1955–3 FEBRUARY 1956   This half-hour children's western was produced by Gene Autry's Flying A Productions, and its central character was Champion, Autry's horse. The human parts were played by Barry Curtis as twelve-year-old Ricky North and Jim Bannon as Uncle Sandy; a German shepherd named Rebel was also featured. The series, which was scheduled opposite ABC's *Rin Tin Tin,* was replaced in midseason by another kids' horse opera, *My Friend Flicka.*

THE ADVENTURES OF FALCON SYNDICATED

1955   A television version of the espionage series which began on radio in 1945. Charles McGraw starred as Mike Waring, an American agent whose code name was The Falcon.

THE ADVENTURES OF FU MANCHU
See DR. FU MANCHU

THE ADVENTURES OF GULLIVER
See GULLIVER

THE ADVENTURES OF HIRAM HOLLIDAY
See HIRAM HOLLIDAY

THE ADVENTURES OF JIM BOWIE
See JIM BOWIE

THE ADVENTURES OF JONNY QUEST
See JONNY QUEST

THE ADVENTURES OF KIT CARSON
See KIT CARSON

THE ADVENTURES OF OZZIE AND HARRIET
See OZZIE AND HARRIET

THE ADVENTURES OF RIN TIN TIN
See RIN TIN TIN

THE ADVENTURES OF ROBIN HOOD
See ROBIN HOOD

THE ADVENTURES OF SIR FRANCIS DRAKE
See SIR FRANCIS DRAKE

THE ADVENTURES OF SIR LANCELOT
See SIR LANCELOT

THE ADVENTURES OF SUPERMAN
See SUPERMAN

THE ADVENTURES OF THE SEA HAWK   SYNDICATED
1958   Caribbean adventure series starring John Howard as John Hawk,
skipper of the *Sea Hawk*.

THE ADVENTURES OF THE SEASPRAY   SYNDICATED
1968   South Pacific adventure series starring Walter Brown as freelance
writer John Wells, skipper of the *Seaspray*. With Gary Gray as son Mike;
Rodney Pearlman as son Noah; and Susanne Haworth as daughter Susan. Produced in Australia.

THE ADVENTURES OF WILLIAM TELL
See WILLIAM TELL

THE ADVOCATES   PBS
5 OCTOBER 1969–23 MAY 1974; 26 JANUARY 1978–9 SEPTEMBER 1979
One of PBS's most popular public affairs programs, *The Advocates* was
essentially a series of debates (usually live) on topical issues. Each week
two speakers, espousing opposite points of view, presented their respective "cases" for or against the proposition at issue and could call "witnesses" to "testify" on their behalf. On many shows during the early
1970s the two sides were taken by Howard Miller, a law professor of liberal bent, and William Rusher, a conservative associated with the *National Review*. Michael Dukakis, who was elected governor of Massachusetts
in 1974, frequently moderated the series in its first years. The show was
the brainchild of Roger Fisher, a professor of international law at Harvard, and was seen locally in Boston before going network in 1969. It was
produced by both KCET, Los Angeles, and WGBH, Boston. Early in
1978 the show returned on a biweekly basis with Marilyn Berger as
moderator.

THE AFFAIRS OF CHINA SMITH
See CHINA SMITH

AFRICAN PATROL   SYNDICATED
1959   John Bentley starred as Inspector Derek of the African Patrol, a
modern-day police force, in this adventure series filmed on location in
Kenya.

AN AGE OF KINGS   SYNDICATED
1961   A limited series of William Shakespeare's historical plays (e.g.,
Richard II, Richard III, Henry IV, Henry V, and *Henry VI*), which were
produced in England and performed by the BBC Repertory Company.
Winner of a Peabody Award in 1962.

AIR POWER   CBS
11 NOVEMBER 1956–5 MAY 1957   CBS's answer to NBC's successful
documentary series *Victory at Sea, Air Power* was a twenty-six-week se-
ries of documentaries about aviation. Because producers Perry Wolff and
Jim Faichney were able to obtain rare German and captured Japanese
film, there was emphasis on aerial warfare during World War II. Walter
Cronkite was the principal narrator; Winston Churchill and Michael
Redgrave served as guest narrators for the "Battle of Britain" segment.
The series was rerun in 1958 as a summer replacement for *The Twentieth
Century*.

AIR TIME '57   ABC
27 DECEMBER 1956–4 APRIL 1957   Half-hour Thursday-night musical
series hosted by Vaughn Monroe. Sponsored by the United States Air
Force Reserve.

AIRFLYTE THEATRE (NASH AIRFLYTE THEATRE)   CBS
21 SEPTEMBER 1950–15 MARCH 1951   Undistinguished half-hour dramatic anthology series, seen on Thursdays. Typical episodes included: "A
Double-Eyed Deceiver," with Van Heflin (21 September); "Waltz
Dream," with Kitty Carlisle (4 January); and "Peggy," with Joan Bennett (8 February). William Gaxton was the host.

THE AL CAPP SHOW   SYNDICATED
1968   Conservative cartoonist Al Capp, creator of Li'l Abner and Fearless Fosdick, briefly hosted his own ninety-minute talk show.

THE AL HIRT SHOW
See FANFARE; MAKE YOUR OWN KIND OF MUSIC

THE AL MORGAN SHOW   DUMONT
5 SEPTEMBER 1949–30 AUGUST 1951   Half-hour musical variety series
with pianist Al Morgan and the Billy Chandler Trio. Broadcast from
Chicago, the show was directed by Don Cook.

THE AL PEARCE SHOW   CBS
Daytime: 11 FEBRUARY 1952–9 MAY 1952; 30 JUNE 1952–26 SEPTEMBER
1952; *Nighttime:* 3 JULY 1952–4 SEPTEMBER 1952   Comedian Al
Pearce's first television show was a forty-five-minute daytime variety series, which was broadcast live from Hollywood. His second daytime series and his prime-time half-hour show, which replaced *The Burns and
Allen Show* for the summer, both originated from New York. Pearce's
best-remembered character is probably Elmer Blurt, the bumbling door-
to-door salesman.

THE ALAN BURKE SHOW   SYNDICATED
1966   Talk show with the accent on the sensational, presided over by the
acerbic Alan Burke. Burke and Joe Pyne were probably the best-known
practitioners of this peculiar talk show subcategory, which relied more on
a steady flow of crackpots (who were of course subject to vicious personal
attack by the host) for its guests than on showbiz personalities. See also
The Joe Pyne Show.

THE ALAN YOUNG SHOW   CBS
6 APRIL 1950–27 MARCH 1952; 15 FEBRUARY 1953–21 JUNE 1953   One
of television's earliest stars, comedian and mime Alan Young first hosted

a Thursday-night variety show that featured Polly Bergen. Early in 1953 he returned in a Sunday-night slot, which he shared biweekly with Ken Murray. This effort was a situation comedy which featured Mabel Paige. After doing a British variety series in 1958, Young resurfaced in 1961 with *Mister Ed*. When *Mister Ed* folded in 1965, Young left show business to become active in the Christian Science church.

THE ALASKANS   ABC
4 OCTOBER 1959–25 SEPTEMBER 1960   One of the many Warner Brothers adventure series, this was set in Alaska during the Gold Rush of 1898 (as the theme song went, "Got the fever, got the fever—gold fever!"). With Roger Moore as Silky Harris; Dorothy Provine as Rocky Shaw; and Jeff York (he'd played Mike Fink on the Davy Crockett episodes of *Disneyland*) as Reno McKee.

THE ALCOA HOUR/ALCOA THEATRE   NBC
14 OCTOBER 1955–19 SEPTEMBER 1960   This dramatic anthology series alternated with *Goodyear Theatre* during its five-season run. Four Star Films produced both series. *The Alcoa Hour,* the first of several dramatic series sponsored by the aluminum company, was shown on Sunday nights during the 1955–1956 and 1956–1957 seasons. In 1957 a thirty-minute format was adopted, and *Alcoa Theatre* was seen on Mondays for the next three seasons. Among the major stars who appeared were Laurence Harvey (in his first major TV role, "The Small Servant," 30 October 1955), Charles Boyer (three appearances), Jack Lemmon (four), David Niven (four), Jane Powell (two), and Robert Ryan (four).

ALCOA PREMIERE   ABC
10 OCTOBER 1961–12 SEPTEMBER 1963   Dramatic anthology series hosted by Fred Astaire. Most segments were one hour, although there were some half-hour shows. Episodes included: "People Need People," with Arthur Kennedy and Lee Marvin (10 October 1961); "The Jail," with John Gavin (his first major TV role, 6 February 1962); and "The Voice of Charlie Pont," with Diana Hyland and Robert Redford (25 October 1962; Redford's only Emmy nomination was for this performance).

ALCOA PRESENTS
See ONE STEP BEYOND

THE ALDRICH FAMILY   NBC
2 OCTOBER 1949–29 MAY 1953   A favorite on radio since the late 1930s, *The Aldrich Family* was NBC's first successful television sitcom. Five actors played typical American teenager Henry Aldrich on TV: Bob Casey (1949–1950), Richard Tyler (1950–1951), Henry Girard (1951–1952), Kenneth Nelson (spring 1952), and Bobby Ellis (1952–1953). Also fea-

tured were House Jameson (the only member of the original radio cast to make the transition to TV) as his father, Sam; Lois Wilson (1949–1950), Nancy Carroll (1950–1951), Lois Wilson (again), and Barbara Robbins (1951–1953) as his mother, Alice ("Henry! Henry Aldrich!"); June Dayton (1949–1951) and Mary Malone (1951–1953) as his sister, Mary; Jackie Kelk (1949–1951), Robert Barry (1951–1952), and Jackie Grimes (1952–1953) as his best friend, Homer Brown; and Loretta Leversee (1952–1953) as his girlfriend, Eleanor. Paul Newman, in one of his earliest TV roles, also appeared occasionally during the 1952–1953 season. The series was created and written by Clifford Goldsmith (the characters first appeared in his play, *What A Life!*), produced and directed by Roger Kay.

ALFRED HITCHCOCK PRESENTS/THE ALFRED HITCHCOCK HOUR

2 OCTOBER 1955–25 SEPTEMBER 1960 (CBS); 27 SEPTEMBER 1960–18 SEPTEMBER 1962 (NBC); 20 SEPTEMBER 1962–18 SEPTEMBER 1964 (CBS); 5 OCTOBER 1964–6 SEPTEMBER 1965 (NBC) Alfred Hitchcock, who had been directing films for three decades by 1955, entered television that fall as host of a half-hour anthology series of mysteries and melodramas. At the beginning of each episode Hitchcock's silhouette was seen filling the famous line drawing of his profile. The camera would then pan to Hitchcock himself, who would introduce the evening's story with a few well-chosen witty remarks; the set on which he appeared either bore a connection to the plot or was a spoof of a popular commercial. The opening remarks (which were filmed in French and German as well as English) typically ended with a barb at the sponsor. After the inevitable commercial, the episode ran. Suspense and surprise endings were the trademarks of the series. Hitchcock reappeared at the end of each show, sometimes to tie up loose ends, sometimes to assure viewers that the killer had been apprehended ("a necessary gesture to morality," as Hitchcock told *TV Guide*). In 1962 the show returned to CBS, expanded to one hour, and was retitled *The Alfred Hitchcock Hour*. Although Hitchcock hosted every episode, he directed only twenty of the several hundred shows. Between 1957 and 1959 several episodes were directed by Robert Altman, who went on to direct such notable films as *M*A*S*H* and *Nashville*. Among the many stars who made multiple appearances over the ten-year run of the series were Barbara Baxley (six appearances), Barbara Bel Geddes (four), Pat Collinge (six), Mildred Dunnock (four), Robert H. Harris (eight), Paul Hartman (five), Robert Horton (five), Henry Jones (four), Brian Keith (five), Hugh Marlowe (four), Ralph Meeker (four), Gary Merrill (seven), Claude Rains (four), Gena Rowlands (four), Phyllis Thaxter (eight), Cara Williams (four) and Dick York (five). Other notable guest appearances included those by Cloris Leachman ("Premonition," 9 October 1955), Joanne Woodward ("Momentum," 24 May 1956), Steve McQueen ("Human Interest Story," 24 May 1959; "Man

from the South," with Peter Lorre, 3 January 1960), Michael J. Pollard ("Anniversary Gift," 1 November 1959, his first major TV role), Dick Van Dyke ("Craig's Will," 6 March 1960), Judy Canova ("Party Line," 29 May 1960, her first TV dramatic appearance), Robert Redford ("The Right Kind of Medicine," 19 December 1961; "A Piece of the Action," 20 September 1962), Katharine Ross ("The Dividing Wall," 6 December 1963) and Peter Fonda ("The Return of Verge Likens," 5 October 1964).

ALIAS SMITH AND JONES   ABC

21 JANUARY 1971–13 JANUARY 1973   A breezy western featuring two outlaws who try to earn amnesty for themselves by assuming new identities and going straight for a year ("Only you and me and the governor'll know!"). With Peter Duel (he'd spelled his last name Deuel on *Love on a Rooftop*) as Hannibal Heyes, alias Joshua Smith; Ben Murphy as Kid Curry, alias Thaddeus Jones. On 30 December 1971, Duel shot and killed himself after watching the show at his home. He was replaced by Roger Davis on 3 February 1972.

ALICE   CBS

29 SEPTEMBER 1976–   Situation comedy based on the 1975 movie, *Alice Doesn't Live Here Any More,* about a recently widowed woman in her mid-thirties who, with her twelve-year-old son, moves to Phoenix. An aspiring singer, she gets a "temporary" job as a waitress in a diner, attends college at night, and hopes for the big break. With Linda Lavin as Alice Hyatt; Philip McKeon as son Tommy; Vic Tayback (repeating his film role) as Mel Sharples, short-tempered owner of Mel's Diner; Polly Holliday as Flo Castleberry, the brassy, man-hungry waitress; Beth Howland as Vera Gorman, the mousy, scatterbrained waitress; and Marvin Kaplan (1978–   ) as Henry, a regular customer. In March 1980 Diane Ladd (who had played Flo in the movie) joined the cast as Belle, replacing Holliday. Created by Robert Getchell.

THE ALICE PEARCE SHOW   ABC

28 JANUARY 1949–11 MARCH 1949   Alice Pearce, who would later become famous as Gladys Kravitz, the suspicious neighbor on *Bewitched,* broke into television with her own fifteen-minute musical show, broadcast 9:45 on Friday evenings. Accompanied by pianist and songwriter Mark Lawrence, she sang such novelty numbers as "I'm in Love with a Coaxial Cable."

ALKALI IKE   CBS

17 APRIL 1950–11 MAY 1950   A fifteen-minute puppet show with a western theme, *Alkali Ike* was seen after the evening news once or twice a week. Ventriloquist Al Robinson was assisted by Beverly Fite and the Slim Jackson Quartet. Barry Wood produced the series.

ALL ABOARD   CBS

19 OCTOBER 1952–11 JANUARY 1953   Fifteen-minute interview show
hosted by Skeets Minton.

ALL ABOUT FACES   SYNDICATED

1971   Richard Hayes hosted this lackluster game show, similar in format to Gene Rayburn's *The Amateur's Guide to Love* and similar in title
to Ben Alexander's *About Faces*. On this one, celebrity pairs were shown
brief film sequences and tried to predict their outcome.

ALL AROUND THE TOWN   CBS

18 JUNE 1951–7 AUGUST 1952   Hosted by Mike Wallace and Buff Cobb,
this half-hour series examined goings-on in New York City. Originally
seen three afternoons a week, the show moved to prime time in November 1951.

ALL IN THE FAMILY (ARCHIE BUNKER'S PLACE)   CBS

12 JANUARY 1971–   Because of its impact on American audiences and on the style of television comedy, *All in the Family* is perhaps
the single most influential program in the history of broadcasting. In
terms of production techniques, the series added nothing new; in some
ways it represented a return to the old days of television: one basic set, a
small cast, and little reliance on guest stars. *I Love Lucy,* TV's first
smash hit sitcom, was the first to be filmed before a live audience; *All
in the Family* was the first sitcom to be videotaped, and, unlike the
vast majority of sitcoms of the 1960s, it was performed before a live
audience.

It was in story develpment and character treatment that *All in the
Family* broke new ground. It was the first situation comedy to deal open-
ly with bigotry, prejudice, and politics. "Hot" issues such as abortion,
birth control, mate-swapping, menopause, and homosexuality were handled successfully on the show. "Taboo" words, such as "spic," "hebe,"
and "spade" were uttered. And throughout it all, audiences laughed. The
show's immense popularity with all segments of the population demonstrated that it had broad appeal and indicated that American audiences
of the 1970s were sophisticated enough to appreciate well-produced, well-
written, and well-acted topical comedy. Studies showed that, by 1973, the
face of central character Archie Bunker was the most widely recognized
in America; phrases such as "Stifle yourself!" "Dingbat!" and "Meat-
head!" were part of the American vocabulary.

The men responsible for *All in the Family* were Norman Lear and his
partner Alàn "Bud" Yorkin, two motion picture producer-directors with
considerable television experience. Lear had been a comedy writer in the
early 1950s, then a director, and later a producer ("The TV Guide
Awards Show" in 1962, "Henry Fonda and the Family" in 1963, *The*

Andy Williams Show in 1965–1966); Yorkin had directed many shows at NBC (including *The Colgate Comedy Hour, The Dinah Shore Show, The Tony Martin Show, Tennessee Ernie Ford,* and *The George Gobel Show*) and directed and produced Fred Astaire's 1958 and 1959 specials. Together or separately during the 1960s they made such films as *Come Blow Your Horn* (Lear producer, Yorkin director), *Never Too Late* (Yorkin director), *Divorce American Style* (Lear producer, Yorkin director) and *The Night They Raided Minsky's* (Lear producer). Lear and Yorkin dissolved their partnership in 1971; both have remained active in television production.

All in the Family was on the drawing board as early as 1968, shortly after Lear learned of a hit series on British television, *Till Death Us Do Part.* Created by Johnny Speight, it told of a British family of modest means, with bigoted father and live-in son-in-law. Lear bought the American rights to the series, wrote a script, and convinced ABC to finance a pilot. With Carroll O'Connor and Jean Stapleton in the lead roles, a pilot was made; the show was called *Those Were the Days.* But ABC, unhappy with the concept even after a second pilot, let its option lapse. CBS executives then saw the pilot, and the network grabbed the series. Rob Reiner and Sally Struthers were brought in for the supporting roles as production began. At 9:30 p.m. (EST) on Tuesday, January 12, 1971, the show premiered. It was prefaced by an announcement: "The program you are about to see is *All in the Family.* It seeks to throw a humorous spotlight on our frailties, prejudices, and concerns. By making them a source of laughter we hope to show—in a mature fashion—just how absurd they are."

Those who watched the premiere (it was fifty-fourth in the weekly Nielsen ratings) apparently liked what they saw and told their friends. By summer, the show was number one. In the fall it was moved to Saturdays at 8 p.m., the slot it occupied for the next four seasons. It was there that America learned to love the people of *All in the Family.*

Carroll O'Connor, a character actor of much experience but little previous recognition, caught Lear's eye when he appeared in a 1968 film, *What Did You Do in the War, Daddy?* Lear was certain that O'Connor would be just right for the role of Archie Bunker, a bigoted, right-wing, lower-middle-class, high-school educated, white Protestant with a tendency to run off at the mouth. Archie lived in Queens (704 Houser Street) with his wife, daughter, and son-in-law, and until 1976 worked as a loading dock foreman at Prendergast Tool and Die Company. As O'Connor explained his role to *TV Guide,* "Archie's dilemma is coping with a world that is changing in front of him. . . . But he won't get to the root of the problem, because the root of the problem is himself, and he doesn't know it."

Jean Stapleton, also a relatively unheralded character player, was well known to Lear and Yorkin: In Yorkin's film, *Never Too Late,* she played a woman in her forties named Edith who learned she was pregnant; she also costarred in Lear's movie, *Cold Turkey,* filmed in 1970. As Archie's devoted wife, Edith Bunker, she is patient, tolerant, even-tempered, and honest, though perhaps a bit confused at times. Unlike Archie, Edith is able to cope with the changes that life brings.

Two virtual unknowns filled out the main cast. Sally Struthers, with brief TV comedy experience from the Smothers Brothers' 1970 summer show and Tim Conway's 1970 fall series, played the Bunkers' only child, Gloria, who, though liberal in outlook, loved her parents. She worked part-time as a salesclerk to help support her husband, Mike Stivic. Rob Reiner, son of Carl Reiner, one of television's most creative funny people, played Mike, a student with a big appetite and a big mouth. Vocally liberal, he enjoyed baiting Archie. As the series progressed, Mike finally finished college and got a job as an instructor. He and Gloria then moved next door and had a baby; little Joey Stivic (played by Jason Draeger, and later by Cory Miller) was born in January 1976 (a 1976 episode caused some consternation at the network when it showed Archie changing a naked baby boy).

Other principal characters over the seasons have included: Michael Evans (to January 1975) as Lionel Jefferson, Mike and Gloria's black friend; Isabel Sanford (who first appeared on 2 March 1971 and became a regular in 1972) as Louise Jefferson, Lionel's mom; Mel Stewart (1972–1974) as Henry Jefferson, Lionel's uncle; and Sherman Hemsley (1974–January 1975) as George Jefferson, Lionel's dad. In January 1975 the Jeffersons, who had become the Bunkers' next-door neighbors, moved out of the neighborhood and into their own series. In 1973 Betty Garrett and Vincent Gardenia joined the cast as Irene and Frank Lorenzo, the Bunkers' other next-door neighbors. Gardenia left after one season, Garrett after three. In the fall of 1976 the Bunkers rented out their now spare bedroom (the kids having moved into the Jeffersons' old house) for the season to Teresa Betancourt (played by Liz Torres), a Puerto Rican hospital worker. In the fall of 1977, a year after his promotion to a dispatcher's job at the plant, Archie quit his job to become his own boss: he bought Kelsey's, his favorite local watering hole, and renamed it Archie's Place. Added to the cast were Jason Wingreen as Harry, the bartender; Allan Melvin as Archie's neighbor, Barney Hefner; and Danny Dayton as Archie's pal Hank.

Both Rob Reiner and Sally Struthers announced their plans to leave the show at the end of the 1977–1978 season; in the season finale viewers learned that Mike Stivic had landed a teaching job at a distant university, forcing the Stivics to move away. As *All in the Family*'s ninth season began in the fall of 1978, Archie and Edith found themselves alone together, but only temporarily, as Danielle Brisebois (who had been in the cast of *Annie* on Broadway) was introduced as Stephanie Mills, a distant niece of Edith's who was dropped off—indefinitely—at the Bunkers' by her vagabond father.

More changes occurred in the fall of 1979. The show's title was changed to *Archie Bunker's Place*, as the action shifted from the Bunker household to Archie's bar. O'Connor, Brisebois, Melvin, and Dayton remained as regulars, with Stapleton scheduled to make a number of guest appearances during the season. Martin Balsam joined the cast as Archie's new business partner, Murray Klein; Bill Quinn appeared regularly as the blind Mr. Van Ranseleer, a regular customer; Anne Meara was the new chef, Veronica Rooney; and Guerin Barry and Dino Scofield played her nephew Fred, the waiter.

All in the Family's opening theme song, "Those Were the Days," was written by Lee Adams and Charles Strouse and sung by O'Connor and Stapleton. The closing instrumental theme, "Remembering You," was composed by O'Connor and Roger Kellaway. The show's spinoffs have included *Maude* (1972–1978; *Maude*'s star, Beatrice Arthur, appeared as Edith's cousin on 11 December 1971) and *The Jeffersons* (January 1975–). Other series developed by Norman Lear and/or Bud Yorkin have included *All That Glitters, All's Fair, Good Times, Grady, Hot L Baltimore, Mary Hartman, Mary Hartman, One Day at a Time,* and *Sanford and Son,* among others.

ALL MY CHILDREN   ABC

5 JANUARY 1970–   Created by veteran serial writer Agnes Nixon (*Search for Tomorrow, One Life to Live,* and *Another World*), *All My Children* has become ABC's highest-rated soap opera. Serial buffs generally agree that the show tends to emphasize the traditional themes of love and romance a bit more strongly than most of the other soaps. Set in Pine Valley, a town within driving distance of New York City, its central families are the Tylers and the Martins. Principal players have included: Hugh Franklin as Dr. Charles Tyler, a prominent physician; Ruth Warrick as his concerned wife, Phoebe Tyler; Paul Dumont and Peter White as their son Lincoln; Diana De Vegh, Joanna Miles, and Judith Barcroft as their daughter, Ann; Jack Stauffer, Chris Hubbell, Gregory Chase, and Richard Van Fleet as Charles's grandson (by a former marriage), Dr. Chuck Tyler, who was orphaned during infancy; Rosemary Prinz (1970) as Lincoln's wife, Amy, who left Linc after news was spread that she had had an illegitimate child; Susan Lucci as Erica Kane, the resident busybody who spread the news; Larry Keith (1970–1978) as Nick Davis, the man with whom Amy had an affair; Richard Hatch and Nick Benedict as Phillip Brent, son of Amy and Nick; Mary Fickett as Amy's sister, Ruth Brent, who raised young Phillip; Mark Dawson as Ruth's husband, Ted Brent, who was killed in a car crash; Karen Gorney, Stephanie Braxton, Karen Gorney (again), and Nancy Frangione as

Tara Martin, Phil's girlfriend, who was abandoned by Phil after he contracted amnesia and left town (he later returned, interrupting Tara and Chuck's wedding); Ray MacDonnell as Tara's father, Dr. Joseph Martin, also a prominent physician, who married Ruth Brent; Deborah Solomon as Sydney Scott, who opened a boutique with Ann Tyler; Christopher Wines, Charles Frank, Robert Perault, and James O'Sullivan as Jeff Martin, Tara's brother, who was ensnared by Erica Kane (Erica subsequently underwent the first legal abortion on a TV soap opera); Ken Rabat and William Mooney as Joe Martin's brother, lawyer Paul Martin, who married Ann Tyler after her brief marriage to Nick Davis; Ian Miller Washam and Brian Lima as little Phillip Tyler, son of Tara and Phil, who was raised by Tara and Chuck Tyler; Biff McGuire and John Devlin as modeling agent Jason Maxwell, who caused Erica to divorce Jeff and was later murdered; Jacqueline Boslow and Susan Blanchard as nurse Mary Kennicott, Jeff's second wife; Frances Heflin as Erica's mother, Mona Kane, Jason's murderer; Francesca James as Kitty Shea, who married Nick Davis; Eileen Letchworth as Margo Flax, who married Paul Martin after his divorce from Ann; Dan Hamilton as drug dealer Hal Short, Kitty Shea's former husband; Paulette Breen and Susan Plantt-Winston as Margo's daughter, Claudette Montgomery; Eileen Herlie as Mrs. Myrtle Lum, a woman hired by Phoebe Tyler to pose as Kitty's long lost mother; Paul Gleason as ex-doctor David Thornton, with whom Ruth Martin fell in love; John Danelle as Dr. Franklin Grant, a black physican who settled in Pine Valley; Avis MacArthur and Lisa Wilkinson as his wife (and later his ex-wife), Nancy Grant; Pat Dixon as nurse Carolyn Murray, who became Frank's second wife; Francesca Poston and Candice Early as Donna Beck, a prostitute who was rehabilitated by Chuck Tyler and later married him; Christine Thomas, Kate Harrington, and Kay Campbell as Kate Martin, mother of Joe and Paul Martin; Marilyn Chris as Edie Hoffman; Michael Shannon as Bill Hoffman; Maureen Mooney as Stacy Coles; Bruce Gray as Wyatt Coles; Daren Kelly as Danny Kennicott; Elissa Leeds and Julia Barr as Brooke English; Matthew Anton and John E. Dunn as Tad Gardner; Reuben Green as Clay Watson; Dawn Marie Boyle as Dottie Thornton; Matthew Cowles as Billy Clyde Tuggle; Larry Fleischman as Benny Sago; Sandy Gabriel as Edna Thornton; William Griffis as Harlan Tucker, who married Mona Kane; Steven James as Carl Blair; Mark LaMura as Mark Dalton; Kathleen Noone as Ellen Shepherd; Tricia Pursley (later known as Tricia P. Hawkins) as Devon Shepherd; Gil Rogers as Ray Gardner; Richard Shoberg as Tom Cudahy, who married Erica; Robin Strasser as Dr. Christina Karras; Paula Trueman (1977–1978) as Maggie Flanagan.

More recent comings and goings have included those of Kathleen Dezina as Estelle LaTour; Francesca James as Kelly Cole, twin sister of Kitty Cole (killed off in 1977); Jeff Magee as Wally McFadden; Ross Petty and Warren Burton as Eddie Dorrance; Bob Hover as Adrian Shepherd;

Harry Boda as Mel Jacobi; David Pendleton as Dr. Russ Anderson; Fred Porcelli as Freddy; Judith Roberts as Lettie Jean.

In an unusual guest appearance, Carol Burnett turned up as Mrs. Johnson, a hospital patient, on 16 March 1976; *All My Children* is her favorite soap opera. The show, which expanded from thirty to sixty minutes on 25 April 1977, is produced by Bud Kloss.

ALL THAT GLITTERS   SYNDICATED
18 APRIL 1977–15 JULY 1977   The success of *Mary Hartman, Mary Hartman* prompted Norman Lear to develop a second soap opera which, like *Mary Hartman,* was shown in most markets in a late-night time slot. The setting of the short-lived effort was the Globatron Corporation, a conglomerate in which all the key positions were held by women and the secretarial slots were filled by men. The cast included: Lois Nettleton as executive Christina Stockwood; Chuck McCann as her stay-at-home spouse, Bert Stockwood; Anita Gillette as Nancy Bankston; Wes Parker as Glen Bankston, an aspiring actor; Barbara Baxley as L. W. Carruthers, the chairwoman of the board; Vanessa Brown as Peggy Horner; Louise Shaffer as Andrea Martin; David Haskell as Michael McFarland; Linda Gray as model Linda Murkland, a transsexual; Jessica Walter as agent Joan Hamlyn; Eileen Brennan as Ma Packer; Marte Boyle Slout as Grace Smith; and Gary Sandy as Dan Kincaid, the secretary with "the cutest little buns in the corporation." Stephanie Stills was the executive producer, Viva Knight the producer.

ALLAKAZAM
See THE MAGIC LAND OF ALLAKAZAM

ALLEN LUDDEN'S GALLERY   SYNDICATED
1969   Allen Ludden was one of a number of game show hosts who took a stab at the talk show format during the late 1960s. After a brief run, Ludden returned to the quizmaster's desk.

THE ALL-NEW SUPERFRIENDS HOUR
See THE SUPER FRIENDS

ALL'S FAIR   CBS
20 SEPTEMBER 1976–15 AUGUST 1977   Unlike most of Norman Lear's earlier comedies, *All's Fair* was set neither in a typical town nor in a typical household. Here, in Washington, D.C., a conservative political columnist, forty-nine, fell in love with a feminist freelance photographer, twenty-three. Their differences in age and outlook provided the tension; the Washington setting provided the topicality. With Richard Crenna (a sitcom veteran who had made only a few TV appearances after 1966) as

syndicated columnist Richard Barrington; Bernadette Peters (in her first series role) as photographer Charlotte (Charley) Drake; J. A. Preston as Al Brooks, Barrington's black but equally conservative assistant; Judy Kahan as Ginger Livingston, Charley's roommate (when Charley was not at Richard's), a secretary; Lee Chamberlin as Lucy Daniels, a CBS-TV newswoman and Al's female companion (they got married early in 1977); Jack Dodson as bumbling Senator Wayne Joplin (constituency unspecified), a friend of Barrington's; Michael Keaton as Lanny Wolfe, a presidential joke writer.

ALL-STAR ANYTHING GOES
See ALMOST ANYTHING GOES

ALL-STAR GOLF
ABC/NBC

12 OCTOBER 1957–29 APRIL 1961 (ABC); 4 OCTOBER 1961–23 MARCH 1963 (NBC) A weekend series of head-to-head golf matches, hosted for most of its run by Jimmy Demaret.

ALL-STAR NEWS
ABC

9 OCTOBER 1952–30 AUGUST 1953 ABC's innovative news show began as a five-nights-a-week effort, with a full hour of news (compared with the fifteen-minute newscasts on NBC and CBS) on four of those evenings. By January of 1953, however, *All-Star News* had been trimmed to just one hour on Sunday nights. The show relied not on a single anchorman, but rather on live reports from ABC correspondents all over the country. Regular news broadcasts resumed on ABC in the fall of 1953: see *ABC News.*

ALL-STAR REVUE
NBC

8 SEPTEMBER 1951–18 APRIL 1953 A variety hour that preceded *Your Show of Shows* on Saturday nights for two seasons. There were many guest hosts, but those who appeared with regularity included Ezio Pinza, Jimmy Durante, Ed Wynn, Danny Thomas, George Jessel, Tallulah Bankhead (who made five appearances during the second season), and finally, Martha Raye. In the fall of 1953 Martha Raye's monthly replacements for *Your Show of Shows* were entitled *All-Star Revue* before the title was changed to *The Martha Raye Show* in December. See also *Four Star Revue.*

ALL STAR SECRETS
NBC

8 JANUARY 1979–10 AUGUST 1979 A straightforward daytime game show hosted by Bob Eubanks, *All Star Secrets* featured three contestants and a panel of five guest celebrities. At the outset of each round the host revealed a "secret" held by one of the celebs; contestants won money by correctly guessing the holder of the secret.

ALMOST ANYTHING GOES   ABC
31 JULY 1975–28 AUGUST 1975; 24 JANUARY 1976–9 MAY 1976
ALL-STAR ANYTHING GOES   SYNDICATED
1977   A raucous hour game show, *Almost Anything Goes* was modeled
after a British series, *It's a Knockout.* In the American version teams
from three small towns, selected by local civic groups, competed in various zany stunts (such as negotiating obstacle courses, or trying to carry
loaves of bread across a greased beam suspended over a pool of water).
Each show was shot on location at one of the competing towns. No prizes
were awarded to the competitors; civic pride, and the chance to appear
on nationwide TV, motivated the participants. Reporting the festivities
were Charlie Jones and Lynn Shackleford; the on-the-field correspondents were Dick Whittington (1975) and Regis Philbin (1976). Bob Banner and Beryl Vertue were the executive producers. *All-Star Anything
Goes,* which was introduced a year later, was played similarly, except that
the teams were composed of celebrities; the half-hour show was hosted by
Bill Boggs. Bill Healy handled the play-by-play, and Judy Abercrombie
kept score. See also *Junior Almost Anything Goes.*

ALUMNI FUN   ABC/CBS
20 JANUARY 1963–28 APRIL 1963 (ABC); 12 JANUARY 1964–5 APRIL
1964 (CBS); 10 JANUARY 1965–28 MARCH 1965 (CBS); 23 JANUARY
1966–7 MAY 1966 (CBS)   This weekly game show, an earlier version of
which had been on radio, featured two teams, each composed of famous
alumni from the same college or university. The winning team would return the following week to face a new team of challengers. The show was
usually seen on Sunday afternoons, following the completion of the professional football season. John K. M. McCaffery hosted during the first
season; Peter Lind Hayes was the host during the other seasons.

THE ALVIN SHOW   CBS
4 OCTOBER 1961–12 SEPTEMBER 1962   ABC introduced prime-time cartoon programs in 1960 with *Bugs Bunny* and *The Flintstones.* CBS followed suit in 1961 with this effort, which featured three singing
chipmunks (known as The Chipmunks, oddly enough) and their song-
writer-manager, David Seville. The Chipmunks had gained real-life fame
in 1958 when songwriter Ross Bagdasarian (who used the name David
Seville and wrote such hits as "The Witch Doctor") wrote a novelty
Christmas number and recorded it for Liberty records. As a gimmick
Bagdasarian used three speeded-up vocal tracks and named his high-
pitched hitmakers The Chipmunks. The record was a smash. In the song
the three characters were named Alvin, Simon, and Theodore. In his
book, *Rock On,* Norm Nite notes that Bagdasarian named them after
Liberty executives Al Bennett and Si Warnoker and recording engineer

Ted Keep. When the series came to television Bagdasarian continued to supply the main characters' voices; an additional segment featured the adventures of inventor Clyde Crashcup, with voice supplied by Shepard Menken. Though the series fared poorly on prime time (it was opposite *Wagon Train*), it lasted three seasons (1962–1965) on Saturday mornings. The series returned, in reruns, to NBC's Saturday morning schedule in March of 1979.

THE AMATEUR HOUR
See TED MACK'S ORIGINAL AMATEUR HOUR

THE AMATEUR'S GUIDE TO LOVE   CBS
27 MARCH 1972–23 JUNE 1972 Gene Rayburn hosted this daytime game show which involved a panel of three celebrities, two studio contestants, and a videotaped sequence. First, the celebs ("The Guidebook Panel") watched part of the videotaped sequence, in which the contestants became involved in a sexy or amorous situation. The tape was stopped prior to its conclusion and the Guidebook Panel voted on how the contestants should have reacted to the situation. The tape was then resumed; if the contestants reacted as the panel predicted, they won money. The show's credits carried the following disclaimer: "Studio interviews are discussed with panel and guests in advance."

THE AMAZING CHAN AND THE CHAN CLAN   CBS
9 SEPTEMBER 1972–22 SEPTEMBER 1974 Charlie Chan's second television incarnation was in cartoon form, produced by Hanna-Barbera, shown on Saturdays during the first season and Sundays during the second. The inscrutable detective was assisted by his ten children. The voice of Charlie was supplied by Keye Luke, who had played number-one son (to Warner Oland's Charlie) in the Chan films of the 1930s. See also *Charlie Chan.*

THE AMAZING MR. MALONE   ABC
24 SEPTEMBER 1951–10 MARCH 1952 A short-lived television version of the radio series which premiered in 1948. Lee Tracy starred as John J. Malone, a Chicago criminal defense lawyer.

THE AMAZING POLGAR   CBS
16 SEPTEMBER 1949–28 OCTOBER 1949 This ten-minute show, seen Fridays after the evening news, was probably television's first show to deal with hypnotism. Each week Dr. Franz Polgar demonstrated his hypnotic prowess upon selected members of the studio audience. Chuck Lewin produced the series.

THE AMAZING SPIDER-MAN   CBS
5 APRIL 1978–3 MAY 1978 Like *The Incredible Hulk* and *Wonder Woman, The Amazing Spider-Man* was an hour adventure series based on a comic book character. The series starred Nicholas Hammond as Peter Parker, a reporter for the New York *Bugle* who, as the result of a mysterious spider bite, could transform himself into Spider-Man; Spider-Man's arachnid powers include the ability to walk along walls and ceilings, and to cast ropelike lines between buildings. Also featured were Robert F. Simon as his boss, Mr. Jameson; Chip Fields as Rita, another newspaper employee; and Michael Pataki as Captain Barbera of the New York Police Department. Charles Fries and Dan Goodman were the executive producers of the series, a single episode of which was introduced in the fall of 1977. After a five-week trial run in the spring of 1978, it was seen on an irregular basis, and a new character was added: Ellen Bry as Julie, a photographer.

THE AMAZING TALES OF   SYNDICATED
HANS CHRISTIAN ANDERSEN
1954 A series for children, based on the writings of the Danish fabulist. Hosted by George and Gene Bernard.

THE AMAZING THREE   SYNDICATED
1967 Cartoon series in which three intergalactic beings were sent to Earth to determine whether it should be destroyed. Upon their arrival they assumed the identities of a dog, a duck, and a horse and befriended young Kenny Catrer.

THE AMAZING WORLD OF KRESKIN   SYNDICATED
1971 Demonstrations of apparent mind-reading and ESP by the amazing Kreskin, a self-described "mentalist" and frequent talk show guest. Like Dunninger, the leading TV mentalist of the 1950s, Kreskin used just one name and never divulged his secrets.

AMERICA   NBC/PBS
14 NOVEMBER 1972–15 MAY 1973 (NBC); 17 SEPTEMBER 1974–18 MARCH 1975 (PBS) Alistair Cooke's highly acclaimed "personal history" of the United States was produced by Michael Gill for BBC and Time-Life Films. It was originally telecast as thirteen hours, each focusing on a given topic, on alternate Tuesdays. In 1974, it was presented on PBS as a series of twenty-six half hours, with new introductions and conclusions by host Cooke.

AMERICA ALIVE!   NBC
24 JULY 1978–5 JANUARY 1979 Broadcast live, this hour magazine show was hosted by Jack Linkletter, who had hosted a similar show eigh-

teen years earlier (see *On the Go*). Linkletter's traveling cohosts included Pat Mitchell, Bruce Jenner, and Janet Langhart. Other regular contributors included David Sheehan (films), Virginia Graham (gossip and interviews), David Horowitz (consumer affairs), Dick Orkin and Bert Berdis (comedy), and Dr. William H. Masters and Virginia Johnson (sex and health). Woody Fraser was the executive producer.

AMERICA SPEAKS   NBC
2 JULY 1951–24 AUGUST 1951   A summer replacement for *The Bert Parks Show,* this daytime documentary series examined the American economy.

AMERICA 2NIGHT
See FERNWOOD 2-NIGHT

THE AMERICAN ADVENTURE   SYNDICATED
1960   A series of thirteen 15-minute films on American government and patriotism.

AMERICAN BANDSTAND   ABC
5 AUGUST 1957–   ABC's longest running series actually began as a local show in Philadelphia in 1952. Then called *Bandstand,* it was hosted by Bob Horn. The set resembled a record shop, and the show featured records, film clips of popular singers, and a live audience of local teenagers who danced while the records played. Dick Clark, then a disc jockey on a Philadelphia radio station, took over as host in 1956. The show soon attracted network attention, as it was the highest-rated program in its time slot in the Philadelphia area. Sixty-seven ABC affiliates carried the show starting in the summer of 1957; some carried it for the full ninety minutes, others for only thirty or sixty minutes. For the next six years the show was telecast weekday afternoons from the studios of WFIL-TV in Philadelphia. A prime-time version also surfaced for thirteen weeks in the fall of 1957. Clark, who was twenty-six when the show first went network, kept the format simple: The new set contained little but a set of bleachers for the kids to sit on when they weren't dancing, a raised podium for the host, an autograph table for guest stars, and a signboard listing the week's top ten hits.

Kids (and quite a few adults) watched the show to see other kids dance; many of the 200 or so teenagers who filled the studio each day were regulars, and some received considerable fan mail. The show also provided the chance for performers to do their newest hits. Over the years almost every major rock star appeared at least once (two notable exceptions were Elvis Presley and Rick Nelson). On the 1957 Thanksgiving show, for example, two New York teenagers who called themselves Tom and Jerry sang their hit record, "Hey, Schoolgirl." They are better known today as Paul Simon and Art Garfunkel. Because the show was broadcast from Philadelphia during those years, Philadelphia artists showed up frequently: Frankie Avalon, Bobby Rydell, Chubby Checker, Fabian, and James Darren all guested dozens of times.

Clark was a shrewd businessman, and by the end of 1957 he had invested in various music publishing and record distributing ventures. He later put together road shows—the *Dick Clark Caravan of Stars* toured the country (by bus) many times. Clark's involvement in such activities, though profitable, almost cut short his career as a TV personality, as the "payola" scandal broke in 1959. A Congressional subcommittee investigating "payola"—the payment of money or other favors to get a new record played on radio—called Clark to testify in 1960. By that time, Clark, at network insistence, had divested himself of his interests in music publishing and record distributing outfits. He steadfastly denied ever having received payment to play a song on *American Bandstand* and also tried to show that certain songs in which he had a financial interest were not played disproportionately often on the show. Clark emerged from the hearings relatively unscathed and, unlike many less fortunate disc jockeys, continued to host his show. *Bandstand* continued to run weekday afternoons until 30 August 1963, when it was switched to Saturday afternoons. In the spring of 1964 the show moved to Los Angeles, where it has remained. There Clark established Dick Clark Productions, successfully promoted many concerts, and also developed such TV series as *Where the Action Is* and *It's Happening.*

In sum, *American Bandstand* should be noted not only as one of television's longest-running musical series, but also as the first network series devoted exclusively to rock-and-roll music.

AN AMERICAN FAMILY PBS

11 JANUARY 1973–29 MARCH 1973 A controversial documentary series chronicling the lives of the members of the Loud family of Santa Barbara, California, *An American Family* was shown in twelve hour-long installments. Producer Craig Gilbert and his two assistants spent seven months with the Louds in 1971 and shot some 300 hours of film of the seven Louds—husband Bill, president of American Western Foundries, his wife Pat, and their five children, Lance, Kevin, Grant, Delilah, and Michele. The footage that finally emerged on television was sometimes banal, sometimes boring, and sometimes riveting. In the second episode, viewers saw Pat meeting Lance in New York's Greenwich Village and learning of his involvement in the local homosexual scene. The eighth and ninth episodes concerned the breakup of the Louds' marriage, as Pat decided to file for a divorce, and Bill moved out of the house (the two were divorced in 1972). The Louds themselves criticized the series, maintaining that selective editing of 300 hours into twelve-hour segments had painted a grossly distorted picture of their lives.

THE AMERICAN FORUM OF THE AIR   NBC
4 FEBRUARY 1950–15 SEPTEMBER 1957 This Sunday-afternoon public affairs program featured debates on topical issues. Theodore Granik, who introduced the series on radio in 1937, moderated. Toward the end of its run the series alternated with *Youth Wants to Know.*

THE AMERICAN GIRLS   CBS
23 SEPTEMBER 1978–10 NOVEMBER 1978 Hour-long dramatic series about two field researchers for *The American Report,* a television news-magazine. With Priscilla Barnes as Becky Tomkins, a veteran staffer; Debra Clinger as her new partner, Amy Waddell, a former college reporter who landed the job because she had once obtained an interview with President Nixon; David Spielberg as Francis X. Casey, their producer. Harve Bennett and Harris Kattleman were the executive producers.

AMERICAN HORSE AND HORSEMAN   SYNDICATED
1973 Dale Robertson hosted this equestrian documentary series.

THE AMERICAN HOUR
See THE MOTOROLA TV HOUR

AMERICAN INVENTORY   NBC
1 JULY 1951–16 JANUARY 1955 Panel discussions and documentary films were the staples of this public affairs program, which was seen Sunday afternoons for most of its run.

AMERICAN LIFESTYLE   SYNDICATED
1972 E. G. Marshall narrated this documentary series, which often presented biographies of famous Americans.

AMERICAN RELIGIOUS TOWN HALL   ABC/SYNDICATED
4 MARCH 1956–9 JUNE 1957 (ABC); 1970–   (SYNDICATED) Religious and moral topics are debated on this panel show. The ABC version, which was seen Sunday afternoons, was moderated by James A. Pike. The syndicated version, based in Dallas, is moderated by Bishop A. A. Leisky.

AMERICAN SONG   NBC
15 APRIL 1948–21 FEBRUARY 1949 A twenty-minute musical series broadcast once or twice a week before the evening newsreel, *American Song* featured singer Paul Arnold and dancers Nelle Fisher and Ray Harrison.

THE AMERICAN SPORTSMAN   ABC
31 JANUARY 1965–   Curt Gowdy hosts this outdoor series,
on which celebrities and athletes go hunting and fishing. Executive producer: Roone Arledge. Produced by Curt Gowdy, Neil Cunningham, and
Pat Smith.

THE AMERICAN WEEK   CBS
4 APRIL 1954–10 OCTOBER 1954   Sunday-afternoon news review with
Eric Sevareid.

THE AMERICAN WEST   SYNDICATED
1966   Travelogue hosted by Jack Smith.

AMERICANA
See BEN GRAUER'S AMERICANA GUIDE

THE AMERICANS   NBC
23 JANUARY 1961–11 SEPTEMBER 1961   The story of two brothers, Virginia farmers, fighting on opposite sides during the Civil War. With Darryl Hickman as Corporal Ben Canfield, fighting for the Union, and Dick
Davalos as Corporal Jeff Canfield, fighting for the Confederacy. Robert
Redford guest starred in one episode, "The Coward" (8 May). A midseason replacement for *Riverboat.*

AMERICA'S GREATEST BANDS   CBS
25 JUNE 1955–24 SEPTEMBER 1955   Bandleader Paul Whiteman reintro-
duced the Big Band era of the 1930s on this Saturday-night hour, a summer replacement for *The Jackie Gleason Show.* Most of the bands which
had survived the era guested on the show.

AMERICA'S HEALTH   ABC
20 AUGUST 1951–6 MARCH 1952   A series of public interest films on
health and medicine.

AMERICA'S TOWN MEETING   ABC
5 OCTOBER 1948–8 MARCH 1949; 27 JANUARY 1952–6 JULY 1952   Public affairs discussion program which featured guest speakers and audience
debate. George V. Denny, who originated the show on radio in 1935,
hosted the series in 1948 and 1952, John Daly in 1949.

THE AMES BROTHERS SHOW   SYNDICATED
1955   Fifteen-minute musical series starring the Ames Brothers (Joe,
Gene, Vic, and Ed), who began recording in 1949. Youngest brother Ed

went on to record as a solo artist and later appeared as Mingo in *Daniel Boone.*

AMOS AND ANDY   CBS

28 JUNE 1951–11 JUNE 1953   Amos and Andy, the immensely popular black characters created on radio in 1928 by white dialecticians Freeman Gosden and Charles Correll, were brought to television in 1951. CBS is reported to have paid Gosden and Correll $1 million each for the rights to the series. All the television roles were filled by black performers: Tim Moore as George (Kingfish) Stevens, a scheming con man and president of the Mystic Knights of the Sea, a fraternal order; Spencer Williams as Andrew H. Brown, Kingfish's trusting friend and usual mark; Alvin Childress as Amos Jones, a level-headed cabdriver (for the Fresh Air Cab Co.); Ernestine Wade as Sapphire Stevens, the Kingfish's nagging wife; Amanda Randolph as Mama, Sapphire's mother; Johnny Lee as Algonquin J. Calhoun, a fast-talking lawyer; Nick O'Demus as Lightnin', the janitor at the lodge. Theme: "The Perfect Song." Gosden and Correll supervised the production; Charles Barton directed most of the episodes.

Although the series lasted only two seasons, it was widely syndicated until 1966, when pressure from civil rights groups prompted CBS to withdraw the series from syndication. The basis of their complaints was that the characterizations were stereotyped and only served to reinforce the feelings of prejudice harbored by white Americans. Whether the characterizations presented a more objectionable stereotype than those of *Sanford and Son* is for the sociologists to debate. In any event, it seems unlikely that *Amos and Andy* will be reshown. Its historical significance should not be overlooked: It was the first television dramatic series with an all-black cast, and the only one until *Sanford and Son* in 1971. Indeed, it was not until 1965 that a black performer (Bill Cosby) costarred as a regular in a dramatic series, *I Spy.*

AMOS BURKE, SECRET AGENT
See BURKE'S LAW

AMY PRENTISS   NBC

1 DECEMBER 1974–6 JULY 1975   One segment of the *NBC Sunday Mystery Movie,* alternating with *McCloud, Columbo,* and *McMillan and Wife.* Jessica Walter starred as widow Amy Prentiss, chief of detectives for the San Francisco police department; Art Metrano as Detective Roy Pena; Steve Sandor as Sergeant Tony Russell; and Gwenn Mitchell as Joan Carter, her secretary. Produced by Cy Chermak for Universal Television.

AND EVERYTHING NICE   DUMONT

8 MARCH 1949–9 JANUARY 1950   Maxine Barratt hosted this weekly talk show for women.

AND HERE'S THE SHOW   NBC

9 JULY 1955–24 SEPTEMBER 1955 A summer replacement for *The George Gobel Show,* this half-hour variety series was a showcase for new talent. Hosted by Ransom Sherman, it featured a young comedian named Jonathan Winters, and the Double-Daters: Stephanie Antie, Kay O'Grady, Tommy Knox, and Ted Canterbury.

THE ANDROS TARGETS   CBS

31 JANUARY 1977–9 JULY 1977 Hour adventure series about a team of investigative journalists working for the New York *Forum,* a great metropolitan daily newspaper. With James Sutorius as Mike Andros; Pamela Reed as Sandi Farrell; Roy Poole as Chet Reynolds; and Ted Beniades as Wayne Hillman. Bob Sweeney and Larry Rosen were the executive producers.

ANDY
See THE ANDY WILLIAMS SHOW

THE ANDY GRIFFITH SHOW   CBS

3 OCTOBER 1960–16 SEPTEMBER 1968 The first, and probably the best, of the rural-oriented comedies brought to TV by James C. Aubrey, then president of CBS-TV. Its success engendered later hits such as *The Beverly Hillbillies, Petticoat Junction,* and *Green Acres,* as well as *Gomer Pyle, U.S.M.C.,* a spinoff. It starred Andy Griffith, a low-key comedian from North Carolina who had starred in "No Time for Sergeants" on *The U.S. Steel Hour* and later on Broadway. Here, Griffith played widower Andy Taylor, sheriff of Mayberry, North Carolina; Don Knotts (1960–1965) as his cousin Barney Fife, the zealous but inept deputy sheriff; six-year-old Ronny Howard as Opie, Andy's son; Frances Bavier as Andy's aunt, Bee Taylor, who lived in and helped care for Opie. The townspeople included Jim Nabors (1960–1964) as Gomer Pyle, gas pump jockey; Howard McNear as Floyd Lawson, the barber; Paul Hartman as Emmet Clark, a handyman; Jack Dodson as Howard Sprague, the town clerk; Elinor Donahue (1960–1961) as Elly Walker, drugstore salesclerk; Betty Lynn as Thelma Lou, Barney's girlfriend; Aneta Corsaut (1964–1967) as schoolteacher Helen Crump, Andy's girlfriend; Hal Smith as Otis Campbell, the town drunk.

When Nabors left in 1964 for his own series *(Gomer Pyle),* George Lindsey joined the cast as Goober Pyle, Gomer's cousin. In 1965, Knotts, who had won five Emmys for his portrayal of Deputy Fife, left the series; it was explained that Fife became a detective in Raleigh. Replacing him as deputy was Warren Ferguson, played by Jack Burns. By 1968 Griffith, too, had decided to leave the series. During the last season Andy Taylor married Helen Crump. Joining the cast were Ken Berry as farmer and town councilman Sam Jones, and Arlene Golonka as Millie Hutchins.

After Griffith's departure the series continued for three more seasons as *Mayberry, R.F.D.* (see that title). *The Andy Griffith Show* was syndicated as *Andy of Mayberry.*

THE ANDY WILLIAMS SHOW   NBC/ABC/CBS/SYNDICATED

2 JULY 1957–5 SEPTEMBER 1957 (NBC); 3 JULY 1958–25 SEPTEMBER 1958 (ABC); 7 JULY 1959–22 SEPTEMBER 1959 (CBS); 27 SEPTEMBER 1962–3 SEPTEMBER 1967 (NBC); 20 SEPTEMBER 1969–17 JULY 1971 (NBC); 1976 (SYNDICATED)   Singer Andy Williams began his musical career in his teens as one of the Four Williams Brothers, who sang behind Kay Thompson. The group disbanded in 1952, and in 1954 Williams became a featured vocalist on the *Tonight* show, joining Steve Lawrence and Eydie Gormé. In 1957 he appeared in the first of several shows that bear his name; *The Andy Williams-June Valli Show* was a twice-weekly, fifteen-minute series, a summer replacement for *The Jonathan Winters Show* and *The Dinah Shore Show.* June Valli, Williams's co-host, had been a winner on Arthur Godfrey's *Talent Scouts* and had been featured on *Your Hit Parade* and *Stop the Music;* she and Williams had appeared together in "Five Stars for Springtime," a 1957 NBC special.

In 1958 Williams's show, titled *The Chevy Showroom,* was a summer replacement for *The Pat Boone Show;* Dick Van Dyke and the Bob Hamilton Trio were regulars. In 1959 Williams moved to his third network and his third summer series, a replacement for *The Garry Moore Show.* In 1962, Williams was finally given a fall series on NBC; the hour show lasted five seasons and featured The New Christy Minstrels and the Osmond Brothers. His third NBC series, which premiered in 1969, featured comics Charlie Callas and Irwin Corey, along with Janos Prohaska (as the Cookie Bear); the hour show lasted another two seasons. In 1976 Williams hosted a syndicated series, entitled *Andy.* The half-hour show featured puppeteer Wayland Flowers; Pierre Cossette was the executive producer.

ANDY'S GANG   NBC

20 AUGUST 1955–31 DECEMBER 1960   *Andy's Gang* was the successor to *Smilin' Ed's Gang* and was so retitled when gravel-voiced Andy Devine took over as host following the death of Smilin' Ed McConnell. The rest of the gang remained with the show, including Midnight the Cat, Squeaky the Mouse, and the mischievous Froggy the Gremlin ("Plunk your magic twanger, Froggy!"). Filmed sequences were also part of the program; the adventures of Gunga Ram, an Indian boy, were often shown, starring Nino Marcel as Gunga.

ANGEL   CBS

6 OCTOBER 1960–20 SEPTEMBER 1961   Domestic sticom about an American architect married to a Frenchwoman. With Marshall Thomp-

son as Johnny Smith; Annie Farge as Angel Smith; Doris Singleton as neighbor Susie; and Don Keefer as Susie's husband George. Produced by Jess Oppenheimer.

ANGIE   ABC
8 FEBRUARY 1979–   Half-hour sitcom about a Philadelphia waitress who met and married a wealthy pediatrician. With Donna Pescow as Angie Falco, a waitress at the Liberty Coffee Shop; Robert Hays as Dr. Brad Benson; Sharon Spelman as Joyce Benson, Brad's thrice-divorced and insufferable older sister; Tammy Lauren (spring 1979) as Hillary, Joyce's daughter; Debralee Scott as Marie Falco, Angie's younger sister; Diane Robin as waitress DiDi Malloy; and Doris Roberts as Angie's mother, Theresa Falco, a newsstand operator. Executive producers: Dale McRaven and Bob Ellison for Paramount TV.

ANIMAL CLINIC   ABC
19 AUGUST 1950–13 JANUARY 1951   This early Saturday morning series focused on animal care and behavior. Broadcast from Chicago, it was hosted by a veterinarian, Dr. Wesley A. Young, who was assisted by trainer Oscar Franzen and Don Driscoll.

ANIMAL SECRETS   NBC
15 OCTOBER 1966–8 APRIL 1967   Half-hour documentary series on animal behavior, hosted by Loren C. Eisley.

ANIMAL WORLD (ANIMAL KINGDOM)   NBC/CBS/ABC/SYNDICATED
16 JUNE 1968–1 SEPTEMBER 1968 (NBC); 8 MAY 1969–18 SEPTEMBER 1969 (CBS); 30 APRIL 1970–17 SEPTEMBER 1970 (ABC); 11 JULY 1971–12 SEPTEMBER 1971 (CBS); 1973–   (SYNDICATED)   Narrated by Bill Burrud, *Animal World* was a series of half-hour wildlife documentaries which frequently found its way onto network schedules as a summer replacement. Since 1973 the show has been available in syndication. Charles Sutton was the executive producer for Bill Burrud Productions, Inc.

ANIMALS, ANIMALS, ANIMALS   ABC
12 SEPTEMBER 1976–   This Sunday-morning show about animals is narrated by Hal Linden, star of *Barney Miller.*

THE ANN SOTHERN SHOW   CBS
6 OCTOBER 1958–25 SEPTEMBER 1961   A new format for Ann Sothern, last seen as Susie, a private secretary. In this sitcom Sothern played Kathleen (Katy) O'Connor, assistant manager of the Bartley House, a New York hotel. The original cast included Ernest Truex as Jason McCauley,

the manager; Ann Tyrrell as Olive Smith, Katy's secretary; Jack Mullaney as Johnny Wallace, the bellhop; Jacques Scott as Paul Martine, the desk clerk; and Reta Shaw as Flora McCauley. In March 1959 all the cast members except for Tyrrell were jettisoned, and virtually the entire cast from the old *Private Secretary* series was brought in: Don Porter as James Devery, the manager; Ken Berry as Woody, the bellhop; Louis Nye (1960–1961) as Dr. Delbert Gray, the hotel dentist; and Jesse White as Oscar Pudney, the newsstand operator.

ANNA AND THE KING   CBS
17 SEPTEMBER 1972– 31 DECEMBER 1972   Anna Leonowens's true-life adventures in nineteenth-century Siam were the subject of a book, a play, and two films before this television series. Despite lavish sets (including backdrops from the 1956 film, *The King and I*) and the presence of Yul Brynner (recreating his film role), the show went nowhere. With Yul Brynner as the King of Siam; Samantha Eggar as Anna Owens, the American schoolteacher hired by the King to educate his children; Keye Luke as Kralahome, the King's officious aide; Eric Shea as Louis, Anna's son; Brian Tochi as Prince Chula, the crown prince; and Lisa Lu as Lady Thiang, the King's number-one wife.

ANNIE OAKLEY   SYNDICATED
1952–1956   Children's western, set in the town of Diablo. With Gail Davis as Annie Oakley, gun-toting rancher; Brad Johnson as Sheriff Lofty Craig; and Jimmy Hawkins as Tagg, Annie's kid brother. Shelley Fabares, later to star in *The Donna Reed Show,* appeared occasionally. Davis, a skilled rider (her horse was called Target) and a crack shot, did most of her own stunt work. The series, the first western to star a woman, was produced by Gene Autry's Flying A Productions.

THE ANNIVERSARY GAME   SYNDICATED
1970   Al Hamel hosted this game show which featured three married couples. Most of the games involved one person attempting to predict whether his or her spouse would successfully perform a stunt.

ANOTHER DAY   CBS
8 APRIL 1978–29 APRIL 1978   Domestic sitcom about a married couple, both of whom held down full-time jobs, their two children, and her mother-in-law. With David Groh as Don Gardner, an advertising executive; Joan Hackett as Ginny Gardner, who worked at an insurance company; Hope Summers as Don's live-in mother, Olive Gardner; Lisa Lindgren as their daughter, Kelly; and Al Eisenmann as their son, Mark. Created by James Komack, the half-hour series was produced by Paul Mason. Paul Williams composed and sang the show's theme.

ANOTHER WORLD   NBC

4 MAY 1964–   Another of the several successful serials created by Irna Phillips, *Another World* has made history: In 1970 it became
the first soap opera to engender a spinoff (though the offspring, *Somerset,*
bore little resemblance to the parent), and on 6 January 1975 it became
the first soap opera to expand to a full hour. (*Days of Our Lives, As the
World Turns, All My Children, The Guiding Light, General Hospital,* and
One Life to Live later followed suit.) *Another World* has consistently
ranked among the top-rated daytime serials, and in general, its story lines
have emphasized psychological themes; as Irna Phillips explained in an
interview, the serial depicts the difference between "the world of events
we live in and the world of feelings and dreams that we strive for." Phillips left the series late in the 1960s and was succeeded by Robert Cene-
della and Agnes Nixon; Harding Lemay was the head writer during most
of the 1970s, and Robert Rauch has produced the show for Procter and
Gamble. *Another World* is set in Bay City, and the large cast has included: John Beal (1964), Leon Janney (1964–1965), Shepperd Strudwick
(1965–1970), and Hugh Marlowe (1970–   ) as accountant Jim Matthews, husband and father of three children; Virginia Dwyer (1964–1975)
as his wife, Mary Matthews; Susan Trustman (1964–1966) and Beverly
Penberthy (1966–   ) as their elder daughter, Pat Matthews; Joey
Trent (1964–1967), Sam Groom, Bob Hover, and David Bailey as their
son, Dr. Russ Matthews; Jacqueline Courtney (1964–1976) and Susan
Harney (1976–   ) as their younger daughter, Alice Matthews; Sara
Cunningham (1964), Audra Lindley (1964–1970), Nancy Wickwire
(1970–1973), and Irene Dailey (1973–   ) as Jim and Mary's sister-in-
law, Liz Matthews (in the first scene on the 1964 premiere Liz, whose
husband had just died, was in tears); Joe Gallison (1964–1968) as Liz's
son, lawyer Bill Matthews, who drowned in 1968; Liza Chapman as
Liz's daughter, Janet Matthews; Fran Sharon and Lisa Cameron as Liz's
daughter, Susan Matthews; Vera Allen as Grandma Matthews; Nicholas
Pryor as Pat Matthews's boyfriend, Tom Baxter, who talked her into
having an abortion and was later killed by her; William Prince as Ken
Baxter; Michael Ryan as lawyer John Randolph, who defended Pat and
later married her (they were divorced in 1976); Ariane Munker (to 1976)
and Adrienne Wallace (1977–   ) as Marianne Randolph, daughter of
John and Pat; Gaye Huston and Barbara Rodell as John's daughter from
a previous marriage, Lee Randolph, who got into LSD and died in a car
crash; Gary Pillar as lawyer Mike Bauer (visiting from another Irna Phillips's serial, *The Guiding Light*), a colleague of John's; Carol Roux as
Melinda Palmer, who was also accused of murder and was defended by
Bill Matthews, whom she later married; Antony Ponzini as Danny Fargo, a smalltime crook who had been married to Melissa; Constance Ford
as Ada Davis Downs; Harry Bellaver as her second husband, Ernie
Downs; Jordan Charney as Ada's brother, Sam Lucas; Ann

Wedgeworth as Lahoma Vane, who married Sam (Sam and Lahoma later moved to *Somerset* when that spinoff was created); Robin Strasser, Margaret Impert, and Victoria Wyndham as Rachel Davis, Ada's daughter, who married Russ Matthews and later divorced him; George Reinholt (1968–1975) as Steven Frame, who married Alice Matthews, then married Rachel Davis, and then remarried Alice before his death in a helicopter accident; Victoria Thompson and Christine Jones as Janice Frame, Steven's sister; John Fitzpatrick and Leon Russom (1977–) as Willis Frame, Steven's brother; Charles Baxter as Fred Douglas, who married Susan; Robert Milli as Wayne Addison, who was interested in Liz Matthews; Val Dufour as District Attorney Walter Curtin, who killed Wayne Addison; Judith Barcroft as Lenore Moore Curtin, Walter's wife, who was indicted for Addison's murder; Scott Firestone and Dennis McKiernan as Wally Curtin, son of Walter and Lenore; Muriel Williams as Helen Moore, Lenore's mother; Janice Young as Bernice Addison; Bobby Doran and Tim Holcum (1978–) as Jamie Frame, son of Rachel and Steven Frame; Steven Bolster as Ted Clark, who became Rachel's second husband; Leonie Norton as nurse Cindy Clark, Ted's sister, who married Russ Matthews on her deathbed; Walter Matthews as Gerald Davis, Rachel's father; Janet Ward as Belle Clark; Beverly Owen as Dr. Paula McCrae; James Douglas as writer Eliot Carrington; Beverlee McKinsey as Iris Carrington, his estranged wife; Michael Hammett and Jim Poyner (1978–) as Dennis Carrington, Iris's son; Donald Madden as Dr. Kurt Landis, Iris's boyfriend; Anne Meacham as Iris's secretary, Louise Goddard; Nick Coster as architect Robert Delaney, who married Lenore Curtin and later married Iris Carrington; Robert Emhardt and Douglass Watson as Mac Cory, father of Iris Carrington, who became Rachel Davis's fourth husband; Charles Durning and Dolph Sweet as Lieutenant Gil McGowan, who married Rachel's mother, Ada Davis Downs; Chris Allport as Tim McGowan; Doris Belack as Madge Murray, a friend of Ada's; Ann Sheridan as Cathryn Corning, mother of Melinda Palmer; Colgate Salisbury as David Thornton, a friend of Lee Randolph's; Beverlee McKinsey (who later played Iris Carrington) and Tresa Hughes as Emmy Ordway, older sister of Steven Frame; Jeanne Lange as architect Carol Lamont; John Getz as her coworker, Neil Johnson; John Considine, Jr., as lawyer Vic Hastings; Roberta Maxwell and Kathryn Walker as lawyer Barbara Weaver; Cathy Greene as Sally Spencer, adopted daughter of the widowed Alice Matthews Frame; Jacqueline Brooks as Sally's grandmother, Beatrice Gordon, housekeeper for Mac and Rachel Cory; Ted Shackelford and Gary Carpenter as Beatrice's son, Raymond Gordon, who fell in love with Alice Frame; David Ackroyd as Dr. David Gilchrist; Gail Brown as Clarice Hobson; Ralph Camargo as Judge Merrill; Toni Kalem and Maeve Kinkead as Angie Perini; Christopher J. Brown and Lionel Johnston as Michael Randolph; Robert Kya-Hill as Frank Chadwick; Micki Grant as Peggy Nolan; Andrew Jarkowsky as Mark Venable; Vera Moore as Linda Metcalf; Rosetta Le-Noire as Mrs. Metcalf; James Preston as Ray Scott; Terry Alexander as Zach Richards; Jane Alice Brandon as Harriet Sullivan; William Roerick as Dr. Richard Gavin; James Luisi as Phil Wainwright; John Braden as Rocky Olson; Maia Danziger as Glenda Toland; Michael Goodwin and Paul Tulley as Scott Bradley; Rob Gibbons as Mel Lafferty; Elaine Kerr as Loretta Simpson; Laurie Heinemann as Sharlene Watts Matthews; Caroline McWilliams as Tracy DeWitt; Kelly Monaghan as Ken Palmer; Anna Shaler as Phyllis; Karin Wolfe as Pam Sloan; Dorothy Blackburn as Louella Watson; Jennifer Leak as Olive Gordon; Rolanda Mendels as Molly Ordway; Roberts Blossom as Sven Petersen; Pamela Brook as Corinne Seton; Danielle Jean Burns as Nancy McGowan; Richard Dunne as Daryll Stevens; Dan Hamilton as Jeff Stone; Carol Mayo Jenkins as Vera Finley; Barry Jenner as Evan Webster; Dorothy Lyman as Gwen Parrish; Joseph Maher and John Tillenger as Brooks; Eric Roberts as Ted Bancroft; Paul Stevens as Brian Bancroft; William Russ and Joe Hindy as Burt McGowan; Helen Stenborg as Helga Lindemann; Barbara Eda-Young as Regine Lindemann; Patricia Estrin as Joan Barnard; Ned Schmidtke as Greg Barnard; Jay Ingram as Cal Zimmerman; Arthur E. Jones as Claude Kelley; Lynn Lowry as Doris Bennett; Lynn Milgrim as Susan Shearer; Jay Morran as Vince (Otis) Frame; Christina Pickles as Countess Elena DePoulignac; Tom Rolfing as Cliff Tanner; Fred J. Scollay as Charlie Hobson; Peter Ratray as Quentin Ames; Vicky Dawson as Eileen Sampson; Ray Liotta as Joey Perrini; Kathleen Widdoes as Rose Perrini; Laurie Bartram as Karen Campbell; Eric Conger as Buzz Winslow; Leora Dana as Sylvie Kosloff; Robert Gibson as Ray Barry; Trish Hawkins as Mimi; Laura Malone as Blaine Frame; Brian Murray as Dan Shearer; Gretchen Oehler as Vivian; Rick Porter as Larry Ewing.

On 5 March 1979 *Another World* again made soap opera history when it became the first serial to expand to ninety minutes a day.

ANSWER YES OR NO   NBC
30 APRIL 1950–23 JULY 1950 Playwright Moss Hart hosted this Sunday-night game show on which a celebrity panel tried to predict whether contestants would answer yes or no to getting involved in a hypothetical situation.

ANSWERS FOR AMERICANS   ABC
11 NOVEMBER 1953–24 FEBRUARY 1954 Wednesday-evening public affairs show, moderated by Deven Garrity. The panel included General Frank Howley, Professor John K. Norton, and Hardy Burt.

ANYBODY CAN PLAY (ANYONE CAN PLAY)   ABC
6 JULY 1958–8 DECEMBER 1958 George Fenneman hosted this night-time game show on which four contestants sought to identify a hidden

object. The show was originally entitled *Anybody Can Play* and, for reasons unknown, was retitled *Anyone Can Play*.

ANYONE CAN WIN CBS
14 JULY 1953–1 SEPTEMBER 1953 Al Capp hosted this prime-time game show, which was seen biweekly for most of its short run. On each show four celebrity panelists competed in a question-and-answer segment; three of the celebs were fully visible to viewers, while the fourth wore the mask of a Capp cartoon character, Hairless Joe. Members of the studio audience could back any of the celebrities; those who backed the panelist who correctly answered the most questions split $2,000 among themselves. Periodically through the show, calls were placed to home viewers, who were given the opportunity to identify the masked panelist.

ANYWHERE, U.S.A. ABC
9 NOVEMBER 1952–14 DECEMBER 1952 A lighthearted look at health and nutrition, hosted by Eddie Dowling.

APPLE PIE ABC
23 SEPTEMBER 1978–7 OCTOBER 1978 Half-hour sitcom, set in 1933 in Kansas City, about a woman who put together a "family" by placing classified ads in the newspaper. With Rue McClanahan as Ginger-Nell Hollyhock, a hairdresser; Jack Gilford as the blind and feisty Grandpa; Caitlin O'Heaney as the daughter, Anna Marie; Derrel Maury as the son, Junior; and Dabney Coleman as Eddie Murtaugh, the man of the house. Charlie Hauck produced this short-lived show for Norman Lear's T. A. T. Communications.

APPLE'S WAY CBS
10 FEBRUARY 1974–12 JANUARY 1975 A Los Angeles architect returns to his hometown (Appleton, Iowa) with his family. With Ronny Cox as George Apple; Frances Lee McCain as Barbara Apple; Vincent Van Patten as son Paul; Patti Cohoon as daughter Cathy; Franny Michel (February 1974–September 1974) and Kristy McNichol (September 1974– January 1975) as daughter Patricia; Eric Olson as son Steven; and Malcolm Atterbury as Grandpa (Alden Apple). Created by Earl Hamner, the series was supposed to be a contemporary version of *The Waltons*. Executive producers: Lee Rich and Earl Hamner.

APPOINTMENT WITH ADVENTURE CBS
3 APRIL 1955–1 APRIL 1956 Half-hour dramatic anthology series.

THE AQUANAUTS CBS
14 SEPTEMBER 1960–22 FEBRUARY 1961 Ivan Tors, producer of *Sea Hunt*, produced this hour-long adventure series which featured not one,

but two divers. Originally featured were Keith Larsen as Drake Andrews and Jeremy Slate as Larry Lahr. A sinus operation necessitated Larsen's withdrawal from the show in midseason, and he was replaced by Ron Ely, as Mike Madison, on 25 January. It was explained that Drake Andrews had decided to rejoin the Navy. Charles Thompson was occasionally featured as the Captain. In March the show's format and title were changed (see *Malibu Run*).

ARA'S SPORTS WORLD SYNDICATED
1976 Sports series hosted by Ara Parseghian, former football coach at Notre Dame.

ARCHER NBC
30 JANUARY 1975–13 MARCH 1975 Brian Keith starred as Lew Archer, the private eye created by Ross Macdonald. With John P. Ryan as Lieutenant Barney Brighton. Executive producer: David Carp. Produced by Jack Miller and Leonard B. Kaufman. The pilot for the series, "The Underground Man," was televised 6 May 1974 on NBC.

THE ARCHIE SHOW CBS
14 SEPTEMBER 1968–30 AUGUST 1969
THE ARCHIE COMEDY HOUR CBS
6 SEPTEMBER 1969–5 SEPTEMBER 1970
ARCHIE'S FUNHOUSE CBS
12 SEPTEMBER 1970–4 SEPTEMBER 1971
ARCHIE'S TV FUNNIES CBS
11 SEPTEMBER 1971–1 SEPTEMBER 1973
EVERYTHING'S ARCHIE CBS
8 SEPTEMBER 1973–26 JANUARY 1974
THE U.S. OF ARCHIE CBS
7 SEPTEMBER 1974–5 SEPTEMBER 1976
THE NEW ARCHIE SABRINA HOUR NBC
10 SEPTEMBER 1977–12 NOVEMBER 1977
THE BANG-SHANG LALAPALOOZA SHOW NBC
19 NOVEMBER 1977–28 JANUARY 1978 Bob Montana's cartoon high schoolers have been a fixture on Saturday-morning TV for a decade, though the gang—including Archie Andrews, Jughead Jones, Veronica Lodge, Betty Cooper, and all the rest—have been featured in a different format almost every season. The early years of the series emphasized music, and the Archies (as the assemblage of anonymous studio musicians was called) released several records; one, "Sugar Sugar," was a monster hit. After one season *The Archie Show,* a half-hour vehicle that introduced the Riverdale revelers to television, gave way to *The Archie Comedy Hour.* Archie and his pals now shared space with Sabrina, the teenage witch. (In later years, Sabrina would be featured in her own shows, and

even later would be reunited with Archie in a joint hour.) In 1970, *Archie's Funhouse,* back to a half hour, premiered (Sabrina had gone off to her own show with the Groovie Goolies). A year later came *Archie's TV Funnies,* a half-hour show in which Archie and the crew ran a television station. This was the first format which lasted more than one season. It was replaced by *Everything's Archie,* which in turn was replaced by *The U.S. of Archie* in 1974, as the group prepared for the Bicentennial. After a season's absence (1976–1977), Archie returned in 1977 on NBC, in *The New Archie Sabrina Hour.* Archie and Sabrina parted company again after only a few weeks, as the hour was broken into two half-hour shows, *The Bang-Shang Lalapalooza Show* (featuring the Archie gang) and *Super Witch* (featuring Sabrina). Both were dropped in midseason.

ARCHIE BUNKER'S PLACE
See ALL IN THE FAMILY

ARE YOU POSITIVE   NBC
6 JULY 1952–24 AUGUST 1952   Bill Stern first hosted this Sunday game show, on which sports personalities tried to guess the identities of other famous athletes from blownup negatives. Stern was succeeded by Frank Coniff late in July.

ARK II   CBS
11 SEPTEMBER 1976–13 NOVEMBER 1977; 16 SEPTEMBER 1978–25 AUGUST 1979   Weekend daytime series for children, set in the twenty-fifth century, in which the Ark II, a traveling repository of scientific knowledge, and its youthful crew attempted to save a civilization ravaged by global war and ecological plunder. Its mission: "To bring the hope of a new future to mankind." With Terry Lester as Jonah, the captain; Jean Marie Hon as Ruth; José Flores as Samuel; and Adam the talking chimp.

THE ARLENE FRANCIS SHOW   NBC
12 AUGUST 1957–21 FEBRUARY 1958   The successor to *Home,* the ambitious magazine of the air hosted by Arlene Francis. This thirty-minute daytime show was a blend of chitchat and features.

ARMCHAIR DETECTIVE   CBS
6 JULY 1949–28 SEPTEMBER 1949   John Milton Kennedy hosted this early game show in which studio contestants tried to solve mysteries acted out on stage.

THE ARMED FORCES HOUR   NBC/DUMONT
30 OCTOBER 1949–11 JUNE 1950 (NBC); 4 FEBRUARY 1951–6 MAY 1951 (DUMONT)   One of the first television series supplied by the United States government, *The Armed Forces Hour* was produced by the Depart-

ment of Defense. Broadcast from Washington, it emphasized the process of the unification of the separate service branches. Segments were culled from the estimated 500 million feet of film already on hand. Production of the series (which, despite its title, was only a thirty-minute show) was supervised by Major Robert P. Keim (USAF) and Lieutenant Benjamin S. Greenberg (USNR) of the Public Information Office of the Department of Defense.

ARMSTRONG CIRCLE THEATER (CIRCLE THEATER) NBC/CBS
6 JUNE 1950–25 JUNE 1957 (NBC); 2 OCTOBER 1957–28 AUGUST 1963 (CBS) This high-quality anthology series specialized in dramatizations of actual events, but a few documentaries were also broadcast. It began as a half-hour weekly series and was more commonly known as the *Circle Theater*. In 1955, a one-hour format was adopted, and the series began a biweekly run, alternating with *Playwrights '56* (1955–1956), *The Kaiser Aluminum Hour* (1956–1957), and on CBS, *The U.S. Steel Hour* (1957–1963). John Cameron Swayze hosted the show on NBC, Douglas Edwards, Ron Cochran and Henry Hamilton on CBS. David Susskind served as executive producer for several seasons. Many stars played their first major television dramatic roles in this series, including John Cassavetes ("Ladder of Lies," 1 February 1955); Robert Duvall ("The Jailbreak," 14 October 1959); Anne Jackson ("Johnny Pickup," 28 August 1951); and Telly Savalas ("House of Cards," 18 February 1959).

ARNIE CBS
19 SEPTEMBER 1970–9 SEPTEMBER 1972 The story of a loading dock foreman who is suddenly named Director of Product Improvement at Continental Flange became a run-of-the-mill sitcom that barely lasted two seasons. With Herschel Bernardi as new executive Arnie Nuvo; Sue Ane Langdon as Lillian, his wife; Stephanie Steele as teenage daughter Andrea; Del Russel as teenage son Richard; Roger Bowen as Hamilton Majors, Jr., top banana at Continental Flange; Herb Voland as Neil Oglivie, company VP; Olan Soule as executive Fred Springer; Tom Pedi as Julius, Arnie's pal from the loading dock; and Charles Nelson Reilly (1971–1972) as next-door neighbor Randy Robinson (TV's "Giddyap Gourmet").

AROUND THE TOWN NBC
7 JANUARY 1950–18 FEBRUARY 1950 Not to be confused with CBS' *All Around the Town,* this Saturday-night series was emceed by Bob Stanton and was broadcast from various locations in New York City.

AROUND THE WORLD IN 80 DAYS NBC
9 SEPTEMBER 1972–1 SEPTEMBER 1973 Saturday-morning cartoon show based loosely on the Jules Verne novel. Produced in Australia.

ARREST AND TRIAL ABC
15 SEPTEMBER 1963–6 SEPTEMBER 1964   A ninety-minute crime show, with half the show spent catching the crook and half spent convicting him. With Ben Gazzara as Sergeant Nick Anderson; Chuck Connors as Public Defender John Egan; John Larch as Prosecutor Jerry Miller; Roger Perry as Detective Kirby; and Noah Keen as Bone.

THE ARROW SHOW NBC
17 DECEMBER 1948–19 MAY 1949   Phil Silvers first hosted this Thursday-night half-hour variety show, until he landed a starring role in the Broadway musical, *High Button Shoes.* Hank Ladd succeeded Silvers as host. Rod Erickson produced the series.

THE ART FORD SHOW (IN RECORD TIME) NBC
4 AUGUST 1951–15 SEPTEMBER 1951   On this summer replacement for *One Man's Family,* a celebrity quiz was sandwiched around musical numbers. New York disc jockey Art Ford hosted the series.

THE ART LINKLETTER SHOW NBC
18 FEBRUARY 1963–16 SEPTEMBER 1963   Half-hour prime-time show hosted by Art Linkletter on which celebrity guests attempted to predict the outcome of a situation shown on film, performed either by unsuspecting participants or by the Art Linkletter Players. Some segments involved audience participation. Linkletter was one of the few personalities to have hosted series simultaneously on two networks: Both this series and Linkletter's earlier *People Are Funny* were seen on NBC, while *Art Linkletter's House Party* enjoyed a long run on CBS.

ART LINKLETTER'S HOUSE PARTY (THE LINKLETTER SHOW) CBS
1 SEPTEMBER 1952–5 SEPTEMBER 1969   Television's longest-running daytime variety show began on radio in 1944. When the easygoing Linkletter first brought his blend of talk and audience participation to television, it was aired at 2:45 p.m. (EST). By February 1953, it had been moved back to the 2:30 p.m. slot, where it remained for fifteen years. In 1968 the show was retitled *The Linkletter Show* and given a morning slot. During its first TV season the sound portion was replayed on CBS radio immediately following the telecast. The most memorable feature of the series was the daily interview with four young schoolchildren, who were seated on a raised platform. Their "unrehearsed" remarks were the fodder for a series of books by Linkletter, the first of which was *Kids Say the Darndest Things.*

ARTHUR GODFREY AND HIS FRIENDS CBS
12 JANUARY 1949–26 JUNE 1957

ARTHUR GODFREY AND HIS UKULELE CBS

4 APRIL 1950–30 JUNE 1950

ARTHUR GODFREY TIME CBS

7 JANUARY 1952–24 APRIL 1959

THE ARTHUR GODFREY SHOW CBS

23 SEPTEMBER 1958–28 APRIL 1959   Born in 1903, Arthur Godfrey began his broadcasting career on radio in 1930 at the CBS affiliate in Washington, D.C. Before long he was working for CBS radio in New York. During those years he developed his easygoing, straightforward, low-key style; his show, a blend of musical numbers and relaxed comedy, was a perennial hit. Godfrey had little discernible talent; though he could pluck the ukulele a bit, he was neither an accomplished singer nor a skilled actor. But he was a shrewd judge of commercial talent, a superb salesman, and a hard worker; these qualities helped make him an effective catalyst on the air.

In 1948 Godfrey entered television as the host of *Talent Scouts,* a long-running Monday-night showcase for amateur and professional talent. He soon became one of the most popular—and ubiquitous—personalities on television. Early in 1949 he could also be seen on Wednesday nights, hosting *Arthur Godfrey and His Friends,* an hour-long variety series which lasted eight seasons. For a brief period in 1950 Godfrey hosted a third prime-time series, *Arthur Godfrey and His Ukulele,* a fifteen-minute show seen after the news on Tuesday evenings. During the entire period the seemingly inexhaustible Godfrey continued to do a daytime radio show.

Beginning in 1952 the hour-long Monday-through-Thursday daytime radio show—*Arthur Godfrey Time*—was televised. Godfrey was again hosting three television series. Though he maintained that hectic pace for several seasons, Godfrey was often in great pain. A 1931 auto accident left him with injuries from which he never fully recovered: a broken pelvis, two broken kneecaps, one broken hip, and one permanently damaged hip. Godfrey's bouts with pain and depression have been cited as a cause of his mercurial temperament and as a reason for the fact that few of his stage "Friends" remained with the show for long, other than announcer Tony Marvin.

A large number of "Friends" shared the stage with Godfrey over the years: Carmel Quinn, Janette Davis, Bill Lawrence, Julius LaRosa, Marion Marlowe, Frank Parker, LuAnn Simms, Haleloke, The McGuire Sisters (Phyllis, Christine, and Dorothy), The Chordettes, The Mariners (one of the few integrated vocal groups that regularly appeared on TV), Pat Boone, Anita Bryant, and Johnny Nash, to name only a few. Many, like Boone, Nash, and the McGuire Sisters, were discovered on *Talent Scouts* and later joined the Godfrey troupe (the regulars appeared on both *Arthur Godfrey and His Friends* and on *Arthur Godfrey Time*). Several left voluntarily to pursue solo careers; some were quietly fired by the boss. But only one—LaRosa—was fired publicly, in what was one of the most widely publicized incidents in television history.

Julius LaRosa, a kid who could sing, was in the Navy when Godfrey heard him during a visit to Pensacola, Florida. Impressed with LaRosa, Godfrey arranged for him to come to New York in the fall of 1951. After LaRosa's second appearance on the show (Christmas 1951), Godfrey announced to his viewers that when "Julie" left the Navy, he could go to work for Godfrey. By the spring of 1952 LaRosa was a regular, and a popular one. His television exposure helped launch a recording career: His first record, "Anywhere I Wander," released in January 1953, sold 750,000 copies. By the middle of 1953 LaRosa's fan mail outstripped Godfrey's.

Meanwhile, Godfrey was sidelined with a hip operation. When he returned to the show in the fall, he detected an aura of laziness and cockiness among some of his regulars. The first of the last straws came when LaRosa missed a ballet rehearsal (upon his return, Godfrey had ordered ballet lessons for the cast); Godfrey abruptly yanked LaRosa from the next day's broadcast. LaRosa, understandably upset and unable to reach Godfrey directly, deepened his own grave by hiring an agent (Godfrey didn't deal with agents).

On Monday, October 19, 1953, the boom was lowered on an unsuspecting LaRosa. Godfrey brought LaRosa on for the last spot on the morning show. After innocuously asking whether LaRosa thought doing the show "was a pain in the neck," he bade him do his song. At the conclusion of the number, Godfrey announced, "That, folks, was Julie's swan song," and closed the show. LaRosa is reported to have been unaware that he'd just been fired, because he didn't know what "swan song" meant. Later that week, Godfrey also fired his musical director, Archie Bleyer, who was a partner with LaRosa in a record company. Bleyer was replaced by Paul Farber.

At that time Godfrey's popularity was probably at its zenith. In his book, *CBS: Reflections in a Bloodshot Eye,* Robert Metz states that the Godfrey shows generated 12 percent of CBS's television revenues. After the LaRosa incident, however, Godfrey's popularity began to slip. The press had a field day; at a press conference Godfrey said that LaRosa had shown "a lack of humility," a statement Godfrey now regrets.

Godfrey continued his three shows until 1957, when competition from ABC's *Disneyland* knocked off *Arthur Godfrey and His Friends. Talent Scouts* lasted one more season, while *Arthur Godfrey Time* continued during the day. In the fall of 1958 Godfrey returned with a half-hour Tuesday offering, *The Arthur Godfrey Show.* In 1959 Godfrey decided to leave television when he learned he had lung cancer. In a tearful farewell to his daytime audience, Godfrey explained that he didn't want viewers to see him waste away. The operation proved successful (a lung was removed), and Godfrey returned briefly in 1960 as cohost of *Candid Camera.* He didn't last long, and he is seen infrequently nowadays. See also *Candid Camera; Talent Scouts; Your All-American College Show.*

THE ARTHUR MURRAY PARTY   ABC/DUMONT/CBS/NBC
20 JULY 1950–7 SEPTEMBER 1950 (ABC); 15 OCTOBER 1950–11 MARCH 1951 (DUMONT); 2 APRIL 1951–25 JUNE 1951 (ABC); 19 SEPTEMBER 1951–11 MAY 1952 (ABC); 11 JULY 1952–29 AUGUST 1952 (CBS); 12 OCTOBER 1952–26 APRIL 1953 (DUMONT); 28 JUNE 1953–4 OCTOBER 1953 (CBS); 12 OCTOBER 1953–12 APRIL 1954 (NBC); 15 JUNE 1954–14 SEPTEMBER 1954 (NBC); 28 JUNE 1955–13 SEPTEMBER 1955 (NBC); 5 APRIL 1956–27 SEPTEMBER 1956 (CBS); 9 APRIL 1957–16 SEPTEMBER 1957 (NBC); 29 SEPTEMBER 1958–6 SEPTEMBER 1960 (NBC)   One of the handful of shows broadcast over all four major commercial networks, *The Arthur Murray Party* most often surfaced as a summer replacement series, sometimes as a half-hour show and sometimes as a full hour. Ballroom dancing was the subject of the show, which was hosted by Kathryn Murray, wife of Arthur Murray, founder of the dancing schools which bear his name. Most shows featured songs, comedy sketches, and dance contests.

AS THE WORLD TURNS   CBS
2 APRIL 1956–   *As the World Turns* and *The Edge of Night,* which premiered the same day, were daytime television's first thirty-minute serials. *World* was created by Irna Phillips, the prolific writer whose career began in radio and who was responsible for *The Guiding Light* and *The Brighter Day,* as well as many other soaps. For much of its run *World* has been the highest rated daytime show; its success spawned a short-lived prime-time serial, *Our Private World,* which failed to catch on as ABC's *Peyton Place* had a season earlier. Ted Corday produced the series for many years. Joe Willmore currently produces it, and Walter Gorman directs. Irna Phillips wrote for the show during its first few years and returned to it in 1972. She continued to write for it until shortly before her death in 1974. Robert Soderberg and Edith Sommer are now the head writers. On 1 December 1975, *World* expanded to a full hour.

Set in the Midwestern town of Oakdale, *World* originally contrasted two families: the middle-class Hughes family and the upwardly mobile Lowells. Today, almost all of the Lowells have been written out of the show, but most of the Hughes clan remains in Oakdale. When *World* unfolded in 1956, viewers were introduced to the main characters: Chris and Nancy Hughes and their three children (Don, Penny, and Bob); Jim and Claire Lowell and their daughter, Ellen, best friend of Penny Hughes. Featured were Don MacLaughlin as lawyer Chris Hughes and Helen Wagner as his wife, Nancy; MacLaughlin and Wagner are the only original cast members remaining as of 1980. Also featured were Hal Studer, Richard Holland, Jim Noble, Peter Brandon, Martin West and

Conrad Fowkes as Don Hughes; Rosemary Prinz as Penny Hughes (written out of the show in 1967); Bobby Alford, Ronnie Welch, and Don Hastings (formerly the Video Ranger on *Captain Video*) as Bob Hughes. Santos Ortega played Grandpa Hughes until his death in 1976.

As the story began, the Hugheses learned that Chris's law partner, Jim Lowell (played by Les Damon), was having an affair with Chris's sister, Edith Hughes (Ruth Warrick). Jim died in 1957, and Edith later married Dr. George Frye (George Petrie). Jim's widow, Claire Lowell (played by Anne Burr until 1960, Nancy Wickwire until 1963, Jone Allison until late in 1963, and Barbara Berjer until 1968), subsequently married Dr. Doug Cassen (Nat Polen) and was again widowed. Her third marriage— to Dr. Michael Shea—ended in divorce, and Claire herself died in a car crash in 1968.

Wendy Drew and Pat Bruder have played the Lowells' daughter, Ellen. Ellen had an affair with Dr. Tim Cole (William Redfield), who died of a blood disease in 1964; custody of their child had been awarded to Dr. David Stewart (Henderson Forsythe) and his wife, Betty (Pat Benoit). Ellen was briefly imprisoned for killing the Stewarts' housekeeper, Franny Brennan (Toni Darnay); by the time of her release, Ellen could marry Dr. Stewart, for Betty had died. Ellen and David raised Ellen's son, Dan Stewart (played by Jeff Rowland, John Colenback, John Reilly, and again by John Colenback), David's son by a previous marriage, Paul Stewart (played by Steve Mines, Michael Hawkins, Marco St. John, and Dean Santoro), and a child of their own: Annie (played by Martina Deignan).

Young Dan Stewart grew up to become a doctor. After learning that Dan had had an affair with an Englishwoman, Elizabeth Talbot (Jane House), Dan's wife Susan (Marie Masters) refused to give him a divorce. Elizabeth married Dan's stepbrother, Paul, who died of a brain tumor shortly afterward. Dan finally succeeded in getting a divorce, but his marriage to the now widowed Elizabeth was brief, for she died after a fall down the stairs at home. Dan, despondent, later left Oakdale with his two daughters: Emily (nicknamed Emmy, she was his daughter by Susan and has been played by Jenny Harris) and Betsy (his daughter by Elizabeth and played by Suzanne Davidson).

Penny Hughes was first widowed in 1959, when her husband Jeff Baker (Mark Rydell) was killed in an auto accident. Sadly, Penny's second husband, a nonpracticing physician named Neil Wade (Michael Lipton), also died in a car crash. Penny eventually moved to England and adopted a Eurasian girl, Amy (played by Irene Yah-Ling Sun).

In 1960, Eileen Fulton joined the series as Lisa Miller, one of soapdom's most hated villainesses. Her first target was Bob Hughes, whom she met at college. Lisa married Bob and bore him a son, Tom. Lisa had an affair with Bruce Elliott (James Pritchett), was divorced from Bob, and left town. When she returned to Oakdale, it was learned that she had married a wealthy oldster and had been widowed. Lisa then married Dr.

Michael Shea (former husband of Claire Lowell) and bore him a son, Chuck (played by Pip Sarser, Willie Rook, and David Perkins). When Michael Shea was found murdered, Tom Hughes, Lisa's son by her first marriage, was implicated but proved to be innocent. Lisa, now widowed, tried unsuccessfully to win back Bob Hughes, her first husband, and later married lawyer Grant Colman, an associate of Chris Hughes (Colman has been played by Konrad Matthaei and James Douglas).

Tom Hughes, son of Bob and Lisa, has been played by Jerry Schaffer, Frankie Michaels, Paul O'Keefe, Peter Galman, and C. David Colson. Tom was briefly interested in Meredith Halliday (Nina Hart) but married Carol Demming (played by Rita McLaughlin, now known as Rita McLaughlin Walter). After that marriage ended in divorce, Tom married Natalie Branning (Judith Chapman).

Tom's father, Bob Hughes, kept active after his divorce from Lisa Miller. He married Sandy McGuire (played by Dagne Crane and Barbara Rucker, among others), whom Ellen Lowell had met while in prison. After a second divorce, Bob married Jennifer Ryan (played by Geraldine Court and Gillian Spencer), a widow, in 1972. Jennifer's son by her earlier marriage, Dr. Rick Ryan (Con Roche), resented the presence of Bob and was responsible for Jennifer leaving Bob. She returned when she learned she was pregnant; their daughter was named Franny (played by Kelly Campbell and Maura Gilligan). In the meantime, Jennifer's sister, Kim Reynolds (played by Kathryn Hays and temporarily by Patty McCormack), came to town, had an affair with Bob, and eventually married Dr. John Dixon (Larry Bryggman). Jennifer died in 1975.

Others who have appeared over the years have included: William Johnstone as Judge Lowell, Jim Lowell's father and founder of Chris Hughes's law firm; Martin Rudy and Anna Minot as Sandy McGuire's parents, Carl and Martha Wilson; Michael Nader as Kevin Thompson, whom Sandy later married; Jerry Lacy as Simon Gilbey, Meredith Halliday's guardian; Charles Siebert as Wally Matthews, a onetime boyfriend of Lisa's; Dennis Cooney as Jay Stallings, another boyfriend of Lisa's who married Carol Demming after her divorce from Tom Hughes; Joyce Van Patten and Virginia Dwyer as Janice Turner, who fell in love with Don Hughes before marrying Carl Whipple (Rod Colbin); Barbara Rodell as Joyce Colman, ex-wife of Grant Colman who later married Don Hughes; Grace Matthews as Grace Baker, mother of Jeff Baker, Penny's first husband; Hal Hamilton and Charles Baxter as Tom Pope, a lawyer in Chris Hughes's firm; Geoffrey Lumb as lawyer Mitchell Drew; Millette Alexander as nurse Sylvia Hill; George Rose as Dr. Prescott; Ben Hayes as Dr. Bruce Baxter; John Swearingen as Dr. Bill Jenkins; Addison Powell as Dr. Flynn; Joan Anderson as nurse Mary Mitchell; Bernie McInerney as Jerry Butler; Ethel Remey and Dorothy Blackburn as Alma Miller, Lisa's mother; Ed Kemmer as lawyer Dick Martin; Bob Hover and Kelly Wood as Brian and Mary Ellison, adoptive parents of Grant Colman;

Anthony Herrera as Mark Galloway; Jean Mazza as Dawn Stewart; Fran Carlon as Julia Burke; Donna Wandrey and Colleen Zenk as Barbara Ryan; Lisa Cameron as Peggy Reagan; Curt Dawson as Ron Talbot; Carmine Stipo and Jill Harmon as Tony and Maria Moreno; Michael Lombardo as Lieutenant Joe Fernando; Michael Finn as Richard Taylor; Christoper Hastings as Peter Burton; and Ted Agress as Luke Peters.

Recent additions to the cast have included: Clarice Blackburn as Marion Connelly; Keith Charles as Ralph Mitchell; John Cypher as Dr. Alexander Keith; Laurel Delmar as Laurie Keaton; Jason Ferguson as Andrew Dixon; Wayne Hudgins as Beau Spencer; Georgiann Johnson as Jane Spencer; Marcia McClain as Dee Stewart; Judith McConnell as Valerie Conway; Ariane Munker as Melinda Gray; Biff Warren as Mark Lewis; Tommy Baudo as Teddy Ellison; Doug Travis as Nick Conway; Leslie Denniston as Karen Parker; Kipp Whitman (1978) as Hank Robinson; Rebecca Hollen as Tina Cornell; Rachel Kelly as Kate; Robert Lipton as Jeff Ward; Dennis Romer as Dr. Doug Campbell.

THE ASCENT OF MAN   PBS
7 JANUARY 1975–1 APRIL 1975   Highbrow series which focused on the development of humankind and how certain scientific discoveries shaped the growth of civilization. Hosted by Dr. Jacob Bronowski, a Polish-born scientist who headed the Council for Biology in Human Affairs at the Salk Institute in California. Jointly produced by Time-Life Films and the BBC, the series was broadcast in England during the 1972–1973 season. Bronowski died shortly before the program premiered in the United States.

ASK WASHINGTON   NBC
11 JANUARY 1954–26 FEBRUARY 1954   Monday-through-Friday public affairs program on which a panel of Washington journalists answered questions sent in by viewers. Replaced by *Home*.

THE ASPHALT JUNGLE   ABC
2 APRIL 1961–24 SEPTEMBER 1961   TV version of the 1950 film, based on the novel by W. R. Burnett. Set in New York. With Jack Warden as Deputy Police Commissioner Matt Gower; Arch Johnson as Captain Gus Honochek; and Bill Smith (later known as William Smith on *Laredo*) as Sergeant Dan Keller. Background music for the hour series was composed by Duke Ellington.

ASSIGNMENT FOREIGN LEGION   CBS
1 OCTOBER 1957–24 DECEMBER 1957   Anthology series depicting the exploits of the French Foreign Legion during World War II. Appearing as a war correspondent, Merle Oberon also hosted the series.

ASSIGNMENT MANHUNT   NBC
14 JULY 1951–1 SEPTEMBER 1951; 5 JULY 1952–23 AUGUST 1952   Produced by Julian Claman, this half-hour crime show starred John Baragrey and was a summer replacement for *Your Hit Parade.*

ASSIGNMENT UNDERWATER   SYNDICATED
1960   Maritime adventure starring Bill Williams as Bill Greer, diver and skipper of *The Lively Lady.* With Diane Mountford as his daughter Patty.

ASSIGNMENT: VIENNA   ABC
28 SEPTEMBER 1972–9 JUNE 1973   This segment of ABC's adventure trilogy, *The Men* (see also *The Delphi Bureau* and *Jigsaw*), starred Robert Conrad as Jake Webster, American undercover agent and owner of a Viennese nightspot; Charles Cioffi as Major Bernard Caldwell, his contact man; and Anton Diffring as Inspector Hoffman of the Austrian police.

THE ASSOCIATES   ABC
23 SEPTEMBER 1979–28 OCTOBER 1979   Half-hour sitcom set at Bass & Marshall, a prestigious Manhattan law firm. With Wilfrid Hyde-White as Emerson Marshall, the highly respected but slightly dotty senior partner; Martin Short as Tucker Kerwin, an idealistic new associate; Alley Mills as wholesome Leslie Dunn, Tucker's office mate; Joe Regalbuto as obnoxious Eliot Streeter, a newly named partner; Shelley Smith as sophisticated Sara James, another new associate; and Tim Thomerson as Johnny Danko, the macho office boy. The series was created by the group responsible for the 1978 hit *Taxi*: Jim Brooks, Stan Daniels, Charlie Hauck, and Ed. Weinberger. The show's musical theme, "The Wall Street Blues," was sung by B. B. King.

ASTROBOY   SYNDICATED
1963   Japanese-produced cartoon series about a robot.

AT HOME AND HOW   ABC
1 JANUARY 1949–27 APRIL 1949   Tips on home improvement were given on this half-hour prime-time show.

THE AT HOME SHOW
See THE MASLAND AT HOME SHOW

AT ISSUE   ABC
12 JULY 1953–24 FEBRUARY 1954   Martin Agronsky hosted this fifteen-minute public affairs program on which he interviewed guests.

THE ATOM ANT SHOW   NBC
2 OCTOBER 1965–2 SEPTEMBER 1967

THE ATOM ANT/SECRET SQUIRREL SHOW
9 SEPTEMBER 1967–31 AUGUST 1968   A super-powered insect was the star of this Hanna-Barbera cartoon show. In 1967, Ant joined forces with Secret Squirrel, the daring rodent who had had his own show for two seasons.

ATOM SQUAD   NBC
6 JULY 1953–22 JANUARY 1954   Science fiction for the kids. Bob Hastings starred as Steve Elliott, head of the Atom Squad, a top-secret planetary defense organization. Bob Courtleigh played Elliott's assistant. The fifteen-minute show was televised live from New York weekdays at 5 p.m.

AUCTION-AIRE   ABC
30 SEPTEMBER 1949–23 JUNE 1950   Home viewers bid labels of the sponsors' products, not cash, to win merchandise on this Friday-night game show. Jack Gregson, a licensed auctioneer, hosted the series, assisted by Charlotte "Rebel" Randall. *Variety* noted in 1949 that an irate viewer telephoned in a bid of "30,000 labels if you'll take the show off the air." The offer was not accepted, as *Auction-Aire* stayed on for another eight months.

AUDUBON WILDLIFE THEATRE   SYNDICATED
1971   Wildlife films.

AUSTIN CITY LIMITS   PBS
1976–   An hour with various country-music artists, produced at KLRN-TV, Austin–San Antonio.

THE AUTHOR MEETS THE CRITICS   NBC/ABC/DUMONT
21 SEPTEMBER 1947–24 JULY 1949 (NBC); 3 OCTOBER 1949–25 SEPTEMBER 1950 (ABC); 10 JANUARY 1952–10 OCTOBER 1954 (DUMONT)   This panel show began on radio in 1946 and came to television a year later. Each week two critics discussed a recently published book during the first segment of the show; one of the critics assailed the book, while the other praised it. During the latter segment the author was given the chance to defend the criticisms or acknowledge the kudos. Martin Stone produced the half-hour show; John K. M. McCaffery was the moderator for most of the show's run, though James Michener and Virgilia Peterson appeared as moderators in 1954.

THE AVENGERS   ABC
28 MARCH–15 SEPTEMBER 1969
THE NEW AVENGERS   CBS
15 SEPTEMBER 1978–23 MARCH 1979   This whimsical British spy series began in 1961 as a more straightforward adventure show: the search by a

husband for his wife's killers. The husband was joined in his search by John Steed (Patrick Macnee), an urbane and sophisticated bon vivant. By 1962 the bereaved husband was gone (he never found the killers), having been replaced by Cathy Gale (Honor Blackman—she played Pussy Galore in *Goldfinger*). By this time Steed and his partner had become government agents.

The early *Avengers* shows were never shown in the United States. American viewers saw only the next incarnation of the series, the adventures of Steed and Mrs. Emma Peel. Played by Diana Rigg, Mrs. Peel was not a secret agent, but rather a talented amateur with a thirst for adventure. She was also one of the most liberated women characters on television during the 1960s. It was established that she was the widow of a test pilot, but her relationship with Steed was never really explained. Though hampered by a limited variety of plots, the show was generally well-written and well-acted. More importantly, it embodied a certain element of style all too infrequent on adventure series: Steed, typically in a three-piece suit and bowler, and Mrs. Peel, often in boots and leather, relentlessly pursued an assortment of psychopaths, robots, and human-eating monsters.

Approximately forty-five Steed-Peel episodes were filmed; the last twenty-four were in color. In "The Forget-Me-Knot" (shown here 20 March 1968), Mrs. Peel learned that her husband had been found alive and decided to rejoin him. Steed then joined forces with agent Tara King. King, played by twenty-year-old Linda Thorson, lacked the appeal of Mrs. Peel, and the Rigg episodes are generally considered to be far superior to the Thorson episodes.

Also appearing was Patrick Newell (1967–1969) as "Mother," Steed's wheelchair-bound boss. Among the many guest stars who appeared were Christopher Lee ("The Cybernauts"), Gordon Jackson ("Castle De'Ath"), Ron Moody ("The Bird Who Knew Too Much"), Donald Sutherland ("The Superlative Seven"), and Peter Cushing ("Return of the Cybernauts"). Produced by Brian Clemens and Albert Fennell.

In the fall of 1978 *The New Avengers* first appeared on American television. Filmed in England in 1977, the hour series again featured Patrick Macnee as British agent John Steed, along with Joanna Lumley as Purdey and Gareth Hunt as Mike Gambit. It was also produced by Brian Clemens and Albert Fennell.

AWAY WE GO   CBS
3 JUNE 1967–2 SEPTEMBER 1967   A summer replacement hour for *The Jackie Gleason Show,* featuring George Carlin, Buddy Greco, and the Buddy Rich Band.

BJ AND THE BEAR
NBC

10 FEBRUARY 1979–   Hour adventure series starring Greg
Evigan as B.J. (Billie Joe) McCay, an independent trucker who rides the
roads with his simian sidekick, a chimp named The Bear. During the
spring of 1979 Claude Akins was occasionally featured as McCay's nemesis, Sheriff Lobo, but in the fall of 1979 Lobo sidled off into his own series (see *The Misadventures of Sheriff Lobo*). Joining the cast were Slim
Pickens as Sergeant Beauregard Wiley; Richard Deacon as Sheriff Masters; Conchata Ferrell as Wilhelmina Johnson (better known as The
Fox), a state cop sent to check up on Wiley and Masters's operation; Janet Louise Johnson as B.J.'s friend, Tommy; and Joshua Shelley as Bullets, operator of the Country Comfort Truck Stop. Executive producers:
Glen A. Larson and Michael Sloan for Glen A. Larson Productions in association with Universal TV.

BAA BAA BLACK SHEEP (BLACK SHEEP SQUADRON)
NBC

21 SEPTEMBER 1976–30 AUGUST 1977; 14 DECEMBER 1977–1 SEPTEM-
BER 1978   Set in the Pacific, this hour-long adventure series was based
on the real-life exploits of Marine Corps Major Gregory "Pappy" Boy-
ington, World War II flying ace, who put together a squadron of misfits
and castoffs from other service outfits and nicknamed it "The Black
Sheep." Featured were Robert Conrad as Major Boyington; Dana Elcar
as his commanding officer, Colonel Lard; Simon Oakland as General
Moore; James Whitmore, Jr., as Captain Gutterman; Robert Ginty as
Lieutenant T. J. Wiley; Dirk Blocker (son of the late Dan Blocker) as
Lieutenant Jerry Bragg; W. K. Stratton as Lieutenant Larry Casey; John
Larroquette as Lieutenant Bob Anderson; Red West as Sergeant Andy
Micklin; Joey Aresco as Hutch; Jeff MacKay as French; and Larry Man-
etti as Boyle. *Baa Baa Black Sheep* was canceled by NBC after one sea-
son but was revived in December, thanks to the lobbying efforts of Robert
Conrad and executive producer Stephen Cannell. When it returned, it
was titled *Black Sheep Squadron*. Several new regulars were added in
February of 1978: Jeb Adams (son of the late Nick Adams) as Lieutenant
Jeb Pruitt; Denise DuBarry as nurse Samantha Green; Nancy Conrad
(daughter of Robert) as Nancy, a nurse; Kathy McCullem as Ellie, a
nurse; and Brianne Leary as Susan, also a nurse (the four nurses were
temporarily assigned to duty at the Squadron's Solomon Islands headquarters).

THE BABY GAME
ABC

1 JANUARY 1968–12 JULY 1968   Daytime game show on which three
couples demonstrated their knowledge of infant behavior by predicting
the outcome of previously filmed sequences involving youngsters. Hosted
by Richard Hayes.

BABY, I'M BACK   CBS

30 JANUARY 1978–12 AUGUST 1978   Situation comedy about a black
man who returns home to his wife and family in Washington, D.C., after
a seven-year absence. With Demond Wilson as Ray Ellis; Denise Nicholas as his wife, Olivia; Tony Holmes as their son, Jordan; Kim Fields as
their daughter, Angie; Helen Martin as Olivia's mother, Luzelle Carter;
and Ed Hall as Olivia's new suitor, Colonel Wallace Dickey, an Army
public relations officer. Lila Garrett and Charlie Fries were the executive
producers; Garrett and Mort Lachman created the series. Sandy Krinski
and Chet Dowling were the producers.

BACHELOR FATHER   CBS/NBC/ABC

15 SEPTEMBER 1957–7 JUNE 1959 (CBS); 18 JUNE 1959–21 SEPTEMBER
1961 (NBC); 3 OCTOBER 1961–25 SEPTEMBER 1962 (ABC)   One of the
few situation comedies to have run on all three networks, *Bachelor Father*
told the story of an unmarried Beverly Hills attorney whose carefree
bachelor life is disrupted when his newly orphaned thirteen-year-old
niece comes to live with him. With John Forsythe as lawyer Bentley
Gregg; Noreen Corcoran as niece Kelly Gregg, daughter of Bentley's sister; Sammee Tong as Peter Tong, the butler; Jimmy Boyd (1958–1962) as
Kelly's boyfriend, Howard Meachum; Bernadette Withers as Kelly's girlfriend, Ginger (she was Ginger Farrell on CBS, Ginger Loomis on NBC,
and Ginger Mitchell on ABC); Whit Bissell (1959–1961) as Ginger's father, Bert Loomis; Alice Backes (1957–1959) as Bentley's secretary,
Vicki; Sue Ane Langdon (1959–1961) as Bentley's secretary, Kitty
Marsh; Victor Sen Yung as Peter's cousin, Charlie Fong; and Jasper, a
neighborhood dog who adopted the Greggs. During its CBS years, *Bachelor Father* alternated on Sundays with *The Jack Benny Program*. Produced at Revue-Universal studios. The pilot for the series, "A New Girl
in His Life," was shown on *General Electric Theater* 26 May 1957.

THE BACHELORS
See IT'S A GREAT LIFE

BACK THAT FACT   ABC

22 OCTOBER 1953–26 NOVEMBER 1953   Comic Joey Adams hosted this
Thursday-night game show, developed by Jack Barry and Dan Enright.
Adams interviewed contestants, who were periodically interrupted by an
offstage voice (supplied by Carl Caruso) asking them to "back that
fact"—to provide proof of any assertion made by them. A contestant who
succeeded in providing the documentation won a prize. Contestants were
escorted onstage by Hope Lange, who would later star in *The Ghost and
Mrs. Muir*. Double-talk comic Al Kelly was also featured on the half-
hour show.

BACKGROUND   NBC

10 OCTOBER 1954–26 JUNE 1955 Joseph C. Harsch produced and hosted this Sunday-afternoon news analysis program.

BACKSTAGE WITH BARRY WOOD   CBS

1 MARCH 1949–24 MAY 1949 Fifteen-minute variety show featuring new talent, hosted by Barry Wood.

BACKSTAIRS AT THE WHITE HOUSE   NBC

29 JANUARY 1979–19 FEBRUARY 1979 Four-part miniseries based on the book by Lillian Rogers Parks and Frances Spatz Leighton, drawn from the careers of Maggie Rogers and Lillian Rogers Parks on the White House staff. With Olivia Cole as Maggie Rogers, hairdresser and maid; Tania Johnson and Leslie Uggams as her daughter, seamstress Lillian Rogers; Louis Gossett, Jr., as Levi, butler and footman; Leslie Nielsen as Ike Hoover, one of their supervisors; Cloris Leachman as Mrs. Jaffray, another of their supervisors; Victor Buono as President Taft; Julie Harris as Nellie Taft; Robert Vaughn as President Wilson; Kim Hunter as Ellen Wilson; Claire Bloom as Edith Galt Wilson; George Kennedy as President Harding; Celeste Holm as Florence Harding; Ed Flanders as President Coolidge; Lee Grant as Grace Coolidge; Larry Gates as President Hoover; Jan Sterling as Lou Hoover; Richard Anderson as President Roosevelt; Eileen Heckart as Eleanor Roosevelt; Harry Morgan as President Truman; Estelle Parsons as Bess Truman; Andrew Duggan as President Eisenhower; and Barbara Barrie as Mamie Eisenhower. Ed Friendly was the executive producer of the nine-hour program for Ed Friendly Productions.

THE BAD NEWS BEARS   CBS

24 MARCH 1979–6 OCTOBER 1979 Half-hour sitcom based on the *Bad News Bears* films, which starred Walter Matthau. The video version featured Jack Warden as Morris Buttermaker, a swimming-pool cleaner who agreed to coach baseball at a school for problem youngsters as an alternative to a prison term; Catherine Hicks as Dr. Emily Rappant, principal of the W. Wendell Weaver School, to which Buttermaker was assigned; J. Brennan Smith as Mike Engelberg, the porcine catcher; Tricia Cast as Amanda Wurlitzer, the star pitcher; Billy Jacoby as Rudi Stein; Corey Feldman as Regi; Sparky Marcus as Ogilvie, the team's manager; Meeno Peluce as Tanner; Shane Butterworth as Lupus; Christoff St. John as Ahmad Abdul Rahim; Gregg Forrest as Kelly; Rad Daly (fall 1979) as Josh; Phillip R. Allen as Roy Turner, coach of the rival Lions. Executive producers: Arthur Silver and Bob Brunner. Producers: John Boni and Norman Stiles. After a shaky start in the fall of 1979, *The Bad News Bears* left the air in October.

BAFFLE NBC

26 MARCH 1973–5 OCTOBER 1973

ALL-STAR BAFFLE NBC

8 OCTOBER 1973–29 MARCH 1974 Dick Enberg hosted this daytime game show on which players attempted to guess words and phrases from successive one-letter clues. The format was almost identical to that of *PDQ*, an earlier game show. *Baffle* featured two teams, each consisting of a celebrity and a contestant; *All-Star Baffle* featured teams consisting of two celebrities.

BAGGY PANTS & THE NITWITS NBC

10 SEPTEMBER 1977–28 OCTOBER 1978 Two segments were presented on this Saturday-morning cartoon show: *Baggy Pants,* the adventures of a Chaplinesque cat (this segment featured no dialogue) and *The Nitwits,* the adventures of Tyrone, a secret agent who came out of retirement, and his wife, Gladys (the two characters were based on those created by Arte Johnson and Ruth Buzzi on *Laugh-In*).

BAILEY'S COMETS CBS

8 SEPTEMBER 1973–30 AUGUST 1975 Children's cartoon show with an unusual format: a teenage roller skating team competing in a global roller derby. The second season consisted entirely of reruns. Produced by David H. DePatie and Friz Freleng.

THE BAILEYS OF BALBOA CBS

24 SEPTEMBER 1964–1 APRIL 1965 Feeble sitcom about a couple of inept charter-boat operators. With Paul Ford as Sam Bailey, skipper of the *Island Princess;* Sterling Holloway as first mate Buck Singleton; John Dehner as Commodore Cecil Wyntoon, their nemesis; Judy Carne as Barbara Wyntoon, his daughter; Les Brown, Jr., as Jim Bailey, Sam's son. Clobbered in the ratings race by *Peyton Place* (ABC) and *Hazel* (NBC), *The Baileys of Balboa* was one of three series developed by actor Keefe Brasselle and sold to CBS without a pilot. See also *The Cara Williams Show* and *The Reporter.*

BALANCE YOUR BUDGET CBS

18 OCTOBER 1952–2 MAY 1953 Bert Parks hosted this prime-time game show on which female contestants competed by trying to solve household budget problems; the winning contestant won the right to choose a key which would open a treasure chest. The biweekly series was produced by Peter Arnell and directed by Sherman Marks; Bert Parks was assisted by Lynn Connor.

BALL FOUR   CBS

22 SEPTEMBER 1976–27 OCTOBER 1976   Situation comedy developed by
Jim Bouton, ex–major leaguer and New York sportscaster whose book,
Ball Four, provided an inside view of professional baseball. Most of the
action on the series seemed to take place in the locker room; perhaps that
explains why *Ball Four* was the first casualty of the 1976–1977 season.
Bouton starred as Jim Barton, pitcher for the hapless Washington Americans. With Ben Davidson as Ben (Rhino) Rhinelander, catcher; Jack So-
mack as manager John (Cappy) Capogrosso; Jack McCutcheon as coach
Harold (Pinky) Pinkney; Sam Wright as outfielder Travis; Jaime Tirelli
as utility man Orlando Lopez; Marco St. John as pitcher Ray Plunk-
ett; David-James Carroll as rookie Westlake; Lenny Schultz as
pitcher Birdman. "Ball Four" theme was composed and sung by Harry
Chapin.

BANACEK   NBC

13 SEPTEMBER 1972–3 SEPTEMBER 1974   One segment of *The NBC
Wednesday Movie.* Starring George Peppard as Banacek, an independent
insurance investigator of Polish descent who works for the Boston Casualty Company on a contingent fee basis. With Murray Matheson as Felix
Mullholland, owner of Mullholland's Rare Book and Print Shop, and
confidante of Banacek; Ralph Manza as Jay Drury, Banacek's chauffeur;
and Christine Belford (1973–1974) as insurance investigator Carlie Kirkland.

THE BANANA SPLITS ADVENTURE HOUR   NBC

7 SEPTEMBER 1968–5 SEPTEMBER 1970   Saturday-morning fare from
Hanna-Barbera Studios, presenting both cartoons and live action. The
live characters were the Banana Splits, a rock-and-roll band made up of
four animals (Drooper, Snorky, Bingo, and Fleegle).

BAND OF AMERICA   NBC

17 OCTOBER 1949–9 JANUARY 1950   Hosted by Paul Lavalle, this Monday-night variety show was simulcast on NBC Radio.

BANDSTAND   NBC

30 JULY 1956–23 NOVEMBER 1956   Bert Parks hosted this live half-hour
daytime variety show. Developed by Billy Goodheart, it featured appearances by guest bands.

THE BANG-SHANG LALAPALOOZA SHOW
See THE ARCHIE SHOW

BANK ON THE STARS   CBS/NBC

20 JUNE 1953–5 SEPTEMBER 1953 (CBS); 15 MAY 1954–21 AUGUST 1954
(NBC) On this Saturday-night game show contestants were quizzed
after viewing clips from newly released movies. Jack Paar hosted in 1953;
Bill Cullen was the first host in 1954, and was succeeded by Jimmy Nelson in July.

BANYON   NBC

15 SEPTEMBER 1972–12 JANUARY 1973 Private eye series, set in Los
Angeles during the 1930s. With Robert Forster as Miles Banyon; Joan
Blondell as Peggy Revere, who ran the secretarial school which supplied
Banyon with temporary help; Richard Jaeckel as Lieutenant Pete
McNeil; and Julie Gregg as friend and singer Abby Graham. The pilot
for the series was telecast 15 March 1971.

THE BARBARA McNAIR SHOW   SYNDICATED

1969–1970 Variety hour with little talk and lots of music, hosted by
Barbara McNair. One of the few series hosted by a black woman.

THE BARBARA STANWYCK SHOW   NBC

19 SEPTEMBER 1960– 11 SEPTEMBER 1962 Half-hour dramatic anthology series hosted by, and frequently starring, Barbara Stanwyck. The success of *The Loretta Young Show* apparently prompted NBC to introduce
this series. Like *The Loretta Young Show, The Barbara Stanwyck Show*
was given a late-evening time slot (10:00 p.m. Mondays), but even against
only moderate competition (*Adventures in Paradise* and *Hennesey*) the
show was not a success. Stanwyck, however, reappeared in 1965 in a
more successful vehicle: *Big Valley.*

BARBARY COAST   ABC

8 SEPTEMBER 1975–9 JANUARY 1976 Limpid western set in San Francisco. Starring William Shatner as Jeff Cable, undercover agent for the
governor of California; and Doug McClure as Cash Conover, owner of
the Golden Gate Casino. With seven-foot-two Richard Kiel as Moose
Moran, useful employee at the casino; Dave Turner as Thumbs, another
employee. Created by Douglas Heyes. Executive producer: Cy Chermak.
The series pilot (starring Shatner and Dennis Cole) was aired on 4 May
1975.

BAREFOOT IN THE PARK   ABC

24 SEPTEMBER 1970–14 JANUARY 1971 The play, written by Neil Simon, was a hit. The movie, starring Jane Fonda and Robert Redford, was
also a success. But the television series was a flop. It told the story of a
black couple, newlyweds, living in a tiny top-floor apartment in lower
Manhattan. With Scoey Mitchlll as lawyer Paul Bratter, an associate at

Kendricks, Keene & Klein; Tracy Reed as his wife, Corie Bratter; Thelma Carpenter as Corie's mother, Mabel Bates, a domestic for a Park Avenue family; Nipsey Russell as friend Honey Robinson, proprietor of Honey Robinson's Pool & Billiard Emporium; Harry Holcombe as Arthur Kendricks, Paul's boss. The series was beset with production problems from the beginning and folded when Scoey Mitchlll was fired after thirteen episodes.

BARETTA — ABC
17 JANUARY 1975–1 JUNE 1978   After *Toma's* Tony Musante announced that he would not return to that series for a second season, the surprised producers subsequently signed Robert Blake to star in a "new" series. Blake, a former child actor whose best-known film role was the psychopathic killer of *In Cold Blood,* starred as Tony Baretta, an unorthodox big city cop who lived in a run-down hotel with his pet cockatoo, Fred, and who was constantly getting in hot water with his superiors. Also featured were Tom Ewell as Billy Truman, desk clerk at the King Edward, Baretta's seedy residence; Dana Elcar (to July 1975) as Lieutenant Shiller, his commanding officer; Edward Grover (1975–1978) as Lieutenant Hal Brubaker, his new commanding officer; Michael D. Roberts as Rooster, his streetwise informant; and Chino Williams as Fats, a gravel-voiced street source. Blake often took an active interest in the production of the series, sometimes to the consternation of the people in charge. Bernard L. Kowalski was executive producer; Jo Swerling, Jr., was the first producer and was succeeded by Ed Waters as supervising producer.

THE BARKLEYS NBC
9 SEPTEMBER 1972–1 SEPTEMBER 1973   Saturday-morning cartoon series about a lower-middle-class family of dogs, patterned on the Bunkers of *All in the Family.*

BARNABY JONES CBS
28 JANUARY 1973–   After a year layoff following the cancellation of *The Beverly Hillbillies* in 1971, Buddy Ebsen returned to television as Barnaby Jones, a soft-spoken, milk-drinking private eye who usually works for insurance companies. Jones came out of semiretirement when his son was murdered. With Lee Meriwether as Betty Jones, his widowed daughter-in-law and assistant; John Carter as Lieutenant Biddle; Mark Shera (1976–   ) as Jedediah Jones, Barnaby's cousin once removed, who came to work for Barnaby after his father was murdered. Executive producer: Quinn Martin.

BARNEY GOOGLE SYNDICATED
1963   A cartoon series based on the popular comic strip created by Billy

DeBeck in the 1920s. His backwoods characters included Barney Google, Snuffy Smith, Loweezy, and Jughead.

BARNEY MILLER ABC

23 JANUARY 1975–   This half-hour situation comedy about a New York City precinct captain and his multiethnic band of officers stars Hal Linden as Captain Barney Miller of the Twelfth Precinct; Barbara Barrie (1975–1976) as his wife, Elizabeth Miller; Abe Vigoda (1975–1977) as deadpan Detective Phil Fish; Max Gail as Sergeant Wojehowicz (Wojo); Gregory Sierra (1975–1976) as Sergeant Chano Amengual; Jack Soo (1975–1979) as Sergeant Nick Yemana; Ron Glass as Detective Ron Harris; James Gregory (fall 1975) as Inspector Luger, the man from headquarters; Steve Landesberg (January 1977–   ) as Detective Arthur Dietrich; Ron Carey (1977–   ) as Officer Levitt; Florence Stanley (1975–1977) as Bernice Fish, Phil's wife. Early episodes also featured Michael Tessier and Anne Wyndham as the Millers' children, Daniel and Rachel. Created by Danny Arnold and Theodore J. Flicker, the series is produced by Chris Hayward and Arne Sultan.

THE BARON ABC

20 JANUARY 1966–14 JULY 1966 Steve Forrest starred as John Mannering, suave American art dealer involved in international intrigue. With Sue Lloyd as his assistant Cordelia; Paul Ferris as his assistant David Marlowe; and Colin Gordon as Mr. Templeton-Green. This hour-long series, a midseason replacement for *The Long Hot Summer,* was produced in England. It was based on the short stories by John Creasey.

BARRIER REEF NBC

11 SEPTEMBER 1971–2 SEPTEMBER 1972 Saturday-morning live-action adventure series, filmed in Australia. With Joe James as Captain Chet King, skipper of the windjammer *Endeavor;* Richard Melkle as marine biologist Joe Francis; and Ken James as Kip, Chet's young son.

THE BASEBALL CORNER ABC

1 JUNE 1958–27 AUGUST 1958 Half-hour series on which host Buddy Blattner interviewed baseball stars and introduced film clips.

BAT MASTERSON NBC

8 OCTOBER 1958–21 SEPTEMBER 1961 Gene Barry starred as Bat Masterson, dapper ex-lawman who roamed the West. Masterson's gimmick was a gold-tipped cane that disguised a sword; he also carried a gun, of course. In real life William Bartley Masterson had been a deputy of Wyatt Earp. Notable guest stars included Dyan Cannon (in her first prime-time appearance, "Lady Luck," 5 November 1959) and William Conrad

("Stampede at Tent City," 29 October 1958, his first TV dramatic appearance). Andy White and Frank Pittman produced the half-hour series for United Artists TV.

BATMAN
ABC

12 JANUARY 1966–14 MARCH 1968   *Batman,* the cartoon crimefighter created by Bob Kane in 1939, came to television with a big splash (and lots of publicity) early in 1966. Originally scheduled as a fall 1966 entry, the show was rushed into production late in 1965 as a midseason replacement. Broadcast twice a week, *Batman* was an immediate hit—both half hours cracked Nielsen's top ten that season, and millions of dollars of *Batman* merchandise was sold to children and adults. But by the fall of 1966 the ratings had already begun to fall off. In the fall of 1967 the show was cut back to once a week, and it passed away quietly in midseason. Unlike *Superman, Batman* was written and played for laughs—it was "camp." Visually, it should be remembered for its frequent use of slanted camera angles and for the use of such words as "Pow!" and "Smash!" that were flashed on the screen during fight scenes. The show starred Adam West, a handsome, athletic type who had been featured on *The Detectives,* as Bruce Wayne, a Gotham City millionaire whose secret identity was Batman, a masked, caped crusader who used sophisticated paraphernalia to capture crooks (unlike Superman, Batman was a mere mortal and possessed no super powers). Burt Ward costarred as Dick Grayson, Wayne's teenaged ward, whose secret identity was Robin (the Boy Wonder), similarly masked and caped. Together, the Dynamic Duo assisted the usually impotent police force and helped keep Gotham City's streets safe for the citizenry. Also featured were Alan Napier as Alfred Pennyworth, Wayne's butler, the only other person who knew of their secret identities; Madge Blake as Dick's aunt, Harriet Cooper; Neil Hamilton as Police Commissioner Gordon, the city official who often dialed the Caped Crusaders on the Batphone; and Stafford Repp as Chief O'Hara. In the fall of 1967 Yvonne Craig joined the cast as Barbara Gordon (daughter of the Commissioner), whose secret identity was Batgirl. She often assisted the Dynamic Duo, though she never learned the identities of Batman and Robin and they never learned hers. Among the many "guest villains" who appeared were Burgess Meredith as The Penguin; Frank Gorshin as The Riddler; Julie Newmar, Lee Meriwether, and Eartha Kitt as Catwoman; George Sanders, Otto Preminger, and Eli Wallach as Mr. Freeze; Victor Buono as King Tut; Cesar Romero as The Joker; Liberace as Chandell; Vincent Price as Egghead; Milton Berle as Louie the Lilac; Tallulah Bankhead as The Black Widow; Ethel Merman as Lola Lasagne; and Pierre Salinger (former press secretary to President Kennedy) as Lucky Pierre. Several of the guest villains appeared more than once—the only character ever killed off on *Batman* was Molly, one

of The Riddler's henchpeople, who was played by Jill St. John. Production of the series was supervised by William Dozier for 20th Century-Fox; Howie Horwitz was the line producer. The *Batman* theme was composed by Neil Hefti.

THE BATMAN/SUPERMAN HOUR   CBS

14 SEPTEMBER 1968–6 SEPTEMBER 1969 Saturday-morning cartoon series featuring the famed crimefighters. Superman and Batman appeared together or separately in several Saturday-morning shows: See also *The Batman/Tarzan Adventure Hour, The New Adventures of Superman, The Super Friends,* and *The Superman/Aquaman Hour.*

THE BATMAN/TARZAN ADVENTURE HOUR   CBS

10 SEPTEMBER 1977–2 SEPTEMBER 1978 One of the many Saturday-morning cartoon shows featuring various permutations of comic book heroes. See also *The Batman/Superman Hour, The New Adventures of Superman, The Super Friends, The Superman/Aquaman Hour,* and *Tarzan, Lord of the Jungle.*

BATTLE LINE   SYNDICATED

1963 Author Jim Bishop narrated World War II film footage on this documentary series.

BATTLE OF THE AGES   DUMONT/CBS

1 JANUARY 1952–17 JUNE 1952 (DUMONT); 6 SEPTEMBER 1952–29 NOVEMBER 1952 (CBS) This prime-time game show was a talent contest between a team of children and a team of adult celebrities. John Reed King hosted the DuMont version; Morey Amsterdam the CBS version; and Norman Brokenshire and Arthur Van Horn were the announcers. The studio audience voted for the more talented team at the end of the show. If the adults won, their winnings were donated to the Actors Fund of America. If the kids won, their winnings went to the Professional Childrens' School. In a rare TV appearance, composer W. C. Handy ("The St. Louis Blues") performed on the DuMont premiere.

BATTLE OF THE PLANETS   SYNDICATED

1978 A science fiction cartoon series, *Battle of the Planets* pitted the G Force, a team of five orphans headquartered at a secret base beneath the Pacific, against invaders from alien galaxies. Jameson Brewer was the executive producer and writer, David Hanson the producer and director for Sandy Frank Films.

BATTLE REPORT   NBC

13 AUGUST 1950–20 APRIL 1952 A weekly report on the Korean con-

flict, broadcast live from Washington, D.C. Produced by Ted Ayers, the show was originally seen Sunday evenings, and was shifted to Sunday afternoons in 1951.

BATTLESTAR GALACTICA   ABC
17 SEPTEMBER 1978–4 AUGUST 1979 An expensive and elaborate science fiction series, *Battlestar Galactica* was obviously inspired by the colossal film *Star Wars* (one of Galactica's producers was John Dykstra, who was responsible for the special effects in *Star Wars*). Hurtling through space in a huge convoy of spacecraft, Galactica's inhabitants were heading toward Earth, trying to avoid annihilation by the Cylons, a mechanical race of beings out to destroy all humanoid forms of civilization. The cast included: Lorne Greene as Adama, commander of the fleet; Richard Hatch as Apollo; Dirk Benedict as Starbuck; Herb Jefferson, Jr., as Boomer; Maren Jensen as Athena; Noah Hathaway as Boxey; Tony Swartz as Jolly; and Terry Carter as Tigh; Glen A. Larson was the executive producer for Universal TV in association with Glen Larson Productions. The show, normally an hour program, kicked off with a three-hour premiere, which, at $3 million, was reported to be the most costly premiere telecast in TV history. See also *Galactica 1980* in the Appendix.

THE BAXTERS   SYNDICATED
1979 An unusual half-hour series, *The Baxters* was created by Hubert Jessup and televised locally for several years on WCVB-TC in Boston before Norman Lear acquired the series in 1979. The first part of the program was an eleven-minute dramatic vignette highlighting a particular problem, which was then the subject of discussion by a studio audience for the remainder of the half hour. The cast of the nationally syndicated version included Anita Gillette as Nancy Baxter; Larry Keith as her husband, Fred Baxter; Derin Altay as daughter Naomi; Terri Lynn Wood as daughter Rachel; and Chris Petersen as son Jonah. Local stations which broadcast *The Baxters* were encouraged to provide their own audiences and moderators, although the audience-discussion portion taped in Los Angeles (where the vignettes were also taped) was made available to stations which chose not to provide a local studio audience.

THE BAY CITY ROLLERS SHOW   NBC
4 NOVEMBER 1978–27 JANUARY 1979 A popular recording group from Scotland, the Bay City Rollers hosted *The Krofft Superstar Hour* from September to late October of 1978, when the series was trimmed to thirty minutes and retitled. The group included Derek Longmuir, Alan Longmuir, Stuart Wood, Eric Faulkner, and Leslie McKeown. Also featured on the live-action show were Billie Hayes, Billy Barty, and Jay Robinson.

77

BE OUR GUEST   CBS

27 JANUARY 1960–JUNE 1960   Hour-long variety series, hosted first by
George DeWitt and Mary Ann Mobley (Miss America of 1958), later by
Keefe Brasselle and Mobley. Music by the Burt Farber orchestra. A mid-
season replacement for *The Lineup*.

THE BEACHCOMBER   SYNDICATED

1962   Cameron Mitchell starred as John Lackland, an American busi-
nessman who forsakes a successful career for the tranquility of a South
Pacific island called Amura. With Don Megowan as Captain Huckabee;
Sebastian Cabot as Commissioner Crippen; and Joan Staley as Linda.

BEACON HILL   CBS

2 SEPTEMBER 1975–18 NOVEMBER 1975   The biggest flop of the 1975–
1976 season, *Beacon Hill* was an expensive, cumbersome and much-bally-
hooed attempt to Americanize *Upstairs Downstairs*, the British export
which had proven popular on PBS. Set in Boston's fashionable Beacon
Hill in 1918, it told the story of a large, wealthy Irish family and their
company of servants. The cast was so large that it was often difficult for
viewers to keep track of the many characters. Some Bostonians noted
also that the series was historically inaccurate, as few Irish families lived
on Beacon Hill at that time, even fewer had so many servants, and no
house on the Hill was as large as the Lassiters' seemed to be. Though
thirteen episodes were taped, two were never televised as CBS decided to
cut its losses after only eleven weeks.

Regulars included Stephen Elliott as Benjamin Lassiter, the hardnosed
head of the clan; Nancy Marchand as his wife, Mary Lassiter, the grande
dame; David Dukes as their embittered son Robert, who lost an arm in
World War I; Kathryn Walker as Fawn, their arty-Bohemian daughter;
Maeve McGuire as their daughter Maude Palmer; Edward Herrmann as
Richard, Maude's boring husband; DeAnn Mears as the Lassiters'
daughter Emily Bullock; Roy Cooper as Trevor, Emily's husband; Linda
Purl as Betsy, Trevor and Emily's eighteen-year-old daughter; Kitty
Winn as Rosamund Lassiter, the Lassiters' youngest daughter; Michael
Nouri as Giorgio Balanci, Fawn's voice teacher and lover; George Rose
as Mr. Hacker, the family butler and head of the servant staff; Beatrice
Straight as his wife, Emmaline Hacker; Paul Rudd as Brian Mallory, the
young chauffeur; David Rounds as Terence O'Hara, Hacker's assistant;
Richard Ward as William Piper, the black cook; Don Blakely as his son
Grant, also a veteran of World War I; Barry Snider as Harry Emmet, a
former servant; Holland Taylor as Marilyn Gardiner, Mrs. Lassiter's sec-
retary; Sydney Swire as Eleanor, a maid; Susan Blanchard as Maureen
Mahaffey, a maid; and Lisa Pelikan as Maureen's sister, Kate Mahaffey,
also a maid. Executive producer: Beryl Vertue. Produced by Jacqueline
Babbin. Music by Marvin Hamlisch.

THE BEAGLES CBS/ABC
10 SEPTEMBER 1966–2 SEPTEMBER 1967 (CBS); 9 SEPTEMBER 1967–7
SEPTEMBER 1968 (ABC) Saturday-morning cartoon series about a pair
of rock-and-rolling dogs. (Not to be confused with *The Beatles.*)

BEANY AND CECIL
See TIME FOR BEANY

BEARCATS! CBS
16 SEPTEMBER 1971–30 DECEMBER 1971 Forgettable adventure series
about two troubleshooters roaming the West, circa 1914, in their Stutz
Bearcat. With Rod Taylor as Hank Brackett; Dennis Cole as Johnny
Reach. The show fared poorly against NBC's *The Flip Wilson Show.*

BEAT THE CLOCK CBS/ABC/SYNDICATED
23 MARCH 1950–12 SEPTEMBER 1958 (CBS); 13 OCTOBER 1958–30 JAN-
UARY 1961 (ABC); 1969–1974 (SYNDICATED); 17 SEPTEMBER 1979–
1 FEBRUARY 1980 (CBS) One of the earliest and most successful game
shows from the fertile minds of Mark Goodson and Bill Todman. On
Beat the Clock couples (usually married couples) were required to perform various stunts within certain time periods (usually less than sixty
seconds). The winning couple was given the chance to try a special stunt
for a large prize; the stunt was quite difficult and would be attempted
weekly until someone was able to perform it. Bud Collyer hosted the network versions, which were seen on prime time over CBS and daily over
CBS and ABC; for many seasons he was assisted by an attractive blonde
known as Roxanne (her real name was Dolores Rosedale). The stunts
were devised by Frank Wayne and Bob Howard and were always pre-
tested by members of the show's staff; in 1952 a young, unemployed actor
got his first job in TV testing stunts and warming up audiences. His name
was James Dean.

A syndicated version of the series appeared in 1969; it was hosted first
by Jack Narz, later by Gene Wood. It was substantially identical to the
network version, except that guest celebrities were on hand to aid the
contestants, and there was no special stunt for the winners to attempt.
Monty Hall hosted the 1979 daytime revival on CBS, on which two couples competed.

THE BEATLES ABC
25 SEPTEMBER 1965–7 SEPTEMBER 1969 Saturday cartoon series starring animated versions of the enormously popular British rock group,
The Beatles (John Lennon, Paul McCartney, George Harrison, and
Ringo Starr). Two Beatles songs were usually "performed" on each episode; the Beatles' speaking voices were supplied by Beatle soundalikes.

One of the few series which featured cartoon characterizations of real-life people.

THE BEAUTIFUL PHYLLIS DILLER SHOW   NBC
15 SEPTEMBER 1968–22 DECEMBER 1968   Variety hour hosted by Phyllis Diller, featuring Norm Crosby and Rip Taylor.

BEHIND CLOSED DOORS   NBC
2 OCTOBER 1958–9 APRIL 1959   Stories on this half-hour anthology series were adapted from the files of Rear Admiral Ellis M. Zacharias, deputy chief of naval intelligence during World War II. Bruce Gordon, as Commander Matson, hosted the show.

BEHIND THE LINES   PBS
1971–1976   Half-hour news analysis show, hosted by Harrison E. Salisbury of *The New York Times,* produced at WNET in New York.

BEHIND THE NEWS   CBS
11 JANUARY 1959–27 SEPTEMBER 1959   CBS newsman Howard K. Smith hosted this Sunday-afternoon news analysis program; William Weston produced it. Smith, who was CBS's Washington correspondent at the time, had joined the network in 1941; in 1961, following a dispute with CBS concerning on-the-air editorializing, Smith left for ABC News.

BELIEVE IT OR NOT   NBC
1 MARCH 1949–5 OCTOBER 1950   This half-hour series usually presented dramatizations of some of the amazing incidents depicted by cartoonist Robert L. Ripley in his "Believe It or Not" newspaper strip. Ripley, who died in 1949, hosted the show for many years on radio and also hosted the first few telecasts. Robert St. John succeeded Ripley as host.

THE BELL TELEPHONE HOUR   NBC
12 JANUARY 1959–14 JUNE 1968   This musical series ran semiregularly for almost ten seasons—sometimes weekly, sometimes biweekly, and sometimes as irregularly scheduled specials. All types of music were preducted the Bell Telephone Orchestra.

BEN CASEY   ABC
2 OCTOBER 1961–21 MARCH 1966   "Man, woman, birth, death, infinity." So began the introduction to *Ben Casey,* which, together with NBC's *Dr. Kildare,* ushered in a new era of doctor shows. Both series lasted five seasons. Vince Edwards starred as Ben Casey, resident neurosurgeon at County General Hospital, seemingly an expert in every known area of medicine. Edwards's good looks and surly disposition (on-camera, anyway) helped make him a heartthrob among the female fans. Other

regulars included Sam Jaffe (1961–1965) as Dr. David Zorba, chief of neurosurgery; Bettye Ackerman (Jaffe's wife) as anesthesiologist Dr. Maggie Graham; Harry Landers as Dr. Ted Hoffman; Nick Dennis as orderly Nick Kanavaras; Jeanne Bates as Nurse Wills; and Franchot Tone (1965–1966) as Dr. Freeland, Zorba's replacement as chief of neurosurgery. Created by James Moser (who also created *Medic*); produced by Matthew Rapf for Bing Crosby Productions.

BEN GRAUER'S AMERICANA QUIZ   NBC
8 DECEMBER 1947–4 JULY 1949   Ben Grauer hosted this prime-time half-hour game show on which contestants were quizzed about American history.

BEN JARROD   NBC
1 APRIL 1963–28 JUNE 1963   This daytime serial told the story of two small-town attorneys. With Michael Ryan as young lawyer Ben Jarrod; Addison Richards as his older partner, John Abbott; and Regina Gleason as Janet Donelli, defendant in a murder case. One of the shortest-running soap operas in television history.

BEN VEREEN—COMIN' AT YA   NBC
7 AUGUST 1975–28 AUGUST 1975   This four-week summer variety hour showcased the multitalented Ben Vereen, star of the Broadway hit, *Pippin*. Vereen later achieved wider fame in television for his portrayal of Chicken George in *Roots*. Other regulars included singer Lola Falana and comedians Arte Johnson, Avery Schreiber, and Liz Torres. Produced by Jaime Rogers and Gene McAvoy.

THE BENNETTS (THE BENNETT STORY)   NBC
6 JULY 1953–8 JANUARY 1954   Another short-lived soap opera about a small-town attorney. This one featured Don Gibson as lawyer Wayne Bennett and Paula Houston as his wife, Nancy. Also featured were Jerry Harvey and Ray Westfall. The setting was the town of Kingsport.

THE BENNY RUBIN SHOW   NBC
29 APRIL 1949–1 JULY 1949   Comedian Benny Rubin, whose career began in vaudeville, starred as a talent agent in this comedy-variety show, which also featured Vinnie Monte as the office boy. Jerry Rosen was the producer.

BENSON   ABC
13 SEPTEMBER 1979–   A spinoff from *Soap*, starring Robert Guillaume as Benson, who left his employ at the Tate residence to manage the household of the state's governor. With James Noble as Governor Gatling, a widower, a cousin of *Soap*'s Jessica Tate;

Inga Swenson as Gretchen Kraus, the Teutonic housekeeper at the governor's mansion; Caroline McWilliams as Marcie Hill, the governor's secretary; Missy Gold as Katie, the governor's precocious daughter; Lewis J. Stadlen as Taylor, the governor's aide. The half-hour show was created by Susan Harris, who was the executive producer of the series together with Paul Junger Witt and Tony Thomas.

BERT D'ANGELO–SUPERSTAR · ABC

21 FEBRUARY 1976–10 JULY 1976   Paul Sorvino starred as Bert D'Angelo, a former New York City police detective who worked in San Francisco. With Robert Pine as Inspector Larry Johnson; Dennis Patrick as Captain Jack Breen. Produced by Mort Fine for Quinn Martin Productions. Filmed on location.

THE BERT PARKS SHOW · NBC/CBS

1 NOVEMBER 1950–11 JANUARY 1952 (NBC); 14 JANUARY 1952–26 JUNE 1952 (CBS)   Although Bert Parks hosted many TV series, this daytime variety show—originally aired three times weekly, later daily—was the only one which bore his name. Other regulars included vocalist Betty Ann Grove, Harold Lang, and the Bobby Sherwood Quintet.

THE BEST IN MYSTERY · NBC

13 JULY 1956–31 AUGUST 1956   Rebroadcasts of the several episodes of *Four Star Playhouse* in which Dick Powell starred as Willie Dante, an ex-gambler who owned Dante's Inferno, a San Francisco nightclub. With Alan Mowbray as Jackson; Herb Vigran as Monte; and Regis Toomey as Lieutenant Waldo. Willie Dante reappeared in 1960, and was played by Howard Duff; see *Dante.* Reruns culled from other series were also broadcast under the title *The Best in Mystery* on CBS during the summers of 1954 and 1955.

THE BEST OF BROADWAY · CBS

15 SEPTEMBER 1954–4 MAY 1955   Martin Manulis produced this series of specials, which replaced *Pabst Blue Ribbon Bouts* every fourth Wednesday for one season. Presentations included: "The Royal Family," with Claudette Colbert (making her TV debut), Helen Hayes and Fredric March (15 September); "The Man Who Came to Dinner," with Buster Keaton, Margaret Hamilton, Joan Bennett, Bert Lahr, and Monty Woolley (13 October); "The Philadelphia Story," with Mary Astor and John Payne (8 December); "Arsenic and Old Lace," with Pat Breslin and Orson Bean (5 January); "The Guardsman," with Margaret Hamilton and Mary Boland (2 March); "Stage Door," with Rhonda Fleming (in her first major TV role, 6 April); and "Broadway," with Martha Hyer (4 May).

THE BEST OF EVERYTHING   ABC
30 MARCH 1970–25 SEPTEMBER 1970   Daytime serial based on the 1959
film about three young career women, all working at Key Publishing
Company, trying to make it in New York City. With Susan Sullivan and
Julie Mannix as April Morrison; Patty McCormack as Linda Warren;
Geraldine Fitzgerald as Violet Jordan; and Gale Sondergaard as Amanda
Key.

THE BEST OF SATURDAY NIGHT LIVE
See NBC'S SATURDAY NIGHT LIVE

THE BEST OF THE POST   SYNDICATED
1957   Dramatic anthology series; episodes were based on stories from
the *Saturday Evening Post.* Produced by MGM.

BEST SELLERS   NBC
30 SEPTEMBER 1976–25 APRIL 1977   The umbrella title for an anthology series made up of several serialized novels. Presentations included: (1)
"Captains and the Kings," Taylor Caldwell's story of three generations
of an influential Irish Catholic family, shown in eight parts. The large
cast included Richard Jordan (Joseph Armagh), Patty Duke Astin (Bernadette Armagh, Joseph's wife), Charles Durning (Ed Healey), Henry
Fonda (Senator Enfield Bassett), Perry King (Joseph's son Rory), Celeste
Holm (Sister Angela), John Houseman (Judge Chisholm), Harvey Jason
(Harry Zeff), Vic Morrow (Tom Hennessey), Barbara Parkins (Marti-
nique), Joanna Pettet (Katherine Hennessey), Ann Sothern (Mrs. Finch),
and Robert Vaughn (Charles Desmond). (2) "Once an Eagle," Anton
Meyer's tale of two soldiers and two wars, shown in seven parts, with
Sam Elliott (Sergeant Sam Damon), Cliff Potts (Lieutenant Courtney
Massengale), Darleen Carr (Tommy Caldwell Damon, Sam's wife), Amy
Irving (Emily Massengale, Courtney's wife), Glenn Ford (Major Cald-
well), Gary Grimes (Jack Devlin), Clu Gulagher (Lieutenant Merrick),
John Saxon (Captain Townshend), and William Windom (General Pul-
leyne). (3) "Seventh Avenue," Norman Bogner's saga of New York's gar-
ment industry, shown in three two-hour segments, featuring Steven Keats
(Jay Blackman), Dori Brenner (Rhoda Gold Blackman, his wife), Anne
Archer (Myrna Gold, Rhoda's sister), Herschel Bernardi (Joe Vitelli),
Jack Gilford (Finkelstein), Alan King (Harry Lee), Ray Milland (Freder-
icks), Paul Sorvino (Dave Shaw), Kristoffer Tabori (Al Blackman), and
William Windom (John Meyers). (4) "The Rhinemann Exchange," a
three-part, 5-hour adaptation of Robert Ludlum's World War II spy
thriller, with Stephen Collins (David Spaulding), Lauren Hutton (Leslie
Hawkewood), José Ferrer (Rhinemann), John Huston (Ambassador
Granville), and Roddy McDowall (Bobby Ballard). Although "Captains

and the Kings" fared well in the ratings, the other serializations did not, and the umbrella concept was scrapped in the spring of 1977.

BETTER LIVING TELEVISION THEATER ABC/DUMONT
21 JUNE 1953–16 AUGUST 1953 (ABC); 21 APRIL 1954–29 AUGUST 1954 (DUMONT) Like *Enterprise U.S.A.* and *Industry on Parade, Better Living Television Theater* was a series of documentaries designed to promote American industry. Fischer Black hosted the half-hour series. Typical of the presentations was the 1954 DuMont premiere, "A Is for Atom: The Story of Nuclear Power."

THE BETTER SEX ABC
18 JULY 1977–13 JANUARY 1978 A Goodson-Todman daytime game show in which a team of six men faced a team of six women. One player was given a question, then handed a card which indicated the correct answer and an incorrect answer; the player read one of those answers to members of the opposite team. Two members of the opposite team had to agree on whether the announced answer was the correct one; if their response was correct, two members of the first team were eliminated. If their response was incorrect, they were eliminated. The first team to eliminate all the members of the opposite team was the winner and split $1,000. The winning team then played against thirty audience members of the opposite sex in a similar format for the chance to win $5,000. Former country and western singer Bill Anderson served as cohost with Sarah Purcell; Purcell was the first woman to emcee a game show in more than twenty years.

THE BETTY CROCKER STAR MATINEE ABC
3 NOVEMBER 1951–26 APRIL 1952 Saturday noontime potpourri of variety, talk and short dramas, hosted by Adelaide Hawley.

THE BETTY FURNESS SHOW
See BY-LINE and PENTHOUSE PARTY ABC

THE BETTY HUTTON SHOW CBS
1 OCTOBER 1959–30 JUNE 1960 One of the most popular film stars of the 1940s (*The Fleet's In, The Miracle of Morgan's Creek,* and *Annie Get Your Gun*), Betty Hutton was unable to make a successful transition to television. Her dramatic debut, "Satins and Spurs" (NBC, 12 September 1954), spurred little excitement. In 1959, she and her former husband, Charles O'Curran, put together this unsuccessful situation comedy in which Hutton played Goldie Appleby, a former showgirl, now a manicurist, who is unexpectedly named executrix of a millionaire's estate and guardian of the three children. Also featured were Richard Miles as Nicky Strickland, Gigi Perreau as Patricia Strickland, and Dennis Joel as

Roy Strickland, Goldie's wards; Joan Shawlee as Goldie's friend, Lorna; Jean Carson as Rosemary, Goldie's roommate; Tom Conway as Howard Seaton, attorney for the estate; and Gavin Muir as Hollister, the butler. Slated against ABC's *The Donna Reed Show* and NBC's *Bat Masterson,* the series perished quietly. Hutton then made a few television appearances (the most recent was a 1965 *Gunsmoke*) and vanished from Hollywood. Early in the 1970s she was discovered washing dishes in a Portsmouth, Rhode Island, rectory.

THE BETTY WHITE SHOW   NBC/ABC
8 FEBRUARY 1954–31 DECEMBER 1954 (NBC); 5 FEBRUARY 1958–30 APRIL 1958 (ABC)   Betty White hosted two shows during the 1950s. The first was a daytime talk show; it was broadcast at lunchtime except during the summer, when it was aired late afternoons. Early in 1958 she returned as host of a prime-time comedy-variety show; regulars included John Dehner, Reta Shaw, Peter Leeds, Johnny Jacobs, and Frank DeVol's orchestra. In 1977 she starred in her own sitcom: see below.

THE BETTY WHITE SHOW   CBS
12 SEPTEMBER 1977–9 JANUARY 1978   After achieving her greatest fame as the delightfully catty Sue Ann Nivens on *The Mary Tyler Moore Show,* Betty White was given her own sitcom in 1977. She starred as Joyce Whitman, the not-too-talented star of TV's *Undercover Woman,* a purely fictional series that bore some resemblance to NBC's *Police Woman.* Also featured were John Hillerman as unemotional John Elliot, Joyce's ex-husband and *Undercover Woman*'s director; Georgia Engel (another *Mary Tyler Moore* alumna) as Joyce's roommate, Mitzi Maloney, recently laid off from her job at the unemployment office; Caren Kaye as voluptuous Tracy Garrett, Joyce's costar; Barney Phillips as timid Fletcher Huff, who played the police chief; Charles Cyphers as Hugo Muncy, Joyce's burly double; Alex Henteloff as Doug Porterfield, a network vice-president who oversaw the production of *Undercover Woman.* Executive producer: Bob Ellison. Produced by Charles Raymond and Dale McRaven for MTM Enterprises.

BETWEEN THE WARS   SYNDICATED
1978   Sixteen half-hour documentaries on American diplomacy, 1919–1941, narrated by Eric Sevareid. Produced by Alan Landsburg Productions.

BEULAH   ABC
3 OCTOBER 1950–22 SEPTEMBER 1953   The first TV dramatic series to star a black performer, *Beulah* told the story of a maid with a heart of gold. The character had been created by a white actor, Marlin Hurt, who played the part on the *Fibber McGee and Molly* radio series and on the

first radio version of *Beulah*, which premiered in 1945 (the character was later played by a second white performer, Bob Corley, before Hattie McDaniel took over the radio role). Television's first Beulah was Ethel Waters, a blues singer and Oscar nominee (for *Pinky*); Hattie McDaniel was scheduled to replace Waters in 1951, but was unable to do so; Louise Beavers took over the role in April 1952. Other regulars included William Post, Jr., as Beulah's employer, New York lawyer Harry Henderson; Ginger Jones (1950–1952) and June Frazee (1952–1953) as Alice Henderson, his wife; Clifford Sales (1950–1952) and Stuffy Singer (1952–1953) as Donnie, their son; Percy (Bud) Harris (1950–1952) and Dooley Wilson (1952–1953; he played Sam in *Casablanca*) as Bill Jackson, Beulah's boyfriend; Butterfly McQueen as Beulah's friend and confidante, Oriole, also a domestic.

THE BEVERLY HILLBILLIES   CBS
26 SEPTEMBER 1962–7 SEPTEMBER 1971 Together with *The Andy Griffith Show*, *The Beverly Hillbillies* was the most successful of the "rural" situation comedies brought to television under the aegis of James T. Aubrey, then president of CBS-TV. Universally blasted by the critics upon its premiere, *Hillbillies* climbed to the number-one spot in the Nielsens by January and remained there through 1964. It was the story of a backwoods family who suddenly became rich beyond description when oil was discovered on their property (located somewhere in Appalachia); they immediately packed their belongings in their decrepit car and headed for California. With Buddy Ebsen (song-and-dance man of the 1930s, and Davy Crockett's sidekick on *Disneyland*) as widower Jed Clampett; Irene Ryan (former vaudevillian) as Granny (Daisy Moses), his crusty mother-in-law; Donna Douglas as Jed's daughter, Elly May; Max Baer, Jr., son of the former heavyweight champion, as Jethro Bodine, Jed's dimwitted nephew; Raymond Bailey as Milburn Drysdale, president of the Commerce Bank of Beverly Hills, custodian of the Clampett funds and neighbor of the Clampetts; Nancy Kulp as Jane Hathaway, Drysdale's officious aide-de-camp; Harriet MacGibbon as Margaret Drysdale, Milburn's snooty wife; Shug Fisher (1965–1967) as Shorty, Elly May's boyfriend; Roger Torrey (1970–1971) as Mark Templeton, another boyfriend; and Stretch as Duke, the Clampett bloodhound. The "Beverly Hillbillies Theme" was played by Lester Flatt and Earl Scruggs, who occasionally appeared as themselves. Also appearing during the 1963–1964 season was Sharon Tate, as bank secretary Janet Trego, in one of her first professional roles. In 1963 *Petticoat Junction* was spun off, and in 1965 *Green Acres* appeared; its premise was the converse of the *Hillbillies*—a city family moves to the hinterlands.

BEWITCHED   ABC
17 SEPTEMBER 1964–1 JULY 1972 Situation comedy in which a win-

some witch, married to a mere mortal, tried to curb her supernatural powers. With Elizabeth Montgomery (daughter of Robert Montgomery) as Samantha Stevens; Dick York (1964–1969) and Dick Sargent (1969–1972) as her husband, Darin, an account executive at McMahon and Tate, a New York advertising agency; Agnes Moorehead as Endora, Samantha's meddlesome mother; David White as Larry Tate, Darin's boss; Alice Pearce (1964–1966) and Sandra Gould (1966–1972) as Gladys Kravitz, a nosy neighbor; George Tobias as her husband, Abner Kravitz; Irene Vernon (1964–1966) and Kasey Rogers (1966–1972) as Louise Tate, Larry's wife; Maurice Evans as Maurice, Samantha's warlock father; Marion Lorne (1964–1968) as Samantha's daffy Aunt Clara; Paul Lynde (1965–1966) as Samantha's Uncle Arthur; and Alice Ghostley (1968–1970) as Esmeralda, also a witch. In 1965 the Stevens' first child, Tabitha, was born; she too had supernatural powers. The part was played by three sets of twins: first, Heidi and Laura Gentry; second, Tamar and Julie Young; third (1966–1972), Diane and Erin Murphy (the part was credited to Erin). In 1970 son Adam was born, played by twins David and Greg Lawrence. In the later seasons, Elizabeth Montgomery also played the part of Serena, Samantha's free-spirited cousin. One of ABC's longest-running sitcoms, the series was created by Sol Saks and produced by William Asher, Montgomery's husband, for Screen Gems. See also *Tabitha*.

BID 'N' BUY CBS
1 JULY 1958–23 SEPTEMBER 1958   Bert Parks hosted this Tuesday-night auction game show, a summer replacement for *The $64,000 Question*.

BIFF BAKER, U.S.A. CBS
6 NOVEMBER 1952–26 MARCH 1953   Cold War espionage series starring Alan Hale, Jr. and Randy Stuart as Biff and Louise Baker, husband-and-wife spy team posing as American importers behind the Iron Curtain. Produced at Revue Studios by Alan Miller.

THE BIG ATTACK
See CITIZEN SOLDIER

THE BIG BANDS SYNDICATED
1966   Half-hour series showcasing some of the big bands that had survived from the 1930s and 1940s.

BIG BATTLES SYNDICATED
1974   A warfare documentary series.

BIG BLUE MARBLE SYNDICATED
1974   Ambitious children's series underwritten by the ITT Corporation. A magazine for kids, with filmed segments showing children around the

world at work and at play. Created and first produced by Harry Fownes, the show was so titled because the Earth, when seen from a satellite, resembles "a big blue marble."

BIG EDDIE   CBS

23 AUGUST 1975–7 NOVEMBER 1975 Abysmal situation comedy about an ex-gangster who went straight as the owner of the Big E sports arena. With Sheldon Leonard as Big Eddie Smith; Sheree North as Honey, his new wife, a former showgirl; Quinn Cummings as Ginger, his perky granddaughter; Alan Oppenheimer as Jesse, his younger brother; Billy Sands as Monte (Bang Bang) Valentine, an ex-jockey, now the cook; and Ralph Wilcox as Raymond McKay, Eddie's black business associate. Created by Bill Persky and Sam Denoff.

THE BIG EVENT   NBC

26 SEPTEMBER 1976–   The umbrella title for assorted movies and specials broadcast frequently throughout the year. Presentations included movies such as "Earthquake" and "Gone with the Wind" (which was the highest-rated single program in TV history at the time—it was later surpassed by one segment of *Roots* and the 1978 Super Bowl), made-for-TV features such as "Sybil," the story of a multiple personality with Sally Field and Joanne Woodward, and "The Moneychangers," and documentaries such as "The Search for the Loch Ness Monster—An Adventure," and "Life Goes to the Movies."

By far the most noteworthy presentation of the 1977–1978 season was "Holocaust," a four-part, nine-and-one-half-hour dramatization of the persecution and extermination of European Jews by the Nazis during World War II. Written by Gerald Green, the drama centered on the lives of the Weiss family, who lived in Berlin. Principal players included Fritz Weaver as Dr. Josef Weiss; Rosemary Harris as his wife, Berta Weiss; James Woods as their elder son, Karl; Meryl Streep as Karl's Christian wife, Inga; Joseph Bottoms as their younger son, Rudi; Blanche Baker as their daughter, Anna; Sam Wanamaker as Josef's brother, Moses; and Michael Moriarty as Erik Dorf, an ambitious Nazi officer. "Holocaust" won eight Emmys in 1978.

The chief "Big Event" of the 1978–1979 season was "Centennial," a twenty-five-hour, $25 million adaptation of James Michener's hefty saga of the West, starring Robert Conrad (Pasquinel), Richard Chamberlain (McKeag), Clint Walker (Joe Bean), Raymond Burr (Bockweiss), Sally Kellerman (Lise), Barbara Carrera (Clay Basket), Richard Crenna (Colonel Skimmerhorn), Chad Everett (Maxwell Mercy), and Alex Karras (Hans Brumbaugh). John Wilder was the producer.

BIG GAME   NBC

13 JUNE 1958–12 SEPTEMBER 1958 On this Friday-night game show

two contestants played a game similar to "Battleships," in which each sought to locate his opponent's game animals on a hidden board. This was the first of several game shows hosted by Tom Kennedy, younger brother of television quizmaster Jack Narz.

BIG HAWAII   NBC
21 SEPTEMBER 1977–30 NOVEMBER 1977 An early casualty of the 1977–1978 season, *Big Hawaii* told the story of modern-day cattle ranchers in the fiftieth state. With Cliff Potts as Mitch Fears; John Dehner as Barrett Fears, his father, the ranch owner; Lucia Stralser as Keke, Barrett's niece; Bill Lucking as Oscar, the foreman; Elizabeth Smith as Lulu (Auntie Lu), the housekeeper; Moe Keale as Garfield; Remi Abellira as Kimo; and Josie Over as Asita. Created by William Wood, with Perry Lafferty as executive producer and William Finnegan as supervising producer. Only seven episodes were telecast.

THE BIG IDEA   DUMONT
15 DECEMBER 1952–22 OCTOBER 1953 Half-hour documentary series on recent inventions. Donn Bennett was the host.

THE BIG ISSUE
See KEEP POSTED

BIG JOHN, LITTLE JOHN   NBC
11 SEPTEMBER 1976–3 SEPTEMBER 1977 Saturday-morning sitcom about a forty-five-year-old science teacher, who, after drinking from a "fountain of youth," changes into a twelve-year-old (and back again) at inopportune times. With Herb Edelman as the adult John Martin (Big John); Robbie Rist as the young John Martin (Little John); Joyce Bulifant as his wife, Marjorie; Mike Darnell as their son, Ricky; and Olive Dunbar as Miss Bertha Bottomly, the school principal. Created by Sherwood Schwartz and Lloyd J. Schwartz.

THE BIG MOMENT   NBC
5 JULY 1957–13 SEPTEMBER 1957 Great moments in sports history were relived on this half-hour series, hosted by former Princeton football star Bud Palmer.

THE BIG PARTY   CBS
8 OCTOBER 1959–31 DECEMBER 1959 *The Big Party* was planned as a series of fifteen variety extravaganzas which would alternate with *Playhouse 90* on Thursdays. The set for each show was a living room, with a party going on. Making his television debut, a nervous Rock Hudson hosted the premiere, which also featured a rare TV appearance by Tallu-

lah Bankhead. The entire concept was scrapped after the New Year's Eve "Big Party" and replaced by a series of variety shows entitled *The Revlon Revue.*

THE BIG PAYOFF
NBC/CBS

Daytime: 31 DECEMBER 1951–27 MARCH 1953 (NBC); 30 MARCH 1953–23 OCTOBER 1959 (CBS) *Nightime:* 29 JUNE 1952–14 SEPTEMBER 1952 (NBC); 21 JUNE 1953–27 SEPTEMBER 1953 (NBC) This long-running game show had several hosts, including Bert Parks, Randy Merriman, Mort Lawrence, and Robert Paige; the principal prizes given away were furs, which were modeled for several seasons by Bess Myerson. Vocalist Betty Ann Grove was later featured on the show, as were Denise Lor and Susan Sayers. In addition to its eight-year daytime run, *The Big Payoff* also surfaced as a prime-time show for two summers, and during the summer of 1953 it became one of the few series to have been carried by two networks at the same time.

THE BIG PICTURE
SYNDICATED

1951–1964 Probably the most widely televised public service program in history, *The Big Picture* was the story of the United States Army, as told by the United States Army. Most of the several hundred half-hour shows were assembled from documentary footage filmed over the years by the Army Signal Corps; occasional scenes, however, were dramatized. The first series of thirteen programs was organized by Lt. Carl Bruton and offered to just one station in Washington, D.C. The experiment proved popular, and production continued under the supervision of William Brown of the Army Pictorial Center. By 1957 the show was carried by more than 350 stations in the United States—it seemed to fill the odd nooks and crannies of practically every station's program schedule. The series was also picked up by the ABC network off and on from 1953 to 1959. See also *Flight; Uncommon Valor.*

THE BIG QUESTION
CBS

9 SEPTEMBER 1951–21 OCTOBER 1951 This Sunday series featured debates on current issues among leading journalists and other experts. Charles Collingwood acted as moderator.

THE BIG RECORD
CBS

18 SEPTEMBER 1957–11 JUNE 1958 Popular recording artists stopped by to sing their hits on this musical variety series, hosted by Patti Page and featuring the Vic Schoen orchestra. The show's one-hour format was cut to a half hour beginning 26 March 1958.

BIG SHAMUS, LITTLE SHAMUS
CBS

29 SEPTEMBER 1979–6 OCTOBER 1979 An early casualty of the 1979–80

season, *Big Shamus, Little Shamus* was an hour crime show about a father-and-son detective team. With Brian Dennehy as Arnie Sutter, house dick at the Hotel Ansonia in Atlantic City; Doug McKeon as Max Sutter, his 13-year-old son; George Wyner as Mr. Korman, the security chief; Kathryn Leigh Scott as Stephanie Marsh; Cynthia Sikes as Jingles, a waitress; Ty Henderson as Jerry, another hotel employee. Terry Hotchner created the series; Lee Rich and Sam H. Rolfe were the executive producers for Lorimar Productions.

THE BIG SHOW
See THE BIG PARTY

THE BIG SHOWDOWN   ABC
23 DECEMBER 1974–4 JULY 1975   Jim Peck hosted this daytime game show on which contestants won points by answering questions. The highest scorer then rolled a special pair of dice for cash. If the dice came up "Show" and "Down," the contestant won the $10,000 top prize. Executive producers: Don Lipp and Ron Greenberg.

THE BIG STORY   NBC
16 SEPTEMBER 1949–28 JUNE 1957   This half-hour anthology series presented stories about courageous journalists. It was hosted first by William Sloane, then by Norman Rose, Ben Grauer, finally by Burgess Meredith.

THE BIG SURPRISE (THE $100,000 BIG SURPRISE)   NBC
8 OCTOBER 1955–2 APRIL 1957   This nighttime game show began as a giveaway show, rewarding good Samaritans with valuable prizes. As big-money game shows began to gain popularity, however, the show changed to a question-and-answer format with a $100,000 top prize. The good Samaritans were replaced by contestants with areas of specialized knowledge; silent film star Francis X. Bushman, for example, won $30,000 as an expert in poetry. Jack Barry was the first host but was fired during the second season; he was replaced by Mike Wallace. Executive producer: Steve Carlin.

BIG TOP   CBS
1 JULY 1950–21 SEPTEMBER 1957   Circus program for kids, broadcast weekends from Camden, New Jersey, by WCAU-TV in Philadelphia. Jack Sterling was the ringmaster; regulars included Ed McMahon (in his first national television appearance) as a clown and strongman Dan Luri. Charles Vanda was the producer.

BIG TOWN   CBS/NBC
5 OCTOBER 1950–16 SEPTEMBER 1954 (CBS); 11 OCTOBER 1954–2 OCTOBER 1956 (NBC)   This popular crime show, which began on radio in

1937 (and, for a time, featured Edward G. Robinson), was set in Big Town, U.S.A., home of the *Illustrated Press,* a crusading daily paper. It first starred Patrick McVey as reporter Steve Wilson, with Mary K. Wells as society columnist Lorelei Kilbourne; Wells was succeeded in 1951 by Julie Stevens, then by Jane Nigh, Beverly Tyler, and, late in 1954, by Trudy Wroe. In the fall of 1954 the series switched networks. Mark Stevens, who had starred in another crime show—*Martin Kane*—during the previous season, took over, not only as the star but also as producer and director. Stevens upgraded Steve Wilson from reporter to managing editor. Barry Kelley was also featured as city editor Charlie Anderson, and in the fall of 1955 Doe Avedon was added as reporter Diane Walker, replacing Lorelei Kilbourne. Grace Kelly was the guest star on the 1950 CBS premiere, entitled "The Pay-Off." *Big Town* was widely syndicated during the 1950s under several titles, including *Byline: Steve Wilson, City Assignment,* and *Heart of the City.* It was telecast live until the spring of 1952.

THE BIG VALLEY ABC
15 SEPTEMBER 1965–19 MAY 1969   ABC's answer to *Bonanza, The Big Valley* told the story of the Barkley family, trying to make a go of it on their 30,000-acre ranch in California's San Joaquin Valley. While the Barkley ranch may not have been as large as the Ponderosa, it boasted a mine, a vineyard, an orange grove, and a black servant. With Barbara Stanwyck as the widowed Victoria Barkley, iron-willed head of the clan; Richard Long as level-headed number one son Jarrod, a lawyer; Peter Breck as hot-headed number two son Nick; Lee Majors as feisty number three son Heath (actually, Heath was the illegitimate half-Indian son of Victoria's husband); Charles Briles (1965–1966) as introspective number four son Eugene; Linda Evans as beautiful daughter Audra; and Napoleon Whiting as servant Silas.

THE BIGELOW SHOW NBC/CBS
14 OCTOBER 1948–7 JULY 1949 (NBC); 5 OCTOBER 1949–28 DECEMBER 1949 (CBS)   Mentalist Joseph Dunninger was featured on this half-hour variety show hosted by ventriloquist Paul Winchell and his star dummy, Jerry Mahoney.

BIGELOW THEATER CBS
10 DECEMBER 1950–3 JUNE 1951
BIGELOW-SANFORD THEATER DUMONT
6 SEPTEMBER 1951–27 DECEMBER 1951   This half-hour dramatic anthology series was seen Sundays on CBS, Thursdays on DuMont. Presentations included: "Charming Billy," with Spring Byington (3 June); "A Man's First Debt," with Lloyd Bridges (27 September); and "TKO," with Richard Jaeckel (25 October, his first major television role).

BIGFOOT AND WILDBOY   ABC

2 JUNE 1979–18 AUGUST 1979   A 'Saturday morning adventure series set in the Pacific Northwest, *Bigfoot and Wildboy* was first seen during the 1977–78 season as one segment of *The Krofft Supershow*. It starred Ray Young as the anthropomorphic Bigfoot and Joe Butcher as Wildboy, a human teenager who had been raised by Bigfoot. Also featured was Yvonne Regalado as their friend, Cindy.

THE BIL BAIRD SHOW   CBS

4 AUGUST 1953–29 OCTOBER 1953   This fifteen-minute puppet show, featuring the creations of Bil and Cora Baird, was seen on Tuesday and Thursday mornings.

THE BILL ANDERSON SHOW   SYNDICATED

1966   Country and western music, hosted by singer Bill Anderson.

THE BILL COSBY SHOW   NBC

14 SEPTEMBER 1969–31 AUGUST 1971   Bill Cosby, the first black actor to costar in an adventure series *(I Spy)*, returned to TV after a year's absence in this low-key situation comedy. In so doing, he became the first black man to star in a comedy series since *Amos and Andy* ceased production in 1953. Cosby played Chet Kincaid, a high school gym teacher. Also featured were Lillian Randolph (1969–1970) and Beah Richards (1970–1971) as his mother, Rose; Lee Weaver as his brother Brian, a garbage collector; De De Young (1969) and Olga James (1969–1971) as Brian's wife, Verna; Donald Livingston as Roger, Brian and Verna's young son; Joyce Bulifant as Mrs. Marsha Patterson, the school guidance counselor; Sid McCoy as Mr. Langford; and Joseph Perry as Max.

THE BILL CULLEN SHOW   CBS

12 FEBRUARY 1953–14 MAY 1953   A fifteen-minute Thursday morning variety show, hosted by Bill Cullen, with Betty Brewer and the Milton DeLugg Trio.

THE BILL DANA SHOW   NBC

22 SEPTEMBER 1963–17 JANUARY 1965   Bill Dana's many appearances on *The Steve Allen Show* as José Jiminez, the easily confused Latin American, led him to his own series. On this Sunday-evening sitcom he continued to play Jiminez, now employed as a bellhop at a New York hotel. Also featured were comic Don Adams (in his first continuing TV role) as Byron Glick, the house dick; Jonathan Harris as the persnickety Mr. Phillips, hotel manager; Gary Crosby as Eddie, a fellow bellhop; and Maggie Peterson as Susie, a waitress in the coffee shop.

THE BILL GOODWIN SHOW NBC

11 SEPTEMBER 1951–27 MARCH 1952 Bill Goodwin left his job as announcer on *The Burns and Allen Show* to host his own half-hour variety show, broadcast Tuesday and Thursday afternoons at 3:30. Regulars included Eileen Barton, Roger Dann, and the Joe Bushkin Trio. Produced and directed by Sherman Marks.

THE BILL GWINN SHOW ABC

5 FEBRUARY 1951–21 APRIL 1952 Hosted by Bill Gwinn, this series began under the title *It Could Happen to You*, on which couples from the studio audience acted out scenes suggested by songs. In April of 1951 the show was retitled *The Bill Gwinn Show*.

BILL MOYERS' JOURNAL PBS

14 NOVEMBER 1972–16 APRIL 1976; 5 FEBRUARY 1979–
Magazine series hosted by Bill Moyers, who served as President Johnson's press secretary during the 1960s. During the 1972–1973 and 1975–1976 seasons Moyers's programs focused on life in America; during the 1974–1975 season Moyers reported on international issues. After a two-and-one-half-year stint with CBS, Moyers returned to PBS in 1979. See also *This Week*.

BILLY CBS

26 FEBRUARY 1979–28 APRIL 1979 Half-hour sitcom hastily scheduled by CBS to replace *Co-Ed Fever*, which the network shelved after just one showing. With Steve Guttenberg as Billy Fisher, a nineteen-year-old who fantasizes a lot; James Gallery as George Fisher, his father; Peggy Pope as Alice Fisher, his mother; Paula Trueman as Gran, his grandmother; Michael Alaimo as Norville Shadrack, Billy's employer, a funeral director; and Bruce Talkington as Arthur Milliken, Billy's coworker. *Billy* was supplied by John Rich Productions.

BILLY BOONE AND COUSIN KIB CBS

9 JULY 1950–27 AUGUST 1950 A summer replacement for *Mr. I. Magination*, this half-hour children's show starred Carroll "Kib" Colby and Patti Milligan. *Billy Boone* was an animated figure whose adventures were drawn by Colby. Judy Dupuy produced the series.

THE BILLY DANIELS SHOW ABC

5 OCTOBER 1952–28 DECEMBER 1952 One of few blacks to host a variety series, singer Billy Daniels ("That Old Black Magic") emceed his own fifteen-minute show on Sunday evenings. Benny Payne and Jimmy Blaine were also featured.

BILLY GRAHAM CRUSADES (HOUR OF DECISION)   ABC/SYNDICATED

30 SEPTEMBER 1951–21 FEBRUARY 1954 (ABC); 1954–
(SYNDICATED)   One of the first evangelists to utilize television, Billy
Graham first appeared on a fifteen-minute series entitled *Hour of Decision.* Since that time, the *Billy Graham Crusades,* taped at cities throughout the world, have been widely telecast, usually as specials.

BILLY JAMES HARGIS AND HIS ALL-AMERICAN KIDS   SYNDICATED

1972   Religious show, featuring the Reverend Billy James Hargis and
several of his youthful followers, known as the All-American Kids.

BILLY ROSE'S PLAYBILL   ABC

3 OCTOBER 1950–27 MARCH 1951   Theatrical producer Billy Rose hosted this half-hour dramatic anthology series.

THE BING CROSBY SHOW   ABC

14 SEPTEMBER 1964–14 JUNE 1965   An established recording and motion picture star, Bing Crosby had made few forays into television before
taking the big plunge with this 1964 sitcom. In it he played Bing Collins,
an architectural designer. Also featured were Beverly Garland as his
wife, Ellie; Diane Sherry as their daughter Janice; Carol Faylen as their
daughter Joyce; and Frank McHugh as the handyman, Willie Walters.
The cast usually performed one or two musical numbers each week. The
series was produced by Steven Gethers for Bing Crosby Productions and
was telecast Mondays immediately preceding *Ben Casey,* another Bing
Crosby Productions venture.

BIOGRAPHY   SYNDICATED

1962   Mike Wallace hosted this self-explanatory documentary series on
which the lives of notables were presented through the use of film clips
and interviews.

THE BIONIC WOMAN   ABC/NBC

14 JANUARY 1976–4 MAY 1977 (ABC); 10 SEPTEMBER 1977–2 SEPTEM-
BER 1978 (NBC)   A spinoff from *The Six Million Dollar Man, The
Bionic Woman* starred Lindsay Wagner, a newcomer to television, as
Jaime Somers. Severely injured in a skydiving mishap, Jaime was outfitted with bionic legs, a bionic right arm, and a bionic right ear. Employed
as an OSI operative, she had the cover occupation of a schoolteacher at
the Ventura Air Force Base school. Also featured were Richard Anderson as OSI topsider Oscar Goldman; Martin E. Brooks as Dr. Rudy
Wells, OSI physician; Sam Chew, Jr., as Mark Russell, another OSI employee; Ford Rainey as Jim; and Martha Scott as Helen. In 1977, the series was dropped by ABC and picked up by NBC; it was one of the few

shows to switch networks during the 1970s. As a result of the switch co-stars Richard Anderson and Martin E. Brooks, who continued to appear on *The Six Million Dollar Man* over at ABC, became two of the very few (if not the only two) performers ever to play the same role simultaneously on two series aired by different networks. Added to the cast in the fall of 1977 was Maximillian, the bionic German shepherd. The series was created by Kenneth Johnson, and its executive producer was Harve Bennett for Universal Television.

BIRDMAN NBC
9 SEPTEMBER 1967–14 SEPTEMBER 1968 Saturday-morning cartoon series produced by Hanna-Barbera, featuring the adventures of Ray Randall (alias Birdman), who is endowed with the usual array of super powers by Ra, the Egyptian sun god, and fought evildoers.

BLACK JOURNAL PBS
1968–1976 Long-running public affairs program focusing on issues of concern to black Americans. Produced and hosted by Tony Brown at New York's WNET, the show was aired in both an hour and a half-hour format. Early in 1976 a talk show format, with guest cohosts, was attempted briefly.

BLACK OMNIBUS SYNDICATED
1973 Talent showcase for black performers, hosted by James Earl Jones.

BLACK PERSPECTIVE ON THE NEWS PBS
1973–1979 Black journalists interview newsmakers on this educational series produced by Acel Moore and Reginald Bryant (who also serves as moderator) for Philadelphia's WHYY-TV.

THE BLACK ROBE NBC
18 MAY 1949–6 APRIL 1950 Created by Phillips Lord (creator of *Gangbusters*), this series recreated court cases. In its early weeks, it was entitled *Police Night Court*. To achieve realism, nonprofessionals were used as witnesses and attorneys. Frankie Thomas, Sr., appeared as the judge, and John Green played the court clerk. The live series was usually seen Thursdays.

BLACK SADDLE NBC/ABC
10 JANUARY 1959–5 SEPTEMBER 1959 (NBC); 2 OCTOBER 1959–30 SEPTEMBER 1960 (ABC) Half-hour western starring Peter Breck as Clay Culhane, a former gunfighter who is now a frontier lawyer. With Russell Johnson as Marshal Gib Scott; Anna Lisa as widow Nora Travers, pro-

prietor of the Marathon Hotel. Set in Latigo, a town in New Mexico Territory. Antony Ellis was the producer.

BLACK SHEEP SQUADRON
See BAA BAA BLACK SHEEP

THE BLACK TULIP   SYNDICATED
1972 Dumas's story, set in seventeenth-century France and Holland, was told in a six-part miniseries produced in England and aired as part of *Family Classics Theatre*. It starred Simon Ward as Cornelius von Baerle, a young Dutchman trying to cultivate the legendary black tulip.

THE BLAIR & RAITT SHOW (THE CHEVY SHOW)   NBC
7 JUNE 1959–20 SEPTEMBER 1959 Janet Blair and John Raitt cohosted this musical variety hour, a summer replacement for *The Dinah Shore Show*.

BLANK CHECK   NBC
6 JANUARY 1975–4 JULY 1975 A dull daytime game show on which panelists tried to outguess each other in selecting digits that form the sum of a "blank check." Executive producer: Jack Barry. Hosted by Art James.

BLANKETY BLANKS   ABC
21 APRIL 1975–27 JUNE 1975 Bill Cullen hosted this short-lived daytime game show on which panelists tried to guess puns. Executive producer: Bob Stewart.

BLANSKY'S BEAUTIES   ABC
12 FEBRUARY 1977–27 JUNE 1977 Following the cancellation of her eponymous series, Nancy Walker was immediately cast in a new sitcom, which was in turn canceled; she thus earned the dubious distinction of starring in two unsuccessful series in a single season. In *Blansky's Beauties* she played Nancy Blansky, the manager and den mother of a troupe of Las Vegas showgirls. Featured were Eddie Mekka (also of *Laverne and Shirley*) as her nephew, Joey DeLuca, the troupe's dance instructor; Scott Baio as Anthony DeLuca, her worldwise twelve-year-old nephew; Lynda Goodfriend as Sunshine (Ethel Akalino), the klutzy showgirl; Caren Kaye as Bambi Benton, the daffy one; Rhonda Bates as Arkansas, the tall one; Taaffe O'Connell as Hillary Prentiss, the one who knew the boss; Bond Gideon as Lovely Carson; Gerri Reddick as Jackie Outlaw; Elaine Bolton as Bridget Muldoon; Jill Owens as Misty Karamazov; Shirley Kirkes as Cochise (Gladys Littlefeather); Antonette Yuskis as Sylvia Silver; George Pentecost as Horace (Stubs) Wilmington, manager of the Oa-

sis Hotel; Pat Morita (on loan from *Happy Days*) as Arnold; and Blackjack the Great Dane. Garry K. Marshall, Bob Brunner, and Arthur Silver created the series; Marshall, Edward K. Milkis, and Thomas L. Miller were the executive producers. Three members of the show's cast turned up in a 1978 sitcom which was also set in Las Vegas: see *Who's Watching the Kids*.

BLIND AMBITION   CBS
20 MAY 1977–23 MAY 1979   A four-part, eight-hour docudrama on Watergate, based on the books *Blind Ambition* by former White House counsel John Dean and *Mo* by Maureen Dean, his wife. Principal players included: Martin Sheen as John Dean; Theresa Russell as Maureen Dean; Rip Torn as Richard Nixon; Lawrence Pressman as H. R. Haldeman; Graham Jarvis as John Ehrlichman; John Randolph as John Mitchell; Christopher Guest as Jeb Magruder; Michael Callan as Chuck Colson; Ed Flanders as Dean's lawyer, Charlie Shaffer. The scenes in the Oval Office between Dean and Nixon were all verbatim extracts from the official White House tapes. George Schaefer and Renée Valente produced the series.

BLIND DATE   ABC/NBC/DUMONT
5 MAY 1949–20 SEPTEMBER 1951 (ABC); 7 JUNE 1952–19 JULY 1952 (NBC); 9 JUNE 1953–15 SEPTEMBER 1953 (DUMONT)   A precursor of *The Dating Game, Blind Date* began on radio in 1943. It was the first TV game show to be hosted by a woman: Arlene Francis (Jan Murray hosted the version in 1953). The format was similar to that of *The Dating Game;* two eligible college men talked with a model, who could not see her hopeful suitors. She then chose one of the men to be her date.

BLONDIE   NBC
4 JANUARY 1957–27 SEPTEMBER 1957   The first of two short-running adaptations of Chic Young's long-running comic strip. With Pamela Britton as Blondie Bumstead, hard-working housewife; Arthur Lake as Dagwood Bumstead, her bumbling husband (Lake had played Dagwood to Penny Singleton's Blondie in a score of movies during the 1940s), an architect; Stuffy Singer as teenage son Alexander; Ann Barnes as preteen daughter Cookie; Florenz Ames as J. C. Dithers, Bumstead's blustery boss, president of Dithers Construction Company; and Hal Peary as next-door neighbor Herb Woodley.

BLONDIE   CBS
26 SEPTEMBER 1968–9 JANUARY 1969   The second attempt at turning the comic strip into a successful series also failed. This effort featured Patricia Harty as Blondie Bumstead; Will Hutchins as Dagwood; Peter Robbins as son Alexander; Pamelyn Ferdin as daughter Cookie; Jim

Backus as boss J. C. Dithers; Henny Backus (Jim's real-life wife) as Cora Dithers; Bryan O'Byrne as neighbor Herb Woodley; and Bobbi Jordan as Tootsie Woodley.

THE BLUE ANGEL CBS
6 JULY 1954–12 OCTOBER 1954   This Tuesday-night variety series was a summer replacement for *See It Now.* Orson Bean and Polly Bergen hosted the series, set at a posh New York nightclub.

THE BLUE ANGELS SYNDICATED
1960   The adventures of the Blue Angels, a precision squadron of four U.S. Navy flyers who tour the country giving exhibitions. With Dennis Cross as Commander Arthur Richards, head of the squadron; Warner Jones as Captain Wilbur Scott; Don Gordon as Lieutenant Hank Bertelli; Mike Galloway as Lieutenant Russ MacDonald; Robert Knapp as crewman Zeke Powers; and Ross Elliott as crewman Cort Ryker. Simeon G. Gallu, Jr., produced the half-hour show.

THE BLUE KNIGHT CBS
17 DECEMBER 1975–27 OCTOBER 1976   Joseph Wambaugh's novel about a veteran cop on the beat was first telecast as an eight-hour mini-series in 1973 (shown on four consecutive nights, 13 November–16 November), starring William Holden as patrolman Bumper Morgan. It was Holden's first serious dramatic role on television (he'd played himself on an *I Love Lucy* episode some eighteen years earlier). Holden was not interested in doing a series, however. George Kennedy was then signed for the part. The series pilot was aired 9 May 1975, and the series itself was selected as a midseason replaement for *Kate McShane.* Although the series was renewed in 1976, competition from ABC's *Charlie's Angels* proved too strong. Also appearing (in the last three episodes) was Barbara Rhoades as Carrie Williams, Bumper's lady friend. Executive producers: Lee Rich and Philip Capice.

BLUE LIGHT ABC
12 JANUARY 1966–31 AUGUST 1966   This half-hour adventure series starred Robert Goulet as David March, a double agent working for the U.S.A. in the intelligence unit of the Third Reich. March's code name was "Blue Light." With Christine Carere as Suzanne Duchard, his confidante.

BLUES BY BARGY CBS
24 JANUARY 1949–6 JULY 1950   Singer-pianist Jeane Bargy was the star of this durable musical show. It was usually broadcast several times a week, sometimes in a fifteen-minute format, other times in a thirty-minute format.

BOB AND CAROL AND TED AND ALICE   ABC
26 SEPTEMBER 1973–7 NOVEMBER 1973 This pale adaptation of the
1969 film comedy about mate swapping was the first fatality of the 1973–
1974 season. With Robert Urich as film director Bob Sanders; Anne Archer as his wife, Carol; David Spielberg as attorney Ted Henderson;
Anita Gillette as his wife, Alice; Jodie Foster as Elizabeth, Ted and Alice's preteen daughter; and Brad Savage as Sean, Bob and Carol's young
son.

THE BOB AND RAY SHOW   NBC
26 NOVEMBER 1951–1 FEBRUARY 1952; 12 JULY 1952–16 AUGUST 1952;
7 OCTOBER 1952–23 JUNE 1953; 27 APRIL 1953–28 SEPTEMBER
1953 Bob (Elliott) and Ray (Goulding), two low-key satirists, first
joined forces on a Boston radio station in the late 1940s. Though they
made several forays into television and continue to make guest appearances (they also did a Broadway show, *The Two and Only,* in 1972), their
unique brand of humor seems best suited to radio. Their first TV program, a fifteen-minute affair, was seen Mondays through Fridays at 7:15
p.m. and featured Audrey Meadows. During the summer of 1952 they
hosted a half-hour show on Saturdays, which featured Cloris Leachman.
In the fall of that year, they were again seen in a fifteen-minute format;
this show, also known as *Club Embassy* or *Club Time,* featured Audrey
Meadows (again) and singer Mindy Carson, who replaced Bob and Ray
as host in midseason. In late April of 1953 they began a second fifteen-
minute show, which was seen Mondays at 7:30 p.m. Bob and Ray later
cohosted a game show, *The Name's the Same,* in 1955, and were regulars
on *Happy Days,* a 1970 summer series.

THE BOB CONSIDINE SHOW   NBC/ABC
20 JANUARY 1951–19 JANUARY 1954 (NBC); 11 JULY 1954–29 AUGUST
1954 (ABC) Syndicated columnist Bob Considine had two network
shows of his own. The first, a fifteen-minute weekly show, featured comments and interviews with guests; it was also known as *On the Line with
Considine.* The second show was seen once a week as a summer replacement for *The Walter Winchell Show.* Considine was later one of the regulars on *Tonight! America After Dark,* the short-lived NBC late-night
show that replaced Steve Allen's *Tonight* show in 1957.

THE BOB CRANE SHOW   NBC
6 MARCH 1975–19 JUNE 1975 Insipid sitcom about a middle-aged man
who decided to go to medical school. With Bob Crane as Bob Wilcox;
Trisha Hart as his wife, Ellie Wilcox; Erica Petal as daughter Pam;
Ronny Graham as Ernest Busso, their eccentric landlord, an inventor;
Jack Fletcher as Lyle Ingersoll, dean of the medical school; Todd Susman

as fellow student Marvin Susman; and James Sutorius as student Jerry Mallory. The half-hour show was produced by Norman S. Powell and Martin Cohan for MTM Enterprises. Bob Crane, a one-time disc jockey who had been featured on *The Donna Reed Show* and had starred in *Hogan's Heroes,* was found murdered in an Arizona hotel room in June of 1978.

THE BOB CROSBY SHOW
CBS/NBC

14 SEPTEMBER 1953–30 AUGUST 1957 (CBS); 14 JUNE 1958–6 SEPTEMBER 1958 (NBC)   Bing's younger brother was a popular bandleader during the 1930s and 1940s; Bob Crosby's Bobcats even appeared on television in 1939. Crosby later hosted several radio shows, including *The Crosby Music Shop* and *The Crosby Night Shift.* The first of the two television series he hosted was a half-hour show, broadcast Monday through Friday; it featured the Modernaires (who had sung with Crosby on radio), Joan O'Brien, Jack Narz, and (in later seasons) Bob's daughter Cathy Crosby. Bob's second series was an hour-long prime-time effort, a summer replacement for *The Perry Como Show;* it featured singer Gretchen Wyler, the Peter Gennaro dancers, the Clay Warnick singers, The Carl Hoff orchestra, and (at the opening and closing) clown Emmett Kelly. Produced by Louis DaPron.

THE BOB CUMMINGS SHOW
See LOVE THAT BOB

THE BOB CUMMINGS SHOW
CBS

5 OCTOBER 1961–1 MARCH 1962   Shortly after the demise of *Love That Bob,* Bob Cummings returned in another situation comedy strikingly similar to the earlier one. This time Bob played Bob Carson, a wealthy girl-crazy adventurer. With Murvyn Vye as Lionel; Roberta Shore as young neighbor "Hank" Geogerty. The series was clobbered in the ratings by NBC's *Dr. Kildare.*

BOB HOPE PRESENTS THE CHRYSLER THEATER
NBC

4 OCTOBER 1963–6 SEPTEMBER 1967   Hour-long dramatic anthology series hosted by Bob Hope. Interspersed throughout each season were *The Bob Hope Specials,* musical or variety hours with Hope and guest stars. Dramatic presentations on the anthology series included Aleksandr Solzhenitzyn's "One Day in the Live of Ivan Denisovich" (8 November 1963); "Double Jeopardy," with a rare television appearance by Lauren Bacall (8 January 1965); "The War and Eric Kurtz," with David Carradine (his first major TV role, 5 March 1965); and "Blind Man's Bluff," with Susan Clark (her first major TV role, 8 February 1967).

THE BOB HOPE SHOW   NBC

12 OCTOBER 1953–22 MAY 1956   One of the world's best-known personalities and America's premier comedian, Bob Hope's regular appearances
on television during the 1950s were on a monthly basis. During the 1952–
1953 season he hosted *The Colgate Comedy Hour* on Sundays every four
weeks; during the 1953–1954 and 1954–1955 seasons he was seen once a
month on Tuesdays, replacing Milton Berle; during the 1955–1956 season he was also seen on Tuesdays, alternating with Milton Berle, Martha
Raye, and Dinah Shore. Hope's famous theme song, "Thanks for the
Memory," was written by Ralph Rainger and Leo Robin.

THE BOB HOWARD SHOW   CBS

2 AUGUST 1948–7 DECEMBER 1950   A fifteen-minute nightly musical series hosted by pianist-singer Bob Howard, the first black performer to
host a network TV program. In those days Howard was billed as "TV's
jive bomber."

THE BOB NEWHART SHOW   NBC

11 OCTOBER 1961–13 JUNE 1962   Bob Newhart, a onetime accountant,
was one of the most successful of the "new wave" of stand-up comics
who appeared on television in the late 1950s. Newhart's trademark was a
telephone; many of his monologues were done as telephone conversations. Nicknamed the "button-down comedian" (because of his button-
down shirts), he headlined a thirty-minute variety series in 1961. It was
adored by the critics, if not by a large viewing audience, and won both an
Emmy and a Peabody award in 1962. Other regulars included Jackie Joseph, Kay Westfall, Jack Grinnage, Mickey Manners, Pearl Shear, June
Ericson, Andy Albin, and announcer Dan Sorkin.

THE BOB NEWHART SHOW   CBS

16 SEPTEMBER 1972–2 SEPTEMBER 1978   Bob Newhart's second eponymous series, his first situation comedy, was a clear success. In it he played
Bob Hartley, a Chicago psychologist. With Suzanne Pleshette as his wife
Emily, a third-grade teacher; Bill Daily as divorced neighbor Howard
Borden, a 747 navigator; Peter Bonerz as orthodontist Jerry Robinson,
whose office is on the same floor as Bob's; Marcia Wallace as their receptionist Carol (Kester) Bondurant; Patricia Smith (1972–1973) as Margaret Hoover, the Hartleys' neighbor; Pat Finley (1974–1976) as Ellen,
Bob's sister; Will MacKenzie (1975–   ) as travel agent Larry Bondurant, who married Carol. For several seasons Bob's therapy group included Jack Riley as paranoid Elliott Carlin; Florida Friebus as kindly Mrs.
Bakerman; John Fiedler as timid Mr. Peterson; Renee Lippin as shy Michelle; and Noam Pitlik as obnoxious Mr. Gianelli. Created by David
Davis and Lorenzo Music. Executive producers (and script supervisors):

Tom Patchett and Jay Tarses (a former comedy team). Produced by MTM Enterprises.

THE BOB SMITH SHOW
See THE GULF ROAD SHOW

BOBBIE GENTRY'S HAPPINESS HOUR
CBS

5 JUNE 1974–26 JUNE 1974   A four-week summer replacement for *The Sonny and Cher Comedy Hour,* hosted by singer Bobbie Gentry, who is probably best known for her 1967 record, "Ode to Billy Joe."

THE BOBBY DARIN AMUSEMENT CO.
NBC

27 JULY 1972–7 SEPTEMBER 1972; 19 JANUARY 1973–27 APRIL 1973   Born Walden Robert Cassotto, Bobby Darin burst on the entertainment scene in 1958 with a hit record: "Splish Splash." After several more hits (including "Mack the Knife"), a marriage to Sandra Dee, and a string of movies, he disappeared from show business in 1967. He returned early in the 1970s and was given his own series in 1972, a summer replacement for *The Dean Martin Show.* The series was revived that winter as a midseason replacement. Regulars included Dick Bakalyan, Steve Landesberg, and Rip Taylor. Stricken as a child with rheumatic fever, Darin had had two artificial valves inserted in his heart in 1971; following open heart surgery to correct a malfunctioning valve, Darin died on December 20, 1973, at the age of thirty-seven.

THE BOBBY GOLDSBORO SHOW
SYNDICATED

1972   Half-hour variety series hosted by pop singer Bobby Goldsboro. The announcer was a frog puppet named Calvin Calaveras. Goldsboro's musical career began as a guitarist for Roy Orbison; his hits have included "See the Funny Little Clown," "Little Things," and "Honey."

THE BOBBY LORD SHOW
SYNDICATED

1966   A half hour of country and western music, hosted by Bobby Lord.

THE BOBBY VINTON SHOW
SYNDICATED

1975–1976   Hosted by singer Bobby Vinton, this half-hour musical variety series was produced in Toronto. Vinton began his recording career as a clarinetist and bandleader but is best known as a vocalist. His hits (dating back to 1962) have included "Roses Are Red," "Blue on Blue," "Blue Velvet," and "My Melody of Love." Executive producers: Allan Blye and Chris Bearde.

BOBO THE HOBO
SYNDICATED

1956   A filmed color anthology series for children, starring a repertory company of puppets. The puppets' limbs were manually controlled, but their jaws and lips were operated by a person wearing a special helmet which electronically transmitted the wearer's jaw and lip movements to the puppets. Samuel H. Evans invented the helmet device and co-produced the series with Lorraine Lester. Brett Morrison supplied the voice of Bobo, leader of the puppet troupe.

BOLD JOURNEY ABC
16 JULY 1956–31 AUGUST 1959 Amateur adventurers narrated films of their daring deeds on this documentary series hosted by John Stephenson (1956–1957) and Jack Douglas (1957–1959).

THE BOLD ONES NBC
14 SEPTEMBER 1969–9 JANUARY 1973 The umbrella title for four different series, each with its own producer: (1) *The Doctors*—the only one of the four to last for the duration—starred E. G. Marshall as Dr. David Craig, founder of the David Craig Institute of Medicine; David Hartman as Dr. Paul Hunter; John Saxon as Dr. Ted Stuart; Julie Adams (1970–1971) as Mrs. David Craig. (2) *The Lawyers* (1969–1972)—Nichols, Darrell & Darrell—with Burl Ives as sly senior partner Walter Nichols; Joseph Campanella as tweedy junior partner Brian Darrell; James Farentino as Brian's swinging brother, Neil Darrell. (3) *The Law Enforcers* (1969–1970) with Leslie Nielsen as Deputy Police Chief Sam Danforth; Hari Rhodes as black District Attorney William Washburn. (4) *The Senator* (1970–1971)—with Hal Holbrook as the idealistic Senator Hays Stowe; Michael Tolan as his aide, Jordan Boyle; Sharon Acker as Erin Stowe, the senator's wife; and Cindy Eilbacher as Norma, their young daughter.

BOLD VENTURE SYNDICATED
1959 Dane Clark starred as adventurer Slate Shannon, skipper of *The Bold Venture,* in this half-hour adventure series set in the Caribbean. With Joan Marshall as Sailor Duval, Shannon's ward and companion.

BON VOYAGE
See TREASURE QUEST

BONANZA NBC
12 SEPTEMBER 1959–16 JANUARY 1973 Second only to *Gunsmoke* among long-running westerns, *Bonanza* was the archetype of the "property" western that dominated the genre during the 1960s. Set in Virginia City, Nevada, it told the story of the Cartwrights, owners of a nearby 600,000-acre (give or take a few) ranch—The Ponderosa (named because of the ponderosa pines growing there). Hardworking, resourceful, and independent, the Cartwrights seemed to devote little time to running the

ranch, despite the fact that their hired help never numbered more than four; obviously, the Cartwrights knew good labor when they saw it. With Canadian actor Lorne Greene as Ben Cartwright, a threetime widower; Pernell Roberts (1959–1965) as eldest son Adam; big Dan Blocker (1959–1972) as son Hoss; Michael Landon (star of the 1957 film, *I Was a Teenage Werewolf*) as youngest son, Little Joe; Victor Sen Yung as Hop Sing, the cook; Ray Teal as Sheriff Roy Coffee, the Virginia City lawman who frequently called on the Cartwrights for assistance; David Canary (1968–1970; 1972–1973) as foreman Mr. Canaday (Candy); Mitch Vogel (1970–1972) as Jamie Hunter, a young runaway taken in by the Cartwrights; and Tim Matheson (1972–1973) as ranch hand Griff King, an ex-con.

Each of the Cartwright sons was a half-brother to the other two; the story of Ben Cartwright's three marriages was told in flashbacks. Adam, born in New England, was the son of Ben's first wife Elizabeth. Hoss was the son of second wife Inger, a woman of Scandinavian extraction who was killed by Indians; Hoss's real name is Eric (*hoss* is Norwegian for "good luck"). Little Joe, the youngest, was the son of Marie, whom Ben met in New Orleans; Marie died as the result of a fall from her horse.

During its first two seasons, *Bonanza* was seen on Saturdays and failed to outdraw CBS's *Perry Mason*. In the fall of 1961, it was scheduled on Sundays at 9 p.m. It remained there for eleven years, ranking consistently among the Top Ten, eventually knocking off *Perry Mason* in 1965–1966. Even after Pernell Roberts quit the series in 1965 (explaining he'd grown tired of the role), the show continued to do well. But two calamitous events in 1972 led to *Bonanza's* cancellation halfway through its fourteenth season: the sudden death of Dan Blocker during the summer and a scheduling change to Tuesdays.

BONINO
NBC

12 SEPTEMBER 1953–26 DECEMBER 1953 An early ethnic situation comedy about an Italian-American opera singer, a widower with several children, who decides to spend more time with his family. With Italian-American opera singer Ezio Pinza as Babbo Bonino; Mary Wickes as Martha, the maid; David Opatoshu as Walter Rogers, Bonino's manager; Conrad Janis as eldest son Edward; Lenka Peterson as daughter Doris; Chet Allen as son Terry; Oliver Andes as son Carlo; Gaye Huston as daughter Francesca; and Van Dyke Parks as son Andrew. Parks grew up to be a rock-music producer and composer and cowrote (with Brian Wilson) the Beach Boys' hits "Heroes and Villains" and "Surf's Up."

BONKERS
SYNDICATED

1978 Comedy-variety half hour starring the Hudson Brothers—Bill, Brett, and Mark—with Bob Monkhouse and the Bonkettes. Produced by Jack Burns for ITC.

THE BONNIE PRUDDEN SHOW   SYNDICATED
1968   Half-hour exercise show, hosted by physical fitness expert Bonnie
Prudden.

BOOK BEAT   PBS
1965–   Hardy half-hour series hosted by Robert Cromie of
the Chicago *Tribune,* featuring interviews with authors.

BOOTS AND SADDLES   SYNDICATED
1957–1959   The adventures of the Fifth Cavalry. With Jack Pickard as
Captain Shank Adams; Patrick McVey as Lieutenant Colonel Hays;
Gardner McKay as Lieutenant Kelly; David Willock as Lieutenant Bin-
ning; John Alderson as Sergeant Bullock; and Michael Hinn as scout
Luke Cummings. Thirty-nine half-hour episodes were filmed by California National Productions.

BORDER PATROL   SYNDICATED
1959   Modern-day adventure series starring Richard Webb (*Captain
Midnight*) as Don Jagger, Deputy Chief of the United States Border Patrol.

BORN FREE   NBC
9 SEPTEMBER 1974–30 DECEMBER 1974   Conservation-minded adventure series set in Kenya. With Gary Collins as game warden George
Adamson; Diana Muldaur as Joy Adamson; Hal Frederick as Makedde,
their scout and assistant. The series was based on Joy Adamson's best-
selling books, *Born Free* and *Living Free,* which told of the Adamsons'
adventures with Elsa the lioness. Created for television by Carl Forman.
Executive producer: David Gerber.

BOSS LADY   NBC
1 JULY 1952–23 SEPTEMBER 1952   Lynn Bari, who began her film career in 1933 at age eighteen, starred as Gwen Allen, the boss of a construction company, in this summer replacement for *Fireside Theatre.*
Also featured were Nicholas Joy as Gwen's father and Lee Patrick as Aggie.

BOSTON BLACKIE   SYNDICATED
1951   Boston Blackie, the criminal-cum-detective made famous in films
by Chester Morris, was played on television by veteran character actor
Kent Taylor. With Lois Collier as his lady friend, Mary Wesley; Frank
Orth as Inspector Faraday. The half-hour series was set in New York,
not Boston. Produced by Ziv TV; directed by Eddie Davis, Sobey Martin,
and George M. Cahan.

BOTH SIDES   ABC
15 MARCH 1953–7 JUNE 1953   A series of debates on public policy issues, moderated by Quincy Howe.

BOURBON STREET BEAT   ABC
5 OCTOBER 1959–26 SEPTEMBER 1960   New Orleans was the setting for
this Warner Brothers hour-long detective series. It starred Richard Long
as Rex Randolph and Andrew Duggan as Cal Calhoun, the owners of
Randolph and Calhoun, Special Services. Also featured were Arlene
Howell as their receptionist, Melody Lee Mercer; Van Williams as their
young assistant, Kenny Madison; and Eddie Cole as Lieutenant Baron.
After *Bourbon Street Beat* expired, Rex Randolph moved West to join *77
Sunset Strip*.

BOWLING HEADLINERS   ABC/DUMONT
26 DECEMBER 1948–30 OCTOBER 1949 (ABC); 13 NOVEMBER 1949–9
APRIL 1950 (DUMONT)   One of network television's first bowling
shows, this half-hour series was hosted by Jimmy Powers during its first
season and by Al Cirillo (who also produced it) during its second season.

BOWLING STARS   ABC/NBC
22 SEPTEMBER 1957–29 DECEMBER 1957 (ABC); 1 OCTOBER 1960–6
MAY 1961 (NBC)   A series of head-to-head matches between professional bowlers. The ABC version, which ran in prime time, was hosted by
"Whispering Joe" Wilson (so named because he spoke softly to avoid dis-
turbing the keglers' concentration). The NBC version, a weekend feature,
was hosted by Bud Palmer. See also *National Bowling Champions*.

BOZO THE CLOWN (BOZO'S BIG TOP)   SYNDICATED
1956–   Not exactly a national series, *Bozo the Clown* is essentially a television "franchise" controlled by Larry Harmon. Bozo was
originally the star of dozens of children's records released by Capitol. In
1956 Harmon bought the TV rights to the character and developed the
idea of a live Bozo (each local station supplying its own) introducing
Bozo cartoons. The idea caught on; by 1966 Bozo could be seen on more
than 240 stations in over forty countries. By that time several dozen stations featured the same Bozo on videotape: Frank Avruch, Boston's
Bozo. Those presentations were usually titled *Bozo's Big Top*.

BRACKEN'S WORLD   NBC
19 SEPTEMBER 1969–25 DECEMBER 1970   Life at Hollywood Century
Studios. With Peter Haskell as producer Kevin Grant; Madlyn Rhue as
his wife, Marjorie; Elizabeth Allen as Laura Deane, who runs a talent

school; Dennis Cole as young leading man David Evans; Karen Jensen as starlet Rachel Holt; Steven Oliver as Brando-type Tom Huston; Laraine Stephens as young leading lady Diane Waring; Linda Harrison as shy young actress Paulette Douglas; Jeanne Cooper as Mrs. Douglas, Paulette's overbearing mother; and Eleanor Parker as Sylvia Caldwell, executive secretary to studio boss John Bracken. During the 1969–1970 season Bracken was unseen; for the second season (Cole and Oliver having left the series) Leslie Nielsen was added to play the now-visible Bracken. The hour show was produced by 20th Century-Fox.

THE BRADY BUNCH ABC
26 SEPTEMBER 1969–30 AUGUST 1974 Harmless sitcom about a widower with three sons who married a widow with three daughters. Featuring Robert Reed as architect Mike Brady; Florence Henderson as Carol Brady; Ann B. Davis as Alice Nelson, their harried housekeeper; Maureen McCormick as Marcia; Barry Williams as Greg; Eve Plumb as Jan; Christopher Knight as Peter; Susan Olsen as Cindy; and Michael Lookinland as Bobby. Robbie Rist was also featured in the last six episodes as Carol's eight-year-old nephew, Oliver, who stayed with the Bradys while his parents were away. Sherwood Schwartz created the series and was its executive producer. The Bunch also turned up in animated form (see *The Brady Kids*) and in a variety format (see *The Brady Bunch Hour*).

THE BRADY BUNCH HOUR ABC
23 JANUARY 1977–25 MAY 1977 A variety hour with some running sketches broadcast irregularly during 1977. With Florence Henderson (Carol), Robert Reed (Mike), Maureen McCormick (Marcia), Barry Williams (Greg), Geri Reischl (Jan), Chris Knight (Peter), Susan Olsen (Cindy), and Michael Lookinland (Bobby).

THE BRADY KIDS ABC
16 SEPTEMBER 1972–31 AUGUST 1974 A Saturday-morning cartoon series. The voices of the six *Brady Bunch* children (McCormick, Williams, Plumb, Knight, Olsen, and Lookinland) were used.

BRAINS AND BRAWN NBC
13 SEPTEMBER 1958–27 DECEMBER 1958 Bifurcated prime-time game show featuring a contest between two teams, each composed of one athlete and one celebrity. Fred Davis hosted the Brain portion, a general knowledge quiz; Jack Lescoulie hosted the Brawn portion, which involved physical exertion.

BRANDED NBC
24 JANUARY 1965–4 SEPTEMBER 1966 A midseason replacement for *The Bill Dana Show.* starring Chuck Connors as Jason McCord, an Army

officer wrongfully court-martialed after the Battle of Bitter Creek (he was the only known survivor) and dishonorably discharged.

BRAVE EAGLE CBS

28 SEPTEMBER 1955–6 JUNE 1956 One of the few westerns told from the Indians' point of view. With Keith Larsen as Brave Eagle, a Cheyenne chief; Kim Winona as Morning Star; Keena Nomkeena (a real Indian) as Keena, Brave Eagle's adopted son; and Bert Wheeler as halfbreed Smokey Joe.

BREAK THE BANK ABC/NBC/CBS/SYNDICATED

22 OCTOBER 1948–23 SEPTEMBER 1949 (ABC); 5 OCTOBER 1949–9 JANUARY 1952 (NBC); 13 JANUARY 1952–1 FEBRUARY 1953 (CBS); 30 MARCH 1953–18 SEPTEMBER 1953 (NBC); 31 JANUARY 1954–20 JUNE 1956 (ABC); 12 APRIL 1976–23 JULY 1976 (ABC); 1976 (SYNDICATED)

BREAK THE $250,000 BANK NBC

9 OCTOBER 1956–29 JANUARY 1957 This durable game show, whose network peregrinations have sometimes been difficult to follow, began on radio in 1945. From 1948 until 1956, it was seen in prime time, except for a brief daytime run on NBC in 1953. Bert Parks hosted the ABC and NBC versions of the show, and Bud Collyer emceed the CBS version. It employed a straightforward question-and-answer format; contestants were quizzed in their chosen areas of specialized knowledge and could answer up to eight questions. Those who answered the first eight questions (one wrong answer was permitted) could then opt to answer a ninth question to "break the bank." Winners were paid on the spot—in cash for small amounts and by check for larger sums. In the fall of 1956 the show returned to NBC, with Parks as host, and was retitled *Break the $250,000 Bank*. On this version contestants were permitted to have their families with them and could call upon one family member to answer one question if the contestant had previously missed it. Joseph Nathan Kane, who wrote the questions used on the show, also served as judge, and Janice Gilbert was featured as the paying teller. In 1976 *Break the Bank* again returned, after an absence of almost two decades. The new format featured a panel of nine celebrities and two contestants. When a question was asked, one celebrity provided the correct answer for it, and one provided a false answer; contestants won money by choosing the one who had answered correctly. Tom Kennedy hosted the short-lived daytime network version, and Jack Barry (whose longtime partner, Dan Enright, produced it) hosted the syndicated version.

BREAKFAST IN HOLLYWOOD NBC

11 JANUARY 1954–5 FEBRUARY 1954 Short-lived morning show broadcast live from Hollywood. Johnny Dugan hosted the festivities, which included songs, chitchat, and audience-participation features.

BREAKFAST PARTY   NBC

7 JANUARY 1952–23 MAY 1952   Mel Martin hosted this half-hour morning variety show, which was broadcast live from Cincinnati.

BREAKING POINT   ABC

16 SEPTEMBER 1963–7 SEPTEMBER 1964   The success of *Ben Casey* led to a proliferation of medical shows; this one (like NBC's *Eleventh Hour*) featured two psychiatrists. With Paul Richards as Dr. McKinley Thompson, resident in psychiatry at York Hospital; Eduard Franz as Dr. Edward Raymer, clinic director. Produced by Bing Crosby Productions (which also produced *Ben Casey*). Robert Redford made one of his last TV appearances in one episode, "Bird and Snake" (7 October).

BRENNER   CBS

6 JUNE 1959–10 OCTOBER 1959   A father-and-son police team. With Edward Binns as Lieutenant Roy Brenner, veteran cop; James Broderick as Officer Ernie Brenner, rookie patrolman. This half-hour series was rebroadcast on CBS as a summer replacement for several seasons.

THE BRIAN KEITH SHOW

See THE LITTLE PEOPLE

BRIDE AND GROOM   CBS/NBC

25 JANUARY 1951–9 OCTOBER 1953 (CBS); 7 DECEMBER 1953–27 AUGUST 1954 (NBC); 1 JULY 1957–10 JANUARY 1958 (NBC)   Couples were married before a live coast-to-coast audience on this daytime show broadcast from New York. John Nelson was the first host of the show; Robert Paige and Byron Palmer cohosted the 1957–1958 version (Palmer was later replaced by Frank Parker).

BRIDGET LOVES BERNIE   CBS

16 SEPTEMBER 1972–8 SEPTEMBER 1973   An updated video version of the long-running Broadway hit, *Abie's Irish Rose,* about a rich Irish girl who marries a poor Jewish boy. Starring Meredith Baxter as Bridget Theresa Mary Coleen Fitzgerald, a young schoolteacher, and David Birney as Bernie Steinberg, an aspiring writer and part-time cabbie. As luck would have it, Baxter and Birney actually did fall in love and were married in 1973. Also featured were David Doyle as Walter Fitzgerald, Bridget's wealthy father, an executive; Audra Lindley as Amy Fitzgerald, Bridget's pompous mother; Harold J. Stone as delicatessen owner Sam Steinberg, Bernie's folksy father; Bibi Osterwald as Sophie Steinberg, Bernie's typically Jewish mother; Robert Sampson as Bridget's brother Mike, a priest; Ned Glass as Bernie's uncle, Moe Plotnick; and William Elliott as Bernie's black friend, Otis Foster. Aired at 8:30 p.m. on Saturdays, be-

tween CBS's monster hits *All in the Family* and *The Mary Tyler Moore Show*, *Bridget Loves Bernie* was one of the highest-rated shows ever to be cancelled after one season. It was widely reported that many Jewish groups had pressured CBS to axe the series, but the network's official explanation was that the show's ratings were not high enough. Too many viewers were switching away from CBS after *All in the Family* and returning for *The Mary Tyler Moore Show*.

BRIGHT PROMISE NBC
29 SEPTEMBER 1969–31 MARCH 1972 A soap opera apparently aimed at a youthful audience, *Bright Promise* was set at Bancroft College, a small Midwestern institution. It featured Dana Andrews as college president Thomas Boswell; Paul Lukather as Professor William Ferguson; Susan Brown as Martha Ferguson; Dabney Coleman as Dr. Tracy Brown; Coleen Gray and Gail Kobe as Ann (Boyd) Jones; Mark Miller as Howard Jones; Pamela Murphy as Sandy Jones Pierce, dropout, adulteress and accused murderer; David Lewis as Henry Pierce; Peter Ratray as Stuart Pierce; Sherry Alberoni as Jody Harper; Richard Eastham as Red Wilson; Anthony Eisley as Charles Diedrich; Regina Gleason as Sylvia Bancroft; and June Vincent as Dr. Amanda Winninger.

THE BRIGHTER DAY CBS
4 JANUARY 1954–28 SEPTEMBER 1962 Another successful soap opera created by Irna Phillips ("The Queen of the Soaps"), *The Brighter Day* began on radio in 1948, where it remained until 1956; from 1954 to 1956, the radio broadcast was an audio repeat of the day's television episode. The serial's central characters were the members of the Dennis family, who had just moved from Three Rivers to New Hope as the video version began. Featured were William Smith (1954–1955) and Blair Davies (1955–1962) as the Reverend Richard Dennis, a widower with five children (the eldest of the children, Liz, was never seen on TV; she had been institutionalized earlier in the series); Brooke Byron and Jayne Heller as Althea Dennis Bigby, second eldest, recently widowed; Hal Holbrook and James Noble as son Grayling Dennis; Lois Nettleton and June Dayton as teenage daughter Patsy Dennis; Mary Linn Beller and Nancy Malone as youngest daughter Barbara (Babby) Dennis; Larry Ward as Doctor Randy Hamilton, who married Patsy; Gloria Hoye and Mary K. Wells as Sandra Talbot, who married Grayling; Mona Bruns as Aunt Emily (Potter), Richard's sister; Paul Langton as Uncle Walter, Richard's brother; Herb Nelson as the Reverend Max Canfield; Muriel Williams as Lydia Herrick; Lori March as Lydia's sister, Lenore; Mark Daniels as Robert Ralston; and Joe Sirola as Peter Nino. Also featured were Patty Duke, John Heath, Harriet MacGibbon, Peter Donat, and Anne Meacham. *The Brighter Day* was televised from New York until 1961, when it moved to Hollywood. Leonard Blair was the producer.

111

BRINGING UP BUDDY CBS

10 OCTOBER 1960–25 SEPTEMBER 1961 Situation comedy about a young bachelor who boards with his two spinster aunts. With Frank Aletter as stockbroker Buddy Flower; Enid Markey as Aunt Violet Flower; and Doro Merande as Aunt Iris Flower.

BROADSIDE ABC

20 SEPTEMBER 1964–5 SEPTEMBER 1965 Essentially a *McHale's Navy* with women, *Broadside* featured four WAVES mechanics assigned to duty at New Caledonia in the South Pacific during World War II. With Kathy Nolan as Lieutenant Anne Morgan, the commanding officer; Joan Staley as Private Roberta Love; Lois Roberts as Private Molly McGuire; Sheila James as Private Selma Kowalski; Edward Andrews as Commander Adrian, the stuffy supervisor of the New Caledonia outpost; Dick Sargent as Lieutenant Maxwell Trotter, Anne Morgan's boyfriend; George Furth as Lieutenant Beasley, Adrian's assistant; Arnold Stang as Stanley Stubbs, the cook; Jimmy Boyd as Marion Butnick, a GI mistakenly assigned to the WAVES. In the fall of 1977 ABC dusted off the format: see *Operation Petticoat.*

BROADWAY GOES LATIN SYNDICATED

1962 Bandleader Edmundo Ros hosted this musical variety series syndicated by ITC.

BROADWAY OPEN HOUSE NBC

29 MAY 1950–24 AUGUST 1951 Network television's first regularly scheduled late-night program was conceived by Sylvester "Pat" Weaver, the NBC VP whose ideas in programming (such as *Today, Ding Dong School, Home,* and *Wide Wide World*) helped shape American television. *Broadway Open House* bore little resemblance to the talk shows which succeeded it; the show was a heavy-handed mixture of vaudeville routines, songs, dances, and sight gags. It was to have been hosted by comedian Don "Creesh" Hornsby (so nicknamed because he yelled "Creesh!" a lot), but Hornsby died of polio two weeks before the premiere. Two veteran comedians were quickly signed up to share the hosting duties: Jerry Lester, "The Heckler of Hecklers," and Morey Amsterdam, a walking repository of jokes who also played the cello. Lester emceed the show three nights each week, Amsterdam the other two nights. Assisting them were announcer Wayne Howell, singers Andy Roberts, Jane Harvey, and David Street, accordionist Milton DeLugg, tap dancer Ray Malone, and a buxom blonde named Jennie Lewis, but better known as Dagmar, who played it dumb. The show went through many changes of personnel, and was trimmed to three nights a week in May of 1951. Its fifteen-month weeknight run demonstrated at least that

there was an audience for late-night TV. Weaver refined his ideas and in 1954 introduced the *Tonight* show (see also that title).

BROADWAY TELEVISION THEATER (BROADWAY THEATER)
SYNDICATED

1952–1954   Adaptations of Broadway plays comprised this hour-long dramatic anthology series.

BROADWAY TO HOLLYWOOD
DUMONT

20 JULY 1949–15 JULY 1954   This half-hour series was one of the most durable shows aired on the DuMont network. It began in 1949 as an all-purpose show and was titled *Broadway to Hollywood Headline Clues*. Hosted by George F. Putnam, it consisted of thirty minutes of news, gossip, celebrity interviews, and a quiz for home viewers. By the fall of 1949, however, *Headline Clues* was made a separate daytime game show, while *Broadway to Hollywood* continued as a prime-time variety show. Bill Slater later hosted the series.

BROKEN ARROW
ABC

25 SEPTEMBER 1956–23 SEPTEMBER 1958   Half-hour western starring Michael Ansara as Cochise, Chief of the Apaches, and John Lupton as Indian Agent Tom Jeffords, a blood brother of Cochise. Filmed at 20th Century-Fox Studios, the series was syndicated under the title *Cochise*.

BRONCO
ABC

20 OCTOBER 1959–13 SEPTEMBER 1960   This hour-long western from Warner Brothers starred Ty Hardin as Bronco Layne, a loner who drifted across the Texas plains after the Civil War. Though *Bronco* existed as a separate series only during the 1959–1960 season, when it alternated with *Sugarfoot,* the character was seen for several seasons on *Cheyenne,* another Warner Brothers western. During the 1958–1959 season, when Clint Walker did not appear on *Cheyenne* because of a contractual dispute, a season of *Bronco* episodes was shown under the *Cheyenne* title. During the 1960–1961 season, *Cheyenne, Bronco,* and *Sugarfoot* episodes were all shown under the *Cheyenne* title (Clint Walker had returned to the show in 1959), and during the 1961–1962 season, *Bronco* and *Cheyenne* shows were aired under the *Cheyenne* banner. See also *Cheyenne; Sugarfoot.*

BRONK
CBS

21 SEPTEMBER 1975–18 JULY 1976   Jack Palance starred as Lieutenant Alexander (Bronk) Bronkov, a police detective specially assigned to the mayor of Ocean City, California. With Joseph Mascolo as Mayor Pete

Santori; Henry Beckman as former cop Harry Mark; Tony King as Sergeant John Webber, Bronk's assistant; and Dina Ousley as Ellen, Bronk's crippled daughter. Executive producer: Bruce Geller, for MGM Television.

THE BROTHERS   CBS
2 OCTOBER 1956–26 MARCH 1957   CBS had high hopes for this situation comedy, which went nowhere. It starred Gale Gordon and Bob Sweeney as brothers Harvey and Gilmore (Gilly) Box, who operated a photography studio in San Francisco. With Nancy Hadley as Marilee Dorf, Gilly's girlfriend; Oliver Blake as her father, Carl Dorf; Barbara Billingsley as Barbara, Harvey's girlfriend; Ann Morris as Dr. Margaret Kleeb; and Frank Orth as Captain Sam Box, the brothers' father.

BROTHERS AND SISTERS   NBC
21 JANUARY 1979–6 APRIL 1979   Half-hour sitcom set at Larry Krandall College, home of the Pi Nu fraternity and the Gamma Iota sorority. With Chris Lemmon (son of Jack Lemmon) as Checko; Randy Brooks as Ronald Holmes, Pi Nu's token black; Jon Cutler as the irrepressible Stanley Zipper; Larry Anderson as Harlan Ramsey, beleaguered president of the frat; Amy Johnston as Mary Lee, Harlan's girlfriend; Mary Crosby (daughter of Bing Crosby) as Suzi Cooper; and Roy Teicher as Seymour, frat brother with a ravenous appetite. Producers: Bob Brunner and Arthur Silver for Universal TV.

THE BROTHERS BRANNAGAN   SYNDICATED
1960   This low-budget half-hour crime show was set in Phoenix and starred Steve Dunne and Mark Roberts as private eyes Mike and Bob Brannagan.

THE BUCCANEERS   CBS
22 SEPTEMBER 1956–14 SEPTEMBER 1957   Set in the Caribbean island of New Providence in 1720, this half-hour adventure series featured Robert Shaw as Captain Dan Tempest, an ex-pirate turned commander of the *Sultana,* who fought evildoers; Peter Hammond as Lieutenant Beamish, second in command; Paul Hansard as crewman Taffy; and Brian Rawlinson as crewman Gaff. The show was filmed at Falmouth, England; the *Sultana* had formerly served as the *Pequod* in the 1956 film *Moby Dick.*

THE BUCK OWENS SHOW   SYNDICATED
1972   A half hour of country and western music, hosted by Buck Owens.

BUCK ROGERS ABC

15 APRIL 1950–30 JANUARY 1951 Better known as a radio serial, *Buck Rogers* enjoyed a brief television run. It starred Kem Dibbs as Buck Rogers, an ordinary American who woke up to find himself in the year 2430; from a cave hidden behind Niagara Falls, he battled intergalactic troublemakers. Also featured were Lou Prentis as Lieutenant Wilma Deering; Harry Southern as Doctor Huer; and Harry Kingston as the evil Black Barney Wade. Babette Henry produced and directed.

BUCK ROGERS IN THE 25TH CENTURY NBC

27 SEPTEMBER 1979– The second television incarnation of *Buck Rogers* was a prime-time hour, which starred Gil Gerard as Captain William "Buck" Rogers, a twentieth-century astronaut who was caught in a time warp and returns to Earth 500 years later, where he assists the Defense Directorate. With Erin Gray as Colonel Wilma Deering, Buck's romantic interest and Tim O'Connor as Dr. Huer. William Conrad narrated the series, which was supplied by Glen Larson Productions in association with Universal TV.

BUCKAROO 500 SYNDICATED

1964 Children's variety program, hosted by Buck Weaver.

BUCKSKIN NBC

3 JULY 1958–14 SEPTEMBER 1959 Set in the town of Buckskin, Montana, during the 1880s, this half-hour western was told from the point of view of a ten-year-old boy. It starred Tommy Nolan as young Jody O'Connell and also featured Sallie Brophy as Annie O'Connell, his widowed mother; Mike Road as Sheriff Tom Sellers; Michael Lipton as Ben Newcomb, the town schoolteacher; and Marjorie Bennett and Shirley Knight as Mrs. Newcomb. In 1958 *Buckskin* was introduced as a summer replacement for *The Tennessee Ernie Ford Show* (Ford owned an interest in the series) and was given its own berth in NBC's fall schedule.

BUFFALO BILL, JR. SYNDICATED

1955 Children's western featuring Dick Jones as Buffalo Bill, Jr., an orphan adopted by a judge and subsequently named marshal of Wileyville, Texas; Nancy Gilbert as Calamity, Bill's younger sister; and Harry Cheshire as Judge Ben Wiley, their guardian, founder of Wileyville. The half-hour series was produced by Gene Autry's Flying A Productions.

THE BUFFALO BILLY SHOW CBS

22 OCTOBER 1950–14 JANUARY 1951 *Buffalo Billy* was the main character in this half-hour Sunday-afternoon puppet show, set in the old West.

BUFORD NBC

3 FEBRUARY 1979–1 SEPTEMBER 1979 Formerly part of *Yogi's Space Race,* Buford the lethargic bloodhound was given his own half-hour cartoon series in midseason.

THE BUGALOOS NBC

12 SEPTEMBER 1970–2 SEPTEMBER 1972 Live-action Saturday-morning series about a witch and a four-insect singing group, The Bugaloos. With Martha Raye as Benita Bizarre, the witch; Carolyn Ellis as Joy; John Philpott as Courage; John McIndoe as I.Q.; and Wayne Laryea as Harmony. Created by Sid and Marty Krofft.

THE BUGS BUNNY SHOW ABC/CBS

28 SEPTEMBER 1960–2 SEPTEMBER 1967 (ABC); 11 SEPTEMBER 1971–1 SEPTEMBER 1973 (CBS); 8 SEPTEMBER 1973–30 AUGUST 1975 (ABC)

THE BUGS BUNNY/ROAD RUNNER HOUR CBS

14 SEPTEMBER 1968–4 SEPTEMBER 1971; 6 SEPTEMBER 1975– One of the world's most popular cartoon characters, Bugs Bunny hopped into prime-time television in 1960 after a long career in animated films. His half-hour show remained in prime time for two seasons and began as a Saturday-morning series in April 1962. Bugs and his Warner Brothers cartoon pals—including Daffy Duck, Sylvester and Tweety, Elmer Fudd, and Yosemite Sam—have appeared in both half-hour and hour formats; in the hour shows Bugs has had to share top billing with the Road Runner, a resourceful bird who always manages to outwit his persistent predator, Wile E. Coyote. The voice of Bugs (and of many of the other characters) is supplied by Mel Blanc.

THE BUICK–BERLE SHOW

See THE MILTON BERLE SHOW

THE BUICK CIRCUS HOUR NBC

7 OCTOBER 1952–16 JUNE 1953 A musical variety hour that replaced Milton Berle's *The Texaco Star Theater* every fourth week. Regulars included Joe E. Brown, Dolores Gray, and John Raitt.

THE BULLWINKLE SHOW NBC/ABC

24 SEPTEMBER 1961–12 SEPTEMBER 1964 (NBC); 20 SEPTEMBER 1964–2 SEPTEMBER 1973 (ABC) Bullwinkle the moose, faithful companion of Rocky the flying squirrel on *Rocky and His Friends,* hosted and starred in his own animated spinoff series; the half-hour show was seen Sunday evenings on NBC for one season, before beginning a long run on weekend mornings, first on NBC, later on ABC. Bill Scott provided the voice of Bullwinkle, and William Conrad narrated the series. Jay Ward was the producer. See also *Rocky and His Friends.*

BURKE'S LAW   ABC

20 SEPTEMBER 1963–31 AUGUST 1965

AMOS BURKE, SECRET AGENT   ABC

15 SEPTEMBER 1965–12 JANUARY 1966   Gene Barry starred as *Amos Burke* in both of these adventure series. In *Burke's Law,* Burke was the debonair police chief of Los Angeles. A swinging bachelor, he was independently wealthy and traveled around town in a chauffeured Rolls Royce. Also featured were Regis Toomey as Detective Lester Hart ("old cop"); Gary Conway as Detective Tim Tilson ("young cop"); Eileen O'Neill as Sergeant Ames; and Leon Lontoc as Henry, Burke's chauffeur. Most episodes were entitled "Who Killed _____?" Many featured cameo appearances by film stars such as William Bendix (30 September 1964, his last TV appearance), Rhonda Fleming ("Who Killed 711?" 9 December 1964, her last appearance to date), Jack Haley ("Who Killed Beau Sparrow?" 27 December 1963), Buster Keaton (8 May 1964, his last TV appearance), Jayne Mansfield (27 March 1964, her last dramatic appearance), ZaSu Pitts (20 September 1963, her last appearance), Frank Sinatra ("Who Killed Wade Walker?" 15 November 1963), and Terry-Thomas ("Who Killed Julian Buck?" 18 October 1963, his first American appearance).

In the fall of 1965 the show's producers decided to make Burke a secret agent (apparently to cash in on the success of NBC's 1964 smash, *The Man from U.N.C.L.E*). All the regulars except for Barry were dropped, and Carl Benton Reid was added as The Man, Burke's superior. The show perished opposite NBC's new hit, *I Spy.*

THE BURNS AND ALLEN SHOW   CBS

12 OCTOBER 1950–22 SEPTEMBER 1958   This long-running comedy series is probably best remembered for the vaudeville routines performed at the end of each show by its stars, George Burns and Gracie Allen ("Say goodnight, Gracie!"). Burns and Allen played themselves on the show, though Burns would frequently talk directly to the camera, to comment on the plot, to analyze Gracie's scatterbrained antics, or to tell a few jokes. Ronnie Burns, their son, also played himself on the show. Also featured were Bea Benaderet as Gracie's friend and neighbor, Blanche Morton. Blanche's husband (and George's accountant), Harry Morton, was originally played by Hal March, then by John Brown, until he was blacklisted by the "red scare" of the early 1950s. The part was later played by Fred Clark and Larry Keating. Bill Goodwin was the show's first announcer, but he left in 1951 to host his own series; Harry Von Zell was brought in to replace him. Ralph Levy produced and directed the half-hour show, which was done live for the first two seasons (all but the first six shows were done in Hollywood). Among the show's writers were Paul Henning (who later developed *The Beverly Hillbillies*), Sid Dorfman, Harvey Helm, and William Burns. In 1958 Gracie Allen retired from

show business. George Burns tried a second comedy series, which was unsuccessful: see *The George Burns Show*.

THE BURNS AND SCHREIBER COMEDY HOUR ABC
30 JUNE 1973–1 SEPTEMBER 1973 Summer variety series cohosted by comedy duo Jack Burns and Avery Schreiber.

BURTON HOLMES TRAVELOG SYNDICATED
1949 A series of fifteen-minute travelogues filmed in America, sponsored by the Santa Fe Railroad. Burton Holmes was the host and narrator.

BUS STOP ABC
1 OCTOBER 1961–25 MARCH 1962 This drama series bore little resemblance to William Inge's play or the 1956 film which had starred Marilyn Monroe. It was billed as a dramatic anthology series with continuing characters. The guest stars, passing through the Sherwood Diner (located in Sunrise, Colorado) were supposed to provide the drama and the regulars the continuity. The Sherwood was the town's bus depot as well. Featured were Marilyn Maxwell as Grace Sherwood, the diner owner; Rhodes Reason as Sheriff Will Mayberry; Richard Anderson as District Attorney Glenn Wagner; and Joan Freeman as waitress Emma Gahringer. Robert Redford guest starred in one episode, "The Covering Darkness" (22 October). The most noteworthy episode, however, was titled "A Lion Walks Among Us," broadcast early in December. Several ABC affiliates refused to carry the episode, which attracted much publicity before it was shown and even more afterward. Universally excoriated for its excessive violence (such as guest star Fabian going after an old man with an axe), it precipitated a Congressional inquiry into violence on television.

BUSTING LOOSE CBS
17 JANUARY 1977–16 NOVEMBER 1977 Situation comedy about a twenty-four-year-old who left his overprotective Jewish parents to start out on his own. With Adam Arkin (son of Alan Arkin) as Lenny Markowitz; Pat Carroll as his mother, Pearl Markowitz; Jack Kruschen as his father, Sam Markowitz; Danny Goldman as his friend, Lester Bellman; Greg Antonacci as his pal, Vinnie Mortabito; Stephen Nathan as his pal, Allan Simmonds; Paul Sylvan as his pal, Woody Warshaw; Barbara Rhoades as his voluptuous neighbor, Melody Feebeck; Ralph Wilcox as Raymond St. Williams, Lenny's coworker; and Paul B. Price as Ralph Cabell, Lenny's boss, owner of the Wearwell Shoe Store. Executive producers: Mark Rothman and Lowell Ganz. Producer: John Thomas Lenox.

BUTCH CASSIDY AND THE SUNDANCE KIDS   NBC

8 SEPTEMBER 1973–31 AUGUST 1974 Saturday-morning cartoon series about a bunch of young government agents posing as a rock-and-roll group.

BUZZY WUZZY   ABC

17 NOVEMBER 1948–8 DECEMBER 1948 Fifteen-minute comedy series starring Jerry Bergen.

BWANA MICHAEL

See THE MICHAELS IN AFRICA

BY POPULAR DEMAND   CBS

2 JULY 1950–22 SEPTEMBER 1950 This half-hour variety series, a summer replacement for *This Is Show Business,* was hosted first by Robert Alda, later by Arlene Francis. It was a Mark Goodson–Bill Todman Production.

BY-LINE   ABC

4 NOVEMBER 1951–16 DECEMBER 1951 Half-hour mystery series, starring Betty Furness as a reporter.

BYLINE

See BIG TOWN

C.B. BEARS   NBC

10 SEPTEMBER 1977–28 JANUARY 1978 Saturday-morning cartoon show featuring a bunch of bears who used citizens' band radios.

CBS CARTOON THEATER   CBS

13 JUNE 1956–5 SEPTEMBER 1956 This little heralded summer show was network television's first prime-time cartoon show, antedating *The Flintstones* by four years. It was hosted by Dick Van Dyke, who introduced "Terrytoons," the animated adventures of such creatures as Heckle and Jeckle (who later got a show of their own), Little Roquefort, Dinky Duck, and Gandy Goose.

THE CBS CHILDREN'S FILM FESTIVAL   CBS

11 SEPTEMBER 1971–26 AUGUST 1978; 19 MAY 1979–25 AUGUST 1979 This Saturday-afternoon series was first introduced in 1967 on an irregular basis and was given a permanent slot four years later. Each week films from around the world of interest to youngsters are aired. The series has been hosted by Fran Allison and her puppet friends, Kukla and Ollie (see also *Kukla, Fran and Ollie*).

3 MAY 1948–   CBS has relied on just two anchormen for
the last three decades: Douglas Edwards and Walter Cronkite. Edwards,
who had worked with CBS radio, hosted local television newscasts in
1947 (Larry LeSueur had preceded him) and continued in that position
for fifteen years; Edwards also hosted *Armstrong Circle Theater* from
1957 to 1961. For most of its run the fifteen-minute newscast was officially titled *Douglas Edwards with the News.* On 30 November 1956, it became the first network news show to be videotaped for rebroadcast in the
Western time zones.

In April of 1962 Walter Cronkite succeeded Edwards as CBS's evening
newscaster (Edwards has continued to do a five-minute daytime newscast). A seasoned journalist, Cronkite had worked for radio station
KCMO in Kansas City before joining the United Press in 1939. Cronkite
covered World War II from several locations in Europe, and on D-Day,
June 6, 1944, he was chosen (by lot) to be the only reporter to cover the
Normandy invasion from the air. After the war he was UP's chief correspondent at the Nuremberg trials; he then worked in Moscow before returning to the United States in 1948. He left UP to become a radio
correspondent for a group of ten Midwestern radio stations, and in 1950
he joined CBS News. For a time he anchored the newscasts on CBS's
Washington affiliate, and in 1952 he was named the network's anchorman for the political conventions (he has anchored every convention
since then, except for the 1964 Democratic convention, when the network experimented with Roger Mudd and Robert Trout in a vain attempt to outdraw NBC's Huntley-Brinkley combination). Cronkite
hosted and narrated several CBS public affairs shows during the 1950s
and early 1960s, including *You Are There, The Morning Show, Air Power,*
and *The Twentieth Century.* He also hosted several news specials, including in-depth interviews with former President Dwight Eisenhower and
with political columnist Walter Lippmann.

Cronkite is not only the anchorman for the network newscast, but also
serves as its "managing editor." The dual position gives him considerable
latitude in the selection, timing, and arrangement of the day's news items.
It was during Cronkite's early days at anchor that the nightly broadcasts
expanded from fifteen to thirty minutes. The first half-hour show was
aired 2 September 1963 (a week ahead of NBC's first expanded newscast)
and featured a special interview with President John Kennedy. Less than
twelve weeks later Cronkite anchored the network's marathon coverage
of Kennedy's death and funeral (CBS was the first of the television networks to report the shooting, interrupting *As the World Turns* at 1:40
p.m. on 22 November 1963, but it was the last to confirm his death an
hour later). Cronkite has also anchored the coverage of almost all of
America's space missions, as well as CBS's day-long coverage of America's bicentennial observance on 4 July 1976. Perhaps his most significant

television reportage were his broadcasts from Vietnam following the 1968 Tet offensive, in which he sadly concluded that Americans had been misled about the course of the conflict and (much to the chagrin of President Johnson) advocated a negotiated withdrawal.

Color broadcasts of the evening news began early in 1966, about two months after NBC's. By the end of the decade, the *CBS Evening News* had recaptured the ratings lead from NBC's *Huntley-Brinkley Report.* According to a poll taken in 1974, Cronkite was America's most trusted newscaster.

From the late 1960s until his retirement in 1977, Eric Sevareid commentated on the evening news. A native North Dakotan, Sevareid joined CBS News at Edward R. Murrow's invitation in 1939 and covered World War II from several locations. From 1946 until 1959 he worked mostly in Washington, where for a time he was CBS's bureau chief. From 1961 until 1964 he hosted a series of CBS News specials entitled, "The Roots of Freedom." Later in 1964 he was named national correspondent for CBS News. Cronkite's conscientious efforts to maintain objectivity and to separate news reporting from news advocacy were epitomized by the show's closing during the Sevareid years. Cronkite's familiar benediction, "And that's the way it is . . ." was deliberately omitted on those evenings when Sevareid's commentary was scheduled as the final item of the *CBS Evening News.*

THE CBS MORNING NEWS
CBS
2 SEPTEMBER 1963– CBS has tried since 1954 to compete successfully with NBC's *Today* show. First came *The Morning Show,* which ran from 1954 to 1957. Then the network experimented briefly with an early-morning variety show hosted by Jimmy Dean (see *The Jimmy Dean Show*). In 1963 the network made yet another attempt. From 1963 until 1969 it aired a twenty-five-minute morning news show which was anchored for several seasons by veteran newsman Mike Wallace. In the fall of 1966 Wallace was succeeded by Joseph Benti, who remained until 28 August 1970. It was during Benti's tenure (on 31 March 1969) that the program was expanded to a full hour. On 31 August 1970, John Hart, who had previously been featured on the show, took over the anchor desk and remained there for almost three years. In an effort to boost ratings the network teamed up a man and a woman in August 1973: Hughes Rudd, gravel-voiced former bureau chief of CBS's Moscow office, and Sally Quinn, a former reporter for the *Washington Post,* who had had no television experience. Quinn's lack of experience was apparent, and by January 1974, she was on her way back to the *Post.* (The full story of her television career, gaffes and all, is told in her book, *We're Going to Make You a Star,* which she dedicated to Hughes Rudd.) Rudd continued at the anchor desk and was soon joined by CBS correspondent Bruce Morton in Washington. Morton and Rudd both left in the fall of

1977 and were replaced by Richard Threlkeld and Lesley Stahl; Rudd continued to appear occasionally as a wry commentator. The show has always emphasized hard news, eschewing the lighter features characteristic of its competitors, *Today* and *Good Morning America.*

On 28 January 1979 CBS expanded its morning show to six days a week, Sundays through Fridays. The new shows were titled *Sunday Morning, Monday Morning,* etc. Bob Schieffer took over as the anchor of the weekday programs, replacing Threlkeld and Stahl; Charles Kuralt, CBS's "on the road" correspondent, was named to host the new Sunday show. To make room for the latter program, which ran ninety minutes, the network dropped three venerable but little watched Sunday series— *Camera Three, Lamp unto My Feet,* and *Look Up and Live*—each of which had been on the air for at least twenty-three years.

CBS REPORTS
CBS

27 OCTOBER 1959–   *CBS Reports* is the umbrella title for most of the documentaries produced by CBS News. Though *CBS Reports* has sometimes been scheduled regularly (e.g., during the 1961–1962 and 1970–1971 seasons), the documentaries have usually been telecast as specials. Fred Friendly, longtime associate of Edward R. Murrow, produced the series for the first several years. The premiere telecast, "Biography of a Missile," was narrated by Murrow. Recent offerings have included "The Best Congress Money Can Buy" (a report on political campaign financing anchored by Dan Rather, broadcast 31 January 1975), "The Guns of Autumn" (a report on hunting and firearms anchored by Rather, 5 September 1975), "The American Assassins" (a four-part series, also hosted by Rather, which examined the Kennedy, King, and Wallace incidents, broadcast between November 1975 and January 1976), and "The Selling of the F-14" (a report on the marketing of a fighter plane to Iran, anchored by Jay L. McMullen and Bill McLaughlin, broadcast 27 August 1976).

CBS SPORTS SPECTACULAR
CBS

3 JANUARY 1960–   The umbrella title for CBS's long-running weekend sports anthology series; in its early seasons the show was titled *Sunday Sports Spectacular.* The Harlem Globetrotters were featured on the premiere.

CBS TELEVISION WORKSHOP
CBS

24 JANUARY 1960–1 MAY 1960; 2 OCTOBER 1960–25 DECEMBER 1960 Broadcast at noon on Sundays, this was an experimental anthology series. Among the presentations were "Tessie Malfitano," with Maureen Stapleton (3 April); "Afterthought," by Guy Parent, described as "a play without actors or dialogue" (1 May); "The Dirtiest Word in the En-

glish Language," with Uta Hagen and Ben Piazza (2 October); and "A Pattern of Words and Music," featuring Joan Baez, John Sebastian, and Lightnin' Hopkins.

CHiPs   NBC
15 SEPTEMBER 1977–   Standard police show about two young motorcycle-riding officers of the California Highway Patrol. With Larry Wilcox as Officer Jonathan Baker; Erik Estrada as Officer Francis "Ponch" Poncherello; Robert Pine as their commanding officer, Sergeant Joe Getraer; Brodie Greer as Baricza; Paul Linke as Grossman; Brianne Leary (1978–1979) as Officer Sandy Cahill; and Randi Oakes (1979–   ) as Officer Bonnie Clark. Produced by Rick Rosner.

C.P.O. SHARKEY   NBC
1 DECEMBER 1976–28 JULY 1978   Service sitcom starring Don Rickles as C.P.O. (Chief Petty Officer) Otto Sharkey, a Navy drill instructor with twenty-four years of experience. Also featured were Harrison Page as C.P.O. Robinson, Sharkey's black colleague; Elizabeth Allen (1976–1977) as Captain Quinlan, his commanding officer; tall Peter Isacksen as Seaman Pruitt; Jeff Hollis as Daniels; David Landsberg as Skolnick; Tom Ruben as Kowalski; Richard Beauchamp as Rodriguez; Phillip Sims as Apodaca; and Barry Pearl as Mignone. In the fall of 1977 two new cast members were added: Richard X. Slattery as Captain Buckner, the new commanding officer; Jonathan Daly as Whipple, his aide. The series was created by Aaron Ruben, who also served as its executive producer; Arnie Rosen was the supervising producer. Though *C.P.O. Sharkey* was not on NBC's 1977 fall schedule, it was quickly resuscitated to replace the faltering *Sanford Arms* in October.

CADE'S COUNTY   CBS
19 SEPTEMBER 1971–4 SEPTEMBER 1972   Glenn Ford starred as Sam Cade, sheriff of Madrid County, in this hour-long adventure series set in the modern-day Southwest. With Edgar Buchanan as Senior Deputy J. J. Jackson; Taylor Lacher as Deputy Arlo Pritchard; Victor Campos as Deputy Rudy Davillo; Peter Ford (Glenn's son) as Pete; and Betty Ann Carr as Betty Ann Sundown, the dispatcher.

CAESAR'S HOUR   NBC
27 SEPTEMBER 1954–25 MAY 1957   After the ninety-minute *Your Show of Shows* left the air in 1954, Sid Caesar returned that fall in a sixty-minute format with most of the old gang. Regulars included Nanette Fabray (1954–1956) and Janet Blair (1956–1957), who played Sid's wife in many sketches; Carl Reiner; Howard Morris; Pat Carroll (who often played Reiner's wife); Shirl Conway; Sandra Deel; Ellen Parker; singer Bill Lew-

is; and pianist Earl Wild. Although the show won five Emmys in 1957, it was canceled because it could not top *The Lawrence Welk Show* in the ratings race.

CAFE DePARIS   DUMONT
17 JANUARY 1949– 4 MARCH 1949   Sylvie St. Clair hosted this fifteen-minute musical series, which was seen on Mondays, Wednesdays, and Fridays. The show, which featured Jacques Aubuchon and the Stan Free Trio, was set in a Paris bistro which St. Clair had inherited.

CAIN'S HUNDRED   NBC
19 SEPTEMBER 1961–11 SEPTEMBER 1962   Mark Richman starred as Nick Cain, a former syndicate lawyer who decided to fight crime; his mission was to apprehend the nation's 100 most dangerous underworld figures. Paul Monash was the creator and executive producer.

CALENDAR   CBS
2 OCTOBER 1961–30 AUGUST 1963   A daytime series, aimed at housewives, which emphasized news and current events. Hosted by Harry Reasoner.

CALIFORNIA FEVER   CBS
25 SEPTEMBER 1979–11 DECEMBER 1979   Hour adventure series about four carefree California teenagers. With Jimmy McNichol as Vince Butler; Marc McClure as Ross Whitman; Michele Tobin as Laurie; and Lorenzo Lamas as Rick, the proprietor of Rick's Place, a Sunset Beach hangout. The series, which was titled *We're Cruisin'* before it reached the air, was created by Dan Polier, Jr., for Warner Brothers TV and Lou-Step Productions.

THE CALIFORNIANS   NBC
24 SEPTEMBER 1957–10 SEPTEMBER 1959   This half-hour western was set in San Francisco during the 1850s. The original stars were Adam Kennedy as Dion Patrick and Sean McClory as Jack McGivern. Dion Patrick was an Irish immigrant who headed West to pan for gold; instead, he ended up in San Francisco and became a vigilante along with Jack McGivern, who ran a general store. By midseason, however, pressure from the show's sponsors, who were uneasy about glorifying vigilantes, caused the producers to drop Adam Kennedy and to introduce a new star. Richard Coogan joined the show in March 1958 as Matt Wayne, a newcomer to San Francisco who bought a saloon and soon became the town's marshal. Sean McClory lasted out the first season but was dropped thereafter; also featured during the first season was Nan Leslie as Mrs. McGivern. Two new regulars were added for the second season: Arthur Fleming (who would later host *Jeopardy*) as Jeremy Pitt, a young lawyer, and Carole Matthews as the widowed Wilma Fansler, who ran a

casino. Robert Bassler produced the show until January 1958, when he was replaced by Felix Feist.

CALL IT MACARONI   SYNDICATED
1975–   Monthly series of half-hour documentaries for children on which groups of children participate in the activity under study. Executive producer: George Moynihan for Westinghouse's Group W Productions.

CALL MR. D
See RICHARD DIAMOND, PRIVATE DETECTIVE

CALL MY BLUFF .   NBC
29 MARCH 1965–24 SEPTEMBER 1965   Bill Leyden hosted this daytime game show on which contestants tried to guess which of three proffered definitions of an esoteric word was the correct one. A Mark Goodson–Bill Todman Production.

CALUCCI'S DEPT.   CBS
14 SEPTEMBER 1973–28 DECEMBER 1973   A half-hour situation comedy created by Renée Taylor and Joseph Bologna. Scheduled at 8:00 p.m. on Fridays, opposite NBC's *Sanford and Son,* it went nowhere. James Coco starred as Joe Calucci, supervisor of a state unemployment office in New York City, who tried to manage a motley crew of nincompoops and deadbeats. With José Perez as Ramon Gonzales; Candy Azzara as Shirley Balukis, Joe's secretary and girlfriend; Peggy Pope as Elaine Fusco; Jack Fletcher as claims adjuster Oscar Cosgrove; Bill Lazarus as Jack Woods; and Bernard Wexler as Walter Frohler.

CALVIN AND THE COLONEL   ABC
3 OCTOBER 1961–22 SEPTEMBER 1962   Freeman Gosden and Charles Correll, who created *Amos and Andy* on radio, provided the voices for this prime-time cartoon series about a bear (Calvin) and a fox (The Colonel) afoot in a big city. Other voices included those of Beatrice Kay as Sister Sue; Virginia Gregg as Maggie Belle; and Paul Frees as Oliver Wendell Clutch.

THE CAMEL CARAVAN (THE VAUGHN MONROE SHOW)   CBS
10 OCTOBER 1950–3 JULY 1951   Singer-bandleader Vaughn Monroe ("Ghost Riders in the Sky") hosted this Tuesday-night musical variety series, sponsored by Camel cigarettes.

CAMEL NEWS CARAVAN
See NBC NEWS

CAMEO THEATER   NBC

14 JUNE 1950–27 SEPTEMBER 1950; 18 JUNE 1951–6 AUGUST 1951; 6 JANUARY 1952–13 APRIL 1952; 3 JULY 1955–21 AUGUST 1955   This undistinguished dramatic anthology series was aired three times as a summer replacement and in 1952 was a midseason replacement for *Leave It to the Girls* on Sundays.

CAMERA THREE   CBS/PBS

22 JANUARY 1956–21 JANUARY 1979 (CBS); 4 OCTOBER 1979–(PBS)   A Sunday-morning fixture for more than twenty years, *Camera Three* has perhaps the loosest format of any television series: anything in the arts or sciences is fair game. Concerts, dramas and interviews are all featured regularly. Developed by Robert Herridge, the series was broadcast locally in New York beginning in 1953. In the fall of 1979 *Camera Three* moved to prime time on PBS.

CAMOUFLAGE   ABC/SYNDICATED

9 JANUARY 1961–16 NOVEMBER 1962 (ABC); 1980 (SYNDICATED)   Daytime game show on which contestants sought to trace the outline of a described object camouflaged within a larger scene on the game board. When a contestant answered a question correctly, a portion of the camouflage was electronically removed from the board. Don Morrow hosted the network version, Tom Campbell the syndicated.

CAMP RUNAMUCK   NBC

17 SEPTEMBER 1965–2 SEPTEMBER 1966   Situation comedy about two summer camps across the lake from each other: Camp Runamuck (for boys) and Camp Divine (for girls). With Arch Roberts as Commander Wivenhoe, child-hating boss of Runamuck; Dave Ketchum as Spiffy, his second in command; Dave Madden as Counselor Pruett; Alice Nunn as Mahalia May Gruenecker, chief counselor at Divine; Nina Wayne (older sister of Carol Wayne) as voluptuous counselor Caprice Yeudleman; Hermione Baddeley as Eulalia Divine, owner of the girls' camp; Frank DeVol and Leonard Stone as Doc; and Mike Wagner as Malden, the cook.

CAMPBELL PLAYHOUSE   NBC

6 JUNE 1952–29 AUGUST 1952   This dramatic anthology series was a summer replacement for *The Aldrich Family*. See also *TV Soundstage*.

CAN DO   NBC

26 NOVEMBER 1956–31 DECEMBER 1956   Robert Alda hosted this Monday-night game show on which contestants tried to predict whether celebrity guests could successfully perform prescribed stunts.

CAN YOU TOP THIS ABC/SYNDICATED
3 OCTOBER 1950–26 MARCH 1951 (ABC); 1970 (SYNDICATED) This show was derived from the radio program of the same title. Jokes sent in by home viewers were read to the audience, and a celebrity panel then tried to "top" the response to that joke by telling a funnier joke on the same subject. Ward Wilson hosted the 1950–1951 network version; Wink Martindale first hosted the syndicated version but was replaced by Dennis James. Morey Amsterdam was a permanent panelist.

CANDID CAMERA ABC/NBC/CBS
10 AUGUST 1948–3 DECEMBER 1948 (ABC) 29 MAY 1949–18 AUGUST 1949 (NBC); 12 SEPTEMBER 1949–25 SEPTEMBER 1950 (CBS); 27 AUGUST 1951–23 MAY 1952 (ABC); 2 JUNE 1953–5 AUGUST 1953 (NBC); 2 OCTOBER 1960–3 SEPTEMBER 1967 (CBS)
THE NEW CANDID CAMERA SYNDICATED
1974–1978 Allen Funt created and hosted this unique, and often hilarious, human interest show on which people were filmed by a hidden camera and were "caught in the act of being themselves." The idea originated when Funt was in the armed services; he surreptitiously recorded servicemen's gripes and broadcast them on Armed Forces Radio. In 1947 Funt took the idea to network radio, and the show appeared as *Candid Microphone.* The filmed version, at first titled *Candid Microphone,* followed one year later. Many of the situations were staged by Funt and his stooges (such as driving a car with no engine into a service station, or posting a guard at the Pennsylvania–Delaware border to inform motorists that Delaware was closed for the day), but other situations were not contrived at all (such as filming a traffic cop at work, or teenage boys combing their hair). Some sequences were edited and set to music. On the early years of *Candid Camera,* Funt was assisted by Jerry Lester. When the show returned in 1960, Funt's cohost was Arthur Godfrey; Godfrey left after one season and was replaced by Durward Kirby for the next five seasons. Bess Myerson was the cohost for the 1966–1967 season. In 1974 Funt returned to television with *The New Candid Camera,* which included not only new segments, but also highlights of the old shows. Phyllis George cohosted the show from 1974 until 1976, when Jo Ann Pflug succeeded her.

CANNON CBS
14 SEPTEMBER 1971–19 SEPTEMBER 1976 This successful crime show starred William Conrad as Frank Cannon, a former cop turned private eye. Though television viewers may not have recognized Conrad's hefty frame before this series, his voice certainly should have been familiar: Conrad was radio's Matt Dillon on *Gunsmoke,* and narrated several television series, including *Rocky and His Friends, The Fugitive,* and *The*

Invaders. A Quinn Martin production, *Cannon* was one of the few series of the 1970s with only one regular.

CANNONBALL   SYNDICATED
1958 A half-hour adventure series about a couple of long-distance truckers (NBC exhumed this concept for its 1974 series, *Movin' On*). With Paul Birch as Mike Malone and William Campbell as his partner, Jerry Austin. Robert Maxwell was the producer.

CAPITOL CAPERS   NBC
1 AUGUST 1949–7 SEPTEMBER 1949 A fifteen-minute musical variety show, broadcast twice a week before the evening news from Washington, D.C. The show featured singer Gene Archer and was also known as *The Gene Archer Show*.

CAPITOL CLOAKROOM   CBS
14 OCTOBER 1949–15 SEPTEMBER 1950 Friday-night public affairs program, with Eric Sevareid, Willard (Bill) Shadel, Griffing Bancroft, and a guest panelist. The show was broadcast live from Washington, D.C.

THE CAPTAIN & TENNILLE   ABC
20 SEPTEMBER 1976–14 MARCH 1977 ABC's answer to Sonny and Cher, The Captain (Daryl Dragon) and Tennille (Toni Tennille, his wife) were given their own musical variety series after a string of hit records, the biggest of which was "Love Will Keep Us Together" (written by Neil Sedaka). The laconic Captain and the toothsome Tennille were both talented musicians (each had worked at one time with the Beach Boys), but neither seemed at ease with the labored comedy sketches which often dominated the series.

CAPTAIN BILLY'S MISSISSIPPI MUSIC HALL   CBS
24 SEPTEMBER 1948–3 DECEMBER 1948 This half-hour musical variety show was set aboard a nineteenth-century riverboat and was hosted by Ralph Dumke as Captain Billy Bryant. Also on board were Johnny Downs, Bibi Osterwald, and Juanita Hall. The series was produced by Paul Killiam and actually premiered (as *Captain Billy's Showboat*) on 16 August 1948, though it was not broadcast weekly until late September.

CAPTAIN DAVID GRIEF   SYNDICATED
1955 These adaptations of the Jack London stories starred Maxwell Reed as Caribbean sailor Captain David Grief and Maureen Hingart as Anura, his permanent passenger.

CAPTAIN GALLANT OF THE FOREIGN LEGION   NBC
13 FEBRUARY 1955–7 DECEMBER 1957 This half-hour adventure series for children starred Buster Crabbe as Captain Michael Gallant, com-

mander of the North African headquarters of the French Foreign Legion. Also featured were Cullen Crabbe (Buster's son) as Cuffy Sanders, an orphan taken in by Captain Gallant after the death of his Legionnaire father; Al "Fuzzy" Knight as Private Fuzzy Knight; and Gilles Queant as Sergeant Du Val. Produced by Serge Glykson, the series was filmed on location from 1954 until 1956, when production was shifted to the politically safer climate of Northern Italy. Syndicated reruns were shown under the title *Foreign Legionnaire*.

CAPTAIN HARTZ AND HIS PETS   SYNDICATED
1954   Ned Locke starred in this children's series, as Captain Hartz, an airline pilot who brought back unusual pets from his travels; Jerry Garvey was also featured as his teenage pal.

CAPTAIN KANGAROO   CBS
3 OCTOBER 1955–   Television's longest-running network children's series. Its star, Bob Keeshan, began his show business career as Clarabell on *Howdy Doody*. After hosting two local shows in New York (*Time for Fun* and *Tinker's Workshop*), he brought this show on the air in 1955, playing Captain Kangaroo, a gentle man so named because of the large pockets of his jacket (the show premiered on the same day as *The Mickey Mouse Club*). In two decades the show has changed little. Stressing gentleness, with a touch of morality and religion, Keeshan has managed to keep its tone calm and its pace even. The show is geared to the individual child watching at home—no children appear in the studio (though some are occasionally featured in filmed segments). But the Captain is not alone; Hugh (Lumpy) Brannum, as Mr. Green Jeans, has been with the show from its early days. Mr. Green Jeans is apparently a farmer (and an amateur inventor); several times a week he introduces animals on the show. For many seasons Cosmo Allegretti has been featured as Dennis, the bumbling apprentice. Allegretti and Brannum also appear in other roles on the show; in addition, Allegretti is the show's chief puppeteer and is thus responsible for such characters as the mischievous Mr. Moose, the introspective Bunny Rabbit, the curious Miss Frog, the quiet Mr. Whispers, and the erudite Word Bird. Cartoons are also featured but have never predominated in the show; one of the most frequently seen cartoons starred Tom Terrific and Mighty Manfred the Wonder Dog. In recent seasons two other humans have been featured: Larry Wall as Mr. Baxter and Debby Weems as Debby. Many guest stars have also appeared on the show. A small sample would include Alan Arkin, Pearl Bailey, Carol Channing, Earl Monroe (of the New York Knicks), Edward Villella, Marlo Thomas, Imogene Coca, Doug Henning, Dick Shawn, and Eli Wallach. For several seasons, the show was seen six mornings a week; it has also been shown as a forty-five-minute series as well as in an hour-long format. During the 1964–1965 season, Keeshan

was also the star of a second children's program, *Mister Mayor* (see that title). Now seen Mondays through Fridays, approximately 120 new shows are taped each year and mixed in with reruns.

Keeshan has been keenly aware of the impact of commercials on young viewers. No cast members deliver commercials on the show, and all advertisements must be approved by the show's executives. In recent seasons Keeshan has put even more distance between the program and the ads: At the end of each segment, a young voice announces, "The Captain will be back after these messages." Currently, the show is produced by Jim Hirschfeld and directed by Peter Birch; Bob Colleary is head writer.

CAPTAIN MIDNIGHT CBS
4 SEPTEMBER 1954–12 MAY 1956   A half-hour adventure series for children, *Captain Midnight* began on radio in 1940 and ran for thirteen years. On TV, Richard Webb starred as Captain Midnight, head of the Secret Squadron, an omnibus crimefighting agency (according to the radio story, Captain Midnight was really Captain Albright, a brave and daring World War I flying ace who returned to his home base after a particularly hazardous mission precisely at the stroke of midnight). Also featured were Sid Melton as Ichabod (Ikky) Mudd, Midnight's none-too-bright assistant, and Olan Soule as Tut (Aristotle Jones), an eccentric scientist who worked for the Secret Squadron. The network version of the series was sponsored by Ovaltine, which had also sponsored the radio show. Because Ovaltine owned the rights to the name "Captain Midnight," when the reruns of the series went into syndication (without Ovaltine's sponsorship) it was seen under the title *Jet Jackson, Flying Commando;* all references in the dialogues to "Captain Midnight" were crudely overdubbed with the words "Jet Jackson."

CAPTAIN NICE NBC
9 JANUARY 1967–28 AUGUST 1967   An imitation *Batman, Captain Nice* was set in Big Town. With William Daniels as Carter Nash, a police chemist who devised a secret formula, one swallow of which turned him into Captain Nice, crimefighter; Alice Ghostley as his mother, Mrs. Nash; and Ann Prentiss as Sergeant Candy Kane, his admirer. (*Captain Nice* should not be confused with *Mr. Terrific*, the CBS imitation *Batman*, which premiered and closed on the same dates as *Captain Nice*.)

CAPTAIN SCARLET AND THE MYSTERONS SYNDICATED
1967   Created by Gerry and Sylvia Anderson, this British children's series was filmed in "Super Marionation," a technique using plastic models operated by very fine wires. Captain Scarlet led the forces of Spectra, an international planetary defense force, against the Mysterons, unseen invaders from Mars.

CAPTAIN VIDEO   DUMONT/SYNDICATED

27 JUNE 1949–1 APRIL 1955 (DUMONT); 1953–1955 (SYNDICATED); 1956 (SYNDICATED)   Television's best-known space serial began in 1949 with Richard Coogan as Captain Video, the ordinary human who led the Video Rangers, a squad of loyal agents which fought terrestrial and extraterrestrial villains during the twenty-second century. Coogan was replaced later in 1949 by Al Hodge, who continued in the role for seven years. Also featured were Don Hastings (who would go on to greater fame in *As the World Turns*) as a teenager, The Video Ranger, the Captain's main assistant; Hal Conklin as Dr. Pauli, the Captain's archenemy; and Tobor the robot ("Tobor" is "robot" spelled backwards), originally a foe but later an ally of the Captain. Guest villains over the years included Ernest Borgnine (as Nargola, one of his first TV roles), Jack Klugman, and Tony Randall.

A scientific genius, Captain Video invented dozens of fantastic gadgets in his secret mountain headquarters, such as the Remote Tele-Carrier, the Cosmic Vibrator, the Opticon Scillometer, and the Astra-Viewer. His first spaceship—the *X-9*—crashed; Video replaced it with the *Galaxy*. Broadcast live from New York for its first six years, *Captain Video* started out as a half-hour show four nights a week; by the fall of 1949 it was on every weeknight. In the fall of 1953 the daily version was cut back to fifteen minutes, and it was finally dropped in 1955. In 1953, however, a second *Captain Video* series had begun, titled *The Secret Files of Captain Video,* which appeared in a half-hour, noncontinuing form. In 1956 Al Hodge returned as the host of a syndicated cartoon show, *Captain Video's Cartoons.* After *Captain Video* left the air, Al Hodge appeared only rarely on television. In March of 1979 he died alone in a New York hotel room.

Written by M. C. Brook, the original *Captain Video* was the first and longest-running of the several TV space shows; it spawned a host of competitors, including *Atom Squad, Captain Midnight* (which was not actually set in outer space), *Commando Cody, Rocky Jones, Space Ranger, Rod Brown of the Rocket Rangers, Space Patrol,* and *Tom Corbett, Space Cadet.*

CAPTAIN Z–RO   SYNDICATED

1955   Children's fantasy series written by and starring Roy Steffens as Captain Z-Ro, inventor of a combination rocket ship and time machine. This device enabled him to travel anywhere in the past, present, or future. The show, which began as a local show in Los Angeles in 1952, also featured Bobby Trumbull as Jet, his teenage assistant.

CAR 54, WHERE ARE YOU?   NBC

17 SEPTEMBER 1961–8 SEPTEMBER 1963   Created by Nat Hiken, who also created *You'll Never Get Rich, Car 54* was the first situation comedy

about police officers. It was also one of the few series of its time to feature a black performer (Nipsey Russell) as a regular. The large cast included Joe E. Ross (he played Ritzik on *You'll Never Get Rich*) as Officer Gunther Toody; Fred Gwynne as his partner, Officer Francis Muldoon; Beatrice Pons as Lucille Toody, Gunther's wife (Pons had played Ritzik's wife on *You'll Never Get Rich;* Ross and Pons thus became the first actor-actress team to play two different married couples on two sitcoms); Al Lewis as Schnauzer; Charlotte Rae as Mrs. Schnauzer; Paul Reed as Captain Block; Nipsey Russell as Officer Anderson; Fred O'Neal as Officer Wallace; Mickey Deems as Officer Fleisher; Al Henderson as Officer O'Hara; Duke Farley as Officer Riley; Hank Garrett as Officer Nicholson; Shelley Burton as Officer Murdock; Jerry Guardino as Officer Antonnucci; Jim Gormley as Officer Nelson; and Joe Warren as Officer Steinmetz.

THE CARA WILLIAMS SHOW   CBS
23 SEPTEMBER 1964–10 SEPTEMBER 1965 Half-hour sitcom about a pair of newlyweds who worked for a company where marriage between employees was forbidden. With Cara Williams as Cara Bridges; Frank Aletter as her husband, Frank Bridges; Jack Sheldon as their neighbor, jazz trumpeter Fletcher Kincaid; Paul Reed as their boss, Damon Burkhardt; Reta Shaw as Mrs. Burkhardt; and Jeanne Arnold as Mary, Burkhardt's secretary. The series was developed by Keefe Brasselle.

CARD SHARKS   NBC
24 APRIL 1978–   Jim Perry hosts this daytime game show, a Mark Goodson-Bill Todman production. Essentially, the object of the game is for the two contestants, each of whom faces a row of five large playing cards, to predict whether the value of the next card would be higher or lower than the one preceding it. The first player to complete the row successfully wins the game, and the winner of two games progresses to the "Money Cards," where, with a $200 stake, the player could theoretically win as much as $28,000. Chester Feldman is the executive producer and Jonathan M. Goodson the producer.

CARIBE   ABC
17 FEBRUARY 1975–11 AUGUST 1975 Standard crime show about a two-man police unit (Caribe Force), operating out of Miami, whose territory spanned the Caribbean. With Stacy Keach as Lieutenant Ben Logan; Carl Franklin as Sergeant Mark Walters; and Robert Mandan as Police Commissioner Ed Rawlings. This Quinn Martin production was filmed on location.

THE CARLTON FREDERICKS SHOW   SYNDICATED
1967 Health and diet were the subjects discussed on this half-hour talk show hosted by nutrition expert Carlton Fredericks.

THE CARMEL MYERS SHOW   ABC

26 JUNE 1951–21 FEBRUARY 1952   Fifteen-minute Tuesday-night interview show, hosted by former silent film star Carmel Myers.

CAROL BURNETT & COMPANY   ABC

18 AUGUST 1979–8 SEPTEMBER 1979   A four-week comedy-variety hour with Carol Burnett, Tim Conway, Vicki Lawrence, Craig Richard Nelson, and Kenneth Mars.

THE CAROL BURNETT SHOW   CBS

11 SEPTEMBER 1967–9 AUGUST 1978   Popular variety hour hosted by Carol Burnett, a physical comedienne who became familiar to audiences during her three seasons on *The Garry Moore Show*. By the fall of 1975, *The Carol Burnett Show* was the second-oldest prime-time series on the air (*Walt Disney* was first). A California native, Burnett moved to New York in the mid-1950s, where she landed a role on Buddy Hackett's 1956 sitcom, *Stanley*. She then guested on several variety shows, including *The Garry Moore Show* (daytime version) and Jack Paar's *Tonight* show, where she brought down the house singing a novelty number, "I Made a Fool of Myself over John Foster Dulles." In 1959 she became a regular on the nighttime version of *The Garry Moore Show;* it was there that she met her husband and future producer, Joe Hamilton. After leaving the Moore show in 1962, she appeared in several specials and also hosted *The Entertainers* in 1964. On her own show she brought together a group of talented supporting players: Harvey Korman, a versatile funny man who had previously been featured on *The Danny Kaye Show;* handsome Lyle Waggoner; and a newcomer named Vicki Lawrence, whose resemblance to Burnett led her to be cast as Burnett's younger sister in many sketches. In 1974 Waggoner left the series; a year later Tim Conway (who had guested frequently on the show) joined as a regular. Korman left in 1977 and was replaced by Dick Van Dyke, who announced his "resignation" from the series in December 1977. In later seasons, the show did not emphasize guest stars, relying instead on the talents of the regulars. Spoofs of movies, especially musicals, had become a staple; other recurring segments included "As the Stomach Turns," a soap opera parody, and "The Family," a group of rural folks who constantly bickered with one another. Most shows began with questions from the studio audience and ended with Burnett tugging her ear. Music was supplied by the Peter Matz Orchestra, with choreography by Ernest Flatt and costumes by Bob Mackie.

THE CAROLYN GILBERT SHOW   ABC

15 FEBRUARY 1950–23 JULY 1950   A fifteen-minute musical variety show hosted by singer Carolyn Gilbert.

133

CARRASCOLENDAS PBS

1972– An educational series for children, presented partly in Spanish and partly in English, set in the village of Carrascolendas. With Harry Frank Porter as Agapito, the Lion; Mike Gomez as Campamocha, the handyman; Dyana Elizondo as Dyana, the Doll; Lizanne Brazell as Pepper, the detective; Agapito Leal as Carrascoles, owner of the village café. Produced under a federal grant at KLRN-TV, San Antonio–Austin, for the Southwest Texas Public Broadcasting Council. Executive producer: Aida Barrera.

CARTER COUNTRY ABC

15 SEPTEMBER 1977–23 AUGUST 1979 The first situation comedy to use the name of a current President in its title, *Carter Country* was set in Clinton Corners, a medium-sized town somewhere in the deep South. With Victor French as Roy Mobey, the white police chief; Kene Holliday as Curtis Baker, his black deputy; Richard Paul as Ted Burnside, the town's spineless mayor; Vernée Watson as Lucille Banks, Burnside's black secretary; Barbara Cason as Cloris, the town's policewoman; Guich Koock as Officer Harley Puckett; Harvey Vernon as Officer DeWitt; and Melanie Griffith (1978–1979) as Tracy. Created by Phil Doran and Douglas Arango. Executive producers: Bud Yorkin, Saul Turteltaub, and Bernie Orenstein.

CARTOON TELETALES ABC

11 AUGUST 1948–24 SEPTEMBER 1950 One of the first children's programs to incorporate the philosophy that television can be a participatory medium, rather than a passive one for its viewers, *Cartoon Teletales* was a Sunday-evening feature which encouraged children to sketch along with artist Chuck Luchsinger as he drew illustrations to accompany stories narrated by his brother, Jack Luchsinger. Featured characters included Pinto the Pony, Cletus the Caterpillar, and Alice the Alligator.

CARTOONIES ABC

13 APRIL 1963–28 SEPTEMBER 1963 Known as *Cartoonsville* in its early weeks, this half-hour Saturday-morning cartoon show was hosted by Paul Winchell and his dummies, Jerry Mahoney and Knucklehead Smith.

CASABLANCA ABC

27 SEPTEMBER 1955–24 APRIL 1956 One segment of *Warner Brothers Presents, Casablanca* alternated with *Cheyenne* and *King's Row* for one season. It was a pale adaptation of the 1941 classic film which had starred Humphrey Bogart and Ingrid Bergman. On television Charles McGraw starred as Rick Jason, the American expatriate who ran a night spot in Casablanca at the outbreak of World War II.

THE CASE OF THE DANGEROUS ROBIN
See DANGEROUS ROBIN

THE CASES OF EDDIE DRAKE DUMONT
6 MARCH 1952–29 MAY 1952 Don Haggerty starred in this half-hour crime show as New York private eye Eddie Drake. Nine episodes were filmed by CBS in 1949, but were never shown on that network. DuMont bought them and filmed four more in 1952, adding Patricia Morrison as Karen Gayle, a criminal psychologist who assisted Drake.

CASEY JONES SYNDICATED
1958 Half-hour adventure series for children, based on the life of the legendary engineer. Alan Hale, Jr., starred as Casey Jones, engineer on the Cannonball Express for the Midwest and Central Railroad. Also featured were Mary Lawrence as his wife, Alice, and Bobby Clark as their son, Casey Jr.

CASPER AND THE ANGELS NBC
22 SEPTEMBER 1979– Half-hour Saturday-morning cartoon show starring Casper the Friendly Ghost. This one is set in the future, with Casper helping out two space officers, Mini and Maxi, and another ghost, Harry Scary.

CASPER, THE FRIENDLY GHOST ABC
5 OCTOBER 1963–27 DECEMBER 1969 Casper, a childlike ghost who tried to help people rather then scare them, was the star of a series of theatrical cartoons produced by Paramount in the 1940s. His half-hour TV series was a mainstay of ABC's Saturday-morning schedule for most of the 1960s. Other characters who appeared with Casper were *Nightmare the Galloping Ghost, Wendy the Good Little Witch,* and *The Ghostly Trio.*

THE CATHOLIC HOUR (GUIDELINE) NBC
4 JANUARY 1953–30 AUGUST 1970 This long-running religious series shared a time slot with *Frontiers of Faith* and *The Eternal Light.* It was produced by NBC in cooperation with the National Council of Catholic Men.

CATTANOOGA CATS ABC
6 SEPTEMBER 1969–4 SEPTEMBER 1971 Another of the many Saturday-morning cartoon shows featuring a rock band composed of animals. Produced by Hanna-Barbera, the series originally included *Motor Mouse* cartoons; in 1970 Motor Mouse was given his own series.

CAVALCADE OF AMERICA (CAVALCADE THEATER) NBC/ABC
1 OCTOBER 1952–24 JUNE 1953 (NBC); 29 SEPTEMBER 1953–23 OCTOBER 1956 (ABC) Presentations on this half-hour anthology series fo-

cused on incidents in American history. During the 1952–1953 season the show alternated biweekly with *The Scott Music Hall,* and during the 1955–1956 season it was known as *DuPont Cavalcade Theater.*

CAVALCADE OF BANDS DUMONT
17 JANUARY 1950–25 SEPTEMBER 1951 This Tuesday-night musical series featuring the Big Bands was hosted first by Fred Robbins, then by Warren Hull, singer Ted Steele, and finally by Buddy Rogers.

CAVALCADE OF STARS DUMONT
4 JUNE 1949–26 SEPTEMBER 1952 One of the longest-running series on the short-lived DuMont network, *Cavalcade of Stars* was an hour of variety. It was hosted by Jack Carter (1949–1950), Jackie Gleason (1950–1952), and Larry Storch (summer 1952). It was here that the first episodes of *The Honeymooners* were broadcast, with Pert Kelton as Alice Kramden. See also *The Jackie Gleason Show.*

CAVALCADE THEATER
See CAVALCADE OF AMERICA

CELANESE THEATRE ABC
3 OCTOBER 1951–25 JUNE 1952 Alex Segal directed this dramatic anthology series. Presentations included: "Ah! Wilderness," with Thomas Mitchell (3 October); "Susan and God," with Wendell Corey (his first major TV role, 17 October); "Anna Christie," with June Havoc (23 January); "The Petrified Forest," with Kim Hunter (20 February); "Brief Moment," with Veronica Lake (6 February); "On Borrowed Time," with Ralph Morgan, Mildred Dunnock, and Billy Gray (25 June; Gray later played Bud in *Father Knows Best*).

CELEBRITY BILLIARDS SYNDICATED
1967 Celebrity guests challenged America's best known pool player, Minnesota Fats (née Rudolph Wanderone, Jr.), on this half-hour series.

CELEBRITY BOWLING SYNDICATED
1971–1978 Two two-celebrity teams competed on the lanes in this sports series. Originally, the show was hosted by Jed Allan and Sherry Kominsky and later by Allan alone. Produced by Joe Siegman and Don Gregory.

CELEBRITY CHALLENGE OF THE SEXES CBS
31 JANUARY 1978–28 FEBRUARY 1978 Lightweight half-hour prime-time series featuring head-to-head competition between male and female celebrities in selected athletic endeavors. Taped at Mission Viejo, California, the series was hosted by CBS sportscaster Tom Brookshier, a one-

time defensive back with the Philadelphia Eagles. Also on hand were McLean Stevenson and Barbara Rhoades, who served as "coaches" for their respective genders. Mel Ferber produced the show; Bernie Hoffman directed it.

CELEBRITY CHARADES SYNDICATED
1979 Assisted by his dummy, Squeaky, ventriloquist Jay Johnson hosted this half-hour game show on which two four-member celebrity teams played charades; the prize money was donated to the team captains' favorite charities.

CELEBRITY COOKS SYNDICATED
1978 Half-hour series from Canada on which celebrities dropped by to cook and chat with host Bruno Gerussi. Derek Smith was the executive producer.

THE CELEBRITY GAME CBS
5 APRIL 1964–13 SEPTEMBER 1964; 8 APRIL 1965–9 SEPTEMBER 1965 Carl Reiner hosted this prime-time game show, which, like *The Hollywood Squares,* involved two contestants and a panel of nine celebrities. A Merrill Heatter–Bob Quigley Production, the show replaced *The Judy Garland Show* in 1964 and *The Baileys of Balboa* in 1965.

CELEBRITY GOLF NBC
25 SEPTEMBER 1960–28 MAY 1961 Half-hour sports show on which Sam Snead teed off against a celebrity challenger, who was given a handicap. Harry Von Zell handled the play-by-play.

CELEBRITY QUIZ
See CELEBRITY TIME

CELEBRITY REVUE SYNDICATED
1976 A variety hour with no regulars, produced in Vancouver.

CELEBRITY SWEEPSTAKES NBC/SYNDICATED
1 APRIL 1974–1 OCTOBER 1976 (NBC); 1974–1977 (SYNDICATED) A game show involving two contestants, six celebrities, and the studio audience. First, host Jim McKrell asked a question; the members of the audience then set the "odds" for each celebrity by voting electronically for the one they thought was most likely to answer correctly. Once the odds were established and posted, one contestant could wager on any of the celebrities; if that celebrity answered correctly, the contestant won money. At the end of the show each contestant could wager "all or none" of his or her winnings on one celebrity. Frequently seen on the celebrity panel were Carol Wayne, Buddy Hackett, Dick Martin, and Joey Bishop.

The NBC daytime version ran for two-and-one-half years, spawning a nighttime syndicated version. Executive producer: Ralph Andrews.

CELEBRITY TALENT SCOUTS
See TALENT SCOUTS

CELEBRITY TENNIS
SYNDICATED
1974–1978   Hosted by Tony Trabert and Bobby Riggs, this series featured four guest celebrities playing doubles.

CELEBRITY TIME (CELEBRITY QUIZ)
ABC/CBS
3 APRIL 1949–26 MARCH 1950 (ABC); 2 APRIL 1950–21 SEPTEMBER 1952 (CBS)   This prime-time series was part game show and part talk show. Conrad Nagel presided over the panel, which often included Ilka Chase, Kyle MacDonnell, and Kitty Carlisle.

CENTENNIAL
See THE BIG EVENT

CENTER STAGE
ABC
1 JUNE 1954–21 SEPTEMBER 1954   A biweekly dramatic anthology series.

CHAIN LETTER
NBC
4 JULY 1966–14 OCTOBER 1966   Jan Murray hosted this daytime game show. It featured two celebrity-and-contestant teams. Each team was given a category, then required to name one-word elements of that category; each word so named had to begin with the final letter of the previous word.

CHALLENGE GOLF
ABC
12 JANUARY 1963–6 APRIL 1963   Thirteen-week series of golf matches in which Arnold Palmer and Gary Player teamed up against a pair of challengers.

THE CHALLENGE OF THE SEXES
CBS
10 JANUARY 1976–20 MARCH 1976; 16 JANUARY 1977–3 APRIL 1977; 8 JANUARY 1978–9 APRIL 1978; 14 JANUARY 1979–15 APRIL 1979   A sports show on which top male and female athletes compete against each other. Hosts have included Vin Scully, Suzy Chaffee, and Phyllis George. See also *Celebrity Challenge of The Sexes.*

THE CHALLENGING SEAS SYNDICATED
1969 Bill Burrud hosted this nautical documentary series.

CHAMPAGNE AND ORCHIDS DUMONT
6 SEPTEMBER 1948–10 JANUARY 1949 Fifteen-minute Monday-night musical show, hosted by Adrienne.

THE CHAMPIONS NBC
10 JUNE 1968–9 SEPTEMBER 1968 This British spy series combined *The Lost Horizon* with *The Man from U.N.C.L.E.* It featured three secret agents, operatives of Nemesis, a Swiss-based law-and-order outfit. On a mission to China, the three were shot down in the Himalayas. There they were taken by an old man to a lost city and endowed with superior sensory and extrasensory powers. With Stuart Damon as Craig Stirling; Alexandra Bastedo as Sharon Macready; William Gaunt as Richard Barrett; and Anthony Nichols as W. L. Tremayne, their boss.

CHAMPIONSHIP BRIDGE WITH CHARLES GOREN ABC/SYNDICATED
18 OCTOBER 1959–10 APRIL 1960 (ABC); 1960–1962 (SYNDICATED) Each week four expert bridge players (all of them Life Masters) played two or three hands of bridge. Charles Goren, America's best-known bridge expert, preselected the hands and analyzed the play from a soundproof booth; Alex Dreier provided the card-by-card commentary. The series, which was seen Sunday afternoons in most areas, was filmed in Chicago.

CHAMPIONSHIP DEBATE NBC
3 FEBRUARY 1962–19 MAY 1962 Broadcast live on Saturday afternoons, this half-hour series featured debates between two two-member teams representing American colleges and universities. Dr. James H. McBath was the moderator.

CHANCE FOR ROMANCE ABC
13 OCTOBER 1958–5 DECEMBER 1958 This daytime show was an early version of *The Dating Game.* John Cameron Swayze hosted.

CHANCE OF A LIFETIME ABC/DUMONT
20 SEPTEMBER 1950–20 AUGUST 1953 (ABC); 11 SEPTEMBER 1953–17 JUNE 1955 (DUMONT); 3 JULY 1955–23 JUNE 1956 (ABC) John Reed King (who also hosted the radio version of the show) was the first host of this lighthearted guessing game; when Dennis James succeeded him in the spring of 1952, the format switched to a talent contest.

THE CHANGING EARTH SYNDICATED
1964 Geology was the subject of this educational series, hosted by Jim McClurg of the University of Michigan.

CHANNING ABC
18 SEPTEMBER 1963–8 APRIL 1964 This dramatic series was set at
Channing College and starred Jason Evers as Joseph Howe, professor of
English, and Henry Jones as Fred Baker, the dean. Jack Laird was the
producer.

CHARADE QUIZ DUMONT
27 NOVEMBER 1947–23 JUNE 1949 One of television's first game shows,
Charade Quiz was the forerunner of *Pantomime Quiz*. Bill Slater hosted
the show, on which a celebrity panel acted out charades submitted by
home viewers.

CHARGE ACCOUNT
See THE JAN MURRAY SHOW

CHARLES BOYER THEATER SYNDICATED
1953 Charles Boyer hosted this half-hour dramatic anthology series.

THE CHARLES FARRELL SHOW CBS
2 JULY 1956–24 SEPTEMBER 1956 A summer replacement for *I Love
Lucy,* this sitcom starred Charlie Farrell (playing himself) as the proprietor of the Racquet Club in Palm Springs, California. With Charles Winninger as Dad, Charlie's crusty father; Richard Deacon as Sherman Hull,
club director; Ann Lee as Doris Mayfield, Charlie's girlfriend; Kathryn
Card as Mrs. Papernow; and Jeff Silver as Rodney.

THE CHARLES RUGGLES SHOW
See THE RUGGLES

THE CHARLEY WEAVER SHOW ABC
(CHARLEY WEAVER'S HOBBY LOBBY)
30 SEPTEMBER 1959–23 MARCH 1960 This prime-time series began
with an unusual format: host Cliff Arquette (as beloved bumpkin Charley
Weaver) interviewed celebrity guests about their hobbies. By midseason
that idea had been scrapped, and a standard comedy-variety format was
adopted.

CHARLIE CHAN SYNDICATED
1958 Earl Derr Biggers's fictional sleuth first came to television in this
half-hour series starring J. Carrol Naish as Charlie Chan and James
Hong as number-one son, Barry. In 1972 the Oriental detective reappeared in cartoon form. See *The Amazing Chan and the Chan Clan*. The
Chan character was based on a Honolulu police detective, Chang Apana.

CHARLIE WILD, PRIVATE DETECTIVE   CBS/ABC/DUMONT

22 DECEMBER 1950–JUNE 1951 (CBS); 11 SEPTEMBER 1951–4 MARCH
1952 (ABC); 13 MARCH 1952–19 JUNE 1952 (DUMONT)   Half-hour
crime show starring Kevin O'Morrison, then John McQuade as New
York private eye Charlie Wild, with Cloris Leachman as Effie Perrine, his
woman Friday. Herbert Brodkin produced the series, and Leonard Valenta directed it.

CHARLIE'S ANGELS   ABC

22 SEPTEMBER 1976–   By far the most popular new show of
the 1976–1977 season, *Charlie's Angels* was an hour crime show with
enormous visual appeal: three stunning young women who often went
braless. The three "Angels" were all police academy graduates who
signed on with Charles Townsend Associates, a private detective agency.
Featured were Kate Jackson (late of *The Rookies*) as Sabrina Duncan;
former Wella Balsam model Farrah Fawcett-Majors (1976–1977) as Jill
Munroe; former Breck girl Jaclyn Smith as Kelly Garrett; David Doyle
as John Bosley, their avuncular associate; and John Forsythe as the voice
of Charlie Townsend, the Angels' unseen boss, who usually communicat-
ed by telephone. In 1977 Farrah Fawcett-Majors decided to leave the series, even though another year remained on her contract. She was
replaced by Cheryl Ladd (the wife of actor David Ladd, she was formerly
known as Cheryl Stoppelmoor when she was featured on *Search*) as Jill's
younger sister, Kris Munroe, also a police academy graduate. Cheryl
Ladd proved every bit as popular with viewers as Farrah Fawcett-Majors
had been; some three million posters of Ladd were sold during the 1977–
1978 season. In the spring of 1978 Fawcett-Majors settled her dispute
with Aaron Spelling and Leonard Goldberg, the executive producers of
the show, by agreeing to appear in six episodes during the 1978–1979 season. Kate Jackson left the show after the third season, and was succeeded
by Shelley Hack as Tiffany Welles.

CHASE   NBC

11 SEPTEMBER 1973–28 AUGUST 1974   Jack Webb produced this crime
show around a special police unit that handled "the tough ones, the ones
nobody wants." With Mitchell Ryan as Captain Chase Reddick, head of
the unit; Wayne Maunder as Detective Sergeant Sam MacCray; Reid
Smith as Officer Norm Hamilton, helicopter ace; Michael Richardson as
Officer Steve Baker, hot-rodder; and Brian Fong as Fred Sing, motorcycle man. In January, Smith, Richardson, and Fong were dropped. Added
to the cast were Gary Crosby as Officer Ed Rice; Craig Gardner as
Officer Tom Wilson; and Albert Reed as Officer Frank Dawson.

THE CHEAP SHOW   SYNDICATED

1978   Raucous game show combining *Truth or Consequences* with *Liars*

Club. Hosted by Dick Martin, the game involved two competing couples and a pair of celebrities. Martin asked a question of the celebrities, one of whom answered correctly, one incorrectly. One member of one couple team then tried to guess which celeb had answered correctly; if the guess proved incorrect, the player's partner was then "punished" with a hosing, pie in the face, or other surefire laugh-getter. Cheap prizes were also given away from time to time by Polly the Prize Lady, and the grand prize award was determined by a rat, Oscar the Wonder Rodent. Chris Bearde and Robert D. Wood were the executive producers.

THE CHEATERS   SYNDICATED
1961   John Ireland starred as John Hunter, insurance fraud investigator for the Eastern Insurance Company, in this half-hour adventure series filmed in England. Also featured was Robert Ayres as his associate, Walter Allen.

CHECKMATE   CBS
17 SEPTEMBER 1960–19 SEPTEMBER 1962   The private eyes who comprised Checkmate, Inc., tried not only to solve crimes but also to prevent them. The hour-long series starred Tony George as Don Corey; Doug McClure as young Jed Sills; Sebastian Cabot as Dr. Carl Hyatt, theoretician and criminologist; and Frank Betts (1961–1962) as Chris Devlin. Notable guest appearances included those by Charles Laughton (in "Terror from the East," 7 January 1961, his last TV role) and Cyd Charisse (in "Dance of Death," 22 April 1961, her first TV dramatic role).

CHEER TELEVISION THEATRE   NBC
30 MAY 1954–27 JUNE 1954   This half-hour filmed dramatic anthology series was produced by MCA-TV and sponsored by Procter & Gamble. It was seen only on the West Coast for a time before going coast-to-coast.

CHER   CBS
16 FEBRUARY 1975–4 JANUARY 1976   After the divorce and the demise of *The Sonny and Cher Comedy Hour* in 1974, Sonny (Bono) was the first to return to television. His ABC series, *The Sonny Comedy Revue,* was gone in thirteen weeks. A few weeks later, Cher returned to host this musical variety series; it did well enough to be renewed. Cher kicked off her new series with a special preview broadcast on 12 February; her guests included Elton John, Flip Wilson, and Bette Midler. In January 1976 Cher left the air, returning a month later with Sonny in *The Sonny and Cher Show* (see that title). Also featured on the *Cher* show was Gailard Sartain. Executive producer: George Schlatter; producers: Lee Miller, Alan Katz, and Don Reo.

CHESTER THE PUP
ABC

7 OCTOBER 1950–30 SEPTEMBER 1951   On this kids' show the adventures of Chester the Pup and his friend Drizzlepuss were sketched onscreen by Sid Stone, as they were narrated by Art Whitefield. The show was originally seen Saturday mornings but switched to Sundays in January.

THE CHESTERFIELD SUPPER CLUB
See THE PERRY COMO SHOW

CHET HUNTLEY REPORTING
NBC

26 OCTOBER 1958–17 SEPTEMBER 1963   For one season, each half of NBC's Huntley-Brinkley news team had his own prime-time news analysis series. *David Brinkley's Journal* premiered in 1961, and its relative success led to the rescheduling of this series from Sunday afternoons to prime time.

CHEVROLET ON BROADWAY
See TELE-THEATRE

CHEVROLET SHOWROOM
ABC

25 SEPTEMBER 1953–12 FEBRUARY 1954   Cesar Romero hosted this half-hour variety show, which featured appearances by guest stars and by the 1954 Chevrolets.

CHEYENNE
ABC

20 SEPTEMBER 1955–13 SEPTEMBER 1963   One of the first series for TV by Warner Brothers, *Cheyenne* was introduced during the 1955–1956 season as one segment of *Warner Brothers Presents*. The hour-long western starred Clint Walker as Cheyenne Bodie, a laconic drifter of mixed descent. During the first season L. Q. Jones was also featured as Smitty, an itinerant mapmaker who accompanied Bodie. *Cheyenne* was the only one of the *Warner Brothers Presents* segments to be renewed; during the 1956–1957 season it alternated with *Conflict,* an anthology series. In its third season (1957–1958) *Cheyenne* alternated with *Sugarfoot,* a new Warner Brothers western, and its subsequent history is closely entwined with that of *Sugarfoot* and a third Warner Brothers western, *Bronco.* In 1958 Walker walked out of the series, but the show continued; Ty Hardin, as Bronco Layne, starred in the series during the 1958–1959 season, as *Cheyenne* again alternated with *Sugarfoot.* By mid-1959 Walker had agreed to return to *Cheyenne;* meanwhile, Hardin had proved popular enough as Bronco to merit his own series. The problem was solved by making *Bronco* a separate series, which alternated with *Sugarfoot* during the 1959–1960 season. During the 1960–1961 season, episodes of *Chey-*

enne, Bronco, and *Sugarfoot* were all shown under the *Cheyenne* title, and during the 1961–1962 season *Cheyenne* and *Bronco* shows were both aired under the *Cheyenne* banner. *Cheyenne,* with Walker alone in the saddle, continued on for another season, leaving the air early in 1963; reruns popped up later that year. See also *Bronco; Sugarfoot.*

CHICAGO JAZZ   NBC
26 NOVEMBER 1949–31 DECEMBER 1949   A short-lived program of jazz music, broadcast live from Chicago. The series was also titled *Sessions.*

THE CHICAGO SYMPHONY CHAMBER ORCHESTRA   ABC
25 SEPTEMBER 1951–18 MARCH 1952   A half-hour program of clasical music.

THE CHICAGO TEDDY BEARS   CBS
17 SEPTEMBER 1971–17 DECEMBER 1971   Set at Linc & Latzi's Speakeasy in Chicago during the 1920s, this sitcom was gone in thirteen weeks. With Dean Jones as Linc McCray; John Banner as Uncle Latzi, his partner; Art Metrano as Big Nick Marr, Linc's cousin, a gangster; Huntz Hall (one of the original Bowery Boys) as Dutch, Nick's henchman; Jamie Farr as henchman Duke; Mickey Shaughnessy as henchman Lefty; Mike Mazurki as Julie, Linc's bouncer; and Marvin Kaplan as Marvin, Linc's accountant.

THE CHICAGOLAND MYSTERY PLAYERS   DUMONT
(THE CHICAGOLAND PLAYERS)
11 SEPTEMBER 1949–23 JULY 1950   Broadcast live from Chicago, this series began as a crime drama, with Gordon Urquhart as criminologist Jeff Hall and Bob Smith as Sergeant Holland. In midseason, the crime format was dropped, and the show became a dramatic anthology series.

CHICO AND THE MAN   NBC
13 SEPTEMBER 1974–21 JULY 1978   A situation comedy set in the barrio of East Los Angeles, *Chico and the Man* told the story of a salty white garage owner and his Mexican-American employee. It starred Jack Albertson, a former vaudevillian, as cantankerous Ed Brown, the last WASP left in the neighborhood, and young Freddie Prinze as Chico Rodriguez, the optimistic, fast-talking Chicano who convinced Ed to hire him. Although the show was the first series set in a Mexican-American neighborhood, it was criticized by many Chicano organizations because there were no Chicanos in the cast (indeed, few Mexican-Americans were involved in any aspect of television production, despite the fact that the large majority of programs are produced in Los Angeles). Freddie Prinze

was of Puerto Rican and Hungarian extraction (a "Hungarican," as he described himself), and José Feliciano, who composed and sang the show's theme, was also of Puerto Rican origin. Additionally, the name "Chico" was considered a derogatory nickname to many Chicanos. To rectify matters, executive producer James Komack soon expanded the cast, adding four new members, including two Mexican-Americans: Isaac Ruiz as Ramon (Mando), Chico's friend, and Rodolfo Hoyos as Rudy, Ed's pal. Also added were Scatman Crothers, a black trouper with fifty years of experience, as Louie Wilson, the garbage collector ("I'm the man who empties your can"), and Bonnie Boland as Mabel, the letter carrier. All but Crothers were gone by the end of the second season. Ronny Graham was seen in 1975–1976 as Reverend Bemis and Della Reese was added in 1976 as Della Rogers, Ed's landlady (she also operated a traveling snack wagon).

Freddie Prinze committed suicide in January 1977, at the age of twenty-two. The young performer had been an overnight success—a high school dropout who first appeared on TV late in 1973, Prinze was the star of a smash hit series less than a year later. Though he played a happy-go-lucky character, Prinze was a troubled young man offstage. In nightclub appearances Prinze often emulated Lenny Bruce, the so-called "sick" comic whose troubles with the law precipitated his death from a drug overdose in 1966. Prinze was briefly engaged to the comic's daughter, Kitty Bruce. Prinze, too, was involved with drugs and was also fascinated by guns. He had remarked to several friends that he did not expect to live to be an old man. On 27 January 1977, a despondent Prinze shot himself in the head; he died two days later.

Despite the tragic death of Prinze, NBC elected to continue the series. In the fall of 1977, twelve-year-old Gabriel Melgar joined the cast as Raul Garcia, a Mexican youngster who sneaked into the trunk of Louie's car when Ed and Louie went fishing in Mexico. Ed proceeded to adopt the boy. Also joining the show was Charo, as Aunt Charo. James Komack, creator of the series, served as its executive producer. Produced by Alan Sacks (1974–1975); Michael Morris (1975–1976) and Ed Scharlach (1975–1976); Jerry Ross (1976–1978) and Charles Stewart (1976–1978).

THE CHICO MARX SHOW
See THE COLLEGE BOWL

THE CHILDREN'S CORNER NBC
20 AUGUST 1955–28 APRIL 1956 This Saturday-morning puppet show for children was cohosted by Josie Carey and Fred Rogers, who later emceed *Mister Rogers' Neighborhood* on PBS. Featured puppets included King Friday and Daniel S. Tiger.

CHILDREN'S SKETCH BOOK   NBC

12 MARCH 1949–4 FEBRUARY 1950 Edith Skinner told stories for young viewers on this half-hour series.

CHILD'S WORLD   ABC

1 NOVEMBER 1948–27 APRIL 1949 Helen Parkhurst hosted this fifteen-minute discussion show, on which groups of children talked about their feelings and problems.

CHINA SMITH (THE AFFAIRS OF CHINA SMITH)   SYNDICATED
(THE NEW ADVENTURES OF CHINA SMITH)

1953 This half-hour filmed series starred Dan Duryea as China Smith, an opportunistic American adventurer living in Singapore. Smith's services were available to the highest bidder.

THE CHISHOLMS   CBS

29 MARCH 1979–19 APRIL 1979 Four-part Western saga of a family that moved from Virginia to Oregon during the mid-1840s. Principal players included: Robert Preston as Hadley Chisholm, head of the clan; Rosemary Harris as Minerva Chisholm, his wife; Ben Murphy as son Will; Brian Kerwin as son Gideon; Jimmy Van Patten as son Bo; Stacey Nelkin as daughter Bonnie Sue; Susan Swift as daughter Annabel; Charles Frank as guide Lester Hackett, who joined up in Louisville. The series was created by David Dortort and developed by Evan Hunter. See also *The Chisholms* in the Appendix.

CHOOSE UP SIDES   NBC

7 JANUARY 1956–31 MARCH 1956 This kids' game show was hosted by Gene Rayburn (who was also the announcer on Steve Allen's *Tonight* show at the same time). Produced by Mark Goodson and Bill Todman, it began in 1953 as a local show in New York, hosted by Dean Miller (later of *December Bride*).

CHOPPER ONE   ABC

17 JANUARY 1974–11 JULY 1974 A half hour of cops and choppers, this series was essentially an updated version of *The Whirlybirds,* TV's first helicopter series. It starred Jim McMullan as Officer Don Burdick and Dirk Benedict as Officer Gil Foley, the two pilots of the Chopper One unit. With Ted Hartley as Captain Ted McKeegan, their commanding officer, and Lew Frizzell as Mitch, the mechanic.

THE CHRISTOPHERS (CHRISTOPHER CLOSEUP)   SYNDICATED

1952–   This long-running religious program was brought to television by the Reverend James Keller, founder of the Christophers, a

Catholic religious group. By the 1970s the show was entitled *Christopher Closeup.* It usually featured interviews and was cohosted by the Reverend Richard Armstrong and Jeanne Glynn, who also served as its executive producer and producer respectively.

CHRONICLE
CBS

2 OCTOBER 1963–25 MARCH 1964   This hour documentary series shared a Wednesday time slot with *CBS Reports.* Richard Siemanowski was the executive producer of the show, which focused on the arts and sciences.

CHRONOLOG
NBC

22 OCTOBER 1971–28 JULY 1972   This monthly newsmagazine was the successor to *First Tuesday;* it was telecast on the fourth Friday of each month. Garrick Utley hosted the two-hour show. In 1974 NBC again revived the concept: see *Weekend.*

CHRYSLER THEATER
See BOB HOPE PRESENTS THE CHRYSLER THEATER

THE CHUCK BARRIS RAH-RAH SHOW
NBC

28 FEBRUARY 1978–11 APRIL 1978   A prime-time variety hour hosted by game show magnate Chuck Barris. The show featured celebrity guest stars as well as acts originally seen on *The Gong Show,* the daytime game show created and hosted by Barris.

CIMARRON CITY
NBC

11 OCTOBER 1958–26 SEPTEMBER 1959   This hour-long western battled CBS's *Have Gun Will Travel* and *Gunsmoke* for one season. It featured George Montgomery as cattleman Matt Rockford, ex-mayor of Cimarron City, Oklahoma; Audrey Totter as Beth Purcell, proprietor of a boardinghouse; and John Smith as blacksmith and Deputy Sheriff Lane Temple. Montgomery's wife—Dinah Shore—guest-starred in one episode ("Cimarron Holiday," 20 December). Norman Jolley and Richard Bartlett were the producers.

CIMARRON STRIP
CBS

7 SEPTEMBER 1967–19 SEPTEMBER 1968   Television's third ninety-minute western (following *The Virginian* and *Wagon Train*) was the second western set in Oklahoma's Cimarron country. This time there was a range war brewing. With Stuart Whitman as Marshal Jim Crown; Randy Boone as Francis Wilde, a young photographer and part-time deputy; Percy Herbert as MacGregor, another deputy; and Jill Townsend as Dulcey Coopersmith, café owner.

CIRCLE   SYNDICATED

1960   Singer Lonnie Sattin hosted this half-hour musical variety series.

CIRCLE OF FEAR   NBC

5 JANUARY 1973–22 JUNE 1973   *Circle of Fear* was the new title given to NBC's *Ghost Story,* following Sebastian Cabot's departure as its host.

CIRCLE THEATER

See ARMSTRONG CIRCLE THEATER

THE CIRCUIT RIDER   ABC

5 MARCH 1951–7 MAY 1951   A filmed religious show presented by America for Christ, Inc., *The Circuit Rider* featured guests, biographies of evangelists and musical selections. Franklyn W. Dyson produced the series.

CIRCUS!   SYNDICATED

1971   Bert Parks hosted this half-hour series, which, like *International Showtime,* presented European circus acts. The series was filmed on location.

CIRCUS BOY   NBC/ABC

23 SEPTEMBER 1956–8 SEPTEMBER 1957 (NBC); 19 SEPTEMBER 1957–11 SEPTEMBER 1958 (ABC)   Children's western from Screen Gems, starring Mickey Braddock as Corky, a youngster whose parents were killed in a high-wire accident; Robert Lowery as Big Tim Champion, the new owner of the circus, and guardian of Corky; Noah Beery, Jr., as Uncle Joey, one of the clowns; and Guinn Williams as Pete, a roustabout. Braddock, later known as Mickey Dolenz (his real name), achieved stardom as one of the Monkees on the show of that title.

CIRCUS TIME   ABC

4 OCTOBER 1956–27 JUNE 1957   Circus and novelty acts were featured on this Thursday-night hour-long series hosted by ventriloquist Paul Winehell and his dummy, Jerry Mahoney.

THE CISCO KID   SYNDICATED

1950   One of the most durable of television's early westerns, *The Cisco Kid* began on radio in 1943. The TV version, from Ziv TV, starred Duncan Renaldo as Cisco and Leo Carillo as his jovial sidekick, Pancho. In the eyes of the law, Cisco and Pancho were desperadoes, wanted for unspecified crimes; in the eyes of the poor and downtrodden, the two were do-gooders who often acted where inept and unscrupulous lawmen would not. The producers' decision to film the series in color proved to be a wise one, for Cisco and Pancho are still seen on many local stations.

CITIZEN SOLDIER (THE BIG ATTACK)   SYNDICATED
1956   Half-hour anthology series which dramatized true-life incidents during World War II and the Korean conflict. Each episode was narrated by the individual whose exploits were the subject of the drama.

CITY DETECTIVE   SYNDICATED
1953   Rod Cameron starred as Lieutenant Bart Grant, tough New York cop, in this half-hour crime show. Late in 1953 *Variety* noted that the series had been sold to 171 stations, a record at the time.

CITY HOSPITAL   CBS
25 MARCH 1952–1 OCTOBER 1953   One of TV's first medical shows, *City Hospital* starred Melville Ruick as Dr. Barton Crane, New York City physician. A real-life drama forced the cancellation of one episode, scheduled for 30 June 1953. During rehearsal that afternoon a man burst into the studio, stabbed a camera operator, and shattered a pitcher over the head of one of the actors. The half-hour series was seen on Tuesdays, alternating with *Crime Syndicated.*

CITY OF ANGELS   NBC
3 FEBRUARY 1976–10 AUGUST 1976   Inspired by the film *Chinatown,* this private eye series was set in Los Angeles during the 1930s. It featured Wayne Rogers (formerly of *M*A*S*H*) as Jake Axminster; Clifton Jones as Lieutenant Murray Quint; Elaine Joyce as Marsha, Jake's secretary; Timmie Rogers as Lester; and Philip Sterling as Michael Brimm. Executive producer: Jo Swerling, Jr. Produced by Philip DeGuere, Jr., and William F. Phillips.

CLAUDIA (CLAUDIA, THE STORY OF A MARRIAGE)   NBC/CBS
6 JANUARY 1952–23 MARCH 1952 (NBC); 31 MARCH 1952–30 JUNE 1952 (CBS)   This situation comedy was based on Rose Franken's stories about a young woman and her romance. With Joan McCracken as newlywed Claudia Naughton; Hugh Reilly as her husband, David Naughton, an architect; and Margaret Wycherly as Mrs. Brown, Claudia's mother.

THE CLEAR HORIZON   CBS
11 JULY 1960–10 MARCH 1961; 26 FEBRUARY 1962–11 JUNE 1962   This soap opera attempted to capitalize on the topicality of the space age; it told the story of astronauts and their families. *The Clear Horizon* was the first daytime serial to originate from Hollywood and was also one of the few programs to reappear after its original cancellation. The cast includ-

ed Ed Kemmer as Captain Roy Selby; Phyllis Avery as his wife, Ann; Craig Curtis; Denise Alexander as Lois; Jimmy Carter (the actor, not the President); Lee Meriwether; Ted Knight; William Roerick as Colonel Adams; Rusty Lane as Sergeant Moseby; and William Allyn as Frank.

THE CLIFF EDWARDS SHOW   CBS

23 MAY 1949–19 SEPTEMBER 1949   Cliff "Ukulele Ike" Edwards hosted this fifteen-minute musical series seen on Mondays, Wednesdays, and Fridays after the network news (sometimes the show was only ten minutes long, preceding the five-minute *Ruthie on the Telephone*). Edwards is better known to the public as the voice of Jiminy Cricket in Walt Disney films.

CLIFFHANGERS   NBC

27 FEBRUARY 1979–1 MAY 1979   An unusual prime-time program, *Cliffhangers* presented chapters from three continuing serials each week. The first three offerings were: "Stop Susan Williams," with Susan Anton as Susan Williams, a news photographer investigating the mysterious death of her brother; "The Secret Empire," a science fiction western with Geoffrey Scott as Marshal Jim Donner, a frontier lawman who accidentally stumbles on a futuristic subterranean society, and Diane Mankoff as Tara, leader of the secret empire; "The Curse of Dracula," with Michael Nouri as the five-hundred-year-old vampire who turns up teaching night courses in history at South Bay College in California, Stephen Johnson as Kurt von Helsing, and Carol Baxter as Mary. Executive producer: Kenneth Johnson for Universal TV.

CLIMAX   CBS

7 OCTOBER 1954–26 JUNE 1958   This hour-long dramatic anthology series began as a live show but soon switched to film. It was cohosted by William Lundigan and Mary Costa. Presentations included: Raymond Chandler's "The Long Goodbye," with Dick Powell (as Philip Marlowe), Cesar Romero, and Teresa Wright (7 October 1954); "The Great Impersonation," with Zsa Zsa Gabor (10 March 1955; her first TV dramatic role); "Fear Strikes Out," with Tab Hunter (as baseball player Jimmy Pearsall; 18 August 1955); "Edge of Terror" with Tom Laughlin (11 September 1955; the first major TV role for Laughlin, later the star of the *Billy Jack* films). *Climax* shared a time slot with *Shower of Stars,* which was seen every fourth week (see also that title).

THE CLOCK   NBC/ABC

16 MAY 1949–31 AUGUST 1951 (NBC); 17 OCTOBER 1951–9 JANUARY 1952 (ABC)   An anthology series of half-hour suspense dramas, *The Clock* was seen sporadically for three seasons. It was derived from the radio show which began in 1946.

CLUB EMBASSY
See THE BOB AND RAY SHOW

CLUB OASIS NBC
28 SEPTEMBER 1957–6 SEPTEMBER 1958 This biweekly variety series, set in a nightclub, alternated with *The Polly Bergen Show*. Each program was hosted by a different guest star until 7 June, when bandleader Spike Jones took over as permanent host.

CLUB SEVEN ABC
12 AUGUST 1948–17 MARCH 1949; 11 SEPTEMBER 1950–28 SEPTEMBER 1951 One of the first programs broadcast from ABC's New York studios, *Club Seven* was a weekly half-hour variety show during the 1948–1949 season, when it was hosted by Johnny Thompson (the show was titled *Thompson's Talent Show* during its early weeks). Tony Bavaar took over as host when the show was revived as a Monday-through-Friday-evening entry during the 1950–1951 season.

CLUB 60 NBC
18 FEBRUARY 1957–27 SEPTEMBER 1957
THE HOWARD MILLER SHOW NBC
30 SEPTEMBER 1957–10 JANUARY 1958 A daytime variety hour broadcast live and in color from Chicago, *Club 60* featured vocalists Mike Douglas, Nancy Wright, and the Mello-Larks. Don Sherwood was the first host, but he was succeeded in March by Dennis James. By late summer Howard Miller took over as host, and late in September the show's title was changed to *The Howard Miller Show*. Music on both programs was supplied by the NBC Orchestra, conducted by Joseph Gallicchio.

CLUB TIME
See THE BOB AND RAY SHOW

CLUE CLUB CBS
14 AUGUST 1976–3 SEPTEMBER 1977; 10 SEPTEMBER 1978–21 JANUARY 1979 Two bloodhounds and a group of teenage sleuths were the main characters on this Hanna-Barbera cartoon show.

CODE R CBS
21 JANUARY 1977–10 JUNE 1977 An unimaginative imitation of NBC's *Emergency!*, *Code R* was a midseason replacement for *Spencer's Pilots*, the unlucky occupant of CBS's least successful time slot, Fridays at 8:00 p.m. *Code R* featured James Houghton as Rick Wilson, chief of the Channel Island fire and rescue unit; Marty Kove as George Baker, unit member; Tom Simcox as Walt Robinson, the island police chief; Susanne Reed as Suzy, the dispatcher and office manager; W. T. Zacha as Harry;

Ben Davidson as Ted Milbank; and Robbie Rundle as Bobby Robinson, Walt's young son. Edwin Self produced the hour series for Warner Brothers.

CODE 3   SYNDICATED
1957   This half-hour crime show was ostensibly based on actual case histories. It was hosted by Richard Travis, who appeared as Assistant Sheriff Barnett; as Barrett explained, "Code 3" meant "get there fast." Additional authenticity was imparted to the series by the appearance of Eugene W. Biscailuz, then sheriff of Los Angeles County, at the conclusion of most episodes.

CO-ED FEVER   CBS
4 FEBRUARY 1979   A hapless half-hour sitcom, *Co-Ed Fever* was pulled from CBS's schedule after its only showing, a special preview following the telecast of the movie *Rocky*. Set at Baxter College, an Eastern women's school which recently admitted men, it featured David Keith as Tucker Davis; Alexa Kenin as Maria (Mousie); Christopher S. Nelson as Doug, a wealthy chap; Cathryn O'Neil as Elizabeth; Michael Pasternak as the zany Gobo; Tacey Philips as Hope; Heather Thomas as Sandi; and Jane Rose as Mrs. Selby, the housemother at Brewster House. Martin Ransohoff was the executive producer for Ransohoff Productions. CBS chose a new sitcom, *Billy*, to replace *Co-Ed Fever* in its midseason lineup.

COKE TIME   NBC
29 APRIL 1953–22 FEBRUARY 1957   Eddie Fisher, a pop star of the early 1950s who later made headlines when he married Debbie Reynolds, then Elizabeth Taylor, hosted this fifteen-minute musical series which was seen Wednesdays and Fridays before the news. Singer Jaye P. Morgan appeared frequently. Fisher's backup group was known as the Echoes: Ralph Brewster, Marilyn Jackson, Norma Zimmer, and Don Williams (Zimmer was later a featured vocalist on *The Lawrence Welk Show*). Coca-Cola sponsored the series.

THE COLGATE COMEDY HOUR   NBC
10 SEPTEMBER 1950–25 DECEMBER 1955   This Sunday-evening variety hour competed successfully with *The Ed Sullivan Show* for its first four seasons. Most shows were comedy-variety hours with guest hosts—Dean Martin and Jerry Lewis appeared dozens of times, and Eddie Cantor, Bob Hope, Donald O'Connor, Jimmy Durante, and Fred Allen also appeared frequently. A few comedy plays and musicals were also televised, such as "Roberta," with Gordon MacRae (10 April 1955). In the fall of 1955 the show was retitled *The Colgate Variety Hour*; when Colgate dropped its sponsorship in midseason, the show continued as *The NBC Comedy Hour* (see also that title).

COLGATE THEATER NBC

3 JANUARY 1949–25 JUNE 1950   Half-hour dramatic anthology series.

COLISEUM CBS

26 JANUARY 1967–1 JUNE 1967   A compendium of European and American circus acts, *Coliseum* was hosted by a different guest star each week. The series was a midseason replacement for *Jericho*.

THE COLLEGE BOWL ABC

2 OCTOBER 1950–26 MARCH 1951   This little-known half-hour variety series was hosted by Chico Marx, who appeared as the operator of the College Bowl, a campus hangout. Andy Williams was also featured on the series.

COLLEGE BOWL CBS/NBC

4 JANUARY 1959–16 JUNE 1963 (CBS); 22 SEPTEMBER 1963–14 JUNE 1970 (NBC)   Each week two four-member teams from America's colleges and universities competed on this fast-paced quiz show; by answering "toss-up" and multiple-part questions the teams amassed points. The winning school was awarded $1,500 in scholarship funds (and the right to return the following week), the losing school $500 in funds. General Electric sponsored the series, which was hosted by Allen Ludden (1959–1962) and Robert Earle (1962–1970); Jack Cleary was the producer.

COLLEGE OF MUSICAL KNOWLEDGE NBC
(KAY KYSER'S KOLLEGE OF MUSICAL KNOWLEDGE)

1 DECEMBER 1949–28 DECEMBER 1950; 4 JULY 1954–12 SEPTEMBER 1954   This popular radio giveaway program came twice to television. The first version was hosted by Kay Kyser ("The Old Perfesser"), who began the show on radio in 1938. Attired in cap and gown, Kyser required contestants to identify songs played by the band and to answer true-false questions incorrectly ("That's wrong, you're right!"). Assisting Kyser was mop-topped Mervyn Bogue, better known to audiences as Ish Kabibble; Mike Douglas was one of the show's featured vocalists. After a four-year absence, the show reappeared in the summer of 1954 with Tennessee Ernie Ford as host; it was then called simply *College of Musical Knowledge*. Assisting Ford were three "cheerleaders": Donna Brown, Spring Mitchell, and Maureen Cassidy.

COLLEGE PRESS CONFERENCE ABC

11 OCTOBER 1954–20 NOVEMBER 1960   Ruth Geri Hagy moderated this half-hour public affairs program on which a panel of college students questioned a newsmaker. During its first season the show was seen Monday nights; thereafter, it was relegated to Sunday afternoons.

COLONEL HUMPHREY FLACK (THE FABULOUS FRAUD)　　　DUMONT
7 OCTOBER 1953–2 JULY 1954　This half-hour situation comedy was based on the stories by Everett Rhodes Castle about a modern-day Robin Hood whose specialty was swindling swindlers. The pilot for the series was shown on *Plymouth Playhouse*. Alan Mowbray starred as Colonel Humphrey Flack, and Frank Jenks was featured as his sidekick, Uthas P. (Patsy) Garvey. A similar story line was later used in such series as *The Rogues* and *Switch*.

COLONEL MARCH　　　SYNDICATED
1954　This British detective series starred Boris Karloff as Colonel March, a Scotland Yard sleuth who wore an eyepatch.

COLT .45　　　ABC
18 OCTOBER 1957–20 SEPTEMBER 1960　Half-hour Western starring Wayde Preston as government agent Christopher Colt, son of the inventor of the famous Colt revolver. Donald May replaced Preston as Christopher's cousin, Sam Colt, Jr., and was in turn replaced when Preston returned to the series early in 1960.

COLUMBO　　　NBC
15 SEPTEMBER 1971–1 SEPTEMBER 1978　Peter Falk starred as Columbo, a nonviolent police lieutenant with no first name, in this popular segment of *The NBC Mystery Movie*. Most shows followed the same formula. The crime (usually murder most foul) was committed at the outset, and the viewing audience learned the identity of the culprit. The fun came from watching Columbo pursue his investigation; his beguilingly inept manner and disheveled appearance often led the villain to underestimate his adversary. It was clear from the questions he asked that Columbo was nobody's fool; by the conclusion of each ninety-minute or two-hour episode, he had snared his quarry. By 1975 Falk was reportedly earning $125,000 per episode, thus ranking him as one of the highest-paid regular performers on television. No new *Columbo*'s were shown during the 1976–1977 season, but four were scheduled for the 1977–1978 season. Created by Richard Levinson and William Link, the character first appeared in two pilots: "Prescription: Murder" (20 February 1968), and "Ransom for A Dead Man" (1 March 1971). See also *Kate Loves a Mystery*.

COMBAT　　　ABC
2 OCTOBER 1962–29 AUGUST 1967　The longest running of the several World War II dramas of the 1960s, *Combat* outlived such rivals as *The Gallant Men, The Rat Patrol, Twelve O'Clock High, Jericho, Convoy,* and *Garrison's Gorillas.* Set in Europe, it told the story of one platoon and fea-

tured Vic Morrow as Sergeant Chip Saunders; Rick Jason as Lieutenant Gil Hanley; Dick Peabody as Littlejohn; Pierre Jalbert as Caje; Steven Rogers (1962–1963) and Conlan Carter (1963–1967) as Doc; Jack Hogan as "Wild Man" Kirby; and Tom Lowell (1963–1967) as Nelson. Gene Levitt produced the series.

COMBAT SERGEANT   ABC
29 JUNE 1956–27 SEPTEMBER 1956   One of the first series set during World War II, *Combat Sergeant* blended actual footage from the North African campaign with dramatic action. Featured were Michael Thomas as Sergeant Nelson; Cliff Clark as General Harrison; Bill Slack as Lieutenant Kruger; and Mara Corday as Corporal Harbin of the WACs.

COME CLOSER   ABC
20 SEPTEMBER 1954–13 DECEMBER 1954   Half-hour game show, played for laughs. Ventriloquist Jimmy Nelson was the host, assisted by his puppets Danny O'Day, Humphrey Higby, and Farful. The series was not carried regularly by the network's New York affiliate.

COMEBACK   SYNDICATED
1979   Like *The Comeback Story*, ABC's 1953 series, this half-hour show presented biographies of people who had faced and overcome great adversities in their lives. James Whitmore was the host.

THE COMEBACK STORY   ABC
2 OCTOBER 1953–5 FEBRUARY 1954   George Jessel first hosted this series which resembled *This Is Your Life. The Comback Story* highlighted dramatic moments from the lives of its guests, all of whom were once-famous personalities. Arlene Francis later hosted the show.

THE COMEDY SHOP   SYNDICATED
1978–   Norm Crosby hosts this half-hour series, a showcase for standup comics, known and unknown. Paul Roth is executive producer.

COMEDY THEATRE   ABC
11 OCTOBER 1949–20 NOVEMBER 1949   An experimental anthology series of six comedies produced by Arch Oboler, the playwright and writer who was active in radio. The series was first seen locally on 23 September over KECA-TV, Los Angeles.

COMEDY TONIGHT   CBS
5 JULY 1970–23 AUGUST 1970   A summer replacement for *The Glen Campbell Goodtime Hour,* this hour comedy-variety series was hosted by Robert Klein and produced in part by Shelley Berman, a prominent

stand-up comic of the early 1960s. Regulars included Marty Barris, Peter Boyle, Barbara Cason, MacIntyre Dixon, Boni Enten, Judy Graubart, Laura Greene, Madeline Kahn, Jerry Lacy, and Lynn Lipton.

COMEDYWORLD (DEAN MARTIN'S COMEDYWORLD)   NBC
6 JUNE 1974–15 AUGUST 1974   *Comedyworld,* a summer replacement for *The Dean Martin Comedy Hour,* was a showcase for comics, known and unknown. Most segments were videotaped on location in various clubs. Jackie Cooper hosted the hour show, which also featured Nipsey Russell and Barbara Feldon as roving "Comedy Correspondents."

COMMAND POST   CBS
14 FEBRUARY 1950–4 APRIL 1950   Of the many shows which did battle with NBC's Milton Berle on Tuesday nights, *Command Post* was among the most unusual—the hour-long show was an experiment conducted by the United States Army to train reservists.

COMMANDO CODY   NBC
16 JULY 1955–8 OCTOBER 1955   This Saturday-morning outer space show starred Judd Holdren as Commando Cody, Sky Marshal of the Universe, and Aline Towne as Joan Albright, his assistant. Cody usually did battle with the Ruler (played by Gregory Gay), whose home base was on Saturn. Commando Cody should not be confused with Commander Corry of *Space Patrol* (see also that title).

COMMENT   NBC
14 JUNE 1954–9 AUGUST 1954; 13 APRIL 1958–10 AUGUST 1958; 24 JANUARY 1971–10 SEPTEMBER 1972   *Comment* first surfaced during the summer of 1954 as a Monday-night series on which NBC news reporters commented on topical issues. The 1958 version of the series was more erudite, featuring discussions with luminaries such as Arnold J. Toynbee and Aldous Huxley (the 1958 dates listed above are those of *Comment*'s Sunday-afternoon run; the show had previously been aired as a "filler" program after the conclusion of NBC's Friday-night boxing telecasts). The 1971–1972 version of *Comment* was again seen on Sundays; hosted by Edwin Newman, it featured interviews with newsmakers.

COMPASS   ABC
23 OCTOBER 1954–11 AUGUST 1957   Half-hour travelogue, broadcast irregularly over a three-year period.

CONCENTRATION   NBC/SYNDICATED
28 JULY 1958–23 MARCH 1973 (NBC); 1973–   (SYNDICATED)   *Concentration* enjoyed the longest run of any network daytime game show; it also enjoyed brief nighttime runs in the fall of 1958 and the

spring of 1961. The TV game was based on the card game and featured two contestants each day, seated opposite a board containing thirty numbered squares. Behind each numbered square was the name of a prize, and behind that was a portion of a rebus puzzle; each prize was listed twice on the board. Contestants took turns naming pairs of numbers, which were then turned to reveal the prizes. If the prizes matched, the two portions of the rebus puzzle were uncovered. The first contestant to solve the rebus won all the prizes he or she had accumulated. Hugh Downs was the first host of the series. During his tenure as host, Downs also continued to appear on the *Tonight* show (until Jack Paar's departure in 1962), and later on the *Today* show (which Downs hosted from 1962 to 1971). Downs relinquished his duties as *Concentration*'s host in 1965, and a string of hosts followed: Jack Barry, Art James, Bill Mazer, Ed McMahon, and finally Bob Clayton (26 September 1969–1973). The syndicated version of the show, substantially identical to the network version, first appeared in 1973 and was hosted by Jack Narz.

CONCERNING MISS MARLOWE   NBC
5 JULY 1954–1 JULY 1955   Another of NBC's unsuccessful daytime serials, *Concerning Miss Marlowe* concerned a forty-year-old actress who lived in New York. Louise Allbritton and Helen Shields were featured as Margaret Marlowe; other regulars included John Raby and (in his first television role) Efrem Zimbalist, Jr.

CONCERT TONIGHT   DUMONT
30 DECEMBER 1953–31 MARCH 1954; 15 SEPTEMBER 1954–6 APRIL 1955   An hour of classical music broadcast from Chicago, featuring the Chicago Symphony.

CONFESSION   ABC
19 JUNE 1958–13 JANUARY 1959   Jack Wyatt hosted this unusual half-hour interview show: Wyatt's guests were convicted criminals, who talked about the crimes they had committed. Law enforcement personnel were also featured on the videotaped show, which originated from Dallas.

CONFIDENTIAL FILE   SYNDICATED
1955–57   Paul Coates narrated this half-hour series, which presented interviews with guests as well as dramatic adaptations of topical subjects, particularly crime and show business.

CONFIDENTIAL FOR WOMEN   ABC
28 MARCH 1966–8 JULY 1966   A daytime series that, like NBC's *Modern Romances,* presented a new five-part story each week. Jane Wyatt (formerly of *Father Knows Best*) narrated and psychiatrist Theodore Isaac Rubin provided daily commentary.

CONFLICT ABC

18 SEPTEMBER 1956–3 SEPTEMBER 1957   Warner Brothers supplied this biweekly anthology series, which alternated with *Cheyenne*. A few *Conflict* segments had been seen during the preceding season on *Warner Brothers Presents*. Personal conflicts were the subjects of the episodes; the series was produced by Jack Barry in cooperation with the National Association for Mental Health. Will Hutchins, later star of *Sugarfoot*, made his television debut in "Stranger on the Road," broadcast 11 December.

CONFLICTS PBS

21 NOVEMBER 1973–16 JANUARY 1974   Dramatic anthology series presented by the Hollywood Television Theatre. Among the presentations were "Me," a two-act play by Gardner McKay (former star of *Adventures in Paradise*) with Richard Dreyfuss and Alison Rose, and "Double Solitaire," a drama with Richard Crenna and Susan Clark.

CONGRESSIONAL REPORT NBC

13 APRIL 1969–31 AUGUST 1969   Bill Monroe was the moderator of this Sunday public interest series on which groups of four members of Congress discussed current issues.

CONNECTIONS PBS

30 SEPTEMBER 1979–2 DECEMBER 1979   A ten-week hour series on the history of technology, hosted by James Burke, and produced by BBC-TV and Time-Life Television.

CONRAD NAGEL THEATER SYNDICATED

1955   Actor Conrad Nagel, whose film career began in 1919, hosted this half-hour dramatic anthology series.

CONSULT DR. BROTHERS

See DR. JOYCE BROTHERS

CONSUMER BUYLINE SYNDICATED

1978   David Horowitz hosts this informational show for consumers, which had been featured on local television in Los Angeles before going national. Lloyd Thaxton, host of several game shows and rock music programs of the 1960s, produces the show.

CONSUMER SURVIVAL KIT PBS

1975–1979   Educational series for consumers on products and services, presented with a light touch. Hosted by Lary Lewman, the show was produced by the Maryland Center for Public Broadcasting.

CONTEST CARNIVAL   CBS

3 JANUARY 1954–18 DECEMBER 1955   Telecast on Sunday mornings from Philadelphia, this talent contest for aspiring young circus performers was hosted by Gene Crane. Also on hand were three puppets—Kernel, Puff, and Carney—and Dave Stephen's band.

THE CONTINENTAL   CBS

22 JANUARY 1952– 17 APRIL 1952   This unusual series starred Renzo Cesana as a suave bachelor (The Continental), who wooed the ladies watching at home; the set featured a table for two, a bottle of champagne, and a rose. The show was aired live on Tuesdays and Thursdays at 11:15 p.m. Cesana later hosted a similar series. See *First Date.*

CONTINENTAL CLASSROOM   NBC

6 OCTOBER 1958–18 DECEMBER 1964   Like CBS's *Sunrise Semester, Continental Classroom* was an early-morning educational series for adults. The first offering was a course on physics taught by Dr. Harvey E. White of the University of California at Berkeley. The half-hour show was produced by NBC in cooperation with the American Association of Colleges for Teacher Education.

CONTINENTAL SHOWCASE   CBS

11 JUNE 1966–10 SEPTEMBER 1966   CBS put together this circus show by reediting tapes of European circus acts supplied by Bavarian Television in Munich. Jim Backus was then added as "host," to introduce the acts and provide a measure of continuity.

CONVERSATIONS WITH ERIC SEVAREID   CBS

13 JULY 1975–7 SEPTEMBER 1975   Public affairs series on which Eric Sevareid conversed with notables such as West German Chancellor Willy Brandt, former ambassador George Kennan, and others.

CONVOY   NBC

17 SEPTEMBER 1965–10 DECEMBER 1965   One of the lesser known World War II series, *Convoy* told the story of a group of 200 American ships heading across the North Atlantic. With John Gavin as Commander Dan Talbot, skipper of the fleet's escort destroyer, a naval officer longing for more action; John Larch as Ben Foster, merchant captain of the fleet's flagship; Linden Chiles as Chief Officer Steve Kirkland; and James Callahan as Lieutenant O'Connell. One of the last NBC shows filmed in black and white, *Convoy* was shot down after thirteen weeks.

COOL McCOOL   NBC

10 SEPTEMBER 1966–31 AUGUST 1968; 17 MAY 1969–30 AUGUST 1969   Saturday-morning cartoon series about a secret agent.

COOL MILLION   NBC
25 OCTOBER 1972–11 JULY 1973   One segment of *The NBC Mystery Movie, Cool Million* alternated with *Banacek* and *Madigan*. It starred James Farentino as private eye Jefferson Keyes, who charged a cool $1 million per assignment, with results guaranteed. Also featured was Adele Mara as Elena, the woman who ran Keyes's answering service.

THE COP AND THE KID   NBC
4 DECEMBER 1975–4 MARCH 1976   In this situation comedy a white bachelor cop became the foster father of a black orphan. With Charles Durning as Officer Frank Murphy; Tierre Turner as young Lucas Adams, his ward; Patsy Kelly as Brigid Murphy, Frank's mother; Sharon Spelman as Mary Goodhew, the school principal; Curtiz Willis as Shortstuff, Lucas's pal; and Eric Laneuville as Mouse, another of Lucas's pals. Jerry Davis created the series and was also its executive producer. Produced by Ben Joelson and Art Baer.

THE CORAL JUNGLE   SYNDICATED
1976   A series of marine documentaries filmed at and around the Great Barrier Reef off the coast of Australia; narrated by Leonard Nimoy.

THE CORNER BAR   ABC
21 JUNE 1972–23 AUGUST 1972; 3 AUGUST 1973–7 SEPTEMBER 1973
   Shown during two summers, this sitcom was set in a New York bar. In 1972 the bar was known as Grant's Toomb, in 1973 it was simply The Corner Bar. The 1972 cast included Gabriel Dell as Harry Grant, the owner of Grant's Toomb; J. J. Barry as cabbie Fred Costello, token bigot; Bill Fiore as Phil Bracken, token drunk; Joe Keyes as Joe the cook, token black; Vincent Schiavelli as Peter Panama, token homosexual; and Shimen Ruskin as waiter Meyer Shapiro, token Jew. The 1973 cast featured Barry, Fiore, and Ruskin from the 1972 crew and newcomers Anne Meara as Mae, the widowed co-owner of The Corner Bar; Eugene Roche as Mae's partner, Frank Flynn; and Ron Carey as actor Donald Hooten. Comedian Alan King was the executive producer, and comedian Howard Morris (one of the second bananas on *Your Show of Shows*) was the producer.

CORONADO 9   SYNDICATED
1959   Rod Cameron, who had played cops on *City Detective* and *State Trooper*, played a private eye—Dan Adams—in this half-hour series set in San Diego. Beverly Garland was also featured. Coronado 9 was Adams's telephone exchange.

CORONET BLUE   CBS
29 MAY 1967–4 SEPTEMBER 1967   This offbeat hour-long series featured an amnesiac searching for his identity. Frank Converse starred as Mi-

chael Alden, a young man who lost his memory following an attempt on his life. Fearful that his assailants may still be pursuing him, Alden's only clue to his past were the words "coronet blue." Also featured were Joe Silver as his new friend, Max, and Brian Bedford as Brother Anthony, a monk who tried to help him. Eleven episodes were filmed in 1965, but CBS decided not to air the show at that time. Although the show proved fairly popular in 1967, production could not have continued because Converse had been signed for a fall series, *N.Y.P.D.* Several prominent guest stars appeared on the program, including Susan Hampshire ("A Time to Be Born," 29 May), Candice Bergen ("The Rebel," her only dramatic role on American television, 19 June), Hal Holbrook (10 July), Alan Alda ("Six Months to Live," 14 August), and disc jockeys Murray the K and Dick Clark ("The Flip Side of Tommy Devon," 4 September). Filmed on location in New York, the series was produced by Herbert Brodkin and directed by Paul Bogart.

COS
ABC

19 SEPTEMBER 1976–31 OCTOBER 1976 An unsuccessful Sunday-evening variety hour aimed principally at children, hosted by Bill Cosby, with help from Charlie Callas, Jeff Altman, Buzzy Linhart, Timothy Thomerson, Marion Ramsey, Mauricio Jarrin, Willie Bobo, and Rod Hull. Chris Bearde was the producer.

COSMOPOLITAN THEATER
DUMONT

2 OCTOBER 1951–25 DECEMBER 1951 This hour-long filmed dramatic anthology series was seen on Tuesday nights. The stories were adapted from those appearing in *Cosmopolitan* magazine.

THE COUNT OF MONTE CRISTO
SYNDICATED

1955 George Dolenz starred as Edmond Dantes, the French patriot who escaped from prison and fled to the isle of Monte Cristo, where he set up shop to battle evildoers; Faith Domergue was also featured as Princess Anne. Hal Roach, Jr., was the executive producer of the half-hour adventure series, which was filmed in Hollywood using the sets from the 1940 film of the same title.

COUNTRY CARNIVAL
SYNDICATED

1969 Half-hour country and western music show, hosted by singer Del Reeves.

COUNTRY MUSIC CARAVAN
SYNDICATED

1966 Half-hour musical show.

COUNTRY MUSIC JUBILEE
See OZARK JUBILEE

COUNTRY STYLE   DUMONT
29 JULY 1950–25 NOVEMBER 1950   One of network television's first country-music programs, *Country Style* was seen for an hour on Saturday nights and was hosted by Peggy Anne Ellis.

COUNTRY STYLE U.S.A.   SYNDICATED
1959   Fifteen-minute country and western musical show hosted by singing serviceman Charlie Applewhite, who had been featured on *The Milton Berle Show* in 1953.

COUNTY FAIR   NBC
22 SEPTEMBER 1958–25 SEPTEMBER 1959   Bert Parks hosted this daytime variety half hour, which was set at a county fair.

A COUPLE OF JOES   ABC
5 AUGUST 1949–12 JULY 1950   This half-hour variety series was cohosted by Joe Bushkin and Joe Rosenfield and featured Warren Hull, Joan Barton, Allyn Edwards, the Milton DeLugg Orchestra (1949), and Mike Reilly's Orchestra (1950), and Morgan the basset hound, owned by producer Richard Gordon.

COURT MARTIAL   ABC
8 APRIL 1966–2 SEPTEMBER 1966   Another World War II series, this one focused on the United States Army Judge Advocate General Corps. With Bradford Dillman as Captain David Young; Peter Graves as Major Frank Whittaker; Kenneth J. Warren as their aide, Sergeant MacCaskey; and Diene Clare as their secretary, Wendy.

COURT OF CURRENT ISSUES   DUMONT
9 FEBRUARY 1948–26 JUNE 1951   This early public affairs program featured debates on topical issues. It was not widely watched because for most of its run it was slotted opposite Milton Berle's *The Texaco Star Theater*.

THE COURT OF LAST RESORT   NBC
4 OCTOBER 1957–11 APRIL 1958   This half-hour series dramatized the work of the Court of Last Resort, a real-life organization, founded in 1948, which was not a court of law but rather a group of seven criminal law experts. Its purpose was to aid defendants whom it believed had been convicted unjustly. The series starred Lyle Bettger as investigator Sam Larsen; Paul Birch appeared occasionally as defense attorney Erle Stanley Gardner (Gardner, of course, is better known as the creator of *Perry Mason*). Jules Goldstone was the producer. The series was rerun on ABC during the 1959–1960 season.

COURTROOM U.S.A. SYNDICATED

1960 Actual court cases were dramatized on this series, which starred Jay Jostyn.

THE COURTSHIP OF EDDIE'S FATHER ABC

17 SEPTEMBER 1969–14 JUNE 1972 In this sitcom, a widower was constantly getting entangled with women, thanks to the persistent matchmaking efforts of his young son. Nevertheless, the two were (in the words of the show's theme song) "best friends." With Bill Bixby as Tom Corbett, editor of *Tomorrow* magazine; Brandon Cruz as son Eddie; Miyoshi Umeki as their Japanese housekeeper, Mrs. Livingston; James Komack as Tom's friend Norman Tinker, the magazine's art director; Kristina Holland as Tina Rickles, Tom's secretary; and Jodie Foster (1970–1972) as Joey Kelly, a schoolmate of Eddie's. Costar Komack also produced the series for MGM-TV (he later created *Chico and the Man* and *Sugar Time!*).

COWBOY G–MEN SYNDICATED

1952 This low-budget western starred Russell Hayden and Jackie Coogan as Pat Gallagher and Stoney Crockett, two nineteenth-century government agents. Lesley Selander directed the series.

COWBOY IN AFRICA ABC

11 SEPTEMBER 1967–16 SEPTEMBER 1968 This adventure series starred Chuck Connors as Jim Sinclair, an American rodeo star who goes to Kenya to assist in an ambitious wildlife management project. With Tom Nardini as John Henry, a Navajo who accompanies Jim; Ronald Howard as Wing Commander Hayes, the wealthy rancher who recruited their services; and Gerald B. Edwards as Samson, a young Kenyan boy who makes friends with the two Americans. The series was filmed largely at Africa, U.S.A., near Los Angeles.

COWBOY THEATRE NBC

15 SEPTEMBER 1956–15 SEPTEMBER 1957 Monty Hall, better known as the host of *Let's Make a Deal*, emceed this weekend series of western films.

THE COWBOYS ABC

6 FEBRUARY 1974–14 AUGUST 1974 Adapted from the 1972 film starring John Wayne, *The Cowboys* was a half-hour western about seven homeless boys who go to work on a ranch owned by a widow. With Jim Davis as Marshal Bill Winter; Diana Douglas as widow Kate Andersen; Moses Gunn as Nightlinger, the black cook and overseer of the boys; Robert Carradine as Slim; A Martinez as Cimarron; Sean Kelly as Jim-

my; Kerry MacLane as Homer; Clint Howard as Steve; Mitch Brown as Hardy; and Clay O'Brien as Weedy. Four of the youngsters—Carradine, Martinez, Kelly, and O'Brien—had appeared in the film (Carradine and Martinez repeated their film roles on television; Kelly had played Bob and O'Brien had played Hardy in the movie).

COWTOWN RODEO   ABC
23 JUNE 1958–8 SEPTEMBER 1958   Half-hour rodeo show, with commentary by Marty Glickman, broadcast from New Jersey.

CRAFTS WITH KATY   SYNDICATED
1971   A half-hour of macrame and decoupage and the like, demonstrated by Katy Dacus.

CRAIG KENNEDY, CRIMINOLOGIST   SYNDICATED
1952   Donald Woods starred as criminologist Craig Kennedy in this little-noted half-hour series. Adrian Weiss produced and directed.

CRASH CORRIGAN'S RANCH   ABC
15 JULY 1950–29 SEPTEMBER 1950   Ray "Crash" Corrigan hosted this summer variety series for children. Corrigan's real-life "ranch," located near Hollywood, was widely used for location filming by many TV western series.

CREATIVE COOKERY   NBC/ABC
10 OCTOBER 1953–3 APRIL 1954 (NBC); 30 AUGUST 1954–25 FEBRUARY 1955 (ABC)   A cooking instruction program broadcast from Chicago, hosted by chef François Pope and his sons, Frank and Robert Pope. The NBC version was seen for an hour on Saturday mornings, while the ABC version ran for 55 minutes on weekdays. Elina Fahrenholz was the producer, Phil Bodwell the director.

CRIME AND PUNISHMENT   SYNDICATED
1961   Like *Confession,* this series featured interviews with convicted criminals as well as with law and corrections officials. The program was hosted by Clete Roberts, with additional commentary provided by criminologist Robert A. McGee. Collier Young was the producer.

CRIME PHOTOGRAPHER   CBS
19 APRIL 1951–5 JUNE 1952   The television version of the radio program originally starred Richard Carlyle as Casey, the gutsy photographer for the *Morning Express,* a New York daily. Carlyle was later replaced by Darren McGavin (in his first starring role on television; McGavin would later play a similar role in *The Night Stalker*). Also featured were Jan

Miner as Annie Williams, Casey's girlfriend (Miner had played the role on radio but is better known to modern viewers as Madge the Manicurst in commercials for Palmolive); John Gibson as Ethelbert, bartender at the Blue Note Café, Casey's favorite hangout (Gibson, too, had played the role on radio); and Bernard Lenrow as Inspector Logan of the New York Police Department, Casey's nemesis. George Harmon Coxe created Casey in a series of novels. Martin Manulis produced the TV series.

CRIME SYNDICATED CBS
18 SEPTEMBER 1951–23 JUNE 1953   This anthology series of crime dramas, supposedly based on true stories, was hosted and narrated by Rudolph Halley, an investigator for the Congressional crime committee chaired by Senator Estes Kefauver. It was produced by Jerry Danzig and directed by John Peyser. The half-hour series began as a weekly effort, then alternated biweekly with *City Hospital* beginning in March 1952.

CRIME WITH FATHER ABC
31 AUGUST 1951–25 JANUARY 1952   Comedy-mystery starring Rusty Lane and Peggy Lobbin as a father-daughter detective team.

CRISIS NBC
5 OCTOBER 1949–28 DECEMBER 1949   Arthur Peterson hosted this unusual half-hour dramatic anthology series, which was broadcast from Chicago. Each week a group of actors reenacted three events from the life of a guest; periodically through the show, host Peterson checked with the guest to see if the dramatizations accurately reflected the incidents.

CRITIC AT LARGE ABC
18 AUGUST 1948–27 APRIL 1949   John Mason Brown was the host of this half-hour series, on which he chatted with guest critics about the arts.

CROCKETT'S VICTORY GARDEN PBS
1976–   Educational series primarily for the urban gardener, hosted until 1979 by James Underwood Crockett. Most of the show is taped at the garden constructed just outside the studio of Boston's WGBH-TV. After Crockett's death, Bob Thomson took over as host.

CROSS CURRENT
See FOREIGN INTRIGUE

CROSSROADS ABC
7 OCTOBER 1955–27 SEPTEMBER 1957   This half-hour dramatic anthology series depicted the work of clergymen.

THE CROSS-WITS   SYNDICATED

1976   On this half-hour game show two teams, each consisting of two celebrities and a noncelebrity captain, scored points by filling in words on a giant crossword puzzle. Jack Clark hosted the series; Ralph Edwards was executive producer.

CROWN THEATRE
See THE GLORIA SWANSON SHOW

CRUNCH AND DES   SYNDICATED

1955   This half-hour adventure series, set in the Bahamas, featured Forrest Tucker as Crunch Adams, owner of the Crunch Adams Charter Boat Service and skipper of the *Poseidon*, and Sandy Kenyon as his partner, Des.

CRUSADE IN EUROPE   ABC

5 MAY 1949–27 OCTOBER 1949   One of the first documentary series filmed especially for television, *Crusade in Europe* was a series of twenty-six half hours based on Dwight Eisenhower's book about the American effort in Europe during World War II. Sponsored by Time, Inc., the series was produced by Richard de Rochemont and narrated by Westbrook Van Voorhis.

THE CRUSADER   CBS

7 OCTOBER 1955–28 DECEMBER 1956   Brian Keith starred as Matt Anders, freelance writer, in this little-remembered adventure series. Dick Lewis was the producer.

CRUSADER RABBIT   SYNDICATED

1949–1957   One of the first cartoon series made especially for television, *Crusader Rabbit* was the brainchild of Jay Ward and his partner, Alexander Anderson. The witty, five-minute segments were produced in color and were in serial form; some stations thus ran a single cartoon each day, while others combined several into a longer show. The stars of the series were Crusader Rabbit, a small but noble adventurer, and Rags the Tiger, his somewhat less intelligent partner. The first set of cartoons was produced between 1948 and 1951; NBC was offered the series in 1949 but declined it. A second set of cartoons was made in 1956; by that time Jay Ward had sold his interest in the show and had begun to develop a new series for television, *Rocky and His Friends* (Rocky and Bullwinkle closely resembled Crusader and Rags). The voices of Crusader and Rags were supplied by Lucille Blass and Verne Loudin respectively.

CURIOSITY SHOP   ABC

11 SEPTEMBER 1971–2 SEPTEMBER 1973   This educational show for

children was a mix of cartoons, filmed segments, and interviews; each hour was devoted to one theme, such as "Tools," "Rules," or "Flight." With Pamelyn Ferdin as Pam; Kerry MacLane as Ralph; John Levin as Gerard; Jerrelyn Fields as Cindy; and Barbara Minkus as Gittel the Witch. Seen on Sunday mornings, the series was created and produced by Chuck Jones.

CURTAIN CALL NBC

20 JUNE 1952–26 SEPTEMBER 1952   This half-hour dramatic anthology series was a summer replacement for *The Dennis Day Show*. Telecasts included: "The Promise," with Carol Bruce (20 June); "The Soul of the Great Bell," with Boris Karloff (27 June); and "Season of Divorce," with Richard Kiley (8 August).

CUSTER (THE LEGEND OF CUSTER) ABC

6 SEPTEMBER 1967–27 DECEMBER 1967   *Custer* was an unsuccessful attempt to tell the story of America's best-known Calvary officer, a flamboyant twenty-eight-year-old who had risen to the rank of major general and was demoted for dereliction of duty; ordered reinstated, he was put in command of the Seventh Regiment of the United States Cavalry, which was stationed at Fort Hays, Kansas. The series was canceled long before the men of the Seventh would have reached the Little Big Horn. With Wayne Maunder as Lieutenant Colonel George A. Custer; Michael Dante as Sioux chief Crazy Horse; Slim Pickens as scout California Joe Milner; Peter Palmer as Sergeant James Bustard, a former Confederate soldier; Robert F. Simon as General A. H. Terry; and Grant Woods as Captain Myles Keogh. Created by Samuel Peeples and David Weisbart.

CUT DUMONT

4 JUNE 1949–18 JUNE 1949   Hosted by Carl Caruso, this hour-long game show featured phone calls to home viewers. If the viewer could identify the subject of the scene being acted out by a group of players on stage, the viewer could try to identify a photograph of a famous personality as it spun on a wheel. After just three weeks the format was modified, and the show was retitled *Spin the Picture* (see that title). Jerry Layton and Wilbur Stark produced the series, and the Alan Logan Trio provided the music.

THE D.A. NBC

17 SEPTEMBER 1971–7 JANUARY 1972   Jack Webb produced this half-hour series in which most of the action took place in the courtroom. With Robert Conrad as Paul Ryan, deputy district attorney in Los Angeles; Harry Morgan as H. M. "Staff" Stafford, chief deputy D.A.; Ned Romero as investigator Bob Ramirez; and Julie Cobb as Katy Benson, deputy public defender.

THE D.A.'S MAN NBC

3 JANUARY 1959–29 AUGUST 1959 John Compton starred as private detective Shannon, the man whom the New York district attorney called on for help when he needed it, in this half-hour crime show. Also featured was Ralph Manza as Al Bonacorsi, Shannon's contact man in the D.A.'s office. Based on the book by James B. Horan and Harold Danforth, the series was produced by Jack Webb's Mark VII, Ltd.

THE DAFFY DUCK SHOW NBC

4 NOVEMBER 1978– Half-hour Saturday-morning cartoon show starring the Warner Brothers character.

DAGMAR'S CANTEEN NBC

22 MARCH 1952–14 JUNE 1952 Broadcast at 12:15 a.m. on Saturday nights, this short-lived fifteen-minute variety series was hosted by Dagmar (Jennie Lewis), late of *Broadway Open House,* and presented talent culled from the armed forces. Ray Malone and Milton DeLugg were also featured.

THE DAKOTAS ABC

7 JANUARY 1963–9 SEPTEMBER 1963 Set in the Dakota Territory, this Warner Brothers western replaced *Cheyenne.* With Larry Ward as Marshal Frank Ragan; Chad Everett as Deputy Del Stark; Jack Elam as Deputy J. D. Smith, a former gunslinger; and Michael Green as Deputy Vance Porter.

DAKTARI CBS

11 JANUARY 1966–15 JANUARY 1969 This African adventure series was set at the Wameru Study Center for Animal Behavior. It featured Marshall Thompson as Dr. Marsh Tracy, a veterinarian and conservationist (*daktari* is the Swahili word for "doctor"); Cheryl Miller as Paula, his daughter; Yale Summers as conservationist Jack Dane; Hari Rhodes as Mike, an African conservationist; Hedley Mattingly as District Officer Hedley, local game warden; Ross Hagen (1968–1969) as hunter Bart Jason; and Erin Moran (1968–1969) as six-year-old Jenny Jones, an orphan taken in by Dr. Tracy. The show's two animal stars—Clarence the crosseyed lion and Judy the chimp—were as popular as its human stars. Like *Cowboy in Africa, Daktari* was filmed at California's Africa, U.S.A., the home for some 500 beasts established by Ralph Helfer and Ivan Tors. Tors, the producer of *Daktari,* had produced the 1965 film, *Clarence the Cross-Eyed Lion* (which featured Thompson and Miller), from which the series was derived.

DALLAS CBS

2 APRIL 1978– An hour dramatic series centering on a wealthy and powerful Texas family, *Dallas* was introduced for a five-week trial run in April of 1978 and won a place on CBS's fall schedule. Principal players include: Jim Davis as John (Jock) Ewing, head of the clan; Barbara Bel Geddes as his wife, Ellie Ewing; Larry Hagman as J. R. Ewing, the hardnosed elder son; Patrick Duffy as Bobby Ewing, the more idealistic younger son; Linda Gray as Sue Ellen Ewing, J. R.'s wife; Victoria Principal as Pamela Ewing, Bobby's wife; Charlene Tilton as Lucy Ewing, Jock's seductive granddaughter; Steve Kanaly as Ray Krebbs, the ranch foreman; Ken Kercheval as Pamela's brother, Cliff Barnes, an aspiring politician; and David Wayne as Digger Barnes, Pamela's father. Lee Rich and Philip Capice are the executive producers; Leonard Katzman the producer for Lorimar Productions. In the fall of 1979 Keenan Wynn succeeded David Wayne as Digger Barnes, and other new cast members were added: Mary Crosby as Kristin, Sue Ellen's sister and J. R.'s secretary (and new romantic interest); Martha Scott as Mrs. Shepard, the nurse for young J. R. Ewing III (son of J. R. and Sue Ellen); and Randolph Powell as Alan Beame, an unscrupulous lawyer.

DAMON RUNYON THEATRE CBS

16 APRIL 1955–30 JUNE 1956 Some of the episodes on this Saturday-night dramatic anthology series were based on the stories of 1920s and 1930s New York written by Damon Runyon (1884–1946).

DAN AUGUST ABC

23 SEPTEMBER 1970–26 AUGUST 1971 Set in Santa Luisa, California, this hour-long crime show starred Burt Reynolds as Detective Lieutenant Dan August, a tough young cop. With Norman Fell as Detective Sergeant Charles Wilentz; Richard Anderson as Chief George Untermeyer; Ned Romero as Detective Joe Rivera; and Ena Hartman as Katy Grant, department secretary. A Quinn Martin Production, the series was rebroadcast on CBS during the summers of 1973 and 1975, after Reynolds had become a major film star (he did *Deliverance* after *Dan August* ceased production).

DAN RAVEN NBC

23 JANUARY 1960–6 JANUARY 1961 Former child film star Skip Homeier was featured as Hollywood cop Lieutenant Dan Raven in this crime show; also featured was Dan Barton as Sergeant Burke, his assistant, and Quinn Redeker as photographer Perry Levitt. The series began as a half-hour show and was expanded to a full hour in the fall of 1960. Bobby Darin guest-starred on the fall premiere.

DANCE FEVER   SYNDICATED
1979 Disco show on which couples competed for a grand prize of
$25,000. The half-hour series, which originated from Los Angeles, was
hosted by Deney Terio, and featured a panel of three guest celebrities,
who judged the contestants. Freeman King was the announcer.

DANCE PARTY
See SATURDAY NIGHT DANCE PARTY

DANGER   CBS
26 SEPTEMBER 1950–31 MAY 1955 A suspense-filled dramatic anthology series. Notable guest appearances included those by Steve Allen ("Five
Minutes to Die," 15 September 1953; "Flamingo," 10 November 1953);
Carroll Baker ("Season for Murder," 29 March 1955); Mildred Dunnock
and James Dean ("Padlocks," 1954); Lee Grant (three appearances in
1952); Grace Kelly ("Prelude to Death," 5 February 1952); Jack Lemmon ("Sparrow Cop," 24 July 1951); Paul Newman ("Knife in the
Dark," 7 December 1954); and Jacqueline Susann ("A Day's Pay," 24
August 1954). The live series originated from New York. The aura of
suspense even permeated the commercial breaks, as announcer Richard
Stark habitually appeared visibly shaken by the drama when he delivered
the commercials.

DANGER IS MY BUSINESS   SYNDICATED
1958 People with dangerous occupations were the subjects of this documentary series hosted by Lieutenant Colonel John D. Craig.

DANGER MAN   CBS
5 APRIL 1961–13 SEPTEMBER 1961 Patrick McGoohan starred as
NATO agent John Drake in this half-hour British import; in 1965,
McGoohan returned as Drake. See *Secret Agent*.

DANGEROUS ASSIGNMENT   SYNDICATED
1952 Brian Donlevy starred as Steve Mitchell, government agent, in
this half-hour adventure series; Donlevy originated the role on radio in
1940. Harold Knox was the producer.

DANGEROUS ROBIN   SYNDICATED
(THE CASE OF THE DANGEROUS ROBIN)
1960 Rick Jason starred as insurance investigator Robin Scott in this
half-hour crime show. A karate expert, Scott eschewed firearms. Also
featured was Jean Blake as Phyllis Collier, his assistant.

DANIEL BOONE   NBC
24 SEPTEMBER 1964–27 AUGUST 1970 A surprisingly successful series

based loosely on the life of the American pioneer who was instrumental in the settlement of Kentucky during the 1770s. Fess Parker, who owned an interest in the show, starred as Daniel Boone; a decade earlier Parker had skyrocketed to stardom in *Disneyland* as Davy Crockett, another American folk hero. Also featured were Ed Ames (1964–1968) as Mingo, Boone's friend, a college-educated Cherokee; Pat Blair as Rebecca Boone, Daniel's wife; Albert Salmi (1964–1965) as Yadkin, Boone's companion; Jimmy Dean (March 1967–1969) as his companion Josh Clements; Roosevelt Grier (1969–1970) as his companion Gabe Cooper, a runaway slave; Darby Hinton as Boone's son, Israel; Veronica Cartwright as Boone's daughter, Jemima; and Dallas McKennon (1968–1970) as his friend, Cincinnatus. In the fall of 1977, CBS made an unsuccessful attempt to revive the character: see *Young Dan'l Boone*.

THE DANNY KAYE SHOW   CBS
25 SEPTEMBER 1963–7 JUNE 1967 Danny Kaye, an all-around entertainer perhaps best known for his work on behalf of UNICEF, hosted his own Wednesday-night variety hour for four seasons. Regulars included Harvey Korman, four-year-old Victoria Meyerink (1963–1964), youngster Laurie Ichino, the Earl Brown Singers, the Tony Charmoli Dancers, and the Paul Weston Orchestra.

THE DANNY THOMAS HOUR   NBC
11 SEPTEMBER 1967–2 SEPTEMBER 1968 An all-purpose hour hosted by Danny Thomas. Presentations included musical programs, comedy and variety hours, and filmed dramas. Several of the latter were noteworthy because they featured appearances by stars seldom seen on American television, such as Geraldine Chaplin ("The Scene," her only American dramatic appearance, 25 September), Horst Buchholz and May Britt ("Fear Is the Chain," 19 February), and Olivia DeHavilland ("The Last Hunters," 29 January).

THE DANNY THOMAS SHOW
See FOUR STAR REVUE; MAKE ROOM FOR DADDY

DANTE   NBC
3 OCTOBER 1960–10 APRIL 1961 This adventure series starred Howard Duff as Willie Dante, the ex-gambler who ran Dante's Inferno, a San Francisco nightspot. With Alan Mowbray as Stewart Styles, the maitre'd; Tom D'Andrea as Biff, Dante's man Friday; Mort Mills as Lieutenant Bob Malone. Dick Powell had previously played Dante on several episodes of *Four Star Playhouse,* which were later rebroadcast under the title *The Best in Mystery* (Alan Mowbray was also featured). This series, however, was clobbered by its competition, *The Andy Griffith Show* and *Adventures in Paradise.*

DARK ADVENTURE   ABC

5 JANUARY 1953–1 JUNE 1953   This half-hour dramatic anthology series was seen on Monday nights; some of the presentations were rebroadcasts of shows aired on other anthologies.

DARK OF NIGHT   DUMONT

3 OCTOBER 1952–1 MAY 1953   This half-hour mystery anthology series was seen on Friday nights. Broadcast live and on location from New York, it was produced and directed by Frank Bunetta.

DARK SHADOWS   ABC

27 JUNE 1966–2 APRIL 1971   This soap opera was a radical departure from other daytime serials: it featured vampires, ghosts, haunted houses, werewolves, and other assorted Gothic surprises. Telecast in a late afternoon time slot, it was especially popular with teenagers. Set at brooding Collins House in Collinsport, Maine (exteriors were actually filmed in Newport, Rhode Island), it told the story of the Collins family. Principal players included Alexandra Moltke as Victoria Winters, a governess sent to take care of young David Collins; Louis Edmonds as Roger Collins, David's father; David Hennessy as David; Joan Bennett as Elizabeth Collins, Roger's sister; Jonathan Frid as Barnabas Collins, a 200-year-old vampire; Grayson Hall as Dr. Julia Hoffman, the physician sent to cure Barnabas who ended up falling in love with him; David Selby as Quentin Collins; Kate Jackson as Daphne Harridge; Lara Parker as Angelique; and Jerry Lacy as Reverend Trask. Toward the end of the show's five-year run the plot grew even thicker as action shifted back and forth between the 1800s and the 1960s; many performers played two roles. Dan Curtis created the serial and produced it with Robert Costello.

DASTARDLY AND MUTTLEY   CBS

13 SEPTEMBER 1969–5 SEPTEMBER 1970   A Saturday-morning cartoon series from Hanna-Barbera about a pair of World War I era aerial racers: Dick Dastardly and his snickering canine companion, Muttley.

A DATE WITH JUDY   ABC

2 JUNE 1951–23 FEBRUARY 1952; 15 JULY 1952–2 OCTOBER 1952; 7 JANUARY 1953–30 SEPTEMBER 1953   *A Date with Judy,* which began on radio in 1941, twice came to television. The 1951 version featured Patricia Crowley (who later starred in *Please Don't Eat the Daisies*) as Judy Foster, all-American teenager; Jimmie Sommer as her goofy boyfriend, Ogden "Oogie" Pringle; Gene O'Donnell as her father, Melvin Foster; Anna Lee as her mother, Dora Foster; and Judson Rees as her kid brother, Randolph. The summer 1952 and 1953 versions featured an entirely new cast, except for Jimmie Sommer: Mary Linn Beller as Judy; John Gibson

as Melvin; Flora Campbell as Dora; and Peter Avramo as Randolph. Both versions of the half-hour sitcom were produced and written by Aleen Leslie.

A DATE WITH LIFE   NBC
10 OCTOBER 1955–29 JUNE 1956   On this fifteen-minute daytime serial a new story was presented every few weeks.

A DATE WITH THE ANGELS   ABC
10 MAY 1957–29 JANUARY 1958   This domestic sitcom starred Betty White as Vickie Angel and Bill Williams as her husband, Gus Angel, an insurance agent. Burt Mustin was also featured as their elderly neighbor, Mr. Finley. Produced by Don Fedderson.

DATELINE: EUROPE
See FOREIGN INTRIGUE

DATELINE: HOLLYWOOD   ABC
3 APRIL 1967–29 SEPTEMBER 1967   Joanna Barnes interviewed celebrities on this daytime series. The show was twenty-five minutes long and was followed by a five-minute series, *Children's Doctor,* with pediatrician Lendon Smith.

THE DATING GAME   ABC
20 DECEMBER 1965–6 JULY 1973
THE NEW DATING GAME   SYNDICATED
1973; 1977–   Jim Lange hosted both the network and syndicated incarnations of this game show, which typically featured one young woman (the "bachelorette") and three young men seated behind a screen, hidden from her view. By asking questions of the men, the bachelorette chose the one she'd most like to go out with. The lucky couple was then sent on a date—with a chaperone, of course. Occasionally the tables were turned: one bachelor would quiz three hopeful young women. The series enjoyed a seven-year daytime run and was also seen during prime time from 1966 to 1970. The syndicated version appeared in 1973 and again in 1977. *The Dating Game* was the first of several game shows developed by Chuck Barris, the best known of which would include *The Newlywed Game* and *The Gong Show.*

DAVE AND CHARLEY   NBC
7 JANUARY 1952–28 MARCH 1952   This fifteen-minute daytime comedy series featured Cliff Arquette (as Charley Weaver) and Dave Willock (as himself).

DAVE ELMAN'S CURIOSITY SHOP   SYNDICATED

1952   Dave Elman hosted this half-hour human interest series, which
was essentially a video version of his popular radio show, *Hobby Lobby*,
on which people with unusual hobbies or talents demonstrated them. See
also *Charley Weaver's Hobby Lobby*.

THE DAVE GARROWAY SHOW   NBC

2 OCTOBER 1953–25 JUNE 1954   In addition to hosting the *Today* show,
Dave Garroway also found time to host this Friday-night half-hour vari-
ety series. Regulars included Jack Haskell, Jill Corey, Shirley Harmer,
Cliff Norton, and dancers Ken Spaulding and Diane Sinclair; Haskell and
Norton had worked previously with Garroway on his first series,
Garroway at Large.

THE DAVE KING SHOW   NBC

27 MAY 1959–23 SEPTEMBER 1959   British singer Dave King hosted this
summer replacement for *The Perry Como Show*.

DAVEY AND GOLIATH   SYNDICATED

1962–   A long-running series of fifteen-minute morality lessons for children. The central characters are young Davey Hanson and
Goliath, his talking dog. *Davey and Goliath* was one of the few series
which employed "pixillation," the process by which small models appear
to move by themselves; this is usually accomplished by shooting a few
frames of film, physically moving each model a fraction of an inch, then
shooting a few more frames, and so on.

DAVID BRINKLEY'S JOURNAL   NBC

11 OCTOBER 1961–26 AUGUST 1963   This highly acclaimed public
affairs program won both an Emmy and a Peabody award in 1962. NBC
newscaster David Brinkley covered a wide variety of topics, heavy and
light, during its two-season run. Brinkley himself appeared live, though
filmed segments were regularly featured. One of the show's researchers
was Marya McLaughlin, who later became an on-camera correspondent
for CBS News.

DAVID CASSIDY—MAN UNDERCOVER   NBC

2 NOVEMBER 1978–18 JANUARY 1979   Hour crime show starring David
Cassidy as Officer Dan Shay, an undercover police officer in Los Angeles,
with Wendy Rastatter as his wife, Joanne Shay; Elizabeth Reddin as their
young daughter, Cindy; Simon Oakland as his commanding officer, Lieutenant Abrams; and Ray Vitte as T. J. Epps. David Gerber was the executive producer for David Gerber Productions in association with
Columbia Pictures TV. A few episodes were telecast during the summer
of 1979.

THE DAVID FROST REVUE   SYNDICATED
1971   A half hour of satirical comedy with host David Frost and regulars Jack Gilford, Marcia Rodd, and George S. Irving.

THE DAVID FROST SHOW   SYNDICATED
7 JULY 1969–14 JULY 1972   A ninety-minute talk show hosted by David Frost, the British television star who became familiar to American audiences on *That Was the Week That Was*. As host, Frost chose not to sit behind a desk, relying instead on a clipboard to hold his notes. Seemingly able to concentrate totally on each guest, he appeared to be equally fascinated by all of them. During the three-year run of his American talk show, Frost continued to appear regularly on London Weekend Television. To accommodate his hectic schedule, the show was taped in New York Mondays through Thursdays (two shows were taped each Wednesday). Frost was then free to commute back to London each weekend. About 750 American shows were taped; among the most famous guests were Elizabeth Taylor and Richard Burton, and Johnny Carson. Music was provided by the Billy Taylor Orchestra; the show's theme was composed by George Martin. The series was syndicated by Westinghouse. After the show ceased production in 1972, Frost was seldom seen on American TV until 1977, when his multipart series of interviews with former President Richard Nixon was shown on many stations.

THE DAVID McLEAN SHOW   SYNDICATED
1970   A short-lived talk show, hosted by David McLean.

THE DAVID NIVEN SHOW   NBC
7 APRIL 1959–15 SEPTEMBER 1959   A half-hour dramatic anthology series, hosted by (and occasionally starring) David Niven. Vincent Fennelly was the producer.

DAVID NIVEN'S WORLD   SYNDICATED
1976   On this documentary series adventurers tried to set records in various fields of endeavor. Hosted by David Niven, the series' executive producer was Aubrey Buxton.

THE DAVID STEINBERG SHOW   CBS
19 JULY 1972–16 AUGUST 1972   A five-week summer variety hour, hosted by comedian David Steinberg. Born in Manitoba, Steinberg was a member of the Second City comedy troupe in Chicago and frequently appeared on the *Tonight* show during the late 1960s. In 1969 he hosted *The Music Scene*.

THE DAVID SUSSKIND SHOW (OPEN END)   SYNDICATED
1958–   This long-running New York-based talk show is

hosted by theatrical and television producer David Susskind. Typically, each show centers around one topic and features four to seven guests, who often seem to spend much of their time interrupting each other. In 1960 Soviet premier Nikita Khrushchev appeared on the program as the sole guest; the interview was generally criticized as dull. The show was originally titled *Open End* because it had no fixed time limit: guests could chatter on as long as they (or Susskind) wished. By the early 1960s a two-hour format was established; this was subsequently reduced to one hour and later expanded to ninety minutes. The show is now seen on educational outlets in many markets.

DAVY CROCKETT
See WALT DISNEY

DAY AT NIGHT   PBS
1974–1975 Half-hour interview series hosted by James Day, former president of New York's educational outlet, WNET.

DAY IN COURT   ABC
13 OCTOBER 1958–24 JUNE 1965 On this half-hour daytime series of courtroom dramas, each case was based on a real case from which the show's writers developed an outline. The actual dialogue was largely improvised by the participants: professional actors portrayed the litigants and witnesses, while real attorneys appeared as the lawyers. The presiding judges were played by Edgar Allan Jones, Jr. (a law professor at UCLA) and by William Gwinn (a former law professor). Created by Selig J. Seligman, the show was televised locally in Los Angeles before going network in 1958.

DAYDREAMING WITH LARAINE
See THE LARAINE DAY SHOW

DAYS OF OUR LIVES   NBC
8 NOVEMBER 1965–   This medically oriented daytime serial premiered as a half-hour show in 1965; in April of 1975 it became TV's second soap opera to expand to a full hour. It was created by Ted Corday, Irna Phillips, and Allan Chase; Corday's wife, Betty Corday, took over as executive producer following her husband's death shortly after the show began. In 1976 she was joined by H. Wesley Kenney as coexecutive producer. Taped at Screen Gems in Hollywood, the series has been produced by Jack Herzberg and Al Rabin. United States Supreme Court Justice Thurgood Marshall is said to be one of *Days'* biggest fans. Set in the town of Salem, the show revolves around the Horton family—Tom and Alice, their five children, and assorted grandchildren. The large cast has included: Macdonald Carey as Dr. Tom Horton, chief of internal

medicine at University Hospital; Frances Reid as his wife, Alice; John Lupton as their eldest son, Dr. Tommy Horton, who was believed missing in action in Korea but turned up in Salem having undergone plastic surgery; Pat Huston and Patricia Barry as their daughter, Addie Olson, who died; John Clarke as their son, Mickey, a lawyer; Marie Cheatham as their daughter, Marie Horton (Marie Horton decided to become a nun and was written out of the show; several years later she returned, played by Kate Woodville); Ed Mallory as their youngest son, Dr. Bill Horton; Floy Dean, Susan Flannery, Susan Oliver (1975–1976), and Rosemary Forsyth (1976–   ) as psychiatrist Dr. Laura Spencer, who married Mickey Horton; Clive Clerk as David Martin; Denise Alexander (1966–1973) and Bennye Gatteys (1973–1976) as Susan Martin, who killed David; Regina Gleason as Kitty Horton, wife of Dr. Tommy Horton; Heather North as Sandy Horton, daughter of Tommy and Kitty; Dick Colla as Tony Craig; Marie Horton's boyfriend; Robert Knapp as Ben Olson, Addie's husband; Charla Doherty (1965–1967), Catherine Dunn (1967–1968), Cathy Ferrar (1968–1969), and Susan Seaforth as Julie Olson, daughter of Addie and Ben (and granddaughter of Tom and Alice Horton); Robert Carraway, Mike Farrell, Robert Hogan, and Ryan MacDonald as Julie's first husband, Scott Banning, who died; Bill Hayes as nightclub owner Doug Williams, who became Julie's second husband in one of TV's biggest weddings on 1 October 1976 (in real life Bill Hayes and Susan Seaforth were married in October 1974); Joyce Easton as Janet Banning, Scott Banning's first wife; Stuart Lee, Alan Decker, John Amour, Dick DeCoit, and Wesley Eure as Michael Horton, son of Mickey and Laura Horton; Flip Mark, James Carroll Jordan, and Stephen Schnetzer as Steve Olson, son of Addie and Ben; Natasha Ryan as Hope Williams, daughter of Doug and Addie Williams (Doug had been married to Addie, Julie's mother, before he married Julie); Stanley Kamel as Eric Peters; Peter Brown as Eric's brother, Dr. Greg Peters; Jeanne Bates as Anne Peters; Herb Nelson as Phil Peters; Mark Tapscott as Bob Anderson, who fell for Julie Olson; Nancy Wickwire (who played the role until her death in 1973) and Corinne Conley as Bob's wife, Phyllis Anderson; Karin Wolfe, Carla Borelli, Nancy Stephens, and Barbara Stanger as Mary Anderson, daughter of Bob and Phyllis; Margaret Mason as Linda Peterson, Mickey Horton's secretary and lover; Victor Holchak as lawyer Jim Phillips, who eventually married Linda; Coleen Gray as Diane Hunter; Jed Allan as lawyer Don Craig; Suzanne Rogers as Maggie Simmons; Kaye Stevens as Jeri Clayton, a singer at Doug Williams's nightclub; Patty Weaver as Trish Clayton, Jeri's daughter; Joe Gallison as Dr. Neal Curtis; Mary Frann as Amanda (Howard) Peters; Jan Jordan as Helen Cantrell, Jim Phillips's secretary; Jeffrey Williams, Steve Doubet, and Richard Guthrie as David Martin Banning, Julie's illegitimate son; Adrienne LaRussa as Brooke Hamilton; Burt Douglas as Sam Monroe; Helen Funai as Kim Douglas; Robert Brubaker as John

Martin; K. T. Stevens as Helen Martin; Mark Miller as Howard Jones; Robert Clary as Robert LeClare; Garry Marshall as Bert Atwater; Jack Denbo as Jack Clayton; Brooke Bundy as Rebecca North; Joan Van Ark as Janene Whitney; John Aniston as Dr..Eric Richard; John Howard as Cliff Peterson; Eloise Hardt as Rita Beacon; Maidie Norman as Gracie Jones; Graham Brown as Jeffrey Jones; Susan Adams as Meredith Marshall; Tina Andrews and Rose Fonseca as Valerie Grant; Ketty Lester as Helen Grant; Michael Dwight-Smith as Danny Grant; Lawrence Cook as Paul Grant; Paul Henry Itkin as Johnny Collins; Mike Warren as Jerry Davis; Fred Beir as Larry Atwood; John Lombardo as Fred Barton; Jocelyn Somers as Jean Barton; Chip Fields as Toni Johnson; Tom Scott as Jim Bradley; Josh Taylor as Chris Kositchek; Deidre Hall as Marlene Evans; Andrea Hall Lovell (Deidre Hall's twin sister) as Samantha Evans, Marlene's twin sister; Fran Ryan as Rosie Carlson; Jenny Sherman as Betty Worth; William H. Bassett as Dr. Walter Griffin; Cindy Fisher as Patti Griffin; Stephen Manley as Billy Barton; Ken Sansom as Dr. Powell; Martha Nix as Janice Horton; Kim Durso as Melissa; Frederic Downs as Hank; Paul Savior as Sam; Tom Brown as Nathaniel Curtis; Dee Carroll as Adele Hamilton; Pauline Myers as Mrs. Jackson; Sid Conrad as Ribitz; Hal Riddle as Max; Ben DiTosti as Ben; Myron Natwick as Rick; Peter Brandon as Dr. Cunningham; Peter MacLean as Dr. Paul Whitman; Gary McGurrin as Roy Hazeltine; Francine York as Lorraine Temple; Elizabeth MacRae as Phyllis Curtis; Tracy Bregman as Donna Craig; Diana Douglas as Mrs. Evans; Corinne Michaels as Joann Barnes; Elizabeth Brooks as Theresa Harper; Gail Johnson as Mimi; Amanda Jones as Dora; Eileen Barnett as Stephanie Woodruff; Meegan King as Pete Curtis; Robin Pohle as Amy Kositchek; Suzanne Zenor as Margo Horton.

DEADLINE   SYNDICATED
1959 An anthology series about journalists, hosted and narrated by Paul Stewart.

DEADLINE FOR ACTION   ABC
8 FEBRUARY 1959–13 SEPTEMBER 1959 Rebroadcasts of those episodes of *Wire Service* which starred Dane Clark as reporter Dan Miller. See *Wire Service.*

DEALER'S CHOICE   SYNDICATED
1973 An audience-participation game show broadcast from Las Vegas. Hosted first by Bob Hastings, later by Jack Clark.

THE DEAN JONES VARIETY HOUR
See WHAT'S IT ALL ABOUT, WORLD

THE DEAN MARTIN COMEDY HOUR
See THE DEAN MARTIN SHOW

DEAN MARTIN PRESENTS MUSIC COUNTRY
See MUSIC COUNTRY

DEAN MARTIN PRESENTS THE GOLDDIGGERS
See THE GOLDDIGGERS

THE DEAN MARTIN SHOW (THE DEAN MARTIN COMEDY HOUR)   NBC
16 SEPTEMBER 1965–24 MAY 1974   A variety hour hosted by Dean
Martin. Few would have predicted that when the comedy team of Dean
Martin and Jerry Lewis broke up in 1956, it would be Martin who would
have the more successful solo career. Martin demonstrated, however,
that he could not only do comedy but could also sing and act; he appeared in more than thirty films after splitting with Lewis. By not taking
himself too seriously, Martin became an enormously popular television
personality. In 1970 it was reported that he and NBC negotiated the largest contract in history between a network and a star. The TV show itself
required little of Martin: he usually spent only one day a week rehearsing
and taping. It was obvious to viewers that Martin was reading from cue
cards (as do most stars on variety shows), but it was equally obvious that
he was having a good time doing the show. Several of the shows were celebrity "roasts," set at a banquet table, in which the guest of honor was
showered with insults by other celebs. Regulars on the series included pianist Ken Lane (1965–1972), Kay Medford, Lou Jacobi, The Golddiggers, Marian Mercer (1971–1972), Tom Bosley (1971–1972), Rodney
Dangerfield (1972–1973), Dom DeLuise (1972–1973), and Nipsey Russell (1972–1974). Among the several attractive young women who assisted Martin in various comedy sketches were Kathi King, Diana Lee, Betty
Rosebrock, Diane Shatz, and Melissa Stafford. Music was provided by Les
Brown and his Band of Renown. Greg Garrison produced the series,
which was entitled *The Dean Martin Comedy Hour* during its final season.

DEAN MARTIN'S COMEDYWORLD
See COMEDYWORLD

DEAR DETECTIVE   CBS
28 MARCH 1979–18 APRIL 1979   Four-week miniseries based on the
French film, *Tendre Poulet.* With Brenda Vaccaro as Sergeant Kate Hudson, a detective with the Los Angeles Police Department; Arlen Dean
Snyder as Richard Wayland, her boyfriend, a professor of Greek philosophy; Ron Silver as Sergeant Schwartz; Michael MacRae as Sergeant
Brock; John Dennis Johnston as Sergeant Clay; Jack L. Ging as Sergeant

Chuck Morris; Lesley Woods as Mrs. Hudson, Kate's mother; Jet Yardum as Lisa, Kate's daughter by a previous marriage. Dean Hargrove and Roland Kibbee were the producers.

DEAR PHOEBE
NBC

10 SEPTEMBER 1954–2 SEPTEMBER 1955 A situation comedy about a former psychology professor who got a job writing the advice-to-the-lovelorn column (under the name Phoebe Goodheart) for a Los Angeles newspaper. With Peter Lawford as Bill Hastings; Marcia Henderson as sports columnist Mickey Riley, his girlfriend; Charles Lane as Mr. Fosdick, the editor; and Joe Corey as Humphrey, the copyboy.

DEATH VALLEY DAYS
SYNDICATED

1952–1970 This long-running series began on radio in 1930; it was one of television's few western anthology series. Approximately twenty new episodes were filmed each year; several were filmed on location at Death Valley. The series was hosted by Stanley Andrews from 1952 to 1965 (as the Old Ranger). Ronald Reagan succeeded him and when Reagan left for politics in 1966, he was replaced by Robert Taylor. In 1968 Taylor was succeeded by Dale Robertson (star of two previous westerns, *Wells Fargo* and *The Iron Horse*). The show was sponsored for many years by Twenty Mule Team Borax. It was originally produced by Darrell McGowan for Gene Autry's Flying A Productions; early episodes were directed by Stuart McGowan.

THE DEBBIE REYNOLDS SHOW
NBC

16 SEPTEMBER 1969–1 SEPTEMBER 1970 This unsuccessful situation comedy was NBC's attempt to rival CBS's 1968 hit, *The Doris Day Show.* Like Doris Day, Debbie Reynolds was a popular and talented film star, and like Day she had not appeared in a dramatic role on television before. Created by Jess Oppenheimer *(I Love Lucy),* the show featured Reynolds as Debbie Thompson, a housewife who longed to become a newspaperwoman; Don Chastain as her husband, Jim Thompson, a sportswriter (note the parallel between this show and *I Love Lucy*—in each the housewife wanted to break into her husband's line of work); Tom Bosley as accountant Bob Landers, their neighbor and Debbie's brother-in-law; Patricia Smith as Bob's wife, Charlotte Landers, Debbie's sister; Bobby Riha as Bruce Landers, Bob and Charlotte's young son; and Billy DeWolfe as accountant Delbert Deloy. Reynolds, who owned a 50 percent interest in the show, had originally been guaranteed a two-year run by NBC. Infuriated by the fact that the show was sponsored by a cigarette manufacturer, she relinquished the second-season guarantee in exchange for the network's agreement to drop the cigarette sponsorship.

DECEMBER BRIDE CBS

4 OCTOBER 1954–24 SEPTEMBER 1959 This domestic sitcom starred Spring Byington as Lily Ruskin, a widow who lived with her daughter and son-in-law; Frances Rafferty as Ruth Henshaw, her daughter; Dean Miller as architect Matt Henshaw, Ruth's husband; Harry Morgan as next-door neighbor Pete Porter, an insurance agent who constantly wisecracked about his wife, Gladys (who was never seen in the flesh); Verna Felton as Lily's comrade, Hilda Crocker. Occasionally featured was Arnold Stang, as Private Marvin Fisher, Pete's brother-in-law. Filmed at Desilu Studios before a live audience, most of the "action" in *December Bride* took place in the Henshaws' living room. Joel Grey guest-starred as Lily's nephew (7 December 1957 and 14 December 1957). In 1960 a spinoff appeared: see *Pete and Gladys*.

DECISION NBC

6 JULY 1958–28 SEPTEMBER 1958 This half-hour dramatic anthology series was a summer replacement for *The Loretta Young Show*. The premiere telecast, "The Virginian," starring James Drury, became a series in 1962.

DECISION: THE CONFLICTS OF HARRY S TRUMAN SYNDICATED

1964 Truman's presidency (1945–1953) was the subject of this half-hour documentary series.

DECOY (POLICEWOMAN DECOY) SYNDICATED

1957 Beverly Garland starred as New York policewoman Casey Jones in this half-hour crime show, apparently the first series to feature a female cop.

THE DEFENDERS CBS

16 SEPTEMBER 1961–9 SEPTEMBER 1965 This high-quality series about a father-and-son defense team attracted much controversy, as well as much critical acclaim during its four-year run. The show regularly dealt with such sensitive issues as euthanasia, abortion, blacklisting, and civil disobedience. Even more atypical was the fact that the defenders occasionally lost a case. The show starred E. G. Marshall as Lawrence Preston: it was the first continuing role for Marshall, one of the most frequently seen performers on television during the 1950s. Robert Reed costarred as his Ivy League son, Kenneth Preston. Also featured were Polly Rowles (1961–1962) as their secretary, Helen Donaldson, and Joan Hackett (1961–1963) as Ken's girlfriend, social worker Joan Miller. Among the many guest stars who appeared were Gene Hackman ("Quality of Mercy," 16 September 1961; "Judgment Eve," 20 April 1963), Martin Sheen ("The Attack," 9 December 1961, his first major TV role),

James Farentino ("The Last Illusion," 9 March 1963, his first major TV role), Jon Voight ("The Brother Killers," 25 May 1963, a rare TV appearance), Ossie Davis (seven appearances), James Earl Jones ("The Non-Violent," 6 June 1964), Robert Redford ("The Siege," 3 December 1964, his last TV dramatic role), and Dustin Hoffman ("A Matter of Law and Disorder," 8 April 1965). The series was created by Reginald Rose, who wrote several of the scripts, including the two-part genesis of the series for *Studio One*, which was entitled "The Defenders" (with Ralph Bellamy and William Shatner, 25 February and 4 March 1957). Other regular writers included Ernest Kinoy and Robert Crean. Produced by Herbert Brodkin, the series was filmed in New York.

DELLA   SYNDICATED
1969   A talk show hosted by singer-actress Della Reese, who began her professional career as a gospel singer and became a pop artist in 1957.

THE DELPHI BUREAU   ABC
5 OCTOBER 1972–1 SEPTEMBER 1973   Part of ABC's trilogy, *The Men,* this segment alternated with *Assignment: Vienna* and *Jigsaw*. It featured Laurence Luckinbill as Glenn Garth Gregory, a secret agent who possessed total recall, and Anne Jeffreys (infrequently seen since *Topper*) as his assistant, Sybil Van Loween.

DELTA HOUSE   ABC
18 JANUARY 1979–28 APRIL 1979   Half-hour sitcom based on *National Lampoon's Animal House*, one of the most successful films of 1978. Students at Pennsylvania's Faber College in 1962, its central characters resided at Delta House, the campus's most hedonistic and socially undesirable fraternity, where they managed to thwart the efforts of the dean (and the upright lads of Omega House) to expel them. With John Vernon as Dean Vernon Wormer; Stephen Furst as Kent (Flounder) Dorfman; Bruce McGill as Daniel (D-Day) Day; Jamie Widdoes as Bob Hoover, Delta's president; Josh Mostel (son of Zero Mostel) as Jim (Blotto) Blutarski, a transfer student, the younger brother of Bluto Blutarski (played by John Belushi in the film); Peter Fox as Eric "Otter" Stratton; Richard Seer as Larry (Pinto) Kroger; Gary Cookson as Doug Niedermeyer of Omega House; Brian Patrick Clarke as Greg Marmalarde of Omega House; Susanna Dalton as Mandy Peppridge; Wendy Goldman as Muffy Jones, Pinto's girlfriend; Peter Kastner as Professor Jennings; Lee Wilkof as Einswin; and Michele Pfeiffer as Bombshell. Vernon, Furst, McGill, and Widdoes had been featured in the motion picture. Executive producers: Matty Simmons and Ivan Reitman for Universal TV in association with Matty Simmons–Ivan Reitman Productions.

DELVECCHIO

CBS

9 SEPTEMBER 1976–17 JULY 1977   This crime show starred Judd Hirsch as Sergeant Dominick Delvecchio, a tough but fair-minded cop who graduated from law school but flunked the bar exam. With Charles Haid as Officer Paul Shonski, his eager-beaver assistant; Michael Conrad as Lieutenant Macavan, his commanding officer; and Mario Gallo as Tomaso Delvecchio, Dom's father, a barber. William Sackheim was the executive producer.

DEMI-TASSE TALES

SYNDICATED

1953   A half-hour dramatic anthology series of little note.

THE DENNIS DAY SHOW
(THE RCA VICTOR SHOW STARRING DENNIS DAY)

NBC

8 FEBRUARY 1952–2 AUGUST 1954   Dennis Day, the singer-actor who worked with Jack Benny for many years, also hosted his own comedy-variety series. Regulars included Cliff Arquette (fall 1952–1954, as Charley Weaver), Hal March (fall 1952–1953), and Jeri Lou James. During the spring of 1952 the show was seen biweekly, alternating with *The Ezio Pinza Show,* also sponsored by RCA. Paul Henning, who later developed *The Beverly Hillbillies,* was the producer.

THE DENNIS JAMES SHOW

ABC

24 SEPTEMBER 1951–15 FEBRUARY 1952   One of television's most ubiquitous performers (he was seen regularly as early as 1938), Dennis James hosted this half-hour daytime variety show as well as countless other programs. It was produced by Aaron Steiner and directed by Lou Sposa (James's brother).

THE DENNIS O'KEEFE SHOW

CBS

22 SEPTEMBER 1959–14 JUNE 1960   This half-hour sitcom featured Dennis O'Keefe as widower Hal Towne, a newspaper columnist; Rickey Kelman as his young son, Randy; Hope Emerson as Sarge, the housekeeper; and Eloise Hardt as Karen. Les Hafner produced the series.

DENNIS THE MENACE

CBS

4 OCTOBER 1959–22 SEPTEMBER 1963   Hank Ketcham's mischievous cartoon character made a successful transition to television in this prime-time series. There were 146 half-hour episodes filmed, with Jay North as young Dennis Mitchell; Herbert Anderson as his father, Henry; Gloria Henry as his mother, Alice; Joseph Kearns (1959–1961) as next-door neighbor George Wilson, the object of many of Dennis's well-intentioned escapades; Sylvia Field (1959–1961) as Martha Wilson, Mr. Wilson's kindly wife; Billy Booth as Dennis's friend Tommy Anderson; Gil Smith

as Dennis's friend Joey MacDonald; and Jeannie Russell as Dennis's sometime friend Margaret Wade. After Kearns's death in 1961, Gale Gordon joined the cast as Mr. Wilson's brother (and the Mitchells' neighbor), John Wilson, and Sara Seegar was added as his wife, Eloise. In real life cartoonist Ketcham has a son named Dennis; the inspiration for the comic strip came one day when Ketcham's wife remarked, "Our son, Dennis, is a menace." Harry Ackerman was the executive producer.

THE DEPUTY
NBC

12 SEPTEMBER 1959–16 SEPTEMBER 1961 Set in Prescott, Arizona, this half-hour western featured Henry Fonda as Marshal Simon Fry; Allen Case as Deputy Clay McCord, a storekeeper; Read Morgan as Sergeant Tasker (Sarge), the one-eyed cavalry officer stationed in town; and Wallace Ford (1959–1960) as Herb Lamson, owner of the general store. Robert Redford made his television debut on one episode of the series ("The Last Gunfight," 30 April 1960).

DEPUTY DAWG
SYNDICATED/NBC

1961 (SYNDICATED); 11 SEPTEMBER 1971–2 SEPTEMBER 1972 (NBC) A cartoon show about a fumbling canine law enforcement officer.

THE DES O'CONNOR SHOW (KRAFT MUSIC HALL)
NBC

20 MAY 1970–2 SEPTEMBER 1970; 2 JUNE 1971–1 SEPTEMBER 1971 A summer variety series taped in London, starring singer Des O'Connor. Other regulars included Jack Douglas, the MacGregor Brothers (1970), and Connie Stevens (1971).

DESILU PLAYHOUSE
CBS

6 OCTOBER 1958–10 JUNE 1960 Desi Arnaz was the host and occasional star of this hour dramatic anthology series, filmed at Desilu Studios. Some episodes of *The Lucy-Desi Comedy Hour* were shown during this time slot (see also *I Love Lucy*).

DESTRY
ABC

14 FEBRUARY 1964–11 SEPTEMBER 1964 This little-watched western replaced *77 Sunset Strip* on Friday nights; it starred John Gavin as Harrison Destry, a loner who sought to prove himself innocent of a trumped-up robbery charge.

DETECTIVE SCHOOL
ABC

31 JULY 1979–24 NOVEMBER 1979 Introduced for a four-week trial run in the summer of 1979, *Detective School* (then titled *Detective School—One Flight Up*) proved popular enough to warrant a spot on

ABC's fall schedule. The half-hour sitcom starred James Gregory as Nick Hannigan, veteran private eye, now the sole instructor at a low-budget school for fledgling gumshoes. Hannigan's class included Randolph Mantooth as Eddie Dawkins; LaWanda Page as Charlene Jenkins; Jo Ann Haris (summer 1979) as Teresa; Melinda Naud (fall 1979) as Maggie; Douglas V. Fowley as Robert Redford; Pat Proft as Leo; and Taylor Negron as Silvio. Executive producers were Bernie Kukoff and Jeff Harris for the Kukoff-Harris Partnership.

THE DETECTIVES (ROBERT TAYLOR'S DETECTIVES)   ABC/NBC
16 OCTOBER 1959–22 SEPTEMBER 1961 (ABC); 29 SEPTEMBER 1961–21 SEPTEMBER 1962 (NBC) This straightforward crime show was set in New York. With Robert Taylor as Captain Matt Holbrook; Tige Andrews as Lieutenant Johnny Russo; Lee Farr as Lieutenant Joe Conway; Russell Thorsen as Lieutenant Otto Lindstrom; Mark Goddard (1960–1962) as Sergeant Chris Ballard; and Adam West (1961–1962) as Sergeant Steve Nelson. The series expanded from a half hour to an hour when it shifted networks in 1961.

DETECTIVE'S DIARY
See MARK SABER

DETECTIVE'S WIFE   CBS
7 JULY 1950–6 OCTOBER 1950 Broadcast live from New York, this comedy-mystery was a summer replacement for *Man Against Crime*. It starred Lynn Bari as Connie Conway, who tried to help her private-eye husband solve his cases, and Donald Curtis as her husband, Adam Conway.

DEVLIN   ABC
7 SEPTEMBER 1974–15 FEBRUARY 1976 Kids' cartoon show about three orphans (Ernie, Tod, and Sandy) who decide to become motorcycle stunt drivers. The Hanna-Barbera production was seen Saturdays during its first season; reruns were shown on Sundays during the second season.

DIAGNOSIS: UNKNOWN   CBS
5 JULY 1960–20 SEPTEMBER 1960 A summer replacement for *The Garry Moore Show, Diagnosis: Unknown* starred Patrick O'Neal as New York police pathologist Dr. Daniel Coffee. Also featured were Chester Morris as Detective Ritter; Phyllis Newman as lab assistant Doris Hudson; Cal Bellini as Dr. Motilal Mookerji, a visiting physician from India; and Martin Huston as Link, the teenage lab assistant.

THE DIAHANN CARROLL SHOW   CBS
14 AUGUST 1976–4 SEPTEMBER 1976 This four-week variety series was a summer replacement for *The Carol Burnett Show*. Diahann Carroll, for-

merly the star of *Julia*, hosted the show. Executive producers: Robert DeLeon and Max Youngstein.

DIAL 999   SYNDICATED

1959 Set at Scotland Yard, this crime show starred Robert Beatty as Inspector Michael Maguire, a Canadian police officer sent to London to learn advanced methods of detection.

THE DIAMOND HEAD GAME   SYNDICATED

1975 Bob Eubanks hosted this game show, taped at Oahu's Kuilima Hotel. Through a series of questions, the field of contestants was gradually reduced until only one remained. That contestant was then placed in a plastic booth ("The Diamond Head Treasure Vault"), where dollar bills of various denominations were blown about. The contestant was given fifteen seconds to fill a "treasure bag" with dollar bills; afterward, Eubanks pulled out up to ten bills from the bag. Those bills were then awarded to the contestant, unless a $1-bill was drawn, in which case the contestant lost everything.

DIANA   NBC

10 SEPTEMBER 1973–7 JANUARY 1974 *Diana* was an unsuccessful vehicle for Diana Rigg, the former star of *The Avengers*. In this comedy she starred as Diana Smythe, a recent divorcée who left London for New York, where she moved into the apartment of her brother, Roger (he was out of the country) and got a job as a fashion coordinator at Buckley's Department Store. Also featured were David Sheiner as Norman Brodnik, her boss; Barbara Barrie as Norman's wife, Norma Brodnik, head of the merchandising department; Richard B. Shull as coworker Howard Tolbrook, a copywriter; Robert Moore as window dresser Marshall Tyler; and Carol Androsky as Diana's neighbor, Holly Green, a model. Executive producer: Leonard Stern.

DICK AND THE DUCHESS   CBS

28 SEPTEMBER 1957–16 MAY 1958 This comedy-mystery was set in London. With Patrick O'Neal as insurance investigator Dick Starrett; Hazel Court as his British wife, Jane Starrett, a duchess; Richard Wattis as Dick's boss, Peter Jamison; and Ronnie Stevens as Rodney, a young man who also worked in Dick's office.

THE DICK CAVETT SHOW   ABC/CBS/PBS

4 MARCH 1968–24 JANUARY 1969; 26 MAY 1969–19 SEPTEMBER 1969; 29 DECEMBER 1969–1 JANUARY 1975 (ABC); 16 AUGUST 1975–6 SEPTEMBER 1975 (CBS); 10 OCTOBER 1977–   (PBS) Though Dick Cavett has hosted several series, he is best known as the host of ABC's late-night show, a noble attempt to compete with Johnny Carson of

NBC. Like Carson, Cavett was raised in Nebraska and was interested in magic as a teenager. After graduating from Yale, Cavett went to New York, hoping to get a job as a writer; he thrust some material into Jack Paar's hand in an NBC corridor and was subsequently hired by Paar. After writing for others, he became a stand-up comic for a while and continued to do summer stock. During the mid-1960s he was occasionally seen as a game show panelist. In 1968 he was given his first series on ABC. It was a daytime talk show and was originally titled *This Morning* before it was changed to *The Dick Cavett Show.* In the summer of 1969 he hosted a thrice-weekly prime-time series on ABC, and later that year he succeeded Joey Bishop as host of the network's late-night talk show. Cavett brought with him the announcer and the bandleader who had worked with him on the earlier shows—Fred Foy (better known as the announcer on *The Lone Ranger*) and drummer Bobby Rosengarten. The show was originally seen five nights a week but was gradually cut back over the years as Cavett's ratings failed to dent Carson's. By January of 1973 the show was seen one week a month, as part of *ABC's Wide World of Entertainment;* by late 1974 the show was seen only twice a month and disappeared altogether on New Year's Day 1975. Perhaps because of Cavett's Yale background and because of his interest in language, he has acquired the image of an "intellectual" host (an image which Cavett himself disputes), and because of it the show probably failed to attract more viewers. Nevertheless, there were some fine moments on the show, such as Lester Maddox's sudden departure after getting into an argument with Cavett, and a verbal brawl between Norman Mailer and Gore Vidal, with Cavett and Janet Flanner caught in the middle. Cavett also made effective use of the one-guest show, managing to lure such elusive talk show guests as Marlon Brando, Katharine Hepburn, and John Lennon and Yoko Ono. In the summer of 1975 Cavett switched networks, hosting a four-week variety series on CBS. Regulars included Leigh French and Marshall Efron; the show was produced by Carole Hart and Bruce Hart. In the fall of 1977 he appeared on PBS in a half-hour talk show on which he returned to his strong suit: one-guest interviews. The show is produced by Cavett's former Yale roommate, Christopher Porterfield.

DICK CLARK PRESENTS THE ROCK AND ROLL YEARS   ABC
28 NOVEMBER 1973–9 JANUARY 1974   On this half-hour series, host Dick Clark reminisced with live guests and introduced film clips of rock performances from the fifties and sixties.

THE DICK CLARK SHOW   ABC
(THE DICK CLARK SATURDAY NIGHT BEECHNUT SHOW)
15 FEBRUARY 1958–10 SEPTEMBER 1960   Dick Clark, who was already hosting *American Bandstand* weekdays, commuted to New York from Philadelphia on weekends to host this half-hour rock-and-roll show,

broadcast live from the Little Theater. Dick's guests on the premiere included Pat Boone, Connie Francis, Jerry Lee Lewis, Johnnie Ray, Chuck Willis, and the Royal Teens. Sponsored by Beechnut Foods.

DICK CLARK'S LIVE WEDNESDAY   NBC
20 SEPTEMBER 1978–27 DECEMBER 1978   The only live prime-time entertainment show of the 1978–1979 season, this hour variety series was hosted by Dick Clark, who also served as its executive producer. The show was seen live only in the East and Midwest and was shown on tape in areas farther west.

DICK CLARK'S WORLD OF TALENT   ABC
27 SEPTEMBER 1959–20 DECEMBER 1959   Dick Clark, one of ABC's most ubiquitous personalities of the time, hosted this half-hour series on which aspiring performers were rated by a celebrity panel; regular panelists included Jack E. Leonard and Zsa Zsa Gabor.

DICK POWELL THEATRE   NBC
26 SEPTEMBER 1961–17 SEPTEMBER 1963   Dick Powell hosted and occasionally starred in some episodes of this hour-long dramatic anthology series. These were the last appearances of Powell, who died in 1963. The most widely acclaimed drama was probably "The Price of Tomatoes," (16 January 1962), Richard Alan Simmons's story of a truck driver (Peter Falk) who picked up a pregnant hitchhiker (Inger Stevens); Falk won an Emmy for his performance.

DICK POWELL'S ZANE GREY THEATER
See ZANE GREY THEATER

DICK TRACY   ABC
13 SEPTEMBER 1950–12 FEBRUARY 1951   One of fiction's most famous cops, Dick Tracy first appeared in the comic strip drawn by Chester Gould. In 1935 he went to radio, and in 1937 a fifteen-chapter movie serial was made starring Ralph Byrd. Byrd played Tracy in several more films before making this television series; his death in 1952 terminated plans to continue production. Tracy, however, reappeared on television in cartoon form in 1961 and in 1971 (where he could be seen on *The Archie Show*).

THE DICK VAN DYKE SHOW   CBS
3 OCTOBER 1961–7 SEPTEMBER 1966   After a shaky first season (the series didn't crack Nielsen's top thirty-five shows), this popular situation comedy became a solid hit. It was one of the first series in which the central characters worked for a television series; both Van Dyke and costar Mary Tyler Moore employed a similar format on their later series (*The*

New Dick Van Dyke Show and *The Mary Tyler Moore Show*). With Dick Van Dyke as Rob Petrie, head writer for *The Alan Brady Show*, a variety series; Mary Tyler Moore as his wife, Laura Petrie, a former dancer; Morey Amsterdam as Buddy Sorrell, wisecracking comedy writer; Rose Marie as Sally Rogers, husband-hunting comedy writer; Richard Deacon as Mel Cooley, producer of *The Alan Brady Show* (and brother-in-law of Alan Brady), the target of many of Buddy's barbs; Carl Reiner as Alan Brady, the vain star; Jerry Paris (who also directed many episodes) as dentist Jerry Helper, the Petries' next-door neighbor in New Rochelle; Ann Morgan Guilbert as Millie Helper, Jerry's wife; Larry Matthews as Richie Petrie, Rob and Laura's young son. Occasionally appearing were Jerry Van Dyke (Dick's brother) as Rob's brother, Stacy Petrie; Peter Oliphant as Freddy Helper, Jerry and Millie's son and Richie's pal; Joan Shawlee as Buddy's wife, Viona (Pickles) Sorrell; Tom Tully and J. Pat O'Malley as Rob's father, Sam Petrie; and Isabel Randolph and Mabel Albertson as Rob's mother, Clara Petrie. Created by Carl Reiner, the pilot for the series (with Reiner as Rob and Barbara Britton as Laura) was broadcast 19 July 1960. Production of the series was supervised by Sheldon Leonard; many episodes were written by Bill Persky and Sam Denoff, who later produced the show.

DIFF'RENT STROKES   NBC
3 NOVEMBER 1978–   Half-hour sitcom set in New York, starring Conrad Bain as Philip Drummond, a Park Avenue millionaire who adopts two orphans from Harlem (the boys' mother had been his housekeeper for many years). With Gary Coleman as Arnold Jackson, his eight-year-old ward; Todd Bridges as Willis Jackson, his thirteen-year-old ward; Charlotte Rae as his housekeeper, Mrs. Garrett; and Dana Plato as his daughter, Kimberley. In January 1980 Nedra Volz succeeded Rae, playing Adelaide the new housekeeper. Bernie Kukoff and Jeff Harris created the series, and Howard Leeds and Herbert Kenwith are the producers for Tandem Productions.

DINAH!   SYNDICATED
1974–   Ninety-minute talk show hosted by Dinah Shore. Featuring a set resembling a living room, the program is seen during the daytime in most markets. Executive producers: Henry Jaffe and Carolyn Raskin. In 1979 the show was retitled *Dinah! & Friends*, as Dinah employed a weekly co-host.

DINAH AND HER NEW BEST FRIENDS   CBS
5 JUNE 1976–31 JULY 1976 This summer replacement for *The Carol Burnett Show* starred Dinah Shore and a group of young professionals: Diana Canova, Bruce Kimmel, Gary Mule Deer, Mike Neun, Leland Palmer, Michael Preminger, Avelio Falana, and Dee Dee Rescher.

Executive producer: Henry Jaffe. Producer: Carolyn Raskin.

THE DINAH SHORE SHOW   NBC
27 NOVEMBER 1951–18 JULY 1957; 20 OCTOBER 1957–1 JUNE 1962
DINAH'S PLACE   NBC
3 AUGUST 1970–26 JULY 1974   One of the few females to host a successful television variety series, Dinah Shore came to TV in 1951 with several
years experience in show business; she had had her own radio series in
1939 (at the age of twenty-two), and had begun making records in 1941.
From 1951 until 1957 she hosted a fifteen-minute musical show, which
was seen once or twice a week before the evening news. For several seasons the show was sponsored by Chevrolet and was known officially as
The Dinah Shore Chevy Show; Shore's backup group during the latter seasons was the Skylarks, who included George Becker, Earl Brown, Joe
Hamilton, Lee Lombard, and Gilda Maiken. During the 1956–1957 season, in addition to her fifteen-minute show, Shore starred in a number of
specials, which were also sponsored by Chevrolet and were scheduled on
Sunday evenings. These specials were the genesis of her second series, an
hour variety show which ran from 1957 to 1962, and was again sponsored by Chevrolet; for most of these five seasons Shore hosted the series
three out of every four weeks, with guest hosts filling in every fourth
week. In 1970, after an eight-year absence, Shore returned to host *Dinah's Place,* a daytime half-hour talk show. After the cancellation of that
show in 1974, she continued to host a talk show: see *Dinah!*

DING DONG SCHOOL   NBC/SYNDICATED
22 DECEMBER 1952–28 DECEMBER 1956 (NBC); 1959 (SYNDICA-
TED)   One of the first educational series for young children, *Ding Dong
School* was seen Mondays through Fridays on NBC. It was presided over
by Dr. Frances Horwich, head of the education department at Roosevelt
College in Chicago; she was better known to viewers, of course, as Miss
Frances. The show was given its title by the three-year-old daughter of
producer Reinald Werrenrath after she watched a test broadcast of the
opening sequence (a hand ringing a small bell). In 1959 a syndicated version appeared.

DINNER DATE   DUMONT
28 JANUARY 1950–29 JULY 1950   Saturday-evening musical show,
broadcast from the Grill Room at New York's Hotel Taft, featuring Vincent Lopez and his orchestra, Ann Warren, and Lee Russell.

DIONE LUCAS' COOKING SHOW   CBS
25 FEBRUARY 1948–29 DECEMBER 1949   One of television's first cooking shows, this prime-time series, hosted by Dione Lucas, was titled *To
the Queen's Taste* in its early weeks.

THE DIPSY DOODLE SHOW   SYNDICATED

1974   An hour-long children's show produced at WJW-TV in Cleveland. Its central character was an animated figure, Dipsy Doodle; also featured were live performers Karen League Barrett, Sandy Faison, Jon Freeman, Michael McGee, Harry Gold, Emil Herrera, and Helene Leonard. Executive producer: Bob Huber.

DIRECTIONS   ABC

13 NOVEMBER 1960–   Sunday-morning religious program produced by the News Public Affairs department of ABC. Executive producer: Sid Darion.

DIRTY SALLY   CBS

11 JANUARY 1974–19 JULY 1974   This light western starred Jeanette Nolan as crusty Sally Fergus, a wandering junk collector, and Dack Rambo as Cyrus Pike, the ex-outlaw with whom she teamed up. Nolan had first appeared as Sally on an episode of *Gunsmoke*.

DISCO MAGIC   SYNDICATED

1978   Half-hour disco music show, taped in Fort Lauderdale and hosted by Evelyn "Champagne" King.

DISCO '77   SYNDICATED

1977   Los Angeles-based disco music series.

THE DISCOPHONIC SCENE   SYNDICATED

1966   Disc jockey Jerry Blavat hosted this hour of rock music. For many years Blavat was the only white DJ on Philadelphia soul station WHAT, where he was known as "The Geater with the Heater."

DISCOVERY   ABC

1 OCTOBER 1962–5 SEPTEMBER 1971   This highbrow series for children, bankrolled by a large investment from ABC, began as a twenty-five-minute weekday series but was unable to attract enough affiliates in that format. In 1963 it switched to Sunday mornings, where it remained for the duration of its run. Historical and cultural themes were emphasized on the program, which was cohosted by Frank Buxton and Virginia Gibson, later by Bill Owen and Gibson. The exact title of the series included the last two digits of the current year (*Discovery '63*, etc.).

DISNEYLAND

See WALT DISNEY

DIVORCE COURT   SYNDICATED

1957–1969   This long-running courtroom drama presented a new case each day. The purpose of the show (according to the announcer, anyway) was "to help stem the rising tide of divorces." Voltaire Perkins portrayed the presiding judge; Bill Walsh and Colin Male were the courtroom-based narrators.

DIVORCE HEARING
SYNDICATED

1958 This unusual documentary series was filmed in Los Angeles; on each program couples discussed marital problems with marriage counselor Dr. Paul Popenoe (the participants were identified by first names or by initials). Dave Walpert produced and directed the half-hour show.

DO IT YOURSELF
NBC

26 JUNE 1955–18 SEPTEMBER 1955 A light approach to home repair was taken on this series, cohosted by Dave Willock and Cliff Arquette (as Charley Weaver). The two had previously been seen on *Dave and Charley.* This Sunday-night series replaced *Mr. Peepers.*

DO YOU KNOW?
CBS

12 OCTOBER 1963–25 APRIL 1964 On this Saturday-afternoon game show for kids, children were quizzed about books they had been assigned to read. Afterward they discussed the books with their authors and with host Robert Maxwell.

DO YOU TRUST YOUR WIFE?
See WHO DO YOU TRUST?

DOBIE GILLIS (THE MANY LOVES OF DOBIE GILLIS)
CBS

29 SEPTEMBER 1959–18 SEPTEMBER 1963 This situation comedy about a girl-crazy teenager was ahead of its time. Its central characters would have felt equally at home in the late sixties: Dobie Gillis, the confused romantic who could never figure out what he wanted from life, and Maynard G. Krebs, his carefree beatnik friend, television's primordial hippie. During the show's four-year run, Dobie and Maynard finished high school, enlisted in the army, and eventually went to junior college. Dwayne Hickman starred as Dobie Gillis; his hair was lightened for the series, apparently to make him look younger (it grew darker as time wore on). When Dobie wasn't at the malt shop trying to impress some sweet young thing, he could be found seated beneath a replica of Rodin's "The Thinker," trying to explain his thoughts to the audience. Bob Denver costarred as Dobie's good buddy, Maynard G. Krebs, a goateed and sweatshirted free spirit who shuddered whenever the word "work" was uttered. Also featured were Frank Faylen as Dobie's father, Herbert T. Gillis, who owned the grocery store over which the Gillises dwelt and whose unrealized dream was that Dobie would come to his senses and

take over the business; Florida Friebus as Dobie's mother, Winnifred Gillis, who seemed to understand Dobie and often interceded between father and son; Stephen Franken as Dobie's wealthy classmate, Chatsworth Osborn, Jr., who found the Gillises boorishly amusing; Doris Packer as Mrs. Chatsworth Osborn, the equally insufferable mother of Chatsworth; Sheila James as classmate Zelda Gilroy, who, confident that she and Dobie were meant for each other, pursued him in vain; William Schallert as Mr. Pomfret, Dobie's English teacher (both at high school and at S. Peter Pryor Junior College); Tuesday Weld (1959–1960) as Thalia Menninger, the unattainable object of Dobie's affections who put him off with an armada of excuses. In the earliest episodes Warren Beatty was seen as Milton Armitage, the boy whom Thalia preferred. Darryl Hickman (Dwayne's brother) appeared occasionally as Dobie's brother Davey Gillis. Michael J. Pollard also appeared briefly as Maynard's cousin; when Denver was drafted in 1960, Pollard was under consideration to replace him, but Denver flunked his physical. Ryan O'Neal made his TV debut on one episode, "The Hunger Strike," which also featured Marlo Thomas (26 January 1960). Created by Max Shulman, the series was produced by Rod Amateau.

DOC
CBS

13 SEPTEMBER 1975–30 OCTOBER 1976   In this situation comedy about a dedicated New York physician, Barnard Hughes starred as Dr. Joe Bogert. During the first season Bogert was a private practitioner with eight grown children. The cast included: Elizabeth Wilson as his wife, Annie Bogert; Mary Wickes as his nurse, Mrs. Beatrice Tully; comic Irwin Corey as cabbie Happy Miller, a frequent patient; Judy Kahan as Laurie Fenner, Joe and Annie's daughter; John Harkins as Fred Fenner, her pompous husband; and Herbie Faye as Mr. Goldman, another patient. For the second season, Bogert (now widowed) worked at the Westside Community Clinic. The 1975–1976 cast was jettisoned (Mary Wickes appeared on the season premiere), and the new regulars included: Audra Lindley as Janet Scott, R.N.; Ray Vitte as lab technician Woody Henderson; Lisa Mordente as receptionist Teresa Ortega; and David Ogden Stiers as clinic director Stanley R. Moss. The series was created by Ed. Weinberger and Stan Daniels, who also served as its executive producers. Produced by Norman Barasch, Carroll Moore, and Paul Wayne for MTM Enterprises, Inc.

DOC CORKLE
NBC

5 OCTOBER 1952–19 OCTOBER 1952   In this situation comedy about a dentist, Eddie Mayehoff starred as Doc Corkle; also featured were Connie Marshall as his daughter, Chester Conklin as his father, Arnold Stang, Hope Emerson, and Billie Burke. The first fatality of the 1952–

1953 season, *Doc Corkle* was replaced after three episodes by a series which had proved popular that summer: *Mr. Peepers*. Lou Place was the producer, Dick Bare the director.

DOC ELLIOT   ABC
10 OCTOBER 1973–14 AUGUST 1974   A dramatic series about a doctor who gave up his lucrative New York practice for life in rural Colorado. With James Franciscus as Dr. Ben Elliot; Neva Patterson as "Mags" Brimble, his landlady; Noah Beery as store owner Barney Weeks; and Bo Hopkins as pilot Eldred McCoy. The series began as a once-a-month replacement for *Owen Marshall* and went weekly in January.

THE DOCTOR   NBC
24 AUGUST 1952–28 JUNE 1953   Warner Anderson hosted this half-hour medical anthology series, which was produced by Marion Parsonnet. Charles Bronson played one of his first major TV roles on one episode, "Take the Odds," seen 18 January 1953.

DR. CHRISTIAN   SYNDICATED
1956   This medical show was based on the film and radio series, which had starred Jean Hersholt. On TV Macdonald Carey starred as small-town physician Dr. Mark Christian, nephew of Dr. Paul Christian, the character Hersholt had played.

DR. DOOLITTLE   NBC
12 SEPTEMBER 1970–2 SEPTEMBER 1972   A Saturday-morning cartoon series about a kindly veterinarian who could talk to the animals, based on the stories by Hugh Lofting and inspired by the 1967 film starring Rex Harrison.

DR. FIX-UM   ABC
3 MAY 1949–6 AUGUST 1950   Host Arthur Youngquist presented tips on home repair on this prime-time show.

DR. FU MANCHU (THE ADVENTURES OF FU MANCHU)   SYNDICATED
1956   The inscrutable Oriental mastermind created by Sax Rohmer almost came to television in 1952; that year a pilot film was made at Fox Movietone Studios in New York with John Carradine as Fu Manchu and Sir Cedric Hardwicke as Detective Nayland Smith, his adversary. In 1956 Fu reappeared, played by Glen Gordon, with Lester Stevens as Nayland Smith.

DR. HUDSON'S SECRET JOURNAL   SYNDICATED
1956–1957   Half-hour dramatic series starring John Howard as Dr. Wayne Hudson, a neurosurgeon at Center Hospital. Also featured were

Olive Blakeney as his housekeeper, Mrs. Grady; Cheryl Galloway as his daughter. Created by Lloyd C. Douglas, the series was produced by Eugene Solow and Brewster Morgan; at least seventy-eight episodes were filmed.

DR. I.Q. ABC
4 NOVEMBER 1953–10 OCTOBER 1954; 15 DECEMBER 1958–23 MARCH 1959 Neither of the television adaptations of this popular radio quiz show fared well. Jay Owen was the first host of the 1953–1954 version. As Dr. I.Q., the Mental Banker, he awarded twenty silver dollars for each question answered correctly by contestants from the studio audience. An Episcopalian minister, James McClain, succeeded Owen during the 1953–1954 season, and Tom Kennedy hosted the show when it was revived four years later as a midseason replacement for *Anybody Can Play.*

DOCTOR IN THE HOUSE SYNDICATED
1971–1974 This British comedy about a group of medical students studying at St. Swithin's Teaching Hospital in London was based on the stories by Richard Gordon (which in turn had formed the basis for the 1953 film). With Barry Evans (1971–1973) as Michael A. Upton; Ernest Clark as Professor Loftus, anatomy instructor; Robin Nedwell (1971–1972; 1973–1974) as Duncan Waring; George Layton as Paul Collier; Jeffrey Davies as Dick Stuart-Clark; Martin Shaw as Huw Evans; Simon Cuff (1971–1972) as David Briddock; Ralph Michael (1971–1972) as The Dean; and Richard O'Sullivan (1972–1974) as Dr. Lawrence Bingham. Filmed between 1969 and 1972, the series was not made available to American markets until 1971. The students had earned their degrees by the second season and left St. Swithin's, only to return (as interns) a year later; it was explained that Upton had gone away to sea.

DOCTOR JOYCE BROTHERS SYNDICATED
(CONSULT DR. BROTHERS) (TELL ME, DR. BROTHERS)
(LIVING EASY WITH DR. JOYCE BROTHERS)
1961; 1964; 1972 Doctor Joyce Brothers, the psychologist who was the first woman to win the top prize on *The $64,000 Question* (her category was boxing), hosted several syndicated series. The first two—*Consult Dr. Brothers* (1961) and *Tell Me, Dr. Brothers* (1964)—focused on human relationships; the third—*Living Easy with Dr. Joyce Brothers* (1972)—was basically a talk show, featuring celebrity guests.

DR. KILDARE NBC
28 SEPTEMBER 1961–30 AUGUST 1966 This popular medical series, like ABC's *Ben Casey,* enjoyed a five-year run. NBC sealed its doom in 1965 by breaking up the show into two half-hour segments. Richard Chamber-

lain starred as Dr. James Kildare, an intern at Blair General Hospital. Raymond Massey costarred as Dr. Leonard Gillespie, the paternal senior staff physician who guided him. Also featured were Jud Taylor as Dr. Gerson; Steven Bell (1965–1966) as Dr. Lowry; Lee Kurty (1965–1966) as Nurse Lawton; and Jean Inness (1965–1966) as Nurse Fain. Norman Felton was the executive producer of the series, which was produced at MGM studio. The *Doctor Kildare* short stories were written by Frederick Schiller Faust, who commonly used the pen name of Max Brand; the inspiration for the stories came from Dr. George Winthrop Fish (1895–1977), a prominent urologist. Several films were made, beginning in 1938, and a radio series appeared in 1939. A second TV series was made in 1972: see *Young Dr. Kildare*.

DOCTOR SIMON LOCKE SYNDICATED
1971 A half-hour medical drama, filmed in Canada. With Jack Albertson as Dr. Andrew Sellers, a general practitioner in the small town of Dixon Mills; Sam Groom as Dr. Simon Locke, the young associate who joined him in the practice; Nuala Fitzgerald as their housekeeper and nurse, Mrs. Louise Winn; and Len Birman as Dan Palmer, local police chief. After one season Doctor Locke left Dixon Mills for the big city: see *Police Surgeon*.

DR. SPOCK NBC
9 OCTOBER 1955–9 AUGUST 1956 Dr. Benjamin Spock, America's most famous pediatrician, advised parents on child care on this Sunday-afternoon series. The show was broadcast from KYW-TV in Cleveland; Spock taught at the Western Reserve University College of Medicine.

DR. WHO SYNDICATED
1970–1973 A popular children's fantasy in its home country, Great Britain, *Dr. Who* first became available in the United States in 1973. Though several actors have played the title role (including Peter Cushing), American audiences have seen only Jon Pertwee and Tom Baker as Dr. Who, a scientist who (like Captain Z-Ro of American TV) developed a machine capable of transporting him to any point in space or time; this useful invention enabled him to battle such creatures as the Daleks, the Cybermen, and the Kreals.

THE DOCTORS NBC
1 APRIL 1963– Created by Orin Tovrov, who wrote the radio serial *Ma Perkins* for many years, *The Doctors* has always been set in and around Hope Memorial Hospital. It began, however, not as a continuing drama but as a daily anthology series in which one of the show's four main characters was featured: Jock Gaynor as Dr. William Scott; Margot Moser as Dr. Elizabeth Hayes; Richard Roat as Dr. Jerry Chan-

dler; Fred J. Scollay as Sam Shafer, the chaplain. The series experimented briefly with a weekly anthology format later in 1963 before switching to its present format (a continuing serial with a large cast) early in 1964. In 1972 *The Doctors* became the first daytime serial to win an Emmy award; in recent years its producers have included Allen Potter, Joseph Stuart, and Jeff Young. Head writers have included Eileen Pollock and Robert Mason Pollock, Margaret DePriest, and Douglas Marland. When *The Doctors* changed formats in 1964 Richard Roat and Fred J. Scollay were retained for a time but were eventually written out as the new characters took over. Principal players in 1964 included: James Pritchett as Dr. Matt Powers, the head of Hope Memorial Hospital (Pritchett had appeared on the show in 1963, playing a corporate president in a single story), who was a widower as the new format got underway; Ann Williams as Dr. Maggie Fielding, who married Matt in 1968 (Ann Williams was replaced by Bethel Leslie in 1965, who was replaced by Lydia Bruce in 1969); Adam Kennedy as Brock Hayden, who was murdered; Ellen McRae (who later changed her name to Ellen Burstyn) as Dr. Kate Bartok; Elizabeth Hubbard as Dr. Althea Davis (Hubbard was replaced by Virginia Vestoff briefly in 1969 but returned to the role); Gerald O'Loughlin as Pete Banas, the hospital custodian; Karl Light as Dave Davis, Althea's ex-husband; Dorothy Blackburn as Nurse Brown; Katherine Meskill as Faith Collins; and Court Benson as Willard Walling. Additional players have included: Charles Braswell and Joseph Campanella as Alec Fielding, Maggie Fielding's first husband; Byron Sanders as Kurt Van Allen, Maggie's second husband; Harry Packwood, Peter Burnell, Michael Landrum, Armand Assante, and John Shearin as Dr. Mike Powers, Matt's son by his first marriage; Pamela Toll (1967–1970) as Liz Wilson, Mike's girlfriend; Morgan Sterne as Keith Wilson, Liz's father; Meg Myles as Harriet Wilson, Liz's mother; Julia Duffy as Penny Davis, daughter of Althea and Dave Davis (their other child, Buddy, died of spinal meningitis); Gerald Gordon as Dr. Nick Bellini, a brain surgeon who was briefly married to Althea Davis; Eileen Kearney and Jennifer Houlton as Greta Van Allen, daughter of Kurt and Maggie (Fielding) Van Allen, subsequently adopted by Matt Powers when he married Maggie; Terry Kiser (1967–1969) as Dr. John Rice; Nancy Donohue as nurse Nancy Bennett; James Shannon as Paul Bennett, Nancy's missing husband; Conrad Roberts as Dr. Simon Harris; Zeida Coles as Anna Ford; Ginger Gerlach as Julie Forrest, who died after a fall down the stairs (not long afterward, Ginger Gerlach died of a drug overdose); Carolee Campbell (1969–1976) and Jada Rowland (1976–   ) as nurse Carolee Simpson; Richard Higgs as Dr. Dan Allison, who married Carolee and later committed suicide, though he attempted to make it look like a murder; David O'Brien as Dr. Steve Aldrich, who was implicated in Dan Allison's death but later married Carolee in 1972; Laryssa Lauret as Dr. Karen Werner, Steve's lover, killed in a plane crash; Keith Blanchard and

Thor Fields as Erich Aldrich, illegitimate son of Steve and Karen; Bobby Hennessy, David Elliott, and Shawn Campbell as Billy Allison, son of Dan and Carolee; Patrick Horgan as psychiatrist Dr. John Morrison, who was murdered; Carol Pfander, Nancy Barrett, and Holly Peters as nurse Kathy Ryker, who committed suicide; Anna Stuart as lab technician Toni Ferra, who married Dr. Mike Powers; Nancy Franklin (who also wrote for the series) as Toni's mother, Barbara Ferra; Paul Henry Itkin as Dr. Vito McCray; Palmer Deane as Dr. Hank Iverson, a black physician; Marie Thomas as Lauri James, Hank's girlfriend; Katherine Squire as Carolee's mother, Emma Simpson; Sally Gracie as Martha Allen; Tara Baker and Bridget Breen as Stephanie Aldrich, daughter of Steve and Carolee; Meg Mundy as Mona Aldrich Croft, Steve Aldrich's mother; Glenn Corbett as Jason Aldrich; Geraldine Court as Dr. Ann Larimer, ex-wife of Steve Aldrich; Gil Gerard as Dr. Alan Stewart, Dr. Matt Powers's nephew; Mary Denham as Margo Stewart; Leslie Ann Ray as Stacy Wells; Lloyd Bremseth as Andy Anderson; Lauren White and Kathy Glass as Mary Jane (M. J.) Match; Alex Sheafe as lawyer Luke McAlister; Dino Narizzano as Dr. Kevin MacIntyre; Chandler Hill Harben as Dr. Rico Bellini; Jess Adams as Webb Sutherland; Thomas Connolly as Dr. Clifford DeSales; Edmund Lyndeck as Dr. Carl Hendryx; Toni Darnay as Vivian Hendryx; Anthony Cannon as Dr. Tom Barrett; Roni Dengel as Dawn Eddington; George Smith as Detective Ernie Cadman; Tammy McDonald as Iris Fonteyne; Matthew Tobin as Rex Everlee; Robert Coppes as Reverend Joe Turner; George Coe as Scott Conrad; Peter Lombard as Dr. Robert Wilson; Lois Smith as Eleanor Conrad; Fanny Spiess and Kathy Eckles as Wendy Conrad; Alan Koss as Alvin Ing; Dale Robinette as Dr. Gil Lawford; Paul Carr as Dr. Paul Sommers; Kathryn Harrold and Kathleen Turner as Nola Dancy Aldrich; Jonathan Hogan as Jerry Dancy; Frank Telfer as Luke Dancy; Elizabeth Lawrence as Virginia Dancy; Jonathan Frakes as Tom Carroll; Jason Matzner as Ricky Manero; Patronia Paley as Dr. Jesse Rawlings; Larry Weber as Barney Dancy; Pamela Lincoln as Doreen Aldrich; Philip English as Colin Wakefield; Melissa Sherman as Judy; Peggy Cass as Sweeney; Dorothy Fielding as Sara Dancy; Martin Shakar as Dr. Speer; John Downes as Michael Paul Powers; Jane Fleiss as Kim; John Newton as Dr. Cummings; Dorian LoPinto as Missy Roberts; Heywood Hale Broun as Cappy Randall; Patricia Hayling as Mrs. Chambers; Count Stovall as Hank Chambers.

THE DOCTORS AND THE NURSES
See THE NURSES

DOCTORS HOSPITAL   NBC
10 SEPTEMBER 1975–14 JANUARY 1976   Hour-long medical series set at Lowell Memorial Hospital. With George Peppard as Dr. Jake Goodwin,

chief of neurosurgery; Zohra Lampert as Dr. Noah Purcell; Victor Campos as Dr. Felipe Ortega; and Albert Paulsen as Dr. Janos Varga. Executive producer: Matthew Rapf. Produced by Jack Laird.

DOCTORS' PRIVATE LIVES   ABC
5 APRIL 1979–26 APRIL 1979   Four-week medical miniseries. With Ed Nelson as Dr. Michael Wise, chief of surgery; John Gavin as Dr. Jeff Latimer, head of the hospital cardiovascular unit; Randolph Powell as Dr. Rick Calder, a young surgeon; Phil Levien as Kenny Wise, Michael's son; Gwen Humble as med student Sheila Castle, a friend of Michael's; Eddie Benton as nurse Diane Curtis; William Smithers as Dr. Trilling; Elinor Donahue as Mona, Michael's ex-wife. James Henerson created the series; David Gerber was the executive producer, Matthew Rapf the producer.

DOG AND CAT   ABC
5 MARCH 1977–14 MAY 1977   Crime drama about a woman police officer assigned to work with a male officer who, at least initially, doubted her abilities. With Kim Basinger as Officer J. Z. Kane; Lou Antonio as Sergeant Jack Ramsey; and Matt Clark as Lieutenant Kipling. Walter Hill created the series; Lawrence Gordon was the executive producer.

DOLLAR A SECOND   DUMONT/NBC/ABC
20 SEPTEMBER 1953–14 JUNE 1954 (DUMONT); 4 JULY 1954–22 AUGUST 1954 (NBC); 1 OCTOBER 1954–24 JUNE 1955 (ABC); 5 JULY 1955–23 AUGUST 1955 (NBC); 2 SEPTEMBER 1955–31 AUGUST 1956 (ABC); 22 JUNE 1957–28 SEPTEMBER 1957 (NBC)   Jan Murray hosted this prime-time game show, which was not unlike *Truth or Consequences.* Contestants earned $1 for each second during which they could answer questions correctly; if they answered incorrectly or were interrupted by the host, they were required to perform a stunt. The show was based on a French radio program, *Cent Francs par Seconde,* created by Jean-Pierre Bloudeau.

THE $1.98 BEAUTY CONTEST   SYNDICATED
1978   This half-hour game show bears the unmistakable marks of a Chuck Barris Production. Hosted by comic Rip Taylor, it is similar to *The Gong Show;* three celebrity panelists watch a group of contestants compete—in talent and swimsuit segments—for the daily prize, $1.98 in cash and a tacky tiara.

DOLLY   SYNDICATED
1976–   A half hour of country and western music, hosted by Dolly Parton, one of the most popular country and western stars of the decade.

THE DOM DeLUISE SHOW CBS

1 MAY 1968–18 SEPTEMBER 1968   Comedian Dom DeLuise hosted this variety hour, a summer replacement for *The Jackie Gleason Show* (though it was televised in a different time slot). Regulars included Carol Arthur (Dom's wife), Marian Mercer, Bill McCutcheon, Paul Dooley, B. S. Pulley, the Gentry Brothers, Dick Lynn, the June Taylor Dancers, and the Sammy Spear Orchestra. Taped in Miami Beach, the show was produced by Ronnie Wayne.

DON ADAMS' SCREEN TEST SYNDICATED

1975   Half-hour game show on which preselected contestants acted out scenes from various motion pictures with celebrity partners. At the end of the show a guest judge (usually a producer or director) selected the best amateur, who was then promised a small role in an upcoming film or television series. Don Adams was host and executive producer. Producer: Marty Pasetta.

DON AMECHE PLAYHOUSE (DON'S MUSICAL PLAYHOUSE) ABC

5 JULY 1951–4 OCTOBER 1951   Half-hour musical comedy series hosted by Don Ameche; it replaced the very similar *Holiday Hotel* on Thursdays.

THE DON HO SHOW ABC

25 OCTOBER 1976–4 MARCH 1977   Half-hour daytime variety series broadcast from various sites in Hawaii and hosted by singer Don Ho.

DON KIRSHNER'S ROCK CONCERT SYNDICATED

1973–   Film clips of various rock-and-roll stars introduced by Don Kirshner, the music publisher and rock impresario responsible for the success of such groups as the Monkees and the Archies. Kirshner also served as executive producer of the series; it was produced by David Yarnell.

THE DON KNOTTS SHOW NBC

15 SEPTEMBER 1970–6 JULY 1971   After years as a supporting player on *The Steve Allen Show* and *The Andy Griffith Show,* Don Knotts took a stab at headlining a variety series. Also featured were Elaine Joyce, Frank Welker, John Dehner, Kenneth Mars, Eddy Carroll, Francis De-Sales, Mickey Deems, Brad Logan, Fay De Witt, Gary Burghoff, and Bob Williams and his dog, Louis. Executive producer: Nick Vanoff. Producer: Bill Harbach. Director: Norman Abbott.

DON McNEILL'S TV CLUB ABC

13 SEPTEMBER 1950–19 DECEMBER 1951

THE BREAKFAST CLUB ABC

22 FEBRUARY 1954–25 FEBRUARY 1955   Don McNeill hosted one of

America's longest-running radio shows: *The Breakfast Club* ran from 1933 to 1968. It was a spontaneous, low-key blend of music, interviews, comedy, and audience participation broadcast weekday mornings from Chicago. In 1950 McNeill brought his show to prime-time television, where it was titled *Don McNeill's TV Club.* Regulars included Fran Allison (of *Kukla, Fran and Ollie* fame), Johnny Desmond, Eileen Parker, Patsy Lee, Sam Cowling, and Eddie Ballantine and his orchestra. The show was produced by George M. Cahan and directed by Grover J. Allen. In 1954 McNeill again tried television, this time on weekday mornings. The show, called *The Breakfast Club,* was simulcast with the radio show.

THE DON RICKLES SHOW   ABC
27 SEPTEMBER 1968–31 JANUARY 1969   An ill-conceived half-hour series, part-game show and part-variety show. Host Don Rickles, known to most audiences strictly as an insult comic (his sobriquet, "The Merchant of Venom," was well deserved), spent most of the show trading insults with celebrity guests. Occasionally he found time to quiz—and insult—contestants from the studio audience. Rickles's considerable talents as a dramatic actor never surfaced on the series, unfortunately. Also featured was Pat McCormick, king-sized comic (and the show's head writer). The show was a Mark Goodson–Bill Todman Production.

THE DON RICKLES SHOW   CBS
14 JANUARY 1972–26 MAY 1972   Don Rickles's second series was a sitcom in which Rickles was cast as Don Robinson, a high-strung executive with Kingston, Cohen & Vanderpool, a New York advertising agency. With Louise Sorel as Barbara Robinson, Don's wife; Erin Moran as Janie, their daughter; Robert Hogan as Don's friend and coworker, Tyler Benedict; Joyce Van Patten as Jean Benedict, Tyler's wife and Barbara's best friend; Barry Gordon as Conrad Musk, aggressive young adman. Executive producer: Sheldon Leonard. Director: Hy Averback.

DONAHUE
See THE PHIL DONAHUE SHOW

THE DONALD O'CONNOR SHOW   NBC
9 OCTOBER 1954–10 SEPTEMBER 1955   This half-hour filmed variety series was seen biweekly, alternating with *The Jimmy Durante Show* on Saturdays. It was hosted by singer-dancer Donald O'Connor, who had earlier hosted *The Colgate Comedy Hour.*

THE DONALD O'CONNOR SHOW   SYNDICATED
1968   Donald O'Connor, the star of countless musical comedies during the 1940s and 1950s, made few appearances on TV after his earlier show

left the air in 1955. He returned briefly in 1968 to host this syndicated talk show.

THE DONNA FARGO SHOW   SYNDICATED
1978   Half-hour country-and-western music show hosted by singer Donna Fargo.

THE DONNA REED SHOW   ABC
24 SEPTEMBER 1958–3 SEPTEMBER 1966   One of the most wholesome sitcoms ever made, *The Donna Reed Show* barely escaped cancellation after its first season. It was moved to Thursdays in 1959, where it remained for seven more seasons; by the end of its run in 1966 it was ABC's third oldest prime-time series. Donna Reed, who won an Academy Award for her performance in *From Here to Eternity* (1955), starred as Donna Stone, all-American housewife and mother. Also featured were Carl Betz as her husband, Alex Stone, a small-town pediatrician; Shelley Fabares (1958–1963) as Mary, their teenage daughter; Paul Petersen as Jeff, their son (he was eleven when the show started and had been one of the original Mouseketeers on *The Mickey Mouse Club*). In 1963 Patty Petersen (Paul's real-life sister) joined the cast as Trisha, an orphan taken in by the Stones. Other regulars included Kathleen Freeman (1958–1960) as Mrs. Wilgus, their nosy neighbor; Harvey Grant as Jeff's pal, Philip; Darryl Richard as Jeff's friend, Smitty; Jimmy Hawkins as Scotty Simpson; Candy Moore (1964–1966) as Bebe Barnes, Jeff's girlfriend; Bob Crane (1963–1965) as Dr. Dave Kelsey, their neighbor; and Ann McCrea (1963–1966) as Midge Kelsey, Dave's wife and Donna's best friend. Both Shelley Fabares and Paul Petersen attempted to launch recording careers on the strength of their popularity; each had a hit or two (Fabares's "Johnny Angel," Petersen's "My Dad" and "She Can't Find Her Keys"), but neither approached the phenomenal success achieved by Rick Nelson of ABC's other long-running sitcom, *Ozzie and Harriet*. *The Donna Reed Show* was produced by Reed's husband, Tony Owen. Among the guest stars who made their first major TV appearances on the series were John Astin ("Mouse at Play," 5 October 1961), James Darren ("April Fool," 1 April 1959), and George Hamilton ("Have Fun," 4 February 1959). Margaret Dumont made a rare television appearance on the show ("Miss Lovelace Comes to Tea," 12 May 1959) as did Buster Keaton ("A Very Merry Christmas," 24 December 1958).

DONNY AND MARIE   ABC
23 JANUARY 1976–19 JANUARY 1979   The first variety hour hosted by a brother-and-sister team: Donny and Marie Osmond, two of the nine talented Osmond children. Both are excellent singers (she, "a little bit country," he, "a little bit rock and roll") as well as competent ice skaters; many routines were done on ice, and the dancing Ice Vanities were regu-

lar performers (the ice routines were dropped in the fall of 1978). Additional regulars included Jim Connell and Hank Garcia. The other Osmond siblings appeared frequently on the show (Donny had sung with his older brothers in the Osmonds). In the fall of 1977 designer Bob Mackie was hired to help dress up Marie's image and plans were undertaken to shift production of the series from Hollywood to Utah, the Osmonds' home state. Executive producer: Raymond Katz. Producers: Sid and Marty Krofft. See also *The Osmond Family Show.*

DON'T CALL ME CHARLIE   NBC
21 SEPTEMBER 1962–25 JANUARY 1963   Forgettable sitcom about an Iowa veterinarian who was drafted and ended up assigned to the Army in Paris. With Josh Peine as Private Judson McKay; John Hubbard as Colonel Charles ("Don't call me Charlie!") Barker; Alan Napier as General Steele; Cully Richards as Sergeant Wozniak; Arte Johnson as Corporal Lefkowitz; Louise Glenn as Selma; Linda Lawson as Pat; and Penny Santon as Madame Fatime.

THE DOODLES WEAVER SHOW   NBC
9 JUNE 1951–1 SEPTEMBER 1951   A half hour of sight gags, costumery, and sound effects hosted by Doodles Weaver and featuring Lois Weaver (his wife) and Red Marshall. Weaver, whose real first name was Winstead, was the brother of NBC executive Sylvester "Pat" Weaver, the creative genius responsible for such shows as *Today* and *Tonight.* This series was a summer replacement for *Your Show of Shows.*

THE DOOR WITH NO NAME   NBC
6 JULY 1951–17 AUGUST 1951   A summer replacement for *Big Story,* this half-hour spy show starred Grant Richards as an American intelligence agent, Doug Carter, and Melville Ruick as his boss. Westbrook Van Voorhis narrated the series. See also *Doorway to Danger.*

DOORWAY TO DANGER   NBC
4 JULY 1952–22 AUGUST 1952; 3 JULY 1953–28 AUGUST 1953   This half-hour spy series was twice a summer replacement for *Big Story.* It starred Roland Winters as secret agent John Randolph and Stacy Harris as agent Doug Carter. See also *The Door with No Name.*

DOORWAY TO FAME   DUMONT
7 MARCH 1949–4 JULY 1949   This half-hour dramatic anthology series was significant because of a technical innovation it utilized: the actors performed in front of a simple black backdrop, while a second camera was trained on miniature sets or on painted backdrops. The two images were then blended in the control room to create the desired illusion.

THE DORIS DAY SHOW   CBS

24 SEPTEMBER 1968–3 SEPTEMBER 1973   Doris Day was one of the few
film stars whose initial entry into television proved successful; her situation comedy lasted five seasons and weathered four formats. Doris Day
starred as Doris Martin in each of them. The first format found Doris, recently widowed, settling down on her uncle's farm with her two young
sons. It featured Denver Pyle (1968–1970) as her uncle, Buck Webb; Tod
Starke (1968–1971) as son Toby; Philip Brown (1968–1971) as son Billy;
James Hampton (1968–1969) as Leroy B. Simpson, Buck's handyman;
Fran Ryan (1968) as Aggie, the first housekeeper; Naomi Stevens (1969)
as Juanita, the second housekeeper. As the second season began, Doris
found work as an executive secretary for *Today's World* magazine. Pyle,
Starke, and Brown remained and new additions to the cast included
McLean Stevenson (1969–1971) as her boss, Michael Nicholson; Rose
Marie (1969–1971) as coworker Myrna Gibbons; Paul Smith (1969–
1971) as Ron Harvey, associate editor; Billy DeWolfe as fussy Willard
Jarvis, Doris's neighbor. For the third season, Doris left the farm (and
Denver Pyle left the series) and moved into an apartment over an Italian
restaurant; joining the series were Kaye Ballard (1970–1971) as Angie
Palucci and Bernie Kopell (1970–1971) as Louie Palucci, the proprietors
of the eatery. The fourth season saw the most dramatic change in format:
Doris became a swinging single. Gone were the kids, as well as Stevenson
and Marie. The final format lasted two seasons, longer than any of the
others. It featured John Dehner (1971–1973) as editor Sy Bennett and
Jackie Joseph (1971–1973) as his secretary, Jackie Parker (Doris had
finally become a reporter). Occasionally appearing was Peter Lawford as
her boyfriend, Dr. Peter Lawrence. Day's son, Terry Melcher, was executive producer of the series.

DOROTHY   CBS

8 AUGUST 1979–29 AUGUST 1979   A four-episode half-hour sitcom set
at the Hannah Huntley School for Girls. With Dorothy Loudon as the di-
vorced music and drama teacher, Dorothy Banks; Russell Nype as Mr.
Foley, the headmaster (and grandson of the founder); Priscilla Morrill as
Lorna Cathcart, the French teacher; Kenneth Gilman as T. Jack Landis,
the biology teacher; Linda Manz as fresh Frankie Sumter, a scholarship
student; Elissa Leeds as Cissy; Susan Brecht as Meredith; and Michele
Greene as Margo. Created by Nick Arnold, Madelyn Davis, and Bob
Carroll, Jr., *Dorothy* should not be confused with NBC's *The Facts of
Life*, another 1979 sitcom set at a girl's boarding school.

DO'S AND DONT'S   ABC

3 JULY 1952–18 SEPTEMBER 1952   Hints on safety were dispensed on
this half-hour public service series.

DOTTO CBS/NBC

Daytime: 6 JANUARY 1958–15 AUGUST 1958 (CBS); *Nighttime:* 1 JULY 1958–19 AUGUST 1958 (NBC) Jack Narz hosted this game show which, like the parlor game, required contestants to identify a figure outlined in dots; by answering questions correctly, contestants saw the lines connecting the dots. *Dotto* is probably better remembered as one of the first series implicated in the quiz show scandals. In August 1958, a standby contestant accidentally happened upon some notes left by another contestant; the notes contained the answers to the questions asked that day. The discovery led to an investigation of game shows by the New York District Attorney and precipitated the cancellation of several series, including *Dotto.*

THE DOTTY MACK SHOW DUMONT/ABC

16 FEBRUARY 1953–25 AUGUST 1953 (DUMONT); 3 SEPTEMBER 1953–3 SEPTEMBER 1956 (ABC) The regulars on this variety series, broadcast from Cincinnati, performed pantomime routines to popular recordings. Surprisingly, the show lasted three years. Assisting former model Dotty Mack were Colin Male and Bob Braun. The DuMont series was originally titled *Girl Alone.*

DOUBLE DARE CBS

13 DECEMBER 1976–29 APRIL 1977 Alex Trebek hosted this daytime game show on which two contestants sought to identify subjects from descriptive clues; the first contestant to identify the subject could then "dare" the opponent to identify the subject from subsequent clues. If the opponent then missed, the first contestant won extra money. The first contestant to win $500 faced "The Spoilers," a panel of three Ph.D.s. If two of the spoilers failed to identify a subject after four clues, the contestant was awarded $5,000. The show was a Mark Goodson–Bill Todman Production.

DOUBLE EXPOSURE CBS

13 MARCH 1961–29 SEPTEMBER 1961 Steve Dunne hosted this daytime game show on which contestants sought to identify a picture hidden beneath a large jigsaw puzzle.

THE DOUBLE LIFE OF HENRY PHYFE ABC

13 JANUARY 1966–1 SEPTEMBER 1966 This situation comedy—a midseason replacement for *O.K. Crackerby!*—was a pale imitation of *Get Smart.* Red Buttons, whose TV appearances had been infrequent since the cancellation of his own series in 1954, starred as Henry Phyfe, a bumbling accountant hired by American intelligence to impersonate a deceased enemy agent known as U-31. Also featured were Fred Clark as

Chief Hannahan, his immediate superior; Parley Baer as Mr. Hamble, Phyfe's boss at the accounting firm; Zeme North as Judy, Phyfe's girl-friend, who is unaware of his double life; and Marge Redmond as Phyfe's landlady, Florence.

DOUBLE OR NOTHING CBS/NBC
6 OCTOBER 1952–2 JULY 1954 (CBS); 5 JUNE 1953–3 JULY 1953 (NBC) One of the many game shows hosted by Bert Parks, *Double or Nothing* began on radio in 1940. Each show featured five contestants in a question-and-answer format; contestants jointly agreed whether to try to double their winnings on the "Double or Nothing" round, and split their earnings evenly. The CBS version was a daytime entry; the NBC version was a prime-time program.

DOUBLE PLAY SYNDICATED
1953 Sports personalities were interviewed by Leo Durocher and his then wife, Laraine Day, on this series.

DOUGH RE MI NBC
24 FEBRUARY 1958–30 DECEMBER 1960 Hosted by Gene Rayburn, this daytime game show was similar to *Name That Tune:* Contestants tried to identify songs after hearing a limited number of notes.

DOUGLAS FAIRBANKS PRESENTS SYNDICATED
1953–1956 Dramatic anthology series hosted by, and occasionally star-ring, Douglas Fairbanks, Jr. Buster Keaton's first dramatic appearance was on this show ("The Awakening"); Christopher Lee, star of countless British horror films, made his American TV debut in an episode entitled "Destination Milan." In some areas, the show was known by another ti-tle, such as the name of the sponsor; in New York, for example, the series was called *Rheingold Theatre.*

DOWN YOU GO DUMONT/CBS/ABC/NBC
30 MAY 1951–27 MAY 1955 (DUMONT); 18 JUNE 1955–3 SEPTEMBER 1955 (CBS); 15 SEPTEMBER 1955–14 JUNE 1956 (ABC); 16 JUNE 1956–8 SEPTEMBER 1956 (NBC) One of the few programs broadcast over all four commercial networks, *Down You Go* was a prime-time game show hosted by Dr. Bergen Evans. The game, played by a panel of celebrities, was similar to "Hangman." The object was to guess a mystery word or phrase. The panel was shown a row of blanks representing the number of letters in the secret word or phrase; panelists then took turns suggesting a letter of the alphabet. A panelist who suggested an incorrect letter was eliminated from the game. Among the many panelists who appeared over the years were Carmelita Pope, Toni Gilman, Robert Breen, Francis

Coughlin, Georgiann Johnson, William Williams, Patricia Cutts, and Arthur Treacher.

DRAGNET

NBC

16 DECEMBER 1951–6 SEPTEMBER 1959; 12 JANUARY 1967–10 SEPTEMBER 1970   One of the most famous (and often lampooned) crime shows in television history, *Dragnet* began on radio in 1949. It starred Jack Webb as Sergeant Joe Friday, a hard-working Los Angeles cop who seemed to have no personal life and no interests other than police work. Civil but not quite courteous (everyone was "ma'am" or "sir"), tireless but not quite overzealous ("It's my job. I'm a cop."), Friday pursued every lead, interviewed every witness ("Just the facts, ma'am"), and eventually apprehended the wrongdoer. Webb, who owned an interest in the series, directed most episodes, and also served as narrator, stressed realism in *Dragnet:* police jargon, paperwork, and intensive investigation characterized the show. Episodes were supposedly based on actual cases; as announcers Hal Gibney and (later) George Fenneman stated at the end of each show: "The story you have just seen is true. The names have been changed to protect the innocent." The emphasis on authenticity also characterized most of the shows which Webb later produced, such as *Adam-12* and *Emergency!*

When *Dragnet* came to TV in 1951, Barton Yarborough was featured as Friday's partner, Sergeant Ben Romero. Yarborough died after three episodes were filmed; for the rest of the first season Barney Phillips was seen as Friday's partner, Sergeant Ed Jacobs. In the fall of 1952 Ben Alexander (a former child star in several Cecil B. DeMille films) replaced Phillips as Friday's sidekick, Officer Frank Smith; Smith's character gave the show a touch of comic relief, offering counterpoint to Friday's matter-of-fact character. By the time *Dragnet* left the air in 1959, Friday and Smith had earned promotions to lieutenant and sergeant respectively.

Eight years later a new version of *Dragnet* returned to NBC as a midseason replacement for *The Hero.* It was titled *Dragnet '67* (and later *Dragnet '68,* etc.). Webb again starred as Sergeant Joe Friday (how he lost his former rank was never explained). Harry Morgan was featured as his partner, Officer Bill Gannon. Many of the shows dealt with topical issues, especially student dissidence and drug use. The show seemed a bit heavy-handed in its second incarnation but lasted two and a half seasons nevertheless. The little details that helped fashion *Dragnet*'s unique style will long be remembered: Walter Schumann's suspenseful theme, the epilog relating the fate of the evening's evildoers, and the chiseling of "Mark VII" (the name of Webb's production company) in stone at the show's conclusion.

DRAW ME A LAUGH

ABC

15 JANUARY 1949–5 FEBRUARY 1949   This short-lived series was part-

variety show and part-game show. The object of the game portion was for cartoonist Mel Casson, a regular, to sketch a cartoon from an idea submitted by a viewer. Simultaneously, a studio contestant attempted to sketch a cartoon, having been given the gag line of the cartoon. A panel then chose the funnier cartoon. The game portion was interspersed with music from folksinger Oscar Brand.

DRAW TO WIN   CBS
22 APRIL 1952–10 JUNE 1952   A Tuesday-night game show which briefly replaced *See It Now.* Henry Morgan hosted the series, on which a panel of four cartoonists tried to identify subjects drawn by home viewers.

DREAM GIRL OF '67   ABC
19 DECEMBER 1966–29 DECEMBER 1967   This daytime game show was a year-long beauty pageant. Each day four young women competed for the "Dream Girl of the Day" title. The four daily winners competed for the weekly title on Fridays; the weekly winners all competed at year's end. Dick Stewart hosted the series until September, when he was replaced by Paul Petersen (formerly of *The Donna Reed Show*).

DREAM HOUSE   ABC
Nighttime: 27 MARCH 1968–19 SEPTEMBER 1968; *Daytime:* 1 APRIL 1968–2 JANUARY 1970   Mike Darrow hosted this game show on which three couples competed in a question-and-answer format; the winning couple was awarded the furnishings for one room of a house. A couple that won seven rooms also won their "dream house": A home, valued at up to $40,000, would be built for them on the site of their choice.

THE DREW PEARSON SHOW   ABC/DUMONT
4 MAY 1952–9 NOVEMBER 1952 (ABC); 24 DECEMBER 1952—18 MARCH 1953 (DUMONT)   A half-hour of commentary by Washington political columnist Drew Pearson. See also *Washington Merry-Go-Round.*

DROODLES   NBC
21 JUNE 1954–24 SEPTEMBER 1954   Roger Price hosted this lighthearted game show on which celebrity panelists tried to think of captions for line drawings submitted by home viewers or sketched by Price himself. The panel included playwright Marc Connelly, Denise Lor, and Carl Reiner. The show was scheduled irregularly during the summer of 1954.

THE DUDLEY DO-RIGHT SHOW   ABC
27 APRIL 1969–6 SEPTEMBER 1970   Sunday-morning cartoon series featuring Dudley Do-Right, the inept Mountie who loved Nell Fenwick, daughter of Inspector Ray K. Fenwick, Dudley's boss. Alas, Dudley's

love was unrequited, for Nell was in love with Dudley's horse, Steed. Jay Ward's cartoon characters originally appeared on *The Bullwinkle Show.*

DUFFY'S TAVERN   SYNDICATED

1954   An unsuccessful attempt to bring a popular radio program to television. Ed Gardner created the series, which ran on radio from 1941 to 1951. Gardner starred as Archie, the manager of Duffy's Tavern, a seedy bar and grille on New York's Third Avenue; Duffy, the owner, was never seen. Also featured were Pattee Chapman as Miss Duffy, Duffy's husband-hunting daughter; Alan Reed as Archie's slow-witted comrade, Charlie Finnegan. The radio series had been as much a showcase for guest stars (such as Bing Crosby and Clifton Fadiman) as a situation comedy; the TV adaptation was merely the latter.

THE DUKE   NBC

2 JULY 1954–10 SEPTEMBER 1954   This summer sitcom had a fairly interesting story line: a boxer with a penchant for the arts suddenly quit the fight game to open a night club. With Paul Gilbert as Duke Zenlee; Allen Jenkins as Johnny, his former trainer; Phyllis Coates (formerly featured on *Superman*) as Gloria, his girlfriend; and Rudy Cromwell as Claude Stroud, his partner in the club.

THE DUKE   NBC

5 APRIL 1979–18 MAY 1979   Miniseries about an aging Chicago boxer who decided to become a private eye. With Robert Conrad (who actually fought professionally in his younger days) as Duke Ramsey; Larry Manetti as Joe Cadillac, a promoter of less than impeccable integrity; Red West as Sergeant Mick O'Brien; Patricia Conwell as Duke's friend, Dedra, a wealthy socialite. Stephen J. Cannell was the executive producer for Stephen J. Cannell Productions in association with Universal TV.

THE DUKES OF HAZZARD   CBS

26 JANUARY 1979–   Hour comedy-adventure series set in Hazzard County, somewhere in the South. With Tom Wopat as Luke Duke; John Schneider as Bo Duke; Catherine Bach as Daisy Duke (the three are cousins); Denver Pyle as wise Uncle Jesse; James Best as Sheriff Rosco Coltrane; Sorrell Booke as Jefferson Davis (Boss) Hogg, the corrupt politician who runs Hazzard County; and Sonny Shroyer as Enos Straight, Coltrane's deputy. Music and narration are supplied by Waylon Jennings. Executive producers: Paul R. Picard and Philip Mandelker for Warner Brothers TV.

THE DUMPLINGS   NBC

28 JANUARY 1976–31 MARCH 1976   One of Norman Lear's most forgettable ventures, this sitcom told the story of a happily married couple who

ran a luncheonette (Dudley's Take-Out) in a New York skyscraper. With James Coco as Joe Dumpling; Geraldine Brooks as Angela Dumpling; George S. Irving as Charles Sweetzer, executive vice president of the Bristol Oil Company, located upstairs; Jane Connell as Norah McKenna, Sweetzer's secretary; George Furth as Frederic Steele; Marcia Rodd as Stephanie, Angela's sister; and Mort Marshall as Cully, the Dumplings' employee. The show was produced by Don Nicholl, Michael Ross, and Bernie West.

DUNDEE AND THE CULHANE   CBS
6 SEPTEMBER 1967–13 DECEMBER 1967   The most interesting feature of this western was probably its title. It starred John Mills as Dundee, a British lawyer who roamed the West with a feisty young American lawyer, The Culhane (played by Sean Garrison). Mike Dann, chief of CBS programming during the 1960s, disclosed in a 1968 *TV Guide* interview that the network had decided to cancel the show before it premiered. Network officials had been pleased with the pilot, but were disappointed after reviewing the scripts for the next several episodes; the decision was made in September to replace it with *The Jonathan Winters Show* in December.

THE DUNNINGER SHOW   NBC/ABC
25 JUNE 1955–10 SEPTEMBER 1955 (NBC); 9 MAY 1956–10 OCTOBER 1956 (ABC)   Master mentalist Joseph Dunninger, who had cohosted *The Bigelow Show* with Paul Winchell some years earlier, hosted two summer shows on which he demonstrated his mind-reading prowess. A reward of $10,000 was offered each week to anyone who could prove that Dunninger was a fake; it was never claimed.

THE DuPONT SHOW STARRING JUNE ALLYSON
See THE JUNE ALLYSON SHOW

DuPONT THEATER   ABC
30 OCTOBER 1956–4 JUNE 1957
THE DuPONT SHOW OF THE MONTH   CBS
29 SEPTEMBER 1957–21 MARCH 1961
THE DuPONT SHOW OF THE WEEK   NBC
17 SEPTEMBER 1961–6 SEPTEMBER 1964   DuPont sponsored an anthology series on each of the three major commercial networks. The first, on ABC, ran for one season in a half-hour weekly format. The second, which lasted four seasons on CBS, was a series of ninety-minute monthly specials. Most of those presentations were of well known novels and plays, including: "A Tale of Two Cities," with Denham Elliott, Gracie Fields, and George C. Scott (in his first major TV role, 27 March 1958); "The Red Mill," with Harpo Marx, Mike Nichols and Elaine May, and

Donald O'Connor (19 April 1958); "Wuthering Heights," with Richard Burton (in his American TV dramatic debut, 9 May 1958); "The Count of Monte Cristo," with Colleen Dewhurst and Hurd Hatfield (28 October 1958); "The Browning Version," with Sir John Gielgud (in his American TV debut, 23 April 1959); "I, Don Quixote," with Lee J. Cobb (from which the musical, *Man of La Mancha,* was adapted, 9 November 1959); "Arrowsmith," with Diane Baker, Ivan Dixon, and Oscar Homolka (17 January 1960); and "Ethan Frome," with Sterling Hayden (18 February 1960). In 1961 DuPont switched its sponsorship to NBC and inaugurated a weekly hour-long format; most of the presentations on this series were dramatizations of real-life incidents, though some documentaries were also shown.

DUSTY'S TRAIL   SYNDICATED
1973   Abysmal sitcom about a Conestoga wagon separated from the rest of the train somewhere in the old West. With Bob Denver as Dusty, the bumbling scout; Forrest Tucker as Callahan, the bumbling wagonmaster; Ivor Francis as Carson Brookhaven, stuffy Bostonian passenger; Lynn Wood as Mrs. Brookhaven, his stuffy wife; Jeannine Riley as Lulu, an aspiring showgirl; Lori Saunders as Betsy, an aspiring schoolteacher (Riley and Saunders were both alumnae of *Petticoat Junction*); and Bill Cort as Andy, a regular guy. Produced by Sherwood Schwartz, the man responsible for Denver's previous venture, *Gilligan's Island.*

DUSTY'S TREEHOUSE   SYNDICATED
1976   Stu Rosen hosted this all-purpose children's show, which consisted of skits, songs, and demonstrations.

DYNOMUTT   ABC
15 JULY 1978–2 SEPTEMBER 1978   Dynomutt, the bionic dog introduced on *The Scooby-Doo/Dynomutt Hour* in 1976, had his own half-hour cartoon show for a few weeks in 1978.

E.S.P.   ABC
11 JULY 1958–22 AUGUST 1958   Vincent Price hosted this short-lived series, which explored the phenomenon of extrasensory perception. Guests related personal experiences and also participated in various tests calculated to demonstrate their putative abilities.

THE EARL WRIGHTSON SHOW
See THE MASLAND AT HOME SHOW

EARN YOUR VACATION   CBS
23 MAY 1954–5 SEPTEMBER 1954   On this prime-time game show contestants competed for the chance to win a vacation to the spot of their

choice. The show had been on radio in 1951. The host of the TV version was a twenty-seven-year old comedian who had had his own local show in Los Angeles: Johnny Carson.

EARTHLAB   SYNDICATED
1971   A science series for kids, hosted by Rex Trailer. Produced at WBZ-TV in Boston.

EAST SIDE, WEST SIDE   CBS
23 SEPTEMBER 1963–14 SEPTEMBER 1964   A dramatic series about social workers. Because of its treatment of many controversial issues, especially race relations, CBS was never able to sell the entire hour to sponsors, and the show barely lasted a season. Network executives were never enthusiastic about the series. A scene from one episode, which showed the white star (George S. Scott) dancing with a black woman, was deleted at network insistence. In retrospect, *East Side, West Side* was probably ahead of its time; TV audiences of 1963 just weren't ready for a hard-hitting series focusing on social problems, especially one in which most of the problems remained unsolved at the hour's end. The show starred George C. Scott as Neil Brock, social worker for the Community Welfare Service, a private agency located in Manhattan; Elizabeth Wilson as Frieda (Hecky) Hechlinger, his boss; Cicely Tyson as the secretary, Jane Porter (Tyson was the first black performer cast in a regular role on a noncomedy series and was also the first to feature an Afro hair style). In midseason the format was changed slightly but ratings failed to improve—Brock went to work for a New York Congressman; Linden Chiles appeared as Representative Hanson. David Susskind was the executive producer of the series, which was shot on location in New York.

EASY ACES   DUMONT
14 DECEMBER 1949–7 JUNE 1950   A television version of the popular radio comedy show which began in 1930. Goodman Ace and his wife, Jane Sherwood Ace, starred as themselves. Goodman Ace was one of radio's foremost comedy writers and later wrote for several television shows, including Milton Berle's *The Texaco Star Theater* and *The Perry Como Show.* Jane Ace was famous for her malaprops. Much of each fifteen-minute program was ad-libbed.

EASY DOES IT   CBS
25 AUGUST 1976–15 SEPTEMBER 1976   A four-week summer variety series starring Frankie Avalon, the Philadelphia rock-and-roller who catapulted to stardom in 1958 with such hits as "De De Dinah" and "Venus." Dick Clark, who had featured Avalon frequently on *American Bandstand,* was the executive producer of this half-hour effort. Avalon's

special guest star on the premiere was Annette Funicello, his costar in several "beach" films of the early 1960s.

ED ALLEN TIME
SYNDICATED
1964   Half-hour exercise show with Ed Allen and his dog, Alice.

THE ED NELSON SHOW
SYNDICATED
1969   A ninety-minute talk show hosted by actor Ed Nelson.

THE ED SULLIVAN SHOW (TOAST OF THE TOWN)
CBS
20 JUNE 1948–6 JUNE 1971   Television's longest-running variety show ran on Sunday nights for twenty-three years. Its host, Ed Sullivan, couldn't sing or dance, but he knew who could, and he signed them for his show. A syndicated newspaper columnist, Sullivan had hosted two radio shows before agreeing to try television in 1948. On camera Sullivan always seemed ill at ease; he regularly fluffed introductions, and his habit of wandering around the stage during the broadcasts was a continual challenge to the show's technical crew. Ironically, Sullivan's mannerisms probably helped launch the careers of many impressionists. Fortunately for those comics, Sullivan was not too vain to poke fun at himself; Frank Fontaine lampooned him as early as 1949. But when Sullivan shared the stage with the most accomplished Sullivan impersonator of all—Will Jordan—the effect was eerily hilarious.

The show began inauspiciously. Although eight acts appeared on the 1948 premiere, the total talent budget was only $475, with headliners Dean Martin and Jerry Lewis (making their TV debut) splitting $200; composers Richard Rodgers and Oscar Hammerstein 2nd also appeared on that broadcast. From the beginning, Ray Bloch and his orchestra provided the music; the June Taylor Dancers also began appearing regularly that summer. It was reported that during the early months of the series CBS offered the show to sponsors with or without Sullivan as emcee; fortunately for the network, none of the sponsors opted against "Old Stone Face," as Sullivan had been described by reviewers.

The format for the show was soon established and was changed very little during the next two decades. Sullivan tried to present something to please everyone each week. Thus a typical evening's fare might include an acrobatic act, a couple of comics, a recording star, an aria by an operatic performer, a film star plugging a new movie, and the introduction of a few notables "in our studio audience" by Sullivan. Occasionally an entire program would be devoted to a single event, such as a biography of playwright Josh Logan, or the appearance of the Moiseyev Dancers, a folk troupe from the Soviet Union. In 1959 Sullivan took a group of American performers to the USSR.

It would take a small book just to catalog the thousands of performers who appeared, ranging from Bob Hope (who made his East Coast TV debut on 26 September 1948) to Albert Schweitzer (filmed playing the organ at his African mission). Other notables who made their television debuts on *The Ed Sullivan Show* (it was officially titled *Toast of the Town* until 1955) were Irving Berlin (15 August 1948), Victor Borge (25 September 1949), Hedy Lamarr (17 September 1950), Walt Disney (8 February 1953), and Fred Astaire and Jane Powell (14 February 1954). Two acts, however, deserve special mention, for they attracted some of the largest television audiences of the time: Elvis Presley and the Beatles.

In the summer of 1956 Presley was signed for three appearances at the unheard-of fee of $50,000. The twenty-one-year-old recording artist had signed with RCA Records earlier that year, and his career was already skyrocketing by that time. For the record, Presley first appeared on 9 September 1956 and performed "Don't Be Cruel," "Love Me Tender," "Reddy Teddy," and "Hound Dog." Charles Laughton was the substitute host that evening. On 28 October, Presley again appeared, singing "Don't Be Cruel," "Love Me Tender," "Love Me," and "Hound Dog." Presley's final appearance was 6 January 1957, when he performed seven numbers: "Hound Dog," "Love Me Tender," "Heartbreak Hotel," "Don't Be Cruel," "Peace in the Valley," "Too Much," and "When My Blue Moon Turns to Gold Again." Two popular misconceptions about the Presley appearances should be dispelled. First, Presley did not make his TV debut on Sullivan's show—he had appeared several times on the Dorsey Brothers' *Stage Show,* as well as on *The Milton Berle Show* and *The Steve Allen Show* (it was reported that Sullivan signed Presley after noting the ratings from his appearance on the Allen show; this act exacerbated the feud between the two men, whose shows were in direct competition with one another). Second, Presley was not photographed only from the waist up; his "lascivious" posturings (which had been the subject of a *TV Guide* editorial during the week of 7 July 1956) were seen in full on the first two Sullivan shows. It was only for the third show, after much furor, that the decision was made to photograph Presley in tight close-ups. After the third appearance, Presley had had enough of television. By that time his film career had begun to look promising, and, except for a brief appearance on a Frank Sinatra special in May 1960, eleven years would pass before he again appeared on TV.

In the fall of 1963 Sullivan signed the Beatles for two appearances for $25,000. At that time the group was a sensation in England and was gaining a sizable reputation throughout Europe. Their first American singles, however, had gone nowhere. By the time of their first appearance on the Sullivan show, all that had changed, thanks in large part to a publicity blitz by Capitol Records. On 9 February 1964 most Americans saw the quartet for the first time (Jack Paar had shown film clips of them on 3 January, and they had also been covered by the network news) as they performed "All My Loving," "She Loves You," "This Boy," and "Till

There Was You." Beatlemania was officially under way on this side of the ocean. After concerts in New York and Washington, they returned a week later to perform six songs. The Beatles' appearances opened the floodgates for a torrent of British rock groups; more important, rock acts became a regular feature of the show for the remainder of its run.

One of the few musical giants of the 1960s who did not appear was Bob Dylan, but not because he wasn't asked. Dylan had been signed for an appearance in 1963 and indicated he intended to perform "Talkin' John Birch Society Blues," a humorous number about a man who begins to look for Communists everywhere. Reportedly Sullivan liked the song when he heard it during rehearsal and voiced no objection. He subsequently informed Dylan that the network brass, fearful of a lawsuit, had vetoed the number. Dylan understandably refused to compromise and declined to appear on the program.

Sullivan's ratings, which had remained fairly steady during the 1950s and 1960s, began to slip in 1968, as *The F.B.I.* and *Walt Disney* made inroads. In 1971 his show was canceled as part of CBS's attempt to acquire a new image as the network for youthful audiences. Sullivan, who had co-produced the show (first with Marlo Lewis, later with his son-in-law, Bob Precht), appeared in a few specials and also hosted one episode of *The ABC Comedy Hour (The Kopykats)*. He died in 1974.

THE ED WYNN SHOW   CBS
6 OCTOBER 1949–4 JULY 1950   CBS's first Los Angeles-based variety show starred Ed Wynn, a trouper who began his career in vaudeville in 1904 and appeared on radio as early as 1922, where he starred in such comedy series as *The Perfect Fool* and *The Fire Chief*. Wynn's guests on television included Leon Errol, Charles Laughton, Andy Devine, and Dinah Shore. Produced by Harlan Thompson and directed by Ralph Levy, the show was seen via kinescopes on the East Coast.

THE ED WYNN SHOW   NBC
25 SEPTEMBER 1958–1 JANUARY 1959   During the mid-1950s Ed Wynn was not often seen on television; he made a triumphant return in 1956, however, on *Playhouse 90*'s "Requiem for a Heavyweight." That performance established him, after fifty years in show business, as a character actor. In this half-hour sitcom he starred as John Beamer, a retired man trying to raise two granddaughters in a small college town. Also featured were Jacklyn O'Donnell as granddaughter Laurie; Sherry Alberoni as granddaughter Midge; and Herb Vigran as Beamer's friend, lawyer Ernie Hinshaw. Ben Feiner, Jr., produced the series and William Russell directed it.

THE EDDIE ALBERT SHOW   CBS
2 MARCH 1953–8 MAY 1953   For nine weeks in 1953 Eddie Albert host-

ed his own half-hour daytime variety show. Also featured were Ellen Hanley and Norman Paris' band.

THE EDDIE CANTOR COMEDY THEATER   SYNDICATED
1955   An anthology series that sometimes featured variety acts and sometimes presented half-hour comedies. Eddie Cantor was the host and occasional star.

THE EDDIE CAPRA MYSTERIES   NBC
8 SEPTEMBER 1978–12 JANUARY 1979   A typical crime show starring Vincent Baggetta as lawyer-sleuth Eddie Capra. With Ken Swofford as his senior partner, J. J. Devlin; Wendy Phillips as his friend and secretary, Lacey Brown; Michael Horton as Capra's junior investigator, Harvey Winchell; and Seven Ann McDonald as Lacey's young daughter, Jennie. Peter S. Fischer was executive producer, James McAdams producer for Universal TV.

THE EDDIE FISHER SHOW   NBC
1 OCTOBER 1957–17 MARCH 1959   After *Coke Time* left the air in February of 1957, Eddie Fisher returned as host of an hour-long variety series that alternated biweekly with *The George Gobel Show*. During the 1957–1958 season Gobel was "permanent guest star" on Fisher's show, and Fisher reciprocated on Gobel's program. Debbie Reynolds, Fisher's wife at the time, also appeared occasionally. Music was provided by the Buddy Bregman Orchestra. Fisher's theme song was "As Long As There's Music," by Sammy Kahn and Jule Styne.

THE EDDY ARNOLD SHOW   CBS/NBC/SYNDICATED/ABC
14 JULY 1952–22 AUGUST 1952 (CBS); 7 JULY 1953–1 OCTOBER 1953 (NBC); 1954–1956 (SYNDICATED); 26 APRIL 1956–26 SEPTEMBER 1956 (ABC)   A popular country-and-western singer for several decades, Eddy Arnold made his television debut on Milton Berle's *Texaco Star Theater* in 1949. In 1952 he hosted the first of his several TV series, a summer replacement for *The Perry Como Show* on CBS which was seen three nights a week after the news. In the summer of 1953 he substituted for Dinah Shore twice a week on NBC. A year later he began a syndicated show, *Eddy Arnold Time,* which originated from Springfield, Missouri. Produced and directed by Ben Park, it featured Betty Johnson, the Gordonaires, Hank Garland, and Roy Wiggins. In 1956 he hosted a live half-hour series on ABC, which featured the Paul Mitchell Quartet and guitarist Chet Atkins.

EDGAR WALLACE MYSTERIES   SYNDICATED
1963   Edgar Wallace, the prolific thriller writer, journalist, and play-

wright, produced and introduced the episodes of this hour-long anthology series.

THE EDGE OF NIGHT CBS/ABC
2 APRIL 1956–28 NOVEMBER 1975 (CBS); 1 DECEMBER 1975–
(ABC) CBS introduced television's first thirty-minute daytime serials, *As the World Turns* and *The Edge of Night,* on the same day; both have proved extremely successful. *The Edge of Night,* so titled because of its late afternoon (4:30 p.m., originally) time slot, was created by Irving Vendig, and, for the first few years, emphasized crime stories and courtroom drama; gradually, however, its story lines have drifted away from crime toward the romantic and sexual themes common to most soap operas. The show's time slot has drifted as well since 1963, when it was first shifted back an hour. In 1975, after two or three years of declining ratings on CBS, *The Edge of Night* became the first daytime serial to shift networks. The show was produced for Procter and Gamble, first by Don Wallace, later by Charles Fisher, and currently by Erwin Nicholson; Henry Slesar is the head writer. Principal players over the past two decades have included: John Larkin (1956–1962; Larkin had previously played *Perry Mason* on radio), Larry Hugo (1962–1971), and Forrest Compton (1971–   ) as lawyer Mike Karr (Karr was an assistant district attorney in Monticello, the town where *Edge* is set, when the show began, but later went into private practice); Teal Ames (1956–1961) as Sarah Lane, who married Mike and was killed in 1961 while saving the life of their daughter; Don Hastings (1956–1960) as Jack Lane, Sarah's brother; Mary Alice Moore as Betty Jean Lane, Jack's wife; Betty Garde and Peggy Allenby as Mattie Lane, Sarah and Jack's mother; Walter Greaza as Winston Grimsley, a widower who married Mattie; Carl Frank and Mandel Kramer as Bill Marceau, Monticello's police chief; Joan Harvey as Judy Marceau, Bill's daughter; Teri Keane (1965–1975) as Martha, Bill's secretary and eventual wife; Heidi Vaughn and Johanna Leister as Phoebe Smith, a troubled teenager adopted by Bill and Martha; Ann Flood (1962–   ) as Nancy Pollock, who became Mike Karr's second wife on 22 April 1963; Ronnie Welch, Sam Groom, and Tony Roberts as Lee Pollock, Nancy's brother; Fran Sharon as Cookie Pollock, Nancy's sister; Ed Kemmer as Malcolm Thomas, who married Cookie and was later murdered; Burt Douglas as Ron Christopher, Cookie's next husband; John Gibson and Allen Nourse as Joe Pollock, Nancy's father; Kay Campbell and Virginia Kaye as Rose Pollock, Nancy's mother; Millette Alexander as Gail Armstrong, Laura Hillyer, and Julie Jamison (Alexander played the three roles at different times—Gail Armstrong was a commercial artist, Laura Hillyer was killed in a car crash, and Julie Jamison was Laura's lookalike, who showed up shortly after Laura's death); Wesley Addy as Hugh Campbell; Ed Holmes as Detective Willie

Bryan; Larry Hagman as lawyer Ed Gibson; Karen Thorsell as Margie Gibson, Ed's sister; Maxine Stuart as Grace O'Leary; Ray MacDonnell as Phil Capice; Mary K. Wells as Louise Capice, Phil's wife, daughter of Winston Grimsley; Conrad Fowkes as Steve Prentiss; Liz Hubbard as Carol Kramer; Val Dufour as André Lazar; Lauren Gilbert as Harry Lane; Lester Rawlins as Orin Hillyer (who was married first to Laura Hillyer, and then to Julie Jamison; both roles were played by the afore-mentioned Millette Alexander); Alberta Grant as Liz Hillyer, Orin's daughter; Millee Taggart as Gerry McGrath, who married Pollock; Keith Charles as disc jockey Rick Oliver, who was murdered by Laura Hillyer; Barry Newman as lawyer John Barnes, a young associate of Mike Karr's; Donald May (1967–1977) as Adam Drake, Mike Karr's law partner; Maeve McGuire and Jayne Bentzen as Nicole Travis, who mar-ried Drake in 1973; Bibi Besch as Susan Forbes, Nicole's onetime partner in a dress shop; William Prince and Cec Linder as Nicole's father, Ben Travis, a crook; Alice Hirson as murder victim Stephanie Martin; Irene Dailey as Pamela Stewart; Richard Clarke as Duane Stewart; Alan Fein-stein as Dr. Jim Fields, who married Liz Hillyer; Emily Prager, Jeannie Ruskin, and Linda Cook as Laurie Ann Karr, daughter of Mike and Sarah Karr; Ted Tinling as Vic Lamont, Laurie's first husband; John La-Gioia as nightclub owner Johnny Dallas, Laurie's second husband; Pat Conwell as Tracey Dallas, Johnny's sister; Alan Gifford as former sena-tor Gordon Whitney; Lois Kibbee as his wife, Geraldine Whitney; An-thony Call as their son Collin Whitney; Lucy Martin as Collin's wife, Tiffany; Bruce Martin as Gordon and Geraldine's other son, Keith Whit-ney (a split personality, Keith was also known as Jonah Lockwood); George Hall as John, the Whitney butler; Mary Hayden as Trudy, the Whitney maid; Hugh Reilly as Simon Jessup; Fred Scollay as Lobo Haines; Francine Beers as Nurse Hubbell; Jay Gregory as Morlock; Eliz-abeth Farley as Kate Reynolds; Nick Pryor and Paul Henry Itkin as Joel Gantry; Ward Costello as Jake Berman; Dorothy Lyman as Elly Jo Ja-mison; Dick Schoberg and John Driver as Kevin Jamison; Dixie Carter as Assistant District Attorney Brandy Henderson; Michael Stroka as Brandy's brother, Dr. Quentin Henderson; Lou Criscuolo as Danny Mi-celli, who married Tracey Dallas; Louise Shaffer as Nicole Travis's cous-in, Serena Faraday (another split personality, Serena was also known as Josie); Doug McKeon as Serena's son, Timmy; Dick Latessa as Noel Douglas; Niles McMaster as Dr. Clay Jordan; Brooks Rogers as Dr. Hugh Lacey; Helena Carroll as Molly O'Connor; Herb Davis as Lieuten-ant Luke Chandler; and Tony Craig as Draper Scott.

Recent additions to the cast have included: Juanin Clay and Sharon Gabet as Raven Alexander Jamison; Louis Turrene as Tony Saxon; Frances Fisher as Deborah Saxon; Denny Albee as Steve Guthrie; Polly Adams as Carol Barclay; Joel Crothers as Miles Cavanaugh; Holland Taylor (1977–1978) as Denise Cavanaugh; Terry Davis as April Cavanaugh Scott; Robin Groves as Maggie; Joe Lambie as Logan Swift; Irving Lee as Calvin Stoner; Kiel Martin as Raney Cooper; Marilyn Randall as Theresa; Dick Callinan as Ray Harper; Micki Grant as Ada Chandler; Dennis Marino as Packy Dietrich; Gwynn Press as Inez Johnson; Dorothy Stinette as Nadine Scott; Eileen Finley as Joannie Collier; Lee Godart as Elliot Dorn; Dan Hamilton as Wade Meecham; Michael Longfield as Tank Jarvis; Ann Williams as Margo Huntington; Susan Yusen as Diana Selkirk; Lori Cardille as Winter Austen; Mel Cobb as Ben Everett; and Wyman Pendleton as Dr. Norwood.

THE EDIE ADAMS SHOW
See HERE'S EDIE

EDITOR'S CHOICE   ABC
18 JUNE 1961–24 SEPTEMBER 1961   Sunday-night public affairs show on which host Fendall Yerxa and others interviewed newsmakers.

EDWARD ARNOLD THEATER   SYNDICATED
1954   Half-hour dramatic anthology series hosted by portly character actor Edward Arnold.

EDWARD THE KING   SYNDICATED
1979   A thirteen-part miniseries based on the life of Edward VII, the son and successor of Queen Victoria. Produced in England in 1975, the American versions of the hour programs were hosted by Robert MacNeil and sponsored by Mobil Oil. With Charles Sturridge and Timothy West as the teenage and adult Edward; Annette Crosbie as Victoria; Robert Hardy as Prince Albert, Edward's father; Deborah Grant and Helen Ryan as Alexandra, Edward's Danish wife; and John Gielgud as Benjamin Disraeli.

EDWIN NEWMAN REPORTING   NBC
5 JUNE 1960–4 SEPTEMBER 1960   Also titled *Time: Present*, this half-hour Sunday series was hosted by Edwin Newman, who was then NBC's Paris correspondent. Newman was subsequently featured on the *Today* show.

THE EGG AND I   CBS
3 SEPTEMBER 1951–1 AUGUST 1952   Television's first comedy serial, *The Egg and I* told the story of a young woman from New York City who married a chicken farmer from upstate. It was based on Betty MacDonald's book, which had been made into a movie in 1947 starring Claudette Colbert. The fifteen-minute series ran five days a week at noon and

starred Pat Kirkland as Betty MacDonald and John Craven as Bob Mac-Donald.

EIGHT IS ENOUGH
ABC

15 MARCH 1977–   A comedy-drama from the producers of *The Waltons, Eight Is Enough* is based on the autobiography of Washington columnist Tom Braden. Set in Sacramento, the hour series stars Dick Van Patten as Tom Bradford, a columnist for the Sacramento *Register.* Diana Hyland costarred as his wife, Joan Bradford; Hyland died of cancer in 1977 after five shows had been filmed, and the series continued with Tom as a widower. The eight Bradford children are played by: Grant Goodeve as David; Lani O'Grady as Mary; Laurie Walters as Joannie; Susan Richardson as Susan; Dianne Kay as Nancy; Willie Aames as Tommy; Connie Newton as Elizabeth; and Adam Rich as Nicholas. In the fall of 1977 Betty Buckley joined the cast as Abby Abbott, a widow hired as a tutor; Abby and Tom were married on 9 November. In the fall of 1979 a double wedding was celebrated: David married Janet McArthur (played by Joan Prather) and Susan married minor-league baseball pitcher Merle Stockwell (played by Brian Patrick Clarke). Also featured are Jennifer Darling as Tom's secretary, Donna; Michael Thoma as Dr. Maxwell; and Virginia Vincent as Daisy Maxwell. Lee Rich and Philip Capice created the series and serve as its executive producers for Lorimar Productions.

EIGHTH MAN
SYNDICATED

1965   Japanese cartoon series about *Tobor the Eighth Man,* a robot imbued with the spirit of Peter Brady, a slain police officer.

87TH PRECINCT
NBC

25 SEPTEMBER 1961–10 SEPTEMBER 1962 Standard New York cop show. With Robert Lansing as Detective Steve Carella; Norman Fell as Detective Meyer Meyer; Gregory Wolcott as Detective Roger Havilland; Ron Harper as Detective Bert Kling; and Gena Rowlands was occasionally featured as Carella's wife, Teddy, a deaf-mute. Executive producer: Hubbell Robinson. The characters were based on those created by Ed McBain.

EISCHIED
NBC

21 SEPTEMBER 1979–27 JANUARY 1980 Hour crime show starring Joe Don Baker as Earl Eischied, the unorthodox chief of detectives of the New York City Police Department, with Alan Oppenheimer as Finnerty; Alan Fudge as Kimbrough; Eddie Egan (a former cop in real life) as Chief Ed Parks; Suzanne Lederer as Carol Wright; Vincent Bufano as Alessi; Joe Cirillo as Malfitano; and Waldo Kitty as P. C., Eischied's cat.

The executive producer was David Gerber for David Gerber Productions and Columbia Pictures TV.

ELDER MICHAUX   DUMONT
17 OCTOBER 1948–9 JANUARY 1949   Probably the first black evangelist to appear regularly on network television, Solomon Lightfoot Michaux hosted his own half-hour religious show, which was broadcast from Washington, D.C.

THE ELECTRIC COMPANY   PBS
1971–1976   Aimed principally at seven- to ten-year-olds, *The Electric Company* emphasized the development of reading skills. Produced by the Children's Television Workshop, its format was similar to that of *Sesame Street,* CTW's notable series for preschoolers. Regulars included Bill Cosby, Rita Moreno, Lee Chamberlin, Jim Boyd, Morgan Freeman, Hattie Winston, Luis Avalos, Judy Graubart, Skip Hinnant, and Danny Seagren.

ELECTRIC IMPRESSIONS   SYNDICATED
1971   Half-hour variety series for young people, hosted by Ron Majers. Syndicated by Westinghouse.

THE ELEVENTH HOUR   NBC
3 OCTOBER 1962–9 SEPTEMBER 1964   NBC followed up its 1961 smash, *Dr. Kildare,* with a second medical series that focused on mental problems. It starred Wendell Corey (1962–1963) as Dr. Theodore Bassett, a court-appointed psychiatrist, and Jack Ging as Dr. Paul Graham, a clinical psychologist. In the fall of 1963 Corey was replaced by Ralph Bellamy, who played psychiatrist Dr. Richard Starke. Norman Felton was the executive producer for MGM.

THE ELGIN HOUR   ABC
5 OCTOBER 1954–14 JUNE 1955   This undistinguished hour-long dramatic anthology series alternated on Tuesdays with *The U.S. Steel Hour.* The premiere telecast, "Flood," starred Robert Cummings and Dorothy Gish.

ELLERY QUEEN   DUMONT/ABC/SYNDICATED/NBC
19 OCTOBER 1950–6 DECEMBER 1951 (DUMONT); 16 DECEMBER 1951–26 NOVEMBER 1952 (ABC); 1954 (SYNDICATED); 26 SEPTEMBER 1958–4 SEPTEMBER 1959 (NBC); 11 SEPTEMBER 1975–19 SEPTEMBER 1976 (NBC)   Ellery Queen, the fictional detective created by two cousins, Frederic Dannay and Manfred Lee, has been played by six actors in five television series. Each series employed the device of having Queen

address the home audience at the show's climax, to see if they had been as skillful as he in identifying the real murderer. The first effort—*The Adventures of Ellery Queen*—was seen originally on the DuMont network and later switched to ABC. Richard Hart was TV's first *Ellery Queen;* he was succeeded in 1951 by Lee Bowman. The 1954 version starred Hugh Marlowe, who had played the part on radio. Florenz Ames was also featured in the first three versions as Ellery's father, Inspector Richard Queen of the New York Police Department. Irving and Norman Pincus produced the half-hour series. In the fall of 1958 the character returned in a sixty-minute format, *The Further Adventures of Ellery Queen;* it lasted one season. George Nader played Ellery Queen until March 1959, when he was replaced by Lee Philips. Televised in color, the show was originally broadcast live from Hollywood and later became one of the first dramatic series to be videotaped. In 1975 NBC revived the character again; the new series, entitled simply *Ellery Queen*, was set in 1947, and the cast included: Jim Hutton as Ellery Queen; David Wayne as his father, Inspector Richard Queen; Tom Reese as Sergeant Velie; John Hillerman as criminologist Simon Brimmer; and Ken Swofford as reporter Frank "Front Page" Flannigan. The 1975 edition was produced by Peter S. Fischer and Michael Rhodes; Richard Levinson and William Link were the executive producers.

EMERGENCY! NBC

22 JANUARY 1972–3 SEPTEMBER 1977   When this series was introduced as a midseason replacement for *The Partners* and *The Good Life,* few people would have predicted that it could withstand the competition from CBS's *All in the Family. Emergency!* lasted, however, because it appealed to a different audience; for several seasons it was the most popular primetime program among viewers aged two to eleven. It was a fast-moving show which depicted the efforts of a team of paramedics assigned to Squad 51 of the Los Angeles County Fire Department; the paramedical team was also associated with nearby Ramparts General Hospital. With Robert Fuller as Dr. Kelly Brackett of the hospital staff; Bobby Troup as Dr. Joe Early of the hospital staff; Julie London (Bobby Troup's wife) as Nurse Dixie McCall; Randolph Mantooth as paramedic John Gage; Kevin Tighe as paramedic Roy DeSoto; Dick Hammer as Captain Henderson; Mike Stoker as fireman-engineer Stoker; Tim Donnelly as fireman Chet Kelly; Marco Lopez as fireman Marco Lopez; Michael Norrell as Captain Stanley; Ron Pinkard as Dr. Morton; and Deidre Hall as Sally. Executive producer: Robert A. Cinader for Jack Webb's Mark VII Productions. On 31 December 1978 a two-hour *Emergency!* was aired on NBC, which consisted mainly of flashbacks.

EMERGENCY + 4 NBC

8 SEPTEMBER 1973–4 SEPTEMBER 1976   Saturday-morning cartoon se-

ries based on *Emergency!* Paramedics DeSoto and Gage from the prime-time series were assisted by four kids: Sally, Randy, Jason, and Matt. The third season consisted entirely of reruns. Produced by Fred Calvert.

EMPIRE (REDIGO)
NBC/ABC

25 SEPTEMBER 1962–31 DECEMBER 1963 (NBC); 22 MARCH 1964–6 SEPTEMBER 1964 (ABC) *Empire* was an hour-long dramatic series set in modern New Mexico. It featured Richard Egan as Jim Redigo, foreman of the Garrett ranch; Anne Seymour as Lucia Garrett, the owner; Terry Moore as her daughter, Connie; Ryan O'Neal as her son, Tal; Warren Vanders as Chuck Davis; Charles Bronson joined the cast in February 1963 as ranch hand Paul Moreno. In the fall of 1963 the format was changed, shortened to a half hour, and retitled *Redigo*. Egan remained as Jim Redigo, who now owned his own spread. The rest of the *Empire* cast was jettisoned; the new regulars included Roger Davis as ranch hand Mike; Rudy Solari as ranch hand Frank; and Elena Verdugo as Gerry, assistant manager of the local hotel. In 1964 ABC reran some of the *Empire* episodes.

ENCOUNTER
ABC

5 OCTOBER 1958–2 NOVEMBER 1958 *Encounter* was an experimental dramatic anthology series; broadcast live from Toronto, the hour-long show was also carried by the Canadian Broadcasting Corporation.

THE END OF THE RAINBOW
NBC

11 JANUARY 1958–15 FEBRUARY 1958 Bob Barker hosted this Saturday-night game show on which contestants were given the chance to realize a lifetime ambition. The short-lived series was a midseason replacement for another game show, *What's It For?*

THE ENGELBERT HUMPERDINCK SHOW
ABC

21 JANUARY 1970–19 SEPTEMBER 1970 An hour-long variety series taped in London and hosted by British pop star Engelbert Humperdinck. Known previously by his real name—Arnold Dorsey—he had enjoyed little success until his manager, Gordon Mills, decided on the name change (the real Engelbert Humperdinck was a nineteenth-century German composer). In 1967, Humperdinck was voted Show Business Personality of the Year in Great Britain.

ENSIGN O'TOOLE
NBC

23 SEPTEMBER 1962–15 SEPTEMBER 1963 Military sitcom, set aboard the destroyer *Appleby* in the Pacific. With Dean Jones as easygoing Ensign O'Toole; Jay C. Flippen as cantankerous Captain Homer Nelson; Jack Albertson as Lieutenant Commander Stoner; Jack Mullaney as Lieutenant Rex St. John; Harvey Lembeck as Seaman DiJulio; Beau

Bridges as Seaman Spicer; and Robert Sorrells as Seaman White. Hy Averback produced and directed for Four Star Films.

ENTERPRISE U.S.A. ABC

19 OCTOBER 1952–8 MARCH 1953; 6 OCTOBER 1954–26 JANUARY 1955 A series of half-hour documentaries on American industry, produced by ABC News and Public Affairs. Though *Enterprise U.S.A.* was a network offering, ABC's New York affiliate did not carry it regularly. The series popped up later on ABC's schedule as a "filler" program.

THE ENTERTAINERS CBS

25 SEPTEMBER 1964–27 MARCH 1965 An unsuccessful variety series. Originally, the idea was to have three rotating hosts: Carol Burnett, Bob Newhart, and Caterina Valente. After the first few weeks, however, the three cohosts usually appeared together. Other regulars included Dom DeLuise, John Davidson, Ruth Buzzi, Don Crichton, and columnist Art Buchwald.

THE ERN WESTMORE SHOW SYNDICATED/ABC

1953 (SYNDICATED); 7 AUGUST 1955–11 SEPTEMBER 1955 (ABC) Advice on make-up for women from beauty consultant Ern Westmore. Westmore's wife, Betty, also appeared on the series, which was seen Sundays over ABC.

ERNIE KOVACS NBC/CBS

14 MAY 1951–29 JUNE 1951 (NBC); 2 JULY 1951–24 AUGUST 1951 (NBC); 4 JANUARY 1952–28 MARCH 1952 (NBC); 30 DECEMBER 1952–14 APRIL 1953 (CBS); 12 DECEMBER 1955–27 JULY 1956 (NBC); 2 JULY 1956–10 SEPTEMBER 1956 (NBC) A brilliant and iconoclastic comedian, Ernie Kovacs pioneered the use of blackouts and trick photography in television comedy. He frequently satirized TV programs and commercials, and introduced his audiences to a host of Kovacsian characters, such as lisping poet Percy Dovetonsils, German disc jockey Wolfgang Sauerbraten, Chinese songwriter Irving Wong, as well as J. Walter Puppybreath and Uncle Gruesome. Many of his shows also featured The Nairobi Trio, a motley group of three instrumentalists dressed in ape suits.

Kovacs grew up in Trenton, New Jersey, but honed his unique skills in Philadelphia, where at one time he found himself hosting three local shows simultaneously: *Three to Get Ready,* a two-hour daily morning show on Philadelphia's channel 3; *Deadline for Dinner,* a lighthearted afternoon cooking show; and *Pick Your Ideal,* a weekly fashion show. His work on *Three to Get Ready,* most of which was improvised, caught the attention of network executives, and in May of 1951 he hosted his first NBC series, *It's Time for Ernie,* a fifteen-minute afternoon effort. In July Kovacs was given a weekday evening slot as a summer replacement for *Kukla, Fran and Ollie;* the thirty-minute show was titled *Ernie in Kovacsland.* Early in 1952 he reappeared on daytime TV as the host of a morning show, *Kovacs on the Korner,* the last of his shows to originate from Philadelphia.

In April of 1952 Kovacs moved to New York to host a local daytime show on WCBS-TV, *Kovacs Unlimited,* which ran until January 1954. In December 1952 the CBS network gave him a prime-time hour series, *The Ernie Kovacs Show.* Billed as "the shortest hour in television," the program was unfortunately scheduled opposite Milton Berle's *Texaco Star Theater* on NBC, and, like most of Berle's competition in those years, folded quickly.

In the spring of 1954 Kovacs moved over to WABD-TV, New York's DuMont outlet, where he hosted a late-night local show for about a year. Late in 1955 he returned to NBC, where he hosted another daytime series; shortly before the daytime show ended its seven-month run, Kovacs began hosting a Monday-night variety hour, which replaced *Caesar's Hour* for the summer.

All of Kovacs's network shows (except *It's Time for Ernie*) featured singer Edie Adams. One of Kovacs's staffers had spotted her on Arthur Godfrey's *Talent Scouts,* where she was an unsuccessful contestant, and recommended her to Kovacs; they were married in 1954. Other regulars on Kovacs's early shows included Andy McKay, Trigger Lund, and Eddie Hatrak. Regulars on the 1956 summer series included Barbara Loden, Peter Hanley, Bill Wendell, Al Kelly, and the Bob Hamilton Dancers.

In addition to the several series mentioned here, Kovacs also filled in twice a week for Steve Allen on the *Tonight* show during the fall of 1956, hosted a game show (see *Take a Good Look*), a motion picture anthology series (see *Silents Please*), and starred in several television specials. The first, and most unusual, of these was a half-hour special broadcast by NBC on 19 January 1957 which featured not a single word of dialogue. Kovacs's final television work was a series of monthly specials carried by the ABC network during 1961 and 1962; these programs, which were videotaped, demonstrated his mastery of the medium. A technical perfectionist, Kovacs conceived a wide array of special effects and thought nothing of spending thousands of dollars on a three- or four-second sequence.

The last Kovacs special was televised 23 January 1962, barely a week after his tragic death in an auto accident while returning home from a party in Beverly Hills. In 1977 excerpts from several of Kovacs's shows were packaged for educational television under the title *The Best of Ernie Kovacs.*

ERROL FLYNN THEATER   SYNDICATED
1957   Half-hour dramatic anthology series hosted by Errol Flynn, the swashbuckling star of dozens of adventure films.

ESCAPE   CBS
5 JANUARY 1950–30 MARCH 1950   This Thursday-night anthology series—usually of thrillers—was derived from the radio show which ran from 1947 to 1954; it was narrated by William Conrad, and produced and directed by Wyllis Cooper.

ESCAPE   NBC
11 FEBRUARY 1973–1 APRIL 1973   Jack Webb produced and narrated this dramatic anthology series purportedly based on true stories of persons enmeshed in do-or-die situations.

ESPECIALLY FOR YOU
See THE ROBERTA QUINLAN SHOW

ESPIONAGE   NBC
2 OCTOBER 1963–2 SEPTEMBER 1964   Produced in England, this anthology series presented spy stories. Herbert Brodkin produced.

ETHEL AND ALBERT   NBC/CBS/ABC
25 APRIL 1953–25 DECEMBER 1954 (NBC); 20 JUNE 1955–26 SEPTEMBER 1955 (CBS); 14 OCTOBER 1955–6 JULY 1956 (ABC)   A low-key situation comedy, *Ethel and Albert* starred Peg Lynch and Alan Bunce as Ethel and Albert Arbuckle, a middle-aged married couple who lived in the town of Sandy Harbor. Lynch created and wrote the series, which began on radio over a local station in Minnesota in 1938 and went network in 1944 (Lynch's radio costar for several years was Richard Widmark). *Ethel and Albert*'s first television exposure was during the 1952–1953 season, when it was telecast as a regular fifteen-minute segment of *The Kate Smith Hour;* in April of 1953 it was given its own half-hour slot on Saturday nights. In 1955 it was carried by CBS as a summer replacement for *December Bride,* and in the fall of 1955 ABC broadcast a filmed version of the show on Fridays.

ETHEL BARRYMORE THEATER   SYNDICATED
1956   Half-hour dramatic anthology series hosted by seventy-seven-year-old Ethel Barrymore, star of stage and screen, and sister of John and Lionel Barrymore.

EVANS AND NOVAK   SYNDICATED
1976   This hour-long series examined political issues in depth. Syndicat-

ed columnists Rowland Evans and Robert Novak hosted the show which was produced in Washington by Gordon Hyatt.

THE EVE ARDEN SHOW
CBS
17 SEPTEMBER 1957–25 MARCH 1958 After the cancellation of *Our Miss Brooks,* Eve Arden returned a year later in this unsuccessful situation comedy, based on Emily Kimbrough's autobiography. Arden starred as Liza Hammond, a widow who made her living as a traveling lecturer. Also featured were Allyn Joslyn as George Howell, her agent; Karen Greene as Mary, her thirteen-year-old, the nonidentical twin sister of Jenny, played by Gail Stone; and Frances Bavier as Nora, the housekeeper who tended the twins while Liza was on the road. Produced by Robert Sparks and Edmund Hartmann, the series was directed by John Rich.

THE EVE HUNTER SHOW
NBC
10 OCTOBER 1951–28 MARCH 1952 Eve Hunter hosted this daily hour interview show for six months during the 1951–1952 season. Because the show was broadcast at one o'clock, few NBC affiliates carried it, choosing instead to carry local programs at that hour. It was not until the late 1970s that NBC again carried a regular network show at one o'clock.

EVENING AT POPS
PBS
12 JULY 1970– A recurring summer series, *Evening at Pops* presents the Boston Pops Orchestra, under the direction of Arthur Fiedler (until his death in 1979), together with guest artists.

EVENING AT SYMPHONY
PBS
6 OCTOBER 1974– An hour of classical music, taped at Symphony Hall in Boston, with the Boston Symphony Orchestra.

AN EVENING WITH
SYNDICATED
1966 An anthology variety series that showcased a different performer each week. There was no regulars.

THE EVERGLADES
SYNDICATED
1961 In this half-hour adventure series Ron Hayes starred as Lincoln Vail, officer of Florida's Everglades County Patrol. Gordon Cosell costarred as Chief Anderson, Vail's commanding officer.

THE EVERLY BROTHERS SHOW
ABC
8 JULY 1970–16 SEPTEMBER 1970 A summer replacement for *The Johnny Cash Show.* The cohosts, Don and Phil Everly, began making records in 1957; their sound, which blended elements of country and rock

music, influenced many artists, including the Beatles. Regulars on the series included Ruth McDevitt and Joe Higgins.

EVERYBODY'S TALKING   ABC
6 FEBRUARY 1967–29 DECEMBER 1967   Daytime game show on which contestants, after watching film clips of people talking, tried to guess what they were talking about. A celebrity panel was on hand to help the players. Lloyd Thaxton hosted the show. A very similar concept was employed in the 1973 game show, *Hollywood's Talking*.

EVERYDAY   SYNDICATED
1978   An hour variety-talk show with two cohosts—Stephanie Edwards and John Bennett Perry—and five other regulars: Anne Bloom, Tom Chapin, Robert Corff, Judy Gibson, and Murray Langston (formerly *The Gong Show*'s "Unknown Comic"). David Salzman was the executive producer for Group W Productions.

EVERYTHING GOES   SYNDICATED
1973   Variety show produced in Canada, cohosted by comedians Norm Crosby and Tom O'Malley.

EVERYTHING'S ARCHIE
See THE ARCHIE SHOW

EVERYTHING'S RELATIVE   SYNDICATED
1965   Jim Hutton hosted this game show, which pitted two families against each other. Individual family members were called on to answer a question or perform a task; the remaining family members then predicted whether the other one would be able to answer or perform correctly.

EVERYWHERE I GO   CBS
7 OCTOBER 1952–6 JANUARY 1953   Dan Seymour hosted this human interest series, which was seen Tuesday and Thursday afternoons. It was one of the first daytime shows to employ production techniques such as backscreen projection, so that a housewife on stage would appear to be standing in her kitchen at home; producer Irv Gitlin described the effect as a "studio without walls." Lloyd Gross directed.

THE EVIL TOUCH   SYNDICATED
1973   An anthology series of half-hour melodramas, hosted by Anthony Quayle. Produced in Canada.

EXCLUSIVE   SYNDICATED
1960   The stories on this half-hour dramatic anthology series were all written by members of the Overseas Press Club of America.

EXCURSION   NBC

13 SEPTEMBER 1953–21 MARCH 1954 Burgess Meredith hosted this wide-ranging Sunday-afternoon documentary series. Some programs were devoted to the arts, some examined foreign cultures, and some featured interviews with such guests as former President Harry S Truman. The show was produced first by Jerry Bragg, and later by Pete Barnum, for the Ford Foundation TV Workshop; Dan Petrie directed.

EXECUTIVE SUITE   CBS

20 SEPTEMBER 1976–11 FEBRUARY 1977 A continuing drama set at the Cardway Corporation, a large conglomerate headquartered in Los Angeles. The large cast included Mitchell Ryan as Dan Walling, concerned corporate president; Sharon Acker as Helen Walling, his wife; Leigh McCloskey as Brian Walling, their prodigal son; Wendy Phillips as Stacey Walling, their radical daughter; Stephen Elliott as Howell Rutledge, reactionary senior vice president; Gwyda DonHowe as Astrid Rutledge, his scheming wife; Byron Morrow as Pearce Newberry, alcoholic VP; Madlyn Rhue as Hilary Madison, the only woman on the board of directors; Percy Rodriguez as Malcolm Gibson, the only black board member; William Smithers as Anderson Galt, philandering VP; Patricia Smith as Leona Galt, his troubled wife; Joan Prather as Glory Dalessio, Anderson Galt's secretary and after-hours companion; Paul Lambert as Tom Dalessio, Glory's father, the plant manager; Brenda Sykes as Summer Johnson, Glory's black roommate who fell in love with Brian Walling; Richard Cox as Mark Desmond, hotshot young executive; Trisha Noble as Yvonne Holland, the woman who purported to be Mark's wife; Carl Weintraub as Harry Ragin, shop steward; and Scott Marlowe as Nick Coslo, an industrial spy. Based loosely on the novel by Cameron Hawley, the show was produced by Don Brinkley and later by Buck Houghton; its executive producers were Norman Felton and Stanley Rubin.

EXPEDITION   ABC

20 SEPTEMBER 1960–23 APRIL 1962 Documentary series that presented modern-day geographical adventures. Hosted by Colonel John D. Craig.

EXPLORING   NBC

13 OCTOBER 1962–17 APRIL 1965; 8 JANUARY 1966–9 APRIL 1966 An educational series for children that explored language, music, mathematics, social studies, and science. Televised Saturdays, the show was hosted by Dr. Albert R. Hibbs, who was assisted by the Ritts Puppets: Magnolia the Ostrich, Albert the Chipmunk and Sir Godfrey Turtle.

EXPLORING GOD'S WORLD   CBS

4 JULY 1954–26 SEPTEMBER 1954 This Sunday-morning series for chil-

dren presented films about natural history. Carrie McCord was the host, and was assisted by youngsters Lydia Jean Shaffer and Glenn Walken.

EYE GUESS

NBC

3 JANUARY 1966–26 SEPTEMBER 1969 This daytime game show tested contestants' abilities to memorize. After observing a board containing the answers to eight upcoming questions for eight seconds, the contestants had to choose the location of the correct answer when the corresponding questions were asked by host Bill Cullen.

EYE ON NEW YORK

CBS

25 DECEMBER 1955–4 NOVEMBER 1956; 9 JUNE 1957–1 SEPTEMBER 1957; 2 MARCH 1958–31 AUGUST 1958; 28 DECEMBER 1958–6 SEPTEMBER 1959 A wide-ranging Sunday-morning documentary series, *Eye on New York* examined the problems, the politics, and the cultural life of New York City. Bill Leonard hosted the half-hour show, which shared a time slot with *The U.N. in Action.*

EYE WITNESS

NBC

30 MARCH 1953–29 JUNE 1953 A half-hour mystery anthology series, broadcast live from New York, *Eye Witness* presented stories about people who had witnessed crimes. Richard Carlson was the first host and was succeeded by Lee Bowman.

THE EYES HAVE IT

NBC

20 NOVEMBER 1948–19 JUNE 1949 Ralph McNair hosted this half-hour game show on which contestants sought to identify photographs.

EYEWITNESS TO HISTORY

CBS

30 SEPTEMBER 1960–26 JULY 1963 Charles Kuralt hosted this Friday-night public affairs program on which the most significant news story (or stories) was reviewed. The show's title was shortened to *Eyewitness* in its last season.

THE EZIO PINZA SHOW
(THE RCA VICTOR SHOW STARRING EZIO PINZA)

NBC

23 NOVEMBER 1951–13 JUNE 1952 Ezio Pinza, the Italian-American opera singer who starred in *South Pacific* on Broadway, made his TV debut in September 1951 as host of *All-Star Revue.* The reaction was so favorable that he was given his own variety series later that fall. The half-hour show was seen weekly until February, when it began alternating bi-weekly with *The Dennis Day Show.* In the fall of 1953, Pinza returned to star in an ethnic sitcom: see *Bonino.*

THE F.B.I.   ABC

19 SEPTEMBER 1965–8 SEPTEMBER 1974   ABC's longest-running crime show was produced with the cooperation of J. Edgar Hoover, Director of the Federal Bureau of Investigation. It starred Efrem Zimbalist, Jr., as Inspector Lewis Erskine, a man of impeccable integrity and little humor; Philip Abbott as Agent Arthur Ward; Stephen Brooks (1965–1967) as Agent Jim Rhodes, boyfriend of Erskine's daughter; Lynn Loring (1965–1966) as Barbara Erskine, Lew's daughter; William Reynolds (1967–1974) as Agent Tom Colby; and Shelly Novack (1973–1974) as Agent Chris Daniels. At the conclusion of some episodes, Zimbalist appeared to broadcast the photograph and description of certain real-life fugitives sought by the FBI.

F. D. R.   ABC

8 JANUARY 1965–10 SEPTEMBER 1965   A series of twenty-seven half hour documentaries on the life of Franklin Delano Roosevelt. Arthur Kennedy served as host and narrator; Charlton Heston read excerpts from Roosevelt's writings. Robert D. Graff and Ben Feiner, Jr., produced the series.

F TROOP   ABC

14 SEPTEMBER 1965–31 AUGUST 1967   A farcical western that featured a crew of bumbling cavalrymen and a complement of inept Indians. With Ken Berry as Captain Wilton Parmenter, assigned to a command at Fort Courage as a promotion following his unintentional instigation of a Union victory during the Civil War; Forrest Tucker as scheming Sergeant Morgan O'Rourke (the Sergeant Bilko of his day); Larry Storch as Corporal Randolph Agarn, O'Rourke's main henchman; Melody Patterson (who was only sixteen when the series began) as Wrangler Jane, the young woman who ran the post store; Edward Everett Horton as Roaring Chicken, medicine man of the Hekawi tribe; and Frank DeKova as Wild Eagle, Hekawi chief. Produced by Hy Averback.

F.Y.I.   CBS

3 JANUARY 1960–25 SEPTEMBER 1960   This series of half-hour documentaries on various subjects was shown Sunday mornings; *F.Y.I.* was an acronym for "For Your Information."

FABIAN OF SCOTLAND YARD   SYNDICATED

1955   Half-hour crime show starring Bruce Seton as Inspector Fabian.

THE FABULOUS FRAUD
See COLONEL HUMPHREY FLACK

THE FABULOUS FUNNIES NBC

9 SEPTEMBER 1978–1 SEPTEMBER 1979 On this Saturday-morning children's show, serious topics such as safety and health care were dealt with by characters from the newspaper comic strips such as Alley Oop, Broom Hilda, The Katzenjammer Kids, Nancy and Sluggo, and Shoe. The executive producers of the half-hour series were Norm Prescott and Lou Scheimer.

THE FACE IS FAMILIAR CBS

7 MAY 1966–3 SEPTEMBER 1966 This Saturday-night game show involved two teams, each consisting of a celebrity and a contestant. The object of the game was to identify the photograph of a famous person; the photo had been cut up into large pieces, scrambled, and covered. By answering questions correctly, contestants were shown the pieces, one by one, and given the chance to identify the subject. The show was hosted by Jack Whitaker, a former weather forecaster for WCAU-TV in Philadelphia, now a CBS sportscaster.

FACE THE FACTS CBS

13 MARCH 1961–29 SEPTEMBER 1961 Red Rowe hosted this daytime game show on which contestants tried to predict the outcome of previously filmed dramatizations of criminal trials.

FACE THE MUSIC CBS

3 MAY 1948–10 DECEMBER 1948 This fifteen-minute musical show was usually seen three nights a week. Featured were singers Johnny Desmond and Shaye Cogan (who was later replaced by Sandra Deel) and the Tony Mottola Trio. Ace Ochs produced the series and Worthington "Tony" Miner directed it.

FACE THE NATION CBS

7 NOVEMBER 1954–20 APRIL 1961; 15 SEPTEMBER 1963– *Face the Nation* is the CBS counterpart of NBC's *Meet the Press:* Newsmakers are interviewed by a panel of journalists. CBS News correspondent George Herman has been the moderator since 1969. The program usually originates from Washington but has been produced at other locations; Soviet Premier Nikita Khrushchev, for example, was interviewed in Moscow in May 1957. Senator Joseph McCarthy was the guest on the 1954 premiere. The series is produced by Mary O. Yates.

THE FACTS OF LIFE NBC

24 AUGUST 1979–14 SEPTEMBER 1979; 14 MARCH 1980–

Spun off from *Diff'rent Strokes,* this half-hour sitcom stars Charlotte Rae as Edna Garrett, who left the Drummond household on *Diff'rent Strokes* to become a temporary housemother at the Eastland School, a prestigious girls' boarding academy. Also featured are John Lawlor as Steven Bradley, the headmaster; Jenny O'Hara as Miss Mahoney; Lisa Whelchel as Blair, a precocious student; Felice Schachter as Nancy; Julie Piecarski as Sue Ann; Julie Anne Haddock as Cindy; Molly Ringwald as Molly; Kim Fields as Tootie; and Mindy Cohn as Natalie. Jerry Mayer produces the series, which should not be confused with *Dorothy,* the CBS comedy set at a girls' boarding school.

FAIR EXCHANGE   CBS
21 SEPTEMBER 1962–28 DECEMBER 1962; 28 MARCH 1963–19 SEPTEMBER 1963 Situation comedy about an American family and a British family who exchanged their teenage daughters for a year. The Yankee family included Eddie Foy, Jr., as Eddie Walker, owner of a New York ticket agency; Audrey Christie as his wife, Dorothy; Lynn Loring as their daughter, Patty; and Flip Mark as their son, Larry. The British family included Victor Maddern as Thomas Finch, owner of a sporting goods store; Diane Chesney as his wife, Sybil; Judy Carne as their daughter, Heather; and Dennis Waterman as their son, Neville. Also featured was Maurice Dallimore as Tom's friend, Willie Shorthouse. Filmed in England and in Hollywood, *Fair Exchange* was one of TV's first hour-long sitcoms. That format proved unwieldy, and the show was canceled in December 1962. Three months later it returned in a half-hour format.

FAIRMEADOWS, U.S.A.   NBC
4 NOVEMBER 1951–27 APRIL 1952 *Fairmeadows, U.S.A.* began as a Sunday-afternoon serial about life in a small town. It featured Howard St. John as John Olcott, owner of a general store; Ruth Matteson as Mrs. Olcott; Hazel Dawn, Jr., as their older daughter; Tom Taylor as their son; Mimi Strongin as their younger daughter, Evvie. In the fall of 1952 the series reappeared with several changes: a new title (*The House in the Garden*), a new time slot (weekday afternoons, as the third quarter hour of *The Kate Smith Hour*), and several new faces, including Lauren Gilbert as John Olcott; Monica Lovett as the older daughter; James Vickery as the older daughter's boyfriend (Ruth Matteson and Tom Taylor were retained). Agnes Ridgeway wrote the series, and Alan Neuman directed it.

FAITH BALDWIN ROMANCE THEATER   ABC
20 JANUARY 1951–20 OCTOBER 1951 This dramatic anthology series, hosted by Faith Baldwin, was shown on Saturday afternoons, usually on a biweekly basis.

FAITH FOR TODAY ABC/SYNDICATED

21 MAY 1950– This long-running religious series, produced in cooperation with the Seventh Day Adventist Church, was hosted for many years by the Reverend William A. Sagal.

THE FALCON
See THE ADVENTURES OF THE FALCON

FAMILY ABC

9 MARCH 1976–13 APRIL 1976; 28 SEPTEMBER 1976–27 APRIL 1979; 24 DECEMBER 1979– The story of a family of five living in Pasadena, *Family* first appeared as a six-part miniseries in the spring of 1976; it proved popular enough to merit a slot in ABC's fall lineup. Generally well written, and always well acted, the show has managed to avoid much of the mawkishness characteristic of other family dramas of the 1970s. *Family* features Sada Thompson as strong but sensitive Kate Lawrence, the mother of three; James Broderick as her husband, Douglas Lawrence, a lawyer; Elaine Heilveil (spring 1976) and Meredith Baxter Birney (fall 1976–) as their spoiled daughter, Nancy Maitland, who was divorced in 1976 and lived in the family's guest house with her young son Timmy while attending law school; Gary Frank as their son Willie, a headstrong youth who quit school and hopes to become a writer; Kristy McNichol as their younger daughter, Buddy (Letitia), an honest and open young teenager adjusting to adolescence; Michael David Shackelford as Timmy, Nancy's toddler. Occasionally featured is John Rubinstein as Nancy's former husband, Jeff Maitland; Rubinstein also composed the show's theme music. The series was created by Jay Presson Allen, and its executive producers are Mike Nichols, Aaron Spelling, and Leonard Goldberg. In the fall of 1978 Quinn Cummings joined the cast as Andrea (Annie) Cooper, an orphan adopted by the Lawrences; Nancy moved into her own apartment, and Willie took over the guest house.

FAMILY AFFAIR CBS

12 SEPTEMBER 1966–9 SEPTEMBER 1971 This saccharine sitcom was salvaged by the cuteness of its two youthful costars. It starred Brian Keith as Manhattan bachelor Bill Davis, an industrial designer who suddenly finds himself guardian of his nephew and his two nieces (the three children had been raised in separate homes after their parents' deaths); Sebastian Cabot as Davis's manservant, Giles French, a formal Briton with neither the interest nor the inclination to look after small children; Cathy Garver as Bill's teenage niece, Cissy; Johnny Whitaker as his nephew, Jody; and Anissa Jones as his niece, Buffy, Jody's twin sister. Also featured were John Williams as Mr. French's brother, Nigel, who

filled in for Giles in the latter's absence; Nancy Walker (1970–1971) as Emily Turner, the cleaning lady; Gregg Fedderson as Gregg Bartlett, Cissy's occasional boyfriend. Young Fedderson was the son of Don Fedderson, executive producer of the series. Following the cancellation of the show in 1971, Johnny Whitaker continued to be seen regularly on TV; he was a regular on *Sigmund and the Sea Monsters* and was featured in several Walt Disney productions. His costar, Anissa Jones, appeared rarely on television; in 1976, she was found dead (from drug-related causes) in her California home.

FAMILY CLASSICS THEATER
The umbrella title of a group of three miniseries. See: *The Black Tulip, Ivanhoe,* and *Little Women.*

THE FAMILY FEUD ABC/SYNDICATED
12 JULY 1976–   (ABC);   1977–   (SYNDICA-TED)   Two five-member family units compete on this game show hosted by Richard Dawson. Basically, the players try to match responses to those given previously by a group of 100 people. A Mark Goodson–Bill Todman Production.

THE FAMILY GAME ABC
19 JUNE 1967–15 DECEMBER 1967   Bob Barker hosted this daytime game show on which three families competed; each family consisted of two parents and two children. The children were asked questions before the telecast; the parents then tried to determine which answers had been given by their respective children.

THE FAMILY GENIUS DUMONT
9 SEPTEMBER 1949–30 SEPTEMBER 1949   Short-lived sitcom about a child prodigy. With Jack Diamond as Tommy Howard, Phyllis Lowe as his mother, and Arthur Edwards as his father. James L. Caddigan and Elwood Hoffman produced the series.

THE FAMILY HOLVAK NBC
7 SEPTEMBER 1975–27 OCTOBER 1975   Glenn Ford's second TV series proved even less successful than his first (*Cade's County*). Presumably inspired by *The Waltons,* it was based on Jack Ferris's novel, *Ramey,* and told the story of a preacher and his family living in the South during the 1930s. Ford starred as the Reverend Tom Holvak; Julie Harris as his wife, Elizabeth; Lance Kerwin as their son, Ramey; Elizabeth Cheshire as their daughter, Julie Mae; Ted Gehring as storekeeper Chester Purdle; Cynthia Hayward as Ida, his helper; and William McKinney as police

deputy Jim Shanks. Executive producers: Roland Kibbee and Dean Hargrove. A few episodes were broadcast over CBS during the summer of 1977.

THE FAMOUS ADVENTURES OF MR. MAGOO
See MR. MAGOO

FAMOUS FIGHTS FROM MADISON SQUARE GARDEN   DUMONT
15 SEPTEMBER 1952–22 DECEMBER 1952   Highlights of famous boxing matches were telecast on this fifteen-minute filmed series.

FAMOUS JURY TRIALS   DUMONT
12 OCTOBER 1949–12 MARCH 1952   Most, but not all, of the action in this dramatic series took place in the courtroom; flashbacks were also used to flesh out the stories. Jim Bender played the prosecuting attorney, and Truman Smith played the defense attorney.

FANFARE   CBS
19 JUNE 1965–11 SEPTEMBER 1965   Trumpeter Al Hirt hosted this variety hour, a summer replacement for *Jackie Gleason and His American Scene Magazine.*

FANGFACE   ABC
9 SEPTEMBER 1978–8 SEPTEMBER 1979   Saturday-morning cartoon show about the adventures of four teenagers, one of whom can turn into a werewolf (*Fangface*). Joe Ruby and Ken Spears were the executive producers for Filmways. See also *The Plasticman Comedy/Adventure Show.*

THE FANTASTIC FOUR   ABC/NBC
9 SEPTEMBER 1967–15 MARCH 1970 (ABC); 9 SEPTEMBER 1978–1 SEPTEMBER 1979 (NBC)   Based on the comic book, *The Fantastic Four* premiered in 1967 as a Hanna-Barbera Production. Each of the four characters had acquired a special power after their rocket ship encountered a radioactive field: Reed Richards could be stretched infinitely, his wife Sue Richards could become invisible, Johnny Storm ("The Human Torch") could ignite himself, and Ben Grimm ("The Thing") was extraordinarily strong. The series returned in 1978, with new producers (David H. DePatie and Friz Freleng) and a new member—Johnny Storm had been replaced by a robot named Herbie.

THE FANTASTIC JOURNEY   NBC
3 FEBRUARY 1977–16 JUNE 1977   In this science fiction series, an expedition investigating the Bermuda Triangle found itself mysteriously transported to what appeared to be another world. In their quest to return to their own time, the three expedition members encountered others who,

for various reasons, also wished to join them. Featured were Jared Martin as Varian, expedition leader; Carl Franklin as Dr. Fred Walters, medical expert; Ike Eisenmann as Scott Jordan, a youngster who could read minds; Katie Saylor as Liana, a mysterious woman who joined them in the first episode; and Roddy McDowall as Jonathan Willoway, a scientist who joined up in the third episode. Bruce Lansbury was the executive producer for Bruce Lansbury Productions, Ltd., in association with Columbia Pictures Television and NBC.

FANTASTIC VOYAGE
ABC

14 SEPTEMBER 1968–6 SEPTEMBER 1970 This weekend cartoon series about four people who could be miniaturized was based loosely on the 1966 film that starred Raquel Welch.

FANTASY ISLAND
ABC

28 JANUARY 1978– This escapist adventure hour stars Ricardo Montalban as Roarke, proprietor of Fantasy Island, a tropical resort where guests can live out their wildest dreams; Herve Villechaize is featured as Roarke's diminutive assistant, Tattoo. Usually, two stories are presented each week, with the action shifting back and forth from fantasy to fantasy. Production of the weekly series was begun after two fairly successful pilot films had been televised. Aaron Spelling and Leonard Goldberg are the executive producers.

FAR OUT SPACE NUTS
CBS

6 SEPTEMBER 1975–4 SEPTEMBER 1976 This live-action sitcom was seen on Saturday mornings. It starred Bob Denver as Junior and Chuck McCann as Barney, two space-center employees who accidentally blasted off while loading food onto a rocket. Also featured were Patty Maloney as Honk, their space pal, and Al Checco. Produced by Sid and Marty Krofft and Al Schwartz.

FARADAY AND COMPANY
NBC

26 SEPTEMBER 1973–13 AUGUST 1974 One segment of *The NBC Wednesday Mystery Movie, Faraday and Company* alternated with *Banacek, The Snoop Sisters,* and *Tenafly.* It featured Dan Dailey as Frank Faraday, a private eye who escapes to the United States after spending twenty-eight years in a Caribbean prison (he'd been framed, of course); James Naughton as Steve Faraday, Frank's new partner, the son Frank had never seen; Geraldine Brooks as Lou Carson, Frank's former secretary and Steve's mother, the woman Frank had intended to marry twenty-eight years before; and Sharon Gless as Holly Barrett, their current secretary and Steve's girlfriend. This appears to have been the first series other than a soap opera in which a parent and an illegitimate child were regular characters.

THE FARMER'S DAUGHTER   ABC

20 SEPTEMBER 1963–2 SEPTEMBER 1966   Sitcom based on the 1947 film about a young woman from Minnesota who becomes the housekeeper for a widowed Congressman in Washington, D.C. With Inger Stevens as Katy Holstrum; William Windom as Congressman Glen Morley; Cathleen Nesbitt as Glen's mother, Agatha Morley, herself the widow of a Congressman; Mickey Sholdar as Glen's son Steve; Rory O'Brien as Glen's son Danny; and Philip Coolidge as Glen's brother, Cooper. Occasionally featured were Walter Sande as Papa Holstrum, Alice Frost as Mama Holstrum, and Nancy DeCarl as Steve's girlfriend, Pam. During the fall of 1965 (1 November), Katy and Glen finally got married. The event was even celebrated in real-life Washington, where Perle Mesta threw a party for 300 guests (including Stevens and Windom).

FASHION MAGIC   CBS

10 NOVEMBER 1950–15 JUNE 1951   Beauty and wardrobe were the topics discussed on this daytime series, which was usually broadcast twice a week. Hosted by Ilka Chase through 20 April, then by Arlene Francis.

FASHION STORY   ABC

4 NOVEMBER 1948–22 FEBRUARY 1949   Host Marilyn Day presented news from the world of fashion on this Thursday-night series. Carl Reiner also appeared.

FASHIONS ON PARADE   DUMONT/ABC

5 FEBRUARY 1948–24 APRIL 1949 (DUMONT); 27 APRIL 1949–29 JUNE 1949 (ABC)   One of television's first fashion programs, *Fashions on Parade* was hosted by Adelaide Hawley. Leon Roth and Charles Caplin produced the series, which was also broadcast under the titles *Television Fashions* and *Fashion Parade*.

FAST DRAW   SYNDICATED

1968   Johnny Gilbert hosted this game show played by two teams, each consisting of a celebrity and a contestant. One partner tried to guess a phrase from sketches drawn by the other partner.

FAT ALBERT AND THE COSBY KIDS   CBS

9 SEPTEMBER 1972–   Bill Cosby hosts this Saturday cartoon series with a humanitarian message. Its central characters—such as Fat Albert, Weird Harold, Mush Mouth, and Donald—are based on the boyhood friends of Cosby, who grew up in Philadelphia. Produced by Norm Prescott and Lou Scheimer; Cosby served as executive producer.

FATHER KNOWS BEST   CBS/NBC

3 OCTOBER 1954–27 MARCH 1955 (CBS); 31 AUGUST 1955–17 SEPTEM-

BER 1958 (NBC); 22 SEPTEMBER 1958–17 SEPTEMBER 1962 (CBS) This durable sitcom began on radio in 1949, starring Robert Young as Jim Anderson, an insurance agent who lived in the town of Springfield with his wife and three children. Originally, Father was somewhat of a bumbler, but by the end of the show's run on radio, he had become wiser and more paternal. Young was the only member of the radio cast to make the transition to television. Joining him on camera were Jane Wyatt as Margaret Anderson, his wife; Elinor Donahue as Betty (or "Princess" to Father), their eldest child; Billy Gray as teenager Bud (Jim, Jr.); Lauren Chapin as Kathy ("Kitten" to Father), the youngest. Natividad Vacio occasionally appeared as gardener Frank Smith ("Fronk"), a newly naturalized American citizen. The show was produced by Eugene B. Rodney, who owned the series together with Young. Despite critical acclaim, the series was dropped after its first twenty-six weeks; one reason for its initial lack of success may have been that few children saw it—it was scheduled at 10:00 on Sundays. The following season it found a new sponsor, a new time, and a new network and became a solid hit. Between 1954 and 1960, there were 203 episodes filmed; reruns were broadcast on CBS for two more seasons and subsequently on ABC. After *Father Knows Best* ceased production, Young, Wyatt, and Donahue continued to appear frequently on television; Young, of course, starred in *Marcus Welby, M.D.* for seven seasons. Gray and Chapin, however, made few TV appearances. On 15 May 1977 the five appeared together in "The Father Knows Best Reunion," on NBC; the slow-moving hour-long special proved disappointing.

FATHER OF THE BRIDE   CBS
29 SEPTEMBER 1961–14 SEPTEMBER 1962 This domestic sitcom was based on the book by Edward Streeter and the 1950 film. The TV version featured Leon Ames as lawyer Stanley Banks, the father of the bride; Ruth Warrick as Ellie Banks, the mother of the bride; Myrna Fahey as Kay Banks, the bride; Rickie Sorensen as Tommy Banks, the bride's kid brother; Burt Metcalfe as Buckley Dunston, Kay's intended; Ransom Sherman as Buckley's father, Herbert Dunston; Lurene Tuttle as Buckley's mother, Doris Dunston. Kay and Buckley became engaged in the premiere episode and were married in midseason. Robert Maxwell was the executive producer.

FAVORITE STORY
See MY FAVORITE STORY

FAY   NBC
4 SEPTEMBER 1975–23 OCTOBER 1975 A remarkably unsuccessful situation comedy about a forty-three-year-old divorcée who got a job as a secretary in a San Francisco law office. With Lee Grant as Fay Stewart;

Joe Silver as Jack Stewart, her ex; Margaret Willock as Linda Baines, Fay's conservative daughter; Stewart Moss as Dr. Elliott Baines, Linda's stuffy husband; Audra Lindley as Lillian, Fay's tactless neighbor; Bill Gerber as lawyer Danny Messina, Fay's boss; Norman Alden as Al Cassidy, Danny's law partner; and Lillian Lehman as Letty Gilmore, Al's black secretary. Created by Susan Harris. Executive producer: Paul Younger Witt. Produced by Jerry Mayer. *Fay*'s theme song was sung by Jaye P. Morgan. Susan Harris later blamed the show's failure on the fact that it had been intended as a sophisticated, adult comedy but had been scheduled by NBC at 8:30 p.m. on Thursdays, smack in the middle of the "family viewing hour." As a result of the scheduling decision, the network ordered many changes in dialogue and characterization, which seriously weakened the show's import.

FAYE AND SKITCH NBC
26 OCTOBER 1953–22 OCTOBER 1954 Faye Emerson and Skitch Henderson (who were married to each other at the time) cohosted this fifteen-minute nightly series of music and chitchat. Johnny Stearns produced and directed it.

THE FAYE EMERSON SHOW CBS/NBC
13 MARCH 1950–9 JULY 1950 (CBS); 22 APRIL 1950–30 AUGUST 1950 (NBC); 26 SEPTEMBER 1950–23 DECEMBER 1950 (CBS) One of network television's first female interviewers, Faye Emerson attracted much attention—and a large number of male viewers—because of the low-cut gowns she wore. She began hosting a local show in New York, which went network in March of 1950; a month later she began a second series, *Fifteen with Faye*, on NBC, thus becoming one of the few performers to appear on two networks simultaneously. Each of her first two series was seen once a week; in the fall of 1950, however, her CBS show was seen three evenings a week. In 1951 she hosted another local show in New York, before returning to network TV with *Faye Emerson's Wonderful Town* (see below).

FAYE EMERSON'S WONDERFUL TOWN CBS
(WONDERFUL TOWN, U.S.A.)
16 JUNE 1951–19 APRIL 1952 Faye Emerson returned to CBS in this half-hour variety series that replaced part of *The Frank Sinatra Show*. Skitch Henderson also appeared on the show, which was broadcast live from a different city each week; Boston was the site of the premiere telecast.

FEAR AND FANCY ABC
13 MAY 1953–2 SEPTEMBER 1953 Half-hour filmed dramatic anthology series that usually featured supernatural stories.

FEARLESS FOSDICK   NBC
1 JUNE 1952–28 SEPTEMBER 1952   Fearless Fosdick, the bumbling cartoon detective created by Al Capp, was the star of this short-lived puppet
show. Other characters included Schmoozer and The Chief.

THE FEATHER AND FATHER GANG   ABC
7 MARCH 1977–6 AUGUST 1977   A pale imitation of CBS's *Switch*, this
hour-long adventure series featured a female lawyer and her dad, an ex-
con man, who combined forces to outwit assorted evildoers. With Stefanie Powers as Toni "Feather" Danton; Harold Gould as her father,
Harry Danton. The "Gang," all of them Harry's henchpeople, included
Frank Delfino as the midget Enzo; Monte Landis as Michael; Joan Shawlee as Margo; and Lewis Charles as Lou. Bill Driskill created the series,
and Larry White was the executive producer.

FEATHER YOUR NEST   NBC
4 OCTOBER 1954–27 JULY 1956   Bud Collyer hosted this daytime game
show on which couples had the chance to win home furnishings; questions were written on feathers that were hidden among the merchandise.
Assisting Collyer at various times were Lou Prentis, Janis Carter, and
Jean Williams.

FEELIN' GOOD   PBS
1974   Produced by the Children's Television Workshop, *Feelin' Good* attempted to educate adults on matters of health care. Two formats were
attempted: The first was in a sixty-minute sitcom-variety form, set at a
club known as Mac's Place. It featured Tex Everhart as Mac; Priscilla
Lopez as Rita; Marjorie Barnes as Melba; Joe Morton as Jason; Ethel
Shutta as Mrs. Stebbins; and Ben Slack as Hank. That format was
scrapped after eleven weeks, and Dick Cavett was brought in to host a
half-hour narrative program.

FELONY SQUAD   ABC
12 SEPTEMBER 1966–31 JANUARY 1969   Half-hour crime show set in
Los Angeles. With Howard Duff as Detective (and later Sergeant) Sam
Stone; Ben Alexander as Sergeant Dan Briggs; Dennis Cole as Detective
Jim Briggs, Dan's son; Frank Maxwell (1966–1967) as Captain Nye; and
Barney Phillips (1967–1969) as Captain Ed Franks. The series was sup-
plied by 20th Century-Fox TV.

FERNWOOD 2-NIGHT   SYNDICATED
4 JULY 1977–30 SEPTEMBER 1977
AMERICA 2NIGHT   SYNDICATED
10 APRIL 1978–18 AUGUST 1978   A satire of talk shows, *Fernwood 2-
Night* was developed by Norman Lear to fill the summer gap between

Mary Hartman, Mary Hartman and *Forever Fernwood.* Set at the studios of Channel 2 in Fernwood, Ohio, it starred Martin Mull as host Barth Gimble, Fred Willard as his half-witted sidekick, Jerry Hubard, and Frank DeVol as Happy Kyne, leader of the show's four-man band, the Mirthmakers. Host Gimble was the twin brother of Garth Gimble, a wife-beater who had impaled himself on an aluminum Christmas tree on *Mary Hartman, Mary Hartman.* Second banana Hubard was the brother-in-law of the station owner, while bandleader Kyne supplemented his income by running a chain of fast-food outlets known as Bun 'n' Run. In real life, Frank DeVol was a talented musician and composer of many TV theme songs, including the song in *Family Affair.* Most of the guests on *Fernwood 2-Night* were purely fictional (such as Fernwood's high school principal, who demonstrated the proper technique for spanking the bottom of a shapely sixteen-year-old), but a few celebrities, such as singer Tom Waits and journalist Harry Shearer, played themselves. *America 2Night* was introduced in the spring of 1978 and was similar in format to its predecessor, except that it was broadcast from Alta Coma, California, "the unfinished furniture capital of the world." Many of *America 2Night*'s guests appeared as themselves; Charlton Heston, for example, was a guest on the premiere.

FESTIVAL OF STARS   NBC
2 JULY 1957–17 SEPTEMBER 1957   Jim Ameche hosted this Tuesday-night series of rebroadcasts from *The Loretta Young Show.*. The episodes that were shown did not feature Young.

FIBBER McGEE AND MOLLY   NBC
15 SEPTEMBER 1959–5 JANUARY 1960   A short-lived version of the popular radio comedy that starred Jim Jordan (who created the show with Don Quinn) and his wife, Marian Jordan. On television Bob Sweeney starred as Fibber McGee, teller of tall tales, and Cathy Lewis played his long-suffering wife, Molly. Also featured were Hal Peary (who originated The Great Gildersleeve on the radio version of *Fibber McGee*) as Mayor Charles LaTrivia, a bombastic politician; Addison Richards as Doctor Gamble; Paul Smith as neighbor Roy Norris; and Barbara Beaird as Teeny, the youngster who lived next door (the McGees, of course, resided at 79 Wistful Vista).

50 GRAND SLAM   NBC
4 OCTOBER 1976–31 DECEMBER 1976   Tom Kennedy hosted this day-time game show on which contestants could earn up to $50,000. The format was somewhat similar to that of *Twenty-One:* Pairs of contestants competed in areas of specialized knowledge or in games. The winner of the first round (which paid $200) could elect to risk his or her winnings on the next round against a new challenger; each new challenger began at

the $200 level, while the champion competed for ever-increasing amounts up to the $50,000 top prize.

54TH STREET REVUE
CBS

5 MAY 1949–25 MARCH 1950   This Thursday-night variety hour, broadcast live from a theater on 54th Street in New York, was a showcase for up-and-coming professionals. The first few shows were hosted by comic Al Bernie; other regulars included Carl Reiner, Jack Sterling, Mort Marshall, Wynn Murray, and dancer Bob Fosse. Reiner, of course, went on to *Your Show of Shows* and later created *The Dick Van Dyke Show;* Fosse choreographed many Broadway hits and later directed the film *Cabaret.* Barry Wood was the executive producer of the series. Ralph Levy, who directed it, later produced and directed *The Burns and Allen Show* and served as executive producer of *The Jack Benny Program.* Original music and lyrics were supplied by Al Selden, who later wrote *Man of La Mancha;* Bill Scudder also provided musical material for the series. Writers included Max Wilk, George Axelrod, and Allen Sherman. The last few shows were hosted by Billy Vine.

THE FIGHT OF THE WEEK
ABC

24 JANUARY 1953–11 SEPTEMBER 1964   ABC's weekly boxing series, which ran continuously for eleven years, was aired under several different titles. From 1953 to 1955 it was known as *The Saturday Night Fights.* In the summer of 1955 it moved to a new day and became *The Wednesday Night Fights.* In the fall of 1960 the series moved back to Saturdays and was retitled *The Fight of the Week;* that title was retained when the show switched to Fridays for its final season. Jack Drees announced the bouts during the early seasons, Don Dunphy during the later ones. The popularity of boxing on television (and in the arenas) took a significant downturn during the early 1960s. One reason for this decline may have been *The Fight of the Week* of 24 March 1962, when Emile Griffith defeated Benny "Kid" Paret for the welterweight championship. Paret was carried unconscious from the ring and later died of his injuries.

THE FILES OF JEFFREY JONES
SYNDICATED

1954   This half-hour crime show starred Don Haggerty as New York private eye Jeffrey Jones and Gloria Henry as reporter "Mike" Malone, his girlfriend. Produced by Lindsley Parsons; directed by Lew Landers.

FIREBALL FUN FOR ALL
NBC

28 JUNE 1949–27 OCTOBER 1949   Ole Olsen and Chic Johnson, the veteran comedy team who starred in *Hellzapoppin* on Broadway, hosted this hour of slapstick and sight gags. Broadcast from the Center Theater in New York, it began as a summer replacement for Milton Berle's *The Texaco Star Theater* on Tuesdays and later shifted to Thursdays before

its cancellation. Produced and directed by Ezra Stone, its writers included Arnold Horwitt, Lew Lipton, Mike Stewart (who later wrote *Hello, Dolly*), and Max Wilk. Also in the cast were June Johnson, Marty May, Bill Hayes, and J. C. Olsen.

FIREBALL XL–5 NBC

5 OCTOBER 1963–25 SEPTEMBER 1965   This Saturday-morning series was one of the first to use "Super Marionation," a technique utilizing fine wires and plastic models developed by Gerry Anderson; the technique was refined in Anderson's later series (*Captain Scarlet and the Mysterons, The Thunderbirds,* etc.). This series was set in Space City; its central character was Colonel Steve Zodiac, who piloted his spacecraft—*Fireball XL-5*—throughout the galaxy.

FIREHOUSE ABC

17 JANUARY 1974–1 AUGUST 1974   This half-hour adventure series was apparently inspired by NBC's *Emergency!* It told the story of the fearless firefighters of Engine Company 23 in Los Angeles. With James Drury as Captain Spike Ryerson; Richard Jaeckel as number two man Hank Myers; Mike DeLano as firefighter Sonny Capito, who doubled as the company cook; Bill Overton as firefighter Cal Dakin, token black; Scott Smith as firefighter Scotty Smith; and Brad David as rookie firefighter Billy DelZell.

FIRESIDE THEATRE NBC

5 APRIL 1949–23 AUGUST 1955   Produced and directed by Frank Wisbar, *Fireside Theatre* was a fixture at 9:00 p.m. on Tuesdays. During the first season fifty-two 15-minute films were presented; thereafter, the series offered thirty-minute dramas. Gene Raymond hosted the show for several seasons; in 1955 Jane Wyman took over as host, and the show's title was changed. See *Jane Wyman Theatre.*

FIRING LINE SYNDICATED/PBS

1966–   William F. Buckley, Jr., the erudite conservative columnist, hosted this political discussion program. The show was broadcast by PBS between 1971 and 1976 and went back into syndication in 1976. Produced and directed by Warren Steibel.

FIRST DATE SYNDICATED

1952   Renzo Cesana, formerly the host of *The Continental,* presided over this unusual program on which he greeted couples who were on their first date together.

THE FIRST HUNDRED YEARS CBS

4 DECEMBER 1950–27 JUNE 1952   CBS's first television soap opera, *The*

First Hundred Years accentuated the lighter side of married life. It starred Jimmy Lydon and Olive Stacey as newlyweds Chris and Connie Thayer; Stacey was later replaced by Anne Sargent. In 1952 CBS replaced the show with a more successful serial: *The Guiding Light.*

FIRST LOOK   NBC
16 OCTOBER 1965–9 APRIL 1966   An educational series for children hosted by singer Oscar Brand and featuring youngsters Sally Sheffield, Jackie Washington, and Neil Jones.

FIRST LOVE   NBC
5 JULY 1954–30 DECEMBER 1955   This soap opera also centered on newlyweds. With Val Dufour as jet engineer Zach James; Patricia Barry as Laurie James; Rosemary Prinz as Penny Hughes; Bob Courtleigh as David; Joe Warren as Phil; Henrietta Moore as Peggy; and Frederic Downs as Andrews.

FIRST PERSON PLAYHOUSE (FIRST PERSON SINGULAR)   NBC
3 JULY 1953–11 SEPTEMBER 1953   In this half-hour dramatic anthology series, a summer replacement for *The Life of Riley,* the camera was the principal character.

FIRST TUESDAY   NBC
7 JANUARY 1969–7 SEPTEMBER 1971; 3 OCTOBER 1972–7 AUGUST 1973   Eliot Frankel produced this news magazine series, televised on the first Tuesday of each month. Sander Vanocur was the original host, but was succeeded by Garrick Utley. From 1969 to 1971 *First Tuesday* was a two-hour series; when it returned to NBC's schedule in the fall of 1972, however, it was trimmed to sixty minutes. The network continued to experiment with the concept of a monthly magazine series during the 1970s: see also *Chronolog* and *Weekend.*

FISH   ABC
5 FEBRUARY 1977–8 JUNE 1978   This half-hour sitcom was a spinoff from *Barney Miller.* Abe Vigoda starred as Phil Fish, who retired from the New York Police Department to run a home for juvenile delinquents. Also featuring Florence Stanley as his devoted wife, Bernice; Barry Gordon as live-in counselor Charlie. The lovable young troublemakers included Lenny Bari as Mike, Denise Miller as Jilly, Todd Bridges as Loomis, Sarah Natoli as Diane Pulaski, and John Cassisi as Victor. Executive producer: Danny Arnold. Produced by Norman Barasch and Roy Kammerman.

FISHING AND HUNTING CLUB   DUMONT
7 OCTOBER 1949–31 MARCH 1950   Half-hour panel show on which the

panelists answered questions about outdoor activities submitted by viewers. Bill Slater was the host, and the panel included former Olympian Gail Borden, author Jeff Bryant, the New York *Mirror* outdoor editor Jim Hurley, and Dave Newell, a former editor of *Field and Stream*. The show was later titled *Sports for All*.

THE FITZPATRICKS CBS

5 SEPTEMBER 1977–10 JANUARY 1978 One of the plethora of family dramas presented during the 1977–1978 season, *The Fitzpatricks* were a middle-class family who lived in Flint, Michigan. With Bert Kramer as steelworker Mike Fitzpatrick; Mariclare Costello as Maggie Fitzpatrick, pregnant with their fifth child; Clark Brandon as son Sean, sixteen; James Vincent McNichol (brother of Kristy McNichol of ABC's *Family*) as son Jack, fifteen; Michele Tobin as daughter Maureen, fourteen; Sean Marshall as son Max, ten; Derek Wills as R. J., Max's best friend, a black; Helen Hunt as teenager Kerry, a neighbor; and Detroit, the family dog. Created by John Sagret Young. Executive producer: Philip Mandelker. Produced by John Cutts.

FIVE FINGERS NBC

3 OCTOBER 1959–9 JANUARY 1960 Cold War spy drama set in Europe; it was based on the 1952 film starring James Mason. With David Hedison (who starred in the 1958 horror film, *The Fly*) as Victor Sebastian, American counterintelligence agent; Luciana Paluzzi as Simone Genet, his gal Friday; and Paul Burke as Robertson, Sebastian's contact man. Herbert Bayard Swope, Jr., was the producer.

FIVE STAR JUBILEE NBC

17 MARCH 1961–22 SEPTEMBER 1961 Broadcast live from Springfield, Missouri, *Five Star Jubilee* was a half-hour country and western music series similar to *Ozark Jubilee*. Five stars shared the hosting chores on an alternating basis: Rex Allen, Snooky Lanson, Tex Ritter, Carl Smith, and Jimmy Wakely. Other regulars included Slim Wilson and His Jubilee Band, the Promenaders, and the Jubilaires.

FIVE-STAR COMEDY ABC

18 MAY 1957–15 JUNE 1957 A five-week comedy show for kids, shown on Saturday afternoons. Guest hosts included Paul Winchell and Jerry Mahoney, Jerry Colonna, and Señor Wences.

FLAME IN THE WIND

See A TIME FOR US

FLASH GORDON SYNDICATED

1957 The television adaptation of the popular movie serial was produced in Germany. It starred Steve Holland as Flash Gordon; Irene Champlin as his assistant, Dale Arden; and Joe Nash as Dr. Alexis Zarkov.

FLASH GORDON NBC
8 SEPTEMBER 1979– Half-hour Saturday-morning cartoon version of the story of Flash Gordon, the astronaut who sought to save Earth from the evildoings of Ming the Merciless. Lou Scheimer and Norm Prescott were the executive producers.

FLATBUSH CBS
26 FEBRUARY 1979–12 MARCH 1979 Half-hour sitcom about the five fun-loving members of a Brooklyn gang known as the Flatbush Fungos. With Joseph Cali as Presto; Adrian Zmed as Socks; Vincent Bufano as Turtle; Randy Stumpf as Joey D; Sandy Helberg as Figgy; Antony Ponzini as Esposito, owner of the pool hall where the boys hung out; and Helen Verbit as Mrs. Fortunato, neighborhood busybody. The series was created by David Epstein for Lorimar Productions. Producers: Philip Capice and Gary Adelson.

FLICK-OUT PBS
5 OCTOBER 1970–27 SEPTEMBER 1971 A showcase for young independent filmmakers.

FLIGHT SYNDICATED
1958 The saga of the United States Air Force, which was hosted by General George C. Kenney. Al Simon was the executive producer for California National Productions.

FLIGHT NUMBER 7 ABC
5 SEPTEMBER 1954–10 SEPTEMBER 1955 A travelogue hosted by Robert McKenzie, *Flight Number 7* relied heavily on aerial photography. The half-hour series was not carried regularly by ABC's New York affiliate.

FLIGHT TO ADVENTURE SYNDICATED
1960 A series of thirty-nine real-life adventure films, which were shot all over the world. Host: Bill Burrud.

FLIGHT TO RHYTHM DUMONT
10 MARCH 1949–22 SEPTEMBER 1949 Musical series hosted by Delora Bueno. The show premiered as a fifteen-minute series under the title *The Delora Bueno Show*; it was retitled when it expanded to thirty minutes in May, and became a musical serial.

THE FLINTSTONES   ABC

30 SEPTEMBER 1960–2 SEPTEMBER 1966   Produced by William Hanna and Joseph Barbera, *The Flintstones* was the first prime-time cartoon series made especially for television; remarkably, it enjoyed a six-year run, far longer than any of the other prime-time cartoon shows. Set in the Stone Age, *The Flintstones* was little more than an animated version of *The Honeymooners*—the voices of the characters were similar to the *Honeymooners*, and the Flintstones' cave even resembled the Kramdens' apartment. The voices were provided by: Alan Reed as Fred Flintstone, quarry worker; Jean vander Pyl as Wilma Flintstone, his wife; Mel Blanc as Barney Rubble, Fred's best friend; Bea Benaderet and Gerry Johnson as Betty Rubble, Fred's wife. Before the series had run its course, Fred and Wilma had a daughter, and Barney and Betty had a son. The two children—Pebbles and Bamm Bamm— were later featured in their own Saturday-morning cartoon series. *The Flintstones* was rerun on Saturday mornings over NBC from 1967 to 1970, and new episodes were aired in 1972 (see *The Flintstones Comedy Hour*). Additionally, *Flintstones* segments were later combined with other Hanna-Barbera properties (such as *The Jetsons, The Banana Splits,* and *Top Cat*) and syndicated under the title *Fred Flintstone and Friends.*

THE FLINTSTONES COMEDY HOUR   CBS

9 SEPTEMBER 1972–1 SEPTEMBER 1973

THE FLINTSTONES SHOW   CBS

8 SEPTEMBER 1973–26 JANUARY 1974

THE NEW FRED AND BARNEY SHOW   NBC

3 FEBRUARY 1979–15 SEPTEMBER 1979

FRED AND BARNEY MEET THE THING   NBC

22 SEPTEMBER 1979–   Episodes of *The Flintstones* and *Pebbles and Bamm Bamm* were shown Saturday mornings on CBS for a season and a half as *The Flintstones Comedy Hour* and *The Flintstones Show.* In 1979 new episodes appeared on NBC as *The New Fred and Barney Show,* and later as *Fred and Barney Meet the Thing* (retitled *Fred and Barney Meet the Shmoo* in December 1979).

THE FLIP WILSON SHOW   NBC

17 SEPTEMBER 1970–27 JUNE 1974   A successful variety hour hosted by a talented black comedian, Flip Wilson. Wilson, whose real first name is Clerow, created and popularized such characters as Geraldine Jones ("What you see is what you get!"), Reverend Leroy (pastor of the Church of What's Happenin' Now), and Freddie Johnson, Wilson's Everyman.

FLIPPER   NBC

19 SEPTEMBER 1964–2 SEPTEMBER 1967   Another aquatic adventure series created by Ivan Tors (*Sea Hunt, The Aquanauts,* etc.). The star of the

show was Flipper, a dolphin who was the seagoing equivalent of Lassie. The human roles were filled by Brian Kelly as Porter Ricks, the Chief Ranger at Coral Key Park, a marine refuge in Florida; Luke Halpin as his son Sandy; Tommy Norden as his son Bud; and Ulla Stromstedt (1965–1966) as Ulla Norstrand, a visiting biochemist. Though Flipper was supposed to be a male dolphin, he was played by a female named Susie.

FLIPSIDE   SYNDICATED
1973   A showcase for rock-and-roll performers with no regulars.

FLOOR SHOW   NBC/CBS
1 JANUARY 1949–1 OCTOBER 1949 (NBC); 13 MAY 1950–24 JUNE 1950 (CBS)   One of the first TV programs to feature jazz musicians, *Floor Show* was hosted by guitarist Eddie Condon. The half-hour show was seen on Saturday nights.

THE FLORIAN ZaBACH SHOW   SYNDICATED
1956   Half-hour variety show hosted by fleet-fingered violinist Florian ZaBach.

THE FLYING DOCTOR   SYNDICATED
1959   Richard Denning starred in this half-hour series as an American physician who served the Australian outback by airplane; Jill Adams co-starred as his nurse. Donald Hyde was executive producer for Associated British Pictures Corporation; Gross-Krasne Productions distributed the series.

THE FLYING FISHERMAN
See GADABOUT GADDIS

FLYING HIGH   CBS
29 SEPTEMBER 1978–23 JANUARY 1979   Hour comedy-drama about a trio of flight attendants working for Sunwest Airlines. With Pat Klous as Marcy Bower; Connie Sellecca as Lisa Benton; Kathryn Witt as Pam Bellagio; and Howard Platt as their pilot, Captain Douglas March. Mark Carliner was the executive producer.

THE FLYING NUN   ABC
7 SEPTEMBER 1967–18 SEPTEMBER 1970   Situation comedy about a novice nun who discovers she can fly. Sally Field starred as Elsie Ethrington, a young woman who joins the Convent San Tanco in Puerto Rico where she is ordained as Sister Bertrille. Because of the trade winds, her light weight, and the lofty coronets worn by members of her order, Sister Bertrille develops the ability to leave the ground. Also featured were Madeline Sherwood as Reverend Mother Plaseato; Marge Redmond as

Sister Jacqueline; Shelley Morrison as Sister Sixto; Alejandro Rey as Carlos Ramirez, owner of a nearby nightspot; and Vito Scotti as Gaspar Formento, local police captain. The half-hour series was a Screen Gems production.

FOLLOW THAT MAN
See MAN AGAINST CRIME

FOLLOW THE LEADER   CBS
7 JULY 1953–18 AUGUST 1953   On this prime-time game show studio contestants tried to reenact scenes demonstrated by the "leader"—hostess Vera Vague.

FOLLOW THE SUN   ABC
17 SEPTEMBER 1961–9 SEPTEMBER 1962   This hour-long adventure series was set in Honolulu; thus, for one season, ABC carried two shows with Hawaiian locales (the other was *Hawaiian Eye*). On this effort, the heroes were freelance writers rather than detectives. With Barry Coe as Ben Gregory; Brett Halsey as Paul Templin; Gary Lockwood as boatsman Eric Jason; Gigi Perreau as their secretary, Katherine Ann Richards; and Jay Lanin as Lieutenant Frank Roper, Honolulu cop.

FOLLOW YOUR HEART   NBC
3 AUGUST 1953–8 JANUARY 1954   A short-lived serial set on Philadelphia's Main Line, *Follow Your Heart* told the story of a society girl who didn't want to marry the man her mother had in mind for her. Created by Elaine Carrington, the series was inspired by Carrington's popular radio serial, *When A Girl Marries*. It starred Sallie Brophy as Julie Fielding; Nancy Sheridan as her mother, Mrs. Fielding; and Grant Richards as Julie's boyfriend, Peter Davis, an FBI agent.

FOOD FOR THOUGHT   SYNDICATED
1956–1961   A daytime talk show hosted by Virginia Graham.

FOODINI THE GREAT   ABC
25 AUGUST 1951–29 DECEMBER 1951   A filmed puppet show created by Hope and Morey Bunin. Its star puppets, a bumbling magician named Foodini and his assistant (Pinhead), first appeared on the Bunins' earlier show, *Lucky Pup*.

FOOTBALL SIDELINES   DUMONT
6 OCTOBER 1952–22 DECEMBER 1952   Sportscaster Harry Wismer narrated highlights of the preceding weekend's football games on this fifteen-minute Monday-night series.

FOOTLIGHTS THEATER   CBS
4 JULY 1952–26 SEPTEMBER 1952; 3 JULY 1953–25 SEPTEMBER
1953 This half-hour dramatic anthology series was seen on Friday
nights. In 1953, it was a summer replacement for *Our Miss Brooks*.

FOR ADULTS ONLY   SYNDICATED
1971 Talk show cohosted by Barbara Howar and Joyce Susskind.

FOR BETTER OR WORSE   CBS
29 JUNE 1959–24 JUNE 1960 A daytime serial that focused on problems
in marriages; stories generally lasted one or two weeks. Dr. James A. Peterson, a professional marriage counselor, served as host and commentator. Dyan Cannon made her television debut on this series.

FOR LOVE OR MONEY   CBS
30 JUNE 1958–2 JANUARY 1959 Bill Nimmo hosted this question-and-
answer daytime game show.

FOR RICHER, FOR POORER   NBC
5 DECEMBER 1977–29 SEPTEMBER 1978 Set in suburban Chicago, *For
Richer, For Poorer* was a revamped version of *Lovers and Friends,* which
had left the air seven months earlier. Both serials were created by Har-
ding Lemay; Paul Rauch was the executive producer of both. The cast in-
cluded most of the principals of *Lovers and Friends,* plus a few new faces:
Darlene Parks as Megan Cushing; Tom Happer as Bill Saxton, whom
Megan was about to marry as the show began; Cynthia Bostick as Connie
Ferguson Saxton; Rod Arrants as Megan's brother, Austin Cushing;
Laurinda Barrett as the widowed Edith Cushing, mother of Megan and
Austin; Albert Stratton as Lester Saxton, Bill's alcoholic father; Patricia
Englund as Lester's wife, Josie Saxton; Flora Plumb as their daughter,
Eleanor Saxton Kimball; Richard Backus as their son, Jason Saxton; Da-
vid Abbott as their son, Bentley Saxton; Breon Gorman as their daugh-
ter, Tessa Saxton; Stephen Joyce as Eleanor's husband, lawyer George
Kimball; Christine Jones as the Saxtons' cousin, Amy Gifford Cushing,
wife of Austin; Charles Bateman as investment banker Roger Hamilton;
David Knapp as his son, lawyer Desmond Hamilton; Julia MacKenzie as
Laurie Brewster Hamilton, Desmond's wife; Robert (Skip) Burton as Lee
Ferguson, Connie's brother; Patricia Barry as Viola Brewster; Anthony
Call as Fred Ballard; Michael Goodwin as Stan Hillmer; Lynne MacLar-
en as Barbara Manners; Roy Poole as Ira Ferguson; Sloane Shelton as
Mildred Quinn; David Laden as Turk; Chu Chu Mulave as Paco; Ste-
phen Burleigh as Frank Damico; Connie LoCurto as Wendy Prescott;
Dennis Romer as Dr. Ray White; and Nancy Snyder as Colleen Griffin.

FOR THE PEOPLE   CBS

31 JANUARY 1965–9 MAY 1965   Herbert Brodkin produced this series about an assistant district attorney in New York City. With William Shatner as David Koster; Howard Da Silva as his boss, Anthony Celese; Jessica Walter as his wife, Phyllis; and Lonny Chapman as Frank Malloy, an investigator for the D.A.'s office. Fortunately for *Star Trek* fans, *For the People* was canceled (though it was highly acclaimed); had the show been renewed for the 1965–1966 season, Shatner would not have been available to begin work on *Star Trek*.

FOR YOU, BLACK WOMAN   SYNDICATED

1977–1978   Public affairs program from Gerber/Carter Productions, hosted by Alice Travis, former cohost of *A.M. New York*, a local show.

FOR YOUR PLEASURE

See GIRL ABOUT TOWN

FORD FESTIVAL (THE JAMES MELTON SHOW)   NBC

5 APRIL 1951–26 JUNE 1952   Singer James Melton hosted this hour-long variety series, which replaced *The Ford Star Revue* on Thursdays.

FORD STAR JUBILEE   CBS

24 SEPTEMBER 1955–3 NOVEMBER 1956   Ford Motor Company sponsored this lavish series of monthly specials, all of which were broadcast in color. Presentations included: "The Judy Garland Show," a variety special which marked her television debut (24 September 1955); "The Caine Mutiny Court-Martial," with Lloyd Nolan, Barry Sullivan, and Frank Lovejoy (19 November; directed by Franklin Schaffner); Noel Coward's "Blithe Spirit," with Lauren Bacall and Noel Coward (in his American TV debut; 14 January); "The Day Lincoln was Shot," with Raymond Massey, Lillian Gish, and Jack Lemmon as John Wilkes Booth (11 February; directed by Delbert Mann); "High Tor," a musical version of the play by Maxwell Anderson, with Bing Crosby and Julie Andrews (in her TV debut; 10 March); "Twentieth Century," with Betty Grable and Orson Welles (7 April); Noel Coward's "This Happy Breed," with Coward and Edna Best (5 May); the first television showing of the 1939 film, *The Wizard of Oz* (3 November 1956).

FORD STAR REVUE   NBC

6 JULY 1950–28 SEPTEMBER 1950; 4 JANUARY 1951–29 MARCH 1951   This hour-long variety series began as a summer replacement for *Kay Kyser's Kollege of Musical Knowledge* and replaced it again that winter. Jack Haley hosted the show which also featured singer Mindy Carson.

FORD STARTIME   NBC

6 OCTOBER 1959–31 MAY 1960   An anthology series of dramatic and variety shows. Presentations included: "The Turn of the Screw," with Ingrid Bergman (her first dramatic role on television, 20 October); "The
Wicked Scheme of Jebal Deeks," with Alec Guinness (his American TV
dramatic debut, 10 November); "Dear Arthur," with Rex Harrison (a
rare television appearance, 22 March); "The Young Juggler," with Tony
Curtis (29 March); "Sing Along with Mitch," the first of Mitch Miller's
sing-along specials (24 May). Sponsored by the Ford Motor Company, all
presentations were done in color.

FORD THEATER (THE FORD TELEVISION THEATER)   CBS/NBC/ABC

17 OCTOBER 1948– 29 JUNE 1951 (CBS); 2 OCTOBER 1952–27 SEPTEM-
BER 1956 (NBC); 3 OCTOBER 1956–26 JUNE 1957 (ABC)   *The Ford
Television Theater* was CBS's first sponsored dramatic anthology series,
beginning in 1948 as a once-a-month effort. By the end of its run the
show had been aired over all three major networks, sometimes as a half
hour and sometimes as an hour, sometimes live and sometimes filmed.
Marc Daniels produced and directed the series when it was aired on CBS;
Jules Bricken later produced and directed it during its NBC run. Among
the many stars who played their first major TV roles on the series were
Ernest Borgnine ("Night Visitor," 29 April 1954), Michael Connors
("Yours for a Dream," 8 April 1954), Vince Edwards ("Garrity's Sons,"
24 March 1955), Barbara Hale ("The Divided Heart," 27 November
1952), Judy Holliday ("She Loves Me Not," 4 November 1949), Robert
Horton ("Portrait of Lydia," 16 December 1954), Tab Hunter ("While
We're Young," 28 April 1955), Peter Lawford ("The Son-In-Law," 30
April 1953), Donna Reed ("Portrait of Lydia"), Gilbert Roland ("The
Arden Woodsman," 14 January 1954), Ann Sheridan ("Malaya Inci-
dent," 18 June 1953), Roger Smith ("Never Lend Money to a Woman,"
19 January 1956), Barry Sullivan ("As the Flame Dies," 19 November
1953), Claire Trevor ("Alias Nora Hale," 31 December 1953), James
Whitmore ("For Value Received," 18 February 1954), Shelley Winters
("Mantrap," 28 January 1954), and Robert Young ("Keep It in the Family," 27 May 1954).

FOREIGN INTRIGUE   SYNDICATED

1951–1955   Sheldon Reynolds produced this half-hour adventure series,
which was filmed in Europe. From 1951 to 1953 the show starred Jerome
Thor and Sydna Scott as Robert Cannon and Helen Davis, reporters for
the *Consolidated News*. During the 1953–1954 season James Daly and
Ann Preville starred as Mike Powers and Pat Bennett, reporters for the
Associated News. The third, and final, version of the series starred Gerald
Mohr as Chris Storm, the American owner of a Vienna hotel. Each of the

three shows was later syndicated under a different title: Those with Thor and Scott were titled *Dateline: Europe,* those with Daly and Preville as *Overseas Adventures,* and those with Mohr as *Cross Current. Foreign Intrigue* also holds the distinction of being the first American series televised in Canada when broadcasting began in that country in 1952.

THE FOREST RANGERS
SYNDICATED

1964 A half-hour adventure series produced in Canada. With Graydon Gould as Ranger Keeley of the Forest Rangers; Michael Zenon as Joe Two Rivers, an Indian; Gordon Pinset as Sergeant Scott; and Rolland Bedard as Uncle Raoul. Also featured were the Junior Rangers, a group of youngsters who helped out the Rangers: Ralph Endersby as Chub; Rex Hagon as Peter; Peter Tully as Mike; George Allen as Ted; Susan Conway as Kathy; and Barbara Pierce as Denise.

FOREVER FERNWOOD
SYNDICATED

1977–1978 Following the departure of Louise Lasser from *Mary Hartman, Mary Hartman,* production of the serial resumed, after a summer hiatus, under this title. Most of the gang from *MH2* returned: Greg Mullavey as Tom Hartman, Mary Kay Place as Loretta Haggers, Graham Jarvis as Charlie Haggers, Dody Goodman as Martha Shumway, Debralee Scott as Cathy Shumway, Claudia Lamb as Heather Hartman, Victor Kilian as Grandpa Larkin, Marian Mercer as Wanda, and Dabney Coleman as Merle Jeeter. Tab Hunter, seldom seen on TV since the early 1960s, replaced Philip Bruns as George Shumway; it was explained that George had accidentally fallen into a chemical vat at work and had undergone plastic surgery. Other cast members included: Shelley Fabares as Eleanor Major; Judy Kahan as Penny; Richard Hatch as T'Harmon; Dennis Burkley as Mac; Severn Darden as Popesco, a balloonist; Joe Penny as Sal; Randall Carver as Jeffrey DeVito; Shelley Berman as Mel Beach; Renée Taylor as Annabelle; Orson Bean as Reverend Brim, Archbishop of Ohio; Skip Young (formerly of *Ozzie and Harriet*) as Freddie Friesen; and James Staley as Dr. Szymon.

THE FORSYTE SAGA
NET

5 OCTOBER 1969–29 MARCH 1970 A twenty-six-part adaptation of John Galsworthy's series of novels, *The Forsyte Saga* was produced in England (in black and white) by the BBC in 1967. Spanning the period from 1879 to 1926, it chronicled the lives of the members of a moderately wealthy English family against a backdrop of Victorian and Edwardian life. Principal players included: Kenneth More as Jolyon (Jo) Forsyte, the heir apparent; Eric Porter as lawyer Soames Forsyte; Nyree Dawn Porter as Irene; Susan Hampshire as Fleur; Margaret Tyzack as Winnifred; Nicholas Pennell as Michael Mont; Joseph O'Connor as Jolyon, Sr. (Old Jo-

lyon); Fay Compton as Aunt Ann; Lana Morris as Helene; Martin Jarvis as Jon Forsyte; Ursula Howells as Frances; and George Woodbridge as Swithin. Donald Wilson was the producer, David Giles and James Cellan Jones the directors.

FOUR JUST MEN   SYNDICATED
1959   Half-hour adventure series filmed largely in Europe. The Four Just Men were former comrades during World War II and later joined forces to combat crime on an international scale; each episode featured just one of the Four Just Men. With Dan Dailey as Tim Collier, an American reporter; Jack Hawkins as Ben Manfred, a British detective; Richard Conte as Jeff Ryder, a French attorney; and Vittorio DeSica as Rico Poccari, an Italian hotelier with connections. Jack Wrather produced the series in association with the J. Arthur Rank Organisation.

FOUR STAR PLAYHOUSE   CBS
25 SEPTEMBER 1952–27 SEPTEMBER 1956   This half-hour dramatic anthology series originally featured appearances by the actors who founded Four Star Films: Dick Powell, Charles Boyer, Joel McCrea, and Rosalind Russell. McCrea and Russell left shortly after the inception of the project and were replaced by David Niven and Ida Lupino. Several episodes starred Dick Powell as Willie Dante, operator of Dante's Inferno, a San Francisco nightspot; these episodes were rebroadcast in 1956 as *The Best in Mystery* (see also that title). Other notable appearances included those by Nigel Bruce (in "A String of Beads," his only U.S. TV role, 21 January 1954), Ronald Colman (in "The Lost Silk Hat," his first TV dramatic appearance, 23 October 1952), and Joan Fontaine (in "The Girl on the Park Bench," her first major dramatic role on television, 3 December 1953).

FOUR STAR REVUE   NBC
4 OCTOBER 1950–18 JULY 1951   This Wednesday-night variety hour featured four rotating hosts: Danny Thomas, Jack Carson, Jimmy Durante, and Ed Wynn. In the fall of 1951, more hosts were added, and the show was retitled *All-Star Revue* (see also that title).

FOUR-IN-ONE   NBC
16 SEPTEMBER 1970–8 SEPTEMBER 1971   The umbrella title for four miniseries introduced by NBC. See: *McCloud; Night Gallery; The Psychiatrist; San Francisco International Airport.*

FOURSQUARE COURT   ABC
16 MARCH 1952–22 JUNE 1952   Norman Brokenshire hosted this unusual panel show on which convicted criminals, all of whom wore masks,

discussed their bad deeds. Other experts in the area of criminal law also participated in the panel discussions. David Lown and Albert T. Knudsen were the producers.

THE FOURTH R   NBC
28 MARCH 1954–26 MAY 1957   The fourth "R" stood for "religion" in this Sunday-morning series, which was produced by several different religious organizations.

FRACTURED FLICKERS   SYNDICATED
1963   Silent films from Hollywood's early days were embellished with "funny" dialogue on this half-hour series hosted by Hans Conried.

FRACTURED PHRASES   NBC
27 SEPTEMBER 1965–31 DECEMBER 1965   Art James hosted this daytime game show on which contestants tried to decipher sayings or titles of books and songs after seeing them spelled phonetically.

THE FRANCES LANGFORD–DON AMECHE SHOW   ABC
10 SEPTEMBER 1951–14 MARCH 1952   Frances Langford and Don Ameche, who played *The Bickersons* on radio, hosted this daytime variety hour. A regular feature of the show was "The Couple Next Door," with Jack Lemmon and Cynthia Stone (Lemmon's wife at the time) as young marrieds; this sketch formed the basis of their 1952 series, *Heaven for Betsy*. Also featured on the Langford-Ameche show were Neil Hamilton and the Tony Romano Orchestra. Produced by Ward Byron.

THE FRANK LEAHY SHOW   ABC
27 SEPTEMBER 1953–6 DECEMBER 1953   Fifteen-minute Sunday-night sports show, hosted by football coach Frank Leahy.

FRANK McGEE: HERE AND NOW   NBC
29 SEPTEMBER 1961–29 DECEMBER 1961   Friday-night news analysis and commentary with NBC correspondent Frank McGee. Chet Hagan produced the series.

THE FRANK SINATRA SHOW   CBS
7 OCTOBER 1950–1 APRIL 1952   Frank Sinatra's first series, a musical variety show, inexplicably failed to catch on during its first season; for the 1951–1952 season, it was cut from an hour to a half hour and scheduled opposite Milton Berle's *The Texaco Star Theater*, where, like virtually all of Berle's competition, it perished. Regulars on the show included Erin O'Brien and comic Ben Blue.

THE FRANK SINATRA SHOW   ABC
18 OCTOBER 1957–27 JUNE 1958   Frank Sinatra's second attempt at a
series proved as unsuccessful as the first. This time he was given free
reign (and a reported $3 million) by ABC. The series was a mixed bag—a
combination of dramatic shows (some of which starred Sinatra, the rest
of which were introduced by him), musical programs, and one or two live
half hours. Despite unimposing competition (CBS's *Mr. Adams and Eve*
and NBC's *M Squad*), the show was canceled after one season.

FRANKENSTEIN JR. AND THE IMPOSSIBLES   CBS
10 SEPTEMBER 1966–7 SEPTEMBER 1968   Saturday-morning cartoon
show from the Hanna-Barbera Studios; Frankenstein Jr. was a giant robot, and the Impossibles were a team of super-powered government
agents. The series was rerun in 1976–1977.

THE FRANKIE CARLE SHOW   NBC
7 AUGUST 1956–29 OCTOBER 1956   Frankie Carle hosted this fifteen-
minute musical series, which preceded the network news. It was first seen
on Tuesdays, later on Mondays, and was officially titled *The Golden
Touch of Frankie Carle.*

FRANKIE LAINE TIME   CBS/SYNDICATED
(THE FRANKIE LAINE SHOW)
20 JULY 1955–7 SEPTEMBER 1955; 1 AUGUST 1956–19 SEPTEMBER 1956
(CBS); 1957 (SYNDICATED)   One of America's most popular singers
during the pre-rock-and-roll years, Frankie Laine twice hosted a summer
replacement series for *Arthur Godfrey and His Friends* on Wednesday
nights entitled *Frankie Laine Time.* In 1957 he hosted a syndicated half-
hour variety program, *The Frankie Laine Show.* Laine is perhaps best remembered by television audiences as the vocalist of the *Rawhide* theme.

FRED AND BARNEY MEET THE THING
See THE FLINTSTONES COMEDY HOUR

THE FRED WARING SHOW   CBS
17 APRIL 1949–30 MAY 1954; 22 JULY 1957–30 AUGUST 1957   Fred
Waring organized his first band in 1920; by 1932 he and his group, the
Pennsylvanians, had their own radio show. Waring's assemblage usually
numbered about sixty-five musicians and singers. Among the featured
performers were Joanne Wheatley, Daisy Bernier, Joe Marino, Keith and
Sylvia Textor, Virginia and Livingston Gearhart, and Hugh Brannum,
who later played Mr. Green Jeans on *Captain Kangaroo.* Waring's first
TV series was a half-hour show, which ran on Sunday nights for most of

its run; it was produced and directed by Bob Banner. Waring's 1957 series was a daytime show, a six-week summer replacement for *The Garry Moore Show* broadcast from Waring's Pennsylvania resort, Shawnee-on-the-Delaware.

THE FREDDY MARTIN SHOW (THE HAZEL BISHOP SHOW) NBC
12 JULY 1951–5 DECEMBER 1951 This half-hour musical series, sponsored by Hazel Bishop cosmetics, was introduced as a summer replacement for *Martin Kane, Private Eye* and was later given another time slot. Bandleader Freddy Martin hosted the series; one of its featured vocalists was Merv Griffin.

FREE COUNTRY ABC
24 JUNE 1978–22 JULY 1978 Half-hour comedy-drama starring Rob Reiner and Judy Kahan as Joseph and Anna Bresner, Lithuanian immigrants who came to America in 1906 and 1909 respectively. The five-part series spanned almost seventy years, and each show was "hosted" by Reiner as the eighty-nine-year-old Joseph. Reiner and Phil Mishkin created the series and were its executive producers; Gareth Davies was the producer. Also featured were Larry Gelman and Renée Lippin as the Bresners' friends, Leo and Ida Gewurtzman.

FREEDOM RINGS CBS
3 MARCH 1953–27 AUGUST 1953 John Beal hosted this audience participation show, on which contestants acted out household problems with members of the show's cast—Alice Ghostley, Malcolm Broderick, Joy Hilton, Chuck Taylor, and Ted Tiller. Applause from the studio audience determined the prizewinning contestants. Lloyd Gross produced the half-hour show, which was seen Tuesday and Thursday afternoons.

THE FRENCH CHEF NET–PBS
1962–1973 Half-hour series on French cooking. Thanks to its host, the irrepressible Julia Child, the show was enjoyed by those not interested in French cuisine as well as by gastronomes. See also *Julia Child & Company.*

FRIENDS ABC
25 MARCH 1979–22 APRIL 1979 Wholesome hour miniseries about three suburban sixth graders. With Charles Aiken as Pete Richards; Jill Whelan as Nancy Wilks; Jarrod Johnson as Randy Summerfield; Andy Romano and Karen Morrow as Pete's parents, Mr. and Mrs. Richards; Roger Robinson and Janet MacLachlan as Randy's parents, Warren and Jane Summerfield; Dennis Redfield as Nancy's divorced father, Mr. Wilks; Charles Lampkin as Randy's grandfather; Alicia Fleer as Cynthia, Pete's sixteen-year-old sister. A. J. Carothers created the series, and Aaron Spelling and Douglas S. Cramer were the executive producers.

FRIENDS AND LOVERS   CBS

14 SEPTEMBER 1974-4 JANUARY 1975 Set in Boston, this situation comedy starred Paul Sand as Robert Dreyfuss, a young man who wins a job as bass violinist with the Boston Symphony Orchestra (the show's official title was *Paul Sand in Friends and Lovers*). Also featured were Michael Pataki as his brother, Charlie Dreyfuss; Penny Marshall as Charlie's wife, Janice; Dick Wesson as Jack Reardon, orchestra manager; Steve Landesberg as Robert's friend, Fred Meyerbach, a violinist; and Craig Richard Nelson as Mason Woodruff, the young conductor. Henry Winkler guest starred in the premiere episode. Like *Bridget Loves Bernie, Friends and Lovers* was scheduled between two blockbusters (*All in the Family* and *The Mary Tyler Moore Show*) and was canceled when it failed to win large enough ratings. Executive producers: James L. Brooks and Allan Burns. Produced by Steve Pritzker for MTM Enterprises.

FRIENDS OF MAN   SYNDICATED

1974 Animals were the subject of this half-hour documentary series narrated by Glenn Ford. Executive producer: John Must. Produced by Tony Bond, Henning Jacobsen, and Rupert McNee.

FROM A BIRD'S EYE VIEW   NBC

29 MARCH 1971-16 AUGUST 1971 This comedy, imported from England, centered around two stewardesses employed by International Airlines. With Millicent Martin as Millie Grover, the British one; Patte Finley as Maggie Ralston, the American one; Peter Jones as Mr. Clyde Beauchamp, their supervisor; and Robert Cawdron as Uncle Bert, Millie's uncle.

FROM THESE ROOTS   NBC

30 JUNE 1958-29 DECEMBER 1961 This daytime serial is fondly remembered by soap opera fans as a high quality show; it was also the spawning ground for a number of performers who went on to play major roles in other soaps. Created by Frank Provo, the series was produced by Paul Lammers and directed by Don Wallace. The cast included: Rod Henrickson and Joseph Macauley as Ben Fraser, editor of the Strathfield *Record;* Ann Flood as Liz Fraser, his daughter, a fiction writer; Frank Marth as Ben Fraser, Jr.; Julie Bovasso and Tresa Hughes as Rose Corelli Fraser, his wife; Len Wayland and Tom Shirley as Dr. Buck Weaver; Billie Lou Watt as Maggie Barker Weaver, his wife; Robert Mandan as playwright David Allen, who married Liz Fraser; Barbara Berjer as Lynn Franklin; Audra Lindley as Laura Tompkins; Millette Alexander as Gloria Saxon; Henderson Forsythe as Jim Benson; Craig Huebing as Tom Jennings; David Sanders as Bruce Crawford; and Vera Allen as Kass, Ben Sr.'s maid.

THE FRONT PAGE   CBS
29 SEPTEMBER 1949–26 JANUARY 1950   Franklin Heller directed this
Thursday-night series, which was based on the film of the same title. John
Daly starred as editor Walter Burns; one week after the show's cancella-
tion, Daly and Heller moved on to a new game show created by Mark
Goodson and Bill Todman called *What's My Line?*

FRONT PAGE DETECTIVE   DUMONT
16 MARCH 1951–19 SEPTEMBER 1952   Edmund Lowe starred as reporter David Chase in this half-hour series. Paula Drew costarred as his girlfriend, a fashion designer. Jerry Fairbanks produced the show, which was
filmed in Los Angeles. A few episodes were broadcast on DuMont in the
fall of 1953.

FRONT ROW CENTER   DUMONT
25 MARCH 1949–2 APRIL 1950   Regulars on this musical variety series
included Phil Leeds, Hal Loman, Joan Fields, and Bibi Osterwald.

FRONT ROW CENTER   CBS
1 JUNE 1955–21 SEPTEMBER 1955; 8 JANUARY 1956–22 APRIL
1956   This dramatic anthology hour, produced and directed by Fletcher
Markle, alternated with *The U.S. Steel Hour* during the summer of 1955,
then reappeared on Sunday afternoons early in 1956. Presentations included: "Dinner at Eight," with Mary Astor, Everett Sloane, Pat O'Bri-
en, and Mary Beth Hughes (1 June); "Ah, Wilderness!" with Leon Ames
and Lillian Hellman (15 June); and "The Human Touch," with Lisa Kirk
(15 April).

FRONTIER   NBC
25 SEPTEMBER 1955–9 SEPTEMBER 1956   Worthington Miner produced
this half-hour western anthology series in which gunplay was deemphasized. Walter Coy served as narrator, and starred in occasional episodes;
the stories were said to have been based on fact.

FRONTIER CIRCUS   CBS
5 OCTOBER 1961–20 SEPTEMBER 1962   The T & T Circus provided the
backdrop for this hour-long western, which featured Chill Wills as Colonel Casey Thompson and John Derek as Ben Travis, coowners of the circus, and Richard Jaeckel as their scout, Tony Gentry.

FRONTIER DOCTOR   SYNDICATED
1958   Rex Allen, star of countless "B" western movies, starred as Dr.
Bill Baxter, a frontier physician in the Arizona Territory.

FRONTIER JUSTICE   CBS
14 JULY 1958–29 SEPTEMBER 1958; 6 JULY 1959–21 SEPTEMBER 1959 This series of rebroadcasts of *Zane Grey Theater* episodes was seen as a summer replacement for *December Bride* in 1958 and for *Make Room for Daddy* in 1959. Lew Ayres hosted in 1958, Melvyn Douglas in 1959.

FRONTIERS OF FAITH   NBC
7 OCTOBER 1951–19 JULY 1970 This long-running religious series was sponsored by the National Council of Churches. For many years it shared a time slot with two other religious programs: *The Catholic Hour* (later known as *Guideline*) and *The Eternal Light.*

FROSTY FROLICS   ABC
19 SEPTEMBER 1951–10 OCTOBER 1951 This four-week series appears to have been the first ice revue series on television; it was produced and directed by Klaus Landsberg. The idea was later employed on such series as *Music on Ice* and *Ice Palace,* and to a limited extent on *Donny and Marie.*

THE FUGITIVE   ABC
17 SEPTEMBER 1963–29 AUGUST 1967 Quinn Martin produced this popular adventure series, which starred David Janssen as Dr. Richard Kimble and Barry Morse as Lieutenant Philip Gerard. Wrongly convicted for the murder of his wife and sentenced to death, Kimble escaped from custody in a train wreck while being transported to prison. He spent the next four years searching for the mysterious one-armed man whom he had seen running from the house the night his wife was murdered. Complicating his search was the fact that he was being relentlessly (if unsuccessfully) pursued by Lieutenant Gerard. The series climaxed in a two-parter shown after the summer reruns in 1967. After learning that the one-armed man had been captured in Los Angeles, Kimble surrendered. Shortly thereafter, the one-armed man escaped from custody; Kimble prevailed upon Gerard to let him track the man down. Kimble found him in a deserted amusement park and chased him to the top of a water tower; there, the one-armed man confessed to the killing just as he was about to throw Kimble from the tower. At that moment, Gerard arrived below and, apparently convinced of Kimble's innocence, shot the one-armed man. Also featured on the series were Bill Raisch as Fred Johnson, the one-armed man and (in the openings and in flashbacks) Diane Brewster as Helen Kimble. William Conrad served as narrator.

FULL CIRCLE   CBS
27 JUNE 1960–10 MARCH 1961 Bill Barrett wrote this little-known daytime serial, which featured Robert Fortier as Gary Donovan, a romantic

drifter, and Dyan Cannon as Lisa Crowder, the young widow with whom he got involved. Also featured were Bill Lundmark as songwriter David Talton; Amzie Strickland as Beth Perce; Jean Byron as Dr. Kit Aldrich; and Byron Foulger as Carter Talton.

THE FUN FACTORY
NBC

14 JUNE 1976–1 OCTOBER 1976   Bobby Van hosted this daytime show, which combined audience-participation games with songs and sketches performed by the regulars: Jane Nelson, Betty Thomas, Deborah Harmon, Doug Steckler, and Dick Blasucci. Executive producers: Ed Fishman and Randall Freer. Produced by David Fishman.

FUN FOR THE MONEY
ABC

17 JUNE 1949–9 DECEMBER 1949   Johnny Olsen hosted this Chicago-based game show on which teams of women and men competed against each other. James Saphier produced the half-hour series, and Ed Skotch directed it.

THE FUNKY PHANTOM
ABC

11 SEPTEMBER 1971–1 SEPTEMBER 1972   Saturday-morning cartoon show about three kids and their pal, a two-hundred-year-old chap who locked himself in a grandfather clock in 1776.

FUNNY BONERS
NBC

27 NOVEMBER 1954–9 JULY 1955   A game show for children, which was seen on Saturday mornings and hosted by ventriloquist Jimmy Weldon and his dummy duck, Webster Webfoot. Broadcast from Hollywood.

FUNNY FACE
CBS

18 SEPTEMBER 1971–11 DECEMBER 1971   This half-hour sitcom starred Sandy Duncan as Sandy Stockton, a student teacher who also did commericals for an ad agency. Also featured were Valorie Armstrong as her friend and neighbor, Alice McCraven, and (in the first few episodes only) Henry Beckman and Kathleen Freeman as Pat and Kate Harwell, Sandy's landlords. Production of the series was discontinued in 1971 when Duncan required eye surgery; she returned to television in 1972 in a slightly different format. See *The Sandy Duncan Show.*

FUNNY MANNS
SYNDICATED

1960   Cliff Norton hosted this series of silent film comedy shorts. Between segments, Norton appeared as any one of several "Mann" characters, such as Mail Mann, Police Mann, or Trash Mann.

THE FUNNY SIDE
NBC

14 SEPTEMBER 1971–7 DECEMBER 1971   On this hour-long comedy se-

ries, a repertory company of five couples explored the funny side of a particular subject each week. Gene Kelly hosted most of the episodes. The players included: Burt Mustin and Queenie Smith as the old couple; Dick Clair and Jenna McMahon as the sophisticated couple; John Amos and Teresa Graves as the black couple; Warren Berlinger and Pat Finley as the blue-collar couple; and Michael Lembeck and Cindy Williams as the young couple. Bill Persky and Sam Denoff were the producers.

FUNNY YOU SHOULD ASK
ABC

28 OCTOBER 1968–27 JUNE 1969 Lloyd Thaxton hosted this daytime game show on which contestants tried to match answers with the celebrities who had supplied them.

THE FURTHER ADVENTURES OF ELLERY QUEEN
See ELLERY QUEEN

FURY
NBC

15 OCTOBER 1955–3 SEPTEMBER 1966 This popular show about a boy and his horse was a Saturday staple for several seasons. Bobby Diamond starred as Joey Newton, a city orphan who was taken into custody by a policeman after a street fight and who was permitted to live on a ranch with the policeman; Peter Graves costarred as Jim Newton, the cop who eventually adopted Joey. Also featured were William Fawcett as Pete, the chief hand at the Broken Wheel Ranch; Roger Mobley as Joey's friend, Packy; and Jimmy Baird as Joey's friend, Pee Wee. Fury, the black horse given to Joey by Jim, was owned and trained by Ralph McCutcheon. There were 114 episodes filmed between 1955 and 1960 and rerun by the network until 1966. The series was syndicated under the title of *Brave Stallion*.

FUTURE COP
ABC

5 MARCH 1977–6 AUGUST 1977 An irregularly scheduled crime show, *Future Cop* starred Ernest Borgnine as Officer Joe Cleaver and John Amos as his partner, Officer Bill Bundy. The two veterans were assigned to break in a rookie officer, a robot supposedly programmed to be the perfect cop. The android, Officer Haven, was played by Michael Shannon. Anthony Wilson and Gary Damsker were the executive producers of the hour series.

THE G.E. COLLEGE BOWL
See COLLEGE BOWL

G.E. THEATER
See GENERAL ELECTRIC THEATER

G.E. TRUE

30 SEPTEMBER 1962–22 SEPTEMBER 1963   Jack Webb served as host
and narrator of this half-hour anthology series; the episodes were based
on stories from *True* magazine. Sponsored by General Electric, the show
occupied the same Sunday slot that *General Electric Theater* held down
for many seasons.

THE GABBY HAYES SHOW
NBC/ABC

11 DECEMBER 1950–1 JANUARY 1954 (NBC); 12 MAY 1956–14 JULY
1956 (ABC)   George "Gabby" Hayes, the grizzled character actor who
appeared in countless western films, showed clips from the old westerns
on both his series. The first was a fifteen-minute show that immediately
preceded *Howdy Doody* weekdays; the second was a half-hour show seen
on Saturday mornings.

GADABOUT GADDIS
SYNDICATED

1950–1965   Roscoe Vernon, better known as Gadabout Gaddis, hosted
this long-running series about fishing.

THE GALAXY GOOF-UPS
See YOGI'S SPACE RACE

THE GALE STORM SHOW
See OH! SUSANNA

THE GALLANT MEN
ABC

5 OCTOBER 1962–14 SEPTEMBER 1963   *The Gallant Men* and *Combat*
ushered in a wave of World War II dramas beginning in 1962. This one
focused on the American campaign in Italy, as seen through the eyes of a
war correspondent. With William Reynolds as Captain James Benedict;
Robert McQueeney as correspondent Conley Wright; Robert Ridgely as
Kimbro; Eddie Fontane as D'Angelo; Richard X. Slattery as McKenna;
Roland LaStarza as Lucavich; Roger Davis as Gibson; and Robert
Gothie as Hanson.

THE GALLERY OF MADAME LIU-TSONG
DUMONT

27 AUGUST 1951–21 NOVEMBER 1951   Anna May Wong starred as Madame Liu-Tsong, owner of an art gallery, in this little-noted half-hour adventure series (Miss Wong's real name was, in fact, Wong Liu-Tsong).

THE GALLOPING GOURMET
SYNDICATED

1969   Graham Kerr, with a glass of wine in hand, presided over this
freewheeling half hour on which gourmet dishes sometimes came out
right and sometimes didn't. The show was produced by Treena Kerr (his

wife) at CJOH-TV, Ottawa. In the 1970s the Kerrs reportedly found religion and gave up wine, even for cooking.

GAMBIT CBS

4 SEPTEMBER 1972–10 DECEMBER 1976   Married couples played blackjack with oversized cards on this daytime game show hosted by Wink Martindale (Elaine Stewart dealt the cards). Executive producers: Merrill Heatter and Bob Quigley.

GAMBLE ON LOVE DUMONT

16 JULY 1954–20 AUGUST 1954   This prime-time quiz show for married couples was originally hosted by Denise Darcel. Ernie Kovacs took over early in August, and shortly thereafter, the show's title and format were changed: see *Time Will Tell.*

THE GAME GAME SYNDICATED

1969   Jim McKrell hosted this game show on which contestants tested their knowledge of psychology against a panel of three celebrities.

GANGBUSTERS NBC

20 MARCH 1952–25 DECEMBER 1952   A crime anthology series, *Gangbusters* was created by Phillips Lord and enjoyed a far longer run on radio (1935–1957) than it did on TV. The stories were based on fact, and the show featured interviews with law enforcement officials. The half-hour show alternated with *Dragnet* on Thursdays. Reruns were syndicated under the title *Captured* and were hosted by Chester Morris.

THE GARLUND TOUCH

See MR. GARLUND

GARRISON'S GORILLAS ABC

5 SEPTEMBER 1967–17 SEPTEMBER 1968   This World War II drama was inspired by the film *The Dirty Dozen*. It starred Ron Harper as Lieutenant Craig Garrison, an Army officer who put together a squad of four men, all of whom were serving time in federal prisons; the men were promised pardons in exchange for their cooperation. With Chris Cary as Goniff, a pickpocket; Rudy Solari as Casino, a thief; Brendon Boone as Chief, a knife-wielding Indian; and Cesare Danova as Actor, a con man. Executive producer: Selig J. Seligman. Produced by Richard Caffey.

GARROWAY AT LARGE NBC

18 JUNE 1949–24 JUNE 1951   This prime-time half-hour musical variety series, broadcast live from Chicago, introduced Dave Garroway to national television audiences. Other regulars included Jack Haskell, Cliff Norton, Connie Russell, Betty Chappel, Jimmy Russell, and Aura

Vainio. The show's trademarks were its spare sets (necessitated by a low budget) and humorous endings (such as Garroway announcing that the show was broadcast from Chicago, "the friendliest city in the world," then turning around to show a knife stuck in his back). Ted Mills produced the series, and Charlie Andrews wrote it. Garroway's theme song, "Sentimental Journey," was later used on the *Today* show.

THE GARRY MOORE SHOW   CBS
26 JUNE 1950–27 JUNE 1958; 30 SEPTEMBER 1958–14 JUNE 1964; 11 SEPTEMBER 1966–8 JANUARY 1967

THE GARRY MOORE EVENING SHOW   CBS
18 OCTOBER 1951–27 DECEMBER 1951 Before coming to television in 1950, Garry Moore had worked on several radio shows, including *Club Matinee*, *Take It Or Leave It*, and *The Jimmy Durante–Garry Moore Show*. It was on *Club Matinee* that he first teamed up with Durward Kirby, who would be his sidekick for many years; it was also on *Club Matinee* that a contest to choose Garry Moore's stage name was held (until then he was known by his real name, Thomas Garrison Morfit).

The first of his several television series began in June 1950; it was originally telecast five evenings per week but moved to weekday afternoons in October. Moore again hosted an evening show in the fall of 1951; lasting only a few weeks, it alternated beweekly with *The Burns and Allen Show*. The daytime show, however, proved durable: It lasted eight years, blending songs and chatter in a low-key, straightforward manner. Moore was neither a singer nor a comedian, but rather a relaxed and congenial host who surrounded himself with a crew of talented performers. In addition to sidekick Kirby, regulars on the daytime show included singers Ken Carson (who had worked with Moore on the *Durante–Moore Show*) and Denise Lor (whom Moore had spotted on *Broadway Open House*). Comedians were regularly featured; among the funny people who made some of their earliest appearances on the show were Don Adams, Kaye Ballard, Wally Cox, George Gobel, Milt Kamen, Don Knotts, Roger Price and his "Droodles" cartoons, Jonathan Winters, and the comedy team of Mickey Ross and Bernie West (Ross and West were later two of the producers of *All in the Family*). Other young performers who appeared on the show included singers Leslie Uggams and Peter Marshall (with his then partner, Tommy Farrell), and a twelve-year-old blonde named Tuesday Weld. Another newcomer was, of course, Carol Burnett, who first appeared on the daytime show in the fall of 1956 and later became a regular on Moore's prime-time series. One of the most notable guests to appear was Frank Lloyd Wright, who, at age eighty-seven, did two shows in 1956.

Not all of Moore's guests were human: Naturalists Ivan Sanderson and Lorraine D'Essen frequently brought unusual animals to the program. The home audience also had the opportunity to "participate" in the show from time to time. In a contest held in 1954, one lucky Ohio family won Durward Kirby for a weekend. On another 1954 broadcast, Moore asked viewers to send one member of the studio audience (a Michigan housewife) a nickel. Within two days the woman had received 48,000 letters, and it was reported that she eventually received more than $12,000 in nickels.

In 1958, Moore announced that he had grown "tired" of the daytime grind and would leave the show. Moore's last regular appearance was on 16 May; Dick Van Dyke and Durward Kirby cohosted the final six weeks. It is small wonder that Moore was tired: in addition to hosting more than 2,000 shows, he had also been hosting *I've Got a Secret* for six years. Apparently, a summer's rest did him a world of good, for he returned to television that fall to host a prime-time variety series. That show held down a Tuesday-night slot for six seasons. Regulars included Durward Kirby, Ken Carson, Denise Lor, Carol Burnett (1959–62), and Marion Lorne; a regular feature each week was a musical salute to "That Wonderful Year 19——." Moore grew tired of that series (and of *I've Got a Secret,* which he had continued to host) in 1964, and briefly retired from show business.

In the fall of 1966 he returned to host a Sunday-night variety series which fared poorly against NBC's *Bonanza*.. Moore's regulars included Durward Kirby, John Byner, Jackie Vernon, Pete Barbutti, and Patsy Elliott.

Moore's daytime series was produced by Herb Sanford and directed for many seasons by Clarence Schimmel. Among the show's writers were Bill Demling, Vinnie Bogert, Marsha Durant, Harold Flender, Chuck Horner, Hank Miles, Charlie Slocum, Aaron Ruben, Roland Scott, and Allan Sherman. Moore's 1958–1964 series was produced by Joe Hamilton and Bob Banner, and the executive producer of the 1966 series was Sylvester "Pat" Weaver.

GAY NINETIES REVUE   ABC
11 AUGUST 1948–14 JANUARY 1949   This musical variety series recreated the early days of vaudeville. It was hosted by eighty-one-year-old Joe Howard, a trouper whose career actually went back to the 1890s; Howard had previously hosted the show on radio.

THE GAYELORD HAUSER SHOW   ABC
31 OCTOBER 1951–25 APRIL 1952   Health and nutrition were the subjects discussed on this daytime show hosted by Gayelord Hauser; it was seen Wednesday and Friday afternoons.

GEMINI MAN   NBC
23 SEPTEMBER 1976–28 OCTOBER 1976   This hour-long adventure series featured a think-tank employee who could become invisible for up to fifteen minutes a day. With Ben Murphy as Sam Casey; Katherine Craw-

ford as Dr. Abby Lawrence; and William Sylvester as Leonard Driscoll, director of Intersect, the think tank. Produced by Harve Bennett, the show was little more than a rewarmed version of *The Invisible Man,* a 1975 NBC series that folded after eleven episodes.

THE GENE AUTRY SHOW CBS
23 JULY 1950–7 AUGUST 1956   One of the first western film stars to begin filming a series especially for television, Gene Autry formed his own production company (Flying A Productions) and made 104 half-hour episodes. He played himself; his sidekick was Pat Buttram. Autry was not a lawman, but often assisted the men with the badges in bringing outlaws to justice. His series proved so successful that it led to a pair of spinoffs: One featured TV's first female western hero (*Annie Oakley*), and the other featured Autry's horse (*The Adventures of Champion*).

GENERAL ELECTRIC GUEST HOUSE
See GUEST HOUSE

GENERAL ELECTRIC SUMMER ORIGINALS ABC
3 JULY 1956–18 SEPTEMBER 1956   Half-hour filmed anthology series. Vivian Blaine starred in the premiere, a musical comedy titled "It's Sunny Again."

GENERAL ELECTRIC THEATER CBS
1 FEBRUARY 1953–16 SEPTEMBER 1962   This popular half-hour dramatic anthology series was seen on Sunday nights; Ronald Reagan hosted the show from 1954 to 1962. Among the major stars who made their television dramatic debuts on the series were Joseph Cotten ("The High Green Wall," 3 October 1954), Alan Ladd ("Committed," 5 December 1954), Fred MacMurray ("Bachelor's Pride," 20 February 1955), James Stewart ("The Windmill," 24 April 1955), Myrna Loy ("It Gives Me Great Pleasure," 3 April 1955), Bette Davis ("With Malice Toward None," 10 March 1957), Anne Baxter ("Bitter Choice," 21 April 1957), Tony Curtis ("Cornada," 10 November 1957), Fred Astaire ("Imp on a Cobweb Leash," 1 December 1957), Sammy Davis, Jr. ("Auf Wiedersehen," 5 October 1958), Peggy Lee ("So Deadly, So Evil," 13 March 1960), and Gene Tierney ("Journey to a Wedding," 27 November 1960). Other notable appearances included those by Joan Crawford ("The Road to Edinburgh," 31 October 1954), Harry Belafonte ("Winner by Decision," 6 November 1955), Rosalind Russell ("The Night Goes On," 18 March 1956), Ernie Kovacs ("The World's Greatest Quarterback," 19 October 1958), Harpo and Chico Marx ("The Incredible Jewel Robbery," 8 March 1959), and Groucho Marx ("The Holdout," 14 January 1962).

GENERAL HOSPITAL   ABC

1 APRIL 1963–   *General Hospital* and *The Doctors*, daytime
television's most prominent medical soap operas, both premiered on the
same day; unlike *The Doctors*, which was an anthology series during its
first few months, *General Hospital* has been a continuing drama from the
beginning. Created by Frank and Doris Hurley, *General Hospital* is set in
the town of Port Charles. The show is currently written by Eileen and
Robert Mason Pollock, who had written *The Doctors* for several years before moving over in 1975; the Pollocks succeeded Jerome and Bridget
Dobson. Tom Donovan became the producer of *General Hospital* in
1975, replacing Jim Young. On 26 July 1976, the serial expanded from
thirty to forty-five minutes, and on 16 January 1978, it expanded again to
a full hour. Two members of the cast have been with the show from the
beginning: John Beradino (a former major league baseball player) as Dr.
Steve Hardy, director of internal medicine at General Hospital, and Emily McLaughlin as nurse Jessie Brewer, his close friend and confidante.
Other longtime cast members include Lucille Wall, who joined in July
1963 as head nurse Lucille March (she left the series in 1976); Rachel
Ames, who joined a year later, as Lucille's sister, nurse Audrey March,
who married Steve Hardy (they were later divorced); and Peter Hansen,
who has played Lee Baldwin since 1965. Other principal players over the
years have included: Roy Thinnes, Rick Falk, Robert Hogan, and Martin
West as Jessie's husband, Dr. Phil Brewer (Phil was thought to have been
killed in a car crash, but surfaced later under the name of Harold Williamson; Phil was finally murdered in 1974); Carolyn Craig as Phil's girlfriend, Cynthia Allison; K. T. Stevens as Steve Hardy's onetime romantic
interest, Peggy Mercer; Allyson Hayes as Priscilla Longworth, who was
also interested in Steve; Patricia Breslin and Elizabeth MacRae as widowed nurse Meg Bentley, who married Lee Baldwin, and later suffered a
nervous breakdown and died; Adrienne Hayes and Indus Arthur as
Meg's stepdaughter, Brooke Clinton, who was murdered; Dean Harens
as Noll Clinton, Brooke's husband; Paul Savior as Dr. Tom Baldwin,
brother of Lee Baldwin; Barry Atwater as Dr. John Prentice, who married Jessie Brewer and was later murdered; Jennifer Billingsley as his
daughter (and murderer), Polly Prentice, who was killed in the car crash
that also involved Phil Brewer; Ed Platt as Dr. Miller (Platt returned to
the show several years later to play another role, Wyatt Chamberlain);
Peggy McCay as nurse Iris Fairchild; Shelby Hiatt as nurse Jane Harland; Ray Girardin as Howie Dawson, who married Jane; Maxine Stuart
and Phyllis Hill as Howie's mother, Mrs. Dawson; Julie Adams as
Howie's girlfriend, Denise Wilton; Jim McKrell as Denise's boyfriend,
Bruce Andrews; Kim Hamilton as Dr. Tracy Adams; Robin Blake as
nurse Judy Clampett; Adolph Caesar as Douglas Burke, a blind patient
who fell for Judy (his eyesight was subsequently restored); Craig Huebing

as psychiatrist Dr. Peter Taylor, who was married briefly to Jessie Brewer (their marriage was annulled when Phil Brewer returned to Port Charles); Valerie Starrett and Brooke Bundy (1977–   ) as Diana Maynard, Peter Taylor's next wife; Sharon DeBord as nurse Sharon McGillis; Peter Kilman as Dr. Henry Pinkham, who married Sharon; Susan Bernard as student nurse Beverly Cleveland, who had an affair with Howie Dawson; Tom Brown as Al Weeks of the hospital maintenance staff, who married head nurse Lucille March in 1972; Doug Lambert and Craig Curtis as Al's son, Eddie Weeks; Jana Taylor as Eddie's girlfriend, Angie Costello; Anne Helm as nurse Mary Briggs; Tom Simcox as Mary's husband, Wade Collins, an ex-con; Denise Alexander (who came to *General Hospital* in 1970 after several years on *Days of Our Lives*) as Dr. Lesley Williams; Don Matheson as Cameron Faulkner, who married Lesley; Stacy Baldwin and Genie Ann Francis as Lesley's illegitimate daughter, Laura Vining; Judy Lewis as Laura's foster mother, Barbara Vining; Jonathan Carter as Laura's foster father, Jason Vining; Deanna Lund as Cameron Faulkner's secretary, Peggy Lowell; Ann Collings as Florence Gray, a patient of Lesley's; Howard Sherman and Eric Server as her husband, Gordon Gray; James Sikking as Dr. James Hobart; Judith McConnell as nurse Augusta McLeod, killer of Phil Brewer; Rod McCary as Dr. Joel Stratton; Linda Cooper as nurse Linda Cooper (a rare instance in which the actress and the role share the same name); Jenny Sherman as Sally Grimes; Augusta Dabney as Caroline Chandler; Ted Eccles as Caroline's son, Bobby Chandler; Kimberly Beck (1973–1975) and Marla Pennington (1975–1976) as nurse Samantha Livingston, who married Bobby; Michelle Conaway as Beth Maynard, sister of Diana Maynard Taylor; Daniel Black as Dr. Kyle Bradley, Beth's boyfriend; Victoria Shaw as Kira Faulkner; Don Clarke and Kin Shriner as Scotty Baldwin, son of the late Meg Baldwin; John Gabriel and James Westmoreland as newspaper reporter Teddy Holmes; Anne Wyndham as Jessie Brewer's niece and ward, Carol Murray; Mark Hamill as Jessie's nephew and ward, Kent Murray; Monica Gayle as Jessie's niece, Kate Marshall; George Chandler as Walter Douglas; Georgia Schmidt as Amy Douglas; Kevin Matthews as Dr. Duncan Stewart; Maida Stevens as Mrs. Andrews; Virginia Ann Lee as Mai Lin, a visiting dancer from the People's Republic of China; Nathan Jung as Won Chu; George Chiang as Ling Wang; Ivan Bonar as Chase Murdock; Betty Ann Rees as Margaret Colson; Jennifer Peters as Martha Taylor; Mark Travis as Felix Buchanan; Mark Miller as Randy Washburn; Louise Fitch as Mrs. Taylor; William Mims as Gus Wheeler; Don Hammer as Lieutenant Adams; Laura Campbell as Pat Lambert; Joseph DiSante as Dr. Gerald Henderson; Richard Eastham as Mr. Livingston; and Burt Douglas as Mac.

More recent additions to the cast have included: Richard Dean Anderson as Dr. Jeff Webber; Jerry Ayres as David Hamilton; Susan Brown as Dr. Gail Adamson; William Bryant as Lamont Corbin; Steve Carlson as

Dr. Gary Lansing; Angela Cheyne as Dorrie Fleming; David Comfort as Tommy Baldwin Hardy; Stuart Damon as Alan Quartermain; Dennis Dinster as Mike Mallon; Lieux Dressler as Mrs. Grant; Gerald Gordon as Dr. Mark Dante; Michael Gregory and Chris Robinson as Dr. Rick Webber; Brett Halsey (1976–1978) as Dr. Adam Streeter; Janice Heiden as Lisa Holbrook, a split personality; Bobbi Jordan as Terri Arnett; Georganne LaPiere (sister of Cher Bono Allman) and Mary O'Brien as Heather Grant; Maria Perschy as Maria Schuller; Patsy Rahn (1976–1977) and Leslie Charleson (1977–   ) as Dr. Monica Webber; William Schreiner as Darren Blythe; Anna Stuart as Dr. Gina Dante; Maggie Sullivan as Katie Corbin, Lamont's wife; Richard Venture as Herbert Behrman; Lee Warrick as Mary Ellen Dante; Lesley Woods as Edna Hadley; Jackie Zeman as Barbara Spencer; Donna Bacalla as Dr. Gina Lansing; Todd Davis as Bryan Phillips; Jane Elliott as Tracy Quartermain; David Lewis as Edward Quartermain; Anna Lee as Lila Quartermain; Jay Gerber as Jim Richardson; Bob Hastings as Burt Ramsey; Frank Maxwell as Dan Rooney; Gail Ramsey as Susan Moore; Richard Sarradet as Howard Lansing; Joan Tompkins as Mrs. Maynard; Christopher Stafford Nelson as Chris; Anthony Geary as Luke Spencer; Joyce Jameson as Colleen Middleton; Craig Littler as Dr. Todd Levine; Susan O'Hanlon as Ann Logan; Chris Pennock as Mitch Williams.

THE GENERATION GAP   ABC

7 FEBRUARY 1969–21 MAY 1969   A team of three adults faced a team of three juveniles on this convoluted prime-time game show; each team had to predict whether the other team would be able to answer questions about the opposite generation. Dennis Wholey first hosted the series and was replaced by Jack Barry.

GENTLE BEN   CBS

10 SEPTEMBER 1967–31 AUGUST 1969   The adventures of a boy and his pet bear (Ben). With Clint Howard as young Mark Wedloe; Dennis Weaver as his father, Tom Wedloe, a game warden in the Florida Everglades; Beth Brickell as his mother, Ellen Wedloe; Jack Morley as Tom's friend, Spencer; and Angelo Rutherford (1968–1969) as Mark's friend, Willie. Ben, the bear, was played by Bruno and trained by Monty Cox. Ivan Tors produced the series; it was filmed on location in Florida.

THE GEORGE BURNS AND GRACIE ALLEN SHOW
See THE BURNS AND ALLEN SHOW

THE GEORGE BURNS SHOW   NBC

21 OCTOBER 1958–14 APRIL 1959   After Gracie Allen retired from show business, George Burns continued the situation comedy, this time on NBC. He continued to play himself, though he now cast himself as a tele-

vision producer. Most of the old gang from *The Burns and Allen Show* remained: Bea Benaderet as Blanche Morton, his secretary; Larry Keating as Harry Morton, his accountant; Ronnie Burns (as himself); and Harry Von Zell as his announcer, always eager to land a dramatic role.

THE GEORGE GOBEL SHOW NBC/CBS

2 OCTOBER 1954–10 MARCH 1959 (NBC); 11 OCTOBER 1959–5 JUNE 1960 (CBS) A casual, folksy, down-home comedian, George Gobel hosted a half-hour comedy-variety series on Saturday nights beginning in 1954; regulars included singer Peggy King and Jeff Donnell, who played his wife, Alice, in many sketches. In the fall of 1957, he moved to Tuesday nights, where he hosted a biweekly hour-long series that alternated with *The Eddie Fisher Show;* Fisher was the "permanent guest star" on the Gobel shows, and Gobel reciprocated on the Fisher broadcasts. Gobel's other regulars included Jeff Donnell (1957–1958), Phyllis Avery (1958–1959, who replaced Donnell as Alice), Shirley Harmer, and the Johnny Mann Singers. In the fall of 1959 Gobel moved to CBS, where he hosted a half-hour variety series that alternated with *The Jack Benny Program* on Sundays; regulars there included Joe Flynn, Anita Bryant, and Harry Von Zell. Gobel's theme song, "Gobelues," was composed by his longtime bandleader, John Scott Trotter.

THE GEORGE HAMILTON IV SHOW ABC

13 APRIL 1959–29 MAY 1959 Country and western singer George Hamilton IV ("A Rose and a Baby Ruth") hosted this half-hour musical series, which was seen weekdays at noon. Originating from Washington, D.C., it featured Roy Clark and Mary Klick.

THE GEORGE JESSEL SHOW ABC

13 SEPTEMBER 1953–11 APRIL 1954 One of several major stars signed up by ABC in 1953, George Jessel, America's "Toastmaster General," hosted a half-hour variety series on Sunday evenings. Hal Sawyer was also featured on the show that was produced by Mannie Manheim. Making one of his earliest television appearances, Buddy Hackett guest starred on the premiere.

GEORGE OF THE JUNGLE ABC

9 SEPTEMBER 1968–6 SEPTEMBER 1970 Jay Ward created this fairly sophisticated Saturday-morning cartoon show. Segments included: "George of the Jungle," with George, a clumsy Tarzan type, Ape, an erudite gorilla, and Shep, George's trusty elephant; "Super Chicken," the story of Henry Cabot Henhouse III, an ordinary fowl who turned into Super Chicken after a swig of Super Sauce, and his pal, Fred the lion; and "Tom Slick," an auto racer who always played fair.

THE GEORGE RAFT CASEBOOK
See I AM THE LAW

GEORGE SANDERS MYSTERY THEATRE   NBC
22 JUNE 1957–14 SEPTEMBER 1957   Suave British actor George Sanders
hosted this half-hour anthology series.

GEORGETOWN UNIVERSITY FORUM   DUMONT
3 JULY 1951–11 OCTOBER 1953   An early public affairs series, produced
at Georgetown University in Washington, D. C.

GEORGIA GIBBS' MILLION RECORD SHOW   NBC
1 JULY 1957–2 SEPTEMBER 1957   "Her Nibs," Georgia Gibbs, hosted
this musical series on which million-sellers were performed. The fifteen-
minute show was seen Mondays preceding the news.

THE GERALD McBOING-BOING SHOW   CBS
16 DECEMBER 1956–10 MARCH 1957; 30 MAY 1958–3 OCTOBER
1958   Gerald McBoing-Boing, the star of several U.P.A. cartoon shorts
who was familiar to moviegoers, first came to television late in 1956 in a
Sunday-afternoon slot. The lad spoke only in sounds, not words; the
voice of Bill Goodwin was employed to interpret McBoing-Boing's utter-
ings. Also featured were two other cartoon segments: "The Twirliger
Twins" and "Dusty of the Circus." When the show was rerun in a Friday-night slot during the summer of 1958, it became one of television's
first prime-time cartoon series, antedating *The Flintstones* by two seasons.

THE GERTRUDE BERG SHOW
See MRS. G. GOES TO COLLEGE

GET CHRISTIE LOVE!   ABC
11 SEPTEMBER 1974–18 JULY 1975   *Laugh-In* alumna Teresa Graves
starred as TV's first black policewoman, Christie Love, in this hour-long
crime show. The series was originally produced by Paul Mason and featured Charles Cioffi as her boss, Lieutenant Matt Reardon of the Special
Investigations Unit of the Los Angeles Police Department; Dennis
Rucker as Lieutenant Steve Belmont; and Andy Romano as Lieutenant
Joe Caruso. In January some changes were made: Glen A. Larson and
Ron Satlof replaced Mason as producers, and Cioffi and Romano were
dropped from the cast. Joining the series were Jack Kelly as her new
boss, Captain Arthur P. Ryan; Michael Pataki as Officer Pete Gallagher;
and Scott Peters as Officer Valencia. In one episode (aired 5 February),
six members of the *Laugh-In* crew guest starred: Arte Johnson, Henry
Gibson, Jo Anne Worley, Judy Carne, Johnny Brown, and Gary Owens.

GET IT TOGETHER   ABC
3 JANUARY 1970–5 SEPTEMBER 1970 This half-hour rock music show
was usually seen on Saturday mornings. It was hosted by Cass Elliott
(formerly of The Mamas and the Papas) and Sam Riddle.

GET SET, GO!   SYNDICATED
1958 Half-hour variety show, with Chuck Richardson and Sue Ane
Langdon.

GET SMART   NBC/CBS
18 SEPTEMBER 1965–13 SEPTEMBER 1969 (NBC); 26 SEPTEMBER 1969–
11 SEPTEMBER 1970 (CBS)   Mel Brooks and Leonard Stern created this
spoof of spy shows, one of few successful sitcoms not centered around a
family. It starred Don Adams as Maxwell Smart, Agent 86 for CON-
TROL, a Washington-based counterintelligence agency. An inept secret
agent, Smart could barely operate the telephone implanted in his shoe;
nevertheless, he and his cohorts usually succeeded in thwarting the operations of KAOS, an organization dedicated to evil. Barbara Feldon, a former winner on *The $64,000 Question,* costarred as Smart's partner, Agent
99 (her real name was Susan Hilton), an intelligent and resourceful
agent. In the fall of 1968, she and Smart became engaged and were married on 16 November; the Smarts had twins during the 1969–1970 season.
Character actor Edward Platt played their boss, known simply as The
Chief. Also featured from time to time were Robert Karvelas as Agent
Larraby; Dick Gautier as Hymie, a robot; and Dave Ketchum as Agent
13. Cocreator Leonard Stern also served as executive producer.

GET THE MESSAGE   ABC
31 MARCH 1964–25 DECEMBER 1964 Frank Buxton hosted this Goodson-Todman daytime game show on which contestants, each teamed
with two celebrities, tried to identify a secret word or phrase from clues
supplied by the celebs.

GETTING TOGETHER   ABC
18 SEPTEMBER 1971–8 JANUARY 1972 This half-hour sitcom about a
couple of young songwriters featured onetime teen idol Bobby Sherman
as Bobby Conway; Wes Stern as his partner Lionel Poindexter; Pat Car-
oll as their landlady, Rita Simon; Jack Burns as Rita's boyfriend, Rudy
Colchek, a cop; and Susan Neher as Jenny, Bobby's kid sister.

THE GHOST AND MRS. MUIR   NBC/ABC
21 SEPTEMBER 1968–6 SEPTEMBER 1969 (NBC); 18 SEPTEMBER 1969–18
SEPTEMBER 1970 (ABC)   This half-hour sitcom starred Hope Lange as
Carolyn Muir, a recently widowed writer who moves with her two children to the town of Schooner Bay in New England and settles into Gull

Cottage, a house that turns out to be haunted by the ghost of an old ship captain; Edward Mulhare as Captain Daniel Gregg, the ghost who proceeds to look out for the best interests of the Muirs after his initial protests; Charles Nelson Reilly as Claymore Gregg, the Captain's mortal nephew; Harlen Carraher as Jonathan Muir, Carolyn's son; Kellie Flanagan as Candy Muir, Carolyn's daughter; Reta Shaw as Martha Grant, their housekeeper, Guy Raymond as Peavey, Martha's friend; and Scruffy, the family dog. Produced by Howard Leeds for 20th Century-Fox TV, the series was based on the 1947 film which starred Rex Harrison and Gene Tierney.

THE GHOST BUSTERS
CBS

6 SEPTEMBER 1975–4 SEPTEMBER 1976 This live-action Saturday-morning series starred Larry Storch as Eddie Spenser and Forrest Tucker as Kong, the "ghost busters" who fought the ghosts of historical villains. Also featured was Bob Burns as Tracy, their gorilla. Created by Mark Richards. Executive producers: Lou Scheimer and Norm Prescott. Produced and directed by Norman Abbott.

GHOST STORY
NBC

15 SEPTEMBER 1972–22 DECEMBER 1972 This anthology of supernatural tales was hosted by Sebastian Cabot, who appeared as Winston Essex, a wealthy gentleman who owned and operated the Mansfield House, his former mansion that had been turned into a hotel. When Cabot departed in 1972, the series continued under the title *Circle of Fear*.

THE GIANT STEP (TAKE A GIANT STEP)
CBS

7 NOVEMBER 1956–29 MAY 1957 Bert Parks hosted this prime-time game show for young people.

GIBBSVILLE
NBC

11 NOVEMBER 1976–30 DECEMBER 1976 This little noticed hour-long dramatic series was based on John O'Hara's short stories about Gibbsville, a Pensylvania mining town. The action—what there was of it—took place during the 1940s. Featured were Gig Young as reporter Ray Whitehead; John Savage as young reporter Jim Malloy; Biff McGuire as Jim's father, Dr. Malloy; Peggy McCay as Jim's mother, Mrs. Malloy; and Bert Remsen as Mr. Pell. The series was originally on NBC's 1976 fall schedule but was displaced at the last minute. It finally surfaced in November, replacing *Gemini Man* in NBC's reshuffled Thursday lineup. David Gerber was the executive producer.

GIDGET
ABC

15 SEPTEMBER 1965–1 SEPTEMBER 1966 Based on the film series, this sitcom starred Sally Field as California teenager Frances "Gidget" Law-

rence. Also featured were Don Porter as her father, Russell Lawrence, a widower; Betty Connor as her older sister, Anne; Peter Deuel as Anne's husband, John, a psychiatrist; and Lynette Winter as Gidget's friend, Larue. The half-hour show was a Screen Gems production.

GIGANTOR
SYNDICATED
1966   Produced in Japan, this cartoon series featured a huge robot (Gigantor) who was controlled by twelve-year-old Jimmy Sparks.

THE GILLETTE CAVALCADE OF SPORTS
NBC
4 SEPTEMBER 1948–24 JUNE 1960   NBC's Friday-night boxing telecast was sponsored by Gillette for most of its run, and the ringside commentary was usually provided by Jimmy Powers. In the early years the fights were broadcast from St. Nicholas Arena in New York, but from the mid-1950s the matches were telecast from anywhere in the country. If the featured fight failed to go the full distance, the remainder of the hour was filled with features, of variable lengths, such as *Greatest Fights of the Century, Great Moments in Sports,* or *Red Barber's Corner.* Summer broadcasts usually consisted of filmed bouts.

GILLIGAN'S ISLAND
CBS
26 SEPTEMBER 1964–4 SEPTEMBER 1967   Situation comedy about seven people left stranded on an uncharted isle in the Pacific after their boat, the *Minnow,* ran aground in a storm. With Bob Denver as Gilligan, the inept first mate; Alan Hale, Jr., as The Skipper (Jonas Grumby); Jim Backus as multimillionaire Thurston Howell III; Natalie Schafer as his wife, Lovey Howell; Tina Louise as movie star Ginger Grant; Russell Johnson as The Professor (Roy Hinkley); and Dawn Wells as working girl Mary Ann Summers. Created and produced by Sherwood Schwartz, the show was generally criticized as inane, but it has proven extremely popular in syndication, especially among young viewers. In 1974 a cartoon version appeared: see *The New Adventures of Gilligan.*

GIRL ABOUT TOWN (FOR YOUR PLEASURE)
(THE KYLE MacDONNELL SHOW)
NBC
15 APRIL 1948–10 SEPTEMBER 1949   Singer Kyle MacDonnell appeared frequently in television's early days, and hosted several series. Her first show was originally seen on Thursdays, and was titled *For Your Pleasure;* by the summer of 1948, however, it had shifted to Wednesdays, and in September it was retitled *Girl About Town;* the twenty-minute series moved to Sundays in February 1949. That summer the show expanded to thirty minutes, moved to Saturday nights, and again assumed the title *For Your Pleasure.*

GIRL ALONE
See THE DOTTY MACK SHOW

THE GIRL FROM U.N.C.L.E. NBC
13 SEPTEMBER 1966–29 AUGUST 1967   This hour-long adventure series was an unsuccessful spinoff from *The Man from U.N.C.L.E.* It starred Stefanie Powers as agent April Dancer; Noel Harrison (son of Rex Harrison) as agent Mark Slate; Leo G. Carroll (duplicating his *Man from U.N.C.L.E.* role) as U.N.C.L.E. chief Alexander Waverly; and Randy Kirby as U.N.C.L.E. trainee Randy Kovacs. Produced by Douglas Benton.

THE GIRL IN MY LIFE ABC
9 JULY 1973–20 DECEMBER 1974   Fred Holliday presided over this half-hour daytime show on which women who had done nice things for people were rewarded. Executive producer: Bill Carruthers. Produced by Brad Lachman.

GIRL OF THE WEEK NBC
9 SEPTEMBER 1948–2 DECEMBER 1948   Sarah Palfrey Cooke hosted this five-minute show, broadcast before the news on Thursday nights, which honored a different woman each week. By November of 1948, however, the show's focus had shifted to honoring only female athletes, and its title was changed to *Sportswoman of the Week*.

GIRL TALK SYNDICATED
1963–1970   This talk show for women was hosted for most of its run by Virginia Graham; Betsy Palmer took over the hosting duties in 1969. The show was produced and directed by Monty Morgan.

THE GIRL WITH SOMETHING EXTRA NBC
14 SEPTEMBER 1973–24 MAY 1974   This sitcom was not unlike *Bewitched*—it featured two newlyweds, one of whom (she) possessed ESP. With Sally Field as Sally Burton; John Davidson as lawyer John Burton; Jack Sheldon as Jerry, John's brother; and Zohra Lampert as Anne, Sally's best friend. Produced by Bob Claver and Bernie Slade.

THE GIRLS
See YOUNG AND GAY

THE GISELE MacKENZIE SHOW NBC
28 SEPTEMBER 1957–29 MARCH 1958   Singer Gisele MacKenzie left *Your Hit Parade* in 1957 to host this half-hour musical variety series, which was produced by Jack Benny's J & M Productions.

GIVE AND TAKE   CBS

20 MARCH 1952–12 JUNE 1952   This unheralded game show, not to be confused with CBS's 1975 show, *Give-N-Take,* was seen on Thursday afternoons for thirteen weeks. Jack Carney produced the question-and answer program, which is notable chiefly because it was the first network TV show in which Bill Cullen, who cohosted it with John Reed King, appeared regularly.

GIVE-N-TAKE   CBS

8 SEPTEMBER 1975–28 NOVEMBER 1975   This half-hour daytime game show was the successor to *Spin-Off.* Four contestants competed for a top prize of $5,000 on the series that was hosted by Jim Lange and produced by Bill Carruthers and Joel Stein.

GLADYS KNIGHT AND THE PIPS   NBC

10 JULY 1975–31 JULY 1975   This four-week summer variety series was hosted by recording group Gladys Knight and the Pips (Edward Patten, William Guest, and Merald "Bubba" Knight, Gladys's brother). The group got together in the 1950s and began making records in 1961, although their first big hit was not until 1967 ("I Heard It Through the Grapevine"). Bob Henry produced the series.

GLAMOUR GIRL   NBC

6 JULY 1953–8 JANUARY 1954   Harry Babbitt hosted this daytime audience participation show; each day four women from the studio audience told why they wanted to be the day's "Glamour Girl"; the winner was given a twenty-four-hour beauty treatment, an assortment of gifts, and a vacation trip. Jack McCoy was the executive producer.

THE GLEN CAMPBELL GOODTIME HOUR   CBS
29 JANUARY 1969–13 JUNE 1972
THE SUMMER BROTHERS SMOTHERS SHOW   CBS

23 JUNE 1968–8 SEPTEMBER 1968   Glen Campbell came to Hollywood from Arkansas in the early 1960s and for several years made his living as a guitarist on recording sessions; in 1965 he toured briefly as a guitarist with the Beach Boys. In 1967 he began appearing regularly on *The Smothers Brothers Comedy Hour,* and in 1968 he hosted their summer replacement series, *The Summer Brothers Smothers Show.* Regulars on that show included Pat Paulsen, Leigh French, singer John Hartford (composer of "Gentle on My Mind," one of Campbell's biggest records), the Louis DaPron dancers, the Jimmy Joyce singers, the Nelson Riddle orchestra, and announcer Bill Thompson. In 1969 he returned to TV as host of *The Glen Campbell Goodtime Hour;* his regulars included Pat Paulsen (1969–1970), Jack Burns (1969–1970), John Hartford, Jerry Reed, Larry McNeeley, the Mike Curb Congregation (1971–1972), the

Ray Charles Singers, the Ron Poindexter dancers, the Marty Paich orchestra, and announcer Eddie Mayehoff. Among the show's writers was comedian Steve Martin.

GLENCANNON   SYNDICATED

1959   This comedy-adventure series was set in the Caribbean and starred Thomas Mitchell as Captain Colin Glencannon, skipper of a freighter, *The Inchcliffe Castle,* and Patrick Allen as Bos'n Hughes. Based on the stories by Guy Gilpatric, the series was produced in England by Gross-Krasne, Ltd.

GLENN MILLER TIME   CBS

10 JULY 1961–11 SEPTEMBER 1961   Vocalist Johnny Desmond and bandleader Ray McKinley (who was the drummer in Glenn Miller's orchestra) cohosted this live, half-hour musical series, which sought to recreate the Big Band Era of the 1940s. Also featured were singers Patty Clark and the Castle Sisters. The show was a summer replacement for *Hennesey.*

THE GLENN REEVES SHOW   SYNDICATED

1966   Country and western singer Glenn Reeves hosted this half-hour musical series.

GLOBAL ZOBEL   SYNDICATED

1961   Myron Zobel hosted this half-hour travelogue.

THE GLORIA SWANSON SHOW   SYNDICATED
(CROWN THEATRE WITH GLORIA SWANSON)

1954   This half-hour dramatic anthology series, hosted by (and occasionally starring) Gloria Swanson, was produced by Bing Crosby Enterprises.

GLYNIS   CBS

25 SEPTEMBER 1963–18 DECEMBER 1963   This sitcom was one of the early fatalities of the 1963–1964 season. It starred Glynis Johns as Glynis Granville, a novelist and amateur detective; Keith Andes as her husband, Keith Granville; George Mathews as Chick Rogers, a retired policeman who occasionally assisted Glynis.

GO (GO-U.S.A.)   NBC

8 SEPTEMBER 1973–4 SEPTEMBER 1976   *Go,* the TV series with the shortest title, was aimed at children. It began in 1973 as a series that explored occupations; in 1975 its title was lengthened (to *Go-U.S.A.*) and its emphasis was shifted to America's bicentennial observance. The Saturday series' executive producer was George A. Heinemann.

GO LUCKY   CBS
15 JULY 1951–2 SEPTEMBER 1951   Jan Murray hosted this game show,
a summer replacement for *This Is Show Business,* on which guest celebrities acted out charades for contestants.

THE GODZILLA POWER HOUR   NBC
8 SEPTEMBER 1978–   A Saturday-morning cartoon series
from Hanna-Barbera Productions, *The Godzilla Power Hour* began as a
sixty-minute show featuring segments of "Godzilla" (who was now a
friendly monster from the depths of the ocean who helped out his friends,
a group of research scientists stationed aboard the *Calico*) and "Jana of
the Jungle" (a female Tarzan). In November of 1978 the show expanded
to ninety minutes and was retitled *Godzilla Super 90,* adding on segments
of *Jonny Quest,* another Hanna-Barbera series. In the fall of 1979 the series was reduced to thirty minutes and titled *The Godzilla Show;* it later
became *The Godzilla Globetrotters Hour.*

THE GO-GO GLOBETROTTERS
See THE HARLEM GLOBETROTTERS

THE GO-GO GOPHERS   CBS
14 SEPTEMBER 1968–6 SEPTEMBER 1969   This Saturday-morning cartoon series was set in the old West and featured two gophers who tried to
fight off the advances of Kit Coyote of the Cavalry.

GOING MY WAY   ABC
3 OCTOBER 1962–11 SEPTEMBER 1963   Based on the 1944 film, this situation comedy starred Gene Kelly as Father Charles O'Malley, a priest assigned to St. Dominic's Parish in Manhattan; Leo G. Carroll as Father
Fitzgibbon, the parish pastor; Dick York as Tom Colwell, the progressive
director of the local community center; and Nydia Westman as Mrs.
Featherstone.

GOING PLACES   ABC
3 JUNE 1956–26 AUGUST 1956   This weekend variety series was broadcast each week from a different city in Flordia. Jack Gregson hosted the
first few shows and was replaced by Merv Griffin.

THE GOLDBERGS   CBS/NBC/DUMONT/SYNDICATED
17 JANUARY 1949–18 JUNE 1951 (CBS); 4 FEBRUARY 1952–14 JULY
1952; 3 JULY 1953–25 SEPTEMBER 1953 (NBC); 13 APRIL 1954–19 OCTO-
BER 1954 (DUMONT); 1954–1955 (SYNDICATED)   Created by Gertrude Berg in 1929, this hit radio show became one of TV's first popular
sitcoms. In addition to writing and producing the show, Gertrude Berg

also starred as Molly Goldberg, the lovable Jewish mother who lived with her family at 1038 East Tremont Avenue in the Bronx. Philip Loeb first played her husband, Jake, a tailor, but was blacklisted during the "Red Scare" of the early 1950s (Loeb committed suicide in 1955); Harold J. Stone took over the role in 1952, and Robert H. Harris (who had previously played Jake's partner, Mendel) played the part from 1953 through 1955. Also featured were Arlene McQuade as their daughter Rosalie; Larry Robinson (1949–1952) and Tom Taylor (1953–1955) as their son Sammy; Eli Mintz (1949–1952 and 1954–1955) and Menasha Skulnik (1953) as Uncle David. From 1949 to 1951 the show was seen on Monday nights. In 1952 it was seen Monday, Wednesday, and Friday evenings in a fifteen-minute format. In 1953 it reverted to a half-hour format. The 1954–1955 syndicated version was also a half-hour series; the Goldbergs, however, had left the Bronx and moved to Haverville, a suburban community. Arnold Stang was featured in the latter version as Seymour, Jake's shipping clerk.

THE GOLDDIGGERS   NBC/SYNDICATED
20 JUNE 1968–5 SEPTEMBER 1968; 17 JULY 1969–11 SEPTEMBER 1969; 16 JULY 1970–10 SEPTEMBER 1970 (NBC); 1971 (SYNDICATED) The Golddiggers were a group of attractive young women put together by producer Greg Garrison. Their show was a summer replacement for *The Dean Martin Show* in 1968, 1969, and 1970; in 1971 they hosted a syndicated series. The show was entitled *Dean Martin Presents the Golddiggers* in 1968 and 1969. The 1968 show was set in the 1930s, and regulars included cohosts Frank Sinatra, Jr., and Joey Heatherton, and Paul Lynde, Barbara Heller, Stanley Myron Handelman, Stu Gilliam, The Times Square Two, Skiles and Henderson, and the Les Brown Orchestra. In 1969 the series was hosted by Lou Rawls, Gail Martin (Dean's daughter), and Paul Lynde; other regulars included Stanley Myron Handelman, Tommy Tune, Albert Brooks, Danny Lockin, Allison McKay, Darleen Carr, and Fiore and Eldridge. The 1970 series was taped in England and titled *The Golddiggers in London;* regulars included Charles Nelson Reilly (the host), Marty Feldman, Tommy Tune, and Julian Chagrin. The 1971 series was entitled simply *The Golddiggers* and featured Charles Nelson Reilly, Jackie Vernon, Barbara Heller, and Alice Ghostley; unlike the summer series, it was only a half hour in length. The composition of the ten-to-twelve member Golddiggers troupe changed from time to time. In 1970 the group consisted of Pauline Antony, Wanda Bailey, Jackie Chidsey, Paula Cinko, Rosetta Cox, Michelle della Fave, Tara Leigh, Susan Lund, Micki McGlone, and Patricia Mickey. A year later, only Chidsey and Lund remained: New arrivals included Jimmi Cannon, Loyita Chapel, Lee Crawford, Liz Kelley, Francie Mendenhall, Nancy Reichert, and Janice Whitby.

GOLDEN WINDOWS NBC
5 JULY 1954–8 APRIL 1955   This daytime serial told the story of an aspiring young singer who moves to New York. It featured Leila Martin as
hopeful vocalist Juliet Goodwin; Grant Sullivan as her boyfriend, Tom
Anderson. Also featured were Herb Patterson as Sheriff Alvin and Joe
DeSantis.

GOLDIE
See THE BETTY HUTTON SHOW

GOLF FOR SWINGERS
See LEE TREVINO'S GOLF FOR SWINGERS

GOMER PYLE, U.S.M.C. CBS
25 SEPTEMBER 1964–19 SEPTEMBER 1969   This military sitcom was a
spinoff from *The Andy Griffith Show*. It starred Jim Nabors as Gomer
Pyle, the naive and trusting gas pump jockey from Mayberry, North
Carolina, who decided to join the Marines. Assigned to Camp Henderson
in California, he served a five-year enlistment as a private. Also featured
were Frank Sutton as the irascible Sergeant Vince Carter, his platoon
leader; Forrest Compton as Colonel Gray, the commanding officer; Ronnie Schell as his buddy, Private Duke Slater; Ted Bessell (1964–1966) as
pal Frankie Lombardi, also a private; Ray Stuart as Corporal Boyle, Carter's aide; Allan Melvin (1967–1969) as Sergeant Hacker; and Elizabeth
MacRae (1967–1969) as Gomer's girlfriend, Lou Ann Poovie, an aspiring
singer. Executive producers: Aaron Ruben and Sheldon Leonard.

THE GONG SHOW NBC/SYNDICATED
14 JUNE 1976–21 July 1978 (NBC); 1976–   (SYNDICA-
TED)   This popular game show took *Ted Mack's Original Amateur
Hour* one step further: A panel of three celebrities judges unusual amateur (and professional) talent acts, and any member of the panel can, by
banging a large gong, terminate any act before completion. Completed
acts are then rated on a one-to-ten scale, and the winning act receives a
cash award—$516.32 on the day show, $712.05 (or sometimes $1,000) on
the syndicated version. The show is a magnet for unusual acts: nose-whis-
tlers, sink players, and singing dogs are all commonplace. Chuck Barris,
who created the show with coproducer Chris Bearde, chose to host the
festivities. It was the first time in front of the microphone for Barris, the
man responsible for *The Dating Game, The Newlywed Game,* and *How's
Your Mother-in-Law* (before that, he'd written "Palisades Park" for singer Freddy Cannon). The syndicated version was hosted for one season by
Gary Owens before Barris assumed those chores as well. Among the celebrities who frequent the panel are Jaye P. Morgan, Rex Reed, Arte
Johnson, Michelle Lee, and Jamie Farr. Siv Aberg keeps score.

GOOBER AND THE GHOST CHASERS   ABC

8 SEPTEMBER 1973–31 AUGUST 1975   On this weekend cartoon show a dog who could become invisible teamed up with some magazine staffers to chase ghosts. Some of the voices were supplied by Paul Winchell (as Goober, the dog), Ronnie Schell, and several members of *The Partridge Family*: Susan Dey, Danny Bonaduce, Brian Forster, and Suzanne Crough. Iwao Takamoto produced the series for Hanna-Barbera Productions, Inc. The second season consisted entirely of reruns.

GOOD COMPANY   ABC

7 SEPTEMBER 1967–21 DECEMBER 1967   Noted trial lawyer F. Lee Bailey (whose clients have included Dr. Sam Sheppard and Patty Hearst) hosted this series in which celebrities were interviewed at their homes. Its resemblance to *Person to Person* may have been more than coincidental: John Aaron produced both series.

GOOD DAY!   SYNDICATED

1976   This Boston-based talk show was cohosted by John Willis and Janet Langhart.

THE GOOD GUYS   CBS

25 SEPTEMBER 1968–23 JANUARY 1970   This low-key sitcom was one of the few shows of the 1960s filmed before a live audience. It starred Herb Edelman as Bert Gramus and Bob Denver as Rufus Butterworth, two childhood friends who buy a diner (Bert's Place) together (Rufus also drove a cab part time), and Joyce Van Patten as Claudia Gramus, Bert's wife. Also featured was Ron Masak as Andy, their friend and patron. The half-hour show was produced by David Susskind's Talent Associates.

GOOD HEAVENS   ABC

29 FEBRUARY 1976–26 JUNE 1976   This irregularly scheduled situation comedy starred Carl Reiner as Mr. Angel, a representative from the afterlife who returns to Earth to grant wishes to deserving people. Created by Bernard Slade, the series was produced by Austin Kalish and Irma Kalish. Carl Reiner also served as executive producer.

THE GOOD LIFE   NBC

18 SEPTEMBER 1971–8 JANUARY 1972   In this sitcom a middle-class couple decided to hire themselves out as a butler and maid to a wealthy family. With Larry Hagman as Albert Miller; Donna Mills as Jane Miller, his wife; David Wayne as their wealthy employer, Charles Dutton; Hermione Baddeley as Grace Dutton, Charles's sister; and Danny Goldman as Nick, Charles's son.

GOOD MORNING!
See THE MORNING SHOW

GOOD MORNING AMERICA   ABC
3 NOVEMBER 1975–   The first show to provide any meaningful competition to NBC's *Today, Good Morning America* is a refined version of ABC's first early morning effort, *A.M. America*. Its format is
similar to that of *Today*, but it is set in a living room rather than a newsroom, and features more soft news segments than *Today*. David Hartman
and Nancy Dussault cohosted the two-hour show until April 1977, when
Sandy Hill succeeded Dussault. Regular contributors have included columnists Jack Anderson, Erma Bombeck, and Rona Barrett, former New
York mayor John Lindsay, comedian Jonathan Winters, video journalist
Geraldo Rivera, editor Helen Gurley Brown, former Olympian Bruce
Jenner and his wife Chrystie, and physicians Dr. Timothy Johnson and
Dr. Lendon Smith. Woody Fraser is the executive producer. In 1980
Sandy Hill became a reporter for the series.

GOOD MORNING WORLD   CBS
5 SEPTEMBER 1967–17 SEPTEMBER 1968   This sitcom was the first to be
set at a radio station. It starred Joby Baker as Dave Lewis and Ronnie
Schell as Larry Clarke, two Los Angeles disc jockeys who cohosted an
early-morning show ("The Lewis and Clarke Show"). Also featured were
Julie Parrish as Linda Lewis, Dave's wife; Billy DeWolfe as station manager Roland B. Hutton, Jr.; Goldie Hawn as Sandy, a neighbor of the
Lewises who was interested in Larry. The series was developed by the
team responsible for *The Dick Van Dyke Show*: Carl Reiner, Sheldon
Leonard, Bill Persky, and Sam Denoff.

GOOD TIMES   CBS
8 FEBRUARY 1974–3 JANUARY 1979; 23 MAY 1979–1 AUGUST
1979   *Good Times* was the first spinoff of a spinoff: it was descended
from *All in the Family* by way of *Maude*. Set in Chicago, it told the story
of a lower-class black family—an often-unemployed father and a mother
trying hard to make ends meet, both hoping to build a better future for
their three children. The show starred Esther Rolle (1974–1977) as Florida Evans, formerly the maid on *Maude;* John Amos (1974–1976) as
James, her husband; Jimmie Walker as J. J. (James, Jr.), their jive-talking
eldest son; BernNadette Stanis as Thelma, their teenage daughter; Ralph
Carter as Michael, their serious-minded younger son; Ja'net DuBois as
their friend and neighbor, Willona Woods; Johnny Brown as Mr. Book-
man, the much-despised building janitor. Amos left the series at the end
of the 1975–1976 season; in the 1976 fall premiere it was explained that
he had found work in Mississippi but had been killed in an auto accident.

Later that season Moses Gunn joined the cast as Carl Dixon, Florida's new romantic interest. When Esther Rolle decided to leave the series as production began for the 1977–1978 season, it was explained that she and Carl had gotten married and had gone to Arizona for Carl's health; the three children remained in Chicago to take care of themselves (with a little help from Willona); Janet Jackson joined the cast as Penny, a battered child who was adopted by Willona. In the fall of 1978 Esther Rolle returned to the show, and Ben Powers joined the cast as former football star Keith Anderson, who married Thelma. *Good Times* was created by Eric Monte and Michael Evans (of *The Jeffersons*). Executive producers have included Norman Lear (1974–1975), Allan Manings (1975–1976), Austin and Irma Kalish (1976–1978), and Norman Paul (1978–1979). Producers have included Allan Manings (1974–1975), Jack Elinson and Norman Paul (1975–1976), Gordon Mitchell and Lloyd Turner (1976–1978), and Sid Dorfman (1978–1979). The series' theme was written by Marilyn and Alan Bergman and Dave Grusin.

GOODYEAR PLAYHOUSE NBC
14 OCTOBER 1951–22 SEPTEMBER 1957 Produced by Fred Coe, *Goodyear Playhouse* was an hour-long dramatic anthology series which, together with several other high-quality shows, comprised television's so-called "Golden Age," an era of original teleplays, usually broadcast live. *Goodyear Playhouse* came to the air in 1951 and shared a Sunday slot first with *Philco Television Playhouse* (until 1955), then with *The Alcoa Hour*. During the 1956–1957 season, *Goodyear* and *Alcoa* also alternated with *The Dinah Shore Show* and *The Bob Hope Show*. Among the many noteworthy presentations were: "October Story," with Julie Harris and Leslie Nielsen (14 October 1951); "Raymond Schindler, Case One," with Rod Steiger (20 January 1952, his first major TV role); "Catch a Falling Star," with Susan Strasberg (28 June 1953, her first major TV role); "The Huntress," with Judy Holliday (14 February 1954, a rare TV appearance); "Guilty Is the Stranger," with Paul Newman (26 September 1954); "The Chivington Raid," with Steve McQueen (27 March 1955); Gore Vidal's "Visit to a Small Planet," with Cyril Ritchard and Dick York (8 May 1955); Paddy Chayefsky's "The Catered Affair," with Thelma Ritter (22 May 1955); Robert Anderson's "All Summer Long," with Raymond Massey and William Shatner (in his first major TV role, 28 October 1956). After this series left the air in 1957, Goodyear sponsored another anthology series: see *Goodyear Theatre*. See also *Philco Television Playhouse*.

GOODYEAR THEATRE NBC
14 OCTOBER 1957–12 SEPTEMBER 1960 This half-hour filmed dramatic anthology series alternated with *Alcoa Theatre;* both were produced by

Four Star Films. Jack Lemmon appeared in four shows during the 1957–1958 season: "Lost and Found;" 14 October; "Voice in the Fog," 11 November; "The Victim," 6 January; and "Disappearance," 9 June.

THE GORDON MacRAE SHOW   NBC
5 MARCH 1956–27 AUGUST 1956   Musical comedy star Gordon MacRae hosted this fifteen-minute musical show, broadcast Monday before the evening news; a vocal group known as The Cheerleaders backed him up.

GOVERNMENT STORY   SYNDICATED
1969   A series of forty half-hour documentaries which examined various aspects of the United States Government. Stephen Horn hosted the series, which was produced by Group W. Paul Long and E. G. Marshall supplied the narration.

THE GOVERNOR AND J.J.   CBS
23 SEPTEMBER 1969–30 DECEMBER 1970   This half-hour sitcom starred Dan Dailey as Governor William Drinkwater, a widower, and Julie Sommars as his daughter, J. J. (Jennifer Jo), who served as his official hostess when she was not working at the zoo. Also featured were James Callahan as Drinkwater's press secretary, George Callison; Neva Patterson as his personal secretary, Maggie McLeod; Nora Marlowe as Sarah, the housekeeper; and Guv, the basset hound. The series was one of the few sixties sitcoms filmed before a live audience.

GRADY   NBC
4 DECEMBER 1975–4 MARCH 1976   In this spinoff from *Sanford and Son*, Whitman Mayo starred as Grady Wilson, who left the Sanfords' Los Angeles neighborhood to move in with his daughter and son-in-law in Santa Monica. With Carol Cole as Ellie Marshall, his daughter; Joe Morton as her husband, Hal, a schoolteacher; Rosanne Katon as Laurie, their daughter; and Haywood Nelson as Haywood, their son. Executive producers: Saul Turteltaub and Bernie Orenstein. Produced by Howard Leeds and Jerry Ross for Bud Yorkin Productions.

GRAND CHANCE ROUNDUP   CBS
17 FEBRUARY 1951–4 AUGUST 1951   A talent contest for young people, *Grand Chance Roundup* was set at a Western ranch, though it was broadcast Saturday mornings from Philadelphia. Gene Crane and Richard Caulk cohosted the show, and Thomas Freebairn-Smith produced it.

THE GRAND JURY   SYNDICATED
1959   This half-hour crime show starred Lyle Bettger as Harry Driscoll and Harold J. Stone as John Kennedy, two grand jury investigators.

THE GRAND OLE OPRY SYNDICATED/ABC
(STARS OF THE GRAND OLE OPRY)
1955–1957 (SYNDICATED); 15 OCTOBER 1955–15 SEPTEMBER 1956 (ABC)   This country and western musical series was filmed at Opryland in Nashville; the show began on radio in 1925 and is still broadcast on WSM every Saturday night. The ABC version was broadcast as a once-a-month replacement for *Ozark Jubilee*.

GRANDPA GOES TO WASHINGTON NBC
7 SEPTEMBER 1978–16 JANUARY 1979   An hour-long comedy-drama about a recently retired college professor who was asked to run for the United States Senate, did so, and won. With Jack Albertson as the irascible but principled new Senator, Josephus (Joe) Kelley; Larry Linville as his son, Kevin Kelley, a two-star general at the Pentagon with whose family Joe moved in; Sue Ane Langdon as Kevin's wife, Rosie Kelley, a health-food fanatic; Michele Tobin as their daughter, Cathleen; Sparky Marcus as their son, Kevin Jr.; and Madge Sinclair as Madge, Joe's secretary. The show was produced by Paramount TV.

GRANDSTAND NBC
21 SEPTEMBER 1975–   *Grandstand* is the title given to the live sports informational broadcasts sandwiched around and amid NBC's major sports telecasts. Hosts have included Bryant Gumbel, Jack Buck, Lee Leonard, Larry Merchant, and Fran Tarkenton. Executive producer: Don Ellis. Produced by Bill Fitts.

THE GRAY GHOST SYNDICATED
1957   This Civil War series starred Tod Andrews as Major John Mosby, a daring Confederate soldier. The character was based on fact: John Mosby was a young lawyer who joined the Forty-Third Battalion of the First Virginia Cavalry and organized an effective guerilla unit. Created and produced by Lindsley Parsons, the series was distributed by CBS Film Sales.

THE GREAT ADVENTURE CBS
27 SEPTEMBER 1963–18 SEPTEMBER 1964   Van Heflin hosted this American historical anthology series, which was produced by John Houseman.

THE GREAT AMERICAN DREAM MACHINE PBS
6 JANUARY 1971–9 FEBRUARY 1972   This unusual, and often irreverent, magazine series incorporated a little bit of everything: interviews, short filmed segments, satirical features, and musical numbers. Regular contributors included Marshall Efron, Andrew Rooney, Nicholas von

Hoffman, Ken Shapiro and Chevy Chase (the two heads who panto-mimed to music at the beginning of each show), and author Studs Terkel (who was usually seen conversing with a few folks at a Chicago bar). A. H. Perlmutter and Jack Willis were the executive producers of the show, which was first seen in a ninety-minute format; in the fall of 1971 it was trimmed to sixty minutes.

GREAT GHOST TALES   NBC
6 JULY 1961–21 SEPTEMBER 1961   Frank Gallop hosted this half-hour color anthology series, which appears to have been the last live dramatic series on commercial television. Richard Thomas (of *The Waltons*) made one of his earliest TV appearances on 24 August in Saki's "Sredni Vash-tar," costarring with Judith Evelyn.

THE GREAT GILDERSLEEVE   SYNDICATED
1955   Throckmorton P. Gildersleeve was created by Harold Peary on radio's *Fibber McGee and Molly.* In 1941, the bombastic politician won his own series; this was one of radio's first spinoffs. Peary played the role until 1950 when Willard Waterman took over. When the series came to television in 1955, Waterman continued to play the role of Gildersleeve, the water commissioner of Summerfield. Also featured were Stephanie Griffin as his niece (and ward), Marjorie Forrester; Ronald Keith as his nephew (and ward), Leroy Forrester; Lillian Randolph as their house-keeper, Birdie Lee Coggins (she had originated the role on radio); Willis Bouchey as Mayor Terwilliger, Gildy's boss; Forrest Lewis as Mr. Pea-vey, the town druggist; Barbara Stuart as Bessie, Gildy's secretary; and Shirley Mitchell as Leila Ransom.

GREAT MYSTERIES   SYNDICATED
1973   An undistinguished half-hour anthology series.

GREAT PERFORMANCES   PBS
1974–   Classical music and dance programs are the primary components of this series produced by Jac Venza at New York's WNET, but some dramatic presentations are also included, most notably "Jennie: Lady Randolph Churchill," a seven-parter starring Lee Remick and writ-ten by Julian Mitchell.

GREAT ROADS OF AMERICA   SYNDICATED
1973   Andy Griffith narrated this half-hour documentary series, which focused on American highways and byways.

THE GREAT TALENT HUNT
See HENRY MORGAN'S GREAT TALENT HUNT

THE GREAT WAR   SYNDICATED

1964   Michael Redgrave narrated this documentary of World War II.

THE GREATEST GIFT   NBC

30 AUGUST 1954–1 JULY 1955   This daytime serial was one of the first
to center around physicians. It starred Anne Burr as Dr. Eve Allen (apparently TV's first woman doctor) and Phillip Foster as Dr. Phil Stone,
her romantic interest. Also featured were Henry Barnard, Joe Draper,
Marion Russell, and Jack Klugman.

THE GREATEST MAN ON EARTH   ABC

3 DECEMBER 1952–19 FEBRUARY 1953   Ted Brown hosted this prime-
time game show on which five male contestants competed; each man had
been "nominated" by a woman, who was also present on stage. The game
consisted of several rounds, in which the men went on a scavenger hunt,
played charades, or tried to fashion a dress from a few yards of material.
One contestant was eliminated after each round, and the man who remained was crowned "The Greatest Man on Earth." The half-hour series
was produced by Walt Framer.

THE GREATEST SHOW ON EARTH   ABC

17 SEPTEMBER 1963–8 SEPTEMBER 1964   This hour-long adventure se-
ries was based on Cecil B. DeMille's 1952 film. The TV version starred
Jack Palance as Johnny Slate, the circus boss, and Stu Erwin as Otto
King, the business manager. Among the guest stars who appeared were
Brenda Vaccaro (in "Don't Look Down, Don't Look Back," 8 October,
her first major TV role), Ruby Keeler (in "The Show Must Go On—To
Orange City," 28 January, a rare TV appearance), and Buster Keaton (in
"You're All Right, Ivy," 28 April, also a rare TV appearance). Stanley
Colbert produced the series.

GREATEST SPORTS LEGENDS   SYNDICATED

1973–   Athletes are the subject of this film and interview series, hosted by Paul Hornung (1973–1976), Reggie Jackson (1976–1977),
and Tom Seaver (1977–   ). Produced by Bert Rotfeld.

GREEN ACRES   CBS

15 SEPTEMBER 1965–7 SEPTEMBER 1971   The format of this situation
comedy, another of the several CBS "rural" shows, was the converse of
The Beverly Hillbillies: A wealthy couple left the big city to live in the
hinterlands. Like *Petticoat Junction, Green Acres* was set in Hooterville,
and many members of the *Junction* cast occasionally appeared on *Acres*
as well. Principals included: Eddie Albert as Oliver Douglas, a New York
lawyer who had always longed for the country life; Eva Gabor as his

fashionable wife, Lisa Douglas, who reluctantly agreed to accompany him; Pat Buttram as Mr. Haney, a fast-talking local who tried to sell the Douglases everything; Tom Lester as Eb Dawson, the Douglases' handyman; Frank Cady as storekeeper Sam Drucker; Alvy Moore as Hank Kimball, the local agricultural agent; Hank Patterson as pig farmer Fred Ziffel, owner of Arnold Ziffel, the smartest pig in town (Arnold was really owned and trained by Frank Inn); Sid Melton as carpenter Alf Monroe; and Mary Grace Canfield as Alf's sister, and partner in the business, Ralph Monroe. Jay Sommers produced the show.

THE GREEN HORNET   ABC
9 SEPTEMBER 1966–14 JULY 1967 Created by George Trendle, *The Green Hornet* first appeared on radio in 1936. His secret identity was that of Britt Reid, editor and publisher of the *Daily Sentinel*; as the masked Green Hornet, he was a dedicated crimefighter. He was also the grandnephew of the Lone Ranger (Trendle also created that masked crimefighter). Reid's secret identity was known only by three people: Kato, his houseboy; Lenore Case, his secretary; and Frank Scanlon, the district attorney. On television Van Williams starred as Britt Reid/The Green Hornet. Also featured were Bruce Lee (later star of countless martial arts films) as Kato; Wende Wagner as Lenore Case (Casey); Walter Brooke as Frank Scanlon; and Lloyd Gough as Mike Axford, a former cop who is now the paper's police reporter. The series, which tried to capitalize on the popularity of *Batman* (another masked crimefighter), was produced by Richard Bluel.

GRIFF   ABC
29 SEPTEMBER 1973–5 JANUARY 1974 This lackluster crime show starred Lorne Greene (late of *Bonanza*) as Wade Griffin, a former cop who became a private eye. With Ben Murphy as his young partner, Mike Murdock; Vic Tayback as Captain Barney Marcus of the Los Angeles Police Department; and Patricia Stich as Gracie Newcombe, Griff and Mike's secretary.

GRINDL   NBC
15 SEPTEMBER 1963–13 SEPTEMBER 1964 Imogene Coca starred as Grindl, a housemaid employed by Mrs. Foster's Domestic Agency, in this half-hour sitcom. James Millhollin was featured as Mr. Foster, her boss at the agency.

THE GROOVIE GOOLIES   CBS/ABC
12 SEPTEMBER 1971–17 SEPTEMBER 1972 (CBS); 25 OCTOBER 1975–5 SEPTEMBER 1976 (ABC) This weekend cartoon series featured a bunch of musical monsters who resided in Horrible Hall. Executive producers: Lou Scheimer and Norm Prescott.

THE GROWING PAYNES DUMONT

20 OCTOBER 1948–3 AUGUST 1949 This early domestic sitcom starred Elaine Stritch and Ed Holmes, and featured David Anderson as their son.

GRUEN GUILD PLAYHOUSE ABC/DUMONT

27 SEPTEMBER 1951–13 DECEMBER 1951 (ABC); 17 JANUARY 1952–7 AUGUST 1952 (DUMONT) This half-hour dramatic anthology series was produced by Leon Fromkess.

GUESS AGAIN CBS

14 JUNE 1951–21 JUNE 1951 Short-lived prime-time game show hosted by Mike Wallace, on which contestants tried to answer questions based on a routine acted out by a celebrity panel. Al Span produced the half-hour show, which was replaced by *Amos and Andy.*

GUESS WHAT? DUMONT

8 JULY 1952–26 AUGUST 1952 Dick Kollmar hosted this Tuesday-night game show on which a celebrity panel tried to identify subjects from clues supplied by the host.

GUESS WHAT HAPPENED NBC

7 AUGUST 1952–21 AUGUST 1952 This Thursday-night current events quiz was hosted by NBC newscaster John Cameron Swayze.

GUEST HOUSE (GENERAL ELECTRIC GUEST HOUSE) CBS

1 JULY 1951–2 SEPTEMBER 1951 A summer replacement for *The Fred Waring Show,* this series blended a celebrity quiz with comedy and music. Oscar Levant and Durward Kirby cohosted the show.

A GUEST IN YOUR HOME NBC

5 MARCH 1951–30 MARCH 1951 This short-lived fifteen-minute daytime series featured poet Edgar Guest and was directed by Frank Jacoby.

GUESTWARD HO! ABC

29 SEPTEMBER 1960–21 SEPTEMBER 1961 Based on the book by Patrick Dennis and Barbara Hooton, this situation comedy told the story of a couple who left New York to buy a dude ranch in New Mexico. With Joanne Dru (sister of *Hollywood Squares'* Peter Marshall) as Babs Hooton; Mark Miller as her husband, Bill; Flip Mark as their son, Brook; J. Carrol Naish as Hawkeye, the local Indian chief; Earle Hodgins as Lonesome, the Hootons' foreman; Jolene Brand as Pink Cloud, Hawkeye's assistant at the trading post; and Tony Montenaro, Jr., as Rocky.

GUIDE RIGHT   DUMONT

25 FEBUARY 1952–5 FEBRUARY 1954 This variety program was produced in cooperation with the United States Army and Air Force recruiting offices. Each show was hosted by a different guest celebrity, and music was provided by the Eastern Air Defense Command Band. Barry Shear directed the show.

GUIDELINE

See THE CATHOLIC HOUR

THE GUIDING LIGHT   CBS

30 JUNE 1952–   *The Guiding Light* began on radio in 1937 and came to television fifteen years later; it was the only radio serial to make a really successful transition to the new medium. Created by Irna Phillips, it went through several changes of leading characters and locations before settling down in the late 1940s to concentrate on the Bauer family, a close-knit German-American family who settled in the town of Springfield. Agnes Nixon (who later created *One Life to Live* and *All My Children*) succeeded Irna Phillips as head writer when Phillips left the show to create *As the World Turns*. In recent years Jerome and Bridget Dobson (who formerly wrote for *General Hospital*) have been the head writers. David Lesan was the producer when *The Guiding Light* first came to TV but was soon succeeded by Lucy Rittenberg, who held the job for more than twenty years; Allen Potter is the current executive producer, Leslie Kwartin the producer. *The Guiding Light* and *Search for Tomorrow* were the last television serials to expand from fifteen to thirty minutes a day (both did so in September 1968); *The Guiding Light* expanded to a full hour on 7 November 1977.

As the action began in 1952, the central characters were the several members of the Bauer clan, and the cast in the early years included: Theo Goetz as Fred (Papa) Bauer, a widower with three grown children (Goetz played the role from 1949 until his death in 1972); Lyle Sudrow (1952–1959) and Ed Bryce (1959–1969) as his son, Bill Bauer, who was killed in an air crash; Charita Bauer as Bill's wife, Bertha (Charita Bauer was the only member of the original television cast still on the show in 1980); Jone Allison (1952) and Ellen Demming as Papa's daughter, Meta (Bauer) (White) Roberts; Lisa Howard as Papa's daughter, Trudy, who moved away to New York with her husband shortly after the TV series began; Glenn Walken (later known as Christopher Walken), Michael Allen, Paul Prokop, Gary Pillar, Bob Pickering, and Don Stewart as lawyer Michael Bauer, son of Bill and Bertha; Bob Gentry and Mart Hulswit as Dr. Ed Bauer, son of Bill and Bertha; Herb Nelson as Joe Roberts, Meta Bauer's second husband; Les Damon, Barnard Hughes, Sydney Walker, and William Roerick as Dr. Bruce Banning, Meta's third husband; Susan Douglas as Kathy Roberts Lang, Joe Roberts's daughter by a prior marriage, who was killed in a car crash in 1958; James Lipton (1953–1962) as Dr. Dick Grant, Kathy's second husband; Whit Connor as Mark Holden, who also married Kathy; Zina Bethune (to 1959), Abigail Kellogg (1959–1961), Nancy Malone (1961–1964), and Gillian Spencer as Kathy's daughter, Robin Lang Holden, who was killed by a truck; Ernest Graves as Alex Bowden, Robin's first husband; Bernie Grant (1957–1971) as Dr. Paul Fletcher, who married Robin after he accidentally shot his first wife; Joan Gray and Elizabeth Hubbard as Anne Fletcher, Paul's unfortunate first wife; Lynne Rogers (1958–1962) as Marie Wallace, who married Dick Grant; Lin Pierson as Alice Holden; Virginia Dwyer and Louise Platt as Ruth Jennings, who later married Mark Holden; Tarry Green as Joey Roberts, Kathy's younger brother; Joseph Campanella as artist Joe Turino; Kay Campbell as Helene Benedict, mother of Anne Fletcher; John Buloff as Henry Benedict, father of Anne Fletcher; Sandy Smith as Julie Conrad, who became Michael Bauer's first wife.

Among the principal players during the 1960s and early 1970s were: Chase Crosley as Jane Fletcher, Paul Fletcher's half sister; Phil Sterling as George Hayes, who married Jane; Bernard Kates as Ben Scott; June Graham as Maggie Scott, his wife and Bill Bauer's secretary; Fran Myers as their daughter Peggy Scott Thorpe; Don Scardino (to 1967) and Erik Howell (1967–   ) as Johnny Fletcher, son of Paul Fletcher, who was murdered in 1968 (Peggy was tried for the crime, but was acquitted); Lynne Adams, Barbara Rodell, and Lynne Adams (again) as Leslie Jackson, who married Ed Bauer in 1967, divorced him in 1970, and married Michael Bauer (Ed's brother) in 1971; Stefan Schnabel as Dr. Stephen Jackson, Leslie's father; Elissa Leeds, Tisch Raye, Robin Mattson (1976–1978) and Katherine Justice (1978–1979) as Hope Bauer, daughter of Ed and Julie Bauer; Caroline McWilliams as Janet Mason; Millette Alexander as Dr. Sara McIntyre Blackford; Ray Fulmer as Lee Gantry, who married Sara; Jan Sterling as Mildred Foss; Victoria Wyndham and Melinda Fee as Charlotte Waring, who was briefly married to Michael Bauer; William Smithers as Stanley Norris, who married Leslie Jackson Bauer and was later murdered; Barbara Berjer (1970–   ) as Barbara Norris, Stanley's ex-wife; Lynn Deerfield and Maureen Garrett (1976–   ) as Holly Norris, daughter of Stanley and Barbara, who married Ed Bauer; Roger Newman as Stanley and Barbara's son, Ken Norris, who married Janet Mason; Ben Hayes, Ed Zimmerman (to 1972) and Anthony Call (1972–1976) as Dr. Joe Werner, who married Sara McIntyre; Nancy Addison as Kit Vestid; Dan Hamilton as David Vestid; David Pendleton as Gil Mehron; Olivia Cole as Deborah Mehron; Mike Durrell as Peter Wexler; Paul Carpinelli as Flip Malone; Grace Matthews as Claudia Dillman; Roger Morden as Dr. Carey; William Beaudine as Dr. King; James Earl Jones as Dr. Jerry Turner; Carol Teitel as Mrs. Ballinger; Jeanne Arnold as Ellen Mason; Chris Sarandon as Tom Halverson; Christina Pickles as Linell Conway; Kate Harrington as Muriel

Conway; Tudi Wiggins as Karen Martin; and Rosetta LeNoire as Mrs. Herbert.

More recent additions to the cast have included: Michael Zaslow as Roger Thorpe; Robert Milli as Adam Thorpe, his father; Jordan Clarke as Dr. Tim Ryan; Maureen Silliman as Pam Chandler; Lenore Kasdorf as Rita Stapleton; Maureen Mooney as Ann Jeffers; T. J. Hargrave as T. J., a runaway taken in by Joe and Sara Werner; Everett McGill as Chad Richards; Gary Hannoch and Robbie Berridge as Freddie Bauer, son of Ed and Leslie Bauer; Lee Richardson as Captain Jim Swanson; Larry Gates as Ira Newton: Graham Jarvis (who later turned up on *Mary Hartman, Mary Hartman*) as Charles Eiler; Madeline Sherwood as Betty Eiler; Barney McFadden as Andy Norris; Gina Foy as Christina Bauer; Tom Aldredge as Victor Kincaid; Laryssa Lauret as Simone Morey Kincaid; Linda McCullough and Marsha Clark as Hilary Kincaid; Ed Bryce (who had formerly played Bill Bauer) as William Morey; Chris Bernau as Alan Spaulding; Lezlie Dalton as Elizabeth Spaulding; Jarrod Ross as Phil Spaulding; Ben Hammer as Max Chapman; Delphi Harrington as Georgene Granger; Janet Gray as Eve Stapleton; Kate Wilkinson as Viola Stapleton; Frank Latimore as Emmet Scott; Shane Nickerson and Dai Stockton as Billy Fletcher; Denise Pence as Katie Parker; Stephen Yates as Ben McFarren; Tom O'Rourke as Dr. Justin Marler; Cindy Pickett as Jacqueline Marler; Curt Dawson as Peter Chapman; Janet Gray as Eve McFarren; Mark Travis as Jerry McFarren; Sofia Landon as Diane Ballard; Gordon Rigsby as Dean Blackford; Jobeth Williams as Brandy Sheloo; Nicholas Kepros as Wilbur Morrison; Kathleen Cullen as Amanda Wexler; Rita Lloyd as Lucille Wexler; and Cheryl Lynn Brown as Christina; Burton Cooper as Dr. Mark Hamilton; Marcus Smythe as Gordon Middleton.

THE GUINNESS GAME   SYNDICATED
1979   An unusual game show on which three contestants try to predict whether a challenger will succeed in an endeavor to break one of the records listed in *The Guinness Book of World Records*. Don Galloway hosts the half-hour show.

GULF PLAYHOUSE   NBC
3 OCTOBER 1952–26 DECEMBER 1952   This half-hour dramatic anthology series was seen on Friday nights.

THE GULF ROAD SHOW   NBC
2 SEPTEMBER 1948–30 JUNE 1949   This half-hour variety show was hosted for most of its run by Bob Smith, who was better known as the emcee of *Howdy Doody;* Dan Seymour also hosted the series for several weeks in 1949.

GULLIVER (THE ADVENTURES OF GULLIVER) ABC

14 SEPTEMBER 1968–5 SEPTEMBER 1970   The adventures of Gary Gulliver, son of Lemuel Gulliver (*the* Gulliver), were chronicled in this Saturday-morning cartoon show; searching for his father, Gary sailed to Lilliput and there befriended the little people.

THE GUMBY SHOW NBC

16 MARCH 1957–16 NOVEMBER 1957   This Saturday-morning kids' show was spun off from *Howdy Doody:* Gumby was first introduced on that show in 1956. .Gumby and his horse, Pokey, were movable clay figures; their adventures, like those of *Davey and Goliath,* were filmed via the process of "pixillation"—shooting a few frames at a time, moving the figures slightly, and shooting a few more frames. *The Gumby Show* was first hosted by Bobby Nicholson, who had played both Clarabell and Cornelius Cobb on *Howdy Doody,* and later by Pinky Lee.

THE GUNS OF WILL SONNETT ABC

8 SEPTEMBER 1968–15 SEPTEMBER 1969   This half-hour western starred Walter Brennan as Will Sonnett, a former Cavalry scout who raised his grandson after the boy's father, Jim Sonnett, ran off and became a gunfighter. Dack Rambo costarred as the grandson, Jeff Sonnett, who now wants to find his father. Together, Will and Jeff roamed the West looking for Jim. Jason Evers appeared occasionally as the wayward Jim.

GUNSLINGER CBS

9 FEBRUARY 1961–14 SEPTEMBER 1961   This hour-long western, a midseason replacement for *The Witness,* starred Tony Young as Cord, an agent for the U.S. Cavalry whose cover was that of a dangerous gunslinger. Also featured were Preston Foster as Captain Zachary Wingate, commanding officer of the post to which Cord was assigned, Fort Scott in New Mexico Territory; John Pickard as Sergeant Major Murdock; Midge Ware as Amber (Amby) Hollister; Charles Gray as Pico McGuire; and Dee Pollock as Billy. Produced by Charles M. Warren.

GUNSMOKE CBS

10 SEPTEMBER 1955–1 SEPTEMBER 1975   Not only was *Gunsmoke* television's longest-running western, it was also televison's longest-running prime-time series with continuing characters. The show began on radio in 1952, with William Conrad (later TV's *Cannon*) as Marshal Matt Dillon, tough lawman of Dodge City, Kansas; the show's producer, Norman Macdonnell, saw Dillon as a fallible antihero, and the show has been described as one of radio's most violent westerns. By 1955 Macdonnell and his associates John Meston and Charles Marquis Warren had decided to bring the show to television. John Wayne was offered the starring role but

turned it down; he recommended a tall, relatively unknown actor for the part—James Arness. Arness, brother of Peter Graves (who began co-starring in *Fury* that season), had appeared in several movies, perhaps most notably in the title role of *The Thing* in 1950. Arness was hired, and three other performers were selected to fill out the cast: Amanda Blake as Kitty Russell, owner of the Long Branch saloon, whose relationship with Dillon was close, though never precisely delineated; Dennis Weaver as Chester B. Goode, Dillon's gimpy-legged deputy; and Milburn Stone as Doc Adams (his first name was Galen), the town's crusty but trusty physician. Stone remained with the show for its entire run (except when sidelined by a heart attack), Blake for nineteen seasons. The show began in 1955 as a half-hour series; John Wayne introduced the premiere episode, explaining to viewers that they were about to see a new kind of western.

The opening sequence that season featured Matt Dillon standing in "Boot Hill," Dodge City's graveyard, where he briefly introduced each episode. In 1956, a new opening sequence was shot, which featured Dillon and an unidentified badman squaring off in Dodge's Main Street (Dillon managed to outdraw the outlaw). The sequence was reshot over the years in part to reflect the expansion of Dodge City. By the 1970s, the gunfight sequence had been replaced by a new opening that featured shots of Dillon riding across the plains.

Gunsmoke became the number-one-rated series in its third season (1957–1958) and remained in that position for four seasons. In the fall of 1961 it expanded from a half hour to an hour, and its ratings declined over the next six years. The first changes in the cast were also made during the early 1960s. Dennis Weaver had made it clear by 1962 that he intended to leave the show; he made two pilots for new series, neither of which sold, and twice returned to *Gunsmoke*. In 1964, his third pilot—*Kentucky Jones*—sold, and he left the show for good that year. Ken Curtis was added that fall as Festus Haggen, a backwoodsman who became the new deputy and who provided the comic relief formerly supplied by Chester (Curtis, who had sung with Tommy Dorsey's orchestra at one time, had appeared as Festus in one or two episodes before becoming a regular).

Meanwhile, the producers had decided to add a fifth central character—a rugged male—in 1962. The role was first filled by Burt Reynolds as Quint Asper, a half-breed blacksmith; Reynolds lasted three seasons. In 1965, Roger Ewing joined the cast as Thad Greenwood, a young townsman; he left after two seasons. In the fall of 1967, Buck Taylor (son of character actor Dub Taylor) was added as gunsmith Newly O'Brian; Taylor, who first played a killer in a two-part episode, stayed with the show. A number of other people were occasionally seen as Dodge City's townsfolk. This group included: James Nusser as Louie Pheeters, the town drunk; Dabbs Greer (1955–1960) as Mr. Jones, a storekeeper; Charles Seel as Barney, the telegraph agent, Hank Patterson (1957–   )

as Hank, the stableman; Howard Culver as Howie, the hotel clerk at the Dodge House; Sarah Selby (1962–1975) as Ma Smalley, boardinghouse owner; Woody Chamblis as Mr. Lathrop, a storekeeper; Roy Roberts as Mr. Bodkin, the banker; Tom Brown as rancher Ed O'Connor; Ted Jordan (1964–1975) as Nathan Burke, the freight agent; Charles Wagenheim as Halligan, another rancher; John Harper as Percy Crump, the undertaker. Glenn Strange also appeared for many seasons as Sam, the bartender at the Long Branch.

Norman Macdonnell produced the series from 1955 until 1964, when differences with the show's other principals—including Arness—led to his departure. Arness gradually acquired more and more influence over the show, although the degree of his dominance is hard to ascertain because Arness almost never spoke to the press and loathed publicity; it is known, however, that the show's production schedule was arranged so that Arness rarely had to work more than three days a week. Macdonnell was succeeded as producer by Philip Leacock, who was in turn succeeded by John Mantley in 1967.

Gunsmoke's ratings had smoldered considerably by the end of the 1966–1967 season, and CBS programmers had decided to cancel it. CBS President William Paley interceded, however, and the decision was made to change its time slot from Saturday to Monday; that decision proved to be a wise one, for *Gunsmoke* zoomed back into Nielsen's top ten in 1967–1968, and remained there for six seasons. In all, 233 half-hour episodes were filmed, and more than 400 hour segments were made (the series was broadcast in color beginning with the 1966–1967 season); from 1961 to 1964, reruns of the half-hour shows were broadcast Tuesdays on CBS, while the hour version ran Saturdays.

THE GUY LOMBARDO SHOW SYNDICATED
1954   Half-hour musical series with Guy Lombardo and His Royal Canadians.

GUY LOMBARDO'S DIAMOND JUBILEE CBS
6 MARCH 1956–12 JUNE 1956   In addition to hosting New Year's Eve festivities for decades, Guy Lombardo and His Royal Canadians were also featured on this half-hour musical series, which replaced *Meet Millie* in 1956; Lombardo's brothers—Carmen, Lebert, and Victor—joined him on the show. One of the regular features was the "Song of Your Life" contest, in which viewers were invited to write, describing how a particular song had affected their lives. Winning contestants appeared on the show and, in addition to winning $1,000, heard the orchestra play their song.

THE GUY MITCHELL SHOW ABC
7 OCTOBER 1957–13 JANUARY 1958   Guy Mitchell, a popular recording

artist of the early 1950s, hosted this Monday-night half-hour musical show, produced in Hollywood; the Van Alexander Orchestra accompanied him. Rock-and-roller Chuck Berry appeared on the show on 16 December.

GYPSY SYNDICATED
1965
THE GYPSY ROSE LEE SHOW SYNDICATED
1958 One of America's foremost burlesque queens, Gypsy Rose Lee hosted two talk shows. The 1958 show was ninety minutes; the 1965 show thirty minutes.

H. R. PUFNSTUF NBC
6 SEPTEMBER 1969–4 SEPTEMBER 1971 A children's fantasy series set at Living Island, with Jack Wild (star of the film *Oliver*) as Jimmy, Billie Hayes as Witchiepoo, and the Sid and Marty Krofft Puppets (one of whom was H. R. Pufnstuf).

HAGGIS BAGGIS NBC
Nighttime: 20 JUNE 1958–29 SEPTEMBER 1958; *Daytime:* 30 JUNE 1958–19 JUNE 1959 Players won merchandise on this game show by identifying photos; each photo was gradually uncovered as questions were answered correctly. Twenty-year-old Jack Linkletter, son of Art Linkletter, hosted the nighttime show, a summer replacement for *The Price Is Right.* The daytime version was hosted first by Fred Robbins, later by Dennis James.

HAIL THE CHAMP ABC
22 DECEMBER 1951–14 JUNE 1952; 27 DECEMBER 1952–20 MAY 1953 Saturday game show for children, on which two teams of youngsters competed in various stunts. Broadcast from Chicago, the show was hosted first by Herb Allen, and later by Howard Roberts with Angel Casey.

HALF THE GEORGE KIRBY COMEDY HOUR SYNDICATED
1972 Impressionist George Kirby hosted this Toronto-based variety half hour. Among the regulars was Steve Martin.

HALLMARK HALL OF FAME NBC
6 JANUARY 1952– One of television's best known dramatic anthology series, *Hallmark Hall of Fame* was a weekly series from 1952 until 1955; since that time it has been seen as a series of specials, with five or six presentations scheduled each season. Sponsored by Hallmark Cards ("When you care enough to send the very best. . ."), it was titled *Hallmark Television Playhouse* during its first two seasons, when it was a

half-hour series. Sarah Churchill was the host, and occasional star, from 1952 until 1955. Mildred Freed Alberg produced the show for many seasons; George Schaefer succeeded her. A small sample of the many programs presented would include: "Hamlet," with Maurice Evans and Ruth Chatterton (26 April 1953); "Moby Dick," with Victor Jory (16 May 1954); "Macbeth," with Maurice Evans, Dame Judith Anderson, and House Jameson (28 November 1954); "Alice in Wonderland," with Eva LaGallienne, Elsa Lanchester, and Reginald Gardiner (23 October 1955); "The Taming of the Shrew," with Maurice Evans and Diane Cilento (18 March 1956); "Born Yesterday," with Mary Martin and Arthur Hill (28 October 1956); "Man and Superman," with Maurice Evans (25 November 1956); "The Green Pastures," with Frederick O'Neal and Eddie "Rochester" Anderson (first broadcast 17 October 1957, it was restaged 23 May 1959); "Twelfth Night," with Maurice Evans, Rosemary Harris, and Piper Laurie (15 December 1957); "Hans Brinker," with Tab Hunter and Basil Rathbone (9 February 1958); "Winterset," with Martin Balsam, George C. Scott, and Piper Laurie (26 October 1959); "A Doll's House," with Julie Harris, Hume Cronyn, Eileen Heckart, and Christopher Plummer (15 November 1959); "The Tempest," with Maurice Evans, Richard Burton, and Lee Remick (3 February 1960); "Captain Brassbound's Conversion," with Christopher Plummer and Robert Redford (2 May 1960); "Give Us Barabbas," with James Daly, Kim Hunter, and Dennis King (26 March 1961); "Victoria Regina," with Julie Harris (30 November 1961); "Cyrano de Bergerac," with Christopher Plummer and Hope Lange (6 December 1962); "Little Moon of Alban," with Julie Harris, Dirk Bogarde, Christopher Plummer, and George Peppard (18 March 1964); "The Fantasticks" with John Davidson and Bert Lahr (18 October 1964); "The Magnificent Yankee," with Alfred Lunt and Lynn Fontanne (28 January 1965); "Anastasia," with Julie Harris (17 March 1967); "The Man Who Came to Dinner," with Orson Welles, Lee Remick, and Don Knotts (29 November 1972); "The Borrowers," with Eddie Albert, Judith Anderson, and Tammy Grimes (14 December 1973); "Brief Encounter," with Richard Burton and Sophia Loren (12 November 1974); "Caesar and Cleopatra," with Alec Guinness and Genevieve Bujold (1 February 1976); "Beauty and the Beast," with George C. Scott and Trish Van Devere (3 December 1976); "The Last Hurrah," with Carroll O'Connor (16 November 1977); "Return Engagement," with Elizabeth Taylor (17 November 1978). Another important television event which was sponsored by Hallmark Cards (though it was not part of the *Hallmark Hall of Fame* series) was the premiere of Gian Carlo Menotti's Christmas opera, "Amahl and the Night Visitors," 24 December 1951. In the spring of 1979 Hallmark Cards announced that, after a twenty-six-year association with NBC, it had scheduled at least one presentation on CBS for the 1979–1980 season.

THE HALLS OF IVY   CBS
19 OCTOBER 1954–13 OCTOBER 1955   The television version of the radio
sitcom was also set at Ivy College in Ivy, U.S.A. It starred Ronald Colman as Dr. William Todhunter Hall, president of the college; Benita
Hume (Colman's wife) as Victoria Cromwell (Vicky) Hall, his wife, former star of the British stage; Herb Butterfield as Dr. Clarence Wellman,
chairman of the trustees; Mary Wickes as Alice, the Halls' housekeeper;
and Ray Collins as Professor Merriweather. Occasionally seen as Ivy students were John Lupton, Jerry Paris, Richard Tyler, and Bob Sands. Created by Don Quinn.

HANDLE WITH CARE
See THE MAIL STORY

HANDS OF MURDER   DUMONT
24 AUGUST 1949–11 DECEMBER 1951   This half-hour mystery anthology series was first titled *Hands of Murder.* In April 1950, the Friday-
night show became known as *Hands of Destiny;* from January through
April of 1951, it was called *Hands of Mystery* and was again known as
Hands of Destiny for the last months of its run. James L. Caddigan was
the producer, Lawrence Menkin the director.

HANDYMAN   SYNDICATED
1955   Norman Brokenshire hosted this home repair show.

HANGING IN   CBS
8 AUGUST 1979–29 AUGUST 1979   Four-week summer sitcom set at
Braddock University, a Southern college. With Bill Macy as Lou Harper,
the new president; Dennis Burkley as Sam Diggs, the hefty dean of ad-
missions; Barbara Rhoades as Maggie Gallagher, the dean of faculty; and
Nedra Volz as Pinky Nolan, Harper's saucy housekeeper. The half-hour
show was a reworked version of *Mr. Dugan,* a sitcom from Norman
Lear's T.A.T. Communications about a black Congressman, which Lear
had decided not to air.

HANK   NBC
17 SEPTEMBER 1965–2 SEPTEMBER 1966   Dick Kallman starred as
Hank Dearborn, a youngster who was forced to quit school when his parents died, leaving him to care for his kid sister; Hank got a job running an
ice cream truck near the campus of Western State University and tried to
sneak into college classes and other official activities. Also featured were
Howard St. John as Dr. Lewis Royal, the registrar, Hank's nemesis;
Lloyd Corrigan as Professor McKillup; Linda Foster as Doris Royal,
Hank's girlfriend, the registrar's daughter; Katie Sweet as Tina, Hank's

sister; Dabbs Greer as Coach Weiss of the track team; and Dorothy Nue-
mann as Miss Mittleman.

THE HANK McCUNE SHOW NBC
9 SEPTEMBER 1950–9 DECEMBER 1950   Half-hour sitcom starring Hank
McCune as the host of a television show, and featuring Larry Keating,
Arthur Q. Bryan, Frank Nelson, Sara Berner, Charles Maxwell, and
Tammy Kiper. Written by Mort Lachman and Cy Rose, the show had
been seen locally in New York in 1949.

THE HANNA-BARBERA HAPPY HOUR NBC
18 APRIL 1978–4 MAY 1978   This hour-long, prime-time variety series
from Hanna-Barbera Productions, the prolific supplier of animated series, was similar in format to *The Muppet Show:* It was hosted by two
puppets, Honey and Sis, and featured celebrity guest stars. The life-sized
puppets were operated from behind by wands, and through the use of the
chroma-key process, the puppets' images were superimposed upon appropriate backgrounds. Joseph Barbera was the executive producer.

HAPPENING '68 ABC
6 JANUARY 1968–20 SEPTEMBER 1969   A Saturday-afternoon rock music show, hosted by Mark Lindsay and Paul Revere and the Raiders. The
show was known simply as *Happening* in 1969. See also *It's Happening.*

HAPPY NBC
8 JUNE 1960–28 SEPTEMBER 1960; 13 JANUARY 1961–8 SEPTEMBER
1961   This trivial sitcom borrowed one idea from *The Peoples' Choice*—
instead of a dog who could think out loud, this one featured a baby who
could think out loud. With Ronnie Burns as Chris Day, manager of a
Palm Springs motel; Yvonne Lime as his wife, Sally; twins David and
Steven Born as Happy (Christopher Hapgood Day), their gifted child;
Lloyd Corrigan as Uncle Charlie, Sally's uncle; Doris Packer as Clara
Mason, a woman who pursued Charlie; Burt Metcalfe as their friend, Joe
Brigham; and Wanda Shannon as Joe's wife, Terry.

HAPPY DAYS CBS
24 JUNE 1970–27 AUGUST 1970   An hour of nostalgia, hosted by Louis
Nye, with Chuck McCann, Bob (Elliott) and Ray (Goulding), and assorted bandleaders from the 1930s.

HAPPY DAYS ABC
15 JANUARY 1974–   This half-hour fifties sitcom was one of
the cornerstones of ABC's dramatic rise to the top of the ratings heap.
After a season and a half of unspectacular ratings, it began to climb in the

fall of 1975; the principal reason given for its rise was the decision of ABC programming chief Fred Silverman (newly arrived from CBS) to emphasize Fonzie, the leather-jacketed character. Another reason may have been that the show was also being taped in front of a live audience. The cast includes Ron Howard (veteran of *The Andy Griffith Show* and star of the 1973 film, *American Graffiti*) as Richie Cunningham, all-American teenager from Milwaukee's Jefferson High; Tom Bosley as Howard Cunningham, his father, who runs a hardware store; Marion Ross as Marion Cunningham, his mother; Erin Moran as Joanie, his kid sister; Gavan O'Herlihy (spring 1974) as his jockish older brother, Chuck; Anson Williams as Warren "Potsie" Webber, Richie's best friend; Henry Winkler as Arthur "Fonzie" Fonzarelli, the epitome of "cool," a guy who knows a lot about cars and girls; Donny Most as Richie's friend, Ralph Malph; Misty Rowe (September 1974–1975) as Wendy, a waitress at Arnold's, the local hangout; Pat Morita (1975–1976) as Arnold (Mitsuo Takahashi), the proprietor; Al Molinaro (1976–   ) as Al DelVecchio, the new proprietor of Arnold's; Scott Baio as Chachi (Charles) Arcola, Fonzie's enterprising young cousin. In 1975, Fonzie moved into the apartment above the Cunninghams' garage; that enabled him to retain his cherished independence, while being able to become involved in almost any situation involving the Cunninghams. In the fall of 1977 Richie, Potsie, and Ralph all began college at the University of Wisconsin in Milwaukee. The series was created by Garry Marshall, whose sister Penny Marshall starred in a *Happy Days* spinoff, *Laverne and Shirley*. Executive producers: Garry Marshall, Thomas L. Miller, and Edward K. Milkis.

HAPPY FELTON'S SPOTLIGHT CLUB   NBC
4 DECEMBER 1954–26 FEBRUARY 1955   Seen on Saturday mornings, this half-hour audience participation show for children was hosted by Happy Felton.

HARBOR COMMAND   SYNDICATED
1957   A half-hour adventure series from Ziv TV, starring Wendell Corey as Captain Ralph Baxter of the United States Coast Guard Harbor Police Command.

HARBOURMASTER (ADVENTURE AT SCOTT ISLAND)   CBS/ABC
26 SEPTEMBER 1957–26 DECEMBER 1957 (CBS); 5 JANUARY 1958–29 JUNE 1958 (ABC)   Set in New England, *Harbourmaster* was dropped by CBS in midseason; ABC then picked up the program, airing it under the title *Adventure at Scott Island*. With Barry Sullivan as Captain David Scott, who ran a boat repair business on Scott Island, a tightly knit island community settled by his forebears; Paul Burke as Jeff Kittredge, Scott's partner; Nina Wilcox as Anna Morrison, proprietor of the Dolphin res-

taurant; Michael Keene as Cap'n Dan, a local oldtimer; and Evan Elliott as Danny, Cap'n Dan's grandson. Suzanne Pleshette made her TV debut in one episode, "Night Rescue," aired 5 December. Exteriors were filmed at Rockport, Mass.

THE HARDY BOYS   ABC
6 SEPTEMBER 1969–5 SEPTEMBER 1970 In this Saturday morning cartoon series, Franklin W. Dixon's youthful sleuths were part of a rock group known as the Hardy Boys.

THE HARDY BOYS/NANCY DREW MYSTERIES   ABC
30 JANUARY 1977–21 JANUARY 1979 *The Hardy Boys Mysteries* and *The Nancy Drew Mysteries* started out as two separate series, alternating biweekly in the same time slot. Early in 1978 the casts merged for the remainder of the season, and in the fall of 1978 *The Hardy Boys Mysteries* continued on alone. Both the Hardy Boys and Nancy Drew were created in 1927 by Edward Stratemeyer, using the pen names Franklin W. Dixon for the Hardy Boys stories and Carolyn Keene for the Nancy Drew stories; his daughter, Harriet Stratemeyer Adams, continued writing the books after his death. *The Hardy Boys* cast included: Parker Stevenson as Frank Hardy; Shaun Cassidy (brother of David Cassidy of *The Partridge Family*) as Joe Hardy; Edmund Gilbert as their father, Fenton Hardy, a private eye; Edith Atwater (to September 1978) as Aunt Gertrude; Lisa Eilbacher (to September 1978) as the boys' friend, Callie Shaw; and Gary Springer (to September 1978) as Chet Morton. The *Nancy Drew* cast included Pamela Sue Martin and Janet Louise Johnson as Nancy Drew (Martin had balked at the idea of merging the two shows and was replaced when the decision to merge was final); William Schallert as Nancy's father, Carson Drew, a criminal lawyer; George O'Hanlon as Ned Nickerson; and Jean Rasey as George Fayne. Glen A. Larson was the executive producer for Glen A. Larson Productions in association with Universal Television.

THE HARLEM GLOBETROTTERS   CBS/NBC
12 SEPTEMBER 1970–2 SEPTEMBER 1972 (CBS); 4 FEBRUARY 1978–2 SEPTEMBER 1978 (NBC) The world famous basketball tricksters came to Saturday-morning television in a Hanna-Barbera cartoon series. Scatman Crothers provided the voice for the Globetrotters' star, Meadowlark Lemon. In 1978 reruns were shown on NBC under the title *The Go-Go Globetrotters*, a two-hour program which also included segments of *CB Bears, The Herculoids,* and *Space Ghost.*

THE HARLEM GLOBETROTTERS POPCORN MACHINE   CBS
7 SEPTEMBER 1974–5 SEPTEMBER 1976 The Harlem Globetrotters again came to weekend television, this time in a live-action format. Sever-

al members of the team were featured: Meadowlark Lemon, Curley Neal, Geese Ausbie, Tex Harrison, Bobby Joe Mason, Marques Haynes, John Smith, Theodis Lee, and Nate Brown. Also featured were young Rodney Allen Rippy and Avery Schreiber (as Mister Evil). Executive producers: Frank Peppiatt and John Aylesworth. Produced by Norman Baer.

HARRIGAN AND SON
ABC

14 OCTOBER 1960–29 SEPTEMBER 1961   Situation comedy about two lawyers, father and son. With Pat O'Brien as Jim Harrigan; Roger Perry as Jim Harrigan, Jr.; Georgine Darcy as Gypsy, Jim Sr.'s secretary; Helen Kleeb as Miss Claridge, Jim Jr.'s secretary.

HARRIS AGAINST THE WORLD
NBC

5 OCTOBER 1964–4 JANUARY 1965   Part Two of NBC's *90 Bristol Court, Harris Against the World* was sandwiched between *Tom, Dick and Mary* and *Karen*: only *Karen* survived the midseason purge. *Harris* featured Jack Klugman as Alan Harris, a businessman constantly battling with life's frustrations; Patricia Barry as Kate Harris, his wife; David Macklin as Billy, their son; Claire Wilcox as Dee Dee, their daughter; Fay DeWitt as Helen Miller, their friend; Sheldon Allman as Norm, Helen's husband; and Guy Raymond as Cliff Murdock, the building handyman.

HARRY O
ABC

12 SEPTEMBER 1974–12 AUGUST 1976   This crime show starred David Janssen as Harry Orwell, a cop who became a private eye after he was shot in the back. Orwell was a low-paid, low-key private eye who often had to take the bus to pursue criminals when his car was laid up and rarely got the better of the bad guy in a fight. Also featured were Henry Darrow (1974–January 1975) as Detective Manny Quinlan of the San Diego police; Anthony Zerbe (January 1975-1976) as Lieutenant K. C. Trench of the Los Angeles police; Paul Tulley (1975–1976) as Sergeant Don Roberts. In the middle of the first season Orwell moved from San Diego to Los Angeles. The first pilot for the series was shown 11 March 1973. Created by Howard Rodman. Executive producer: Jerry Thorpe. Producer: E. Thompson (for Warner Brothers).

HARRY'S GIRLS
NBC

13 SEPTEMBER 1963–3 JANUARY 1964   This situation comedy about an American vaudeville act touring Europe was filmed in southern France. With Larry Blyden as Harry Burns; Dawn Nickerson as Lois; Susan Silo as Rusty; and Diahn Williams as Terry. It was replaced in midseason by *That Was the Week That Was*.

HART TO HART
ABC

22 SEPTEMBER 1979–   Breezy hour adventure series, starring

Robert Wagner and Stefanie Powers as Jonathan and Jennifer Hart, husband-and-wife amateur sleuths in their spare time. (Professionally, Jonathan ran a conglomerate and Jennifer was an author.) Also featured was Lionel Stander as Max, their chauffeur and aide. Aaron Spelling and Leonard Goldberg were the executive producers.

THE HARTMANS (THE HARTMANS AT HOME) NBC
27 FEBRUARY 1949–22 MAY 1949   This Sunday-night sitcom starred Grace and Paul Hartman as themselves.

THE HARVEY KORMAN SHOW ABC
4 APRIL 1978–3 AUGUST 1978   After a onetime telecast on 31 January 1978, *The Harvey Korman Show* began its regular schedule in April. Harvey Korman, who had been featured on *The Carol Burnett Show* for ten years, starred in the half-hour sitcom as actor Harvey Kavanaugh. Also featured were Christine Lahti as his daughter, Maggie, an employee of the Friendly Community Bank; Barry Van Dyke as Maggie's boyfriend and coworker, Stuart Stafford; Milton Selzer as Jake, Harvey's agent. Hal Dresner was the executive producer of the series, and Don Van Atta produced it.

THE HATHAWAYS ABC
6 OCTOBER 1961–31 AUGUST 1962   Situation comedy about a couple who agree to take in a family of performing chimps. With Jack Weston as real estate agent Walter Hathaway; Peggy Cass as his wife, Eleanor; Harvey Lembeck as the chimps' agent, Jerry Roper; and the Marquis Chimps. The half-hour show was a Screen Gems production.

HAVE A HEART DUMONT
3 MAY 1955–14 JUNE 1955   John Reed King hosted this prime-time game show on which two four-member teams, each from a different city or town, competed; all winnings were awarded to charity.

HAVE GUN WILL TRAVEL CBS
14 SEPTEMBER 1957–21 SEPTEMBER 1963   This half-hour western starred Richard Boone as Paladin, a loner who was based at the Hotel Carlton in San Francisco; his professional services—as detective, bodyguard, courier, or whatever—were available to those who requested them. Paladin's business card, which bore the image of a chess knight, read: "Have Gun, Will Travel. Wire Paladin, San Francisco." Kam Tong was also featured as Paladin's servant, Hey Boy, except during the fall of 1959 (when Tong costarred in *Mr. Garlund*) and during the 1960–1961 season, when Lisa Lu was featured as Hey Girl. Boone exercised considerable control over the show; in 1961 *TV Guide* reported that Boone not only had directed several episodes but also exercised script and casting

approval. Whatever the case, Boone's judgments seem to have been right, for the show was a solid hit, ranking in Nielsen's top five during each of its first four seasons. Though the show was extremely popular and was widely syndicated during the 1960s, it is doubtful whether it will ever be seen again, for in 1974, a federal magistrate ruled that a Rhode Island radio performer, Victor De Costa, had actually created the character in the 1940s and was entitled to an accounting of the profits realized from the show.

HAVING BABIES (JULIE FARR, M. D.) ABC
7 MARCH 1978–18 APRIL 1978 *Having Babies* was introduced as an hour-long series after three made-for-TV movies had been telecast; midway through its limited run the show's title was changed to *Julie Farr, M.D.,* as the emphasis shifted from specialized to generalized medical drama. Featured were Susan Sullivan as obstetrician Dr. Julie Farr; Mitchell Ryan as surgeon Dr. Blake Simmons; Dennis Howard as intern Dr. Ron Danvers; and Beverly Todd as Kelly. A few additional episodes were televised during the summer of 1979.

HAWAII FIVE-O CBS
26 SEPTEMBER 1968– TV's longest-running crime show embodies the right mixture of scenery (it was filmed entirely on location) and action. Created by Leonard Freeman (who served as executive producer until his death in 1973), it stars Jack Lord as Steve McGarrett, the no-nonsense head of Five-O, a special investigative unit directly responsible to the governor of Hawaii. Almost all the stories are straight-ahead crime dramas; McGarrett's personal life is rarely explored beyond the fact that he is a bachelor who enjoys sailing. Among those who have been featured are James MacArthur (1968–1979) as Danny ("Dano") Williams, McGarrett's number-one assistant; Kam Fong as Chin Ho Kelly, who was killed off at the end of the 1977–1978 season; Zulu (1968–1972) as Kono; Richard Denning (appearing occasionally) as The Governor (Keith Jameson); Maggi Parker (1968–1969) as May, Steve's secretary; Peggy Ryan (1969–   ) as Jenny Sherman, Steve's secretary; Al Eben as Doc Bergman, the pathologist; Harry Endo as lab expert Che Fong; Al Harrington (1972–1977) as Ben Kokua; Herman Wedemeyer (1972–   ) as Duke Lakela; Douglas Mossman (1974–1975) as Frank Kemana; and Glenn Cannon (1976–1978) as Attorney General John Manicote. Also appearing occasionally was Khigh Deigh as Wo Fat, a mysterious Oriental criminal who is McGarrett's archenemy. In the fall of 1979 three new regulars were added: Bill Smith as James (Kimo) Carew; Sharon Farrell as Lori Wilson; and Moe Keale as Tom (Truck) Tahale. Following producer Freeman's death, Bill Finnegan and Bob Sweeney took over as producers; they were replaced in 1975 by Philip Leacock and Richard Newton, who were in turn succeeded by Douglas

Green and B. W. Sandefur. It is no secret, however, that Jack Lord is actively involved in most aspects of the show's production.

HAWAIIAN EYE
ABC

7 OCTOBER 1959–10 SEPTEMBER 1963   Set in Honolulu, this Warner Brothers detective show was cast in the same mold as *77 Sunset Strip,* the first of Warners' private eye shows. *Hawaiian Eye* originally featured Anthony Eisley as Tracy Steele, a former Honolulu cop; Robert Conrad as Thomas Jefferson (Tom) Lopaka, his partner in Hawaiian Eye; Connie Stevens as Cricket Blake, singer at the Shell Bar of the nearby Hawaiian Village Hotel: Poncie Ponce as Kazuo Kim (Kim), a cabbie; Mel Prestidge as Lieutenant Quon of the Honolulu police. In 1961, Grant Williams joined the cast as Gregg Mackenzie, Tracy and Tom's new partner. Eisley left the series in 1962; for the final season Troy Donahue (late of *SurfSide 6*) was added as Phil Barton, social director of the hotel, and Doug Mossman joined the cast as Moke. Sharp-eyed viewers could have noted Chad Everett in his TV debut ("The Kahuna Curtain," 9 November 1960) and an early appearance by Jack Nicholson ("Total Eclipse," 21 February 1962). William T. Orr was the executive producer of the series.

HAWK
ABC

8 SEPTEMBER 1966–29 DECEMBER 1966   An hour-long crime show starring Burt Reynolds as Detective Lieutenant John Hawk, an Iroquois Indian police officer assigned to the New York City district attorney's office. Also featured were Wayne Grice as Detective Carter, his sometime partner; Leon Janney as Gorten, a newsdealer who doubled as Hawk's street source.

HAWKEYE (HAWKEYE
AND THE LAST OF THE MOHICANS)
SYNDICATED

1957   Produced in Canada, this adventure series was based loosely on James Fenimore Cooper's book. With John Hart as Hawkeye, a white trapper and scout; Lon Chaney, Jr., as Chingachgook, a Mohican, Hawkeye's blood brother.

HAWKINS
CBS

2 OCTOBER 1973–3 SEPTEMBER 1974   James Stewart starred as Billy Jim Hawkins, a plain ol' country lawyer from Beauville, West Virginia, in this hour-long crime show. Veteran character actor Strother Martin costarred as his cousin, R. J. Hawkins, who occasionally did some investigating for Billy Jim. Though the format of the show seemed ideally suited for Stewart's talents (unlike his first series, *The Jimmy Stewart Show*), the series failed to catch on. The show was produced by Arena Productions in association with MGM TV.

HAWKINS FALLS   NBC

Nighttime: 17 JUNE 1950–19 AUGUST 1950; *Daytime:* 2 APRIL 1951–1
JULY 1955   The official title of this serial, in its early days, was *Hawkins
Falls, Pop. 6200.* The evening version was broadcast from Chicago and
was seen Saturdays; the following spring it began a daytime run which
lasted four years. It told of life in a small town (exterior sequences were
filmed at Woodstock, Illinois). The cast included: Bernadine Flynn as
Lona Drewer Carey; Michael Golda as Dr. Floyd Carey, the man she
married; Win Stracke as Laif Flaigle; Ros Twohey as Millie Flaigle; Hel-
en Bernie as Betty Sawtel; Russ Reed as Spec Bassett; and Elmira
Roessler as Elmira Cleebe.

HAZEL   NBC/CBS

28 SEPTEMBER 1961–9 SEPTEMBER 1965 (NBC); 13 SEPTEMBER 1965–5
SEPTEMBER 1966 (CBS)   One of the few successful TV series based on a
comic strip, *Hazel* came to television in 1961, about nineteen years after
her creation by Ted Key (the cartoons were published in *The Saturday
Evening Post*). Shirley Booth, a stage actress who had done little television previously, starred as Hazel Burke, a domestic with a penchant for
getting involved in other people's business. For the first four years of the
series, Hazel was employed by the George Baxter family. Appearing as
the Baxters were Don Defore as George Baxter, a lawyer; Whitney Blake
as his wife, Dorothy Baxter; and Bobby Buntrock as their son, Harold.
Occasionally appearing were Cathy Lewis as George's sister, Deirdre
Thompson; Robert P. Lieb as Harry Thompson, Deirdre's henpecked
husband; Maudie Prickett as Hazel's friend Rosie, also a domestic; Howard Smith as Harvey Griffin, one of George's clients; Norma Varden as
next-door neighbor Harriet Johnson; and Donald Foster as Harriet's husband, Herbert Johnson. When the series shifted networks in 1965, Hazel
was given new employers—the Steve (younger brother of George) Baxter
family. It was explained that George Baxter had been sent to Saudi Ara-
bia on business, and Dorothy had gone with him, but that young Harold
had stayed in town to finish school. Defore and Blake, as well as most of
the semiregulars, left the cast, though Buntrock remained. Added to the
cast were Ray Fulmer as Steve Baxter, a real estate agent; Lynn Borden
as Barbara Baxter, his wife; and Julia Benjamin as Susie, their daughter
(Harold, their nephew, lived with them while his parents were away).
Also added were Mala Powers as Mona Williams, a friend of Barbara's;
Ann Jillian as Millie, Steve's secretary. The series, which cracked Nielsen's top ten in its first season, was produced by James Fonda for Screen
Gems.

THE HAZEL BISHOP SHOW
See THE FREDDY MARTIN SHOW

THE HAZEL SCOTT SHOW DUMONT

3 JULY 1950–29 SEPTEMBER 1950 Pianist Hazel Scott hosted this fifteen-minute musical series, which was seen Mondays, Wednesdays, and Fridays. It was the first network series hosted by a black woman.

HE & SHE CBS

6 SEPTEMBER 1967–18 SEPTEMBER 1968 This unsuccessful sitcom brought together a talented group of players: Richard Benjamin as Dick Hollister, a cartoonist, the creator of "Jetman"; Paula Prentiss (who was married to Benjamin) as Paula Hollister, Dick's wife, who worked for Travelers' Aid in New York; Hamilton Camp as Andrew Hummel, the superintendent of their apartment building; Jack Cassidy as Oscar North, the actor who played Dick's "Jetman" on TV; Kenneth Mars as the Hollisters' neighbor, Harry, a fireman; and Harold Gould as Norman Nugent, Dick's boss. Though the series was scheduled in a good time slot (9:30 Wednesdays, following *The Beverly Hillbillies* and *Green Acres*), audiences seemed to stay away in droves. The half-hour show was produced by Talent Associates.

HE SAID, SHE SAID SYNDICATED

1969 Developed by Mark Goodson and Bill Todman, this game show featured celebrity couples. Husbands and wives were separated, and one set of spouses was asked a question. The object of the game was for the other set of spouses to determine which answers had been given by their respective mates. Joe Garagiola hosted the series.

HEADLINE CLEWS
See BROADWAY TO HOLLYWOOD

HEADLINERS WITH DAVID FROST NBC

31 MAY 1978–5 JULY 1978 David Frost was the host and the executive producer of this hour-long interview series; almost all of the segments were taped, though the introductions and other material were presented live. Frost's guests on the premiere included John Travolta, the Bee Gees, and former CIA director Richard Helms.

HEADMASTER CBS

18 SEPTEMBER 1970–1 JANUARY 1971 Andy Griffith returned to television in this low-key comedy-drama. He played Andy Thompson, headmaster of a coeducational prep school in California. Also featured were Claudette Nevins as his wife, Margaret Thompson, who also taught there; Jerry Van Dyke as athletic coach Jerry Brownell; and Parker Fennelly as Mr. Purdy, the custodian. Aaron Ruben produced the series; the

format was scrapped in midseason, and the show was retitled. See *The New Andy Griffith Show.*

HEART OF THE CITY
See BIG TOWN

HEAVEN FOR BETSY   CBS
30 SEPTEMBER 1952–25 DECEMBER 1952 This fifteen-minute sitcom was seen on Tuesdays and Thursdays following the network news. It starred Jack Lemmon and Cynthia Stone (Lemmon's wife at the time) as newlyweds Pete and Betsy Bell. Lemmon and Stone previously played newlyweds on a 1951–1952 daytime series, *The Frances Langford–Don Ameche Show.*

HEC RAMSEY   NBC
8 OCTOBER 1972–25 AUGUST 1974 This segment of *The NBC Sunday Mystery Movie* starred Richard Boone as Hec Ramsey, a deputy police officer in New Prospect, Oklahoma, at the turn of the century; a former gunslinger, Ramsey now used modern scientific methods to solve cases. Also featured were Rick Lenz as the young police chief, Oliver B. Stamp; Harry Morgan as Doc Coogan, New Prospect's ad hoc physician. Douglas Benton produced the series for Jack Webb's Mark VII Productions.

HECKLE AND JECKLE   SYNDICATED/CBS/NBC
1955 (SYNDICATED); 14 OCTOBER 1956–24 SEPTEMBER 1960 (CBS); 25 SEPTEMBER 1965–3 SEPTEMBER 1966 (CBS); 6 SEPTEMBER 1969–4 SEPTEMBER 1971 (NBC) Heckle and Jeckle, a pair of fast-talking black-birds, were created by Paul Terry and starred in hundreds of theatrical cartoons before coming to television in 1955. Other Terrytoon characters who appeared on the durable TV show were Gandy Goose, Dinky Duck, Little Roquefort, and The Terry Bears. See also *The New Adventures of Mighty Mouse and Heckle and Jeckle.*

THE HECTOR HEATHCOTE SHOW   NBC
5 OCTOBER 1963–25 SEPTEMBER 1965 Saturday-morning cartoon series about a scientist and his time machine. Assisting Heathcote were Hashimoto, a judo-trained mouse, and Sidney, an elephant.

HEE HAW   CBS/SYNDICATED
15 JUNE 1969–7 SEPTEMBER 1969; 17 DECEMBER 1969–13 JULY 1971 (CBS); 1971–   (SYNDICATED) Best described as the country-and-western version of *Laugh-In, Hee Haw* was a fast-paced mixture of songs, skits, blackouts, and corny jokes. It began as a summer series and attracted decent enough ratings to warrant its return that winter. Though it was blasted by the critics, there was no doubt that it had wide

appeal; it ranked a respectable sixteenth when CBS canceled it in 1971 along with rest of the network's rural shows (*The Beverly Hillbillies, Green Acres,* and *The Jim Nabors Show*). A syndicated version of the show appeared that fall and soon was carried by more stations than when it ran on CBS; by 1977 it was the nation's number-one-rated non-network show.

From the beginning, the show was taped in Nashville, first at the studios of WLAC-TV, later at WTVF. The show was taped in assembly-line style during periods lasting several weeks. The segments were then cut, edited, and spliced together to comprise the hour-long programs. The show was the brainchild of two Canadians, Frank Peppiatt and John Aylesworth, who now serve as its executive producers (Sam Lovullo is the producer). The series is cohosted by Buck Owens and Roy Clark. A large stable of regular performers have been featured, including Louis M. ("Grandpa") Jones, Junior Samples, Jeannine Riley, Lulu Roman, David Akeman ("Stringbean"), Sherry Miles, Lisa Todd, Minnie Pearl, Gordie Tapp, Diana Scott, Cathy Baker, unicyclist Zella Lehr, The Hagers, and Barbi Benton. In recent years the nucleus of regulars has included Jones, Samples, The Hagers, Roman, Todd, Pearl, Archie Campbell, Roni Stoneham, George Lindsey, Gunilla Hutton, Harry Cole, Don Harron (as Charlie Farquharson), Misty Rowe, and Gailard Sartain.

THE HEE HAW HONEYS   SYNDICATED
1978–   A half-hour sitcom set at Honey's Club, a small restaurant in Nashville, this series was spun off from *Hee Haw.* With Kenny Price and Lulu Roman as the proprietors, Kenny and Lulu Honey; Misty Rowe and Cathie Lee Johnson as their daughters, Misty and Cathie, who wait on tables and also sing there; and Gailard Sartain as their son, Willy Billy, the cook. A regular feature of the show is the appearance of guest stars from the world of country-and-western music, who stop by to sing a number or two at the club. Sam Lovullo is the executive producer.

THE HELEN O'CONNELL SHOW   NBC
29 MAY 1957–6 SEPTEMBER 1957   Helen O'Connell, who sang with several big bands during the 1940s, hosted this fifteen-minute series, which was seen Wednesdays and Fridays before the evening news.

THE HELEN REDDY SHOW   NBC
28 JUNE 1973–16 AUGUST 1973   Australian-born singer Helen Reddy, who won a Grammy for "I Am Woman," hosted this variety hour, a summer replacement for *The Flip Wilson Show.* Carolyn Raskin produced the series.

HELLO, LARRY   NBC
26 JANUARY 1979–   Half-hour sitcom about a radio talk-

show host who moves from Los Angeles to Portland, Oregon, with his two teenage daughters following the breakup of his marriage. With McLean Stevenson as Larry Alder; Donna Wilkes (spring 1979) and Krista Errickson (fall 1979–   ) as daughter Diane; Kim Richards as daughter Ruthie; Joanna Gleason as Morgan Winslow, Larry's producer; and George Memmoli as Earl, Larry's corpulent engineer. In the fall of 1979 Meadowlark Lemon, formerly of the Harlem Globetrotters, joined the cast (as himself), and John Femia was added as Tommy. It is no coincidence that *Hello, Larry* bears more than a passing resemblance to *One Day at a Time,* for *Larry*'s executive producers—Dick Bensfield and Perry Grant (for Norman Lear's TAT Communications)—had also worked on *One Day at a Time.*

HELP! IT'S THE HAIR BEAR BUNCH   CBS
11 SEPTEMBER 1971–2 SEPTEMBER 1972   Saturday-morning cartoon show from Hanna-Barbera about a bunch of bears living in a zoo.

HENNESEY   CBS
28 SEPTEMBER 1959–17 SEPTEMBER 1962   Situation comedy about a Navy doctor stationed in San Diego. With Jackie Cooper as Lieutenant Charles "Chick" Hennesey; Abby Dalton as his girlfriend, Nurse Martha Hale; Roscoe Karns as his commanding officer, Captain Walter Shafer; James Komack as Navy dentist Harvey Spencer Blair III; and Henry Kulky as Max Bronsky, an orderly who read Spinoza. In the fall of 1961 promotions were handed out: Hennesey became a lieutenant commander, Hale a lieutenant, Shafer an admiral, and Bronsky a chief petty officer. Hennesey and Hale also got married that season. Don McGuire wrote and coproduced the series with Jackie Cooper.

THE HENNY AND ROCKY SHOW   ABC
1 JUNE 1955–31 AUGUST 1955   *The Henny and Rocky Show* was a series of variable length—it was designed to fill out the rest of the hour if and when ABC's Wednesday-night boxing matches ran short. Comedian Henny Youngman and boxer-actor Rocky Graziano cohosted the show, which also featured singer Marion Colby.

HENRY FONDA PRESENTS THE STAR AND THE STORY   SYNDICATED
1955   Half-hour dramatic anthology series hosted by Henry Fonda.

THE HENRY MORGAN SHOW   ABC/NBC
18 APRIL 1948–16 MAY 1948 (ABC); 13 MARCH 1949–22 APRIL 1949 (NBC); 26 JANUARY 1951–15 JUNE 1951 (NBC)   Though comedian Henry Morgan is remembered today mainly as a panelist on game shows such as *I've Got a Secret,* he hosted several shows in television's early days. His 1948 show, titled *On the Corner,* was seen Sunday nights on the

ABC network (though it was carried by the DuMont affiliate in New York). In 1949 he moved to NBC, where he was first given a half hour on Sunday nights; that slot was soon shifted to a fifteen-minute slot on Mondays, Wednesdays, and Fridays, before disappearing altogether in April of that year. Early in 1951 he tried a second series for NBC, a Friday-night half hour called *Henry Morgan's Great Talent Hunt.* A forerunner of *The Gong Show,* the series featured people with unusual talents; assisting Morgan were Arnold Stang and Kaye Ballard. In April 1951 the talent format was scrapped, and Morgan hosted a half-hour comedy-variety show for a few more weeks, which featured Arnold Stang, Pert Kelton, and Art Carney. The principal reason that all of Morgan's series were short-lived was his apparently incurable habit of ridiculing his sponsors; *TV Guide* reported that one advertiser, Life Savers, dropped its sponsorship after one week, following Morgan's tongue-in-cheek accusation that the company was cheating the public by drilling holes in its product.

HERB SHRINER TIME ABC
11 OCTOBER 1951–3 APRIL 1952
THE HERB SHRINER SHOW CBS
2 OCTOBER 1956–4 DECEMBER 1956 Indiana comedian Herb Shriner was first seen on television in 1949, when he hosted a thrice-weekly five-minute show on CBS. In 1951 he hosted his first prime-time variety series, seen Thursdays over ABC. He then hosted a game show, *Two for The Money,* before trying a second variety series in 1956 on CBS.

THE HERCULOIDS CBS
9 SEPTEMBER 1967–30 AUGUST 1969 Saturday-morning cartoon show from Hanna-Barbera featuring several super-powered characters who lived in another galaxy.

HERE COME THE BRIDES ABC
25 SEPTEMBER 1968–18 SEPTEMBER 1970 Based on the film, *Seven Brides for Seven Brothers,* this Screen Gems sitcom was set at a Washington logging camp in the 1870s, where the men arranged to import 100 available women from New Bedford, Massachusetts. With Robert Brown as Jason Bolt, unofficial leader of the camp; David Soul as Joshua Bolt, his brother; Bobby Sherman as Jeremy Bolt, their younger brother; Mark Lenard as Aaron Stempel, operator of the local sawmill; Henry Beckman as Clancey, the boat captain; Joan Blondell as Lottie Hatfield, proprietor of the camp saloon; Bridget Hanley as Candy Pruitt, an eligible bride; Susan Tolsky as Biddie Cloom; Mitzi Hoag as Essie, the schoolteacher; Hoke Howell as Ben Jenkins; Bo Svenson as Big Swede, camp foreman; Eric Chase (1969–1970) as Christopher, Candy's little brother; and Patti Cohoon (1969–1970) as Molly, Candy's little sister.

HERE COME THE DOUBLE-DECKERS ABC

12 SEPTEMBER 1970–17 SEPTEMBER 1972 A British import about a group of youngsters who lived in a reconverted double-decker bus, this half-hour series was seen on weekend mornings. With Michael Auderson as Brains; Gillian Bailey as Billie; Bruce Clark as Sticks; Peter Firth as Scooper; Brinsley Forde as Spring; Debbie Russ as Tiger; and Douglas Simmonds as Doughnut. Also appearing was Melvyn Hayes as their grownup pal, Albert.

HERE COMES THE GRUMP NBC

6 SEPTEMBER 1969–4 SEPTEMBER 1971 Saturday-morning cartoon series reminiscent of *The Wizard of Oz*. Here, a boy (Terry) and his dog (Bib) found themselves in a fantasy land and were commissioned by Princess Dawn to find a magic key secreted by The Grump.

HERE WE GO AGAIN ABC

20 JANUARY 1973–23 JUNE 1973 This situation comedy about divorce failed to make a dent in the ratings of its CBS competitor, *All in the Family*. With Larry Hagman as Richard Evans, a divorced architect who remarried; Diane Baker as Susan Standish, the divorcée whom he married; Dick Gautier as Jerry Standish, Susan's ex, a restaurateur who lived nearby; Nita Talbot as Judy Evans, Richard's ex, who edited a movie magazine; Chris Beaumont as Jeff, Richard and Judy's teenage son (he lived with Judy after the divorce); Leslie Graves and Kim Richards as Cindy and Jan, Jerry and Susan's young daughters (they lived with Richard and Susan). Created by Bob Kaufman; produced by Steve Pritzker for Metromedia.

HERE'S BARBARA SYNDICATED

1969 Barbara Coleman hosted this Washington-based half-hour talk show.

HERE'S EDIE ABC

26 SEPTEMBER 1963–19 MARCH 1964 This half-hour variety series alternated with *The Sid Caesar Show* on Thursdays. It was hosted by singer-comedienne Edie Adams, widow of Ernie Kovacs. Don Chastain was also featured on the show.

HERE'S HOLLYWOOD NBC

26 SEPTEMBER 1960–28 DECEMBER 1962 Celebrity interviews comprised this daytime half-hour show, cohosted by Dean Miller and Jo-ann Jordan; Helen O'Connell later replaced Jordan.

HERE'S LOOKING AT YOU
See THE RICHARD WILLIS SHOW

HERE'S LUCY
CBS

23 SEPTEMBER 1968–2 SEPTEMBER 1974 *Here's Lucy* was the direct successor to *The Lucy Show,* with a slight change in format. It starred Lucille Ball as Lucille Carter, a secretary at her brother-in-law's employment agency; Gale Gordon as Harrison Carter, her brother-in-law and boss, head of the Unique Employment Agency; Lucie Arnaz as her daughter, Kim; Desi Arnaz, Jr. (1968–1971) as her son, Craig; Mary Jane Croft as Mary Jane Lewis, Lucy's friend. Many prominent stars appeared on the series, including Johnny Carson (1 December 1969), Ann-Margret (2 February 1970), Richard Burton and Elizabeth Taylor (14 September 1970), Flip Wilson (13 September 1971 and 6 March 1972), Ginger Rogers (8 November 1971), David Frost (29 November 1971), and Joe Namath (9 October 1972).

THE HERMAN HICKMAN SHOW
NBC

3 OCTOBER 1952–27 MARCH 1953 Fifteen-minute Friday-night sports show hosted by Herman Hickman, who had formerly coached football at Yale.

THE HERO
NBC

8 SEPTEMBER 1966–5 JANUARY 1967 An early casualty of the 1966–1967 season, *The Hero* featured a series-within-a-series format. It starred Richard Mulligan as Sam Garret, star of "Jed Clayton—U.S. Marshal," a hit western, but a clumsy bloke offscreen. Also featured were Mariette Hartley as his wife, Ruth Garret; Bobby Doran as their son, Paul; Victor French as neighbor Fred Gilman; Joey Baio as Fred's son, Burton; and Marc London as Dewey. Leonard Stern created the series and served as its executive producer; Jay Sandrich produced it for Talent Associates.

HEY, JEANNIE
CBS

8 SEPTEMBER 1956–4 MAY 1957 Half-hour sitcom about a Scotswoman who emigrated to New York City. With Jeannie Carson as Jeannie MacLennan; Allen Jenkins as her sponsor, Al Murray, a Brooklyn cabbie; and Jane Dulo as Liz Murray, Al's sister. After arriving in New York, Jeannie moved in with Al and Liz and got a job as a waitress in a donut shop.

HEY LANDLORD
NBC

11 SEPTEMBER 1966–14 MAY 1967 Half-hour sitcom about two young bachelors who own an apartment building. With Will Hutchins as Woody Banner, a would-be writer; Sandy Baron as Chuck Hookstratten, a would-be comic; Pamela Rodgers as tenant Timothy Morgan, a weather forecaster; Michael Constantine as tenant Jack Ellenhorn, a photographer; and Ann Morgan Guilbert as tenant Mrs. Henderson, a fussbudget. Produced by Lee Rich.

HEY MULLIGAN
See THE MICKEY ROONEY SHOW

HIDDEN FACES   NBC
30 DECEMBER 1968–27 JUNE 1969   Short-lived daytime serial which
NBC scheduled opposite CBS's *As the World Turns*. Soap opera buffs
generally agree that it was well written and well acted, but that failure
was inevitable against such strong competition. With Conrad Fowkes as
lawyer Arthur Adams; Gretchen Walther as Dr. Katherine Walker, a
surgeon who left medicine after accidentally killing a patient during an
operation, and who eventually fell in love with Adams. Also featured
were Stephen Joyce, Rita Gam, Tony LoBianco, and Nat Polen.

THE HIGH CHAPARRAL   NBC
10 SEPTEMBER 1967–10 SEPTEMBER 1971   This fairly successful western was produced by David Dortort, who also produced *Bonanza*. Like
Bonanza, The High Chaparral was a "property" western: the two central
families—the Cannons and the Montoyas—were both large landowners
in the Arizona Territory. With Leif Erickson as John Cannon, owner of
the High Chaparral Ranch; Linda Cristal as his wife, Victoria Cannon,
daughter of the Montoyas; Cameron Mitchell as Buck Cannon, John's
brother; Mark Slade as Blue Cannon, John's son and Victoria's stepson;
Frank Silvera (1967–1970) as Don Sebastian Montoya, owner of the
Montoya Ranch and father of Victoria Cannon; Gilbert Roland (1970–
1971) as his brother, Don Domingo de Montoya; and Henry Darrow as
Manolito, Don Sebastian's son. The several ranch hands on the two
ranches included Bob Hoy as Joe, Roberto Conteras as Pedro, Rudy Ramos as Wind, and Rodolfo Acosta as Vasquero.

HIGH FINANCE   CBS
7 JULY 1956–15 DECEMBER 1956   The top prize was $75,000 on this
prime-time current events quiz show, hosted by Dennis James. In September 1956 former boxing champ Joe Louis and his wife Rose appeared,
trying to earn money to defray a hefty federal tax bill.

HIGH HOPES   SYNDICATED
1978   A half-hour serial set in the small college town of Cambridge.
With Bruce Gray as family counselor Neal Chapman; Marianne McIsaac
as Jessie Chapman, his possessive daughter; Nuala Fitzgerald as Paula
Myles, sister of Neal's ex-wife; Barbara Kyle as Trudy Bowen, hostess of
a local talk show; Colin Fox as Walter Telford; Gina Dick as Amy Sper-
ry; Jayne Eastwood as Louise Bates; Jan Muszinski as Dr. Dan Gerard;
Vivian Reis as Norma Stewart; Michael Tait as Michael Stewart; Gordon
Thompson as Mike Stewart, Jr.; Deborah Turnbull as Mrs. Telford; Can-
dace O'Connor as Helen; and Doris Petrie as Meg Chapman, Neal's

mother. Taped in Toronto, the series was written by Winnifred Wolfe and Mort Forer. Dick Cox was the executive producer.

HIGH LOW QUIZ
NBC

4 JULY 1957–12 SEPTEMBER 1957 Contestants battled a panel of experts on this prime-time game show, a summer replacement for *The (Tennessee Ernie) Ford Show,* hosted by Jack Barry. Contestants earned money by matching answers with either the expert with the most correct answers or the expert with the fewest correct answers.

HIGH ROAD (JOHN GUNTHER'S HIGH ROAD)
ABC

7 SEPTEMBER 1959–1 OCTOBER 1960 Prime-time travelogue, hosted by John Gunther.

HIGH ROAD TO DANGER
SYNDICATED

1958 Steve Brodie narrated this half-hour series of films about modern-day adventurers.

HIGH ROLLERS
NBC/SYNDICATED

1 JULY 1974–11 JUNE 1976 (NBC); 1975 (SYNDICATED); 24 APRIL 1978–   (NBC) By answering questions correctly, contestants on this game show earned the chance to acquire prizes in accordance with the roll of a pair of giant dice. Alex Trebek hosts the show, which began as a daytime series on NBC; Ruta Lee rolls the dice on the network version, while Elaine Stewart handled the chore on the 1975 syndicated version. When the series returned to NBC's daytime schedule in 1978, it was titled *The New High Rollers.* Merrill Heatter and Bob Quigley are the executive producers.

HIGHCLIFFE MANOR
NBC

12 APRIL 1979–3 MAY 1979 Comedy melodrama set at a mysterious island, the headquarters of the Blacke Foundation, a research outfit. With Shelley Fabares as Helen Blacke, widow of the foundation's founder; Stephen McHattie as Reverend Glenville; Eugenie Ross-Leming as Frances; Gerald Gordon as Dr. Felix Morger; Audrey Landers as Wendy, secretary to the late Berkeley Blacke; Jenny O'Hara as Rebecca, the housekeeper; Christian Marlowe as Bram Shelley; David Byrd as Dr. Lester; Luis Avalos as Dr. Sanchez; Ernie Hudson as Smythe, valet to the late Mr. Blacke; Harold Sakata as Cheng. Robert Blees created the half-hour series.

HIGHWAY PATROL
SYNDICATED

1955–1959 Very popular crime show produced by Ziv TV, depicting the work of the Highway Patrol, a law enforcement agency analogous to the State Police. Broderick Crawford starred as Captain Dan Matthews, the gravel-voiced chief who seemed to spend most of his time barking "10–4! 10–4!" over the police radio. Narrator: Art Gilmore. The *Highway Patrol* theme was composed by Ray Llewellyn.

THE HILARIOUS HOUSE OF FRIGHTENSTEIN   SYNDICATED
1975 Videotaped children's series hosted by Billy Van.

HIPPODROME   CBS
5 JULY 1966–6 SEPTEMBER 1966   European circus acts were presented on this hour-long series; guest hosts included Woody Allen, Eddie Albert, Trini Lopez, and Tony Randall, among others. This Tuesday-night series should not be confused with *Continental Showcase,* another European circus show aired by CBS that summer on Saturdays.

HIRAM HOLLIDAY (THE ADVENTURES OF HIRAM HOLLIDAY)   NBC
3 OCTOBER 1956–27 FEBRUARY 1957, Half-hour filmed sitcom based on the short stories by Paul Gallico. Wally Cox (formerly of *Mr. Peepers*) starred as Hiram Holliday, a newspaper proofreader who was rewarded with a trip around the world by his employer when he corrected an error in an article, thereby preventing a lawsuit against the paper. Also featured was Ainslie Pryor as his companion, Joel Smith, a reporter sent along with Holliday. Most of the stories involved cases of mistaken identity, or the innocent involvement of mild-mannered Holliday in international intrigue.

HIS HONOR, HOMER BELL
See HOMER BELL

HOGAN'S HEROES   CBS
17 SEPTEMBER 1965–4 JULY 1971   This popular situation comedy demonstrated that a prisoner-of-war camp was as good a site as any for laughs. With Bob Crane as Colonel Robert Hogan, ranking American officer at Stalag 13, a German POW camp; Werner Klemperer as Colonel Wilhelm Klink, its inept commandant; John Banner as Sergeant Schultz, Klink's chief aide; Robert Clary as Corporal Louis LeBeau, a French prisoner; Richard Dawson as Corporal Newkirk, a British prisoner; Ivan Dixon (1965–1969) and Kenneth Washington (1969–1971) as Corporal Kinchloe, an American prisoner; Larry Hovis as Sergeant Carter, another Yankee prisoner; and Sigrid Valdis as Hilda, Klink's secretary. Produced by Ed Feldman for Bing Crosby Productions .

HOLD 'ER NEWT   ABC
11 SEPTEMBER 1950–13 OCTOBER 1950; 26 JANUARY 1952–17 MAY 1952   A puppet show for kids, *Hold 'Er Newt* was first broadcast locally

in June 1950 over WENR-TV in Chicago. In the fall of 1950 it enjoyed a brief Monday-through-Friday network run, and in 1952 it surfaced again on the network's Saturday morning schedule. Don Tennant wrote the show and provided the voice of Newt, who ran a general store in a small town.

HOLD IT PLEASE CBS
8 MAY 1949–22 MAY 1949   Short-lived prime-time game show incorporating both charades and telephone calls to home viewers. The charades were performed by a panel of celebrities, which included Cloris Leachman, Mort Marshall, Bill McGraw, Max Showalt, and Evelyn Ward. Viewers who were telephoned could win a prize if they were able to identify a celebrity's picture which was partially covered. The series was hosted by Gil Fates, who was later the executive producer of several Goodson-Todman game shows, including *What's My Line?* and *To Tell the Truth.*

HOLD THAT NOTE NBC
22 JANUARY 1957–2 APRIL 1957   Bert Parks hosted this Tuesday-night musical quiz show, a midseason replacement for Parks's previous game show, *Break the $250,000 Bank.*

HOLIDAY HANDBOOK ABC
4 APRIL 1958–20 JUNE 1958   Half-hour travelogue.

HOLIDAY HOTEL ABC
23 MARCH 1950–28 JUNE 1951   A musical revue set at the Holiday Hotel in New York. Edward Everett Horton was the first host of the series and was succeeded by Don Ameche (both appeared as the hotel manager). Other regulars included Bill Harrington, Betty Brewer, June Graham, Don Sadler, Bob Dixon, the Bernie Green Orchestra, and the Charles Tate Dancers. See also *Don Ameche Playhouse.*

HOLIDAY LODGE CBS
27 JUNE 1961–8 OCTOBER 1961   This summer replacement for *The Jack Benny Program* starred a pair of Canadian comics, Johnny Wayne and Frank Shuster, as Johnny Miller and Frank Boone, recreation directors at the Holiday Lodge, somewhere in New York's Catskills. Also featured were Maureen Arthur as Dorothy, the desk clerk; Justice Watson as Mr. Harrington, the boss; and Charles Smith as Woodrow, the bellhop.

HOLLYWOOD A GO GO SYNDICATED
1965   One of the raft of rock music shows in the style of *Hullabaloo, Hollywood A Go Go* was hosted by Sam Riddle.

HOLLYWOOD AND THE STARS NBC
30 SEPTEMBER 1963–28 SEPTEMBER 1964   Joseph Cotten hosted and narrated this documentary series about American movies.

HOLLYWOOD BACKSTAGE
See The ERN WESTMORE SHOW; HOLLYWOOD TODAY

HOLLYWOOD CONNECTION SYNDICATED
1977   Game show hosted by Jim Lange on which studio contestants tried to predict how a panel of celebrities would answer questions.

HOLLYWOOD HOUSE ABC
4 DECEMBER 1949–26 FEBRUARY 1950   Half-hour variety show starring Jim Backus and Dick Wesson. Set at a hotel, the series was broadcast from Los Angeles and was produced by Joe Bigelow.

HOLLYWOOD JUNIOR CIRCUS NBC/ABC
25 MARCH 1951–1 JULY 1951 (NBC); 8 SEPTEMBER 1951–19 JANUARY 1952 (ABC)   This circus show for kids was broadcast from Chicago, not Hollywood; the series was seen Sunday afternoons on NBC and Saturday mornings on ABC. Paul Barnes was the ringmaster. Produced by Bill Hyer; directed by George Byrne.

HOLLYWOOD OFF BEAT SYNDICATED/DUMONT/CBS
1952 (SYNDICATED); 7 NOVEMBER 1952–30 JANUARY 1953 (DU-MONT); 16 JUNE 1953–11 AUGUST 1953 (CBS)   Half-hour crime show starring Melvyn Douglas as Steve Randall, a former World War II intelligence agent who became a private eye after he was wrongfully disbarred from the practice of law. Marion Parsonnet produced and directed the series, which was also titled *Steve Randall*.

HOLLYWOOD OPENING NIGHT CBS/NBC
13 JULY 1951–28 MARCH 1952 (CBS); 6 OCTOBER 1952–23 MARCH 1953 (NBC)   Half-hour dramatic anthology series. Among the stars who made their TV dramatic debuts on this West Coast series were Dorothy Lamour ("The Singing Years," 24 November 1952), Ethel Barrymore ("Mysterious Ways," 8 December 1952), and Gloria Swanson ("The Pattern," 16 February 1953).

THE HOLLYWOOD PALACE ABC
4 JANUARY 1964–7 FEBRUARY 1970   This hour-long variety series was a midseason replacement for *The Jerry Lewis Show*. The show was videotaped at the El Capitan Theater in Los Angeles, which was renamed The Hollywood Palace. Each week a different guest host introduced several

acts. Bing Crosby hosted the premiere telecast; his guests included Bob Newhart, Bobby Van, Nancy Wilson, Mickey Rooney, and Gary Crosby. Other notable guest appearances included those by the Rolling Stones (in one of their first American TV appearances, 26 September 1964; Ed Wynn, who had played New York's Palace Theater in 1913, hosted the show), Groucho Marx and Margaret Dumont (in her last TV appearance, 17 April 1965), and Fred Astaire and Rudolf Nureyev (2 October 1965). Executive producer: Nick Vanoff. Producer: Bill Harbach. Director: Grey Lockwood. Music: the Mitchell Ayres Orhcestra (the show's theme was "Put on a Happy Face"). Raquel Welch was featured as the holder of the cards introducing the acts.

HOLLYWOOD PREVIEW
SYNDICATED

1955   Conrad Nagel hosted this series on which previews of recently released motion pictures were shown.

HOLLYWOOD SCREEN TEST
ABC

15 AUGUST 1948–18 MAY 1953   One of the first shows on the ABC network, *Hollywood Screen Test* offered young performers the chance to further their careers by appearing in dramatic stories with well-know stars. Neil Hamilton hosted the series during most of its run; Hurd Hatfield hosted during the 1950–1951 season. The show premiered on 15 April 1948 in Philadelphia.

THE HOLLYWOOD SQUARES
NBC/SYNDICATED

17 OCTOBER 1966–   (NBC); 1972–   (SYNDICATED)   Durable game show hosted by Peter Marshall featuring two contestants and a panel of nine celebrities. The contestants play tic-tac-toe, earning their Xs and Os by stating whether a given celebrity has correctly answered a question (the celebrities are seated in a three-tiered box). Regular panelists over the years have included Paul Lynde (occupant of the center square), Rose Marie, Cliff Arquette (as Charley Weaver), Wally Cox, John Davidson, George Gobel, and many others. The daytime version of the series began in 1966; a nighttime network version was seen in the spring of 1968 and the summer of 1969, and the syndicated version (televised evenings in most markets) premiered in 1972. Executive producers: Merrill Heatter and Bob Quigley. Announcer: Kenny Williams.

HOLLYWOOD SUMMER THEATRE
CBS

3 AUGUST 1956–28 SEPTEMBER 1956   Half-hour filmed dramatic anthology series, hosted by Gene Raymond.

HOLLYWOOD TALENT SCOUTS
See TALENT SCOUTS

HOLLYWOOD TEEN
SYNDICATED
1978   Half-hour talk show hosted by teenager Jimmy McNichol, brother of *Family*'s Kristy McNichol.

HOLLYWOOD TELEVISION THEATRE
PBS
1970–   Dramatic anthology series which presented original plays as well as established dramas. Executive producer: Norman Lloyd for KCET, Los Angeles.

HOLLYWOOD THEATER TIME
ABC
8 OCTOBER 1950–6 OCTOBER 1951   One of the first dramatic anthology series to originate from the West Coast, this half-hour series was seen via kinescopes in the East. The half-hour show was produced by George M. Cahan and Thomas W. Sarnoff.

HOLLYWOOD TODAY
NBC
3 JANUARY 1955–23 SEPTEMBER 1955   *Hollywood Today* began as a daily fifteen-minute show hosted by columnist Sheilah Graham; each week a guest celebrity was featured as her cohost. In the summer of 1955 the show was expanded to thirty minutes and was retitled *Hollywood Backstage;* late in the summer Ern Westmore took over as the show's host (see also *The Search for Beauty*).

HOLLYWOOD'S TALKING
CBS
26 MARCH 1973–22 JUNE 1973   Daytime game show hosted by Geoff Edwards on which three contestants, after watching videotaped sequences in which celebrities spoke a line or two about a subject, tried to guess the subject.

HOLMES AND YOYO
ABC
25 SEPTEMBER 1976–11 DECEMBER 1976   Hapless sitcom about a police detective and his partner, a human-looking robot. With Richard B. Shull as Detective Alexander Holmes; John Schuck as Gregory Yoyonovich, his mechanical partner; Andrea Howard as policewoman Maxine Moon; and Bruce Kirby as Captain Harry Sedford. Created by Jack Sher and Lee Hewitt, the series' executive producer was Leonard Stern, and its producer was Arne Sultan.

HOLOCAUST
See THE BIG EVENT

HOME
NBC
1 MARCH 1954–9 AUGUST 1957   Styled as a "women's magazine of the air," *Home* was an ambitious weekday series developed by Sylvester "Pat" Weaver and intended to be a logical extension of NBC's early-

morning show, *Today*. It was also one of the first NBC programs to be broadcast in color (though not every day). Arlene Francis hosted the series, and, in keeping with *Home*'s magazine format, was billed as editor in chief. In 1955 the group of contributing "editors" included Natalie Cole (fashion and beauty), Katherine Kinne (food), Will Peigelbeck (gardening and home repair), Dr. Ashley Montagu (family affairs), Dorsey Connors (Chicago editor), Esther von Waggoner Tutty (Washington editor), Dr. Leona Baumgartner (health), and Nancyanne Graham (home decorating). At other times the group included Eve Hunter (fashion and beauty), Poppy Cannon (food), Dr. Rose Franzblau (family affairs), and Sydney Smith (home decorating). Also appearing were announcer and sidekick Hugh Downs and singer Johnny Johnston. By 1956 a regular feature of the series, entitled "Hometown U.S.A.," was presented once each week and featured a remote pickup from the town so designated. At that time Fred Freed had become the show's supervising writer or "managing editor."

HOME RUN DERBY   SYNDICATED
1959–1961 Mark Scott hosted this half-hour filmed athletic contest. Each week two big league ballplayers competed head-to-head to see who could hit more home runs.

HOMER BELL   SYNDICATED
1955 Half-hour comedy-western, starring Gene Lockhart as Judge Homer Bell of Spring City. Also featured were Jane Moultrie as Maude, the housekeeper, and Mary Lee Dearring as Casey Bell, Homer's daughter.

HOMEWOOD   PBS
7 OCTOBER 1970–6 JANUARY 1971 Thirteen-week musical series, hosted by Charles Champlin.

HONDO   ABC
8 SEPTEMBER 1967–29 DECEMBER 1967 This Friday-night hour-long western perished opposite NBC's *Star Trek*. Set in the Arizona Territory in 1869, it starred Ralph Taeger as Hondo Lane, an agent for the U.S. Army; Noah Beery, Jr., as Buffalo Baker, his sidekick; Gary Clarke as Captain Richards, Hondo's commanding officer; Kathie Browne as Angie Dow, a widow (Hondo killed her husband); Buddy Foster as Johnny, Angie's young son; and Michael Pate as Vittoro, an Apache chief. Based on the 1953 film starring John Wayne, the television series was produced by Andrew Fenady.

HONESTLY, CELESTE!   CBS
10 OCTOBER 1954–5 DECEMBER 1954 This half-hour sitcom was one of the first casualties of the 1954–1955 season. It starred Celeste Holm as

Celeste Anders, a journalism teacher from a Midwestern college who decided to get a job as a reporter with a New York newspaper. Also featured were Scott McKay as her friend, Bob Wallace; Geoffrey Lumb as Bob's father, Mr. Wallace, editor of the paper; Mary Finney as Mr. Wallace's secretary; and Mike Kellin as Celeste's friend, Marty Gordon, an ex-gangster. When it became apparent early in the fall that the show was in trouble, a young writer named Norman Lear was called in to help out, but his efforts proved unsuccessful.

HONEY WEST
ABC

17 SEPTEMBER 1965–2 SEPTEMBER 1966 Half-hour crime show starring Anne Francis as Honey West, a private eye who took over the business after her father's death. Also featured were John Ericson as her assistant, Sam Bolt; Irene Hervey as her Aunt Meg; and Bruce, her pet ocelot. Francis first appeared as Honey West in an episode of *Burke's Law* aired 21 April 1965. The series was produced by Four Star Films.

THE HONEYMOON RACE
ABC

17 JULY 1967–1 DECEMBER 1967 Bill Malone hosted this daytime game show, produced in Florida, in which three couples went on a scavenger hunt in a supermarket. The show was a revamped version of *Supermarket Sweep* (see also that title).

THE HONEYMOONERS
See THE JACKIE GLEASON SHOW

HONG KONG
ABC

28 SEPTEMBER 1960–20 SEPTEMBER 1961 A 20th Century-Fox adventure series set in the Far East. With Rod Taylor as Glenn Evans, an American journalist based in Hong Kong; Lloyd Bochner as Neil Campbell, Hong Kong's chief of police; Jerald Jann as Ling, Glenn's houseboy; Jack Kruschen as Tully, owner of a bar and grill where Glenn hung out; and Mai Tai Sing as Ching Mei, a waitress.

HONG KONG PHOOEY
ABC/NBC

7 SEPTEMBER 1974–4 SEPTEMBER 1976 (ABC); 4 FEBRUARY 1978–2 SEPTEMBER 1978 (NBC); 8 SEPTEMBER 1979–3 NOVEMBER 1979 (NBC) Hanna-Barbera cartoon series about a crimefighting dog, Penrod Pooch, whose secret identity was that of Hong Kong Phooey. The voice of the lead character was supplied by Scatman Crothers. The series' second season on ABC consisted entirely of reruns, and reruns were again shown when the show popped up on NBC in 1978 and 1979.

HOOTENANNY
ABC

6 APRIL 1963–12 SEPTEMBER 1964 Jack Linkletter hosted television's

first folk music series, broadcast from a different college campus each week. Most of the "folk" music featured was of the commercial type, such as that of the Limeliters and the Chad Mitchell Trio; more controversial folk artists, such as Bob Dylan or Joan Baez, did not appear. According to Pete Seeger's book, *The Incompleat Folksinger,* the word "hootenanny" was coined by Woody Guthrie sometime in the 1940s.

HOPALONG CASSIDY
NBC/SYNDICATED

24 JUNE 1949–23 DECEMBER 1951 (NBC); 1952–1954 (SYNDICATED)
William Boyd first starred as Hopalong Cassidy, a western hero who dressed in black and rode a white horse, in sixty-six movie features filmed between 1935 and 1948. Boyd himself acquired the television rights to the films and edited the features into thirty- and sixty-minute segments; thus, he was in a position to offer a readily available source of action programming to the rapidly expanding postwar television station market. The films proved so popular that Boyd filmed an additional fifty-two episodes especially for TV in 1951–1952.

HOPPITY HOOPER
SYNDICATED

1963   Cartoon series with a frog (Hoppity Hooper), a bear (Fillmore), and a fox (Uncle Waldo).

THE HORACE HEIDT SHOW
CBS

2 OCTOBER 1950–24 SEPTEMBER 1951   Bandleader Horace Heidt, who hosted several radio programs featuring talented amateurs and young professionals, brought the same concept to television in this Monday-night variety series. Heidt returned in 1955 to host another series: see *Show Wagon.*

HORIZONS
ABC

2 DECEMBER 1951–30 DECEMBER 1951; 18 MAY 1952–29 JUNE 1952; 12 DECEMBER 1954–6 MARCH 1955   The 1951 and 1952 editions of *Horizons* were half-hour lectures on selected topics; each lecture was titled "The Future of . . . ." The 1954–1955 version of *Horizons* was a fifteen-minute series which focused on medicine. See also *Medical Horizons.*

HOT CITY
SYNDICATED

1978   Los Angeles-based disco dance show, hosted by Shadoe Stevens, with celebrity guest hosts. Ed Warren was the executive producer of the hour series, Kip Walton the producer and director.

HOT DOG
NBC

12 SEPTEMBER 1970–4 SEPTEMBER 1971   A highly acclaimed Saturday show for kids which explained how things are made; Jonathan Winters, Woody Allen, and Jo Anne Worley did the explaining. Created by Frank

Buxton, *Hot Dog* had Lee Mendelson as executive producer. The show won a Peabody Award in 1971.

HOT FUDGE SHOW
SYNDICATED

1976–   Educational series for children featuring puppets and live actors. Produced by Barry Hurd and Bob Elnicky; distributed by Lexington Broadcast Services.

HOT HERO SANDWICH
NBC

10 NOVEMBER 1979–   Hour variety series for children, broadcast at noon on Saturdays; interviews, sketches, and musical selections are the principal components of the show. Regulars include Paul O'Keefe, Denny Dillon, Matt McCoy, Jarett SmithWrick, L. Michael Craig, Nan-Lynn Nelson, and Vicky Dawson. Bruce Hart and Carole Hart created the show and are its executive producers.

HOT L BALTIMORE
ABC

24 JANUARY 1975–6 JUNE 1975   The first Norman Lear series that ABC picked up was an unsuccessful one. Based on the play by Lanford Wilson, it was set in a rundown hotel and featured an assortment of seedy characters: Conchata Ferrell as April Green, hooker with a heart of gold; Jeannie Linero as Suzy Marta Rocket, hooker with a heart of silver; James Cromwell as Bill Lewis, the desk clerk; Richard Masur as Clifford Ainsley, the manager; Al Freeman, Jr., as Charles Bingham; Lee Bergere as George, an apparent homosexual; Henry Calvert as Gordon, his roommate; Gloria LeRoy as Millie, a waitress; Stan Gottlieb as Mr. Morse, a mean old man; Robin Wilson as Jackie; and Charlotte Rae as Mrs. Bellotti. Executive producer: Rod Parker. Producers: Ron Clark and Gene Marcione.

HOT OFF THE WIRE
See THE JIM BACKUS SHOW

THE HOT SEAT
ABC

18 APRIL 1952–29 DECEMBER 1952   Stuart Scheftel interviewed newsmakers on this half-hour series. James A. Farley and Harold Stassen were Scheftel's guests on the fall premiere.

THE HOT SEAT
ABC

12 JULY 1976–22 OCTOBER 1976   Jim Peck hosted this daytime game show, which involved a type of lie detector. Two married couples competed; one spouse was hooked up to a machine that measured chemical changes in the skin as he or she responded to questions. The other spouse tried to predict the nature of the forthcoming response. Developed by

Merrill Heatter and Bob Quigley, the show's executive producer was Robert Noah.

HOT WHEELS
ABC

6 SEPTEMBER 1969–4 SEPTEMBER 1971   Saturday-morning cartoon show about a group of teenage racers who, it was emphasized, were "responsible" young drivers.

HOTEL BROADWAY
DUMONT

20 JANUARY 1949–17 MARCH 1949   Half-hour variety series hosted by Jeri Blanchard, produced and directed by Harvey Marlowe.

HOTEL COSMOPOLITAN
CBS

19 AUGUST 1957–11 APRIL 1958   This daytime serial replaced *Valiant Lady.* Set in a New York hotel (The Cosmopolitan), it presented episodic, rather than continuing, dramas. Donald Woods (appearing as himself) hosted the series.

HOTEL DE PAREE
CBS

2 OCTOBER 1959–23 SEPTEMBER 1960   In this unlikely titled western, Earl Holliman starred as Sundance, a man recently released from prison who became a partner in a hotel in Georgetown, Colorado. The principal gimmick in the show involved Sundance's hat: the hatband was decorated with shiny oval discs that Sundance could use to temporarily blind his adversaries. Also featured were Jeanette Nolan as Annette Devereaux, his partner in the hotel; Judi Meredith as Monique Devereaux, her niece and Sundance's romantic interest; and Strother Martin as Sundance's pal, Aaron.

THE HOUNDCATS
NBC

9 SEPTEMBER 1972–1 SEPTEMBER 1973   Saturday-morning cartoon show about a cat-and-dog team of secret agents.

HOUR OF POWER
SYNDICATED

1970–   Religious series videotaped at the Garden Grove Community Church in California. Four ministers appear: Raymond Beckering, Calvin Rynbrandt, Robert H. Schuller, and Kenneth Van Wyk.

THE HOUR OF ST. FRANCIS
SYNDICATED

1961   Half-hour religious show that featured dramatizations of moral questions. It was produced in Los Angeles by four Franciscan fathers: Fr. Hugh Noonan, Fr. Edward Henriques, Fr. Terence Cronin, and Fr. Carl Holtsnider.

THE HOUSE IN THE GARDEN
See FAIRMEADOWS, U.S.A.; THE KATE SMITH SHOW

THE HOUSE ON HIGH STREET NBC
28 SEPTEMBER 1959–5 FEBRUARY 1960 One of the first daytime serials to be videotaped, *The House on High Street* presented three- to five-part stories about divorce and juvenile delinquency, ostensibly based on actual case histories. Continuity was provided by Philip Abbott, who played caseworker John Collier. Produced in New York, the series was directed by Lela Swift and written under the supervision of Jim Elward.

HOUSE PARTY
See ART LINKLETTER'S HOUSE PARTY

HOW DID THEY GET THAT WAY?
See WHAT'S ON YOUR MIND

HOW DO YOU RATE CBS
31 MARCH 1958–26 JUNE 1958 Tom Reddy hosted this daytime game show on which a male and a female contestant competed against each other in tests of intelligence and problem solving. A machine called an "Aptigraph" was also used during the contest. The show was seen Monday through Thursday; on Friday the hour-long *Garry Moore Show* took over the time slot.

HOW THE WEST WAS WON ABC
12 FEBRUARY 1978–23 APRIL 1979 This ambitious western, based loosely on the 1962 MGM film, began as a made-for-TV movie entitled *The Macahans,* which was aired 19 January 1976. In 1977 a six-hour sequel, entitled *How the West Was Won,* was broadcast, and in 1978 twenty more hours were presented. The series told the saga of the Macahan clan, several generations of hardy pioneers. Principal players in the 1978 edition included James Arness as Zeb Macahan, former Cavalry scout; Bruce Boxleitner as Luke Macahan, his nephew, an army deserter; Kathryn Holcomb as Laura Macahan; Fionnula Flanagan as Molly Culhane, sister of Zeb's late wife; William Kirby Cullen as Jed Macahan; and Vicki Schreck as Jessie Macahan. John Mantley, who had previously worked with Arness as *Gunsmoke*'s last executive producer, was executive producer of *The Macahans* and *How the West Was Won.* The 1978 series was produced by John G. Stephens and directed by Vincent and Bernard McEveety.

HOW TO CBS
12 JULY 1951–27 AUGUST 1951 A satire on panel shows, *How To* was

hosted by humorist Roger Price. The panel—Anita Martell, Stanley Andrews, and Leonard Stern—suggested unusual solutions to problems posed by contestants. Dick Linkroum and Larry Berns produced the half-hour prime-time show.

HOW TO MARRY A MILLIONAIRE   SYNDICATED
1958–1959 Situation comedy based on the 1953 film (which had starred Marilyn Monroe, Betty Grable, and Lauren Bacall) about three New York career girls, each looking for a wealthy and eligible man. The TV version starred Barbara Eden as Loco Jones, a model; Merry Anders as Michelle (Mike) Page, a secretary; Lori Nelson (1958) as Greta Lindquist, secretary to a stockbroker; and Lisa Gaye (1959) as Gwen Laurel, also a secretary. Produced by 20th Century-Fox.

HOW TO SURVIVE A MARRIAGE   NBC
7 JANUARY 1974–18 APRIL 1975 This fairly controversial daytime serial stressed the problems of coping with divorce and widowhood. It premiered with a ninety-minute episode which featured an explicit bedroom scene between a husband and his mistress. Principal players included: Jennifer Harmon as Chris Kirby, whose marriage was on the rocks; Michael Landrum and Ken Kerchval as Larry Kirby, her philandering husband; Lynn Lowry as Sandra Henderson, Larry's mistress; Rosemary Prinz as Dr. Julie Franklin, a liberated psychiatrist who advised many of the other characters; Fran Brill as Fran Bachman, who became a widow; Allan Miller as her husband, David Bachman; Joan Copeland as Monica Courtland; Peter Brandon as Terry Courtland; Steve Elmore and Berkley Harris as lawyer Peter Willis; Tricia O'Neil as Joan Willis; Suzanne Davidson as Lori Kirby; Paul Vincent as Dr. Charles Maynard; Armand Assante as Johnny McGhee; and Lauren White as Maria McGhee. The series was created by Ann Howard Bailey, though NBC daytime programming chief Lin Bolen also helped formulate it. Allen Potter was the first producer; he was succeeded by Peter Andrews.

HOWARD COSELL SPORTS MAGAZINE   ABC
7 JANUARY 1972–27 APRIL 1975 Fifteen-minute sports show presented during the winter months, hosted by Howard Cosell.

HOWARD K. SMITH   ABC
14 FEBRUARY 1962–16 JUNE 1963 Half-hour news analysis show, hosted by Howard K. Smith, the former CBS correspondent who joined ABC News in 1961.

THE HOWARD MILLER SHOW
See CLUB 60

27 DECEMBER 1947–30 SEPTEMBER 1960 (NBC); 1976 (SYNDICATED)
Television's first popular kids' show premiered late in 1947 and exited
thirteen years—and 2,343 performances—later. It was brought to TV by
Bob Smith, a onetime singer who began hosting a kids' radio show, *Triple
B Ranch,* in New York in 1945. One of the characters Smith created on
that show, Elmer, regularly introduced himself with the phrase, "Well,
howdy doody!" The character was popular with Smith's young listeners,
and when Smith convinced NBC to introduce a puppet show on television, the newly created marionette was named Howdy Doody. The original puppet, crafted by Frank Paris, bore little resemblance to the
freckled, plaid-shirted Howdy that most viewers fondly recall. The first
Howdy, together with his maker, departed from the show after only a few
weeks when puppeteer Paris became enmeshed in contractual difficulties
with NBC. Some months later a new Howdy, designed by two artists who
had worked at Walt Disney Studios, appeared; it was explained that
Howdy, who was then running for the office of president of All the Boys
and Girls (1948 was, after all, a Presidential election year), had undergone "plastic" surgery.

At first Howdy and his friends were seen only once a week for an hour;
the show was then titled *Puppet Playhouse.* After experimenting with a
thrice-weekly format, the show was seen Mondays through Fridays for a
half hour beginning 15 August 1948. From the outset the show was set in
Doodyville, a circus town populated by an assortment of puppets and
people (the circus setting obviously enabled characters to come and go
with relative ease). Each day an audience of children sat in the bleachers,
an area known as the "Peanut Gallery." A typical day's activities might
have included a silent film short, a song or two, some chitchat, and a running story involving the citizens of Doodyville. By 1948 Bob Smith, who
had previously been called "Mr. Smith" by the other characters, became
known as "Buffalo Bob"; he was so named by the Sycapoose Indians, a
friendly tribe which lived near town (in real life, Smith had been born in
Buffalo, N.Y.). Buffalo Bob's principal assistant, and sometime nemesis,
was a voiceless clown named Clarabell, who honked a horn attached to
his belt and carried a seltzer bottle. Clarabell was first played by Bob
Keeshan, an NBC staffer whose jobs included handing props to Buffalo
Bob; it was decided that since Keeshan appeared on camera, he should be
costumed, and thus the Clarabell character was created. For a short time
Keeshan also played Oscar, a professorial chap; when Keeshan left the
series in 1953 to host his own local show (in 1955 he returned to network
TV as Captain Kangaroo), he was replaced by Bobby Nicholson. Nicholson later switched roles to play Cornelius Cobb, Doodyville's storekeep-
er, and Lew Anderson took over as Clarabell. Other humans included:
Chief Thunderthud, an Indian chief who frequently shouted "Kowa-

bunga!" (played by Bill LeCornec); Princess Summerfall Winterspring, a beautiful Indian princess (the character first appeared as a puppet), played by Judy Tyler (who died in an auto accident in 1957) and briefly by Linda Marsh; Bison Bill, who filled in for Buffalo Bob when the latter was ill or on vacation, played by Ted Brown; and Ugly Sam, a wrestler, played by Dayton Allen.

Howdy Doody, of course, was the star puppet, but he had many wooden costars: Phineas T. Bluster, the misanthropic mayor of Doodyville who instigated most of the sinister plots on the show; Dilly Dally, a lame-brained carpenter who was usually duped by Mr. Bluster into doing his dirty work; Flub-a-Dub, a creature made up of parts of eight different animals; Captain Scuttlebutt, a salty seaman who piloted an old scow; John J. Fadoozle, a private eye; Don José Bluster and Hector Hamhock Bluster, Phineas's triplet brothers; Double Doody, Howdy's twin brother; and Heidi Doody, Howdy's sister. Voices were provided by Bob Smith (who prerecorded Howdy's voice and thus could sing duets with the puppet), Dayton Allen (Mr. Bluster), Bill LeCornec (Dilly Dally), and Alan Swift, among others.

The series continued to run five days a week until 1 June 1956. On 16 June 1956, it moved to Saturdays, where it remained for another four years. During that time other characters were added, including the puppet Sandra, a witch. The filmed adventures of Gumby, a movable clay figure, were also incorporated; in 1957 Gumby was given his own series (see *The Gumby Show*). *Howdy Doody* was one of the first regularly scheduled NBC shows to be shown in color; experimental broadcasts were conducted in the summer of 1953, and regular color-casting began 12 September 1955. Robert Muir was the producer of the series; Edward Kean wrote most of the shows between 1947 and 1955, and also wrote the lyrics to "It's Howdy Doody Time" and Clarabell's theme song. Rufus Rose was the chief puppeteer, assisted by Rhoda Mann and Dayton Allen. At the end of the final telecast, Clarabell sadly broke his series-long silence to say, "Goodbye, kids."

In 1970 Buffalo Bob toured the nostalgia circuit, appearing at colleges and universities. In 1976 he returned to host a new version of *Howdy Doody,* which failed to catch on with the children of the 1970s the way its predecessor had with another generation of youngsters almost thirty years earlier.

HOW'S YOUR MOTHER-IN-LAW? ABC

4 DECEMBER 1967–1 MARCH 1968 Chuck Barris created this daytime game show which featured three contestants—each of whom was a mother-in-law, and a panel of three comedians—each of whom joked about his or her mother-in-law; at the end of the show the panel tried to decide

which of the contestants was the "best" mother-in-law. Wink Martindale presided over the festivities.

THE HUCKLEBERRY HOUND SHOW   SYNDICATED

1958   One of the first television cartoon series developed by William Hanna and Joseph Barbera, the founders of Hanna-Barbera Productions, *Huckleberry Hound* featured a lovable mutt who would try anything once. The success of this series led to the creation of dozens of cartoon characters by Hanna-Barbera, the best known of which include Yogi Bear, Quickdraw McGraw, and The Flintstones.

THE HUDSON BROTHERS RAZZLE DAZZLE SHOW   CBS

7 SEPTEMBER 1974–30 AUGUST 1975   After hosting their own prime-time summer series, the Hudson Brothers—Bill (the eldest), Mark, and Brett (the youngest)—next turned up as hosts of a live-action Saturday-morning show for kids. Joining them were Ted Zeigler, Billy Van, Peter Cullen, and Rod Hull. Produced by Chris Bearde and Allan Blye.

THE HUDSON BROTHERS SHOW   CBS

31 JULY 1974–28 AUGUST 1974   This five-week variety series was a summer replacement for *The Sonny and Cher Comedy Hour;* it was hosted by three musical brothers from Oregon—Bill, Mark, and Brett Hudson. Also featured were Ronnie Graham, Gary Owens, Ron Hull, and Stephanie Edwards. Sonny and Cher's producers, Chris Bearde and Allan Blye, also produced this show.

HULLABALOO   NBC

12 JANUARY 1965–29 AUGUST 1966   The relative success of ABC's *Shindig* prompted NBC to introduce its own rock-and-roll series in mid-season. During the spring and summer of 1965, it was an hour-long show; in the fall it moved from Tuesday to Monday and was cut to a half hour. A different guest host was featured each week, together with several acts; a regular feature during the spring of 1965 was a filmed segment (in black and white, unlike the rest of the show) hosted by Brian Epstein, manager of the Beatles, who usually introduced a British act. Movement was supplied by the Hullabaloo Dancers, the best known of which was Lada Edmund, Jr. Gary Smith produced the series; David Winters was the choreographer. Additional music was supplied by the Peter Matz Orchestra.

THE HUMAN JUNGLE   SYNDICATED

1964   This British import starred Herbert Lom as a psychiatrist, Dr. Roger Corder, and featured Michael Johnson as his assistant, Davis.

THE HUNTER   CBS/NBC

3 JULY 1952–24 SEPTEMBER 1952 (CBS); 26 SEPTEMBER 1954–26 DE-

CEMBER 1954 (NBC) Half-hour Cold War spy series. Barry Nelson starred as Bart Adams, American undercover agent, in the CBS version, and Keith Larsen played the role in the NBC version two years later. Filmed in New York, the series was produced by Ed Montagne and directed by Oscar Rudolph.

HUNTER   CBS
18 FEBRUARY 1977–27 MAY 1977 A pallid adventure series which replaced *Executive Suite.* With James Franciscus as James Hunter, a man who ran a bookstore before being selected to be a member of a special team of government operatives; Linda Evans as Marty Shaw, his frequent partner; and Ralph Bellamy as Mr. Baker, his seldom-seen boss. Created by William Blinn.

HUSBANDS, WIVES & LOVERS   CBS
10 MARCH 1978–30 JUNE 1978 Southern California was the setting for this hour-long comedy series about five contemporary couples. The series had a continuing story line, which began with the announcement by one of the couples (the Willises) of their impending separation. Featured were Cynthia Harris as Paula Zuckerman; Stephen Pearlman as her husband, Murray Zuckerman, a traveling salesman; Lynne Marie Stewart as Joy Bellini; Eddie Barth as her formerly married husband, Harry Bellini, a sanitation removal magnate; Ron Rifkin as Ron Willis, a dentist; Jesse Welles as his wife, Helene Willis; Charles Siebert as lawyer Dixon Fielding; Claudette Nevins as his wife, Courtney Fielding; Mark Lonow as Harry's younger brother, Lennie Bellini; and Randee Heller as Rita, the woman who lived with Lennie and managed "Lennie's Denim Boutique" with him. Hal Dresner was the executive producer, and Don Van Atta the producer for 20th Century-Fox Television.

THE HY GARDNER SHOW   SYNDICATED
1965 Ninety-minute talk show, hosted by columnist Hy Gardner.

I AM THE GREATEST: THE ADVENTURES OF MUHAMMAD ALI   NBC
10 SEPTEMBER 1977–21 JANUARY 1978 Saturday-morning cartoon show featuring the voice of the talkative boxing champ. Executive producer: Fred Calvert. Producer: Janis Diamond.

I AM THE LAW   SYNDICATED
1953 Low-budget cop show, starring George Raft (who usually played gangsters in the movies) as Lieutenant George Kirby of the New York Police Department. Executive producer: Pat Costello (brother of Lou Costello). Produced and directed by Jean Yarborough.

I BELIEVE IN MIRACLES SYNDICATED
1966–1976   Half-hour religious program hosted by faith healer Kathryn Kuhlman. Most of the guests were persons who had been cured by Kuhlman. Singer Jimmy McDonald was also a regular.

I COVER TIMES SQUARE ABC
5 OCTOBER 1950–11 JANUARY 1951   Half-hour crime show, starring Harold Huber as newspaper columnist Johnny Warren.

I DREAM OF JEANNIE NBC
18 SEPTEMBER 1965–1 SEPTEMBER 1970   Half-hour sitcom about an Air Force astronaut who, after a crash landing on an uninhabited island, uncorked a bottle and thereby released a beautiful genie named Jeannie. Though popular during its original run and later in syndication, the show was sexist when judged by current standards—Jeannie was always the "slave," and the astronaut the "master." The series starred Barbara Eden as Jeannie; Larry Hagman as Captain (later Major) Tony Nelson, the lucky astronaut; Bill Daily as Captain Roger Healey, Tony's friend, who also knew of Jeannie's existence and magical powers; Hayden Rorke as Colonel Alfred Bellows, a NASA psychiatrist; Emmaline Henry as his wife, Amanda Bellows; and Barton MacLane as General Martin Peterson. During the series' first three seasons, Jeannie and Tony apparently enjoyed a platonic relationship; in the fall of 1968 they were married. In a few of the later episodes Farrah Fawcett could be seen—these were among her first TV appearances. Sidney Sheldon was the creator and executive producer of the series for Screen Gems.

I LED THREE LIVES SYNDICATED
1953–1956   This well-known counterespionage series was based on the real-life adventures of Herbert A. Philbrick, who wrote a best-selling book about his life as a Boston advertising executive by day, as a member of the American Communist Party by night, and as an undercover agent for the FBI after hours. Richard Carlson starred as Philbrick, with Virginia Steffan as his wife, Ann.

I LOVE LUCY CBS
15 OCTOBER 1951–24 JUNE 1957
THE LUCY-DESI COMEDY HOUR CBS
6 NOVEMBER 1957–1 APRIL 1960   Television's first smash hit situation comedy, *I Love Lucy* was the most consistently popular program in TV history: during its six seasons it ranked first for four years, second once, and third once. It was also the first sitcom to be filmed before a live audience; the decision to film the show was fortuitous, not only for its principals (the stars, Desi Arnaz and Lucille Ball, owned the show through their production company, Desilu), but also for subsequent generations of

viewers, as *I Love Lucy* has proven virtually indestructible in reruns. A classic comedy about a bandleader, his wife, and their frumpy neighbors, *I Love Lucy* clicked simply because it was well written and well played.

Desi Arnaz emigrated to Miami from his native Cuba in 1933, the same year that Lucille Ball headed toward Hollywood after a luckless stay in New York. Arnaz drifted into music, landed a job with Xavier Cugat's orchestra, and led his own band before going to Hollywood in 1940 to repeat his stage role in the filmed version of *Too Many Girls*. He met Lucille Ball on the set of the film, and the two were married a few months later. Arnaz appeared in one or two more films before resuming his career as a bandleader, while Lucille Ball continued her film career. By the end of the decade she was starring in a radio sitcom, *My Favorite Husband*, opposite Richard Denning. Its sponsor wanted to take the show to television with the same cast, but Lucy wanted Desi to be her TV costar. The two decided to produce a pilot film, which was the beginning of the *I Love Lucy* series.

The film was made early in 1951. It was directed by Ralph Levy and written by Jess Oppenheimer, Madelyn Pugh, and Bob Carroll—Oppenheimer had produced *My Favorite Husband* and Pugh and Carroll had written it. In the pilot Lucy and Desi played themselves, she a Hollywood actress, he a well-known bandleader (there were no neighbors in the film). The script incorporated some of the vaudeville routines that the two had worked up during the preceding year. The Milton Biow advertising agency showed interest in the concept, and Biow himself suggested that Lucy and Desi not play celebrities, but rather more everyday types. Oppenheimer, Pugh, and Carroll went back to work; Desi would now play Ricky Ricardo, a not-too-successful bandleader working in New York, and Lucy would be Lucy Ricardo, a talentless housewife ever hopeful of breaking into showbiz. The Ricardos would live in a small apartment on East 68th Street, above Fred and Ethel Mertz, their friends (and their landlords). Lucy had originally wanted Gale Gordon and Bea Benaderet, both of whom had been featured on *My Favorite Husband*, to play the Mertzes; Desi, however, decided to hire William Frawley, a sixty-four-year-old character actor with a reputation as a two-fisted drinker, after Frawley suggested himself for the part of Fred. Vivian Vance, a character actress with vaudeville, Broadway, and movie experience, was suggested for the Ethel part by Marc Daniels, who would direct the first season's shows. The casting was inspired; though Frawley cared little for Vance, the two seemed perfect as the down-to-earth Mertzes—Frawley as Ricky's irascible but loyal comrade in the battle of the sexes, and Vance as Lucy's frequent conspirator in her incessant attempts to get on stage.

The new concept for *I Love Lucy* was sold to a sponsor, Philip Morris, and was scheduled on CBS. As neither Lucy nor Desi was willing to relocate in New York and as CBS refused to permit the show to be televised live from Hollywood (because Eastern viewers would thus have to watch poor quality kinescopes of the broadcasts, as there were not yet any coast-to-coast transmission lines), it was decided that the show would be filmed; that way, audiences throughout the country would be assured of high quality reception. The show would be produced by Desilu, the production company that Lucy and Desi had formed in 1950; Jess Oppenheimer was named producer, and Madelyn Pugh and Bob Carroll were the writers. Several mammoth production problems were overcome during the summer of 1951: a soundstage was located, leased, and remodeled to accommodate a studio audience, and, under the guidance of cinematographer Karl Freund, the stage itself was redesigned and the four-camera filming system was developed. A more personal preproduction uncertainty was resolved on 17 July 1951, when Lucy gave birth to their first child, Lucie Arnaz. Filming of *I Love Lucy* began in September.

I Love Lucy premiered on 15 October 1951, to overwhelmingly favorable reviews (the premiere episode, "The Girls Want to Go to a Nightclub," was not the first filmed). By the end of the season it was a smash; the American Research Bureau announced in April 1952 that it had become the first TV program to have been seen in 10 million homes. In May of that year the show made the cover of *Time* magazine. *I Love Lucy* ended its first season third in the seasonal Nielsen ratings.

Production of the second season's show began earlier than usual because Lucy discovered that she was again expecting a child. Desi and Jess Oppenheimer convinced the sponsor to incorporate Lucy's pregnancy into the *I Love Lucy* story line (though the subject of pregnancy had been treated on other TV shows, such as *One Man's Family*, this was the first time that a pregnant woman had played a mother-to-be). Seven of the season's episodes would deal with Lucy's pregnancy; at CBS's insistence, however, the word "pregnant" was forbidden, though the word "expecting" was deemed acceptable. The episode concerning the birth of the baby (to be filmed in November) would be shown on 19 January 1953, and it was decided that the Ricardos' child would be a boy. Arnaz explained that the decision was made mainly for the benefit of little Lucie Arnaz. Her parents felt that Lucie might have been confused if the Ricardos' first child was, like her, a little girl.

The story line proved immensely popular, as *I Love Lucy* became television's top-ranked show, toppling Arthur Godfrey's *Talent Scouts*. As luck would have it, the Ricardos' baby boy (Little Ricky) was born on TV the same day that Lucille Ball gave birth to a son, Desi Arnaz IV (he would later be known as Desi Arnaz, Jr.). News of the events dominated the headlines, crowding out other stories such as the inauguration of President Eisenhower. In April of 1953 young Desi graced the cover of the first issue of *TV Guide*.

I Love Lucy remained the number-one show during its third and fourth seasons, surviving a brief brouhaha in the fall of 1953 when Walter Winchell broadcast the news that in 1936 Lucy had publicly announced her intention to vote Communist (she explained that she had made the statement solely to please her grandfather, and was exonerated by the House Un-American Activities Committee). The episodes of the second, third, and fourth seasons were all directed by William Asher, who would later produce *Bewitched*. Two casting changes occurred: twins Michael and Joseph Mayer played Little Ricky from the fall of 1953 until the spring of 1956, replacing twins Richard and Ronald Simmons, and Jerry Hausner, who had occasionally played Ricky's agent, Jerry, left after the 1953–1954 season.

The series broadened its story line for the fourth season, as Ricky Ricardo landed a part in a movie; twenty-seven episodes of the 1954–1955 season chronicled the Ricardos' and Mertzes' move West. This story line lent itself to the use of big-name guest stars, a device not previously employed on the show. Among the big names who appeared that season were: Tennessee Ernie Ford (who first appeared at the end of the third season, and returned 24 January 1955 as the Ricardos began their trip), William Holden (7 February), Hedda Hopper (14 March), Rock Hudson (25 April), Harpo Marx (9 May, featuring a superb "mirror" scene with Lucy), and Richard Widmark (30 May).

For its fifth season, *I Love Lucy* acquired a new sponsor (General Foods), a new director (James V. Kern), and a second pair of writers (Bob Schiller and Bob Weiskopf). The use of guest stars continued, starting with John Wayne (in his TV dramatic debut, 10 October 1955). Halfway through the season, the Ricardos and the Mertzes were on the move again, this time to Europe. In the ratings race, the show finally slipped to second place, behind *The $64,000 Question*.

Producer Jess Oppenheimer left after the fifth season, and the series' final season began with the Ricardos and the Mertzes back in New York, where Ricky now owned his own nitery. Keith Thibodeaux, a six-year-old drummer whose professional name was Richard Keith, joined the cast as Little Ricky, replacing the Mayer twins. Bob Hope appeared as a guest star (1 October 1956), followed by Orson Welles (15 October) and Elsa Lanchester (12 November). William Asher returned to direct the final thirteen episodes, which depicted the Ricardos' move to suburban Connecticut (Mary Jane Croft and Frank Nelson were seen as their New England neighbors, Betty and Ralph Ramsey). In the last episode of *I Love Lucy*, "The Ricardos Dedicate a Statue," Lucie and Desi Arnaz, Jr., made their only appearances on the show. During its last season *I Love Lucy* reclaimed its number-one ranking (*I Love Lucy* and *The Andy Griffith Show* have been the only TV series to cease production after finishing first in the ratings; however, *The Andy Griffith Show* continued, without Griffith, as *Mayberry R.F.D.*). A total of 180 half-hour episodes were produced, though only 179 were made available for syndication; in his book, *The Story of I Love Lucy,* Bart Andrews notes that the episode of 24 December 1956, in which Fred bought a Christmas tree for Little Ricky, has never been rebroadcast.

From 1957 to 1960, thirteen hour-long shows were filmed, which were shown as *The Lucy-Desi Comedy Hour* and *The Lucille Ball-Desi Arnaz Show.* The first five were telecast as specials during the 1957–1958 season, and the others were broadcast during the *Desilu Playhouse* time slot. The first of these, "Lucy Takes a Cruise to Havana," ran seventy-five minutes, but Desi Arnaz persuaded the sponsor of the succeeding program, *The U.S. Steel Hour,* to permit a fifteen-minute incursion. The last of the thirteen, "Lucy Meets the Moustache," featured Ernie Kovacs and Edie Adams, and was televised 1 April 1960. It was especially poignant, not because it signified the end of the Ricardos and the Mertzes, but because it was filmed after Lucy and Desi had agreed to get divorced.

After their divorce Lucy became the head of Desilu Studios, buying out Desi's interest in 1962; in 1967 the operation was sold to Paramount. Desilu had expanded considerably from a one-show company since it was founded in 1950; Desilu produced many series during the 1950s and 1960s, including *Our Miss Brooks, December Bride, Willy, Those Whiting Girls, It's Always Jan, The Whirlybirds, The Untouchables, Fair Exchange,* and *Glynis.* Desi Arnaz has made few TV appearances since 1960, though he was occasionally featured on *The Mothers-in-Law,* a sitcom he produced. Lucille Ball, who married Gary Morton in 1961, went on to star in a pair of similar sitcoms, *The Lucy Show* and *Here's Lucy,* which together lasted twelve seasons. On 28 November 1976, CBS broadcast a two-hour tribute to her three shows, "CBS Salutes Lucy—The First 25 Years," which included a rare television appearance by CBS's chief executive, William Paley.

I MARRIED JOAN NBC

15 OCTOBER 1952–6 APRIL 1955   Domestic sitcom starring Joan Davis as Joan Stevens and Jim Backus as her husband, Judge Bradley Stevens. Also featured as the Stevens's friends and neighbors over the years were Hal Smith and Geraldine Carr as Charlie and Mabel; Dan Tobin and Sheila Bromley as Kerwin and Janet; Wally Brown and Sally Kelly as Wally and Sally; and Sandra Gould as Mildred Webster. Bing Crosby made a rare guest appearance on the show (25 February 1953), as did oldtime cowboy star Hoot Gibson (16 March 1955). The series was owned by Davis's production company and was produced by Dick Mack and directed by Hal Walker. Ninety-eight half-hours were filmed.

I REMEMBER MAMA
See MAMA

I SEARCH FOR ADVENTURE   SYNDICATED

1957   Another of the several documentary series produced and hosted by Jack Douglas, this half-hour series featured films taken by modern-day adventurers. See also *Bold Journey* and *Seven League Boots*.

I SPY   SYNDICATED

1956   The first of the two series by this title was an anthology of spy dramas, historical and modern, hosted by Raymond Massey (who appeared as Anton the Spymaster).

I SPY   NBC

15 SEPTEMBER 1965–2 SEPTEMBER 1968   The second series which bore this title told the story of two American undercover agents who traveled around the world on various assignments. More significantly, it was the first noncomedy series to star a black actor—Bill Cosby, who played Alexander Scott (better known as Scotty), a Temple graduate, a Rhodes Scholar, and a spy whose cover was that of the trainer of a tennis pro. Cosby's white costar was Robert Culp, who played Kelly Robinson, a Princeton-educated secret agent who masqueraded as the tennis pro. Filmed largely on location all over the world, *I Spy* was produced by Sheldon Leonard, Mort Fine, and David Friedkin.

THE ICE PALACE   CBS

23 MAY 1971–25 JULY 1971   A variety hour with guest hosts, guest acts, and a group of talented skaters which included Billy Chappell, Linda Carbonetto, Tim Wood, and the Bob Turk Ice Dancers.

ICHABOD AND ME   CBS

26 SEPTEMBER 1961–18 SEPTEMBER 1962   Low-key sitcom created by Joe Connelly and Bob Mosher. With Robert Sterling as Bob Major, a New Yorker who purchased a New England newspaper and moved to Phippsboro with his son; George Chandler as Ichabod Adams, the man from whom Major bought the paper; Jimmy Mathers (younger brother of *Leave It to Beaver*'s Jerry Mathers) as Benjie, Bob's young son; Christine White as Abigail Adams, Ichabod's daughter, Bob's girlfriend; Reta Shaw as Livvy, Bob's housekeeper; and Guy Raymond as Martin, a typically taciturn New England townsman. The pilot for the series, entitled "Adams' Apples," was shown on *General Electric Theater* in 1960.

I'D LIKE TO SEE   NBC

5 NOVEMBER 1948–29 MARCH 1949   Host Ray Morgan introduced film shorts on subjects suggested by home viewers on this Tuesday-night half-hour series.

IDENTIFY   ABC
14 FEBRUARY 1949–9 MAY 1949 Bob Elson hosted this prime-time
sports quiz show.

IF YOU HAD A MILLION
See THE MILLIONAIRE

THE IGOR CASSINI SHOW   DUMONT
25 OCTOBER 1953–28 FEBRUARY 1954 Columnist Igor Cassini (who
wrote under the name of Cholly Knickerbocker) hosted this Sunday-
night celebrity-interview series.

THE ILKA CHASE SHOW   CBS
16 FEBRUARY 1950–10 AUGUST 1950 Fifteen-minute Thursday-night
series hosted by fashionable Ilka Chase. It was also titled *Glamour-Go-
Round*.

I'LL BET   NBC
29 MARCH 1965–24 SEPTEMBER 1965 On this daytime game show hosted by Jack Narz, one spouse tried to predict whether the other spouse
would be able to answer a question correctly. In 1971 a syndicated version of the show appeared under the title *It's Your Bet* (see that title).

I'LL BUY THAT   CBS
15 JUNE 1953–17 DECEMBER 1953 Mike Wallace hosted this twice-
weekly daytime game show on which studio contestants tried to identify
items sent in by home viewers. A celebrity panel was on hand to assist the
contestants.

THE ILONA MASSEY SHOW   DUMONT
1 NOVEMBER 1954–3 JANUARY 1955 Half-hour variety show, hosted by
Hungarian-born actress Ilona Massey.

I'M DICKENS, HE'S FENSTER   ABC
28 SEPTEMBER 1962–13 SEPTEMBER 1963 A pair of zany carpenters
were the central characters in this sitcom. With John Astin as Harry
Dickens; Marty Ingels as Arch Fenster; Emmaline Henry as Kate Dickens, Harry's wife; Dave Ketchum as Mel, their occasional helper; Harry
Beckman as Mulligan, another helper; Frank DeVol as Mr. Bannister,
their boss; and Noam Pitlik as Bentley. Leonard Stern was the producer.

THE IMMORTAL   ABC
24 SEPTEMBER 1970–14 JANUARY 1971; 12 MAY 1971–8 SEPTEMBER
1971 An hour-long adventure series starring Chris George as Ben Richards, an automobile test driver who discovered that his blood contained

certain miraculous antibodies that could make him live forever. Ben searched for his long-lost brother, Jason, in the hope that he, too, had the same kind of blood. Also featured were David Brian as Arthur Maitland, a rich old man who, having once refused a transfusion of Richards's blood, pursued Richards; Don Knight as Fletcher, the man Maitland hired to track Richards down. Tony Wilson was the executive producer of the series, which was based loosely on James Gunn's novel, *The Immortals.* Canceled in midseason, reruns were broadcast later in 1971, replacing *The Johnny Cash Show.*

THE IMOGENE COCA SHOW
NBC

2 OCTOBER 1954–25 JUNE 1955 After several seasons as second banana to Sid Caesar on *Your Show of Shows,* Imogene Coca was given her own half-hour comedy show in 1954 (Sid Caesar having gone on to *Caesar's Hour*), which lasted a season. Regulars included David Burns, Billy DeWolfe, Ruth Donnelly, Hal March, and Bibi Osterwald.

IMUS, PLUS
SYNDICATED

1978 Ninety-minute talk show hosted by former New York disc jockey Don Imus. Henri Bollinger and Robert Yamin were the executive producers, Hal Parets the producer.

IN PERFORMANCE AT WOLF TRAP
PBS

1974– Videotaped performances of artists (mainly musicians and dancers) performing at Wolf Trap Park Farm in Arlington, Virginia. Produced at WETA-TV, Washington.

IN RECORD TIME
See THE ART FORD SHOW

IN SEARCH OF
SYNDICATED

1976– Half-hour documentary series which explores strange phenomena, lost civilizations, and the like, narrated by *Star Trek*'s Leonard Nimoy. Jim McGinn and Alan Landsburg are the executive producers, Robert L. Long the series producer.

IN SESSION
SYNDICATED

1974 Musical series on which assorted rockers rapped and rocked. Phil Everly, the younger half of the Everly Brothers, hosted.

IN THE BEGINNING
CBS

20 SEPTEMBER 1978–18 OCTOBER 1978 Half-hour sitcom about a conservative Irish priest who was teamed up with a streetwise nun and assigned to open a storefront mission in a tough inner-city neighborhood. With McLean Stevenson as Father Daniel M. Cleary; Priscilla Lopez as

his coworker, Sister Agnes; Priscilla Morrill as Sister Lillian; Olivia Barash as Willie; Bobby Ellerbee as Jerome Rockefeller; and Jack Dodson as Monsignor Barlow. Mort Lachman was the executive producer for Norman Lear's T.A.T. Communications.

IN THE FIRST PERSON CBS
29 JANUARY 1949–10 OCTOBER 1950 Fifteen-minute interview and commentary series hosted by journalist Quincy Howe.

IN THE MORGAN MANNER ABC
1 MARCH 1950–23 JULY 1950 Bandleader Russ Morgan hosted his own half-hour musical variety series, which was usually seen Sunday afternoons. In the summer of 1956 Morgan hosted a second series: see *The Russ Morgan Show.*

IN THE PARK CBS
9 DECEMBER 1951–31 MAY 1953 This children's show was seen Sunday mornings. It was hosted by Bill Sears and his puppet friends: Calvin the Crow, Sir Geoffrey the Giraffe, Magnolia the Ostrich, and Albert the Chipmunk. Paul Ritts and Mary Holliday handled the puppets.

THE INA RAY HUTTON SHOW NBC
4 JULY 1956–5 SEPTEMBER 1956 No male guests or regulars appeared on this half-hour musical variety series, hosted by Ina Ray Hutton. Hutton, who put together her first "all-girl" band in 1935, assembled a new crew in the early 1950s for her local show in Los Angeles. Purex sponsored the show nationally for one summer. Some of Hutton's musicians included Margaret Rinker on drums, Lois Cronin on trombone, Helen Hammond on trumpet, Mickey Anderson on clarinet, and Deedie Ball on piano.

INCH HIGH, PRIVATE EYE NBC
8 SEPTEMBER 1973–31 AUGUST 1974 Saturday-morning cartoon series about a very small detective.

THE INCREDIBLE HULK CBS
10 MARCH 1978– After two popular made-for-TV movies, *The Incredible Hulk* was given a weekly spot in March 1978. The series, based on the Marvel Comics character, stars Bill Bixby as Dr. David Banner, a research scientist who is accidentally exposed to an overdose of gamma rays; as a result, Banner finds himself transformed into a green-skinned, white-eyed behemoth (The Incredible Hulk) whenever he becomes enraged. Also featured are former Mr. America Lou Ferrigno as

Banner's awesome but inarticulate alter ego, and Jack Colvin as Jack McGee, a reporter for the *National Register* who is out to expose the Hulk. Kenneth Johnson is the executive producer, and James D. Parriott and Chuck Bowman the producers, for Universal Television.

INDUSTRY ON PARADE SYNDICATED
1950–1958 Long-running series of fifteen-minute films on American industry, produced by the National Association of Manufacturers. The series won a Peabody Award in 1954.

INFORMATION PLEASE CBS
29 JUNE 1952–21 SEPTEMBER 1952 Created by Dan Golenpaul, *Information Please* ran on radio from 1938 to 1948; its television run was considerably shorter, replacing *The Fred Waring Show* for one summer. The format of the game show remained unchanged when it came to television: Viewers were invited to submit questions and won prizes if they succeeded in stumping the celebrity panel. Clifton Fadiman, the show's host on radio, continued as the moderator; permanent panelists included Franklin P. Adams, New York newspaper columnist, and John Kieran, sportswriter for *The New York Times.* Two guest celebrities completed the panel.

THE INNER FLAME
See PORTIA FACES LIFE

THE INNER SANCTUM SYNDICATED
1954 *The Inner Sanctum,* an anthology series of creepy tales, began on radio in 1941. Its trademark, on radio and television, was a squeaking door, the entrance to the "inner sanctum." Paul McGrath, who had hosted the show for several years on radio, was heard (but not seen) as the host, Mr. Raymond.

INNER SPACE SYNDICATED
1974 The underwater photography of Ron and Valerie Taylor was featured on this documentary series hosted by William Shatner.

THE INQUIRING MIND SYNDICATED
1965 An educational series produced at the University of Michigan; research work of Michigan scientists was examined. John Arthur Hanson hosted the program.

INSIDE DETECTIVE
See ROCKY KING, DETECTIVE

INSIDE U.S.A. WITH CHEVROLET CBS

29 SEPTEMBER 1949–16 MARCH 1950 This half-hour variety show, co-hosted by Peter Lind Hayes and Mary Healy (his wife), was seen biweekly on Thursdays. It alternated first with *Sugar Hill Times,* then with *Romance.*

INSIGHT SYNDICATED

1961– Widely syndicated religious program that presents modern-day morality lessons. Ellwood E. Kieser, a Paulist priest, is its host and executive producer.

INTERFACE PBS

1969–1975 Half-hour public affairs series hosted and produced by Tony Batten for WETA-TV, Washington.

INTERNATIONAL DETECTIVE SYNDICATED

1959 Stories on this half-hour crime show were supposedly adapted from the files of the William J. Burns Agency. Arthur Fleming starred as Ken Franklin, a Burns Agent. Fleming later shortened his first name to Art and became famous as the host of *Jeopardy.* Filmed in England, the series was produced by Eddie Sutherland for Official Films.

INTERNATIONAL PLAYHOUSE DUMONT

30 MAY 1951–14 NOVEMBER 1951 Dramatic anthology series that presented short foreign films and other foreign-made dramatic stories.

INTERNATIONAL SHOWTIME NBC

15 SEPTEMBER 1961–10 SEPTEMBER 1965 European circuses were showcased on this Friday-night series, hosted by Don Ameche.

THE INTERNS CBS

18 SEPTEMBER 1970–10 SEPTEMBER 1971 Based on the movie of the same title, *The Interns* was an undistinguished medical series about a group of young doctors and a crusty hospital director—all of whom worked at New North Hospital. With Broderick Crawford as Peter Goldstone, the director; Mike Farrell as Sam Marsh; Elaine Giftos as Bobbe Marsh, his wife (a nonphysician); Christopher Stone as Jim "Pooch" Hardin; Sandra Smith as Lydia Thorpe; Hal Frederick as Cal Baron; and Stephen Brooks as Greg Pettit.

INTERPOL CALLING SYNDICATED

1959 Charles Korvin starred as Inspector Duval of Interpol, an international law enforcement organization, in this British import. Jack Wrather produced the half-hour series in association with the J. Arthur Rank Organisation.

THE INVADERS   ABC

10 JANUARY 1967–17 SEPTEMBER 1968   An imaginative adventure series about visitors from space. Roy Thinnes starred as David Vincent, an architect who, having taken a wrong turn on the highway, witnessed the landing of a spacecraft. Returning to the spot the following morning, he found no clues, but subsequent attempts on his life convinced him that somebody—or something—was after him. Gradually, Vincent learned that the Earth had indeed been visited by aliens, creatures capable of assuming human form; their native world was dying, and they were searching for new areas to colonize. Thereafter, Vincent spent most of his time trying to convince other people of the aliens' existence and trying to ferret out the aliens; some aliens were easy to spot because their little fingers were splayed, and all aliens when killed simply dematerialized into red dust. In December of 1967, Kent Smith joined the series as Edgar Scoville, another true believer. A total of forty-three episodes, all in color, were made. Executive producer: Quinn Martin. Creator: Larry Cohen. Producer: Alan A. Armer.

THE INVESTIGATOR   NBC

3 JUNE 1958–2 SEPTEMBER 1958   This live, color adventure series was a summer replacement for *The George Gobel–Eddie Fisher Show*. It starred Lonny Chapman as Jeff Prior, private eye, and Howard St. John as Lloyd Prior, his father, a former reporter.

THE INVESTIGATORS   CBS

5 OCTOBER 1961–28 DECEMBER 1961   Insurance investigators were the central characters in this crime show. With James Franciscus as Russ Andrews; James Philbrook as Steve Banks; Mary Murphy as Maggie Peters; Al Austin as Bill Davis; and June Kenney as Polly, the secretary.

THE INVISIBLE MAN   CBS

4 NOVEMBER 1958–27 JANUARY 1959   H. G. Wells's classic tale of a young scientist who accidentally ingested a formula which made him invisible was the basis of this British import. The scientist's name was Peter Brady, but the name of the actor who portrayed him (his voice was audible and his clothing was, of course, visible) was never disclosed. Also featured were Lisa Daniely as Diane, his sister; Deborah Watling as Sally, his niece; and Ernest Clark as Sir Charles, a member of the British Cabinet. Thirteen half-hour episodes were seen over CBS. Ralph Smart produced the show for Official Films in cooperation with CBS-TV.

THE INVISIBLE MAN   NBC

8 SEPTEMBER 1975–19 JANUARY 1976   The second TV version of H. G. Wells's story was made in America. It starred David McCallum as Dr. Daniel Westin, a research scientist for the Klae Corporation, a West

Coast think tank, who cooked up a formula that rendered him invisible. Westin was outfitted with a special plastic mask that was a replica of his old face; thus, McCallum was quite visible to viewers. Also featured were Melinda Fee as Kate Westin, his wife; Craig Stevens as Walter Carlson, his boss. Harve Bennett was the executive producer of the series, Leslie Stevens its producer. Though the show failed to catch on, NBC apparently thought there was merit in the concept, for they introduced the very similar *Gemini Man* the following season. Undaunted when the show was canceled in midseason, NBC brought on *The Man from Atlantis* in 1977; it, too, proved unsuccessful.

INVITATION TO MURDER
See EDGAR WALLACE MYSTERIES

IRON HORSE ABC
12 SEPTEMBER 1966–6 JANUARY 1968   This hour-long western focused on the construction of the Buffalo Pass & Scalplock Railroad. It featured Dale Robertson as Ben Calhoun, the owner; Gary Collins as Dave Tarrant, the engineer; Bob Random as Barnabas Rogers; Roger Torrey as Nils Torvald; and Ellen McRae (1966–1967) as Julie Parsons. Produced by Screen Gems.

IRONSIDE NBC
14 SEPTEMBER 1967–16 JANUARY 1975   Raymond Burr returned to television one year after the demise of *Perry Mason* in another successful crime show. This time he played Robert T. Ironside, Chief of Detectives for the San Francisco Police Department, who was paralyzed from the waist down by a would-be assassin's bullet. Assisting him were Don Galloway as Lieutenant Ed Brown; Barbara Anderson (1967–1971) as Policewoman Eve Whitfield; Don Mitchell as Mark Sanger, Ironside's personal assistant, an ex-con attending law school; Gene Lyons as Commissioner Dennis Randall; Elizabeth Baur (1971–1975) as Officer Fran Belding; and Joan Pringle (1974–1975) as Diana Sanger, Mark's wife. Executive producer: Joel Rogosin.

ISIS CBS
6 SEPTEMBER 1975–2 SEPTEMBER 1978   *Isis,* a live-action Saturday-morning show, was introduced in 1975 as one half of *The Shazam!/Isis Hour,* where it remained for two seasons. When *Shazam!* left the air in 1977, *Isis* continued under the title *The Secrets of Isis.* The half-hour adventure series starred JoAnna Cameron as Andrea Thomas, a mild-mannered high school science teacher who learned the secrets of Isis, an Egyptian goddess, and could transform herself into the super-powered Isis. Also featured were Brian Cutler as schoolteacher Rick Mason and

Joanna Pang as student Cindy Lee. Lou Scheimer and Norm Prescott were the executive producers of the series. See also *Shazam!*

THE ISLANDERS
ABC

2 OCTOBER 1960–26 MARCH 1961   Intended as a companion series to *Adventures in Paradise,* this Warner Brothers adventure show was also set in the South Pacific. It starred William Reynolds and James Philbrook as Sandy Wade and Zack Malloy, coowners of a one-plane airline service. Also featured were Diane Brewster as Willy Vandeveer, the office manager; Roy Wright as Shipwreck Callahan, an island personality; and Daria Massey as Naja. The series was replaced in midseason by *The Asphalt Jungle.*

ISSUES AND ANSWERS
ABC

27 NOVEMBER 1960–   Newsmakers are interviewed by journalists on this public affairs program, ABC's counterpart of CBS's *Face the Nation* and NBC's venerable *Meet the Press.* In its earliest weeks the series was entitled *ABC Press Conference.* The series is currently produced by Peggy Whedon.

IT COULD BE YOU
NBC

4 JUNE 1956–29 DECEMBER 1961   Bill Leyden hosted this audience participation show. A regular feature involved three members of the audience, one of whom would be reunited with a long-lost friend or loved one. Wendell Niles was the announcer on the series, which enjoyed a five-year daytime run and was also seen evenings during the summers of 1958 and 1961 and during the entire 1959–1960 season. Ralph Edwards created the show.

IT HAPPENED IN SPORTS
NBC

3 JULY 1953–19 JANUARY 1954   Fifteen-minute sports documentary series.

IT IS WRITTEN
SYNDICATED

1975–   Half-hour religious discussion show, hosted by George Vandeman and produced by the Seventh Day Adventist Church.

IT PAYS TO BE IGNORANT
CBS/NBC/SYNDICATED

6 JUNE 1949–19 SEPTEMBER 1949 (CBS); 5 JULY 1951–27 SEPTEMBER 1951 (NBC); 1973 (SYNDICATED)   *It Pays to Be Ignorant* was a spoof of game shows and was popular on radio during the 1940s. The celebrity panel tried to avoid answering such stumpers as "What beverage is made from tea leaves?" On television the show first surfaced as a summer replacement for Arthur Godfrey's *Talent Scouts* in 1949 and was seen in

1951 as a summer replacement for Groucho Marx's *You Bet Your Life*. The radio and television versions were hosted by Tom Howard, the father-in-law of the show's creator, Bob Howell. The panel, also carried over from radio, consisted of veteran troupers Harry McNaughton, Lulu McConnell, and George Shelton (Shelton and Howard had been partners in vaudeville). In 1973 a revamped syndicated version appeared, featuring host Joe Flynn and panelists Jo Anne Worley, Charles Nelson Reilly, and Billy Baxter.

IT PAYS TO BE MARRIED   NBC
4 JULY 1955–28 OCTOBER 1955 Married couples competed for cash on this question-and-answer daytime game show, hosted by Bill Goodwin. It was replaced by *Matinee Theater*. Stefan Hatos (who later produced *Let's Make a Deal* with Monty Hall) created the show with Henry Hoople.

IT SEEMS LIKE YESTERDAY   SYNDICATED
1953 Radio newscaster H. V. Kaltenborn narrated old newsreels on this documentary series.

IT TAKES A THIEF   ABC
9 JANUARY 1968–14 SEPTEMBER 1970 Light adventure series starring Robert Wagner as Alexander Mundy, a suave thief who was released from prison on condition that he undertake certain sensitive missions requiring his skills for the government. Malachi Throne costarred as Noah Bain, chief of the S.I.A., the government agency which hired Mundy. Fred Astaire appeared occasionally as Alex's father, Alistair Mundy, a master thief. The show was produced by Universal TV.

IT TAKES TWO   NBC
31 MARCH 1969–31 JULY 1970 Daytime game show hosted by Vin Scully, featuring three celebrities and their spouses. Questions that called for mathematical answers were asked. The object of the game was for selected members of the studio audience to determine which couple's answers came the closest to the correct answer.

IT WAS A VERY GOOD YEAR   ABC
10 MAY 1971–30 AUGUST 1971 Mel Tormé hosted this nostalgic look at selected years from the twentieth century; each week a different year was highlighted through the use of film clips and songs.

IT'S A BUSINESS   DUMONT
19 MARCH 1952–21 MAY 1952 A situation comedy with a Tin Pan Alley setting, *It's a Business* starred Bob Haymes and Leo DeLyon as song publishers and Dorothy Loudon as their secretary. The half-hour series

was produced by Paul Rosen, directed by Frank Bunetta, and written by Bob Weiskopf (who later produced *Maude*).

IT'S A GREAT LIFE
NBC

7 SEPTEMBER 1954–3 JUNE 1956   Situation comedy about two ex-GI's who moved to California and took a furnished apartment. With William Bishop as Denny Davis; Michael O'Shea as Steve Connors; Frances Bavier as Mrs. Amy Morgan, their landlady; James Dunn as Amy's Uncle Earl; and Harry Harvey as Mr. Russell, a neighbor. The show was written and produced by Ray Singer and Dick Chevillat; it was syndicated under the title *The Bachelors*.

IT'S A HIT
CBS

1 JUNE 1957–21 SEPTEMBER 1957   Happy Felton hosted this Saturday-morning quiz show for children. Each week two teams of youngsters competed; each squad was managed by a sports personality.

IT'S A MAN'S WORLD
NBC

17 SEPTEMBER 1962–28 JANUARY 1963   Half-hour sitcom about three male college students living together on a houseboat moored on the Ohio River. With Ted Bessell as Tom (Tom-Tom) DeWitt; Glenn Corbett as Wes Macauley; Randy Boone as Vern Hodges; Mike Burns as Howie, Wes's orphaned kid brother who also lived with them; Jan Norris as Irene; Kate Murtagh as Mrs. Dodson; Jeanine Cashell as Alma Jean; Ann Schuler as Nora; and Harry Harvey, Sr., as Mr. Stott, owner of the gas station where Wes worked.

IT'S A PROBLEM
NBC

16 OCTOBER 1951–13 OCTOBER 1952   A daytime panel show, hosted by Ben Grauer. Each day a single topic relating to family life was discussed. Fannie Hurst and Helen Parkhurst were permanent panelists; in August of 1952 Parkhurst was succeeded by Alice Thompson, editor-publisher of *Seventeen* magazine. Broadcast live from New York, the half-hour series was originally titled *What's Your Problem?*.

IT'S A SMALL WORLD
DUMONT

27 JUNE 1953–27 JULY 1953   Half-hour travelogue.

IT'S A WONDERFUL WORLD
SYNDICATED

1963   Half-hour travelogue hosted by John Cameron Swayze.

IT'S ABOUT TIME
ABC

4 MARCH 1954–25 MARCH 1954   Short-lived prime-time game show hosted by Dr. Bergen Evans. Studio contestants were quizzed on historical events.

IT'S ABOUT TIME   CBS
11 SEPTEMBER 1966–27 AUGUST 1967   This sitcom took its stars on a journey to the Stone Age and back again. It starred Frank Aletter as Captain Glenn McDivitt (Mac) and Jack Mullaney as Hector, two astronauts who broke through the time barrier and landed in a prehistoric world where they met and befriended a Stone Age family; in midseason they brought the family with them into the modern era. The Stone Agers included Imogene Coca as Shad; Joe E. Ross as Gronk, her mate; Pat Cardi as Breer, their son; Mary Grace as Mlor, their daughter; Cliff Norton as Boss, the unfriendly leader of the cave people; Kathleen Freeman as Mrs. Boss; Mike Mazurki as Clon, Boss's henchman. Frank Wilcox joined the cast in midseason as General Morley, Mac and Hector's commanding officer.

IT'S ACADEMIC   SYNDICATED
1963-1966   A game show for high-schoolers, not unlike *College Bowl*. The show was essentially a franchised series, like *Bozo the Clown* or *Romper Room*; each participating station selected its own emcee and scheduled meets between local schools. Each week three 4-member high school teams competed.

IT'S ALEC TEMPLETON TIME   DUMONT
3 JUNE 1955–26 AUGUST 1955   Half-hour musical series hosted by Alec Templeton, the blind, British-born pianist who specialized in playing popular tunes in the style of classical composers.

IT'S ALWAYS JAN   CBS
10 SEPTEMBER 1955–30 JUNE 1956   Situation comedy about three New York career girls, presumably inspired by the film *How to Marry a Millionaire*. With Janis Paige as Jan Stewart, nightclub singer; Patricia Bright as Pat Murphy, a secretary; Merry Anders as Val Marlowe, a model; Jeri Lou James as Josie Stewart, Jan's daughter (Jan was a war widow); Arte Johnson as Stanley Schreiber, delivery boy for the local delicatessen; and Sid Melton as Harry Cooper, Jan's agent. Merry Anders went on to appear in the TV version of *How to Marry a Millionaire*.

IT'S ANYBODY'S GUESS   NBC
13 JUNE 1977–30 SEPTEMBER 1977   Daytime game show hosted by Monty Hall. Two contestants tried to predict whether a panel of five members of the studio audience would supply a preselected answer to a particular question. If the contestant predicted correctly, he or she won one point; if the guess was incorrect, the contestant's opponent won the point. If one of the five panelists gave the preselected answer, he or she also won a prize. The show was a Stefan Hatos–Monty Hall Production.

Jay Stewart, Hall's longtime sidekick on *Let's Make a Deal,* was the announcer.

IT'S FUN TO KNOW
CBS

23 APRIL 1951–22 JUNE 1951   A Monday-through-Friday educational series for children, hosted by Dorothy Engel Clark. Mondays were devoted to history, Tuesdays to crafts, Wednesdays to science, Thursdays to drawing, and Fridays to dancing. The half-hour show was produced by Frederick Kugel.

IT'S HAPPENING
ABC

15 JULY 1968–25 OCTOBER 1968   This short-lived daytime musical series replaced the short-lived game show, *Wedding Party.* It was hosted by Mark Lindsay and his band (Paul Revere and the Raiders), and featured guest appearances by rock stars. A weekend version also appeared: see *Happening '68.*

IT'S MAGIC
CBS

31 JULY 1955–4 SEPTEMBER 1955   A summer replacement for *Lassie,* *It's Magic* featured guest prestidigitators each week. Paul Tripp (formerly of *Mr. I. Magination*) hosted the series.

IT'S NEWS TO ME
CBS

2 JULY 1951–27 AUGUST 1954   The format of this prime-time game show was similar to that of *Liars Club*—contestants had to choose which of four celebrity panelists was telling the truth. The subject of the game was current events; after being shown a clue to a recent news story, three of the panelists suggested the wrong event, while one named the correct event associated with the clue. The show was seen sporadically for three years and was hosted at various times by newsmen John Daly, Walter Cronkite, and Quincy Howe.

IT'S POLKA TIME
ABC

13 JULY 1956–24 SEPTEMBER 1957   Polka music and dancing from Chicago, hosted by Bruno "Junior" Zielinski, with Stan Wolowic's Band, The Polka Chips (singers), Carolyn DeZurik, and the Kanal Siodmy Dancers.

IT'S YOUR BET
SYNDICATED

1970–1972   This game show was the descendant of *I'll Bet;* the show featured two celebrities and their spouses, and the object was for one spouse to predict whether the other would be able to answer a question correctly. The several hosts included Hal March (seldom seen on TV after the demise of *The $64,000 Question*), Tom Kennedy, Dick Gautier, and Lyle Waggoner.

IT'S YOUR BUSINESS   SYNDICATED
1979   A series of half-hour debates on public-policy issues, moderated by Karna Small, and broadcast from Washington, D.C., under the auspices of the U.S. Chamber of Commerce.

IVAN THE TERRIBLE   CBS
21 AUGUST 1976–18 SEPTEMBER 1976   Forgettable five-week summer sitcom about a group of nine Muscovites living in a small apartment. With Lou Jacobi as Ivan Petrovsky; Maria Karnilova as Olga Petrovsky, his wife; Phil Leeds as Vladimir, Olga's former husband; Matthew Barry as Sascha, Ivan's son; Despo as Tatiana; Alan Cauldwell as Nikolai; Carolina Kava as Sonya; Christopher Hewett as Federov; Nana Tucker as Svetlana, Ivan's mother-in-law; and Manuel Martinez as Raoul. Alan King was the executive producer.

IVANHOE   SYNDICATED
1958   This British adventure series, based on Sir Walter's Scott's novel, starred Roger Moore as Ivanhoe, a youthful and noble knight and crusader.

IVANHOE   SYNDICATED
1972   The second incarnation of Sir Walter Scott's novel was serialized in ten chapters as part of *Family Classics Theater* and starred Eric Flynn (son of Errol Flynn) as Ivanhoe.

I'VE GOT A SECRET   CBS/SYNDICATED
19 JUNE 1952–3 APRIL 1967 (CBS); 1972 (SYNDICATED); 15 JUNE 1976–6 JULY 1976 (CBS)   On this popular prime-time game show the celebrity panelists tried to guess the guests' secrets. The guest whispered his secret to the host, and the secret was superimposed on the screen for the home audience. Top prize on the 1952–1967 network version was only $80 (and a carton of Winstons), so the show was played mainly for laughs; each week a celebrity guest also came on to try to stump the panel. Garry Moore hosted the show from 1952 until 1964, when he was succeeded by Steve Allen. Often seen on the celebrity panel were Bill Cullen, Betsy Palmer, Henry Morgan, Bess Myerson, Steve Allen, and Jayne Meadows. Steve Allen also hosted the 1972 syndicated version; Bill Cullen emceed the 1976 network version. The show was a Mark Goodson–Bill Todman Production.

JABBERJAW   ABC
11 SEPTEMBER 1976–3 SEPTEMBER 1978   Weekend cartoon series about a giant shark (Jabberjaw) who was the drummer for a rock group known

as the Neptunes. The creature was later featured on *Yogi's Space Race:* see *Yogi Bear.*

THE JACK BENNY PROGRAM
CBS/NBC

28 OCTOBER 1950–15 SEPTEMBER 1964 (CBS); 25 SEPTEMBER 1964–10 SEPTEMBER 1965 (NBC)   One of America's best-loved comedians, Jack Benny proved almost as durable on television as he had on radio. His half-hour show transcended the boundary between variety and situation comedy—some shows featured guest stars who sang or danced, and other shows consisted of just one sketch, performed by Benny and his company of regulars.

Benny entered television cautiously, testing the waters with four shows spread out during the 1950–1951 season; the following season he appeared six times, and gradually increased his appearances to twenty in 1954–1955, and to thirty-nine by 1960–1961. Benny succeeded in landing many top stars on his shows; guests during the first season included Ken Murray (28 October 1950), Frank Sinatra (28 January 1951), Claudette Colbert and Basil Rathbone (1 April 1951). A young comedian named Johnny Carson, newly arrived in Los Angeles, made one of his earliest national appearances in 1952. Marilyn Monroe and Humphrey Bogart made their TV debuts during the 1953–1954 season, and it is reported that Benny came close to signing the elusive Clark Gable for a guest shot.

From the beginning Benny relied heavily on a group of supporting players, many of whom had been with him for years on radio. The group included Eddie Anderson as his gravel-voiced valet, Rochester Van Jones; hefty Don Wilson as his announcer; singer Dennis Day; Mel Blanc (the voice of Bugs Bunny) as his violin teacher; Mary Livingstone (Benny's wife); and Frank Nelson as the man who said "Yeeeeesssss!" Occasionally seen were Hy Averback, Bea Benaderet, Barry Gordon (as the boyhood Jack Benny), Sandra Gould, Burt Mustin (as the guard of Benny's vaults), Benny Rubin, Herb Vigran, and Dale White (as Don Wilson's son, Harlow).

For most of its run on CBS the show was seen on Sundays, alternating with *This Is Show Business* through January 1953; from February 1953 through 1957 it alternated with Ann Sothern's sitcom, *Private Secretary.* It then shared a slot with *Bachelor Father* for two seasons and with *The George Gobel Show* for one season. In the fall of 1960 it first appeared as a weekly series and moved to Tuesdays in 1962. When CBS dropped the show in 1964, NBC, the network that had lost Benny to CBS in 1949, picked it up and scheduled it on Fridays; the show did poorly and was canceled after one season. Thereafter Benny headlined several specials and frequently appeared on talk shows. The executive producer of his show (for the first several seasons) was Ralph Levy, and its producer was Hilliard Marks, Benny's brother-in-law. Principal writers included Sam Perrin, George Balzer, Hal Goldman, and Al Gordon.

THE JACK CARSON SHOW NBC

22 OCTOBER 1954–11 MARCH 1955 Comedian Jack Carson, who often hosted such variety hours as *The Colgate Comedy Hour* and *All-Star Revue,* also had his own half-hour series in 1954, which was scheduled as an occasional replacement for *The Red Buttons Show* on Fridays.

JACK CARTER AND COMPANY ABC

12 MARCH 1949–21 APRIL 1949 This half-hour variety show featured comedian Jack Carter, comedienne Elaine Stritch, Sonny King, and Rowena Rollin. Kenny Lyons was the producer and Sean Dillon the director.

THE JACK CARTER SHOW
See ALL-STAR REVUE

THE JACK LA LANNE SHOW SYNDICATED

1956–1970 America's foremost physical fitness enthusiast, Jack La Lanne hosted a long-running exercise program, aimed principally at women viewers. He had hosted a local exercise show in San Francisco for five years before moving to Los Angeles in 1956.

JACK LONDON STORIES
See CAPTAIN DAVID GRIEF

THE JACK PAAR SHOW CBS

13 NOVEMBER 1953–2 JULY 1954; 17 JULY 1954–4 SEPTEMBER 1954; 4 JULY 1955–25 MAY 1956 Before succeeding Steve Allen as host of the *Tonight* show in 1957, Jack Paar had gained considerable experience as host of several daytime shows (he also emceed a quiz show, *Bank on the Stars*). The first of the daytime series was seen Friday mornings as a weekly replacement for *Arthur Godfrey Time.* It featured singers Edith Adams (later known as Edie Adams), Richard Hayes, and Jack Haskell, pianist José Melis (an old Army buddy of Paar's), and the Pupi Campo Orchestra. In July of 1954 he and his crew moved to a Saturday-evening slot, and in August Paar moved to an earlier time slot, succeeding Walter Cronkite as host of *The Morning Show* (see also that title), CBS's answer to the *Today* show. After a year on that show, Paar surfaced in an afternoon slot, hosting a Monday-through-Friday half hour. It featured Adams, Haskell, Melis, and announcer Hal Simms.

THE JACK PAAR SHOW (THE JACK PAAR PROGRAM) NBC

21 SEPTEMBER 1962–10 SEPTEMBER 1965 After leaving the daily grind of the *Tonight* show in March 1962, Jack Paar returned that fall as host of a Friday-night variety series. Frequent guests included British humorist Alexander King and American comedian Jonathan Winters; music

was provided by the José Melis Orchestra. Paar's program was the first American variety show to present the Beatles—film clips of the foursome were shown on 3 January 1964, more than a month before the group's famous "debut" on *The Ed Sullivan Show.*

JACK PAAR TONITE   ABC

8 JANUARY 1973–16 NOVEMBER 1973   Jack Paar returned to late night TV after an eleven-year absence on a one-week-per-month basis; his ninety-minute talk show was part of ABC's umbrella series, *ABC's Wide World of Entertainment.* Peggy Cass was Paar's announcer and sidekick. Freddie Prinze, the future star of *Chico and the Man,* made his TV debut on 18 October.

JACK THE RIPPER   SYNDICATED

1974   This British miniseries was a fictional reopening of the series of murders that shocked London in the 1880s; two modern-day detectives, using the sophisticated techniques of twentieth-century criminology, tried to solve the crimes. Sebastian Cabot hosted the series, which featured Alan Stratford-Johns as Detective Chief Superintendent Barlow and Frank Windsor as Detective Chief Superintendent Watt.

THE JACKIE GLEASON SHOW (THE HONEYMOONERS)   CBS
(JACKIE GLEASON AND HIS AMERICAN SCENE MAGAZINE)

20 SEPTEMBER 1952–22 JUNE 1957; 3 OCTOBER 1958–2 JANUARY 1959; 3 FEBRUARY 1961–24 MARCH 1961; 29 SEPTEMBER 1962–12 SEPTEMBER 1970   Jackie Gleason, television's rotund showman, was a fixture on CBS for most of two decades. His series-within-a-series, *The Honeymooners,* was one of TV's all-time classic comedies, and its syndicated reruns thrive today. With experience in vaudeville, Broadway, and films already under his considerable belt, Gleason entered television in 1949 in the first version of *The Life of Riley* (dropped by NBC after twenty-six weeks, it reappeared in 1953 with William Bendix). The following season he began to appear regularly on *Cavalcade of Stars,* a variety hour broadcast on the DuMont network. There Gleason introduced to television audiences many of the characters he had developed: the insufferably wealthy Reggie Van Gleason III, The Poor Soul, Joe the Bartender, Charley the Loudmouth, Rudy the Repairman, Pedro the Mexican, Stanley R. Sogg, Fenwick Babbitt, Father and Son, The Ham, and Rum Dum. He also introduced a running sketch entitled "The Honeymooners," which was an immediate hit with viewers. *Cavalcade of Stars* soon became one of the most popular shows on the limited DuMont network, and Gleason attracted the attention of CBS. In 1952 he accepted CBS's offer to star in his own variety hour. The network originally planned to schedule Gleason either on Tuesdays opposite Milton Berle on NBC or on Saturdays opposite Sid Caesar's *Your Show of Shows.* Shortly before the start of the

1952 season, however, the network decided to put the show into an earlier slot on Saturdays, where it remained for the next five years. From 1952 until 1955, the show ran a full hour; each one started with a production number staged by the June Taylor Dancers, following which "The Great One" (Gleason) made his entrance. During his short monologue Gleason managed to interject some of his favorite phrases—"How sweet it is," "And away we go," or "A little traveling music please."

The main event of the evening filled the second half hour—the *Honeymooners* sketch. These were usually done with little rehearsal (Gleason was well known as a quick study), but the chemistry among the players was strong enough to overcome any difficulty that might arise on stage. Gleason played Ralph Kramden, a New York bus driver living in a small apartment with his wife of fifteen years. Audrey Meadows costarred as his weary wife, Alice (the part was first played by Pert Kelton on *Cavalcade of Stars*). Art Carney, a comic and character actor with some television experience, provided the perfect foil for Kramden as Ralph's friend and upstairs neighbor, Ed Norton, a city sewer worker. Norton's apparent dimwittedness was balanced by a certain grace and imperturbability, and these qualities offset Kramden's impatience and hot temper. Joyce Randolph rounded out the foursome as Norton's doting wife, and Alice's best friend, Trixie Norton.

Almost all of the action took place on a sparsely furnished set: the Kramdens' living room contained little more than a bureau, table and chairs, sink, stove, and icebox. Rarely did additional characters appear (Joyce Randolph did not even appear in some sketches), and rarely were any needed; the timing and interaction of the regulars worked almost magically.

During the 1955–1956 season thirty-nine *Honeymooners* were filmed before a live audience. These half hours, produced at the rate of two a week, were scheduled Saturdays at 8:30. The show returned to an hour variety format (with a *Honeymooners* sketch) in the fall of 1956. The show finally left the air in June of 1957 (Gleason himself missed the last three shows). In the fall of 1958 he returned in a live half-hour series scheduled on Fridays. That effort, which also featured Buddy Hackett, vanished in midseason. Gleason was again seen Friday nights in 1961 as host of a game show, *You're in the Picture.* One of the biggest flops in TV history, the show was axed—by Gleason—after a single week. Gleason appeared the following week and apologized to viewers for "that bomb." Early in February the show was retitled *The Jackie Gleason Show* and continued for a few weeks as a half-hour talk show.

In the fall of 1962 Gleason was back to a Saturday slot, which he occupied for another eight seasons. From 1962 to 1966 it was called *Jackie Gleason and His American Scene Magazine,* and featured topical comedy sketches as well as musical numbers. One of Gleason's characters, Joe the Bartender, appeared regularly. Addressing the camera as his patron,

("Hiya, Mr. Dunahy!"), Joe told a few jokes before calling out the tipsy Crazy Guggenham from the back room. Guggenham, played by Frank Fontaine, traded quips with Joe and then sang a song. Sue Ane Langdon, later to costar in *Arnie,* was also featured regularly, and singer Wayne Newton made some of his earliest television appearances on the show.

In 1966 Gleason moved the operation to Miami Beach (where he could indulge in his favorite pastime, golf, all year round). The "magazine" concept was dropped, and the show was retitled *The Jackie Gleason Show.* For the first time in almost a decade, production of *The Honeymooners* was resumed. Gleason was reunited with Art Carney; Sheila MacRae and Jane Kean were added to play Alice and Trixie. Many of these later *Honeymooners* sketches ran a full hour, and the accent was now on music. Lyn Duddy and Jerry Bresler composed several original numbers a week for the show, many of which were performed by the *Honeymooners* crew. Jack Philbin was executive producer of the series, and Ronald Wayne produced it. Frank Bunetta was the director.

Gleason has made few TV appearances since 1970, though some *Honeymooners* episodes were rerun on CBS during the winter of 1970–1971. On 2 February 1976, he was again reunited with Art Carney, Audrey Meadows, and Jane Kean in an ABC special, "The Honeymooners—The Second Honeymoon," celebrating the Kramdens' twenty-fifth television anniversary.

JACKPOT
NBC

7 JANUARY 1974–26 SEPTEMBER 1975 Daytime game show on which fifteen contestants, chosen from the studio audience, competed for a top prize of $50,000 by trying to answer riddles. Geoff Edwards was the host, and Bob Stewart was the executive producer.

JACKPOT BOWLING STARRING MILTON BERLE
NBC

19 SEPTEMBER 1960–13 MARCH 1961 Having signed a thirty-year contract with NBC in 1951, Milton Berle starred in two series after *The Milton Berle Show* left the air in 1956. The first was the *Kraft Music Hall* in 1958, and the second was this half-hour sports series, broadcast live from Legion Lanes in Hollywood. Each week two competitors tried to bowl as many strikes as possible; veteran sportscaster Chick Hearn handled the play by play, and Berle sandwiched comedy bits between frames. Produced by Buddy Arnold and directed by Dave Brown, the show was dropped after twenty-six weeks.

THE JACKSON 5IVE
ABC

11 SEPTEMBER 1971–1 SEPTEMBER 1973 Saturday-morning cartoon series about the Jackson Five, a real-life rock group from Gary, Indiana, discovered in 1968 by Diana Ross. The voices of the five Jackson brothers—Michael, Marlon, Jackie, Tito, and Jermaine—were used.

THE JACKSONS   CBS

16 JUNE 1976–7 JULY 1976; 26 JANUARY 1977–9 MARCH 1977   The Jacksons, several of whom had previously been seen in cartoon form on TV, hosted a half-hour variety series which first appeared during the summer of 1976 and resurfaced briefly early in 1977. Eight of the nine Jackson children appeared on the show—brothers Michael, Marlon, Jackie, Tito, and Randy, and sisters Maureen (Rebie), La Toya, and Janet; brother Jermaine, an original member of The Jackson Five, had left the group previously to pursue a solo recording career. Additional regulars included Jim Samuels and Marty Cohen on the 1976 show, and Johnny Dark on the 1977 show. The Jacksons danced at least as well as they sang—choreography was handled by Anita Mann. Their father, Joe Jackson, was executive producer of the series with Richard Arons.

THE JACOBS BROTHERS   SYNDICATED

1975   Religious music with a country flavor, performed by the Jacobs Brothers Quartet.

JACQUELINE SUSANN'S OPEN DOOR   DUMONT

7 MAY 1951–18 JUNE 1951   Though Jacqueline Susann is best remembered for her novels, she also appeared frequently on television in its early days; she was married to producer Irving Mansfield and was a regular on *The Morey Amsterdam Show* in 1948. In 1951 she hosted her own show, *Jacqueline Susann's Open Door,* a late-night weekly program on which she interviewed celebrities and also introduced persons who were looking for jobs. George Scheck produced the series. In 1952 she was featured on a daytime game show, *Your Surprise Store,* and in 1953 she hosted a local talk show in New York.

JACQUES FRAY'S MUSIC ROOM   ABC

19 FEBRUARY 1949–9 OCTOBER 1949   Sunday-night half-hour musical series, hosted by Jacques Fray.

JAMBO   NBC

6 SEPTEMBER 1967–4 SEPTEMBER 1971   Saturday-morning series of animal films and stories, hosted and narrated by Marshall Thompson, formerly the star of *Daktari;* assisting Thompson was another *Daktari* alumna, Judy the chimp.

JAMES AT 15 (JAMES AT 16)   NBC

27 OCTOBER 1977–27 JULY 1978   Family drama about a teenager who moved from Oregon to suburban Boston with his family. With Lance Kerwin as James Hunter; Linden Chiles as his father, Paul, a college professor; Lynn Carlin as his mother, Joan; David Hubbard as Sly (Ludwig Hazeltine), James's jive-talking black friend; Susan Myers as Marlene, Ja-

mes's intellectual friend; Kim Richards as James's sister, Sandy; and Deirdre Berthrong as James's sister Kathy. The show's first executive producers, Martin Manulis and Joe Hardy, were replaced in December 1977 by Ron Rubin. Its head writer, novelist Dan Wakefield, quit the show in a dispute with the network on the treatment of the show aired 9 February 1978 (on that date the title was changed to *James at 16*), in which young James had a love affair with a Swedish exchange student.

JAMES BEARD   SYNDICATED
1963   Cooking show hosted by chef James Beard.

THE JAMES MASON SHOW   SYNDICATED
1956   A half hour of dramatic readings performed by James Mason, Pamela Mason (his wife at the time), and Richard Burton.

THE JAMES MELTON SHOW
See FORD FESTIVAL

JAMIE   ABC
5 OCTOBER 1953–4 OCTOBER 1954   Brandon De Wilde, the child actor who was featured in the movie *Shane* in 1953, starred as eleven-year-old Jamie McHummer in this family sitcom. Young Jamie had just moved in with relatives as the show began—his parents had been killed. Also featured were Ernest Truex as Grandpa McHummer; Polly Rowles as Aunt Laurie, a widow; and Kathy Nolan as Cousin Liz, Laurie's daughter. Julian Claman was the producer.

THE JAN MURRAY SHOW (CHARGE ACCOUNT)   NBC
5 SEPTEMBER 1960–28 SEPTEMBER 1962   On this daytime game show, hosted by Jan Murray, players competed for the right to purchase prizes by forming words out of a group of sixteen letters.

JANE FROMAN'S U.S.A. CANTEEN (THE JANE FROMAN SHOW)   CBS
18 OCTOBER 1952–23 JUNE 1955   *Jane Froman's U.S.A. Canteen* was first seen as a half-hour series on Saturdays; talented members of the armed services appeared with Froman, who was billed as "The Sweetheart of the Armed Forces." The Saturday show lasted about two months. Beginning 30 December 1952, the show was trimmed to fifteen minutes and shown Tuesdays and Thursdays following the network news. By late 1953 the series had been retitled *The Jane Froman Show,* and by the end of its run in 1955 it was seen only on Thursdays.

THE JANE PICKENS SHOW   ABC
31 JANUARY 1954–5 SEPTEMBER 1954   Fifteen-minute Sunday-night musical series hosted by singer Jane Pickens, who had been a featured vo-

calist on such radio programs as *Ben Bernie, The Old Maestro,* and *The Chamber Music Society of Lower Basin Street.*

JANE WYMAN THEATER   NBC
(JANE WYMAN PRESENTS THE FIRESIDE THEATRE)
30 AUGUST 1955–29 MAY 1958   Actress Jane Wyman made a successful transition to television, taking over as host of *Fireside Theatre* in 1955; Wyman also starred in about one-half of the episodes that season and co-produced the show with William Asher. She co-owned the production company, Lewman Productions, with Music Corporation of America. By the second season the title was shortened to *Jane Wyman Theater.* During the summer of 1957 Wyman hosted *Jane Wyman's Summer Play-house* on NBC, an anthology series which consisted of rebroadcasts from other anthology series.

JANET DEAN, REGISTERED NURSE   SYNDICATED
1954   The first TV series about a nurse starred Ella Raines as Janet Dean, a New York practitioner. The thirty-nine half hours were produced by Joan Mary Harrison.

JASON OF STAR COMMAND   CBS
15 SEPTEMBER 1979–22 DECEMBER 1979   One segment of *Tarzan and the Super 7, Jason of Star Command* became a separate series in 1979. The Saturday noontime show featured Craig Littler as Jason, space explorer; Charlie Dell as the Professor; Sid Haig as Dragos, the villain; John Russell as the Commander; and Tamara Dobson as Samantha, Jason's frequent comrade. Arthur H. Nadel created, produced, and directed.

THE JAYE P. MORGAN SHOW   NBC
13 JUNE 1956–31 AUGUST 1956   Singer Jaye P. Morgan hosted her own fifteen-minute musical series, a summer replacement for Eddie Fisher's *Coke Time* on Wednesdays and Fridays. Assisting her were her four brothers—Bob, Charlie, Dick, and Duke—with whom she had sung as a teenager.

JAZZ SCENE, U.S.A.   SYNDICATED
1963   Half-hour series on American jazz, featuring performances by and interviews with jazz artists. Oscar Brown, Jr., hosted the series.

THE JEAN ARTHUR SHOW   CBS
12 SEPTEMBER 1966–5 DECEMBER 1966   The star of many motion picture comedies during the 1930s and 1940s, Jean Arthur came out of retirement to do this short-lived sitcom about a pair of lawyers, mother and son. She played Patricia Marshall, a widow. Also featured were Ron Harper as her son, Paul Marshall; Richard Conte as Richie Wells, an ex-

gangster interested in the elder Marshall; and Leonard Stone as Morton. Producer: Richard Quine.

THE JEAN CARROLL SHOW
ABC

4 NOVEMBER 1953–6 JANUARY 1954 This half-hour sitcom starred Jean Carroll as a New York housewife, Lynn Loring as her daughter, Alan Carney as her husband, and Alice Pearce as their neighbor. The series, which was also known as *Take It from Me,* was produced and directed by Alan Dinehart and written by Coleman Jacoby and Arnie Rosen.

JEAN SHEPHERD'S AMERICA
PBS

1971 Thirteen-part series of whimsical essays on aspects of American culture and life-style, hosted by Jean Shepherd. Produced by Fred Barzyk for WGBH-TV, Boston.

JEANNE WOLF WITH ...
PBS

1974–1975 Half-hour talk show, produced and hosted by Jeanne Wolf at WPBT-TV, Miami.

JEANNIE
CBS

8 SEPTEMBER 1973–30 AUGUST 1975 A Saturday-morning cartoon spinoff from *I Dream of Jeannie;* the animated Jeannie was discovered not by an astronaut, but by a high school student, Corey Anders. From Hanna-Barbera Productions.

JEFFERSON DRUM
NBC

25 APRIL 1958–23 APRIL 1959 Half-hour western about a crusading newspaper editor. With Jeff Richards as Jefferson Drum, a man who headed for San Francisco after his wife was murdered and his newspaper destroyed in another town; on his way West Drum stopped in the town of Jubilee and decided to take over its paper when he learned that the former publisher had been murdered. Also featured were Eugene Martin as his young son, Joey; Cyril Delevanti as the old typesetter, Lucius Coin; and Robert J. Stevenson as Big Ed, Drum's friend. *Jefferson Drum* was one of the few dramatic series put together by game show producers Mark Goodson and Bill Todman.

THE JEFFERSONS
CBS

18 JANUARY 1975–   In this spinoff from *All in the Family,* the Bunkers' black neighbors—the Jeffersons—moved from Queens to Manhattan's East Side. The half-hour sitcom stars Sherman Hemsley as George Jefferson, owner of a chain of successful cleaning stores, and a short-tempered, know-it-all bigot, and Isabel Sanford as Louise Jefferson, his tolerant and forgiving wife. Mike Evans played their son, Lionel, until September of 1975, when he was succeeded by Damon Evans (no re-

lation); and Zara Cully played George's doting mother, Mama Jefferson, until her death early in 1978. Also featured are Franklin Cover and Roxie Roker as Tom and Helen Willis, the Jeffersons' neighbors (the Willises were the first racially mixed married couple to be featured on a prime-time series); Berlinda Tolbert as Jenny Willis, their daughter; Paul Benedict as Harry Bentley, an eccentric neighbor employed as a United Nations translator; Marla Gibbs (1976–) as Florence Johnston, the Jeffersons' sassy maid; Ned Wertimer (1976–) as Ralph, the obsequious doorman; Ernest Harden, Jr., (1977–1978) as Marcus Wilson, a young man employed at one of George's stores; and Jay Hammer (1978–1979) as Allan Willis, Tom's son. In December of 1976 Lionel and Jenny were married; though Damon Evans left the show in the fall of 1978, Berlinda Tolbert continued to appear. Mike Evans returned to play Lionel in the fall of 1979. *The Jeffersons* was created by Don Nicholl, Michael Ross, and Bernie West (who also serve as its executive producers) and was developed by Norman Lear.

JEOPARDY NBC/SYNDICATED
30 MARCH 1964–3 JANUARY 1975 (NBC); 1974 (SYNDICATED); 2 OCTOBER 1978–2 MARCH 1979 (NBC) This "answer and question" game show enjoyed a long daytime run on NBC. Art Fleming hosted the series, on which three contestants competed for cash by supplying the correct questions to answers uncovered on a board of thirty squares, containing five answers in each of six categories. At the end of the show ("Final Jeopardy"), contestants could wager up to all of their winnings on one answer. The series was developed by Merv Griffin and produced by his production company. The 1978 version of the series was similar to the earlier version; three contestants competed in the first round, but only two contestants moved on to the second round. The "final jeopardy" round was also modified so that only one player participated.

JERICHO CBS
15 SEPTEMBER 1966–19 JANUARY 1967 One of the lesser known World War II dramas, *Jericho* featured a trio of Allied agents who usually worked behind German lines. With Don Francks as Franklin Shepard, an American who was an expert in psychological warfare; John Leyton as Nicholas Gage, a Britisher whose specialty was demolition; and Marino Mase as Jean-Gaston André, a Frenchman whose forte was munitions. Dan Melnick and Norman Felton produced the hour-long series.

THE JERRY COLONNA SHOW ABC
28 MAY 1951–17 NOVEMBER 1951 Half-hour variety series hosted by Jerry Colonna, a mustachioed comic who had worked with Bob Hope on the latter's radio series.

JERRY FALWELL   SYNDICATED

1971–   Evangelist Jerry Falwell appears in a half-hour religious program, which is usually taped at one of his revival meetings. The show has also been broadcast under the title *The Old-Time Gospel Hour*.

THE JERRY LESTER SHOW   ABC

28 SEPTEMBER 1953–14 MAY 1954   Jerry Lester, the comedian who had hosted *Broadway Open House,* later hosted his own daytime show. Also featured were singer and violinist Leon Belasco, and vocalists Lorenzo Fuller, Kathy Collin, and Ellie Russell. The hour-long show was produced by Vernon Becker and Milton Stanson.

THE JERRY LEWIS SHOW   ABC/NBC

21 SEPTEMBER 1963–21 DECEMBER 1963 (ABC); 12 SEPTEMBER 1967–27 MAY 1969 (NBC)   After breaking up with partner Dean Martin in 1956, Jerry Lewis appeared little on TV for the next seven years, concentrating instead on films. In 1963 it was reported that he had signed a five-year, $35-million deal with ABC; that fall he hosted a live, two-hour variety-talk show, which proved to be an enormous failure. In 1967 he returned to host an hour-long variety show on NBC, which was somewhat more successful; Bob Finkel produced it.

THE JERRY REED WHEN YOU'RE HOT YOU'RE HOT HOUR   CBS

20 JUNE 1972–25 JULY 1972   A summer replacement for *The Glen Campbell Goodtime Hour,* hosted by country and western singer Jerry Reed, whose record, "When You're Hot, You're Hot," was a hit a year earlier. Other regulars included John Twomey, Spencer Quinn, Cal Wilson, Norman Andrews, and eighty-three-year-old Merie Earle.

JERRY VISITS   SYNDICATED

1971–1973 Celebrities were interviewed in their homes by Jerry Dunphy on this half-hour talk show.

JET JACKSON
See CAPTAIN MIDNIGHT

THE JETSONS   ABC/CBS/NBC

Nighttime: 23 SEPTEMBER 1962–8 SEPTEMBER 1963 (ABC); *Daytime:* 21 SEPTEMBER 1963–18 APRIL 1964 (ABC); 26 SEPTEMBER 1964–18 SEPTEMBER 1965 (CBS); 2 OCTOBER 1965–2 SEPTEMBER 1967 (NBC); 13 SEPTEMBER 1969–5 SEPTEMBER 1970 (CBS); 11 SEPTEMBER 1971–31 AUGUST 1975 (NBC); 3 FEBRUARY 1979–3 NOVEMBER 1979 (NBC)   This durable cartoon series was the Space Age counterpart of Hanna-Barbera's Stone Age smash, *The Flintstones;* the Jetsons—

George, Jane, Judy, and Elroy—lived in the ultramodern world of the twenty-first century. The series was seen in prime time over ABC for one season and on Saturday mornings over all three networks for many seasons thereafter. The voices of the Jetsons were provided by the Hanna-Barbera regulars: George O'Hanlon as George, Penny Singleton as Jane, Janet Waldo as Judy, Daws Butler as Elroy, and Don Messick as Astro, the family dog.

JEWELER'S SHOWCASE   SYNDICATED
(YOUR JEWELER'S SHOWCASE)
1952   This half-hour dramatic anthology series was sponsored by the International Silver Company and the Hamilton Watch Company.

JIGSAW   ABC
21 SEPTEMBER 1972–11 AUGUST 1973   One segment of ABC's adventure trilogy, *The Men, Jigsaw* alternated with *Assignment: Vienna* and *The Delphi Bureau*. It starred James Wainwright as Lieutenant Frank Dain, an investigator for the California bureau of missing persons.

JIGSAW JOHN   NBC
2 FEBRUARY 1976–13 SEPTEMBER 1976   Crime show based on the exploits of real-life police investigator John St. John. With Jack Warden as John St. John, Los Angeles cop; Alan Feinstein as Sam Donner, his partner; Pippa Scott as Maggie Hearn, John's friend, a schoolteacher; Marjorie Bennett as Mrs. Cooley; and James Hong as Frank Chen. The hour-long series was created by Al Martinez, and produced by Ronald Austin and James Buchanan.

THE JIM BACKUS SHOW (HOT OFF THE WIRE)   SYNDICATED
1960   Situation comedy starring Jim Backus as John Michael (Mike) O'Toole, editor of a newspaper struggling to keep afloat; Nita Talbot as Dora, his gal Friday; and Bobs Watson as Sidney, the office boy.

JIM BOWIE (THE ADVENTURES OF JIM BOWIE)   ABC
7 SEPTEMBER 1956–29 AUGUST 1958   Half-hour western starring Scott Forbes as Jim Bowie, the nineteenth-century American adventurer who invented the knife that bears his name. Criticism of the frequent use of the knife on the series led to a cutback of violence on *Jim Bowie.* Though Forbes (who was British by birth) was the only regular on the show, he did not appear in all the episodes. Louis Edelman produced the series.

THE JIM NABORS HOUR   CBS
25 SEPTEMBER 1969–20 MAY 1971   Hour-long variety series hosted by Jim Nabors, the singer-comedian who got his start on *The Andy Griffith Show* and later starred in a spinoff, *Gomer Pyle, U.S.M.C.* Nabors

brought with him a couple of his *Gomer Pyle* costars, Frank Sutton and Ronnie Schell. Also on hand were Karen Morrow and the Nabors Kids. Richard O. Linke was the executive producer.

THE JIM NABORS SHOW   SYNDICATED

1978   Talk show hosted by Jim Nabors. Executive producers: Carolyn Raskin and Larry Thompson. Producers: Ken Harris and Charles Colarusso.

THE JIM STAFFORD SHOW   ABC

30 JULY 1975–3 SEPTEMBER 1975   Six-week summer variety series starring Jim Stafford, a country singer who had had a minor hit with "My Girl Bill." Other regulars included Valerie Curtin, Tom Biener, Deborah Allen, Richard Stahl, Phil MacKenzie, Jeanne Sheffield, and Cyndi Wood. Executive producers: Phil Gernhard and Tony Scotti. Producers: Rich Eustis and Al Rogers.

JIM THOMAS OUTDOORS   SYNDICATED

1976   A series for sportsmen, with emphasis on hunting and fishing, hosted by Jim Thomas.

THE JIMMIE RODGERS SHOW   NBC/CBS

31 MARCH 1959–8 SEPTEMBER 1959 (NBC); 16 JUNE 1969–1 SEPTEMBER 1969 (CBS)   Country and western singer Jimmie Rodgers ("Honeycomb" was his biggest hit, recorded in 1957) hosted two variety series. The first was a half-hour show, which featured Connie Francis, the Kirby Stone Four, The Clay Warnick Singers, and the Buddy Morrow Orchestra. The second, an hour-long series, was a summer replacement for *The Carol Burnett Show,* and featured *Burnett* regulars Vicki Lawrence and Lyle Waggoner, plus Don Crichton, Bill Fanning, Nancy Austin, the Burgundy Street Singers, and the Frank Comstock Orchestra.

THE JIMMY DEAN SHOW   CBS/ABC/SYNDICATED

Daytime: 8 APRIL 1957–26 JUNE 1959 (CBS); *Nighttime:* 22 JUNE 1957–14 SEPTEMBER 1957 (CBS); 19 SEPTEMBER 1963–1 APRIL 1966 (ABC); 1974 (SYNDICATED)   Country and western singer Jimmy Dean first hosted a local show on WTOP-TV in Washington, D.C. He attracted network attention and was given a daytime spot in the spring of 1957—the early-morning show originated from Washington and was aired six days a week for part of its two-year run. During the summer of 1957 Dean hosted a Saturday-night variety show, returning to the daytime grind that fall. Assisting him were Jan Crockett, Mary Klick, Jo Davis, ventriloquist Alex Houston, the Texas Wildcats, the Country Lads, the Noteworthies, and the Joel Herron Orchestra. In 1963 Dean hosted a prime-time hour variety series on ABC, which lasted three seasons. Regulars included Karen Morrow, Molly Bee, Chuck McCann, the Chuck Cassey Singers, and Rowlf the Muppet, the first of the puppet creations of Jim Henson to be featured on national TV (Rowlf was operated by Jim Henson and Frank Oznowicz).

JIMMY DURANTE PRESENTS THE LENNON SISTERS HOUR ABC
26 SEPTEMBER 1969–4 JULY 1970   Hour-long variety series starring seventy-six-year-old Jimmy Durante and the singing Lennon Sisters (Dianne, Janet, Kathy, and Peggy), who were featured on *The Lawrence Welk Show* for many years. Executive producer: Harold Cohen. Producers: Bernie Kukoff and Jeff Harris.

THE JIMMY DURANTE SHOW NBC
2 OCTOBER 1954–23 JUNE 1956   This half-hour variety show was seen on Saturday nights; during its first season it alternated with *The Donald O'Connor Show*. Joining "The Schnozz" were three of his long-time compatriots—Eddie Jackson, his former vaudeville partner (together with the late Lou Clayton), pianist Jules Buffano, and drummer Jack Roth. The show was set at the Club Durant, and also featured the Durante Girls.

JIMMY HUGHES, ROOKIE COP DUMONT
8 MAY 1953–3 JULY 1953   Half-hour crime show starring William Redfield as Jimmy Hughes, a young Korean War veteran who joined the New York police force, hoping to find the slayers of his father, also a cop. The cast also included Rusty Lane as Inspector Ferguson, Jimmy's mentor, and Wendy Drew as Jimmy's sister. Barry Shear directed the series.

THE JIMMY STEWART SHOW NBC
19 SEPTEMBER 1971–27 AUGUST 1972   Situation comedy starring Jimmy Stewart as Jim Howard, professor of anthropology at Josiah Kessel College, a man caught in the generation gap. Also featured were Julie Adams as his wife, Martha Howard; Jonathan Daly as P. J. Howard, their twenty-nine-year-old son; Ellen Geer as Wendy, P. J.'s wife; Kirby Furlong as Jake, P. J. and Wendy's eight-year-old son; Dennis Larson as Teddy, Jim and Martha's eight-year-old son and Jake's uncle; and John McGiver as Luther Quince, a faculty colleague of Jim's. Like many other major film stars, Jimmy Stewart seemed unable to find the right vehicle for himself on TV; neither this show nor his second series—*Hawkins*—caught on with viewers. Warner Brothers produced the series.

JIMMY SWAGGART SYNDICATED
1977–   Half-hour religious show hosted by evangelist Jimmy Swaggart and produced by the Jimmy Swaggart Evangelistic Association in Baton Rouge, Louisiana.

THE JO STAFFORD SHOW
CBS/SYNDICATED

2 FEBRUARY 1954–28 JUNE 1955 (CBS); 1962 (SYNDICATED) Jo Stafford, whose recording career began in 1944 (her biggest hit was probably "You Belong to Me" in 1952), hosted a fifteen-minute musical show seen Tuesdays after the network news. She was backed up by the Starlighters, and music was provided by the orchestra led by her husband, Paul Weston. In 1962 she hosted a second musical series, taped in London, and distributed by ITC.

THE JOAN EDWARDS SHOW
DUMONT

4 JULY 1950–24 OCTOBER 1950 A twice-weekly, fifteen-minute musical series hosted by Joan Edwards. Martin Goodman was the producer, Dick Sandwick the director.

THE JOAN RIVERS SHOW (THAT SHOW)
SYNDICATED

1969 Half-hour talk show hosted by comedienne Joan Rivers; typically, each show featured a celebrity guest and someone with an unusual hobby or talent.

JOANNE CARSON'S V.I.P.'S
SYNDICATED

1973 Half-hour talk show set in a kitchen, hosted by Joanne Carson, the second wife (and second ex-wife) of America's foremost talk show host, Johnny Carson.

JOE AND MABEL
CBS

20 SEPTEMBER 1955–25 SEPTEMBER 1956 Half-hour filmed sitcom about a New York cabbie and his marriage-minded girlfriend. With Larry Blyden as Joe Sparton; Nita Talbot as Mabel Stooler, a manicurist; Luella Gear as Mrs. Stooler, Mabel's mother; Michael Mann as Sherman Stooler, Mabel's brother; and Shirl Conway as Dolly, a friend of Mabel's. Alex Gottlieb was producer and head writer of the show, which was directed by Ezra Stone (he'd played Henry Aldrich on radio) and packaged by David Susskind. The show was seen for only a few weeks during the fall of 1955, returning to the air 26 June 1956.

JOE AND SONS
CBS

9 SEPTEMBER 1975–13 JANUARY 1976 The only TV series set in Erie, Pennsylvania, *Joe and Sons* was a situation comedy about a widower and his two sons. With Richard Castellano as Joe Vitale, who ran a screw press; Barry Miller as Mark, the older son; Jimmy Baio as Nick, the younger son; Jerry Stiller as Gus Duzik, Joe's buddy; Bobbi Jordan as Estelle, Joe's neighbor; and Florence Stanley as Josephine, Joe's sister. Executive producer: Douglas S. Cramer. Producers: Bernie Kukoff and Jeff Harris.

JOE AND VALERIE   NBC

24 APRIL 1978–10 MAY 1978; 5 JANUARY 1979–19 JANUARY 1979 A
half-hour sitcom, *Joe and Valerie* surfaced for two short runs. The 1978
version took its cue from the film *Saturday Night Fever* and featured
disco sequences; the 1979 version abandoned the disco element and con-
centrated on the wedding plans of the two principals. With Paul Regina
as Joe Pizo, a young Brooklynite; Char Fontane as Valerie Sweetzer, his
dancing partner and fiancée; David Elliott as Joe's pal Paulie, a hearse
driver; Bill Beyers (1978) and Lloyd Alann (1979) as Joe's friend Frank;
Robert Costanzo as Joe's widowed father, Vince Pizo, a plumber; Pat
Benson (1978) and Arlene Golonka (1979) as Valerie's divorced mother,
Stella Sweetzer; and Donna Ponterotto as Valerie's friend, Thelma. Linda
Hope (daughter of Bob Hope) was the executive producer.

JOE FORRESTER   NBC

9 SEPTEMBER 1975–30 AUGUST 1976 An hour-long cop show which,
like CBS's *The Blue Knight,* told the story of a veteran patrolman. With
Lloyd Bridges as Officer Joe Forrester; Eddie Egan (a former New York
cop) as Sergeant Bernie Vincent; Pat Crowley as Georgia Cameron, Joe's
romantic interest; Dwan Smith as Jolene Jackson, one of Joe's street in-
formants; and Taylor Lacher as Detective Will Carson. On 6 May 1975,
the pilot for the series, "The Return of Joe Forrester," was shown on *Police Story.* David Gerber was executive producer of the series, which was
produced by Mark Rodgers and James H. Brown.

JOE GARAGIOLA'S MEMORY GAME   NBC

15 FEBRUARY 1971–30 JULY 1971 Daytime game show on which the
five contestants were shown lists of questions and answers, and then
quizzed by host Joe Garagiola.

THE JOE NAMATH SHOW   SYNDICATED

1969 Short-lived talk show cohosted by Joe Namath (then quarterback
for the New York Jets) and sportswriter Dick Schaap.

THE JOE PALOOKA STORY   SYNDICATED

1954 Ham Fisher's cartoon pugilist came to life briefly on television in
this low-budget syndicated series. It featured Joe Kirkwood, Jr., as Joe
Palooka, the honest and upright, if not quick-witted, boxing champ;
Cathy Downs as Ann Howe, his girlfriend; Sid Tomack as his manager,
Knobby Walsh; and "Slapsie" Maxie Rosenbloom as his pal, Humphrey
Pennyworth.

THE JOE PYNE SHOW   SYNDICATED

1965–1967 Characterized by its host as a "fist-in-the-mouth" talk show,
The Joe Pyne Show was a two-hour parade of eccentrics, crackpots, and

controversial guests. Chain-smoking Joe Pyne delighted in insulting most of his guests, as well as members of the studio audience, who were given the chance to state their views at the outset of each show. Pyne began his show locally in Los Angeles on KTTV and attracted attention from the beginning. During the Watts riots of 1965, a black militant guested; Pyne opened his desk drawer to reveal a revolver, whereupon the guest drew back his coat to show that he, too, was armed. Another guest, wanted by the police, was arrested on camera. George Lincoln Rockwell, head of the American Nazi Party, and Marguerite Oswald, mother of Lee Harvey Oswald, also appeared on the show. Robert Hayward was the producer.

JOEY AND DAD

CBS

6 JULY 1975–27 JULY 1975   A four-week summer replacement for *Cher*, starring singer-dancer Joey Heatherton and her father, Ray Heatherton, who was better known to many New Yorkers as host of a 1950s kids' show, *The Merry Mailman.* Other regulars included Henny Youngman, Pat Paulsen, and Pat Proft. Executive producers: Allan Blye and Bob Einstein. Producers: Bob Arnott, Coslough Johnson, and Stan Jacobson.

THE JOEY BISHOP SHOW

NBC/CBS

20 SEPTEMBER 1961–5 SEPTEMBER 1964 (NBC); 27 SEPTEMBER 1964–7 SEPTEMBER 1965 (CBS)   This situation comedy, produced by Danny Thomas's Bellmar Productions, changed both formats and networks during its four-year run. The pilot for the series, "Everything Happens to Me," was aired on Thomas's *Make Room for Daddy* on 27 March 1961. During the 1961–1962 season Joey played Joey Barnes, a publicist; he was unmarried. Also featured were Joe Flynn as Frank, his brother-in-law; Marlo Thomas (in her first continuing role) as Stella, Joey's sister, an aspiring actress; Virginia Vincent as his sister Betty; Warren Berlinger as his brother, Larry; Madge Blake as his mother, the widowed Mrs. Barnes; John Griggs as J. R. Willoughby, his boss; and Nancy Hadley as Barbara, Joey's girlfriend. A new format was adopted for the second season, and the show was retitled *The New Joey Bishop Show.* Bishop continued to play Joey Barnes, but Barnes was now a married man, employed as a nightclub comedian. Gone were all the old regulars, and joining the cast were Abby Dalton as his wife, Ellie; Guy Marks (1962–1963) as his manager, Freddy; Corbett Monica as Larry, his writer; Joe Besser as Mr. Jillson, his landlord; and Mary Treen (1963–1965) as Hilda, the nurse for Joey and Ellie's baby boy, Joey Jr. (played by Matthew David Smith). The second format lasted three seasons—two on NBC and one on CBS.

THE JOEY BISHOP SHOW

ABC

17 APRIL 1967–26 DECEMBER 1969   Comedian Joey Bishop took over the host's chair on ABC's late night talk show in 1967; the chair had first been occupied by Les Crane (when the show was known as *The Les*

Crane Show), and later by a succession of guest hosts (when it was called *Nightlife*). Though Bishop had had considerable experience as a talk show host, having substituted many times for NBC's Johnny Carson, he was unable to lure enough viewers away from the *Tonight* show; late in 1969 Bishop was succeeded by Dick Cavett. Bishop's sidekick for the two-and-a-half-year run was Regis Philbin, with music provided by Johnny Mann and His Merry Men.

THE JOHN BYNER COMEDY HOUR   CBS
1 AUGUST 1972–29 AUGUST 1972   Five-week summer variety hour hosted by comedian John Byner, featuring Patty Deutsch, R. G. Brown, Linda Sublette, Gary Miller, and Dennis Flannigan.

THE JOHN DAVIDSON SHOW   NBC/ABC
(THE KRAFT SUMMER MUSIC HALL)
6 JUNE 1966–29 AUGUST 1966 (NBC); 30 MAY 1969–5 SEPTEMBER 1969 (ABC); 24 MAY 1976–14 JUNE 1976 (NBC)   Singer John Davidson has hosted three prime-time variety hours. The first was titled *The Kraft Summer Music Hall* and featured George Carlin, the Lively Set, the 5 King Cousins, and Jackie and Gayle. The latter two shows were both known as *The John Davidson Show*. The 1969 show was taped in London and featured Rich Little, Mireille Mathieu, and Amy McDonald. The 1976 show featured comedian Pete Barbutti; its executive producers were Alan Bernard and Dick Clark.

THE JOHN FORSYTHE SHOW   NBC
13 SEPTEMBER 1965–29 AUGUST 1966   *The John Forsythe Show* began as a situation comedy, starring John Forsythe as Major John Foster, an Air Force veteran who inherited the Foster School for Girls from his late Aunt Victoria. Also featured were Elsa Lanchester as Miss Culver, the principal; Ann B. Davis as Miss Wilson, the gym teacher; Guy Marks as Ed Robbins, John's aide, formerly a sergeant. The students included Pamelyn Ferdin as Pamela; Darleen Carr as Kathy; Page Forsythe (John's daughter) as Marcia; Brook Forsythe (also John's daughter) as Norma Jean; Peggy Lipton (later of *Mod Squad*) as Joanna; Tracy Stratford as Susan; and Sara Ballantine as Janice. In midseason that format was scrapped, and the show changed from a sitcom to a spy show. It was explained that Major Foster had been "recalled" to active duty and had become a secret agent; all the regulars except for John Forsythe and Guy Marks were dropped. Peter Kortner produced the series.

THE JOHN GARY SHOW   CBS/SYNDICATED
22 JUNE 1966–7 SEPTEMBER 1966 (CBS); 1968 (SYNDICATED)   The first of pop singer John Gary's variety hours was a summer replacement for *The Danny Kaye Show* and featured the Mitchell Ayres Orchestra, the

Jimmy Joyce Singers, and the Jack Regas Dancers. The second show was a syndicated effort and featured Sammy Spear's Orchestra.

THE JOHNNY CARSON SHOW
CBS

30 JUNE 1955–29 MARCH 1956; 28 MAY 1956–28 SEPTEMBER 1956 Johnny Carson, who later became famous as the host of the *Tonight* show, also hosted two game shows (*Earn Your Vacation* and *Who Do You Trust*) as well as these two variety shows. The first show, a Thursday-night half-hour series, featured Jill Corey, Virginia Gibson, and Barbara Ruick. Broadcast from Hollywood, it went through several changes of directors and writers before expiring after thirty-nine weeks. Carson, aged thirty, then hosted a daytime half-hour show which replaced *The Robert Q. Lewis Show.* Also featured were Glenn Turnbull, Betty Holt, Tommy Leonetti, and the New Yorkers. Both programs showcased the young comedian's puckish style and frequently featured parodies of current films and commercials.

THE JOHNNY CASH SHOW
ABC

7 JUNE 1969–27 SEPTEMBER 1969; 21 JANUARY 1970–5 MAY 1971

JOHNNY CASH AND FRIENDS
CBS

29 AUGUST 1976–19 SEPTEMBER 1976 Both of Johnny Cash's variety series were taped at the Grand Ole Opry in Nashville. The first—*The Johnny Cash Show*—was introduced as a summer series and returned later as a midseason replacement. In addition to Cash it featured June Carter Cash (his wife), Carl Perkins, The Carter Family, the Statler Brothers, and the Tennessee Three. The second show—*Johnny Cash and Friends*—was a summer series and featured Cash, June Carter Cash, Steve Martin, Jim Varney, and Howard Mann. It was produced by Joseph Cates.

THE JOHNNY DUGAN SHOW
NBC

19 MAY 1952–5 SEPTEMBER 1952 Daytime variety half-hour, broadcast from Hollywood, featuring singers Johnny Dugan, Barbara Logan, and Arch Presby.

THE JOHNNY JOHNSTON SHOW
CBS

22 JANUARY 1951–9 FEBRUARY 1951 Short-lived, forty-five-minute daytime variety show with singers Johnny Johnston and Rosemary Clooney.

JOHNNY JUPITER
DUMONT/ABC

21 MARCH 1953–13 JUNE 1953 (DUMONT); 5 SEPTEMBER 1953–29 MAY 1954 (ABC) On this imaginative kids' show an Earthling was able to communicate with the inhabitants of Jupiter. On the DuMont version, Vaughn Taylor starred as Ernest P. Duckweather, a television studio jan-

itor who stumbled upon interplanetary TV. On the ABC version Wright King played Duckweather, who was then employed as a store clerk whose hobby was electronics. Jerry Coopersmith wrote and produced the series; Frank Bunetta directed. The Jupiterians were all puppets: Johnny Jupiter, B-12, and Major Domo, B-12's robot. Carl Harms was the puppeteer, and Gilbert Mack supplied the voices. Also featured on the latter version were Pat Peardon as Duckweather's girlfriend, and Cliff Hall as her father, Duckweather's boss.

JOHNNY MIDNIGHT SYNDICATED
1960 Standard crime show starring Edmond O'Brien as New York private eye Johnny Midnight. Also featured were Arthur Batanides as Sergeant Olivera; Barney Phillips as Lieutenant Geller; and Yuki Shimoda as Aki, Midnight's manservant. Jack Chertok produced the series.

JOHNNY OLSEN'S RUMPUS ROOM DUMONT
17 JANUARY 1949–4 JULY 1952 Daytime variety and audience participation show hosted by Johnny Olsen. Olsen is better remembered as the announcer on numerous game shows, including *What's My Line?* and *I've Got a Secret.*

JOHNNY RINGO CBS
1 OCTOBER 1959–29 SEPTEMBER 1960 Half-hour western starring Don Durant as Johnny Ringo, an ex-gunslinger who became the sheriff of an Arizona town and toted a seven-shooter. Also featured were Mark Goddard as his young deputy, Cully; Karen Sharpe as Ringo's girlfriend, Laura Thomas; and Terence de Marney as oldtimer Case Thomas, Laura's father, owner of the general store (Sharpe and de Marney were dropped from the cast in March 1960). Aaron Spelling produced the series for Four Star Films.

JOHNNY STACCATO
See STACCATO

THE JOHNS HOPKINS SCIENCE REVIEW DUMONT
3 OCTOBER 1950–20 APRIL 1953
JOHNS HOPKINS FILE 7 SYNDICATED
1956–1958 Lynn Poole, faculty member of Johns Hopkins University, hosted both of these public affairs shows, which were produced at WAAM-TV in Baltimore.

THE JOKER'S WILD CBS/SYNDICATED
4 SEPTEMBER 1972–13 JUNE 1975 (CBS); 1976– (SYNDICA-TED) Jack Barry hosts this game show on which two contestants take turns spinning devices that resemble slot machines and have the chance

to answer questions worth $50, $100, or $150. The first player to win $500 then has the chance to go for as much as $25,000. Barry's longtime partner, Dan Enright, is the executive producer of the series, which had a three-year daytime run on CBS before going into syndication. In 1980 a children's version appeared in syndication, titled *Joker! Joker!! Joker!!!*

THE JONATHAN WINTERS SHOW

NBC/CBS

2 OCTOBER 1956–25 JUNE 1957 (NBC); 27 DECEMBER 1967–22 MAY 1969 (CBS) Jonathan Winters, an inventive and improvisational funny man, appeared on many variety shows during the early 1950s, including *The Garry Moore Show* and *Tonight*. In 1955 he was a regular on a summer variety series, *And Here's the Show*. In the fall of 1956 he was given his own fifteen-minute show on Tuesdays before the evening news; this was the first network entertainment series to use videotape regularly. Late in 1967 he returned as host of a Wednesday-night variety hour, which replaced *Dundee and the Culhane*. Joining him were Abby Dalton (who often played his wife in sketches), Cliff Arquette (as Charley Weaver), Pamela Rodgers, Alice Ghostley, and Paul Lynde. Winters later starred in a syndicated show: see *The Wacky World of Jonathan Winters*.

JONNY QUEST
(THE ADVENTURES OF JONNY QUEST)

ABC/CBS/NBC

18 SEPTEMBER 1964–9 SEPTEMBER 1965 (ABC); 9 SEPTEMBER 1967–5 SEPTEMBER 1970 (CBS); 11 SEPTEMBER 1971–2 SEPTEMBER 1972 (NBC); 8 SEPTEMBER 1979–3 NOVEMBER 1979 (NBC) Hanna-Barbera cartoon series about a young boy—Jonny Quest—who accompanied his father, Dr. Benton Quest, a famous detective, on global adventures. Tim Matheson provided the voice of Jonny; John Stephenson was the voice of Benton. Like several other Hanna-Barbera shows (*The Jetsons, Top Cat,* etc.), *Jonny Quest* was seen in prime time on ABC, and on Saturday mornings over the other networks.

THE JOSEPH COTTEN SHOW
See ON TRIAL

JOSEPH SCHILDKRAUT PRESENTS

DUMONT

28 OCTOBER 1953–21 JANUARY 1954 Half-hour filmed dramatic anthology series hosted by, and occasionally starring, Austrian-born actor Joseph Schildkraut. Ray Benson produced the show and Barry Shear directed it.

JOSIE AND THE PUSSYCATS
(JOSIE AND THE PUSSYCATS IN OUTER SPACE)

CBS/NBC

12 SEPTEMBER 1970–31 AUGUST 1974 (CBS); 6 SEPTEMBER 1975–4 SEPTEMBER 1976 (NBC) Hanna-Barbera Saturday-morning cartoon show

about an all female rock group. From 1972 to 1974, the show was known as *Josie and the Pussycats in Outer Space*—in which the group accidentally blasted off into space.

JOURNEY THROUGH LIFE · CBS
30 MARCH 1953–2 APRIL 1954 Tom Reddy hosted this daytime show on which married couples talked about their lives together.

JOURNEY TO ADVENTURE · SYNDICATED
1954– Gunther Less hosts this long-running half-hour travelogue. The series is produced by Sheridan-Elson Communications, using film from around the world, and is distributed by B. R. Syndication.

JOURNEY TO THE CENTER OF THE EARTH · ABC
9 SEPTEMBER 1967–6 SEPTEMBER 1969 Saturday-morning cartoon show derived from Jules Verne's inner space novel.

JOURNEY TO THE UNKNOWN · ABC
26 SEPTEMBER 1968–30 JANUARY 1969 Undistinguished science fiction anthology hour, produced in England.

JUBILEE U.S.A.
See OZARK JUBILEE

JUDD FOR THE DEFENSE · ABC
8 SEPTEMBER 1967–19 SEPTEMBER 1969 Standard courtroom drama, starring Carl Betz as lawyer Clinton Judd and Stephen Young as his associate, Ben Caldwell. Executive producer: Paul Monash.

JUDGE FOR YOURSELF (THE FRED ALLEN SHOW) · NBC
18 AUGUST 1953–11 MAY 1954 Prime-time game show that began with Fred Allen as host and featured a panel of three celebrities and three members of the studio audience which judged talent acts; during its early weeks it was also known as *The Fred Allen Show*. In January the format was changed as Dennis James took over the hosting duties: The panel rated songs, which were performed by Kitty Kallen and Bob Carroll and the Skylarks. The series was a Mark Goodson–Bill Todman Production.

JUDGE ROY BEAN · SYNDICATED
1956 Half-hour western set in Langtry, Texas, a town named for actress Lillie Langtry. Starring Edgar Buchanan as Judge Roy Bean, "the law west of the Pecos." With Jack Beutel as Jeff Sanders, his right-hand man; Jackie Loughery as Lettie, his niece; and Russell Hayden as Steve, a Texas ranger.

THE JUDY GARLAND SHOW

CBS

29 SEPTEMBER 1963–29 MARCH 1964   CBS had high hopes for this musical hour, but backstage problems and competition from NBC's *Bonanza* (the number-two-rated show that season) combined to ensure its doom. Much was done to keep the star happy—Judy Garland's dressing room even had a yellow brick road painted on it. Taping began in June 1963 with George Schlatter as executive producer; network officials, however, were unhappy after watching previews of the first shows, and Schlatter was replaced after five hours had been completed (the shows were not broadcast in the order in which they had been taped). Norman Jewison, who had produced and directed many musical-comedy specials, became the new executive produucer and Gary Smith the new producer. Mort Lindsey lasted through the entire season as musical director, but Mel Tormé, an old friend of Garland's who had been hired to do her vocal arrangements, left in the winter after Bobby Cole had been brought aboard. Despite the production problems, there were several noteworthy shows, including one which featured Ethel Merman and Barbra Streisand, another with Danny Kaye, one with Garland's two daughters (Lorna Luft and Liza Minnelli), and one or two solo concerts. Mel Tormé also appeared occasionally, and Jerry Van Dyke was featured as a regular.

THE JUDY LYNN SHOW

SYNDICATED

1969–1971   Half-hour country-and-western music show, hosted by singer Judy Lynn.

JUDY SPLINTERS

NBC

13 JUNE 1949–30 JUNE 1950   This weekday puppet show originated from Los Angeles. The puppeteer, Shirley Dinsdale, was TV's first Emmy winner.

JUKE-BOX

SYNDICATED

1978   Half-hour rock music show hosted by Twiggy, the famous fashion model of the 1960s.

JUKEBOX JURY

ABC/SYNDICATED

13 SEPTEMBER 1953–28 MARCH 1954 (ABC); 1959 (SYNDICATED)   Peter Potter hosted this game show on which a celebrity panel rated new records and predicted whether each recording would be a hit or a miss. For many years the show was seen locally in Los Angeles.

JULIA

NBC

17 SEPTEMBER 1968–25 MAY 1971   The first TV series since *Beulah* to star a black woman, *Julia* was a half-hour situation comedy about a widowed nurse trying to raise her young son. Diahann Carroll, a singer with

motion picture experience, starred as Julia Baker; her husband, an Air Force pilot, had been killed in Vietnam, and she took a job as a nurse at an aerospace company in Los Angeles. Also featured were Marc Copage (who was six when the show began) as her son, Corey; Lloyd Nolan as Dr. Morton Chegley, her boss; Lurene Tuttle as Hannah Yarby, chief nurse at the plant; Michael Link as Earl J. Waggedorn, Corey's best friend; Betty Beaird as Marie Waggedorn, Earl's mom; Hank Brandt as Leonard Waggedorn, Earl's dad; Eddie Quillan as Eddie Edwards, a plant employee; Mary Wickes as Melba Chegley, Dr. Chegley's wife; Ned Glass as Julia's landlord, Sol Cooper; Alison Mills (1968–1969) as Carol Deering, a mother's helper who assisted Julia; Virginia Capers (1968–1969) as Mrs. Deering, Carol's mother; Paul Winfield (1969–1970) as Julia's occasional boyfriend, Paul Cameron; Fred Williamson (1970–1971) as Julia's boyfriend, Steve Bruce, a widower; Stephanie James as Kim, Steve's four-year-old daughter; Janear Hines (1970–1971) as babysitter Roberta; and Richard Steele (1970–1971) as Richard, a friend of Corey's. Produced by Hal Kanter for 20th Century-Fox.

JULIA CHILD & COMPANY   PBS
7 OCTOBER 1978–   Half-hour cooking show, hosted by Julia Child, the star of *The French Chef*.

THE JULIE ANDREWS HOUR   ABC
13 SEPTEMBER 1972–28 APRIL 1973 Unsuccessful variety hour hosted by musical comedy star Julie Andrews and featuring Alice Ghostley and Rich Little. Produced by Nick Vanoff, the show was packaged by British impressario Sir Lew Grade's ITC operation.

THE JULIUS LaROSA SHOW   CBS/NBC
27 JUNE 1955–23 SEPTEMBER 1955 (CBS); 14 JULY 1956–4 AUGUST 1956; 15 JUNE 1957–7 SEPTEMBER 1957 (NBC) After his dismissal from *Arthur Godfrey Time*, singer Julius LaRosa made guest appearances on many shows and hosted his own variety shows for three summers. In 1955 he was seen for fifteen minutes on Mondays, Wednesdays, and Fridays following the network news, backed by the Debutones. In 1956 and 1957, he replaced Perry Como for the summer.

THE JUNE ALLYSON SHOW   CBS
(THE DuPONT SHOW STARRING JUNE ALLYSON)
21 SEPTEMBER 1959–12 JUNE 1961 Half-hour dramatic anthology series hosted by, and occasionally featuring, June Allyson. The series was filmed at Four Star Films, a studio founded by Allyson's husband, Dick Powell, and others. Notable guest appearances included those by Ginger Rogers ("The Tender Shoot," 19 October 1959) and Harpo Marx ("Silent Panic," 22 December 1960, one of his last TV appearances).

THE JUNE HAVOC SHOW   SYNDICATED
1964   Hour-long talk show hosted by June Havoc (sister of Gypsy Rose Lee).

JUNGLE BOY (ADVENTURES OF A JUNGLE BOY)   SYNDICATED
1958   Filmed on location in Kenya, this children's adventure series starred fourteen-year-old Michael Carr Hartley as Boy, the only survivor of a plane crash in Africa, who generally fended for himself in the wilds. Also on hand was Ronald Adam as Dr. Laurence, a research scientist.

JUNGLE JIM   SYNDICATED
1955   Not to be confused with *Ramar of the Jungle, Jungle Jim* was based on the comic strip and starred former Olympian Johnny Weissmuller as an African guide. Also featured were Martin Huston as Skipper, his son; Norman Fredric as Kassim, his aide (Fredric was later known as Dean Fredericks and starred in *Steve Canyon*); and Tamba the chimp.

JUNGLE MACABRE   SYNDICATED
1953   A series of fifteen-minute wildlife films.

JUNIOR ALMOST ANYTHING GOES   ABC
11 SEPTEMBER 1976–4 SEPTEMBER 1977   Kids' game show, based on *Almost Anything Goes,* featuring teams of children representing different localities. Hosted by Soupy Sales.

JUNIOR HI-JINX   CBS
2 MARCH 1952–25 MAY 1952   Sunday-morning children's show hosted by Warren Wright and his puppet, Willie the Worm. The show was seen locally in Philadelphia for several seasons in addition to its brief network run.

JUNIOR PRESS CONFERENCE   ABC
23 NOVEMBER 1952–8 NOVEMBER 1953   A public affairs program for young people on which newsmakers were quizzed by a panel of children. Similar shows were also presented by the other networks: see, for example, *The New York Times Youth Forum* and *Youth Wants to Know.*

JUST FRIENDS   CBS
4 MARCH 1979–11 AUGUST 1979   Officially titled *Stockard Channing in Just Friends,* this half-hour sitcom starred Stockard Channing as Susan Hughes, a woman who left her husband in Boston to find a new life for herself in Los Angeles. Also featured were Mimi Kennedy as her sister, Victoria; Gerrit Graham as Leonard Scribner, her new neighbor; Lou Criscuolo as Milt D'Angelo, owner of the Beverly Hills Fountain of

Youth Health Spa, where Susan got a job; Albert Insinnia as Angelo D'Angelo, Milt's son; and Sydney Goldsmith as Coral, a coworker at the health spa. Executive producer: David Debin for Little Bear Productions. Though *Just Friends* left the air in August 1979, it remained in production as a potential midseason replacement.

THE JUST GENERATION
PBS

1 OCTOBER 1972–24 DECEMBER 1972   Thirteen-part informational series on the law, hosted by Howard Miller, with help from the Ace Trucking Company.

JUSTICE
NBC

8 APRIL 1954–25 MARCH 1956   Half-hour dramatic series about lawyers for the Legal Aid Society of New York. With Dane Clark (1954–1955) and William Prince (1955–1956) as Richard Adams; and Gary Merrill (1954–1955) as Jason Tyler.

JUVENILE JURY
NBC/CBS/SYNDICATED

3 APRIL 1947–28 SEPTEMBER 1953 (NBC); 11 OCTOBER 1953–14 SEPTEMBER 1954 (CBS); 2 JANUARY 1955–27 MARCH 1955 (NBC); 1970 (SYNDICATED)   A panel of youngsters dispensed unrehearsed advice to questions sent in by viewers. Jack Barry, who created the series and brought it to radio in 1946, hosted the several television versions and produced it with his partner, Dan Enright. The duo later went into game shows, producing such programs as *Twenty-One, Tic Tac Dough,* and *The Joker's Wild.* Barry also hosted a popular children's show during the 1950s: see *Winky Dink and You.*

THE KAISER ALUMINUM HOUR
NBC

3 JULY 1956–18 JUNE 1957   This hour-long dramatic anthology series alternated with *Armstrong Circle Theater* on Tuesdays and is one of the several dramatic shows which comprised TV's so-called "Golden Age." During its one-season run, it employed the directing talents of men such as Worthington Miner, Franklin Schaffner, Fielder Cook, and George Roy Hill. Notable presentations included: "The Army Game," with Paul Newman, Philip Abbott, and George Grizzard (3 July); a modern version of "Antigone," with Claude Rains and Marisa Pavan (11 September); Steven Gethers's "The Rag Jungle," with Paul Newman (20 November); and "The Deadly Silence," with Harry Guardino (21 May).

KALEIDOSCOPE
SYNDICATED

1953   John Kieran hosted this fifteen-minute series of films about science and nature.

KALEIDOSCOPE
NBC

2 NOVEMBER 1958–17 MAY 1959 This wide-ranging Sunday-afternoon series was described by the network as "an ambitious new experimental series." Some shows were produced by the NBC news department, others by the program department. Former *Twenty-One* winner Charles Van Doren hosted the series, which alternated biweekly with *Omnibus.*

THE KALLIKAKS
NBC

3 AUGUST 1977–31 AUGUST 1977 Uninspired sitcom about a family which moved from Appalachia to California. With David Huddleston as J. T. Kallikak, gas station proprietor; Edie McClurg as Venus, his wife; Patrick J. Petersen as Junior, their son; Bonnie Ebsen as Bobbi Lou, their daughter, who worked at a nearby fried chicken stand; and Peter Palmer as Oscar, J. T.'s employee. Created by Roger Price and Stanley Ralph Ross, the series was produced by George Yanok.

KAREN
NBC

5 OCTOBER 1964–30 AUGUST 1965 *Karen* began as one segment of *90 Bristol Court,* a troika of sitcoms all set at the same apartment complex. *Karen*'s two cotenants—*Harris Against the World* and *Tom, Dick and Mary*—were both evicted by the network in midseason, and *Karen* continued alone for the remainder of the year. The show featured Debbie Watson as typical teenager Karen Scott; Richard Denning as her dad, Steve; Mary LaRoche as her mom, Barbara; Gina Gillespie as her little sister, Mimi; Bernadette Withers as her friend Janis; Trudi Ames as her friend Candy; Teddy Quinn as her friend Peter; and Murray MacLeod as her friend Spider. Guy Raymond, as Cliff Murdock, the building handyman, was featured in all three segments of *90 Bristol Court.* Richard Dreyfuss, later to star in such colossal films as *American Graffiti, Jaws,* and *Close Encounters of the Third Kind,* was also featured occasionally as David, another of Karen's many friends.

KAREN
ABC

30 JANUARY 1975–19 JUNE 1975 Topical sitcom, set in Washington, D.C. With Karen Valentine as Karen Angelo, a young lobbyist for Open America, a progressive citizens' lobby; Dena Dietrich as Dena Madison, one of her coworkers; Charles Lane as irascible Dale Busch, the head of Open America (Denver Pyle played Busch in the premiere episode); Will Seltzer as Adam Cooperman, the office boy; Aldine King as Karen's roommate, Cissy Peterson, an FBI agent; Oliver Clark as Jerry Siegel, a neighbor; Alix Elias as Cheryl Siegel, Jerry's wife; and Joseph Stern as Ernie Stone, a friend of Karen's. Executive producers: Gene Reynolds and Larry Gelbart (producers of *M*A*S*H*) for 20th Century-Fox.

KATE LOVES A MYSTERY (MRS. COLUMBO)   NBC

26 FEBRUARY 1979–29 MARCH 1979; 9 AUGUST 1979–6 SEPTEMBER 1979; 18 OCTOBER 1979–6 DECEMBER 1979   An hour crime show starring Kate Mulgrew as Kate Columbo, wife of Lieutenant Columbo (the character played by Peter Falk on *Columbo;* Columbo's wife was never seen on his series, and he was never seen on hers), a part-time reporter for the *Weekly Advertiser* and an amateur sleuth. The show premiered under the title *Mrs. Columbo* in February 1979, and underwent several changes of title between September and October. It was first changed to *Kate Columbo,* then to *Kate the Detective,* before *Kate Loves a Mystery* was selected just before the October return date. Also featured were Lili Haydn as Jenny, the Columbos' young daughter; Henry Jones as Mr. Alden, publisher of the newspaper; and Don Stroud (fall 1979–   ) as Sergeant Varick. The series was produced by Universal TV.

KATE McSHANE   CBS

10 SEPTEMBER 1975–12 NOVEMBER 1975   An early fatality of the 1975–1976 season, *Kate McShane* perished opposite ABC's *Starsky and Hutch.* It starred Anne Meara as Kate McShane, a gutsy lawyer; Sean McClory as Pat McShane, her father, an ex-cop who worked as Kate's investigator; and Charles Haid as Edmond McShane, her brother, a Jesuit priest who doubled as a law professor. E. Jack Neuman, who created the series, was its executive producer; Robert Stambler and Robert Foster produced it. The pilot was televised 11 April 1975.

THE KATE SMITH HOUR   NBC
25 SEPTEMBER 1950–18 JUNE 1954
THE KATE SMITH EVENING HOUR   NBC
19 SEPTEMBER 1951–11 JUNE 1952
THE KATE SMITH SHOW   CBS

25 JANUARY 1960–18 JULY 1960   Kate Smith, the solid singer who was the butt of countless "fat" jokes throughout her show business career, hosted several radio programs from 1930 through 1951. Her first, and most successful, television program—*The Kate Smith Hour*—premiered in 1950 and ran four years in a late afternoon slot, Mondays through Fridays. Appearing with her was her long-time manager, Ted Collins, who also produced the show with Barry Wood. The show was usually divided into discrete fifteen-minute segments, the composition of which changed over the years. Typical segments included "The Cracker Barrel," in which guests were interviewed; "America Sings," in which Smith and her guests performed musical numbers; "The House in the Garden," a continuing drama which was an outgrowth of *Fairmeadows, U.S.A.* (see also that title); "The World of Mr. Sweeney," a continuing comedy which later became a separate series (see also that title); "Ethel and Albert," a do-

mestic comedy which also became a separate series (see also that title). Kate Smith also hosted two prime-time series. The first, entitled *The Kate Smith Evening Hour,* was seen on Wednesdays during the 1951–1952 season; like the daytime show, it was directed by Greg Garrison, who later produced *The Dean Martin Show.* In 1960 she hosted a half-hour variety series on CBS, which also featured the Harry Simeone Chorus. After that she made a few guest appearances. She attracted attention in 1976 when she sang "God Bless America" at the Philadelphia Flyers' ice hockey games.

THE KATHI NORRIS SHOW

NBC

1 MAY 1950–9 OCTOBER 1951   Daytime talk show, primarily for women, hosted by Kathi Norris.

THE KATHRYN KUHLMAN SHOW
See I BELIEVE IN MIRACLES

KAY KYSER'S KOLLEGE OF MUSICAL KNOWLEDGE
See COLLEGE OF MUSICAL KNOWLEDGE

KAZ

CBS

10 SEPTEMBER 1978–19 AUGUST 1979   An hour crime show set in Los Angeles, starring Ron Leibman as Martin Kazinski, a lawyer who earned his degree the hard way—while serving time in prison. Also featured were Patrick O'Neal as Samuel Bennett, the successful attorney who agreed to hire Kaz; Mark Withers as Peter Colcourt, a junior partner at Bennett's firm; Edith Atwater as Mrs. Fogel, the firm's chief secretary; Linda Carlson as Kaz's friend, newspaper reporter Katie McKenna; Dick O'Neill as Malloy, Kaz's streetwise friend; Gloria LeRoy as Mary Parnell, owner of the Starting Gate, a nightspot where Kaz relaxed by playing the drums; and George Wyner as Frank Revko, an assistant district attorney. Ron Leibman and Don Carlos Dunaway created the series; Lee Rich and Marc Merson were the executive producers for Lorimar Productions.

THE KEANE BROTHERS SHOW

CBS

12 AUGUST 1977–2 SEPTEMBER 1977   Four-week half-hour musical variety series, aimed principally at young viewers. Its hosts, brothers Tom and John Keane, aged thirteen and twelve, were reportedly the youngest people ever to host a prime-time series; both were talented musicians and singers. Also on hand were the Anita Mann Dancers. Pierre Cossette was the series' executive producer, Darryl Hickman its producer. The show was created by Woody Kling and developed by Don Kirshner with Norman Lear.

KEEFE BRASSELLE'S VARIETY GARDEN   CBS

25 JUNE 1963–17 SEPTEMBER 1963   Keefe Brasselle hosted this variety hour, a summer replacement for *The Garry Moore Show.* Regulars included Ann B. Davis, French singer Noelle Adam, former boxer Rocky Graziano, the Bill Foster Dancers, and Charles Sanford's Orchestra. Brasselle later developed three series for CBS in 1964 (*The Baileys of Balboa, The Cara Williams Show,* and *The Reporter*) before retiring from show business.

KEEP IT IN THE FAMILY   ABC

12 OCTOBER 1957–8 FEBRUARY 1958   Each week on this Saturday-night quiz show, two five-member families competed against each other. Keefe Brasselle was the first host but was succeeded by Bill Nimmo.

KEEP ON TRUCKIN'   ABC

12 JULY 1975–2 AUGUST 1975   Four-week summer comedy-variety series hosted by impressionist Fred Travalena and featuring a group of newcomers: Franklin Ajaye, Rhonda Bates, Kathrine Baumann, Jeannine Burnier, Didi Conn, Charles Fleischer, Wayland Flowers, Larry Ragland, Marion Ramsey, Rhilo, Jack Riley (he played Mr. Carlin on *The Bob Newhart Show*), Gailard Sartain, and Richard Lee Sung. Frank Peppiatt and John Aylesworth produced the series.

KEEP POSTED   DUMONT

9 OCTOBER 1951–18 JANUARY 1954   Topical issues were debated on this half-hour public affairs program, which was developed by Lawrence Spivak and moderated by Martha Rountree. The show was titled *Keep Posted* for its first two seasons, when it was sponsored by the *Saturday Evening Post* magazine. In May of 1953, after the *Post* dropped its sponsorship, the show was retitled *The Big Issue.*

KEEP TALKING   CBS/ABC

8 JULY 1958–24 JUNE 1959 (CBS); 29 OCTOBER 1959–3 MAY 1960 (ABC)   This prime-time game show featured two teams of celebrities; each team was provided with a secret phrase that was supposed to be inserted into a dialogue improvised by the competitors. At the end of each round, each team tried to identify the secret phrase given to the opponents. Monty Hall was the first host of the series; he was succeeded late in 1958 by Carl Reiner, who was in turn succeeded by Merv Griffin when the show switched networks. Often seen on the celebrity panel were Morey Amsterdam, Joey Bishop, Peggy Cass, Pat Carroll, Ilka Chase, and Danny Dayton.

THE KELLY MONTEITH SHOW   CBS

16 JUNE 1976–7 JULY 1976   Four-week half-hour variety series hosted
by comedian Kelly Monteith, also featuring Nellie Bellflower and Harry
Corden. Executive producer: Robert Tamplin. Producer: Ed Simmons.

KEN BERRY'S WOW   ABC

15 JULY 1972–12 AUGUST 1972   Five-week summer variety hour showcasing the singing and dancing talents of Ken Berry, former star of *Mayberry R.F.D.* Other regulars included Teri Garr, Billy Van, Laura Lacey,
Don Lane, Steve Martin, the New Seekers, the Jaime Rogers Dancers,
and the Jimmy Dale Orchestra. Alan Blye and Chris Bearde, producers
of *The Sonny and Cher Comedy Hour,* created the show.

THE KEN MURRAY SHOW   CBS

15 APRIL 1950–7 JUNE 1952; 8 FEBRUARY 1953–14 JUNE 1953
Vaudevillian Ken Murray hosted an hour-long variety show on Saturday
nights for two seasons; early in 1953 he returned to host a half-hour show
on Sundays, which alternated with *The Alan Young Show.* Also on hand
were comedienne Laurie Anders ("Ah love the wide open spaces!"),
Darla Hood (1950–1951, former star of the "Our Gang" comedies),
Anita Gordon (1951–1952), Art Lund, Johnny Johnston, and the Glamourlovelies.

KENTUCKY JONES   NBC

19 SEPTEMBER 1964–11 SEPTEMBER 1965   Dennis Weaver left the
Gunsmoke fold to star in this comedy-drama; he played Kentucky Jones,
a widowed veterinarian who became the guardian of a ten-year-old Chinese orphan. Also featured were Ricky Der as his ward, Dwight Eisenhower (Ike) Wong; Harry Morgan as Seldom Jackson, a former jockey who
assisted Dr. Jones on his ranch; Cherylene Lee as Annie Ng, Ike's friend;
Arthur Wong as Mr. Ng, her father; Keye Luke as Mr. Wong, a friend of
Dr. Jones; and Nancy Rennick as Miss Thorncroft, Ike's teacher.

KEY TO THE AGES   DUMONT

27 FEBRUARY 1955–22 MAY 1955   Half-hour cultural show hosted by
Dr. Theodore Low. Broadcast from Baltimore, the show received much
help from the Walters Art Gallery and the Enoch Pratt Free Library.

KEY TO THE MISSING   DUMONT

4 JULY 1948–23 SEPTEMBER 1949   Archdale Jones, "the finder of lost
persons," hosted this half-hour documentary series, on which he interviewed people who were searching for long-lost friends and relatives.

KEYHOLE   SYNDICATED
1961   A series of half-hour documentaries and pseudo-documentaries filmed all over the world, produced and narrated by Jack Douglas. Distributed by Ziv TV.

KHAN!   CBS
7 FEBRUARY 1975–28 FEBRUARY 1975   This hour-long crime show lasted only four weeks. It featured Khigh Dhiegh (who had played Wo Fat, Steve McGarrett's archenemy, on *Hawaii Five-O*) as Khan, a private detective in San Francisco's Chinatown; Vic Tayback as Lieutenant Gubbins of the San Francisco police; Irene Yah-Ling Sun as Khan's daughter, Anna, a biophysics student at San Francisco State; and Evan Kim as Kim, Khan's son. Laurence Heath produced the series.

KID GLOVES   CBS
24 FEBRUARY 1951–18 AUGUST 1951   Broadcast from Philadelphia, *Kid Gloves* was a boxing show for very young boxers. Each week boys aged three and up fought each other in abbreviated three-round contests (each round lasted only thirty seconds). Bill Sears and John "Ox" Da Groza hosted the series, which was produced and directed by Alan Bergman.

KID POWER   ABC
16 SEPTEMBER 1972–1 SEPTEMBER 1974   Cartoon series based on the comic strip *Wee Pals*. The show was seen Saturday mornings during the 1972–1973 season, and reruns were broadcast Sunday mornings during the 1973–1974 season.

KIDS AND COMPANY   DUMONT
1 SEPTEMBER 1951–1 JUNE 1952   Saturday-morning kids' show cohosted by Johnny Olsen (who was also hosting *Johnny Olsen's Rumpus Room* five days a week) and cartoonist Ham Fisher, creator of *Joe Palooka*.

KIDS ARE PEOPLE TOO   ABC
10 SEPTEMBER 1978–   Sunday-morning magazine series for children, hosted by Bob McAllister until January 1979, when Michael Young took over.

THE KIDS FROM C.A.P.E.R.   NBC
11 SEPTEMBER 1976–3 SEPTEMBER 1977   Live-action Saturday kids' show about the four young operatives of C.A.P.E.R. (Civilian Authority for the Protection of Everyone Regardless). With John Lansing as Doc; Steve Bonino as P. T.; Cosie Costa as Bugs; and Biff Warren as Doomsday. Don Kirshner and Alan Landsburg produced the series.

KIDSWORLD SYNDICATED
1978 A half-hour magazine series for children, produced by the Behrens Company.

KIERNAN'S CORNER ABC
16 AUGUST 1948–25 APRIL 1949 Half-hour interview show hosted by Walter Kiernan.

THE KILLY CHALLENGE SYNDICATED
1969–1970 On this filmed sports series, former Olympic skiing champion Jean-Claude Killy faced challengers in head-to-head races for prizes of $10,000.

KIMBA THE FRIENDLY LION SYNDICATED
1967 Japanese-produced cartoon series about a white lion, Kimba, benevolent ruler of an African kingdom.

THE KING FAMILY SHOW ABC
23 JANUARY 1965–8 JANUARY 1966; 12 MARCH 1969–10 SEPTEMBER 1969 This wholesome musical show featured the several dozen members of the King clan, none of whom was named King—all were descended from William King Driggs, who organized a family musical group in the 1930s. Three of his daughters—Maxine, Alyce, and Luise—later toured professionally as the King Sisters. After regrouping at a family reunion, the clan put on a show at Brigham Young University, which eventually led to an appearance on *The Hollywood Palace* and, later, to the first *King Family Show,* an hour-long series that replaced *The Outer Limits* early in 1965. The show was revived in 1969, this time in a half-hour version, to replace *Turn-On;* by that time thirty-six Kings appeared on camera, and one member—Tina Cole—was also a regular on *My Three Sons.*

KING KONG ABC
10 SEPTEMBER 1966–31 AUGUST 1969 Saturday-morning cartoon series in which the giant ape was friendly and battled evil together with Professor Bond and his children; reruns were shown on Sunday mornings during the 1968–1969 season.

KING LEONARDO NBC
15 OCTOBER 1960–28 SEPTEMBER 1963 Saturday-morning cartoon series about King Leonardo, beneficent leonine ruler of a peaceable African kingdom, and his pal, Odie Cologne, a skunk; together they battled two sinister villains, Biggy Rat and Itchy Brother. For part of its network run the show was titled *King Leonardo and His Short Subjects,* and in syndication it was known as *The King and Odie.*

KING OF DIAMONDS   SYNDICATED
1961   Half-hour adventure series from Ziv TV, starring Broderick
Crawford as Johnny King, chief of security for the diamond industry.
Also featured was Ray Hamilton as his right-hand man, Casey O'Brien.

KING OF KENSINGTON   SYNDICATED
1976   Canadian sitcom, presumably inspired by *All in the Family*. With
Al Waxman as Larry King, typical blue-collar worker; Fiona Reid as
Kathy, his wife; and Helene Winston as Gladys, Larry's live-in mother.
Created and developed by Perry Rosemond.

KINGDOM OF THE SEA   SYNDICATED
1957   Half-hour documentaries about marine life, narrated by Robert
Stevenson.

KING'S CROSSROADS   ABC
10 OCTOBER 1951–5 OCTOBER 1952   Film shorts, hosted by Carl King.

KING'S ROW   ABC
13 SEPTEMBER 1955–17 JANUARY 1956   *King's Row* was one segment of
Warner Brothers Presents, which with *Casablanca* and *Cheyenne,* heralded Warner Brothers' entry into TV series production; only *Cheyenne*
survived the first season. *King's Row,* set in a town of that name at the
turn of the century, starred twenty-eight-year-old Jack Kelly (later star of
Maverick) as Dr. Parris Mitchell, a psychiatrist. Also featured were Victor Jory as his mentor, Dr. Tower; Robert Horton as Drake; and Nan
Leslie as Randy. Only seven or eight episodes were aired.

KINGSTON: CONFIDENTIAL   NBC
23 MARCH 1977–10 AUGUST 1977   Hour-long adventure series starring
Raymond Burr as R. B. Kingston, a senior journalist for the Frazier
News Group, a San Francisco–based consortium of newspapers and
broadcasters. With Art Hindle as Tony Marino, a young reporter; Pamela Hensley as Beth Kelly, another young reporter; and Linda Galloway as
Linda, Kingston's secretary. Executive producer: David Victor.

THE KIRBY STONE QUINTET   CBS
9 NOVEMBER 1949–23 JUNE 1950   Instrumental selections were played
by the Kirby Stone Quintet on this fifteen-minute series that was seen several times a week at 7 p.m.

KIT CARSON (THE ADVENTURES OF KIT CARSON)   SYNDICATED
1951   Bill Williams starred as Kit Carson, the famous scout, in this half-
hour western from Revue Productions; Don Diamond costarred as his

sidekick, El Toro. The series was directed by Richard Irving and Norman Lloyd.

KITTY FOYLE   NBC
13 JANUARY 1958–27 JUNE 1958   Daytime serial about an Irish secretary from Philadelphia who fell for a wealthy fellow; the series started on radio in 1942. On TV Kathleen Murray starred as Kitty Foyle. Also featured were Judy Lewis (as her friend, Molly Scharf), Billy Redfield, Ralph Dunne (as Kitty's father), Ginger MacManus, Marie Worsham, Lee Bergere, and eleven-year-old Patty Duke. Both the radio and TV versions were derived from the story by Christopher Morley.

KLONDIKE   NBC
10 OCTOBER 1960–13 FEBRUARY 1961   Low-budget adventure series set in Skagway, Alaska, during the Gold Rush of 1898. With Ralph Taeger as Mike Halliday, a young adventurer; Mari Blanchard as Kathy O'Hara, hotel owner; James Coburn as Jeff Durain, a fast-talking adventurer; and Joi Lansing as Goldie. In midseason the format was drastically changed—Taeger and Coburn were retained but were moved up to the twentieth century and south to Mexico: see *Acapulco*. William Conrad produced the series.

KNOCKOUT   NBC
3 OCTOBER 1977–21 APRIL 1978   Daytime game show hosted by Arte Johnson and featuring three contestants. The object of the game was to score the word "Knockout" by winning the eight letters one or two at a time. A player earned one letter by identifying the one item among four which did not belong with the others; the player could then earn additional letters by identifying the common feature of the items or by successfully challenging another player to do so. The winning contestant then played a bonus round for a top prize of $5,000. The show was a Ralph Edwards Production.

KOBBS CORNER   CBS
22 SEPTEMBER 1948–15 JUNE 1949   Wednesday-night half-hour variety series set at a general store, run by host Hope Emerson. In its earliest weeks the show was titled *Korn Kobblers*.

KODIAK   ABC
13 SEPTEMBER 1974–11 OCTOBER 1974   One of the first casualties of the 1974–1975 season, *Kodiak* was clobbered in the ratings by *Sanford and Son*. It starred Clint Walker (seldom seen on TV since his days as Cheyenne) as Cal McKay, an Alaskan cop nicknamed "Kodiak." Also featured were Abner Biberman as Abraham Lincoln Imhook, his Eskimo

partner; Maggie Blye as Mandy, the dispatcher. Stan Shpetner, who created the series with Anthony Lawrence, was the producer.

KOJAK CBS

24 OCTOBER 1973–15 APRIL 1978   An internationally popular crime show, *Kojak* starred Telly Savalas as Lieutenant Theo Kojak, a savvy but incorruptible cop assigned to Manhattan South. Savalas first played the role in a 1973 TV movie, *The Marcus-Nelson Murders,* written by Abby Mann; the movie was based on the Wylie-Hoffert murders, which occurred in 1963. Savalas, who had often played heavies before landing the Kojak role, first appeared on television in an episode of the *Armstrong Circle Theater* in 1959; before that he had worked as a producer at WABC in New York, and had also assisted casting directors in locating foreign-speaking performers. Though he had much television and film experience (including an Academy Award nomination as Best Supporting Actor in *The Bird Man of Alcatraz*), it was not until his role as the Tootsie Pop–sucking Kojak that he became a superstar. Other regulars on the series included Kevin Dobson as Detective Bobby Crocker, Kojak's earnest right-hand man; Dan Frazer as Detective Captain Frank McNeil, his weary boss; George Savalas (Telly's brother) as Detective Stavros (George was billed as Demosthenes—his middle name—during the first two seasons); Mark Russell as Detective Saperstein; Vince Conti as Detective Rizzo; and Borah Silver as Detective Prince. Matthew Rapf was the executive producer and Jack Laird the supervising producer for Universal Television.

KOLCHAK: THE NIGHT STALKER
See THE NIGHT STALKER

THE KOPYKATS
See THE ABC COMEDY HOUR

KORG: 70,000 B.C. ABC

7 SEPTEMBER 1974–31 AUGUST 1975   Essentially a Neanderthal version of *The Waltons, Korg: 70,000 B.C.* was a live-action Saturday-morning show from Hanna-Barbera Productions about a Stone Age family of modest means. With Jim Malinda as Korg; Bill Ewing as Bok; Naomi Pollack as Mara; Christopher Man as Tane; Charles Morteo as Tor; and Janelle Pransky as Ree. Burgess Meredith narrated.

THE KRAFT MUSIC HALL NBC

8 OCTOBER 1958–20 MAY 1959; 13 SEPTEMBER 1967–12 MAY 1971   Kraft Foods sponsored this musical variety program. During the 1958–1959 season it was a half-hour show, hosted by Milton Berle. From 1959 until 1963 Kraft continued to sponsor musical variety shows, but

they were known more commonly by other titles: see *The Dave King Show* and *The Perry Como Show*. The 1967 version of *The Kraft Music Hall* was an hour show, which lasted four seasons. It was hosted by a guest celebrity each week, except during the summer of 1969, when Tony Sandler and Ralph Young cohosted it; Judy Carne was also featured on that summer series. Don Ho hosted the show during the latter weeks of the summer of 1969.

KRAFT SUSPENSE THEATRE   NBC

10 OCTOBER 1963–9 SEPTEMBER 1965   Hour-long mystery anthology series, sponsored by Kraft Foods. Katharine Ross made her TV dramatic debut in one episode, "Are There Any More Out There Like You?" (7 November 1963).

KRAFT TELEVISION THEATRE   NBC/ABC

7 MAY 1947–1 OCTOBER 1958 (NBC); 15 OCTOBER 1953–6 JANUARY 1955 (ABC)   *Kraft Television Theatre* best epitomizes television's Golden Age, an era when live, often original dramas were the rule, not the exception. The principal reason for the growth of original drama on TV was the unavailability of most plays—the major motion picture studios owned the rights to most plays not in the public domain and steadfastly refused to permit those works to be aired over a potentially competitive medium. Thus, the path was open for young writers to submit original scripts to the producers of TV's dramatic anthology series, and writers such as Rod Serling, Paddy Chayefsky, Reginald Rose, and Tad Mosel (to name only a few) immediately began to fill the void. Similarly, there was a need for directors, too; newcomers such as George Roy Hill, John Frankenheimer, and Fielder Cook (again, to name only a few) were soon directing telecasts regularly. Finally, there arose a need for talented performers—men and women who could learn their lines quickly, take direction, and perform their roles in a small, hot studio before an audience of machines and technicians. A small sample of the 650 plays presented on *Kraft* (summer reruns were unknown) indicates the large number of stars who appeared, many in their first starring role on television: "Double Door," with John Baragrey (7 May 1947); "Feathers in a Gale," with George Reeves (9 August 1950); "A Play for Mary," with Bramwell Fletcher (23 May 1951); "Ben Franklin," with Jocelyn Brando (30 May 1951); "The Easy Mark," with Jack Lemmon (5 September 1951); "Six by Six," with George Reeves (6 August 1952); "Duet," with Jack Lemmon (28 January 1953); "Snooksie," with Jack Lemmon (18 February 1953); "Double in Ivory," with Beverly Whitney and Lee Remick (in her first major TV appearance, 9 September 1953); "To Live in Peace," with Anne Bancroft (her first major TV role, 16 December 1953); "The Missing Years," with Mary Astor and Tony Perkins (their first major TV roles, 3 February 1954); "Alice in Wonderland," with Robin Morgan as Alice, accompa-

nied by Edgar Bergen and Charlie McCarthy, Art Carney (as The Mad Hatter), Ernest Truex (The White Knight), and Blanche Yurka (Queen of Hearts) (5 May 1954); "Romeo and Juliet," with Liam Sullivan and sixteen-year-old Susan Strasberg (9 June 1954); "A Connecticut Yankee in King Arthur's Court," with Edgar Bergen and Victor Jory (8 July 1954); "Strangers in Hiding," with Bradford Dillman (his first starring role, 29 December 1954); Rod Serling's "Patterns," with Ed Begley, Richard Kiley, and Everett Sloane (first telecast 12 January 1955, the drama was so highly acclaimed that it was repeated—live—four weeks later); "The Emperor Jones," with Ossie Davis, Everett Sloane, and Rex Ingram (23 February 1955); "The Diamond as Big as the Ritz," with Lee Remick, Elizabeth Montgomery, Signe Hasso, and George Macready (aired 28 September 1955, marking *Kraft*'s five-hundredth broadcast); "A Profile in Courage," with James Whitmore (16 May 1956; the drama was introduced by then Senator John F. Kennedy, from whose book the story was adapted); "Flying Object at Three O'Clock High," with George Peppard (20 June 1956, his first major TV role); "The Singin' Idol," with Tommy Sands and Fred Clark (30 January 1957); "Night of the Plague," with Maggie Smith (20 March 1957, her first American TV role); "Drummer Man," with Sal Mineo (1 May 1957); "The Curly-Headed Kid," with Warren Beatty (26 June 1957, his first major TV role); "The Big Heist," with Patty Duke (her first major role, 13 November 1957); and "The Sea is Boiling Hot," with Sessue Hayakawa and Earl Holliman (12 March 1958). *Kraft Television Theatre* was seen on Wednesdays for eleven seasons on NBC; Kraft also sponsored a second hour, under the same title, over ABC for a season and a half on Thursdays beginning in 1953.

THE KREISLER BANDSTAND ABC
21 MARCH 1951–20 JUNE 1951 A half-hour musical series hosted by Fred Robbins and sponsored by the Jacques Kreisler Manufacturing Company, makers of watchbands. Benny Goodman's orchestra appeared on the premiere. Dick Gordon and George Foley produced the show, and Perry Lafferty directed it.

THE KROFFT SUPERSHOW ABC
11 SEPTEMBER 1976–2 SEPTEMBER 1978
THE KROFFT SUPERSTAR HOUR NBC
9 SEPTEMBER 1978–28 OCTOBER 1978 *The Krofft Supershow* began as a ninety-minute program, but was trimmed to sixty minutes in December of 1976. It was hosted by a rock band assembled for the show, Kaptain Kool and the Kongs: Michael Lembeck as Kaptain Kool, Debbie Clinger as Superchick, Mickey McMell as Turkey, and Louise Duart as Nashville. The foursome introduced the several segments that comprised the

series. During the 1976–1977 season the segments included: "Electra-Woman and Dynagirl," the adventures of two female reporters who could turn into superheroes, with Deidre Hall as Mara/Electra-Woman, Judy Strangis as Lori/Dynagirl; and Norman Alden as Frank; "Wonderbug," the adventures of a fantastic automobile, with John Anthony Bailey, David Levy, and Carol Anne Sefflinger; "Dr. Shrinker," the adventures of a group of miniaturized moppets, with Jay Robinson as Dr. Shrinker, Billy Barty as Hugo, Ted Eccles, Jeff McKay, and Susan Lawrence; and "The Lost Saucer," a 1975–1976 series that was reedited for the Krofft show. For the 1977–1978 season the "Wonderbug" segment was retained, and two new ones were added: "Magic Mongo," the adventures of an inept genie; and "Bigfoot and Wildboy," the adventures of an apelike creature and a human teenager. In the fall of 1978 *The Krofft Superstar Hour* appeared on NBC; the hour musical and variety show was hosted by the Bay City Rollers, a popular recording group from Scotland. Late in October that series left the air, though the Bay City Rollers continued in a show of their own: see *The Bay City Rollers Show*. The Krofft shows were produced by Sid and Marty Krofft, two brothers who started out as puppeteers, and who had previously produced several TV shows, including *H. R. Pufnstuf, Lidsville,* and *Far Out Space Nuts.*

THE KUDA BUX SHOW   CBS

25 MARCH 1950–24 JUNE 1950 Saturday-night show starring Kuda Bux, the mysterious Hindu wizard who could perform wondrous feats while blindfolded. Also featured were Janet Tyler and announcer Rex Marshall.

KUKLA, FRAN AND OLLIE   NBC/ABC/PBS

29 NOVEMBER 1948–13 JUNE 1954 (NBC); 6 SEPTEMBER 1954–30 AUGUST 1957 (ABC); 25 SEPTEMBER 1961–22 JUNE 1962 (NBC); 1969–1971 (PBS) A long-running children's series that was equally popular with adults, *Kukla, Fran and Ollie* featured the puppets of Burr Tillstrom and their human friend, Fran Allison. Tillstrom began creating his characters in the 1930s; one of the first puppets he crafted was Kukla (the Russian word for "doll"), a bald puppet with a big nose and a high voice. Before long an entire troupe of Kuklapolitans was in existence; the group included Ollie (short for Oliver J. Dragon), a kindly dragon with one tooth, Fletcher Rabbit, Cecil Bill, Buelah the Witch, Colonel Crackie, Madame Ooglepuss, Dolores Dragon, and many others. The Kuklapolitans appeared on television as early as 1939, and by 1947 they were regularly featured on local TV in Chicago. Late in 1948 *Kukla, Fran and Ollie* (Fran Allison, who continued to work with *Don McNeill's Breakfast Club* radio show, had been added) began over NBC's Midwest network;

the show was first seen in the East on 12 January 1949, after the completion of New York-to-Chicago transmission lines. The show was seen daily for several seasons before switching to Sunday afternoons. From 1954 to 1957 it was again broadcast daily over ABC. In the fall of 1961 the puppets again appeared, this time in a five-minute daily show; the series, which did not include Fran Allison, was titled *Burr Tillstrom's Kukla and Ollie*. Finally, the show was revived (with Fran Allison) over educational television, where it ran for two seasons. Most of the shows were done without scripts, except for a number of fairly elaborate productions, such as a puppet version of "The Mikado." Tillstrom himself provided the voices of Kukla and Ollie. Beulah Zachary, after whom Buelah the Witch was named, produced the first NBC version and the ABC version of the show.

KUNG FU   ABC
1 OCTOBER 1972–28 JUNE 1975 Highly stylized western starring David Carradine as Kwai Chang Caine, a soft-spoken drifter who eschewed violence, but when given no other choice utilized his prodigious talents in the martial arts. Caine, who was half Chinese, had studied to become a Shaolin priest in China but was forced to leave China after killing a man there. The series was notable for its use of slow motion, especially in fight sequences, and flashbacks showing the young Caine learning the discipline required by the martial arts. The flashback sequences featured Keye Luke as Master Po; Philip Ahn as Master Kan; and Radames Pera as the young Caine (known affectionately to Master Po as "Grasshopper"). The series was created by Ed Spielman and developed by Herman Miller, who produced it with Alex Beaton; Jerry Thorpe was executive producer.

KUP'S SHOW   SYNDICATED/PBS
1962–1975 (SYNDICATED); 1975–   (PBS) Chicago newspaper columnist Irv Kupcinet was seen on local television as early as 1952; by 1958 he was host of an open-ended talk show in Chicago. It was trimmed to an hour when it went into national syndication in 1962; thirteen years later the show was picked up by PBS. Paul Frumkin has produced the show for many seasons.

THE KYLE MACDONNELL SHOW
See GIRL ABOUT TOWN

LADIES BE SEATED   ABC
22 APRIL 1949–17 JUNE 1949 This half-hour prime-time game show featured female contestants, who competed in dance contests and in question-and-answer segments. It was hosted by Tom Moore and Phil Patton, and produced by Greg Garrison and Phil Patton.

LADIES BEFORE GENTLEMEN   DUMONT

28 FEBRUARY 1951–2 MAY 1951   This prime-time panel show was the
converse of *Leave It to the Girls:* Each week a panel of male celebrities
confronted a lone female guest, whose task was to defend the feminine
point of view on the subjects discussed. Ken Roberts hosted the series,
and Henry Misrock produced it.

LADIES' CHOICE   NBC

8 JUNE 1953–25 SEPTEMBER 1953   Johnny Dugan hosted this late-afternoon half-hour variety series, on which guest performers were selected by
women's organizations.

LADIES' DATE   DUMONT

13 OCTOBER 1952–31 JULY 1953   Bruce Mayer hosted this afternoon audience-participation and variety show.

THE LADY NEXT DOOR   NBC

9 MARCH 1949–14 SEPTEMBER 1949   Stories for children, as told by
Madge Tucker, were presented on this early-evening series seen on
Wednesdays.

THE LAMBS GAMBOL   NBC

27 FEBRUARY 1949–22 MAY 1949   This half-hour variety series featured
performances by members of the Lambs Club, a show business fraternal
order, as well as by other guest stars. It was produced by Herb Leder and
directed by Tom McDermott.

LAMP UNTO MY FEET   CBS

21 NOVEMBER 1948–21 JANUARY 1979   This Sunday-morning religious
program was second to *Meet the Press* as TV's longest-running network
program. It featured programs on cultural as well as religious themes;
Pamela Ilott produced the show for CBS News.

LANCELOT LINK, SECRET CHIMP   ABC

12 SEPTEMBER 1970–2 SEPTEMBER 1972   Saturday-morning filmed series about a group of simian secret agents; human voices were dubbed
over. Lancelot Link was the principal primate, though a rock band
known as the Evolution Revolution was also featured. The series was
shown in an hour format during its first season, and in a half-hour format
during the second season.

LANCER   CBS

24 SEPTEMBER 1968–23 JUNE 1970   This hour-long western was an imitation of *Bonanza.* It starred Andrew Duggan as Murdoch Lancer, twice-

widowed California rancher; James Stacy as Johnny Lancer, his hot-headed son; Wayne Maunder as Scott Lancer, his college-educated son, Johnny's half brother; Elizabeth Baur as Teresa O'Brien, Murdoch's ward (daughter of his late foreman); and Paul Brinegar as Jelly Hoskins, the current foreman. Samuel Peeples created the series, which was produced by Alan A. Armer for 20th Century-Fox. Reruns were broadcast during the summer of 1971.

LAND OF THE GIANTS   ABC

22 SEPTEMBER 1968–6 SEPTEMBER 1970   Science fiction series about a group of Earthlings aboard the *Spindrift*, on a flight from Los Angeles to London on June 12, 1983. The aircraft crash lands in a strange world where everything is a dozen times larger than on Earth, and the survivors found themselves hunted by giants. With Gary Conway as Captain Steve Burton; Don Marshall as copilot Dan Erickson; Deanna Lund as Valerie Scott; Don Matheson as the wealthy Mark Wilson; Heather Young as flight attendant Betty Hamilton; Kurt Kasznar as the unscrupulous Alexander Fitzhugh; Stefan Arngrim as youngster Barry Lockridge; and Kevin Hagen as Inspector Kobick, the giant in charge of apprehending the little people. Irwin Allen was executive producer of the series, which was reportedly budgeted at the then astronomical figure of $250,000 per episode.

LAND OF THE LOST   NBC

7 SEPTEMBER 1974–20 NOVEMBER 1976; 4 FEBRUARY 1978–2 SEPTEM-BER 1978   Innovative, live-action Saturday-morning show about a forest ranger and his two children who, caught in a time warp, found themselves in a prehistoric world. With Spencer Milligan as ranger Rick Marshall; Wesley Eure as Will, his son; Kathy Coleman as Holly, his daughter; Philip Paley as Cha-Ka, one of the Pakuni people, an apelike race discovered by the visitors; Sharon Baird and Joe Giamalva as other Pakunis; and Dave Greenwood, Bill Laimbeer, and John Lambert as Sleestacks, a race of reptilian creatures. Sid and Marty Krofft produced the series, which returned early in 1978.

LANIGAN'S RABBI   NBC

30 JANUARY 1977–3 JULY 1977   This crime show surfaced irregularly in 1977. Based on Harry Kemelman's novel, *Friday the Rabbi Slept Late*, it featured Art Carney as Paul Lanigan, big city police chief; Bruce Solomon as Rabbi David Small, Lanigan's occasional partner and consultant; Janis Paige as Kate Lanigan, Paul's wife; Janet Margolin as Miriam Small, the Rabbi's wife; Barbara Carney as Bobbie Whittaker; and Robert Doyle as Osgood. The pilot for the series was telecast 17 June 1976. Leonard B. Stern was executive producer.

THE LANNY ROSS SHOW   NBC

1 APRIL 1948–4 AUGUST 1949 Lanny Ross, who had been featured on such radio series as *The Maxwell House Show Boat* and *Your Hit Parade,* hosted one of television's first network variety shows. Sponsored by Swift, the half-hour series was also known as *The Swift Show.* Martha Logan and Sandra Gahle were also featured; Lee Cooley was the producer.

THE LARAINE DAY SHOW   ABC

5 MAY 1951–18 AUGUST 1951

DAYDREAMING WITH LARAINE   ABC

17 MAY 1951–19 JULY 1951 Laraine Day hosted two interview shows in 1951. The first, titled *The Laraine Day Show,* was a half-hour series broadcast on Saturday afternoons; it featured Ruth Woodner and the Bill Harrington Trio. The second series, *Daydreaming with Laraine,* was a fifteen-minute show aired on Thursday evenings; it featured interviews with sports personalities (at the time Day was married to Leo Durocher, then manager of the New York Giants baseball team). *The Laraine Day Show* was produced by Ted Kneeland, while *Daydreaming with Laraine* was produced by Ward Byron.

LARAMIE   NBC

15 SEPTEMBER 1959–17 SEPTEMBER 1963 Hour-long western set in Laramie, Wyoming. With John Smith as Slim Sherman and Robert Fuller as Jess Harper, partners in a ranch who supplemented their income by operating a stagecoach station on the premises. Also featured were Hoagy Carmichael (1959–1960) as Jonesy, their chief ranch hand; Bobby Crawford, Jr. (older brother of *The Rifleman*'s Johnny Crawford) as Andy Sherman, Slim's brother; Don Durant (1960–1963) as Gandy, a ranch hand; Arch Johnson (1960–1963) as Wellman, another ranch hand; Dennis Holmes (1961–1963) as Mike, a young orphan who moved in; and Spring Byington (1961–1963) as Daisy Cooper, the housekeeper.

LAREDO   NBC

16 SEPTEMBER 1965–1 SEPTEMBER 1967 Light western about a group of Texas Rangers who spent as much time fighting among themselves as they did fighting desperadoes. With Neville Brand as Reese Bennett; Peter Brown (formerly of *The Lawman*) as Chad Cooper; William Smith as Joe Riley; Philip Carey as Captain Parmalee, their harried commanding officer; and Robert Wolders (1966–1967) as rookie ranger Erik Hunter. The series was produced by Universal TV.

THE LARRY KANE SHOW   SYNDICATED

1971 Rock-and-roll performers guest starred on this hour program hosted by Philadelphia disc jockey Larry Kane.

THE LARRY STORCH SHOW   CBS

11 JULY 1953–12 SEPTEMBER 1953   Larry Storch hosted this variety hour, which was a summer replacement for *The Jackie Gleason Show*. Like Gleason, Storch had earlier hosted *Cavalcade of Stars* on the Du-Mont network.

THE LAS VEGAS SHOW   SYNDICATED

1967   *The Las Vegas Show*, a nightly two-hour talkfest broadcast live from Las Vegas, premiered 1 May 1967, and was supposed to be the cornerstone of a "fourth network," The United Network. Hosted by Bill Dana, the show disappeared after a few weeks, together with the plans for the new network.

LASH OF THE WEST   ABC

4 JANUARY 1953–9 MAY 1953   Fifteen-minute series on which western star Lash LaRue demonstrated skills such as using the bullwhip (LaRue's trademark).

LASSIE   CBS/SYNDICATED

12 SEPTEMBER 1954–12 SEPTEMBER 1971 (CBS); 1971–1974 (SYNDICATED)   Lassie, the daring and resourceful collie owned and trained by Rudd Weatherwax, had starred both in films and on radio before coming to TV in 1954. Over the next two decades the dog survived many changes in format and cast and never seemed to age; actually, over the years Lassie was played by at least six different dogs, all of them males, and other Lassies were used for special shots or difficult stunts. For her first three seasons Lassie lived on the Miller farm near the town of Calverton; the cast then included Tommy Rettig as Jeff Miller; Jan Clayton as Ellen Miller, his widowed mother; George Cleveland as Gramps (George Miller), Jeff's granddad; Donald Keeler (nephew of actress Ruby Keeler) as Jeff's best friend, Porky Brockway; and Paul Maxey as Matt Brockway, Porky's father. By 1957 young Rettig had outgrown the role—that fall the Millers suddenly moved to the city and entrusted Lassie to the care of a young orphan, recently adopted by a Calverton couple. The new cast included Jon Provost as Timmy Martin; Cloris Leachman as his mother, Ruth Martin; Jon Shepodd as Paul Martin, his father; and George Chandler as Uncle Petrie. Leachman and Shepodd lasted only one season as Timmy's parents; they were replaced in 1958 by June Lockhart and Hugh Reilly (again as Ruth and Paul Martin). Other regulars included Todd Ferrell as Boomer Bates, Timmy's pal; Andy Clyde as old-timer Cully, also a friend of Timmy's. By 1964 the show's owners—The Wrather Corporation—had decided on another change; it was explained that the Martins had decided to move to Australia, and since dogs entering that country had to be quarantined for six months, Lassie would be better off with a new owner. Robert Bray stepped in as Corey

Stewart, a forest ranger (Bray had actually been introduced in a five-parter during the 1963–1964 season to test audience reaction). Freed from the farm format, Lassie could now become involved in a wider variety of outdoor adventures. Bray departed in 1968, and for the last three years of the network run and the first year of syndication there were no human regulars—Lassie was a freelance troubleshooter. For the final two years of syndication, Lassie returned to a farm (a ranch, actually), run by Keith Holden (played by Larry Wilcox). A cartoon version of the show was also seen during the 1973 and 1974 seasons: see *Lassie's Rescue Rangers.* The earlier versions of the series were syndicated under different titles: the episodes starring Tommy Rettig were titled *Jeff's Collie,* and those with Jon Provost were titled *Timmy and Lassie.*

LASSIE'S RESCUE RANGERS   ABC
8 SEPTEMBER 1973–30 AUGUST 1975   Ecology-oriented weekend cartoon series based, of course, on *Lassie.* The cartoon Lassie was the boss of a group of animals dedicated to saving the environment. Norm Prescott and Lou Scheimer produced the series.

THE LAST OF THE MOHICANS
See HAWKEYE AND THE LAST OF THE MOHICANS

LAST OF THE WILD   SYNDICATED
(LORNE GREENE'S LAST OF THE WILD)
1974   Half-hour documentaries about wildlife, narrated by Lorne Greene. From Ivan Tors Productions.

THE LAST RESORT   CBS
19 SEPTEMBER 1979–   Half-hour sitcom about a group of college kids working at a resort hotel. With Larry Breeding as Michael Lerner, premed student; Stephanie Faracy as Gail Collins, the pastry chef; Zane Lasky as Duane Kaminsky; Walter Olkewicz as Zach Comstock; John Fujioka as Kevin, the cook; Ray Underwood as rich kid Jeffrey Barron; Robert Costanzo as Murray, the maitre 'd; and Dorothy Konrad as Mrs. Trilling, one of the guests. Gary David Goldberg created and produced the show, which got off to a slow start and was pulled from the schedule after three weeks; it returned in December.

THE LAST WORD   CBS
6 JANUARY 1957–18 OCTOBER 1959   The English language was the topic of discussion on this Sunday-afternoon panel show. Each week a panel of three celebrities or authorities discussed questions submitted by viewers about the language. Fred Freed produced the highbrow half hour, and John Mason Brown was featured as a permanent panelist. Dr. Bergen Evans was the moderator.

THE LATE SUMMER, EARLY FALL BERT CONVY SHOW   CBS

25 AUGUST 1976–15 SEPTEMBER 1976 Four-week half-hour summer variety series hosted by Bert Convy, with Henry Polic II, Sallie James, Lenny Schultz (as "The Bionic Chicken"), Marty Barris, and Donna Ponterotto. Executive producer: Howard Hinderstein.

LAUGH LINE   NBC

16 APRIL 1959–11 JUNE 1959 On this Thursday-night game show hosted by Dick Van Dyke, celebrity panelists were required to supply captions to cartoons. Panelists over the several weeks included Dorothy Loudon, Mike Nichols and Elaine May, Pat Harrington, Jr. (as Guido Panzini), Shelley Berman, Roger Price, and Orson Bean.

LAUGH-IN   NBC

22 JANUARY 1968–14 MAY 1973 Hosted by the comedy duo of Dan Rowan and Dick Martin (the show's official title was *Rowan and Martin's Laugh-In*), *Laugh-In* was a fast-moving hour of sight gags, one-liners, short skits, and blackouts. The show was an immediate hit and did much to speed up the pace of TV comedy shows. It relied little on the talents of guest stars, though many celebrities made cameo appearances (including Richard Nixon, who uttered "Sock it to me?" in a 1968 show); instead, a large company of regulars, including many who were new to television, carried the show, and above all, kept it moving. The program seemed to operate on the premise that if enough gags could be crammed into an hour, only a small proportion needed to be genuinely funny for the show to succeed, and at the very least, the viewers could not complain of boredom. Thanks to *Laugh-In,* such phrases as "Ring my chimes," "Look that up in your Funk & Wagnall's," and "You bet your bippy" joined the American vocabulary, at least temporarily. Among the many regulars on the show were Dennis Allen, Chelsea Brown, Ruth Buzzi, Johnny Brown, Judy Carne, Ann Elder, Byron Gilliam, Henry Gibson, Richard Dawson, Teresa Graves, Larry Hovis, Arte Johnson, Goldie Hawn, Jeremy Lloyd, Gary Owens, Dave Madden, Lily Tomlin, Nancie Phillips, Pamela Rodgers, Alan Sues, Barbara Sharma, and Jo Anne Worley. In 1972 several new faces were added, including Patti Deutsch, Sarah Kennedy, Donna Jean Young, Jud Strunk, Brian Bessler, Todd Bass, Willie Tyler, and the Burbank Quickies. George Schlatter and Ed Friendly were the executive producers until 1971 when Paul Keyes succeeded them. In the fall of 1977 *Laugh-In* (minus hosts Rowan and Martin) returned to NBC as a series of specials, headlined by guest stars.

LAUGHS FOR SALE   ABC

20 OCTOBER 1963–22 DECEMBER 1963 On this half-hour series a panel of comedians performed material submitted by aspiring comedy writers,

after which the material was discussed and evaluated. Hal March hosted the show, which was hastily scheduled to replace *100 Grand*, a game show axed after only three weeks.

LAVERNE AND SHIRLEY — ABC

27 JANUARY 1976– This situation comedy, spun off from *Happy Days*, is one of the few spinoffs that proved as popular as the originating series. Like *Happy Days*, it is set in Milwaukee during the 1950s. It stars Penny Marshall as Laverne DeFazio and Cindy Williams as Shirley Feeney, two young women who work together at a brewery and live together in a basement apartment. Also featured are Phil Foster as Frank DeFazio, Laverne's father, owner of a pizzeria; David L. Lander as Squiggy (Andrew Squigman), their dim-witted friend and coworker; Michael McKean as Lenny Kolowski, another friend and coworker, Squiggy's inseparable pal; Betty Garrett (September 1976–   ) as Laverne and Shirley's landlady, Edna Babish, who married Frank in 1979; and Eddie Mekka as Carmine Ragusa, another friend of the two. Executive producers: Garry Marshall (brother of Penny), Thomas L. Miller, and Edward K. Milkis.

THE LAW AND MR. JONES — ABC

7 OCTOBER 1960–22 SEPTEMBER 1961 Half-hour crime show starring James Whitmore as idealistic attorney Abraham Lincoln Jones. With Janet DeGore as his secretary, Marsha Spear; Conlan Carter as his law clerk, C. E. Carruthers. Sy Gomberg created and produced the series.

THE LAW OF THE PLAINSMAN — NBC

1 OCTOBER 1959–22 SEPTEMBER 1960 Half-hour western starring Michael Ansara as Sam Buckhart, a United States Marshal in the Arizona Territory; Buckhart, an Apache, had befriended a Cavalry officer and was educated at Harvard. Also featured were Robert Harland as his deputy, Billy Lordan; Gina Gillespie as his adopted daughter, Tess. Reruns were shown on ABC in 1962. Peter Packer produced the program.

THE LAWBREAKERS — SYNDICATED

1963 Documentary series about real-life criminals, narrated by Lee Marvin.

THE LAWLESS YEARS — NBC

16 APRIL 1959–3 SEPTEMBER 1959; 12 MAY 1961–22 SEPTEMBER 1961 *The Lawless Years* was the first crime show set in the 1920s, antedating *The Untouchables* by a half season. James Gregory starred as Barney Ruditsky, a New York police detective; Robert Karnes was featured as Max, his sidekick. Jack Chertok was the producer.

THE LAWMAN ABC

5 OCTOBER 1958–9 OCTOBER 1962 Half-hour western from Warner Brothers starring John Russell as Marshal Dan Troop of Laramie, Wyoming; Peter Brown as his deputy, Johnnie McKay; Bek Nelson (1958–1959) as Dru Lemp, owner of the Blue Bonnet Cafe; Barbara Long (1959) as Julie Tate, editor of the Laramie newspaper, and Peggie Castle (1959–1962) as Lily Merrill, proprietor of the Birdcage Saloon.

THE LAWRENCE WELK SHOW ABC/SYNDICATED

2 JULY 1955–4 SEPTEMBER 1971 (ABC); 1971–
(SYNDICATED)

LAWRENCE WELK'S TOP TUNES AND NEW TALENT ABC

8 OCTOBER 1956–2 JUNE 1958

THE PLYMOUTH SHOW STARRING LAWRENCE WELK ABC
(LAWRENCE WELK'S LITTLE BAND)

10 SEPTEMBER 1958–27 MAY 1959 One of TV's most durable musical series, *The Lawrence Welk Show* has presented middle-of-the-road music ("champagne music," in Welk's words) for more than two decades. It is also one of few series to be aired on more stations in its syndicated form than when it ran on the ABC network. Welk, an accordionist and bandleader, has kept the format simple and predictable—lots of music, a little dancing, and few guest stars. Numbers are performed by the members of Welk's television family. That large group has included the Lennon Sisters (Dianne, Peggy, Kathy, and Janet), Alice Lon, Norma Zimmer, Tanya Falan, Arthur Duncan, Joe Feeney, Guy Hovis, Jim Roberts, Raina English, Larry Hooper, Jerry Burke, and former Mouseketeer Bobby Burgess. A fixture on ABC's Saturday-night schedule for sixteen seasons, the show was known as *The Dodge Dancing Party* in its first years. From 1956 to 1959 Welk was seen twice a week on ABC; *Lawrence Welk's Top Tunes and New Talent* ran on Monday nights for two seasons, and *The Plymouth Show Starring Lawrence Welk*—which featured a ten-piece orchestra comprised of children, known as Lawrence Welk's Little Band—was seen on Wednesdays during the 1958–1959 season.

THE LAZARUS SYNDROME ABC

4 SEPTEMBER 1979–16 OCTOBER 1979 Hour medical drama starring Louis Gossett, Jr., as Dr. Macarthur (Mac) St. Clair, a cardiologist and chief of staff at Webster Memorial Hospital; Ronald Hunter as Joe Hamill, an ex-reporter who became the hospital's administrator; Sheila Frazier as Gloria St. Clair, Mac's wife; and Peggy McCay as Stacy, Hamill's secretary. Created by William Blinn (who served as executive producer with Jerry Thorpe), the series was pulled from ABC's schedule in October 1979 for "retooling," and was set to return later in the season. The term "Lazarus syndrome" refers to the belief by patients that physicians are capable of solving all the patients' problems.

LEAVE IT TO BEAVER

CBS/ABC

4 OCTOBER 1957–17 SEPTEMBER 1958 (CBS); 2 OCTOBER 1958–12 SEPTEMBER 1963 (ABC)   This family sitcom centered around the Cleaver family of Mayfield. With Hugh Beaumont as Ward Cleaver, an accountant and a patient, understanding father; Barbara Billingsley as June Cleaver, a well-dressed housewife and a patient, understanding mother; Tony Dow as their older son, Wally, an all-American kid; and Jerry Mathers as their younger son, Theodore, better known as The Beaver. In almost all of the 234 half-hours Beaver's well-intentioned efforts to do good managed to backfire, landing him in some kind of trouble; Mathers's cuteness (particularly in the early seasons) and his natural acting style helped distinguish the show from other 1950s family sitcoms. Also featured were Ken Osmond as Wally's crafty friend, Eddie Haskell, whose obsequious attitude toward Mr. and Mrs. Cleaver belied his contempt of them (and Beaver); Frank Bank as Wally's chunky friend, Clarence "Lumpy" Rutherford; Richard Deacon as Lumpy's father, Fred Rutherford, Ward's boss; Diane Brewster as Miss Canfield, Beaver's second-grade teacher at the Grant Avenue Elementary School; Sue Randall as Miss Landers, Beaver's third-grade teacher; Doris Packer as Mrs. Rayburn, the school principal; Rusty Stevens as Larry Mondello, one of Beaver's friends; Madge Blake as Mrs. Mondello, Larry's mom; and Burt Mustin as Gus, the old-timer at the fire station. Other friends of Beaver's over the years included Stanley Fafara as Whitey Whitney; Stephen Talbot as Gilbert Bates; Richard Correll as Richard Rickover; Tiger Fafara as Tooey; Buddy Hart as Chester; and Jeri Weil as Judy Hensler, Beaver's nemesis at school. The series was created, written, and produced by Joe Connelly and Bob Mosher, who had written for *Amos and Andy*.

LEAVE IT TO LARRY

CBS

14 OCTOBER 1952–23 DECEMBER 1952   Eddie Albert starred in this half-hour sitcom as Larry, a bumbling shoe salesman who worked in his father-in-law's store. Ed Begley appeared as his boss and father-in-law, and Katharine Bard was featured as his wife. Leo Solomon produced the series, and Mervyn Nelson and Allen Reisner directed it. The show was little noted and certainly little watched, for it was scheduled opposite Milton Berle's *The Texaco Star Theater* on Tuesdays.

LEAVE IT TO THE GIRLS

NBC/ABC

27 APRIL 1949–30 DECEMBER 1951 (NBC); 3 OCTOBER 1953–27 MARCH 1954 (ABC)   This early talk show began on radio in 1945. Each week a panel of female celebrities met to air the women's point of view on a certain subject (usually one of a romantic nature). Also on hand was a lone male guest, whose job it was to defend the men's point of view. Maggi McNellis hosted the show for most of its run, and Martha Rountree, who also produced *Meet the Press,* produced it.

LEE TREVINO'S GOLF FOR SWINGERS   SYNDICATED
1972   Half-hour game show on which celebrities played three holes with golf pro Lee Trevino.

THE LEFTOVER REVUE   NBC
17 SEPTEMBER 1951–9 NOVEMBER 1951   Half-hour daytime variety series hosted by Wayne Howell.

THE LEGEND OF CUSTER
See CUSTER

THE LEGEND OF JESSE JAMES   ABC
13 SEPTEMBER 1965–5 SEPTEMBER 1966   Jesse James, the notorious frontier outlaw, was portrayed as a nineteenth-century Robin Hood in this unsuccessful half-hour western; according to the series, Jesse and his brother Frank robbed trains only to repay local folks whose property had been confiscated by the railroad barons, who had even hassled their mother when she balked at turning over her ranch. The show featured Chris Jones as Jesse James; Allen Case as his brother, Frank; Ann Doran as their mother, Mrs. James; and Robert J. Wilke as Marshal Sam Corbett, the lawman who vainly pursued them. The series was produced by 20th Century-Fox TV.

LEROY JENKINS
See REVIVAL OF AMERICA CRUSADE

THE LES CRANE SHOW   ABC
9 NOVEMBER 1964–5 MARCH 1965   ABC's first attempt at a late-night talk show was hosted by Les Crane; the show featured a "shotgun" microphone which enabled members of the studio audience to talk to Crane's guests. After four months the network decided to go with a series of guest hosts, and the show was retitled *Nightlife.*

THE LESLIE UGGAMS SHOW   CBS
26 SEPTEMBER 1969–14 DECEMBER 1969   Leslie Uggams, who had previously been featured on *Sing Along with Mitch,* became the first black woman since Hazel Scott to host a network variety series. It fared poorly against NBC's *Bonanza,* as did most of the CBS shows scheduled in that time slot during the 1960s. Other regulars included Johnny Brown, Alison Mills, Lillian Hayman, and Lincoln Kilpatrick; a regular feature was "Sugar Hill," a running sketch about a poor black family. Saul Ilson and Ernest Chambers, who had previously produced *The Smothers Brothers Comedy Hour,* produced the series.

LET THERE BE STARS
ABC

16 OCTOBER 1949–27 NOVEMBER 1949 A half-hour revue from Hollywood, produced by Leighton Brill and William Trinz. Among the many regulars who appeared was a young singer-comedian named Peter Marshall, who would become the host of *Hollywood Squares* in 1966.

LET'S DANCE
ABC

18 SEPTEMBER 1954–16 OCTOBER 1954 Ballroom dancing was featured on this musical hour, broadcast live from both New York and Chicago, with music supplied by guest bands. Ralph Mooney hosted the New York portion, Art Mooney the Chicago segment.

LET'S MAKE A DEAL
NBC/ABC/SYNDICATED

30 DECEMBER 1963–27 DECEMBER 1968 (NBC); 30 DECEMBER 1968–9 JULY 1976 (ABC); 1971–1976 (SYNDICATED) One of TV's best-known game shows, *Let's Make a Deal* required no skill, no dexterity, and no knowledge of its contestants. Each day, thirty-one members of the studio audience (many of whom were dressed in ridiculous outfits) were selected to sit in the "trading area" up front; some of those people then had the chance to "make a deal" with "TV's big dealer," host Monty Hall. Theoretically, the traders were supposed to have brought something of their own to trade, but over the years even this requirement was virtually abandoned. If selected by Hall, each trader was presented with a choice—whether to take one prize or another. Sometimes one prize would be described fully while the other remained hidden inside a box or behind a door; sometimes neither prize would be described; sometimes cash (in stated or unstated amounts) would be offered against a merchandise prize; and sometimes one of the prizes would be worthless—they were known as "zonks." And there lay the show's appeal. A player could be given, for example, $1,000 in cash, trade the money for what proved to be a mink coat, and decide to trade the coat—only to end up with a wheelbarrow. At the end of each show the two players who had won the most were given the chance to trade their winnings for the day's "Big Deal." Each player selected one of three doors and won what was behind it; there were no "zonks" at this level, and the Big Deal, concealed behind one of the doors, was usually worth at least $10,000. Monty Hall, who developed and produced the show with his partner, Stefan Hatos, was the perfect host for the show. Monty kept the show moving while he treated the outrageously garbed and occasionally greedy contestants courteously; it is hard to imagine anyone else but Hall working the trading area as skillfully. Hall was assisted by announcer Jay Stewart and model Carol Merrill. More than 3,800 shows were done over a thirteen-year span; at the final show, taped in Nevada shortly before Christmas 1976, there were no zonks.

LET'S PLAY POST OFFICE   NBC
27 SEPTEMBER 1965–1 JULY 1966   Don Morrow hosted this daytime
game show on which contestants tried to identify the "authors" of ficti-
tious letters read aloud a line at a time.

LET'S SEE   ABC
14 JULY 1955–1 SEPTEMBER 1955   John Reed King hosted this summertime panel show.

LET'S TAKE A TRIP   CBS
17 APRIL 1955–23 FEBRUARY 1958   Sunday series for children on which
Sonny Fox and two children paid visits to interesting places. Fox was assisted first by youngsters Pud Flanagan and Ginger MacManus; in 1957
they were succeeded by Joan Terrace and Jimmy Walṣh. Jim Colligan
succeeded Steve Fleischman as producer of the New York-based series.

A LETTER TO LORETTA
See THE LORETTA YOUNG SHOW

LETTERS TO LAUGH-IN   NBC
29 SEPTEMBER 1969–26 DECEMBER 1969   This daytime game show was
an unusual spinoff from *Laugh-In.* Host Gary Owens, the announcer of
Laugh-In, presided over the program on which a panel of four guest celebrities read jokes submitted to *Laugh-In* by home viewers; judges from
the studio audience then rated the jokes.

LEWISOHN STADIUM CONCERT   ABC
26 JUNE 1950–7 AUGUST 1950   A summer replacement for *Robert
Montgomery Presents* featuring the New York Philharmonic Symphony
Orchestra in concert with guest artists. Ben Grauer was the announcer.

LIARS CLUB   SYNDICATED
1969; 1975–   Game show featuring two contestants, four celebrities, and a group of unusual objects. Three of the four celebrities sug-
gest a false definition or description of the object, while the fourth
describes it correctly. The contestants try to figure out who is telling the
truth. Rod Serling hosted the 1969 version; Bill Armstrong was the first
host of the later version and was succeeded by Allen Ludden. The show is
a Ralph Andrews Production.

THE LIBERACE SHOW   NBC/SYNDICATED/ABC/CBS
1 JULY 1952–28 AUGUST 1952 (NBC); 1953–1955 (SYNDICATED); 13
OCTOBER 1958–10 APRIL 1959 (ABC); 15 JULY 1969–16 SEPTEMBER
1969 (CBS)   Liberace, the flamboyant pianist best remembered for his
sequined wardrobe and the candelabra atop his instrument, hosted sever-

al television programs. The first was a fifteen-minute series which replaced *The Dinah Shore Show* on Tuesdays and Thursdays during the summer of 1952. It was well enough received so that Liberace decided to try a syndicated, half-hour show, which proved to be enormously popular; both of the early series also featured Liberace's brother, George, as violinist and orchestra leader. Illness forced him to curtail his schedule in 1955, but he returned to television in 1958 to host a half-hour daytime show on ABC; it featured Joan O'Brien, Erin O'Brien, Dick Roman, Steve Dunne, and the Gordon Robinson Orchestra. Liberace hosted a British series in 1960, and his 1969 summer series, shown in this country, was produced in London; the hour show featured Richard Wattis and Georgina Moon. Born Wladziu Valentino Liberace, he preferred to use just one name.

LIDSVILLE
ABC

11 SEPTEMBER 1971–1 SEPTEMBER 1973   Sid and Marty Krofft were the executive producers of this Saturday-morning live-action kids' show. It starred Butch Patrick as Mark, a youngster who found himself in Lidsville, a mysterious world of hats. Also featured were Charles Nelson Reilly as the evil Whoo Doo, and Billie Hayes as the good Weenie the Genie.

THE LIEUTENANT
NBC

14 SEPTEMBER 1963–5 SEPTEMBER 1964   Hour-long dramatic series set at Camp Pendleton in California. With Gary Lockwood as Lieutenant William Rice, U.S.M.C.; Robert Vaughn as his commanding officer, Captain Raymond Rambridge; Steven Franken as Lieutenant Sam Panosian; Carmen Phillips as Lily, Rambridge's secretary; Henry Beckman as Barker; Richard Anderson as Hiland; John Milford as Kagey; and Don Penny as Harris. Norman Felton was the executive producer of the series, which was created and produced by Gene Roddenberry, who later created *Star Trek.*

THE LIFE AND LEGEND OF WYATT EARP
See WYATT EARP

THE LIFE AND TIMES OF GRIZZLY ADAMS
NBC

9 FEBRUARY 1977–26 JULY 1978   Set in the nineteenth century, *The Life and Times of Grizzly Adams* was an hour-long adventure series aimed principally at children. It starred Dan Haggerty as James (Grizzly) Adams; accused of a crime he never committed, Adams escaped to the northwest wilderness to live by himself, in harmony with nature. He fished, but did not hunt, and wore only cloth garments. His best friend was a large grizzly bear called Ben (played by a real bear known as Bozo). Adams also had one or two human acquaintances—Denver Pyle as Mad Jack, who also served as the show's narrator, and Don Shanks as

Nakuma, Adams's Indian blood brother. Charles E. Sellier, Jr., was the executive producer of the series, which was produced by Leonard B. Kaufman and Jim Simmons. The TV show was based on the film of the same title, which had starred Haggerty and been produced by Sellier.

LIFE AROUND US   SYNDICATED
1971   A series of half-hour documentaries on biology from Time-Life Films.

LIFE BEGINS AT EIGHTY   NBC/ABC/DUMONT
13 JANUARY 1950–25 AUGUST 1950 (NBC); 3 OCTOBER 1950–10 MARCH 1952 (ABC); 21 MARCH 1952–24 JULY 1955 (DUMONT); 31 JULY 1955–25 FEBRUARY 1956 (ABC)   Produced and hosted by Jack Barry, this panel show was the converse of Barry's previous effort, *Juvenile Jury;* a panel of octogenarians dispensed advice on topics submitted by viewers. Regular panelists included Fred Stein and Georgiana Carhart, who had also been featured on the radio version.

LIFE IS WORTH LIVING   DUMONT
12 FEBRUARY 1952–26 APRIL 1955
MISSION TO THE WORLD   ABC
13 OCTOBER 1955–8 APRIL 1957   *Life Is Worth Living* and *Mission to the World* were the titles of the two network shows hosted by Bishop Fulton J. Sheen; they were among the few religious shows ever aired during prime time. *Life Is Worth Living* was scheduled opposite Milton Berle's *The Texaco Star Theater*, but, unlike most of Berle's competition, managed to attract enough viewers to warrant its continuation. Frank Bunetta, who later directed *The Jackie Gleason Show*, directed *Life Is Worth Living*.

THE LIFE OF LEONARDO DA VINCI   CBS/PBS
13 AUGUST 1972–10 SEPTEMBER 1972 (CBS); 20 NOVEMBER 1974–18 DECEMBER 1974 (PBS)   Five-part miniseries on the life of Leonardo Da Vinci. Produced by RAI, Italy's state-owned network, it starred Phillipe Leroy as Leonardo, Alberto Fiorini and Arduino Paolini as the younger Leonardo, and Bruno Cirino as Michelangelo. Giulio Bosetti served as the guide and narrator for the series, and Ben Gazzara introduced the episodes on PBS.

THE LIFE OF RILEY   NBC
4 OCTOBER 1949–28 MARCH 1950; 2 JANUARY 1953–22 AUGUST 1958
This family sitcom began on radio in 1944 and twice came to television. More than any other comedy of the 1950s, it resembled *All in the Family,* as both shows centered around a blue-collar husband and father who fre-

quently found life a bit too perplexing (or, as Riley put it, "What a revoltin' development this is!"). The first, and less well known, TV version starred Jackie Gleason as Chester A. Riley, a riveter at Stevenson Aircraft in Los Angeles; Rosemary DeCamp as his wife, Peg; Gloria Winters as their daughter, Babs; Lanny Rees as their son, Chester A. Riley, Jr. (Junior); Sid Tomack as Riley's friend and coworker, Jim Gillis; and John Brown as the neighborhood undertaker, Digby "Digger" O'Dell. The series was produced by Irving Brecher, Reuben Ship, and Alan Lipscot, and directed by Herbert I. Leeds. Though Gleason won an Emmy for his performance, the show was dropped after twenty-six weeks. Early in 1953 it returned, however, and stayed for more than five years. The second version starred William Bendix (who had played the part on radio) as Chester A. Riley; Marjorie Reynolds as wife Peg; Lugene Sanders as daughter Babs; Wesley Morgan as Junior; Tom D'Andrea as Gillis; Gloria Blondell as Gillis's wife, Honeybee; Gregory Marshall as Egbert Gillis, son of Jim and Honeybee; Henry Kulky as Riley's friend and coworker, dim-witted Otto Schmidlap; and Sterling Holloway as Riley's eccentric friend, Waldo Binney, an amateur inventor. In the fall of 1955 the Gillises, who had lived in the Rileys' next-door cottage, were dropped from the series, as Tom D'Andrea had signed to appear in a new sitcom, *The Soldiers.* George O'Hanlon and Florence Sundstrom joined the cast as their new neighbors, Calvin and Belle Dudley. They in turn were dropped after the 1955–1956 season as D'Andrea and Blondell returned. Tom McKnight produced the second television version.

LIFE WITH BUSTER KEATON
SYNDICATED

1951 Buster Keaton, star of many silent film comedies, filmed this half-hour series when he was in his late fifties; in most of the stories he appeared as a clerk in a sporting goods shop.

LIFE WITH ELIZABETH
SYNDICATED

1953–1954 Domestic sitcom starring Betty White and Del Moore as newlyweds Elizabeth and Alvin White. Don Fedderson produced the series in association with Guild Films.

LIFE WITH FATHER
CBS

22 NOVEMBER 1953–5 JULY 1955 *Life with Father* began as a series of essays by Clarence Day, Jr., which appeared in *Harper's Magazine* and later in *The New Yorker.* A best-selling book ensued, followed shortly by a tremendously successful Broadway play which ran for eight years. The TV version of the comedy was not especially popular, however. Set at the turn of the century, it starred Leon Ames as Clarence Day, Sr., a prosperous banker and an old-fashioned patriarch, and Lurene Tuttle as his wife, Vinnie. Also featured were Steve Terrell and Ralph Reed as the eldest son, Clarence Jr.; Freddie Leiston as second son John; Ronald Keith as

third son Whitney; Harvey Grant as youngest son Harlan; and Dorothy Bernard (the only member of the cast who had been in the play) as Margaret, the maid. Ezra Stone, who had played Henry Aldrich on radio, produced the half-hour series. At the insistence of Mrs. Clarence Day, Jr., who served as a special consultant to the show, all of the members of the television Day family had to have red hair (as they had had in real life), even though the show was broadcast in black and white.

LIFE WITH LINKLETTER
ABC/NBC

6 OCTOBER 1950–25 APRIL 1952 (ABC); 29 DECEMBER 1969–25 SEPTEMBER 1970 (NBC)   Art Linkletter's first television series, *Life with Linkletter,* was a prime-time version of *Art Linkletter's House Party,* which began on radio in 1945 and came to TV in 1952; like *House Party,* it featured audience-participation games and interviews with schoolchildren. It was produced by John Guedel and directed by Stuart Phelps. In 1969, after *House Party* had left the air, Linkletter and his son cohosted a daytime show on NBC, also entitled *Life with Linkletter.*

LIFE WITH LUIGI
CBS

22 SEPTEMBER 1952–29 DECEMBER 1952; 9 APRIL 1953–4 JUNE 1953   This ethnic sitcom began on radio in 1948. Set in Chicago, it starred J. Carrol Naish as Luigi Basco, an Italian immigrant who opened a small antique store and hoped to become an American citizen; Alan Reed as Luigi's sponsor, Pasquale, proprietor of Pasquale's Spaghetti Palace; Jody Gilbert as Rosa, Pasquale's portly daughter, whom Pasquale hoped would marry Luigi; Mary Shipp as Miss Spalding, Luigi's night-school teacher; Ken Peters as Olson, one of Luigi's classmates; Joe Forte as Horowitz, another classmate; and Sig Ruman as Schultz, another classmate. Except for Sig Ruman, all the cast members had played the roles on radio. Dropped in midseason, the show reappeared briefly in the spring of 1953 with different principals: Vito Scotti as Luigi, Thomas Gomez as Pasquale, and Muriel Landers as Rosa. Produced by Cy Howard, the show was directed by Mac Benoff.

LIFELINE
NBC

7 SEPTEMBER 1978–30 DECEMBER 1978   One of the most unusual prime-time shows of the decade, *Lifeline* was an hour documentary series about the medical profession. Each week the cameras followed a doctor around; much of the action took place in operating rooms. Thomas Moore and Robert Fuisz, M.D., were the executive producers, Jackson Beck the narrator.

LIGHTS, CAMERA, ACTION!
NBC

4 JULY 1950–20 AUGUST 1950   Half-hour talent show, hosted by Walter Wolfe King.

LIGHTS OUT   NBC
12 JULY 1949–29 SEPTEMBER 1952   This anthology series of thriller and
suspense dramas ran for three years on television, considerably less than
the twelve-year run enjoyed by the radio version under the supervision of
Wyllis Cooper and, later, Arch Oboler. Jack LaRue was the first TV host;
he was succeeded by Frank Gallop. A sampling of the half-hour presentations includes: "Faithful Heart," with Anne Francis (10 April 1950);
"Beware this Woman," with Veronica Lake (4 December 1950); "The
House of Dust," with Anthony Quinn and Nina Foch (5 February 1951);
and "The Hollow Man," with William Bendix (29 September 1952).

LILIAS, YOGA AND YOU   PBS
1974–1977   Half-hour physical-and-mental exercise program, hosted by
Lilias Folan and produced by WCET-TV, Cincinnati.

THE LILLI PALMER SHOW   CBS
29 MARCH 1951–28 JUNE 1951   Lilli Palmer interviewed celebrities on
this fifteen-minute show, seen Thursdays.

LILLI PALMER THEATRE   SYNDICATED
1956   Half-hour dramatic anthology series hosted by actress Lilli Palmer.

THE LINEUP   CBS
1 OCTOBER 1954–20 JANUARY 1960   Crime show filmed partly on location in San Francisco and later syndicated under the title *San Francisco
Beat*. With Warner Anderson as Lieutenant Ben Guthrie; Tom Tully
(1954–1959) as Inspector Matt Grebb; they were later joined by Marshall
Reed as Inspector Fred Asher. In the fall of 1959 the show expanded to
one hour and several new cast members were added: Rachel Ames as policewoman Sandy McAllister; Tod Burton as Inspector Charlie Summers;
William Leslie as Inspector Dan Delaney; and Skip Ward as Officer Peter
Larkin. The series was a Desilu production.

LINUS THE LIONHEARTED   CBS
26 SEPTEMBER 1964–3 SEPTEMBER 1966   Saturday-morning cartoon
show set in Africa. Voices included those of Sheldon Leonard as Linus,
the king; Carl Reiner as Sascha Grouse and Dinny Kangaroo; Jonathan
Winters as The Giant; and Ed Graham (the series' producer) as The
Mockingbird. Other characters included Rory Raccoon, So-Hi, Billie
Bird, and Lovable Truly.

LITTLE HOUSE ON THE PRAIRIE   NBC
11 SEPTEMBER 1974–   Laura Ingalls Wilder's "Little
House" books form the basis for this hour family drama set during the
1870s. The show, one of NBC's few mainstays during the 1970s, is under

the almost total control of Michael Landon, who is not only its star and executive producer, but also a frequent writer and director. For its first four seasons the show was set in Walnut Grove, Minnesota, and the cast included: Michael Landon as farmer Charles Ingalls; Karen Grassle as his wife, Caroline Ingalls; Melissa Sue Anderson as their eldest daughter, Mary; Melissa Gilbert as their second daughter, Laura, from whose point of view the stories are told; twins Lindsay and Sidney Greenbush as Carrie, the third daughter (a fourth daughter, Grace, was born in 1977 and is played by the Turnbeaugh twins); Victor French (1974–1977) as Mr. Edwards; Bonnie Bartlett (1974–1977) as Grace Edwards; Richard Bull as storekeeper Nels Oleson; Katherine MacGregor as his wife, Harriet Oleson; Jonathan Gilbert as their son, Willie; Alison Arngrim as their nasty daughter, Nellie; Charlotte Stewart (1974–1977) as Miss Beadle, the schoolteacher; Dabbs Greer as Reverend Robert Alden; Tracie Savage as Laura's friend, Christy; Ted Gehring (1975–1976) as banker Ebenezer Sprague; Kevin Hagen (1976–1977) as Dr. Baker; Merlin Olsen (1977–) as Jonathan Garvey; Hersha Parady (1977–) as his wife, schoolteacher Alice Garvey; and Patrick Laborteaux (1977–) as their son, Andy. At the end of the 1977–1978 season Mary, the eldest Ingalls daughter, went blind as the result of a progressive disease (the same event occurred in Laura Ingalls Wilder's book), and Linwood Boomer joined the cast as Adam Kendall, Mary's teacher. Mary accepted Adam's offer to help him teach at a school for blind children in the Dakota Territory, and, at the outset of the 1978–1979 season the entire Ingalls family moved from Walnut Grove to Winoka, Dakota. By some strange coincidence, the Oleson and Garvey families also relocated in Winoka. A new cast member was added as well: Matthew Laborteaux (foster brother of Patrick Laborteaux) as Albert, a street urchin who is adopted by the Ingalls. Later in the season, the three families returned to Walnut Grove, and Mary married Adam. In the fall of 1979 Dean Butler joined the cast as Almanzo Wilder, Laura's future husband, and Lucy Lee Flippen appeared as schoolmarm Eliza Jane Wilder.

THE LITTLE PEOPLE (THE BRIAN KEITH SHOW) NBC
15 SEPTEMBER 1972–30 AUGUST 1974 Forgettable sitcom about a pediatrician in Hawaii. With Brian Keith as Dr. Sean Jamison; Shelley Fabares as his daughter and partner, Dr. Anne Jamison; Victoria Young (Brian Keith's wife) as Puni, their nurse; Michael Gray as Ronnie Collins, a student doctor working with them; Stephen Hague as Alfred, a pesky neighborhood youngster; Sean Tyler Hall as Stewart, a friend of Alfred's; and Moe Keale as Officer O'Shaughnessy. In the fall of 1973 the title was changed from The Little People to The Brian Keith Show, and two new cast members were added: Nancy Kulp as Mrs. Millard Gruber, the landlady; Roger Bowen as Dr. Spencer Chaffee, an allergist. Bruce Johnson produced the series.

THE LITTLE REVUE ABC
4 SEPTEMBER 1949–11 DECEMBER 1949; 17 MARCH 1950–28 APRIL 1950 Half-hour musical variety show, featuring Bill Sherry, Gloria Van, Nancy Evans, and Dick Larkin. The series was seen Sundays in 1949 and Fridays in 1950. It was one of the few variety shows of the era on which there was no studio audience.

THE LITTLE SHOW NBC/ABC
27 JUNE 1950–22 NOVEMBER 1951 (NBC); 3 APRIL 1953–19 JUNE 1953 (ABC) Fifteen-minute musical show hosted by John Conte; it was seen Tuesdays and Thursdays before the network news on NBC, Friday nights over ABC.

LITTLE VIC SYNDICATED
1977 Six-part miniseries about a horse (Little Vic) and the orphaned black teenager who trained and rode him. With Joey Green as Gilly Walker, the series was produced by Linda Marmelstein.

LITTLE WOMEN SYNDICATED
1972 Louisa May Alcott's classic book became a nine-part miniseries, televised as part of *Family Classics Theatre*. Produced in England, it featured Stephanie Bidmead as Mrs. March; Sara Craze as Beth; Angela Down as Jo; Janina Faye as Amy; and Jo Rowbottom as Meg.

LITTLE WOMEN NBC
8 FEBRUARY 1979–8 MARCH 1979 Hour dramatic series which began where Louisa May Alcott's classic novel left off. With Jessica Harper as Jo March; Eve Plumb as Lissa; Ann Dusenberry as Amy; Susan Walden as Meg; Dorothy McGuire as Marmee; William Schallert as Reverend March; Richard Gilliland as Laurie; Virginia Gregg as Hannah; David Ackroyd as Friedrich Bhaer, Jo's fiancé; Mildred Natwick as Aunt March; and Robert Young as Mr. Laurence. Executive producer: David Victor for Universal TV.

THE LITTLEST HOBO SYNDICATED
1963 This Canadian-produced series was one of few shows without a human regular. The Littlest Hobo was a German shepherd named London who wandered about and helped out people with problems.

LIVE LIKE A MILLIONAIRE CBS/ABC
5 JANUARY 1951–14 MARCH 1952 (CBS); 25 OCTOBER 1952–7 FEBRUARY 1953 (ABC) On this prime-time talent show all the acts were parents, who were introduced by their children. John Nelson and Jack McCoy hosted the series.

THE LIVELY ONES   NBC
26 JULY 1962–13 SEPTEMBER 1962; 25 JULY 1963–12 SEPTEMBER
1963   Hosted by Vic Damone, this half-hour musical variety show was a
summer replacement for *Hazel* for two seasons. Produced by Barry
Shear, the show also featured Quinn O'Hara as Smitty, Gloria Neil as
Melvin, Joan Staley as Tiger, and Shirley Yelm as Charley. Music was
provided by Jerry Fielding's orchestra. Many of the segments were taped
on location at unusual sites throughout the country.

LIVING EASY WITH DR. JOYCE BROTHERS
See DR. JOYCE BROTHERS

THE LLOYD BRIDGES SHOW   CBS
11 SEPTEMBER 1962–3 SEPTEMBER 1963   Half-hour dramatic anthology
series hosted by former *Sea Hunt* star Lloyd Bridges, who portrayed
writer Adam Shepherd from September until January. In January the
show became a straightforward anthology series hosted by Bridges. His
two sons, Beau and Jeff, appeared occasionally on the show. Aaron Spelling was the producer.

THE LLOYD THAXTON SHOW   SYNDICATED
1964   An hour of rock music, hosted by disc jockey Lloyd Thaxton.

LOCK UP   SYNDICATED
1959   Low-budget crime show from Ziv TV, with Macdonald Carey as
defense attorney Herbert L. Maris and John Doucette as his legman,
Weston.

LOGAN'S RUN   CBS
16 SEPTEMBER 1977–16 JANUARY 1978   This science fiction series was
based on the movie of the same title. It starred Gregory Harrison as Logan 5, a young man who chose to escape from the Domed City, a futuristic society in which life was pleasurable, but in which all inhabitants were
"terminated" when they reached age thirty. Also featured were Heather
Menzies as Jessica 6, a young woman who escaped with him; Donald
Moffat as Rem, their android companion; and Randy Powell as Francis
7, the man sent to apprehend them (he was promised a seat on the secret
council of elders, a group of persons who were permitted to live beyond
thirty and who, unknown to the rest of the populace, actually ran the
Domed City). Despite the enormous popularity of contemporaneous sci-fi
films like *Star Wars* and *Close Encounters of the Third Kind, Logan's Run*
ended in midseason after only a few episodes. Ivan Goff and Ben Roberts
were the executive producers; Leonard Katzman was the producer.

THE LONE RANGER   ABC

15 SEPTEMBER 1949–12 SEPTEMBER 1957   One of television's most popular westerns, *The Lone Ranger* was created for radio in 1933 by George
W. Trendle. Clayton Moore starred in most of the 221 half twenty-six epi-
Lone Ranger, though John Hart played the part in at least twenty-six episodes filmed between 1951 and 1953. Jay Silverheels costarred as Tonto,
his faithful Indian companion. At least once each year the "original" episode was telecast, which explained the origins of the character. In brief,
the Lone Ranger was really a Texas Ranger named John Reid, who was
the only survivor of an ambush by Butch Cavendish's Hole in the Wall
Gang. Nursed back to health by Tonto (coincidentally, the two had been
childhood friends), he vowed to help bring justice to the West and
donned a mask (originally, to fool the Cavendish gang). Armed with silver bullets, he shot only to wound, not to kill. In the later episodes Chuck
Courtney was also featured as the Lone Ranger's nephew, Dan Reid; on
his horse, Victor, he sometimes rode with his uncle (astride Silver) and
Tonto (on Scout). Faithful viewers never seemed to mind that, wherever
they traveled throughout the West, the Lone Ranger and Tonto always
seemed to camp near the same set of rocks, "just outside of town." From
their campground Tonto might venture into town, posing as an ignorant
Redskin in order to overhear the bad guys, or the Lone Ranger might
don one of his several disguises (which, of course, enabled him to shed his
mask): The Oldtimer, a Swedish immigrant; José, a bandito; Don Pedro
O'Sullivan, a Mexican Irishman; or "Professor" Horatio Tucker, seller of
patent medicines. As many of the shows were filmed in color, the show is
still seen in syndication in many local areas. A cartoon version also appeared (see below). *The Lone Ranger*'s classic introduction ("A fiery
horse with the speed of light . . .") was read by announcer Fred Foy to
the strains of Rossini's "William Tell Overture." Clayton Moore continued to make public appearances as the Lone Ranger for many years, but
in 1979 Lone Ranger Television, Inc., a subsidiary of the Wrather Corporation, obtained a court injunction prohibiting Moore from wearing his
mask in public. The Wrather Corporation had recently made a Lone
Ranger feature film with an actor other than Moore.

THE LONE RANGER   CBS

10 SEPTEMBER 1966–6 SEPTEMBER 1969   This cartoon version of the
long-running western was seen on Saturday mornings for three seasons.

THE LONE WOLF (STREETS OF DANGER)   SYNDICATED

1955   Half-hour adventure series starring Louis Hayward as Mike Lan-
yard (The Lone Wolf), globe-trotting private eye. Based on the stories by
Louis Joseph Vance, the show had been featured on radio in 1948.

THE LONER   CBS

18 SEPTEMBER 1965–30 APRIL 1966 Created and produced by Rod
Serling, this half-hour western starred Lloyd Bridges as William Colton,
a Union soldier disillusioned by the Civil War who decided to head West
after Appomattox and who helped out people along the way.

THE LONG HOT SUMMER   ABC

16 SEPTEMBER 1965–13 JULY 1966 After ABC introduced a successful
prime-time serial—*Peyton Place*—in 1964, it followed suit a year later
with *The Long Hot Summer*. The hour-long show was based on the film
of the same title, which in turn was based on William Faulkner's *The
Hamlet*. Set in the Southern town of Frenchman's Bend, it told the story
of Ben Quick, a drifter who returned to the town and found it was run by
one man, Will Varner; Quick fell in love with Varner's daughter and attempted to clear the good name of his late father, who was suspected of
murder. Principal characters included: Roy Thinnes as Ben Quick; Edmond O'Brien (to January 1966) and Dan O'Herlihy (after January) as
Will Varner; Nancy Malone as Clara Varner, Will's daughter; Lana
Wood as Eula Varner, Clara's younger sister; Paul Geary as Jody Varner,
their brother; Paul Bryar as Sheriff Harve Anders; John Kerr as Duane
Galloway; Ruth Roman as Minnie, Will Varner's lady friend; Harold
Gould as Bo Chamberlain; Wayne Rogers as Curley; Josie Lloyd as Agnes; Tish Sterling as Susan; Charles Lampkin as Andrew; Jason Wingreen as Dr. Clark; William Mims as Ruddabaw; and Warren
Kemmerling as Lucas Taney. Frank Glicksman produced the series for
20th Century-Fox TV.

LONG JOHN SILVER   SYNDICATED

1955 Robert Newton recreated the role of Long John Silver, goodheart-
ed pirate, which he had first played in the 1950 film, *Treasure Island*. Set
during the 1700s on the island of Porto Bello, the half-hour series was
filmed in Sydney, Australia. Also featured were Kit Taylor as young Jim
Hawkins, his unofficial ward; Connie Gilchrist as Purity, the proprietor
of Long John's favorite pub.

LONGSTREET   ABC

16 SEPTEMBER 1971–10 AUGUST 1972 This hour-long crime show
starred James Franciscus as Michael Longstreet, a New Orleans insurance investigator who was blinded in an attempt on his life in which his
wife was killed. Seeking no sympathy from anyone, Longstreet, with a little help from his friends and his seeing-eye dog, Pax, a white German
shepherd, continued at his job, solving mysteries week after week. Also
featured were Marlyn Mason as Nikki Bell, his Braille instructor and
companion; Peter Mark Richman (formerly known as Mark Richman) as
Duke Paige of the Great Pacific Casualty Company, Longstreet's em-

ployer; and Ann Doran as Mrs. Kingston, Longstreet's housekeeper. Stirling Silliphant was the executive producer for Paramount TV.

LOOK HERE
NBC

15 SEPTEMBER 1957–4 MAY 1958 NBC correspondent Martin Agronsky interviewed newsmakers on this live public affairs program, aired Sunday afternoons. Agronsky's first guest was Secretary of State John Foster Dulles.

LOOK UP AND LIVE
CBS

3 JANUARY 1954–21 JANUARY 1979 This long-running religious show was a Sunday-morning fixture for two dozen years. In the early years, the Reverend Lawrence McMaster frequently appeared, and Merv Griffin hosted the show briefly in 1955. In later years, however, there was no fixed format, since different religious and cultural themes were explored. Pamela Ilott, director of religious programming for CBS News, was executive producer.

THE LORENZO AND HENRIETTA MUSIC SHOW
SYNDICATED

1976 Short-lived talk show cohosted by Lorenzo Music (producer and voice of Carlton on *Rhoda*) and his wife, Henrietta Music.

THE LORETTA YOUNG SHOW (A LETTER TO LORETTA)
NBC

20 SEPTEMBER 1953–10 SEPTEMBER 1961 Hosted by, and frequently starring, Loretta Young, this half-hour dramatic anthology series was seen Sunday nights at 10:00 p.m. It is probably best remembered for Young's fashions, and her swirling entrance through a door at the beginning of each episode. During its first season the show was titled *A Letter to Loretta;* Young read a letter supposedly written by a viewer which served as an introduction to the evening's presentation. In 1954 that device was dropped. It was reported in 1972 that Young had been awarded $559,000 in a suit against NBC for the network's violation of her contract in permitting syndicated reruns of the series to be shown with her outdated fashions and hairstyles. John Newland, who later hosted *One Step Beyond,* appeared many times, and also directed several shows.

LOST IN SPACE
CBS

15 SEPTEMBER 1965–11 SEPTEMBER 1968 Science fiction series about the Space Family Robinson. Dispatched by the United States government in 1997 to colonize a planet in Alpha Centauri, the Robinsons' spacecraft was thrown hopelessly off course by a stowaway. With Guy Williams as Dr. John Robinson, astrophysicist; June Lockhart as Maureen Robinson, his wife; Marta Kristen as Judy, their elder daughter; Billy Mumy as Will, their son; Angela Cartwright as Penny, their youngest child; Mark Goddard as Don West, the pilot; Jonathan Harris as the stowaway, Dr.

Zachary Smith, an enemy agent who was to have sabotaged the craft on the launching pad; and Bob May as The Robot. Irwin Allen created the series and was also its executive producer; eighty-three hour episodes were filmed.

THE LOST SAUCER   ABC
6 SEPTEMBER 1975–4 SEPTEMBER 1976   Live-action Saturday-morning show about two extraplanetary creatures who inadvertently pick up a boy and his babysitter while visiting Earth. With Ruth Buzzi as Fi; Jim Nabors as Fum; Alice Playten as Alice, the babysitter; and Jarrod Johnson as Jerry, the boy. Produced by Sid and Marty Krofft, the series was later shown as one segment of *The Krofft Supershow*.

LOTSA LUCK   NBC
10 SEPTEMBER 1973–24 MAY 1974   Blue-collar sitcom based on the British series, *On the Buses*. With Dom DeLuise as Stanley Belmont, lost-and-found clerk for a New York bus company; Kathleen Freeman as his mother, Iris Belmont; Beverly Sanders as his sister, Olive Swan; Wynn Irwin as Olive's unemployed husband, Arthur Swan; and Jack Knight as the Belmonts' neighbor, Bummy Pfitzer, a bus driver. The show was created by three alumni of *The Dick Van Dyke Show:* Carl Reiner, Bill Persky, and Sam Denoff.

LOU GRANT   CBS
20 SEPTEMBER 1977–   In this hour-long series Edward Asner continues to play the part he had created on *The Mary Tyler Moore Show*—Lou Grant, who, having lost his job at WJM in Minneapolis, moved to Los Angeles and got a new job as city editor of the Los Angeles *Tribune*. While it is not uncommon for characters to be spun off from one series to another, this appears to have been the first instance in which a character left a situation comedy to headline a dramatic series. Also featured are Mason Adams as managing editor Charlie Hume, an old friend of Lou's; Nancy Marchand as Margaret Pynchon, owner and publisher of the *Tribune*; Jack Bannon as Art Donovan, assistant city editor; Robert Walden as scrappy young reporter Joe Rossi; and Daryl Anderson as Dennis (Animal) Price. In the earliest episodes Rebecca Balding was also featured as Carla, another young reporter, but she was replaced by Linda Kelsey as reporter Billie Newman. Executive producers: James L. Brooks, Allan Burns, and Gene Reynolds.

LOVE, AMERICAN STYLE   ABC
29 SEPTEMBER 1969–11 JANUARY 1974   A rarity in television programming, *Love, American Style* was a comedy anthology series; each week two or three stories of mixed lengths were televised, and short blackouts were aired between them. The group which performed the blackouts usu-

ally numbered about eight, and from time to time included Bill Callaway, Buzz Cooper, Phyllis Elizabeth Davis, Jaki DeMar, Mary Grover, James Hampton, Stuart Margolin, Lynne Marta, Barbara Minkus, Bernie Kopell, Tracy Reed, and Richard Williams. Arnold Margolin and Jim Parker were the show's executive producers for most of its run. Writers included Frank Buxton, Jerry Rannow, Greg Strangis, Ed Scharlach, and Doug Tibbles. The show was broadcast in an hour-long format except during the 1970–1971 season, when it was a half hour. In the fall of 1977 ABC revived the concept: see *The Love Boat.*

LOVE AND MARRIAGE
NBC

21 SEPTEMBER 1959–25 JANUARY 1960   Featured in this half-hour sitcom were William Demarest as Bill Harris, owner of a music publishing company in shaky financial condition; Stubby Kaye as Stubby Wilson, his promo man; Kay Armen as Sophie, the secretary; Jeanne Bal as Pat Baker, Bill's daughter, who tried to bring new talent to the firm; Murray Hamilton as her husband, Steve Baker, a lawyer; Susan Reilly as their daughter, Susan; and Jeannie Lynn as their daughter, Jenny.

THE LOVE BOAT
ABC

24 SEPTEMBER 1977–   One of the most popular new shows of the 1977–1978 season, *The Love Boat* followed the format of *Love, American Style,* featuring guest stars in comedy vignettes; unlike *Love, American Style,* the stories are intertwined rather than telecast consecutively. All the action takes place aboard *The Pacific Princess,* a cruise ship. The ship's crew, who are the only regulars on the series, include Gavin MacLeod as Captain Merrill Stubing; Bernie Kopell as Doc (Adam Bricker), the ship's doctor; Fred Grandy as Burl (Gopher) Smith, assistant purser; Ted Lange as Isaac Washington, the bartender; and Lauren Tewes as Julie McCoy, social director. In the fall of 1979 Jill Whelan was added as Vickie, Stubing's illegitimate daughter. Aaron Spelling and Douglas S. Cramer are the executive producers; Henry Colman, Gordon Farr, and Lynne Farr are the producers.

THE LOVE EXPERTS
SYNDICATED

1978   A game show not unlike *The Amateur's Guide to Love,* this series featured a panel of four celebrities who gave advice to contestants on matters of love and romance. At the end of each show the panel selected the contestant who had posed the most interesting "love problem"; the lucky player then won a prize. Bill Cullen hosted the half-hour show.

LOVE IS A MANY SPLENDORED THING
CBS

18 SEPTEMBER 1967–23 MARCH 1973   Another of the daytime serials developed by Irna Phillips, *Love Is a Many Splendored Thing* was intended to be a continuation of the 1955 film, which had starred William Hold-

en and Jennifer Jones. Its central theme at first involved interracial romance; when the network insisted that that theme be dropped, Phillips quit. Under new writers, story lines veered toward political intrigue. Principal players included Nancy Hsueh as Mia Elliott, the daughter of an American father and an Asian mother who, as the series began, came to San Francisco to study medicine; Nicholas Pryor as Paul Bradley, Mia's first romantic interest; Robert Milli and Ron Hale as Dr. Jim Abbott, Mia's second romantic interest; Sam Wade, David Birney, Michael Hawkins, Vincent Cannon, and Tom Fuccello as Mark Elliott, Mia's cousin; Grace Albertson and Gloria Hoye as Mark's mother, Helen Elliott; Leslie Charleson and Bibi Besch as Iris Donnelly, Mark's girlfriend; Robert Burr and Albert Stratton as Lieutenant Tom Donnelly, Iris's brother; Shawn Campbell as Ricky Donnelly, Tom's son; Beverlee McKinsey as Martha Donnelly, Tom's estranged wife (who was also known as Julie Richards); Berkeley Harris as Jim Whitman, Martha's boyfriend; Donna Mills, Veleka Gray, and Barbara Stanger as Laura Donnelly, sister of Iris and Tom, who eventually married Mark Elliott; Judson Laire as Dr. Will Donnelly, father of Iris, Tom, and Laura; Ed Power and Brett Halsey as Spence Garrison, an aspiring politician who became involved with Iris; Susan Browning as Nancy Garrison, Spence's wife; Don Gantry as Senator Alfred E. Preston; John Carpenter as millionaire Walter Travis, Preston's backer; Leon Russom as Joe Taylor, a former employee of Travis; Andrea Marcovicci as Betsy Chernak, who married Joe Taylor; Vincent Baggetta as Dr. Peter Chernak, Betsy's brother; and Diana Douglas as Lily Chernak, widowed mother of Peter and Betsy, who eventually married Dr. Will Donnelly.

LOVE OF LIFE CBS

24 SEPTEMBER 1951–1 FEBRUARY 1980 Only three weeks younger than TV's senior serial (*Search for Tomorrow*), *Love of Life* enjoyed a run of twenty-eight years. It was created by John Hess for The Biow Company but was sold to CBS in the early 1960s. Roy Winsor was its first executive producer, Charles Schenck its first producer. In recent years Darryl Hickman (a former child actor and brother of Dwayne Hickman) was the executive producer, with Jean Arley the producer. Larry Auerbach was the director from the beginning (though Jerry Evans and John Desmond codirected with him during the 1970s). Recent head writers included Claire Labine and Paul Avila Mayer (who subsequently created *Ryan's Hope*), Margaret DePriest, Paul Schneider, and Gabrielle Upton. *Love of Life* premiered as a fifteen-minute show and was then set in the town of Barrowsville. It was expanded to thirty minutes on 14 April 1958, and was trimmed to a twenty-five-minute format in 1962. Over the years, the action shifted away from Barrowsville to the nearby town of Rosehill. The story originally centered around two sisters—noble, long-suffering Vanessa Dale and amoral, opportunistic Margaret (Meg) Dale. After

Meg was written out of the story in the late 1950s, the story lines diffused as younger characters were introduced; Meg was brought back, however, late in 1973 by then head writers Labine and Mayer. The large cast has included: Peggy McCay (1951–1955), Bonnie Bartlett (1955–1959) and Audrey Peters (1959) as Vanessa Dale; Jean McBride (1951–1956) and Tudi Wiggins (who joined the cast in 1973, when the role was revived after a seventeen-year absence) as Margaret Dale Harper Aleata; Jane Rose (1951–1956) and Joanna Roos (who took the role in 1968, when the character returned after a long absence) as Sarah Dale, mother of Van and Meg; Ed Jerome as Will Dale, father of Van and Meg; Paul Potter as Charles Harper, Meg's first husband; Dennis Parnell (1951–1957), Tommy White (1957–1958), Christopher Reeve (1968–1976), and Chandler Hill Harben (1976–   ) as Benno, the son of Meg and Charles Harper, who was known as "Beanie" in his youth and, when he returned to the show after some ten years, as "Ben"; Joe Allen, Jr., as Miles Pardee, an unsavory boyfriend of Meg's who was found murdered; Ronald Long as lawyer Evans Baker; Richard Coogan as lawyer Paul Raven, who married Van in 1954 and was reported kiled in 1958 (actually, Paul lived, though he was stricken with amnesia: played by Robert Burr, he showed up in 1971 under the name of Matt Corby; he was later jailed and died); Bonnie Bartlett (1951) and Hildy Parks (1951–1956) as Van's roommate, Ellie Crown (Bartlett later played Van herself); Marie Kenney as Mrs. Rivers; Joanna Roos as Althea Raven, Paul's mother (Roos returned to the show as Sarah Dale); Virginia Robinson as Judith Lodge Raven, Paul's first wife; Steven Gethers as casino owner Hal Craig; Donald Symington as Jack Andrews, Meg's second husband; Lauren Gilbert as Tom Craythorne, Meg's third husband; Ann Loring as actress Tammy Forrest; Gene Peterson as Noel Penn; Ron Tomme (1959–   ) as Bruce Sterling, who married Van, divorced her, and married her again in 1972; Jimmy Bayer, Dan Ferrone (to 1966), Dennis Cooney (1966–1969), and John Fink (1969–1970) as Alan Sterling, Bruce's son by a former marriage; Nina Reader (to 1961), Lee Lawson (1961–1965), and Zina Bethune as Barbara Sterling, Bruce's daughter by a former marriage; Helene Dumas (1959–1977) as Vivian Carlson, mother of Bruce's former wife; Tom Shirley (1959–1961) and Jack Stamberger (1961–1970) as Henry Carlson, father of Bruce's former wife and head of a paper company; Ron Jackson as Dr. Tony Vento, Barbara Sterling's first husband; Kimetha Laurie as Cindy Craythorne, Tom Craythorne's daughter; Gene Pelligrini as Link Porter; Joan Copeland as Link's wife, Maggie Porter, and her twin, Kay Logan; John Straub as Guy Latimer; Paul Savior (1961–1966), Michael Ebert, Edward Moore, and Jerry Lacy (1971–1978) as his son, Rick Latimer, who became Barbara Sterling's second husband; Fred Stewart (1966–1971) and Charles White (1971–1973) as Alex Caldwell, who married Sarah Dale after Will Dale died; Eileen Letchworth as Sharon Ferris; Marie Masters as Hester Ferris, her daughter; Robert Alda as Jason Ferris, Sharon's husband; Stan Watt and Jonathan Moore as bookdealer Charles Lamont, next-door neighbor of Van and Bruce Sterling; Diane Rousseau as Diana Lamont, his wife (and ex-wife); Gene Bua as Bill Prentiss, son of Charles Lamont, who died in 1972 of a blood disease; Toni Bull as Tess Krakauer, Bill's wife; Frances Sternhagen and Jocelyn Brando as Mrs. Krakauer, Tess's mother; Alan York as Mickey Krakauer; Byron Sanders as John Randolph, who was married briefly to Tess and turned up murdered in 1970; Lawrence Weber as Richard Rollins, Randolph's killer; Renée Roy as Clair Bridgeman; Cathy Bacon as Sally Bridgeman, her daughter; Lincoln Kilpatrick as Joe Bond; Darlene Cotton as his wife, Rita Bond (the Bonds were the first black couple on *Love of Life*); Leonie Norton and Sally Stark as singer Kate Swanson; Drew Snyder as Dr. Dan Phillips, who married Kate and was later killed in a crash; Keith Charles as Kate's next husband, Dr. Ted Chandler, who ran a sex clinic; Michael Glaser and Tony LoBianco as Dr. Joe Corelli (Glaser, later known as Paul Michael Glaser, starred in *Starsky and Hutch*); Paul McGrath as Larry Andrews; Roy Scheider, Ben Piazza, and Roy Shuman as Jonas Falk; Bonnie Bedelia as Sandy Porter; Jessica Walter as Julia Moreno; David Rounds as Philip Holden; John Gabriel and George Kane as Link Morrison; Nancy Marchand as Vinnie Phillips; Douglass Watson as Lloyd Phillips; Polly Rowles as Helen Hunt; Shirley Blanc as Dr. Lederer; David Sabin as Dr. Peck; Carl Betz as Collie Jordan; Shari Freels as Daisy Allen; Ja'net DuBois as Loretta Allen; Joe Silver as Larry Prince; Brian Brownlee as Jack Bendarik; Phil Sterling as Dr. Westheimer; Cindy Grover as Stacy Corby, daughter of Matt Corby (Matt was really Van's long-lost husband, Paul Raven); Don Warfield and Ray Wise as Jamie Rollins, a lawyer who married Diana Lamont; Deborah Courtney (1973–1977) and Roxanne Gregory (1977–1978) as Caroline (Cal) Aleata, daughter of Meg Dale Aleata; Charles Baxter as Jeff Hart, the corrupt mayor of Rosehill who married Meg Dale Aleata after her return; Brian Farrell as David Hart, his son; Elizabeth Kemp as Betsy Crawford, who married Ben Harper after his return; Birgitta Tolksdorf (1974–   ) as Arlene Lovett, Ben's previous wife; Peg Murray as Carrie Lovett, her mother; Leon B. Stevens as Dr. Kreisinger; Nancy MacKay and Season Hubley as nurse Candy Lowe; Richard Cox as Bobby Mackey, who tried to defraud Tess and was murdered; Richard McKensie as Walter Morgan, Bobby's partner and killer; Michael Fairman as Phil Waterman; Ed Crowley as Howie Howells; John Aniston as Edouard Aleata; Pamela Lincoln as Felicia Fleming, who married Charles Lamont (in real life, Pamela Lincoln was married to *Love of Life*'s executive producer, Darryl Hickman); David Carlton Stambaugh as Hank Latimer, son of Rick and Barbara Latimer; Oren Jay, Raymond Cass, and Trip Randall as Johnny Prentiss, son of Bill and Tess Prentiss; Romola Robb Allrud as Linda Crawford; Kenneth McMillan as James

Crawford; Chris Chase as Connie Loomis; Earle Hyman as Dr. Paul Bryson; Marsha Mason as Judith Cole; Natalie Schafer as Augusta Rolland; Geraldine Brooks as Arden Delecort; Renne Jarrett as Eileen McCallion; Stephen Elliott as Paul Ailey; Bert Convy as Gene Hamilton; Lloyd Battista as Roy Slater; Peter Brouwer as Joe Cusack; Michael Allinson as Ian Russell; Amy Gibson as Lynn Henderson; Veleka Gray as Mia Marriott; Ron Harper as Andrew Marriott; Richard Council as Michael Blake; Corinne Neuchateau as Mary Owens; Elaine Grove as Wendy Hayes; Sherry Rooney as Dory Patton; Danielle Cusson as Susie Ryker; Robert McCone as Danny Ryker; Michael Kennedy as Kevin Patten; Jessica Rooney as Kirsten Patten; Jack Marks as Leon Matthews; Donald Warfield (again) as Bert; Martin Zurla as T. J. Brogger; Gretchen Walther as Faith Manning; Elizabeth Stack as Cherie Manning; Ted Leplat as Elliott Lang; Chris Marlowe as Andrew Marriott, Jr.; Richard Fasciano as Dr. Paul Graham; Peter Gatto as Tony Alphonso; Ann Spangler McCarthy as Bambi Brewster; Margo McKenna as Elizabeth Lang; Shepperd Strudwick as Timothy McCauley; Jake Turner as Zachary Bly; Richard K. Weber as Dr. Tom Crawford.

In addition, according to Ron Lackmann's book, *TV Soap Opera Almanac,* other roles have been played by such notables as Martin Balsam, Warren Beatty, Damon Evans, Peter Falk, and Anne Jackson.

LOVE ON A ROOFTOP   ABC

13 SEPTEMBER 1966–31 AUGUST 1967   Domestic sitcom about two newlyweds who moved into a tiny top-floor apartment in San Francisco. With Judy Carne as Julie Willis, an art student; Peter Deuel (he later shortened his last name to Duel) as her husband, Dave Willis, an architect; Rich Little as their neighbor, Stan Parker; Barbara Bostock as Carol Parker, Stan's wife; Herb Voland as Julie's father, Fred Hammond, owner of a string of used car lots; Edith Atwater as Julie's mother, Phyllis Hammond; and Lillian Adams as the Willises' landlady, Mrs. Lewis. E. W. Swackhamer produced and directed the series, which was rerun on ABC during the summer of 1971.

LOVE STORY   DUMONT

20 APRIL 1954–29 JUNE 1954   Half-hour dramatic anthology series, produced by David Lowe.

LOVE STORY   CBS

31 OCTOBER 1955–30 MARCH 1956   Jack Smith, assisted by Pat Meikle, hosted this daytime game show on which newlyweds or to-be-weds competed in a quiz segment for the chance to win a trip to Paris. Smith and Meikle had previously worked together on *Welcome Travelers,* a human interest show which had occupied the same time slot.

LOVE STORY   NBC

3 OCTOBER 1973–2 JANUARY 1974   This dramatic anthology series died
in midseason, having been slotted opposite *Kojak*.

LOVE THAT BOB   NBC/CBS

2 JANUARY 1955–25 SEPTEMBER 1955 (NBC); 1 SEPTEMBER 1955–19
SEPTEMBER 1957 (CBS); 24 SEPTEMBER 1957–15 SEPTEMBER 1959
(NBC)   Popular half-hour sitcom starring Bob Cummings as Bob Col-
lins, a girl-crazy photographer ("Hold it—I think you're gonna like this
picture!"). With Ann B. Davis as his gal Friday, Schultzy (short for
Charmaine Schultz); Rosemary DeCamp as Margaret MacDonald, Bob's
widowed sister; Dwayne Hickman as Chuck MacDonald, her teenage
son; Joi Lansing as Shirley Swanson, the buxom model who chased after
Bob; Nancy Kulp as Pamela Livingstone, a local birdwatcher; King
Donovan as Harvey Helm, Bob's Air Force buddy; Mary Lawrence as
Harvey's wife, Ruth; Charles Herbert as Tommy Helm, their son; and
Marjorie Bennett as Mrs. Neemeyer, a neighbor.

LOVE THAT JILL   ABC

20 JANUARY 1958–28 APRIL 1958   Half-hour sitcom starring Anne
Jeffreys as Jill Johnson and Robert Sterling as Jack Gibson, owners of rival modeling agencies in New York. The two had previously worked together in *Topper*. Also featured on *Love That Jill* were Barbara Nichols
as Ginger, one of Jill's models, and James Lydon as Richard, Jill's secretary. Alex Gottlieb produced the series.

LOVE THY NEIGHBOR   ABC

15 JUNE 1973–19 SEPTEMBER 1973   Predictable ethnic sitcom about a
white-collar black couple who moved in next door to a blue-collar white
couple. With Harrison Page and Janet MacLachlan as Ferguson and
Jackie Bruce, the black couple; Ron Masak and Joyce Bulifant as Charlie
and Peggy Wilson; and Milt Kamen as Murray Bronson, another employee at Turner Electronics, where Ferguson and Charlie both worked.

LOVERS AND FRIENDS   NBC

3 JANUARY 1977–6 MAY 1977   Created by Harding Lemay, this short-
lived daytime serial was set in Point Clair, a fashionable suburb of Chicago, where dwelt two families: the Cushings, an aristocratic family who
had lived there for generations, and the Saxtons, a family of humbler origins who had just moved in from a less prestigious suburb. The cast included: Ron Randell as Richard Cushing, a wealthy stockbroker; Nancy
Marchand as his wife, Edith Slocum Cushing; Rod Arrants as their son,
Austin, a dropout; Patricia Estrin as Megan Cushing, their daughter;
Dianne Harper as Laurie Brewster, Austin's girlfriend; David Knapp as
Desmond Hamilton, Megan's fiancé; John Heffernan as Lester Saxton, a

reformed alcoholic; Patricia Englund as his wife, Josie; Flora Plumb as Eleanor Saxton Kimball, their elder daughter; Bob Purvey as Rhett Saxton, their eldest son, who fell in love with Megan Cushing; Richard Backus as Jason Saxton, their second eldest son; David Abbott as Bentley Saxton, their youngest son; Vicky Dawson as Tessa Saxton, their younger daughter; Stephen Joyce as lawyer George Kimball, husband of Eleanor; Christine Jones as Amy Gifford, cousin of the Saxton kids; Margaret Barker as Sophia Slocum, mother of Edith Cushing; Karen Philipp as Barbara Manners, an employee and after-hours companion of Richard Cushing; and Susan Foster as Connie Ferguson, sometime girlfriend of Rhett Saxton. Paul Rauch, a former daytime programming executive at CBS, was executive producer of the series. Late in 1977 a revamped version of the serial reappeared on NBC: see *For Richer, for Poorer*.

LOVES ME, LOVES ME NOT
CBS

20 MARCH 1977–27 APRIL 1977   Courtship was the theme of this sitcom which starred Kenneth Gilman and Susan Dey as Dick Phillips and Jane Benson. Also featured were Art Metrano as Tom, Dick's boss (Dick was a reporter); Phyllis Glick as Sue, Jane's friend. Created by Susan Harris, the show was produced by Paul Younger Witt and Tony Thomas.

LUCAN
ABC

12 SEPTEMBER 1977–4 DECEMBER 1978   An irregularly scheduled adventure series starring Kevin Brophy as Lucan, a boy who had lived with wolves in the woods of Minnesota until he was ten, and who, as a teenager, searched for his real identity. Also featured were John Randolph as Dr. Hoagland, a research scientist at the university to which the boy had been taken for study, and from which he escaped, and Don Gordon as Prentiss, a modern-day bounty hunter hired by the university to find the boy.

LUCAS TANNER
NBC

11 SEPTEMBER 1974–20 AUGUST 1975   Family drama starring David Hartman as Lucas Tanner, a sportswriter who decided to become a schoolteacher after his wife and son were killed in an automobile accident; Tanner managed to find a position in the English department at Harry S Truman Memorial High School in Webster Groves, Missouri. Also featured were Rosemary Murphy (to January 1975) as Mrs. Margaret Blumenthal, the principal; John Randolph (from January 1975) as John Hamilton, the new principal; Robbie Rist as Glendon, the youngster who lived next door to Tanner; Alan Abelew as Jaytee, one of Tanner's students; Trish Soodik as Cindy, another student; Kimberley Beck as Terry, a student; and Michael Dwight-Smith as Wally, a student. David Victor was executive producer of the series, which was produced by Jay Benson.

LUCKY PAIR SYNDICATED
1969 Celebrities and studio contestants teamed up on this game show hosted by Richard Dawson.

LUCKY PARTNERS NBC
30 JUNE 1958–22 AUGUST 1958 On this little-known daytime game show, hosted by Carl Cordell, members of the studio audience tried to match serial numbers on dollar bills with those of on-stage contestants. Home viewers could also participate. The show was bumped from NBC's schedule after only a few weeks to make room for another game show, *Concentration.*

LUCKY PUP (THE ADVENTURES OF LUCKY PUP) CBS
23 AUGUST 1948–23 JUNE 1951 This fifteen-minute puppet show was seen early weekday evenings for most of its run. It featured Doris Brown and the puppets of Hope and Morey Bunin. Two of the puppets, Pinhead and Foodini, later had their own series: see *Foodini the Great.*

LUCKY STRIKE THEATER
See ROBERT MONTGOMERY PRESENTS

THE LUCY SHOW CBS
1 OCTOBER 1962–16 SEPTEMBER 1968 Lucille Ball returned to the air, without her ex-husband Desi Arnaz, in this half-hour sitcom. She remained on the air for the next twelve seasons (the last six were as star of *Here's Lucy*). On *The Lucy Show* she played Lucy Carmichael, a recently widowed bank secretary. Originally she worked at the First National Bank in Danfield, Connecticut, and the show also featured Vivian Vance (her crony from *I Love Lucy*) as her pal and cotenant, Vivian Bagley; Jimmy Garrett as Lucy's son, Jerry; Candy Moore as Lucy's daughter, Chris; Ralph Hart as Vivian's son, Sherman; Dick Martin as Lucy's friend, Harry; and Charles Lane as cantankerous Mr. Barnsdahl, Lucy's boss. In the fall of 1963 Gale Gordon replaced Lane as Lucy's new, but equally cantankerous, boss, Theodore J. Mooney. In the fall of 1965 all the supporting players (except for Gordon) were dropped, and the new format found Lucy as a bank secretary in San Francisco. Joining the cast were Roy Roberts as bank president Harrison Cheever, and Mary Jane Croft as Lucy's friend, Mary Jane Lewis.

LUX PLAYHOUSE CBS
3 OCTOBER 1958–18 SEPTEMBER 1959 This half-hour dramatic anthology series shared a time slot with *Schlitz Playhouse of Stars* for one season.

THE LUX SHOW STARRING ROSEMARY CLOONEY   NBC

26 SEPTEMBER 1957–19 JUNE 1958   After sponsoring a dramatic series
for seven seasons, the makers of Lux detergent decided to sponsor a musical variety show. Pop singer Rosemary Clooney, who had previously
hosted her own syndicated show, headlined the half hour, which also featured the Modernaires and the Frank DeVol Orchestra. Rosemary
Clooney's theme song was "Tenderly," composed by Lloyd Gross.

LUX VIDEO THEATRE   CBS/NBC

2 OCTOBER 1950–24 JUNE 1954 (CBS); 26 AUGUST 1954–12 SEPTEMBER
1957 (NBC)   This half-hour dramatic anthology series was the television
counterpart of *Lux Radio Theatre,* the popular radio anthology series
which began in 1934. During the 1954–1955 season it was hosted by
James Mason, who was succeeded by Otto Kruger and Gordon MacRae.
Notable guest appearances included those by Robert Stack (in "Inside
Story," one of his earliest TV roles, 18 June 1951), Peter Lorre ("The
Taste," his first major TV role, 31 March 1952), Grace Kelly ("A Message for Janice," 29 September 1952), Edward G. Robinson ("Witness for
the Prosecution," his TV dramatic debut, 17 September 1953), Barbara
Rush ("Gavin's Darling," her first major role, 22 April 1954), James Arness ("The Chase," his first major TV role, 30 December 1954), and Esther Williams ("The Armed Venus," a rare TV appearance, 23 May
1957).

M*A*S*H   CBS

17 SEPTEMBER 1972–   . Robert Altman's 1970 film was the
basis for this Korean War sitcom. One of the most popular shows of the
1970s, it has lasted longer than the war in which it is set. The action takes
place not along the front lines, but at the 4077th M*A*S*H (Mobile
Army Surgical Hospital) Unit a few miles away. With Alan Alda as Captain Benjamin Franklin (Hawkeye) Pierce, a surgeon from Maine whose
disdain for rules and regulations is matched by his skill with a scalpel, his
quick wit, and a sense of compassion; Wayne Rogers (1972–1975) as
Captain John F. X. (Trapper John) McIntire, Hawkeye's tentmate, also a
skilled surgeon and every bit as rambunctious as Pierce; McLean Stevenson (1972–1975) as Lieutenant Colonel Henry Blake, the easygoing commanding officer who generally preferred to avoid the exercise of
authority; Loretta Swit as Major Margaret (Hot Lips) Houlihan, commanding officer of the nurses; Larry Linville (1972–1977) as Major Frank
Burns, the by-the-book zealot who was the butt of many of Hawkeye and
Trapper John's practical jokes; Gary Burghoff (1972–1979) as Corporal
Walter (Radar) O'Reilly, the naive but efficient company clerk; Jamie
Farr as Corporal Max Klinger, an enlisted man who, hoping to win his
discharge from the Army on psychiatric grounds, usually wears dresses

while on duty. Of that group only Burghoff had been featured in the movie; in the earliest episodes a few other regulars were also featured, but most had been phased out by the end of the first season: Tim Brown (who had also been featured in the movie) as Spearchucker Jones, a football star who was also a physician; Odessa Cleveland as Lieutenant Ginger Ballis, a nurse; Karen Philipp as Lieutenant Maggie Dish, also a nurse; and G. Wood as General Hammond. The first company chaplain, Father John Mulcahy, was played by George Morgan; he was succeeded in midseason by William Christopher as Father Francis Mulcahy, who has remained with the series.

At the end of the third season Stevenson and Rogers left the show—Stevenson's character, Colonel Blake, was killed in a plane crash on the final show that year. In the fall of 1975 two new faces joined the cast: Harry Morgan as Colonel Sherman Potter, the new commanding officer, a surprisingly tolerant fellow for a career man; and Mike Farrell as Captain B. J. Hunnicutt, Hawkeye's new tentmate, another gifted surgeon who also loves a good practical joke. During the 1974–1975 season Loudon Wainwright III was occasionally featured as Captain Calvin Spaulding. At the end of the 1976–1977 season Major Houlihan, who had had a not-so-secret affair with Major Burns for most of the past five seasons, finally got married—to Lieutenant Colonel Donald Penobscot (played by Beeson Carroll), an officer stationed at headquarters; they were later divorced. Larry Linville, who played Burns, left the show in 1977 and was succeeded by David Ogden Stiers as Major Charles Emerson Winchester, a stuffy but technically adept surgeon. The series was produced for several seasons by Gene Reynolds and Larry Gelbart and is currently produced by Burt Metcalfe. More than any other service comedy, *M*A*S*H* has depicted the futility—and the horror—of war.

THE M & M CANDY CARNIVAL   CBS
6 JANUARY 1952–28 JUNE 1953   Gene Crane hosted this Sunday-afternoon talent contest, broadcast from Philadelphia and sponsored by the manufacturers of M & M candy. In 1954 Crane returned as host of a similar program: see *Contest Carnival*.

M-G-M PARADE   ABC
14 SEPTEMBER 1955–2 MAY 1956   ABC, which had succeeded in persuading Warner Brothers to produce a TV series in 1955 (see *Warner Brothers Presents*), also succeeded in landing a second major film studio—Metro-Goldwyn-Mayer. George Murphy hosted the half-hour series that presented clips from vintage films, biographies of stars, and previews of upcoming motion pictures.

M SQUAD   NBC
20 SEPTEMBER 1957–13 SEPTEMBER 1960   Half-hour crime show star-

ring Lee Marvin (who also owned a 50 percent interest in the show) as Lieutenant Frank Ballinger, a Chicago plainclothesman assigned to M Squad, a unit that mainly investigated homicides. Paul Newlan was also featured as his superior, Captain Grey. Burt Reynolds played one of his first major TV roles in one episode, "The Teacher," aired 2 January 1959.

M. V. P. SYNDICATED
1971 Sports-oriented talk show hosted by Cincinnati Reds' catcher Johnny Bench, who was named the National League's M.V.P. (Most Valuable Player) in 1972.

THE MAC DAVIS SHOW NBC
11 JULY 1974–29 AUGUST 1974; 19 DECEMBER 1974–22 MAY 1975; 18 MARCH 1976–17 JUNE 1976 Singer Mac Davis hosted three hour variety shows. The first one was a summer replacement for *The Flip Wilson Show;* the second one was activated to replace *Sierra* late in 1974. Sandy Gallin was its executive producer, and Arnie Rosen and Bob Ellison produced it. Davis's third show appeared in the spring of the following season, with Gary Smith and Dwight Hemion as executive producers, and Mike Post and Steve Binder as producers. Regulars included mimes Shields and Yarnell, who later hosted their own variety series (see also *Shields and Yarnell*).

THE MacKENZIES OF PARADISE COVE ABC
27 MARCH 1979–18 MAY 1979 Irregularly scheduled hour series about five orphans who hooked up with an adventurer in Hawaii. With Clu Gulagher as Cuda Webber, the orphans' adopted guardian; Lory Walsh as Bridget MacKenzie; Shawn Stevens as Kevin MacKenzie, her twin brother; Sean Marshall as Michael MacKenzie; Randi Kiger as Celia MacKenzie; Keith Mitchell as Timothy MacKenzie; Harry Chang as Barney, a friend of Cuda's; Moe Keale as Big Ben, another pal of Cuda's. Jerry Thorpe and William Blinn were the producers.

MACKENZIE'S RAIDERS SYNDICATED
1958 Half-hour western starring Richard Carlson as Colonel Ranald Mackenzie, a cavalry officer who headed an outfit that operated along the Mexican border during the 1870s.

THE MacNEIL–LEHRER REPORT PBS
5 JANUARY 1976– A nightly news analysis series, this half-hour show began in 1975 as a local show in New York; it went network in January 1976. It was originally hosted solely by Robert MacNeil (it was then known as *The Robert MacNeil Report*), a native Canadian who had previously worked for CBC (the Canadian Broadcasting Corporation), BBC, NBC, and the Reuters News Agency. In the fall of 1976

MacNeil was joined by cohost Jim Lehrer, who reported from Washington (MacNeil remained in New York). Early in 1978 the two were joined by Charlayne Hunter-Gault.

MADE IN AMERICA   CBS
5 APRIL 1964–3 MAY 1964   Robert Maxwell hosted this prime-time game show on which a celebrity panel tried to figure out the identities of guests, all of whom were self-made millionaires. The short-lived series replaced half of *The Judy Garland Show* and was in turn replaced by reruns of *Brenner*.

MADIGAN   NBC
20 SEPTEMBER 1972–22 AUGUST 1973   This ninety-minute crime show was one segment of *The NBC Wednesday Mystery Movie* and alternated with *Banacek* and *Cool Million*. It starred Richard Widmark, a major film star whose television appearances have been extremely infrequent, as Sergeant Dan Madigan, a typically tough New York cop. Dean Hargrove and Roland Kibbee produced the series for Universal Television.

MAGGIE AND THE BEAUTIFUL MACHINE   PBS
1972–1975   Half-hour exercise program hosted by Maggie Lettwin. The show was seen locally on WGBH-TV, Boston, for three seasons before going network in 1972.

MAGGI'S PRIVATE WIRE   NBC
12 APRIL 1949–2 JULY 1949   Fifteen-minute interview show, hosted by Maggi McNellis.

MAGIC CIRCUS   SYNDICATED
1972   An hour of magic, sponsored by Pillsbury, starring Mark Wilson, Nani Darnell, and Rebo the Clown. The trio had previously been featured on Wilson's network magic show, *The Magic Land of Allakazam*.

THE MAGIC CLOWN   NBC
11 SEPTEMBER 1949–27 JUNE 1954   This fifteen-minute kids' show was seen on Sunday mornings and starred a magician known as Zovella. The series was written and produced by Al Garry.

THE MAGIC COTTAGE   DUMONT
18 JULY 1949–12 SEPTEMBER 1952   Pat Meikle hosted this Monday-through-Friday kids' show.

THE MAGIC EYE   SYNDICATED
1959   Scientific topics were explored on this educational show for children.

THE MAGIC LAND OF ALLAKAZAM
CBS/ABC

1 OCTOBER 1960–22 SEPTEMBER 1962 (CBS); 29 SEPTEMBER 1962–28 DECEMBER 1963 (ABC); 25 APRIL 1964–12 DECEMBER 1964 (ABC) Magician Mark Wilson hosted this Saturday kids' show, which blended magic tricks and illusions with a fantasy story line. Wilson's wife, Nani Darnell, and their son Mike, who was seven when the show began, were also featured, as were Rebo the Clown (played by Bev Bergerson) and the King of Allakazam (played by Bob Towner). Wilson himself was the executive producer of the series, and Dan Whitman was its producer. Many of the principals later appeared in Wilson's 1972 syndicated show, *Magic Circus.*

MAGIC MIDWAY
NBC

22 SEPTEMBER 1962–16 MARCH 1963 Claude Kirchner, who had hosted *Super Circus* for several years during the 1950s, returned as ringmaster of this Saturday-morning circus show for children. Also featured were Bonnie Lee and Lou Stein. The show was sponsored by Marx Toys.

THE MAGIC OF MARK WILSON
SYNDICATED

1978 Half-hour magic show, with illusionist Mark Wilson (formerly host of *The Magic Land of Allakazam*), Nani Darnell, and Greg Wilson, Mark's son.

THE MAGIC RANCH
ABC

30 SEPTEMBER 1961–17 DECEMBER 1961 Don Alan hosted this Saturday-morning kids' show, which was set at a dude ranch. Alan's guests included not only professional magicians, but also talented junior illusionists. George B. Anderson produced the series that was telecast from Chicago.

THE MAGIC SLATE
NBC

2 JUNE 1950–25 AUGUST 1950; 21 JANUARY 1951–24 JUNE 1951 Plays for children were presented on this half-hour series shown on alternate Fridays in 1950, and alternate Sunday afternoons in 1951.

THE MAGICIAN
NBC

2 OCTOBER 1973–20 MAY 1974 Bill Bixby starred in this nonviolent crime show as Anthony Blake, a wealthy nightclub magician who used his talents offstage to solve crimes. Also featured were Keene Curtis as Max Pomeroy, his manager; Todd Crespi as Dennis, Max's young son; and Jim Watkins as Jerry Anderson, pilot of Blake's full-size jet plane. Bixby, who performed his own tricks on the show, was coached by illusionist Mark Wilson (star of *The Magic Land of Allakazam*). The series began as a monthly show and went to a weekly slot in midseason; it was produced by Paramount TV.

THE MAGILLA GORILLA SHOW SYNDICATED/ABC
1964–1965 (SYNDICATED); 1 JANUARY 1966–2 SEPTEMBER 1967
(ABC) Principal characters on this half-hour cartoon show from Hanna-Barbera Productions were Magilla Gorilla, an enormous ape who lived in Peebles' Pet Shop, Mr. Peebles, and Ogee, a little girl. Additional segments included "Ricochet Rabbit and Droopalong Coyote," "Mushmouse and Punkin' Puss," and "Breezly and Sneezly," a polar bear and seal duo.

MAGNAVOX THEATER CBS
15 SEPTEMBER 1950–15 DECEMBER 1950 Friday-night hour-long dramatic anthology series.

THE MAGNIFICENT MARBLE MACHINE NBC
7 JULY 1975–11 JUNE 1976 A daytime game show that tried to capitalize on the pinball-machine craze. Art James hosted the show on which celebrity-and-contestant pairs played a word game with the winning pair earning the opportunity to play a giant pinball machine for prizes. In January 1976 the format was changed to include only celebrity players. Robert Noah was executive producer of the series for Heatter-Quigley Productions.

THE MAIL STORY ABC
7 OCTOBER 1954–30 DECEMBER 1954 Half-hour dramatic anthology series about the United States Post Office. Postmaster General Arthur Summerfield introduced the premiere telecast. The show was also seen under the title *Handle with Care.*

THE MAIN EVENT SYNDICATED
1961 Former heavyweight champion Rocky Marciano introduced film clips of classic fights and interviewed boxing greats on this half-hour sports series.

MAJOR ADAMS
See WAGON TRAIN

MAJOR DEL CONWAY OF THE FLYING TIGERS DUMONT
14 APRIL 1951–26 MAY 1951; 29 JULY 1951–2 MARCH 1952 Eric Fleming first starred as Major Del Conway, an American agent whose cover was that of a pilot for the Flying Tigers Airline. When the show returned in July 1951, Ed Peck was the new Major Conway. Bern Hoffman was also featured in the half-hour series. In real life, the Flying Tigers Airline was a cargo airline founded by General Claire L. Chennault during the late 1940s.

MAJORITY RULES   ABC
2 SEPTEMBER 1949–30 JULY 1950   Hosted by Ed Prentiss, this prime-time game show featured a panel of three contestants. When the panel was asked a question, at least two panelists had to agree on an answer.

MAKE A FACE   ABC
2 OCTOBER 1961–30 MARCH 1962; 29 SEPTEMBER 1962–22 DECEMBER 1962   Bob Clayton hosted this game show on which contestants were required to assemble pictures of famous persons; the pictures had been cut up and placed on moving belts in front of the contestants. Art Baer produced the series, which was first seen Mondays through Fridays; in the fall of 1962 a children's version was seen Saturdays.

MAKE A WISH   ABC
12 SEPTEMBER 1971–5 SEPTEMBER 1976   Tom Chapin hosted this highly acclaimed Sunday-morning educational series for children. During the early seasons two themes were explored each week through songs, films, and interviews. During the final season the nation's bicentennial observance was emphasized, and songs were provided by Harry Chapin (Tom's brother). Lester Cooper was the executive producer, director, and head writer of the series.

MAKE ME LAUGH   ABC/SYNDICATED
20 MARCH 1958–12 JUNE 1958 (ABC); 1979 (SYNDICATED)   Robert Q. Lewis hosted the network version of this unusual game show on which contestants earned money by keeping a straight face. Each week three comedians were on hand, each of whom was given one minute to try to break up the contestant; a contestant won one dollar for each second of non-smiling. Johnny Stearns produced and directed the prime-time series, and Renny Peterson escorted the contestants. *TV Guide* reported in 1958 that some comedians were reluctant to appear on the show because they felt their popularity might suffer if the contestants succeeded in remaining stonefaced. Twenty-one years later a syndicated version of *Make Me Laugh* surfaced, with Bobby Van as host.

MAKE MINE MUSIC   CBS
13 DECEMBER 1948–19 MAY 1949   Carole Coleman, Bill Skipper, and Larry Douglas were featured on this fifteen-minute musical show, which was seen after the network news on certain weeknights.

MAKE ROOM FOR DADDY (THE DANNY THOMAS SHOW)   ABC/CBS
29 SEPTEMBER 1953–18 JULY 1957 (ABC); 7 OCTOBER 1957–14 SEPTEMBER 1964 (CBS)   One of the few situation comedies to last more than a decade, *Make Room for Daddy* starred Danny Thomas, a nightclub sing-

er and comedian, as Danny Williams, a nightclub singer and comedian. During the show's first three seasons, Danny was married and had two children. Jean Hagen played his wife, Margaret, with Sherry Jackson as eleven-year-old Terry and Rusty Hamer as seven-year-old Rusty. Also featured were Amanda Randolph as Louise, the housekeeper; Horace McMahon (1953–1954) as Danny's agent, Phil Arnold; Jesse White (1954–1957) as his agent, Jesse Leeds; Sid Melton as Charlie Halper, owner of the Copa Club; Ben Lessy as Ben, Danny's pianist; Mary Wickes as Liz O'Neal, Danny's publicist; Hans Conried as Uncle Tonoose, Danny's wacky Lebanese relation; and Nan Bryant (1955–1956) as Danny's mother-in-law. Jean Hagen left the series at the end of the 1955–1956 season, and in the fall of 1956 the title was changed to *The Danny Thomas Show*. Danny was a widower during the 1956–1957 season, but in the spring of 1957 Marjorie Lord was introduced as Kathy O'Hara, a widowed nurse who came to take care of Rusty when he contracted the measles. Lelani Sorenson was also introduced as Patty, Kathy's six-year-old daughter. When the show switched networks in the fall of 1957, Danny and Kathy were married, but Angela Cartwright had been added as Kathy's daughter Linda, replacing Lelani Sorenson. Also joining the cast were Sheldon Leonard as Phil Arnold, Danny's agent; Pat Harrington, Jr., as Pat Hannigan, Terry's boyfriend and eventual husband; and Pat Carroll (1961–1964) as Bunny Halper, Charlie's wife. In 1960 Penny Parker replaced Sherry Jackson as daughter Terry. Many of the principals were reunited in two specials aired in 1967 and 1969, and in 1970 the crew reappeared in a new sitcom: see *Make Room for Granddaddy*.

MAKE ROOM FOR GRANDDADDY · ABC
23 SEPTEMBER 1970–2 SEPTEMBER 1971 A sequel to *Make Room for Daddy,* this half-hour sitcom again featured Danny Thomas as Danny Williams, who had become a grandfather sometime between the two series. Many of the old *Make Room for Daddy* troupe were also on hand: Marjorie Lord as Danny's wife, Kathy; Rusty Hamer as Rusty, now a med student; Angela Cartwright as Linda, now at boarding school; Sid Melton as Charlie Halper, now Danny's agent; and Hans Conried as the still-wacky Uncle Tonoose. Sherry Jackson was seen in the premiere episode as Danny's older daughter, Terry Johnson, who wanted to leave her young son with Danny and Kathy while she visited her serviceman-husband in Japan. Other regulars included Michael Hughes as Michael, Terry's son; Rosey Grier as Rosey Robbins, Danny's pianist; and Stanley Myron Handelman as Henry, the elevator operator in Danny's apartment building. Jana Taylor was occasionally featured as Rusty's wife, Susan. Richard Crenna, former star of *The Real McCoys,* produced the show.

MAKE THAT SPARE · ABC
15 OCTOBER 1960–11 SEPTEMBER 1964 A bowling series of variable

length, *Make That Spare* was seen immediately following *The Fight of the Week; Make That Spare* filled out the hour time slot and began whenever the boxing match ended. Johnny Johnston hosted the series except during the 1961–1962 season, when Win Elliott took over.

MAKE THE CONNECTION
NBC

7 JULY 1955–29 SEPTEMBER 1955   Mark Goodson and Bill Todman produced this prime-time game show on which a celebrity panel tried to figure out how the lives of two contestants had crossed. Jim McKay, in his first network appearance, hosted the series in its early weeks; he was succeeded by Gene Rayburn. The celebrity panelists were Betty White, Gene Glavan, Eddie Bracken, and a guest celebrity.

MAKE YOUR OWN KIND OF MUSIC
NBC

20 JULY 1971–7 SEPTEMBER 1971   This summer variety hour was hosted by the Carpenters—sister Karen and brother Richard—and also featured trumpeter Al Hirt, singer Mark Lindsay (formerly of Paul Revere and the Raiders), comics (Tom) Patchett and (Jay) Tarses (who later became the executive producers of *The Bob Newhart Show*) and The New Doodletown Pipers.

MAKIN' IT
ABC

1 FEBRUARY 1979–16 MARCH 1979   Half-hour sitcom with a disco flavor, set in Passaic, New Jersey. With David Naughton as college student Billy Manucci; Greg Antonacci as his older brother, Tony Manucci, star dancer at the Inferno, Passaic's hottest disco; Ellen Travolta as their mother, Dorothy Manucci; Lou Antonio as their father, Joseph Manucci; Denise Miller as their younger sister, Tina Manucci; Rebecca Balding as Corky Crandall, Billy's girlfriend, a receptionist at the William Morris Agency; Ralph Seymour as Billy's pal, Kingfish; Gary Prendergast as Billy's pal, Bernard; Wendy Hoffman as Suzanne, Bernard's girlfriend; Diane Robin as Felice, Kingfish's girlfriend; and Jennifer Perrito as Ivy, a waitress at the ice cream store where Billy works part time. The show was created by Mark Rothman, Lowell Ganz and Garry Marshall.

MAKING THINGS GROW
PBS

1970–1975   Half-hour series for indoor and outdoor gardeners, hosted by Thalassa Cruso and produced at WGBH-TV, Boston.

MAL'BU RUN
CBS

1 MARCH 1961–27 SEPTEMBER 1961   Produced by Ivan Tors, *Malibu Run* was a revamped version of *The Aquanauts*. It starred Jeremy Slate as Larry Lahr and Ron Ely as Mike Madison; both had been featured in *The Aquanauts*, but on *Malibu Run* they seemed to spend a little more time on land trying to solve crimes.

MALIBU U. ABC

21 JULY 1967–1 SEPTEMBER 1967   Rick Nelson hosted this half-hour summer musical series; Nelson was the "dean" of a "college" located on the beach at Malibu. Other regulars included Australian singer Robie Porter and the Bob Banas Dancers.

MAMA CBS

1 JULY 1949–27 JULY 1956; 16 DECEMBER 1956–17 MARCH 1957   One of TV's first popular sitcoms, *Mama* was based on John Van Druten's play, *I Remember Mama,* which was in turn derived from Kathryn Forbes's book, *Mama's Bank Account.* The series told the story of the Hansens, a closely knit Norwegian family living on San Francisco's Steiner Street in 1917. Featured were Peggy Wood as Marta (Mama) Hansen; Judson Laire as Lars (Papa) Hansen, a carpenter; Rosemary Rice as elder daughter Katrin, whose off-screen voice introduced each episode; Dick Van Patten as son Nels; Iris Mann (1949–1950) and Robin Morgan (1950–1956) as younger daughter Dagmar; Ruth Gates as Aunt Jenny, Mama's older sister; Malcolm Keen as Uncle Chris; Carl Frank as Uncle Gunnar; Alice Frost as Aunt Trina, Mama's younger sister; and Kevin Coughlin (1954–1957) as T. R. Ryan. From 1949 through the summer of 1956, the show was done live. After its cancellation in 1956, public demand prompted CBS to revive the series that winter. The second version was filmed and lasted only thirteen weeks. By that time daughter Katrin had become a secretary, and son Nels had become a medical student. Toni Campbell joined the cast as daughter Dagmar, replacing Robin Morgan (who had been featured on *The Quiz Kids* and later became active in the women's movement). The half-hour series was originally produced and directed by Ralph Nelson and was later produced by Carol Irwin.

MAN AGAINST CRIME CBS/DUMONT/NBC

7 OCTOBER 1949–2 OCTOBER 1953 (CBS); 11 OCTOBER 1953–4 APRIL 1954 (DUMONT); 18 OCTOBER 1953–4 JULY 1954 (NBC); 1 JULY 1956–26 AUGUST 1956 (NBC)   Ralph Bellamy originally starred in this half-hour crime show as Mike Barnett, a New York City private eye who didn't use a gun. When Bellamy took a vacation during the summer of 1951, Robert Preston filled in for him, playing Mike's brother, Pat. During the 1953–1954 season both NBC and DuMont carried the series. In 1956 NBC briefly revived the series as a live summer replacement for *The Loretta Young Show.* This version starred Frank Lovejoy as Mike Barnett, who was no longer unarmed. The Bellamy episodes were widely syndicated under the title *Follow That Man.* Larry Klee created the series.

THE MAN AND THE CHALLENGE

NBC

12 SEPTEMBER 1959–3 SEPTEMBER 1960   Ivan Tors produced this half-hour adventure series, starring George Nader as Dr. Glenn Barton, a research scientist for the Institute of Human Factors, an agency that conducted experiments designed to measure human endurance.

THE MAN AND THE CITY

ABC

15 SEPTEMBER 1971–5 JANUARY 1972   An unsuccessful hour-long dramatic series that starred Anthony Quinn as Thomas Jefferson Alcala, a widower, mayor of a Southwestern city. Also featured were Mike Farrell as Andy Hays, his aide, and Mala Powers as Marian Crane, his secretary. The show was produced by Universal TV.

THE MAN BEHIND THE BADGE

CBS

11 OCTOBER 1953–3 OCTOBER 1954   Charles Bickford was host and narrator of this half-hour crime anthology series. Stories were based on true incidents, and Bickford introduced real-life law enforcement officers on the show. Jerry Robinson was the producer.

A MAN CALLED SHENANDOAH

ABC

13 SEPTEMBER 1965–5 SEPTEMBER 1966   Robert Horton starred in this half-hour western as an amnesiac who called himself Shenandoah. Nursed back to health after having been shot, Shenandoah wandered around the West trying to get his head together. E. Jack Neuman created the series and was its executive producer; Fred Freiberger produced it for MGM TV.

A MAN CALLED SLOANE

NBC

22 SEPTEMBER 1979–22 DECEMBER 1979   Hour adventure series starring Robert Conrad as counterintelligence agent Thomas Remington Sloane III, an employee of UNIT. With Ji-Tu Cumbuka as his aide, Torque, who was conveniently equipped with a metal right hand; Dan O'Herlihy as The Director; Karen Purcill as Kelly, another UNIT employee; and Michele Carey as the voice of Effie, the UNIT computer. Cliff Gould created the show for QM Productions.

THE MAN CALLED X

SYNDICATED

1956   Barry Sullivan starred as Ken Thurston, a globe-trotting United States intelligence agent whose code name was "X." The series, which began on radio in 1944, was produced and directed by Eddie Davis. Ladislas Farago, a real-life intelligence agent and successful author, was technical supervisor.

THE MAN FROM ATLANTIS

22 SEPTEMBER 1977–2 MAY 1978   Apparently undaunted by the failure of *The Invisible Man* in 1975 and the failure of *Gemini Man* in 1976, NBC made a third attempt to introduce an hour-long adventure series featuring a man with super-human powers; like its predecessors, *The Man from Atlantis* sank in midseason, though it resurfaced briefly later in 1978. It starred Patrick Duffy as Mark Harris, an unusual fellow who was apparently a survivor of the lost continent of Atlantis. Equipped with webbed hands and feet, and with the ability to breathe underwater, Harris worked with the Foundation for Oceanic Research. Also featured were Belinda J. Montgomery as Dr. Elizabeth Merrill, a Foundation scientist; Alan Fudge as C. W. Crawford, another Foundation employee; and Victor Buono as Mr. Schubert, the archvillain whose schemes were thwarted by Harris. As Harris, Patrick Duffy wore latex webbing and full-eye green contact lenses in order to look authentically Atlantean. Herbert F. Solow was the executive producer of the series, and Herman Miller the producer.

THE MAN FROM BLACKHAWK

ABC

9 OCTOBER 1959–23 SEPTEMBER 1960   Robert Rockwell (formerly of *Our Miss Brooks*) starred in this half-hour western as Sam Logan, an investigator for the Blackhawk Insurance Company, which was headquartered in Chicago.

MAN FROM INTERPOL

NBC

30 JANUARY 1960–22 OCTOBER 1960   Filmed in Europe, this half-hour crime show starred Richard Wyler as Anthony Smith, a special agent assigned to Interpol, the international police organization. John Longden was also featured as Superintendent Mercer. Edward and Harry Danziger produced the series, which was a midseason replacement for *It Could Be You.*

THE MAN FROM U.N.C.L.E.

NBC

22 SEPTEMBER 1964–15 JANUARY 1968   This lighthearted hour-long spy show was inspired by the James Bond stories. Bond's creator, Ian Fleming, had been consulted by Norman Felton, the series' executive producer, and had agreed to let Felton use the name of a character who had appeared in *Goldfinger* (Fleming had little else to do with the show, as he died of a heart attack in 1964). The character, Napoleon Solo, was an underworld chieftain who had been killed off in the book, but on television Solo was a stalwart secret agent. Robert Vaughn starred as Napoleon Solo, and David McCallum costarred as his partner, Illya Kuryakin; Leo G. Carroll rounded out the cast as Alexander Waverly, head of U.N.C.L.E. (the United Network Command for Law and Enforcement), an international crime fighting organization based in New York. Most of

the episodes were titled "The _____ Affair," and the recurring theme of the stories was that the U.N.C.L.E. agents required the help of an ordinary citizen each week. A spinoff, *The Girl from U.N.C.L.E.*, was introduced in 1966 and lasted one season (see also that title). Though *The Man from U.N.C.L.E.* lasted four seasons and is widely remembered today, it is surprising to note that it cracked Nielsen's Top Twenty only in its second season. It should also be noted that the show was scheduled in a different time slot each autumn.

MAN IN A SUITCASE   ABC
3 MAY 1968–20 SEPTEMBER 1968   Filmed in England, this hour-long adventure show starred Richard Bradford as John McGill, an American adventurer for hire.

MAN OF THE WEEK   CBS
26 AUGUST 1951–10 OCTOBER 1954   On this Sunday-afternoon public affairs program a different male guest was interviewed each week. Vice President Alben W. Barkley was the guest on the premiere. The series was the antecedent of CBS's long-running interview show, *Face the Nation*.

MAN OF THE WORLD   SYNDICATED
1962   Produced in England and distributed by ITC, *Man of the World* was an adventure series, starring Craig Stevens (late of *Peter Gunn*) as Michael Strait, an American freelance writer.

THE MAN WHO NEVER WAS   ABC
7 SEPTEMBER 1966–4 JANUARY 1967   Half-hour spy show about a secret agent who masqueraded through Europe under the identity of a multimillionaire. Robert Lansing starred as Peter Murphy, an American agent who had escaped from East Berlin with the East German authorities hot on his trail. Murphy stumbled onto the estate of wealthy Mark Wainwright, who turned out to be Murphy's exact double. Wainwright was killed by the East Germans, and Murphy, with the cooperation of Wainwright's widow, assumed his identity. Also featured were Dana Wynter as Eva Wainwright, Mark's widow; Alex Davion as Roger Berry, Mark's suspicious half brother; Murray Hamilton as Jack Forbes, Murphy's commanding officer; and Paul Stewart as Grant, another American agent. The series was filmed on location; John Newland was the executive producer.

MAN WITH A CAMERA   ABC
10 OCTOBER 1958–29 FEBRUARY 1960   Essentially an updated version of *Casey, Crime Photographer*, this half-hour crime show starred Charles Bronson as Mike Kovac, a freelance photographer who helped the cops

solve crimes. James Flavin was also featured as Lieutenant Donovan, Kovac's contact on the New York City police force.

MAN WITHOUT A GUN   SYNDICATED
1959   Half-hour western from 20th Century-Fox, starring Rex Reason as crusading newspaper editor Adam MacLean, a man hoping to prove the supremacy of the pen over the sword in the Old West. Also on hand was Mort Mills as Marshal Tallman, in case things got out of hand. Created by Peter Packer, the series was set in Yellowstone, Dakota Territory.

THE MANCINI GENERATION   SYNDICATED
1972   Half-hour musical show with Henry Mancini and his orchestra. A gifted composer and arranger, Mancini wrote the theme to *Peter Gunn* and to films such as *The Pink Panther* and *Breakfast at Tiffany's.*

MANHATTAN HONEYMOON   ABC
22 FEBRUARY 1954–30 APRIL 1954   Neva Patterson hosted this daytime game show on which the winning couple was awarded a trip to New York.

MANHATTAN SHOWCASE   CBS
28 FEBRUARY 1949–16 JUNE 1949   This fifteen-minute talent show was hosted by Johnny Downs and Helen Gallagher, and featured the music of the Tony Mottola Trio. The thrice-weekly show had previously been known as *Places, Please,* when it was hosted by Barry Wood (see also that title).

MANHATTAN SPOTLIGHT   DUMONT
17 JANUARY 1949–20 APRIL 1951   Fifteen-minute Monday-through-Friday interview show hosted by Charles Tranum.

THE MANHATTAN TRANSFER   CBS
10 AUGUST 1975–31 AUGUST 1975   Four-week summer variety hour showcasing the Manhattan Transfer, a slick vocal group whose musical tastes ranged from the harmonies of the 1940s to the heavy hits of the present day. The foursome consisted of Alan Paul, Janis Siegel, Tim Hauser, and Laurel Masse. Archie Hahn was also featured on the series.

MANHUNT   SYNDICATED
1959   Half-hour crime show with Victor Jory as Lieutenant Howard Finucane of the San Diego Police Department and Patrick McVey as police reporter Ben Andrews. The show was a Screen Gems production.

THE MANHUNTER   CBS
11 SEPTEMBER 1974–9 APRIL 1975   Hour-long crime show set in Idaho

during the 1930s, with Ken Howard as Dave Barrett, amateur crime-fighter and nonamateur farmer. Also seen were Hilary Thompson as Elizabeth Barrett, his sister; Robert Hogan as Sheriff Paul Tate; Ford Rainey as James Barrett, Dave's father; and Claudia Bryar as Mary Barrett, Dave's mother. Quinn Martin was the executive producer.

MANNIX
CBS

16 SEPTEMBER 1967–27 AUGUST 1975   This popular hour-long crime show starred Mike Connors as Joe Mannix, Los Angeles private eye. During the first season Mannix worked for Intertect, an ultramodern, computerized organization, and Joe Campanella was featured as Lew Wickersham, his boss. As the second season began, however, Mannix had left Intertect and set up his own shop at 17 Paseo Verdes in West Los Angeles. Gail Fisher joined the cast as Peggy Fair, his black secretary. Occasionally featured were Robert Reed as Lieutenant Adam Tobias and Ward Wood as Lieutenant Art Malcolm. Bruce Geller was the executive producer for Paramount TV.

MAN'S HERITAGE
SYNDICATED

1956   Raymond Massey recited Bible stories on this half-hour series.

MANTRAP
SYNDICATED

1971   A reworking of the 1950s panel show *Leave It to the Girls, Mantrap* featured a panel of three female celebrities who grilled a male guest each week. Al Hamel was the moderator of the series and frequent panelists included Chelsea Brown, Selma Diamond, Margot Kidder, Phyllis Kirk, Sue Lyon, Meredith MacRae, Jaye P. Morgan, Jan Sterling, Jacqueline Susann, and Carol Wayne.

MANY HAPPY RETURNS
CBS

21 SEPTEMBER 1964–12 APRIL 1965   Half-hour sitcom set at Krockmeyer's Department Store in Los Angeles. With John McGiver as Walter Burnley, manager of the complaint department; Russell Collins as store manager Owen Sharp; Elinor Donahue as Burnley's daughter, Joan Randall; Mark Goddard as Bob, Joan's husband; Elena Verdugo as store worker Lynn Hall; Mickey Manners as employee Joe Foley; Jesslyn Fax as employee Wilma Fritter; Richard Collier as Harry; Arte Johnson as Virgil Slamm; and Jerome Cowan as store owner J. L. Fox.

THE MARCH OF TIME THROUGH THE YEARS
ABC

23 FEBRUARY 1951–27 AUGUST 1951; 8 OCTOBER 1952–10 DECEMBER 1952   *March of Time,* which ran on radio from 1931 to 1945, was revived for television in 1951. John Daly hosted the series that year, introducing not only vintage newsreels and other documentary film footage, but also live guests. Westbrook Van Voorhis, who had narrated the show

through most of its radio run, was the host in 1952. Arthur Tourtellot and Dick Krolik produced the half-hour series, and Fred Feldkamp directed it.

MARCUS WELBY, M.D. ABC

23 SEPTEMBER 1969–11 MAY 1976   A popular medical show, starring Robert Young as Dr. Marcus Welby, Southern California's kindliest physician. Welby, whose very name ("well-be") suggested good health, had offices at his house in Santa Monica and also became associated with the Family Practice Center at Lang Memorial Hospital. Also featured were James Brolin as Dr. Steven Kiley, Welby's young associate who made his house calls by motorcycle; Elena Verdugo as Consuelo Lopez, their receptionist and nurse; Sharon Gless (1974–1975) as Kathleen Faverty, a nurse; and Pamela Hensley (1975–1976) as Janet Blake, the hospital public relations director who married Kiley in October 1975. David Victor was executive producer of the series for Universal.

THE MARGE AND GOWER CHAMPION SHOW NBC

31 MARCH 1957–9 JUNE 1957   Marge and Gower Champion, a popular husband-and-wife dance team during the 1950s, played themselves in this half-hour sitcom, which blended song and dance into a story line. Also featured were Jack Whiting as Marge's father, the couple's agent; drummer Buddy Rich as Cozy, a drummer; and Peg LaCentra as Amanda, a singer.

MARGE AND JEFF DUMONT

21 SEPTEMBER 1953–24 SEPTEMBER 1954   This fifteen-minute domestic sitcom was seen weekday evenings at 7:15. It starred Marge Greene and Jess Cain as Manhattan newlyweds Marge and Jeff Green. Marge Greene also wrote the series, which was produced by Ernest Walling and directed by Leonard Valenta.

MARGIE ABC

12 OCTOBER 1961–31 AUGUST 1962   One of the three series set in the 1920s or 1930s that ran on ABC during the 1961–1962 season (the other two were *The Roaring Twenties* and *The Untouchables*), *Margie* was a half-hour sitcom about a teenage girl growing up in New England. With Cynthia Pepper as Margie Clayton; Dave Willock as her father, Harvey Clayton; Wesley Tackitt as her mother, Nora Clayton; Hollis Irving as Aunt Phoebe; Billy Hummert and Johnny Bangert as her brother, Cornell; Tommy Ivo as her boyfriend, Heywood Botts; Dick Gering as her occasional boyfriend, Johnny Green; and Penny Parker as her best friend, Maybelle Jackson.

THE MARILYN McCOO & BILLY DAVIS, JR. SHOW   CBS

15 JUNE 1977–20 JULY 1977   Six-week summer variety series hosted by singers Marilyn McCoo and Billy Davis, Jr. Both McCoo and Davis, who were married to each other, had sung with the Fifth Dimension. Dick Broder was the executive producer.

MARINE BOY   SYNDICATED

1966   Japanese-produced cartoon series about Marine Boy, a diminutive agent for the Ocean Patrol who helped save the world from sea monsters.

MARK SABER   ABC/NBC

5 OCTOBER 1951–30 JUNE 1954 (ABC); 16 MARCH 1957–23 SEPTEMBER 1961 (NBC)   Mark Saber was the central character in two quite different series. In the first series, Tom Conway starred as Inspector Mark Saber of the New York City Homicide Squad, and James Burke costarred as Sergeant Tim Maloney. Produced by Roland Reed Productions, the half-hour filmed series was shown under several titles during its three-year run, including *Mark Saber Mystery Theatre, Inspector Mark Saber,* and *Homicide Squad.* The second *Mark Saber* series was produced in England by Edward J. Danziger and Harry Lee Danziger, and starred a one-armed actor, Donald Gray, as Mark Saber; in this version Saber was a former chief inspector at Scotland Yard who had become a private detective. Also featured were Michael Balfour as Barney O'Keefe; Diana Decker as Stephanie Ames; Colin Tapley as Inspector Parker; Neil McCallum as Pete Paulson; Garry Thorne as Eddie Wells; and Robert Arden as Bob Page. The series ran for four years in a Saturday-afternoon slot on NBC under the title *Detective's Diary,* and also surfaced in prime-time slots on NBC between 1957 and 1960. (It should be noted that the final episodes of *Detective's Diary* were reruns of *Man from Interpol,* starring Richard Wyler.)

MARKHAM   CBS

2 MAY 1959–22 SEPTEMBER 1960   Half-hour crime show starring Ray Milland as Roy Markham, a combination lawyer and private eye, with Simon Scott as John Riggs, his boss. Joe Sistrom and Warren Duff were the producers.

MARLO AND THE MAGIC MOVIE MACHINE   SYNDICATED

1977–   Kids' show hosted by Laurie Faso as Marlo, operator of the Magic Movie Machine, a talking computer that could be programmed to show old newsreels and film shorts as well as baby pictures of celebrities. Taped at WFSB-TV in Hartford, the show was first seen in an hour-long format, but was later trimmed to a half hour. Mert Koplin provided the voice of the Machine.

THE MARRIAGE
NBC

1 JULY 1954–19 AUGUST 1954   One of the first prime-time programs broadcast in color, *The Marriage* was a half-hour comedy-drama starring Hume Cronyn and Jessica Tandy (who were husband and wife in real life) as Ben and Liz Marriott. Ben was a lawyer, and he and Liz lived in New York with their two children, Emily (played by Susan Strasberg and Natalie Trundy) and Pete (Malcolm Broderick). William Redfield also appeared as Emily's boyfriend, Bobby Logan.

MARRIED: THE FIRST YEAR
CBS

28 FEBRUARY 1979–21 MARCH 1979   Hour dramatic series about the trials and tribulations of a young married couple. With Leigh McCloskey as Billy Baker; Cindy Grover as his wife, Joanna Huffman; K Callan as Cathy; Claudette Nevins as Barbara; Christine Belford as Aunt Emily; Stephanie Kramer as Sharon; Gigi Vorgan as Cookie; Stephen Manley as Donny; Jennifer McAllister as Millie; and Stanley Grover as Bert.

MARSHAL DILLON
See GUNSMOKE

THE MARSHAL OF GUNSIGHT PASS
ABC

12 MARCH 1950–30 SEPTEMBER 1950   Half-hour western for children starring Russell Hayden.

MARSHALL EFRON'S ILLUSTRATED,
SIMPLIFIED AND PAINLESS SUNDAY SCHOOL
CBS

9 DECEMBER 1973–28 AUGUST 1977   Marshall Efron, formerly a regular on PBS's *The Great American Dream Machine,* hosted a multipart religious series for young children, which CBS broadcast on Sunday mornings from time to time between 1973 and 1977. Pamela Ilott was the executive producer, Ted Holmes the director.

THE MARSHALL PLAN IN ACTION
ABC

23 JULY 1950–30 DECEMBER 1951   One of the first documentary series filmed especially for television, *The Marshall Plan in Action* was filmed largely in Europe, showing the results of the $12 billion postwar reconstruction program developed by Secretary of State George C. Marshall. The series was developed by Robert Saudek, who would later help develop *Omnibus* for the Ford Foundation.

THE MARTHA RAYE SHOW
NBC

20 MARCH 1954–29 MAY 1956   Comedienne Martha Raye began appearing regularly on television in 1951 as occasional host of *All-Star Revue.* By the fall of 1953, when *All-Star Revue* had become a once-a-month replacement for Sid Caesar's *Your Show of Shows,* Raye was its regular

host; in March of 1954 that show's title was officially changed to *The Martha Raye Show*. During the 1954–1955 and 1955–1956 seasons, her show was seen Tuesday nights as a monthly replacement for *The Milton Berle Show*. Raye's sidekick on most of the shows was former boxer Rocky Graziano.

THE MARTHA WRIGHT SHOW
See THE PACKARD SHOWROOM

MARTIN AGRONSKY: EVENING EDITION PBS
1971–1976   Half-hour nightly news analysis program hosted by Martin Agronsky, produced at WETA-TV, Washington, D.C.

THE MARTIN BLOCK SHOW ABC
17 SEPTEMBER 1956–31 DECEMBER 1957   A half-hour daytime variety series, hosted by New York disc jockey Martin Block.

MARTIN KANE, PRIVATE EYE NBC/SYNDICATED
1 SEPTEMBER 1949–17 JUNE 1954 (NBC); 1958 (SYNDICATED)   One of the first fictional detectives to move from radio to television, *Martin Kane* was played by four actors on the latter medium. William Gargan was the first Martin Kane, a tough private eye who worked in New York; Gargan had been a private investigator before turning to show business and had played the role on radio. After two seasons Gargan had decided to become a producer and left the series. Lloyd Nolan took over the role on 31 August 1951, and played it for one season; Lee Tracy succeeded him in 1952. During its first four seasons the show was done live, and the commercial—for a cigarette manufacturer—was worked into the story: Kane, for example, would stop at his favorite newsstand (it was usually operated by Horace McMahon) and ask for the sponsor's brand. In the fall of 1953, a filmed version of the series, entitled *The New Adventures of Martin Kane,* appeared, with Mark Stevens in the title role; the show was filmed in Europe and lasted a single season. In 1958 Gargan again played Kane in a second series filmed in Europe (from United Artists), entitled *The Return of Martin Kane.*

THE MARTY FELDMAN COMEDY MACHINE ABC
12 APRIL 1972–23 AUGUST 1972   Segments of this comedy show were taped in England and edited into half hours for American viewing. Marty Feldman, pop-eyed British comedian, was the host and star of the series. Animations were done by Terry Gilliam of *Monty Python's Flying Circus.*

MARTY ROBBINS' SPOTLIGHT SYNDICATED
1977   Taped in Nashville, this half-hour series was essentially a version of *This Is Your Life* for stars of country music. Singer Marty Robbins hosted the show.

443

MARY CBS

24 SEPTEMBER 1978–8 OCTOBER 1978   An hour variety show starring Mary Tyler Moore, *Mary* opened to lackluster ratings and dismal reviews, and was abruptly pulled off the air after only three showings (several more shows had already been taped, but were never broadcast). Also featured on the series were Dick Shawn, Jim Hampton, Judy Kahan, Michael Keaton, Swoosie Kurtz, and David Letterman; Tom Patchett and Jay Tarses were the producers for MTM Enterprises. Following the show's cancellation, a new producer (Perry Lafferty) was brought in, and a new Mary Tyler Moore series was scheduled to be introduced in mid-season: see *The Mary Tyler Moore Hour.*

THE MARY HARTLINE CHILDREN'S SHOW ABC

12 FEBRUARY 1951–15 JUNE 1951   Mary Hartline, who was also seen on *Super Circus,* hosted this half-hour kids' show, which was seen Monday through Friday at 5 p.m.

MARY HARTMAN, MARY HARTMAN SYNDICATED

1976–1977   Developed by Norman Lear, this half-hour serial was part parody and part soap opera. Set in Fernwood, Ohio, the first season began with a mass murder and culminated with the heroine's crackup on a television talk show. Louise Lasser starred as Mary Hartman, the pigtailed, gingham-frocked Ohio housewife who lived in a world where television commercials were as meaningful as personal experiences, and who tried to remain calm while her daughter was held hostage by a mass murderer, her husband was impotent, her father disappeared, and her best friend was paralyzed. Other principals included Greg Mullavey as her husband Tom Hartman, an assembly-line worker whose emotional development was arrested during adolescence; Dody Goodman as Martha Shumway, Mary's addled mother; Philip Bruns as George Shumway, Mary's father; Debralee Scott as Cathy Shumway, Mary's active younger sister; Claudia Lamb as Heather Hartman, Tom and Mary's sullen daughter; Victor Kilian as Mary's grandfather, Raymond Larkin, the "Fernwood Flasher"; Bruce Solomon as Sergeant Dennis Foley, the Fernwood cop who eventually convinced Mary to have an affair with him; Mary Kay Place as Mary's best friend, Loretta Haggers, an aspiring country and western singer; Graham Jarvis as Charlie Haggers, Loretta's husband and Tom's coworker; Sparky Marcus as eight-year-old Jimmy Joe Jeeter, a child evangelist who was electrocuted when a TV set fell into his bathtub; Dabney Coleman as Merle Jeeter, Jimmy Joe's father; and Marian Mercer as Wanda Rittenhouse, wife of a Fernwood politician. After 325 episodes Louise Lasser decided to leave the show; after a summer hiatus (during which *Fernwood 2-Night,* a TV talk show spoof, was telecast), production resumed with most of the other principals under the title *Forever Fernwood. Mary Hartman, Mary Hartman* was created by Gail Parent, Ann Marcus, Jerry Adelman, and Daniel Gregory Browne.

MARY KAY AND JOHNNY DUMONT/NBC/CBS
18 NOVEMBER 1947–24 AUGUST 1948 (DUMONT); 10 OCTOBER 1948–13 FEBRUARY 1949 (NBC); 23 FEBRUARY 1949–1 JUNE 1949 (CBS); 13 JUNE 1949–11 MARCH 1950 (NBC) One of TV's first domestic sitcoms, *Mary Kay and Johnny* starred Mary Kay and Johnny Stearns as themselves. Broadcast live from Philadelphia, and later from New York, the series was shown in a fifteen-minute weekly format on the DuMont network, and then in a half-hour weekly format except during the summer of 1949, when it was seen for fifteen minutes five nights a week.

THE MARY MARGARET McBRIDE SHOW NBC
21 SEPTEMBER 1948–14 DECEMBER 1948 One of radio's best-known female interviewers and saleswomen, Mary Margaret McBride also hosted her own half-hour television interview show for thirteen weeks.

THE MARY TYLER MOORE HOUR CBS
4 MARCH 1979–6 MAY 1979 An hour comedy-variety series which surfaced in midseason, following the demise of Mary Tyler Moore's ill-fated fall effort, *Mary*. In the new show Mary Tyler Moore starred as Mary McKinnon, star of her own variety show. Also featured were Michael Keaton as Kenneth Christy, the studio gofer; Michael Lombard as Mary's producer, Harry Sinclair; Ron Rifkin as her director, Artie Miller; and Joyce Van Patten as Mary's secretary and assistant, Iris Chapman. Perry Lafferty produced the series for MTM Enterprises.

THE MARY TYLER MOORE SHOW CBS
19 SEPTEMBER 1970–3 SEPTEMBER 1977 This highly successful sitcom starred Mary Tyler Moore, who was well known to television audiences as Laura Petrie on *The Dick Van Dyke Show*. Here she played Mary Richards, a single woman of thirty or so who settled in Minneapolis after calling it quits with her boyfriend (as originally conceived, Mary was to have been a divorcée, but this idea was abandoned). Mary landed a job as associate producer of the evening news at WJM-TV, Channel 12, Minneapolis's lowest-rated station, and found herself a small apartment. In most of the 168 episodes Mary Richards was the center of the storm, the calm, level-headed professional with whom an assortment of zany characters (all played by gifted performers) interacted. That group originally included Edward Asner (whose previous TV roles had largely been limited to heavies) as gruff Lou Grant, Mary's boss, the producer of the news show; Gavin MacLeod as Murray Slaughter, the quick-witted news writer; Ted Knight as Ted Baxter, the dense and self-centered anchorman;

Valerie Harper (1970–1974) as Mary's upstairs neighbor, Rhoda Morgenstern, a window dresser; and Cloris Leachman as Mary's high-strung landlady, Phyllis Lindstrom. Occasionally featured were John Amos (1970–1973) as Gordy Howard, the weatherman; Lisa Gerritsen (1970–1974) as Phyllis's daughter, Bess; Nancy Walker (1970–1974) as Rhoda's undersized but overbearing mother, Ida Morgenstern; and Harold Gould (1970–1974) as Rhoda's father, Martin Morgenstern. In the fall of 1973 Georgia Engel joined the cast as Georgette Franklin, Ted Baxter's naive girlfriend; in the fall of 1975 she and Ted were married, and in the fall of 1976 they had a baby, Mary Lou. In the fall of 1974 Betty White was added as Sue Ann Nivens, the man-hungry "Happy Homemaker" of Channel 12; Sheree North was also seen occasionally that season as Charlene McGuire, Lou Grant's girlfriend (Lou's wife had left him earlier). In the fall of 1975 Mary Richards moved from her old apartment to a high rise; her former landlady had left for San Francisco and a show of her own.

In its seven-year run *The Mary Tyler Moore Show* spawned two spinoffs, *Rhoda* and *Phyllis*, and when production ceased in 1977, many of the remaining regulars found work that fall in new series: Betty White and Georgia Engel on *The Betty White Show*, Edward Asner on *Lou Grant*, and Gavin MacLeod as the skipper of *The Love Boat*. All of those series, except for *The Love Boat*, were produced by MTM Enterprises, the production company established by Mary Tyler Moore and her husband, Grant Tinker. James L. Brooks and Allan Burns were the executive producers of *The Mary Tyler Moore Show*, Ed. Weinberger and Stan Daniels the producers. The show's theme song, "Love Is All Around," was composed by Pat Williams and sung by Sonny Curtis.

THE MASK   ABC
10 JANUARY 1954–16 MAY 1954 An hour-long crime show starring Gary Merrill and William Prince as brothers Walter and Peter Guilfoyle, attorneys at law. Paul Newman guest starred in one episode, "The Party Night," 11 April. Both Merrill and Prince were again featured as attorneys in *Justice*, an NBC series.

THE MASLAND AT HOME SHOW   CBS/ABC
14 SEPTEMBER 1949–7 JUNE 1950 (CBS); 30 AUGUST 1951–21 FEBRUARY 1952 (ABC) Masland Carpets sponsored this fifteen-minute musical series, which featured vocalist Earl Wrightson and the Norman Paris Trio. It was seen Wednesdays after the news on CBS and Thursday nights over ABC.

MASQUERADE PARTY   NBC/CBS/ABC/SYNDICATED
14 JULY 1952–25 AUGUST 1952 (NBC); 22 JUNE 1953–14 SEPTEMBER 1953 (CBS); 21 JUNE 1954–27 SEPTEMBER 1954 (CBS); 29 SEPTEMBER

1954–29 DECEMBER 1956 (ABC); 6 MARCH 1957–4 SEPTEMBER 1957 (NBC); 4 AUGUST 1958–15 SEPTEMBER 1958 (CBS); 2 OCTOBER 1958–24 SEPTEMBER 1959 (NBC); 26 OCTOBER 1959–18 JANUARY 1960 (CBS); 29 JANUARY 1960–23 SEPTEMBER 1960 (NBC); 1974 (SYNDICATED) This durable game show was seen throughout the 1950s, most frequently as a summer replacement. The object of the game was for a panel of celebrities to guess the identity of guest celebrities, who always appeared in elaborate costumes and heavy makeup. The show had several hosts through the years, including Bud Collyer (1952), Douglas Edwards (1953), Peter Donald (1954–1956), Eddie Bracken (1957), Robert Q. Lewis (1958), and Bert Parks (the 1958–1959 and 1960 NBC shows). After a fourteen-year absence *Masquerade Party* reappeared briefly as a syndicated offering in 1974; Stefan Hatos and Monty Hall were the executive producers, Richard Dawson was the host, and the celebrity panel included Bill Bixby, Nipsey Russell, and Lee Meriwether. On the syndicated version two members of the studio audience were also given the chance to guess the identity of the mystery guests.

MASTERPIECE PLAYHOUSE
NBC

23 JULY 1950–3 SEPTEMBER 1950   A summer replacement for *Philco Television Playhouse, Masterpiece Playhouse* presented hour-long versions of well-known dramatic works such as "Hedda Gabler," with Jessica Tandy and Walter Abel (23 July); "Richard III," with William Windom and Blanche Yurka (30 July); "Six Characters in Search of an Author," with Joseph Schildkraut and Betty Field (13 August); and "Uncle Vanya," with Walter Abel, Eva Gabor, and Boris Karloff (3 September).

MASTERPIECE THEATRE
PBS

10 JANUARY 1971–   *Masterpiece Theatre* has been one of public television's most popular dramatic anthology series; most of its presentations have been multipart serializations, adapted from literary works or from original screenplays. Funded by a grant from Mobil Oil, the show is hosted by Alistair Cooke. All of the presentations are produced in Great Britain, most of them by the BBC. During the first season presentations included: "The First Churchills," a twelve-part adaptation of Sir Winston Churchill's *Marlborough, His Life and Times,* with John Neville, Susan Hampshire, John Westbrook, James Villiers, and Moira Redmond; Henry James's "The Spoils of Poynton," a four-parter with Pauline Jameson, Ian Ogilvy, and Diane Fletcher; Dostoevsky's "The Possessed," in six parts, with Keith Bell, Rosalie Crutchley, Joseph O'Conor, and Anne Stallybrass; a four-part adaptation of Balzac's "Pere Goriot," with Andrew Keir, David Dundas, Michael Goodliffe, and June Ritchie.

Seven offerings were telecast during the 1971–1972 season: Thomas Hardy's "Jude the Obscure," in six parts, with Robert Powell, Fiona

Walker, Alex Marshall, and Daphne Heard; a two-part adaptation of Dostoevsky's "The Gambler," with Dame Edith Evans; Tolstoy's "Resurrection," in four parts, with Alan Dobie, Bridget Turner, and Clifford Parrish; a one-part, two-hour telecast of Stella Gibson's "Cold Comfort Farm," with Sarah Badel, Alistair Sim, and Rosalie Crutchley; "The Six Wives of Henry VIII," a repeat of the six-part miniseries originally broadcast on CBS (see also that title); "Elizabeth R," a six-parter starring Glenda Jackson as Queen Elizabeth I; an eight-part adaptation of James Fenimore Cooper's "The Last of the Mohicans," with Andrew Crawford, Kenneth Ives, Patricia Maynard, Richard Warwick, and Philip Madoc.

Six novels were serialized during the 1972–1973 season: Thackeray's "Vanity Fair," in five parts, with Susan Hampshire, Dyson Lovell, Barbara Cooper, and John Moffatt; Balzac's "Cousin Bette," in five parts, with Margaret Tyzack, Colin Baker, Thorley Walters and Helen Mirren; Wilkie Collins's "The Moonstone," in five parts, with Vivien Heilbron, Robin Ellis, Martin Jarvis, and Peter Sallis; Thomas Hughes's "Tom Brown's Schooldays," in five parts, with Simon Turner, Anthony Murphy, Gerald Flood, John Paul, and Valerie Holliman; Aldous Huxley's "Point Counter Point," in five parts, with Lyndon Brook, Tristam Jellinek, Valerie Gearon, and David Graham; Henry James's "The Golden Bowl," in six parts, with Barry Morse, Jill Townsend, Daniel Massey, and Gayle Hunnicutt.

During the 1973–1974 season five dramas were introduced, including "Upstairs Downstairs," the longest-running and most popular drama in the *Masterpiece Theatre* repertoire. The season's first four presentations included: Dorothy Sayers's "Clouds of Witness," in five parts, with Ian Carmichael, Glyn Houston, and Rachel Herbert; N. J. Crisp's "The Man Who Was Hunting Himself," in three parts, with Donald Burton, Carol Austin, David Savile, and Conrad Phillips; Sayers's "The Unpleasantness at the Bellona Club," in four parts, with Ian Carmichael, Derek Newark, and John Quentin; and a one-shot presentation of H. E. Bates's "The Little Farm," with Bryan Marshall, Barbara Ewing, and Michael Elphick. On 6 January 1974 the first of the season's thirteen episodes of "Upstairs Downstairs" premiered. Created by Jean Marsh and Eileen Atkins, the series was produced by London Weekend Television. It told the story of the members of a wealthy London family and their several servants; between 1974 and 1977 some fifty-five episodes were telecast on *Masterpiece Theatre,* spanning the first three decades of the twentieth century (ten earlier episodes, covering the late 1890s, were never shown in America). Principal players included: David Langton as Richard Bellamy, head of the clan, member of Parliament; Simon Williams as his son, James; Meg Wynn Owen as Hazel, James's wife; Leslie-Anne Down as Georgina Worsley, Richard Bellamy's ward; Gordon Jackson as Hudson, the dutiful butler; Jean Marsh as Rose, the maid; Angela Baddeley as Mrs. Bridges, the cook; Christopher Beeny as Edward, the footman; Jenny Tomasin as Ruby, the scullery maid; and Jacqueline Tong as Daisy, the maid.

On the fifth season of *Masterpiece Theatre* (1974–1975) five selections were presented: Dorothy Sayers's "Murder Must Advertise," in four parts, with Ian Carmichael, Rachel Herbert, Mark Eden, and Bridget Armstrong; thirteen more episodes of "Upstairs Downstairs"; "Country Matters," a miniseries of four one-episode playlets; a six-part miniseries, "Vienna 1900: Games with Love and Death," in which five stories by Arthur Schnitzler were adapted; Dorothy Sayers's "The Nine Tailors," in four parts, with Ian Carmichael, Glyn Houston, Donald Eccles, and Keith Drinkel.

Another five presentations made up the 1975–1976 season: the six-part "Shoulder to Shoulder," with Sian Phillips, Patricia Quinn, Angela Down, and Georgia Brown; "Notorious Woman," a seven-part dramatization of the life of George Sand, with Rosemary Harris and George Chakiris; another thirteen episodes of "Upstairs Downstairs"; a three-part adaptation of Somerset Maugham's "Cakes and Ale," with Judy Cornwell, Michael Hordern, and Mike Pratt; a six-part adaptation of Lewis Grassic Gibbon's "Sunset Song," with Vivien Heilbron, Andrew Keir, Edith Macarthur, and James Grant.

Presentations in the 1976–1977 season included: Gustave Flaubert's "Madame Bovary," in four parts, with Francesca Annis and Tom Conti; Richard Llewellyn's "How Green Was My Valley," in six parts, with Stanley Baker, Sian Phillips, and Nerys Hughes; Dorothy Sayers's "Five Red Herrings," in four parts, with Ian Carmichael, Glyn Houston, John Junkin, and Ian Ireland; the final sixteen episodes of "Upstairs Downstairs"; the sixteen-part "Poldark," adapted from Winston Graham's novels, with Robin Ellis, Clive Francis, Norma Streader, and Angharad Rees.

The 1977–1978 season began early (28 August) with the ten-part "Dickens of London," from Yorkshire Television, with Roy Dotrice, Diana Coupland, Karen Dotrice, and Richard Leech. Later presentations included: the thirteen-part "I, Claudius," adapted from Robert Graves's historical novels, with Derek Jacobi, Sian Phillips, Brian Blessed, and John Paul; a ten-part adaptation of Tolstoy's "Anna Karenina," with Nicola Pagett, Stuart Wilson, Davyd Harries, and Robert Swann; and Dickens's "Our Mutual Friend," with Andrew Ray, Jack Wild, Lesley Dunlop, and Duncan Lamont.

The 1978–1979 season led off with a seven-part adaptation of Thomas Hardy's "The Mayor of Casterbridge," with Alan Bates. Subsequent presentations included fifteen segments of "The Duchess of Duke Street," with Gemma Jones; "Country Matters," in four parts, with Meg Owens; and thirteen episodes of "Lillie," starring Francesca Annis as actress Lillie Langtry.

Scheduled for the 1979–1980 season were: "Kean," a two-parter with

Anthony Hopkins as actor Edmund Kean; twelve episodes of "Love for Lydia," starring Mel Martin; "Prince Regent"; fifteen more episodes of "The Duchess of Duke Street"; "Disraeli, Portrait of a Romantic"; and "Lillie."

MASTERS OF MAGIC
CBS

16 FEBRUARY 1949–11 MAY 1949   One of TV's first magic shows, *Masters of Magic* was a fifteen-minute show seen on Wednesdays after the network news. Originally titled *Now You See It,* the show was emceed by Andre Baruch and produced by Sherman H. Dreyer Productions.

THE MATCH GAME
NBC/CBS/SYNDICATED

31 DECEMBER 1962–20 SEPTEMBER 1969 (NBC); 2 JULY 1973–20 APRIL 1979 (CBS); 1975–   (SYNDICATED)   All of the incarnations of this Goodson-Todman game show have been hosted by Gene Rayburn. On the NBC version, entitled simply *The Match Game,* two three-member teams, each consisting of a celebrity and two contestants, competed; the object of the game was to fill in the blank in a sentence read by the host, and contestants who matched answers with their teammates won money. On the CBS version, which added the last two digits of the year to the title (*Match Game '73,* etc.), and on the syndicated version (titled *Match Game PM*), two contestants played with a panel of six celebrities, and contestants won points for each celebrity whose answer matched theirs.

MATINEE THEATER
NBC

31 OCTOBER 1955–27 JUNE 1958   John Conte hosted this ambitious anthology series—each weekday afternoon a new drama was presented live and in color. Some 7,000 actors were used in some 650 productions, but the series never attracted large audiences. Albert McCleery was the producer.

THE MATT DENNIS SHOW
NBC

27 JUNE 1955–29 AUGUST 1955   Pianist Matt Dennis hosted this fifteen-minute summer musical series.

MATT HELM
ABC

20 SEPTEMBER 1975–3 JANUARY 1976   Uninspired hour-long crime show, starring Tony Franciosa as Matt Helm, a high-living former government agent who became a private detective in Los Angeles. Also featured were Laraine Stephens as his friend, Claire Kronski, a lawyer; Gene Evans as Sergeant Hanrahan of the L. A. police; and Jeff Donnell (seldom seen on TV since her days on *The George Gobel Show*) as Ethel, operator of Helm's answering service. Charles FitzSimmons and Ken Pettus

produced the series. The character was created by Donald Hamilton and played by Dean Martin in several films during the 1960s.

MATT LINCOLN   ABC
24 SEPTEMBER 1970–14 JANUARY 1971   Vincent Edwards, who had played a neurosurgeon on *Ben Casey,* returned to television as Matt Lincoln, a community psychiatrist, in this forgettable hour series. Also featured were Chelsea Brown as Tag, Michael Larrain as Kevin, June Harding as Ann, and Felton Perry as Jimmy.

MATTY'S FUNDAY FUNNIES   ABC
11 OCTOBER 1959–30 DECEMBER 1961   A half-hour cartoon series sponsored by Mattel Toys, *Matty's Funday Funnies* was seen on Sunday afternoons during the 1959–1960 season, and on Friday nights during the 1960–1961 season. The cartoons were from Harvey Films, and segments included "Casper the Friendly Ghost," "Little Audrey," and "Baby Huey." Hosting the show were two animated characters known as Matty and Sisterbelle. In the fall of 1961 the series shifted to early Saturday evenings, and early in 1962 a new set of cartoons was introduced: see *Time for Beany.*

MAUDE   CBS
12 SEPTEMBER 1972–29 APRIL 1978   First introduced on *All in the Family* as Edith Bunker's cousin, Maude Findlay proved herself every bit as vocal and opinionated—on the liberal side—as her reactionary in-law. Beatrice Arthur starred as Maude Findlay, a loud, liberal middle-aged woman living with her fourth husband in suburban Tuckahoe. Also featured were Bill Macy as Walter Findlay, her current husband, owner of Findlay's Friendly Appliances; Adrienne Barbeau as Carol Traynor, Maude's divorced daughter (by one of her previous marriages), who lived with the Findlays; Conrad Bain as their conservative neighbor, Dr. Arthur Harmon; Rue McClanahan (1973–1978) as Arthur's wife, Vivian Harmon, Maude's best friend; Brian Morrison (1972–1977) and Kraig Metzinger (1977–1978) as Philip, Carol's son; Esther Rolle (1972–1974) as Florida Evans, Maude's black maid; and John Amos (1972–1974) as James Evans, Florida's husband. Rolle and Amos left the series in January of 1974 to star in their own series, *Good Times.* Hermione Baddeley then joined the cast as Mrs. Nell Naugatuck, an English maid. J. Pat O'Malley was added in 1975 as grave digger Bert Beasley, who courted Mrs. Naugatuck (a widow) and married her in 1977. In the fall of 1977, Marlene Warfield joined the series as Maude's third maid, Victoria Butterfield, a Caribbean native. Created by Norman Lear, the series fared well, cracking Nielsen's Top Ten in each of its first four seasons. But ratings had slipped drastically by the 1977–1978 season, and in March of

1978 Beatrice Arthur announced she would be leaving the show. Rod Parker, who produced the show for several seasons, became executive producer in 1975, succeeding Norman Lear. In 1977 Parker was coexecutive producer with Hal Cooper, and Charlie Hauck was the producer. The show's theme, "And Then There's Maude," composed by Marilyn Bergman, Alan Bergman, and Dave Grusin, was sung by Donny Hathaway.

MAURICE WOODRUFF PREDICTS   SYNDICATED
1969   Hour-long talk show hosted by seer Maurice Woodruff.

MAVERICK   ABC
22 SEPTEMBER 1957–8 JULY 1962   This popular hour-long western originally starred James Garner as Bret Maverick, an unconventional western hero who preferred chicanery to combat and a card table to a covered wagon. Garner was to have been the only star, but when it became obvious to the show's executives after a few weeks that production was hopelessly behind schedule, a second Maverick was introduced: Jack Kelly as Bret's equally devious brother, Bart Maverick. Kelly first appeared on 10 November 1957, and starred in about one third of that season's episodes (the Kelly episodes were produced by a separate production crew). By 1960 Kelly and Garner were featured more or less equally, and in some episodes they appeared together. Garner left the series after the 1960–1961 season, and Kelly starred in virtually all of the final season's shows. Occasionally featured were Roger Moore (1960–1962) as Beau Maverick, their English cousin; Robert Colbert (1961–1962) as brother Brent Maverick; and Diane Brewster as their friend, Samantha Crawford, an accomplished swindler in her own right. *Maverick* is best remembered for its light touch, and for its parodies of other westerns, such as "Gunshy," a lampoon of *Gunsmoke,* and "Three Queens Full," a takeoff on *Bonanza.* William L. Stewart produced the series for Warner Brothers. See also *Young Maverick.*

MAYA   NBC
16 SEPTEMBER 1967–10 FEBRUARY 1968   Hour-long adventure series about an American boy searching for his missing father, a big game hunter, in the jungles of India. With Jay North as Terry Bowen; Sajid Than as Raji, a native lad who joined up with Terry; and Maya, Raji's pet elephant. Frank King was executive producer of the series, which was filmed entirely on location.

MAYBERRY, R.F.D.   CBS
23 SEPTEMBER 1968–6 SEPTEMBER 1971   This half-hour sitcom was the direct successor of *The Andy Griffith Show.* With Ken Berry as Sam Jones, farmer and town councillor in Mayberry, North Carolina; Buddy

Foster as his son, Mike; Frances Bavier (1968–1970) as Aunt Bee Taylor, their housekeeper; Alice Ghostley (1970–1971) as Alice, the housekeeper; Arlene Golonka as Millie Swanson, girlfriend of widower Sam; George Lindsey as Goober Pyle, slow-witted gas pump jockey; Paul Hartman as Emmett Clark, owner of the town repair shop; Mary Lansing as Martha Clark, Emmett's wife; and Jack Dodson as Howard Sprague, the county clerk. Andy Griffith and Richard O. Linke were the executive producers of the series.

MAYOR OF HOLLYWOOD
NBC
29 JUNE 1952–18 SEPTEMBER 1952   Walter O'Keefe interviewed celebrity guests in Hollywood on this twice-weekly half-hour summer series.

MAYOR OF THE TOWN
SYNDICATED
1954   Thomas Mitchell starred as Mayor Russell of Springdale in this short-lived television version of the series that ran on radio from 1942 to 1949. Also featured were Kathleen Freeman as his housekeeper, Marilly, and David Saber as his ward, Butch.

McCLOUD
NBC
16 SEPTEMBER 1970–28 AUGUST 1977   This crime show began in 1970 as one segment of NBC's *Four-In-One*. In the fall of 1971 it expanded from an hour to ninety minutes and was featured as one segment of *The NBC Mystery Movie* on Wednesdays. The following year it moved to Sunday, as one segment of *The NBC Sunday Mystery Movie*, where it remained for the next five years; some features were two hours, others ninety minutes. Dennis Weaver starred as Sam McCloud, a deputy marshal from Taos, New Mexico, on assignment in New York to learn sophisticated crimefighting techniques. Also featured were J. D. Cannon as the Chief of Detectives, Peter B. Clifford; Terry Carter as Sergeant Joe Broadhurst; Ken Lynch as gravel-voiced Sergeant Grover; and Diana Muldaur as Chris Coughlin, McCloud's female friend. The pilot for the series, "McCloud: Who Killed Miss U.S.A.?" was televised 17 February 1970. Glen A. Larson was executive producer of the series for Universal Television.

McCOY
NBC
5 OCTOBER 1975–28 MARCH 1976   One segment of *The NBC Sunday Mystery Movie, McCoy* shared a slot with *McCloud, Columbo,* and *McMillan and Wife.* Created by Roland Kibbee and Dean Hargrove, it starred Tony Curtis as McCoy, a con artist with a heart of gold, and Roscoe Lee Browne as his associate, Gideon Gibbs.

McDUFF, THE TALKING DOG
NBC
11 SEPTEMBER 1976–20 NOVEMBER 1976   Abysmal live-action Satur-

day-morning series about a ghostly English sheepdog (McDuff) and a veterinarian, the only person who could see or communicate with him. The human roles were played by Walter Willison as veterinarian Calvin Campbell; Gordon Jump as next-door neighbor Amos Ferguson; Monty Margetts as Mrs. Osgood, Calvin's nurse and housekeeper; Johnnie Collins III as Ferguson's nephew, Squeaky; and Michelle Stacy as Kimmy. The voice of McDuff was supplied by Jack Lester. William Raynor and Myles Wilder created, produced, and wrote the half-hour series.

McHALE'S NAVY ABC

11 OCTOBER 1962–30 AUGUST 1966 This popular service sitcom was set on a South Pacific island during World War II for its first three seasons. It featured Ernest Borgnine as Lieutenant Commander Quinton McHale, skipper of PT–73 and commanding officer of a squadron of goof-offs, gamblers, and nincompoops; Joe Flynn as blustery Captain Wallace Binghamton, McHale's meddlesome superior; Tim Conway as Ensign Chuck Parker, the bumbling klutz whom Binghamton assigned to the squadron in the vain hope that he could whip it into shape. The rest of the crew included Carl Ballantine as Lester Gruber; Gary Vinson as "Christy" Christopher; Bob Hastings as Lieutenant Carpenter, Binghamton's aide; Billy Sands as "Tinker" Bell; Gavin MacLeod (1962–1964) as Happy Haines; Edson Stroll as Virgil Edwards; John Wright as Willy Moss; and Yoshio Yoda as Fuji, a Japanese POW who served as the squadron's cook. Occasionally seen were Roy Roberts as Admiral Rogers; Jacques Aubuchon as Tali Urulu, the local chieftain; Jane Dulo (1962–1964) as Nurse Molly Turner. At the outset of the fourth season Binghamton, McHale and company (including Fuji) were transferred to Italy and assigned to duty near the town of Voltafiore. Joining the cast were Henry Beckman as Colonel Harrigan; Simon Scott as General Bronson; Jay Novello as Mayor Lugatto; and Dick Wilson as Dino Barone, one of the locals. One of TV's longer-lasting military comedies, *McHale's Navy* is still widely seen in syndication.

McKEEVER AND THE COLONEL NBC

23 SEPTEMBER 1962–16 JUNE 1963 Half-hour sitcom set at Westfield Academy, a boys' military school. With Scott Lane as Cadet Gary McKeever, a fun-loving youngster; Allyn Joslyn as Colonel Harvey T. Blackwell, the head of the academy; Jackie Coogan as Sergeant Barnes; Elisabeth Fraser as Mrs. Warner, the academy dietician; Johnny Eimen as Monk, one of McKeever's pals; and Keith Taylor as Tubby, another of McKeever's pals. R. Allen Saffian and Harvey Bullock created the series, and Billy Friedberg produced it.

THE McLEAN STEVENSON SHOW NBC

1 DECEMBER 1976–9 MARCH 1977 Half-hour sitcom with McLean Ste-

venson as Max Ferguson, a Chicago hardware dealer; Barbara Stuart as Peggy Ferguson, his wife; Steve Nevil as Chris, their live-at-home son in his twenties; Ayn Ruymen as Janet, their recently divorced daughter; David Hollander as Janet's son David; Jason Whitney as Janet's son Jason; Madge West as Grandma ("Gram"); Andrew Parks as Allan; and Sandra Kerns as Susan. Monty Hall was the executive producer of the series, and Paul Williams composed the show's theme music.

McMILLAN AND WIFE
NBC

29 SEPTEMBER 1971–21 AUGUST 1977   *McMillan and Wife* premiered in 1971 as one segment of *The NBC Mystery Movie* on Wednesdays. In 1972 it moved to Sundays and was featured as one segment of *The NBC Sunday Mystery Movie* for the next five years. It starred Rock Hudson in his first dramatic role on television as Stewart McMillan, Commissioner of Police in San Francisco. Susan St. James costarred as his wife, Sally McMillan, who usually became involved in her husband's cases. Also featured during the first five seasons were John Schuck as Sergeant Charles Enright, McMillan's chief aide, and Nancy Walker as Mildred, the McMillans' housekeeper. At the end of the 1975–1976 season St. James, Schuck, and Walker all left the series (Schuck to star in *Holmes and Yoyo*, Walker to star in *The Nancy Walker Show*). For the final season, the title was shortened to *McMillan*, and McMillan was now a widower. Martha Raye joined the cast as Agatha, McMillan's new housekeeper, and Richard Gilliland was featured as his aide, Sergeant DiMaggio. The pilot for the series, "Once upon a Dead Man," was telecast 17 September 1971. Leonard B. Stern was executive producer of the series for Universal Television.

ME AND THE CHIMP
CBS

13 JANUARY 1972–18 MAY 1972   One of the most dismal failures of the 1972–1973 season, *Me and the Chimp* somehow limped through nineteen weeks before its well-deserved cancellation. Created by Garry Marshall and Tom Miller (who later worked together on *Happy Days* and *Laverne and Shirley*), it told the story of a dentist who was persuaded by his two children to take in a runaway chimpanzee. With Ted Bessell as dentist Mike Reynolds; Anita Gillette as his wife, Liz; Scott Kolden as their son, Scott; and Kami Cotler (who landed a role on *The Waltons* a few months later) as their daughter, Kitty. Buttons, the chimp, was played by a three-and-a-half-year-old primate named Jackie.

MEDALLION THEATRE
CBS

11 JULY 1953–3 APRIL 1954   This half-hour dramatic anthology series was seen on Saturday nights. Presentations included: "The Decision at Arrowsmith," with Henry Fonda (his first major TV dramatic role, 11 July); "The Grand Cross of the Crescent," with Jack Lemmon (25 July);

"The Man Who Liked Dickens," with Claude Rains (his first major TV dramatic role, 1 August); "Dear Cynthia," with Janet Gaynor (her first major TV dramatic role, 28 November); and "A Day in Town," with Charlton Heston (12 December).

MEDIC
NBC

13 SEPTEMBER 1954–19 NOVEMBER 1956   One of TV's first medical anthology shows, *Medic* was created by James Moser (who later worked on *Ben Casey*) and produced by Worthington Miner (who formerly produced *Studio One*). As Dr. Konrad Styner, Richard Boone hosted the series and starred in many of the stories. Filmed in cooperation with the Los Angeles County Medical Association, *Medic* presented both historical and contemporary medical dramas; it was the first television series to show the birth of a baby (26 September and 3 October 1955). Among the guest stars who played some of their earliest TV roles on the show were Dennis Hopper ("Boy in the Storm," 3 January 1955), John Saxon ("Walk with Lions," 12 September 1955), and Robert Vaughn ("Black Friday," 21 November 1955).

MEDICAL CENTER
CBS

24 SEPTEMBER 1969–6 SEPTEMBER 1976   Hardy hour-long medical drama, with James Daly as Dr. Paul Lochner, chief of staff at the University Medical Center in Los Angeles; Chad Everett as Dr. Joe Gannon, his young colleague, a skilled surgeon and accurate diagnostician. Occasionally featured were Jayne Meadows as Nurse Chambers; Audrey Totter (1972–1976) as Nurse Wilcox; Chris Hutson (1973–1975) as Nurse Courtland; and Barbara Baldavin (1973–1975) as Nurse Holmby. O. J. Simpson and Cicely Tyson guest-starred in the premiere telecast, "The Last Ten Yards." Frank Glicksman and Al C. Ward were the executive producers.

MEDICAL HORIZONS
ABC

12 SEPTEMBER 1955–9 JUNE 1957   Don Goddard hosted this half-hour documentary series on medical technology and health care.

MEDICAL STORY
NBC

4 SEPTEMBER 1975–8 JANUARY 1976   Short-lived hour-long medical anthology series. Abby Mann was the executive producer, Christopher Morgan the producer.

MEDIX
SYNDICATED

1971–1978   Half-hour public affairs program on health care, hosted by Mario Machado (1971–1977) and Stephanie Edwards (1977–1978). Distributed by Dave Bell Ax Associates, the series was produced in cooperation with the Los Angeles County Medical Association.

MEET BETTY FURNESS CBS

2 JANUARY 1953–3 JULY 1953   Betty Furness hosted this fifteen-minute talk show, which was seen Friday mornings. Set in a living room and kitchen, the show was produced by Lester Lewis.

MEET CORLISS ARCHER CBS/SYNDICATED

13 JULY 1951–10 AUGUST 1951 (CBS); 26 JANUARY 1952–29 MARCH 1952 (CBS); 1954 (SYNDICATED)   Neither of the TV versions of this adolescent sitcom was as successful as the radio version, which ran from 1943 to 1955, and was based on F. Hugh Herbert's play, *Kiss and Tell.* The show surfaced on television briefly in 1951, in what was apparently a trial run, and was revived early in 1952. It starred Lugene Sanders as Corliss Archer, a headstrong teenager (Sanders played the part on radio for a time and later played Babs on *The Life of Riley*). Also featured were Fred Shields as her father, Harry Archer, an insurance agent; Frieda Inescort as her mother, Janet Archer; and Bobby Ellis as Dexter Franklin, Corliss's boyfriend. When the series resurfaced in 1954, only Bobby Ellis remained from the first TV cast. Ann Baker was now seen as Corliss, with John Eldredge as Harry and Mary Brian as Janet. Also featured was Ken Christy as Dexter's father, Mr. Franklin. The 1954 series was filmed and was widely syndicated during the 1950s.

MEET McGRAW NBC

2 JULY 1957–24 JUNE 1958   This half-hour crime show starred Frank Lovejoy as McGraw, a private eye with no first name; as Lovejoy put it at the beginning of each episode, "This is McGraw, just McGraw. It's enough of a name for a man like McGraw." Lovejoy first played the part on an episode of *Four Star Playhouse,* "Meet McGraw," aired 25 February 1954. Angie Dickinson guest-starred on one of the early episodes, broadcast 9 July 1957. The series was rerun on ABC during part of the 1958–1959 season. The show's theme, "One for My Baby," was written by Harold Arlen and Johnny Mercer.

MEET ME AT THE ZOO CBS

10 JANUARY 1953–30 MAY 1953   This half-hour educational series for children was broadcast from the Philadelphia Zoo. Each week host Jack Whitaker (who later became a CBS sportscaster) brought three young visitors along to chat with zoo director Freeman Shelly and meet the zoo's residents. Glen Bernard directed the show, which was aired Saturdays.

MEET MILLIE CBS

25 OCTOBER 1952–28 FEBRUARY 1956   The misadventures of a Manhattan secretary were the subject of this half-hour sitcom. With Elena Verdugo as Millie Bronson; Florence Halop as her widowed mother, Mrs.

Bronson, eager to find a husband for her daughter; Ross Ford as J. R. (Johnny) Boone, Jr., the boss's son, Millie's occasional romantic interest; Earl Ross and Roland Winters as J. R. Boone, Sr., Millie's boss; Marvin Kaplan as Alfred, the young man who lived next door; and Ray Montgomery (1955–1956) as Jack. Though *Meet Millie* was set in New York, it was one of the first series broadcast from CBS's Television City facility in Hollywood.

MEET MR. McNULTY/MEET MR. McNUTLEY
See THE RAY MILLAND SHOW

MEET THE BOSS   DUMONT
10 JUNE 1952–12 MAY 1953   Leaders of American industry were profiled on this half-hour series. Bill Cunningham, the first host, was succeeded by Robert Sullivan.

MEET THE CHAMPIONS   NBC
21 JULY 1956–12 JANUARY 1957   Jack Lescoulie interviewed athletes on this fifteen-minute Saturday-evening series.

MEET THE MASTERS   NBC
24 FEBRUARY 1952–4 MAY 1952   This half-hour series of classical music was seen on alternate Sunday afternoons. Violinist Jascha Heifetz was the guest on the premiere.

MEET THE PRESS   NBC
6 NOVEMBER 1947–   Network television's oldest program has changed little since its inception: Each week a well-known guest, usually a political figure, is grilled by four journalists. The show was created by Martha Rountree, who brought it to radio in 1945; Lawrence E. Spivak, then editor of *American Mercury* magazine, was a permanent panelist from the earliest days, and producer Rountree also served as moderator. In 1953 Spivak bought out Rountree's interest in the show, and Ned Brooks succeeded her as moderator. By the early 1960s Spivak himself had become moderator and remained there until 1975. Spivak decided to retire from the show in November of that year, and the guest on Spivak's last regular show (an hour-long special aired 9 November, commemorating the series' twenty-eighth anniversary on television) was President Gerald Ford; it was the first time that an incumbent President had appeared on the program. NBC newsman Bill Monroe is currently the moderator.

MEET THE PROFESSOR   ABC
5 FEBRUARY 1961–14 MAY 1961   A Sunday-afternoon show with an academic flavor. Each week Dr. Harold Taylor, former president of

Sarah Lawrence College, interviewed a guest from the world of education.

MEET THE VEEP   NBC
1 FEBRUARY 1953–1 SEPTEMBER 1953   Alben W. Barkley, former Vice President under Harry S Truman, chatted with Earl Goodwin on this public affairs program. It began as a half-hour show on Sundays and later switched to fifteen minutes on Fridays, then Tuesdays.

MEET YOUR CONGRESS   NBC/DUMONT
1 JULY 1949–12 NOVEMBER 1949 (NBC); 8 JULY 1953–4 JULY 1954 (DUMONT)   Broadcast from Washington, this public affairs program was moderated by Blair Moody; each week four Congressional representatives, two from each party, discussed topical issues. Charles Christiansen produced the half-hour series.

MEET YOUR COVER GIRL   CBS
24 OCTOBER 1950–1 NOVEMBER 1951   Robin Chandler interviewed guest models on this half-hour daytime series.

MEETING OF MINDS   PBS
10 JANUARY 1977–   An unusual talk show created and hosted by versatile Steve Allen, *Meeting of Minds* features guests not from the present, but from the past. Each week four or five historical figures (played by actors) get together and discuss matters past, present, and future. Steve Allen's "guests" on the premiere included Cleopatra (played by Jayne Meadows, Allen's wife), Thomas Aquinas (Peter Bromilow), Thomas Paine (Joe Sirola), and Theodore Roosevelt (Joe Earley). The hour series won a Peabody Award for the year 1977.

MEL & SUSAN TOGETHER   ABC
22 APRIL 1978–13 MAY 1978   Four-week variety show hosted by country and western singer Mel Tillis and former Miss California Susan Anton. The executive producers of the half-hour series were Merrill and Alan Osmond, and the show was taped at the Osmonds' production facilities in Orem, Utah.

THE MEL MARTIN SHOW
See BREAKFAST PARTY

THE MEL TORMÉ SHOW   CBS
17 SEPTEMBER 1951–21 AUGUST 1952   One of the first shows to be broadcast in color, *The Mel Tormé Show* was a half-hour daytime musical variety show. Assisting Tormé were singers Ellen Martin and Peggy

King, comedienne Kaye Ballard, Haitian dancer Jean Leon Dustine, and a French sketch artist known as Monsieur Crayon.

THE MELBA MOORE–CLIFTON DAVIS SHOW   CBS
7 JUNE 1972–5 JULY 1972 A five-week summer replacement for *The Carol Burnett Show,* this musical variety hour was cohosted by Melba Moore and her husband, Clifton Davis. Also on hand were Timmie Rogers, Ron Carey, Dick Libertini, and Liz Torres.

MELODY, HARMONY & RHYTHM   NBC
13 DECEMBER 1949–16 FEBRUARY 1950 Broadcast from Philadelphia on Tuesdays and Thursdays before the network news, this fifteen-minute show featured the music of the Tony DeSimone Trio and singers Carol Reed and Lynne Barrett.

MELODY STREET   DUMONT
23 SEPTEMBER 1953–5 FEBRUARY 1954 Half-hour musical variety series hosted by Elliott Lawrence.

MELODY TOUR   ABC
8 JULY 1954–30 SEPTEMBER 1954 This half-hour musical revue was set in a different locale each week. It featured pianist Stan Freeman, soprano Nancy Kenyon, baritones Norman Scott and Robert Rounseville, dancers Nellie Fisher, Jonathan Lucas, and Peter Gladke, and comedienne Jorie Remes.

THE MEN   ABC
21 SEPTEMBER 1972–1 SEPTEMBER 1973 *The Men* was the umbrella title for three alternating hour-long adventure series: see *Assignment: Vienna, The Delphi Bureau,* and *Jigsaw.*

MEN AT LAW
See THE STOREFRONT LAWYERS

MEN IN CRISIS   SYNDICATED
1965 Edmond O'Brien narrated this half-hour biographical series, which focused on great decision makers. The show was produced and directed by Alan Landsburg.

MEN INTO SPACE   CBS
30 SEPTEMBER 1959–7 SEPTEMBER 1960 The first of the post-Sputnik space shows, *Men into Space* was filmed with the cooperation of the Department of Defense, which retained script approval. Thus, the show dealt with space travel in a fairly plausible fashion and avoided the use of aliens, monsters, and secret weapons. Thirty-eight half-hour episodes

were filmed, with William Lundigan as Colonel Ed McCawley, American space pioneer. Occasionally featured were Joyce Taylor as his wife, Mary, and Tyler McVey as General Norgath. Lewis Rachmil produced the series.

MEN OF ANNAPOLIS   SYNDICATED
1957   Produced by Ziv TV, *Men of Annapolis* was a companion piece to Ziv's 1956 service academy show, *West Point.* The half-hour anthology series was filmed largely on location at the United States Naval Academy in Annapolis, Maryland.

MENASHA THE MAGNIFICENT   NBC
3 JULY 1950–11 SEPTEMBER 1950   Half-hour sitcom starring Menasha Skulnik as a restaurant manager. Skulnik had previously played Uncle David on the radio version of *The Goldbergs* and joined the television cast of that series in 1953. Produced by Martin Goodman, the show was given a weekly slot some months after the pilot, "Magnificent Menasha," was telecast on 20 February 1950.

THE MEREDITH WILLSON SHOW   NBC
31 JULY 1949–21 AUGUST 1949   Half-hour musical variety series hosted by bandleader-composer Meredith Willson. Also featured were the Talking People, a five-member vocal group. Bill Brown produced and directed the series.

THE MERV GRIFFIN SHOW   NBC/SYNDICATED/CBS
1 OCTOBER 1962–29 MARCH 1963 (NBC); 1965–1969 (SYNDICATED); 18 AUGUST 1969–11 FEBRUARY 1972 (CBS); 1972–   (SYNDICATED)   Merv Griffin has hosted talk shows almost continuously since 1962. Before that he had been featured on several series, first as a singer, later as a game show host (*The Freddy Martin Show, Going Places, Keep Talking, Play Your Hunch, The Robert Q. Lewis Show,* and *Song Snapshots on a Summer Holiday*). On 1 October 1962, the day that Johnny Carson took over as host of the *Tonight* show, Griffin began hosting an afternoon talk show on NBC; the fifty-five-minute daily show lasted twenty-six weeks. After developing two game shows—*Jeopardy* and *Word for Word* (he also emceed the latter)—Griffin again hosted a talk show. This effort, syndicated by Westinghouse, was seen on weekday afternoons in most markets and fared well enough to attract the attention of CBS. At that time CBS, which had not previously aired a late-night talk show, was interested in finding someone to challenge Johnny Carson at 11:30 p.m. The network signed Griffin to a lucrative contract and renovated the Cort Theater in New York especially for the new show. Griffin's guests on the 1969 premiere included Woody Allen, Hedy Lamarr, Moms Mabley, Ted Sorensen, and Leslie Uggams. Also on hand

were announcer Arthur Treacher and the Mort Lindsey Orchestra, both of whom had been with Griffin on the Westinghouse show. In March of 1970 antiwar activist Abbie Hoffman came on the show wearing a red, white, and blue shirt that resembled the American flag. The network, skittish about possible political repercussions, decided to air the tape, but arranged to have Hoffman's image electronically obscured; when the program was broadcast, Griffin and his other guests could be seen clearly, while Hoffman's voice emanated from within a jumble of lines. Although the incident attracted some controversy, it did little to bolster the show's ratings; the network continued to have difficulty in lining up enough affiliates to mount a serious challenge to Carson (many local stations found that running old movies against the *Tonight* show was more profitable). In September of 1970, the show moved from New York to Los Angeles, but to no avail. Griffin and CBS called it quits early in 1972; later that year, after negotiating again with Westinghouse, Griffin signed with Metromedia and began hosting his second syndicated talk show. This show, like the Westinghouse show, is seen on weekday afternoons in most markets. Directed by Dick Carson, brother of Johnny Carson (and former director of the *Tonight* show), it has proven to be Griffin's most successful effort.

METROPOLITAN OPERA AUDITIONS OF THE AIR ABC
15 JANUARY 1952–1 APRIL 1952   Viewers had the rare opportunity to watch auditions for the Metropolitan Opera Company on this prime-time half-hour series. Milton Cross, "the voice of the Met," hosted the show.

MIAMI UNDERCOVER SYNDICATED
1961   Low-budget half-hour crime show starring Lee Bowman as Jeff Thompson, a private eye employed by the Miami Hotel Owners Association, and Rocky Graziano as his partner, Rocky.

MICHAEL SHAYNE NBC
30 SEPTEMBER 1960–22 SEPTEMBER 1961   Michael Shayne, the private eye created by Brett Halliday (the pen name of Davis Dresser), first appeared on radio in 1944. The television series, which ran a full hour, was set in Miami Beach and featured Richard Denning as Michael Shayne; Jerry Paris as reporter Tim O'Rourke; Patricia Donahue and Margie Regan as Shayne's secretary, Lucy Hamilton; Gary Clarke as Dick, Lucy's younger brother; and Herbert Rudley as Lieutenant Gentry, Miami Beach cop.

THE MICHAELS IN AFRICA SYNDICATED
1960   A series of documentaries filmed in Africa, hosted by George and Marjorie Michael.

MICKEY ABC

16 SEPTEMBER 1964–13 JANUARY 1965   Unsuccessful half-hour sitcom starring Mickey Rooney as Mickey Grady, a Midwestern businessman who inherited a hotel in Newport Beach, California, from his late uncle. With Emmaline Henry as his wife, Nora; Timmy Rooney (Mickey's real-life son) as their son Tim; Brian Nash as their son Buddy; Sammee Tong as Sammy Ling, manager of the hotel; and Alan Reed as Mr. Swidler, owner of a nearby gas station.

THE MICKEY MOUSE CLUB ABC

3 OCTOBER 1955–24 SEPTEMBER 1959

THE NEW MICKEY MOUSE CLUB SYNDICATED

1977   The second television series from Walt Disney Studios, *The Mickey Mouse Club* was introduced as a Monday-through-Friday show a year after *Disneyland* premiered. The filmed show was seen for an hour a day during its first two seasons and was trimmed to a half-hour in the fall of 1957. Unlike other popular children's shows of the day, *The Mickey Mouse Club* did not use a studio audience, and, instead of a sole adult host (such as Pinky Lee or Buffalo Bob Smith), it employed a group of child performers; the T-shirted, mouse-hatted company was known, of course, as the Mouseketeers.

Though the format of each day's show was approximately the same (a typical hour usually consisted of a newsreel or other short documentary film, a production number or sketch, an episode of a filmed serial, and a Disney cartoon), the show for each day of the week was constructed around a general theme. Monday was "Fun with Music Day," on which original musical numbers were performed; Tuesday was "Guest Star Day," featuring appearances by celebrities; Wednesday was "Anything Can Happen Day," on which a potpourri of features was presented; Thursday was "Circus Day," which featured a cartoon appearance by Jiminy Cricket followed by stunts and games involving the Mouseketeers; Friday was "Talent Roundup Day," on which talented youngsters performed and were then made "Honorary Mouseketeers." During the show's first two seasons, a short, child-oriented newsreel was shown three times a week.

The thread that held the show together was the Mouseketeers, who sang, danced, starred in the filmed serials, introduced the cartoons, and provided an audience for the guest stars and talent acts. Twenty-four youngsters were featured regularly during the first season: Nancy Abbate, Sharon Baird, Billie Jean Beanblossom, Bobby Burgess, Lonnie Burr, Tommy Cole, Johnny Crawford, Dennis Day, Dickie Dodd, Mary Espinosa, Annette Funicello, Darlene Gillespie, Judy Harriet, John Lee Johann, Bonni Lou Kern, Carl "Cubby" O'Brien, Karen Pendleton, Mary Sartori, Bronson Scott, Michael Smith, Ronnie Steiner, Mark Sutherland,

Doreen Tracey, and Don Underhill. Three other youngsters were featured on the earliest shows, but left after only a few weeks: Paul Petersen (who later was featured on *The Donna Reed Show*), and Tim and Mickey Rooney, Jr. (sons of actor Mickey Rooney). Two adults, similarly hatted and shirted, rounded out the cast: Jimmie Dodd, an actor and songwriter who was, in effect, the show's host and Roy Williams ("The Big Mouseketeer"), a veteran Disney writer and animator; it was Williams who designed the Club hat.

Only ten of the first two dozen Mouseketeers returned for the 1956–1957 season: Sharon, Bobby, Lonnie, Tommy, Dennis, Annette, Darlene, Cubby, Karen, and Doreen. Seven new Mouseketeers were added: Sherry Allen, Eileen Diamond, Cheryl Holdridge, Charley Laney, Larry Larsen, Jay-Jay Solari, and Margene Storey. Again, ten of that group returned for the remaining seasons (the shows seen during the fourth season were actually produced in 1958): Sharon, Bobby, Lonnie, Tommy, Annette, Darlene, Cubby, Karen, Doreen, and Cheryl. Four newcomers were added: Don Agrati (later known as Don Grady when he was featured on *My Three Sons*), Bonnie Lynn Fields, Linda Hughes, and Lynn Ready. Other youngsters were featured as Mouseketeers from time to time, especially those who appeared in the serials.

The Mickey Mouse Club was one of the few children's shows that presented made-for-TV serials. Several features were produced, most of which consisted of fifteen to thirty episodes. Among the more popular cliff-hangers were: "Corky and White Shadow," with Darlene Gillespie, Buddy Ebsen, and Lloyd Corrigan; "The Hardy Boys: The Mystery of the Applegate Treasure," with Tim Considine, Tommy Kirk, and Florenz Ames (a sequel, "The Hardy Boys: The Mystery of Ghost Farm," was also produced); "Clint and Mac," with Neil Wolfe and Jonathan Bailey; "Annette," with Annette Funicello, Tim Considine, and Roberta Shore. The most popular of the serials, however, was "The Adventures of Spin and Marty," the story of two boys at the Triple R Ranch, a western summer camp; it featured Tim Considine (as Spin Evans), David Stollery (as Marty Markham), J. Pat O'Malley, and Roy Barcroft. "Spin and Marty" was introduced during the 1955–1956 season, and two sequels were produced.

Produced by Bill Walsh, the series left ABC in the fall of 1959 after a four-year run. Reruns were syndicated in 1962 and again in 1975. In the fall of 1976 the series was revived, as production began on *The New Mickey Mouse Club*. This version was a half-hour series, and was videotaped. A new group of Mouseketeers (that included black and Asian–American faces) was formed, which included: Pop Attmore, Scott Craig, Nita DiGiampaolo, Mindy Feldman, Angelo Florez, Allison Fonte, Shawnte Northcutte, Kelly Parsons, Julie Piekarski, Todd Turquand, Lisa Whelchel, and Curtis Wong. Ron Miller was the executive producer.

THE MICKEY ROONEY SHOW
NBC

28 AUGUST 1954–4 JUNE 1955 Also seen under the title *Hey Mulligan,* this half-hour filmed sitcom starred Mickey Rooney as Mickey Mulligan, a TV studio page, aspiring to become a performer. Also featured were Regis Toomey as his father, Mr. Mulligan, a cop; Claire Carleton as his mother, Mrs. Mulligan, a former burlesque queen; Carla Belenda as his girlfriend; Joey Forman as his pal Freddie; and John Hubbard as his boss.

MICKIE FINN'S
NBC

21 APRIL 1966–1 SEPTEMBER 1966 Half-hour musical variety series co-hosted by Fred Finn and his wife, Mickie Finn. The show, which had a gay nineties flavor, was taped at a replica of the Finns' San Diego nightclub, where Fred led the band while Mickie played the banjo.

THE MIDNIGHT SPECIAL
NBC

2 FEBRUARY 1973– Network television's first regularly scheduled attempt at late-late night programming, *The Midnight Special* is a ninety-minute rock music show, which runs from 1:00 a.m. to 2:30 a.m. on Fridays. Helen Reddy hosted the premiere telecast and also served as regular host from 1975 to 1977. America's legendary disc jockey Wolfman Jack is the announcer. Burt Sugarman is the executive producer.

MIDWEST HAYRIDE
SYNDICATED/NBC

1951–1961 *Midwest Hayride,* also known as *Midwestern Hayride,* was a long-running country and western music show that was filmed (and later taped) on location throughout the nation. It was hosted by Willie Thall (1951–1955), Hugh Cherry (1955–1956), and Paul Dixon (1957–1961). The syndicated show was occasionally picked up by one of the major networks as a summer replacement; it was seen on NBC during the summers of 1951, 1952, 1954, 1955, and 1959, and on ABC during the summers of 1957 and 1958. NBC also carried the show during the 1955–1956 season.

THE MIGHTY MOUSE PLAYHOUSE
CBS

10 DECEMBER 1955–2 SEPTEMBER 1967 The star of this long-running Saturday-morning cartoon show was Mighty Mouse, a caped crimefighter who was the rodent equivalent of Superman. Although other segments were also telecast on the series, such as "The Adventures of Gandy Goose," the Mighty Mouse episodes are the best remembered, primarily because of their operatic style. From late October 1966 through 1967, the show was seen under the title *Mighty Heroes.* See also *The New Adventures of Mighty Mouse and Heckle and Jeckle.*

MIKE AND BUFF   CBS

20 AUGUST 1951–27 FEBRUARY 1953   Mike Wallace and Buff Cobb,
who was Wallace's wife at the time, cohosted one of CBS's first color
shows in 1951. The experimental telecasts were conducted weekday
mornings, and in its earliest days their show was called *Two Sleepy People*. By November of 1951, the show had been retitled *Mike and Buff* and
was seen—in black and white—on weekday afternoons, where it remained for the next fifteen months.

THE MIKE DOUGLAS SHOW   SYNDICATED

1963–   Mike Douglas has without doubt hosted more nationally televised talk shows than anyone; in February of 1978 *The Mike
Douglas Show*, which began as a local show in 1961, celebrated its
4,000th broadcast. Like Merv Griffin, whose syndicated talk show is
Douglas's chief competition in many markets, Douglas started out as a
singer, and he was a featured vocalist on such shows as *College of Musical Knowledge* and *Club 60*. From 1953 to 1955 he hosted his own show
in Chicago, a daytime variety series titled *Hi Ladies*. In 1961 he began
hosting a daily ninety-minute talk show in Cleveland, which (with
changes in locale) has remained on the air for nineteen years. From the
beginning Douglas has been joined each week by a celebrity cohost (the
first was Carmel Quinn). By 1963 *The Mike Douglas Show* was syndicated nationally, and in 1965 the operation was moved to Philadelphia,
where it remained for thirteen years; during that time it was the only major syndicated show to originate from that city. Most of Douglas's guests
came from New York, which was a two-hour limousine drive from Philadelphia. In the fall of 1978, however, Douglas left Philadelphia for good,
moving his show to Los Angeles, primarily because of the comparative
ease of booking guests on the West Coast. Douglas's first producer was
Woody Frazer; subsequent producers have included Jack Reilly, Brad
Lachman, and (in Los Angeles) Vince Calandra and E. V. DiMassa. *The
Mike Douglas Show* was the first syndicated talk show to win an Emmy
(the award was made in 1967). Douglas's distributor, Group W, planned
to drop the show in mid-1980, but Douglas managed to find a new
distributor.

MIKE HAMMER   SYNDICATED

1958   Mike Hammer, the gritty private eye created by Mickey Spillane,
was played by Darren McGavin in this half-hour show. Seventy-eight
episodes were filmed.

THE MIKE WALLACE INTERVIEW   ABC

28 APRIL 1957–14 SEPTEMBER 1958   Mike Wallace interviewed a single
guest each week on this half-hour series. Though Wallace is best known
today as one of *60 Minutes*' hard-hitting reporters, his earliest TV appear-

ances were as the cohost of a daytime variety show (see *Mike and Buff*) and as emcee of a game show (see *The Big Surprise*). He honed his interviewing techniques during the mid-1950s on a local show in New York, *Nightbeat,* which led to this nationally televised series.

THE MILLIONAIRE
CBS

19 JANUARY 1955–28 SEPTEMBER 1960   Essentially an anthology series, *The Millionaire* starred Marvin Miller as Michael Anthony, executive secretary to a reclusive multibillionaire whose hobby was giving away a million dollars to persons he had never met. Typically, the show began with Anthony being summoned to the study of his employer, John Beresford Tipton, at "Silverstone," Tipton's 60,000-acre estate. After a brief conversation, Tipton (whose face was never shown to viewers) gave Anthony a cashier's check together with instructions on its delivery. Anthony would track down the donee and present the check, explaining to the recipient that the million dollars was tax free, the donor wished to remain anonymous, and the donee merely had to agree never to divulge the exact amount of the check or the circumstances under which it was received (except to his or her spouse, if the donee should marry). Anthony then disappeared, leaving the recipient richer, if not wiser. The voice of the benevolent Mr. Tipton was supplied by Paul Frees. Don Fedderson, the producer of the series, disclosed in a 1955 *TV Guide* interview that Tipton's name was "a composite of Fedderson's home town, his wife's home town, and his lawyer's first name." Fedderson also managed to include his wife, Tido Fedderson, as an uncredited extra in almost every episode. *TV Guide* later reported that Marvin Miller regularly received requests from people who wanted their own check for a million dollars. Miller's customary reply was to send each person a "check" for "a million dollars' worth of good luck." The half-hour series was syndicated under the title *If You Had a Million.* On 19 December 1978 CBS televised a two-hour made-for-TV movie based on the series; titled "The Millionaire," it featured Robert Quarry as Michael Anthony.

THE MILTON BERLE SHOW (THE TEXACO STAR THEATER)
NBC

21 SEPTEMBER 1948–9 JUNE 1953

THE BUICK–BERLE SHOW
NBC

29 SEPTEMBER 1953–14 JUNE 1955

THE MILTON BERLE SHOW
NBC

27 SEPTEMBER 1955–5 JUNE 1956

THE KRAFT MUSIC HALL
NBC

8 OCTOBER 1958–13 MAY 1959

THE MILTON BERLE SHOW
ABC

9 SEPTEMBER 1966–6 JANUARY 1967   Milton Berle was television's first superstar. His first series, *The Texaco Star Theater,* was the most popular variety show in video history; its phenomenal success proved that TV was

more than a toy and that it could (and would) compete effectively with stage and screen as an entertainment medium. Berle's sobriquet, "Mr. Television," was fully deserved.

Though he is remembered today chiefly as a television entertainer, Berle had an extensive background in vaudeville, films, and radio; he was five years old when he first appeared on stage. He was also one of the first persons to appear on television, having participated in some experimental broadcasts in 1929 and 1933. During the 1940s Berle hosted several radio shows, the last of which were *The Philip Morris Playhouse,* a 1947 anthology series of comedies, and *The Texaco Star Theater,* a comedy-variety show. Among the writers on the latter show were Nat Hiken, Aaron Ruben, and brothers Danny and Neil Simon.

By the spring of 1948 Texaco had become interested in sponsoring a variety show on television. Several prospective hosts, including Berle, "auditioned" on Tuesday nights during the summer of 1948; Berle first hosted the program on 8 June, with guests Pearl Bailey, Harry Richman, Bill "Bojangles" Robinson, and Señor Wences. Pleased with Berle's performance, Texaco chose him as permanent host of the show. Berle's guests on the fall premiere (21 September) included Phil Silvers, Evelyn Knight, Stan Fisher, Smith and Dale, Park and Clifford, and the Four Carters.

The new show was an immediate smash, scoring ratings as high as eighty during its first season. Theater and nightclub attendance dwindled on Tuesdays, as people gathered at the homes of friends who owned television sets. Many of those people soon bought sets of their own—set ownership passed the million mark early in 1949 and doubled later that year. The millions who tuned in on Tuesdays saw broad comedy; Berle, who was actively involved with every aspect of the show's production, capitalized on the visual impact of the medium, relying heavily on outlandish costumes (many of which were designed by his sister, Rosalind) and sight gags. Laughter from the studio audience was further guaranteed by the presence of Berle's mother at almost every telecast. Guest stars were featured each week, and most programs concluded with a musical sketch. Woody Kling and Buddy Arnold, who wrote the show's theme, "We're the Men from Texaco," composed hundreds of numbers for the program. Also featured from the earliest days was vaudevillian Sid Stone, who, as a pitchman, delivered the commercials.

Berle continued to do the radio version during the 1948–1949 season and also found time to host the first telethon on 4 April 1949, for the Damon Runyon Cancer Fund. After a summer's rest he returned to TV (but not to radio) in the fall of 1949. The show continued to top the ratings and again dominated Tuesday-night viewing. Ad-libbing at the end of one show that season, Berle referred to himself as "Uncle Miltie," a nickname that endeared him to younger viewers. *The Texaco Star Theater* continued as TV's number-one show in its third season (1950–1951), though the margin between it and its competition was lessening. In 1951 Berle signed a thirty-year contract with NBC, which guaranteed him an annual income of $200,000 whether he worked or not.

In the fall of 1951, as *Texaco*'s fourth season began, Berle cut back his schedule, hosting the show three out of every four weeks. The show was finally surpassed in the ratings (by Arthur Godfrey's *Talent Scouts*); Berle attributed the decline to the fact that he was appearing less regularly, but in all probability the show's popularity would have tapered off anyway. In the fall of 1952, Berle's last show with Texaco as his sponsor, several changes were made. Veteran radio writer Goodman Ace was brought in as head writer, and several new writers were added, including Selma Diamond, George Foster, Mort Greene, and Jay Burton. Greg Garrison, a young director with several years' experience in the medium, was also hired. A new "show-within-a-show" format was introduced—Berle played himself, the star of a TV variety show, and was joined by a group of regulars: Ruth Gilbert as his secretary, Max, Fred Clark as his agent, and Arnold Stang as Francis the stagehand. Ventriloquist Jimmy Nelson as his dummy, Danny O'Day, handled the commercials.

In spite of all the changes, the show's ratings continued to slip (*Texaco Star Theater* finished fifth that year), and Texaco dropped its sponsorship of the Berle show at the end of the 1952–1953 season (Texaco sponsored a Saturday-night show in the fall of 1953 on NBC, with Jimmy Durante and Donald O'Connor alternating as hosts). Buick, however, picked up the Tuesday-night slot in the fall of 1953; *The Buick–Berle Show* ran for two seasons, continuing with the same format that had been introduced in the fall of 1952. Singers Charlie Applewhite and Connie Russell also joined the cast.

Buick decided to switch its allegiance to CBS—and Jackie Gleason—in 1955. Berle moved his operation from New York to Hollywood that summer and hosted an hour show on Tuesdays—*The Milton Berle Show*—for one more season. It was one of the first color variety shows broadcast from the West Coast. One of the guests on the final telecast in 1956 was Elvis Presley. Though Berle's Tuesday-night shows came to an end in 1956, he continued to be seen throughout the next decade. In the fall of 1958 he hosted *The Kraft Music Hall,* a half-hour variety show on Wednesday nights (see also that title). In the fall of 1960 he hosted an unsuccessful sports show, *Jackpot Bowling Starring Milton Berle* (see that title). In 1965 Berle renegotiated his thirty-year contract with NBC; annual payments were reduced to $120,000, and Berle received the right to appear on other networks. In the fall of 1966 Berle hosted a Friday-night variety hour on ABC, which was canceled in midseason. Produced by Bill Dana, the show also featured Donna Loren, Bobby Rydell, and Irving Benson as an offstage heckler. Berle has also made several dramatic appearances in such series as *The Mod Squad, Mannix,* and *Batman* (as Louie the Lilac), and has guest-starred on dozens of variety shows. On 26

March 1978, almost thirty years after he first stepped into thousands of television homes, Milton Berle was honored in a celebrity-studded, televised special, "A Tribute to Milton Berle"; he was also given a special award at the 1978–1977 Emmy Awards show.

MILTON THE MONSTER   ABC
9 OCTOBER 1965–2 SEPTEMBER 1967   Saturday-morning cartoon show starring Milton the Monster, a lovable denizen of Transylvania's Horrible Hill.

MIND YOUR MANNERS   NBC
24 JUNE 1951–2 MARCH 1952   Allen Ludden, who would later host such shows as *College Bowl* and *Password,* was the moderator of this Sunday-afternoon public affairs program on which teenaged panelists discussed current events.

MINDREADERS   NBC
13 AUGUST 1979–11 JANUARY 1980   Dick Martin presided over this daytime game show of "hunch and ESP." The game involved a team of four women and a team of four men, each captained by a celebrity; each of the several rounds required the players to predict how their teammates, or a panel of studio-audience members, would respond to a personal or hypothetical question.

MIRROR THEATER (REVLON MIRROR THEATER)   NBC/CBS
23 JUNE 1953–1 SEPTEMBER 1953 (NBC); 19 SEPTEMBER 1953–5 DECEMBER 1953 (CBS)   Sponsored by Revlon, this half-hour dramatic anthology series was hosted by Robin Chandler. It was seen Tuesdays on NBC during the summer of 1953, then shifted to Saturdays on CBS that fall. Presentations included: "The Little Wife," with Eddie Albert (23 June); "Salt of the Earth," with Richard Kiley (30 June); "Because I Love Him," with Joan Crawford (her first major TV role, 19 September); and "Uncle Jack," with Jack Haley (28 November). Donald Davis and Dorothy Mathews produced the series, and Daniel Petrie directed it. The NBC version was broadcast live from New York; the CBS version was on film from Hollywood.

THE MISADVENTURES OF SHERIFF LOBO   NBC
18 SEPTEMBER 1979–   Hour adventure series spun off from *BJ and the Bear,* starring Claude Akins as the slightly corrupt Sheriff Elroy S. Lobo, with Mills Watson as Deputy Perkins; Brian Kerwin as Deputy Birdie; Leann Hunley as Sarah; Cyd Crampton as Rose; and Janet Lynn Curtis as Margaret Ellen. Executive producer is Glen A. Larson.

MISS SUSAN

NBC

12 MARCH 1951–28 DECEMBER 1951 This unusual soap opera starred Susan Peters, an actress who was paralyzed from the waist down as the result of a hunting accident in 1945. On the show she appeared as herself and played a wheelchair-bound lawyer who had just moved back to her hometown, Martinsville, Ohio. Also featured on the series were Mark Roberts, Robert McQueeney, Katharine Grill, Natalie Priest, and John Lormer. The daily, fifteen-minute show was broadcast live from Philadelphia, where it was written by William Kendal Clarke and produced and directed by Kenneth Buckridge.

MISS WINSLOW & SON

CBS

28 MARCH 1979–2 MAY 1979 Half-hour sitcom based on the British series *Miss Jones & Son*. With Darleen Carr as artist Susan Winslow, mother of a son by a man with whom she had lived for two years but who left her for South America (she named the baby Edmund Hillary Winslow, after the man who first scaled Mount Everest); Roscoe Lee Browne as Harold Neistadter, her neighbor; Elliott Reid as her father, Warren Winslow, a pharmacist; Sarah Marshall as her mother, Evelyn Winslow; William Bogert as Mr. Callahan, her boss. Ted Bergmann and Don Taffner were the executive producers for T.T.C. Productions.

MISSING LINKS

NBC/ABC

9 SEPTEMBER 1963–27 MARCH 1964 (NBC); 30 MARCH 1964–25 DECEMBER 1964 (ABC) Daytime game show on which contestants tried to predict the ability of celebrity guests to supply the missing words to a story previously read aloud. The show, a Mark Goodson–Bill Todman Production, was hosted by Ed McMahon on NBC and Dick Clark on ABC.

MISSION: IMPOSSIBLE

CBS

17 SEPTEMBER 1966–8 SEPTEMBER 1973 Bruce Geller was the executive producer of this durable hour-long adventure series, which depicted the exploits of the I.M.F. (Impossible Missions Force), a government agency that undertook extremely hazardous or intricate espionage missions. Typically, the I.M.F. leader received his instructions on a miniature tape recorder ("Your mission, Jim, should you decide to accept it"), which self-destructed after its message had been conveyed. After assembling his crew of experts, the leader explained to them the nature of the project, usually with the help of films or photos. The first head of the I.M.F. was Dan Briggs, played by Steven Hill. He was replaced, however, after one season, ostensibly because of the difficulty of accommodating the show's production schedule to the preferences of Hill, an Orthodox Jew, who declined to work after sundown Fridays and on Saturdays. The new leader of the I.M.F. was Jim Phelps, played by Peter Graves, who re-

mained with the show for the rest of its run. The rest of the I.M.F. crew included: Martin Landau (1966–1969) as Rollin Hand, an expert at disguises; Barbara Bain (1966–1969) as Cinnamon Carter, who could turn on the charm when needed; Greg Morris as Barney Collier, ace mechanic and electronics technician; and Peter Lupus as hefty Willy Armitage, resident strong man. Landau and Bain (who was married to Landau) quit the show after three seasons in a dispute over budget cuts. Leonard Nimoy was added in the fall of 1969 as Paris, the new master of disguise; Nimoy left the show after two seasons. Other additions to the crew included: Lesley Warren (1970–1971) as Dana Lambert; Sam Elliott (1970–1971) as Doug; Lynda Day George (1971–1972) as Casey; and Barbara Anderson (1972–1973) as Mimi Davis.

MISSION: MAGIC! ABC
8 SEPTEMBER 1973–31 AUGUST 1974 Saturday-morning cartoon show about a group of six high school students and their teacher, who traveled together to lands of fantasy.

MISSION TO THE WORLD
See LIFE IS WORTH LIVING

MISSUS GOES A-SHOPPING CBS
19 NOVEMBER 1947–12 JANUARY 1949 CBS's first commercial daytime series was an audience participation show, broadcast live from various Manhattan supermarkets. John Reed King was the original host. Toward the end of its run the show was retitled *This Is the Missus* and was hosted by Bud Collyer.

MR. ADAMS AND EVE CBS
4 JANUARY 1957–23 SEPTEMBER 1958 Half-hour sitcom with Howard Duff as film star Howard Adams and Ida Lupino as his wife, film star Eve Adams (known professionally as Eve Drake). Also featured were Hayden Rorke as Steve, their agent; Olive Carey as Elsie, their housekeeper; Alan Reed as J. B. Hafter, the head of the studio; and Larry Dobkin as their director. Sixty-eight episodes were produced. Collier Young, former husband of Ida Lupino, was the executive producer.

MR. AND MRS. JIMMY CARROLL DUMONT
18 OCTOBER 1950–13 APRIL 1951 Fifteen-minute twice-weekly variety program, cohosted by Jimmy and Rita Carroll.

MR. AND MRS. NORTH CBS/NBC
3 OCTOBER 1952–25 SEPTEMBER 1953 (CBS); 26 JANUARY 1954–20 JULY 1954 (NBC) *Mr. and Mrs. North* began on radio as a situation

comedy, but by 1942 it had shifted to a lighthearted murder mystery show. A "pilot" program was telecast 4 July 1949, starring Joseph Allen, Jr. and Mary Lou Taylor, but it was not until 1952 that production of a TV series got underway. Produced by John W. Loveton and directed by Ralph Murphy, the filmed, half-hour series starred Richard Denning as Jerry North, a publisher, and Barbara Britton as his wife, Pamela North, a New York couple who seemed to stumble on an unsolved murder every week. Also featured was Francis DeSales as Lieutenant Bill Weigand. Both the radio and the television series were based on the stories written by Richard and Frances Lockridge.

MR. ARSENIC
ABC

8 MAY 1952–26 JUNE 1952 Half-hour mystery anthology series hosted by Burton Turkus, author of *Murder, Inc.*

MR. BLACK
ABC

19 SEPTEMBER 1949–7 NOVEMBER 1949 This Monday-night mystery anthology series was hosted by Anthony Christopher as Mr. Black, a mysterious soul who was seen each week in his cobweb-shrouded study. Broadcast from Chicago, the half-hour series was written by Bill Ballanger and directed by Tony Rizzo.

MR. BROADWAY
CBS

26 SEPTEMBER 1964–26 DECEMBER 1964 Garson Kanin created this unsuccessful hour-long adventure series, which starred Craig Stevens as New York public relations man Mike Bell. Also featured were Lani Miyazaki as Toki, his assistant; Horace McMahon as Hank McClure, his contact at the police department. David Susskind and Daniel Melnick produced the series, and Dave Brubeck supplied music. The thirteen episodes included rare guest appearances by Liza Minnelli (in her first TV dramatic role, "Nightingale for Sale," 24 October), Sandy Dennis ("Don't Mention My Name in Sheboygan," 7 November), and Lauren Bacall ("Something to Sing About," 19 December).

MR. CHIPS
SYNDICATED

1976 Bill Brown and Don McGowan cohosted this series aimed at the do-it-yourselfer.

MR. CITIZEN
ABC

20 APRIL 1955–20 JULY 1955 Allyn Edwards hosted this unusual anthology series, which depicted real-life incidents in which ordinary citizens had come to the assistance of those in need. A prominent American presented the "Mister Citizen Award" each week to the person whose efforts had been cited that week.

MR. DEEDS GOES TO TOWN   ABC

26 SEPTEMBER 1969–16 JANUARY 1970   The television adaptation of
Frank Capra's 1936 film starred Monte Markham as Longfellow Deeds, a
newspaper publisher from the small town of Mandrake Falls who inherited a huge corporation from his late uncle. Also on hand were Pat Harrington, Jr., as Tony Lawrence, his aide; Ivor Barry as George the butler;
and Herb Voland as Henry Masterson, chairman of the board of Deeds
Enterprises. The half-hour sitcom was pounded by *Hogan's Heroes* and
The Name of the Game and was dropped at midseason.

MR. DISTRICT ATTORNEY   ABC/SYNDICATED

1 OCTOBER 1951–23 JUNE 1952 (ABC); 1954 (SYNDICATED)   Created by Ed Byron, *Mr. District Attorney* began on radio in 1939 and twice
came to television. Jay Jostyn, who had taken over the role on radio in
1940, was the first D.A. and was known simply as "The D.A." or
"Chief." (Thomas E. Dewey, New York's district attorney during the
1930s, and presidential contender in 1948, was reported to have been
the model for the role.) Also featured were Vicki Vola as Miss Miller, the
D.A.'s secretary and Len Doyle as Detective Harrington, an investigator
for the D.A.'s office. In 1954 Ziv TV revived the series with David Brian
in the lead role; by this time the D.A. had a name—Paul Garrett. Jackie
Loughery now played his secretary, Miss Miller. The 1951–1952 series,
which was seen on alternate Mondays, was produced and directed by Ed
Byron.

MISTER ED   SYNDICATED/CBS

1961 (SYNDICATED); 1 OCTOBER 1961–4 SEPTEMBER 1966 (CBS)
Half-hour sitcom about a talking horse. With Alan Young as Wilbur
Post, an architect who discovered the horse, Mister Ed, in the barn of
their new house and also discovered that he was the only person to whom
the horse deigned to talk; Connie Hines as Carol Post, Wilbur's wife;
Larry Keating (1961–1964) as next-door neighbor Roger Addison; Edna
Skinner (1961–1964) as Roger's wife, Kay Addison; Leon Ames (1964–
1966) as next-door neighbor Gordon Kirkwood; and Florence MacMichael (1964–1966) as Gordon's wife, Winnie Kirkwood. The voice of Ed
was provided by former western star Allan "Rocky" Lane. Al Simon was
executive producer of the series, and Arthur Lubin the producer–
director.

MR. EXECUTIVE   SYNDICATED

1954   Host Westbrook Van Voorhis interviewed leading American in-
dustrialists on this half-hour documentary series.

MR. GARLUND   CBS

7 OCTOBER 1960–13 JANUARY 1961   This light adventure series starred

Charles Quinlivan as Frank Garlund, a young tycoon whose origins were uncertain. Also featured were Kam Tong as Kam Chang, his foster brother, and Philip Ahn as Po Chang, the Chinese businessman who raised Garlund. In November of 1960 the show's title was changed to *The Garlund Touch,* but under either title the show proved weak competition for *77 Sunset Strip* and *The Bell Telephone Hour.*

MR. I. MAGINATION   CBS
29 MAY 1949–28 JUNE 1952   This half-hour children's show was partly educational and partly fantasy. As Mr. I. Magination, Paul Tripp hosted the series, which was set in Imagination Town, a place where any child's wish could come true. The show was produced by Worthington Miner, Irving Pincus, and Norman Pincus.

MR. LUCKY   CBS
24 OCTOBER 1959–3 SEPTEMBER 1960   This half-hour adventure series was based on the 1943 film that had starred Cary Grant. On TV John Vivyan starred as Mr. Lucky, owner of the *Fortuna,* a casino ship moored off the California coast. Ross Martin costarred as Andamo, Lucky's man Friday, and Pippa Scott played Lucky's girlfriend, Maggie Shank-Rutherford. The show was a Blake Edwards production, and music was supplied by Henry Mancini.

MR. MAGOO   NBC/CBS
19 SEPTEMBER 1964–21 AUGUST 1965 (NBC); 10 SEPTEMBER 1977–12 NOVEMBER 1977 (CBS); 10 SEPTEMBER 1978–21 JANUARY 1979 (CBS)   Mr. Magoo, the myopic star of hundreds of theatrical cartoons, had his own full-length prime-time series on NBC for one season. Officially titled *The Famous Adventures of Mr. Magoo,* the series each week cast Magoo in a different role—usually, a historical figure. In the fall of 1977 Magoo showed up in a half-hour Saturday-morning cartoon show on CBS, titled *What's New Mister Magoo,* in which he was teamed up with McBaker, a nearsighted dog. The show was rerun the following season. Jim Backus supplied Magoo's voice.

MISTER MAYOR   CBS
26 SEPTEMBER 1964–18 SEPTEMBER 1965   This Saturday-morning kids' show featured Bob Keeshan (who played Captain Kangaroo weekday mornings) as Mister Mayor, Jane Connell as Aunt Maud and Miss Melissa, and Rollo the hippopotamus.

MR. NOVAK   NBC
24 SEPTEMBER 1963–31 AUGUST 1965   Hour-long dramatic series set at Jefferson High School in Los Angeles. With James Franciscus as John Novak, English teacher; Dean Jagger (to December 1964) as Albert

Vane, the principal; Burgess Meredith as Martin Woodridge, Vane's successor as principal; Steven Franken (1963–1964) as Mr. Allen, French teacher; Jeanne Bal (1963–1964) as Jean Pagano, assistant vice principal; Donald Barry (1963–1964) as Mr. Galo; Marian Collier as Miss Scott; Vince Howard as Pete Butler; André Phillippe as Mr. Johns; Stephen Roberts as Mr. Peeples; Kathleen Ellis as Mrs. Floyd; Marjorie Corley as Miss Dorsey; Phyllis Avery (1964–1965) as Ruth Wilkinson, girls' vice principal; Bill Zuckert (1964–1965) as Mr. Bradwell; David Sheiner (1964–1965) as Paul Webb; Peter Hansen (1964–1965) as Mr. Parkson; and Irene Tedrow (1965) as Mrs. Ring. E. Jack Neuman was executive producer for MGM.

MR. PEEPERS   NBC
3 JULY 1952–12 JUNE 1955   Broadcast live from New York, this low-key situation comedy starred a young comedian named Wally Cox as Robinson J. Peepers, a mild-mannered science teacher at Jefferson Junior High. The talented cast also included Tony Randall as Peepers' pal, English teacher Harvey Weskitt; Georgiann Johnson as Marge Weskitt, Harvey's wife; Patricia Benoit as Nancy Remington, the school nurse who married Peepers on 23 May 1954; Marion Lorne as Mrs. Gurney, Peepers' daffy landlady; Reta Shaw as Aunt Lil; Jack Warden as Coach; Ernest Truex as Mr. Remington, Nancy's father; and Sylvia Field as Mrs. Remington, Nancy's mother. The half-hour series was created especially for Cox by David Swift in association with producer Fred Coe. The show was introduced as a summer replacement, but found a place on NBC's 1952 fall schedule when *Doc Corkle,* a Sunday-night sitcom, bombed.

MR. PIPER   SYNDICATED
1962   This children's show was hosted by Alan Crofoot as Mr. Piper; produced in England, it was distributed by ITC.

MR. ROBERTS   NBC
17 SEPTEMBER 1965–2 SEPTEMBER 1966   The remake of the 1955 film starred Roger Smith as Lieutenant Douglas Roberts, a Naval officer assigned to duty in the South Pacific aboard the *Reluctant,* a cargo ship. Desperate to be transferred to a ship that would see some action, Mr. Roberts found his efforts thwarted by the captain. Also featured were Richard X. Slattery as Captain John Morton; Steve Harmon as Ensign Frank Pulver; George Ives as Doc; Ronald Starr as Seaman Mannion; Richard Sinatra as Seaman D'Angelo; Ray Reese as Seaman Reber; and John McCook as Seaman Stefanowski. James Komack produced the half-hour comedy.

MISTER ROGERS' NEIGHBORHOOD   PBS
22 MAY 1967–   Public television's longest-running children's

program is hosted by Fred Rogers, a Presbyterian minister from Pittsburgh. Rogers had previously worked on a 1955 network kids' show, *The Children's Corner*, but is best known as the host of this series of 460 half hours. Through the use of puppets, guests, and musical numbers, Rogers and his crew have gently taught young viewers to handle problems such as impatience and anger, and minor crises such as the death of a pet. Other regulars on the show have included Betty Aberlin, Betsy Nadas, Joe Negri, David Newell, Don Brockett, François Clemmons, Robert Trow, Audrey Roth, Elsie Neal, and Yoshi Ito. The show was produced at WQED-TV, Pittsburgh, and Rogers was the executive producer. Production ceased in 1975, but resumed in 1979.

MR. SMITH GOES TO WASHINGTON
ABC

29 SEPTEMBER 1962–30 MARCH 1963 Half-hour sitcom based on the 1939 film that starred James Stewart. On TV Fess Parker starred as Eugene Smith, an honest but unsophisticated politician from a rural state who was elected to a Senate vacancy following the death of the incumbent. Also featured were Sandra Warner as Pat Smith, his wife; Red Foley as the Senator's Uncle Cooter; Rita Lynn as his secretary, Miss Kelly; and Stan Irwin as the chauffeur, Arnie.

MR. T AND TINA
ABC

25 SEPTEMBER 1976–30 OCTOBER 1976 This half-hour sitcom was one of the first casualties of the 1976–1977 season: only five episodes were shown. Produced by James Komack, the show starred Pat Morita as Taro Takahashi, a widowed Japanese inventor who moved to Chicago with his children; Susan Blanchard as Tina Kelly, a young woman from Nebraska hired by Mr. T as governess for the children; Pat Suzuki as Michi, Mr. T's sister-in-law; Jerry Fujikawa as Uncle Matsu; June Angela as Sachi, Mr. T's young daughter; Eugene Profanato as Aki, Mr. T's young son; Ted Lange as Mr. Harvard, the handyman; and Miriam Byrd-Nethery as Miss Llewellyn, the landlady.

MR. TERRIFIC
CBS

9 JANUARY 1967–28 AUGUST 1967 This insignificant half-hour sitcom, an imitation *Batman*, featured Stephen Strimpell as Stanley Beamish, the owner of a service station in Washington, D.C., who was on call as an agent for the Bureau of Special Projects. Beamish could take a pill developed by the Bureau, which gave him an hour's worth of super powers and turned him into Mr. Terrific, a caped crusader. Also on hand were Dick Gautier as Hal, Beamish's friend; John McGiver as Barton J. Reed, director of the Bureau; and Paul Smith as Harley Trent, another Bureau agent. Jack Arnold produced the series, which should not be confused with *Captain Nice*, a similar spoof that ran on NBC at the same time

(Strimpell had tested for *Captain Nice* before landing the role on *Mr. Terrific*).

MR. WIZARD
NBC

3 MARCH 1951–4 JULY 1965; 11 SEPTEMBER 1971–2 SEPTEMBER 1972   On this long-running educational series for children, Don Herbert (as Mr. Wizard) explained the principles of science and showed how to perform various experiments. Each week a dutifully amazed boy or girl was on hand to marvel at Mr. Wizard's revelations. The series ran continuously for fourteen years and returned six years later for one season. Broadcast from Chicago, it was produced by Jules Pewowar.

MRS. COLUMBO
See KATE LOVES A MYSTERY

MRS. G GOES TO COLLEGE
CBS

4 OCTOBER 1961–5 APRIL 1962   This half-hour sitcom starred Gertrude Berg, the creator and star of *The Goldbergs,* as Sarah Green, a widow who decided to go to college. Also featured were Sir Cedric Hardwicke as Professor Crayton; Skip Ward as freshman Joe Caldwell; Marion Ross (later to star in *Happy Days*) as Sarah's daughter, Susan; Leo Penn as Sarah's son, Jerry; Mary Wickes as Maxfield, Sarah's landlady; Paul Smith as George Howell; and Karyn Kupcinet as Carol. Though the show's title was changed in midseason to *The Gertrude Berg Show,* the ratings did not improve; Hy Averback produced the series.

MRS. ROOSEVELT MEETS THE PUBLIC
NBC

12 FEBRUARY 1950–15 JULY 1951   Sunday-afternoon panel discussion show moderated by Eleanor Roosevelt. Produced by Roger Muir, the series was originally titled *Today with Mrs. Roosevelt.*

MIXED DOUBLES
NBC

5 AUGUST 1949–12 NOVEMBER 1949   Carleton E. Morse produced, wrote, and directed this half-hour sitcom about two newlywed couples who lived next door to each other in a New York apartment building. The cast included Billy Idelson, Ada Friedman, Eddy Firestone, and Rhoda Williams.

MOBILE ONE
ABC

12 SEPTEMBER 1975–29 DECEMBER 1975   Hour-long adventure series with Jackie Cooper as Peter Campbell, news reporter for KONE-TV, a West Coast station; Julie Gregg as Maggie Spencer, the producer; and Mark Wheeler as Doug McKnight, Campbell's camera operator. Jack Webb was the executive producer of the series, which was created by James M. Miller.

MOBY DICK AND THE MIGHTY MIGHTOR CBS

9 SEPTEMBER 1967–6 SEPTEMBER 1969 Saturday-morning cartoon show from Hanna-Barbera Productions. The two segments depicted the adventures of Moby Dick, a great white whale, and The Mighty Mightor, the super-powered alter ego of a boy named Tor.

THE MOD SQUAD ABC

24 SEPTEMBER 1968–23 AUGUST 1973 Hour-long crime show about three young people who comprised the Mod Squad, an undercover unit of the Los Angeles Police Department. With Michael Cole as Pete Cochrane; Clarence Williams III as Linc Hayes; Peggy Lipton as Julie Barnes; and Tige Andrews as Captain Adam Greer, their boss, the only other officer who knew of their identities. Aaron Spelling was the producer. The four principals were reunited in a two-hour made-for-TV movie, "The Return of Mod Squad," broadcast 18 May 1979 on ABC.

MODERN ROMANCES NBC

4 OCTOBER 1954–19 SEPTEMBER 1958 A new five-part story was introduced each week on this fifteen-minute weekday series. Martha Scott was usually on hand as host and narrator, though guest celebrities also dropped by to introduce the weekly story.

THE MOHAWK SHOWROOM

See THE MORTON DOWNEY SHOW; THE ROBERTA QUINLAN SHOW

THE MOLLY PICON SHOW ABC

1 MARCH 1949–12 APRIL 1949 Half-hour variety series hosted by Yiddish actress Molly Picon.

MOMENT OF FEAR NBC

1 JULY 1960–23 SEPTEMBER 1960 First seen during the summer of 1960, this half-hour anthology of thrillers was broadcast live. NBC also televised reruns of other anthology series under the title *Moment of Fear* during the summers of 1964 and 1965.

MOMENT OF TRUTH NBC

4 JANUARY 1965–5 NOVEMBER 1965 This half-hour daytime serial was produced in Toronto and was set in an Ontario college town. Principal players included: Douglass Watson as Dr. Bob Wallace, a psychologist; Louise King as his wife, Nancy Wallace; Sandra Scott as Lila, Nancy's sister; Robert Goodier as Walter Leeds; Lynne Gorman as his wife, Wilma Leeds; Stephen Levy as Jack Williams; Barbara Pierce as Sheila; Michael Dodds as Johnny; Toby Tarnow as Carol; Lucy Warner as Helen Gould; Mira Pawluk as Barbara Harris; Peter Donat as Vince Conway;

Ann Campbell as Diane; Alan Bly as Arthur; John Bethune as Dr. Gil Bennett; Ivor Barry as Dr. Russell Wingate; Fernande Giroux as Monique; John Horton as Eric; Chris Wiggins as Dexter; and Anne Collings as Kathy. After a ten-month run the half-hour series was replaced by *Days of Our Lives*.

MOMENTS OF MUSIC ABC
24 JULY 1951–11 SEPTEMBER 1951   A fifteen-minute filmed musical interlude.

MONA McCLUSKEY NBC
16 SEPTEMBER 1965–14 APRIL 1966   Half-hour sitcom about a glamorous movie star struggling to make ends meet on the salary of her serviceman husband. With Juliet Prowse as Mona Carroll McCluskey (known professionally as Mona Jackson); Denny Miller as her husband, Sergeant Mike McCluskey of the U.S. Air Force; Herbert Rudley as General Crone; Bartlett Robinson as Mr. Caldwell, Mona's producer; Robert Strauss as Sergeant Stan Gruzewsky, a friend of Mike's; Elena Verdugo as Alice, Stan's girlfriend; and Frank Wilcox as General Somers. George Burns produced the series.

THE MONEY MAZE ABC
23 DECEMBER 1974–4 JULY 1975   On this daytime game show, hosted by Nick Clooney, contestants first answered questions; the winning contestant then tried to guide his or her spouse through a maze for prizes. Don Lipp was the producer.

THE MONKEES NBC
12 SEPTEMBER 1966–19 AUGUST 1968   This half-hour comedy featured a rock-and-roll group that was supposed to be the American version of the Beatles (even the names of the two groups were similar plays on words); the loosely structured show was obviously inspired by the Beatles' films, *A Hard Day's Night* and *Help*. Open auditions were held for the four roles, and more than 400 actors were tested by producers Bert Schneider and Robert Rafelson. Four young men were finally selected: Micky Dolenz, Davy Jones, Mike Nesmith, and Peter Tork. Dolenz had had prior television experience: he had starred in *Circus Boy* (under the name of Mickey Braddock). Nesmith and Tork had had prior musical experience, while Jones had been a jockey in England, his native country. The four spent most of the summer of 1966 learning improvisational acting techniques (the producers wanted spontaneity) and had little time to learn to play music together. Their first records, which they lip-synched on the show, were produced by Don Kirshner, and, except for some of the vocal parts, were actually performed by studio sidemen. Nevertheless, because of the weekly exposure given the group, the early records were

tremendously popular: more than eight million Monkees albums had been sold by the end of 1966. By 1967, however, Dolenz, Jones, Nesmith, and Tork, after a heated meeting with Kirshner, secured the right to perform their own music. Their third album, "Headquarters," produced without Kirshner, also proved successful. Their TV series, though popular with younger viewers, was hurt by competition from *Gunsmoke* in its second season and was dropped in 1968; reruns were shown Saturdays on CBS and later on ABC. Mike Nesmith remained in the music business, primarily as a songwriter (he wrote "Different Drum" for Linda Ronstadt and the Stone Poneys). Davy Jones and Micky Dolenz teamed up in 1975 with Tommy Boyce and Bobby Hart (who had written such Monkees's hits as "Last Train to Clarksville"), but the group went nowhere.

THE MONROES ABC

7 SEPTEMBER 1966–30 AUGUST 1967   Hour-long western about a pioneer family headed for Wyoming; when the parents drowned in the first episode, the children decided to go on and set up a homestead on the land their father had marked out years earlier. With Michael Anderson, Jr., as Clayt Monroe, the eldest; Barbara Hershey as Kathy Monroe; Keith Schultz as Jefferson (Big Twin) Monroe; Kevin Schultz as Fenimore (Little Twin) Monroe; Tammy Locke as Amy Monroe, the youngest; Ron Soble as Jim, an Indian whom the Monroes befriended; Liam Sullivan as Major Mapoy, an evil land dealer; Jim Westmoreland as Ruel; and Ben Johnson as Sleeve.

MONSTER SQUAD NBC

11 SEPTEMBER 1976–3 SEPTEMBER 1977   Live-action Saturday-morning kids' show about a night watchman in a wax museum who could summon the resident monsters to help him fight crimes. With Fred Grandy as Walter, the watchman; Henry Polic II as Dracula; Buck Kartalian as Wolfman; and Michael Lane as Frankenstein.

THE MONTEFUSCOS NBC

4 SEPTEMBER 1975–23 OCTOBER 1975   Together with *Fay,* another ill-fated Thursday-night sitcom, *The Montefuscos* was the first casualty of the 1975–1976 season. The story of a big Italian-American family living in Connecticut, it featured Joe Sirola as Tony (Papa) Montefusco; Naomi Stevens as Rose (Mama) Montefusco; Ron Carey as their son, Frank, a dentist; Phoebe Dorin as Frank's wife, Theresa; Sal Viscuso as their son, Nunzio, an actor; John Aprea as their son, Joey, a priest; Linda Dano as Angelina, their daughter; Bill Cort as Jim Cooney, Angie's husband; Damon Raskin as Anthony Patrick Cooney, Jim and Angie's son; Dominique Pinassi as Gina, Frank and Theresa's daughter; Jeff Palladini as Anthony Carmine, Frank and Theresa's son; and Robby Paris as Jerome, Frank and Theresa's second son. Bill Persky and Sam Denoff created the

show and were its executive producers; Don Van Atta and Bill Idelson produced it.

MONTY NASH   SYNDICATED

1971   Half-hour crime show starring Harry Guardino as government investigator Monty Nash.

MONTY PYTHON'S FLYING CIRCUS   PBS

1974–1977   Produced for the BBC and aired in Great Britain from 1969 to 1971, *Monty Python's Flying Circus* was not made available in the United States until 1974. The half-hour series consisted of skits (some filmed, some videotaped), blackouts, and animated sequences, vaguely unified by a common comic thread. Though the show was sometimes uneven, its best moments were probably those which satirized television programming—boring talk shows and pretentious documentaries were favorite targets of the Python troupe. Six young men comprised the group, though only five—Graham Chapman, John Cleese, Eric Idle, Terry Jones, and Michael Palin—appeared on camera regularly. The sixth member and the sole American, Terry Gilliam, designed the animated sequences. Ian MacNaughton produced the show.

THE MOREY AMSTERDAM SHOW   CBS/DUMONT

17 DECEMBER 1948–7 MARCH 1949 (CBS); 21 APRIL 1949–12 OCTOBER 1950 (DUMONT)   Morey Amsterdam, the cello-stroking comic with a joke on any subject, hosted a half-hour comedy–variety series which began on CBS and later moved to the DuMont network. The CBS version was set at a nightspot known as the Golden Goose Café and featured Art Carney (in one of his earliest TV roles) as Charlie the waiter and Jacqueline Susann (who would later write several best-selling novels) as Lola the cigarette girl. Susann's husband, Irving Mansfield, produced and directed the show. The DuMont version was set at the Silver Swan Café and featured Art Carney as Newton the waiter and singer Vic Damone. Amsterdam later cohosted *Broadway Open House* and appeared on *The Dick Van Dyke Show*.

MORK & MINDY   ABC

14 SEPTEMBER 1978–   A half-hour sitcom from the *Happy Days* people (the lead character was introduced on a *Happy Days* episode), *Mork & Mindy* stars Robin Williams as Mork, an alien, and Pam Dawber as Mindy McConnell, the young woman he meets. Mork, a humorous humanoid, was unpopular on his home planet, Ork, where emotions had been bred out of the citizenry; dispatched to Earth to learn more about its backward ways, Mork's aircraft lands in Boulder, Colorado, and Mork persuades Mindy to let him stay with her while they learn more about each other. Featured during the first season were Conrad

Janis as Frederick McConnell, Mindy's father, owner of a music store; Elizabeth Kerr as Mindy's grandmother, Cora Hudson, who worked at the store; Jeffrey Jacquet as Eugene, a hip young black music student; and Ralph James as the voice of Orson, Mork's Orkian mentor. The series was created by Garry K. Marshall, Joe Glauberg, and Dale McRaven; Garry K. Marshall and Tony Marshall are the executive producers. In the fall of 1979 Janis, Kerr, and Jacquet let the series, and three new regulars were added: Jay Thomas as Remo DaVinci and Gina Hecht as his sister, Jean DaVinci, owners of the New York Delicatessen; and Jim Staahl as Mindy's cousin, Nelson Flavor.

MORNING
See CBS MORNING NEWS

MORNING COURT   ABC
10 OCTOBER 1960–12 MAY 1961   This half-hour daytime entry presented simulated court cases and was a companion to ABC's longer-running courtroom show, *Day in Court.* William Gwinn and Georgianna Hardy presided over the morning sessions.

THE MORNING SHOW   CBS
15 MARCH 1954–5 APRIL 1957   An unsuccessful attempt to compete with NBC's *Today* show, *The Morning Show* went through several changes of personnel during its three low-rated years. CBS newsman Walter Cronkite, who was then hosting *You Are There,* was the first host; Charles Collingwood read the news, and other features were handled by Estelle Parsons, Jack Lyman, and the Bil and Cora Baird Puppets. Cronkite had left by the summer of 1954, and on 16 August, Jack Paar replaced him. Paar had previously hosted a weekly daytime show, and he brought with him most of the regulars from that series: pianist Jose Melis, Pupi Campo and his Orchestra, and singer Edie Adams. Betty Clooney and Charlie Applewhite also joined *The Morning Show* when Paar took over, and Charles Collingwood and the Baird Puppets also remained. By November of 1954, the Baird Puppets were gone, and when Paar took a brief vacation that winter, a young comedian named Johnny Carson filled in. Paar lasted until June 1955, and was succeeded briefly by John Henry Faulk, the folksy humorist who was blacklisted a few months later (and who subsequently won a libel suit against his accusers). Faulk was succeeded late in 1955 by Dick Van Dyke. Van Dyke's regulars included singers Merv Griffin and Sandy Stewart. Will Rogers, Jr., was the last host of the series, and when he took over on 20 February 1956, the show's title was changed to *Good Morning.* Before the show left the air fourteen months later, its title was again changed to *The Will Rogers, Jr. Show.* The network later introduced *The Jimmy Dean Show* at the same hour (7 a.m.) as *The Morning Show,* but shifted Dean to a later time slot

after a few weeks. The idea of a morning show was shelved until 1963, when *The CBS Morning News* was introduced. *The Morning Show* began as a two-hour program and was reduced to one hour on 3 October 1955, when *Captain Kangaroo* premiered in the 8 a.m. slot. Among the writers for *The Morning Show* was Barbara Walters, who would later cohost *Today*.

MORNING STAR   **NBC**
27 SEPTEMBER 1965–1 JULY 1966   This daytime serial starred Elizabeth Perry as Katy Elliott, a fashion designer who moved to New York from New England after her fiancé had been killed. Also featured were Adrienne Ellis as Jan; Nina Roman as Liz; Olive Dunbar as Ann Burton; Edward Mallory as Bill Porter; Ed Prentiss as Uncle Ed; Sheila Bromley as Aunt Milly; and Burt Douglas as Gregory Ross.

THE MORTON DOWNEY SHOW   **NBC**
2 MAY 1949–9 DECEMBER 1949   Irish tenor Morton Downey hosted his own fifteen-minute musical show three nights a week; it was officially titled *Mohawk Showroom* and featured Carmen Mastren's Orchestra and announcer Bob Stanton. See also *The Roberta Quinlan Show.*

MOSES THE LAWGIVER   **CBS**
21 JUNE 1975–2 AUGUST 1975   This six-part miniseries bout the life of Moses was filmed in Israel. An Italian–English production, it featured Burt Lancaster as Moses, Irene Papas as Zipporah, Anthony Quayle as Aaron, and Laurent Terzieff as Pharaoh.

THE MOST DEADLY GAME   **ABC**
10 OCTOBER 1970–16 JANUARY 1971   Hour-long crime show with three ace criminologists: Ralph Bellamy as Ethan Arcane; Yvette Mimieux as Vanessa Smith; and George Maharis as Jonathan Croft. The series was produced by Mort Fine, David Friedkin, and Joan Harrison and was developed by Aaron Spelling.

MOST WANTED   **ABC**
16 OCTOBER 1976–20 AUGUST 1977   Hour-long crime show about a special unit of the Los Angeles Police Department that went after the big crooks. With Robert Stack as Captain Link Evers; Shelly Novack as Charlie Benson; and Jo Ann Harris as Kate Manners. Quinn Martin, John Wilder, and Paul King were the executive producers.

MOTHER'S DAY   **ABC**
13 OCTOBER 1958–2 JANUARY 1959   Dick Van Dyke hosted this daytime game show; each day three mothers competed at household tasks for the chance to win prizes.

THE MOTHERS-IN-LAW
NBC

10 SEPTEMBER 1967–7 SEPTEMBER 1969 Half-hour sitcom about two next-door neighbors whose children intermarried. With Eve Arden as Eve Hubbard; Herbert Rudley as her husband, Herb Hubbard, a lawyer; Roger C. Carmel (1967–1968) and Richard Deacon (1968–1969) as Roger Buell, a TV writer; Kaye Ballard as his wife, Kaye Buell; Jerry Fogel as Roger and Kaye's son, Jerry Buell; and Deborah Walley as Eve and Herb's daughter, Suzie, who married Jerry and lived with him in the Hubbard garage. Desi Arnaz, the executive producer of the series, also appeared occasionally as bullfighter Raphael del Gado.

MOTOR MOUSE
ABC

12 SEPTEMBER 1970–4 SEPTEMBER 1971 Formerly featured on *Cattanooga Cats,* Motor Mouse headlined his own show for one season. The Saturday-morning cartoon show was a Hanna-Barbera production.

THE MOTOROLA TV HOUR
ABC

3 NOVEMBER 1953–18 MAY 1954 Sponsored by Motorola, this hourlong dramatic anthology series alternated on Tuesdays with *The U.S. Steel Hour.* Presentations included: "Outlaw's Reckoning," with Eddie Albert and Jane Wyatt (3 November); "Westward the Sun," with Brian Keith (in his first major TV role, 17 November); "The Brandenburg Gate," with Jack Palance and Maria Riva (1 December); "The Thirteen Clocks," with John Raitt (29 December); and "Love Song," with Oscar Homolka and Lisa Kirk (4 May).

THE MOUSE FACTORY
SYNDICATED

1972 Old Walt Disney cartoons and film clips were presented on this half-hour series aimed principally at children. Each show was hosted and narrated by a guest celebrity.

THE MOVIE GAME
SYNDICATED

1969–1970 Films were the subject of this game show. First hosted by Sonny Fox, it featured two three-member teams, each consisting of two stars and one contestant. When Larry Blyden succeeded Fox as host, the format was changed slightly—to two panels of three stars each, playing for a home viewer. Hollywood columnist Army Archerd was also featured on both versions.

MOVIELAND QUIZ
ABC

19 AUGUST 1948–26 OCTOBER 1948 The questions on this half-hour prime-time game show were based on film clips from old movies that were shown to the show's contestants. Arthur Q. Bryan, the first emcee, was succeeded by Ralph Dumke.

MOVIN' ON NBC

12 SEPTEMBER 1974–14 SEPTEMBER 1976   Hour-long adventure series about a couple of truckers: Claude Akins as gritty Sonny Pruett, and Frank Converse as Will Chandler, an idealistic fellow who had attended law school. During the second season a second pair of truckers was added: Rosey Grier as Benjy and Art Metrano as Moose. Like *Route 66,* a highway adventure show of the 1960s, *Movin' On* was filmed on location all over the United States. Philip D'Antoni and Barry Weitz were the executive producers.

MUGGSY NBC

11 SEPTEMBER 1976–2 APRIL 1977   Taped in Bridgeport, Connecticut, this half-hour Saturday-morning childrens' show starred Sarah McDonnell as Muggsy, a teenager. Also featured were Ben Masters as Nick, her half-brother; Star-Shemah as Clytemnestra, her friend; Donny Cooper as T. P.; Paul Michael as Gus; and Jimmy McCann as Li'l Man. George A. Heinemann was the executive producer, and Joseph F. Callo the producer.

MULLIGAN'S STEW NBC

25 OCTOBER 1977–13 DECEMBER 1977   The story of "nine people and two bathrooms," *Mulligan's Stew* was a short-lived family drama. Mr. and Mrs. Mulligan had not only their own three kids to care for, but also four nieces and nephews whose parents had been killed in a plane crash in Hawaii. With Lawrence Pressman as Mike Mulligan, a high school teacher and football coach; Elinor Donahue as Jane Mulligan, his wife; Johnny Doran as Mark, their elder son; Julie Anne Haddock as their daughter, Melinda; K. C. Martel as Jimmy, their younger son; Christopher Ciampa as Adam (Moose) Friedman, their nephew; Suzanne Crough as Stevie Friedman, their niece; Lory Kochheim as Polly Friedman, their niece; and Sunshine Lee as Kimmy Nguyen Friedman, their youngest niece, a Vietnamese orphan whom the Friedmans had adopted. Joanna Lee produced the hour series.

THE MUNSTERS CBS

24 SEPTEMBER 1964–1 SEPTEMBER 1966   Like *The Addams Family,* which premiered on ABC in 1964 and ran for two seasons, *The Munsters* was a half-hour sitcom about a motley family of misfits. With Fred Gwynne as Herman Munster, a six-foot ten-inch funeral director who resembled Frankenstein's monster; Yvonne DeCarlo as his vampirish wife, Lily Munster; Beverly Owen (to December 1964) and Pat Priest (from January 1965) as their attractive niece, Marilyn Munster, considered by the rest of the clan to be the abnormal one; Al Lewis as Lily's ancient father, Grandpa; and Butch Patrick as Edward Wolfgang (Eddie) Munster,

Herman and Lily's lycanthropic young son. Joe Connelly and Bob Mosher, who had worked together on *Leave It to Beaver,* created the series for Universal Television.

THE MUPPET SHOW   SYNDICATED
1976–   The Muppets, the lovable puppets created by Jim Henson and company, star in their own half-hour comedy-variety show. Each week a guest celebrity is also on hand to assist master of ceremonies Kermit the Frog. Taped in England and syndicated in many foreign countries, the show is produced by Jack Burns.

MUSIC BINGO   NBC/ABC
29 MAY 1958–11 SEPTEMBER 1958 (NBC); 5 DECEMBER 1958–1 JANUARY 1960 (ABC)   Two contestants played a version of bingo on this game show. By correctly identifying a song, a contestant won a square on a giant bingo board. Johnny Gilbert hosted the series, which was introduced as a prime-time show over NBC and moved to a daytime slot when it switched networks.

MUSIC COUNTRY   NBC
26 JULY 1973–6 SEPTEMBER 1973; 17 JANUARY 1974–16 MAY 1974   Taped in Nashville, *Music Country* was an hour of country music, all performed by guest artists. The show's official title was *Dean Martin Presents Music Country.*

MUSIC '55   CBS
12 JULY 1955–13 SEPTEMBER 1955   Bandleader Stan Kenton hosted this half-hour musical variety series.

MUSIC FOR A SPRING NIGHT
See MUSIC FOR A SUMMER NIGHT

MUSIC FOR A SUMMER NIGHT   ABC
3 JUNE 1959–21 SEPTEMBER 1959; 2 MARCH 1960–21 SEPTEMBER 1960   This musical variety show featured guest artists and the music of Glenn Osser's Orchestra. From March to May of 1960 it was titled *Music for a Spring Night.*

MUSIC FROM CEDAR GROVE   ABC
23 MAY 1953–26 SEPTEMBER 1953   This hour-long musical variety series was broadcast from Frank Dailey's Meadowbrook in Cedar Grove, New Jersey (the show was also titled *Music from Meadowbrook*). Bill Williams was the emcee, and music was provided by Ralph Marterie's Orchestra.

MUSIC FROM CHICAGO   DUMONT

15 APRIL 1951–17 JUNE 1951 Another of the several Chicago-based music and variety shows, this one was broadcast on Sundays over the DuMont network. See also *Chicago Jazz*; *Chicago Symphony Chamber Orchestra*; *Concert Tonight*; *The Music Room*; *Music in Velvet*; *Sing-Co-Pation*; and *Vaudeo Varieties*.

MUSIC HALL AMERICA   SYNDICATED

1976 Hour-long country music series, taped in Nashville.

MUSIC IN VELVET   ABC

16 JANUARY 1949–17 APRIL 1949; 15 JULY 1951–28 OCTOBER 1951 Broadcast from Chicago, *Music in Velvet* was first seen in the Midwest in 1948 and was one of the first shows to be televised live in the East after coaxial cable facilities linking Chicago and New York became operational early in 1949. Don Lindley and the Velveteers were featured on the 1949 version, which was produced and directed by Ed Skotch. Rex Maupin and his orchestra were featured on the 1951 version of the half-hour show.

MUSIC ON ICE   NBC

8 MAY 1960–11 SEPTEMBER 1960 This frosty summer variety show, taped somewhere in Brooklyn, was hosted by singer Johnny Desmond and featured skater Jacqueline du Bief, the singing Skip-Jacks, the dancing Blades, and the Bob Boucher Orchestra.

THE MUSIC SCENE   ABC

22 SEPTEMBER 1969–12 JANUARY 1970 This popular music series featured appearances by guest artists from the rock and folk scene. The forty-five-minute series preceded *The New People,* another forty-five-minute series, on Monday nights. It was hosted by comedian David Steinberg, and the resident troupe of performers included Chris Bokeno, Larry Hankin, Paul Reid Roman, Christopher Ross, and Lily Tomlin (who joined *Laugh-In* shortly after the series folded). Stan Harris and Ken Fritz were the producers.

THE MUSIC SHOP   NBC

11 JANUARY 1959–8 MARCH 1959 Half-hour musical variety show, hosted by bandleader Buddy Bregman. Rock-and-roller Richie Valens made a rare TV appearance on the premiere, just three weeks before his death in a plane crash.

THE MUSIC SHOW   DUMONT

19 MAY 1953–17 OCTOBER 1954 Broadcast from Chicago, this half-hour series presented light classical and popular selections without com-

mercial interruptions. Robert Trendler conducted the orchestra, and vocalists included Mike Douglas, Henri Noel, Jackie Van, and Eleanore Warner. J. E. Faraghan produced the series and Barry McKinley directed it.

MUSICAL CHAIRS   NBC
9 JULY 1955–17 SEPTEMBER 1955   The first of the two programs by this title was a prime-time game show hosted by Bill Leyden *(It Could Be You),* who quizzed a celebrity panel on musical subjects. The panel included Mel Blanc, singer Peggy King, lyricist Johnny Mercer, and trumpeter Bobby Troup.

MUSICAL CHAIRS   CBS
16 JUNE 1975–31 OCTOBER 1975   The second of the two shows titled *Musical Chairs* was a daytime game show hosted by singer Adam Wade. Contestants listened to songs and then tried to select the next line of the song from three choices shown to them. Produced by Bill W. Chastain, Jr., *Musical Chairs* is notable in that it was the first game show emceed by a black performer.

MUSICAL COMEDY TIME   NBC
2 OCTOBER 1950–19 MARCH 1951   This Monday-night anthology series shared a time slot with *Robert Montgomery Presents.* Presentations included: "Anything Goes," with Martha Raye (2 October); "Babes in Toyland," with Dennis King (25 December); "No No Nanette," with Jackie Gleason and Ann Crowley (5 March); and "Flying High," with Bert Lahr (19 March).

MUSICAL MERRY-GO-ROUND   NBC
2 OCTOBER 1947–25 MARCH 1949   Twenty-minute musical variety show hosted by Jack Kilty.

MUSICAL MINIATURES   NBC
10 MAY 1948–12 JANUARY 1949   A twenty-minute musical series with no regulars, broadcast two or three times a week before the evening newsreel. The show was also aired under the titles *Topical Tunes* and *Musical Almanac.* It was also seen irregularly later in 1949.

MY FAVORITE HUSBAND   CBS
12 SEPTEMBER 1953–27 DECEMBER 1955   This domestic sitcom, starring Lucille Ball, came to radio in 1948 and lasted three seasons there. It was resurrected for TV in 1953. Because Lucille Ball was then starring in *I Love Lucy,* Joan Caulfield was chosen for the part of Liz Cooper, the scatterbrained wife of George Cooper, a Manhattan banker; Barry Nelson costarred as George. Also featured were Alix Talton as neighbor

Myra Cobb and Bob Sweeney as her husband, Gilmore Cobb. In the fall of 1955 Vanessa Brown replaced Joan Caulfield as Liz Cooper, and Alix Talton was seen as neighbor Myra Shepard; Bob Sweeney also left the series and Gale Gordon (who had been featured in the radio version) joined the TV cast as Myra's husband, Oliver Shepard. The half-hour show was directed by George Cahan, who was the husband of costar Talton. The latter episodes were rerun on CBS during the summer of 1957.

MY FAVORITE MARTIAN   CBS
29 SEPTEMBER 1963–4 SEPTEMBER 1966 Half-hour sitcom about a Martian whose spaceship crash landed on Earth and who moved in with the reporter who witnessed the crash landing. With Bill Bixby as Tim O'Hara, reporter for the Los Angeles *Sun;* Ray Walston as the Martian, who took the name Martin O'Hara (Tim's uncle) when he settled in; Pamela Britton as Mrs. Lorelei Brown, Tim's befuddled landlady; and Alan Hewitt as Bill Brennan, a Los Angeles cop. Jack Chertok produced the series. See also *My Favorite Martians.*

MY FAVORITE MARTIANS   CBS
8 SEPTEMBER 1973–30 AUGUST 1975 This Saturday-morning cartoon show was derived from the 1963 sitcom, *My Favorite Martian.* In the cartoon version, there were three Martians who were discovered by two Earthlings. Norm Prescott and Lou Scheimer produced the series.

MY FAVORITE STORY   SYNDICATED
1953–1954 This half-hour filmed dramatic anthology series was hosted by Adolphe Menjou.

MY FRIEND FLICKA   CBS
10 FEBRUARY 1956–1 FEBRUARY 1957 *My Friend Flicka,* a half-hour western based on Mary O'Hara's book, was the first filmed series from 20th Century-Fox. Set at the Goose Bar Ranch in Montana at the turn of the century, it featured Johnny Washbrook as Ken McLaughlin; Gene Evans as his father, Rob McLaughlin; Anita Louise as his mother, Nell McLaughlin; and Frank Ferguson as Gus the ranch hand. Flicka, Ken's equine companion, was played by an Arabian sorrel named Wahama. The thirty-nine half-hour episodes were filmed in color.

MY FRIEND IRMA   CBS
8 JANUARY 1952–25 JUNE 1954 Created by Cy Howard, *My Friend Irma* began on radio in 1947 and ran for seven years. The television adaptation was less successful, even though most of the members of the radio cast recreated their roles for TV. The half-hour sitcom starred Marie Wilson as Irma Peterson, a not-too-bright legal secretary living in a New

York boardinghouse; Cathy Lewis (1952–1953) as her roommate, Jane Stacey, a level-headed young woman who, like George Burns on *The Burns and Allen Show,* addressed the viewing audience directly from time to time during the show; Sid Tomack (1952–1953) as Al, Irma's boyfriend, a scheming con man; Brooks West as Richard Rhinelander III, Jane's wealthy boyfriend; Gloria Gordon as Mrs. O'Reilly, proprietor of the boardinghouse; Donald McBride as Mr. Clyde, Irma's boss; and Richard Eyer as Bobby, Irma's young nephew. In the fall of 1953 Mary Shipp succeeded Cathy Lewis as Irma's new roommate, newspaper reporter Kay Foster, and Hal March replaced Sid Tomack as Irma's new boyfriend, Joe. The series was produced by Nat Perrin and directed by Richard Whorf; in the fall of 1952 it became the first series to be broadcast from CBS's Television City facility in Hollywood.

MY FRIEND TONY   NBC
5 JANUARY 1969–31 AUGUST 1969   Hour-long crime show with James Whitmore as Professor John Woodruff, teacher of criminology and private detective, and Enzo Cerusico as Tony Novello, Woodruff's partner, an Italian whom Woodruff had met during World War II. Sheldon Leonard created the series and was its executive producer.

MY HERO   NBC
8 NOVEMBER 1952–1 AUGUST 1953   Half-hour sitcom starring Bob Cummings as Bob Beanblossom, an inept real estate salesman; John Litel as Mr. Thackery, his boss; and Julie Bishop as Thackery's secretary and Beanblossom's girlfriend, Julie Marshall. Produced by Mort Green for Don Sharpe Enterprises, *My Hero* was the first of several sitcoms for Cummings: see also *The Bob Cummings Show, Love That Bob,* and *My Living Doll.*

MY LITTLE MARGIE   CBS/NBC
16 JUNE 1952–30 JULY 1953 (CBS); 2 SEPTEMBER 1953–24 AUGUST 1955 (NBC)   Half-hour sitcom about a womanizing widower and his meddlesome daughter. With Gale Storm as Margie Albright; Charles Farrell as her father, Vern Albright; Don Hayden as Margie's boyfriend, Freddie Wilson; Clarence Kolb as Vern's boss, George Honeywell, president of Honeywell & Todd; Hillary Brooke (1952–1954) as Vern's frequent girlfriend, Roberta Townsend; Gertrude Hoffman as their kindly old neighbor, Mrs. Odetts; and Willie Best as Charlie, the elevator operator in their New York apartment house. Produced by Hal Roach, Jr., and Roland Reed, the series was first introduced as a summer replacement for *I Love Lucy* and found a place on CBS's fall schedule for one season before shifting networks. A radio version was also introduced in 1952. The 126 TV episodes were widely syndicated throughout the 1950s and 1960s.

MY LIVING DOLL   CBS

27 SEPTEMBER 1964–8 SEPTEMBER 1965   Half-hour sitcom about a psychiatrist and his live-in patient, a female robot. With Bob Cummings as Dr. Bob McDonald; Julie Newmar as Rhoda, the government-built robot (Project AF709); Jack Mullaney as Dr. Peter Robinson, a colleague of McDonald's; Doris Dowling as Irene McDonald, Bob's sister, who also lived at home with Bob and Rhoda; and Nora Marlowe as Mrs. Moffat. Bob Cummings quit the series after twenty-one episodes, and Dr. Robinson became Rhoda's caretaker for the remaining shows (it was explained that Dr. McDonald had been sent to Pakistan).

MY MOTHER THE CAR   NBC

14 SEPTEMBER 1965–6 SEPTEMBER 1966   Universally blasted as one of the feeblest sitcoms of the decade, *My Mother the Car* told the story of a man who heard his late mother's voice emanating from a 1928 Porter. With Jerry Van Dyke as lawyer Dave Crabtree; Maggie Pierce as his wife, Barbara Crabtree; Cindy Eilbacher as their daughter, Cindy; Randy Whipple as their son, Randy; Avery Schreiber as the evil Captain Manzini, an antique automobile collector desperate to add the 1928 Porter to his collection; and Ann Sothern as the voice of Dave's mother, Gladys. Created by Allan Burns and Chris Hayward, the half-hour series was produced by Rod Amateau.

MY PARTNER THE GHOST   SYNDICATED

1973   Produced in England, this lighthearted crime show featured Mike Pratt as private eye Jeff Randall; Kenneth Cope as Marty Hopkirk, Jeff's former partner who was killed on the job but who returned as a ghost (visible only to Randall) to help his associate; and Annette Andre as Marty's widow, Jean Hopkirk, who worked as Randall's secretary.

MY SISTER EILEEN   CBS

5 OCTOBER 1960–12 APRIL 1961   Ruth McKinney's book was the subject of two movies and this half-hour comedy series. With Elaine Stritch as Ruth Sherwood, magazine writer; Shirley Bonne as her sister, Eileen Sherwood, an actress; Leon Belasco as Mr. Appopolous, their Greenwich Village landlord; Rose Marie as Bertha, a friend of theirs; Jack Weston as Chick Adams, a reporter; Stubby Kaye as Marty, Eileen's agent; and Raymond Bailey as Mr. D. X. Beaumont, Ruth's boss.

MY SON JEEP   NBC

4 JULY 1953–22 SEPTEMBER 1953   Half-hour sitcom about a widower and his young son. With Jeffrey Lynn as Doc Allison; Martin Huston as his son, Jeep; Anne Sargent as Barbara, Doc's receptionist and secretary; Betty Lou Keim as Jeep's older sister, Peggy; and Leona Powers as the

housekeeper. Though regular broadcasting of the series did not begin until July, a "sneak preview" was telecast 3 June 1953.

MY THREE SONS
ABC/CBS

29 SEPTEMBER 1960–2 SEPTEMBER 1965 (ABC); 16 SEPTEMBER 1965–24 AUGUST 1972 (CBS)   Second only to *Ozzie and Harriet* as network television's longest-running situation comedy, *My Three Sons* starred Fred MacMurray as widower Steve Douglas, a West Coast aerodynamics engineer trying to raise three boys. His first "three sons" were played by Tim Considine as Mike, the eldest; Don Grady (a onetime Mouseketeer) as Robbie; and Stanley Livingston as Chip, the youngest. Also featured was William Frawley as the boys' grandfather, "Bub" O'Casey, who also resided in the Douglas household. In the fall of 1963 Meredith MacRae joined the cast as Mike's girlfriend, Sally Morrison. Midway through the 1964–1965 season William Frawley left the series for health reasons, and William Demarest was brought in as Charley O'Casey, the boys' live-in uncle. Several more changes took place in the fall of 1965 as *My Three Sons* shifted networks: eldest son Mike married Sally, and the two were written out of the series; a new "son" joined the household: Ernie, a bespectacled orphan, was adopted by Steve. The role was played by Barry Livingston, younger brother of costar Stanley Livingston. Tina Cole joined the crew a year later as Robbie's girlfriend, Katie Miller; she and Robbie subsequently got married, continued to live at home, and eventually had triplets. The three youngest Douglases—Charlie, Steve, and Robbie, Jr.—were played by Michael, Daniel, and Joseph Todd. In the fall of 1969 Steve Douglas remarried. His new wife, Barbara Harper (played by Beverly Garland), had been one of Ernie's high school teachers; Barbara was a widow and the mother of a small daughter, Dodie (played by Dawn Lyn). In the fall of 1970 Ronnie Troup joined the cast as Polly Williams, a college classmate of Chip (the original youngest son); she and Chip were married that year. Don Fedderson was the executive producer of the series.

MY TRUE STORY
ABC

5 MAY 1950–22 SEPTEMBER 1950   Produced in cooperation with *True Story* magazine, this half-hour dramatic anthology series presented stories based on the ostensibly true accounts from the periodical. The television show was not nearly as successful as the radio adaptation, which ran from 1943 to 1961. Charles Powers was the producer and director of the television version.

MY WORLD AND WELCOME TO IT
NBC

15 SEPTEMBER 1969–7 SEPTEMBER 1970   This whimsical sitcom was based loosely on the life and writings of humorist James Thurber. It

starred William Windom as John Monroe, a writer and cartoonist for *Manhattanite* magazine who, like Walter Mitty, frequently fantasized about what life could be like; animated sequences were regularly employed to depict Monroe's daydreams and other diversions. Also featured were Joan Hotchkis as Monroe's wife, Ellen; Lisa Gerritsen as their daughter, Lydia; and Harold J. Stone as Monroe's boss, Hamilton Greeley. Henry Morgan was occasionally featured as Monroe's colleague, Phil Jensen (the character was reportedly inspired by that of Robert Benchley). Sheldon Leonard was the executive producer of the half-hour series, and Danny Arnold produced it.

MYSTERIES OF CHINATOWN   ABC
4 DECEMBER 1949–23 OCTOBER 1950   One of the first ABC shows telecast from Hollywood, *Mysteries of Chinatown* was a half-hour crime show set in San Francisco's Chinatown. The cast included Robert Bice, Spencer Chan, Herb Ellis, and Cy Kendall. Ray Buffum produced the series and Richard Goggin directed it.

THE MYSTERY CHEF   NBC
1 MARCH 1949–29 JUNE 1949   One of NBC's first daytime programs, this cooking show was broadcast from Philadelphia, where it was hosted by John MacPherson, the "Mystery Chef." First seen on Tuesday and Thursday afternoons, the show later shifted to Wednesdays.

THE NBC COMEDY HOUR   NBC
8 JANUARY 1956–10 JUNE 1956   The successor to *The Colgate Comedy Hour, The NBC Comedy Hour* was a Sunday-night variety show hosted by a different guest star each week, except during the spring of 1956, when Gale Storm was the permanent host.

NBC DRAMATIC THEATRE   NBC
17 APRIL 1949–10 JULY 1949   Also known as *NBC Repertory Theatre*, this hour anthology series was a temporary replacement for *Philco Television Playhouse*. Vaughn Taylor starred in the premiere telecast, "Mr. Mergenthwirker's Lobblies."

NBC FOLLIES   NBC
13 SEPTEMBER 1973–27 DECEMBER 1973   Thursday-night variety hour, hosted by Sammy Davis, Jr. Mickey Rooney was featured in most of the shows.

THE NBC MYSTERY MOVIE/   NBC
THE NBC SUNDAY MYSTERY MOVIE/THE NBC WEDNESDAY MOVIE
These were the umbrella titles for the several multipart series that ran on NBC between 1971 and 1977. The composition changed slightly each

year. In the fall of 1971 *The NBC Mystery Movie* included *Columbo, McCloud,* and *McMillan and Wife.* Two umbrella series were featured in the fall of 1972: *The NBC Sunday Mystery Movie* (*Columbo, McCloud, McMillan and Wife,* and *Hec Ramsey*) and *The NBC Wednesday Mystery Movie,* which introduced three new crime shows: *Banacek, Cool Million,* and *Madigan.* The composition of *The NBC Sunday Mystery Movie* remained intact during the 1973–1974 season, but *The NBC Wednesday Movie* presented *Banacek* and three newcomers: *Faraday and Company, The Snoop Sisters,* and *Tenafly.* By the fall of 1974 *The NBC Wednesday Movie* was gone entirely, but *The NBC Sunday Mystery Movie* carried on for three more seasons. *Columbo, McCloud,* and *McMillan and Wife* shared space with a new fourth member each season—*Amy Prentiss* in 1974–1975, *McCoy* in 1975–1976, and *Quincy* in 1976–1977 (*Quincy* was given its own regular slot partway through the 1976–1977 season). See individual titles for details.

NBC NEWS   NBC
16 FEBRUARY 1948–   Nightly newscasts on the NBC television network began in February 1948 with *The Camel Newsreel Theatre,* a ten-minute Fox Movietone Newsreel sponsored by Camel Cigarettes; earlier, the network had experimented with a fifteen-minute weekly newscast, *NBC Television Newsroom* (also known as *The Esso Newsreel*). *The Camel Newsreel Theatre* lasted a year; on 14 February 1949 John Cameron Swayze took the helm of *The Camel News Caravan,* a nightly fifteen-minute broadcast. Like most of television's early newscasters, Swayze had worked in radio for several years before switching to the new medium. There was little on-the-spot reportage on *The Camel News Caravan;* the newscasts consisted mainly of Swayze reading the evening's news. Swayze anchored the Monday-through-Friday broadcasts for more than seven and one-half years (during the 1949–1950 season NBC also carried a Saturday-evening newscast, anchored by Leon Pearson); he later hosted a game show *(Chance for Romance)* and served as commercial spokesman for Timex watches. In 1954 *The Camel News Caravan* became the first network news show to be broadcast in color (though regular colorcasting did not begin until 15 November 1965).

On 29 October 1956 *The Camel News Caravan* was succeeded by *The Huntley-Brinkley Report,* a fifteen-minute newscast coanchored by Chet Huntley and David Brinkley, two NBC newsmen who had been paired up that summer to host the network's coverage of the political conventions. Huntley, a Westerner, had worked for several radio stations before joining CBS News in 1939. From 1951 to 1955 he worked for ABC News, earning a Peabody Award in 1953 for his radio reporting; in 1955 he joined NBC. Brinkley, a Southerner, joined NBC News in 1943 after a stint with the United Press, and served as a local reporter in Washington during the early 1950s. *The Huntley-Brinkley Report* soon became television's top-rated news show, and remained in that position for most of its fourteen-year run. Huntley and Brinkley complemented each other almost perfectly, with Huntley's no-nonsense toughness neatly offset by Brinkley's dry and wry wit. Their familiar closing exchange—"Good night, Chet/Good night, David"—was suggested by producer Reuven Frank in order to provide a touch of warmth to the newscast. In real life, however, the two saw little of each other, for Huntley was usually based in New York while Brinkley generally broadcast from Washington. NBC followed CBS's lead in expanding its newscasts from fifteen to thirty minutes in 1963; NBC's initial half-hour show was on 9 September, just a week after CBS's. In 1970 Huntley announced his retirement, and the final *Huntley-Brinkley Report* was broadcast 31 July 1970. Huntley died in 1974.

After Huntley's departure, the newscast was retitled *NBC Nightly News,* and seven-nights-a-week broadcasts were inaugurated. The weeknight newscasts were first anchored solely by David Brinkley, but in August of 1971 John Chancellor became the new anchorman. Chancellor, who joined NBC News in 1950, had been a floor correspondent at the 1956 political conventions (when Huntley and Brinkley were upstairs), and later served as a correspondent in Vienna, London, and Moscow before succeeding Dave Garroway as host of the *Today* show in 1961; in 1964 Chancellor took a leave of absence from NBC to head the Voice of America. Throughout the 1970s Brinkley and Chancellor have been teamed together, though Brinkley's role has fluctuated between coanchor and commentator. In October 1979 Brinkley left the coanchor position, and no longer appeared regularly.

In the fall of 1977 a new feature was introduced on the weeknight broadcasts; titled "Segment 3," it is essentially an in-depth feature which usually runs more than four minutes. Most of these segments are investigative reports, though some light features have been included; NBC reported in 1978 that viewer interest in the segments has been strong.

NBC NOVELS FOR TELEVISION   NBC
14 FEBRUARY 1979–21 MARCH 1979   An umbrella title for a group of miniseries, each of which was based on a best-selling novel. The show led off with "From Here to Eternity," an adaptation of James Jones's novel, set in Hawaii in 1941. The three-parter featured William Devane as Sergeant Milt Warden; Roy Thinnes as his commanding officer, Captain Holmes; Natalie Wood as Karen Holmes, his wife; Steve Railsback as Private Robert E. Lee Prewitt; Kim Basinger as Lorene, a prostitute; and Peter Boyle as Fatso Judson. The second miniseries was "Studs Lonigan," a three-parter based on James T. Farrell's trilogy chronicling the coming of age of a tough young man in Chicago during the 1920s. Featured were Dan Shor and Harry Hamlin as Studs Lonigan; Charles

Durning as his father; Colleen Dewhurst as his mother; and Lisa Pelikan as Lucy, his girlfriend.

NBC REPORTS
NBC

12 SEPTEMBER 1972–4 SEPTEMBER 1973   A series of news documentaries, *NBC Reports* shared a time slot on Tuesdays with *First Tuesday* and *America.*

NBC SPORTS IN ACTION
NBC

17 JANUARY 1965–5 JUNE 1966   This sports anthology series, hosted by Jim Simpson, was seen both on Sunday afternoons and in prime time.

NBC'S SATURDAY NIGHT LIVE
NBC

11 OCTOBER 1975–   NBC introduced this freewheeling ninety-minute comedy-variety show into what appeared to be an unpromising time slot—11:30 p.m. on Saturdays (the slot had previously been occupied by reruns of *The Tonight Show*). To the surpise of almost everyone, the show took off, and in some ways it represented the boldest leap in television comedy since Sid Caesar's *Your Show of Shows,* which had held down an earlier slot on Saturdays two decades before. One of the few live network entertainment programs of any kind, the show is presented on three Saturdays a month. Each week a guest host emcees the show, backed up by a stock company of regulars: Chevy Chase, Dan Aykroyd, John Belushi, Jane Curtin, Garrett Morris, Laraine Newman, and Gilda Radner (Chase left the series in the fall of 1976 and was later replaced by Bill Murray; Aykroyd and Belushi left after the 1978–1979 season). The members of this talented group were virtual newcomers to television (though Chase had been featured on *The Great American Dream Machine* and Morris had appeared regularly on a 1973 sitcom, *Roll Out!*). Several of the others, along with a number of the show's writers, had been featured in various productions under the auspices of *National Lampoon* magazine. George Carlin was the first guest host, but the show has not always relied on show business regulars for its hosts—among the more unusual emcees have been Presidential press secretary Ron Nessen (17 April 1976), consumer advocate Ralph Nader (15 January 1977), and Georgia legislator Julian Bond (9 April 1977). Regular segments have included "Weekend Update," a news satire first presented by Chevy Chase, later by Jane Curtin and Dan Aykroyd; "The Coneheads," the story of a family from another planet trying to blend inconspicuously into American society; "Samurai Warrior," the adventures of an Oriental swordsman (played by John Belushi). Some of the comedy presented on the show has been criticized as being in poor taste, but that criticism can be made of almost any variety series in television history (Arthur Godfrey was regularly condemned in the late 1940s for his

"blue" material). *NBC's Saturday Night Live* was developed by network vice president Dick Ebersol, who was its executive producer during the 1975–1976 season. Lorne Michaels, who began his career as a writer on *Laugh-In,* has been the producer. The show was originally titled *NBC's Saturday Night*—the word *Live* was officially added in May of 1977. The stable of writers has included Aykroyd, Belushi, Chase, Morris, and Murray, together with Anne Beatts, Tom Davis, Al Franken, producer Michaels, Marilyn Suzanne Miller, Michael O'Donoghue, Herb Sargent, Tom Schiller, Rosie Shuster, and Alan Zweibel. The show's announcer is Don Pardo, whose mellifluous voice is most closely associated with *The Price Is Right.* In the fall of 1979 the series came to prime time; beginning 24 October, edited reruns were shown Wednesdays at 10 p.m. as *The Best of Saturday Night Live.*

N.E.T. FESTIVAL NET/PBS
6 DECEMBER 1967–29 SEPTEMBER 1970 Umbrella title for a series of American- and foreign-produced hour-long programs devoted to the arts.

N.E.T. JOURNAL NET/PBS
OCTOBER 1966–21 SEPTEMBER 1970 Umbrella title for a series of documentaries.

N.E.T. PLAYHOUSE NET/PBS
9 OCTOBER 1966–24 JANUARY 1972 Dramatic anthology series. The premiere telecast was "Ten Blocks on the Camino Real" by Tennessee Williams.

N.F.L. MONDAY NIGHT FOOTBALL ABC
21 SEPTEMBER 1970–   ABC took a gamble in 1970 when it chose to experiment with coverage of a professional football game on Monday nights during the fall; professional football had not been played regularly on that night previously. It was reported that the network paid $8 million for the Monday-night rights, but the gamble seems to have paid off. Each season a trio of commentators has handled the play-by-play. Keith Jackson, Don Meredith, and ABC's ubiquitous sportscaster, Howard Cosell, handled the chores during the 1970–1971 season. In the fall of 1971 former New York Giants running back Frank Gifford replaced Jackson, joining Meredith and Cosell; that group stayed together for two more seasons. In the fall of 1974 Meredith left to try his hand at acting and was replaced by former defensive back Fred Williamson; Williamson was replaced later that season by Alex Karras, an ex-lineman for the Detroit Lions. Karras, Gifford, and Cosell were featured during the 1975 and 1976 seasons as well. In the fall of 1977, however, Don Meredith returned, replacing Karras. Fran Tarkenton was added in the fall of 1979.

N.O.P.D.

1956   *N.O.P.D.* stood for the New Orleans Police Department in this low-budget crime show, starring Stacy Harris as Detective Beaujac and Lou Sirgo as Detective Conroy, who was on leave from the department. Frank Phares produced the series, which was filmed on location; thirty-nine episodes were made.

N.Y.P.D.

5 SEPTEMBER 1967–16 SEPTEMBER 1969   One of the last dramatic series to be filmed on location in New York, *N.Y.P.D.* was produced by Talent Associates and was filmed with the cooperation of the real N.Y.P.D., the New York Police Department. Most of the filming was done with 16-millimeter cameras. The half-hour show starred Jack Warden as Detective Lieutenant Mike Haines; Frank Converse as Detective Johnny Corso; and Robert Hooks as Detective Jeff Ward.

NAKED CITY

30 SEPTEMBER 1958–29 SEPTEMBER 1959; 12 OCTOBER 1960–11 SEPTEMBER 1963   Filmed entirely on location in New York, this popular crime show began as a half-hour series in 1958 and ran for one season. It returned after a season's absence in an hour-long format, which ran for three seasons. The first cast included James Franciscus as Detective Jim Halloran of the Sixty-fifth Precinct; John McIntire as Lieutenant Dan Muldoon, his superior; and Harry Bellaver as Sergeant Frank Arcaro. Suzanne Storrs was occasionally featured as Halloran's wife, Janet. McIntire left the series in March of 1959 and was replaced by Horace McMahon as Lieutenant Mike Parker. When *Naked City* returned in the fall of 1960, Bellaver and McMahon returned with it, Paul Burke was introduced as Detective Adam Flint, and Nancy Malone was featured as Flint's girlfriend, Libby. *Naked City*'s famous tag line ("There are eight million stories in the naked city; this has been one of them") was first used in the 1948 film from which the series was derived. The title of the film and the series was taken from a book of photographs published by Arthur H. Fellig, better known as "Weegee." Herbert B. Leonard was the executive producer of the series, and some of the many guest stars who appeared were Robert Redford ("Tombstone for a Derelict," 5 April 1961), Dustin Hoffman ("Sweet Prince of Delancey Street," 7 June 1961, his first major TV role), Peter Fonda ("The Night the Saints Lost Their Halos," 17 January 1962, his first major TV role), Sandy Dennis ("Idylls of a Running Back," 26 September 1962, her first major TV role), and Jon Voight ("Alive and Still a Second Lieutenant," 6 March 1963, his first major TV role).

NAKIA

21 SEPTEMBER 1974–28 DECEMBER 1974   Hour-long crime show star-

ring Robert Forster as Nakia Parker, a Navajo who was a deputy sheriff in New Mexico. With Arthur Kennedy as Sheriff Sam Jericho; Taylor Lacher as Hubbell Martin, another deputy; and Gloria DeHaven as Irene James, also a deputy. Charles Larson was executive producer of the series, which was filmed largely on location.

THE NAME DROPPERS NBC
29 SEPTEMBER 1969–27 MARCH 1970 Daytime game show cohosted by Los Angeles disc jockeys Al Lohman and Roger Barkley. The object of the game was for selected members of the studio audience to determine which of the three celebrity guest panelists was related to the "name dropper," a guest who described his or her relationship to the celebrity (without, of course, divulging which of the celebs was the "correct" relative).

THE NAME OF THE GAME NBC
20 SEPTEMBER 1968–10 SEPTEMBER 1971 This ninety-minute crime show was a tripartite series: Each of the three stars appeared every third week. It starred Gene Barry as Glenn Howard, publisher of *Crime* magazine; Tony Franciosa as investigative correspondent Jeff Dillon; Robert Stack as senior editor Dan Farrell, a former FBI agent. Also featured were Susan St. James as Peggy Maxwell, their research assistant; Ben Murphy (1968–1970) as Dan's assistant, Joe Sample; Cliff Potter as Andy Hill, a young correspondent; and Mark Miller as reporter Ross Craig. Each of the three costars selected his own producer: Richard Irving produced the Barry episodes, E. Jack Neuman (and, later, Leslie Stevens) the Franciosa episodes, and David Victor the Stack episodes. In a 1969 article *TV Guide* reported that the series was the most expensive in the history of television, budgeted at $400,000 per episode. The pilot for the series, "Fame Is the Name of the Game," starring Tony Franciosa and Susan St. James, was telecast 26 November 1966.

NAME THAT TUNE NBC/CBS/SYNDICATED
6 JULY 1953–14 JUNE 1954 (NBC); 2 SEPTEMBER 1954–19 OCTOBER 1959 (CBS); 1970 (SYNDICATED); 29 JULY 1974–3 JANUARY 1975 (NBC); 1974–   (SYNDICATED); 3 JANUARY 1977–10 JUNE 1977 (NBC) The best known of the musical identification game shows, *Name That Tune* has been presented in several different formats over the years. Created by Harry Salter, the show first appeared as a prime-time series in the summer of 1953, with Red Benson as host. When it switched networks the following season, Bill Cullen became the host; he was succeeded in 1955 by George DeWitt. At that time the show featured two contestants, who stood at one side of the stage while the orchestra played a musical selection; the contestant who could identify it then raced across the stage and rang a bell (female contestants were placed closer to the bell

than male contestants). The winner of that round then tried to identify several songs within a specified time period. After an eleven-year absence a syndicated version of the show appeared in 1970 with Richard Hayes as host. In 1974 both a new network and a new syndicated version appeared. The network version was a daytime show, hosted by Dennis James; the syndicated show was emceed by Tom Kennedy. Both versions added two new features: the "Bid-a-Note" round, in which the contestants challenged each other to identify a song from as few notes as possible, and the "Golden Medley," in which the winning contestant tried to identify seven songs in thirty seconds. In 1976 the syndicated version was retitled *The $100,000 Name That Tune*—a contestant who won the "Golden Medley" could return to try to identify a "mystery tune" for a grand prize of $10,000 a year for the next ten years. When the series was revived for network television again in 1977, Tom Kennedy hosted; top prize on that daytime effort was $25,000. In the fall of 1977 vocalist Cathie Lee Johnson was added to the syndicated version and a playoff system was devised to award the grand prize. Ralph Edwards was the executive producer of the 1970s versions.

THE NAME'S THE SAME ABC
5 DECEMBER 1951–7 OCTOBER 1955   On this prime-time game show a celebrity panel tried to discern the names of the contestants; each contestant's name was the same as that of a well-known personality or famous event. The show was first hosted by Robert Q. Lewis, and then by Dennis James, Clifton Fadiman, and finally by Bob (Elliott) and Ray (Goulding).

NANCY NBC
17 SEPTEMBER 1970–7 JANUARY 1971   Insipid sitcom about the daughter of the President, who, while vacationing in Iowa, met and married a Center City veterinarian. With Renne Jarrett as Nancy Smith; John Fink as Adam Hudson, the vet; Celeste Holm as Abby Townsend, Nancy's official chaperone (and the press secretary of the President's wife); Robert F. Simon as Adam's Uncle Everett; William Bassett as Agent Turner of the Secret Service; Ernesto Macias as Agent Rodriquez; and Eddie Applegate as Willie, a local reporter. Sidney Sheldon created and produced the half-hour series.

NANCY DREW MYSTERIES
See THE HARDY BOYS/NANCY DREW MYSTERIES

THE NANCY WALKER SHOW ABC
30 SEPTEMBER 1976–23 DECEMBER 1976   Half-hour sitcom starring Nancy Walker as Nancy Kitteridge, a Hollywood talent agent. Also featured were William Daniels as her husband, Kenneth Kitteridge, a Merchant Marine commander who had just retired after being at sea for most

of their twenty-nine years of marriage; Beverly Archer as their forlorn daughter, Loraine; and Ken Olfson as Terry Folsom, their gay boarder, a struggling actor. Produced by Norman Lear's T.A.T. Communications, the series was canceled in midseason. Walker returned a few weeks later in a new (and equally unsuccessful) sitcom, *Blansky's Beauties*.

NANNY AND THE PROFESSOR ABC
21 JANUARY 1970–27 DECEMBER 1971   Half-hour sitcom starring Juliet Mills as Phoebe Figalilly, better known as Nanny, housekeeper and governess to a widowed professor and his three children. Gifted with mysterious powers, Nanny attributed her abilities to "a little bit of faith and lots of love." Also featured were Richard Long as Professor Howard Everett; David Doremus as son Hal; Trent Lehman as son Butch; and Kim Richards as daughter Prudence. Elsa Lanchester joined the cast in the fall of 1971 as Nanny's Aunt Henrietta. Charles B. FitzSimmons produced the series.

NASHVILLE 99 CBS
1 APRIL 1977–22 APRIL 1977   Hour-long crime show starring Claude Akins as Lieutenant Stoney Huff of the Nashville Police Department. With Jerry Reed as his sidekick, Detective Trace Mayne; Lucille Benson as Stoney's mother, Birdie Huff. Ernie Frankel created the miniseries and was its executive producer.

NASHVILLE ON THE ROAD SYNDICATED
1976   Country and western music show, taped on location around the country.

THE NAT KING COLE SHOW NBC
5 NOVEMBER 1956–24 JUNE 1957; 2 JULY 1957–17 DECEMBER 1957   Nat King Cole, the popular black pianist and singer, appeared frequently as a guest star on variety shows during the 1950s. In the fall of 1956 he was given his own fifteen-minute show, broadcast on Mondays before the network news. In the summer of 1957 he was shifted to a half-hour slot on Tuesdays at 10:00 p.m., and in September he was given the 7:30 p.m. slot that night. The Nelson Riddle Orchestra and the Randy Van Horne Singers were featured on all three shows. Sadly, Cole's show failed to attract a nationwide sponsor and was dropped in midseason. Though it was reported that potential sponsors feared a Southern boycott, it should be noted that several NBC affiliates in the North as well as the South declined to carry the show. Cole's show is sometimes described as the first network variety program hosted by a black performer, but in fact Cole was preceded by Bob Howard, Hazel Scott, and Billy Daniels. In any event, it was not until 1966 that a black performer—Sammy Davis, Jr.—again hosted a network variety series.

NATIONAL BARN DANCE

ABC

21 FEBRUARY 1949–7 NOVEMBER 1949 Also known as *ABC Barn Dance,* this half-hour musical series was the television version of the long-running radio series that began locally in Chicago in 1924 and was broadcast nationally beginning in 1933. John Dolce hosted most of the television broadcasts.

NATIONAL BOWLING CHAMPIONS

NBC

8 APRIL 1956–24 MARCH 1957 Late-night series of head-to-head bowling matches between two professionals. Broadcast from Chicago, the show was hosted by "Whispering Joe" Wilson. See also *Bowling Stars.*

NATIONAL GEOGRAPHIC SPECIALS

CBS/ABC/PBS

1964–1973 (CBS); 1973–1975 (ABC); 1975– (PBS) Produced in cooperation with the National Geographic Society, this long-running series of specials on biological, historical, and cultural subjects was first produced by Wolper Productions, later by Metromedia, and again by Wolper. Approximately four new specials are produced each year. Joseph Campanella narrated many of the specials on CBS, and E. G. Marshall has narrated most of those on PBS.

NATIONAL VELVET

NBC

18 SEPTEMBER 1960–10 SEPTEMBER 1962 Based on the 1944 film (which had starred Elizabeth Taylor) about a young girl who trained her horse for the Grand National Steeplechase, this half-hour dramatic series starred Lori Martin as Velvet Brown; Arthur Space as her father, Herbert Brown; Ann Doran as her mother, Martha Brown; James McCallion as Mi Taylor, the Browns' handyman; Carole Wells as Edwina, Velvet's sister; and Joey Scott as Donald, Velvet's brother. Rudy Abel produced the series.

THE NATION'S FUTURE

NBC

12 NOVEMBER 1960–16 SEPTEMBER 1961 John K. M. McCaffery was the moderator of this Saturday-night public affairs program, which presented debates on topical issues. Edwin Newman succeeded McCaffery as moderator in June 1961. Irving Gitlin was the producer.

THE NATURE OF THINGS

NBC

5 FEBRUARY 1948–29 MARCH 1954 One of television's first science shows, this fifteen-minute series was hosted by astronomer Dr. Roy K. Marshall, director of the Fels Planetarium at Philadelphia's Franklin Institute.

NAVY LOG

CBS/ABC

20 SEPTEMBER 1955–25 SEPTEMBER 1956 (CBS); 17 OCTOBER 1956–25 SEPTEMBER 1958 (ABC) A half-hour anthology series about Navy life,

Navy Log was produced by Simeon G. Gallu, Jr. The show's opening, in which 2,000 sailors formed the words "Navy Log," was filmed aboard the U.S.S. *Hancock*. James Cagney made a very rare TV appearance as host of one episode, "The Lonely Watch," aired 9 January 1958; the episode starred Clint Eastwood, in one of his first television roles.

NEEDLES AND PINS NBC
21 SEPTEMBER 1973–28 DECEMBER 1973 Half-hour sitcom set in New York's garment district. With Deirdre Lenihan (a newcomer to television) as Wendy Nelson, a designer from Nebraska who got a job at Lorelei Fashions; Norman Fell as her boss, Nathan Davidson; Louis Nye as Davidson's dilettante brother-in-law, Harry Karp; Sandra Deel as Sonia Baker, the bookkeeper; Bernie Kopell as Charlie Miller, the salesman; Larry Gelman as Max Popkin, the cutter; Alex Henteloff as Myron, the patternmaker; and Milton Selzer as Singer, Davidson's chief competitor. David Gerber was executive producer of the series, and Hy Averback produced and directed it.

THE NEIGHBORS ABC
29 DECEMBER 1975–9 APRIL 1976 Silly game show on which five neighbors exchanged gossip about each other for the chance to win prizes. Regis Philbin, assisted by Jane Nelson, was the host, and Bill Carruthers the executive producer of this short-lived daytime show.

NEVER TOO YOUNG ABC
27 SEPTEMBER 1965–24 JUNE 1966 This daytime serial focused on a group of active teenagers and their harried parents. Set at Malibu Beach, the cast included: Michael Blodgett as Tad; Cindy Carol as Susan; Pat Connolly as Barbara; Tony Dow (late of *Leave It to Beaver*) as Chet; Robin Grace as Joy; John Lupton as Frank; Tommy Rettig (formerly of *Lassie*) as JoJo; David Watson as Alfie; and Patrice Wymore as Rhoda. Though *Never Too Young* failed in its attempt to attract teenaged viewers to a continuing drama, its successor in the late-afternoon time slot—*Dark Shadows*—performed admirably.

THE NEW ADVENTURES OF CHARLIE CHAN
See CHARLIE CHAN

THE NEW ADVENTURES OF CHINA SMITH
See CHINA SMITH

THE NEW ADVENTURES OF GILLIGAN ABC
7 SEPTEMBER 1974–4 SEPTEMBER 1976 Saturday-morning cartoon show based on the 1964 sitcom, *Gilligan's Island* (see also that title). Five members of the *Gilligan's Island* cast—Bob Denver, Alan Hale, Jim

Backus, Natalie Schafer, and Russell Johnson—lent their voices to the animated production, and two new voices—those of Jane Webb and Jane Edwards—were added. Norm Prescott and Lou Scheimer were the executive producers.

THE NEW ADVENTURES OF HUCKLEBERRY FINN NBC
15 SEPTEMBER 1968–7 SEPTEMBER 1969 This half-hour Sunday-night series bore almost no resemblance to Mark Twain's classic. The series combined live action with animated sequences, and its premise was that Huck, Tom, Becky, and Joe had been caught in a time warp and were trying to find their way through time and space back to Missouri. With Kevin Schultz as Tom Sawyer; Michael Shea as Huck Finn; Lu Ann Haslam as Becky Thatcher; and Ted Cassidy as Injun Joe. The show was a Hanna-Barbera production.

THE NEW ADVENTURES OF MIGHTY MOUSE AND
HECKLE AND JECKLE CBS
8 SEPTEMBER 1979–   Mighty Mouse, the caped rodent who left network TV in 1967, returned in a series of new cartoon adventures, in which he battled his nemesis, Oilcan Harry, to save the honor of Pearl Pureheart. Other segments on the Saturday-morning series included new adventures of Heckle and Jeckle, the mischievous crows, and Quacula, a vampirish duck. See also *Heckle and Jeckle*; *The Mighty Mouse Playhouse*.

THE NEW ANDY GRIFFITH SHOW CBS
8 JANUARY 1971–21 MAY 1971 *The New Andy Griffith Show* was the title given to the series that began in the fall of 1970 as *Headmaster* and changed formats in midseason. Griffith had played an educator on *Headmaster*; in the new format he played a role more similar to that he'd played on *The Andy Griffith Show*—the mayor of a small town in North Carolina. Featured were Andy Griffith as Andy Sawyer; Lee Meriwether as his wife, Lee Sawyer; Marty McCall as their son, T. J.; Lori Ann Rutherford as their daughter, Lori; Glen Ash as town councilman Buff McKnight; and Ann Morgan Guilbert as Nora, Lee's unmarried sister.

THE NEW ARCHIE SABRINA HOUR
See THE ARCHIE SHOW

THE NEW AVENGERS
See THE AVENGERS

THE NEW BILL COSBY SHOW CBS
11 SEPTEMBER 1972–7 MAY 1973 Hour-long variety show hosted by comedian Bill Cosby and featuring Lola Falana, Foster Brooks, Oscar de-

Gruy, and Susan Tolsky. Quincy Jones conducted the orchestra, and the Donald McKayle Dancers were also featured.

THE NEW BREED ABC

3 OCTOBER 1961–25 SEPTEMBER 1962 The heroes of this hour-long crime show were the men of Los Angeles's Metropolitan Squad: Leslie Nielsen as Lieutenant Price Adams, the squad leader; Greg Roman as Officer Pete Garcia; John Clarke as Officer Joe Huddleston; John Beradino as Sergeant Vince Cavelli; and Byron Morrow as Captain Gregory, Adams's commanding officer.

THE NEW CANDID CAMERA
See CANDID CAMERA

THE NEW CHRISTY MINSTRELS SHOW NBC

6 AUGUST 1964–10 SEPTEMBER 1964 A summer replacement for *Hazel,* this half-hour musical variety show featured the New Christy Minstrels, a wholesome folk troupe organized in 1962 by Randy Sparks; the name was taken from the Christy Minstrels, a nineteenth-century American singing group founded by Edwin P. Christy. In 1964 the New Christy Minstrels included: Karen Gunderson, Barry Kane, Barry McGuire, Art Podell, Paul Potash, Larry Ramos, Clarence Treat, Ann White, and Nick Woods. Gary Smith produced the five-week series, and Al deCaprio directed it.

THE NEW DATING GAME
See THE DATING GAME

THE NEW DICK VAN DYKE SHOW CBS

18 SEPTEMBER 1971–2 SEPTEMBER 1974 Created by Carl Reiner (the man responsible for *The Dick Van Dyke Show*), this half-hour sitcom went through two formats in its three seasons. In both formats Dick Van Dyke starred as Dick Preston and Hope Lange costarred as his wife, Jenny Preston; Angela Powell was also featured as their daughter, Annie. For the first two seasons the show was set in Phoenix (and was actually produced there), where Dick Preston was host of a local television talk show. The cast also included Marty Brill as Dick's manager, Bernie Davis; Nancy Dussault as Bernie's wife, Carol Davis; Fannie Flagg as Mike, Dick's sister and secretary; David Doyle as Ted Atwater, the station manager; and Michael Shea as Lucas Preston, Dick and Jenny's college-age son. In the fall of 1973 the Prestons moved to Hollywood, where Dick landed a role as Dr. Brad Fairmont on a soap opera entitled "Those Who Care." The new cast included: Richard Dawson as their neighbor, Richard Richardson, a television star; Chita Rivera as his wife, Connie Richardson; Dick Van Patten as Max, producer of "Those Who Care";

Henry Darrow as Alex, the stage manager; Barry Gordon as Dennis Whitehead, one of the writers; and Barbara Rush as Dick's costar on "Those Who Care," Margot Brighton.

THE NEW FRED AND BARNEY SHOW
See THE FLINTSTONES

THE NEW HIGH ROLLERS
See HIGH ROLLERS

THE NEW JOEY BISHOP SHOW
See THE JOEY BISHOP SHOW

A NEW KIND OF FAMILY   ABC
16 SEPTEMBER 1979–21 OCTOBER 1979   One of the first casualties of the 1979–1980 season, this was a half-hour comedy about two families—a widow with three kids, and a divorcee with one child—who ended up renting the same house. With Eileen Brennan as Kit Flanagan, the widow, who moved west from New York; Gwynne Gilford as Abby Stone, the divorcée, who was starting law school; David Hollander as Andy Flanagan; Lauri Hendler as Hillary Flanagan; Rob Lowe as Tony Flanagan; Connie Ann Hearn as Jill Stone; and Chuck McCann as next-door neighbor Harold Zimmerman. Margie Gordon and Jane Eisner created the series and were its executive producers. A few episodes were later shown, with Telma Hopkins (replacing Gilford) as Jessie Ashton, and Janet Jackson as her daughter, JoJo.

THE NEW LAND   ABC
14 SEPTEMBER 1974–19 OCTOBER 1974   This hour-long family drama, set in Minnesota in 1858, collapsed early in the season under competition from CBS's *All in the Family* and NBC's *Emergency!* It featured Scott Thomas as Christian Larsen, the head of a family of Swedish immigrants; Bonnie Bedelia as his wife, Anna Larsen; Todd Lookinland as their son, Tuliff; Debbie Lytton as their daughter, Annaliese; Kurt Russell as Christian's brother, Bo Larsen; Donald Moffat as Lundstrom; Gwen Arner as Molly, Lundstrom's wife; and Lew Frizzell as Murdock. William Blinn was the executive producer and Philip Leacock the producer for Warner Brothers Television.

THE NEW LORETTA YOUNG SHOW   CBS
24 SEPTEMBER 1962–18 MARCH 1963   Loretta Young starred in this continuing comedy-drama as Christine Massey, a recently widowed writer with seven children who got a job with a New York magazine; in the last episode Christine married her editor. Also featured were James Philbrook as Paul Belzer, the editor; Celia Kaye as Marnie, the oldest child;

Dack Rambo as Peter; Dirk Rambo as Peter's twin brother, Paul; Beverly Washburn as Vickie; Carol Sydes as Binkie; Sandy Descher as Judy; and Tracy Stratford as Maria, the youngest.

THE NEW MICKEY MOUSE CLUB
See THE MICKEY MOUSE CLUB

THE NEW PEOPLE
ABC

22 SEPTEMBER 1969–12 JANUARY 1970   This forty-five-minute continuing drama was the companion to *The Music Scene,* a forty-five-minute variety series that preceded it on Mondays. *The New People* told the implausible story of a planeload of American young people who crash landed on a remote Pacific island; the island was conveniently outfitted with structures, supplies, and provisions, because it had been designated as a nuclear test site but abandoned before any tests were ever made. The cast included: Peter Ratray as George, the unofficial leader of the group; Tiffany Bolling as Susan; Zooey Hall as Bob Lee; Jill Jaress as Ginny; David Moses as Washington; Dennis Olivieri as Stanley; Clive Clerk as Jack; and Donna Bacalla as Wendy. Though the youngsters were supposedly isolated from the rest of the world, guest stars managed to appear almost every week; one of them was Richard Dreyfuss, who was featured in the 29 September episode. Aaron Spelling and Harold Gast were the producers.

THE NEW PERRY MASON
CBS

16 SEPTEMBER 1973–27 JANUARY 1974   An unsuccessful remake of television's most famous courtroom show, *The New Perry Mason* lasted about one-twentieth as long as the old *Perry Mason.* The new cast included Monte Markham as Perry Mason; Sharon Acker as his secretary, Della Street; Albert Stratton as investigator Paul Drake; Harry Guardino as prosecutor Hamilton Burger; Dane Clark as Lieutenant Arthur Tragg; and Brett Somers as Perry's receptionist, Gertie. Ernie Frankel and Art Seid, who had both been associated with the old *Perry Mason,* were the producers of the new version for 20th Century-Fox Television.

THE NEW PHIL SILVERS SHOW
CBS

28 SEPTEMBER 1963–27 JUNE 1964   Phil Silvers's "new" show was a lot like his "old" show, *You'll Never Get Rich.* In this half-hour sitcom he played Harry Grafton, a plant foreman for a large corporation. Always on the lookout for a get-rich-quick scheme, Grafton and his crew of stooges never seemed to find the elusive pot of gold. The cast also included: Stafford Repp as Grafton's boss, Mr. Brink; Jim Shane as Lester; Herbie Faye (who had also played one of the enlistees on *You'll Never Get Rich*) as Waluska; Steve Mitchell as Starkey; Bob Williams as Bob; Bud-

dy Lester as Nick; Pat Renella as Roxy; and Norm Grabowski as Grabowski. In February of 1964 three new cast members were added as Grafton moved in with his widowed sister: Elena Verdugo as his sister, Audrey; Sandy Descher as her daughter, Susan; and Ronnie Dapo as Andy, Audrey's son.

THE NEW SHMOO
NBC

22 SEPTEMBER 1979–1 DECEMBER 1979   Al Capp's amorphous cartoon creation came to Saturday morning television in this half-hour cartoon series. The Shmoo assisted three teenage journalists who investigated phenomena for Mighty Mysteries Comics. In December 1979 the show became part of the ninety-minute *Fred and Barney Meet the New Schmoo*.

THE NEW TEMPERATURES RISING SHOW
See TEMPERATURES RISING

THE NEW THREE STOOGES
SYNDICATED

1966   The cartoon adventures of the Three Stooges—Moe, Larry, and Curly. See also *The Skatebirds.*

THE NEW TIC TAC DOUGH
See TIC TAC DOUGH

THE NEW TREASURE HUNT
See TREASURE HUNT

THE NEW TRUTH OR CONSEQUENCES
See TRUTH OR CONSEQUENCES

NEW YORK CONFIDENTIAL
SYNDICATED

1959   Half-hour crime show starring Lee Tracy as crimefighting reporter Lee Cochran.

THE NEW YORK TIMES YOUTH FORUM
DUMONT

14 SEPTEMBER 1952–14 JUNE 1953   This Sunday-evening public affairs program for young people was produced by Al Hollander and moderated by Dorothy Gordon.

NEW ZOO REVUE
SYNDICATED

1972–1975   This half-hour children's show was seen daily in most markets. Created by Barbara Atlas and Douglas Momary (who also appeared as Doug), it introduced viewers to cultural and educational themes principally through musical numbers. Other cast members included Emily

Peden as Emily Jo; Yanco Inone as Freddie the Frog; Larri Thomas as Henrietta the Hippo; and Sharon Baird as Charlie the Owl. Stephen W. Jahn was the executive producer.

THE NEWCOMERS   CBS
12 JULY 1971–6 SEPTEMBER 1971   A summer replacement for *The Carol Burnett Show,* this lackluster variety hour was hosted by Dave Garroway and featured a group of young professionals: singers David Arlen, Cynthia Clawson, Raul Perez, Gay Perkins, Peggy Sears, and the Californians; comics Joey Garza, Rodney Winfield, and the Good Humor Company.

THE NEWLYWED GAME   ABC/SYNDICATED
11 JULY 1966–20 DECEMBER 1974 (ABC); 1977–   (SYNDICATED)   Bob Eubanks hosts this tasteless but highly successful game show on which four newly married couples compete for prizes. One set of spouses is sent offstage while the remaining set is asked questions and predicts the responses that the offstage spouses will make when asked the same question. Couples whose answers match win points. The durable series, which ran for eight years in a daytime slot, was also seen in prime time on occasion between 1967 and 1971 (it usually showed up as a midseason or summer replacement). The show is created by Chuck Barris, the man responsible for *The Dating Game* and *The Gong Show.*

THE NEWS AND ITS MEANING   CBS
27 AUGUST 1950–24 SEPTEMBER 1950   Five-week, Sunday-night news analysis series hosted by John Daly, who later became head of ABC's news division.

NEWSWEEK VIEWS THE NEWS   DUMONT
7 NOVEMBER 1948–22 MAY 1950   On this prime-time public affairs program, members of the board of editors of *Newsweek* magazine met to discuss the views and to interview guests. Ernest K. Lindley was the moderator. The show was originally titled *Newsweek Analysis.*

THE NEXT STEP BEYOND   SYNDICATED
1978   A revival of *One Step Beyond,* ABC's 1960s anthology series, *The Next Step Beyond* dwelt on the occult and the supernatural. John Newland returned as host and director, with Collier Young the executive producer, Alan J. Factor producer, and Merwin Gerard writer.

NICHOLS   NBC
16 SEPTEMBER 1971–1 AUGUST 1972   Set in Nichols, Arizona, in 1914, this lighthearted western starred James Garner as Nichols, a drifter who returned to his hometown and reluctantly became the sheriff; on the last

first-run episode, Nichols was killed, but was replaced by his twin brother. Also featured were Neva Patterson as Ma Ketcham; Margot Kidder as Ruth, the barmaid; John Beck as Ketcham, Ma's son, Ruth's boyfriend; Stuart Margolin as Mitchell, Nichols's deputy; and Paul Hampton as Johnson. Produced by Garner's company, Cherokee Productions, the show was officially titled *James Garner as Nichols* after October 1971.

THE NICK KENNY SHOW
NBC

18 JULY 1951–1 JANUARY 1952 Nick Kenny, radio editor for the New York *Mirror,* hosted a late-night, fifteen-minute series on which he read poetry, sang a few songs, and interviewed guests.

NIGHT COURT
SYNDICATED

1961 Half-hour courtroom drama show, with Jay Jostyn as the presiding judge of a big-city night court session.

NIGHT EDITOR
DUMONT

14 MARCH 1954–8 SEPTEMBER 1954 An unusual fifteen-minute show, *Night Editor* was a series of dramas written, narrated, and starring Hal Burdick. Burdick appeared as the night editor of a newspaper, and began to tell the evening's story; as the tale progressed, Burdick himself then acted out some of the segments as he narrated. Ward Byron produced the show, and Dick Sandwick directed it.

NIGHT GALLERY
NBC

16 DECEMBER 1970–14 JANUARY 1973 This anthology series of supernatural tales was introduced in 1970 as one segment of NBC's *Four-in-One.* In the fall of 1971 it was given its own slot. Rod Serling hosted the show from an art-gallery setting. In the fall of 1972 the show was cut back from sixty to thirty minutes, and *Night Gallery* vanished in the middle of its third season. Among the many directors who worked on the show was twenty-one-year-old Steven Spielberg, who later directed such colossal films as *Jaws* and *Close Encounters of the Third Kind.*

THE NIGHT STALKER
ABC

13 SEPTEMBER 1974–30 AUGUST 1975 This hour-long fantasy series starred Darren McGavin as Carl Kolchak, a gritty reporter for the Independent News Service who stalked a new and mysterious murderer each week, whether it be Jack the Ripper, a swamp monster, a vampire, a werewolf, or an invisible force. Also featured were Simon Oakland as Kolchak's disbelieving boss, Tony Vincenzo; Jack Grinnage as Ron Updyke, another reporter for I.N.S.; Ruth McDevitt as Emily Cowles, author of the advice-to-the-lovelorn column; John Fiedler as Gordy Spangler; and Carol Ann Susi as Monique Marmelstein. The series was ordered into production after two successful made-for-TV movies, "The

Night Stalker" (17 March 1972) and "The Night Strangler" (16 January 1973). Twenty one-hour episodes were filmed; Darren McGavin was executive producer, and Paul Playdon and Cy Chermak the producers.

NIGHTLIFE   ABC

8 MARCH 1965–12 NOVEMBER 1965   This late-night talk show was the successor to *The Les Crane Show,* ABC's first attempt to compete with NBC's Johnny Carson. The show featured a different guest host each week for the first few months, but by late June Les Crane was back in the host's chair, assisted by Nipsey Russell and the Elliott Lawrence Orchestra.

90 BRISTOL COURT   NBC

5 OCTOBER 1964–4 JANUARY 1965   *90 Bristol Court* was the umbrella title for three half-hour situation comedies, all set at the same apartment complex in Southern California, and all aired back-to-back on Mondays: *Karen; Tom, Dick and Mary;* and *Harris Against the World.* Guy Raymond was featured on all three shows as Cliff Murdock, the handyman. Produced by Revue Studios, it is probably not coincidental that the initials of the umbrella series were NBC. See also *Karen*; *Tom, Dick and Mary*; and *Harris Against the World.*

NO TIME FOR SERGEANTS   ABC

14 SEPTEMBER 1964–6 SEPTEMBER 1965   *No Time for Sergeants* was a half-hour sitcom based on the movie of the same title, which was based on the play of the same title, which was based on the television show of the same title broadcast on *The U.S. Steel Hour* 15 March 1955 (it starred Andy Griffith, who repeated his role on stage and on film). The television series starred Sammy Jackson as Private Will Stockdale, a Southern lad assigned to Andrews Air Force Base. Also featured were Kevin O'Neal as Private Ben Whitledge; Harry Hickox as Sergeant King; Hayden Rorke as Colonel Farnsworth; Paul Smith as Captain Martin; Laurie Sibbald as Milly Anderson, Stockdale's girlfriend; Andy Clyde as Grandpa Jim Anderson, Milly's grandfather; Michael McDonald as Private Langdon; George Murdock as Krupnick; Greg Benedict as Private Blanchard; and Joey Tata as Private Neddick. The Warner Brothers series, as well as the film, the play, and the original telecast, were all based on Mac Hyman's story.

NO WARNING!   NBC

6 APRIL 1958–7 SEPTEMBER 1958   *No Warning!* was the title given to this series of half-hour suspense dramas produced by Al Simon. Simon had produced a similar series the preceding season, entitled *Panic!,* and nine *Panic!* episodes were rerun on *No Warning!* along with fourteen originals. Westbrook Van Voorhis returned as host and narrator.

NOAH'S ARK NBC

18 SEPTEMBER 1956–26 FEBRUARY 1957 Jack Webb produced this half-hour dramatic series about a pair of veterinarians. It featured Paul Burke as young Dr. Noah McCann; Vic Rodman as Dr. Sam Rinehart, Noah's mentor, who was confined to a wheelchair; and May Winn as their receptionist and nurse, Liz Clark. The series was filmed in color.

NORBY NBC

5 JANUARY 1955–6 APRIL 1955 This half-hour sitcom starred David Wayne as Pearson Norby, vice president of the First National Bank in Pearl River, New York. Also featured were Joan Lorring as his wife, Helen Norby; Susan Hallaran as their daughter, Diane; Evan Elliott as their son, Hank; Paul Ford as the bank president; Ralph Dunn as another vice president; Janice Mars as the switchboard operator; and Carol Veazie as Maude Endless. Created by David Swift, the series was the first television show sponsored by Eastman Kodak. It was filmed in color, and exteriors were actually shot in Pearl River, New York. The show's time slot (Wednesdays at 7 p.m., a slot which relatively few network affiliates made available for network broadcasts) was probably the chief factor behind its early cancellation.

NORMAN CORWIN PRESENTS SYNDICATED

1971 Half-hour dramatic anthology series produced and hosted by Norman Corwin, one of radio's most prolific writers and directors.

NORTHWEST PASSAGE NBC

14 SEPTEMBER 1958–8 SEPTEMBER 1959 This half-hour adventure series told the story of Rogers' Rangers during the French and Indian War. Set in upstate (or upcolony) New York in 1754, it starred Keith Larsen as Major Robert Rogers; Buddy Ebsen as Sergeant Hunk Marriner; and Don Burnett as Ensign Towne. The show was produced by MGM TV.

NOT FOR HIRE SYNDICATED

1959 Set in Hawaii, this half-hour crime show starred Ralph Meeker as Sergeant Steve Dekker, a criminal investigator for the United States Army. Also featured were Norman Alden, Ken Drake, and Herb Ellis. John Florea produced and directed.

NOT FOR PUBLICATION DUMONT

27 APRIL 1951–27 AUGUST 1951; 21 DECEMBER 1951–27 MAY 1952 William Adler first starred in this dramatic series as Collins, an investigative reporter for the New York *Ledger*. When the show began in April of 1951, it was a fifteen-minute series, but it returned to the air in December in a half-hour format, with Jerome Cowan as Collins.

NOT FOR WOMEN ONLY   SYNDICATED

1971–   Half-hour daytime talk show. First hosted by Barbara
Walters, the show began as a local show in New York, titled *For Women
Only.* Hugh Downs later became cohost, and in 1976 Polly Bergen and
Frank Field took over as cohosts.

NOTHING BUT THE BEST   NBC

7 JULY 1953–13 SEPTEMBER 1953   Eddie Albert hosted this half-hour
summer variety series.

NOTRE DAME FOOTBALL   ABC

27 SEPTEMBER 1953–29 NOVEMBER 1953   Broadcast Sunday nights,
this seventy-five-minute series consisted of films of the previous day's
football game between Notre Dame and its opponent. Harry Wismer did
the play-by-play.

NOVA   PBS

3 MARCH 1974–   High-quality series of filmed documentaries on scientific subjects. Produced at WGBH-TV, Boston, the show receives the cooperation of the American Association for the Advancement
of Science. Most programs are sixty minutes, though some ninety-minute
shows have been aired.

NOW AND THEN   CBS

1 AUGUST 1954–5 SEPTEMBER 1954; 16 JANUARY 1955–26 JUNE 1955
Dr. Frank Baxter, professor of English literature at the University of
Southern California, hosted this half-hour Sunday afternoon series of lectures on literature. The show was first televised locally in Los Angeles,
and at that time USC offered college credit for the televised course. Dr.
Baxter later hosted many television documentaries, including the highly
acclaimed "Bell Science Series."

NOW YOU SEE IT   CBS

1 APRIL 1974–13 JUNE 1975   On this daytime game show contestants
tried to find words hidden within a grid of letters. Jack Narz hosted the
show, and Frank Wayne (who created it) was the executive producer for
Goodson-Todman Productions.

NUMBER PLEASE   ABC

31 JANUARY 1961–29 DECEMBER 1961   Hosted by Bud Collyer, this
daytime game show was similar to the word game, Hangman. The show
was a Goodson-Todman production.

THE NURSES   CBS

27 SEPTEMBER 1962–7 SEPTEMBER 1965   This hour-long medical drama was produced in New York by Herbert Brodkin. It starred Shirl Con-

way as Nurse Liz Thorpe, a supervising nurse at Alden Hospital; Zina Bethune as Nurse Gail Lucas, new to the job; Edward Binns as Dr. Kiley; and Stephen Brooks as Dr. Lowry. In the fall of 1964 two new male leads were signed to beef up the show, and the show's title was changed to *The Doctors and the Nurses*. Joining the cast were Michael Tolan as Dr. Alexander Tazinski and Joseph Campanella as Dr. Ted Steffen. Alan Alda made a rare guest appearance on the series ("Many a Sullivan," 17 January 1963), as did Dustin Hoffman ("The Heroine," 4 May 1965). A daytime serial based on the show ran on ABC beginning in 1965 (see below).

THE NURSES
ABC

27 SEPTEMBER 1965–31 MARCH 1967 This half-hour daytime serial was based on the prime-time series of the same title. The cast included: Mary Fickett as Nurse Liz Thorpe; Melinda Plank as Nurse Gail Lucas; Carol Gainer as Donna; Patricia Hyland as Brenda; Judson Laire as Jaimie MacLeod; Mimi Turque as Sandy Feigin; Polly Rowles as Mrs. Grossberg; Darryl Wells as Mike; Arthur Franz as Hugh; Nicholas Pryor as Ken; Dick McMurray as Jake; Sally Gracie as Pat; Joan Wetmore as Martha; and Nat Polen as Dr. Crager.

THE O. HENRY PLAYHOUSE
SYNDICATED

1957 The works of O. Henry (the pen name of William Sidney Porter) were the subjects of this half-hour dramatic anthology series, hosted by Thomas Mitchell as O. Henry.

O. K. CRACKERBY!
ABC

16 SEPTEMBER 1965–6 JANUARY 1966 Created by Cleveland Amory and Abe Burrows, this half-hour sitcom starred Burl Ives as O. K. Crackerby, a folksy Oklahoman who happened to be the richest man in the world. Also featured were Hal Buckley as St. John Quincy, the Harvard-educated tutor to widower Crackerby's children; Joel Davison as O. K.'s son Hobart; Brooke Adams as O. K.'s daughter Cynthia; Brian Corcoran as O. K., Jr.; Laraine Stephens as Susan Wentworth; and Dick Foran as Slim.

O. S. S.
ABC

26 SEPTEMBER 1957–17 MARCH 1958 Stories on this half-hour spy series were gleaned from the files of the O.S.S. (Office of Strategic Services), the American intelligence unit active during World War II. Produced in England by former O.S.S. officer William Eliscu, the half-hour series starred Ron Randell as Captain Frank Hawthorn and Lionel Murton as The Chief.

THE OBJECT IS   ABC
30 DECEMBER 1963–27 MARCH 1964   Dick Clark hosted this daytime
game show on which a panel of six, including three celebrities and three
studio contestants, tried to identify the names of famous personalities
from "object" clues.

OCCASIONAL WIFE   NBC
13 SEPTEMBER 1966–29 AUGUST 1967   Half-hour sitcom from Screen
Gems about a young bachelor who landed a job with a company that
hired only married men; to overcome the obstacle, he arranged with another tenant in his apartment building, a female art student, to pose as his
wife when needed. With Michael Callan as Peter Christopher; Patricia
Harty as Greta Patterson; Jack Collins as Peter's boss, Mr. Brahms,
president of Brahms Baby Food Company; Joan Tompkins as Mrs.
Brahms; and Bryan O'Byrne as Man-in-Middle, the unlucky tenant
whose apartment was between Peter's seventh-floor place and Greta's
ninth-floor pad. Sara Seegar was occasionally featured as Peter's mother,
and Vince Scully narrated the episodes.

THE ODD COUPLE   ABC
24 SEPTEMBER 1970–4 JULY 1975   Based on Neil Simon's play, this
half-hour sitcom told the story of a fastidious photographer who shared
an apartment with a sloppy sportswriter; the two men had been childhood friends and had renewed their acquaintance after their respective
divorces. With Tony Randall as tidy Felix Unger; Jack Klugman as
messy Oscar Madison. The only other regular who remained with the
show for its entire run was Al Molinaro as one of their poker-playing
pals, Murray Greshler, a New York cop. Others who came and went included Garry Walberg, Ryan MacDonald, and Larry Gelman as poker
pals Speed, Roy, and Vinnie; Monica Evans and Carole Shelley as Cecily
and Gwen Pigeon, their daffy neighbors for the first half of the first season; Joan Hotchkis as Oscar's first female friend, Dr. Nancy Cunningham; Elinor Donahue (1972–1975) as Miriam Welby, their neighbor and
Felix's female friend; Penny Marshall (1973–1975) as Myrna Werner, Oscar's secretary; Brett Somers (Jack Klugman's real-life wife) as Blanche,
Oscar's ex-wife; and Janis Hansen as Gloria, Felix's ex-wife. Garry Marshall and Sheldon Keller were the executive producers of the series for
Paramount Television. A cartoon version of the show also ran for one
season: see *The Oddball Couple*.

THE ODDBALL COUPLE   ABC
6 SEPTEMBER 1975–3 SEPTEMBER 1977   This Saturday-morning cartoon show was inspired by *The Odd Couple;* its central characters were
Spiffy, a neat cat, and Fleabag, a messy dog, who shared an office as re-

porters. Produced by David H. DePatie and Friz Freleng, the show consisted entirely of reruns during its second season.

ODYSSEY
CBS

6 JANUARY 1957–2 JUNE 1957   This half-hour educational series for children was seen Sunday afternoons. Hosted by CBS newsman Charles Collingwood, it was filmed on location throughout the country and was produced in cooperation with local museums and historical societies; the premiere telecast, for example, was based in Virginia City, Nevada, and told the story of the Comstock Lode. Irving Gitlin was the executive producer, and Fred Freed was script editor for most of the show's run.

OF ALL THINGS
CBS

23 JULY 1956–24 AUGUST 1956   This daytime variety show was a summer replacement for *The Garry Moore Show*. It was hosted by Faye Emerson and featured singers Ilene Woods and Jack Haskell.

OF LANDS AND SEAS
SYNDICATED

1969   Travelogue, hosted by Colonel John D. Craig.

OF MANY THINGS
ABC

5 OCTOBER 1953–11 JANUARY 1954   Half-hour panel discussion show hosted by Dr. Bergen Evans. The series was not carried regularly by ABC's New York affiliate.

OFF TO SEE THE WIZARD
ABC

8 SEPTEMBER 1967–20 SEPTEMBER 1968   This prime-time hour was an anthology series of films for children. It was hosted by cartoon characters from *The Wizard of Oz*. Though the series only lasted a year, ABC revived the concept of a children's anthology show in the 1970s when it introduced *The ABC Afterschool Special*.

OFFICIAL DETECTIVE
SYNDICATED

1957   Produced in cooperation with *Official Detective* magazine, this half-hour crime show was based on the radio series that began in 1946. Everett Sloane hosted the anthology show on television.

OH, BOY!
ABC

16 JULY 1959–3 SEPTEMBER 1959   This British pop music show was imported by ABC for a brief summer run. Regularly featured were such early British rockers as Cliff Richard and Marty Wilde, and one of the 1959 guest stars was Tony Sheridan, who subsequently recorded several sides with the Beatles. Tony Hall hosted the series, and music was supplied by the house band, Lord Rockingham's XI, under the direction of Harry

Robinson. The half-hour series was produced by Jack Good, who later helped develop ABC's American rock series, *Shindig*. Apparently, *Oh, Boy!* was something less than a smash in this country; reviewing it for the New York *Herald Tribune*, critic Sid Bakal described it as "an appalling piece of trash."

OH, KAY! ABC

24 FEBRUARY 1951–18 AUGUST 1951 This half-hour variety show was broadcast live from Chicago on Saturday mornings. It was hosted by Kay Westfall and featured Jim Dimitri and David LeWinter. Dan Schuffman produced and directed it.

OH! SUSANNA CBS/ABC

29 SEPTEMBER 1956–11 APRIL 1959 (CBS); 1 OCTOBER 1959–24 MARCH 1960 (ABC) Half-hour sitcom starring Gale Storm as Susanna Pomeroy, social director of the S.S. *Ocean Queen*, a cruise ship. Also featured were ZaSu Pitts as her cohort, Elvira (Nugey) Nugent, the ship's beautician; Roy Roberts as Captain Huxley; James Fairfax as Cedric, the first mate; Ray Montgomery as the ship's doctor; and Joe Cranston as the purser. Created by Lee Karson, the series was produced by Hal Roach, Jr. The series was titled *Oh! Susanna* during its first two seasons on CBS; in the fall of 1958 it was retitled *The Gale Storm Show*. Ninety-nine episodes were shown on CBS between 1956 and 1959; in the spring of 1959 ABC acquired the rights to the show and began showing reruns in the daytime; an additional twenty-six first-run episodes were telecast in prime time on ABC during the 1959–1960 season.

OH, THOSE BELLS! CBS

8 MARCH 1962–31 MAY 1962 This half-hour sitcom starred the Wiere brothers (Herbert, Harry, and Sylvester), a German-born comedy trio, as Herbert, Harry, and Sylvester Bell, three employees at a Hollywood theatrical supply house. Also featured were Henry Norell as their boss, Mr. Slocum; Carol Byron as Kitty, the secretary; and Reta Shaw as the Bells's landlady. Ben Brady produced the series of thirteen episodes, which were filmed in 1960.

O'HARA, UNITED STATES TREASURY CBS

17 SEPTEMBER 1971–8 SEPTEMBER 1972 Jack Webb produced this hour-long crime show, which starred David Janssen as Treasury Agent Jim O'Hara.

OKAY MOTHER DUMONT

1 NOVEMBER 1948–6 JULY 1951 One of TV's first daytime shows, *Okay Mother* was an audience participation and variety show hosted by Dennis James.

THE OLD AMERICAN BARN DANCE   DUMONT
5 JULY 1953–13 SEPTEMBER 1953   Bill Bailey hosted this half-hour
country and western music show. Among the regulars were Pee Wee
King and Tennessee Ernie Ford (who was billed merely as Tennessee
Ernie).

OLD FASHIONED MEETING   ABC
8 OCTOBER 1950–1 APRIL 1951   Half-hour Sunday-night religious series.

OLDSMOBILE MUSIC THEATRE   NBC
26 MARCH 1959–7 MAY 1959   Bill Hayes and Florence Henderson cohosted this live, half-hour anthology series. Most presentations were
musicals.

THE OLDSMOBILE SHOW
See THE PATTI PAGE SHOW

THE OLD-TIME GOSPEL HOUR
See JERRY FALWELL

OMNIBUS   CBS/ABC/NBC
9 NOVEMBER 1952–1 APRIL 1956 (CBS); 7 OCTOBER 1956–31 MARCH
1957 (ABC); 20 OCTOBER 1957–10 MAY 1959 (NBC)   *Omnibus* was the
first major television project underwritten by the Ford Foundation,
which in turn offered the show to commercial advertisers. During its seven-year run it was carried by each of the three main commercial networks
and was usually telecast Sunday afternoons. Hosted by Alistair Cooke,
British by birth but American by choice, the aptly titled series presented
everything from dramas to musicals to documentaries; each program
usually contained several segments. Presentations during the first season
included James Agee's "Mr. Lincoln," a continuing story that starred
Royal Dano as Abraham Lincoln; three Maxwell Anderson plays; Chek-
hov's "The Bear," with June Havoc and Michael Redgrave (4 January);
"Die Fledermaus," with Eugene Ormandy conducting the Metropolitan
Opera Orchestra (1 February); Agnes DeMille's ballet, "Three Virgins
and the Devil" (broadcast 22 March, the title was changed, at network
insistence, to "Three Maidens and the Devil"); and Shaw's "Arms and
the Man," with Nanette Fabray and Jean-Pierre Aumont (3 May). A
small sample of highlights from later seasons would include selections
from the Broadway hit "Oklahoma!" by the original cast (4 October
1953); "King Lear," with Orson Welles in his television dramatic debut
(18 October 1953); concerts conducted by Leonard Bernstein (frequent
throughout the 1954–1955 and 1955–1956 seasons); documentary films
from undersea explorer Jacques Cousteau (featured during the 1956–
1957 season); "Oedipus Rex," with Christopher Plummer (6 January

1957); "The Empty Chair," with George C. Scott and Peter Ustinov (7 December 1958); and Gilbert and Sullivan's "H.M.S. Pinafore," with Cyril Ritchard (10 May 1959). *Omnibus* was first produced by Robert Saudek and was later produced by Fred Rickey. A few additional programs were televised on NBC during the 1960–1961 season on an irregular basis.

ON BROADWAY TONIGHT   CBS
8 JULY 1964–16 SEPTEMBER 1964; 1 JANUARY 1965–12 MARCH 1965
Hour-long variety show hosted by Rudy Vallee; promising young professionals were regularly featured. Irving Mansfield produced the series, which was introduced as a summer replacement for *The Danny Kaye Show*.

ON GUARD   ABC
28 APRIL 1952–29 MAY 1954   A series of half-hour documentary films on America's armed forces, *On Guard* was one of several "filler" shows scheduled by ABC during the 1950s. Few of the network's affiliates bothered to carry such dry programming, opting instead to carry a syndicated or locally produced show during the time slot when series like *On Guard* were offered.

ON OUR OWN   CBS
9 OCTOBER 1977–20 AUGUST 1978   Half-hour sitcom about two young women who shared an apartment and worked at a Manhattan advertising agency. With Lynnie Greene as Maria Teresa Bonino; Bess Armstrong as her coworker and roommate, Julia Peters; Gretchen Wyler as their boss at Bedford Advertising, Toni McBain; Dixie Carter as copywriter April Baxter; Dan Resin as salesman Craig Boatwright; and John Christopher Jones as producer Eddie Barnes. David Susskind was the executive producer of the series, which was created by Bob Randall and produced by Sam Denoff. *On Our Own* was the only prime-time dramatic series produced in New York during the 1977–1978 season.

ON PARADE   NBC
24 JULY 1964–18 SEPTEMBER 1964   This half-hour variety series, which had no regulars, was produced in Canada by Norman Sawdawie.

ON STAGE   SYNDICATED
1970–1972   This Canadian-produced hour-long anthology series was also seen in the United States; some shows were aired on NBC as specials.

ON THE BOARDWALK ABC

30 MAY 1954–1 AUGUST 1954 Broadcast from Steel Pier in Atlantic City, New Jersey, this talent show was hosted by bandleader Paul Whiteman.

ON THE GO CBS

27 APRIL 1959–8 JULY 1960 Jack Linkletter, son of Art Linkletter, hosted this daytime variety show from locations throughout the country. The videotaped half-hour series was produced by William Kayden.

ON THE LINE WITH CONSIDINE

See THE BOB CONSIDINE SHOW

ON THE ROCKS ABC

11 SEPTEMBER 1975–17 MAY 1976 Based on a British sitcom entitled *Porridge*, this half-hour series was set at Alamesa Prison. The show stirred some controversy late in 1975, when the National Association for Justice asked ABC to cancel the series on the grounds that it painted too rosy a picture of prison life. The network refused to cancel the program at that time, and it was later reported that the show was a hit at many real-life prisons. The show starred José Perez as inmate Hector Fuentes; Bobby Sandler as Nicky Palik; Hal Williams as DeMott; Rick Hurst as Cleaver; Jack Grimes as Baxter; Mel Stewart as Mr. Gibson, one of the officers; Tom Poston as Mr. Sullivan, another officer; and Logan Ramsey as The Warden. Created by Dick Clement and Ian La Frenais, the series was produced by John Rich.

ON TRIAL ABC

22 NOVEMBER 1948–1 JULY 1952 On the first of the two series titled *On Trial,* issues of public importance were formally debated each week.

ON TRIAL NBC

14 SEPTEMBER 1956–13 SEPTEMBER 1957 The second of the two series titled *On Trial* was an anthology series of courtroom dramas, hosted by (and occasionally starring) Joseph Cotten. In March 1957 the series was retitled *The Joseph Cotten Show.*

ON YOUR ACCOUNT NBC/CBS

8 JUNE 1953–2 JULY 1954 (NBC); 5 JULY 1954–30 MARCH 1956 (CBS) This daytime game show was similar to *Strike It Rich* and *Queen for a Day:* Contestants related their hard-luck stories to a panel, which selected the most deserving candidate at the end of the show. The contestants also earned money by answering questions. The half-hour series was hosted at various times by Eddie Albert, Dennis James, and Win Elliott.

ON YOUR MARK   ABC
23 SEPTEMBER 1961–30 DECEMBER 1961   This Saturday-morning game
show for children was hosted by Sonny Fox, with help from Johnny Olsen. Lloyd Gross produced and directed it.

ON YOUR WAY   DUMONT/ABC
9 SEPTEMBER 1953–20 JANUARY 1954 (DUMONT); 23 JANUARY 1954–
17 APRIL 1954 (ABC)   This nighttime game show began as a quiz show
and was first hosted by Bud Collyer. The premise of the show was that
the contestants were trying to go somewhere; the contestant who answered the most questions correctly won a trip to his or her destination.
When the show switched networks in 1954, it also changed formats and
hosts: John Reed King and Kathy Godfrey (sister of Arthur Godfrey) cohosted the show on ABC, and the quiz format was scrapped in favor of a
talent contest.

ONCE UPON A CLASSIC   PBS
9 OCTOBER 1976–   Half-hour dramatic anthology series for
children, which has presented original stories as well as adaptations of
classic tales.

ONCE UPON A TUNE   DUMONT
6 MARCH 1951–15 MAY 1951   This hour-long series presented original
musicals. Bob Loewi was the producer and Sid Frank the writer.

ONE DAY AT A TIME   CBS
16 DECEMBER 1975–   Half-hour sitcom, set in Indianapolis,
about a recently divorced woman trying to raise two teenaged daughters.
With Bonnie Franklin as divorcée Ann Romano, who works at an ad
agency; Mackenzie Phillips as elder daughter Julie Cooper; Valerie Bertinelli as younger daughter Barbara Cooper; Pat Harrington as macho
Dwayne Schneider, superintendent of their apartment building; Richard
Masur (to November 1976) as lawyer and neighbor David Kane, Ann's
sometime boyfriend; and Mary Louise Wilson (1976–1977) as neighbor
Ginny Wrobliki, a brassy cocktail waitress. Created by Whitney Blake
and Allan Manings, the show was developed by Norman Lear. Mort
Lachman and Lila Garrett were the executive producers during the first
season and were succeeded in 1976 by Norman Paul and Jack Elinson.
Dick Bensfield and Perry Grant are the producers, and the show's theme
was composed by Jeff Barry and Nancy Barry. In the fall of 1979 Michael
Lembeck costarred as Julie's husband, Max Horvath, a flight attendant.

THE $1.98 BEAUTY CONTEST
See THE $1.98 BEAUTY CONTEST under *dollar*

ONE HAPPY FAMILY   NBC
13 JANUARY 1961–15 SEPTEMBER 1961   Half-hour sitcom about three
generations living under one roof. With Dick Sargent and Jody Warner
as newlyweds Dick and Penny Cooper; Chick Chandler and Elisabeth
Fraser as Penny's parents, Barney and Mildred Hogan; and Jack Kirkwood and Cheerio Meredith as Charley and Lovey Hackett, Penny's
grandparents.

100 GRAND   ABC
15 SEPTEMBER 1963–29 SEPTEMBER 1963   One of the shortest-lived
game shows in TV history, *100 Grand* was axed after only three airings.
Jack Clark hosted the big money, prime-time show, on which an amateur
faced a panel of experts and tried to answer questions posed by them.

THE $100,000 BIG SURPRISE
See THE BIG SURPRISE

THE $100,000 NAME THAT TUNE
See NAME THAT TUNE

THE $128,000 QUESTION   SYNDICATED
1976–1978   *The $128,000 Question* was a remake of the big-money game
show of the 1950s, *The $64,000 Question*, presumably adjusted for infla-
tion. Like the old show, the new version featured contestants who were
experts in a particular field of knowledge. Contestants started at the $64
level, and by answering successive questions correctly, could double their
money up to $512. The next question was worth $1,000, and the values of
the remaining questions again doubled, up to the limit of $128,000. Mike
Darrow hosted the show during its first season and was succeeded by
Alex Trebek in 1977. Steve Carlin was the executive producer. See also
The $64,000 Question.

ONE IN A MILLION   ABC
3 APRIL 1967–16 JUNE 1967   Danny O'Neil hosted this short-lived daytime game show on which contestants tried to guess the unusual secrets
held in common by a guest panel.

ONE LIFE TO LIVE   ABC
15 JULY 1968–   This daytime serial was created by Agnes
Nixon, who served her apprenticeship on Irna Phillips's *The Guiding
Light* and *As the World Turns,* and who later created *All My Children.*
Set in the suburban town of Llanview, *One Life to Live* stressed ethnic situations from the beginning—Jews, WASP's, Poles, and blacks are all well
represented. One story line was taped on location at New York's Odyssey

House, a drug rehabilitation center. Sold by Nixon to ABC, *One Life to Live* has been produced by Doris Quinlan, and Gordon Russell has been the head writer. The show expanded from thirty to forty-five minutes on 26 July 1976, and expanded again to sixty minutes on 16 January 1978. The cast has included: Ernest Graves and Shepperd Strudwick as widower Victor Lord, a newspaper publisher; Gillian Spencer (1968–1971) and Erika Slezak (1971–   ) as his daughter, Victoria Lord (Vicky was a split personality for a time and her *alter ego* was Nikki Smith); Trish Van Devere and Lynn Benesch as his daughter, Meredith Lord, who died after being surprised by a burglar; Lee Patterson as reporter Joe Riley, who married Vicky (they were later divorced and subsequently remarried); Patricia Rose and Alice Hirson as Eileen Riley Siegel, Joe's sister; Allan Miller as lawyer Dave Siegel, Eileen's husband, who died of a heart attack; Lee Warrick and Leonie Norton as their daughter, Julie Siegel; Bill Fowler and Tom Berenger as their son, Timmy Siegel, who died in a fall; David Snell and Jack Ryland as Julie's boyfriend, Jack Lawson; Doris Belack (1968–1977) and Kathleen Maguire (1977–   ) as Anna Wolek; Antony Ponzini (1968–1975), Jordan Charney (1975–1977) and Michael Ingram (1977–   ) as Anna's brother, Vince Wolek; Paul Tulley, James Storm, and Michael Storm (brother of James Storm) as Anna's brother, Dr. Larry Wolek, whose second wife was Meredith Lord; Niki Flacks, Kathryn Breech, and Judith Light as nurse Karen Martin, Larry Wolek's first wife; Terry Logan as murder victim Dr. Ted Hale; Joe Gallison (1968–1970) as Tom Edwards; Jan Chasmar as Amy, an orphan; Justin McDonough as District Attorney Bill Kimbrough; Donald Moffat and Norman Rose as Dr. Marcus Polk, who cured Vicky Lord's personality disorder; Ellen Holly as Carla Gray, a light-skinned black who tried to pass for white (and called herself Carla Benari), but later married a black police officer; Lillian Hayman as Sadie Gray, Carla's mother; Peter DeAnda as Dr. Pryce Trainor, a black physician who was interested in Carla; Robert Milli and Nat Polen as Dr. James Craig, a white physician who was also interested in Carla, but later married Anna Wolek; Cathy Burns, Amy Levitt, Jane Alice Brandon, Dorrie Kavanaugh, and Jennifer Harmon (1975–   ) as Cathy Craig, daughter of James Craig, who became involved with drugs; John Cullum as Artie Duncan, who was murdered by the drug-crazed Cathy; Bernie Grant as Steve Burke, who married Vicky Lord Riley (Vicky thought her first husband, Joe, had been killed in a car crash, but he later turned up alive and remarried Vicky); Millee Taggart as Millie Parks; Francesca James as murder victim Marcy Wade; Jack Crowder as Lieutenant Jack Neal; Tom Lee Jones as Dr. Mark Toland, who married Julie Siegel; Marilyn Chris and Lee Lawson as waitress Wanda Webb, who wed Vince Wolek; Katherine Glass as Jenny Wolek, a novitiate nun who left her order to marry Timmy Siegel just before his death; Nancy Pinkerton (to 1977) and Claire Malis (1977–   ) as Dr. Dorian Cramer, who married Victor

Lord; Al Freeman, Jr., as Lieutenant Ed Hall, who married Carla Gray; Laurence Fishburne as Joshua West, a youngster adopted by Ed and Carla; George Reinholt (1975–1977) and Philip MacHale (1977–   ) as Victor Lord's long-lost illegitimate son, Tony Harris; Jacquie Courtney (1975–   ) as Pat Kendall; Stephen Austin as Brian Kendall, illegitimate son of Tony and Pat; Neail Holland and Eddie Moran as young Danny Wolek, son of Larry and Meredith; Lisa Richards as Susan Barry; Donald Madden as John Douglas; Rod Browning as Ben Farmer; Lani Miyazaki as Michiko; Herb Davis as Bert Skelly; Christine Jones as Sheila Rafferty; Patricia Pearcy and Jane Badler as Melinda Cramer; Jeffrey Pomerantz as Dr. Peter Janssen; Farley Granger (1976–1977) and Anthony George (1977–   ) as Dr. Will Vernon; Teri Keane as Naomi Vernon; Jameson Parker as Brad Vernon; Julie Montgomery as Samantha Vernon; Vance Jeffries as Matthew McAllister; Morgan Melis as Kevin Riley; Roger Rathburn as Alan Bennett; Jackie Zeman as Lana McLain; Gerald Anthony as Marco Dane; Kathleen Devine as Pamela Shepard; Tom Fuccello as Paul Kendall; Stuart Germain as Ethan Allen Bottomly; Sally Gracie as Ina Hopkins; Margaret Klenck as Edwina Lewis; David Reilly as Richard Abbott; Jill Voight as Rebecca Lee Hunt; Marshall Borden as Luke Jackson; Arthur Burghardt as Dr. Jack Scott; Byron Sanders as Talbot Huddleston; Andrea Evans as Tina Clayton; Stephen Bolster as Roger Landover; Joan Copeland as Gwendolyn Abbott; Linda Dano as Gretel Cummings; Paul Joynt as Greg Huddleston; John Mansfield as Adam Brewster; Lori March as Mrs. Huddleston; Nancy Snyder as Katrina.

Guest stars on *One Life to Live* have included Dr. Joyce Brothers (as herself), Walter Slezak (as Laszlo Braedeker, godfather of Vicky Lord, who was played by his real-life daughter), and John Beradino (repeating his *General Hospital* role as Dr. Steve Hardy).

ONE MAN'S EXPERIENCE   DUMONT

6 OCTOBER 1952–10 APRIL 1953   Literary classics—those that depicted the struggles of men—were serialized each week on this fifteen-minute daytime show. When the series began in 1952, it was telecast back to back with a female-oriented series, *One Woman's Experience.* Early in 1953 the title was changed to *One Man's Story,* and the series was seen on an alternating basis with *One Woman's Story.*

ONE MAN'S FAMILY   NBC

4 NOVEMBER 1949–21 JUNE 1952; 1 MARCH 1954–1 APRIL 1955   Created by Carleton E. Morse, *One Man's Family* was one of radio's most popular continuing dramas; its twenty-seven-year run began in 1932. The show twice came to television, but neither version was particularly popular. The first version was a prime-time show; the cast included Bert Lytell as Henry Barbour, head of the clan, a wealthy stockbroker who lived in

San Francisco's Sea Cliff area; Marjorie Gateson as his wife, Frances (Fanny) Barbour; Russell Thorsen as Paul, the eldest of their five children, a writer and aviator; Patricia Robbins and Lillian Schaaf as their daughter Hazel; Nancy Franklin and Eva Marie Saint as their daughter Claudia; Billy Idelson and James Lee as their son Clifford, Claudia's twin; Arthur Casell and Robert Wigginton as their son Jack; Walter Brooke as Hazel's husband, Bill Herbert; Susan Shaw as Beth Holly, Paul's female friend; Madaline Belgard as Teddy Lawton, Paul's adopted daughter; Tony Randall as Mac; Jim Boles as Joe. In the fall of 1951 at least one member of the Barbour clan was shown pregnant; this pregnancy, which predated Lucy Ricardo's on *I Love Lucy,* was probably the first involving a continuing character on a prime-time television series. The show, which was done live, was also the first NBC series to use rear-screen projection. In the spring of 1954 the show returned to TV as a daily fifteen-minute serial. At that time the cast included Theodore van Eltz as Henry; Mary Adams as Fanny; Linda Leighton as Hazel; Anne Whitfield as Claudia; Martin Dean as Jack; Jack Edwards as Johnny Roberts, Claudia's boyfriend; and Emerson Treacy as Dr. Thompson.

ONE MINUTE PLEASE   DUMONT
6 JULY 1954–17 FEBRUARY 1955   John K. M. McCaffery first hosted this prime-time game show, based on a British series, on which celebrity panelists were required to extemporize for sixty seconds on a given subject. Allyn Edwards succeeded McCaffery in November 1954.

ONE OF A KIND   CBS
12 JANUARY 1964–29 MARCH 1964   Harry Reasoner hosted this Sunday-afternoon series of twelve filmed documentaries on subjects of general interest.

ONE STEP BEYOND   ABC
20 JANUARY 1959–3 OCTOBER 1961   John Newland directed and hosted this anthology series of tales of the occult and supernatural; the stories were said to have been based on true incidents. Sponsored by Alcoa, the series was also titled *Alcoa Presents.* A total of ninety-four half-hour episodes were filmed, with Collier Young as producer. Merwin Gerard created the series. In 1978 Newland, Young, and Gerard again combined forces to produce a syndicated successor: see *The Next Step Beyond.*

1,2,3—GO!   NBC
8 OCTOBER 1961–27 MAY 1962   This educational series for children was seen early on Sunday evenings. Each week cohosts Jack Lescoulie and ten-year-old Richard Thomas (who would star in *The Waltons* eleven years later) explored subjects of interest to young people. Irving Gitlin produced the half-hour series.

ONE WOMAN'S EXPERIENCE   DUMONT
6 OCTOBER 1952–3 APRIL 1953   This fifteen-minute daytime show serialized classics from literature that emphasized the stories of women. It
was introduced in 1952 together with its counterpart, *One Man's Experience;* early in 1953 the shows' titles were changed to *One Man's Story* and
One Woman's Story, and the two were seen on an alternating basis.

THE O'NEILLS   DUMONT
6 SEPTEMBER 1949–10 JANUARY 1950   A once-a-week serial, *The
O'Neills* was a short-lived TV version of the radio soap opera that ran
from 1934 to 1943. It featured Vera Allen as Mrs. O'Neill, a widow; Ian
Martin as Uncle Bill; Janice Gilbert as Mrs. O'Neill's daughter, Peggy;
Michael Lauson as son Danny O'Neill; Ben Fishbein as family friend
Morris Levy, a hardware dealer in the town of Royalton; and Celia Bud-
kin as his wife, Trudy Levy.

OPEN END
See THE DAVID SUSSKIND SHOW

OPEN HEARING   ABC
1 FEBRUARY 1954–1 JULY 1954; 3 FEBRUARY 1957–4 SEPTEMBER
1960   John Secondari was the host and moderator of this half-hour public affairs program; it was seen on Sunday afternoons during most of its
run, though it surfaced in prime time during the 1957–1958 season.

OPERA CAMEOS   DUMONT
8 NOVEMBER 1953–9 JANUARY 1955   Excerpts from operas were presented on this half-hour series. Giovanni Martinelli was the host and narrator of the series, which began as a local show in New York in 1950.

OPERA VS. JAZZ   ABC
25 MAY 1953–21 SEPTEMBER 1953   Though billed as a "symposium,"
this half-hour series featured little in the way of debate or discussion on
jazz or classical music, but instead presented selections from the two
genres. Nancy Kenyon was the host, or "moderator," of the series, and
Alan Dale and Jan Peerce were regularly featured. Fred Heider produced
the series, and Charles Dubin directed it.

OPERATION ENTERTAINMENT   ABC
5 JANUARY 1968–26 APRIL 1968; 27 SEPTEMBER 1968–31 JANUARY
1969   This hour-long variety show was staged at a different military base
each week and was hosted by a guest star. Regulars included Jim Lange,
the Operation Entertainment Girls, and the Terry Gibbs Band. Chuck
Barris produced the series.

OPERATION INFORMATION   DUMONT
17 JULY 1952–18 SEPTEMBER 1952   This public service series sought to inform veterans of their rights. See also *Operation Success* (1948–1949 version).

OPERATION NEPTUNE   NBC
28 JUNE 1953–16 AUGUST 1953   Created by Maurice Brockhausen, this Sunday-evening children's adventure series starred Tod Griffin as Commander Bill Hollister, skipper of an American submarine, who battled deep-sea evildoers. Richard Holland costarred as Dink.

OPERATION PETTICOAT   ABC
17 SEPTEMBER 1977–26 OCTOBER 1978   The story of a group of Army nurses stationed aboard a pink submarine during World War II, *Operation Petticoat* was based on the 1959 film of the same title. During the 1977–1978 season the large cast included: John Astin as Lieutenant Commander Matthew Sherman, skipper of the *Sea Tiger;* Richard Gilliland as Lieutenant Nick Holden, the crafty supply officer; Yvonne Wilder as Major Barbara Hayward, chief of the nurses; Melinda Naud as Lieutenant Dolores Crandall; Dorrie Thomson as Lieutenant Colfax; Jamie Lee Curtis as Lieutenant Barbara Duran; Bond Gideon as Lieutenant Claire Reid; Richard Brestoff as Yeoman Hunkle; Christopher J. Brown as Ensign Stovall; Kraig Cassity as Seaman Dooley; Wayne Long as Chief Herbert Molumphrey; Richard Marion as Williams; Michael Mazes as Chief Sam Gossett; Jack Murdock as Tostin; Peter Schuck as Seaman Horwich; Raymond Singer as Watson; Jim Varney as Seaman "Doom and Gloom" Broom; and Jesse Dizon as Ramon Galardo. Leonard B. Stern was the executive producer, David J. O'Connell and Si Rose the producers for Universal. When the show returned for its abortive second season, it featured new producers (Jeff Harris and Bernie Kukoff were the new executive producers, Michael Rhodes the new producer) and an almost entirely new cast. Only Melinda Naud, Richard Brestoff, and Jim Varney remained from the first season, and the new faces included: Robert Hogan as the new skipper, Commander Haller; Randolph Mantooth as Lieutenant Bender, the executive officer; Jo Ann Pflug as Lieutenant O'Hara; Hilary Thompson as Lieutenant Wheeler; Warren Berlinger as Stanley Dobritch; Fred Kareman as Doplos; and Scott McGinnis as Dixon.

OPERATION: RUNAWAY
See THE RUNAWAYS

OPERATION SUCCESS   DUMONT
21 SEPTEMBER 1948–19 OCTOBER 1948; 27 JANUARY 1949–16 JUNE 1949   A public service show in the truest sense of the term, *Operation*

Success was produced by the DuMont network in cooperation with the Veterans Administration. Its goal was to find jobs for disabled veterans. Veterans, doctors, training officers, and guidance officers all appeared on the show, and employers were asked to telephone in with job offers. Apparently, *Operation Success* was a success—late in 1948 a spokesman for the VA noted that, as a result of the first series, requests for disabled veterans' services had "almost doubled."

OPERATION SUCCESS
SYNDICATED

1955   Quentin Reynolds interviewed successful business executives on this half-hour public affairs program.

ORAL ROBERTS
SYNDICATED

1955–   One of television's best-known evangelists, Oral Roberts began his own series in 1955. The half-hour program is currently entitled *Oral Roberts and You.*

THE ORCHID AWARD
ABC

24 MAY 1953–24 JANUARY 1954   Each week on this fifteen-minute series a celebrity guest was honored. Ronald Reagan hosted the premiere telecast from Hollywood, presenting the "Orchid Award" to Rosemary Clooney. Thereafter the show was broadcast from New York, with Bert Lytell as host, until July, when Donald Woods became the New York host and Ronald Reagan the Los Angeles host. Harold Romm produced the series and Robert Finkel directed it. *Variety* noted in 1953 that *The Orchid Award* was the first show under ABC's new corporate structure to have been fully sold to sponsors before its premiere.

THE OREGON TRAIL
NBC

21 SEPTEMBER 1977–30 NOVEMBER 1977   Only six episodes of this hour-long western were telecast. Set along the Oregon Trail in 1842, it starred Rod Taylor as widower Evan Thorpe, a member of the wagon party who became the leader in the first episode. Also featured were Andrew Stevens as Andrew, his seventeen-year-old son; Tony Becker as William, his twelve-year-old son; Gina Marie Smika as Rachel, his seven-year-old daughter; Darleen Carr as Margaret Devlin, one of the passengers; and Charles Napier as Luther Sprague, the scout recruited by Thorpe in the first episode. Michael Gleason was the executive producer, Richard Collins the supervising producer, and Carl Vitale the producer for Universal. The pilot for the series was telecast 10 January 1976.

ORIENT EXPRESS
SYNDICATED

1953   Most of the stories on this half-hour filmed dramatic anthology series were set in Europe.

THE OSMOND FAMILY SHOW   ABC

28 JANUARY 1979–27 MAY 1979 An hour variety show, the successor
to *Donny and Marie, The Osmond Family Show* featured the performing
members of the Osmond clan: Donny, Marie, Alan, Wayne, Jay, Merrill,
and Jimmy.

THE OSMONDS   ABC

9 SEPTEMBER 1972–1 SEPTEMBER 1974 Saturday-morning cartoon
show inspired by the real-life singing group, The Osmond Brothers. The
animated series told the story of a globe-trotting musical group, who
were goodwill ambassadors for the United States. The voices of the several Osmond Brothers—Merrill, Wayne, Alan, Jay, Donny, and Jimmy—
were used. Reruns were shown Sunday mornings during the second
season.

OTHER PEOPLE OTHER PLACES   SYNDICATED

1974 Travelogue, hosted by Peter Graves.

OUR AMERICAN HERITAGE   NBC

1959–1961 Broadcast as a series of specials, this American historical
anthology series was produced by Mildred Freed Alberg in cooperation
with *American Heritage* magazine.

OUR FIVE DAUGHTERS   NBC

2 JANUARY 1962–28 SEPTEMBER 1962 This short-lived daytime serial
centered on the lives of the five girls in the Lee family. Featured were Esther Ralston as Helen Lee, their mother; Michael Keene as Jim Lee, their
father; Patricia Allison as daughter Barbara; Iris Joyce as daughter Marjorie; Nuella Dierking as daughter Jane; Wynne Miller as daughter Mary;
and Jacquie Courtney as daughter Ann.

OUR GOODLY HERITAGE   CBS

16 NOVEMBER 1952–26 JANUARY 1958 Williams Rush Baer of New
York University hosted this Sunday-morning Bible study show.

OUR MAN HIGGINS   ABC

3 OCTOBER 1962–11 SEPTEMBER 1963 Half-hour sitcom about a British
butler inherited by the American branch of the MacRobert clan. With
Stanley Holloway as Higgins; Frank Maxwell as Duncan MacRobert;
Audrey Totter as his wife, Alice MacRobert; Ricky Kelman as their son,
Tommy; K. C. Butts as their son, Dinghy; and Regina Groves as their
daughter, Joannie.

OUR MISS BROOKS   CBS

3 OCTOBER 1952–21 SEPTEMBER 1956 *Our Miss Brooks,* a situation
comedy about a high school English teacher, began on radio in 1948;

when it moved to television in 1952, most of the radio cast came with it: Eve Arden as Connie Brooks, Madison High's favorite educator; Gale Gordon as blustery Osgood Conklin, the principal; Richard Crenna as high-voiced Walter Denton, the student who usually drove Miss Brooks to school; Gloria McMillan as Walter's girlfriend, Harriet Conklin, the principal's daughter; and Jane Morgan as Miss Brooks's landlady, Mrs. Margaret Davis. Robert Rockwell, the only regular who had not been one of the original radio cast, was seen as biology teacher Philip Boynton, Miss Brooks's shy and elusive quarry. In the fall of 1955 the show's format changed slightly—Madison High was torn down to make room for a new highway, and Miss Brooks and Mr. Conklin found jobs at a private elementary school (on the radio version of the show, everyone remained at Madison High through the season). Eve Arden, Gale Gordon, and Jane Morgan remained from the old cast, and several newcomers were added: Nana Bryant as Mrs. Nestor, owner of Mrs. Nestor's School; Bob Sweeney as Oliver Munsey, Mrs. Nestor's brother; Ricky Vera as Benny Romero, a troublesome ten-year-old. Gene Barry was seen during the first half of the 1955–1956 season as Gene Talbot, the physical education teacher, one of Miss Brooks's romantic interests, but he was replaced in midseason when Robert Rockwell returned as Mr. Boynton. William Ching also appeared that season as athletic director Clint Albright, another romantic interest. In midseason, Isabel Randolph, as Mrs. Nestor's sister-in-law, also named Mrs. Nestor, succeeded Nana Bryant and took over as owner of the school. The half-hour series was produced by Larry Berns and directed by Al Lewis.

OUR PLACE   CBS

2 JULY 1967–3 SEPTEMBER 1967 A summer replacement for *The Smothers Brothers Comedy Hour, Our Place* was actually hosted by Rowlf the Muppet, one of puppeteer Jim Henson's first creations (Rowlf had previously been featured on *The Jimmy Dean Show*). The comedy duo of Jack Burns and Avery Schreiber provided human company for Rowlf, and the Doodletown Pipers were also featured. Bill Angelos and Buz Kohan wrote and produced the hour series.

OUR PRIVATE WORLD   CBS

5 MAY 1965–10 SEPTEMBER 1965 To compete with ABC's popular prime-time soap opera *Peyton Place,* CBS attempted a spinoff from its popular daytime serial, *As the World Turns. Our Private World* was seen on Wednesday and Friday nights. As the show opened, Lisa Hughes (played by Eileen Fulton for several years on *As the World Turns*) moved to New York after a divorce. Other members of the evening cast included Sandra Smith as Sandy, who was facing a trial for murder as the series closed; Julienne Marie as Eve; Robert Drivas as Brad, Eve's boyfriend; Geraldine Fitzgerald as Helen; Pamela Murphy as Franny; Sam Groom

as Tom; David O'Brien as Dr. Tony Larson; Nicholas Coster as John; Ken Tobey as Dick; Cathy Dunn as Pat; and Michael Strong as Sergeant Clark.

OUR SECRET WEAPON: THE TRUTH   DUMONT
22 OCTOBER 1950–17 APRIL 1951   Half-hour panel discussion show which focused on exposing Communist propaganda. The discussions were usually moderated by Ralph De Toledano and Leo Cherne.

OUT OF THE BLUE   ABC
9 SEPTEMBER 1979–21 OCTOBER 1979   Half-hour sitcom about a probationary angel who was sent to Earth to help out a family of five orphaned kids in Chicago. With Jimmy Brogan as Random, the angel who lived in a vacant room in the household and found a job as a high-school science teacher; Dixie Carter as Marion McLemore, the aunt of the five orphans who was taking care of them; Tammy Lauren as orphan Stacey Richards; Jason Keller as Jason Richards; Shane Keller (twin brother of Jason Keller) as Shane Richards; and Eileen Heckart as The Boss Angel, Random's supervisor. Thomas L. Miller and Robert L. Boyett created the series, which perished after a few weeks along with *A New Kind of Family.* Austin Kalish and Irma Kalish were the executive producers.

OUT OF THE FOG   ABC
7 APRIL 1952–22 SEPTEMBER 1952   Half-hour filmed mystery anthology series.

OUT OF THIS WORLD   SYNDICATED
1959   Half-hour series of lectures and experiments on scientific topics. Host Dr. Daniel Q. Posin was occasionally assisted by his cat, Minerva.

OUT ON THE FARM   NBC
11 JULY 1954–21 NOVEMBER 1954   This half-hour documentary series examined life on an American farm. Televised Sunday afternoons, the show was filmed at the Wilbert Landmeier farm near Cloverdale, Illinois. Eddy Arnold was the host.

OUT THERE   CBS
28 OCTOBER 1951–13 JANUARY 1952   One of TV's first science fiction anthology series, *Out There* was also one of the first shows to mix filmed special effects with live action. The half-hour series, seen Sunday evenings, was produced by John Haggodd; Donald Davis was executive producer.

THE OUTCASTS   ABC
23 SEPTEMBER 1968–15 SEPTEMBER 1969   Hour-long western about two bounty hunters, one black and one white, who joined forces after the

Civil War. With Don Murray as Earl Corey, a former slaveowner; Otis Young as Jemal David, a former slave. Hugh Benson was the executive producer of the series, and Jon Epstein the producer for Screen Gems.

OUTDOORS WITH KEN CALLAWAY
SYNDICATED
1975 Half-hour series for hunters and fishermen, hosted by Ken Callaway.

THE OUTER LIMITS
ABC
16 SEPTEMBER 1963–16 JANUARY 1965 Leslie Stevens was the creator and executive producer of this hour-long science fiction anthology series. Most of the forty-nine filmed episodes involved contact with extraterrestrial life forms. Joseph Stefano produced the show during the first season and Ben Brady during the second.

THE OUTLAWS
NBC
29 SEPTEMBER 1960–13 SEPTEMBER 1962 Set in Stillwater, Oklahoma Territory, this hour-long western starred Barton MacLane as Marshal Frank Caine. Also featured were Don Collier as Deputy Will Foreman; Jock Gaynor as Deputy Heck Martin; Bruce Yarnell (1961–1962) as Deputy Chalk Breeson; Judy Lewis (daughter of Loretta Young) (1961–1962) as Connie, Will's girlfriend; and Slim Pickens (1961–1962) as Slim.

OUTLOOK
NBC
1 APRIL 1956–19 OCTOBER 1958 Half-hour news analysis show, hosted by Chet Huntley. In the fall of 1958 the series, which was seen on Sunday afternoons or evenings, was retitled *Chet Huntley Reporting* (see also that title).

OUTRAGEOUS OPINIONS
SYNDICATED
1967 Half-hour talk show hosted by Helen Gurley Brown, editor of *Cosmopolitan* magazine.

OUTSIDE THE U.S.A.
ABC
1 SEPTEMBER 1955–3 JUNE 1956 Travelogue, hosted by Quincy Howe.

THE OUTSIDER
NBC
18 SEPTEMBER 1968–3 SEPTEMBER 1969 Hour-long crime show starring Darren McGavin as David Ross, an unarmed private detective recently released from prison (he'd killed a man, but it wasn't his fault). Roy Huggins was executive producer of the series.

OVER EASY
PBS
1977– Produced under a grant from the United States Department of Health, Education and Welfare, *Over Easy* is a daily, half-

hour public affairs program for older Americans. Hugh Downs hosts the series, produced at KQED-TV, San Francisco.

OVERLAND TRAIL
NBC

7 FEBRUARY 1960–11 SEPTEMBER 1960 Hour-long western starring William Bendix as Fred Kelly, superintendent of the Overland Stage Company, and Doug McClure as "Flip" Flippen, his sidekick. The series should not be confused with ABC's 1960 effort, *Stagecoach West*.

OVERSEAS PRESS CLUB
CBS

2 OCTOBER 1949–25 JUNE 1950 This Sunday-afternoon public affairs program featured panel discussions by members of the Overseas Press Club of America.

OWEN MARSHALL: COUNSELOR AT LAW
ABC

16 SEPTEMBER 1971–24 AUGUST 1974 This hour-long dramatic show starred Arthur Hill as Owen Marshall, a widowed attorney who practiced in Santa Barbara. Also featured were Lee Majors (1971–1973) as his associate, Jess Brandon; Joan Darling as his secretary, Frieda Krause; Christine Matchett as his twelve-year-old daughter, Melissa; Reni Santoni (fall 1973–January 1974) as his new associate, Danny Paterno; and David Soul (January 1974– August 1974) as his newest associate, Ted Warrick. David Victor was executive producer for Universal Television.

OZARK JUBILEE
ABC

22 JANUARY 1955–21 NOVEMBER 1961 Red Foley hosted this country and western music show, which originated from Springfield, Missouri, for most of its run. Among the many regulars over the years were Smiley Burnette, Bobby Lord, Wanda Jackson, and Brenda Lee (who was only ten years old when she became a regular in 1956), Webb Pierce, Suzi Arden, Uncle Cyp and Aunt Sap Brasfield, The Tall Timber Trio, and The Promenaders. Hank Garland composed the show's theme song, "Sugarfoot Rag." The show was titled *Country Music Jubilee* during the 1957–1958 season, and *Jubilee U.S.A.* thereafter; in the fall of 1959 it was reduced from one hour to thirty minutes. The show left ABC's regular schedule in the spring of 1960, but returned later as a replacement series.

OZMOE
ABC

6 MARCH 1951–12 APRIL 1951 Principal characters on this twice-weekly puppet show included a monkey named Ozmoe, a leprechaun named Rhoderick Dhon't, a mermaid known as Misty Waters, Poe the Crow, Sam the Clam, Throckmorton the sea serpent, and Horatio, a caterpillar. The several puppets were made of latex and were operated by gears; they were created by Henry Banks, who produced the show, and Skip Weshner, who wrote it.

OZZIE AND HARRIET

10 OCTOBER 1952–3 SEPTEMBER 1966   Television's longest-running situation comedy was a family affair—Ozzie Nelson created it, directed it, wrote it (together with his brother Don Nelson, Bill Davenport, and Ben Gershman), and starred in it with his wife and two sons. Nelson had graduated from Rutgers with a law degree, but his first love was music; he led a popular dance band in the early 1930s, and in 1935 he married Harriet Hilliard, the band's singer. Harriet Hilliard, born Peggy Lou Snyder, had grown up in show business. In 1944 they introduced a radio sitcom, *The Adventures of Ozzie and Harriet,* in which they played themselves. On the show, and in real life, they had two young sons, David and Ricky (born Eric), but the boys' parts were played by child actors during the show's first five seasons; in March 1949 David and Ricky began playing themselves. The four Nelsons also starred in a 1950 film, *Here Come the Nelsons.* The radio show lasted until 1954.

The television series was also officially titled *The Adventures of Ozzie and Harriet,* but the title seems a misnomer; it is hard to imagine a series less adventuresome than *Ozzie and Harriet*—Ozzie seemed to spend all his time at home or in his yard (he was never at work and his occupation on the show—if he had one—was never revealed, much less the subject of an episode), and Harriet could usually be found in the kitchen. The show's real drawing cards were the boys, especially Ricky, who was able to capitalize on weekly television exposure to become one of rock and roll's biggest stars. Rick (as he preferred to be called in his teens) first sang on 10 April 1957, in an episode titled "Rick the Drummer." He performed Fats Domino's "I'm Walkin'," which became his first record for the Verve label. Rick's singing career really took off in the fall of 1957, when "Be-Bop Baby," his first record on the Imperial label, topped the million mark. Thereafter he performed at least one number on almost every episode of *Ozzie and Harriet;* his regular backup musicians included guitarist James Burton, pianist Ray Johnson, bassist Joe Osborne, and drummer Richie Frost.

Of course, not all of the action centered around young Rick. A small host of friends and neighbors was around throughout the years to give Ozzie an occasional hand, whether it involved planning a fishing trip or mowing the lawn. The supporting cast included: Don DeFore (1952–1961) as "Thorny" Thornberry; Parley Baer as Darby; Lyle Talbot as Joe Randolph; Mary Jane Croft as Joe's wife, Clara Randolph; and Frank Cady as Doc Williams. Sons David and Rick also acquired a number of friends, particularly after they started attending college in the late 1950s (on the show, both David and Rick became lawyers). Among them were: Skip Young as Wally Plumstead; Charlene Salerno as Wally's girlfriend, Ginger; Connie Harper as David and Rick's secretary, Miss Edwards; Sean Morgan as Sean (he also played a friend named Bruce); Greg Dawson as Greg; Karl George (known earlier as Karl Kindberg) as Dink;

Jack Wagner as Jack; James Stacy as Fred; Kent McWhirter as Kent (McWhirter was later known as Kent McCord when he starred on *Adam-12*); Tracy Stratford as Betty; Ivan Bonar as Dean Hopkins, the college dean; and Melinda Plowman as Melinda. Finally, David and Rick's real-life wives also joined the cast. June Blair, who married David in 1961, joined the cast that year (though she played David's girlfriend for one season), and Rick's wife, Kris Nelson, joined in 1963.

Ozzie and Harriet left the air in 1966 after a fourteen-year TV run; the Nelsons made few television appearances after that, until 1973 when Ozzie and Harriet starred in a syndicated sitcom, *Ozzie's Girls* (see below). David, who had long been interested in behind-the-scenes work, produced the show. Rick continued his musical career, and in 1973 released a bittersweet song, "Garden Party," in which he expressed a desire to leave the past behind him; he has also made a few guest appearances in dramatic series such as *Owen Marshall: Counselor at Law* and *McCloud*.

OZZIE'S GIRLS   SYNDICATED
1973   On this limp sequel to *Ozzie and Harriet,* the elder Nelsons decided to rent out the boys' old room to two college girls. Ozzie and Harriet Nelson played themselves, and Susan Sennett and Brenda Sykes played the two coeds, Susie Hamilton and Brenda MacKenzie (Brenda was known as Jennifer for some reason in the first episodes). David Nelson produced the half-hour series.

PBL   NET
5 NOVEMBER 1967–25 MAY 1969   An ambitious Sunday-evening magazine series, *PBL* stood for "Public Broadcasting Laboratory," and was chiefly funded by the Ford Foundation. Edward F. Morgan was the chief correspondent for the series, which was scheduled biweekly during the 1967–1968 season and weekly during the 1968–1969 season; most shows were two hours long.

P.D.Q.   SYNDICATED
1965–1969   On this game show 2 two-member teams competed; one member of the team was placed in an isolation booth and tried to identify a word or phrase as his partner placed letters from the word or phrase on a rack. The show was hosted by Dennis James and later by Bill Cullen. A network version of the show appeared in 1973: see *Baffle.*

P.M. EAST—P.M. WEST   SYNDICATED
1961–1962   This ninety-minute nightly talk show was videotaped in New York and San Francisco. The first hour, from New York, was co-hosted by Mike Wallace and Joyce Davidson, and the last half hour, from San Francisco, was emceed by Terrence O'Flaherty.

P.M. PLAYHOUSE
See THE PHILIP MORRIS PLAYHOUSE

THE P.T.L. CLUB   SYNDICATED
1975–   "P.T.L." stands for "Praise the Lord" on this widely
syndicated religious talk show. Based in Charlotte, North Carolina, the
two-hour daily program is hosted by Reverend James Bakker and features Henry Harrison. The show is sponsored by contributions from viewers.

PABST BLUE RIBBON BOUTS   CBS
28 OCTOBER 1948–25 MAY 1955   CBS's weekly boxing series was seen
on Wednesday nights and was sponsored by Pabst Breweries for most of
its run. Russ Hodges was the ringside announcer for several seasons, and
Bill Nimmo was the commercial spokesman.

THE PACKARD SHOWROOM   ABC
18 APRIL 1954–5 DECEMBER 1954   Sponsored by Packard automobiles,
this fifteen-minute Sunday-night musical series was hosted by Martha
Wright and featured trumpeter Bobby Hackett.

PADDY THE PELICAN   ABC
11 SEPTEMBER 1950–13 OCTOBER 1950   Broadcast from Chicago on
weekday afternoons, this fifteen-minute children's show starred a pelican
named Paddy, who appeared both in animated form and as a puppet.
Mary Frances Desmond was also featured as Pam.

THE PALLISERS   PBS
31 JANUARY 1977–27 JUNE 1977   A twenty-two-part adaptation of six
novels by Anthony Trollope, *The Pallisers* concerned a wealthy English
family living in the Victorian era. Principal players included: Susan
Hampshire as Lady Glencora Palliser; Philip Latham as her husband,
Plantagenet Palliser, M.P.; Barry Justice as Burgo Fitzgerald, for whom
Glencora developed a penchant ; Donal McCann as Phineas Finn, an ambitious Irish M.P.; Roland Culver as The Duke of Omnium; Caroline
Mortimer as Alice Vavasor; Gary Watson as George Vavasor; Anna
Massey as Lady Laura Standish; Fabia Drake as Countess Midlothan;
and Rachel Herbert as Lady Dumbello. The series was jointly produced
by the BBC and Time-Life Television; Sir John Gielgud introduced the
episodes.

THE PAMELA MASON SHOW   SYNDICATED
1965   Talk show hosted by Pamela Mason, former wife of James Mason.

PANHANDLE PETE AND JENNIFER NBC

18 SEPTEMBER 1950–28 JUNE 1951 This late-afternoon children's show was set at a western ranch; featured were Panhandle Pete, a dummy operated by Jennifer Holt, and Johnny Coons (who later hosted his own kids' show). The fifteen-minute series was originally seen Mondays through Fridays but was later cut back to Tuesdays and Thursdays.

PANIC! NBC

5 MARCH 1957–17 SEPTEMBER 1957 Westbrook Van Voorhis hosted this half-hour anthology series of suspenseful dramas. Al Simon was the producer. See also *No Warning!*

PANTOMIME QUIZ
(STUMP THE STARS) CBS/NBC/DUMONT/ABC/SYNDICATED

4 OCTOBER 1949–20 AUGUST 1951 (CBS); 2 JANUARY 1952–26 MARCH 1952 (NBC); 4 JULY 1952–28 AUGUST 1953 (CBS); 20 OCTOBER 1953–13 APRIL 1954 (DUMONT); 9 JULY 1954–27 AUGUST 1954 (CBS); 22 JANUARY 1955–6 MARCH 1955 (ABC); 8 JULY 1955–6 SEPTEMBER 1957 (CBS); 8 APRIL 1958–21 SEPTEMBER 1959 (ABC); 17 SEPTEMBER 1962–16 SEPTEMBER 1963 (CBS); 1968–1970 (SYNDICATED) One of television's most durable prime-time game shows, *Pantomime Quiz* began as a local show in Los Angeles in 1948 and won an Emmy that season. A year later the series went nationwide. The format was simple: two teams, each with four celebrities, played charades. One member of the team acted out the charade (all of which were suggested by home viewers) and the other three teammates were required to guess it within two minutes; the team with the lower total elapsed time was the winner. Mike Stokey produced and hosted the half-hour show, which was often scheduled as a midseason or summer replacement throughout the 1950s. In 1958 the celebrity teams consisted of Howard Morris, Carol Burnett, Milt Kamen, and a guest versus Stubby Kaye, Denise Darcel, Tom Poston, and a guest. In 1962 the show returned, after a three-year absence, in the same format but with a new title: *Stump the Stars.* Regular panelists at that time included Sebastian Cabot, Robert Clary, Hans Conried, Beverly Garland, Stubby Kaye, Ruta Lee, Richard Long, Ross Martin, and Tommy Noonan. On the syndicated version, also titled *Stump the Stars,* regulars included Sebastian Cabot, Roger C. Carmel, Beverly Garland, Stubby Kaye, Deanna Lund, Ross Martin, and Dick Patterson.

THE PAPER CHASE CBS

19 SEPTEMBER 1978–17 JULY 1979 Hour dramatic series based on John Jay Osborn, Jr.'s novel (which was made into a movie in 1973), *The Paper Chase* was highly acclaimed but little watched. Set at a prestigious but unnamed Eastern law school, it starred John Houseman (repeating his

film role) as the awesomely autocratic Professor Charles W. Kingsfield, Jr., who strove to make his students think like lawyers in his contracts class, and James Stephens as James T. Hart, a first-year student from the Midwest who strove to learn all he could from the course. Hart's classmates were played by Tom Fitzsimmons as Franklin Ford, son of a prominent lawyer; Robert Ginty as Thomas Anderson; James Keane as Willis Bell; Jonathan Segal (to January 1979) as Jonathan Brooks, who left school after a cheating incident; and Francine Tacker as Elizabeth Logan. Deka Beaudine was also featured in the first episode (and credited for many weeks) as Asheley, Brooks's wife. Occasionally featured were Betty Harford as Mrs. Nottingham, Kingsfield's officious secretary, and Charles Hallahan as Ernie, proprietor of the pizza joint where Hart worked part time. The series was developed for television by James Bridges; Robert C. Thompson was the executive producer for 20th Century-Fox TV.

PAPER MOON   ABC
12 SEPTEMBER 1974–2 JANUARY 1975   Based on Peter Bogdanovich's 1973 film, this half-hour sitcom starred Chris Connelly as Moze Pray, an itinerant con artist who worked the Midwest during the 1930s, and Jodie Foster as Addie Pray, an eleven-year-old waif who, convinced that Moze was her father, teamed up with him. Anthony Wilson was the executive producer and Robert Stambler the producer for Paramount Television.

PARADISE BAY   NBC
27 SEPTEMBER 1965–1 JULY 1966   Set in Paradise Bay, California, this half-hour daytime serial featured Keith Andes as Jeff Morgan, manager of a radio station; Marion Ross as Mary Morgan, his wife; Heather North as their daughter, Kitty; Walter Brooke as newspaper editor Walter Montgomery; Paulle Clark as Charlotte Baxter; Dennis Cole as Duke Spalding; and Steven Mines as Fred.

PARADISE ISLAND   SYNDICATED
1949   Starring Danny O'Neil and Anne Sterling, this fifteen-minute variety show was filmed at Churubusco Studios in Mexico City by Jerry Fairbanks Productions; the series, which featured the music of Everett Hoagland and his orchestra, was produced in Mexico to reduce costs and to circumvent regulations imposed on domestic productions by the American Federation of Musicians.

THE PARENT GAME   SYNDICATED
1972   Clark Race hosted this game show on which three married couples were asked questions about child behavior and tried to select the response that a child psychologist had determined was the correct one.

PARIS   CBS

29 SEPTEMBER 1979–15 JANUARY 1980 Hour crime show starring
James Earl Jones as Los Angeles police detective, Captain Woodrow
"Woody" Paris, with Lee Chamberlin as his wife, Barbara, a nurse; Hank
Garrett as Deputy Chief Jerome Bench; Cecilia Hart as Sergeant Stacy
Erickson; Jake Mitchell as Charlie Bogart; Frank Ramirez as Ernesto;
and Michael Warren as Willie Miller. Steven Bochco created the series
and was the executive producer for MTM Enterprises.

PARIS CAVALCADE OF FASHIONS   NBC

11 NOVEMBER 1948–6 JANUARY 1949 One of TV's first fashion series,
this fifteen-minute show was hosted first by Faye Emerson, later by Julie
Gibson.

PARIS PRECINCT   SYNDICATED

1955 Filmed in Paris, this half-hour crime show was based on the files
of Sûreté, the French national police agency. Featured were Louis Jourdan as Inspector Bolbec and Claude Dauphin as Inspector Beaumont.

PARIS 7000   ABC

22 JANUARY 1970–4 JUNE 1970 When *The Survivors,* ABC's ambitious
and costly attempt to serialize a novel, failed in midseason, George Hamilton, who had starred in *The Survivors,* was inserted into a new, hastily
concocted format. On *Paris 7000* Hamilton played Jack Brennan, an employee of the United States Department of State assigned to the American consulate in Paris. Also featured were Jacques Aubuchon as Jules
Maurois, head of Sûreté, the French national police agency, and Gene
Raymond as Robert Stevens, Brennan's occasional sidekick.

PAROLE   SYNDICATED

1958 Actual parole hearings, filmed at American prisons, were presented on this half-hour documentary series, produced and directed by Fred
Becker.

THE PARTNERS   NBC

18 SEPTEMBER 1971–8 JANUARY 1972 Slated opposite CBS's *All in the
Family,* this half-hour sitcom about two wacky detectives was canceled in
midseason (a few reruns were shown during the summer of 1972). It
starred Don Adams as Detective Sergeant Lenny Crooke; Rupert Crosse
as his black partner, Detective Sergeant George Robinson; John Doucette
as their commanding officer, Captain Andrews; and Dick Van Patten as
Sergeant Higgenbottom.

THE PARTRIDGE FAMILY   ABC

25 SEPTEMBER 1970–31 AUGUST 1974 Popular with younger viewers,
The Partridge Family was a half-hour sitcom about a fatherless family of

six who decided to become a rock-and-roll band. Featured were Shirley Jones as Shirley Partridge; David Cassidy as Keith; Susan Dey as Laurie; Danny Bonaduce as Danny; Jeremy Gelbwaks (1970–1971) and Brian Forster (1971–1974) as Chris; Suzanne Crough as Tracy; and Dave Madden as their manager, Reuben Kincaid. In the fall of 1973 the show was moved from its Friday slot to Saturdays, opposite *All in the Family* and *Emergency!*, where its ratings sagged quickly. Two youngsters were added to the cast that season: Ricky Segall as Ricky Stevens, the little boy who lived next door; Alan Bursky as Alan, Reuben's nephew. *The Partridge Family* helped establish David Cassidy (stepson of Shirley Jones) as a teen idol, and millions of Partridge Family records were sold. On record, however, only the voices of Jones and Cassidy from the TV cast were used, with the rest of the vocals supplied by studio musicians. Bob Claver was executive producer of the series. See also *Partridge Family: 2200 A.D.*

PARTRIDGE FAMILY: 2200 A.D.   CBS
7 SEPTEMBER 1974–8 MARCH 1975   A cartoon sequel to *The Partridge Family,* this Saturday-morning show found the rock-and-rolling Partridges in space. The voices of Susan Dey, Danny Bonaduce, Brian Forster, Suzanne Crough, and Dave Madden from the prime-time show were used. Iwao Takamoto was the producer for Hanna-Barbera Productions.

PARTY TIME AT CLUB ROMA   NBC
14 OCTOBER 1950–6 JANUARY 1951   A Saturday-night audience-participation show, this series was hosted by Ben Alexander (who later costarred with Jack Webb on *Dragnet*). It started out as a quiz and stunt show before shifting formats to a talent contest.

PASS THE BUCK   CBS
3 APRIL 1978–30 JUNE 1978   Bill Cullen hosted this daytime game show on which four contestants competed. During the first round each contestant was required to supply an answer to a general question (e.g., name a word that rhymes with "blink"), and contestants who failed to make a timely response were exiled to the "bullpen" until only one contestant remained. The survivor then played a second round, alone, in which the top prize was $5,000. The executive producer of the short-lived series was Bob Stewart.

PASSPORT TO DANGER   SYNDICATED
1954–1955   Half-hour adventure series starring Cesar Romero as Steve McQuinn, a diplomatic courier. Hal Roach, Jr., produced the show.

PASSWORD   CBS/SYNDICATED/ABC/NBC
2 OCTOBER 1961–15 SEPTEMBER 1967 (CBS); 1967–1969 (SYNDICATED); 5 APRIL 1971–27 JUNE 1975 (ABC); 8 JANUARY 1979–

(NBC)   A durable game show, *Password* has been hosted by Allen Ludden and has appeared in several different formats. Originally the game was played by two 2-member teams; one member of each team was shown the "password," and sought to have her or his partner guess the password by providing one-word clues. If the password was guessed after the first clue, the successful team was awarded ten points; if the word was guessed after two clues, the team was given nine points, and so on. The first team to score twenty-five points won the game and proceeded to the "lightning round," where a player won $50 for each of five words that she or he could identify within sixty seconds. A Mark Goodson–Bill Todman Production, *Password* enjoyed a six-year daytime run on CBS, and was seen in prime time as well, usually surfacing as a midseason replacement. Late in 1974, during *Password*'s daytime run on ABC, the show was retitled *Password Allstars* and featured six celebrities instead of the celebrity-and-contestant pairs previously used. In January of 1979 the series appeared on NBC's daytime schedule; titled *Password Plus,* it again featured two celebrity-and-contestant teams. The teams no longer played for points, however; players won money not by guessing the passwords, but rather by guessing a second word or phrase suggested by each series of passwords.

THE PASTOR   SYNDICATED
1955   This religious anthology series was hosted by Dr. Robert E. Goodrich, Jr., of the First Methodist Church in Dallas. Each show was a drama depicting the life of a minister.

THE PAT BOONE SHOW   ABC/NBC/SYNDICATED
3 OCTOBER 1957–23 JUNE 1960 (ABC); 17 OCTOBER 1966–30 JUNE 1967 (NBC); 1969 (SYNDICATED)   Pat Boone, the cleancut singer who became a regular on Arthur Godfrey's *Talent Scouts* in 1954, hosted three shows of his own. The first, on ABC, was a prime-time half-hour variety series and featured the McGuire Sisters and the Mort Lindsey Orchestra. The second was a daytime half-hour variety and talk show on NBC and featured the Paul Smith Orchestra. The third, a ninety-minute talk show, was titled *Pat Boone in Hollywood.*

PAT PAULSEN'S HALF A COMEDY HOUR   ABC
22 JANUARY 1970–16 APRIL 1970   Pat Paulsen, the deadpan comedian who had been featured on *The Smothers Brothers Comedy Hour,* hosted his own half-hour comedy series, which also featured Pepe Brown, Bob Einstein, Sherry Miles, Vanetta Rogers, George Spell, and the Denny Vaughn Orchestra. Former vice president Hubert Humphrey guested on the premiere.

THE PATRICE MUNSEL SHOW   ABC

18 OCTOBER 1957–13 JUNE 1958   Opera star Patrice Munsel turned to popular music in her half-hour variety show. Also featured were the Martin Quartet and the Charles Sanford Orchestra. Munsel's husband, Bob Schuler, was the executive producer, and the show's theme, "Breezy and Easy," was composed by Hugh Martin.

THE PATRICIA BOWMAN SHOW   CBS

11 AUGUST 1951–3 NOVEMBER 1951   Fifteen-minute Saturday-evening variety show hosted by dancer Patricia Bowman.

PATROL CAR   SYNDICATED

1958   Produced in Canada, this half-hour crime show starred Bruce Seton.

THE PATTI PAGE SHOW   SYNDICATED/NBC/ABC

1955–1956 (SYNDICATED); 16 JUNE 1956–7 JULY 1956 (NBC); 24 SEPTEMBER 1958–16 MARCH 1959 (ABC)   Patti Page, born Clara Ann Fowler, began making records in 1948 and became one of the biggest pop singers of the 1950s. She hosted several television series during that decade, beginning in 1952 with *The Scott Music Hall* (see that title). In 1955 she began a fifteen-minute musical series, which was widely syndicated, featuring the Page Five Singers and the Jack Rael Orchestra (Rael was her longtime musical director). In the summer of 1956 she hosted a four-week summer replacement for *The Perry Como Show;* the hour series, broadcast in color, featured the Jack Rael Orchestra and the Spellbinders. During the 1957–1958 season she hosted *The Big Record,* a series designed to compete with *Your Hit Parade* (see also those titles). In the fall of 1958 she hosted a half-hour variety series, also known as *The Oldsmobile Show,* which featured Rocky Cole, The Jerry Packer Singers, and the Vic Schoen Orchestra. The latter series was produced by Ted Mills.

THE PATTY DUKE SHOW   ABC

18 SEPTEMBER 1963–31 AUGUST 1966   When Patty Duke was given her own series in 1963 at the age of seventeen, she was the youngest person in television history to have a prime-time series named after herself. Before that, however, she had had considerable experience in both television (as a guest star and as a regular, on *Kitty Foyle*) and on stage (most notably in *The Miracle Worker* on Broadway). In the series she played identical cousins, Patty and Cathy Lane; Patty was a typically outgoing American teenager, and Cathy, who was living with Patty's family while her father was overseas, was a reserved and artistic English lass. Also featured were William Schallert as Patty's father, Martin Lane, a magazine editor; Jean

Byron as Patty's mother, Natalie Lane; Paul O'Keefe as Patty's younger brother, Ross; and Eddie Applegate as Richard Harrison, Patty's boyfriend. Occasionally seen were John McGiver (1963–1964) as Martin's boss, J. R. Castle; Kitty Sullivan as Patty's archrival, Sue Ellen Turner; Skip Hinnant as Ted, Cathy's sometime boyfriend; Alberta Grant as Maggie; Robyn Miller as Roz; and Kelly Wood as Gloria.

THE PAUL ARNOLD SHOW CBS
24 OCTOBER 1949–23 JUNE 1950 This fifteen-minute musical series, hosted by singer Paul Arnold, was seen several nights a week before CBS's evening newscast.

THE PAUL DIXON SHOW ABC/DUMONT/SYNDICATED
8 AUGUST 1951–4 SEPTEMBER 1952 (ABC); 29 SEPTEMBER 1952–8 APRIL 1955 (DUMONT); 1973 (SYNDICATED) Paul Dixon, a popular television personality in Cincinnati, hosted three nationally distributed programs. The first was a Thursday-night variety hour, on which regulars Dotty Mack and Wanda Lewis pantomimed routines to popular recordings (Dotty Mack later did the same thing on her own ABC series). Jack Taylor produced the series, and Lee Hornback directed it. In the fall of 1952 Dixon hosted a daytime series on the DuMont network, which became one of that network's longest-running daytime shows; it again featured Wanda Lewis and Dotty Mack and was produced by Dick Perry. After a long absence from national television, Dixon returned in 1973 as host of a half-hour talk show that also featured Coleen Sharp and Bonnie Lou.

THE PAUL HARTMAN SHOW
See PRIDE OF THE FAMILY

THE PAUL LYNDE SHOW ABC
13 SEPTEMBER 1972–8 SEPTEMBER 1973 Half-hour sitcom starring Paul Lynde as high-strung lawyer Paul Simms, with Elizabeth Allen as his wife, Martha Simms; Jane Actman as their daughter, Barbara; John Calvin as Barbara's husband, Howie Dickerson, an obnoxious genius who was unemployed and lived with the elder Simmses; Pamelyn Ferdin as Sally, Paul and Martha's younger daughter; Herb Voland as T. J. McNish, Paul's law partner; James Gregory as T. R. Scott, another law partner; and Allison McKay as Alice, Paul's secretary. William Asher was executive producer of the series.

PAUL SAND IN FRIENDS AND LOVERS
See FRIENDS AND LOVERS

THE PAUL WHITEMAN CLUB
See TV TEEN CLUB

THE PAUL WHITEMAN REVUE   ABC
6 NOVEMBER 1949–30 MARCH 1952   Bandleader Paul Whiteman hosted
this half-hour musical variety show for three seasons; Linda Romay and
Joe Young were also on hand. While Whiteman vacationed during the
summer of 1951, Earl Wrightson and Maureen Cannon filled in (the series was then titled *Paul Whiteman's Goodyear Summertime Revue*).
Whiteman also hosted several other series: see *America's Greatest Bands,
On the Boardwalk,* and *TV Teen Club.*

PAUL WINCHELL AND JERRY MAHONEY   NBC/ABC/SYNDICATED
18 SEPTEMBER 1950–23 MAY 1954; 20 NOVEMBER 1954–25 FEBRUARY
1956 (NBC); 29 SEPTEMBER 1957–3 APRIL 1960 (ABC); 1965 (SYNDI-
CATED)   Ventriloquist Paul Winchell constructed his most famous
dummy, Jerry Mahoney, when he was a teenager. The two appeared on
radio, first on *Major Bowes' Original Amateur Hour,* and later on their
own short-lived series in 1943. Winchell and Mahoney began appearing
regularly on TV as early as 1947, and in 1948 Winchell cohosted a prime-
time series known as *The Bigelow Show* (see also that title) with mentalist
Dunninger (the two had previously worked together on stage). In the fall
of 1950 Winchell and Mahoney were given their own prime-time series,
which ran for four years on NBC. For the first three seasons the show
was titled *The Speidel Show* and was essentially a comedy-variety series
that also featured Knucklehead Smiff, a dim-witted dummy created by
Winchell, Dorothy Claire, Hilda Vaughn, and Jimmy Blaine. In 1952 a
quiz segment was incorporated into the series. Titled "What's My
Name?" and hosted by Ted Brown, the segment required contestants to
try to identify a famous person from clues suggested by Winchell and his
crew. "What's My Name?" was also featured during the series' fourth
season, when the show shifted to a Sunday-evening time slot. In the fall
of 1954 Winchell and Mahoney moved from prime time to Saturday
mornings on NBC, where their half-hour show featured a live audience
and Mary Ellen Terry; occasionally seen in 1956 was a young comedienne named Carol Burnett, in her earliest TV appearances. In the fall
of 1956 Winchell and company moved to ABC, where they hosted *Circus
Time* for one season (see also that title), before beginning *The Paul Winchell Show* in the fall of 1957; *The Paul Winchell Show* was aimed principally at younger viewers and was usually seen Sunday afternoons. It
featured Frank Fontaine and the Milton DeLugg Orchestra. After that
show left the air in 1960, Winchell was seen less frequently on TV,
though he did host a Saturday-morning cartoon show in 1963 (see *Cartoonies*), an hour syndicated show in 1965 titled *Winchell and Mahoney*

Time, and a children's game show in 1972 (see *Runaround*). Winchell had studied medicine intermittently, and in 1962 he developed a blood storage system and followed that a year later with an artificial heart; since that time Winchell's primary interest has been medical technology rather than show business.

PAULINE FREDERICK'S GUEST BOOK ABC
15 AUGUST 1948–30 MARCH 1949 A fifteen-minute interview series hosted by Pauline Frederick, who later became the United Nations correspondent for NBC News.

PAY CARDS SYNDICATED
1968 On this game show, hosted by Art James, three players attempted to build poker hands by acquiring cards from a twenty-card board.

THE PEARL BAILEY SHOW ABC
23 JANUARY 1971–8 MAY 1971 ABC had high hopes for this hour-long variety show, hosted by the incomparable Pearl Bailey, but even against unimpressive competition the show failed to catch on. Taped at the Hollywood Palace, the show was produced by Bob Finkel and featured the Allan Davies Singers, the Robert Sidney Dancers, and the orchestra of Louis Bellson (Bailey's husband).

PEBBLES AND BAMM BAMM CBS
11 SEPTEMBER 1971–4 SEPTEMBER 1976 Spun off from *The Flintstones, Pebbles and Bamm Bamm* was seen as a separate series during the 1971–1972 season and again from 1974 to 1976; from 1972 to 1974 it was part of *The Flintstones Comedy Hour.* See also *The Flintstones.*

PECK'S BAD GIRL CBS
5 MAY 1959–4 AUGUST 1959 Patty McCormack, who had made a big splash in *The Bad Seed* on stage and on film, played a mischievous twelve-year-old named Torey Peck in this half-hour sitcom. Also featured were Wendell Corey as her father, attorney Steven Peck; Marsha Hunt as her mother, Jennifer Peck; Roy Ferrell as her little brother, Roger; and Reba Waters as her friend, Francesca. Norman Felton was the executive producer of the series and Stanley Rubin the producer. The show was rerun on CBS during the summer of 1960.

THE PEE WEE KING SHOW ABC
23 MAY 1955–5 SEPTEMBER 1955 Regulars on this Cincinnati-based half-hour country and western music show included Pee Wee King, Redd Stewart, Little Eller Long, Neal Burris, Bonnie Sloan, Mitchell Torak, and Lulabelle and Scotty.

PENNY TO A MILLION   ABC

4 MAY 1955–19 OCTOBER 1955 Bill Goodwin hosted this prime-time game show, which featured two teams of five; any panelist who answered a question incorrectly was eliminated, until only one panelist from each side remained. Those two players then had the chance to go for the show's top prize of $10,000 (a million cents). Herb Wolf produced the show.

PENTAGON   DUMONT

6 MAY 1951–24 NOVEMBER 1952 The progress of the Korean War was the principal subject of discussion on this half-hour public affairs show, DuMont's counterpart of NBC's *Battle Report*.

PENTAGON U.S.A.   CBS

6 AUGUST 1953–1 OCTOBER 1953 A half-hour crime show depicting the exploits of the officers of the Criminal Investigation Division of the United States Army, starring Addison Richards (as The Colonel) and Edward Binns. The series was to have been titled *Corridor D. Pentagon;* that title was changed to *Pentagon Confidential,* which was in turn changed to *Pentagon U.S.A.* just before the show premiered. William Dozier was the executive producer, Alex March the producer.

PENTHOUSE PARTY   ABC

15 SEPTEMBER 1950–8 JUNE 1951 Betty Furness hosted this half-hour variety show, which also featured Don Cherry.

PENTHOUSE PLAYERS   ABC

20 MARCH 1949–23 OCTOBER 1949 Half-hour Sunday-night dramatic anthology series.

PEOPLE   NBC

21 AUGUST 1955–9 OCTOBER 1955 Morgan Beatty narrated this Sunday-afternoon series of live and filmed human interest segments.

PEOPLE   CBS

18 SEPTEMBER 1978–11 NOVEMBER 1978 A half-hour magazine series, based on *People* magazine. The segments, almost all of which were three minutes or less, included peeks at celebrities and a few human interest features. Phyllis George, Miss America of 1971, was the host; some interviews were handled by correspondent Mark Shaw. David Susskind was executive producer for Time-Life TV.

PEOPLE ARE FUNNY   NBC

19 SEPTEMBER 1954–2 APRIL 1961 Art Linkletter hosted this half-hour show, which combined stunts and audience participation features. A reg-

ular feature for several seasons was a Univac computer, which tried to match eligible young men and women. Reruns were shown after 1958.

PEOPLE WILL TALK · NBC
1 JULY 1963–27 DECEMBER 1963 The format of this daytime game show, hosted by Dennis James, was not unlike that of *The Celebrity Game*—contestants tried to predict how members of a studio audience panel would respond to yes-or-no questions. The show was a Merrill Heatter–Bob Quigley Production.

THE PEOPLES' CHOICE · NBC
6 OCTOBER 1955–25 SEPTEMBER 1958 Jackie Cooper starred in this half-hour sitcom as Socrates (Sock) Miller, a government naturalist who became a city councilor in New City, Oklahoma and sold houses in a real estate development there. Also featured were Pat Breslin as Amanda (Mandy) Peoples, Sock's girlfriend (and later his wife); Paul Maxey as New City's mayor and Mandy's corpulent father, John Peoples; Margaret Irving as Sock's Aunt Gus; Leonid Kinskey as Pierre, an artist pal of Sock's; and Dick Wesson (1957–1958) as Rollo, another friend of Sock's. The "gimmick" on the show was a talking basset hound named Cleo, who made droll comments (with the help of Mary Jane Croft, who provided the voice) from time to time during each episode.

PEOPLE'S PLATFORM · CBS
17 AUGUST 1948–18 AUGUST 1950 Charles Collingwood was the moderator of this early public affairs program. The show, which originated on radio in 1938, featured a panel of experts discussing a topical subject.

PEPSI-COLA PLAYHOUSE · ABC
2 OCTOBER 1953–26 JUNE 1955 This half-hour dramatic anthology series was filmed at Revue Studios. Arlene Dahl was the first host of the series; she was succeeded by Anita Colby and later by Polly Bergen. Robert G. Walker was the director.

THE PERFECT MATCH · SYNDICATED
1967 Dick Enberg hosted this game show, which was similar in format to *The Dating Game:* three women and three men participated, and a computer had previously matched up the three couples. Those who chose their computer-assigned matches won a cash prize.

THE PERILS OF PENELOPE PITSTOP · CBS
13 SEPTEMBER 1969–5 SEPTEMBER 1970 A female auto racer named Penelope Pitstop was the central character in this Saturday-morning cartoon show from Hanna-Barbera Productions.

THE PERRY COMO SHOW   NBC/CBS
(THE CHESTERFIELD SUPPER CLUB)/(THE KRAFT MUSIC HALL)

24 DECEMBER 1948–4 JUNE 1950 (NBC); 2 OCTOBER 1950–24 JUNE
1955 (CBS); 17 SEPTEMBER 1955–12 JUNE 1963 (NBC)   Perry Como
was a barber before he began singing professionally in 1933. In 1944, the
year his first record was released, he appeared on radio in *The Chester-
field Supper Club;* when that show came to television late in 1948, Como
came with it and has remained on television for three decades. *The Ches-
terfield Supper Club,* which also featured the Mitchell Ayres Orchestra
and the Fontane Sisters, was originally seen on Friday nights but soon
shifted to a half-hour slot on Sundays, opposite Ed Sullivan's *Toast of the
Town.* In the fall of 1950 Como shifted to CBS, where he hosted his own
show for the next five seasons; the fifteen-minute program was seen Mondays, Wednesdays, and Fridays following the network news. Also featured were the Mitchell Ayres Orchestra and the Fontane Sisters,
together with announcer Frank Gallop. In the fall of 1955 Como returned to NBC, where he hosted a weekly hour show for the next eight
years; from 1955 to 1959 it was seen Saturdays and was titled *The Perry
Como Show.* From 1959 to 1963 it was seen Wednesdays and was titled
The Kraft Music Hall (*The Kraft Music Hall* had previously been hosted
by Milton Berle, and the series returned in 1967; see also that title). The
Mitchell Ayres Orchestra and Frank Gallop were again featured, along
with the Ray Charles Singers and the Louis DaPron Dancers (later, the
Peter Gennaro Dancers). Como's theme song, "Dream Along with Me,"
was composed by Carl Sigman. For several seasons the show was produced by Bob Finkel, directed by Grey Lockwood, with Goodman Ace
as head writer. Though he has not hosted a weekly series since 1963,
Como has regularly appeared in specials since then.

PERRY MASON   CBS

21 SEPTEMBER 1957–4 SEPTEMBER 1966   Perry Mason, one of fiction's
most successful criminal lawyers, was created by Erle Stanley Gardner
(who was himself an attorney) in 1933. Though the character was featured in dozens of novels, several films, a radio serial that ran for twelve
years, and two television series, Raymond Burr's portrayal of the Los
Angeles lawyer in the nine-year run of the first *Perry Mason* TV series
overshadows all the others.

After the radio series left the air in 1955, Gardner formed a partnership—Paisano Productions—with his agent, Cornwall Jackson; Jackson's
wife, Gail Patrick Jackson, a former actress who had attended law
school, was hired as executive producer, and Ben Brady, who was also an
attorney, was hired as producer. Though Gardner did no writing for the
show, he exercised script approval and helped insure that the quality of
the show met his expectations.

Several actors were considered for the leading role before Raymond Burr was chosen. Among the also-rans were William Hopper, Richard Carlson, Fred MacMurray, and Efrem Zimbalist, Jr. Burr, who had starred in the movie *Godzilla* and had played heavies in several other films, originally tested for the role of prosecuting attorney Hamilton Burger. Burr's Mason was an aggressive advocate blessed with superb powers of deductive reasoning. Usually it took no more than a quick pause and a short breath for Burr's Mason to piece together an intricate sequence of events from a few sketchy facts. Typically, Mason's clients found themselves linked by a chain of circumstantial evidence to a murder ("But, Mr. Mason, he was dead when I got there!"). Some hapless clients were even convinced that they had, in fact, committed the crime; all, however, were grateful for Mason's uncanny ability to secure an in-court confession (usually on the witness stand, but occasionally from the spectators' area) from the real culprit.

Perry Mason first cracked Nielsen's Top Twenty series in its second season, when it ranked nineteenth. It climbed as high as fifth in 1961–1962 before the ratings began to taper off. Not all of the credit for the series' success belongs to Burr; a popular and talented supporting cast was an integral part of the show. Though four other regulars were featured in most episodes, only two of them were featured continuously through the nine-year run: Barbara Hale as Della Street, Mason's cool and efficient private secretary, and William Hopper (son of Hollywood columnist Hedda Hopper) as private detective Paul Drake, Mason's tireless investigator. William Talman, as prosecutor Hamilton Burger, was Mason's usual courtroom foe, but was not featured continuously: Talman had been arrested at a wild Hollywood party early in 1960 and was seen only occasionally during the 1960–1961 season. Mason also handled cases outside the Los Angeles area from time to time, which, of course, pitted him against other prosecutors; all of them, however, were as unsuccessful as Burger in obtaining convictions against Mason's clients. Rounding out the long-term supporting cast was veteran character actor Raymond Collins, who played Lieutenant Arthur Tragg, the grim homicide officer from the Los Angeles Police Department from 1957 to 1964; Collins died in 1965. A few other players were also featured occasionally: Wesley Lau (1961–1965) as Lieutenant Anderson, a colleague of Tragg's; Richard Anderson (1965–1966) as Lieutenant Steve Drumm, Tragg's successor; Lee Miller (1965–1966) as Lieutenant Brice; Carl Held (1961–1962) as David Gideon, an associate of Paul Drake's; and Connie Cezon as the rarely seen Gertie, Mason's switchboard operator and receptionist. Even Burr himself was not featured in every show; Walter Pidgeon substituted for him, as attorney Sherman Hatfield, on 28 February 1963, and Michael Connors filled in, as attorney Joe Kelly, on 5 November 1964.

Almost all of the episodes followed the same format. Most featured alliterative titles (such as the premiere, "The Case of the Restless Redhead"; "The Case of the Treacherous Toupee," with Robert Redford, 17 September 1960; and "The Case of the Bountiful Beauty," with Ryan O'Neal, 6 February 1964). The action was usually confined to the first thirty minutes (the identity of the killer was never divulged to the viewers), and the courtroom segment comprised the second half hour. Strictly speaking, few of the courtroom proceedings were actually trials. Most were styled as "evidentiary hearings"; by using that technique, the producers saved the expense of hiring twelve extras to play jurors. Though Mason seemed to elicit a confession from the guilty party week after week, it is probably not accurate to say that he won every case; in at least one episode, "The Case of the Deadly Verdict," telecast during the fall of 1963, a jury returned a guilty verdict.

Approximately 271 hour episodes were produced between 1957 and 1966. On the last first-run episode, "The Case of the Final Fade-Out" (telecast 22 May 1966), Mason's creator, Erle Stanley Gardner, appeared as the judge. The *Perry Mason* theme music, one of TV's best remembered signatures, was composed by Fred Steiner. Reruns of the series were widely syndicated after 1966, and by 1973 CBS was interested in reviving the series. The new version, titled *The New Perry Mason,* was gone in fourteen weeks (see also that title).

PERRY PRESENTS NBC

13 JUNE 1959–5 SEPTEMBER 1959   A summer replacement for *The Perry Como Show,* this hour-long musical show was broadcast in color and was hosted by singers Tony Bennett, Teresa Brewer, and Jaye P. Morgan. Other regulars included the Four Lads, the Modernaires, the Louis DaPron Dancers, and the Mitchell Ayres Orchestra.

PERSON TO PERSON CBS

2 OCTOBER 1953–23 SEPTEMBER 1960; 23 JUNE 1961–15 SEPTEMBER 1961   *Person to Person,* a prime-time interview show, made effective use of television's technological advances. Thanks to coast-to-coast coaxial cable, celebrities and newsmakers could be interviewed—live—almost anywhere in North America. Each week on *Person to Person* two interviews were conducted; the interviewees were usually seen in their homes, while the host (Edward R. Murrow from 1953 to 1959, then Charles Collingwood) remained in a studio in New York, watching the guests on a monitor. On the 1953 premiere Murrow first "visited" Leopold Stokowski and Gloria Vanderbilt, and then dropped in on Brooklyn Dodgers' catcher Roy Campanella. Among the most famous of those interviewed was Marilyn Monroe, whose television appearances were indeed infrequent; Monroe was interviewed at the home of friends in Connecticut on 8 April 1955. For most of its run *Person to Person* was produced by Edward R. Murrow, Jesse Zousmer, and John Aaron.

PERSONAL APPEARANCE THEATER ABC

27 OCTOBER 1951–23 MAY 1952   Half-hour dramatic anthology series.

PERSONALITY NBC

30 JULY 1967–26 SEPTEMBER 1969   A panel of three celebrities was featured on this daytime game show hosted by Larry Blyden. The game was played in three rounds, during which the celebs tried to determine (a) how the other two celebs responded to various personal and topical questions, (b) how members of the public had predicted that the celebrity himself or herself would answer, and (c) how another celebrity (who appeared in a prerecorded sequence) responded to each of three questions. Bob Stewart created and produced the series.

PERSONALITY PUZZLE ABC

19 MARCH 1953–25 JUNE 1953   A biweekly prime-time game show, *Personality Puzzle* was similar to *What's My Line?* A celebrity panel tried to guess the identity of a guest celebrity from articles of the guest's clothing or from other props associated with the person. Robert Alda was the host.

PERSPECTIVE ABC

6 NOVEMBER 1952–6 APRIL 1953   Produced by the ABC Public Affairs Department in cooperation with the New York Bar Association, this prime-time public affairs program had no moderator. Featured on the premiere were Lester B. Pearson and Dean Rusk (then president of the Rockefeller Foundation). The half-hour series was directed by Edward Nugent.

THE PERSUADERS ABC

18 SEPTEMBER 1971–14 JUNE 1972   This hour-long adventure series, produced in Europe by England's Associated Television Corporation (ATV), starred Tony Curtis and Roger Moore as two wealthy playboys, Danny Wilde and Lord Brett Sinclair. According to the story line, they were sent to investigate various matters at the behest of Judge Fulton, a retired jurist (played by Laurence Naismith). The show's Saturday-night slot probably helped to keep the ratings down, and it vanished after only one season. Robert S. Baker was the creator and producer for ATV.

THE PET SET SYNDICATED

1971   Betty White hosted this half-hour series on which celebrities dropped by with their pets.

THE PET SHOP DUMONT

1 DECEMBER 1951–14 MARCH 1953   Gail Compton hosted this prime-time series on pets and pet care, with help from her eight-year-old daughter, Gay.

PETE AND GLADYS   CBS

19 SEPTEMBER 1960–10 SEPTEMBER 1962   Parke Levy was the executive producer of this half-hour sitcom, a spinoff from *December Bride*. It starred Harry Morgan as wisecracking insurance agent Pete Porter and Cara Williams as his daffy wife, Gladys Porter; Morgan had played Pete on *December Bride* but his wife Gladys had never been seen on that series. Also featured were Verna Felton, who repeated her *December Bride* role as Hilda Crocker; Alvy Moore as Howie, Pete and Gladys's friend and neighbor; Barbara Stuart as Howie's wife, Alice; Peter Leeds as neighbor George Colton; Shirley Mitchell as his wife, Janet; Ernest Truex as Pop, Gladys's father; Barry Kelley as Pete's boss, Mr. Slocum; Helen Kleeb and Lurene Tuttle as his wife, Mrs. Slocum; Gale Gordon (1961–1962) as Pete's Uncle Paul; Joe Mantell (1961–1962) as neighbor Ernie Briggs; and Mina Kolb (1961–1962) as his wife, Peggy.

PETE KELLY'S BLUES   NBC

31 MARCH 1959–4 SEPTEMBER 1959   A half-hour crime show set in Kansas City during the 1920s, starring William Reynolds as Pete Kelly, a cornetist and bandleader at a local speakeasy who also found time to help people in distress. Also featured were Fred Eisley (later known as Anthony Eisley) as Johnny Cassiano, a tough Kansas City cop; Connee Boswell as Savannah Brown, singer at the club; and Phil Gordon as George Lupo, owner of the club. Jack Webb, who had starred in the 1951 radio series and the 1955 film on which the TV series was based, produced and directed the show. Webb was himself a jazz fan and employed an eight-piece band, headed by Dick Cathcart, to provide the music for the series.

PETER GUNN   NBC/ABC

22 SEPTEMBER 1958–26 SEPTEMBER 1960 (NBC); 3 OCTOBER 1960–25 SEPTEMBER 1961 (ABC)   This half-hour crime show is probably best remembered for its driving jazz theme, composed by Henry Mancini. It starred Craig Stevens as Peter Gunn, a smooth private eye who sported a brush cut and hung out at a nightspot known as Mother's. Also featured were Herschel Bernardi as Lieutenant Jacoby; Lola Albright as Gunn's romantic interest, Edie Hart, the singer at Mother's; and Hope Emerson (1958–1959) and Minerva Urecal (1959–1961) as Mother, the clubowner. Occasionally seen during the third season were Bill Chadney as Emmett and James Lamphier as Leslie. Blake Edwards produced the series.

THE PETER LIND HAYES SHOW   NBC/ABC

23 NOVEMBER 1950–29 MARCH 1951 (NBC); 13 OCTOBER 1958–10 APRIL 1959 (ABC)   Peter Lind Hayes, together with his wife, Mary Healy, hosted two variety shows. The first was a prime-time show, seen Thursday nights during the 1950–1951 season. The second was a half-hour daytime series that also featured Anita Bryant, Don Cherry, and the

553

Four Voices. Hayes and Healy later costarred in a situation comedy: see *Peter Loves Mary*.

PETER LOVES MARY   NBC
12 OCTOBER 1960–31 MAY 1961   This half-hour sitcom starred Peter Lind Hayes and Mary Healy (who were married in real life) as Peter and Mary Lindsey, a showbiz couple living in suburban Oakdell, Connecticut. Also featured were Merry Martin as their daughter, Leslie; Gil Smith as their son, Steve; and Bea Benaderet as their housekeeper, Wilma.

THE PETER MARSHALL VARIETY SHOW   SYNDICATED
1976   Peter Marshall, better known as host of *Hollywood Squares*, also hosted his own ninety-minute variety series, which also featured Rod Gist and Denny Evans and Chapter 5. David Salzman was the executive producer of the show, which was distributed by Westinghouse Broadcasting.

THE PETER POTAMUS SHOW   ABC
2 JANUARY 1966–24 DECEMBER 1967   The star of this Sunday-morning cartoon series from Hanna-Barbera Productions was Peter Potamus, a purple hippo, who roamed the world with his aide, So So, an ape. Segments of "Breezly and Sneezly," also telecast on Hanna-Barbera's *Magilla Gorilla* series, were included as well.

PETER POTTER'S JUKE BOX JURY
See JUKEBOX JURY

PETROCELLI   NBC
11 SEPTEMBER 1974–3 MARCH 1976   This hour-long crime show starred Barry Newman as Anthony Petrocelli, a criminal lawyer who gave up his big-city practice to settle in the Southwestern town of San Remo. Susan Howard costarred as his wife, Maggie Petrocelli, and Albert Salmi was seen as his right-hand man, Pete Ritter. Thomas L. Miller and Edward K. Milkis were the executive producers of the show, which was filmed in Tucson, Arizona.

PETTICOAT JUNCTION   CBS
24 SEPTEMBER 1963–12 SEPTEMBER 1970   CBS introduced this rural sitcom one year after *The Beverly Hillbillies*, which had been the number one show of the 1962–1963 season; *Petticoat Junction* proved to be the most popular new show of the 1963–1964 season, ranking fourth that year. Though its ratings declined sharply after the first year, the show enjoyed a seven-year run and was one of CBS's mainstays during the decade. Paul Henning, who had created *The Beverly Hillbillies*, was also the

creator and executive producer of *Petticoat Junction;* the half-hour series was produced by Dick Wesson. The large cast included: Bea Benaderet (1963–1968) as Kate Bradley, the widowed owner of the Shady Rest Hotel in Hooterville, terminus of the Cannonball, an ancient steam train; Edgar Buchanan as Joseph P. (Uncle Joe) Carson, the uncle of Kate's three eligible daughters; Linda Kaye as daughter Betty Jo (Kaye, the boss's daughter, was also known as Linda Kaye Henning later in the series); Pat Woodell (1963–1965) and Lori Saunders (1965–1970) as daughter Bobbie Jo; Jeannine Riley (1963–1965), Gunilla Hutton (1965–1966), and Meredith MacRae (1966–1970) as daughter Billie Jo; Charles Lane as Homer Bedloe, the railroad man who schemed to scrap the Cannonball; Smiley Burnette as engineer Charley Pratt; Rufe Davis as engineer Floyd Smoot; Byron Foulger as engineer Wendell Gibbs; Regis Toomey as Doc Stuart; Mike Minor (1966–1970) as Steve Elliott, Betty Jo's boyfriend and eventual husband; Elvia Allman (1966–1970) as Selma Plout, the woman who hoped to wrest Steve Elliott away from Betty Jo for her own daughter; Lynette Winter (1966–1970) as Selma's daughter, Henrietta Plout; June Lockhart (1968–1970) as Dr. Janet Craig, a physician (in essence, Lockhart replaced Bea Benaderet, who had died in 1968); and Jonathan Daly (1969–1970) as game warden Orrin Pike, Bobbie Jo's boyfriend. Other regulars included members of the cast of *Green Acres,* another Paul Henning series which was also set in Hooterville (see also that title).

PEYTON PLACE   ABC

15 SEPTEMBER 1964–2 JUNE 1969 *Peyton Place* was television's first prime-time serial since its earliest days and was the only successful primetime soap opera in the medium's history. Based on Grace Metalious's enormously popular novel, which had been made into a movie in 1957, it premiered in 1964 amid much fanfare. It was telecast twice a week during the 1964–1965 season, and both segments cracked Nielsen's Top Twenty that year; as the 1965–1966 season began, telecasts were pushed up to three times weekly, but the show's ratings had already begun to fade. The show was reduced to twice a week thereafter and lasted three more seasons. The basic theme of the show involved sexual goings-on in the lives of the residents of Peyton Place, a small New England town. The huge cast included: Mia Farrow as Allison MacKenzie; Ryan O'Neal as Rodney Harrington; Dorothy Malone as Constance MacKenzie Carson; Tim O'Connor as Elliott Carson; Frank Ferguson as Eli Carson; Steven Oliver as Lee Webber; Chris Connelly as Norman Harrington; Pat Morrow as Rita Jacks; Barbara Parkins as Betty Anderson; John Kerr as Fowler; George Macready as Martin Peyton; Ruth Warrick as Hannah Cord; James Douglas as Steven Cord; Leigh Taylor–Young as Rachel Welles; Lana Wood as Sandy Webber; Ed Nelson as Dr. Michael Rossi; Dan Duryea as Eddie; Gena Rowlands as Adrienne; Paul Langton as Leslie

Harrington; Joyce Jillson as Jill; Warner Anderson as Matthew Swain; Heather Angel as Mrs. Dowell; Ruby Dee as Alma Miles; Lee Grant as Stella; Diana Hyland as Susan Winter; Kent Smith as Dr. Morton; and Mariette Hartley as Clair. Paul Monash produced the series for 20th Century-Fox Television. In 1972 a daytime version was introduced: see *Return to Peyton Place*.

THE PHIL DONAHUE SHOW
SYNDICATED

1970–   Phil Donahue began hosting a local talk show in Dayton, Ohio, in 1967; by 1970 it was syndicated nationally, and the number of stations carrying the show increased steadily through the 1970s. By 1977 Donahue had shifted his base of operations to Chicago and the show became known simply as *Donahue*. The hour-long show, which features questions from the studio audience, has been produced by Patricia McMillen and distributed by Multimedia; Richard Mincer has been the executive producer.

THE PHIL SILVERS SHOW
See THE ARROW SHOW; THE NEW PHIL SILVERS SHOW; YOU'LL NEVER GET RICH

PHILCO TELEVISION PLAYHOUSE
NBC

3 OCTOBER 1948–2 OCTOBER 1955   One of the best known of the several dramatic anthology series that comprised television's so-called "Golden Age," *Philco Television Playhouse* was produced by Fred Coe, who was twenty-nine when the series began in 1948. Like the other dramatic shows, *Philco* was a training ground for young writers and directors as well as for performers. *Philco* held down a Sunday slot for its entire seven-year run; from 1951 to 1955 it shared sponsorship with Goodyear on a biweekly basis (both shows were produced by Coe). A representative selection of offerings illustrates the variety of material presented on *Philco:* "Dinner at Eight," with Peggy Wood, Dennis King, Mary Boland, and Vicki Cummings (3 October 1948); "The Late Christopher Bean," with Lillian Gish (in her TV debut, 6 February 1949); "The Story of Mary Surratt," with Dorothy Gish (in her TV debut, 13 February 1949); "Ann Rutledge," with Grace Kelly (12 February 1950); "Nocturne," with Cloris Leachman (2 April 1950); "Leaf Out of a Book," with Grace Kelly (31 December 1950); "No Medals on Pop," with Brandon DeWilde (in his first major TV role, 11 March 1951); "The Basket Weaver," with Walter Matthau (in his first major TV role, 20 April 1952); "A Little Something in Reserve," with Tony Randall (10 May 1953); Paddy Chayefsky's "Marty," with Rod Steiger and Nancy Marchand (directed by Delbert Mann, 24 May 1953); "The Way of the Eagle," with Grace Kelly (in her last dramatic appearance on TV, 7 June 1953); "Statute of Limitations," with Barbara Baxley and Martin Balsam (in his first major

TV role, 21 February 1954); "The Dancers," with Joanne Woodward (7 March 1954); "Run Like a Thief," with James Dean, Kurt Kasznar, Gusti Huber, and Barbara O'Neill (5 September 1954); Robert Alan Aurthur's "Shadow of the Champ," with Eli Wallach, Jack Warden, and Lee Grant (20 March 1955); and Robert Alan Aurthur's "A Man Is Ten Feet Tall," with Sidney Poitier (in a rare television appearance, 2 October 1955). See also *Goodyear Playhouse*.

PHILIP MARLOWE   ABC
29 SEPTEMBER 1959–29 MARCH 1960   Raymond Chandler's fictional sleuth, Philip Marlowe, was played by Philip Carey on this half-hour crime show.

THE PHILIP MORRIS PLAYHOUSE   CBS
8 OCTOBER 1953–4 MARCH 1954   This half-hour filmed dramatic anthology series was hastily ordered by sponsor Philip Morris after its first offering in that time slot, *Pentagon Confidential,* was blasted by the critics. Kent Smith hosted the series, which was also known as *P.M. Playhouse.*

PHOTOCRIME   ABC
21 SEPTEMBER 1949–28 DECEMBER 1949   Inspector Cobb (played by Chuck Webster) was the chief character on this half-hour Wednesday-night crime show.

PHOTOPLAY TIME
See THE WENDY BARRIE SHOW

PHYLLIS   CBS
8 SEPTEMBER 1975–30 AUGUST 1977   In this spinoff from *The Mary Tyler Moore Show,* Cloris Leachman starred as Phyllis Lindstrom; as her own series began, Phyllis had just been widowed and had left Minneapolis with her daughter for San Francisco, where she moved in with her late husband's mother and *her* second husband. The original cast also included Jane Rose as Phyllis's mother-in-law, Audrey Dexter; Henry Jones as Audrey's husband, Judge Jonathan Dexter; Lisa Gerritsen as Phyllis's teenage daughter, Bess; Barbara Colby (who was found murdered after three episodes had been filmed) and Liz Torres as Julie Erskine, the owner of a photography studio where Phyllis found work as a secretary; and Richard Schaal as Leo Heatherton, a photographer who worked at the studio. Judith Lowry became a regular during the first season as Jonathan's crusty and outspoken eighty-seven-year-old mother, Sally (Mother) Dexter. Liz Torres and Richard Schaal left the cast after one season, as Phyllis got a new job as a secretary at the San Francisco Board of Supervisors. Joining the cast were Carmine Caridi as supervisor Dan Va-

lenti; John Lawlor as supervisor Leonard Marsh; and Garn Stephens as fellow secretary Harriet Hastings. In the fall of 1976 Mother Dexter married eighty-nine-year-old Arthur Lanson, played by Burt Mustin (Judith Lowry, who played Mother Dexter, had died two weeks before the episode was telecast). In the spring of 1977 Phyllis's daughter Bess married Dan Valenti's nephew, Mark (played by Craig Wasson). Ed. Weinberger and Stan Daniels were the executive producers of the half-hour series for MTM Enterprises.

THE PHYLLIS DILLER SHOW
See THE BEAUTIFUL PHYLLIS DILLER SHOW; THE PRUITTS OF SOUTHAMPTON

PICCADILLY CIRCUS   PBS
19 JANUARY 1976–11 SEPTEMBER 1977   Telecast monthly, *Piccadilly Circus* was the umbrella title for a potpourri of programs from Great Britain: dramas, comedies, and documentaries were all presented. The series was funded by a grant from Mobil Oil.

PICCADILLY PALACE   ABC
20 MAY 1967–9 SEPTEMBER 1967   A summer replacement for *The Hollywood Palace,* this hour-long variety series was taped at London's Piccadilly Palace and hosted by Millicent Martin. Other regulars included comics Eric Morecombe and Ernie Wise, The Paddy Stone Dancers, and The Michael Sammes Singers. Colin Clews produced the series and directed it with Philip Casson.

PICK AND PAT   ABC
20 JANUARY 1949–17 MARCH 1949   This short-lived variety hour was no doubt the only TV series that regularly featured minstrel acts. Guest minstrels joined regulars Pick and Pat each week; also on hand were comedian and host Jack Carter and singer Mary Small. Ed Wolfe produced the show and Fred Carr directed it. By the end of the show's run, Jack Carter had begun hosting his own variety show: see *Jack Carter and Company.*

PICTURE THIS   CBS
25 JUNE 1963–17 SEPTEMBER 1963   This prime-time game show, a summer replacement for *The Jack Benny Program,* was hosted by Jerry Van Dyke. It featured two teams, each consisting of a celebrity and a contestant; one member of the team tried to get the other to identify a secret phrase by suggesting that his or her teammate draw clues.

THE PINK PANTHER SHOW   NBC/ABC
6 SEPTEMBER 1969–2 SEPTEMBER 1978 (NBC); 9 SEPTEMBER 1978–1

SEPTEMBER 1979 (ABC)   One of NBC's longest-running cartoon shows, *The Pink Panther Show,* starring the character created by Blake Edwards (who produced the Pink Panther films), began in 1969 as a half-hour series. In the fall of 1976 it expanded to ninety minutes and was retitled *The Pink Panther Laugh & ½ Hour & ½ Show.* Joining the suave but silent feline were segments of other cartoons, such as "The Ant and the Aardvark," "Inspector Clouseau," "Misterjaw," and "Texas Toads." In the fall of 1977 the series reverted to thirty minutes and was titled *The Think Pink Panther Show.* It shifted networks a year later, continuing under the title *The All-New Pink Panther Show.* The series were produced by David H. DePatie and Friz Freleng.

THE PINKY LEE SHOW   NBC
19 APRIL 1950–9 NOVEMBER 1950; 4 JANUARY 1954–11 MAY 1956   Though he is best remembered as the host of a daily children's show, Pinky Lee's first TV series was a prime-time variety show telecast in 1950. A year later he cohosted *Those Two,* a fifteen-minute musical variety series that lasted a year and a half. His most successful show began early in 1954, and, in most areas, was broadcast immediately preceding *Howdy Doody* (during the 1955–1956 season it was also seen Saturday mornings). On the half-hour show Lee, in hat and checkered coat, sang, danced, and told stories. Also featured were Roberta Shore, Mel Koontz, Barbara Luke, Jimmy Brown, and Jane Howard. After the show left the air in 1956, Lee was rarely seen on national television, though he hosted local shows in Los Angeles in 1964 and 1966.

PIP THE PIPER   ABC/NBC
25 DECEMBER 1960–28 MAY 1961 (ABC); 24 JUNE 1961–22 SEPTEMBER 1962 (NBC)   This children's fantasy series was set in Pipertown, a city in the clouds where musical instruments grew on trees. Featured were Jack Spear as Pip the Piper; Phyllis Spear as Miss Merry Note; and Lucian Kaminsky as The Leader (and other roles). The show was seen first on Saturdays and later on Sundays during its ABC run and exclusively on Saturdays during its NBC run.

PISTOLS 'N' PETTICOATS   CBS
17 SEPTEMBER 1966–26 AUGUST 1967   One of the first CBS shows regularly broadcast in color, *Pistols 'n' Petticoats* was a half-hour comedy western. Set in Wretched, Colorado, it featured Ann Sheridan as gun-toting widow Henrietta Hanks; Ruth McDevitt as gun-toting Grandma Hanks, her mother; Douglas V. Fowley as Andrew (Grandpa) Hanks, her father; Carole Wells as Henrietta's daughter, Lucy Hanks; and Gary Vinson as Wretched's bumbling sheriff, Harold Sikes. Occasionally featured were Robert Lowery as land baron Buss Courtney; Lon Chaney, Jr., as Chief Eagle Shadow; Marc Cavell as Gray Hawk; Alex Henteloff

as Little Bear; and Bowser, the Hanks' pet wolf. Joe Connelly produced the series.

PLACE THE FACE   NBC/CBS
2 JULY 1953–20 AUGUST 1953 (NBC); 27 AUGUST 1953–26 AUGUST 1954 (CBS); 25 SEPTEMBER 1954–25 DECEMBER 1954 (NBC); 28 JUNE 1955–13 SEPTEMBER 1955 (NBC)   On this prime-time game show contestants tried to identify persons from their past who were brought to the studio and seated opposite them. Jack Smith was the first host of the series and was succeeded by Bill Cullen, who went on to emcee many more game shows.

PLACES, PLEASE   CBS
5 JULY 1948–25 FEBRUARY 1949   Barry Wood produced and hosted this early-evening talent show, which was broadcast two or three times a week. When Wood left in February of 1949, the show was retitled *Manhattan Showcase* (see also that title).

THE PLAINCLOTHESMAN   DUMONT
12 OCTOBER 1949–12 SEPTEMBER 1954   One of the longer-running shows on the DuMont network, *The Plainclothesman* was a half-hour crime show that starred Ken Lynch as The Lieutenant; Lynch's face was never seen on camera, as the show employed the subjective camera technique. Jack Orrison was also featured (and was seen as well) as Sergeant Brady.

PLANET OF THE APES   CBS
13 SEPTEMBER 1974–27 DECEMBER 1974   Based on the movie of the same title, this hour-long sci-fi series chronicled the adventures of two American astronauts who stumbled into a time warp and were hurtled 2,000 years into the future, where they found the Earth ruled by English-speaking apes, who treated the planet's humans as chattels. With Ron Harper as astronaut Alan Virdon; James Naughton as astronaut Pete Burke; Roddy McDowall as Galen, an inquisitive ape who befriended the visitors; Booth Colman as Zaius, leader of the apes; and Mark Lenard as Urko, Zaius's right-hand simian. Herbert Hirschman was the executive producer, and Stan Hough the producer for 20th Century-Fox Television. See also *Return to the Planet of the Apes*.

THE PLASTICMAN COMEDY/ADVENTURE SHOW   ABC
15 SEPTEMBER 1979–   Segments on this two-hour Saturday-morning cartoon show included "Plasticman," the adventures of the "superfantastic highly elastic" superhero and his pals Penny and Hulahula; and "Mighty Man and Yukk," the adventures of the world's smallest superhero and the world's ugliest dog. Two other episodes involved "Rick-

ety Rocket," a talking spaceship and four teenage detectives; and "Fangface and Fangpuss" (*Fangface* had been a separate series during the 1978–1979 season).

THE PLAY OF THE WEEK
SYNDICATED

1959–1961   *The Play of the Week* was a New York–based dramatic anthology series that relied heavily on talent from Broadway. Among the presentations were: Graham Greene's "The Power and the Glory," John Steinbeck's "Burning Bright," Jean Anouilh's "The Waltz of the Toreadors," "Black Monday," with Robert Redford, Eugene O'Neill's "The Iceman Cometh" (also with Redford), and "The Closing Door," with George Segal (in one of his earliest television appearances). Underwritten by Standard Oil of New Jersey, the series' executive producer was David Susskind.

PLAY YOUR HUNCH
CBS/ABC/NBC

30 JUNE 1958–2 JANUARY 1959 (CBS); 5 JANUARY 1959–8 MAY 1959 (ABC); 7 DECEMBER 1959–26 SEPTEMBER 1963 (NBC)   One of the few game shows to have been aired by all three networks, *Play Your Hunch* was somewhat similar to *To Tell the Truth:* contestants tried to guess which of three objects or situations (labeled X, Y, and Z) was the real one. The show was seen during the daytime on all three networks and was also seen at night in 1960 and 1962 on NBC. It was hosted by Richard Hayes, Gene Rayburn, Merv Griffin, and Robert Q. Lewis.

PLAYBOY AFTER DARK
SYNDICATED

1969   The second of the two variety shows hosted by Hugh Hefner, publisher of *Playboy* magazine, *Playboy After Dark* was set at a party—Hefner contrived to bump into his guests and always managed to persuade them to sing a number or tell a few jokes. The Checkmates and several Playboy Bunnies were regularly featured. See also *Playboy's Penthouse*.

PLAYBOY'S PENTHOUSE
SYNDICATED

1959–1960   Hugh Hefner, publisher of *Playboy* magazine, tried his hand at hosting a variety show in 1959 (ten years before *Penthouse* magazine first appeared on the newsstand). Taped at WBKB-TV in Chicago, it was set at a party. Ten years later Hefner again tried a TV show: see *Playboy After Dark*.

PLAYHOUSE 90
CBS

4 OCTOBER 1956–18 MAY 1960   Generally regarded as the most ambitious of television's dramatic anthology series, *Playhouse 90* presented a ninety-minute drama each week during its first three seasons. It was broadcast as a series of specials during the 1959–1960 season, and reruns were aired in 1961. More than one hundred plays were presented, includ-

ing some of TV's best-known original works, such as "Requiem for a Heavyweight" and "The Miracle Worker." With Martin Manulis as its first producer, *Playhouse 90* premiered in 1956 with a Rod Serling screenplay, "Forbidden Area," featuring Charlton Heston, Tab Hunter, Diana Lynn, Vincent Price, and Jackie Coogan. The following week it presented the widely acclaimed "Requiem for a Heavyweight"; written by Serling and directed by Ralph Nelson, it starred Jack Palance as Mountain McClintock, a broken-down boxer, Keenan Wynn (as his manager), Kim Hunter, and Ed Wynn. "Requiem" won an Emmy for best single program of the season, and Palance also won an Emmy for his performance (*Playhouse 90* itself also won, as best new series). Several more top-notch plays were broadcast that season, including: "Eloise," with Evelyn Rudie, Ethel Barrymore, Louis Jourdan, and Kay Thompson (22 November); "So Soon to Die," with Richard Basehart (in his first dramatic role on TV, 17 January); "The Miracle Worker," with Patty McCormack, Teresa Wright, and Burl Ives (written by William Gibson, directed by Arthur Penn, and televised 7 February, it subsequently ran on Broadway, and a filmed version was made in 1962); "Charley's Aunt," with Jeanette MacDonald (in a rare television appearance) and Art Carney (28 March); "Three Men on a Horse," with Carol Channing (in a rare TV dramatic appearance) and Johnny Carson (in his first TV dramatic role, 18 April); "Child of Trouble," with Lillian Roth (in a rare TV appearance, 2 May); "Without Incident," with Errol Flynn (also making a rare appearance, 6 June). The quality of the presentations remained high through the rest of *Playhouse 90*'s run. A representative sampling would include the following from the 1957–1958 season: "The Dark Side of the Earth," with Earl Holliman, Kim Hunter, and Dean Jagger (19 September); "The 80 Yard Run," with Paul Newman (in his last TV dramatic role) and Joanne Woodward (16 January); "No Time at All," with Jack Haley (13 February); "The Male Animal," with Andy Griffith (13 March). From the 1958–1959 season: "The Days of Wine and Roses," with Charles Bickford, Piper Laurie, and Cliff Robertson (2 October); Joseph Conrad's "Heart of Darkness," with Oscar Homolka and Eartha Kitt (6 November); "Face of a Hero," with Jack Lemmon (in his last TV dramatic role until 1976; 1 January); "Child of Our Time," with Maximilian Schell and Bobby Crawford, Jr. (5 February); Ernest Hemingway's "For Whom the Bell Tolls," with Jason Robards, Jr., Maria Schell, Nehemiah Persoff, Maureen Stapleton, Steven Hill, and Eli Wallach (adapted by A. E. Hotchner and directed by John Frankenheimer, it was broadcast in two parts on 12 March and 19 March); Abby Mann's "Judgment at Nuremburg," with Claude Rains, Melvyn Douglas, and Maximilian Schell (16 April). From the 1959–1960 season: "Misalliance," with Claire Bloom (29 October); "Alas, Babylon," with Dana Andrews, Don Murray, Kim Hunter, Barbara Rush, and Burt Reynolds (David Shaw adapted it from Pat Frank's novel, and Robert Stevens directed; it was aired 3 April);

"Journey to the Day," with Mike Nichols (22 April); "In the Presence of Mine Enemies," with Charles Laughton, Arthur Kennedy, and Robert Redford (18 May).

THE PLAY'S THE THING
CBS

17 MARCH 1950–30 JUNE 1950 This Friday-night dramatic anthology hour replaced another anthology series, *Theatre Hour.*

PLAYWRIGHTS '56
NBC

4 OCTOBER 1955–19 JUNE 1956 Fred Coe produced this dramatic anthology hour, which shared a slot on Tuesdays with *Armstrong Circle Theater;* it was also known as *The Playwright Hour.* Presentations included: "The Battler," with Phyllis Kirk and Paul Newman (18 October); "Lost," with Steven Hill (17 January); and "Flight," with Kim Stanley (28 February).

PLEASE DON'T EAT THE DAISIES
NBC

14 SEPTEMBER 1965–2 SEPTEMBER 1967 Based on Jean Kerr's book (which was made into a movie in 1960, starring Doris Day), this half-hour sitcom was set in the town of Ridgemont. It featured Patricia Crowley as freelance writer Joan Nash, suburban wife and mother of four boys; Mark Miller as her husband, Jim Nash, a college professor; Kim Tyler as their son Kyle; Brian Nash as their son Joel; Jeff and Joe Fithian as their twin sons Trevor and Tracy; King Donovan as neighbor Herb Thornton, a lawyer; Shirley Mitchell as his wife, Marge Thornton; and Lord Nelson as the Nash family sheepdog, Ladadog. Paul West produced the series for MGM.

PLEASE STAND BY
SYNDICATED

1978 Half-hour sitcom about an oil executive who quit his job to run a small television station in the boondocks. With Richard Schaal as Frank Lambert; Elinor Donahue as his wife, Carol Lambert; Bryan Scott as their son, Rocky; Marcie Barkin as Vicki James; Stephen Michael Schwartz as David; and Darian Mathias as Susan. Bob Banner and Ed Warren were the executive producers.

PLYMOUTH PLAYHOUSE
See ABC ALBUM

POLICE CALL
SYNDICATED

1955 An undistinguished anthology series of twenty-six half-hour crime shows, *Police Call* was distributed by MCA-TV.

POLICE STORY
CBS

4 APRIL 1952–26 SEPTEMBER 1952 This early police anthology series, which premiered more than twenty years before Joseph Wambaugh's *Po-*

lice Story (see below), was a half-hour show that dramatized incidents taken from police files throughout the nation. Norman Rose narrated the series, Jerome Robinson produced it, and David Rich directed.

POLICE STORY
NBC

2 OCTOBER 1973–23 AUGUST 1977   One of the few successful anthology series of the 1970s, *Police Story* was created by Joseph Wambaugh, a Los Angeles police officer who wrote such police novels as *The New Centurions* and *Black Marble*. As production consultant for the series, Wambaugh tried to insure that it depicted police life more realistically than most other crime shows. Stanley Kallis was the first executive producer of the series and was succeeded in 1976 by David Gerber; Christopher Morgan was the producer until 1975, when he was succeeded by Liam O'Brien and Carl Pingitore. The pilots for two other police shows were televised on *Police Story: Joe Forrester* and *Police Woman*. Though *Police Story* ceased to be seen as a weekly series in the summer of 1977, a few new episodes were shown as specials during the 1977–1978 season.

POLICE SURGEON
SYNDICATED

1972–1973   On this half-hour crime show, Sam Groom again played Dr. Simon Locke; Groom had played the part a season earlier on *Dr. Simon Locke*, in which the title character was a small-town physician. In this series Locke had become a surgeon with the medical unit of a big-city police department. Also featured was Larry D. Mann as Lieutenant Jack Gordon. Wilton Schiller was the executive producer, and Chester Krumholz the producer of the series, which was filmed in Toronto.

POLICE WOMAN
NBC

13 SEPTEMBER 1974–30 AUGUST 1978   This hour-long crime show starred Angie Dickinson as Sergeant Pepper Anderson, an attractive divorcée who was an undercover officer for the criminal conspiracy division of the Los Angeles Police Department. Also featured were Earl Holliman as her frequent companion (both on and off duty), Sergeant Bill Crowley; Charles Dierkop as Detective Pete Royster; and Ed Bernard as Detective Joe Styles. David Gerber was the executive producer and Douglas Benton was the producer. The pilot for the series, entitled "The Gamble," was televised on *Police Story* on 26 March 1974; it featured Dickinson as Lisa Beaumont and Bert Convy as Crowley, with Dierkop and Bernard in their later roles.

POLITICS ON TRIAL
ABC

11 SEPTEMBER 1952–30 OCTOBER 1952   Issues relating to the 1952 presidential campaign were debated in a mock courtroom setting by opposing sides on this half-hour prime-time show.

564

POLKA-GO-ROUND   ABC

23 JUNE 1958–28 SEPTEMBER 1959   ABC's second attempt at a polka
series (the first was *It's Polka Time*) was hosted by Bob Lewandowski
and broadcast from Chicago. Other regulars included Carolyn DeZurik
(who had also been featured on *It's Polka Time*), Lou Prohut, Georgia
Drake, Tom Fouts and the Singing Waiters, the Polka Rounders, and the
Chaine Dancers. The show was seen Monday nights in both hour and
half-hour versions.

THE POLLY BERGEN SHOW   NBC

21 SEPTEMBER 1957–31 MAY 1958   Polly Bergen hosted her own variety
series for one season; the half-hour show alternated biweekly with *Club
Oasis* and featured the orchestra of Luther Henderson, Jr., and the Peter
Gennaro Dancers. The show's theme song, "The Party's Over," was
composed by Jule Styne.

PONDEROSA
See BONANZA

POND'S THEATER   ABC

13 JANUARY 1955–7 JULY 1955   *Pond's Theater* was the new title for the
Thursday-night dramatic anthology series sponsored by Kraft Foods
from October 1953 to 6 January 1955 (Kraft continued to sponsor *Kraft
Television Theatre* on NBC, however). Sidney Poitier played his first major dramatic role on television in one episode of *Pond's Theater,* "The
Fascinating Stranger," broadcast 23 June; Booth Tarkington's story was
adapted by Elizabeth Hart. Paul Lammers produced and directed the
hour series.

PONY EXPRESS   SYNDICATED

1959   Half-hour western with Grant Sullivan as Brett Clark, roving investigator for the Pony Express; Bill Cord as Tom Clyde; and Don Dorell
as Donovan.

POP! GOES THE COUNTRY   SYNDICATED

1974   Ralph Emery hosted this half-hour country and western music
show. Bill Graham was the executive producer and J. Reginald Dunlap
the producer.

POPEYE   SYNDICATED
1958–1963
THE ALL-NEW POPEYE HOUR   CBS

9 SEPTEMBER 1978–   *Popeye,* the spinach-eating sailor created by Max Fleischer in the 1930s, starred in more than 250 cartoons
made for theatrical release; in most of them he tangled with the villain

Bluto to save his girlfriend Olive Oyl. Between 1958 and 1963 an additional 200 cartoons were produced, in many of which Popeye faced a villain named Brutus, who closely resembled Bluto. The cartoons were shown individually by some stations, as part of a local cartoon show, or were strung together to comprise a full half-hour. In the fall of 1978 Popeye came to network television for the first time in *The All-New Popeye Hour*.

POPI CBS
20 JANUARY 1976–24 AUGUST 1976 This half-hour sitcom about a Puerto Rican widower and his two sons was a midseason replacement for *Joe and Sons,* a half-hour sitcom about an Italian widower and his two sons. *Popi* featured Hector Elizondo as Abraham (Popi) Rodriguez, a widowed handyman who lived in New York with his two boys; Anthony Perez as Junior, the older son; Dennis Vasquez as Luis, the younger son; Edith Diaz as Lupe, their neighbor; and Lou Criscuolo as Mr. Maggio. Created by Tina Pine and Lester Pine, the series was based on the 1969 film of the same title; the pilot was shown on CBS 2 May 1975. Herbert B. Leonard was the executive producer, and Don Van Atta was the producer.

THE POPSICLE PARADE OF STARS CBS
15 MAY 1950–17 JULY 1950 This fifteen-minute Monday-evening variety show was hosted by a different guest star each week. Among the headliners were Paul Winchell (22 May), Arthur Godfrey (29 May), Martha Raye (3 July), and Groucho Marx (17 July).

THE PORKY PIG SHOW ABC
13 SEPTEMBER 1964–3 SEPTEMBER 1966 Porky Pig, Warner Brothers' stuttering swine, had his own weekend cartoon show for two seasons. The half-hour series also featured other Warner Brothers cartoons, such as "Bugs Bunny," "Daffy Duck," and "Sylvester and Tweety."

THE PORTER WAGONER SHOW SYNDICATED
1960– One of TV's longest-running country and western music shows, this half-hour show has been hosted by singer Porter Wagoner for two decades. Bill Graham has been the executive producer and J. Reginald Dunlap the producer.

PORTIA FACES LIFE CBS
5 APRIL 1954–1 JULY 1955 *Portia Faces Life* began on radio in 1940 and came to television fourteen years later. The fifteen-minute daily serial starred Frances Reid and Fran Carlon as Portia Blake Manning, a successful attorney. Also featured were Karl Swenson and Donald Woods as

her husband, Walter Manning; Charles Taylor as their son, Dick; Ginger MacManus and Renne Jarrett as their daughter, Shirley; and Patrick O'Neal as Portia's brother, Carl. The serial was also seen under the title *The Inner Flame.*

PORTRAIT
CBS

9 AUGUST 1963–13 SEPTEMBER 1963   CBS newsman Charles Collingwood interviewed celebrities and newsmakers on this Friday-night half-hour series, which replaced *Eyewitness.* Peter Sellers was the guest on the premiere.

THE POWER OF WOMEN
DUMONT

1 JULY 1952–11 NOVEMBER 1952   Half-hour public affairs discussion program for women, moderated first by Vivien Kellems, later by Mrs. John G. Lee.

THE PRACTICE
NBC

30 JANUARY 1976–26 JANUARY 1977   Half-hour sitcom starring Danny Thomas as Dr. Jules Bedford, a crusty but compassionate physician practicing on New York's West Side. Also featured were David Spielberg as Dr. David Bedford, his less idealistic son; Dena Dietrich as Nurse Molly Gibbons; Shelley Fabares as Jenny Bedford, David's wife; Didi Conn as Helen, the receptionist; Allen Price as Paul, David and Jenny's son; Damon Raskin as Tony, David and Jenny's other son; Sam Laws as Nate; John Byner (spring 1976) as Dr. Roland Caine; and Mike Evans (fall 1976) as Lenny. Produced by Danny Thomas Productions in association with MGM and NBC, the series' executive producer was Paul Younger Witt, and its supervising producer was Tony Thomas.

THE PRACTICE TEE
NBC

5 AUGUST 1949–9 SEPTEMBER 1949   Broadcast from Cleveland, this fifteen-minute Friday-night show was hosted by William P. Barbour, resident pro at the Sleepy Hollow Country Club, who showed golfers at home how to improve their games.

PRESENTING SUSAN ANTON
NBC

26 APRIL 1979–17 MAY 1979   Four-week musical variety hour starring Susan Anton, with Jack Fletcher and Jack Knight. Jack Stein was the executive producer, Ernest Chambers the producer.

PRESIDENTIAL TIMBER
CBS

4 APRIL 1952–27 JUNE 1952   On this Friday-night public affairs program, air time was made available to any announced candidate for the Presidency. Robert Trout moderated the series, which was produced by

David Zellman and directed by Don Hewitt (who later became the executive producer of CBS's *60 Minutes*).

PRESS CONFERENCE
ABC/NBC

2 FEBRUARY 1955–11 SEPTEMBER 1955 (ABC); 4 JULY 1956–26 SEPTEMBER 1956 (NBC); 28 OCTOBER 1956–15 JULY 1957 (ABC) The 1955 version of this public affairs program presented filmed coverage of President Eisenhower's news conferences. The 1956 and 1957 versions were panel shows on which guest journalists grilled newsmakers. Martha Rountree, who had previously produced NBC's *Meet the Press,* was the moderator of the latter versions.

PRESS CORRESPONDENTS PANEL
CBS

10 APRIL 1949–22 MAY 1949 Current events were discussed by groups of journalists on this half-hour Sunday-evening program.

PREVIEW
CBS

7 MARCH 1949–5 SEPTEMBER 1949 *Preview* was a Monday-night potpourri of features, hosted by the husband-and-wife team of Tex McCrary and Jinx Falkenburg.

THE PRICE IS RIGHT
NBC/ABC/SYNDICATED/CBS

26 NOVEMBER 1956–6 SEPTEMBER 1963 (NBC); 9 SEPTEMBER 1963–3 SEPTEMBER 1965 (ABC); 1972– (SYNDICATED); 4 SEPTEMBER 1972– (CBS) More merchandise has probably been given away on this game show than on any other show except *Let's Make a Deal.* The series, a Mark Goodson–Bill Todman production, has been seen in several different formats, on network and in syndication, in prime time and in the daytime. In the fall of 1956 the show began a nine-year daytime run, with Bill Cullen as host. The format was fairly rigid then; each day four contestants were featured, all seated behind "tote" machines (manufactured by the American Totalizator Corporation). After being shown an item of merchandise, the contestants bid on it, and the prize was awarded to the contestant who had bid the highest without going over the manufacturer's suggested list price. For most items, each contestant's bid had to be higher than the previous contestant's, and the players were constantly exhorted from the studio audience to stop bidding, or "freeze." Occasionally, an item would be a "one-bid" item, in which the contestants could bid just once, and, in some cases, each successive bid had to be a certain dollar amount higher than the preceding bid. The show ran for seven years on NBC and was also seen during prime time from 1957 to 1963; in the fall of 1963 it moved to ABC, where it ran for two more years in a daytime slot and was also seen briefly in prime time. Announcer Don Pardo was also on hand to introduce the host and to describe the wares. After a seven-year hiatus two versions of

the show resurfaced in 1972; both were known briefly as *The New Price Is Right.* A syndicated version, hosted by Dennis James, is seen in prime time in most markets; the network version, broadcast daily, is hosted by Bob Barker, and in November 1975 it became the first regularly scheduled daytime game show to expand to an hour. On both of the latter versions the format is less rigid; several different price-guessing games are employed, rather than the single form of bidding formerly used.

PRIDE OF THE FAMILY   ABC
2 OCTOBER 1953–24 SEPTEMBER 1954   Half-hour sitcom starring Paul Hartman as Albie Morrison, head of the advertising department of the local paper. With Fay Wray as his wife, Catherine Morrison; Natalie Wood as their teenage daughter, Ann; and Bobby Hyatt as their son, Junior. Bob Finkel directed the series for Revue Productions.

PRIME TIME SUNDAY (PRIME TIME SATURDAY)   NBC
24 JUNE 1979–   A weekly magazine series, *Prime Time Sunday* is the successor to *Weekend.* Tom Snyder, host of NBC's *Tomorrow,* is the host of the hour show, which is broadcast live with taped segments. Jack Perkins is a regular contributor. Paul Friedman left his job as executive producer of the *Today* show to head up the production team for *Prime Time Sunday.* In December 1979 the show moved to Saturday and was suitably retitled.

PRIMUS   SYNDICATED
1971   Essentially an updated version of *Sea Hunt, Primus* starred Robert Brown as oceanographer Carter Primus, with Will Kuluva as his assistant, Charlie Kingman, and Eva Renzi as assistant Toni Hyden. Primus and his cohorts floated about in such craft as *Big Kate,* a sort of underwater robot, and *Pegasus,* a smaller craft used for underwater photography.

PRINCE PLANET   SYNDICATED
1966   Another of the several Japanese-produced cartoon series of the late 1960s, Prince Planet was a young lad from another galaxy who came to Earth to fight wrongdoers.

PRINCETON '55   NBC
2 JANUARY 1955–27 MARCH 1955   This Sunday-afternoon public affairs program was produced at Princeton University; it began as a local show the previous year (when it was titled *Princeton '54*), before going network in January. The 1955 premiere show was titled "Communists and Who They Are," while Robert Frost was featured the following week, on "Enjoyment of Poetry." Steve Krantz was the executive producer, and Harry Olesker was the producer.

THE PRISONER CBS

1 JUNE 1968–21 SEPTEMBER 1968; 29 MAY 1969–11 SEPTEMBER
1969   Regarded by many buffs as the finest dramatic series ever broadcast, *The Prisoner* was certainly one of the most imaginative and enigmat-
ic shows in TV history. The hour series was the brainchild of Patrick
McGoohan, who was its star and executive producer, as well as the writer
and director of several episodes. As *The Prisoner* unfolded, McGoohan,
who had previously played John Drake on *Secret Agent,* found himself
living in a mysterious, self-contained cosmopolitan community known
simply as "the village." Most of the village's inhabitants were known
merely by numbers—McGoohan was Number 6, and in the opening episode he met Number 2, who explained to him that he had been transported to the village because the information stored in his head had made him
too valuable "outside" (though McGoohan never referred to himself by
name, it was strongly implied from the opening sequence and from a
fleeting reference in one episode, that Number 6 was in fact John Drake,
who, for one reason or another, had left the intelligence service). Thus
Number 6 gradually realized that he was a prisoner, though his prison
was an idyllic place with plenty of green fields and parks, recreational activities, and even a butler (the mute manservant was played by Angelo
Muscat). Nevertheless, Number 6 was determined to preserve his individ-
uality, and through most of the seventeen episodes, he either tried to escape from the village or to learn the identity of Number 1, the person
assumed to run the village. His attempts to escape were always thwarted
by large white balloonlike spheres, known as "rovers." In the final episode, "Fall Out" (written by McGoohan), Number 6 ultimately earned
the right not to be called by a number and learned that *he* had been Number 1; as the episode closed, he was seen driving away from the village toward London. In real life, "the village," where almost all of the action
took place, was a resort in North Wales called the Hotel Portmeirion, designed by Sir Clough Williams-Ellis.

PRIVATE SECRETARY CBS/NBC

1 FEBRUARY 1953–10 SEPTEMBER 1957 (CBS); 20 JUNE 1953–5 SEP-
TEMBER 1953 (NBC); 26 JUNE 1954–4 SEPTEMBER 1954 (NBC)   Half-
hour sitcom starring Ann Sothern as brassy Susie MacNamara, a private
secretary. With Don Porter as her boss, theatrical agent Peter Sands;
Ann Tyrrell as Susie's confidante, switchboard operator Violet Praskins;
Jesse White as rival agent Cagey Calhoun; and Joan Banks as Susie's
friend Sylvia. In the later seasons Louis Nye and Ken Berry appeared as
Delbert and Woody. Jack Chertok produced the series and Christian
Nyby directed it. On CBS *Private Secretary* alternated biweekly with *The
Jack Benny Program*; during the summers of 1953 and 1954 NBC carried
reruns of *Private Secretary* as a replacement for *Your Hit Parade*. The se-
ries was syndicated under the title *Susie*.

PRIZE PARTY   CBS

6 DECEMBER 1948–17 JUNE 1949   Bill Slater hosted this Friday-night game show on which the contestants performed stunts. Its full title was *The Messing Prize Party,* as its sponsor was Messing Bakeries.

PRIZE PERFORMANCE   CBS

3 JULY 1950–12 SEPTEMBER 1950   This summer replacement show was a talent showcase for aspiring young performers. Arlene Francis was the host, and Cedric Adams and Peter Donald were regular panelists.

PRO BOWLERS' TOUR   ABC

6 JANUARY 1962–   Long-running sports show, usually seen Saturday afternoons; each week a bowling tournament is telecast live. Chris Schenkel and Jack Buck were the original commentators, and Schenkel has remained with the series through most of its run.

PRO FOOTBALL HIGHLIGHTS   ABC/DUMONT

15 SEPTEMBER 1950–8 DECEMBER 1950 (ABC); 24 SEPTEMBER 1952–17 DECEMBER 1952; 1 OCTOBER 1953–17 DECEMBER 1953 (DU-MONT)   Half-hour wrap-up of pro football news. Because the show was broadcast from New York, much of the show centered around the local eleven, the New York Giants. Joe Hasel hosted the show in 1950, and was succeeded by Steve Owen (the Giants' coach) in 1952 and 1953.

PRODUCERS' SHOWCASE   NBC

18 OCTOBER 1954–24 JUNE 1957   One of the most costly of the several high-quality dramatic anthology series, *Producers' Showcase,* under the supervision of Fred Coe, was seen approximately once a month. Some of television's most notable single programs were presented on the highly acclaimed series. Among them were: "Tonight at 8:30," with Trevor Howard and Ginger Rogers (both making their TV dramatic debuts, 18 October 1954); "State of the Union," with Nina Foch, Joseph Cotten, and Margaret Sullavan (directed by Arthur Penn, it was aired 15 November 1954); the extraordinarily popular telecast of "Peter Pan," with Mary Martin and Cyril Ritchard (directed by Jerome Robbins, it was first aired 7 March 1955, and was restaged 9 January 1956); Sidney Kingsley's "Darkness at Noon," with Joseph Wiseman, Lee J. Cobb, Nehemiah Persoff, and Ruth Roman (directed by Delbert Mann, it was broadcast 2 May 1955); Robert Sherwood's "The Petrified Forest," with Humphrey Bogart (in his only dramatic appearance on television, recreating the role of Duke Mantee, which he had played on stage and on film), Henry Fonda, Lauren Bacall, Jack Klugman, and Richard Jaeckel (30 May 1955); a musical version of Thornton Wilder's "Our Town," with Paul Newman and Frank Sinatra (19 September 1955); "The Barretts of Wim-

pole Street," with Katharine Cornell (in her TV debut), Anthony Quayle, and Nancy Coleman (2 April 1956); Sidney Howard's "Dodsworth," with Fredric March, Florence Eldridge, and Claire Trevor (30 April 1956); "The Lord Don't Play Favorites," with Louis Armstrong, Buster Keaton, Kay Starr, and Dick Haymes (17 September 1956); "Jack and the Beanstalk," with Joel Grey, Celeste Holm, Cyril Ritchard, and Peggy King (12 November 1956); Anatole Litvak's "Mayerling," with Audrey Hepburn, Mel Ferrer, Raymond Massey, Diana Wynyard, Judith Evelyn, Basil Sydney, Nehemiah Persoff, Lorne Greene, Nancy Marchand, Monique Van Vooren, Sorrell Booke, and Suzy Parker (4 February 1957); "The Great Sebastians," starring Alfred Lunt and Lynn Fontanne in their television debut (1 April 1957). *Producers' Showcase* almost succeeded in landing Marilyn Monroe, who, had she taken the part, would have made her TV dramatic debut in "Lysistrata" sometime in 1956; after much consideration, she turned down the offer and never appeared in a dramatic role on television.

PRODUCTION FOR FREEDOM
ABC
22 JUNE 1952–21 SEPTEMBER 1952   Sunday-night series of films about American industry. See also *Enterprise U.S.A.*; *Industry on Parade*.

PROFESSIONAL FATHER
CBS
8 JANUARY 1955–2 JULY 1955   Half-hour sitcom starring Steve Dunne as Dr. Tom Wilson, a child psychologist who has trouble raising his own kids at home; Barbara Billingsley as his wife, Helen Wilson; Ted Marc as their son, Twig; Beverly Washburn as their daughter, Kit; Phyllis Coates as their neighbor, Madge; Joseph Kearns as Madge's husband, Fred; Ann O'Neal as the Wilsons' housekeeper, Nana; and Arthur Q. Bryan as Mr. Boggs, the neighborhood handyman. Harry Kronman produced the series, and Sherman Marks directed it.

PROFILES IN COURAGE
NBC
8 NOVEMBER 1964–9 MAY 1965   An anthology series based on John F. Kennedy's 1956 book about American political leaders who faced difficult decisions. Robert Saudek was executive producer of the half-hour series, and Theodore H. Sorenson and Allan Nevins served as special consultants.

PROGRAM PLAYHOUSE
DUMONT
22 JUNE 1949–14 SEPTEMBER 1949   James L. Caddigan produced this live half-hour anthology series. The premiere telecast, "The Timid Soul," was based on H. T. Webster's comic strip and starred Ernest Truex as Caspar Milquetoast.

PROJECT U.F.O.

NBC

19 FEBRUARY 1978–4 JANUARY 1979   On this hour-long science fiction series a team of Air Force investigators tracked down reports of sightings of unidentified flying objects and of contact with alien beings. Featured were William Jordan as Major Jake Gatlin; Caskey Swaim as Staff Sergeant Harry Fitz; and Aldine King as Libby. Jack Webb, the executive producer and narrator of the series, obtained information from the United States government on nearly 13,000 sightings of unidentified flying objects, some of which were used as the bases for the episodes. William T. Coleman, who headed an Air Force investigation project in the early 1960s, was the producer. In the fall of 1978 Edward Winter joined the cast as Captain Ben Ryan, replacing William Jordan.

THE PROTECTORS

SYNDICATED

1972–1974   Filmed in Europe, this widely syndicated half-hour adventure series followed the activities of the Protectors, an elite crew of private eyes. Featured were Robert Vaughn as Harry Rule; Nyree Dawn Porter as Contessa Caroline di Contini; and Tony Anholt as Paul Buchet.

PRUDENTIAL FAMILY THEATER

CBS

10 OCTOBER 1950–27 MARCH 1951   This hour-long dramatic anthology series was seen on Tuesday nights, opposite Milton Berle's *The Texaco Star Theater,* where it alternated biweekly with *Sure As Fate.* Presentations included: "The Barretts of Wimpole Street," with Helen Hayes and Bethel Leslie (5 December); "Over 21," with Ruth Gordon (19 December); "Burlesque," with Bert Lahr (2 January); "Berkeley Square," with Richard Greene and Grace Kelly (13 February); and "Ruggles of Red Gap," with Cyril Ritchard, Glenda Farrell, and Walter Abel (27 February).

THE PRUITTS OF SOUTHAMPTON

ABC

6 SEPTEMBER 1966–1 SEPTEMBER 1967   Phyllis Diller's attempt at a situation comedy was unsuccessful. She starred as Phyllis Pruitt, a Long Island socialite who had to make a rapid transition from luxury to poverty when she learned she owed millions in back taxes. Also featured were Reginald Gardiner as eighty-one-year-old Uncle Ned; Grady Sutton as Sturgis, the butler; Pam Freeman as her daughter, Stephanie; Lisa Loring as her daughter, Suzy; and Richard Deacon as Mr. Baldwin, the Internal Revenue Service agent. In midseason the format was changed slightly, and the show was retitled; on 13 January *The Phyllis Diller Show* premiered, and the Pruitts' mansion was now a boardinghouse. Added to the cast were three new regulars: John Astin as Rudy Pruitt; Marty Ingels as Norman Krump; and Gypsy Rose Lee as Regina. David Levy was the executive producer of the series for Filmways.

THE PSYCHIATRIST NBC
3 FEBRUARY 1971–1 SEPTEMBER 1971 The concluding segment of
NBC's *Four-in-One, The Psychiatrist* starred Roy Thinnes as Dr. James
Whitman, a Los Angeles analyst, and Luther Adler as his colleague, Dr.
Bernard Altman.

PUBLIC DEFENDER CBS
11 MARCH 1954–23 JUNE 1955 This half-hour crime show starred Reed
Hadley (formerly the star of *Racket Squad*) as public defender Bart
Matthews.

PUBLIC PROSECUTOR SYNDICATED/DUMONT
1947–1948 (SYNDICATED); 6 SEPTEMBER 1951–28 FEBRUARY 1952
(DUMONT) The first filmed series made especially for television, *Public Prosecutor* was a series of twenty-six 17½-minute mysteries starring
John Howard as a prosecuting attorney, with Anne Gwynne as his assistant and Walter Sande as a police lieutenant. When the DuMont network
obtained the series in 1951, it turned the program into a panel show in order to fill a thirty-minute time slot. Each week three guest panelists—
mystery buffs or amateur sleuths—watched an episode (along with the
home audience), which was halted just before the climax; each panelist
then tried to guess the identity of the guilty party. Warren Hull served as
the host of the DuMont version of the show. Other local stations which
bought *Public Prosecutor* rarely bothered to employ a panel or a host,
preferring instead to pad the rest of the half-hour slot with extra commercials. *Public Prosecutor* was produced by Jerry Fairbanks for Jerry Fairbanks Productions.

PULITZER PRIZE PLAYHOUSE ABC
6 OCTOBER 1950–29 JUNE 1951; 2 JANUARY 1952–4 JUNE 1952 Presen-
tations on this hour-long dramatic anthology series were adapted from
Pulitzer Prize–winning stories. Included were: Emlyn Williams's "The
Late Christopher Bean," with Helen Hayes (in her TV debut) and
Charles Dingle (27 October 1950); "The Magnificent Ambersons" (based
on the novel by Booth Tarkington), with Ruth Hussey (3 November
1950); Sidney Howard's "The Silver Cord," with Joanne Dru and Dame
Judith Anderson (26 January 1951); and "The Happy Journey," with
Jack Lemmon (4 May 1951).

PULSE OF THE CITY DUMONT
15 SEPTEMBER 1953–9 MARCH 1954 Fifteen-minute dramatic anthology series.

PURSUIT CBS
22 OCTOBER 1958–14 JANUARY 1959 This hour-long anthology series
of thrillers should not be confused with any of the other similarly titled

suspense anthologies of the period, such as *Climax, Moment of Fear, Panic!,* and *Suspicion.*

Q. E. D.   ABC
3 APRIL 1951–25 SEPTEMBER 1951   Fred Uttal hosted this prime-time game show on which a celebrity panel tried to solve mystery stories submitted by home viewers.

QUADRANGLE   CBS
14 MARCH 1949–22 APRIL 1949   Ralph Levy produced and directed this fifteen-minute talent show, which was set at a campus drugstore.

QUARK   NBC
24 FEBRUARY 1978–14 APRIL 1978   This half-hour science fiction comedy show starred Richard Benjamin as Adam Quark, commander of a garbage scow for the United Galaxy Sanitation Patrol. The cast also included: Timothy Thomerson as Gene Jean, his androgynous assistant; Richard Kelton as Ficus, a boring but talkative plant; twins Tricia and Cyb Barnstable as Betty I and Betty II (Betty II was cloned from Betty I); Conrad Janis as Palindrome, Quark's boss back at Perma One, the space center; Alan Caillou as The Head, Palindrome's boss; and Bobby Porter as Andy, the cowardly robot aboard Quark's ship. David Gerber was the executive producer for Columbia Pictures TV, with Mace Neufeld the coexecutive producer and Bruce Johnson the producer.

THE QUEEN AND I   CBS
16 JANUARY 1969–1 MAY 1969   Situation comedy set aboard the *Amsterdam Queen,* an ocean liner that had seen better days. Featured were Larry Storch as opportunistic Mr. Duffy, the first mate; Billy DeWolfe as First Officer Nelson; Carl Ballantine as Seaman Becker; Pat Morita as Barney Cook; Dave Willock as Ozzie; Barbara Stuart as Wilma; Dave Morick as Max Kowalski; Liam Dunn as Captain Washburn; and Reginald Owen as the ship's owner, Commodore Dodds.

QUEEN FOR A DAY   NBC/ABC/SYNDICATED
3 JANUARY 1956–2 SEPTEMBER 1960 (NBC); 28 SEPTEMBER 1960–2 OCTOBER 1964 (ABC); 1970 (SYNDICATED)   Possibly the most maudlin game show ever broadcast, *Queen for a Day* awarded merchandise prizes to the contestant who could evoke the most sympathy from the studio audience. The show began on radio in 1945 (as *Queen for Today*), and when Jack Bailey became its host later that year, the show settled into a format that changed little over the next nineteen years. Each day four or five women were chosen from the studio audience to appear on stage; one by one each contestant then stated what she most needed and why she needed it. At the end of the show the studio audience then voted, by its ap-

plause, who should become that day's "queen." The winner was crowned and throned and given her desired prize, as well as other merchandise. Though not all of the contestants told sob stories (one contestant merely wanted to trade places with emcee Jack Bailey for a day, and another wanted her nails filed by Bailey), a tear-jerking narrative was most likely to reap lots of applause. *Queen for a Day* came to daytime TV in 1956 and soon became the top-rated daytime show; in July of 1956 it was expanded from a half hour to forty-five minutes (in 1958 it reverted to a half hour). The show was based in Hollywood, though Bailey also took the show on the road from time to time; Jeanne Cagney was also featured as the show's fashion commentator. In 1970 the series was revived briefly for syndication with Dick Curtis as host.

THE QUEST
NBC

22 SEPTEMBER 1976–29 DECEMBER 1976 One of the few westerns introduced during the 1970s, *The Quest* starred Kurt Russell and Tim Matheson as brothers Morgan and Quentin Beaudine; the two had been separated at an early age—Morgan had been captured by Indians and raised by the Cheyennes, while Quentin was raised by an aunt and attended medical school. Finally reunited, they joined forces to search for their younger sister, who they believed was still a captive of the Cheyennes. Unfortunately, the series never really got off the ground, for it was scheduled opposite *Charlie's Angels* and vanished in midseason. Tracy Keenan Wynn created the series; David Gerber was the executive producer and Mark Rodgers and James H. Brown the producers. The pilot for the series, titled "Quest," was aired 13 May 1976.

QUEST FOR ADVENTURE
ABC

22 JULY 1957–2 SEPTEMBER 1957 A summer series of assorted human interest and informational films.

QUICK AS A FLASH
ABC

12 MARCH 1953–25 FEBRUARY 1954 Bobby Sherwood hosted this prime-time game show. A panel of two men faced a panel of two women; the object of the game was to guess a phrase or personality suggested by a specially prepared film clip. Charles B. Moss and Dick Lewis were the producers. The radio version of the series, which used a different format, ran from 1944 to 1951.

QUICK ON THE DRAW
DUMONT

8 JANUARY 1952–9 DECEMBER 1952 On this prime-time game show contestants tried to guess phrases suggested by drawings. Robin Chandler hosted the series and Bob Dunn did the sketching. *Quick on the Draw* should not be confused with other cartoon-oriented game shows of TV's

early days, such as *Draw Me a Laugh* and *Draw to Win*. The show premiered locally in New York on 27 May 1950.

QUICKDRAW McGRAW   SYNDICATED
1959–1962   Segments featured on this widely syndicated Hanna-Barbera cartoon series included "Quickdraw McGraw," the adventures of a bumbling equine marshal; "Snagglepuss," an inept lion ("Heavenths to Mergatroid!") and "Augie Doggie and Doggie Daddy," father-and-son canines.

QUINCY   NBC
3 OCTOBER 1976–   *Quincy,* a medically oriented crime show, began as one segment of *The NBC Sunday Mystery Movie* and became a weekly series early in 1977. Jack Klugman stars as Quincy, a medical examiner for the Los Angeles County Coroner's Office. Also featured are John S. Ragin as Dr. Robert J. Asten, the coroner; Garry Walberg as Lieutenant Frank Monahan, police liaison; Robert Ito as Sam Fujiyama, one of Quincy's assistants; Val Bisoglio as Danny Tovo, another assistant; Joseph Roman as Sergeant Brill; and Lynnette Mettey (1976–1977) as Quincy's female companion, Lee Potter. Glen Larson, the executive producer, created the series with Robert S. O'Neil, the supervising producer. Late in 1977 Jack Klugman caused a minor stir among television writers when he complained publicly of the dearth of high-quality scripts (Klugman himself had done some writing for TV, which included at least one episode of *Kraft Television Theatre*).

THE QUIZ KIDS   NBC/CBS
6 JULY 1949–2 NOVEMBER 1951 (NBC); 7 JULY 1952–18 AUGUST 1952 (NBC); 17 JANUARY 1953–8 NOVEMBER 1953 (CBS); 12 JANUARY 1956–27 SEPTEMBER 1956 (CBS)   *The Quiz Kids* began on radio in 1940 and ran for thirteen years. Originating from Chicago, it featured a panel of five child prodigies who fielded questions submitted by viewers; the ages of the panelists usually ranged from six to sixteen, and three or four youngsters generally stayed on the show for weeks or months (the fifth seat was occupied by a guest child). Joe Kelly, who hosted the radio version, was also the first host on television; he was succeeded by Clifton Fadiman. Packaged by Lou Cowan, the prime-time game show was produced by Rachael Stevenson.

QUIZZING THE NEWS   ABC
11 AUGUST 1948–5 MARCH 1949   One of ABC's first network programs, *Quizzing the News* was a prime-time game show on which a celebrity panel tried to guess a topical news story from cartoons. Allen Prescott was the host and Robert Brenner the producer.

THE RCA VICTOR SHOW
See THE DENNIS DAY SHOW; THE EZIO PINZA SHOW

R.C.M.P. SYNDICATED
1960 This Canadian crime show centered on the Royal Canadian Mounted Police. Featured were Gilles Pelletier as Corporal Jacques Gagnier; Don Francks as Constable Bill Mitchell; and John Perkins as Constable Frank Scott. The show's producers proudly boasted that the series was actually endorsed by the real R.C.M.P.

R.F.D. AMERICA NBC
26 MAY 1949–15 SEPTEMBER 1949 Chicago-based educational series on farming and gardening, hosted by Bob Murphy.

THE RACERS SYNDICATED
1976– Half-hour filmed series on auto racing, narrated by Curt Gowdy.

RACKET SQUAD SYNDICATED/CBS
1950 (SYNDICATED); 7 JUNE 1951–28 SEPTEMBER 1953 (CBS) One of television's first classic crime shows, *Racket Squad* starred Reed Hadley as Captain John Braddock, tireless investigator for San Francisco's Racket Squad, who tracked down a wide variety of flimflammers and con artists. The half-hour show was produced by Hal Roach, Jr., and Carroll Case and directed by Jim Tinling.

RAFFERTY CBS
5 SEPTEMBER 1977–28 NOVEMBER 1977 One of the early casualties of the 1977–1978 season, *Rafferty* was an hour-long medical drama starring Patrick McGoohan as flinty Dr. Sidney Rafferty, a general practitioner with a gift for diagnosis. Also featured were Millie Slavin as Vera Wales, his receptionist; John Getz as Dr. Daniel Gentry, his young associate. Created by James Lee, the show was produced by Norman S. Powell and Robert Van Scoyk; Jerry Thorpe was executive producer.

RAMAR OF THE JUNGLE SYNDICATED
1952–1953 Jon Hall starred in this widely syndicated children's adventure series as Dr. Tom Reynolds, a physician and scientist who worked in the "jungles" of Kenya, where he was known to the local folk as "Ramar." Also featured were Ray Montgomery as his colleague, Professor Howard Ogden; James Fairfax; and M'Lisa McClure. Harry S. Rothschild and Leon Fromkess produced the series.

RANCH PARTY SYNDICATED
1958 Regulars on this half-hour country and western music series in-

cluded host Tex Ritter, Bonnie Guitar, Johnny Cash, Tex Williams, Bobby Helms, Ray Price, and Smiley Burnette.

THE RANGE RIDER   SYNDICATED
1951–1953   Aimed principally at children, this half-hour western starred Jock Mahoney as The Range Rider, a wandering good guy, and Dick Jones as his youthful sidekick, Dick West. The series was produced by Louis Gray for Gene Autry's Flying A Productions.

RANGO   ABC
13 JANUARY 1967–1 SEPTEMBER 1967   Comedy-western with Tim Conway as Rango, an inept Texas Ranger; Norman Alden as Captain Horton, his commanding officer; and Guy Marks as Pink Cloud, his Indian scout.

THE RANSOM SHERMAN SHOW   NBC
3 JULY 1950–25 AUGUST 1950   A summer replacement for *Kukla, Fran and Ollie,* this half-hour musical variety show was hosted by Ransom Sherman and featured singers Nancy Wright and Johnny Bradford.

THE RAT PATROL   ABC
12 SEPTEMBER 1966–16 SEPTEMBER 1968   One of the several World War II dramas of the 1960s, *The Rat Patrol* lasted two seasons. Created by Tom Gries, the series was based on the exploits of a British armored car outfit known as the Long Range Desert Group, which harassed Rommel's Afrika Korps during the war. On television, the unit became an American squad, featuring Christopher George as Sergeant Sam Troy; Gary Raymond as Sergeant Jack Moffitt; Lawrence Casey as Private Mark Hitchcock; Justin Tarr as Private Tully Pettigrew; and Hans Gudegast as Captain Hans Dietrich of the Afrika Korps (Gudegast later changed his name to Eric Braeden). The first few episodes were filmed in Spain; despite production difficulties, the show was one of the more popular new series of the 1966–1967 season and was renewed. Stanley Shpetner was the first producer of the half-hour series but was replaced by Lee Rich.

RAWHIDE   CBS
9 JANUARY 1959–4 JANUARY 1966   *Rawhide,* like *Wagon Train,* was a western on the move; *Rawhide*'s passengers, however, were cattle, as the theme of the show was the long drive from North Texas to Sedalia, Kansas. Featured on the hour show were: Eric Fleming (1959–1965) as Gil Favor, the trail boss; Clint Eastwood as Rowdy Yates, the ramrod (Eastwood, one of the few regulars to remain with the show for its entire run, became the trail boss in the fall of 1965 when Fleming left the show); Jim Murdock (1959–1965) as Mushy; Paul Brinegar as Wishbone, the

cook; Steve Raines as Quince; Rocky Shahan (1959–1965) as Joe Scarlett; Sheb Wooley (1961–1965) as scout Pete Nolan; Robert Cabal (1962–1965) as Hey Soos (pronounced and spelled "Hey Soos," the character's Spanish name was undoubtedly Jesus); John Ireland (1965–1966) as Jed Colby; David Watson (1965–1966) as Ian Cabot; Raymond St. Jacques (1965–1966) as Simon Blake (St. Jacques thereby became the first black actor to be regularly featured on a western series). *Rawhide*'s producers and executive producers seemed to change even more often than the cast. The succession of executives included Charles Marquis Warren, who created the series, and was succeeded in 1961 by Endre Bohem; Bohem was replaced a year later by Vincent Fennelly, who was subsequently replaced by Bernard Kowalski and Bruce Geller. Endre Bohem then returned, only to be succeeded by Ben Brady.

THE RAY ANTHONY SHOW SYNDICATED/ABC
1956 (SYNDICATED); 12 OCTOBER 1956–3 MAY 1957 (ABC); 1969 (SYNDICATED) Bandleader Ray Anthony formed his own group in the mid-1940s and made records throughout the 1950s. His first television program was a summer replacement for *The Perry Como Show:* see *TV's Top Tunes*. In 1956 he hosted his own syndicated series, which was later picked up by ABC; it featured the Four Freshmen, Don Durant, Med Flory, and football coach Frank Leahy. Anthony's then wife, actress Mamie Van Doren, also appeared occasionally. In 1969 he hosted a second musical variety series, also titled *The Ray Anthony Show*. It featured singer Vicki Carr.

THE RAY BOLGER SHOW ABC
8 OCTOBER 1953–10 JUNE 1955 *The Ray Bolger Show,* which was originally entitled *Where's Raymond,* was a situation comedy with plenty of song and dance thrown in; this format enabled Ray Bolger to play himself—Bolger starred as Ray Wallace, a Broadway star living in suburbia. The 1953–1954 cast included Richard Erdman as Pete Morrisey, his landlord, along with Allyn Joslyn, Claire Dubrey, Frances Karath, and Betty Lynn. The 1954–1955 cast included Richard Erdman and several new faces: Marjie Millar as Susan, an aspiring writer from Iowa who became Ray's girlfriend; Charles Cantor as Ray's pal Artie Herman; Christine Nelson as Katy; Sylvia Lewis; and Maureen Stephenson. Jerry Bresler produced the series, and Marc Daniels directed it.

THE RAY MILLAND SHOW CBS
17 SEPTEMBER 1953–30 SEPTEMBER 1955 This half-hour sitcom premiered in the fall of 1953 under the title *Meet Mr. McNutley*; it starred Ray Milland as Ray McNutley, eccentric professor at Lynnhaven, a women's college, and Phyllis Avery as Peggy McNutley, his down-to-earth wife. Also featured were Minerva Urecal as Dean Bradley, Lynnha-

ven's formidable head; Gordon Jones as Pete Thompson; and Jacqueline DeWitt as Pete's wife, Ruth Thompson. After a summer hiatus, the show returned with a slightly changed format and a new title: *The Ray Milland Show*. Milland now played Ray McNulty, a somewhat less eccentric professor who taught at Comstock College (the show was subtitled *Meet Mr. McNulty*). Phyllis Avery was again featured as his wife, Peggy McNulty, but her character became more wacky to counterbalance Ray's shift in character. Lloyd Corrigan rounded out the cast as Dean Dodsworth, Comstock's head. A total of eighty half-hours were filmed for Revue Studios; Joe Connelly and Bob Mosher wrote and produced the series.

THE RAY STEVENS SHOW   NBC

20 JUNE 1970–8 AUGUST 1970   A summer replacement for *The Andy Williams Show,* this hour-long musical variety series was taped in Toronto and hosted by Ray Stevens, who during the 1960s, had recorded several popular novelty records, such as "Ahab the Arab," "Harry the Hairy Ape," and "Gitarzan." Also on hand were British pop star Lulu, American singer Cass Elliott (formerly of The Mamas and the Papas), Steve Martin, Billy Van, Dick Curtis, Carol Robinson, and Solari & Carr.

RAZZMATAZZ   CBS

5 NOVEMBER 1977–   A newsmagazine for children, broadcast irregularly on Saturday mornings and hosted first by Barry Bostwick. Brian Tochi took over as host during the 1978–1979 season.

REACH FOR THE STARS   NBC

2 JANUARY 1967–31 MARCH 1967   Bill Mazer hosted this short-lived daytime game show, on which contestants were required to answer questions and to perform stunts.

READING OUT LOUD   SYNDICATED

1960   Famous people read literature to children on this Westinghouse series.

READING ROOM   CBS

22 SEPTEMBER 1962–16 MARCH 1963   Saturday-afternoon educational show for children, on which a panel of youngsters each week discussed a book with its author. Ned Hoopes was the host and moderator.

THE REAL McCOYS   ABC/CBS

3 OCTOBER 1957–20 SEPTEMBER 1962 (ABC); 30 SEPTEMBER 1962–22 SEPTEMBER 1963 (CBS)   *The Real McCoys* was TV's first successful rural sitcom, antedating *The Andy Griffith Show* and *The Beverly Hillbillies* by several seasons; during its five seasons on ABC it was one of the network's most popular programs, ranking as high as fifth in the Nielsen

seasonal averages for the 1960–1961 season. Featured were: Walter Brennan as Grandpa Amos McCoy, the head of the family, all of whom lived in rural northern California; Richard Crenna as his grandson, Luke McCoy; Kathy Nolan (1957–1962) as Luke's wife, Kate (called "Sugar Babe" by Luke); Michael Winkelman as Little Luke McCoy, an orphaned grandson of Amos; Lydia Reed as Hassie, Little Luke's older sister; Tony Martinez as Pepino Garcia, the McCoys' hired hand; Andy Clyde as George MacMichael, Amos's sometime friend and occasional enemy; and Madge Blake as Flora MacMichael, George's sister. Irving Pincus was the executive producer of the series, and Danny Arnold was the producer.

REAL PEOPLE NBC
18 APRIL 1979–23 MAY 1979; 25 JULY 1979–   Introduced as a short-flight series in the spring of 1979, *Real People* earned a place on NBC's fall schedule. The hour show is part live and part videotape and emphasizes light features on non-celebrities. The original hosts included Fred Willard, Sara Purcell, John Barbour, Skip Stephenson, and Bill Rafferty. In the fall of 1979 the group included Purcell, Barbour, Stephenson, Rafferty, and Byron Allen. George Schlatter is the executive producer.

REALITIES PBS
5 OCTOBER 1970–20 SEPTEMBER 1971   Umbrella title for a series of independently produced documentaries.

THE REASONER REPORT ABC
24 FEBRUARY 1973–28 JUNE 1975   ABC newsman Harry Reasoner hosted this news analysis and commentary program, seen on weekends. Albert T. Primo was executive producer for ABC News.

THE REBEL ABC
4 OCTOBER 1959–17 SEPTEMBER 1961   This half-hour western was billed as more cerebral than most, but whether it really was more intellectual was a matter of opinion. Nick Adams starred as Johnny Yuma, a former Confederate soldier who "roamed through the West," presumably searching for an inner peace. *The Rebel*'s familiar theme song was sung by Johnny Cash. The show was produced by Goodson-Todman Productions (one of the few nongame shows produced by that outfit) in association with Celestial Productions and Fen-Ker-Ada Productions.

REBOP PBS
1976–1979   A half-hour series aimed at preteenagers, *Rebop* consisted mainly of filmed segments about children of many different cultural and ethnic backgrounds. Topper Carew was executive producer for WGBH-

TV, Boston. LeVar Burton, star of *Roots,* became the host in the fall of 1978.

REBOUND
ABC/DUMONT

8 FEBRUARY 1952–30 MAY 1952 (ABC); 5 DECEMBER 1952–16 JANUARY 1953 (DUMONT)   An undistinguished half-hour dramatic anthology series. Lee Marvin played his first major TV dramatic role on one episode, "The Mine," aired 29 February.

THE REBUS GAME
ABC

29 MARCH 1965–24 SEPTEMBER 1965   Jack Linkletter hosted this daytime game show, which featured two 2-member teams. The object of the game was for one player to guess a word or phrase from drawings sketched by his or her partner.

REBUTTAL
CBS

12 JUNE 1960–4 SEPTEMBER 1960   Sunday-afternoon series of debates between teams from colleges and universities, moderated by Jack Kennedy.

RED BARBER'S CLUB HOUSE
CBS

2 JULY 1949–18 FEBRUARY 1950; 12 SEPTEMBER 1953–12 DECEMBER 1953   This Saturday-evening sports show was hosted by veteran sportscaster Red Barber; produced by John Peyser and John Derr, the show was simulcast on radio in 1950. The 1953 show, titled *Peak of the Sports News,* was seen Saturday evenings.

THE RED BUTTONS SHOW
CBS/NBC

14 OCTOBER 1952–14 JUNE 1954 (CBS); 1 OCTOBER 1954–27 MAY 1955 (NBC)   Though it is scarcely recalled today, *The Red Buttons Show* was hailed almost universally as the most promising new show of the 1952–1953 season (Buttons even appeared on the cover of *Time* magazine that season). But by the end of its second season, after several changes in format and writers, the show's popularity had sagged considerably, and it was dropped by CBS. NBC picked up the show for the 1954–1955 season (where it was slated on Friday nights, with *The Jack Carson Show* occupying the slot approximately every fourth week), but it did even less well. Buttons had had considerable experience as a burlesque comedian, and his show began as a comedy-variety show; it was introduced by his familiar theme song, "The Ho Ho Song." The half-hour series was produced by Jess Kimmell and directed by Peter Kass. Other regulars included Dorothy Joliffe (who often played his wife in sketches), Joe Silver, Jeanne Carson, Sara Seegar, Jimmy Little, Ralph Stanley, Sammy Birch, and the Elliott Lawrence Orchestra. By the end of the 1953–1954 season, however, the show had become a situation comedy and remained a sitcom when

it switched networks that fall. In the new format Buttons played himself, a television comedian, and Phyllis Kirk played his wife; Paul Lynde, a newcomer to TV, was also featured as a network vice president. After the demise of his series, Buttons continued to appear in dramatic roles on television and on film, winning an Academy Award in 1957 for his performance in *Sayonara*. Buttons later starred in a 1966 sitcom: see *The Double Life of Henry Phyfe*.

THE RED HAND GANG   NBC

10 SEPTEMBER 1977–21 JANUARY 1978 Five juvenile detectives were the central characters in this live-action Saturday-morning show. Featured were Matthew Laborteaux as Frankie; J. R. Miller as J. R.; Jolie Newman as Joanne; James Bond as Doc; and Johnny Brogna as Li'l Bill.

THE RED ROWE SHOW   CBS

16 NOVEMBER 1959–8 JULY 1960 Red Rowe hosted a daytime variety series of little note, which featured Bill Cunningham and Peggy Taylor.

THE RED SKELTON SHOW   NBC/CBS

30 SEPTEMBER 1951–21 JUNE 1953 (NBC); 22 SEPTEMBER 1953–23 JUNE 1970 (CBS); 14 SEPTEMBER 1970–29 AUGUST 1971 (NBC) One of television's most popular comedians, Red Skelton hosted his own series for twenty years, seventeen of them on CBS. Active in show business from boyhood, Skelton had extensive experience in vaudeville before he began his own radio series in 1941. On that show, which lasted until 1953, Skelton developed most of the characters that he would later bring to television—Junior (the Mean Widdle Kid), Freddie the Freeloader, Clem Kadiddlehopper, George Appleby, Sheriff Deadeye, Willy Lump Lump, Cauliflower McPugg, Cookie the Sailor, San Fernando Red, Bolivar Shagnasty, and others. As Skelton's real comedic talents were in the realm of pantomime, pratfalls, and sight gags, his television series proved to be even more popular than the radio show had been—unlike many other radio comedians, Skelton was able to bring something more to television than his voice. Skelton's first NBC series, which he produced with Freeman Keyes, was a half-hour program seen on Sunday evenings; it ranked fourth overall that year, just behind *I Love Lucy*. In the fall of 1953 Skelton moved to a Tuesday-night slot on CBS, where he remained until 1970. The CBS show, which expanded to an hour in the fall of 1962, cracked Nielsen's Top Twenty in its third season and remained there until its cancellation (*The Red Skelton Hour* ranked seventh in its final year on CBS, but, because of rising production costs, had become only marginally profitable to the network). One of Skelton's writers in the early seasons on CBS was Johnny Carson; Carson unexpectedly got a big break one day in 1954, when he was summoned on a few hours' notice to fill in for Skelton, who had knocked himself unconscious during rehearsal. Car-

son, whose previous on-camera experience had been limited to a local show and a summertime game show, performed admirably and was given his own show by CBS in 1955. Skelton, an inveterate ad-libber, delighted in breaking up his guest stars, and very few comedy sketches appeared to have been performed precisely as written. Musical groups were also featured on the series; the Rolling Stones made one of their earliest American television appearances on 22 September 1964. Skelton's final series, on NBC, was a half-hour comedy-variety show with a large cast of regulars, including Jan Arvan, Elsie Baker, Jackson Bostwick, Yvonne Ewald, Chanin Hale, Dorothy Love, John Magruder, Ida Mae McKenzie, Janos Prohaska, Peggy Rea, Mike Wagner, and the Burgundy Street Singers. The David Rose Orchestra was long associated with Skelton's shows. Vice President Spiro Agnew appeared on the 1970 premiere of the series.

THE REDD FOXX COMEDY HOUR ABC
15 SEPTEMBER 1977–26 JANUARY 1978 Redd Foxx left *Sanford and Son* to star in his own hour comedy-variety show. The series had a few bright moments but was generally uneven and was dropped in midseason. Regulars included Slappy White, Damita Jo, LaWanda Page, Hal Smith, Billy Barty, Bill Saluga (as Raymond J. Johnson), and "Iron Jaw" Wilson. Redd Foxx was the executive producer, Allan Blye and Bob Einstein the producers.

REDIGO
See EMPIRE

THE REEL GAME ABC
18 JANUARY 1971–3 MAY 1971 Jack Barry hosted this prime-time game show on which three contestants competed. The questions concerned famous people and events, and the answers were "verified" by showing newsreel or other documentary film footage.

THE REGIS PHILBIN SHOW SYNDICATED
1964–1965 Regis Philbin succeeded Steve Allen as host of Westinghouse's syndicated ninety-minute talk show. Philbin had earlier hosted *Philbin's People*, a talk show telecast in New York and Los Angeles, and later became Joey Bishop's sidekick on *The Joey Bishop Show*.

THE RELUCTANT DRAGON AND MR. TOAD ABC
12 SEPTEMBER 1970–3 SEPTEMBER 1972 Weekend cartoon series based loosely on *The Wind in the Willows*. The Reluctant Dragon was named Tobias and was featured in one segment, while Mr. Toad was the main character in his own segment. Both creatures were originally featured in stories by Kenneth Grahame.

REMEMBER THIS DATE

NBC

14 NOVEMBER 1950–28 JUNE 1951   Bill Stern hosted this audience participation game show, which was seen Tuesday and Thursday afternoons.

RENDEZVOUS

ABC

13 FEBRUARY 1952–5 MARCH 1952   Ilona Massey starred in this half-hour adventure series as the owner of a nightclub in Nazi-occupied Paris during World War II.

RENDEZVOUS

SYNDICATED

1958   Charles Drake hosted this half-hour dramatic anthology series.

RENDEZVOUS WITH MUSIC

NBC

11 JULY 1950–8 AUGUST 1950   Half-hour musical series featuring Carol Reed, Don Gallagher, and the Tony DeSimone Trio. See also *Melody, Harmony & Rhythm.*

REPORT CARD FOR PARENTS

DUMONT

1 DECEMBER 1952–2 FEBRUARY 1953   Half-hour prime-time discussion show on child behavior and education.

THE REPORTER

CBS

25 SEPTEMBER 1964–18 DECEMBER 1964   The *New York Globe* was the setting for this hour-long dramatic series. Featured were Harry Guardino as reporter Danny Taylor; Gary Merrill as city editor Lou Sheldon; George O'Hanlon as Danny's pal, cabbie Artie Burns; and Remo Pisani as bartender Ike Dawson. Created by Jerome Weidman, the series was developed by Keefe Brasselle.

RESCUE 8

SYNDICATED

1958   This half-hour series about a pair of rescue workers was the antecedent of NBC's *Emergency!* It starred Jim Davis as Wes Cameron and Lang Jeffries as Skip Johnson.

THE RESTLESS GUN

NBC

23 SEPTEMBER 1957–14 SEPTEMBER 1959   This half-hour western from Revue Studios starred John Payne as Vint Bonner, a Civil War veteran who roamed the West. Dan Blocker, who later starred in *Bonanza,* made his first TV appearance in a 1957 episode, "The Child" (23 December), and James Coburn played his first major role in a 1958 show, "Take Me Home" (29 December). Bonner's mount, Scar, was played by a horse named John Henry.

RETURN TO PEYTON PLACE

NBC

3 APRIL 1972–4 JANUARY 1974   This half-hour daytime serial picked up

where *Peyton Place,* ABC's prime-time soap opera, had left off three years earlier. Though *Peyton Place* had been popular with viewers, *Return to Peyton Place* never really caught on; one reason for its lack of success may have been that viewers had identified too strongly with the stars of *Peyton Place* (such as Mia Farrow, Ryan O'Neal, and Ed Nelson), none of whom appeared on the daytime sequel. Principal players on the daytime version included: Kathy Glass as Allison MacKenzie; Bettye Ackerman and Susan Brown as her mother, Constance MacKenzie Carson; Warren Stevens as Elliot Carson, her husband; Guy Stockwell as Dr. Michael Rossi; Joe Gallison as Steven Cord; Mary K. Wells as Hannah Cord; Lawrence Casey and Yale Summers as Rodney Harrington; Ron Russell as Norman Harrington; Patricia Morrow as Rita Jacks Harrington; Julie Parrish and Lynn Loring as Betty Anderson Harrington; Evelyn Scott as Ada Jacks; John Levin as young Matthew Carson; John Hoyt as Martin Peyton; Frank Ferguson as Eli Carson; Dino Fantini as Gino Panzini; and Ben Andrews as Benny Tate.

RETURN TO THE PLANET OF THE APES   NBC
6 SEPTEMBER 1975–4 SEPTEMBER 1976 This Saturday-morning cartoon show was based on the *Planet of the Apes* films and television series. David H. DePatie and Friz Freleng were the producers.

REVIVAL OF AMERICA CRUSADE   SYNDICATED
1975–   Half-hour religious show, with evangelist and faith healer Leroy Jenkins.

THE REVLON REVUE   CBS
28 JANUARY 1960–16 JUNE 1960 *The Revlon Revue* was the scaled down successor to *The Big Party,* CBS's lavish ninety-minute variety series that was dropped in midseason. *The Revlon Revue* was an hour show and had no regulars; Mickey Rooney, Dick Shawn, Patachou, Joey Forman, and Bob Crewe appeared on the premiere, and Maurice Chevalier was the guest star on the second show. The last several shows were titled *The Revlon Spring Music Festival.* Abe Burrows was the executive producer.

REX HUMBARD   SYNDICATED
1952–   One of America's best known evangelists, Rex Humbard began his television broadcasts in Akron in 1952; by the early 1970s his program was seen on approximately 350 stations. In recent years the show has been titled *The Rex Humbard World Outreach Ministry* and is taped at the Cathedral of Tomorrow in Cuyahoga Falls, Ohio. Regulars include the Rex Humbard Family Singers, with Maude Aimee Humbard (Rex's wife) and Elizabeth Humbard (his daughter) featured as soloists. The show's executive producer is Rex Humbard, Jr.

RHODA   CBS

9 SEPTEMBER 1974–9 DECEMBER 1978   Valerie Harper starred in this
spinoff from *The Mary Tyler Moore Show* as Rhoda Morgenstern. On her
own show, Rhoda returned to her native New York from Minneapolis,
got a job, and finally found a fella. David Groh costarred as her new boyfriend, Joe Gerard, owner of the New York Wrecking Company, a demolition outfit; Joe had previously been married and was the father of a ten-
year-old son. Rhoda and Joe were married in the series' eighth episode
and lived in the same apartment building as Rhoda's younger sister,
Brenda (played by Julie Kavner), a bank teller. Also featured during the
first season were Nancy Walker as Rhoda's meddlesome mother, Ida
Morgenstern; Harold Gould as Rhoda's father, Martin Morgenstern;
Lorenzo Music (*Rhoda*'s coproducer) as the heard-but-not seen Carlton
the Doorman. Rhoda and Joe stayed married through the series' second
season, as a few new regulars began to be seen: Richard Masur as Brenda's sometime boyfriend, Nick Lobo, a thick-headed accordionist; Wes
Stern as Brenda's friend Lenny Fiedler; Barbara Sharma as Rhoda's high
school classmate Myrna Morgenstein, who became Rhoda's employee in
her freelance window-dressing business; and Scoey Mitchlll as Joe's employee, Justin Culp. By the beginning of the third season, however, it was
decided that Rhoda and Joe should separate, and early in the fall of 1976
the two agreed to a trial separation. Joe moved out, and Rhoda moved to
a smaller apartment in the same building; Nancy Walker (who was then
starring in her own series, *The Nancy Walker Show*) and Harold Gould
were gone from the series (it was explained that Rhoda's folks had decided to take a motor trip around the country), and Masur, Stern, Sharma,
and Mitchlll were no longer seen as regulars. More new faces were added,
however: Ron Silver as Gary Levy, an aggressive young schlep who ran a
boutique and who agreed to swap apartments with Rhoda; Anne Meara
as Rhoda's friend, Sally Gallagher, an airline stewardess; Michael DeLano as Johnny Venture, a minimally talented but very macho lounge singer newly arrived from Las Vegas, who fell for Rhoda. More changes took
place at the outset of the fourth season, as Rhoda and Joe were finally divorced. David Groh, who had appeared infrequently during the 1976–
1977 season, was dropped entirely; Nancy Walker returned after a season's absence; Rhoda got a new job, with a theatrical costume supply
house; and three new players were added, joining Harper, Kavner, Music, Silver, and DeLano: Kenneth McMillan as Rhoda's gruff boss, Jack
Doyle; Rafael Campos as Doyle's other employee, Ramón Diaz; and Ray
Buktenica as Brenda's boyfriend, Benny Goodwin. DeLano, Silver and
Campos left the show at the end of the 1977–1978 season, and, as the
1978–1979 season began, Rhoda's mother, Ida Morgenstern, was suddenly single: her husband had left her. Nancy Lane also joined the cast in the
fall of 1978 as Tina Molinari, Jack Doyle's third employee. James L.
Brooks and Allan Burns were the executive producers of *Rhoda* from

1974 until 1978, when Charlotte Brown became the new executive producer for MTM Enterprises.

RHYME AND REASON   ABC
7 JULY 1975–9 JULY 1976   Hosted by Bob Eubanks, this daytime game show was essentially a poetic version of *The Match Game*—two contestants tried to guess which word would be rhymed to an open-ended couplet by the panel of six celebrities. Steven Friedman was the executive producer for W. T. Naud Productions, Inc.

RHYTHM RODEO   DUMONT
30 JULY 1950–31 DECEMBER 1950   Half-hour musical series, hosted by Art Jarrett.

THE RICH LITTLE SHOW   NBC
2 FEBRUARY 1976–19 JULY 1976   Impressionist Rich Little hosted his own hour-long comedy-variety series. Other regulars included Charlotte Rae, R. G. Brown, Julie McWhirter, Joe Baker, and Mel Bishop. Jerry Goldstein was executive producer for Little's production company, Dudley Enterprises (Dudley, Little's English sheepdog, appeared at the show's conclusion).

RICH MAN, POOR MAN   ABC
1 FEBRUARY 1976–15 MARCH 1976; 21 SEPTEMBER 1976–8 MARCH 1977   *Rich Man, Poor Man* was introduced early in 1976 as a twelve-hour serialization of Irwin Shaw's novel, which chronicled the lives of the Jordache family from 1945 to 1965. The series was a smash hit, ranking third in the seasonal Nielsens and reaping twenty-three Emmy nominations. In the fall of 1976 ABC introduced *Rich Man, Poor Man—Book II,* a twenty-one-part continuation of the Shaw novel (Shaw himself had virtually nothing to do with *Book II*), which fared less well. The cast of *Book I* (as the original twelve-hour adaptation came to be called when it was rerun in May and June of 1977) included: Peter Strauss as Rudy Jordache; Nick Nolte as Tom Jordache, his brother; Edward Asner as Axel Jordache, their father; Dorothy McGuire as Mary Jordache, their mother; Susan Blakely as Julie Prescott; Bill Bixby as Willie Abbott; Robert Reed as Teddy Boylan; Ray Milland as Duncan Calderwood; Kim Darby as Virginia Calderwood; Talia Shire as Teresa Santoro; Lawrence Pressman as Bill Benton; and Kay Lenz as Kate. The cast of *Book II* included only a few of the principals from *Book I*—Peter Strauss as Rudy, Kay Lenz as Kate, and (in the first episode only) Susan Blakely as Julie. The remainder of the *Book II* cast included: Gregg Henry as Wesley Jordache, Tom's son; James Carroll Jordan as Billy Abbott, Julie's son; Susan Sullivan as Maggie Porter; William Smith as Anthony Falconetti; Dimitra Arliss as Marie Falconetti; Sorrell Booke as Phil Greeneberg;

Peter Haskell as Charles Estep; Laraine Stephens as Claire Estep; Penny Peyser as Ramona Scott; John Anderson as Scotty; Peter Donat as Arthur Raymond; Cassie Yates as Annie Adams; Barry Sullivan as Senator Paxton; G. D. Spradlin as Senator Dillon; and Philip Abbott as John Franklin. Harve Bennett was the executive producer and Jon Epstein the producer of *Book I;* Michael Gleason was executive producer and Epstein the producer of *Book II.* Both books were produced for Universal Television. In sum, the phenomenal success of *Book I* led to a boom in the programming of serialized novels and other stories on prime-time network television.

THE RICHARD BOONE SHOW   NBC
24 SEPTEMBER 1963–15 SEPTEMBER 1964   This hour program was a television rarity—a dramatic anthology series with an in-house repertory company. Richard Boone, formerly of *Have Gun Will Travel,* was both host and performer. The rest of the company included Robert Blake, Lloyd Bochner, Laura Devon, June Harding, Bethel Leslie, Harry Morgan, Jeanette Nolan, Ford Rainey, Warren Stevens, and Guy Stockwell. The show was a Goodson-Todman Production in association with Classic Films and NBC.

RICHARD DIAMOND, PRIVATE DETECTIVE   CBS/NBC
1 JULY 1957–30 SEPTEMBER 1957; 2 JANUARY 1958–25 SEPTEMBER 1958; 15 FEBRUARY 1959–20 SEPTEMBER 1959 (CBS); 5 OCTOBER 1959–6 SEPTEMBER 1960 (NBC)   *Richard Diamond, Private Detective* was first a radio series; introduced in 1949, it starred Dick Powell. The TV version, which bore little resemblance to the radio show, was produced by Four Star Films and starred unsmiling David Janssen as Richard Diamond. One of the first TV private eyes to have a telephone in his car, Diamond checked in regularly with Sam, the woman who ran his answering service. Sam's face was never seen on camera, but her legs were displayed prominently; the part was played by Mary Tyler Moore (known then as Mary Moore) until May of 1959, when Roxanne Brooks took over the role. Also featured were Regis Toomey (1957–1958) as Lieutenant McGough; Russ Conway (1959) as Lieutenant Kile; and Barbara Bain (1959, in her first major television role) as Karen Wells, Diamond's girlfriend. The half-hour series was first introduced as a summer replacement for *December Bride;* in 1958 it returned as a midseason replacement for *Harbourmaster,* and in 1959 it took over the slot formerly occupied by *The $64,000 Challenge.* In syndication the show was titled *Call Mr. D.*

THE RICHARD HARKNESS SHOW   NBC
7 JANUARY 1948–5 JANUARY 1949   Richard Harkness interviewed newsmakers on this fifteen-minute public affairs series.

THE RICHARD PRYOR SHOW   NBC

13 SEPTEMBER 1977–20 OCTOBER 1977   *The Richard Pryor Show,* which could have been one of the brightest spots of the 1977–1978 season, never really got off the ground for a number of reasons. It starred Richard Pryor, a gifted actor and an inventive but unorthodox comedian; Pryor's humor was unmistakably aimed at adult audiences, yet the show was broadcast during the so-called family hour (8 p.m. to 9 p.m. on the East Coast). Even worse, NBC scheduled it opposite ABC's *Happy Days* and *Laverne and Shirley,* two of the top-rated shows of the previous season. Finally, Pryor became involved with the network in a dispute involving censorship; a sequence showing Pryor apparently nude (though he was wearing a body stocking), while explaining that he had relinquished nothing to get his own series, was ordered deleted by the network. Pryor himself decided to halt production of the series shortly after the incident, and only five shows (including a rerun of his spring 1977 special) were broadcast. Other regulars on the short-lived series included Allegra Allison, Sandra Bernhart, Victor Delapp, Argus Hamilton, Jimmy Martinez, Paul Mooney, Tim Reid, Marsha Warfield, Robin Williams, and "Detroit" John Witherspoon. Burt Sugarman was the executive producer and Rocco Urbisci and John Moffitt the producers.

THE RICHARD WILLIS SHOW   NBC

8 OCTOBER 1951–15 FEBRUARY 1957   Makeup artist Richard Willis dispensed advice on beauty and grooming to women on this daytime series, which was originally titled *Here's Looking at You.*

RICHIE BROCKELMAN, PRIVATE EYE   NBC

17 MARCH 1978–14 APRIL 1978   This hour-long crime show was a five-week replacement for *The Rockford Files.* Featured were Dennis Dugan as Richie Brockelman, a private eye in his early twenties; Robert Hogan as Sergeant Ted Coppersmith, his police contact; Barbara Bosson as Sharon Deterson, Brockelman's female friend and assistant. The character was first introduced in a 1976 made-for-TV movie, *Richie Brockelman: The Missing 24 Hours*, and was again introduced on an episode of *The Rockford Files* broadcast 10 March 1978. Stephen J. Cannell and Steven Bochco created the series and were its executive producers; Peter S. Fischer was the producer. Reruns were shown during the summer of 1978.

RIDDLE ME THIS   CBS

5 DECEMBER 1948–13 MARCH 1949   Conrad Nagel hosted this Sunday-night game show, the subject of which was riddles. Celebrity panelists included John Daly and Ilka Chase. See also *Celebrity Time.*

THE RIFLEMAN ABC

30 SEPTEMBER 1958–1 JULY 1963 Chuck Connors starred in this half-hour western as Lucas McCain, a widower trying to raise his young son on a ranch outside North Fork, New Mexico; unfortunately, McCain had little time to concentrate on ranching, as he was constantly called on to use his prowess with a .44 Winchester rifle to rid North Fork of assorted undesirables. Also featured were Johnny Crawford as his son, Mark; Paul Fix as North Fork's ineffective marshal, Micah Torrance; Bill Quinn as Sweeney, the bartender; Hope Summers as storekeeper Hattie Denton; Joan Taylor as Millie Scott, proprietor of the general store; and Pat Blair (1962–1963) as Lou Mallory, the hotelkeeper. *The Rifleman* was the most popular new series of the 1958–1959 season, ranking fourth overall in the seasonal Nielsens; though it lasted four more years, it never equalled the success of the first season. In retrospect *The Rifleman* seems a bit more somber than most of the other westerns of the time; one reason for the series' grim tone may have been that some episodes were directed by Sam Peckinpah, who later became noted for his direction of violent western films. *The Rifleman* was produced by Arthur Gardner, Arnold Laven, and Jules Levy for Four Star Films.

RIN TIN TIN ABC

15 OCTOBER 1954–28 AUGUST 1959 *Rin Tin Tin,* TV's best-known German shepherd, was the star of this half-hour western. The dog and his young master, a boy named Rusty, were the only survivors of an Indian raid on a wagon train and were taken in by the members of the 101st Cavalry. The humans in the cast included: Lee Aaker as Rusty, who was commissioned a corporal in the first episode (Rin Tin Tin was made a private); Jim L. Brown as Lieutenant Ripley (Rip) Masters; Joe Sawyer as Sergeant Biff O'Hara; and Rand Brooks as Corporal Boone. Herbert B. Leonard produced the series, and William Beaudine directed it; the 164 episodes were filmed at Crash Corrigan's movie ranch in California. The original Rin Tin Tin was a veteran of the German Army in World World War I and had starred in several silent films during the 1920s; *Rin Tin Tin* had also been a radio series (once in 1930 and again in 1955). The TV Rin Tin Tin was owned by Lee Duncan.

RIPCORD SYNDICATED

1962 The central characters in this half-hour adventure series were a pair of parachutists who operated Ripcord, Inc., a skydiving school. Larry Pennell and Ken Curtis starred as partners Ted McKeever and Jim Buckley. Maurice Unger and Leon Benson produced the series for United Artists.

RIVERBOAT NBC

13 SEPTEMBER 1959–16 JANUARY 1961 This hour-long adventure se-

ries starred Darren McGavin as Grey Holden, captain of the *Enterprise,* a riverboat which plied the Mississippi River during the 1840s. Also on board were Burt Reynolds (1959–1960, in his first continuing role) as pilot Ben Frazer; Noah Beery (1960–1961) as pilot Bill Blake; Dick Wessel as Carney; Jack Lambert as Joshua; Mike McGreevey as Chip; John Mitchum as Pickalong; and Bart Patton as Terry. A total of forty-four episodes were produced.

ROAD OF LIFE   CBS

13 DECEMBER 1954–1 JULY 1955   One of radio's most popular serials, *Road of Life* was created by Irna Phillips in 1937 and lasted until 1959; the television version was far less successful. It starred Don MacLaughlin as Dr. Jim Brent, a surgeon. Also featured in the TV cast were Barbara Becker, Virginia Dwyer, Elspeth Eric, Harry Holcombe, Hollis Irving, Michael Kane, Elizabeth Lawrence, and Bill Lipton. Nelson Case was the narrator, and John Egan was the producer.

THE ROAD RUNNER SHOW   CBS/ABC

2 SEPTEMBER 1967–7 SEPTEMBER 1968 (CBS); 11 SEPTEMBER 1971–2 SEPTEMBER 1972 (ABC)   The Road Runner, the resourceful bird who constantly outwitted his pursuer, Wile E. Coyote, had his own Saturday-morning cartoon show for two seasons. At other times he has shared a show with Bugs Bunny, which has usually been titled *The Bugs Bunny/Road Runner Hour.* See also *Bugs Bunny.*

ROAD TO REALITY   ABC

17 OCTOBER 1960–31 MARCH 1961   A therapy group was the setting of this half-hour daytime serial, which starred John Beal as psychoanalyst Dr. Lewis.

THE ROAD WEST   NBC

12 SEPTEMBER 1966–28 AUGUST 1967   An undistinguished hour-long western from Universal Television, *The Road West* was the story of a pioneer family who settled in Kansas. Featured were Barry Sullivan as Ben Pride; Kathryn Hays as Elizabeth Pride, his wife; Andrew Prine as their son, Tim; Brenda Scott as their daughter, Midge (Prine and Scott had been married in 1965 but were divorced when production of the series began); Kelly Corcoran as their son, Kip; Glenn Corbett as Chance Reynolds, Elizabeth's brother; and Charles Seel as Tom (Grandpa) Pride, Ben's father.

ROALD DAHL'S TALES OF THE UNEXPECTED   SYNDICATED

1979   This British-produced half-hour anthology series, on which most of the presentations were written by Roald Dahl, should not be confused with the 1952 anthology series, *The Unexpected*, or with the 1977 anthology series, *Tales of the Unexpected*.

ROAR OF THE RAILS CBS

26 OCTOBER 1948–14 DECEMBER 1948; 24 OCTOBER 1949–12 DECEMBER 1949   A fifteen-minute series on railroading, sponsored by the A. C. Gilbert Company. See also *Tales of the Red Caboose*.

THE ROARING TWENTIES ABC

15 OCTOBER 1960–21 SEPTEMBER 1962   Set in New York during the 1920s, this hour-long adventure series tried to capitalize on the success of *The Untouchables,* which was also set in the Prohibition era. *The Roaring Twenties,* however, was considerably less violent and considerably less popular. Featured were Dorothy Provine as Pinky Pinkham, singer at the Charleston Club; Donald May as Pat Garrison, reporter for the New York *Record;* Rex Reason as Scott Norris, also a *Record* reporter; John Dehner as reporter Duke Williams; Mike Road as Lieutenant Joe Switoski, New York cop; Gary Vinson as Chris Higby, the *Record*'s copyboy; and James Flavin as Howard.

THE ROBBINS NEST ABC

29 SEPTEMBER 1950–22 DECEMBER 1950   Fifteen-minute Friday-night variety show, hosted by Fred Robbins.

ROBERT HERRIDGE THEATRE SYNDICATED

1961   This half-hour dramatic-anthology series was seen on many educational stations.

ROBERT MONTGOMERY PRESENTS NBC

30 JANUARY 1950–24 JUNE 1957   Another of television's high-quality dramatic anthology series, this hour show was produced and hosted by actor Robert Montgomery, who occasionally starred in the presentations. A sampling of the shows broadcast would include: "Victoria Regina," with Helen Hayes (30 January 1950); "Arrowsmith," with Van Heflin (9 October 1950); "The Philadelphia Story," with Barbara Bel Geddes (4 December 1950); "Rise Up and Walk," with Kim Hunter (4 February 1952); "Penny," with Joanne Woodward (in her first major TV role, 9 June 1952); "Dinah, Kip, and Mr. Barlow," with Jack Lemmon (23 February 1953); "Harvest," with Ed Begley, Dorothy Gish, Vaughn Taylor, and James Dean (23 November 1953); "Wages of Fear," with Louis Jourdan (3 May 1954); "The Great Gatsby," with Phyllis Kirk, John Newland, and Gena Rowlands (11 April 1955); "Soldier from the Wars Returning," with James Cagney (in the first of his few television appearances, 10 September 1956); "Return Visit," with Peter Falk (in his first

major TV role, 13 May 1957). In its first seasons *Robert Montgomery Presents* was also known as *Lucky Strike Theater.* During the summer months between seasons, Montgomery introduced a repertory company, whose productions were presented under titles such as *Montgomery's Summer Stock* or *The Robert Montgomery Summer Theater.* A regular performer in these companies was Montgomery's daughter, Elizabeth Montgomery, who had made her TV debut in a 1951 episode of *Robert Montgomery Presents,* "Top Secret" (broadcast 3 December). In the summer of 1954 the company consisted of Elizabeth Montgomery, Jan Miner (better known in later years as Madge, the manicurist in Palmolive commercials), John Newland, Anne Seymour, Cliff Robertson, and Vaughn Taylor. In the summer of 1956 the group included Elizabeth Montgomery, John Gibson, Tom Middleton, and Mary K. Wells. Robert Montgomery became a media consultant for President Eisenhower during the 1950s and in 1969 became president of the Lincoln Center Repertory Theater.

THE ROBERT Q. LEWIS SHOW
CBS
16 JULY 1950–7 JANUARY 1951; 16 OCTOBER 1950–19 JANUARY 1951; 11 JANUARY 1954– 25 MAY 1956   Robert Q. Lewis, frequently seen during the 1950s as a game-show host and substitute emcee, hosted a prime-time show and two daytime variety series of his own. The prime-time show was a fifteen-minute interview program seen Sundays. The first daytime series, titled *Robert Q's Matinee,* was a forty-five-minute daily show that ran only fourteen weeks. The second, titled *The Robert Q. Lewis Show,* was much more successful, lasting more than two years. Among the many regulars on the half-hour show were Jaye P. Morgan, Jan Arden, Betty Clooney, Jane Wilson, Lois Hunt and Earl Wrightson, Merv Griffin, Julann Wright (who later married Griffin), The Chordettes, dancer-choreographer Don Liberto, and announcer Lee Vines.

THE ROBERT RIPLEY SHOW
See BELIEVE IT OR NOT

ROBERT TAYLOR'S DETECTIVES
See THE DETECTIVES

THE ROBERTA QUINLAN SHOW
NBC
3 MAY 1949–23 NOVEMBER 1951   Singer Roberta Quinlan hosted her own fifteen-minute musical series of two and a half years; it was seen two or three nights a week before the evening news. In 1949 her show, telecast Tuesdays and Thursdays, was actually part of *The Mohawk Showroom*—singer Morton Downey hosted the series on the other three weeknights.

ROBIN HOOD   CBS

26 SEPTEMBER 1955–22 SEPTEMBER 1958   Officially titled *The Adventures of Robin Hood,* this British import told the story of the legendary twelfth-century hero who, together with his band of men, stole from the rich and gave to the poor; on TV most of Robin's exploits involved attempts to oust Prince John, the hated ruler of Nottingham. The half-hour series starred Richard Greene as Robin Hood and featured Alexander Gauge as Friar Tuck; Archie Duncan and Rufus Cruikshank as Little John; Bernadette O'Farrell (1955–1957) and Patricia Driscoll (1957–1958) as Maid Marian, Robin's apparent romantic interest; Paul Eddington as Will Scarlett; Alan Wheatley as the hapless Sheriff of Nottingham; and Donald Pleasance as Prince John. In 1967 an updated cartoon version appeared: see *Rocket Robin Hood.*

ROCKET ROBIN HOOD   SYNDICATED

1967   In this futuristic cartoon version of the Robin Hood legend, Rocket Robin Hood and his band of spacemen were stationed aboard Sherwood Asteroid in the thirtieth century.

THE ROCKFORD FILES   NBC

13 SEPTEMBER 1974–   James Garner stars in this hour-long crime show as Jim Rockford, a private eye recently released from prison (for a crime he never committed) who lives in a trailer in Malibu. Also featured are Noah Beery as Joe Rockford, his semiretired father; Joe Santos as Sergeant Dennis Becker of the Los Angeles Police; Gretchen Corbett (1974–1978) as defense attorney Beth Davenport; and Stuart Margolin as Angel Martin. Bo Hopkins was featured during the 1978–1979 season as disbarred attorney John Cooper. Created by Roy Huggins and Stephen J. Cannell, the series' executive producer is Meta Rosenberg.

ROCKY AND HIS FRIENDS   ABC

19 NOVEMBER 1959–14 SEPTEMBER 1961   Jay Ward created this popular cartoon series, whose stars were a flying squirrel, Rocky (short for Rocket J. Squirrel) and a dim-witted moose, Bullwinkle. The two battled Mr. Big and his henchpeople, Boris Badenov and Natasha, in a series of adventures. Other segments on the half-hour series included "Fractured Fairy Tales," narrated by Edward Everett Horton, "Bullwinkle's Corner," a poetry segment, and the adventures of Sherman and Mr. Peabody, a boy and a pedantic dog who traveled through time via Peabody's invention, the Wayback Machine. Ward's show attracted a cult following, as had his earlier cartoon series, *Crusader Rabbit* (which also featured a diminutive hero and a not-too-bright sidekick). Ward later created *George of the Jungle* for Saturday morning consumption. See also *The Bullwinkle Show.*

ROCKY JONES, SPACE RANGER

NBC

27 FEBRUARY 1954–17 APRIL 1954 *Rocky Jones* was probably the shortest lived of the several children's space shows of the early 1950s. The half-hour show, set in the twenty-first century, featured Richard Crane as Rocky Jones, Captain of the Space Rangers; Sally Mansfield as Vena Ray; Scotty Becket as Winky; Maurice Cass as Professor Newton; Robert Lydon as Bobby; Leonard Penn as Griff; Charles Meredith as Drake; Frank Pulaski as Darganto; and Bill Hudson as Clark.

ROCKY KING, DETECTIVE

DUMONT

14 JANUARY 1950–26 DECEMBER 1954 This early crime show starred Roscoe Karns as Rocky King, a hardworking New York City police inspector; Todd Karns costarred as his assistant, Sergeant Hart. Rocky's wife, Mabel, was also a regular, though the character was only heard and never seen. The half-hour series was produced by Lawrence Menkin and Charles Spear and was originally titled *Rocky King, Inside Detective.*

ROD BROWN OF THE ROCKET RANGERS

CBS

10 APRIL 1953–29 MAY 1954 This Saturday-morning space opera was notable mainly because it starred Cliff Robertson (in one of his earliest television roles) as Rod Brown, a member of the Rocket Rangers, one of the several interplanetary defense organizations featured on shows of the genre. Also featured were Bruce Hall as Ranger Frank Boyle and Jack Weston as Ranger Wilbur ("Wormsey") Wormser. William Dozier was the executive producer.

THE ROGER MILLER SHOW

NBC

12 SEPTEMBER 1966–26 DECEMBER 1966 Country and western singer Roger Miller ("King of the Road," "Chug-a-Lug," etc.) hosted his own half-hour musical variety series; music was provided by the Eddie Karam Orchestra.

ROGER RAMJET

SYNDICATED

1965 Cartoon series about a research scientist (Roger Ramjet), who developed a pill that endowed him with great strength for limited periods of time.

THE ROGUES

NBC

13 SEPTEMBER 1964–5 SEPTEMBER 1965 The central characters in this light adventure hour were a family of fair-minded felons whose specialty was swindling swindlers and conning con artists. The concept had been used before on television, in *Colonel Humphrey Flack,* and was later employed on such series as *Switch* and *The Feather and Father Gang. The Rogues* was a product of Four Star Television and featured David Niven

as Alexander (Alec) Fleming; Charles Boyer as Marcel St. Clair, Alec's French cousin; Gig Young as Tony Fleming, Alec's American cousin; Gladys Cooper as Auntie Margaret, Alec's aunt; and Robert Coote as Timmy Fleming, an English cousin. John Williams was occasionally seen as Inspector Briscoe of Scotland Yard.

ROLL OUT!
CBS

5 OCTOBER 1973–4 JANUARY 1974 *Roll Out!* was a short-lived service sitcom about a predominantly black supply outfit (the 5050th) headquartered in France during World War II. The cast included: Stu Gilliam as Corporal Sweet Williams; Hilly Hicks as Private Jed Brooks; Val Bisoglio as Captain Rocco Calvelli; Ed Begley, Jr., as Lieutenant Robert Chapman; Mel Stewart as Sergeant B. J. Bryant; Penny Santon as Madame Delacourt, a restaurateur; Garrett Morris (later to join *NBC's Saturday Night Live*) as Wheels; Darrow Igus as Jersey; Rod Gist as Phone Booth; and Theodore Wilson as High Strung.

ROLLERGIRLS
NBC

24 APRIL 1978–10 MAY 1978 Created by James Komack, this half-hour sitcom, four episodes of which were shown, dwelt on a women's roller skating team, the Pittsburgh Pitts. Featured were Rhonda Bates as Mongo Sue Lampert; Candy Ann Brown as J. B. Johnson; Marcy Hanson as Honey Bee Novak; Marilyn Tokuda as Pipeline Akira; Terry Kiser as their hustling manager, Don Mitchell; and James Murtaugh as the team's radio announcer, Howie.

ROLLIN' ON THE RIVER
SYNDICATED

1971–1973 This half-hour musical variety series was hosted by singer Kenny Rogers and his group, the First Edition. In the fall of 1972 the show's title was changed to *Rollin' with Kenny Rogers and the First Edition;* both versions of the show were set aboard a riverboat.

ROMAN HOLIDAY
NBC

9 SEPTEMBER 1972–1 SEPTEMBER 1973 This Hanna-Barbera cartoon show was set about halfway between two of Hanna-Barbera's best known shows, *The Flintstones* (set in the Stone Age) and *The Jetsons* (set in the twenty-first century); *Roman Holiday* was set in first-century Rome, and its central characters were the Holiday family.

ROMANCE
CBS

3 NOVEMBER 1949–12 JANUARY 1950 Also known as *Theater of Romance,* this half-hour anthology series of romantic stories alternated on Thursday nights with *Inside U.S.A.,* replacing *Sugar Hill Times,* a short-lived all-black variety show. Robert Stevens produced and directed.

ROMPER ROOM   SYNDICATED

1954–   Like *Bozo the Clown, Romper Room* is really a franchised program, rather than a syndicated one: local stations are free to
use their hosts. The idea was developed in the early 1950s by Bert Claster
and his wife, Nancy, who originated the show in Baltimore. As the show
grew more popular, the Clasters offered to train the local *Romper Room*
teachers. By the late 1950s more than 100 stations aired the show, most
of which employed their own teachers. In 1977 *Variety* noted that *Romper Room* was televised in forty-six American markets, twenty-nine of
which used Chicago's Miss Sally as host; in real life Miss Sally is Sally
Claster Gelbard, the daughter of Bert and Nancy Claster.

THE ROOKIES   ABC

11 SEPTEMBER 1972–29 JUNE 1976   Straightforward crime show about
three young police recruits. Featured were Gerald S. O'Loughlin as Lieutenant Ed Ryker, the commanding officer; Michael Ontkean (1972–1974)
as Willie Gillis; Georg Stanford Brown as Terry Webster; Sam Melville
as Mike Danko; Kate Jackson as nurse Jill Danko, Mike's wife; and
Bruce Fairbairn (1974–1976) as Chris Owens. The executive producers of
the hour series were Aaron Spelling and Leonard Goldberg; Spelling and
Goldberg had previously produced a successful crime show about three
young plainclothes officers, *The Mod Squad,* and later produced a very
successful crime show about three female private eyes, *Charlie's Angels.*

ROOM FOR ONE MORE   ABC

27 JANUARY 1962–22 SEPTEMBER 1962   Half-hour sitcom about a family with four children—two natural and two foster. With Andrew Duggan as George Rose; Peggy McCay as his wife, Anna Rose; Anna Capri
as daughter Mary, age sixteen; Timothy Rooney as son Jeff, age fourteen;
Carol Nicholson as daughter Laurie, age ten; Ronnie Dapo as son Flip,
age nine; Jack Albertson as neighbor Walter Burton; and Maxine Stuart
as his wife, Ruth Burton. Ed Jurist produced the series.

ROOM 222   ABC

17 SEPTEMBER 1969–11 JANUARY 1974   *Room 222* was a half-hour
comedy-drama set at Walt Whitman High School, an integrated school
in Los Angeles (exteriors for the series were actually shot at Los Angeles
High). The cast included: Lloyd Haynes (who had been a production assistant for the Heatter-Quigley game shows before landing acting jobs) as
Pete Dixon, black American history teacher; Karen Valentine as chipper
Alice Johnson, a student teacher in the English department; Michael
Constantine as Seymour Kaufman, Walt Whitman's good-natured principal; and Denise Nicholas as Liz McIntyre, a black guidance counselor,
and Dixon's female friend. Regular students included: Howard Rice as
Richie Lane; Ta-Tanisha (1969–1972) as Pam; Heshimu as Jason Allen;

Judy Strangis as Helen Loomis; David Joliffe as Bernie; Carol Green as Kim; and Ty Henderson as Cleon. James L. Brooks created the series, which was produced and directed by Gene Reynolds.

ROOTIE KAZOOTIE NBC/ABC
9 DECEMBER 1950–1 NOVEMBER 1952 (NBC); 22 DECEMBER 1952–7 MAY 1954 (ABC) Todd Russell hosted this half-hour children's show, set at the Rootie Kazootie Club. The show featured puppets (such as Rootie Kazootie, Gala Poochie, Polka Dottie, El Squeako, and Poison Zoomack), along with games and prizes for the studio audience. John Vee was also featured on the series, and the puppets were handled by Paul Ashley and Frank Milano. The show was seen Saturdays over NBC, and weekday evenings over ABC; the latter version was written and produced by Steve Carlin.

ROOTS ABC
23 JANUARY 1977–30 JANUARY 1977 One of the most remarkable achievements in television history, *Roots* was a twelve-hour adaptation, telecast on eight consecutive nights, of Alex Haley's moving story about his search for his African ancestors. *Roots* was the highest-rated series of all time—all eight telecasts ranked among the thirteen highest-rated single programs of all time, and the final segment topped all shows with a 51.1 rating and a 71 share. The A. C. Nielsen Company estimated that some 130 million viewers watched at least part of *Roots.* The adaptation of Haley's story was simple and straightforward—it began with the capture of Kunta Kinte in West Africa by slave traders and ended a century and a half later in Tennessee. Principal players in the large cast included: LeVar Burton (a college student appearing in his first television role) as Kunta Kinte; John Amos as Toby, as Kunta Kinte came to be called in later life; Louis Gossett, Jr., as Fiddler; Leslie Uggams as Kizzy; Ben Vereen as Chicken George; Cicely Tyson as Binta; Edward Asner as Captain Davies; Ralph Waite as Slater; Lorne Greene as John Reynolds; Lynda Day George as Mrs. Reynolds; Robert Reed as William Reynolds; Chuck Connors as Tom Moore; John Schuck as Ordell; George Hamilton as Stephen Bennett; Lloyd Bridges as Evan Brent; Scatman Crothers as Mingo; Lillian Randolph as Sister Sara; Richard Roundtree as Sam Bennett; Georg Stanford Brown as Tom; and Hilly Hicks as Lewis. David L. Wolper was the executive producer of *Roots,* which was nominated for about thirty-seven Emmys. Stan Margulies was the producer; Marvin Chomsky, John Erman, David Greene, and Gilbert Moses directed it. William Blinn was the script supervisor, and Alex Haley served as consultant.

ROOTS: THE NEXT GENERATIONS ABC
18 FEBRUARY 1979–25 FEBRUARY 1979 A seven-night, twelve-hour,

$18-million-sequel to *Roots, Roots: The Next Generations* (commonly knows as *Roots II*) chronicled the saga of author Alex Haley's ancestors from 1882 to 1967. Although *Roots II* did not utterly dominate the ratings as had *Roots I*, the miniseries proved highly popular—the seven telecasts all ranked within the week's top eleven programs. Principal players included: Avon Long as Chicken George Moore (Ben Vereen had played the role in *Roots I*); Georg Stanford Brown as Tom Harvey (repeating his *Roots I* role); Lynne Moody as his wife, Irene Harvey (also repeating from *Roots I*); Henry Fonda as Colonel Warner, the local political boss; Richard Thomas as his son, Jim Warner, who was disowned when he married a black woman; Marc Singer as Andy Warner, who succeeded his father as the political boss; Olivia de Havilland as Mrs. Warner, the Colonel's wife; Paul Koslo as Earl Crowther, Andy's hatchet man; Bever-Leigh Banfield and Beah Richards as Cynthia Harvey, daughter of Tom and Irene; Stan Shaw as Will Palmer, who married Cynthia (Will and Cynthia were Alex Haley's grandparents); Harry Morgan as Bob Campbell, Will's employer; Irene Cara as Bertha Palmer, daughter of Will and Cynthia; Dorian Harewood as Simon Haley, who married Bertha; Ruby Dee as Queen Haley, Simon's mother; Paul Winfield as Dr. Huguley, dean of the college where Simon Haley landed a teaching job; Christoff St. John, Damon Evans, and James Earl Jones as Alex Haley, son of Simon and Bertha; Debbie Allen as Nan, Haley's wife; Al Freeman, Jr., as Malcolm X, the charismatic Black Muslim whose autobiography was "told to" Haley; Marlon Brando (in his first TV dramatic role in thirty years) as George Lincoln Rockwell, leader of the American Nazi Party, whom Haley interviewed for *Playboy* magazine. The miniseries culminated with Haley's trip to West Africa, where a *griot,* or oral historian, told him of the disappearance of Kunta Kinte some 200 years before. *Roots: The Next Generations* was produced by Stan Margulies; David L. Wolper was the executive producer.

THE ROPERS
ABC

13 MARCH 1979–17 APRIL 1979; 15 SEPTEMBER 1979– A spinoff from *Three's Company, The Ropers* stars Audra Lindley and Norman Fell as Helen and Stanley Roper, who have moved into a condominium development. Also featured are Jeffrey Tambor as their new neighbor, Jeffrey P. Brookes III; Patricia McCormack as his wife, Anne Brookes; Evan Cohen as their young son, David, Louise Vallance (January 1980–   ) as Jenny Ballinger, the Ropers' boarder. Don Nicholl, Michael Ross, and Bernie West are the executive producers.

THE ROSEMARY CLOONEY SHOW
SYNDICATED

1956–1957 Rosemary Clooney, pop singer of the 1950s, hosted this series of thirty-nine half-hour variety shows, which also featured the Hi-Lo's (Bob Morse, Clark Burrows, Gene Puerling, and Bob Strasen) and

Nelson Riddle's orchestra. In the fall of 1957 Clooney hosted her own network series: see *The Lux Show Starring Rosemary Clooney.*

ROSETTI AND RYAN   NBC

22 SEPTEMBER 1977–10 NOVEMBER 1977   This hour-long crime show vanished early in the 1977–1978 season. It featured Tony Roberts as lawyer Joe Rosetti, the dashing half of a successful defense team; Squire Fridell as his more serious partner, Frank Ryan, a former cop; Jane Elliott as Assistant District Attorney Jessica Hornesby; Ruth Manning as Emma; Randi Oakes as Georgia; and Dick O'Neill as Judge Praetor D. Hardcastle. Leonard B. Stern was the executive producer, Don M. Mankiewicz and Gordon Cotler the supervising producers, and Jerry Davis the producer for Universal Television.

THE ROSEY GRIER SHOW   SYNDICATED

1969   Former professional football star Roosevelt Grier hosted his own half-hour talk show for a brief time.

ROUGH RIDERS   ABC

2 OCTOBER 1958–24 SEPTEMBER 1959   An implausible western about three Civil War veterans—two Union soldiers and one Confederate soldier—who teamed up after the war. With Kent Taylor as Captain Flagg; Jan Merlin (the ex-Confederate) as Lieutenant Kirby; and Peter Whitney as Sergeant Sinclair.

THE ROUNDERS   ABC

6 SEPTEMBER 1966–3 JANUARY 1967   Short-lived sitcom about a couple of cowpokes at a Texas cattle ranch. With Ron Hayes as Ben Jones; Patrick Wayne (son of John Wayne) as Howdy Lewis; Chill Wills as Jim Ed Love, owner of the J. L. Ranch; Janis Hansen as Sally, Ben's girlfriend; Bobbi Jordan as Ada, Howdy's girlfriend; Jason Wingreen as Shorty; James Bowen Brown as Luke; and Walker Edmiston as Regan. Ed Adamson produced the half-hour series for MGM.

ROUTE 66   CBS

7 OCTOBER 1960–18 SEPTEMBER 1964   *Route 66,* an hour-long adventure series about two guys tooling around the country in a 1960 Corvette, was filmed on location throughout America. Featured were Martin Milner as Tod Stiles and George Maharis (1960–1962) as Buzz Murdock; in the fall of 1962 Glenn Corbett succeeded Maharis as Tod's partner, Lincoln Case. Notable guest appearances on the series included those by Alan Alda ("Soda Pop and Paper Flags," 31 May 1963); Joey Heatherton (in her first TV dramatic role, "Three Sides," 18 November 1960); Robert Redford ("First Class Mouliak," 20 October 1961); and Rod Steiger

("Welcome to the Wedding," 8 November 1963). Herbert B. Leonard was the executive producer of the series for Screen Gems.

THE ROWAN AND MARTIN SHOW   NBC
16 JUNE 1966–8 SEPTEMBER 1966 A summer replacement for *The Dean Martin Show, The Rowan and Martin Show* was an hour-long variety series cohosted by comedians Dan Rowan and Dick Martin. Also on hand were Lainie Kazan, Frankie Randall, Judi Rolin, Dom DeLuise, the Wisa D'Orso Dancers, and Les Brown and his band. Rowan and Martin are, of course, better known as the hosts of *Laugh-In* (see also that title).

THE ROY DOTY SHOW   DUMONT
10 MAY 1953–4 OCTOBER 1953 Sunday-morning children's show, hosted by Roy Doty, who drew sketches and told stories.

THE ROY ROGERS AND DALE EVANS SHOW   ABC
29 SEPTEMBER 1962–22 DECEMBER 1963 Roy Rogers and Dale Evans, who had previously starred in a western, *The Roy Rogers Show,* cohosted this Saturday-night variety hour. Also featured were Cliff Arquette, Pat Brady, Cathie Taylor, and the Sons of the Pioneers.

THE ROY ROGERS SHOW   NBC
30 DECEMBER 1951–23 JUNE 1957 One of the most popular of TV's early westerns, especially with younger viewers, this half-hour show, set in the present, starred Roy Rogers and his wife, Dale Evans, as themselves. Pat Brady was featured as Rogers's jeep-driving sidekick (the jeep was named Nelliebelle), and the Sons of the Pioneers, the singing group with which Rogers (then known as Leonard Slye) broke into show business, were also on hand. Rogers rode Trigger, a trained horse (which Rogers had stuffed after its death), while Evans rode Buttercup; rounding out the animal cast was Bullet, a German shepherd. Some 101 episodes were produced by Rogers' own company, Roy Rogers Productions.

ROYAL PLAYHOUSE   DUMONT
12 APRIL 1951–12 JULY 1951; 3 APRIL 1952–26 JUNE 1952 This half-hour dramatic anthology series was seen on Thursday nights.

RUFF AND REDDY   NBC
14 DECEMBER 1957–26 SEPTEMBER 1964 *Ruff and Reddy* was the first network television series from Hanna-Barbera Productions. William Hanna and Joseph Barbera, who had created the *Tom and Jerry* cartoons early in the 1940s, formed their television partnership in 1957 and went on to produce some 100 series, most of which were animated. *Ruff and*

Reddy was a Saturday-morning half-hour show and featured the adventures of a cat (Ruff) and dog (Reddy) team. The show was first hosted by Jimmy Blaine and later by Bob Cottle. The success of *Ruff and Reddy* soon led to such well-known Hanna-Barbera shows as *The Flintstones, Huckleberry Hound, The Jetsons,* and *Quickdraw McGraw.*

THE RUGGLES   ABC
3 NOVEMBER 1949–5 JUNE 1952   Kinescoped in Hollywood, this half-hour sitcom starred Charles Ruggles as himself, Erin O'Brien Moore and Ruth Tedrow as his wife, and Margaret Kerry as their daughter. Robert Raisbeck was the producer.

RUN, BUDDY, RUN   CBS
12 SEPTEMBER 1966–2 JANUARY 1967   Jack Sheldon starred in this half-hour sitcom as Buddy Overstreet, a mild-mannered accountant who was forced to flee his pursuers from The Syndicate after he overheard mobsters discussing "Chicken Little" in a steam room. Also featured were Bruce Gordon as Mr. Devere, syndicate chieftain; Jim Connell as Junior, Devere's son; Nick Georgiade as Wendell, one of Devere's henchmen; and Gregg Palmer as Harry, another henchman.

RUN FOR YOUR LIFE   NBC
13 SEPTEMBER 1965–11 SEPTEMBER 1968   Roy Huggins, who developed *The Fugitive,* also developed and produced this hour series about a man on the run. It starred Ben Gazzara as Paul Bryan, a lawyer who learned that he had no more than two years to live and decided to spend his remaining time traveling around and assisting others. Though Bryan was told in the initial episode that he had only two years, the series managed to stay on the air for three.

RUN, JOE, RUN   NBC
7 SEPTEMBER 1974–4 SEPTEMBER 1976   This unusual live-action Saturday-morning series combined *Lassie* with *The Fugitive.* Its central character was a German shepherd named Joe, who, while undergoing training for the Army K-9 Corps, was wrongly accused of attacking his master and ran away; each week Joe found time to help out someone in distress. During the first season Arch Whiting was featured as Joe's master, Sergeant William Corey, who vainly pursued Joe to let him know that he had been exonerated. During the second season Joe teamed up with a young hiker named Josh McCoy (played by Chad States). Joe was played by Heinrich of Midvale. The half-hour series was produced by Robert Williams and Bill Schwartz the first season, and by Dick O'Connor the second season for William P. D'Angelo Productions, Inc.

RUNAROUND
NBC

9 SEPTEMBER 1972–1 SEPTEMBER 1973 Paul Winchell hosted this Saturday-morning game show for children, on which nine youngsters competed; when questions were asked, the players were supposed to run to certain squares onstage, which represented possible answers to the questions.

THE RUNAWAYS (OPERATION: RUNAWAY)
NBC

27 APRIL 1978–18 MAY 1978; 29 MAY 1979–4 SEPTEMBER 1979 An hour dramatic series about a psychologist whose specialty was tracking down runaways and convincing them to return home, the show premiered in 1978 as a short-run series, titled *Operation: Runaway*. It starred Robert Reed as psychologist David McKay, with Karen Machon as his friend Karen Wingate, dean of women at the college where McKay's office was located; Michael Biehn as Mark Johnson, David's ward; and Ruth Cox as Susan. The show had been scheduled for NBC's fall 1978 schedule, but was yanked in August of 1978; it finally reappeared in May of 1979 entitled *The Runaways* and starring Alan Feinstein as psychologist Steve Arizzio. Karen Machon and Michael Biehn were retained from the 1978 cast, and two new faces were added: James Callahan as Sergeant Hal Grady, and Patti Cohoon as Debbie Shaw. The series was a QM Production.

RUSS HODGES' SCOREBOARD
DUMONT

14 APRIL 1948–22 APRIL 1949 Fifteen-minute nightly sports report by veteran sportscaster Russ Hodges.

THE RUSS MORGAN SHOW
CBS

7 JULY 1956–1 SEPTEMBER 1956 This Saturday-night half-hour musical variety series was hosted by bandleader Russ Morgan and featured singer Helen O'Connell.

RUTH LYONS' 50 CLUB
NBC

1 OCTOBER 1951–5 SEPTEMBER 1952 Broadcast from Cincinnati, this half-hour daytime variety show was hosted by Ruth Lyons and featured singers Bill Thall and Dick Noel.

RUTHIE ON THE TELEPHONE
CBS

7 AUGUST 1949–5 NOVEMBER 1949 A five-minute filmed comedy series, *Ruthie on the Telephone* starred Ruth Gilbert as Ruthie and Philip Reed as the unwilling recipient of her telephone calls. The show was seen five nights a week at 7:55.

RYAN'S HOPE
ABC

7 JULY 1975– One of the few daytime serials to be set in a large metropolis, Ryan's Hope is named after a fictional tavern located on

Manhattan's West Side; most of the action takes place there or at Riverside Hospital, to which most of the show's medical people are affiliated. The half-hour show was created by Claire Labine and Paul Avila Mayer. The original cast included: Faith Catlin as Dr. Faith Coleridge; Justin Deas as Dr. Bucky Carter; Bernard Barrow as Johnny Ryan, founder of Ryan's Hope; Helen Gallagher as his wife, Maeve Ryan; Michael Hawkins as Frank Ryan, their eldest son; Ilene Kristen as Delia Ryan, Frank's wife; Malcolm Groome as Dr. Pat Ryan, Johnny and Maeve's younger son; Kate Mulgrew as Mary Ryan, Johnny and Maeve's daughter; Diana Van Der Vlis as Dr. Nell Beaulac; John Gabriel as her husband, Seneca Beaulac; Frank Latimore as Dr. Ed Coleridge, Faith's father, an old friend of Johnny Ryan; Nancy Addison as Jillian Coleridge, Ed's adopted daughter; Ronald Hale as Ed's son, Dr. Roger Coleridge, who had an affair with Delia Ryan; Michael Levin as reporter Jack Fenelli, who fell for Mary Ryan; Michael Fairman as the unscrupulous Nick Szabo; Earl Hindman as Bob Reid; Hannibal Penney, Jr., as Clem Moultrie; and Rosalinda Guerra as Ramona Gonzalez. Subsequent additions to the cast have included: Nancy Barrett (who replaced Faith Catlin), Catherine Hicks and Karen Ann Morris as Dr. Faith Coleridge; Andrew Robinson (who replaced Michael Hawkins) and Daniel Hugh–Kelly as Frank Ryan; Mary Carney (who replaced Kate Mulgrew), Kathleen Tolan, and Nicolette Goulet as Mary Ryan Fenelli; Tom MacGreevey as Tom Desmond, who married Faith; Julie Barr as Renie Szabo; Dennis Jay Higgins as Sam Crowell; John Perkins as Father McShane; Rosetta LeNoire as Miriam George; Jose Aleman as Angel Nieves; Ana Alicia Ortiz as Alicia Nieves; Louise Shaffer as Rae Woodward; Jadrian Steele as Little John Ryan; Fat Thomas as Jumbo Marino; Lisa Suttan, Megan McCracken and Nana Tucker as Nancy Feldman; John Blazo (who replaced Malcolm Groome) as Dr. Pat Ryan; Sarah Felder as Siobhan Ryan; Pauline Flanagan as Annie Colleary; Patrick Horgan as Thatcher Ross.

Claire Labine and Paul Avila Mayer also serve as the executive producers and head writers of *Ryan's Hope*. Robert Costello is the producer; Lela Swift and Jerry Evans are the directors.

S.S. TELECRUISE   ABC
28 APRIL 1951–2 JUNE 1951 This two-hour Saturday-morning variety show began locally in Philadelphia before going network for a few weeks in 1951. Hosted by "Cap'n" Jack Steck, it featured the Dave Appell Trio, baritone Eddie Roecker, Bon Bon, and Carol Wynne. The show's musical numbers were performed in front of photographs of exotic places.

S.W.A.T.   ABC
24 FEBRUARY 1975–29 JUNE 1976 Generally criticized as one of the most violent shows of the decade, *S.W.A.T.* was the story of the Special

Weapons and Tactics team, an elite unit of police officers stationed somewhere in California. Featured were Steve Forrest as Lieutenant Dan "Hondo" Harrelson, the leader; Rod Perry as Sergeant David "Deacon" Kay, second in command; Robert Urich as Officer James Street; Mark Shera as Officer Dominic Luca; and James Coleman as Officer T. J. McCabe. Created by Robert Hamner, *S.W.A.T.*'s executive producers were Aaron Spelling and Leonard Goldberg; the pilot for the series was telecast 17 February 1975, as one episode of *The Rookies,* another Spelling-Goldberg Production.

SABER OF LONDON
See MARK SABER

SABRINA, THE TEENAGE WITCH
CBS

12 SEPTEMBER 1970–31 AUGUST 1974   Sabrina, a teenage witch, was first introduced on *The Archie Show,* but in the fall of 1970 she was given her own hour cartoon series; that season the show was titled *Sabrina and the Groovie Goolies.* In the fall of 1971 the show was reduced to thirty minutes and retitled *Sabrina, the Teenage Witch* (*The Groovie Goolies* were given their own series that year, too). Sabrina was later reunited with Archie and Company on *The Archie Comedy Hour* and *The New Archie Sabrina Hour.* In the fall of 1977 she was again featured on her own series: see *Super Witch.* See also *The Archie Show; The Groovie Goolies.*

SAFARI TO ADVENTURE
SYNDICATED

1971–1973   Bill Burrud served as host and narrator of this half-hour series of nature films.

SAFARILAND
SYNDICATED

1963   Half-hour African travelogue, narrated by Jim Stewart.

SAILOR OF FORTUNE
SYNDICATED

1957   Lorne Greene starred in this Canadian-produced half-hour adventure series as freighter captain Grant (Mitch) Mitchell.

THE SAINT
SYNDICATED/NBC/CBS

1963–1966 (SYNDICATED) 21 MAY 1967–3 SEPTEMBER 1967; 17 FEBRUARY 1968–14 SEPTEMBER 1968; 18 APRIL 1969–SEPTEMBER 1969 (NBC); 21 DECEMBER 1979–   (CBS)   The Saint, as fictional detective Simon Templar was sometimes known, was created by Leslie Charteris in a series of novels. The first television version, which starred Roger Moore as Simon Templar, was produced in England by ITC. Also featured were Winsley Pithey, Norman Pitt, and Ivor Dean as Inspector Teal of Scotland Yard. The CBS version, titled *Return of the Saint,* starred Ian Ogilvy.

SAINTS AND SINNERS   NBC

17 SEPTEMBER 1962–28 JANUARY 1963   This hour-long dramatic series
was set at a newspaper, the New York *Record* (the same paper had been
featured in *The Roaring Twenties*). It starred Nick Adams as Nick Alexander, a reporter, and featured John Larkin as city editor Mark Grainger;
Richard Erdman as Klugie, the photographer; Robert F. Simon as copy
editor Dave Tobiak; and Barbara Rush as Washington correspondent Liz
Hogan.

SALE OF THE CENTURY   NBC/SYNDICATED

29 SEPTEMBER 1969–13 JULY 1973 (NBC); 1973 (SYNDICATED)   *Sale*
of the Century was a merchandise giveaway show on which the contestants, by answering simple questions, won the right to "buy" proffered
prizes at very low prices. The show had a four-year daytime run on NBC
before going into syndication. Jack Kelly hosted the series until August
of 1971, when affable Joe Garagiola succeeded him.

SALLY   NBC

15 SEPTEMBER 1957–30 MARCH 1958   *Sally* was a half-hour sitcom
about a former salesclerk who was invited to accompany a slightly daffy
widow on a trip around the world. It starred Joan Caulfield as Sally
Truesdale and Marion Lorne as her patron, Myrtle Banford. By February of 1958, the two had returned home, and Sally went back to her job at
the Banford and Bleacher Department Store. Three new regulars were
added for the last few episodes: Gale Gordon as Bascomb Bleacher, Sr.,
manager of the store; Johnny Desmond as Jim Kendall; and Arte Johnson as Junior Bleacher. *Sally* was the first filmed series produced by Paramount Television.

SALTY   SYNDICATED

1974   An innocuous half-hour adventure series about two boys and
Salty, their pet sea lion. With Mark Slade and Johnny Doran as brothers
Taylor and Tim Reed, who were rescued in the hurricane that claimed
their parents' lives; Julius Harris as Clancy Ames, their rescuer, owner of
the Cove Marina; and Vincent Dale as Tim's pal, Rod Porterfield. Filmed
in the Bahamas, the series was produced by Kobi Jaeger.

SALVAGE 1   ABC

29 JANUARY 1979–11 NOVEMBER 1979   Hour adventure series starring
Andy Griffith as Harry Broderick, a junk dealer with high aspirations;
each week he and his crew embark on a salvage expedition of epic pro-
portions (in the pilot film, for example, they built a rocket and flew to the
moon to retrieve the debris left behind by the astronauts). Also featured
are Joel Higgins as Skip Carmichael, a former astronaut; Trish Stewart as

Melanie Slozar, a fuel expert; J. Jay Saunders as Mack; and Richard Jaeckel as Jack Klinger, a federal agent who keeps an eye on Broderick. Executive producers: Harve Bennett and Harris Katleman for Bennett-Katleman Productions in association with Columbia Pictures TV. Though the show did not appear on ABC's schedule for the fall of 1979, it resurfaced as a replacement series for *Out of the Blue* and *A New Kind of Family.*

SAM   CBS
14 MARCH 1978–18 APRIL 1978   Sam was a Labrador retriever assigned to the Los Angeles Police Department in this half-hour crime show from Jack Webb's Mark VII Ltd. Also featured were Mark Harmon as Officer Mike Breen and Len Wayland as Officer Clagett. The pilot for the series was aired 24 May 1977.

SAM BENEDICT   NBC
15 SEPTEMBER 1962–7 SEPTEMBER 1963   An hour-long crime show about a San Francisco defense attorney. With Edmond O'Brien as Sam Benedict; Richard Rust as his young associate, Hank Tabor; and Joan Tompkins as his secretary, Trudy Warner. William Froug produced the series for MGM.

THE SAM LEVENSON SHOW   CBS
27 JANUARY 1951–30 JUNE 1951; 10 FEBRUARY 1952–10 JUNE 1952; 27 APRIL 1959–25 SEPTEMBER 1959   Humorist Sam Levenson hosted three shows of his own. On the first, which was seen on Saturday nights, celebrity guests appeared with their children and discussed the trials and tribulations of child raising. The second *Sam Levenson Show* was a half-hour variety series, which began on Sunday nights but later shifted to Tuesdays. Levenson's third series was a daytime show which replaced *Arthur Godfrey Time* when Godfrey had to undergo surgery; this half-hour series was produced by Charles Andrews.

SAMMY AND COMPANY   SYNDICATED
1975–1977   Sammy Davis, Jr., hosted this ninety-minute variety series; other regulars included Johnny Brown, Kay Dingle, Joyce Jillson, Avery Schreiber, and announcer William B. Williams. Pierre Cossette was executive producer of the series, which was taped in New York, Las Vegas, and Los Angeles.

THE SAMMY DAVIS, JR. SHOW   NBC
7 JANUARY 1966–22 APRIL 1966   The first variety show of the decade to be hosted by a black performer, *The Sammy Davis, Jr. Show* unfortunately inherited the Friday slot formerly occupied by *Convoy* and, despite an impressive guest list (Richard Burton and Elizabeth Taylor on the pre-

miere, Judy Garland on two other shows), failed to attract decent ratings. Also featured were the Lester Wilson Dancers and the George Rhodes Orchestra.

THE SAMMY KAYE SHOW
CBS/NBC/ABC

28 JULY 1951–19 JULY 1952 (CBS); 8 AUGUST 1953–5 SEPTEMBER 1953 (NBC); 20 SEPTEMBER 1958–13 JUNE 1959 (ABC)   Bandleader Sammy Kaye hosted three Saturday-night musical programs. All were half-hour shows; the first was an early evening show on CBS; the second, on NBC, was seen at 8 p.m.; and the third, originally titled *Sammy Kaye's Music from Manhattan,* was scheduled at 10 p.m. on ABC. The latter show also featured singers Ray Michaels, Lynn Roberts, Larry Ellis, and Hank Kanui, plus Kaye's seventeen-piece band. Kaye also hosted a musical game show: see *So You Want to Lead a Band.*

SAMSON AND GOLIATH
NBC

9 SEPTEMBER 1967–7 SEPTEMBER 1968   On this Saturday-morning cartoon show from Hanna-Barbera Productions, a boy named Samson and his dog, Goliath, could, when the need arose, transform themselves into a superhero and a lion, respectively.

SAN FRANCISCO BEAT
See THE LINEUP

SAN FRANCISCO INTERNATIONAL AIRPORT
NBC

28 OCTOBER 1970–25 AUGUST 1971   The second segment of NBC's *Four-in-One* umbrella program, this hour show was, obviously, set at a big-city airport. Featured were Lloyd Bridges as Jim Conrad, the manager; Clu Gulagher as security chief Bob Hatten; Barbara Siegel as Suzie, Jim's daughter; and Barbara Werle as Jim's secretary, June.

SAN FRANCISCO MIX
PBS

6 OCTOBER 1970–29 JUNE 1971   Each program of this twenty-six-week series focused on a single topic or theme. Richard Moore was the producer, and the regulars included Taula Lawrence, Tom Dahlgren, John Sharp, Victor Wong, and Virginia Anderson.

THE SAN PEDRO BEACH BUMS
ABC

19 SEPTEMBER 1977–19 DECEMBER 1977   An unsuccessful attempt at an hour sitcom, *The San Pedro Beach Bums* were a group of five guys who lived on an old boat in the San Pedro (Calif.) harbor: Chris Murney as Buddy Binder; Stuart Pankin as Stuf; John Mark Robinson as Dancer (Ed McClory); Darryl McCullough as Moose; and Christopher DeRose as Boychick. Also featured were Christoff St. John as Ralphie; Susan Mullen as Suzy; and Lisa Reeves as Margo. Aaron Spelling and Douglas

S. Cramer were the executive producers; the pilot for the series, "The San Pedro Bums," was telecast 13 May 1977.

SANDY DREAMS   ABC

7 OCTOBER 1950–2 DECEMBER 1950   The principal character in this Saturday-evening children's show was a girl named Sandy, who was transported to the fantasy land of her dreams each week.

THE SANDY DUNCAN SHOW   CBS

17 SEPTEMBER 1972–31 DECEMBER 1972   Sandy Duncan, who had formerly been featured in *Funny Face,* returned in this half-hour sitcom with a faintly different format. Duncan starred as Sandy Stockton, a U.C.L.A. student, a part-time secretary, and an occasional star of commercials. Also featured were Marian Mercer as Kay Fox, her neighbor; Tom Bosley as Bert Quinn, her boss at the Quinn and Cohen Advertising Agency; Pam Zarit as Hilary, the receptionist; Eric Christmas as Ben Hampton, the handyman in Sandy's apartment building; and M. Emmet Walsh as Alex Lembeck, a motorcycle cop who was a neighbor of Sandy's.

SANFORD AND SON   NBC

14 JANUARY 1972–2 SEPTEMBER 1977   *Sanford and Son,* the second TV series developed by then partners Norman Lear and Bud Yorkin, was NBC's most popular prime-time series for four seasons (1972–1973 through 1975–1976). Lear and Yorkin acquired the rights to a British series, *Steptoe and Son,* and Americanized it by casting it with black performers. The half-hour sitcom starred veteran comedian Redd Foxx as cantankerous Fred Sanford, a widowed junk dealer living in Los Angeles (Foxx, whose real name was John Sanford, had seldom been seen on television before the series), and Demond Wilson as his devoted but restless son, Lamont Sanford. Foxx also brought in some of his contemporaries to work on the show, such as Whitman Mayo, who appeared as Grady Wilson (and later received his own show, *Grady*), Slappy White, who played Melvin, and LaWanda Page, who played Aunt Esther, the sister of Fred's late wife Elizabeth and the butt of many of Fred's jokes. Also featured were Gregory Sierra (1972–1974) as Julio, a friend of Lamont's; Nathaniel Taylor as Rollo; Raymond Allen as Uncle Woody; Don Bexley as Bubba Hoover; Lynn Hamilton as Donna Harris, Fred's female friend; Howard Platt as Hoppy, a local police officer; Hal Williams as Smitty, another cop; Pat Morita (1975–1976) as Ah Chew; Marlene Clark as Janet; and Edward Crawford as Roger. By the end of the 1976–1977 season, both Foxx and Wilson had decided to leave the series—Foxx signed with ABC and hosted his own variety show (see *The Redd Foxx Comedy Hour*) and Wilson turned up in a midseason sitcom (see *Baby, I'm Back*). NBC, however, decided to salvage what it could from the old show and

introduced *Sanford Arms* in the fall of 1977 (see below). Bud Yorkin was the executive producer of *Sanford and Son* and Aaron Ruben was its first producer; Ruben was succeeded by coproducers Saul Turteltaub and Bernie Orenstein.

SANFORD ARMS NBC

16 SEPTEMBER 1977–14 OCTOBER 1977   *Sanford Arms,* NBC's attempt to keep *Sanford and Son* going after the departures of Redd Foxx and Demond Wilson, proved to be one of the first cancellations of the 1977–1978 season. As *Sanford Arms* opened, it was explained that Fred and Lamont Sanford had moved to Phoenix, and that their house and the place next door had been bought. Featured were Teddy Wilson as Phil Wheeler, the new purchaser, who planned to convert the place next door to a rooming house and to use the Sanford place as his home and office; Tina Andrews as Angie Wheeler, Phil's twenty-year-old daughter; John Earl as Nat Wheeler, Phil's twelve-year-old son; Bebe Drake-Hooks as Jeannie, Phil's girlfriend; Don Bexley as Bubba Hoover; LaWanda Page as Esther, who collected the mortgage payments for Fred Sanford; and Whitman Mayo as Grady Wilson. Bud Yorkin, Bernie Orenstein, and Saul Turteltaub (all of whom had worked on *Sanford and Son*) were the executive producers of *Sanford Arms* and Woody Kling was its producer.

SARA CBS

13 FEBRUARY 1976–30 JULY 1976   Based on a novel by Marian Cockrell, *Sara* was an hour-long western about an Eastern schoolteacher who came to Independence, Colorado, in the 1870s. The cast included Brenda Vaccaro as Sara Yarnell; Bert Kramer as Emmet Ferguson, a townsman who was also a member of the school board; Albert Stratton as Martin Pope, newspaper publisher; William Wintersole as banker George Bailey, another school board member; Mariclare Costello as Julia Bailey, his wife; Louise Latham as Sara's landlady, Martha Higgins; William Phipps as Claude Barstow, the third member of the school board; Kraig Metzinger as Georgie Bailey, son of George and Julia, one of Sara's students; Debbie Lytton as Debbie Higgins, Martha's daughter, another student; and Hallie Morgan as Emma Higgins, Debbie's sister, another student. George Eckstein was the executive producer and Richard Collins the producer, for Universal Television.

THE SARAH CHURCHILL SHOW CBS

7 OCTOBER 1951–30 DECEMBER 1951   Fifteen-minute interview show hosted by Sarah Churchill and sponsored by Hallmark Cards. Early in 1952 Hallmark and Churchill moved to NBC, as Churchill became the first host of *Hallmark Hall of Fame.*

SARGE NBC

21 SEPTEMBER 1971–11 JANUARY 1972 George Kennedy starred in this hour dramatic series as Samuel Patrick ("Sarge") Cavanaugh, a former police officer who decided to become a Catholic priest after his wife was murdered; he was assigned to a parish in San Diego. Also featured were Sallie Shockley as Valerie, his secretary; Ramon Bieri as Lieutenant Barney Varick; and Harold Sakata (better remembered as Oddjob in the movie *Goldfinger*) as Kenji Takichi, the volunteer athletic director for the parish youth. The pilot for the series, "Sarge: The Badge or the Cross," was televised 22 February 1971.

SATELLITE POLICE
See SPACE PATROL

SATURDAY NIGHT AT THE GARDEN DUMONT

7 OCTOBER 1950–31 MARCH 1951 Live coverage of events at New York's Madison Square Garden was offered on this Saturday-night series.

SATURDAY NIGHT DANCE PARTY NBC

7 JUNE 1952–30 AUGUST 1952 Jerry Lester, formerly the host of *Broadway Open House*, emceed this variety hour, a summer replacement for Sid Caesar's *Your Show of Shows*.

THE SATURDAY NIGHT FIGHTS
See THE FIGHT OF THE WEEK

SATURDAY NIGHT JAMBOREE NBC

4 DECEMBER 1948–2 JULY 1949 Country and western music, broadcast from New York.

SATURDAY NIGHT LIVE WITH HOWARD COSELL ABC

20 SEPTEMBER 1975–17 JANUARY 1976 Not to be confused with *NBC's Saturday Night Live*, which also premiered in the fall of 1975, this hour-long variety show was seen in prime time and was hosted by ABC sportscaster Howard Cosell. The show originated from New York, with pick-ups from other parts of the country. Roone Arledge was the executive producer, and Rupert Hitzig was the producer. Among Cosell's regulars was Bill Murray, who later turned up on *NBC's Saturday Night Live*.

THE SATURDAY NIGHT REVUE NBC

6 JUNE 1953–5 SEPTEMBER 1953; 12 JUNE 1954–18 SEPTEMBER 1954 *The Saturday Night Revue* was twice a summer replacement for Sid Caesar's *Your Show of Shows*. Hoagy Carmichael was the host in 1953 and Eddie Albert in 1954, with Alan Young and Ben Blue alternating biweek-

ly as guest stars. The latter version also featured Pat Carroll and the Sauter-Finnegan Band and was produced by Ernie Glucksman.

SATURDAY PROM   NBC
15 OCTOBER 1960–1 APRIL 1961 Merv Griffin hosted this half-hour music show for teens, which was telecast early on Saturday evenings.

SATURDAY ROUNDUP   NBC
16 JUNE 1951–1 SEPTEMBER 1951 Kermit Maynard, younger brother of Ken Maynard, starred in this unusual western series. Maynard did not play a continuing character, but rather a different character each week.

SATURDAY SPORTS MIRROR   CBS
14 JULY 1956–15 SEPTEMBER 1956 Cohosts Jack Drees and Bill Hickey presented news from the world of sports and interviews with athletes on this half-hour Saturday-evening series.

SATURDAY SQUARE   NBC
7 JANUARY 1950–18 FEBRUARY 1950 This short-lived prime-time variety series, broadcast from Chicago, was produced by Ted Mills and Norman Felton. The setting was a city block in downtown Chicago.

SAWYER VIEWS HOLLYWOOD   ABC
14 APRIL 1951–31 AUGUST 1951 Hal Sawyer hosted this half-hour variety and interview program.

SAY IT WITH ACTING   NBC/ABC
14 AUGUST 1949–24 SEPTEMBER 1950 (NBC); 7 SEPTEMBER 1951–22 FEBRUARY 1952 (ABC) Ben Grauer hosted this game show, on which teams from Broadway shows played charades. See also *Act It Out.*

SAY WHEN   NBC
2 JANUARY 1961–26 MARCH 1965 This merchandise giveaway show from Goodson-Todman Productions was similar in format to *The Price Is Right*—contestants could choose items of merchandise, and the object of the game was to choose a set of items that totaled closest to a preset dollar amount. The player whose bid was closer won whatever he or she had chosen. Art James hosted the series and was assisted by Ruth Hasely.

THE SCARLET LETTER   PBS
2 APRIL 1979–5 APRIL 1979 A meticulous but labored adaptation of Nathaniel Hawthorne's 1850 novel, *The Scarlet Letter* was telecast in four consecutive hour installments. Principal players included Meg Foster as Hester Prynne, the convicted adulteress who was condemned to

wear the letter A on her dress forever (inexplicably, the letter used on the series was gold, not scarlet); John Heard as her lover, the Reverend Arthur Dimmesdale; Kevin Conway as Hester's husband, Roger Chillingworth. Herbert Hirschman was the executive producer of the series, which was filmed largely in Rhode Island. Rick Hauser produced and directed.

THE SCARLET PIMPERNEL
SYNDICATED

1958   This half-hour adventure series, a European import, was based on Baroness Orczy's novel and starred Marius Goring as The Scarlet Pimpernel, hero of the French Revolution.

SCENE 70
SYNDICATED

1969   Jay Reynolds hosted this hour-long rock music show.

THE SCHAEFER CENTURY THEATRE
SYNDICATED

1952   Filmed half-hour dramatic anthology series. Natalie Wood made her first major TV appearance on one episode, "Playmates."

SCHLITZ PLAYHOUSE OF STARS
CBS

5 OCTOBER 1951–27 MARCH 1959   This long-running half-hour dramatic anthology series was hosted for several seasons by Irene Dunne and later by Robert Paige. A sampling of presentations would include: "Not a Chance," with Helen Hayes (5 October 1951); "Never Wave at a WAC," with Rosalind Russell (19 October 1951); "Dark Fleece," with Anthony Quinn (21 December 1951); "Double Exposure," with Amanda Blake (in her first major TV role, 15 August 1952); "Four Things He'd Do," with Lee Van Cleef (in his first major TV role, 5 February 1954); "The Long Trail," with Anthony Quinn (19 November 1954); "The Unlighted Road," with James Dean (in his last dramatic appearance on television, 6 May 1955); "Bandit's Hideout," with Anthony Quinn (in his last TV appearance until 1971, 7 October 1955); "The Life You Save," with Gene Kelly (in his TV dramatic debut, 1 March 1957); "Carriage from Britain," with Janet Leigh (her first dramatic role on American television, 8 March 1957); "The Restless Gun," with John Payne (telecast 29 March 1957, this was the pilot for the series of the same title); and "Old Spanish Custom," with Dolores Del Rio (7 June 1957).

THE SCHOOL HOUSE
DUMONT

18 JANUARY 1949–12 APRIL 1949   This Tuesday-night revue featured Kenny Delmar and Arnold Stang.

SCIENCE ALL-STARS
ABC

12 JANUARY 1964–26 APRIL 1964; 10 JANUARY 1965–25 APRIL 1965

Don Morrow hosted this Sunday-afternoon show on which youngsters demonstrated their own science projects and talked with guest scientists.

SCIENCE CIRCUS ABC
4 JULY 1949–12 SEPTEMBER 1949   A half-hour of scientific experiments, hosted by Bob Brown.

SCIENCE FICTION THEATER SYNDICATED
1955–1956   Truman Bradley hosted this science fiction anthology show. The half-hour series was one of the first shows produced by Ivan Tors, who later developed *Sea Hunt, Flipper,* and other such shows.

SCOOBY-DOO CBS/ABC
13 SEPTEMBER 1969–7 AUGUST 1976 (CBS); 11 SEPTEMBER 1976– (ABC)   This Saturday-morning cartoon show from Hanna-Barbera Productions about a cowardly Great Dane (Scooby-Doo) and four teenage sleuths (Daphne, Freddy, Shaggy, and Velma) has been seen in several different formats over the years. It premiered in 1969 as a half-hour series, *Scooby-Doo, Where Are You?,* which ran for three years. In the fall of 1972 it expanded to an hour and was titled *The New Scooby-Doo Movies.* In the fall of 1974 reruns of *Scooby-Doo, Where Are You?* were shown under the latter title. The series switched networks in 1976 and became known as *The Scooby-Doo/Dynomutt Hour,* as a new segment was added: the adventures of Dynomutt, bionic dog who battled crime together with the Blue Falcon. In the fall of 1977 the series expanded to two hours, and several cartoon segments were shown under the title *Scooby's All-Star Laff-A-Lympics.* In the fall of 1978 Scooby starred in two Saturday cartoon shows on ABC: the half-hour *Scooby-Doo, Where Are You?,* followed later in the morning by the ninety-minute *Scooby's All-Stars,* the new title for the *Laff-A-Lympics.* In the fall of 1979 Scooby returned to a single program, teaming up with his feisty nephew in *Scooby and Scrappy-Doo.*

SCOTLAND YARD ABC
17 NOVEMBER 1957–3 OCTOBER 1958   Produced in England, this half-hour filmed series was based on case histories from Scotland Yard and was hosted by British author and criminologist Edgar Lustgarten.

SCOTT ISLAND
See HARBOURMASTER

THE SCOTT MUSIC HALL NBC
8 OCTOBER 1952–26 AUGUST 1953   Scott Paper Company sponsored this biweekly half-hour musical variety series, hosted by Patti Page and featuring Frank Fontaine and Mary Ellen Terry.

SCREEN DIRECTORS PLAYHOUSE   NBC

5 OCTOBER 1955–26 SEPTEMBER 1956   Members of the Screen Directors Guild directed the presentations on this half-hour dramatic anthology series. Among the major stars who appeared on the series were John Wayne (in "Rookie of the Year," 7 December, his only real dramatic role on TV), Robert Ryan (in "Lincoln's Doctor's Bag," 14 December, his first TV dramatic role), Jeanette MacDonald (in "The Prima Donna," 1 February, a rare television appearance), Buster Keaton (in "The Silent Partner," 21 March), and Errol Flynn (in "The Sword of Villon," 4 April, his first TV dramatic role).

SEA HUNT   SYNDICATED

1957–1961   Lloyd Bridges starred as underwater adventurer Mike Nelson in this half-hour series, one of the most widely syndicated shows of its time. Ivan Tors produced the series.

SEALAB 2020   NBC

9 SEPTEMBER 1972–1 SEPTEMBER 1973   Half-hour Saturday-morning cartoon series from Hanna-Barbera Productions about a group of oceanauts.

THE SEARCH   CBS

17 OCTOBER 1954–27 SEPTEMBER 1955   Charles Romine hosted this Sunday-afternoon public affairs program; most of the shows were filmed at American colleges and universities. Irv Gitlin produced the series, which resurfaced briefly in the summers of 1957 and 1958 with Eric Sevareid as host.

SEARCH   NBC

13 SEPTEMBER 1972–29 AUGUST 1973   An hour-long adventure series about three agents for Probe, a division of World Securities Corporation, a Washington-based outfit. The Probe agents, equipped with ultramodern scientific gadgets (such as miniaturized receivers implanted in their ears), could be hired to search for anything. The principals included Hugh O'Brian as Hugh Lockwood; Tony Franciosa as Nick Bianco; Doug McClure as C. R. Grover; Burgess Meredith as B. C. Cameron, head of the Probe unit; and Ford Rainey as Dr. Barnett, the research director. The three stars seldom appeared together—O'Brian was featured in about half of the episodes, and Franciosa and McClure split up the remaining half. Among the lesser Probe agents who were occasionally featured were Angel Tompkins as Gloria Harding; Byron Chung as Kuroda; Albert Popwell as Griffin; Ron Castro as Carlos; and Cheryl Stoppelmoor (later known as Cheryl Ladd of *Charlie's Angels* fame) as Amy. Leslie Stevens was the executive producer.

SEARCH AND RESCUE: THE ALPHA TEAM NBC

10 SEPTEMBER 1977–28 JANUARY 1978 The Alpha Ranch, a wildlife preserve, was the setting for this Saturday-morning series about a pair of young rescuers. Featured were: Michael J. Reynolds as Bob; Donann Cavin as Katy; and Michael Kane as Uncle Jack. Levy Lehman produced the half-hour series.

THE SEARCH FOR BEAUTY NBC

26 SEPTEMBER 1955–9 DECEMBER 1955 Makeup consultant Ern Westmore interviewed celebrity guests and dispensed advice on beauty to members of the studio audience on this half-hour daytime show. Late in the summer Westmore had become the host of a daytime show called *Hollywood Backstage,* and this series continued in that time slot.

SEARCH FOR THE NILE NBC

25 JANUARY 1972–29 FEBRUARY 1972 This six-hour dramatization of the efforts by members of the Royal Geographic Society to discover the source of the Nile was produced by the BBC and filmed in Africa; it was run by NBC as a five-part miniseries. James Mason narrated the show, and the principal cast included: Kenneth Haigh as Sir Richard Burton; John Quentin as John Hanning Speke; Ian McCulloch as Captain James Grant; Norman Rossington as Samuel Baker; Catherine Schell as Florence Baker; Keith Buckley as Henry Morgan Stanley; and Michael Gough as David Livingstone.

SEARCH FOR TOMORROW CBS

3 SEPTEMBER 1951– *Search for Tomorrow* holds several television records: not only is it TV's longest-running serial (edging out *Love of Life* by a scant three weeks), but it is also TV's longest-running daytime show of any kind, with more than 7,300 shows telecast by the end of 1979. In addition, Mary Stuart, who has starred in *Search for Tomorrow* from the beginning, has played a continuing role in a series, longer than any other performer (though costar Larry Haines, who joined the show late in 1951 and was still on board in 1979, can claim a close second). *Search for Tomorrow* was created by Roy Winsor, who served as its first executive producer; Charles Irving was the first producer (and the first director). Later producers have included Frank Dodge, Bernie Sofronski, and Mary-Ellis Bunim. Agnes Nixon was the first head writer, but was succeeded late in 1951 by Irving Vendig. Recent head writers have included Ann Marcus and Peggy O'Shea. It began as a fifteen-minute serial and was one of the last to expand to thirty minutes, having done so in September 1968; the show has been broadcast in color since April of 1967.

Search for Tomorrow is set in the town of Henderson, and its central character is Joanne Gardner Barron Tate Vincente, a considerate and compassionate woman who has been married three times and widowed three times; the part has been played by Mary Stuart since the show's inception. Other principal players over the many years have included: Johnny Sylvester as Joanne's first husband, Keith Barron, who died in a car crash (Johnny Sylvester was later known as John Sylvester White and was featured on *Welcome Back, Kotter*); Lynn Loring (1951–1961), Abigail Kellog (1961–1964); Patricia Harty (1964–1965), Trish Van Devere (briefly in 1965), Gretchen Walther (1965–1966), Melissa Murphy (1966–1967), Melinda Plank (1967–1969), and Leigh Lassen (1969–1974) as their daughter, Patti Barron; Cliff Hall as Victor Barron, Keith's father; Bess Johnson as Irene Barron, Keith's mother; Harry Holcombe and Eric Dressler as Frank Gardner, Joanne's father; Melba Rae (1951–1971) as Joanne's best friend, Marge Bergman; Larry Haines as Marge's husband, Stu Bergman; Ellen Spencer, Sandy Robinson (to 1961), Fran Sharon (1961–1966), Marian Hailey, and Millie Taggart as their daughter, Janet Bergman, Patti Barron's best friend; Peter Broderick, Ray Bellaran, and John James as their son, Tommy Bergman; Joanna Roos and Nydia Westman as Jessie Bergman; Peter Lazar as Jimmy Bergman; Coe Norton as Dr. Ned Hilton, who befriended Joanne after her first husband's death; Terry O'Sullivan (1955–1966) and Karl Weber (briefly in 1956) as Arthur Tate, who became Joanne's second husband on 18 May 1955, and died of a heart attack in 1966; Mary Patton as Sue, who masqueraded as her twin sister, Hazel Tate, Arthur Tate's ex-wife; Jeffrey Krolik (son of Mary Stuart in real life) as Duncan Eric Tate, the son of Joanne and Arthur Tate who died in infancy; George Petrie and Frank Overton as lawyer Nathan Walsh; Lee Grant, Nita Talbot, and Constance Ford as Rose Peabody; Don Knotts as Rose's mute brother, Wilbur Peabody; Marion Brash as Eunice, Joanne's widowed sister; Larry Hugo as Rex Twining, who married Eunice; Doris Dalton as Cornelia Simmons, Arthur Tate's aunt; Vicki Vola as Harriet Baxter, Cornelia's housekeeper; Nina Reader and Ann Pearson as Allison Simmons, Cornelia's sister; Tom Carlin, Donald Madden, and David O'Brien as Fred Metcalf, who married Allison; Katherine Meskill as Agnes Metcalf, Fred's mother; Tony Ray and George Maharis as Joanne's nephew, Bud Gardner, who married Janet Bergman; Martin Brooks, Philip Abbott, and Ron Hussman as Dr. Dan Walton, who also married Janet; Denise Nickerson, Kathy Beller, Meg Bennett, Hope Busby, and Sherry Mathis as Liza Walton, daughter of Dan and Janet Walton; Robert Mandan, George Gaynes, and Roy Shuman as Sam Reynolds, who romanced Joanne for several years after Arthur Tate's death but never married her; Virginia Gilmore and Joan Copeland as Andrea Whiting, Sam's ex-wife; Dino Narizzano, Jeff Pomerantz, and Dino Narizzano (again) as Len Whiting, son of Sam and Andrea, who married Patti Barron; Freida Altman as Mrs. Miller; Carl Low as Dr. Bob Rogers; Pamela Murphy, Louise Shaffer, and Kathryn Walker as Emily Rogers, Bob's daughter; Ken Kercheval as Nick Hunter, who married Emily; Ken Harvey as lawyer Doug Martin, who married Eunice; John Napier and Michael Wagner as Cliff Williams; Martin Brooks as Dr. Everett Moore; Lenka Peterson as Isabelle Kittridge Moore; Geoffrey Lumb as Mr. Crane; Selena Longo as Tracy Ellen; Jill Clayburgh as Grace Bolton, who died of a brain tumor; Kelly Wood as Lauri Leshinsky; Christopher Lowe as Erik, Lauri's son; Peter Simon and Peter Ratray as Scott Phillips, who married Lauri; Lilia Skala as Mrs. Leshinsky, Lauri's mother; Courtney Sherman as Kathy Parker, who later married Scott Phillips; John Cunningham as Dr. Wade Collins, a psychiatrist who married Janet Bergman Gardner Walton; Natalie Schafer as Helen Collins; Ralph Clanton as William Collins; Brett Halsey as Clay Collins; Val Dufour as lawyer John Wyatt, who married Eunice Martin; Pat Stanley as Marion, Wyatt's secretary; Kipp Osborne as George, and Susan Sarandon as Sarah, a pair of drifters who murdered Sam Reynolds; Anthony George as Dr. Tony Vincente, who became Joanne's third husband and died of a heart attack in 1975; Jeannie Carson as Marcy Vincente, Tony's ex-wife; Hal Linden as Larry Carter; Michael Shannon as Jim McCarren; Frank Schofield and Stephen Elliott as John Austin; Billie Lou Watt as Ellie Harper, housekeeper for widower Stu Bergman; Linda Bove as Melissa Hayley, a deaf woman who was taken in by Joanne and Tony Vincente (Bove herself was a member of the National Theater of the Deaf); Robert Phelps as Dr. Matt Weldon, who married Melissa; Robin Eisenmann and Morgan Fairchild as Jennifer Phillips, Scott Phillips's ex-wife; Tommy Norden, John Driver, Richard Lohman, and Stephen Burleigh as Gary Walton, son of Janet and Dan Walton; Anne Revere as Agnes Lake; Michael Nouri as Steve Kaslo, who moved in with Liza Walton; Pamela Miller and Anne Wyndham (1975–) as Steve's sister, Amy Kaslo; Mike Durrell as Mike Kaslo; Tom Ewell as Bill Lang; Wayne Rogers as Slim Davis; David Ford as murder victim Carl Devlin; Andrew Jarkowsky as Frank Ross; Byron Sanders as Dr. Walter Osmond; Joe Morton as Dr. James Foster; Gene Fanning as Dr. Lew Brown; Barbara Monte-Britton as Dr. Maria Pettit; Camille Yarbrough as Terry Benjamin; James Hainesworth as Jay Benjamin; Michael Maitland, Gary Tomlin, Steve Nisbet, and Joel Higgins as Bruce Carson; Robert Burr as Mr. McCrady; Dale Robinette as Dave Wilkins; Andrea McArdle (who left the show to star in the musical, *Annie*) and Lisa Peluso as Wendy Wilkins; Katherine Squire as Raney Wesner; Kathleen Deniza as Karen Dehner; Virginia Martin as Connie Schultz; Amy Arutt as Susie Martin; Vera Allen as Ida Weston; Sharon Spelman as Paula Markham; Delphi Harrington as Leslie Halliday; Marie Cheatham as Stephanie Wilkins Wyatt, a nurse; Stephen Joyce as Sam Hunter; Vince O'Brien as Hal Conrad; Lewis Arlt as United States Marshal David Sutton (also known as David Sloane); Lane Binkley as Robin Kennemer; Gayle Pines and Marilyn McIntyre as Caroline Hanley Walton; Allison Argo as Cindy French; Kevin Kline as Woody Reed; Bob

Rockwell as Dr. Greg Hartford; Tina Orr as Meredith Hartford; Drew Snyder as Ralph Heywood; Michael Sivy as Howard Horton; Robert Heitman as William Mandell; Dana Ivey as Maria Thompson; Stacy Moran as Suzie Wyatt; Lenka Peterson (in her second role) as Evelyn Reed; Leslie Ann Ray as Donna Davis; Neil Billingsley as Danny Walton; Lisa Buck as Kylie Halliday; George Shannon as Chance Halliday; Jack Ryland as Lonnie Garrison; Chris Loomis as Buck Peterson; Verna Pierce as Sharon Peterson; Vincent Stewart as Jackie Peterson; John Aniston as Martin Tourneur; Rod Arrants as Travis Sentell; Megan Bagot as Laine Adamson; Chris Goutmas as Marc D'Antoni; Marcia McCabe as Sunny McClure; William Robertson as Greg Tourneur; Tucker Smallwood as Bobby Stuart.

SEAWAY   SYNDICATED
1965   Produced in Canada in 1965 but not made available in the United States until later, this hour adventure series starred Stephen Young as Nick King, a security agent working along the St. Lawrence Seaway, and Austin Willis as Admiral Fox, his boss, the head of the Ship Owners Association.

SECOND CHANCE   ABC
7 MARCH 1977–15 JULY 1977   Jim Peck hosted this daytime game show on which three contestants competed; after writing down their answers to various questions, contestants were shown three possible answers (including the correct one) and were permitted to change their answer. After each round the contestants took a spin at the prize board, where they could win cash and prizes or lose everything. Bill Carruthers, who created the series with Jan McCormack, was the executive producer.

SECOND CITY T.V.   SYNDICATED
1977   This half-hour videotaped series satirized television. Featured were: John Candy, Joe Flaherty, Eugene Levy, Andrea Martin, Catherine O'Hara, Harold Ramis, and Dave Thomas. Bernard Sahlins was the producer.

THE SECOND HUNDRED YEARS   ABC
6 SEPTEMBER 1967–19 SEPTEMBER 1968   Monte Markham played dual roles in this half-hour sitcom—Luke Carpenter, a gold prospector who was frozen in an avalanche in 1900 and who miraculously thawed out, unharmed, after a second avalanche in 1967, and Ken Carpenter, Luke's thirty-three-year-old grandson, who looked exactly like him. Arthur O'Connell costarred as sixty-seven-year-old Edwin Carpenter, Luke's son and Ken's father. Luke came to live with Edwin and Ken, while the Army, for security reasons, struggled to keep secret the fact of Luke's discovery. Also featured were Frank Maxwell as Colonel Garroway and

Bridget Hanley as Nurse Anderson; Karen Black, in one of her first TV roles, appeared occasionally as Garroway's hippie daughter, Marcia. Harry Ackerman was the executive producer and Bob Claver the producer for Screen Gems.

SECRET AGENT   CBS
5 APRIL 1961–13 SEPTEMBER 1961; 3 APRIL 1965–11 SEPTEMBER 1965; 4 DECEMBER 1965–10 SEPTEMBER 1966 Patrick McGoohan starred in this adventure series as John Drake, a comparatively moral intelligence agent who refused to carry a gun and who avoided violence when possible. The series was produced in England by ATV; thirty-nine half-hour episodes were filmed in 1961, and the series was televised there and here as *Danger Man,* in which Drake was a NATO agent. The series was revived in 1965 in an hour format, under the title *Secret Agent,* with Drake now working for British intelligence. The show's theme, "Secret Agent," was composed by P. F. Sloan and Steve Barri, and sung by Johnny Rivers.

SECRET FILE, U.S.A.   SYNDICATED
1955 Filmed principally in Amsterdam, this half-hour Cold War spy show starred Robert Alda as Major William Morgan of Army Intelligence and Lois Hensen as Colonel Custer.

THE SECRET LIVES OF WALDO KITTY   NBC
6 SEPTEMBER 1975–4 SEPTEMBER 1976 This live and animated Saturday-morning series was inspired by the *Walter Mitty* stories. Waldo Kitty was a daydreaming cat who fantasized about saving his girlfriend, Felicia, from the clutches of his nemesis, Tyrone the bulldog. Howard Morris was the voice of Waldo, Jane Webb that of Felicia, and Allan Melvin that of Tyrone. Lou Scheimer and Norm Prescott were the executive producers.

SECRET SQUIRREL   NBC
2 OCTOBER 1965–2 SEPTEMBER 1967 Secret Squirrel, a Hanna-Barbera cartoon character, had his own Saturday-morning series for two seasons before joining forces with Atom Ant in the fall of 1967. Secret Squirrel was accompanied on his missions by Morocco Mole; other animated segments included "Winnie Witch" and "Squiddly Diddly," an octopus. See also *Atom Ant.*

THE SECRET STORM   CBS
1 FEBRUARY 1954–8 FEBRUARY 1974 *The Secret Storm* was created by Roy Winsor, who had previously developed *Search for Tomorrow.* For many years it was produced by Gloria Monty; Joe Manetta produced it during the later seasons. The story lines centered on the comings and go-

ings of the Ames family of Woodbridge until the late 1960s, when the show was sold by American Home Products to CBS; successive sets of writers managed to kill off almost all of the Ameses, and *The Secret Storm,* which had been television's most popular daytime serial at one time, left the air in 1974 after a run of twenty years and a week. It had begun as a fifteen-minute show and had expanded to thirty minutes in 1962. Principal players included: Peter Hobbs (1954–1960), Cec Linder (1960–1964), Ward Costello (1964–1966), and Lawrence Weber (1966–1968) as Peter Ames, a father of three who was widowed during the first week of the story when his wife, Ellen, was hit by a car; Jean Mowry, Rachel Taylor, Mary Foskett, and Judy Lewis as Susan Ames, his elder daughter; Robert Morse, Warren Berlinger, Wayne Tippitt, Peter White, and Stephen Bolster as Jerry Ames, his son; Jada Rowland, Beverly Lunsford, and Lynne Adams as Amy Ames, his younger daughter (Rowland played the role from 1954 until 1974, but not continuously); Russell Hicks as Judge J. T. Tyrell, father of the late Ellen Ames; Marjorie Gateson and Eleanor Phelps as Grace Tyrell, Ellen's mother; Haila Stoddard as Pauline, Ellen's sister; Virginia Dwyer as Jane Edwards, the Ames' housekeeper; Ed Bryce as Bruce Edwards, her estranged husband; James Vickery (1957–1965) as Alan Dunbar, who married Susan Ames and later bought the town newspaper; Donny Melvin as Peter Dunbar; Joan Hotchkis and June Graham as Myra Lake, one of Amy's schoolteachers, who married Peter Ames in 1959; Carl King as Bryan Fuller, who married Pauline and later divorced her; Frank Sutton as reporter Joe Sullivan; Jane McArthur as Nancy Hewlett; Jim Pritchett as Jeff Nichols; Don Galloway, David O'Brien, and Ed Griffith as Kip Rysdale, a boyfriend of Amy's; John Baragrey as Arthur Rysdale, Kip's father; Polly Childs as Kate Lodge, who married Jerry Ames and was later found murdered; Pamela Raymond as Hope, who later married Jerry; Lori March as Valerie Hill, who married Peter Ames; Bibi Besch as Janet Hill, Valerie's daughter; Roy Scheider, Justin McDonough, and Ed Winter as Bob Hill, Valerie's son; Diana Muldaur as Ann Wicker; Nick Coster, Jed Allan, Ed Kemmer, Ryan MacDonald, Conrad Fowkes, and Linden Chiles as Paul Britton, who married Amy Ames; Julie Wilson as Brooke Lawrence, who was accidentally killed by Valerie; Jane Rose as Aggie Parsons; Jacqueline Brooks as Ursula Winthrop; Robert Sherwood as Doug Winthrop; Jack Ryland, Robert Loggia, and Laurence Luckinbill as Frank Carver, who married Susan Ames Dunbar; Keith Charles as Nick Kane; Christina Crawford (daughter of Joan Crawford) as Joann Kane; Jeffrey Lynn as Charlie Clemens; Marla Adams as Belle Clemens, who married Paul Britton; Diane Dell, Terry Falis, and Judy Safran as Lisa Britton, daughter of Paul and Amy Britton; Bernie Barrow as Dan Kincaid, who married Belle Clemens; David Ackroyd and Dennis Cooney as Kevin Kincaid, Dan's son; Barbara Rodell as Jill Stevens Clayborne; Peter MacLean as her husband, Hugh Clayborne, who was killed with her in a plane crash; Joel Crothers as Ken Stevens, Jill's brother; James Grover as Clay Stevens, his son; Stephanie Braxton as Lauri Reddin; David Gale as Mark Reddin, who left the priesthood to marry Lauri, but later returned to it while Lauri married Ken Stevens; Frances Sternhagen as Jesse Reddin; Gary Sandy as Stacey Reddin; Troy Donahue (seldom seen on TV since he starred in *SurfSide 6*) as Keefer, a drug dealer; Jennifer Darling as Iris Sims, Keefer's girlfriend; Gordon Rigsby and Alexander Scourby as Dr. Ian Northcote, who married Valerie Hill Ames; Terry Kiser as Cory Boucher; James Storm as Sean Childers, Jr.; Jeff Pomerantz and Keith Charles as Dr. Brian Neeves; Audre Johnston as nurse Martha Ann Ashley; Dan Hamilton as Robert Landers, son of Dan Kincaid; Ellen Barber and Audrey Landers as Joanna Morrison; Sidney Walker as Monsignor Quinn; Joe Ponazecki as Reilly; Patrick Fox as Phil; Madeline Sherwood as Carmen; Richard Venture as Tom Gregory; Sue Ann Gilfillan as Lurene Post; Roberta Royce as Freddie; Susan Sudert as Charlotte; Philip Bruns as Julius Klepner; Mary K. Wells as Nola Hallister; Diane Ladd as Kitty Styles; Scott Medford as Jonathan Styles; and Nicholas Lewis as Tim Brannigan.

THE SECRETS OF ISIS
See ISIS

SECRETS OF THE DEEP   SYNDICATED
1974   Former astronaut Scott Carpenter hosted this half-hour documentary series about oceans and marine life.

SEE IT NOW   CBS
18 NOVEMBER 1951–7 JULY 1958   Though it was not television's first public affairs program, *See It Now* was surely its most significant. Through careful preparation, thoughtful production, and skillful editing, it demonstrated that television could present to the viewer something more, something deeper, than a mere interview or newsreel. As Alexander Kendrick noted in his book, *Prime Time: The Life of Edward R. Murrow, See It Now* was the first public affairs show to use its own film footage instead of newsreel or file footage; no interview was rehearsed and nothing was dubbed. *See It Now* also pioneered the use of field producers, who supervised the filming on location.

See It Now was jointly produced by Edward R. Murrow (who also hosted the series) and Fred W. Friendly. The two had previously collaborated on two projects: "I Can Hear It Now," a series of three record albums, narrated by Murrow, of "aural history" from 1919 to 1949, and *Hear It Now*, a CBS radio news analysis show. Murrow and Friendly were deeply committed to a high-quality television program; though Murrow continued to do a nightly news show on CBS radio, *See It Now*'s weekly schedule gave Murrow and Friendly time to assemble material and to focus the presentation. The producers hoped that *See It Now* would not only show a news event but would explain to the viewer why it happened. Though a sponsor—Alcoa—had been acquired, the advertising fees paid for only a small fraction of the show's cost; the remainder was absorbed by the network.

The show premiered 18 November 1951; the opening showed, on a split screen, San Francisco's Golden Gate Bridge and New York's Brooklyn Bridge, in the first live commercial coast-to-coast broadcast (the first coast-to-coast broadcast had been on 4 September, when President Truman addressed the Japanese Peace Treaty Conference in San Francisco). Many of the early shows focused on the Korean War, but few stirred any real controversy. It was during *See It Now*'s third season, as the series began to examine the anti-Communist fervor of the time, that the program grew to full maturity. The first notable broadcast of the season took place on 20 October 1953, with the telecast of "The Case Against Milo Radulovich, AO589839." Radulovich, an Air Force lieutenant, had been ordered dismissed from the service because his father, a Serbian immigrant, and sister were said to be Communist sympathizers; following the broadcast, Secretary of the Air Force Harold E. Talbott reviewed the case and ordered Radulovich reinstated. The program was widely hailed as the best single program of the year, and Murrow won an Emmy as most outstanding personality of 1953. Though CBS never pressured Friendly or Murrow to refrain from airing the program, neither the network nor the sponsor would agree to advertise it; Murrow and Friendly put up $1,500 of their own money to purchase an ad in the *New York Times*.

Another significant broadcast from 1953 was titled "Argument in Indianapolis." Shown on 24 November, it examined the refusal by the Indianapolis chapter of the American Legion to permit its meeting hall to be used by the American Civil Liberties Union. The single most important show of the season, however, was shown on 9 March 1954; the untitled half hour, which had been months in preparation, was a series of film clips of Senator Joseph McCarthy, the bombastic demagogue who most embodied the anti-Communist hysteria. The clips showed McCarthy as a shallow and callous man whose stock in trade included conflicting statements, misstatements, and half-truths. The following week's program showed a second half hour of McCarthy, principally of his recent questioning of Annie Lee Moss, an alleged subversive who was employed by the State Department. On 6 April McCarthy accepted Murrow's offer of equal time; McCarthy's appearance on that show probably did as much to weaken his own credibility as the two earlier shows. McCarthy concluded his rebuttal with these remarks: "Now ordinarily I would not take time out from the important work at hand to answer Murrow. However, in this case I feel justified in doing so because Murrow is a symbol, the leader and cleverest of the jackal pack which is always found at the throat of anyone who dares to expose individual Communists and traitors." At a subsequent press conference Murrow uttered his now-famous response: "Who has helped the Communist cause and who has served his country better, Senator McCarthy or I? I would like to be remembered by the answer to that question." After the broadcasts, opposition to McCarthy strengthened; though McCarthy's subcommittee conducted several more weeks of investigations (which ABC and DuMont covered live), McCarthy was censured by the Senate late in 1954, and his influence diminished rapidly.

During the 1954–1955 season *See It Now* presented several noteworthy programs, including a report on *Brown* v. *Board of Education,* the Supreme Court's historic school desegregation decision; stories on the changing face of Africa and the Middle East; "A Conversation with J. Robert Oppenheimer," who had previously been labeled a security risk; and a two-part series on tobacco and lung cancer (Murrow, a chain smoker, lost a lung to cancer and died of a brain tumor in 1965). At the end of the season, *See It Now* lost both its sponsor and its prime-time slot; the reasons for the losses are not entirely clear, but it has been suggested that Alcoa withdrew its sponsorship as a result of pressure following a May 1955 report on a small Texas newspaper that had uncovered a major land scandal (Alcoa was then expanding its Texas operations). The loss of the time slot was principally due to the introduction of *The $64,000 Question* into the preceding half hour on 7 June 1955; network executives no doubt felt that a runaway hit such as that could serve as an effective lead-in to a more popular type of show.

From the fall of 1955 until the summer of 1958, *See It Now* was broadcast as a series of specials, most of which were in a sixty-minute format; some CBS insiders by that time referred to the show as "See It Now and Then." This latter group of broadcasts ranged from "The Secret Life of Danny Kaye" to an interview with Chinese premier Chou En-Lai (filmed in Rangoon, the meeting was arranged by Burma's premier, U Nu). The final telecast, on 7 July 1958, was a report on postwar Germany, entitled "Watch on the Ruhr."

Though *See It Now* left the air in 1958, its legacy has survived. In 1959 the network introduced *CBS Reports;* though not always a regularly scheduled program, it has presented a number of hard-hitting news documentaries. In 1968 CBS introduced *60 Minutes,* which gradually built up a large audience; its executive producer is Don Hewitt, who directed *See It Now* for several years, and one of its principal producers is Joe Wershba, who was a staff reporter on *See It Now.*

SEE THE PROS   SYNDICATED
1958   Former West Point football star Glenn Davis interviewed professional footballers on this half-hour series.

THE SEEKING HEART CBS

5 JULY 1954–10 DECEMBER 1954   A medically oriented soap opera. The cast of the fifteen-minute daily serial included Judith Braun, Flora Campbell, Scott Forbes (who later turned up in *Jim Bowie*), Dorothy Lovett, and James Yarborough. *Road of Life* replaced *The Seeking Heart* in December of 1954.

SEMINAR ABC

11 OCTOBER 1952–3 JANUARY 1953   In this early experiment in educational television, the camera sat in on an actual course in American civilization, taught at Columbia University by Professor Donald Bigelow. Erik Barnouw, Jack Pacey, and Dorothy Oshlag produced the Saturday-evening series, and Alex Segal directed it.

SERGEANT PRESTON OF THE YUKON CBS

29 SEPTEMBER 1955–25 SEPTEMBER 1958   This half-hour adventure series, which ran on radio from 1947 to 1955, starred Richard Simmons as Sergeant Preston of the Royal Canadian Mounted Police; astride his horse, Rex, and accompanied by his faithful canine companion, King, Preston seemed to spend most of his time by himself, trudging through the snow to apprehend fugitives. The character was created by George W. Trendle, who had previously conceived *The Lone Ranger* and *The Green Hornet*. The series was filmed principally at Ashcroft, Colorado, and was produced by the Wrather Corporation; Von Reznicek's "Donna Diana Overture" was used as the theme music. Richard Simmons, the star of the show, later revealed in an interview that Sergeant Preston's first name was Frank, though he added that the first name was never used on the air.

SERPICO NBC

24 SEPTEMBER 1976–28 JANUARY 1977   This unsuccessful hour-long crime show was based on Peter Maas's biography of Frank Serpico, an unorthodox New York cop (the book had been made into a movie in 1974, starring Al Pacino). On TV David Birney starred as the uncorruptible Frank Serpico, with Tom Atkins as Lieutenant Tom Sullivan. Emmet G. Lavery was executive producer for Emmet G. Lavery Productions in association with Paramount Television and NBC-TV.

SESAME STREET NET–PBS

10 NOVEMBER 1969–   The most important children's show in the history of television, *Sesame Street* proved to be not only informative, but also phenomenally successful. It was developed by Joan Ganz Cooney, executive director of the Children's Television Workshop, a company established in 1967 to produce the series with financial support from the United States Office of Education, the Ford Foundation, and the

627

Carnegie Corporation. The show is set along a city street because it was primarily targeted at inner-city preschoolers (fortunately, *Sesame Street* proved popular with children of all backgrounds). Through a skillful blending of skits, songs, puppetry, and animation, *Sesame Street* has managed to teach letters, numbers, and grammatical concepts in a totally entertaining fashion. Most shows are "sponsored" by particular letters or numbers, which are presented as "commercials." *Sesame Street*'s human performers have included: Loretta Long as Susan; Matt Robinson and Roscoe Orman as Gordon; Bob McGrath as Bob; Will Lee as Mr. Hooper; Northern J. Calloway as David; Emilio Delgado as Luis; and Sonia Manzano as Maria. Equally important are the Muppets, the talented group of expressive puppets created by Jim Henson: Ernie, Bert, Oscar the Grouch, The Cookie Monster, and Big Bird (who is not really a puppet, but rather a life-size figure played by Frank Oz and later by Carroll Spinney). Songs for the series have been composed by Jeff Moss and Joe Raposo.

SEVEN AT ELEVEN   NBC
28 MAY 1951–27 JUNE 1951   Broadcast Mondays and Wednesdays at 11 p.m., *Seven at Eleven* alternated with *Broadway Open House,* which was cut back from five nights a week to three after Jerry Lester left the show. The seven regulars were host George DeWitt, singers Denise Lor, Betty Luster, and Jack Stanton, bandleader Milton DeLugg, comic Sid Gould, and the show's unidentified floor manager.

700 CLUB   SYNDICATED
1976–   Based in Virginia Beach, this syndicated daily religious talk show is hosted by Pat Robertson, president of the Christian Broadcasting Network.

SEVEN KEYS   ABC
3 APRIL 1961–27 MARCH 1964   Jack Narz hosted this daytime game show on which two contestants attempted to advance along a board of squares by identifying pictures on the squares. The winner of the game won a key and was awarded the furnishings for one room of a house. A person who stayed on the show long enough to win seven keys won a fully furnished house.

SEVEN LEAGUE BOOTS   SYNDICATED
1959   Another of the several travelogues hosted by Jack Douglas.

THE SEVEN LIVELY ARTS   CBS
3 NOVEMBER 1957–16 FEBRUARY 1958   This ambitious Sunday-afternoon show was supposed to compete with *Omnibus* (which had left CBS in 1956), but never did; thanks to a disastrous premiere, the show never

really had a chance to get off the ground. John Crosby, television critic for the New York *Herald Tribune,* was the host of the series. Among the varied presentations were: "The Changing Ways of Love," by S. J. Perelman, with Perelman, Piper Laurie, Jason Robards, Jr., Rip Torn, Mike Wallace, and Dick York (3 November); "The World of Nick Adams," adapted by A. E. Hotchner from Hemingway's story, with Steven Hill, William Marshall, and Eli Wallach (10 November); "Here Is New York" narrated by E. G. Marshall (15 December); "Hollywood Around the World," a look at the film industry (29 December). Blues singer Billie Holiday also made a rare television appearance on the series. The executive producer of the hour show was John Houseman.

THE SEVENTH SENSE   SYNDICATED
1978   Jim Peck hosted this interview series, which attempted to probe the subconscious minds of those interviewed through the use of hypnosis. Elroy Schwartz, a hypnotist, was the producer.

77 SUNSET STRIP   ABC
10 OCTOBER 1958–9 SEPTEMBER 1964   Warner Brothers' best-known detective show starred Efrem Zimbalist, Jr., and Roger Smith as Stu Bailey and Jeff Spencer, two private eyes whose offices were located at 77 Sunset Strip in Hollywood; Zimbalist had first played his role in an episode of Warner Brothers' anthology show, *Conflict,* titled "Anything for Money" (aired 23 July 1957). Edd Byrnes costarred in *77 Sunset Strip* as Gerald Lloyd Kookson III, better known as Kookie; the character, a hiptalking parking lot attendant at Dino's Lodge next door, was not intended to be a recurring one, but public reaction (chiefly from teenage girls) was so strong that Byrnes was given a regular role. Because of a contract dispute, Byrnes did not appear on the series during most of the 1959–1960 season; shortly after his return (in May of 1960), however, Kookie became a private eye, working with Bailey and Spencer (in Byrnes's absence, Troy Donahue had played the parking lot attendant in several 1959 episodes; Donahue later starred in *SurfSide 6*). Also featured were Jacqueline Beer (Miss France of 1954) as Suzanne Fabray, the receptionist and switchboard operator; Louis Quinn as Roscoe (introduced in the third episode), a horse-playing contact man who hung out at the office; and Byron Keith as Lieutenant Gilmore of the Los Angeles police. In 1960 Richard Long joined the cast as detective Rex Randolph (Long had played the same part a year earlier on Warner Brothers' *Bourbon Street Beat*), and in 1961 Robert Logan was added as J. R. Hale, the new parking lot attendant who usually spoke in abbreviations. Major changes took place in the fall of 1963 as all the regulars except for Zimbalist were dropped; Zimbalist continued as Stu Bailey, but his offices were no longer at 77 Sunset Strip; Joan Staley was added as his secretary, Hannah. The series left the air for a few weeks in February 1964 but returned (in re-

runs) in April of that year. Production was handled first by Roy Huggins, later by Howie Horwitz, and finally by William Conrad (who later starred in *Cannon*). The success of *77 Sunset Strip* spawned several other Warner Brothers hours (*Bourbon Street Beat* and *Hawaiian Eye* in 1959, *SurfSide 6* in 1960), but none of them was as popular as the first of the line.

77TH BENGAL LANCERS
NBC

21 OCTOBER 1956–2 JUNE 1957 This half-hour adventure series was set in India at Fort Oghora, headquarters of the Seventy-seventh Bengal Lancers during the late nineteenth century. The show, a Screen Gems production, featured Warren Stevens as Lieutenant Rhodes; Philip Carey as Lieutenant Storm; and John Sutton and Patrick Whyte as Colonel Standish.

SHA NA NA
SYNDICATED

1977– A successful half-hour musical series, *Sha Na Na* is named for its hosts, a ten-member aggregation dedicated to reviving interest in the music of the 1950s, the Golden Era of rock and roll. The group was founded at Columbia University in 1968, when the members of the Kingsmen, a campus singing group, began to include hits of the fifties in their repertoire; the name "Sha Na Na" was taken from the background chant of the Silhouettes' 1958 classic, "Get a Job." By 1977 the group included Lenny Baker, Johnny Contardo, Denny Greene, Jocko Marcellino, Danny (Dirty Dan) McBride, Chico Ryan, (Screamin') Scott Simon, Scott Powell (also known as Tony Santini), Don York, and muscle-flexing Jon (Bowser) Bauman, the unofficial leader of the gang (Denny, Jocko, Tony, and Don are original members). Among those featured on the show have been Jane Dulo, Pamela Myers, Avery Schreiber (1977–1978), Kenneth Mars, and Soupy Sales (1978–   ). Pierre Cossette is the executive producer, and Bernard Rothman and Jack Wohl are the producers.

SHADOW OF THE CLOAK
DUMONT

6 JUNE 1951–20 MARCH 1952 This half-hour spy show starred Helmut Dantine as Peter House, an agent for International Security Intelligence. Roger Gerry produced the series.

SHAFT
CBS

9 OCTOBER 1973–20 AUGUST 1974 This ninety-minute crime show shared a Tuesday slot with *Hawkins* and with *The New CBS Tuesday Movie*. Richard Roundtree starred as John Shaft, a slick and successful black private eye who worked in New York, and Ed Barth costarred as Lieutenant Al Rossi. The TV series was considerably less violent than the

1971 film (which had also starred Roundtree) on which it was based. Allan Balter and William Read Woodfield produced the series for MGM.

SHAKESPEARE ON TV
SYNDICATED
1954   This lecture series was presented by Dr. Frank Baxter of the University of Southern California.

THE SHAKESPEARE PLAYS
PBS
14 FEBRUARY 1979–   One of the most ambitious projects in broadcasting history, *The Shakespeare Plays* is a six-year effort by the BBC (with financial assistance from Exxon, Morgan Guaranty Trust Company and Metropolitan Life Insurance) to produce all thirty-seven of William Shakespeare's plays. "Julius Caesar" was the first of the works to be broadcast (the plays will not be produced in chronological order).

SHANE
ABC
10 SEPTEMBER 1966–31 DECEMBER 1966   Based on the 1953 film, this hour-long western starred David Carradine as Shane, a drifting gunman who signed on as a hired hand with the Starrett family and helped them save their farm from the clutches of an evil land baron. Also featured were Jill Ireland as widow Marian Starrett, owner of the place; Chris Shea as her young son, Joey; Tom Tully as Tom Starrett, her father-in-law; Bert Freed as Rufe Ryker, the land baron; and Sam Gilman as Grafton, Ryker's henchman. Herbert Brodkin was the executive producer.

SHANNON
SYNDICATED
1961   George Nader starred in this half-hour crime show as Joe Shannon, insurance investigator for the Transport Bonding & Surety Company; Regis Toomey was featured as his boss, Bill Cochran. Jerry Briskin produced the series for Screen Gems.

THE SHARI LEWIS SHOW
NBC
1 OCTOBER 1960–28 SEPTEMBER 1963   Saturday-morning puppet show hosted by Shari Lewis and her puppets, Lamb Chop, Hush Puppy, and Charlie Horse. Also featured were Jackie Warner as Jum-Pup, Ronald Radd as Mr. Goodfellow, and Clive Russell. Robert Scherer was the producer.

THE SHARI SHOW
SYNDICATED
1975   Half-hour puppet show hosted by Shari Lewis. See also *The Shari Lewis Show*.

SHAZAM!
CBS
1 SEPTEMBER 1974–3 SEPTEMBER 1977   Based on the Marvel Comics

character, this live-action Saturday-morning series featured Michael Gray as Billy Batson, a young man who could transform himself into Captain Marvel, the World's Mightiest Mortal, by uttering the word "Shazam!" (Shazam was an acronym for the six immortal elders—Soloman, Hercules, Atlas, Zeus, Achilles, and Mercury—who selected Batson and chose to endow him with rare powers). Also featured were Les Tremayne as Mentor, Batson's traveling companion; John Davey (1974–1976) and Jackson Bostwick (1976–1977) as Captain Marvel. Lou Scheimer and Norm Prescott were the executive producers of the half-hour series; during its last two seasons *Shazam!* was one-half of *The Shazam!/Isis Hour.* (see also *Isis*).

SHAZZAN! CBS
9 SEPTEMBER 1967–6 SEPTEMBER 1969 Not to be confused with *Shazam!,* this half-hour cartoon show from Hanna-Barbera Productions featured a pair of twins (Chuck and Nancy) who were transported back to the time of the Arabian Nights. Shazzan was a giant genie at their disposal.

SHEBANG SYNDICATED
1965 Another of the several rock-and-roll shows that followed in the wake of *Hullabaloo* and *Shindig.*

SHEENA, QUEEN OF THE JUNGLE SYNDICATED
1955 Based on the comic strip, this half-hour children's adventure series starred Irish McCalla as Sheena, the leopard-tunicked jungle denizen who was the female counterpart of Tarzan. Christian Drake was also featured as her friend Bob, a trader, and Chim the chimpanzee was on hand to keep Sheena company. The twenty-six episodes were filmed in Mexico by Nassour Studios.

THE SHEILA MacRAE SHOW SYNDICATED
1971 Half-hour talk show hosted by Sheila MacRae, with help from her daughters Meredith and Heather MacRae.

THE SHEILAH GRAHAM SHOW NBC
20 JANUARY 1951–14 JULY 1951 Hollywood gossip columnist Sheilah Graham hosted her own fifteen-minute show on Saturday nights. In 1955 she hosted a daytime show: see *Hollywood Today.*

SHELL'S WONDERFUL WORLD OF GOLF NBC
20 JANUARY 1963–28 FEBRUARY 1970 Weekend series of golf matches filmed at courses throughout the world. Sponsored by Shell Oil, the show was hosted by Gene Sarazen and George Rogers.

SHENANIGANS ABC

26 SEPTEMBER 1964–20 MARCH 1965 A Saturday-morning game show
for kids, hosted by Stubby Kaye.

SHERIFF OF COCHISE (U.S. MARSHAL) SYNDICATED

1956–1958 John Bromfield starred in both of these half-hour crime
shows as modern-day law enforcement officer Frank Morgan. In the first
thirty-nine episodes, syndicated as *Sheriff of Cochise* or *Man from Cochise,* Morgan was the sheriff of Cochise County, Arizona. In the latter
thirty-nine shows, syndicated as *U.S. Marshal,* Morgan was a federal
marshal working in Arizona. Stan Jones was also featured as Deputy Olson. Mort Briskin was the producer and writer.

SHERLOCK HOLMES SYNDICATED

1954 Ronald Howard starred as Sherlock Holmes, fiction's most famous sleuth, in this series of thirty-nine half hours. Also featured were H.
Marion-Crawford as his faithful companion, Dr. John H. Watson, and
Archie Duncan as Inspector Lestrade. The series was filmed in France
and produced by Sheldon Reynolds, who also directed most of the episodes; some of the stories were based on Arthur Conan Doyle's works,
and others were newly written.

SHIELDS AND YARNELL CBS

13 JUNE 1977–25 JULY 1977; 31 JANUARY 1978–28 MARCH 1978 This
half-hour variety series was cohosted by Robert Shields and Lorene Yarnell, a husband-and-wife mime team who were plucked from the streets
of San Francisco for the show. Other regulars included Ted Zeigler and
Joanna Cassidy in 1977, and Gailard Sartain and John Bloom in 1978.
Shields and Yarnell's best-known sketch was "The Clinkers," an inept
bionic couple. Steve Binder was the executive producer and director,
Frank Peppiatt and John Aylesworth the producers.

SHINDIG ABC

16 SEPTEMBER 1964–8 JANUARY 1966 West Coast disc jockey Jimmy
O'Neill was the host of this prime-time rock-and-roll show, which predated NBC's *Hullabaloo* by a few months and spawned a host of syndicated competitors. *Shindig* was probably a cut above the rest, if for no
other reason than that it was broadcast live (usually) and the acts actually performed on stage, rather than lip-synching to a recording. Several
acts were regularly featured on *Shindig,* such as Bobby Sherman, The
Righteous Brothers (Bill Medley and Bob Hatfield, who weren't brothers
at all), The Wellingtons, The Blossoms (featuring Darlene Love and Fan-
ita James), Glen Campbell, and Donna Loren. The composition of the
house combo, the Shindogs, changed periodically but included James

Burton, Delaney Bramlett, Chuck Blackwell, Joey Cooper, Glen Hardin, Don Preston, and Leon Russell. The Ray Pohlman Band was also featured, as were the Shindigger Dancers, choreographed by Andre Tayir. Several shows were produced in England, including one with the Beatles (telecast 7 October 1964). The lineup on the 1965 fall premiere (16 September) included the Rolling Stones, the Kinks, the Byrds, and the Everly Brothers; the Who made their American TV debut on the show later that year (2 October). *Shindig* was introduced as a half-hour show in the fall of 1964 and expanded to an hour in January 1965. In the fall of 1965 it was broken into two half hours, scheduled Thursdays and Saturdays, and was bumped in midseason to make room for *Batman*. *Shindig* was developed by Jack Good, a British producer who had put together several such shows in England (one of which, *Oh, Boy!*, was carried briefly by ABC). Leon I. Mirell was the executive producer and Dean Whitmore the producer.

SHIRLEY   NBC
26 OCTOBER 1979–25 JANUARY 1980   Hour comedy-drama about a widow and her children who moved from New York City to Lake Tahoe, starring Shirley Jones as Shirley Miller, with Patrick Wayne as her friend Lew; Peter Barton as Shirley's stepson, Bill; Rosanna Arquette as her daughter Debra; Bret Shryer as her son, Hemm; Tracey Gold as her daughter Michelle; John McIntyre as Dutch McHenry, a crusty local character; Ann Doran as Charlotte McHenry, Dutch's ex-wife, the Millers' housekeeper; Cynthia Eilbacher as Tracy, Debra's friend; and Oregano, the family dog.

SHIRLEY TEMPLE'S STORYBOOK   NBC/ABC
12 JANUARY 1958–21 DECEMBER 1958 (NBC); 12 JANUARY 1959–21 DECEMBER 1959 (ABC)
SHIRLEY TEMPLE THEATRE   NBC
18 SEPTEMBER 1960–10 SEPTEMBER 1961   Shirley Temple, who has appeared rarely on television, served as host, narrator, and occasional star of these children's anthology series. Presentations included: "Beauty and the Beast," with Charlton Heston (12 January 1958); "Rumpelstiltskin," with Kurt Kasznar (2 February 1958); "Rapunzel," with Carol Lynley and Agnes Moorehead (27 October 1958); "Mother Goose," with Elsa Lanchester (21 December 1958); "The Land of Oz," with Shirley Temple (as Princess Ozma) and Jonathan Winters (18 September 1960); "Babes in Toyland," with Jonathan Winters (25 December 1960). *Shirley Temple's Storybook,* introduced on NBC, was broadcast as a series of specials, usually on Sundays; reruns were shown on ABC in 1959, when the show was seen on occasional Mondays. *Shirley Temple Theatre* was a weekly series, scheduled on Sundays; William H. Brown, Jr., was its executive producer, and William Asher produced it.

SHIRLEY'S WORLD
ABC

15 SEPTEMBER 1971–5 JANUARY 1972 Another example of an unsuccessful TV series featuring a major film star, *Shirley's World* was an expensive half-hour situation comedy, produced in England (by ITC) and filmed on location around the world. It starred Shirley MacLaine as photojournalist Shirley Logan, on assignment for *World Illustrated* magazine, and featured John Gregson as her editor, Dennis Croft. Sheldon Leonard was the producer.

SHIVAREE
SYNDICATED

1965 Gene Weed hosted this half-hour rock-and-roll show, an imitation *Shindig* or *Hullabaloo*.

SHOOT FOR THE STARS
NBC

3 JANUARY 1977–30 SEPTEMBER 1977 Geoff Edwards hosted this daytime game show, a phrase identification game that was played similarly to *The $20,000 Pyramid* and featured two celebrity-and-contestant teams. Bob Stewart was the executive producer.

SHORT SHORT DRAMAS
NBC

30 SEPTEMBER 1952–9 APRIL 1953 Ruth Woods hosted this fifteen-minute anthology series, seen Tuesday and Thursday evenings at 7:15.

SHOTGUN SLADE
SYNDICATED

1959 Half-hour western starring Scott Brady as Shotgun Slade.

THE SHOW
PBS

11 JANUARY 1970–12 JULY 1970 Variety series for young people hosted by Bob Walsh (who also produced it) and singer Donal Leace. Each week a studio audience of about twenty-five young people was on hand to talk with the performing guests.

SHOW BUSINESS, INC
NBC

10 MARCH 1949–4 SEPTEMBER 1949 This half-hour variety show was first hosted by New York *News* columnist Danton Walker; Dick Kollmar took over as emcee in June, and the show was later titled *Broadway Scrapbook* and *Broadway Spotlight*.

THE SHOW GOES ON
CBS

19 JANUARY 1950–23 FEBRUARY 1952 Robert Q. Lewis hosted this prime-time talent show, on which talent buyers—agents, producers, and stars—dropped by to audition and hire promising young hopefuls. Lester Gottlieb produced the half-hour series, and Alex Leftwich directed it.

SHOW STREET   SYNDICATED

1964   Phyllis Diller hosted this half-hour talent show.

SHOW WAGON   NBC

8 JANUARY 1955–1 OCTOBER 1955   Officially known as *The Swift Show Wagon*, this variety show featured Horace Heidt and the American Way and was presented from a different American city each week, utilizing local talent. Jerry Brown produced the half-hour series.

SHOWCASE '68   NBC

11 JUNE 1968–3 SEPTEMBER 1968   Disc jockey Lloyd Thaxton hosted this half-hour variety series that featured new professional talent. Most shows were taped at American colleges and universities, and the ten weekly winners (who included Julie Budd, Andrea Marcovicci, the Chambers Brothers, Sly and the Family Stone, and the American Breed) competed on the finale at the Ohio State Fair in Columbus.

SHOWDOWN   NBC

4 JULY 1966–14 OCTOBER 1966   The only interesting feature of this daytime game show, hosted by Joe Pyne, was that it featured breakaway seats, so that contestants who missed a question would fall to the floor.

SHOWER OF STARS   CBS

30 SEPTEMBER 1954–17 APRIL 1958   *Shower of Stars*, a once-a-month replacement for *Climax* on Thursdays, was the catchall title for a wide variety of presentations. Most shows were variety spectaculars, such as the 1954 premiere, which featured Betty Grable, Mario Lanza, and bandleader Harry James (Grable's husband), though some dramatic shows were aired, such as Dickens's "A Christmas Carol," with Fredric March (3 December 1954). William Lundigan, who also hosted *Climax*, was the first master of ceremonies and was succeeded by Jack Benny.

SHOWOFFS   ABC

30 JUNE 1975–26 DECEMBER 1975   On this daytime game show from Goodson-Todman Productions, teams consisting of two celebrities and a contestant tried to pantomime words to one another. Larry Blyden was to have hosted the series, but he died just before production; Bobby Van was selected to replace him.

SHOWTIME   CBS

11 JUNE 1968–17 SEPTEMBER 1968   Produced in England, this hour-long variety series was hosted by a guest celebrity each week; the show was a summer replacement for *The Red Skelton Hour*.

636

SHOWTIME U.S.A.　　　　　　　　　　　　　　　　　　　　　ABC
1 OCTOBER 1950–24 JUNE 1951　Vinton Freedley was the usual host of
this half-hour series, on which scenes from current Broadway plays were
performed by the cast members.

SID CAESAR INVITES YOU　　　　　　　　　　　　　　　　　ABC
26 JANUARY 1958–25 MAY 1958　This half-hour comedy show briefly
reunited Sid Caesar and Imogene Coca, who had worked together on
Your Show of Shows. Paul Reed, Milt Kamen, Carl Reiner, and Howard
Morris were also on hand, but the Sunday-night show failed to catch on.

SID CAESAR PRESENTS　　　　　　　　　　　　　　　　　　NBC
4 JULY 1955–12 SEPTEMBER 1955　A summer replacement for *Caesar's
Hour,* this hour-long variety show was produced by Sid Caesar and directed by Carl Reiner. Among the regulars were Sid Gould, Barbara
Nichols, and Cliff Norton.

THE SID CAESAR SHOW　　　　　　　　　　　　　　　　　　ABC
19 SEPTEMBER 1963–12 MARCH 1964　The last of the several comedy-
variety shows hosted by Sid Caesar, this series was a half-hour program
that alternated biweekly with *Here's Edie.* Other regulars included Gisele
MacKenzie, Joey Forman, and Charlotte Rae. See also *Caesar's Hour;
Sid Caesar Invites You;* and *Your Show of Shows.*

SIERRA　　　　　　　　　　　　　　　　　　　　　　　　NBC
12 SEPTEMBER 1974–12 DECEMBER 1974　This hour-long adventure series from Jack Webb's Mark VII, Ltd., was set at Sierra National Park
and told the story of a dedicated group of park rangers; like the members
of the *Emergency!* team, they seemed to spend most of their time rescuing
people. Featured were James C. Richardson as Tim Cassidy; Ernest
Thompson as Matt Harper; Susan Foster as Julie Beck; Mike Warren as
P. J. Lewis; and Jack Hogan as Jack Moore, the chief ranger. Scheduled
on Thursdays, *Sierra* proved to be no match for CBS's *The Waltons* and
was gone in thirteen weeks. Robert A. Cinader was the executive producer, Bruce Johnson the producer.

SIGMUND AND THE SEA MONSTERS　　　　　　　　　　　　NBC
8 SEPTEMBER 1973–18 OCTOBER 1975　On this live-action Saturday-
morning series two brothers took in a refugee sea monster (Sigmund) and
helped him elude the other members of his monstrous family. With Billy
Barty as Sigmund Ooz; Johnny Whitaker as Johnny Stuart; Scott Kolden
as Scott Stuart; Mary Wickes as Zelda, the Stuart family's housekeeper;
Rip Taylor as Sheldon the Sea Genie; Fran Ryan as Gertrude; and
Sparky Marcus as Shelby. Si Rose was the executive producer for Sid and
Marty Krofft Productions.

THE SILENT FORCE ABC

21 SEPTEMBER 1970–11 JANUARY 1971 Bruce Geller was the executive producer of this half-hour crime show about a trio of federal undercover agents. With Ed Nelson as Ward Fuller; Lynda Day (later known as Lynda Day George after her marriage to Chris George) as Amelia Cole; and Percy Rodriguez as Jason Hart.

THE SILENT SERVICE SYNDICATED

1957 This half-hour anthology series about submarine warfare was hosted by Rear Admiral (Ret.) Thomas M. Dykers.

SILENTS PLEASE ABC

4 AUGUST 1960–5 OCTOBER 1961 Host Ernie Kovacs introduced clips from vintage silent movies on this half-hour documentary series.

THE SILVER SWAN CAFE
See THE MOREY AMSTERDAM SHOW

SILVER THEATER CBS

3 OCTOBER 1949–10 JULY 1950 This dramatic anthology series, sponsored by the International Silver Company, began on radio in 1938; Conrad Nagel hosted the half-hour television version, which ran on Monday nights. Representative presentations included: "Farewell Supper," with Charles Korvin (31 October); "The First Show of 1950," with George Reeves (2 January); "My Brother's Keeper," with Ward Bond and Glenn Corbett (20 February); "Minor Incident," with Nancy Kelly (10 April); "Papa Romani," with William Frawley, Margaret Hamilton, and Chico Marx (15 May); and "My Heart's in the Highlands," with Howard Da Silva (12 June).

SING ALONG CBS

4 JUNE 1958–9 JULY 1958 This short-lived half-hour musical series predated *Sing Along with Mitch* by some three years. As on *Sing Along with Mitch,* the lyrics to the songs performed on stage were shown at the bottom of viewers' home screens so that everyone could sing along. Jim Lowe hosted the series and featured vocalists included Tina Robin, Florence Henderson, and Somethin' Smith and the Redheads.

SING ALONG WITH MITCH NBC

27 JANUARY 1961–21 APRIL 1961; 28 SEPTEMBER 1961–21 SEPTEMBER 1964 Home viewers were able to participate in this hour-long musical series, as the lyrics to the songs were superimposed at the bottom of their screens; viewers were invited to "follow the bouncing ball" as it moved from one lyric to the next. Goateed composer-arranger Mitch Miller led

the Sing-Along Gang, an on-stage aggregation of about two dozen. Among the featured vocalists were Leslie Uggams, Diana Trask, Barbara McNair, and Gloria Lambert. *Sing Along with Mitch* was introduced on *Ford Startime* in 1960 and had a limited run in the spring of 1961, alternating with *The Bell Telephone Hour,* before going weekly in the fall of that year. Reruns were exhumed in the spring of 1966 to replace the faltering *Sammy Davis, Jr. Show.* Bill Hobin produced and directed the series.

SING IT AGAIN
CBS

7 OCTOBER 1950–23 JUNE 1951 *Sing It Again* ran on CBS radio for two years before coming to television. The Saturday-night game show featured contestants from the studio audience who tried to identify songs from a few notes; phone calls were also placed to home viewers, who were given the chance to identify a "mystery voice." Dan Seymour hosted the hour show until February, when Jan Murray took over.

SING-CO-PATION
ABC

23 JANUARY 1949–30 OCTOBER 1949 Fifteen-minute musical-variety program, broadcast on Sunday night from Chicago. Subsequently titled *Serenade*, the show was hosted first by Dolores Marshall, later by Joanelle James.

THE SINGING LADY
ABC

12 AUGUST 1948–6 AUGUST 1950; 27 SEPTEMBER 1953–21 MARCH 1954 "The Singing Lady" was Ireene Wicker, who began this children's series on radio in 1931; the Suzarri Marionettes were also featured. The 1948–1950 series was seen Sunday evenings; the 1953–1954 series, titled *Ireene Wicker Storytime,* was seen Sunday mornings.

SIR FRANCIS DRAKE
NBC

24 JUNE 1962–9 SEPTEMBER 1962 Produced in Great Britain, this half-hour adventure series starred Terence Morgan as Sir Francis Drake, commander of *The Golden Hind.* Jean Kent was featured as Queen Elizabeth I.

SIR LANCELOT
NBC

24 SEPTEMBER 1956–24 JUNE 1957 This British import followed *Robin Hood* one season later. Featured were William Russell as Sir Lancelot; Ronald Leigh-Hunt as King Arthur; Jane Hylton as Queen Guinevere; Cyril Smith as Merlin; and Bobby Scroggins as Brian the Squire. Scheduled opposite *The Burns and Allen Show* and *The Danny Thomas Show,* the half-hour swashbuckler was dropped after one season. Dallas Bower produced the series.

SIROTA'S COURT   NBC

1 DECEMBER 1976–20 APRIL 1977   This half-hour sitcom came and
went almost unnoticed, as it was scheduled irregularly during the middle
of the 1976–1977 season. Featured were Michael Constantine as Judge
Matthew J. Sirota, magistrate of a big city night court; Cynthia Harris as
Maureen O'Connor, the court clerk; Kathleen Miller as public defender
Gail Goodman; Ted Ross as defense attorney Sawyer Dabney; Fred Wil-
lard as assistant district attorney H. R. Nugent; and Owen Bush as John
Belson, the bailiff. Harvey Miller and Peter Engel were the producers.

SIT OR MISS   ABC

6 AUGUST 1950–29 OCTOBER 1950   Half-hour game show on which five
contestants played a form of musical chairs, with quizzes and stunts
thrown in as well. Kay Westfall and George Sotos cohosted the series,
which offered a top prize of $75.

THE SIX MILLION DOLLAR MAN   ABC

20 OCTOBER 1973–6 MARCH 1978   *The Six Million Dollar Man* was introduced as a monthly feature on *The ABC Suspense Movie* before becoming a weekly series in January of 1974. It starred Lee Majors as Steve
Austin, an American astronaut who was severely injured in a training
mishap and who was rebuilt (at a cost of $6 million) by the Office of Stra-
tegic Information, a government agency. Equipped with two bionic legs, a
bionic arm, and a bionic eye, Austin was far stronger than any mere mortal and was employed by the O.S.I. to undertake an assortment of deli-
cate missions. Also featured were Richard Anderson as Oscar Goldman,
an O.S.I. topsider; Alan Oppenheimer and Martin E. Brooks as Dr.
Rudy Wells, an O.S.I. physician. The series was very popular with younger viewers, and a spinoff was introduced in January of 1976; see *The
Bionic Woman.* The pilot for *The Six Million Dollar Man* was telecast 7
March 1973, and was based on *Cyborg,* a novel by Martin Caidin. Harve
Bennett was executive producer of the series for Harve Bennett Productions in association with Universal Television.

THE SIX WIVES OF HENRY VIII   CBS

1 AUGUST 1971–5 SEPTEMBER 1971   CBS imported this six-part historical miniseries from England. Each of the six 90-minute stories centered
on one of King Henry's marriages. Keith Michell starred as Henry VIII.
His wives were played by: Annette Crosbie as Catherine of Aragon,
whom Henry divorced; Dorothy Tutin as Anne Boleyn, who was behead-
ed; Anne Stallybrass as Jane Seymour, who died after giving birth to
Henry's long awaited male heir; Elvi Hale as Anne of Cleves, whom Henry divorced; Angela Pleasence as Catherine Howard, who was also be-
headed; and Rosalie Crutchley as Catherine Parr, who survived Henry.

Anthony Quayle narrated the series when it was telecast on CBS; the show was rerun on PBS's *Masterpiece Theatre* in 1972.

THE SIXTH SENSE
ABC

15 JANUARY 1972–30 DECEMBER 1972 This hour-long dramatic series purported to examine the occult and the supernatural. It starred Gary Collins as Dr. Michael Rhodes, a trained parapsychologist, researcher, and college instructor; also featured was Catherine Ferrar as his assistant, Nancy Murphy. Stan Shpetner was the producer.

60 MINUTES
CBS

24 SEPTEMBER 1968– An hour newsmagazine with a strong emphasis on investigative reporting, *60 Minutes* began in 1968 as a bi-weekly show, alternating on Tuesdays with *CBS Reports*. In the fall of 1971 it shifted to Sunday evenings but was often preempted by professional football games and was later seen only during the winter and spring. In the fall of 1975 it finally became a weekly series, and its ratings have steadily improved to the point where *60 Minutes* is the highest-rated public affairs program in television history. A typical show consists of two or three features, each separately produced but put together under the careful supervision of executive producer Don Hewitt. From 1968 until 1970 the show was cohosted by veteran CBS newsmen Mike Wallace and Harry Reasoner; when Reasoner left CBS for ABC, he was replaced by Morley Safer, a Canadian-born CBS correspondent who had been its bureau chief in Saigon and in London. In the fall of 1975 Dan Rather, who had been the network's White House correspondent, joined Wallace and Safer. Another regular feature of *60 Minutes* was "Point/Counterpoint," a segment on which liberal and conservative viewpoints on topical issues have been vocally, if not intensively, exchanged; conservative columnist James J. Kilpatrick originally did battle with liberal Nicholas von Hoffman and jousted with Shana Alexander until 1979, when the feature was dropped. Among the best-known stories covered by *60 Minutes* were those concerning ITT lobbyist Dita Beard, Howard Hughes's supposed biographer Clifford Irving, and Colonel Anthony Herbert, whose claims that certain Vietnam war atrocities had been covered up were disputed by other officers. Herbert's libel suit went all the way to the Supreme Court, which ruled in 1979 that Herbert was entitled to question *60 Minutes'* producers as to their state of mind and motives in presenting the story. Mike Wallace also did two one-hour interviews with former Nixon aide H. R. Haldeman (these were technically broadcast as specials, but were scheduled in *60 Minutes'* time slot); Wallace and his producers were criticized when it was learned that Haldeman had been paid (some estimates ranged as high as $100,000) for the appearances. In the fall of 1978, Harry Reasoner returned to CBS News and rejoined *60 Minutes*: a new regular feature, "A Few Minutes with Andy Rooney," was also added.

THE $64,000 CHALLENGE   CBS

8 APRIL 1956–14 SEPTEMBER 1958   The first TV game show spunoff from another TV game show, *The $64,000 Challenge* offered alumni of *The $64,000 Question* the chance to win even more money; contestants who had won at least $8,000 on *Question* were eligible to compete on *Challenge*, where they faced two challengers in their chosen field of knowledge. Big winners included Myrt Power, Leonard Ross, Dr. Joyce Brothers, Billy Pearson, Gino Prato, Teddy Nadler, and Michael Della-Rocca. Sonny Fox was the first host of *Challenge*, but he was abruptly replaced by Ralph Story in September of 1956. Among the young women who escorted the contestants on and off stage (such assistants were known as "elbow grabbers") were Doris Wiss, Lisa Laughlin, and Pat Donovan. Along with most of television's big money prime-time game shows, *The $64,000 Challenge* was canceled in September of 1958 as the heat of the game show scandals intensified; the show had been scheduled to shift to NBC beginning 18 September 1958, but it never reached the air.

THE $64,000 QUESTION   CBS

7 JUNE 1955–9 NOVEMBER 1958   The first of prime-time television's big money game shows, *The $64,000 Question* premiered in the summer of 1955 and became an instant hit; three years later it passed away unceremoniously amidst the quiz show scandals of 1958. The object of the game was for contestants, each of whom was an expert in a particular field of knowledge, to double their money each time they answered a question correctly; the questions, of course, became increasingly harder as the stakes grew larger, and an incorrect answer at any point ended the game. The first question was worth a dollar, and the stakes doubled up to the tenth question, worth $512. The next question was worth an even $1,000, and the stakes again began to double progressively. To heighten the suspense at the higher levels, players were placed in isolation booths onstage for the question-and-answer sessions, and, if they answered correctly, returned the following week to compete at the next level (a player could always elect to stop after any level, but few of them chose to do so). Thus, on any given show, some contestants would be starting out at the lowest levels while others were announcing their decisions to return the following week to try for more big money. A player who chose to try for the $64,000 question was permitted to bring an expert along, but if neither the player nor the expert answered the question correctly, the player left the show with $4,000. Hal March was the host of the series and was assisted by Lynn Dollar, who escorted the contestants into the isolation booth (Pat Donovan succeeded her in 1958). Dr. Bergen Evans compiled the questions and served as the judge. The first $64,000 winner was a captain in the Marines, Richard S. McCutchen; his area of expertise was gastronomy. Dr. Joyce Brothers, a psychologist who later hosted several TV

shows of her own, was the second big winner; her category was boxing. Actress Barbara Feldon, later seen on *Get Smart,* won the top prize for her knowledge of Shakespeare, and dancer-choreographer Geoffrey Holder won $16,000 on the show. Other well-known winners included ten-year-old Rob Strom (science), Myrt Power (baseball), Dr. Alexander Sas-Jaworsky (history), jockey Billy Pearson (art), Gloria Lockerman (spelling), Gino Prato (opera), police officer Redmond O'Hanlon (Shakespeare), and Teddy Nadler, one of the biggest money winners in television history; after his appearances on *The $64,000 Question*'s sister show, *The $64,000 Challenge* (see also that title), Nadler had won $264,000. As a gag, Jack Benny once appeared on the show but elected to quit after winning the first dollar. *The $64,000 Question* was packaged by Louis G. Cowan, who sold out his interest in the show shortly after it began and later became a CBS executive; Revlon sponsored the series, and Steve Carlin produced it. Though no specific allegations against *The $64,000 Question* were ever substantiated during the game show investigations of 1958 and 1959, the series was dropped along with almost all other prime-time game shows. In 1976 a syndicated version, adjusted for inflation, reappeared: see *The $128,000 Question.*

THE SKATEBIRDS
CBS
10 SEPTEMBER 1977–21 JANUARY 1978 Three skateboarding birds (played by actors) were the hosts of this Saturday-morning hour. The Skatebirds introduced three cartoon segments ("The Robonic Stooges," "Wonder Wheels," and "Woofer and Wimper") and a live-action segment ("Mystery Island"). Trimmed to a half hour in midseason, the series continued under the title *The Three Robonic Stooges.*

THE SKIP FARRELL SHOW
ABC
17 JANUARY 1949–28 AUGUST 1949 Half-hour variety series hosted by Skip Farrell and featuring Joanelle James.

SKIPPY
SYNDICATED
1969 A kangaroo named Skippy was the marsupial star of this Australian import; Skippy, wounded and apparently orphaned, had been taken in by a park ranger and his two sons. The human roles were played by Ed Deveraux as Matt Hammond; Garry Pankhurst as Sonny; Ken James as Mark; and Liza Goddard as Clancy, a young woman who boarded with the Goddards. Officially titled *Skippy the Bush Kangaroo,* the half hour series was filmed on location in Australia's Waratah National Park and was sponsored in this country by Kellogg cereals.

SKY HAWKS
ABC
6 SEPTEMBER 1969–4 SEPTEMBER 1971 Saturday-morning cartoon se-

ries about the members of the Wilson family, who ran Sky Hawks, Incorporated, an all-purpose air service.

SKY KING
NBC

16 SEPTEMBER 1951–26 OCTOBER 1952 Kirby Grant starred in this half-hour adventure series for children as Sky King, the airborne owner of the Flying Crown Ranch; King used his plane, *The Songbird,* not only to patrol his spread but also to rescue the trapped and to capture fugitives. Also featured were Gloria Winters as Penny, King's niece; Ron Hagerthy as Clipper, King's nephew; Norman Ollstead as Bob Carey; and Gary Hunley as Mickey. The series began on radio in 1947, and the TV version was rerun on both ABC and CBS after its initial run on NBC. It was supplied by Jack Chertok Productions.

THE SKY'S THE LIMIT
NBC

1 NOVEMBER 1954–1 JUNE 1956 A daytime game show, *The Sky's the Limit* was hosted first by Gene Rayburn and later by Monty Hall; Hope Lange and Marilyn Cantor were on hand as assistants. The show, which involved both stunts and quizzes, began as a fifteen-minute series but expanded to thirty minutes in the summer of 1955.

SLATTERY'S PEOPLE
CBS

21 SEPTEMBER 1964–26 NOVEMBER 1965 Richard Crenna starred in this hour-long dramatic series as Slattery, the idealistic leader of the minority party in the legislature of an unnamed state. Also featured during the first season were Paul Geary as his aide, Johnny Ramos; Maxine Stuart as B. J. Clawson; Edward Asner as politican Frank Radcliff; and Tol Avery as Metcalf. For the show's abortive second season Slattery acquired not only a new supporting cast but also a first name—Jim. New regulars included Alejandro Rey as aide Mike Valera; Kathie Browne as TV newscaster Liz Andrews; and Francine York as Wendy Wendowski. Matthew Rapf produced the series for Bing Crosby Productions.

SLEEPY JOE
ABC/SYNDICATED

3 OCTOBER 1949–28 OCTOBER 1949 (ABC); 1951 (SYNDICATED) Originally a radio series, *Sleepy Joe* was created by Jimmy Scribner, the dialectician who had created *The Johnson Family* on radio in 1934. *Sleepy Joe* first came to television as a local series over KTSL-TV in Los Angeles. On that version Scribner appeared in blackface as Sleepy Joe, an Uncle Remus–type character who spun yarns at the request of a little girl named Gayle (played by Gayle Scribner, Jimmy's daughter). The ABC and syndicated versions of the show were filmed puppet programs, however, with voices supplied by Scribner.

SMALL FRY CLUB   DUMONT

11 MARCH 1947–15 JUNE 1951 Network television's first successful children's program, *Small Fry Club* was broadcast every weekday evening for most of its run. "Big Brother" Bob Emery hosted the program, which employed most of the devices featured in subsequent kids' shows—cartoons, silent films, puppets, skits, songs, and demonstrations.

SMALL WORLD   CBS

12 OCTOBER 1958–5 APRIL 1959 On this Sunday-afternoon public affairs program, host Edward R. Murrow conversed with three guests; the show was not unlike *Person to Person,* as Murrow remained in New York while his guests were filmed on location throughout the world. On the premiere Murrow chatted with Indian premier Jawarhalal Nehru, former governor Thomas E. Dewey, and Aldous Huxley. Other guest threesomes included Hyman Rickover, Rebecca West, and Mark Van Doren (2 November), and Noel Coward, James Thurber, and Siobhan McKenna (29 March). Murrow produced the show with Fred W. Friendly and had planned to have Eric Sevareid host it; the network, however, insisted that Murrow take the job. The show was broadcast during the 1959–1960 season as a series of specials.

SMILIN' ED'S GANG   NBC/CBS/ABC

26 AUGUST 1950–19 MAY 1951 (NBC); 11 AUGUST 1951–11 APRIL 1953 (CBS); 22 AUGUST 1953–16 APRIL 1955 (ABC); 23 APRIL 1955–13 AUGUST 1955 (NBC) Smilin' Ed McConnell began this popular children's show on radio in 1943 and brought it to television seven years later; the show was a mixture of stories, filmed segments and onstage antics with McConnell and his unpredictable puppets: Midnight the Cat, Squeekie the Mouse, and Froggie the Gremlin. Frank Ferrin produced and directed the series, which was produced in Hollywood and sponsored by Buster Brown Shoes (it was originally titled *The Buster Brown TV Show With Smilin' Ed McConnell and the Buster Brown Gang*). When McConnell died in 1955, Andy Devine took over as host, and the show was retitled *Andy's Gang* (see also that title).

THE SMITH FAMILY   ABC

20 JANUARY 1971–5 JANUARY 1972; 12 APRIL 1972–14 JUNE 1972 Half-hour comedy-drama about a Los Angeles police officer and his family. With Henry Fonda as Detective Sergeant Chad Smith, a twenty-five-year veteran; Janet Blair as his wife, Betty Smith; Darleen Carr as their elder daughter, Cindy, a college student; Ronny Howard as their teenage son, Bob; and Michael-James Wixted as their younger son, Brian (who inexplicably spoke with a British accent). Don Fedderson was the executive producer of the series.

THE SMITHSONIAN   NBC
15 OCTOBER 1966–8 APRIL 1967   Bill Ryan hosted this Saturday afternoon informational series for children, which was filmed at the Smithsonian Institution in Washington, D.C., and on location.

THE SMOKEY BEAR SHOW   ABC
6 SEPTEMBER 1969–5 SEPTEMBER 1971   Weekend cartoon series starring Smokey the Bear, the animated version of the real Smokey, who had
been saved from a forest fire as a cub and spent the rest of his days in the
National Zoo in Washington. One of the first of the conservation-oriented
cartoon shows, *The Smokey Bear Show* was seen Saturdays during its first
season; reruns were shown Sundays the following year.

THE SMOTHERS BROTHERS COMEDY HOUR   CBS
5 FEBRUARY 1967–8 JUNE 1969
THE SMOTHERS BROTHERS SUMMER SHOW   ABC
15 JULY 1970–16 SEPTEMBER 1970
TOM SMOTHERS' ORGANIC PRIME TIME SPACE RIDE   SYNDICATED
1971
THE SMOTHERS BROTHERS SHOW   NBC
13 JANUARY 1975–26 MAY 1975   Brothers Tom and Dick Smothers,
who cohosted *The Smothers Brothers Comedy Hour* on CBS, battled the
network over the program content for two years, and finally lost their
show. Though the series was planned to appeal to the under-thirty generation, its open criticism of the Vietnam War and the Johnson administration created a dilemma for an understandably sensitive network; the
dilemma was solved by canceling the show less than 100 days into the
Nixon administration. To most of its audience, *The Smothers Brothers
Comedy Hour* was a breath of fresh air, but to CBS the Smothers Brothers seemed to be in the wrong place at the wrong time with the wrong
things to say.

The brothers were singing together at San Jose State College as early as
1959, and made their network TV debut on Jack Paar's *Tonight* show. In
1965 they were involved in a trivial sitcom (see *The Smothers Brothers
Show* below); though their first series was unsuccessful, CBS did not lose
interest. When network research suggested that a variety show with appeal to the fifteen-to-thirty age group could compete with NBC's *Bonanza* on Sundays (previous CBS casualties in the 9 p.m. slot included *The
Judy Garland Show, My Living Doll, The Joey Bishop Show, Perry Mason,*
and *The Garry Moore Show*), CBS executives contacted Tom Smothers,
who negotiated a twenty-six-week contract for a variety series. *The
Smothers Brothers Comedy Hour* premiered in February 1967 and ranked
a surprising sixteenth over the remainder of the season (during the 1967–
1968 season the show slipped to eighteenth but succeeded in toppling *Bonanza* from first to sixth).

646

On camera, Tom Smothers, the funny one (and the older one), seemed to be an inarticulate bumbler. Off camera, though, Tom was keenly involved with almost every aspect of the production; the show went through several producers (including Saul Ilson, Ernie Chambers, and Allan Blye) and at least six directors. More importantly, it was Tom who sought to use the show not only to introduce little-known performers to national audiences but also to provide a forum for the expression of political and critical viewpoints seldom expressed on a variety show. Though brother Dick shared Tom's sentiments, he preferred to let Tom take charge; Dick was less interested in show business and the media than Tom; he spent as much time as he could pursuing his real passions—automobile collecting and racing.

Censorship problems arose almost immediately and persisted throughout the Smothers' seventy-one-show run on CBS. Unlike most disputes between performers and networks over program material, the Smothers' disputes usually involved neither lines nor words (though the use of the word "mindblowing" was forbidden), but entire segments. Among the battles which the brothers lost and won were: a skit on film censorship with Tom Smothers and Elaine May, deleted; Pete Seeger's performance on the fall 1967 premiere of "Waist Deep in the Big Muddy," a song with antiwar overtones, deleted (the appearance marked Seeger's return to network television after being blacklisted in the 1950s; Seeger was permitted to perform the number on a later show); a special 1968 Mother's Day message (which concluded with the words, "Please talk peace"), deleted; Harry Belafonte singing in front of a filmed montage of disturbances at the 1968 Democratic convention in Chicago, deleted; an interview with Dr. Benjamin Spock, who had been convicted of aiding draft evaders, deleted. The Smothers Brothers also received a lot of hate mail, particularly for their frequent use of black performers on the show.

After the telecast of 27 October 1968 (from which a David Steinberg "sermonette" had generated much critical mail), CBS took the then unusual step of demanding that a tape of each upcoming show be prescreened for network affiliates by closed circuit. When Tom Smothers failed to deliver one tape until a day before air time, CBS yanked the show and did not broadcast it until three weeks later (on that show, Joan Baez dedicated a song to her husband, David Harris, then serving a jail sentence for draft evasion).

In spite of the constant conflicts, CBS announced its decision to renew *The Smothers Brothers Comedy Hour* on 14 March 1969. Less than two weeks later Tom Smothers attended the National Broadcasters Association convention in Washington, where he sought support from liberal Congressmen and other officials, such as FCC Commissioner Nicholas Johnson. Undoubtedly, Smothers's appearance in Washington worried the network, which would hardly have welcomed any government investigation. On 3 April 1969, Bob Wood, president of CBS Television, telegraphed Smothers that the show was canceled; ostensibly, the reason was that Smothers had failed to deliver a tape on time, though Smothers insisted that timely delivery had been made (the Smothers' guests on that show were David Steinberg, Dan Rowan, and Nancy Wilson). *TV Guide* ran a special editorial in its 19 April issue, characterizing CBS's decision to axe the show "wise, determined, and wholly justified," and citing the network's responsibility to the American public.

Neither ABC nor NBC expressed interest in signing the Smothers Brothers immediately after their cancellation, and *The Smothers Brothers Comedy Hour* left the air quietly in June 1969; it was replaced by *Hee Haw*. ABC signed the two for a summer series a year later; *The Smothers Brothers Summer Show* was a toned-down variety hour and attracted little, if any, controversy. Tom Smothers later starred in an ill-conceived comedy half hour known as *Tom Smothers' Organic Prime Time Space Ride*, which also featured comics Hudson and Landry. In 1975 Tom and Dick returned to network TV as hosts of *The Smothers Brothers Show*, a toothless effort; Joe Hamilton was the executive producer of the variety hour.

Many of the regulars on the Smothers Brothers' shows have become major stars. Among the more successful from *The Smothers Brothers Comedy Hour* crew were comedian Pat Paulsen (who campaigned for the Presidency in 1968), singers Glen Campbell and John Hartford, writer-composer Mason Williams, Bob Einstein (who often appeared as Officer Judy, the humorless cop, and later produced *The Redd Foxx Comedy Hour* with Allan Blye), and Steve Martin (who began as a writer for the show, but occasionally appeared on camera). Other regulars included Leigh French, Jennifer Warren, and Don Wyatt. Regulars on the Smothers' 1970 summer series included Spencer Quinn and Sally Struthers, who later starred in *All in the Family*. Regulars on the 1975 show included Pat Paulsen, Bob Einstein, and Don Novello.

THE SMOTHERS BROTHERS SHOW   CBS

17 SEPTEMBER 1965–9 SEPTEMBER 1966   This first of the several series starring brothers Tom and Dick Smothers was a half-hour situation comedy in which they played themselves. Tom Smothers was a probationary angel assigned to return to Earth and help people there, while Dick Smothers was a publishing executive who was forced to share his apartment with his late sibling. Also featured were Roland Winters as Dick's boss, Leonard J. Costello; Harriet MacGibbon as Mrs. Costello; Marilyn Scott as their daughter, Diane Costello; and Ann Elder as Janet, Dick's girlfriend. Neither of the Smothers Brothers was happy with the show; both felt that the situation comedy format was not the right showcase for their talents. The filmed series was originally produced by Phil Sharp for Four Star Films. See also *The Smothers Brothers Comedy Hour*.

SNAP JUDGMENT · NBC
3 APRIL 1967–28 MARCH 1969   This Goodson-Todman daytime game
show was similar in format to *Password;* Ed McMahon was the first host,
and was succeeded by Gene Rayburn.

SNARKY PARKER CBS
9 JANUARY 1950–29 SEPTEMBER 1950   The Bil and Cora Baird Puppets
were the stars of this fifteen-minute children's serial with a western setting. Snarky Parker and his horse, Heathcliffe, were the principal characters. Officially titled *Life with Snarky Parker,* and usually broadcast four
evenings a week, the show was directed by Yul Brynner, whose stage and
film career took off after *Snarky Parker* left the air.

THE SNOOKY LANSON SHOW NBC
17 JULY 1956–13 SEPTEMBER 1956   Snooky Lanson, who was regularly
featured on *Your Hit Parade,* hosted this summer replacement for the *Dinah Shore Show.* The fifteen-minute musical series was officially titled
Chevrolet on Broadway and also featured the Mello-Larks.

THE SNOOP SISTERS NBC
19 DECEMBER 1973–20 AUGUST 1974   One segment of *The NBC
Wednesday Movie, The Snoop Sisters* starred Helen Hayes and Mildred
Natwick as sisters Ernesta and Gwendolin Snoop, who wrote mystery
stories and solved real mysteries as well. Also featured were Lou Antonio
as their friend Barney, an ex-con; Bert Convy as their nephew, Lieutenant Steve Ostrowski, a New York cop. Six episodes were filmed.

SO THIS IS HOLLYWOOD NBC
1 JANUARY 1955–19 AUGUST 1955   Half-hour sitcom about two young
women trying to make it in show business. With Mitzi Green as Queenie
Dugan, an aspiring stunt woman; Virginia Gibson as Kim Tracey, an aspiring actress; Jimmy Lydon as Kim's agent and boyfriend, Andy Boone;
Gordon Jones as Queenie's boyfriend, stunt man Hubie Dodd; and Peggy
Knudsen as April Adams, the actress for whom Queenie became a stand-
in. The filmed series was produced by Ed Beloin and directed by Richard
Bare.

SO YOU WANT TO LEAD A BAND ABC
5 AUGUST 1954–27 JANUARY 1955   Bandleader Sammy Kaye hosted
this half-hour musical series, on which members of the studio audience
were given a chance to conduct the band; the audience selected the winning amateur conductor by its applause, and the lucky contestant won a
prize. Featured vocalists included Barbara Benson and Jeffrey Clay.

SOAP ABC

13 SEPTEMBER 1977–　　　　This prime-time comedy serial barely made it to the air because of protests lodged before its premiere by an assortment of religious and ethnic groups; ABC's excessive and exaggerated publicity doubtless precipitated the onslaught of complaints, most of which died down after the show came to the air. Though the plot deals with impotence, transsexualism, extramarital affairs, and organized crime, *Soap* is no more sensational than Norman Lear's pioneer serial, *Mary Hartman, Mary Hartman.* Set in Dunn's River, Connecticut, it tells the story of the wealthy Tate family and the middle-class Campbell family. Principal players include: Katherine Helmond as Jessica Tate, a free-thinking socialite who was convicted of murder during the first season; Robert Mandan as Chester Tate, her philandering husband; Jennifer Salt as their daughter Eunice; Diana Canova as their daughter Corinne; Jimmy Baio as their son, Billy; Robert Guillaume (1977–1979) as Benson, the family's cook; Cathryn Damon as Mary Campbell, Jessica's sister; Richard Mulligan as Burt Campbell, her second husband; Ted Wass as Mary's macho son, Danny, who became involved with organized crime; Billy Crystal as Mary's son, Jodie Dallas, who intended to change his gender; Richard Libertini as The Godfather; Katherine Reynolds as Claire; Robert Urich (1977–1978) as Peter; Arthur Peterson as Grandpa Tate, a veteran who is unaware that the war is over; Roscoe Lee Browne (March 1980–　　) as Saunders, the new butler; and Jay Johnson as Chuck. Rod Roddy is the announcer. Susan Harris created, produced, and wrote the half-hour series. See also *Benson.*

SOAP BOX THEATER ABC

1 JULY 1950–3 DECEMBER 1950　Half-hour dramatic anthology series.

THE SOAP FACTORY SYNDICATED

1978　A half hour of disco dancing, taped at the Soap Factory in Palisades Park, New Jersey. Paul Harriss was the host of the series, and David Bergman the executive producer.

SOLDIER PARADE ABC

14 JULY 1954–8 SEPTEMBER 1955　This Army talent show was hosted at various times by Gisele MacKenzie, Arlene Francis, and Martha Wright. Richard Hayes, then an Army private, was the cohost. The half-hour show grew out of an earlier military talent show, *Talent Patrol* (see also that title).

THE SOLDIERS NBC

25 JUNE 1955–3 SEPTEMBER 1955　Half-hour sitcom starring Hal March and Tom D'Andrea as a couple of Army privates. Bud Yorkin produced and directed.

SOLDIERS OF FORTUNE   SYNDICATED

1955   Half-hour adventure series with John Russell as Tim Kelly and
Chick Chandler as Toubo Smith, a pair of freewheeling troubleshooters.
The show was produced at Revue Studios.

SOMERSET   NBC

30 MARCH 1970–31 DECEMBER 1976   Though *Somerset* was the first serial spin-off from another serial, it had little in common with its parent,
Another World, even though it was titled *Another World/Somerset* at
first. Though some of the characters from *Another World* traveled back
and forth from Bay City to Somerset, *Somerset*'s principal characters
were developed independently. While *Another World*'s story lines centered on psychological and romantic themes, *Somerset*'s emphasized
crime and intrigue; the principal reason for the difference was that *Somerset*'s first head writer was Henry Slesar, who had previously worked on
The Edge of Night (all three soaps were owned by Procter and Gamble).
Subsequent head writers included Roy Winsor and Russell Kubec.

The two main characters who emigrated from Bay City to Somerset (a
town of 25,000) as the series premiered were lawyer Sam Lucas (played
by Jordan Charney) and his wife, Lahoma Vane Lucas (played by Ann
Wedgeworth); Missy Matthews (played by Carol Roux), another Bay
City resident, was also featured in the early months. Other members of
the cast included: Ed Kemmer as Ben Grant, Sam's law partner, who
died in a plane crash; Georgann Johnson as his wife, Ellen Bishop Grant,
who later fell for a much younger man; Ralph Clanton as Jasper Delaney,
owner of Delaney Brands, a major industry in Somerset; Len Gochman
as his son, Peter Delaney; Nick Coster as his son, Robert Delaney; Dorothy Stinette as his daughter, Laura Delaney Cooper; Marie Wallace as
Robert's wife, India Delaney; Paul Sparer as Laura's husband, Rex Cooper; Doug Chapin, Ernest Thompson, and Barry Jenner as Laura's son,
Tony Cooper; Fred J. Scollay as Ike Harding (also known as Harry Wil-
son), Tony's real father, and the murderer of Jasper Delaney; Susan Mac-
Donald as Jill Grant, daughter of Ben and Ellen Grant; Ron Martin and
Tom Calloway as David Grant, Jill's twin brother; Dick Schoberg as
Mitch Farmer, who married Jill and later died; Alan Gifford as Judge
Brad Bishop, Ellen Grant's father; Phil Sterling as Rafe Carter; Walter
Matthews as Gerald Davis; Alice Hirson as Marsha Davis; Wynne Miller
as nightclub singer Jessica Buchanan; Gary Sandy as Randy Buchanan;
Gene Fanning and George Coe as Leo Kurtz, who became the owner of
Delaney Brands; Michael Lipton as Leo's brother, Dr. Stanley Kurtz;
Renne Jarrett, Meg Wittner, and Fawne Harriman as Leo's daughter,
Ginger Kurtz, who married Tony Cooper; Lois Smith as the deranged
Zoe Cannel; Joel Crothers as her husband, Julian Cannel; Harriet Hall as
Andrea Moore, whom Zoe tried to poison; Chris Pennock as Andrea's
brother, Dana Moore; Lois Kibbee as their mother, Emily Moore; Frank

Schofield as Zoe's father, Philip Matson, who married Emily Moore; Jay Gregory as Zoe's brother, Carter Matson, whom Zoe murdered; Diahn Williams as Chrystal Ames, also killed by Zoe; Marc Alaimo as Virgil Paris, plant manager at Delaney Brands; Bibi Besch as Eve Lawrence, fiancée of Judge Bishop; Audrey Landers as Eve's daughter, Heather Lawrence Kane; James O'Sullivan as Dr. Jerry Kane, Heather's husband; Gary Swanson as reporter Greg Mercer, Heather's half brother; Stanley Grover as Mark Mercer; Judith Searle as Edith Mercer, Mark's wife; Joseph Julian as Vic Kirby; Ed Winter as Chuck Hillman; Melinda Plank as Danny Cotsworth; Dortha Duckworth as Rowena Standish; Peter MacLean as Scott MacKensie; Glenn Zachar as Skipper MacKensie; Bill Hunt as Bill Greeley; Polly Rowles as Freida Lang; Tina Sloan as Kate Cannel, who became the second wife of Julian Cannel; Eugene Smith as Lieutenant Will Price; Ted Danson as lawyer Tom Conway; James Congdon as Ned Paisley; Veleka Gray as Ned's sister, Victoria Paisley; Gloria Hoye as Dr. Teri Martin, who married Stanley Kurtz; Sean Ward as Joey Cooper; Bernard Grant as Dan Briskin; Molly Picon as Sarah Briskin; Nancy Pinkerton as Karen MacMillan; Abby Lewis as Lena Andrews; Elizabeth Lowry as Marge; Helen Funai as Lyling Sun; Jane Rose as Becky Winkler; Ellen Barber as Marion Parker; Bruce Gray as Warren Parker; Matthew Greene as Bobby Hansen; Lou Jacobi as Mac Wells; Jameson Parker as Dale Robinson, the younger man who became involved with widow Ellen Grant; and Gene Bua as Steve Slade.

SOMERSET MAUGHAM THEATRE

CBS/NBC

18 OCTOBER 1950–28 MARCH 1951 (CBS); 2 APRIL 1951–10 DECEMBER 1951 (NBC)   W. Somerset Maugham hosted this anthology series of adaptations of Maugham stories. The show began on CBS as a half-hour series and was kinescoped for presentation on those CBS affiliates that did not have direct transmission lines to the New York station from which the program originated; when it shifted networks in April of 1951 it expanded to an hour, was seen biweekly (alternating with *Robert Montgomery Presents*), and was presented only in live form. The latter change enabled several more Maugham stories to be presented on television, since, in the absence of a kinescope transcription, there was no longer any legal dispute with the owners of the film rights to those stories. Among the stories presented were: "The Dream," with Joan Bennett (14 February 1951); "The Moon and Sixpence," with Lee J. Cobb (30 April 1951); and "Cakes and Ale," with June Havoc (28 May 1951). The CBS version of the series was also titled *Teller of Tales*.

SOMETHING ELSE

SYNDICATED

1970   Half-hour musical variety show, hosted by John Byner and later by John Hartford.

SONG AND DANCE   NBC
7 JANUARY 1949–14 JUNE 1949   Irregularly scheduled prime-time musical series, hosted by Roberta Quinlan.

SONG AT TWILIGHT   NBC
3 JULY 1951–31 AUGUST 1951   This fifteen-minute musical series was hosted by Bob Carroll, then by Buddy Greco, and finally by Johnny Andrews. A summer replacement for John Conte's *The Little Show* and *The Roberta Quinlan Show,* the Monday-through-Friday program was produced by Richard Schneider. It was originally titled *Songs at Twilight.*

SONG SNAPSHOTS ON A SUMMER HOLIDAY   CBS
24 JUNE 1954–9 SEPTEMBER 1954   A summer replacement for *The Jane Froman Show,* this fifteen-minute musical series was cohosted by Merv Griffin and Betty Ann Grove.

SONGS FOR SALE   CBS
4 JULY 1950–1 SEPTEMBER 1950; 30 JUNE 1951–28 JUNE 1952   On this hour-long musical show compositions by amateur songwriters were performed by guest vocalists and were then judged by a panel of music business professionals. The series, which also ran on radio, was hosted by Jan Murray in 1950; Steve Allen was the host when the show returned to TV in the summer of 1951. Al Span was the producer, Bob Bleyer the director.

SONGTIME   ABC
6 OCTOBER 1951–17 MAY 1952   Jack Wyrtzen sang religious songs on this weekly show, broadcast Saturdays at 11 p.m.

THE SONNY AND CHER COMEDY HOUR   CBS
1 AUGUST 1971–5 SEPTEMBER 1971; 27 DECEMBER 1971–29 MAY 1974
THE SONNY AND CHER SHOW   CBS
1 FEBRUARY 1976–29 AUGUST 1977   *The Sonny and Cher Comedy Hour* was introduced as a summer variety show and found a place in the network's schedule in midseason. By the 1973–1974 season it was television's top-rated variety series. Unfortunately, after nine years of marriage, Sonny (born Salvatore Bono) and Cher (born Cherilyn LaPiere) were divorced in 1974, and the show came to an end. Each of them later hosted their own variety series (*The Sonny Comedy Revue* and *Cher*), neither of which was particularly successful; finally, in 1976, they were reunited, at least on camera, in *The Sonny and Cher Show,* and became the first divorced couple to cohost a variety series. The two had met in the mid-1960s, when Sonny was an occasional songwriter and studio

musician (he played percussion at many of Phil Spector's recording sessions) and Cher was an aspiring singer. Their first records, released under the name Caesar and Cleo, went nowhere, but in 1965 "I Got You Babe," released under their own names, was a smash (and subsequently became their theme song on their TV shows). After a few years of relative obscurity in the late 1960s, Sonny persevered in getting them their summer show; its freshness and slick production insured its chances of renewal. The show was produced by Chris Bearde and Allan Blye, and Cher's elaborate costumes were designed by Bob Mackie. The show also made effective use of such videotape tricks as chroma-key, a process by which one image can be superimposed upon another. Other regulars on *The Sonny and Cher Comedy Hour* included their daughter Chastity Bono, Peter Cullen, Freeman King, Teri Garr, Ted Zeigler, Billy Van, and Murray Langston (who later appeared as "The Unknown Comic" on *The Gong Show*). Nick Vanoff was the executive producer of *The Sonny and Cher Show,* and Frank Peppiatt and Phil Hahn were the producers. Regulars on that show included Ted Zeigler, the mime team of Shields and Yarnell (who later cohosted their own show), Billy Van, and Gailard Sartain. See also *Cher; The Sonny Comedy Revue.*

THE SONNY COMEDY REVUE   ABC
22 SEPTEMBER 1974–29 DECEMBER 1974   Following the breakup of his marriage to Cher, and the cancellation of *The Sonny and Cher Comedy Hour* on CBS, Sonny Bono tried to go it alone as host of a comedy hour on ABC. The effort, produced by Allan Blye and Chris Bearde (who had worked on *The Sonny and Cher Comedy Hour*), was unsuccessful. Other regulars included Freeman King, Billy Van, Ted Zeigler, Peter Cullen, Murray Langston, and Teri Garr. Sonny and Cher were later reunited on *The Sonny and Cher Show.*

THE SONNY KENDIS SHOW   CBS
18 APRIL 1949–6 JANUARY 1950   Sonny Kendis hosted this musical series, seen once or twice a week before or after the evening news. It was seen in both a ten-minute and fifteen-minute format.

SONS AND DAUGHTERS   CBS
11 SEPTEMBER 1974–6 NOVEMBER 1974   A high school drama set at Southwest High in Stockton, California, during the 1950s, *Sons and Daughters* was presumably inspired by the 1973 film *American Graffiti.* The hour series featured Gary Frank as Jeff Reed, all-American boy; Glynnis O'Connor as Anita Cramer, all-American girl, Jeff's girlfriend; Jay W. MacIntosh as Lucille Reed, Jeff's recently widowed mother; John S. Ragin as Walter Cramer, Anita's father; Jan Shutan as Ruth Cramer, Anita's mother; Michael Morgan as Danny Reed, Jeff's younger brother; Debralee Scott as Evie; Laura Siegel as Mary Anne; Scott Colomby as

Stash; Barry Livingston as Moose; Lionel Johnston as Charlie; and Christopher Nelson as Cody. David Levinson was the executive producer, and Michael Gleason the producer, for Universal Television.

SOUL! PBS
1970–1975   An hour-long variety series featuring black musicians, singers, and dancers; produced at WNET-TV, New York.

SOUL TRAIN SYNDICATED
1971–   Essentially the black counterpart of *American Bandstand, Soul Train* features a group of about seventy black teenagers who dance to the music and listen to assorted recording artists who drop by to lip-synch their newest hits. The hour series was created and is produced and hosted by Don Cornelius. The show began in 1970 as a local series in Chicago and later moved to Hollywood.

SOUND-OFF TIME NBC
14 OCTOBER 1951–6 JANUARY 1952   Half-hour comedy-variety show, with three rotating hosts: Bob Hope, Jerry Lester, and Fred Allen.

SOUNDSTAGE PBS
12 NOVEMBER 1974–   A series of hour concerts by popular musical acts, produced at WTTW-TV, Chicago.

THE SOUPY SALES SHOW ABC/SYNDICATED
4 JULY 1955–26 AUGUST 1955 (ABC); 3 OCTOBER 1959–25 JUNE 1960 (ABC); 3 DECEMBER 1960–25 MARCH 1961 (ABC); 26 JANUARY 1962– 13 APRIL 1962 (ABC); 1965–1967 (SYNDICATED); 1979 (SYNDICATED)   Soupy Sales has hosted a plethora of children's shows, both local and national. His first effort was *Soupy's On,* a local show in Detroit that began in 1953; the show caught ABC's attention, and in 1955 Sales hosted his first network program, *The Soupy Sales Show.* It originated from Detroit and was seen weekday evenings for eight weeks. Sales then headed to Los Angeles and hosted a local show there for several years before returning to network TV in the fall of 1959 with a Saturday-morning show, which lasted until 1961 (with one six-month interruption). Early in 1962 Sales hosted a Friday evening show on ABC, and in 1964 he began a daily local show in New York, which was offered in syndication a year later. In 1979 Sales again hosted a syndicated half-hour show, produced in Hollywood. All of his shows have incorporated a combination of features—jokes, puns, songs, silent films, and sketches with an assortment of puppets, including White Fang, Black Tooth, Marilyn MonWolf, Herman the Flea, and Pookie the Lion. Pie-throwing was also a regular feature—Sales no doubt holds the world's record for receiving pies in the face. Sales's offbeat humor occasionally got him in trouble; *The New York*

Times reported in January 1965 that Sales had been suspended for one week by WNEW-TV after asking his young viewers to go to their parents' wallets and send him "those little green pieces of paper." It was noted that although the incident had been intended as a joke, it could have been misinterpreted by certain members of Sales's audience.

THE SOUTHERNAIRES ABC
19 SEPTEMBER 1948–21 NOVEMBER 1948 Half-hour prime-time musical series starring a vocal quartet known as the Southernaires.

SPACE ACADEMY CBS
11 SEPTEMBER 1977–1 SEPTEMBER 1979 This half-hour Saturday-morning series was set at the Space Academy, an artificial planetoid founded in Star Year 3732 as a training school for young space explorers. Featured were Jonathan Harris as Commander Gampu, the three-hundred-year-old head of the Academy; Pamelyn Ferdin as Laura; Ty Henderson as Paul; Ric Carrott as Chris; Pam Cooper as Adrian; Brian Tochi as Tee Gai; Eric Greene as Loki, the junior cadet; and Peepo the robot. Norm Prescott and Lou Scheimer were the executive producers.

SPACE CADET
See TOM CORBETT, SPACE CADET

SPACE GHOST CBS/NBC
10 SEPTEMBER 1966–7 SEPTEMBER 1968 (CBS); 27 NOVEMBER 1976–3 SEPTEMBER 1977 (NBC) Half-hour Saturday-morning cartoon series from Hanna-Barbera Productions about a galactic hero whose magic belt rendered him invisible. Space Ghost was assisted in his exploits by two teenagers, Jan and Jayce. Gary Owens provided the voice of Space Ghost. The series ran for two seasons on CBS and returned in the fall of 1976 on NBC to replace *Land of the Lost,* where it was shown under the title *Space Ghost/Frankenstein Jr.,* and included segments of *Frankenstein Jr. and the Impossibles,* another 1966 cartoon series from Hanna-Barbera.

SPACE KIDETTES NBC
10 SEPTEMBER 1966–2 SEPTEMBER 1967 Another cartoon series from Hanna-Barbera Productions, *Space Kidettes* featured a group of teenage space rangers.

SPACE: 1999 SYNDICATED
1975–1977 Produced in England, this hour-long science fiction series told the story of the 311 inhabitants of Moonbase Alpha, a lunar space colony. As the result of a tremendous nuclear explosion (caused by the storage of radioactive wastes on the dark side of the moon), the moon—

with the surprised colonists aboard—was sent out of its orbit and careening into space. Featured were Martin Landau as Commander John Koenig; Barbara Bain as Dr. Helena Russell, research scientist; Barry Morse (1975–1976) as Professor Victor Bergman; Roy Dotrice as Commissioner Simmonds, Koenig's commanding officer, who was visiting Moonbase Alpha when the explosion occurred; Nick Tate as First Lieutenant Alan Carter; Zienia Merton as communications officer Sandra Benes; Anton Phillips as medical officer Dr. Bob Mathias; Clifton Jones (1975–1976) as David Kano; and Prentis Hancock (1975–1976) as Paul Morrow. In the fall of 1976 Catherine Schell joined the cast as Moonbase Alpha's scientific officer and resident alien, Maya, who could transform herself into any kind of creature at will; Tony Anholt also joined the cast as First Officer Tony Verdeschi. Gerry Anderson (who had previously worked on such series as *Fireball XL-5* and *Thunderbirds*) was the executive producer. Sylvia Anderson, his wife, was producer during the first season, and Fred Freiberger (who had worked on *Star Trek*) was producer during the second season.

SPACE PATROL   ABC
11 SEPTEMBER 1950–26 FEBRUARY 1955 One of the longer-running children's space shows of the early 1950s, *Space Patrol* was set in the thirtieth century. It featured Ed Kemmer as Commander Buzz Corry; Lyn Osborn as his assistant, Cadet Happy; Ken Mayer as Major Robbie Robertson; Norman Jolley as the Secretary General of the United Planets; Virginia Hewitt as Carol, the Secretary General's daughter; Nina Bara as Tonga, a onetime enemy who became an ally. *Space Patrol* began as a fifteen-minute daily series but shifted to a once-a-week, half-hour format late in 1951. Jack Narz, who later hosted several game shows, was the announcer. Mike Mosser produced the series, and Dik Darley directed.

SPACE SENTINELS
See THE YOUNG SENTINELS

SPARRING PARTNERS   ABC
8 APRIL 1949–13 MAY 1949 Prime-time game show hosted by Walter Kiernan, on which three men competed against three women in a question-and-answer format.

SPEAKEASY   SYNDICATED
1964 Host Chip Monck rapped with rock stars on this hour series.

SPECIAL AGENT 7   SYNDICATED
1958 Half-hour crime show starring Lloyd Nolan as Conroy, an agent for the Treasury Department.

SPECIAL EDITION   SYNDICATED

1977 Barbara Feldon hosted this documentary series, the segments of which were filmed versions of various nonfiction magazine articles. Alan Sloan produced the series.

SPEED BUGGY   CBS/ABC/NBC

8 SEPTEMBER 1973–30 AUGUST 1975 (CBS); 6 SEPTEMBER 1975–4 SEPTEMBER 1976 (ABC); 27 NOVEMBER 1976–3 SEPTEMBER 1977 (NBC); 28 JANUARY 1978–2 SEPTEMBER 1978 (CBS) A seemingly indestructible cartoon series from Hanna-Barbera Productions, Speed Buggy was a flying car that carried three teenage passengers: Debbie, Mark, and Tinker. Mel Blanc provided the voice of Speed Buggy.

SPEED RACER   SYNDICATED

1967 Japanese-produced cartoon series about a race-car driver.

THE SPEIDEL SHOW
See PAUL WINCHELL AND JERRY MAHONEY

SPENCER'S PILOTS   CBS

17 SEPTEMBER 1976–19 NOVEMBER 1976 An unimpressive adventure series about charter pilots working for Spencer Aviation. *Spencer's Pilots* was scheduled Fridays at 8 p.m., a slot which CBS found difficult to fill successfully for most of the 1970s. Only six episodes were televised. Featured were Gene Evans as Spencer Parish; Christopher Stone as Cass Garrett; Todd Susmàn as Stan Lewis; Margaret Impert as Linda Dann, a pilot and secretary; and Britt Leach as Mickey "Wig" Wiggins, the mechanic. The hour series was created and produced by Larry Rosen; Bob Sweeney and Edward H. Feldman were the executive producers for CBS Television.

SPIDERMAN   ABC

9 SEPTEMBER 1967–30 AUGUST 1969; 22 MARCH 1970–6 SEPTEMBER 1970 Half-hour cartoon series based on the Marvel Comics superhero, Spiderman, who in real life was Peter Parker, a college freshman who was bitten by a radioactive arachnid and who acquired the power to spin webs. The series was seen Saturday mornings for two years, and reruns were shown on Sunday mornings in 1970. In 1978 a filmed series based on the same character appeared: see *The Amazing Spider-Man.*

SPIDER-WOMAN   ABC

22 SEPTEMBER 1979–   Saturday-morning cartoon show starring Jessica Drew, editor-publisher of *Justice* magazine, who

had been bitten by a poisonous spider as a child and had been treated with an experimental serum that endowed her with arachnid powers.

THE SPIKE JONES SHOW   NBC/CBS
2 JANUARY 1954–8 MAY 1954 (NBC); 2 APRIL 1957–27 AUGUST 1957 (CBS); 1 AUGUST 1960–19 SEPTEMBER 1960 (CBS); 17 JULY 1961–25 SEPTEMBER 1961 (CBS) Bandleader Spike Jones hosted several half-hour comedy-variety shows; all of them featured Jones, singer Helen Grayco (his wife), and Jones's band, The City Slickers. Born Lindley Armstrong Jones, the bandleader injected a great deal of humor and slapstick into his shows—unusual musical instruments and pies in the face were commonplace. Jones is perhaps best remembered for his recording of "Der Führer's Face," popular during World War II.

SPIN THE PICTURE   DUMONT
25 JUNE 1949–4 FEBRUARY 1950 Kathi Norris hosted this early game show on which telephone calls were placed to home viewers, who were then given the opportunity to identify a celebrity from a rapidly revolving photograph. The hour series replaced a similar game show called *Cut.*

SPIN-OFF   CBS
16 JUNE 1975–5 SEPTEMBER 1975 Jim Lange was the host of this short-lived daytime game show, on which the contestants played an automated version of poker. Nick Nicholson and E. Roger Muir were the executive producers.

SPLIT PERSONALITY   NBC
28 SEPTEMBER 1959–5 FEBRUARY 1960 Tom Poston hosted this daytime game show from Goodson-Todman Productions. Contestants attempted to identify celebrities from clues read by the host.

SPLIT SECOND   ABC
20 MARCH 1972–27 JUNE 1975 Tom Kennedy hosted this fast-moving daytime quiz show. Each day three contestants competed for money; a player won a greater sum if he or she was the only person to answer a particular question correctly. At the end of the show the top money winner chose one of five automobiles that were on display; if the car started (only one of them did), the contestant won it. If not, the contestant returned the following day to compete again (if the same contestant won the second day, one of the five cars would be eliminated; thus, a contestant who won five shows automatically received a car). Stu Billet was the executive producer for Stefan Hatos–Monty Hall Productions.

THE SPORTS CAMERA   ABC
12 SEPTEMBER 1950–14 JUNE 1952 Half-hour series of sports films.

SPORTS CHALLENGE   SYNDICATED
1971–1973 Dick Enberg hosted this sports quiz show, which featured two 3-member teams composed of athletes.

SPORTS CLUB   SYNDICATED
1958 Sports interview show hosted by former pro football star Elroy "Crazy Legs" Hirsch.

SPORTS FOCUS   ABC
3 JUNE 1957–12 SEPTEMBER 1958 Monday-through-Friday sports commentary show, hosted by Howard Cosell.

SPORTSMEN'S QUIZ   CBS
26 APRIL 1948–2 MAY 1949 This five-minute, once-a-week sports quiz was sponsored by *Sports Afield* magazine.

SPORTSWOMAN OF THE WEEK
See GIRL OF THE WEEK

SPORTSWORLD   NBC
22 JANUARY 1978–   *SportsWorld* is the umbrella title for NBC's weekend sports anthology series, similar in concept to *ABC's Wide World of Sports*.

SPOTLIGHT   CBS
4 JULY 1967–29 AUGUST 1967 This Tuesday-night summer variety hour had no regulars, other than the Lionel Blair Dancers and the Jack Parnell Orchestra. It was taped in London and produced and directed by Jon Scoffield.

SPOTLIGHT ON SPORTS   NBC
8 JULY 1950–3 SEPTEMBER 1950 Bill Stern hosted this half-hour prime-time sports-interview show. During its later weeks the show was titled *The Bill Stern Show*.

THE SQUARE WORLD OF ED BUTLER   SYNDICATED
1970 Half-hour talk show hosted by Ed Butler.

STACCATO   NBC/ABC
10 SEPTEMBER 1959–24 MARCH 1960 (NBC); 27 MARCH 1960–25 SEPTEMBER 1960 (ABC) John Cassavetes starred in this half-hour crime show as New York private eye Johnny Staccato, a former jazz pianist. Also featured was Eduardo Ciannelli as Waldo, owner of the club where Staccato usually hung out. Panned by most critics as an imitation *Peter Gunn* (perhaps with a touch of *Pete Kelly's Blues* thrown in), *Staccato*

was dropped in midseason by NBC; ABC then showed reruns for twenty-six weeks.

STAGE A NUMBER

DUMONT

10 SEPTEMBER 1952–20 MAY 1953 This prime-time talent program showcased not only aspiring performers, but also fledgling writers, directors, choreographers, and other backstage people. The two best presentations, as selected by a celebrity panel, were invited to return to the show the following week. Bill Wendell hosted the series, and Roger Gerry produced it.

STAGE DOOR

CBS

7 FEBRUARY 1950–28 MARCH 1950 This short-lived Tuesday-night half-hour series starred Louise Allbritton as an aspiring actress and also featured Scott McKay and Tom Pedi. It was produced by Carol Irwin and directed by Barry Kroeger.

STAGE ENTRANCE

DUMONT

2 MAY 1951–2 MARCH 1952 Columnist Earl Wilson hosted this fifteen-minute variety and interview series; it was produced by Tod Hammerstein and directed by Bill Seaman.

STAGE 7

CBS

30 JANUARY 1955–25 SEPTEMBER 1955 An undistinguished half-hour dramatic anthology series. Don Rickles played his first TV dramatic role on one show, "A Note of Fear," broadcast 15 May. Warren Lewis produced the series.

STAGE SHOW

CBS

3 JULY 1954–18 SEPTEMBER 1954; 1 OCTOBER 1955–22 SEPTEMBER 1956 *Stage Show* was a musical variety series cohosted by bandleaders Tommy and Jimmy Dorsey. It was introduced, in an hour format, in 1954 as a summer replacement for *The Jackie Gleason Show* (Gleason was its executive producer). Gleason resurrected the show in the fall of 1955, trimmed it to thirty minutes, and scheduled it immediately preceding his own show on Saturdays (Gleason, too, cut back to a half-hour format that season, as he had decided to do only *The Honeymooners,* instead of a full-hour variety show). Jack Carter, who guested frequently on the show, became the permanent emcee early in 1956 in an effort to boost ratings. It was on *Stage Show* that Elvis Presley, barely twenty-one, made his first national television appearances. Elvis first appeared on the show 28 January 1956, performing "Blue Suede Shoes" and "Heartbreak Hotel" (his first record for RCA); public reaction was strong, and Presley made five more appearances on *Stage Show* over the following eight weeks.

STAGE 13   CBS
19 APRIL 1950–28 JUNE 1950   Wyllis Cooper produced and directed
this suspense anthology series.

STAGE TWO REVUE   ABC
30 JULY 1950–24 SEPTEMBER 1950   Half-hour Sunday-night variety series, hosted by Georgia Lee.

STAGECOACH WEST   ABC
4 OCTOBER 1960–26 SEPTEMBER 1961   This hour-long western borrowed heavily from *Wagon Train* and *Overland Trail*. It featured Wayne
Rogers as stagecoach driver Luke Perry; Robert Bray as driver Simon
Kane; and Richard Eyer as Simon's young son, Davey.

STAINED GLASS WINDOWS   ABC
26 SEPTEMBER 1948–2 OCTOBER 1949   ABC's first religious program,
Stained Glass Windows was a filmed-series broadcast for fifteen or thirty
minutes on Sunday evenings.

STAND BY FOR CRIME   ABC
22 JANUARY 1949–27 AUGUST 1949   Thirty-minute murder mysteries
were presented on this series; at the climax of the show a guest "detective" tried to guess the identity of the killer. Telephone calls from home
viewers were also aired during the show. The series was produced in Chicago by Greg Garrison.

STAND UP AND BE COUNTED   CBS
28 MAY 1956–6 SEPTEMBER 1957   On this unusual daytime audience
participation show, preselected guests appeared and related a problem to
the studio audience. Possible solutions to the problem were then suggested by members of the studio audience, who strode to the "rail of justice"
to air their views. The entire audience then voted on the best solution
propounded by the panel. One of television's few twenty-minute series,
Stand Up and Be Counted was hosted by Bob Russell.

STAND UP AND CHEER   SYNDICATED
1971   On this half-hour musical series host Johnny Mann, together with
the Johnny Mann Singers and assorted guests, sang the praises of the
good old U.S.A.

STANLEY   NBC
24 SEPTEMBER 1956–11 MARCH 1957   Buddy Hackett starred in this
half-hour sitcom as Stanley, manager of a newsstand at a New York hotel. Also featured were Carol Burnett as Celia, his girlfriend; Frederic To-
zere as Mr. Phillips, manager of the hotel; Tom Pedi; and Danny Dayton.

Produced and directed by Max Liebman, the show was broadcast live from New York; the premiere episode was written by Billy Friedberg and Neil Simon.

STAR BLAZER
SYNDICATED

1979   A fifty-two-part series of half-hour cartoon shows made in Japan and set in outer space. The series was shown in Japan under the title *Space Cruiser Yamato*.

STAR NIGHT
NBC

25 FEBRUARY 1951–2 SEPTEMBER 1951   Bill Stern and Candy Jones co-hosted this half-hour audience participation and variety series.

STAR OF THE FAMILY
CBS

22 SEPTEMBER 1950–26 JUNE 1952   The celebrity guests who appeared on this half-hour variety show were supposedly "nominated" by letters submitted by members of their families. Morton Downey hosted the series during the 1950–1951 season, and Peter Lind Hayes and Mary Healy were the cohosts during the 1951–1952 season.

STAR STAGE
NBC

8 SEPTEMBER 1955–7 SEPTEMBER 1956   A Friday-night half-hour filmed dramatic anthology series of little note. Louise Beavers and Betty Grable costarred in one presentation, "Cleopatra Collins," broadcast 9 March.

STAR TIME
DUMONT

5 SEPTEMBER 1950–27 FEBRUARY 1951   An hour-long variety series co-hosted by Frances Langford and Don Ameche, also featuring the Benny Goodman Sextet and Lew Parker.

STAR TONIGHT
ABC

3 FEBRUARY 1955–9 AUGUST 1956   The format of this half-hour dramatic anthology series was similar to that of *Hollywood Screen Test*—each week an unknown actor was teamed up with established professionals. Jacqueline Holt, for example, was showcased on the premiere. The series was produced by Harry Herrmann and was broadcast live from New York in 1955; by 1956 the series was filmed.

STAR TREK
NBC

8 SEPTEMBER 1966–2 SEPTEMBER 1969   One of the few series to prove more popular in syndication than in its three-year network run, *Star Trek* acquired a fiercely loyal cult following. Its devoted fans were almost certainly responsible for securing the show's renewal for a third season on

NBC, and later wrote more than one million letters to the network protesting its cancellation. Surprisingly, the fans (commonly known as "Trekkies") remained loyal as the reruns went into syndication; several fans' conventions have been held, and more *Star Trek* merchandise has been sold during the 1970s than during the late 1960s. For these reasons, *Star Trek* should probably be considered television's most popular adult science fiction series. Set in the twenty-second century aboard the starship *Enterprise, Star Trek*'s voyagers were commissioned by the United Federation of Planets to embark on a five-year mission to "seek out new life and new civilizations." Many of the seventy-eight episodes stressed the differences between humankind, an obviously imperfect but essentially noble species, and the other life forms, which ranged from gaseous beings to remarkably similar humanoids.

Though the *Enterprise* was designed to be staffed by a crew of 400, there were only eight principals in the cast: William Shatner as Captain James Kirk; Leonard Nimoy as Science Officer Spock, an extremely intelligent but coldly unemotional creature born of a Vulcanian father and an Earthling mother; DeForest Kelley as Dr. Leonard "Bones" McCoy, the medical officer; James Doohan as Montgomery Scott (Scotty), the chief engineer; Nichelle Nichols as Lieutenant Uhura, the communications officer; George Takei as Mr. Sulu, one of the navigators; Majel Barrett as Christine Chapel, chief nurse; and Walter Koenig (1967–1969) as Ensign Chekov, another navigator. During the first season Grace Lee Whitney was occasionally featured as Yeoman Janice Rand. *Star Trek* was created by Gene Roddenberry, who also served as executive producer. Gene Coon was the first producer and was succeeded by John Meredyth Lucas and Fred Freiberger. Special effects (which Roddenberry wisely refrained from overemphasizing) were created by the Howard Anderson Company, Film Effects of Hollywood, John Rugg, and the Westheimer Company. The pilot for the series (which starred Jeffrey Hunter as Captain Pike) was never televised in its entirety, though footage from it was used on a two-part episode, "The Menagerie." In 1973 an animated version of the series was introduced: see below.

STAR TREK NBC

8 SEPTEMBER 1973–30 AUGUST 1975 The Saturday-morning cartoon version of the 1966–1969 science fiction series (see above) featured the voices of seven of *Star Trek*'s principals: William Shatner, Leonard Nimoy, DeForest Kelly, Nichelle Nichols, George Takei, Majel Barrett, and James Doohan. Many of the episodes were based on stories originally televised on the prime-time show. Norm Prescott and Lou Scheimer produced the half-hour series.

THE STARLAND VOCAL BAND SHOW CBS

31 JULY 1977–2 SEPTEMBER 1977 A limited-run half-hour variety se-

ries hosted by the Starland Vocal Band (Bill Danoff, Taffy Danoff, Jon Carroll, and Margot Chapman) and taped on location at several sites, including Washington, D.C. Additional regulars included Phil Proctor and Peter Bergman (formerly of the Firesign Theater), Washington satirist Mark Russell, Jeff Altman, and Dave Letterman. The Starland Vocal Band was given the summer series primarily on the strong showing of one hit record, "Afternoon Delight." Jerry Weintraub was the executive producer, and Al Rogers was the producer.

STARLIGHT THEATER   CBS
2 APRIL 1950–4 OCTOBER 1951   A half-hour dramatic anthology series produced by Robert Stevens and directed by John Peyser. During the 1950–1951 season it alternated biweekly with *The Burns and Allen Show*.

STARLIT TIME   DUMONT
9 APRIL 1950–19 NOVEMBER 1950   This Sunday-night musical revue was the successor to *Front Row Center* and retained many of its regulars. *Starlit Time* featured Phil Hanna, Bill Williams, Allen Prescott, Gordon Dillworth, Bibi Osterwald, Holly Harris, and the Cy Coleman Trio. Bela Lugosi made a very rare guest appearance on the show (21 May).

STARLOST   SYNDICATED
1973   Created by Harlan Ellison and produced in Canada, this hour-long science fiction series was set in the twenty-eighth century. Traveling through space in a large spacecraft were the three principals: Keir Dullea as Devon, Gay Rowan as Rachel (Devon's beloved), and Robin Ward as Garth (the man who had intended to marry Rachel).

STARRING BORIS KARLOFF   ABC
22 SEPTEMBER 1949–15 DECEMBER 1949   Boris Karloff hosted and occasionally starred in this half-hour mystery anthology series, which was directed by Alex Segal.

STARS IN KHAKI AND BLUE   NBC
13 SEPTEMBER 1952–27 SEPTEMBER 1952   Wendy Barrie hosted this prime-time talent show for members of the Armed Forces. Craig G. Allen directed the half-hour series.

STARS OF JAZZ   ABC
18 APRIL 1958–30 NOVEMBER 1958   Half-hour musical series, hosted by trumpeter Bobby Troup, and featuring guest artists from the world of jazz.

STARS ON PARADE   DUMONT
4 NOVEMBER 1953–30 JUNE 1954   Half-hour prime-time variety show

featuring talent from the armed forces, as well as civilian acts. Don Russell was the first host of the show, but was succeeded by Bobby Sherwood on the third telecast.

STARS OVER HOLLYWOOD   NBC
6 SEPTEMBER 1950–29 AUGUST 1951 This half-hour filmed dramatic anthology series was seen on Wednesday nights.

STARSKY AND HUTCH   ABC
10 SEPTEMBER 1975–21 AUGUST 1979 A popular, and comparatively violent, hour-long crime show about a pair of undercover cops. With Paul Michael Glaser as Dave Starsky; David Soul as his partner, Ken Hutchinson; Bernie Hamilton as their commanding officer, Captain Harold Dobey; and Antonio Fargas as their street contact, Huggy Bear. William Blinn created the series, and Aaron Spelling and Leonard Goldberg were the executive producers.

STATE TROOPER   SYNDICATED
1957 Half-hour crime show starring Rod Cameron as Nevada State Trooper Rod Blake. Much of the series was filmed in Las Vegas.

STEP THIS WAY   ABC/SYNDICATED
9 JULY 1955–14 APRIL 1956 (ABC); 1966 (SYNDICATED) *Step This Way* was a half-hour dance contest. The 1955 version was hosted by Bobby Sherwood and featured the Nat Brandwynne Orchestra. The 1966 version was hosted by Gretchen Wyler and featured singer Jim Lucas; music was supplied by Warren Covington and his band, and later by Ray McKinley and his band.

STEVE ALLEN PRESENTS   NBC
STEVE LAWRENCE AND EYDIE GORMÉ
13 JULY 1958–31 AUGUST 1958 Steve Lawrence and Eydie Gormé, who had been featured vocalists on Steve Allen's *Tonight* show, were given their own series in 1958, a summer replacement for Steve Allen's Sunday-night variety show. Also featured were Gene Rayburn, the Artie Malvin Singers, and the Jack Kane Orchestra.

THE STEVE ALLEN SHOW   CBS/NBC/ABC/SYNDICATED
25 DECEMBER 1950–22 FEBRUARY 1952 (CBS); 17 JULY 1952–28 AUGUST 1952 (CBS); 24 JUNE 1956–6 JUNE 1960 (NBC); 27 SEPTEMBER 1961–27 DECEMBER 1961 (ABC); 1962–1964 (SYNDICATED); 14 JUNE 1967–16 AUGUST 1967 (CBS); 1967–1969 (SYNDICATED); 1976 (SYNDICATED) Steve Allen is not only one of the busiest performers in television, but he is also one of the most versatile people in show business.

In addition to hosting several TV series, he has also starred in films (*The Benny Goodman Story*), on Broadway (*The Pink Elephant*), and in summer stock (*The Fourposter*), has written at least a dozen books and several television scripts, has composed hundreds of songs (to win a bet with singer Frankie Laine, he once "composed" 350 songs in one week), has played several musical instruments, and has had time left over to deliver an occasional lecture or do a little sculpture.

In 1948 Allen was working at KNX radio in Los Angeles, where his late-night radio show began to attract a studio audience and unscheduled visits by celebrities; it was here that Allen first began to interview members of the studio audience, a device he has continued to use effectively in most of his TV shows. Allen also hosted a radio giveaway show, *Earn Your Vacation* (Johnny Carson would later emcee the TV version). In 1950 he was brought East to New York for the first of his TV shows. *The Steve Allen Show* began as an evening show, broadcast Mondays through Fridays at 7 p.m. After thirteen weeks he moved to a daytime slot, and the show remained on the air for another year; the show was directed by Fred Kelly, and in 1952 featured singer Peggy Lee, announcer Bern Bennett, and a llama named Llemuel. By the time the daytime show left the air, Allen had substituted for Arthur Godfrey on *Talent Scouts* and had hosted a prime-time musical show, *Songs for Sale*. During the summer of 1952 he hosted a prime-time half-hour show on alternate Thursdays. In 1953 he hosted *Talent Patrol* on ABC and later began a local late-night talk show; in the summer of 1954 Allen's local show went network, and the *Tonight* show was born.

The nightly pace of the *Tonight* show did not seem to slow Allen down, however. In the summer of 1956 he agreed to host a variety show opposite *The Ed Sullivan Show* on Sunday nights. The second *Steve Allen Show* premiered on 24 June, with guests Kim Novak, Sammy Davis, Jr., Dane Clark, Wally Cox, Vincent Price, and Bambi Linn and Rod Alexander. Elvis Presley also appeared that summer, and Allen's use of big name guest stars provoked a long-running feud between Sullivan and Allen. Though both shows were variety hours, the difference between them was considerable, as Allen's hour emphasized humor. Allen assembled a talented group of young funny men, who appeared in the well-remembered "Man in the Street" sequences and in the other comedy sketches. Over the years the group included Don Knotts, Tom Poston, Louis Nye, Gabe Dell, Pat Harrington, Jr., Dayton Allen, Cal Howard, and Bill Dana. Allen's writers at the time included Leonard Stern, Stan Burns, Herb Sargent, Bill Dana, Don Hinkley, Arne Sultan, and Marvin Worth.

Though the Sunday-night show rarely outdrew Sullivan's show on a weekly basis, it did succeed in making a significant dent in Sullivan's ratings; *The Ed Sullivan Show* slipped from the second top-rated show during the 1956–1957 season to the nineteenth during the next season. Allen, who gave up his *Tonight* show hosting chores early in 1957, later took his variety show to the West Coast; during the 1959–1960 season the show was seen on Monday nights.

After a season's absence Allen returned to TV, this time on ABC. *The New Steve Allen Show* was a lot like the old Steve Allen show and featured Louis Nye, Don Knotts, Pat Harrington, Jr., Gabe Dell, and Dayton Allen; slotted on Wednesdays opposite *Wagon Train,* it was gone in thirteen weeks. A year later Allen returned to the talk-show format, hosting a daily ninety-minute show for Westinghouse; in many markets the show was scheduled opposite the *Tonight* show that Allen had started eight years earlier (Johnny Carson had since taken over as host). Allen later hosted *I've Got A Secret* for three seasons, and in the summer of 1967 he emceed *The Steve Allen Comedy Hour;* that series featured Jayne Meadows (Steve's wife), Louis Nye, Ruth Buzzi, John Byner, Ron Carey, and the Terry Gibbs Band. Toward the end of 1967 he again hosted a syndicated, ninety-minute talk show. He later hosted a series of musical performances for educational television, *The Sounds of Summer,* and in 1972 he presided over the short-lived syndicated revival of *I've Got a Secret.* In 1976 he again returned to the syndication arena as the host of *Steve Allen's Laughback;* on that ninety-minute show Allen, Jayne Meadows, and guests reminisced over kinescopes and film clips of Allen's old shows. Allen also wrote and hosted a series for PBS, *Meeting of Minds,* a kind of historical talk show on which actors, appearing as historical figures from different eras, discussed issues. See also *I've Got A Secret; Songs for Sale; Talent Patrol; Tonight;* and *What's My Line?*

STEVE CANYON NBC
13 SEPTEMBER 1958–8 SEPTEMBER 1959   Steve Canyon, the fearless Air Force pilot created by cartoonist Milton Caniff in 1948, came to life for one season. Produced by David Haft and Michael Meshekoff, the half-hour series was set at Big Thunder Air Force Base and starred Dean Fredericks (who actually resembled the cartoon prototype) as Lieutenant Colonel Stevenson B. Canyon. Jerry Paris was occasionally seen as Major Willie Williston, and Abel Fernandez appeared as Police Chief Hagedorn.

STEVE DONOVAN, WESTERN MARSHAL SYNDICATED
1955   Half-hour western set in Wyoming during the 1870s, with Doug Kennedy as Marshal Steve Donovan and Eddy Waller as his young sidekick, Rusty Lee. The series was also shown under the title *Western Marshal.*

THE STEVE LAWRENCE AND EYDIE GORMÉ SHOW
See STEVE ALLEN PRESENTS STEVE LAWRENCE AND EYDIE GORMÉ

THE STEVE LAWRENCE SHOW

CBS

13 SEPTEMBER 1965–13 DECEMBER 1965   Steve Lawrence's Monday-night variety hour lasted only thirteen weeks. Other regulars included comics Charles Nelson Reilly and Betty Walker, the Pussycat Dancers, the Dick Williams Singers, and the Joe Guercio Orchestra. The series was taped principally in New York.

STINGRAY

SYNDICATED

1965   Stingray was another of the half-hour puppet adventure shows produced in England by Gerry and Sylvia Anderson (creators of *Fireball XL-5, Supercar,* and *Thunderbirds*); all utilized a process known as Su-permarionation. *Stingray* was set aboard a futuristic submarine, whose crew battled the usual assortment of wrongdoers, despots, and invaders.

STOCK CAR DERBY

NBC

28 JANUARY 1950–11 MARCH 1950   This late-night series offered cover-age of the races from the Kingsbridge Armory in the Bronx; Herb Shel-don provided the commentary.

STOCKARD CHANNING IN JUST FRIENDS
See JUST FRIENDS

STONEY BURKE

ABC

1 OCTOBER 1962–2 SEPTEMBER 1963   One of two modern-day westerns introduced in 1962 (*Wide Country* was the other), Stoney Burke starred Jack Lord in the title role as a rodeo performer. Also featured were Bruce Dern as E. J. Stocker; Bill Hart as Red; Warren Oates as Ves Painter; and Robert Dowdell as Cody Bristol. Leslie Stevens produced the hour-long series for Daystar Productions.

STOP ME IF YOU'VE HEARD THIS ONE

NBC

5 MARCH 1948–22 APRIL 1949   Half-hour game show, based on the ra-dio program, on which celebrity panelists tried to supply punch lines to jokes submitted by home viewers. Ira Skutch produced the show, which was hosted first by Ted Brown, and later by Leon Janney. Panelists in-cluded Lew Lahr, Morey Amsterdam, Cal Tinney, Mae Questel, and Benny Rubin.

STOP THE MUSIC

ABC

5 MAY 1949–24 APRIL 1952; 7 SEPTEMBER 1954–14 JUNE 1956   A prime-time game show, *Stop the Music* came to television a year after it began on radio. For most of its run it was hosted by Bert Parks, though Dennis James filled in occasionally. The game involved identification of songs by members of the studio audience and by home viewers, who were telephoned during the broadcast. Featured vocalists over the years in-

cluded Kay Armen, Jimmy Blaine, Betty Ann Grove, Estelle Loring, Jaye P. Morgan, and June Valli; rounding out the group of regulars were dancers Sonja and Courtney Van Horne, cartoonist Chuck Luchsinger, and the orchestra of Harry Salter. Louis G. Cowan, who later developed *The $64,000 Question,* packaged the half-hour series.

THE STOREFRONT LAWYERS (MEN AT LAW) CBS
16 SEPTEMBER 1970–1 SEPTEMBER 1971 This hour-long dramatic series began with three stars: Robert Foxworth as David Hanson, Sheila Larken as Deborah Sullivan, and David Arkin as Gabe Kaye. The three were members of a Los Angeles law firm but also operated Neighborhood Legal Services, a nonprofit law clinic. In midseason the format was changed slightly, the show was retitled *Men at Law,* and Gerald S. O'Loughlin was added as attorney Devlin McNeil, a senior partner at Horton, Troy, McNeil, and Carroll. Leonard Freeman was the executive producer.

STORIES OF THE CENTURY SYNDICATED
1954 Half-hour western about a pair of detectives for the Southwestern Railroad. With Jim Davis as Matt Clark; Mary Castle as his first partner, Frankie Adams; Kristine Miller as his second partner, Jonesy. *Stories of the Century* was one of the first syndicated series to win a major Emmy award; it was named the best western or adventure series of 1954.

THE STORK CLUB CBS/ABC
7 JULY 1950–31 OCTOBER 1953 (CBS); 11 SEPTEMBER 1954–24 JULY 1955 (ABC) Sherman Billingsley hosted this variety show, set at The Stork Club, a fictional bistro; Billingsley, who also produced the series, appeared as its proprietor. Peter Lind Hayes and Mary Healy were also featured in the early weeks. *The Stork Club* began as a fifteen-minute show and was first telecast five nights a week. In January 1951 it was cut back to twice weekly, and in the fall of 1952 it became a once-a-week, half-hour show.

STORY FOR AMERICANS CBS
6 JULY 1952–2 NOVEMBER 1952 A Sunday-afternoon anthology series that dramatized incidents from American history.

THE STORY OF ... SYNDICATED
1962 A half-hour anthology series from David Wolper Productions and United Artists, *The Story Of* . . . was advertised as a "semidocumentary." John Willis narrated the filmed series.

STORY THEATER

DUMONT/NBC

24 NOVEMBER 1950–11 MAY 1951 (DUMONT); 24 JUNE 1951–17 SEPTEMBER 1951 (NBC)   Half-hour filmed dramatic anthology series.

STORY THEATRE

SYNDICATED

1971   *Story Theatre* was an unusual anthology series, based on the Broadway show of the same title. The half-hour show featured a large repertory company, the members of which acted out various fables, parables, and other stories. Paul Sills directed both the stage and the television versions; the series was taped in British Columbia. Among the members of the repertory company who went on to appear in other series were Peter Bonerz (*The Bob Newhart Show*), Paul Sand (*Friends and Lovers*), and Richard Schaal (*Phyllis*).

THE STORYBOOK SQUARES

NBC

4 JANUARY 1969–30 AUGUST 1969   *The Storybook Squares* was a children's edition of *The Hollywood Squares;* the Saturday-morning show was hosted by Peter Marshall. The principal difference was that the nine celebrity panelists were costumed on *The Storybook Squares.*

STRAIGHTAWAY

ABC

6 OCTOBER 1961–4 JULY 1962   This half-hour adventure series starred Brian Kelly as Scott Ross and John Ashley as Clipper Hamilton, the partners who ran the Straightaway Garage, an exclusive garage for race car drivers and other exciting people. The series was beset with production problems, having gone through three producers before the first episode was televised; Joe Shaftel was the fourth producer.

STRANGE PARADISE

SYNDICATED

1969   One of television's few syndicated serials, *Strange Paradise* was an imitation of *Dark Shadows.* Set at Maljardin Island, a mysterious Caribbean isle, its story lines dealt with voodoo, communication with spirits, and family curses. The cast included: Colin Fox as Jean Paul Desmond, owner of Desmond Hall, and as Jacques Eloi Des Mondes, an ancestor; Tudi Wiggins as his wife, Erica Desmond, who died—once—and returned to life; Dawn Greenhalgh as Erica's sister, Dr. Alison Carr, a visitor to Maljardin; Jon Granik as Dan Forrest; Bruce Gray as artist Tim Stanton; Sylvia Feigel as Holly Marshall; Paisley Maxwell as Holly's mother, Elizabeth Marshall; Dan MacDonald as Reverend Matt Dawson; Costee Lee as Raxl, an island priestess; Kurt Schiegl as Quito; Patricia Collins as Huaco; Peg Dixon as Ada; Pat Moffat as Irene; Jack Creley as Laslo; Lucy Warner as Emily; David Wells as Cort; and Neil Dainard as Philip. Videotaped in color, the half-hour series was produced in Canada.

STRANGE REPORT NBC

8 JANUARY 1971–10 SEPTEMBER 1971 British import about a trio of criminologists, with Anthony Quayle as widower Adam Strange; Kaz Garas as Ham Gynt; and Anneke Wills as Evelyn McClain. The hour series was a midseason replacement for *Bracken's World*.

STRANGE STORIES SYNDICATED

1956 Edward Arnold hosted this half-hour anthology series of supernatural tales.

THE STRANGER DUMONT

25 JUNE 1954–11 FEBRUARY 1955 Frank Telford produced and directed this half-hour series, which is reminiscent of *The Millionaire*. It starred Bob Carroll as The Stranger, a mysterious individual who appeared each week to help someone in distress.

THE STRAUSS FAMILY ABC

5 MAY 1973–16 JUNE 1973 ABC imported this seven-part series from England. It traced the lives of the famous composers over a seventy-five-year period. Principal players included: Eric Woolfe as Johann Strauss, Sr.; Anne Stallybrass as Anna, his wife; Stuart Wilson as Johann Strauss, Jr.; Barbara Ferris as Emilie; Derek Jacobi as Lanner; Lynn Farleigh as Adele; and Tony Anholt as Eduard.

STRAWHAT MATINEE NBC

25 JUNE 1951–7 SEPTEMBER 1951 A summer replacement for *The Kate Smith Show*, *Strawhat Matinee* was broadcast from Cincinnati and featured country-and-western music. Principal vocalists included Mel Martin, Rosemary Olberding, and Dick and Pat.

THE STRAWHATTERS DUMONT

27 MAY 1953–9 SEPTEMBER 1953; 23 JUNE 1954–8 SEPTEMBER 1954 Johnny Olsen hosted this summer variety show, broadcast from Palisades Park, New Jersey. The half-hour series was produced by Roger Gerry and directed by Frank Bunetta.

STREET PEOPLE SYNDICATED

1971 A half-hour series with almost no format—host Mal Sharpe merely interviewed people, or asked them to tell jokes or sing or whatever; the show was filmed on location throughout the United States.

STREETS OF DANGER

See THE LONE WOLF

THE STREETS OF SAN FRANCISCO   ABC

16 SEPTEMBER 1972–23 JUNE 1977   This hour-long crime show was filmed entirely on location in San Francisco. It starred Karl Malden as Detective Lieutenant Mike Stone, a streetwise veteran; Michael Douglas as his young partner, Inspector Steve Keller; and Lee Harris as Lieutenant Lessing. Michael Douglas left the show at the outset of the 1976–1977 season (it was explained that he had decided to pursue a teaching career), and Richard Hatch was added in the fall of 1976 as Stone's new partner, Inspector Dan Robbins. The series was developed by Edward Hume and was based on a novel by Carolyn Weston. Quinn Martin was the executive producer.

STRIKE IT RICH   CBS

7 MAY 1951–3 JANUARY 1958   *Strike It Rich*, which began on radio in 1947, was a game show not unlike *Queen for a Day*. Each day a succession of needy people came on; whoever told the most woeful story (as determined by the studio audience) was the day's winner. The show also featured a perfunctory quiz segment, and the "Heart Line," where viewers could call in with offers of aid for any of the contestants. The show aroused the wrath of the New York City Welfare Department early in 1954, when it was disclosed that in 1953 some fifty-five families had come to New York, hoping to get on the show, and had remained in New York and gone on welfare. *Strike It Rich* was hosted by Warren Hull; the daytime version of the half-hour series ran from May 1951 to January 1958, while a nighttime version was broadcast between July 1951 and January 1955. Walt Framer was the producer.

STRUCK BY LIGHTNING   CBS

19 SEPTEMBER 1979–3 OCTOBER 1979   A short-lived sitcom that was pulled from the air after only three showings, *Struck By Lightning* was set at the Brightwater Inn in Maine, where Frankenstein's monster worked as the handyman. The half-hour series featured Jeffrey Kramer as Ted Stein, a science teacher from Boston who inherited the inn from his late grandfather and subsequently learned that he was a descendant of *the* Frankensteins; Jack Elam as Frank, the 231-year-old monster; Millie Slavin as Nora, who worked at the inn and had expected to inherit it; Bill Erwin as Glenn, one of the inn's guests; Jeff Cotler as Brian, Nora's young son; and Richard Stahl as Walt Calvin, the local realtor. Arthur Fellows and Terry Keegan were the executive producers.

STRYKER OF SCOTLAND YARD   SYNDICATED

1957   Half-hour crime show from England, starring Clifford Evans as Inspector Robert Stryker of Scotland Yard.

THE STU ERWIN SHOW   ABC

21 OCTOBER 1950–13 APRIL 1955   One of TV's first filmed sitcoms, *The Stu Erwin Show* helped set the pace for dozens of comedies to come—it featured a bumbling father, his loving and level-headed wife, and two irrepressible kids. Stu Erwin (playing himself) starred as the principal of Hamilton High School. Also on hand were June Collyer (Erwin's real-life wife and Bud Collyer's sister) as his wife, June Erwin; Ann Todd and Merry Anders as their older daughter, Joyce; Sheila James as their younger daughter, Jackie; Martin Milner as Joyce's boyfriend (and husband in the final season), Jimmy Clark; and Willie Best as Willie, the Erwins' handyman. Produced by Hal Roach, Jr., the half-hour series was aired under several other titles during its network run and later in syndication—*Life with the Erwins, The New Stu Erwin Show,* and *The Trouble with Father.*

STUDIO 57   DUMONT/SYNDICATED

21 SEPTEMBER 1954–26 JULY 1955 (DUMONT); 1955–1956 (SYNDICATED)   A half-hour dramatic anthology series from Revue Studios.

STUDIO ONE   CBS

7 NOVEMBER 1948–29 SEPTEMBER 1958   *Studio One* was one of the oldest, and most highly acclaimed, of the several dramatic anthology series that comprised television's "Golden Age." The hour-long series was produced by Worthington "Tony" Miner from 1948 until 1952, and was later produced by Herbert Brodkin. Many directors worked on *Studio One* at one time or another, but Franklin Schaffner and Paul Nickell, who alternated biweekly during part of the show's ten-year-run, were especially closely associated with it. Other prominent directors who were involved with *Studio One* included Yul Brynner, George Roy Hill, Sidney Lumet, and Robert Mulligan. *Studio One* was broadcast live from New York until January of 1958, when production shifted to the West Coast (and the show was retitled *Studio One in Hollywood*); the show left the air a few months later. A sampling of the many presentations from *Studio One* would include: "The Storm," with Margaret Sullavan (7 November 1948); a 1949 production of "Mary Poppins," with Mary Wickes, E. G. Marshall, and Valerie Cossart; "Of Human Bondage," with Charlton Heston and Felicia Montealegre (Maugham's story was adapted by Sumner Locke Elliott, and broadcast 21 November 1949); "The Rockingham Tea Set," with Grace Kelly (23 January 1950); "The Taming of the Shrew," with Charlton Heston and Lisa Kirk (5 June 1950); "Macbeth," with Charlton Heston and Judith Evelyn (22 October 1951); "The Kill," with Grace Kelly (22 September 1952); "The Laugh Maker," with Jackie Gleason (18 May 1953, in a rare dramatic appearance); "Sentence of Death," with James Dean (in one of his first major TV roles, broadcast 17 August 1953 on *Summer Studio One*); "A Handful of Diamonds," with

Lorne Greene (in his first major TV role, 19 April 1954); "Sue Ellen," with Inger Stevens (in her first major TV role, 9 August 1954); Reginald Rose's "Twelve Angry Men," with Edward Arnold, John Beal, Walter Abel, Bart Burns, Robert Cummings, Paul Hartman, Lee Philips, Joseph Sweeney, Franchot Tone, George Voskovec, and Will West (broadcast 20 September 1954, the drama was later made into a movie); "A Picture in the Paper," with Jason Robards, Jr. (in his first major TV role, 9 May 1955); "For the Defense," with Mike Wallace (in a rare dramatic role, 27 June 1955); "Dino," with Sal Mineo (written by Reginald Rose, broadcast 2 January 1956); Reginald Rose's "The Defender," with Ralph Bellamy, William Shatner, and Steve McQueen (broadcast in two parts on 25 February and 4 March 1957, the drama was the basis for *The Defenders,* a 1961 series); "The Mother Bit," with Peter Falk (10 June 1957); and "The Night America Trembled," with Warren Beatty (in a rare TV appearance, 9 September 1957).

STUDIO SEE   PBS
25 JANUARY 1977–3 AUGUST 1979   Half-hour magazine series aimed principally at young people between ten and fifteen; filmed on location, the show included poetry readings, original animation, and filmed segments. Jayne Adair created the show.

STUDS' PLACE   NBC/ABC
26 NOVEMBER 1949–24 AUGUST 1950 (NBC); 13 OCTOBER 1950–24 DECEMBER 1951 (ABC)   This half-hour comedy was set at Studs' Place, a corner bar and grille in a Chicago neighborhood. Most of the dialogue was improvised by the regulars: Studs Terkel as the owner, Beverly Younger as Grace the waitress, Win Stracke, Chet Roble, and Philip Lord. Developed by Charles Andrews, the show was produced and directed in Chicago by Ben Park and Dan Petrie.

STUMP THE AUTHORS   ABC
15 JANUARY 1949–2 APRIL 1949   Another of the several Chicago-based shows that were broadcast back East after the opening of the coaxial cable in 1949, *Stump the Authors* was a Saturday-night panel series on which professional writers tried to extemporize on various subjects.

STUMP THE STARS
See PANTOMIME QUIZ

STUMPERS   NBC
4 OCTOBER 1976–31 DECEMBER 1976   Allen Ludden hosted this daytime game show that was quite similar to *Password,* which Ludden had also hosted. Two teams, each with a celebrity and a contestant, compet-

ed, trying to identify words from various three-word clues supplied by their partner. The winning team then had the chance to identify ten words within one minute for a large cash prize. Lin Bolen, former chief of daytime programming for NBC-TV, was the executive producer.

SUGAR TIME!   ABC
13 AUGUST 1977–29 MAY 1978   Half-hour sitcom about a female rock-and-roll trio known as "Sugar." With Barbi Benton as Maxx; Marianne Black as Maggie Barton; Didi Carr as Diane; Wynn Irwin as Al Marks; Mark Winkworth as Paul Landson; and Charles Fleischer as Lightnin' Jack Rappaport. Created by James Komack and developed by Hank Bradford, the series had a four-week run in the summer of 1977 and was seen irregularly thereafter. Komack was the executive producer; Bradford and Martin Cohan were the producers. Paul Williams supervised the music.

SUGARFOOT   ABC
17 SEPTEMBER 1957–20 SEPTEMBER 1960   An hour western from Warner Brothers starring Will Hutchins as Tom (Sugarfoot) Brewster, a naive, sarsaparilla-drinking Easterner who headed West, intending to become a lawyer. Introduced in the fall of 1957, Sugarfoot alternated with *Cheyenne* for its first two seasons, then alternated with *Bronco* for one season; a few more *Sugarfoot* episodes were telecast under the *Cheyenne* title during the 1960–1961 season. See also *Bronco; Cheyenne.* William T. Orr was the executive producer, and Carroll Case the producer.

THE SUMMER BROTHERS SMOTHERS SHOW
See THE GLEN CAMPBELL GOODTIME HOUR

SUMMER CAMP   SYNDICATED
1977   Half-hour educational series for children, emphasizing instruction in arts and crafts, produced by the YMCA.

SUMMER SCHOOL   CBS
6 JULY 1953–4 SEPTEMBER 1953   Monday-through-Friday educational series for young children. Broadcast from Philadelphia every afternoon at 4:00, the half-hour show featured guest teachers rather than regular instructors.

SUMMERTIME U.S.A.   CBS
7 JULY 1953–27 AUGUST 1953   A summer replacement for *The Jane Froman Show, Summertime U.S.A.* was a twice-weekly, fifteen-minute musical series cohosted by Teresa Brewer and Mel Tormé.

SUNDAY   NBC

27 OCTOBER 1963–11 JULY 1965 *Sunday* was a Sunday-afternoon news-magazine hosted by Frank Blair. Regular contributors included Joe Garagiola (sports), Ray Scherer (politics), Richard Schickel (books), and William K. Zinsser (films).

SUNDAY AT HOME   NBC

10 JULY 1949–31 JULY 1949 The several members of the Pickard Family were the stars of this fifteen-minute musical show, one of the first Hollywood-based programs to be kinescoped for broadcast in the East.

SUNDAY AT THE BRONX ZOO   ABC

11 JUNE 1950–17 SEPTEMBER 1950 This self-explanatory children's show was hosted by William Bridges, with assistance from Durward Kirby.

SUNDAY DATE   NBC

21 AUGUST 1949–9 OCTOBER 1949 Hosted by Helen Lee, this fifteen-minute Sunday musical series was set at a café.

THE SUNDAY MYSTERY HOUR   NBC

29 MAY 1960–25 SEPTEMBER 1960; 2 JULY 1961–17 SEPTEMBER 1961 This summer anthology hour was hosted by Walter Slezak. The show was presented live and in color during the summer of 1960, but the 1961 fare consisted of reruns. Among the presentations were "Murder Me Nicely," with Everett Sloane (3 July 1960), and "Trial by Fury," with Agnes Moorehead (7 August 1960).

SUNRISE SEMESTER   CBS

23 SEPTEMBER 1963– An early-morning educational series, *Sunrise Semester* was CBS's answer to NBC's *Continental Classroom.* It began in 1957 as a local show in New York and went network six years later. Each year several college-level courses are presented by members of the faculty of New York University. The half-hour show is currently produced by Roy Allen for WCBS-TV, New York. During the summers, courses are offered under the title *Summer Semester.*

SUNSHINE   NBC

6 MARCH 1975–19 JUNE 1975 Offbeat sitcom about a recently widowed young musician, trying to raise his young stepdaughter in Vancouver. Featured were Cliff DeYoung as Sam Hayden; Elizabeth Cheshire as his stepdaughter, Jill Hayden; Bill Mumy as Sam's musician friend, Weaver; Corey Fischer as Givits, another musician who formed a trio with Sam and Weaver; and Meg Foster as their friend, Nora. The half-hour series

was based on a journal excerpted in the Los Angeles *Times,* which was made into a TV-movie shown on CBS on 9 November 1973. The series was produced by George Eckstein for Universal Television.

THE SUPER   ABC

21 JUNE 1972–23 AUGUST 1972 Half-hour summer sitcom starring Richard S. Castellano as Joe Girelli, the harried superintendent of a New York City apartment building. Also featured were Ardell Sheridan as his wife, Francesca Girelli; B. Kirby, Jr., as their son, Anthony; Margaret E. Castellano (Richard's daughter) as their daughter, Joanne; Ed Peck as Officer Clark, a tenant; Virginia Vincent as his wife, Dottie Clark; Janet Brandt as Mrs. Stein; and Louis Basile as Louie. The series was created by Rob Reiner and Phil Mishkin (who appeared as Joe's brother, Frankie), and produced and directed by Alan Rafkin.

SUPER CIRCUS   ABC

16 JANUARY 1949–3 JUNE 1956 This long-running circus show was aimed principally at children. It was broadcast from Chicago from 1949 to 1955, where it was hosted by ringmaster Claude Kirchner and his assistant, Mary Hartline. Also on hand were three clowns: Cliffy Sobier as Cliffy, Bardy Patton and Sandy Dobritch as Scampy, and Nicky Francis as Nicky. In 1955 the show moved to New York, and Jerry Colonna took over as ringmaster, assisted by baton twirler Sandy Wirth. Jack Gibney produced the series.

SUPER FRIENDS   ABC

8 SEPTEMBER 1973–30 AUGUST 1975; 21 FEBRUARY 1976–4 SEPTEMBER 1976; 4 DECEMBER 1976–   *Super Friends,* a Hanna-Barbera cartoon series, depicts the adventures of the members of the Justice League of America—Superman, Batman and Robin, Aquaman, Wonder Woman, Marvin, Wendy, and Wonder Dog. Several of the group had previously been seen in other series, such as *The Superman/Aquaman Hour* or *The Batman/Tarzan Adventure Hour.* In the fall of 1977 the show expanded from thirty to sixty minutes and was retitled *The All-New Superfriends Hour.* In the fall of 1978 it continued under a new title, *Challenge of the Superfriends,* as the members of the Justice League of America battled emissaries of the Legion of Doom. In 1979 it continued as *The World's Greatest Superfriends.*

SUPER GHOSTS   NBC

27 JULY 1952–21 SEPTEMBER 1952; 19 JULY 1953–6 SEPTEMBER 1953 Hosted by Dr. Bergen Evans, this prime-time summer game show was broadcast from Chicago. The game was similar to Hangman— each successive panelist named a letter of the alphabet, and the object of the game was to avoid completing a word. The 1952 panel included Dr.

Irving Lee of Northwestern University, former drama critic Robert Pollak, housewife Shirl Stern, and a guest panelist.

THE SUPER GLOBETROTTERS   NBC
8 SEPTEMBER 1979–1 DECEMBER 1979   Saturday-morning cartoon series featuring the animated antics of the Harlem Globetrotters. See also *The Harlem Globetrotters; The Godzilla Power Hour.*

SUPER PRESIDENT   NBC
9 SEPTEMBER 1967–28 DECEMBER 1968   The central character in this half-hour Saturday cartoon show was James Norcross, President of the United States, who possessed the ability to transform himself into almost anything.

THE SUPER 6   NBC
10 SEPTEMBER 1966–31 AUGUST 1969   Half-hour cartoon show about a half-dozen crimefighters.

SUPER WITCH   NBC
19 NOVEMBER 1977–28 JANUARY 1978   *Super Witch* was the title given to the episodes of *Sabrina the Teenage Witch* when *The New Archie-Sabrina Hour* was broken up in midseason. See also *The Archie Show; The Groovie Goolies;* and *Sabrina, the Teenage Witch.*

SUPERCAR   SYNDICATED
1961   One of the first children's series developed by Gerry and Sylvia Anderson, *Supercar* was a marionette show which centered on Mike Mercury, driver of Supercar, a very versatile vehicle. The Andersons later refined their technique in such series as *Fireball XL-5, Stingray,* and *Thunderbirds.*

SUPERMAN   SYNDICATED
1951–1957   One of fiction's best known heroes, *Superman* was created by Jerry Siegel and Joe Shuster and first appeared in the June 1938 issue of "Action Comics." This humanlike creature had been sent to Earth as an infant by his parents, who discovered that their native planet, Krypton, was about to be destroyed. The boy was raised in a small town by the Kent family and took the name Clark Kent. He soon discovered that he possessed "powers and abilities far beyond those of mortal men." His senses of sight and hearing were extraordinarily acute, he was incredibly strong, and best of all, he was virtually indestructible (certain particles of Kryptonite, which apparently reached Earth from the exploding planet, could render Superman ineffective, however). Fortunately, he vowed to use his gifts for the good of humanity, fighting "a never-ending battle for truth, justice, and the American way." When he grew up, he moved to

Metropolis and got a job as a reporter for the *Daily Planet.* As a reporter, Kent was in a position to learn immediately of impending catastrophes, major crimes, and other compelling situations in which the presence of Superman might be needed.

The Superman character appeared not only in comic books, but also in a radio series beginning in 1940 (on which Bud Collyer played the lead), in a series of feature-length cartoons produced between 1941 and 1943, in two 15-chapter movie serials made in 1948 and 1950 (both of which starred Kirk Alyn), and in a full-length film, *Superman and the Mole Men,* made in 1951 (a second, lavishly produced picture was released late in 1978). Aside from the comic books, the character is most closely associated with the 104 half-hour television episodes, produced between 1951 and 1957, starring George Reeves (Reeves had played Superman in the 1951 motion picture; the film was later edited into a two-part TV story). Still widely syndicated today, *Superman*'s reruns are rivaled in popularity only by those of *I Love Lucy.*

As production of the first twenty-six episodes began in the summer of 1951, the cast included (in addition to Reeves) Phyllis Coates as Lois Lane, another *Daily Planet* reporter, who was infatuated with Superman but cared little for Kent (none of the show's principals ever realized that the two were one and the same, though in one 1955 episode, "The Wedding of Superman," Lois dreamed not only that she married Superman, but also that Kent revealed his true identity to her); Jack Larson as the *Planet*'s cub reporter, Jimmy Olsen; John Hamilton as the *Planet*'s apoplectic editor, Perry White; and Robert Shayne as Inspector William Henderson of the Metropolis police. The 1951 episodes were produced by Robert Maxwell and Bernard Luber, and directed by Lee Sholem and Tommy Carr; though they were somewhat more violent than the remaining episodes (the only on-screen murders were committed during the first twenty-six shows), they set the tone for the run of the series—a low budget, a hectic production schedule, a small guest cast, and lots of stock footage. In spite of the cost cutting, the stock sequences of Superman in flight (production of which was supervised by Thol "Si" Simonson) and the other frequently used special effects, such as Superman crashing through a brick wall (he rarely used the door), were quite effective for the time. Because of the production schedule, parts of several episodes were filmed at the same time (*Superman* was one of the first TV shows to employ this technique); this explains the fact that Clark, Lois, Jimmy, and Perry often seemed to wear the same set of clothes week after week.

Though twenty-six episodes had been completed by the end of 1951, the series was not made available to any broadcasting stations until early in 1953. By that time Kellogg's Cereals had agreed to sponsor the series. Production of *Superman* resumed in May 1953, and a second set of twenty-six episodes was filmed. Whitney Ellsworth was now the producer (and would remain so) and, as Phyllis Coates had accepted other offers,

Noel Neill was signed to play Lois Lane (Neill had previously played the part in the fifteen-chapter serials). These episodes were directed by Tommy Carr and George Blair. By now the character had become extremely popular, and all kinds of Superman merchandise flooded the market; Reeves himself did several successful promotional tours.

Production slowed down to a more leisurely pace in 1954, as only thirteen new episodes were produced (this schedule continued for the next three years); the most significant change was that the show was now being filmed in color. The majority of the final fifty-two episodes were directed by Harry Gerstad, Phil Ford, and George Blair, though Reeves himself directed three shows. In one of the 1957 episodes, "The Big Forget," Clark Kent actually did reveal his identity to Lois, Perry, and Jimmy, but thanks to an antimemory vapor developed by eccentric Professor Pepperwinkle (played by Phillips Tead), the three immediately forgot what they had witnessed.

In June of 1959, two years after production ceased, George Reeves shot and killed himself; he left no note, and the reasons for his death remain conjectural. Because of his close identity with the Superman character, Reeves did have trouble finding suitable work after 1957, but, according to Gary Grossman's book, *Superman—Serial to Cereal,* Reeves had several offers pending at the time of his death. Another possible explanation is that Reeves, who had been in a serious auto accident two weeks earlier, may have taken his life while under the influence of alcohol and pain killers. Sadly, Reeves, who often lamented that he wished he'd had a few adult fans among the *Superman* viewers, did not live long enough to watch his audiences grow up.

Though no major guest stars appeared on *Superman,* several struggling young performers played some of their first television roles on the series. Among them were: Claude Akins ("Peril By Sea," 1955), Hugh Beaumont ("The Big Squeeze," 1953), John Beradino ("The Unlucky Number,"1955), Paul Burke ("My Friend Superman," 1953, and "The Phantom Ring," 1955), Chuck Connors ("Flight to the North," 1954), and Joi Lansing ("Superman's Wife," 1957). In 1966 an animated version of *Superman* first appeared on television: see below.

SUPERMAN
CBS

10 SEPTEMBER 1966–7 SEPTEMBER 1968 *Superman* first appeared in a Saturday-morning cartoon series in the fall of 1966—the show, produced by Allen Ducovny, was titled *The New Adventures of Superman* during the 1966–1967 season. The half-hour show featured "Superman" and "Superboy" cartoon segments. In the fall of 1967, Superman shared an hour program with Aquaman, but retained top billing as the show was titled *The Superman-Aquaman Hour.* Superman continued to be seen on Saturday mornings after 1968 but no longer commanded top billing: see *The Batman-Superman Hour* and *Super Friends.*

SUPERMARKET SWEEP ABC

20 DECEMBER 1965–14 JULY 1967 A daytime game show taped at supermarkets throughout the country, *Supermarket Sweep* gave contestant couples the chance to load their shopping carts with merchandise for a limited period of time; the couple whose total was the highest was declared the winner and got to keep the goods and return the next day. Bill Malone hosted the half-hour show.

SUPERSONIC SYNDICATED

1976 Half-hour series of performances by rock stars.

THE SUPERSTARS ABC

27 JANUARY 1974–3 MARCH 1974; 5 JANUARY 1975–23 MARCH 1975; 11 JANUARY 1976–4 APRIL 1976; 2 JANUARY 1977–27 MARCH 1977; 8 JANUARY 1978–26 MARCH 1978; 14 JANUARY 1979–1 APRIL 1979; 20 JANUARY 1980– A Sunday-afternoon sports show, *The Superstars* features professional athletes, who compete against each other in a variety of athletic endeavors (no competitor is permitted to participate in the sport of his or her profession, however). On some shows teams of athletes compete, and these programs are broadcast under the title *The Superteams.* Keith Jackson is the principal commentator, but he is assisted from time to time by Al Michaels, Donna De Varona, O. J. Simpson, Reggie Jackson, Billie Jean King, Bruce Jenner, Hilary Hilton, Andrea Kirby, and Frank Gifford. *The Superstars* proved surprisingly popular with viewers and spawned a host of similar shows—specials such as "Battle of the Network Stars" and "Us vs. the World," and series such as *The Challenge of the Sexes* and *Celebrity Challenge of the Sexes;* the term "trashsport" was coined to describe the genre.

SUPERSTARS OF ROCK SYNDICATED

1973 Wolfman Jack interviewed rock stars on this half-hour series.

SUPERTRAIN NBC

7 FEBRUARY 1979–28 JULY 1979 An anthology series set aboard an atomic-powered train which traveled from coast to coast in 36 hours, *Supertrain* was an expensive flop. Its lavish set (one of the most expensive ever produced for television) failed to captivate viewers, and its uncertain vacillation between comedy and adventure also seemed to discourage large audiences. The Supertrain itself featured a disco, gymnasium, and swimming pool; and the original train crew included: Edward Andrews as Harry Flood, the conductor; Patrick Collins as Dave Noonan, the passenger relations officer; Robert Alda as Dr. Lewis; Nita Talbot as Rose Casey; Harrison Page as porter George Boone; Michael DeLano as bartender Lou Atkins; Charlie Brill as Robert the hairdresser; Aarika Wells as exercise attendant Gilda; William Nuckols as exercise attendant Wal-

ly; Anthony Palmer as T. C., the chief engineer. Dan Curtis, *Supertrain*'s first executive producer, was replaced by Robert Stambler in March 1979, and *Supertrain* left the air for a few weeks for retooling. It returned with a slimmed-down cast: from the original cast only Andrews, Page, and Alda remained, and Ilene Graff was added as social director Penny Whitaker, along with Joey Aresco as executive operations officer Wayne Randall. The changes were of no avail.

SURE AS FATE   CBS
4 JULY 1950–3 APRIL 1951   Half-hour mystery anthology series, narrated by Paul Lukas.

SURF'S UP   SYNDICATED
1966   Stan Richards hosted this half-hour documentary series, which presented color film footage of surfing and skateboarding activities at the nation's beaches.

SURFSIDE 6   ABC
3 OCTOBER 1960–24 SEPTEMBER 1962   This Warner Brothers detective series was set in Miami Beach; except for its locale, it was virtually identical to Warners' other hour-long detective shows, *77 Sunset Strip* and *Hawaiian Eye*. SurfSide 6 was the address of a trio of private eyes, whose houseboat was anchored next to a Miami Beach hotel. Featured were Troy Donahue as Sandy Winfield II; Van Williams as Ken Madison; Lee Patterson as Dave Thorne; Diane McBain as their friend, Daphne Dutton; Margarita Sierra as nightclub singer Cha Cha O'Brien; Donald Barry (1960–1961) as Lieutenant Snedigar; Richard Crane (1961–1962) as Lieutenant Plehn; and Mousie Garner as Mousie.

SURVIVAL   SYNDICATED
1964   *Survival* was a series of thirty-eight half-hours, mostly containing documentary film footage on famous disasters. James Whitmore narrated the series, and Sherman Grinberg produced it.

THE SURVIVORS   ABC
29 SEPTEMBER 1969–12 JANUARY 1970   One of the biggest flops of the decade, *The Survivors* was an expensive hour series created by novelist Harold Robbins. Shot on location around the world, it told a seamy tale of sex, wealth, and power for its fifteen-week run. The series was a success only for Robbins, who had wisely insisted on a guarantee of $500,000 regardless of the show's duration. The cast included: Ralph Bellamy as Baylor Carlyle, wealthy investor; George Hamilton as his son, Duncan Carlyle; Lana Turner as his daughter, Tracy Hastings; Kevin McCarthy as Philip Hastings, Tracy's husband; Rossano Brazzi as Riakos; Robert Viharo as Miguel Santerra, a South American revolutionary; Jan-Michael

Vincent as Jeffrey, Tracy's son; Diana Muldaur as Belle, Baylor's secretary; Louise Sorel as Jean Vale; Kathy Cannon as Sheila; Donna Bacalla as Marguerita, Miguel's sister; Robert Lipton as Tom; Clu Gulagher as Senator Jennings; and Louis Hayward as Jonathan. After the show was dropped in midseason, Universal Television, which produced the series, developed a new show for George Hamilton, which premiered in a new time slot shortly afterward. See *Paris 7000*. Reruns of *The Survivors* were shown in that timeslot during the summer of 1970.

THE SUSAN RAYE SHOW   DUMONT
2 OCTOBER 1950–20 NOVEMBER 1950   Fifteen-minute musical show hosted by Susan Raye.

SUSAN'S SHOW   CBS
4 MAY 1957–18 JANUARY 1958   Twelve-year-old Susan Heinkel hosted her own children's show on Saturday mornings; it was set in a fantasy land known as Wonderville. The half-hour show originated from Chicago (where it began as a local show in 1956) and was produced by Paul L. Frumkin.

SUSIE
See PRIVATE SECRETARY

SUSPENSE   CBS
1 MARCH 1949–17 AUGUST 1954; 25 MARCH 1964–9 SEPTEMBER 1964
Suspense was a half-hour anthology series of thrillers, based on the radio series that ran from 1942 to 1962. The TV series aroused some controversy late in 1949, when an episode showing a woman drinking blood precipitated an outcry over violence and gore on television. Bela Lugosi made a rare television appearance in one episode (11 October 1949), and Boris Karloff starred in an early adaptation of "The Monkey's Paw" the same year (17 May). Other unusual guest appearances included those by Jacqueline Susann ("Pigeons in the Cave," 21 July 1953) and Mike Wallace (7 July 1953). One of the earliest televised Sherlock Holmes stories was presented on *Suspense*. "The Adventure of the Black Baronet," written by Adrian Conan Doyle and John Dickson Carr, starring Basil Rathbone and Martyn Green, was broadcast 26 May 1953. Bob Stevens produced and directed the first incarnation of *Suspense*. Sebastian Cabot hosted the 1964 version, which replaced *Tell It to the Camera*.

SUSPICION   NBC
30 SEPTEMBER 1957–22 SEPTEMBER 1958   An hour-long suspense anthology series of little note, *Suspicion* was hosted first by Dennis O'Keefe, and later by Walter Abel. Reruns were shown on NBC during the summer of 1959.

SWEEPSTAKES   NBC
26 JANUARY 1979–30 MARCH 1979   An hour anthology series focusing
on several of the finalists in a state lottery with the grand prize of a million dollars. Edd Byrnes appeared as the sweepstakes m.c. Executive producer: Robert Dozier for Miller-Milkis Productions in association with
Paramount TV.

THE SWIFT SHOW WAGON
See SHOW WAGON

SWINGIN' COUNTRY   NBC
4 JULY 1966–30 DECEMBER 1966   Regulars on this twenty-five minute
daytime country-and-western music show included Rusty Draper, Roy
Clark, and Molly Bee.

SWISS FAMILY ROBINSON   ABC
14 SEPTEMBER 1975–11 APRIL 1976   Based on Johann Wyss's novel,
this hour-long adventure series told the story of a family marooned on a
tropic isle. With Martin Milner as Karl Robinson; Pat Delany as his wife,
Lotte Robinson; Willie Aames as their son Fred; Eric Olson as their son
Ernie; Cameron Mitchell as Jeremiah Worth, a shipwrecked sea captain;
and Helen Hunt as Helga Wagner, a teenager adopted by the Robinsons.
Irwin Allen produced the series.

THE SWISS FAMILY ROBINSON   SYNDICATED
1976   This Canadian import was similar to the 1975 network show, except that it was a half-hour series. Featured were Chris Wiggins as Johann Robinson; Diana Leblanc as his wife, Elizabeth Robinson; Ricky
O'Neill as their son, Franz; Heather Graham as their daughter, Marie;
Michael Duhig as their son, Ernest; and Bruno, the dog. Gerald Mayer
produced the series.

SWITCH   CBS
9 SEPTEMBER 1975–3 SEPTEMBER 1978   An hour-long adventure series
about an ex-cop and an ex-con who teamed up as private investigators;
their specialty, like that of *The Rogues,* was fleecing the fleecers and out-
conning the con artists. The show starred Eddie Albert as Frank Mac-
Bride, the ex-cop, and Robert Wagner as Peterson T. (Pete) Ryan, the ex-
con. Also featured were Sharon Gless as their receptionist and assistant,
Maggie; Charlie Callas as Malcolm Argos, an occasional helper; William
Bryant (1976–1978) as Lieutenant Shilton; and James Hong (1977–1978)
as Wang, Malcolm's cook. Glen A. Larson was the executive producer
during the first season, Matthew Rapf during the second, and Jon Epstein
during the third, for Glen Larson Productions in association with Universal Television.

THE SWORD OF FREEDOM   SYNDICATED

·1957   Half-hour adventure series imported from Europe and set during
the Italian Renaissance. Edmund Purdom starred as Marco del Monte, a
painter and freedom fighter who battled the Medici family. Also featured
were Martin Benson as the Duke de' Medici, Adrienne Corri as Angelica;
Kenneth Hyde as Machiavelli.

SWORD OF JUSTICE   NBC

9 SEPTEMBER 1978–31 DECEMBER 1978   An hour-long crime show starring Dack Rambo as Jack Cole, a man who served three years in prison
on a trumped-up embezzlement charge after his father's death and who
vowed upon his release to go after those wrongdoers whom the law
couldn't touch; while in prison Cole learned all he could about such subjects as lock-picking and bugging in order to facilitate his crimefighting
career. Also featured were Bert Rosario as Hector Ramirez, Cole's former cellmate and present partner, and Alex Courtney as Arthur Woods,
the federal agent who was always a step or two behind Cole and Ramirez.
Glen A. Larson was the executive producer.

SYLVESTER AND TWEETY   CBS

11 SEPTEMBER 1976–3 SEPTEMBER 1977   Though Warner Brothers'
most famous cat-and-bird twosome had been featured on several earlier
cartoon shows, it was not until 1976 that Sylvester ("Thufferin' thucko-
tash!") and Tweety ("I taut I taw a puddy tat!") starred in a series of their
own. Mel Blanc provided the voices of the two characters in the half-
hour Saturday-morning show.

SZYSZNYK   CBS

1 AUGUST 1977–29 AUGUST 1977; 7 DECEMBER 1977–25 JANUARY
1978   *Szysznyk* starred Ned Beatty as Nick Szysznyk, a twenty-seven-
year Marine Corps veteran who became the supervisor of the Northeast
Community Center in Washington, D.C. The half-hour sitcom also fea-
tured Leonard Barr as Leonard Kriegler, the custodian; Olivia Cole as
Ms. Harrison, the district supervisor; Susan Lanier (summer 1977) as
Sandi Chandler, the nursery school instructor; Thomas Carter as Ray
Gun; Scott Colomby as Tony; Barry Miller as Fortwengler; and Jarrod
Johnson as Ralph. Jerry Weintraub was the executive producer, Rich
Eustis and Michael Elias the producers. Writers Jim Mulligan and Ron
Landry created the series, which languished at the bottom of the ratings
when it returned in December of 1977.

T.H.E. CAT   NBC

16 SEPTEMBER 1966–1 SEPTEMBER 1967   Half-hour adventure series
starring Robert Loggia as T.H.E. (Thomas Hewitt Edward) Cat, a for-

mer cat burglar who turned to crimefighting. Also on hand were R. G. Armstrong as Captain McAllister, and Robert Carricart as Pepe, proprietor of the Casa del Gato (House of the Cat), the club where Cat's services could be obtained. Robert Loggia had played another catlike character previously on *Walt Disney Presents,* when he played western hero Elfego Baca, "the man with nine lives." *T.H.E. Cat* was produced by Boris Sagal.

TV AUCTION   ABC
10 JULY 1954–28 AUGUST 1954   Sid Stone hosted this fifteen-minute series on which viewers were invited to submit bids on merchandise featured on stage.

TV GENERAL STORE   ABC
14 JUNE 1953–12 JULY 1953   On this Sunday-morning hour series, cohosts Dave and Judy Clark offered merchandise for sale to viewers.

TV HOUR
See THE MOTOROLA TV HOUR

TV READERS DIGEST   ABC
17 JANUARY 1955–9 JULY 1956   The presentations on this filmed half-hour dramatic anthology series were adapted from stories appearing in *Readers Digest* magazine. The series was produced by Chester Erskine, directed by William Beaudine, and hosted first by Hugh Reilly, then by Gene Raymond.

TV SCREEN MAGAZINE   NBC
8 JANUARY 1948–30 APRIL 1949   One of television's first magazine shows, *TV Screen Magazine* was a potpourri of features, including interviews, musical numbers, and fashion shows. It was originally hosted by John K. M. McCaffery (editor of *American Mercury*) and Millicent Fenwick (an editor of *Vogue*). Ray Forrest, who had been the announcer on the early shows, later took over as host.

TV SHOPPER   DUMONT
1 NOVEMBER 1948–1 DECEMBER 1950   Kathi Norris, who hosted this early daytime series for most of its run, dispensed shopping hints to housewives.

TV SOUNDSTAGE   NBC
10 JULY 1953–3 SEPTEMBER 1954   Half-hour dramatic anthology series. James Dean appeared in one program, "Life Sentence," broadcast 16 October 1953.

TV TEEN CLUB   ABC

2 APRIL 1949–28 MARCH 1954   Bandleader Paul Whiteman hosted this
talent show for young people, broadcast from Philadelphia. Nancy Lewis,
June Keegan, and Maureen Cannon were also featured, and seven-year-
old Leslie Uggams appeared on the show in 1950. The show, which was
also titled *Paul Whiteman's TV Teen Club,* was produced by Jack Steck
and directed by Herb Horton.

TV TWIN DOUBLE   SYNDICATED

1977   George DeWitt hosted this syndicated game show on which home
viewers could win prizes based on the results of previously filmed horse
races. Local sponsors who purchased the series arranged to distribute the
race tickets required for viewer participation. Jack O'Hara announced
the races and Laura Lane assisted George DeWitt.

TV'S TOP TUNES   CBS

2 JULY 1951–17 AUGUST 1951; 29 JUNE 1953–21 AUGUST 1953; 28 JUNE
1954–20 AUGUST 1954; 9 JULY 1955–3 SEPTEMBER 1955   *TV's Top
Tunes* was a frequent summer replacement series. In 1951, 1953, and
1954 it was seen Mondays, Wednesdays, and Fridays in a fifteen-minute
format as a replacement for *The Perry Como Show;* it was hosted by Peggy Lee and Mel Tormé in 1951, Helen O'Connell and Bob Eberle in 1953,
and Ray Anthony in 1954. The 1955 version was a half-hour series,
shown on Saturdays; produced and directed by Lee Cooley, it was hosted
by Julius LaRosa and featured the Mitchell Ayres Orchestra.

THE TAB HUNTER SHOW   NBC

18 SEPTEMBER 1960–10 SEPTEMBER 1961   Tab Hunter starred as fun-
loving cartoonist Paul Morgan, creator of the *Bachelor at Large* strip, in
this half-hour sitcom. Also featured were Richard Erdman as his bachelor pal Peter Fairfield and Jerome Cowan as Paul's publisher, John
Larsen.

TABITHA   ABC

10 SEPTEMBER 1977–25 AUGUST 1978   This irregularly scheduled com-
edy series was a sequel to *Bewitched,* and starred Lisa Hartman as Ta-
bitha Stevens, the now grown daughter of *Bewitched*'s Samantha Stevens.
Also featured were David Ankrum as Tabitha's mortal brother, Adam;
Robert Urich as Paul Thurston, star of the TV talk show for which Ta-
bitha worked as a production assistant; and Mel Stewart as Marvin,
Thurston's producer. Jerry Mayer was the executive producer and Bob
Stambler the producer.

TAG THE GAG   NBC

13 AUGUST 1951–27 AUGUST 1951   Hal Block hosted this short-lived

prime-time game show on which guest panelists tried to supply the punch lines to jokes acted out in charade form.

TAKE A CHANCE NBC
1 OCTOBER 1950–24 DECEMBER 1950   Don Ameche hosted this prime-time half-hour quiz show.

TAKE A GIANT STEP NBC
11 SEPTEMBER 1971–2 SEPTEMBER 1972
TALKING WITH A GIANT NBC
9 SEPTEMBER 1972–1 SEPTEMBER 1973   *Take a Giant Step* was an unusual Saturday-morning show. Developed by George Heinemann, NBC's vice president for children's programming, the hour series featured a group of seven- to fourteen-year-olds who, with the help of staff researchers, put together a program that centered on a particular theme each week. In 1972 the concept was revised, but the new version, titled *Talking with a Giant,* was equally ignored by young viewers; the half-hour show featured a guest celebrity who was interviewed by a panel of youngsters. Gloria Peropat and Giovanna Nigro produced and directed *Take a Giant Step.*

TAKE A GOOD LOOK ABC
22 OCTOBER 1959–16 MARCH 1961   Ernie Kovacs hosted this half-hour prime-time game show. At the beginning of the first season, the show involved two contestants, who tried to identify famous newsmakers from documentary clues. By early 1960, a panel format had been substituted and three celebrities tried to identify a celebrity guest from clues suggested in a skit performed by Kovacs, Bobby Lauher, and Peggy Connelly. Frequent panelists included Edie Adams, Hans Conried, Ben Alexander, Cesar Romero, and Carl Reiner.

TAKE A GUESS CBS
11 JUNE 1953–10 SEPTEMBER 1953   A summer replacement for *The Burns and Allen Show, Take A Guess* was a half-hour game show emceed by John K. M. McCaffery. Contestants tried to identify a secret phrase, with help from a celebrity panel that consisted of John Crawford, Dorothy Hart, Ernie Kovacs, and Margaret Lindsay.

TAKE IT FROM ME
See THE JEAN CARROLL SHOW

TAKE MY ADVICE NBC
5 JANUARY 1976–11 JUNE 1976   Kelly Lange hosted this daytime series on which celebrities and their spouses suggested answers to problems

submitted by viewers. The twenty-five-minute show was produced by Mark Massari for Burt Sugarman Productions.

TAKE TWO   ABC
5 MAY 1963–11 AUGUST 1963   Don McNeill hosted this Sunday-afternoon game show on which celebrities were paired with noncelebrity contestants. The object of the game was to determine the common feature of two photographs from an array of four photos.

TALENT JACKPOT   DUMONT
19 JULY 1949–23 AUGUST 1949   Vinton Freedley and Bud Collyer cohosted this five-week prime-time talent show on which five acts competed. Each act could win a "jackpot" of as much as $250, based on the amount of applause the act received from the studio audience. The evening's top winner received not only his or her own jackpot, but whatever was left in the other acts' jackpots.

TALENT PATROL   ABC
19 JANUARY 1953–28 JUNE 1954   Contestants on this half-hour talent show were selected from the nation's armed forces. Steve Allen was the first host of the series and was succeeded by Arlene Francis. See also *Soldier Parade.*

TALENT SCOUTS   CBS
6 DECEMBER 1948–28 JULY 1958; 1 AUGUST 1960–26 SEPTEMBER 1960; 3 JULY 1962–11 SEPTEMBER 1962; 2 JULY 1963–17 SEPTEMBER 1963; 22 JUNE 1965–7 SEPTEMBER 1965; 20 DECEMBER 1965–5 SEPTEMBER 1966   This long-running prime-time talent show, on which celebrity guests introduced amateur or young professional talent, was hosted first by Arthur Godfrey, who began the show on radio in 1946. From 1948 to 1958 it was a weekly show; when Godfrey was unavailable due to illness or other commitments, substitute hosts such as Steve Allen or Robert Q. Lewis filled in. Beginning in 1960 it was seen as a summer replacement series for several years and was titled *Celebrity Talent Scouts* or *Hollywood Talent Scouts;* Sam Levenson hosted it in 1960, Jim Backus in 1962, Merv Griffin in 1963, and Art Linkletter in 1965. Linkletter also hosted the show when it was revived later in 1965 as a midseason replacement. Among the many future stars who were introduced on *Talent Scouts* were Pat Boone, Shari Lewis, the McGuire Sisters, Carmel Quinn, and June Valli.

TALENT SEARCH   NBC
15 FEBRUARY 1950–6 SEPTEMBER 1951   Skitch Henderson hosted this half-hour talent show.

THE TALENT SHOP   DUMONT
13 OCTOBER 1951–29 MARCH 1952   A half-hour talent show for young
people, *The Talent Shop* was set at a New York City drugstore and was
hosted by Fred Robbins and Pat Adair.

TALENT VARIETIES   ABC
28 JUNE 1955–1 NOVEMBER 1955· Slim Wilson hosted this country-and-
western talent show. Broadcast from Springfield, Missouri, the half-hour
series was produced and directed by Bill Ring.

TALES OF THE BLACK CAT   SYNDICATED
1950   Half-hour filmed suspense anthology series, hosted by James
Monks and his cat, Thanatopsis.

TALES OF THE CITY   CBS
· 25 JUNE 1953–17 SEPTEMBER 1953   A summer replacement for *Four
Star Playhouse,* this half-hour dramatic anthology series was hosted by
Ben Hecht and was officially titled *Willys Theatre Presenting Ben Hecht's
Tales of the City.*

TALES OF THE RED CABOOSE   ABC
22 OCTOBER 1948–14 JANUARY 1949   Fifteen-minute prime-time series,
sponsored by Lionel Trains, which consisted of films of model railroads.
Dan Magee was the host. See also *Roar of the Rails.*

TALES OF THE SEVENTY-SEVENTH BENGAL LANCERS
See 77TH BENGAL LANCERS

TALES OF THE TEXAS RANGERS   CBS
3 SEPTEMBER 1955–25 MAY 1957   This half-hour western from Screen
Gems starred Willard Parker as Jace Pearson and Harry Lauter as Clay
Morgan, a pair of Texas Rangers. The most interesting feature of the
show was that the stories were not confined to any one era of Texas history; Pearson and Morgan could be seen battling villains from the 1850s
one week and tracking down desperadoes from the 1950s the following
week. The series, which was seen Saturday mornings on CBS, was later
rerun on ABC.

TALES OF THE UNEXPECTED   NBC
2 FEBRUARY 1977–24 AUGUST 1977   This hour-long suspense anthology
series was first slated opposite ABC's *Charlie's Angels* and was later seen
on an irregular basis. Narrated by William Conrad, the series was produced by John Wilder for Quinn Martin Productions.

TALES OF THE VIKINGS
See THE VIKINGS

TALES OF TOMORROW   ABC
3 AUGUST 1951–12 JUNE 1953   Science fiction and supernatural tales
were presented on this half-hour anthology series. A sample of presentations would include: "The Last Man on Earth," with Cloris Leachman
(31 August 1951); "Frankenstein," with Lon Chaney, Jr. (18 January
1952); "Memento," with Boris Karloff (22 February 1952); "Flight Over-
due," with Veronica Lake (28 March 1952); "Black Planet," with Leslie
Nielsen (16 May 1952); and "Two-Faced," with Richard Kiley (31 January 1953).

TALES OF WELLS FARGO
See WELLS FARGO

TALKING WITH A GIANT
See TAKE A GIANT STEP

THE TALL MAN   NBC
10 SEPTEMBER 1960–1 SEPTEMBER 1962   This fanciful western starred
Barry Sullivan as New Mexico Deputy Sheriff Pat Garrett and Clu Gulagher as William H. Bonney, better known as Billy the Kid; on the series
Billy was not depicted as a sadistic murderer, but rather as a misguided
chap who occasionally helped out Garrett. The half-hour show was created and produced by Samuel Peeples.

TALLAHASSEE 7000   SYNDICATED
1961   Walter Matthau starred in this half-hour crime show as Lex Rogers, special agent for the Florida Sheriffs Bureau. The twenty-six episodes
were filmed on location in Florida.

TAMMY   ABC
17 SEPTEMBER 1965–15 JULY 1966   This half-hour sitcom was based on
the *Tammy* films, and starred Debbie Watson as Tammy Tarleton, a
young Southern lass who left her family's houseboat to become private
secretary to a wealthy plantation owner. Also featured were Frank
McGrath as Uncle Lucius Tarleton; Denver Pyle as Grandpa (Mordecai)
Tarleton; Dennis Robertson as Cousin Cletus; Donald Woods as her employer, John Brent; Doris Packer as Mrs. Brent; Jay Sheffield as Steven
Brent, John's son; George Furth as Dwayne Witt; Dorothy Green as Lavinia Tate, a local widow who had hoped to have her daughter hired for
Tammy's job; Linda Marshall as Gloria Tate, Lavinia's daughter, and
David Macklin as Peter Tate, Lavinia's son.

THE TAMMY GRIMES SHOW   ABC

8 SEPTEMBER 1966–29 SEPTEMBER 1966   The first fatality of the 1966–1967 season, *The Tammy Grimes Show* was an ill-conceived half-hour sitcom that starred musical comedy star Tammy Grimes as Tamantha Ward, a madcap heiress. Also featured were Dick Sargent as her parsimonious twin brother, Terence Ward; Hiram Sherman as their thrifty Uncle Simon, a banker; and Maudie Prickett as Mrs. Ratchett, the housekeeper. The series was canceled after four episodes had been televised, though ten shows had actually been completed by that time. William Dozier was the executive producer for Greenway Productions in association with 20th Century-Fox; Richard Whorf and Alex Gottlieb were the producers.

TARGET   SYNDICATED

1958   Adolphe Menjou hosted, and occasionally starred in, this series of half-hour dramas from Ziv TV.

TARGET: THE CORRUPTORS   ABC

29 SEPTEMBER 1961–21 SEPTEMBER 1962   Stephen McNally starred in this hour crime show as crusading newspaper columnist Paul Marino, who tracked down and exposed racketeers; Robert Harland costarred as his investigator, Jack Flood. Leonard Ackerman and John Burrows produced the series, and Gene Roddenberry (who later created *Star Trek*) supplied at least one script.

TARZAN   NBC

8 SEPTEMBER 1966–13 SEPTEMBER 1968   Edgar Rice Burroughs's famous jungle character, who had been featured in films decades earlier, finally came to television (without Jane) in 1966. The hour adventure series starred Ron Ely as Tarzan, who was born Lord Greystoke, but who preferred jungle life. Also featured were Manuel Padilla, Jr., as young Jai, who, like Tarzan, was a jungle orphan; Alan Caillou as Jason Flood, Jai's tutor; and Rockne Tarkington as Rao, a veterinarian. Filmed on location in Brazil and Mexico, the show was produced by Banner Productions.

TARZAN, LORD OF THE JUNGLE   CBS
11 SEPTEMBER 1976–3 SEPTEMBER 1977
TARZAN AND THE SUPER 7   CBS
9 SEPTEMBER 1978–   Edgar Rice Burroughs's character was featured not only in a live-action prime-time series (see above), but also in cartoon form on Saturday mornings. *Tarzan, Lord of the Jungle* was a half-hour show, which ran for one season. In the fall of 1977 Tarzan teamed up with Batman in *The Batman/Tarzan Adventure Hour* (see that title), and in the fall of 1978 Tarzan regained top billing in *Tarzan and*

the Super 7, a ninety-minute show with seven segments: "Tarzan," "Batman and Robin," "The Freedom Force" (a group of superheroes including Hercules, Isis, Super Samurai, Merlin, and Sinbad), "Superstretch and Microwoman" (a husband-and-wife team), "Moray & Manta" (a pair of underwater crimefighters), "Web Woman," and "Jason of Star Command." The latter segment was a live-action feature set in outer space with Craig Littler as Jason, a young trainee with Star Command, a galactic police force; Sid Haig as Dragos, the archvillain; Susan O'Hanlon; Charlie Dell; and James Doohan. Norm Prescott and Lou Scheimer are the executive producers of both *Tarzan, Lord of the Jungle* and *Tarzan and the Super 7.* See also *Jason of Star Command.*

TATE NBC
8 JUNE 1960–28 SEPTEMBER 1960 This summer western starred David McLean as Tate, a one-armed gunslinger (his bad arm was encased in leather). Robert Redford made two guest appearances on the half-hour show, in "The Bounty Hunter" (22 June) and "Comanche Scalps" (10 August).

TATTLETALES CBS/SYNDICATED
18 FEBRUARY 1974–31 MARCH 1978 (CBS); 1977 (SYNDICATED)
Bert Convy hosted this game show on which three celebrity couples competed, each playing for one-third of the studio audience; the spouses were separated while one set of partners was asked questions. Couples won points by matching responses correctly. *Tattletales,* which enjoyed a four-year daytime run on CBS, plus a syndicated version, was a Mark Goodson–Bill Todman Production.

TAXI ABC
12 SEPTEMBER 1978– A half-hour sitcom set at the Sunshine Cab Company in New York, *Taxi* was created by four former *Mary Tyler Moore* staffers—Ed. Weinberger, David Davis, Stan Daniels, and James L. Brooks. With Judd Hirsch as Alex Reiger, a career cabbie; Jeff Conaway as Bobby Wheeler, a would-be actor; Tony Danza as Tony Banta, a hopeful boxer; Danny DeVito as the dyspeptic dispatcher, Louis DiPalma; Marilu Henner as Elaine Nardo, an aspiring art dealer; Randall Carver (1978–1979) as John Burns, a passenger who decided to become a cabbie; and Andy Kaufman as Latka Gravas, the mechanic hoping to learn the English language. In 1979 Christopher Lloyd joined the cast as "Reverend" Jim Ignatowski, a survivor of the psychedelic sixties. The show's four creators also serve as its executive producers.

THE TED KNIGHT SHOW CBS
8 APRIL 1978–13 MAY 1978 Disappointing sitcom starring Ted Knight as Roger Dennis, operator of a New York City escort service. His em-

ployees included: Fawne Harriman as Honey; Cissy Colpitts as Graziella; Tanya Boyd as Phil; Janice Kent as Cheryl; Ellen Regan as Irma; Deborah Harmon as Joy; and Iris Adrian as Dottie, Roger's salty secretary. Also featured were Normann Burton as Roger's brother, Burt, and Thomas Leopold as Roger's son, Winston. The series was created by Lowell Ganz and Mark Rothman, who also served as its executive producers; Martin Cohan and David W. Duclon were the producers. The pilot for the half-hour series was televised on *Busting Loose.*

TED MACK'S FAMILY HOUR   ABC
7 JANUARY 1951–25 NOVEMBER 1951   Ted Mack hosted this Sunday-evening variety half hour, which also featured singer Andy Roberts and announcer Dennis James.

TED MACK'S MATINEE   NBC
4 APRIL 1955–28 OCTOBER 1955   This half-hour daytime variety show was hosted by Ted Mack and featured Elise Rhodes, Beth Parks, Dick Lee, and the Honey Dreamers. A regular feature of the program awarded prizes to wives who wrote in to praise their husbands. Louis Graham produced the series.

TED MACK'S ORIGINAL AMATEUR HOUR   DUMONT/NBC/ABC/CBS
18 JANUARY 1948–25 SEPTEMBER 1949 (DUMONT); 4 OCTOBER 1949–11 SEPTEMBER 1954 (NBC); 30 OCTOBER 1955–23 JUNE 1957 (ABC); 1 JULY 1957–4 OCTOBER 1958 (NBC); 1 MAY 1959–9 OCTOBER 1959 (CBS); 7 MARCH 1960–26 SEPTEMBER 1960 (ABC); 2 OCTOBER 1960–27 SEPTEMBER 1970 (CBS)   Television's most famous talent show was a direct descendant of radio's best-known talent show, *Major Bowes' Original Amateur Hour,* which began in 1934; Major Edward Bowes hosted the radio program from 1934 until his death in 1946. A year later Ted Mack, who had directed the auditions for the Bowes show, took over as host and brought the show to television (the radio version lasted until 1952). The show, which was originally titled *Major Bowes' Original Amateur Hour* even on TV, was seen sporadically in 1947, with regularly scheduled broadcasts beginning in 1948. It was one of the few programs to have been broadcast on all four commercial networks. For most of its long run it was a half-hour series; it was a prime-time show from 1948 until 1960, when it began a lengthy Sunday-afternoon run on CBS. The format of the show was simple and straightforward, changing little over the years: each week a number of amateur performers displayed their talents, and the viewing audience was invited to vote—by postcard—for their favorite act.

THE TED STEELE SHOW   NBC/DUMONT/CBS
29 SEPTEMBER 1948–29 OCTOBER 1948 (NBC); 27 FEBRUARY 1949–12

JULY 1949 (DUMONT); 6 JUNE 1949–8 JULY 1949 (CBS); 10 OCTOBER 1949–28 APRIL 1950 (CBS)   Singer Ted Steele hosted several musical variety shows. He first hosted a prime-time show on NBC. His DuMont series was seen in both daytime and prime-time versions, and before it was over he had begun a daytime show on CBS. In the fall of 1949 his CBS daytime series was seen Mondays through Fridays at 5 p.m.

TEEN TIME TUNES   DUMONT
7 MARCH 1949–15 JULY 1949   Fifteen-minute Monday-through-Friday-evening musical show, featuring the music of the Alan Logan Trio.

TEENAGE BOOK CLUB   ABC
13 AUGUST 1948–29 OCTOBER 1948   Half-hour panel show featuring discussions on current books of interest to teenagers.

TELECOMICS   SYNDICATED/NBC
1949 (SYNDICATED); 18 SEPTEMBER 1950–30 MARCH 1951 (NBC)
Produced by Vallee Video, *Telecomics* included some of the first cartoons made especially for television. Among the first segments were: "Brother Goose," "Joey and Jug," "Rick Rack, Special Agent," and "Sa-Lih." When the series was picked up by NBC (and broadcast under the title *NBC Comics*) segments included "Danny March," "Johnny and Mr. Do-Right," "Kid Champion," and "Space Barton."

TELEDRAMA   SYNDICATED
1952   Half-hour dramatic anthology series.

TELEPHONE TIME   CBS/ABC
8 APRIL 1956–31 MARCH 1957 (CBS); 4 JUNE 1957–1 APRIL 1958 (ABC)   The stories on this half-hour filmed dramatic anthology series were based on true incidents. Jerry Stagg produced the series, which was hosted by John Nesbitt on CBS and by Dr. Frank Baxter on ABC.

TELESPORTS DIGEST   SYNDICATED
1953   Harry Wismer hosted this sports series, on which films of the past week's top athletic events were shown.

TELE-THEATRE   NBC
27 SEPTEMBER 1948–26 JUNE 1950   A half-hour dramatic anthology series, *Tele-Theatre* was sponsored by Chevrolet and was titled *Chevrolet on Broadway* in its early weeks. Vic McLeod was the producer.

TELEVISION RECITAL HALL   NBC
1 JULY 1951–21 AUGUST 1953; 9 AUGUST 1954–6 SEPTEMBER

1954 This highbrow musical series, on which classical performers appeared, began as a summer replacement for *The Colgate Comedy Hour* and later shifted to Sunday afternoons. During the summer of 1954 it was seen in prime time. Charles Polacheck produced the series.

TELL IT TO GROUCHO CBS

11 JANUARY 1962–31 MAY 1962   *Tell It to Groucho,* a half-hour midseason replacement series, was similar in format to *You Bet Your Life,* except that the quiz segment was emphasized even less. Two contestants appeared and were perfectly free to state their problems or air their gripes during the interview with host Groucho Marx. A top prize of $500 was available in the quiz segment to a contestant who could identify a photograph of a celebrity that appeared for a split second. Jack Wheeler and Patty Harmon served as Groucho's assistants and George Fenneman was the announcer; Bernie Smith produced the show. See also *Tell It to the Camera; You Bet Your Life.*

TELL IT TO THE CAMERA CBS

25 DECEMBER 1963–18 MARCH 1964   *Tell It to the Camera* was hastily devised as a midseason replacement for *Glynis* on Wednesdays. People on the street were invited to state their opinions, thoughts, or complaints to the camera. Red Rowe hosted the half-hour series, which was taped on location throughout the United States; Allen Funt was the producer.

TELL ME, DR. BROTHERS
See DR. JOYCE BROTHERS

TELLER OF TALES
See SOMERSET MAUGHAM THEATRE

THE TELLTALE CLUE CBS

8 JULY 1954–23 SEPTEMBER 1954   Half-hour crime show starring Anthony Ross as Detective Richard Hale of the New York Police Department.

TEMPERATURES RISING ABC

12 SEPTEMBER 1972–8 JANUARY 1974   Half-hour sitcom set at Capitol General Hospital in Washington, D.C. During the 1972–1973 season the cast included: Cleavon Little as Dr. Jerry Noland; James Whitmore as Dr. Vincent Campanelli; Joan Van Ark as Nurse Annie Carlisle; Reva Rose as Nurse Mildred MacInerney; and Nancy Fox as Nurse Ellen Turner. In the fall of 1973 the show was retitled *The New Temperatures Rising Show;* only Cleavon Little was retained from the previous cast. The new regulars included: Paul Lynde as Dr. Paul Mercy, the hospital

administrator; Sudie Bond as Agatha, Paul's mother, owner of the hospital; Alice Ghostley as Edwina, Paul's sister; Jeff Morrow as Dr. Lloyd Axton; Barbara Cason as Nurse Tillis; Jennifer Darling as Nurse Winchester; and John Dehner as Dr. Claver. William Asher was the executive producer of the series.

TEMPLE HOUSTON NBC
19 SEPTEMBER 1963–10 SEPTEMBER 1964 This hour western starred Jeffrey Hunter as lawyer Temple Houston, son of Sam Houston. Jack Elam played his sidekick, George Taggart, a former gunslinger, and Mary Wickes played Ida Goff.

TEMPTATION ABC
4 DECEMBER 1967–1 MARCH 1968 Art James hosted this daytime game show, which combined a question-and-answer segment with a merchandise-swapping segment.

THE $10,000 PYRAMID (THE $20,000 PYRAMID) CBS/ABC
26 MARCH 1973–29 MARCH 1974 (CBS); 6 MAY 1974– (ABC)
THE $25,000 PYRAMID SYNDICATED
1974– On this half-hour game show from Bob Stewart Productions, two teams, each with a celebrity and a contestant, compete in a two-part word game. In the first part players try to get their partners to identify a list of words in a given category by supplying definitions to those words. The team with the higher score after three rounds then progresses to the second part of the game, where the procedure is reversed: by naming elements of a listed category, one player tries to get the other to identify the category; the top prize at the second level was originally $10,000 on the network version, but was increased to $20,000 on 19 January 1976, as the show was retitled *The $20,000 Pyramid*. The top prize on the syndicated version has remained steady at $25,000. Dick Clark has hosted the network version, Bill Cullen the syndicated version.

TEN WHO DARED SYNDICATED
1977 Ten-part historical documentary series on great explorers. Produced by the BBC in cooperation with Time-Life Films, the hour series was sponsored by Mobil Oil. Among the explorers whose lives were dramatized were Columbus, Pizarro, Cook, von Humboldt, Jedediah Smith, Mary Kingsley, and Roald Amundsen. Anthony Quinn was the host and narrator.

TENAFLY NBC
10 OCTOBER 1973–6 AUGUST 1974 One segment of *The NBC Wednesday Movie, Tenafly* alternated for one season with *Banacek, Faraday and*

Company, and *The Snoop Sisters.* It starred James McEachin as Harry Tenafly, a decidedly unflashy black private eye who worked in Los Angeles. Also featured were Lillian Lehman as his wife, Ruth Tenafly; David Huddleston as Lieutenant Church; Rosanna Huffman as his secretary, Lorrie; and Paul Jackson as his son, Herb.

THE TENNESSEE ERNIE FORD SHOW NBC/ABC

3 JANUARY 1955–28 JUNE 1957 (NBC); 4 OCTOBER 1956–29 JUNE 1961 (NBC); 2 APRIL 1962–26 MARCH 1965 (ABC) Tennessee Ernie Ford, best known as a country-and-western singer and folksy humorist, was actually born in Tennessee; by the early 1950s, however, he had moved West and was hosting a local show in Los Angeles called *Hometown Jamboree.* In 1954 he emceed a revival of Kay Kyser's *College of Musical Knowledge,* and a few months later he began hosting the first of his three network variety shows. The first was a half-hour daytime series, which also featured Molly Bee. The second, which started in the fall of 1956, was a Thursday-night half-hour series (when it was sponsored by the Ford Motor Company, it was known simply as *The Ford Show*); it featured the Top Twenty, Harry Geller's Orchestra, and the Voices of Walter Schumann. Ford's third series was a half-hour daytime show on ABC, which featured Dick Noel and Anita Gordon. His NBC shows were produced and directed by Bud Yorkin, who later teamed up with Norman Lear on *All in the Family.* Ford's ABC show was produced and directed by William Burch.

TENNESSEE TUXEDO CBS

5 OCTOBER 1963–3 SEPTEMBER 1966 Segments on this Saturday-morning cartoon show included "Tennessee Tuxedo," a penguin, "The Hunter," the story of a beagle tracking a fox, "Tutor the Turtle," and "The World of Commander McBragg."

TERRY AND THE PIRATES SYNDICATED

1952 This half-hour adventure series, based on the comic strip, starred John Baer as Terry Lee, an American colonel searching for a gold mine in the Far East; also featured were Gloria Saunders as his nemesis, The Dragon Lady, and William Tracy as Hotshot Charlie. The series was produced by Don Sharpe Enterprises.

THE TEXAN CBS

29 SEPTEMBER 1958–12 SEPTEMBER 1960 This half-hour western starred Rory Calhoun as Bill Longley, a fast-drawing drifter. Calhoun and Vic Orsatti were the executive producers, and Jerry Stagg was the producer.

TEXAS RODEO   NBC

30 APRIL 1959–2 JULY 1959   Half-hour rodeo show videotaped in Houston. L. N. Sikes and Bob Gray were the producers.

THE TEXAS WHEELERS   ABC

13 SEPTEMBER 1974–4 OCTOBER 1974; 26 JUNE 1975–31 JULY 1975
The Texas Wheelers was the first casualty of the 1974–1975 season, axed after only four episodes (though a few additional shows were broadcast during the summer of 1975). The half-hour comedy starred Jack Elam as Zack Wheeler, a lazy opportunist who hoped to live off his four children. Also featured were Gary Busey as his oldest son, Truckie; Mark Hamill as second son Doobie; Karen Oberdiear as daughter Boo; Tony Decker as youngest son T. J.; Lisa Eilbacher as Boo's friend, Sally; Bill Burton as Bud; and Dennis Burkley as Herb. Dale McRaven was the executive producer and Chris Hayward the producer for MTM Enterprises.

THAT GIRL   ABC

8 SEPTEMBER 1966–10 SEPTEMBER 1971   Marlo Thomas, daughter of Danny Thomas, starred in this half-hour sitcom as Ann Marie, an aspiring young actress living in New York; Ted Bessell costarred as her boyfriend, Don Hollinger, a writer for *Newsview* magazine (the two were finally engaged in the fall of 1970). Also featured were Lew Parker as Ann's father, Lew Marie, who owned a French restaurant in Brewster, New York, and Rosemary DeCamp as Ann's mother, Helen Marie. A considerable number of performers appeared from time to time on the show, including: Bonnie Scott as Ann's neighbor, Judy Bessemer; Dabney Coleman as Judy's husband, Leon Bessemer, an obstetrician; George Carlin (1966–1967) as Ann's agent, George Lester; Ronnie Schell (1967–1968) as agent Harvey Peck; Morty Gunty as agent Sandy Stone; Billy DeWolfe (1966–1968) as Ann's acting coach, Jules Benedict; Bernie Kopell as Don's pal, Jerry Meyer (Kopell later played pal Jerry Bauman); Alice Borden as Ruth Bauman, Jerry's wife; Reva Rose as Ann's friend, Marcy; Frank Faylen as Don's father, Bert Hollinger; and Mabel Albertson as Don's mother, Mildred Hollinger. *That Girl* was created by Bill Persky and Sam Denoff, who had both previously written for *The Dick Van Dyke Show.*

THAT GOOD OLE NASHVILLE MUSIC   SYNDICATED

1972   Half-hour country-and-western music show.

THAT REMINDS ME   ABC

13 AUGUST 1948–1 OCTOBER 1948   Half-hour Friday-night talk show with Walter Kiernan and Harold Hoffman, former governor of New Jersey (Hoffman was later one of the original panelists on *What's My Line?*).

THAT SHOW
See THE JOAN RIVERS SHOW

THAT WAS THE WEEK THAT WAS NBC
10 JANUARY 1964–4 MAY 1965 *That Was the Week That Was*, commonly abbreviated to *TW3*, was based on a British series created by Ned Sherrin. The half-hour series satirized current events, but the American version was never as well received as its British counterpart. Among the regulars on the American version were David Frost, Elliott Reid, Henry Morgan, Phyllis Newman, Buck Henry, Pat Englund, Doro Merande, Burr Tillstrom's puppets, Skitch Henderson's Orchestra, and vocalist Nancy Ames. Leland Hayward was the executive producer, and Marshall Jamison was the producer; among the writers were Saul Turteltaub, Robert Emmett, and Gerald Gardner. The show was first introduced as a special in November 1963 and became a weekly series in January, replacing *Harry's Girls*.

THAT WONDERFUL GUY ABC
4 JANUARY 1950–28 APRIL 1950 This early musical comedy series starred Jack Lemmon as Harold, a young songwriter-actor who got a job as the manservant of a crotchety drama critic; Neil Hamilton played the drama critic and Cynthia Stone (whom Lemmon later married) played Harold's girlfriend. Bernard Green's orchestra was also featured. Broadcast live, the half-hour series was produced by Charles Irving and directed by Babette Henry.

THAT'S HOLLYWOOD! SYNDICATED
1977–   This half-hour documentary series consists of film clips from the archives of 20th Century-Fox. Jack Haley, Jr. (who put together the nostalgic film, *That's Entertainment*) is the executive producer, Draper Lewis the writer and producer, and Tom Bosley the narrator.

THAT'S LIFE ABC
24 SEPTEMBER 1968–20 MAY 1969 One of television's few musical comedy series, *That's Life* starred Robert Morse as Robert Dickson and E. J. (short for Edra Jeanne) Peaker as Gloria Quigley, who, as the show progressed, got married and had a child. Also featured were Shelley Berman as Gloria's father, Mr. Quigley, and Kay Medford as her mother, Mrs. Quigley. Liza Minnelli made a rare guest appearance on 17 December.

THAT'S MY BOY CBS
10 APRIL 1954–1 JANUARY 1955 Half-hour sitcom starring Eddie Mayehoff as Jarrin' Jack Jackson, a former college football star; Rochelle Hudson as his wife, Alice Jackson; and Gil Stratton, Jr., as their son, Ju-

nior, a bookish lad who tried to resist his father's continual efforts to interest him in athletics. The series was based on the motion picture of the same title, in which Mayehoff had starred with Dean Martin and Jerry Lewis.

THAT'S MY MAMA ABC
4 SEPTEMBER 1974–24 DECEMBER 1975 Set in Washington, D.C., *That's My Mama* told the story of a black family and their friends. Featured were Theresa Merritt as Eloise (Mama) Curtis, a widow; Clifton Davis as her bachelor son, Clifton Curtis, operator of a barber shop; Lynn Moody (1974–spring 1975) and Joan Pringle (fall 1975) as her daughter, Tracy; Lisle Wilson as Tracy's husband, Leonard Taylor; Theodore Wilson as Earl Chambers, the local mail carrier; Jester Hairston as Wildcat, a jive-talking dude; Ted Lange as Clifton's friend, Junior; and DeForest Covan as Josh. Created by Dan T. Bradley and Allan Rice, the half-hour sitcom was a Blye-Beard Production.

THAT'S O'TOOLE ABC
13 MARCH 1949–5 JUNE 1949 Broadcast from Chicago, this half-hour show was aimed at the do-it-yourselfer and featured Arthur Peterson as handyman Tinker O'Toole and Norma Ransome as his wife.

THEATER IN AMERICA PBS
1974–1977 A dramatic anthology series of variable length, *Theater in America* presented fourteen to twenty-two plays per season, which were performed by several repertory companies. The series was produced by WNET-TV, New York.

THEATER OF ROMANCE
See ROMANCE

THEATER OF THE MIND NBC
14 JULY 1949–15 SEPTEMBER 1949 *Theater of the Mind* was a half-hour anthology series of psychological dramas. Each story was followed by a panel discussion moderated by Dr. Houston Peterson and featuring Dr. Marina Farnum, Dr. Edward Strecher, and Claire Savage Littledale, editor of *Parents* magazine. The series was produced and written by Ann Marlowe.

THEATRE HOUR CBS
7 OCTOBER 1949–10 MARCH 1950 This hour-long dramatic anthology series was seen on Friday nights.

THEN CAME BRONSON NBC
17 SEPTEMBER 1969–9 SEPTEMBER 1970 Michael Parks starred in this

hour adventure series as Jim Bronson, a disillusioned young man riding around the country on his motorcycle. The series was produced by MGM TV.

THERE'S ONE IN EVERY FAMILY
CBS

29 SEPTEMBER 1952–12 JUNE 1953 John Reed King hosted this daytime game show that featured contestants who possessed unusual abilities. Richard Levine produced the show, and James Sheldon directed it.

THESE ARE MY CHILDREN
NBC

31 JANUARY 1949–4 MARCH 1949 One of TV's first daytime serials, *These Are My Children* was created by Irna Phillips, who later achieved success with *The Guiding Light, As the World Turns,* and *Another World.* Directed by Norman Felton, the fifteen-minute show was broadcast live from Chicago. The cast included Alma Platts (as a widow), Joan Alt, Jane Brooksmith, George Kluge, Eloise Kunner, and Martha McCain.

THESE ARE THE DAYS
ABC

7 SEPTEMBER 1974–5 SEPTEMBER 1976 This Hanna-Barbera cartoon series capitalized on the popularity of *The Waltons.* Set in a small town at the turn of the century, it depicted the lives of the members of the Day family and their friends and neighbors. The show was seen Saturday mornings during its first season; reruns were shown Sunday mornings during the second season.

THEY STAND ACCUSED
DUMONT

11 SEPTEMBER 1949–5 OCTOBER 1952; 9 SEPTEMBER 1954–30 DECEMBER 1954 On this hour-long anthology series actual court cases were re-enacted. Broadcast live from Chicago, the show featured Chicago attorney Charles Johnston as the judge and Harry Creighton as the announcer. The jurors were chosen from the studio audience, and the verdict was theirs alone. Originally titled *Cross Question,* the show was directed by Sheldon Cooper and written by William C. Wines, an Illinois assistant attorney general.

THEY'RE OFF
DUMONT

7 JULY 1949–18 AUGUST 1949 Prime-time game show modeled after a horse race.

THICKER THAN WATER
ABC

13 JUNE 1973–8 AUGUST 1973 Based on the British series, *Nearest and Dearest,* this half-hour sitcom told the story of a squabbling brother and sister who were each promised a $75,000 inheritance if they agreed to run the family pickle factory for five years. With Julie Harris as Nellie Paine; Richard Long as Ernie Paine; Malcolm Atterbury as their father, Jonas

Paine, who believed that his demise was imminent; Jessica Myerson as Cousin Lily; Lou Fant as Cousin Walter; and Pat Cranshaw as longtime employee Bert Taylor.

THE THIN MAN   NBC
20 SEPTEMBER 1957–26 JUNE 1959   Half-hour crime show based on the Dashiell Hammett novel and the film series. With Peter Lawford as New York private eye Nick Charles; Phyllis Kirk as his wife and frequent partner in crime-solving, Nora Charles; Jack Albertson as Lieutenant Evans; and Asta as Asta, the Charles' pet terrier. The series was produced by MGM TV.

THINK FAST   ABC
26 MARCH 1949–8 OCTOBER 1950   Celebrity panelists tried to outtalk each other on this prime-time game show by extemporizing on subjects suggested by the host. Mason Gross was the first emcee and was succeeded by Gypsy Rose Lee. Robert Kennings produced the half-hour series.

THE THINK PINK PANTHER SHOW
See THE PINK PANTHER SHOW

THE THIRD MAN   SYNDICATED
1959–1960   Graham Greene's adventure novel was made into a movie in 1949 and a radio series in 1950. Almost a decade later it came to television, where Michael Rennie starred as Harry Lime, international troubleshooter (James Mason had previously been considered for the part); Jonathan Harris was also featured as Lime's assistant, Bradford Webster. Vernon Burns was executive producer of the half-hour series, filmed both in Hollywood and on location in Europe.

13 QUEENS BLVD.   ABC
20 MARCH 1979–17 APRIL 1979; 10 JULY 1979–24 JULY 1979   An adult sitcom set in a Queens apartment building. The spring cast included Eileen Brennan as Felicia Winters; Jerry Van Dyke as her husband, Steven Winters; Marcia Rodd as her divorced friend and neighbor, Elaine Dowling; Helen Page Camp as her widowed friend and neighbor, Millie Capestro; and Louise Williams as Millie's daughter, Jill Capestro. The summer cast included Brennan, Camp, and Williams, along with Frances Lee McCain as Lois, Felicia's sister-in-law, and Karen Rushmore as Camille. Richard Baer created the half-hour show, which was developed by Bud Yorkin, Bernie Orenstein, and Saul Turteltaub.

30 MINUTES   CBS
16 SEPTEMBER 1978–   A junior edition of *60 Minutes,* this

Saturday-afternoon newsmagazine for young people is cohosted by Betsy Aaron and Christopher Glenn.

THIRTY MINUTES WITH   PBS
12 JANUARY 1971–21 MAY 1973   Half-hour interview show, hosted by Washington political analyst Elizabeth Drew.

THIS COULD BE YOU
See THE BILL GWINN SHOW

THIS IS ALICE   SYNDICATED
1958   Half-hour family sitcom. With Patty Ann Gerrity as nine-year-old Alice Holliday; Tom Farrell as her father; Phyllis Coates as her mother; Stephen Wootton as her brother; and Leigh Snowden as her friend, Betty Lou. Set in Atlanta, the series was produced and directed by Sidney Salkow.

THIS IS CHARLES LAUGHTON   SYNDICATED
1953   A series of dramatic readings by British actor Charles Laughton; the series marked his American TV debut.

THIS IS GALEN DRAKE   ABC
12 JANUARY 1957–11 MAY 1957   Half-hour variety show for children hosted by Galen Drake.

THIS IS MUSIC   DUMONT/ABC
29 NOVEMBER 1951–9 OCTOBER 1952 (DUMONT); 6 JUNE 1958–21 MAY 1959 (ABC)   On this half-hour musical series the show's regulars pantomimed to popular musical recordings. Regulars on the DuMont version of the series, which was broadcast from Chicago, included Alexander Gray and Colin Male. Regulars on the ABC version included Ramona Burnett, Bob Shreve, Gail Johnson, and Bob Smith.

THIS IS SHOW BUSINESS   CBS/NBC
15 JULY 1949–9 MARCH 1954 (CBS); 26 JUNE 1956–11 SEPTEMBER 1956 (NBC)   On this half-hour variety show guest celebrities dropped by to visit a celebrity panel; in theory, anyway, the guests were supposed to present a problem to the panelists, who could then offer their advice on solving it. By the fall of 1953, however, this requirement had been abandoned. Clifton Fadiman hosted the series, and the CBS panel regularly included Sam Levenson, Abe Burrows, and George S. Kaufman, who was suspended from the show as the result of viewer complaints after he remarked on the broadcast of 21 December 1952, "Let's make this one program on which no one sings 'Silent Night'!" In 1956, when the series

was revived on NBC, the panel included Abe Burrows, Walter Slezak, and Jacqueline Susann. Irving Mansfield (Susann's husband) produced the series, and Byron Paul directed it.

THIS IS THE ANSWER   SYNDICATED
1959–1961   Religious program produced by the Southern Baptist Convention.

THIS IS THE LIFE   SYNDICATED
1952–   This long-running religious show presents dramas dealing with contemporary problems. In the early seasons it centered on the Fisher family of Middleburg, and the regular cast included Forrest Taylor, Onslow Stevens, Nan Boardman, Randy Stuart, Michael Hall, and David Kasday. In more recent times, however, it has relied on guest stars. The show is produced under the auspices of the Lutheran Church, Missouri Synod, in cooperation with the National Council of Churches of Christ. The half-hour series was also carried by ABC and DuMont in 1952 and 1953.

THIS IS TOM JONES   ABC
7 FEBRUARY 1969–15 JANUARY 1971   Welsh singer Tom Jones hosted his own musical variety hour, which also featured Big Jim Sullivan, The Ace Trucking Company, the Norman Maen Dancers, and the Johnnie Spence Orchestra.

THIS IS YOUR LIFE   NBC/SYNDICATED
1 OCTOBER 1952–10 SEPTEMBER 1961(NBC); 1970 (SYNDICATED)
Ralph Edwards hosted this sentimental human interest show, which he began on radio in 1948. Each week a special guest was lured to the studio by a ruse, and then surprised as Edwards announced, "This is your life!" Long-lost friends and relatives materialized during the ensuing half hour to relive long-forgotten incidents in the past. Most of Edwards's guests were celebrities, but some of his most effective shows centered on ordinary people. One program featured a rare television appearance by Stan Laurel and Oliver Hardy; another, honoring educator Laurence C. Jones, generated more than $700,000 in contributions toward the endowment of Piney Woods (Miss.) College, after Edwards suggested that viewers send Dr. Jones a dollar for the fund. One of the very few guests who was not pleasantly surprised by the evening's festivities was Lowell Thomas, who said, "This is a sinister conspiracy!" and refused to crack a smile during the whole show.

THIS IS YOUR MUSIC   SYNDICATED
1955   Half-hour variety show, featuring Joan Weldon and Byron Palmer, among others.

THIS MAN DAWSON　　　　　　　　　　　　　　　SYNDICATED

1959　Half-hour crime show starring Keith Andes as Colonel Frank Dawson, a former Marine officer who took over a big city police department. William Conrad and Elliott Lewis produced the show for Ziv TV.

THIS MORNING

See THE DICK CAVETT SHOW

THIS OLD HOUSE　　　　　　　　　　　　　　　　PBS

1979　Thirteen-part instructional series on refurbishing an old house. The house, located in the Dorchester section of Boston, was sold at auction in June of 1979 to raise funds for WGBH-TV, Boston's educational outlet.

THIS WEEK　　　　　　　　　　　　　　　　　　PBS

6 OCTOBER 1971–26 JUNE 1972　Half-hour show, with no fixed format, hosted by Bill Moyers. See also *Bill Moyers' Journal*.

THIS WEEK IN SPORTS　　　　　　　　　　　　　CBS

20 SEPTEMBER 1949–13 DECEMBER 1949　Fifteen-minute sports newsreel.

THOSE ENDEARING YOUNG CHARMS　　　　　　　　NBC

30 DECEMBER 1951–26 JUNE 1952　A comedy series, *Those Endearing Young Charms* told the story of the Charms, a family living in a small New England town. Featured were Maurice Copeland and Betty Arnold as Mr. and Mrs. Charm, Clarence Hartzell as the eccentric uncle, Gerald Garvey as the son, and Pat Matthews as the daughter. Ben Park produced and directed the half-hour show, broadcast live from Chicago.

THOSE TWO　　　　　　　　　　　　　　　　　NBC

26 NOVEMBER 1951–24 APRIL 1953　Pinky Lee cohosted this musical variety show with Vivian Blaine until May 1952, when Martha Stewart succeeded her. The fifteen-minute show was seen Mondays, Wednesdays, and Fridays before the evening news.

THOSE WHITING GIRLS　　　　　　　　　　　　　CBS

4 JULY 1955–26 SEPTEMBER 1955; 1 JULY 1957–30 SEPTEMBER 1957 This half-hour sitcom was twice a summer replacement for *I Love Lucy;* it was created by two of *Lucy*'s writers, Madelyn Pugh and Bob Carroll, Jr. Sisters Barbara and Margaret Whiting played themselves, Barbara an actress and Margaret a singer. Also featured were Mabel Albertson as their mother, Mrs. Whiting; Jerry Paris as Margaret's accompanist Artie; Beverly Long as their friend, Olive; and Kathy Nolan (1957) as their friend, Penny.

THREE ABOUT TOWN ABC
11 AUGUST 1948–20 OCTOBER 1948 One of ABC's first network programs, this fifteen-minute musical series was hosted by singer Betsi Allison.

THE THREE FLAMES SHOW NBC
13 JUNE 1949–20 AUGUST 1949 This summer musical series starred the Three Flames, a black trio. The group had previously been featured on a daytime show seen locally in New York, and later appeared on *Washington Square*.

3 FOR THE MONEY NBC
29 SEPTEMBER 1975–28 NOVEMBER 1975 Two 3-member teams matched wits on this daytime game show; each was composed of a celebrity captain and two contestants. A Stefan Hatos–Monty Hall Production, the show was hosted by Dick Enberg.

THREE FOR THE ROAD CBS
14 SEPTEMBER 1975–30 NOVEMBER 1975 A Sunday-evening family drama about a widowed photographer and his two sons who traveled around the country in their camper, the "Zebec." With Alex Rocco as Pete Karras; Vincent Van Patten as son John; Leif Garrett as son Endy (short for Endicott). Jerry McNeely was the executive producer for MTM Enterprises.

3 GIRLS 3 NBC
30 MARCH 1977–29 JUNE 1977 *3 Girls 3,* an imaginative variety hour that introduced three unknowns, was highly acclaimed but suffered from a lack of publicity and poor scheduling—one hour was shown in March, the remaining three in June. Gary Smith and Dwight Hemion were the executive producers, and the three stars were Debbie Allen, Ellen Foley, and Mimi Kennedy.

THE THREE MUSKETEERS SYNDICATED
1956 Half-hour adventure series produced in Europe, based on Alexandre Dumas's classic novel. With Jeff Stone as D'Artagnan; Paul Campbell as Aramis; Peter Trent as Porthos; Alan Furlan as Sasquinet; and Sebastian Cabot as the Count de Brisemont.

THREE ON A MATCH NBC
2 AUGUST 1971–28 JUNE 1974 Bill Cullen hosted this daytime game show on which three contestants competed for money by answering true-false questions, then got to spend it on the prize board.

THE THREE ROBONIC STOOGES   CBS

28 JANUARY 1978–2 SEPTEMBER 1978   Half-hour cartoon series which
began as one segment of *The Skatebirds.*

THREE STEPS TO HEAVEN   NBC

3 AUGUST 1953–31 DECEMBER 1954   Daytime serial about a young
woman who left the small town where she grew up to become a model in
New York City. With Kathleen Maguire, Phyllis Hill, and Diana Douglas as model Poco Thurmond; Gene Blakely and Mark Roberts as Poco's
boyfriend, Bill Morgan; Lori March as Jennifer; Ginger MacManus as
Angela; Laurie Vendig as Alice; Walter Brooke; and Joe Brown, Jr. Adrian Samish was the producer and Irving Vendig was the writer.

THREE'S A CROWD   SYNDICATED

1979   Half-hour game show from Chuck Barris Productions which
sought to answer the age-old question: Who knows a man better, his wife
or his secretary? First, three husbands were asked a series of questions;
their secretaries then came onstage and were asked the same questions.
Finally the three wives were brought on and asked the questions. If the
three secretaries scored more matches, they split $1000; if the three wives
had more matches, they divided up the prize. Jim Peck was the host.

THREE'S COMPANY   CBS

18 MAY 1950–29 SEPTEMBER 1950   This fifteen-minute musical series,
seen Tuesdays and Thursdays following the network news, featured Cy
Walters, Stan Freeman, and Judy Lynn.

THREE'S COMPANY   ABC

15 MARCH 1977–21 APRIL 1977; 11 AUGUST 1977–   This sex
comedy, based on a British show called *Man About the House,* was introduced as a limited series in the spring of 1977 and returned to stay a few
months later; it wound up as the third top-rated show for the 1977–1978
season. Set in Los Angeles, it tells the tale of a young man sharing an
apartment with two young women; the landlord, mistakenly believing the
man to be homosexual, permitted the arrangement. Created and produced by Don Nicholl, Michael Ross, and Bernie West, the half-hour series features: John Ritter as Jack Tripper; Joyce DeWitt as Janet Wood,
the sensible one; Suzanne Somers as Chrissy Snow, the daffy one; Norman Fell (1977–1979) as the apparently impotent landlord, Stanley Roper; Audra Lindley (1977–1979) as his sex-starved wife, Helen Roper; and
Richard Kline (1978–   ) as Jack's friend, Larry. In the fall of 1979
Don Knotts was added as the new landlord, Ralph Furley, and Ann
Wedgeworth appeared as neighbor Lana Shields. See also *The Ropers.*

THRILL HUNTERS   SYNDICATED

1966   A series of half-hour films about people with exciting occupations or hobbies, *Thrill Hunters* was hosted by Bill Burrud, and was thus distinguishable from such shows as *Danger Is My Business* and *The Thrillseekers*.

THRILLER   NBC

13 SEPTEMBER 1960–9 JULY 1962   Boris Karloff was the host and occasional star in this anthology series of crime and horror stories. Hubbell Robinson was the executive producer of the hour show for Revue Studios. Fletcher Markle, the original producer, and James P. Cavanaugh, the story editor, were replaced after eight episodes by producers Maxwell Shane and William Frye. A total of sixty-seven episodes were produced.

THE THRILLSEEKERS   SYNDICATED

1973   Chuck Connors hosted this half-hour series, which profiled persons with dangerous occupations and interests.

THROUGH THE CRYSTAL BALL   CBS

18 APRIL 1949–4 JULY 1949   Mime Jimmy Savo hosted this fantasy series for children for several weeks. Produced and directed by Paul Belanger, it was one of the first series to feature pantomime. The later shows were variety programs, rather than fantasies.

THROUGH THE CURTAIN   ABC

21 OCTOBER 1953–24 FEBRUARY 1954   This fifteen-minute prime-time public affairs program was hosted by George Hamilton Combs. It consisted of interviews with people who had been behind the Iron Curtain and digests of press reports from Communist news agencies.

THROUGH WENDY'S WINDOW
See THE WENDY BARRIE SHOW

THUNDER   NBC

10 SEPTEMBER 1977–2 SEPTEMBER 1978   The central character in this live-action Saturday-morning show was a wild black stallion named Thunder, the equine equivalent of Lassie. The human roles were filled by: Clint Ritchie as rancher Bill Williams; Melissa Converse as his wife, Anne Williams, a veterinarian; Melora Hardin as their daughter, Cindy; Justin Randi as their son, Willie. Thunder and Cupcake, the mule ridden by Cindy and Willie, were owned by Bobby Davenport. The half-hour series was created and produced by Irving Cummings and Charles Marion for Charles Fries Productions.

THUNDERBIRDS   SYNDICATED

1967   Another of the marionette adventure series developed in England
by Gerry Anderson, *Thunderbirds* was the most highly sophisticated of
Anderson's efforts. Anderson had by now refined the technique of super-
marionation, a process using wires and electric devices to manipulate the
marionettes, which he had previously used on such shows as *Fireball XL-
5* and *Supercar. Thunderbirds,* produced in hour-long form, told the story
of a group of twenty-first-century space heroes.

TIC TAC DOUGH   NBC

30 JULY 1956–30 OCTOBER 1959

THE NEW TIC TAC DOUGH   CBS/SYNDICATED

3 JULY 1978–1 SEPTEMBER 1978 (CBS); 1978 (SYNDICATED)   Two
contestants played tic-tac-toe on this game show. The game board was divided into nine categories; one of the players selected a category, and a
question was read. Whoever answered correctly won the square, and then
selected another category; the winner of the game then faced a new challenger. *Tic Tac Dough* was seen in both daytime and prime-time versions;
the latter ran from September 1957 to December 1958, and was hosted
for most of its run by Jay Jackson. The daytime version, which ran for
more than three years, was hosted by Jack Barry, Gene Rayburn, and
Bill Wendell. Nineteen years later two versions of *The New Tic Tac
Dough* surfaced, both hosted by Wink Martindale. The network version
was seen during the daytime on CBS, while the syndicated version was
shown evenings in most markets. Both reincarnations were basically similar to the original version of the show.

TIGHTROPE!   CBS

8 SEPTEMBER 1959–13 SEPTEMBER 1960   Half-hour crime show starring Michael Connors as an undercover police agent who hid his gun in
the small of his back. In the earliest episodes Connors's character had no
name, but by late autumn the character was christened Nick Stone. Clarence Greene and Russell Rouse produced the series.

THE TIM CONWAY COMEDY HOUR   CBS

20 SEPTEMBER 1970–13 DECEMBER 1970   Tim Conway's second 1970
show was a variety hour, but it was even less successful than his previous
effort. Conway did, however, line up an impressive list of regulars:
McLean Stevenson, Sally Struthers, Art Metrano, Bonnie Boland, singers
Belland and Somerville (during the 1950s Bruce Belland had sung with
the Four Preps and Dave Somerville with the Diamonds), the Tom Hansen Dancers, the Jimmy Joyce Singers, and announcer Ernie Anderson.

THE TIM CONWAY SHOW   CBS

30 JANUARY 1970–19 JUNE 1970   The first of Tim Conway's two 1970
series was a half-hour sitcom in which he was reunited with his *McHale's*

Navy costar, Joe Flynn. They played Tim "Spud" Barrett and Herb Kenworth, owners and crew of the one-plane Anytime Anyplace Airlines. Also aboard were Anne Seymour as Mrs. Crawford, owner of the local airport; Johnnie Collins III as her son, Ronnie; Fabian Dean as Harry, operator of the airport burger stand; and Emily Banks as Becky, a Crawford employee and Spud's romantic interest.

TIME EXPRESS CBS
26 APRIL 1979–17 MAY 1979 Four-week fantasy series set aboard a mysterious train on which passengers personally selected by "the head of the line" were given the opportunity to return to an incident from their past. With Vincent Price as Jason Winters and Coral Brown as Margaret Winters, the on-board hosts; Woodrow Parfrey as the Ticket Agent; William Edward Phipps as E. Patrick Callahan, the engineer; James Reynolds as Robert Jefferson (R.J.) Walker, the conductor. Ivan Goff and Ben Roberts created the series and were the executive producers; Leonard B. Kaufman was the producer.

TIME FOR BEANY SYNDICATED
1950–1955
THE BEANY AND CECIL SHOW ABC
6 JANUARY 1962–19 DECEMBER 1964 Beany and Cecil, two characters created by Bob Clampett, first appeared nationally in a fifteen-minute puppet show broadcast from Hollywood. Beany was a little boy who sailed the high seas aboard the *Leakin' Lena* with his uncle, Captain Horatio K. Huffenpuff; Cecil was a sea serpent (and a seasick one at that) who was, at first, visible only to Beany, but who later revealed himself to the Captain as well. In their travels the trio encountered a host of unusual characters, such as Tearalong the Dotted Lion and The Staring Herring, but their most persistent nemesis was Dishonest John. The creator of the series, Bob Clampett, was an animator for Warner Brothers who dabbled in puppetry. Cecil, whom Clampett had created several years earlier, was introduced on a local show in Los Angeles in 1948; the show soon acquired a sizable audience and attracted the attention of Paramount Television, which offered it nationwide in 1950. Stan Freberg provided the voice of the Captain; Daws Butler (later the voice of Huckleberry Hound, Quickdraw McGraw, and Yogi Bear) that of Beany; and Clampett himself that of Cecil. Clampett's characters later appeared in a half-hour cartoon series which was carried by ABC for several years. Originally sponsored by Mattel Toys, the latter series was titled *Matty's Funnies with Beany and Cecil* in its early weeks.

TIME FOR REFLECTION DUMONT
30 APRIL 1950–14 JANUARY 1951 David Ross read poetry on this fifteen-minute Sunday-evening show.

A TIME FOR US   ABC
28 DECEMBER 1964–16 DECEMBER 1966   This half-hour daytime serial
premiered in 1964 under the title *Flame in the Wind* and was renamed in
June of 1965. Set in the town of Havilland, its stories centered on young
people. The cast included: Beverly Hayes as Jane Driscoll; Joanna Miles
as her sister, Linda Driscoll, an aspiring actress; Ray Poole as their father, Al Driscoll, a contractor; Lenka Peterson as their mother, Martha
Driscoll; Gordon Gray and Tom Fielding as Steve Reynolds, the romantic interest of both Jane and Linda; Maggie Hayes as Roxanne Reynolds;
Walter Coy as Roxanne's father, Jason Farrell; Ian Berger as Doug Colton; Morgan Sterne as Tony Gray; Josephine Nichols as Louise; Conrad
Fowkes as Paul; Elaine Hyman as Fran; Terry Logan as Dave, a medical
student; Lesley Woods as Miriam Bentley; and Kathleen Maguire as
Kate Austin.

A TIME TO LIVE   NBC
5 JULY 1954–31 DECEMBER 1954   This fifteen-minute daytime serial
starred Pat Sully and Larry Kerr as journalists Kathy Byron and Don
Riker.

TIME TO REMEMBER   SYNDICATED
1963   Half-hour filmed documentary series on great historical events of
the twentieth century.

THE TIME TUNNEL   ABC
9 SEPTEMBER 1966–1 SEPTEMBER 1967   Hour-long science fiction series
about two research scientists who, working on a government-sponsored
project, developed a time machine by which they could be transported
into the past or the future. With James Darren as Dr. Tony Newman;
Robert Colbert as Dr. Doug Phillips; Whit Bissell as Lieutenant General
Heywood Kirk, project supervisor; John Zaremba as Dr. Raymond
Swain; Lee Meriwether as Dr. Ann MacGregor; and Wesley Lau as Master Sergeant Jiggs, the security officer. The series was created by Irwin
Allen, who was also its executive producer (Allen also developed *Land of
the Giants, Lost in Space,* and *Voyage to the Bottom of the Sea*). Special
effects were supervised by Bill Abbott, who won an Emmy for his
services.

TIME WILL TELL   DUMONT
27 AUGUST 1954–15 OCTOBER 1954   Ernie Kovacs hosted this short-
lived prime-time game show.

TIN PAN ALLEY TV   ABC
28 APRIL 1950–29 SEPTEMBER 1950   Each week this half-hour variety
show featured the music of a guest composer. Regulars included Johnny

Desmond, Gloria Van, Chet Roble, Montero and Yvonne, the Vision-aires, and the Rex Maupin Orchestra. Broadcast from Chicago, the show was produced by Fred Killan and Tim Morrow.

TO ROME WITH LOVE   CBS
28 SEPTEMBER 1969–1 SEPTEMBER 1971   Half-hour sitcom about a wid-owed professor and his three daughters, all of whom moved to Rome when he was hired to teach at an American school there. With John For-sythe as Professor Mike Endicott; Joyce Menges as daughter Alison; Su-san Neher as daughter Penny; Melanie Fullerton as daughter Pokey; Kay Medford (1969–1970) as Aunt Harriet; Walter Brennan (1970–1971) as Andy Pruitt, the girls' maternal grandfather; Peggy Mondo as Mama Vi-tale, the landlady; Vito Scotti as cabbie Gino Mancini; and Gerald Mi-chenaud as Penny's pal, Nico. Don Fedderson was the executive producer.

TO SAY THE LEAST   NBC
3 OCTOBER 1977–21 APRIL 1978   Daytime game show hosted by Tom Kennedy on which two 2-member teams (each with a celebrity and a player) played a word game. The half-hour show was from Heatter-Quig-ley Productions.

TO TELL THE TRUTH   CBS/SYNDICATED
Nighttime: 18 DECEMBER 1956–5 SEPTEMBER 1966 (CBS); 12 DECEM-BER 1966–22 MAY 1967 (CBS); *Daytime:* 18 JUNE 1962–6 SEPTEMBER 1968 (CBS); 1969–1977 (SYNDICATED)   One of TV's most popular game shows, *To Tell the Truth* was developed by Mark Goodson and Bill Todman, who also put together *What's My Line?, I've Got a Secret, The Match Game,* and a host of other game shows. The format was simple—a panel of four celebrities tried to determine which of three guests, each claiming to be the same person, was telling the truth. The three guests stood at center stage while an affidavit, reciting the story of the real claimant, was read aloud; the guests were then seated, and the panelists took turns questioning them. The two impostors were free to lie, but the real claimant was sworn to tell the truth. At the conclusion of the ques-tioning each panelist voted separately, and the identity of the claimant was revealed ("Will the real _____ please stand up?"). The three guests then split a cash award, calculated on the number of incorrect votes. Because the identity of the real claimant was not revealed to the viewing audience until the end of the questioning, viewers were able to play the game along with the panelists. *To Tell the Truth* began in 1956 as a prime-time show. The title was changed shortly before the premiere from *Nothing But the Truth.* The celebrity panel on the premiere includ-ed Polly Bergen, Dick Van Dyke, Hildy Parks, and John Cameron Swayze. Other panelists who appeared frequently on the network ver-

sions were Tom Poston, Kitty Carlisle, Peggy Cass, Orson Bean, and Phyllis Newman. Bud Collyer hosted both the prime-time and the daytime versions on CBS. The syndicated version, which began in 1969, was hosted by Garry Moore until 1977, when Joe Garagiola took over for the last few shows; the celebrity regulars on that version were Kitty Carlisle, Peggy Cass, and Bill Cullen, plus a guest celeb.

TO THE QUEEN'S TASTE
See DIONE LUCAS' COOKING SHOW

TOAST OF THE TOWN
See THE ED SULLIVAN SHOW

TODAY   NBC
14 JANUARY 1952–   Network television's first early-morning program, *Today* survived a shaky start to become one of the most profitable shows in history. Though it is not network television's longest-running daytime series (*Search for Tomorrow* predated it), because of its two-hours-per-weekday slot it has occupied more total air time—some 15,000 hours—than any other single show. In its early years, *Today* was actually telecast for three hours a day, though only two hours were carried by any affiliate; the show's first hour was seen from 7 to 8 a.m. only in the East, and was recreated—live—for the Midwest after the second East Coast hour (by late 1958, when high-quality videotape had become available, the show was broadcast to other parts of the country on a delayed basis, and the extra hour was no longer necessary).

The show was the brainchild of Sylvester "Pat" Weaver, one of the most creative executives in the history of broadcasting. Weaver realized that television was more than radio with pictures and sought to develop new kinds of programs to capitalize on television's unique qualities. One of his first concepts was the Saturday-night comedy program which became *Your Show of Shows*. He is also credited with developing the special entertainment broadcast, which he called the "spectacular." In addition to the *Today* show, Weaver also developed *Home, Tonight,* and *Wide Wide World*.

Weaver saw the *Today* show as a program that few people would watch from beginning to end; instead, it was to be designed so that viewers could eat breakfast and get ready for school or work without devoting all of their time and attention to the television set. A news summary was given every half hour, and the other segments (chiefly consisting of sports, weather, interviews, and features) were kept short. As early-morning broadcasting was then virtually unknown (even daytime broadcasting was a rarity in some parts of the country), Weaver sought to make the show attractive to local stations by offering them a share of *Today's* network advertising revenues plus several minutes of commercial time each

715

hour (the latter feature soon became standardized, as most affiliates "cut away" for a five-minute local newscast at twenty-five minutes past each hour).

The man chosen to host the show was Dave Garroway. Though he started out as a radio newscaster in Pittsburgh, he did not attract attention until he began hosting a variety series, *Garroway at Large,* over WMAQ-TV in Chicago. Garroway was not Weaver's first choice for the *Today* job, but his relaxed, conversational manner on camera convinced Weaver that he would be just right for a waking audience. Chosen to assist Garroway were Jack Lescoulie, to handle sports and light features, and Jim Fleming, to read the news.

The show premiered on 14 January 1952, a week behind schedule, in its own studio on the ground floor of the RCA Exhibition Hall on West Forty-ninth Street in New York. A large plate-glass window enabled passersby to see the show and to be seen as the cameras periodically panned it (President Harry S Truman, who liked to take a morning walk wherever he stayed, was once maneuvered into camera range for an abortive interview). Teletape machines, telephones, and a row of clocks showing the time in selected cities throughout the world dominated the set. The show opened with just one sponsor (the Kiplinger Newsletter), thirty-one affiliates, and poor reviews—most of the critics thought that the show was poorly paced and that its human performers seemed overwhelmed by its gadgetry. These early problems were gradually worked out, and the use of electronics was deemphasized; Garroway, Lescoulie, and company even began to appear in skits to help give the show a lighter touch. By the end of 1952 *Today* had managed to pick up a few new sponsors and a few more affiliates.

The year 1953 proved to be a signal year for *Today,* as it attracted large audiences and began to make money. One reason for its change of fortune was an aggressive sales staff, but an equally important factor in boosting ratings was a chimpanzee named J. Fred Muggs, whose antics helped lure hundreds of thousands of children, and their parents, to the screen. Owned by trainer Buddy Menella and Roy Waldron, Muggs was ten months old when he came to the show early in 1953; he soon became one of America's most popular animal celebrities and went on several personal appearance tours (he was especially in demand to dedicate supermarkets). Muggs was never popular with the show's staff, but the same could be said of several of *Today*'s human regulars. Having become increasingly hard to handle, Muggs was dropped after four years (the press release announcing his departure stated that he was leaving to "extend his personal horizons"). He was briefly succeeded by another chimp named Mr. Kokomo.

Shortly after Muggs's arrival in 1953, newscaster Jim Fleming announced his departure; he was replaced by Frank Blair, who remained with *Today* for twenty-two years, longer than anyone else connected with the show. It was also in 1953 that *Today* began to feature a woman regularly. The "Today Girl," as she was called for many years, originally had few responsibilities, but the role gradually expanded so that by 1974 Barbara Walters, the incumbent, had become a full-fledged cohost. The first "Today Girls," however, were shapely young women who were featured just for the day. The first permanent "Today Girl" was a program staffer whose duties included reading the temperature and a one-word description of the weather in America's major cities; she left the show in 1954 for a more promising career on stage and in films. Her name was Estelle Parsons. Among the other women who appeared during Garroway's tenure were Lee Ann Meriwether (Miss America of 1955), who left the show late in 1956 (she is currently a regular on *Barnaby Jones*), singer Helen O'Connell (1956–1958), game show panelist Betsy Palmer (1958–1959), actress Florence Henderson (1959–1960), former Miss Rheingold Robbin Bain (1960), journalist Beryl Pfizer (1960–1961), and actress Anita Colby (1961). Physical fitness expert Bonnie Prudden and learned Charles Van Doren (a big winner on *Twenty-One*) also appeared regularly during the late 1950s.

In 1958, partly to accommodate Dave Garroway's busy schedule (he was hosting *Wide Wide World* on TV and doing several NBC radio broadcasts), the *Today* show began to be taped a day in advance (the news segments, of course, continued to be done live), a practice that continued on and off for the next four years. Despite the change of schedule, Garroway became more difficult to work with, and after the death of his second wife in April of 1961, he decided to leave the show. In July of that year, after more than nine years as host of *Today* (which was by then titled *The Dave Garroway Today Show*), Garroway closed the show for the last time with his familiar "Peace" signoff, to the accompaniment of Lionel Hampton's version of "Sentimental Journey." Garroway made few appearances on network TV thereafter; he was a guest on *Today*'s fifteenth and twenty-fifth anniversary shows, and also hosted *The Newcomers* in 1971 on CBS. Following Garroway's departure, *Today* turned more stolid under new host John Chancellor. A veteran newsman, Chancellor never really felt at home in the role, and lasted only fourteen months. Garroway's second banana, Jack Lescoulie, had also left the show, and Chancellor's regulars included Edwin Newman, who was brought in to read the news, Louise King, the new "Today Girl," and a disgruntled Frank Blair, who found himself in the unwanted role of sidekick (the four even appeared in skits from time to time, an idea revived to make the show less wooden).

Chancellor's successor was Hugh Downs, who took over in October 1962; Downs thus became the only person to have been a regular on all three of Pat Weaver's weekday programming concepts, *Home, Tonight,* and *Today.* Downs also continued to host a daytime game show, *Concentration,* for the first few years of his *Today* tenure. Frank Blair returned to the news desk; Jack Lescoulie also came back to the show that year, but left within twelve months. Though Downs and his producer, Al Morgan, feuded from 1962 to 1968 (when Morgan was dropped at Downs's insistence), *Today*'s ratings remained steady. During this time the show often originated in places other than New York (the practice had actually started with Garroway), and, with the advent of communications satellites, telecasts from Europe were introduced. It was also during Downs's term as host that Barbara Walters began appearing regularly. Walters had previously worked for CBS's *The Morning Show,* an ineffective competitor of *Today,* and was hired as a freelance writer by *Today*'s then producer, Fred Freed, in 1961. She was pressed into on-camera service for the funeral of President John Kennedy in November 1963, and thereafter was used regularly on the show. Finally, in 1964 she was selected to succeed actress Maureen O'Sullivan as the next in the series of "Today Girls." O'Sullivan, who had replaced Pat Fontaine, found it difficult to work with Downs and was dropped after only a few months. Walters soon established herself as a first-rate interviewer; always well prepared, she sometimes joined Downs in questioning guests. *Variety* later hailed her presence on the show as "a victory of brains over mannequin beauty." In 1964 Judith Crist and Aline Saarinen also began to appear regularly, reviewing films and art respectively. By 1967 Joe Garagiola had also signed on as a regular. A onetime second-string catcher for the St. Louis Cardinals, the affable Garagiola had been an NBC sportscaster; his quick wit helped offset Downs's tendency toward longwindedness.

Having outlasted producer Morgan, Downs departed from *Today* on 11 October 1971, concluding a reign only slightly shorter than Garroway's. Downs's successor, Frank McGee, signaled another shift toward the stolid. McGee was a tough, well-respected newsman who had worked in Oklahoma City, Montgomery, Washington, and New York. McGee was not well liked by the *Today* staff. Though he and Barbara Walters appeared to get along on camera, relations between the two were strained—McGee insisted on opening and closing the show himself and also reserved the right to ask the first question of any guest slated to be interviewed by Walters. Whether the rift between the two would have widened will never be known, however, as McGee died of bone cancer in April of 1974, after only two and one-half years on the job.

McGee's replacement, chosen with Barbara Walters's approval, was Jim Hartz. Like McGee, Hartz hailed from Oklahoma (he had delivered the eulogy at McGee's funeral); Hartz had hosted a local newscast in New York beginning in 1965, when he was just twenty-four. Apparently Hartz was never very popular with viewers, for *Today*'s ratings began to decline appreciably during his brief tenure. When Barbara Walters, who was now the official cohost of the show, left the show in June of 1976 for ABC, Hartz too was dropped. It was during Hartz's short stay that

Frank Blair left the show; his last newscast was on 14 March 1975, and he was succeeded by Lew Wood. Joe Garagiola had also left the show by this time and was succeeded by bushy-haired Gene Shalit. A former publicity agent, Shalit had originally reviewed films for *Today,* but by 1974 he was the new number two.

Jim Hartz was succeeded by Tom Brokaw on 29 August 1976; like Chancellor and McGee, Brokaw was an experienced newsman who had worked in Omaha, Atlanta, Los Angeles, and at the White House during the final days of the Nixon administration. Brokaw, however, was not as humorless as his newsmen predecessors. Shortly before Brokaw's arrival, Floyd Kalber was hired to read the news (Lew Wood stayed with the show, but did only the weather; Wood left in the spring of 1978 and was succeeded by Bob Ryan).

An intensive search was undertaken to fill the void left by Barbara Walters. Six women were tested on the air for the job—Cassie Mackin, Betty Rollin, Linda Ellerbee, Kelly Lange, Betty Furness, and Jane Pauley. Pauley was finally selected. Born in 1950, Pauley was barely older than the show itself; she had previously worked in Indianapolis and at WMAQ-TV in Chicago (the same station that Garroway had worked for almost thirty years before). By the end of 1977, *Today's* ratings, which had deteriorated for several years (due in part to competition from ABC's *Good Morning, America*) finally turned around. Tom Brokaw, Jane Pauley, Gene Shalit, Floyd Kalber, and Bob Ryan comprised the show's regular crew; several other people also appeared occasionally, including Betty Furness (reporting on consumer affairs), Dr. Art Ulene (health care), and Edwin Newman (language). In May of 1979 talk-show host Phil Donahue became a regular contributor to the show. Floyd Kalber left during the summer of 1979 and was succeeded by Tony Guida; in the fall of 1979 Guida began to do assignment reporting, and Brokaw and Pauley read the news.

Today's producers have included: Mort Weiner (with Dick Pinkham as the first executive producer), Jac Hein, Bob Bendick, Shad Northshield, Fred Freed, Northshield (again), Al Morgan, Stuart Schulberg, Paul Friedman, and, most recently, Joe Bartelme. The show's theme song until 1978, "This Is Today," was composed by Ray Ellis. Late in 1978, in a copyright infringement suit, a federal court ruled that Ellis's composition bore too close a resemblance to "Day by Day," a song from the musical *Godspell.* Ellis then composed and recorded a new theme for the series.

TODAY IS OURS   NBC
30 JUNE 1958–26 DECEMBER 1958 Half-hour daytime serial about a divorced woman. With Patricia Benoit as Laura Manning, assistant principal of Bolton Central High School; Peter Lazar as her young son, Mickey; Patrick O'Neal as architect Glenn Turner, who fell for Laura;

and Joyce Lear as Glenn's wife. When *Today Is Ours* left the air after six months, its central characters were blended into the opening story line of its successor, *Young Dr. Malone.*

TODAY ON THE FARM   NBC
1 OCTOBER 1960–11 MARCH 1961   Broadcast live at 7 a.m. on Saturday mornings, this half-hour show was geared toward the American farmer. Eddy Arnold hosted the show, and other regulars included Mal Hansen (agricultural news), Carmelita Pope (women's features), and Joe Slattery (weather).

TODAY WITH MRS. ROOSEVELT
See MRS. ROOSEVELT MEETS THE PUBLIC

TOM AND JERRY   CBS
25 SEPTEMBER 1965–17 SEPTEMBER 1972; 6 SEPTEMBER 1975–3 SEP-TEMBER 1978   Tom and Jerry, the cat-and-mouse cartoon characters created by William Hanna and Joseph Barbera in the 1940s, came to tele-vision (with new episodes) in 1965; in 1975 they shared an hour with a 30-foot purple gorilla in *The New Tom and Jerry/Grape Ape Show,* and in 1976 they hooked up with a dog in *The Tom and Jerry/Grape Ape/Mum-bly Show,* another Saturday-morning hour show; by December of 1976, the Grape Ape had departed, and the show continued in a half-hour for-mat as *The Tom and Jerry/Mumbly Show.* Reruns were shown Sunday mornings under *The Grape Ape* title during the 1977–1978 season.

TOM CORBETT, SPACE CADET   CBS/ABC/NBC/DUMONT
2 OCTOBER 1950–29 DECEMBER 1950 (CBS); 1 JANUARY 1951–26 SEP-TEMBER 1952 (ABC); 7 JULY 1951–8 SEPTEMBER 1951 (NBC); 29 AU-GUST 1953–22 MAY 1954 (DUMONT); 11 DECEMBER 1954–25 JUNE 1955 (NBC)   This durable space opera was not only one of the few shows to have run on all four commercial networks, but it was also one of the very few shows to have run on two networks simultaneously; this oc-curred in 1951, when the show was seen Saturday mornings on NBC and three weekday evenings on ABC. Set during the 2350s at the Space Acad-emy, a training school for Solar Guards, the show starred Frankie Thom-as as Tom Corbett, a hopeful cadet. Also on hand were Edward Bryce as Captain Strong; Jan Merlin as Cadet Roger Manning; Jack Grimes as Cadet T. J. Thistle; and Al Markim as Astro, a Venusian crewman aboard the *Polaris,* the Academy's training ship. The series premiered as a fifteen-minute, thrice-weekly show on CBS, and continued in that for-mat on ABC; the NBC and DuMont versions were half-hour shows, tele-cast on Saturday mornings.

TOM, DICK AND MARY
5 OCTOBER 1964–4 JANUARY 1965 The third segment of *90 Bristol Court,* NBC's unsuccessful attempt to set three sitcoms at the same California apartment complex, *Tom, Dick and Mary* told the story of a young married couple who moved in with a swinging bachelor. With Don Galloway as Tom Gentry, an intern; Joyce Bulifant as his wife, Mary Gentry; Steve Franken as their roommate, Dick Moran, also an intern; John Hoyt as Dr. Krevoy, chief of staff at the hospital; J. Edward McKinley as Horace; and Guy Raymond as Cliff Murdock, the handyman. See also *Harris Against the World; Karen.*

THE TOM EWELL SHOW CBS
27 SEPTEMBER 1960–18 JULY 1961 Tom Ewell, who had costarred with Marilyn Monroe in *The Seven Year Itch,* starred in this half-hour sitcom as Tom Potter, a real estate agent who was surrounded by women at home. Also featured were Marilyn Erskine as his wife, Fran; Mabel Albertson as Fran's mother, Irene (Grandma); Cindy Robbins as Tom and Fran's daughter, Carol; Sherry Alberoni as daughter Debbie; and Eileen Chesis as daughter Cissy.

THE TOM JONES SHOW
See THIS IS TOM JONES

THE TOM KENNEDY SHOW SYNDICATED
1970 Though Tom Kennedy is best known as a game-show host (*Big Game, Name That Tune, Split Second, You Don't Say,* etc.), he also hosted this short-lived hour talk show; its official title was *The Real Tom Kennedy Show,* and it also featured comic Foster Brooks.

TOM TERRIFIC
See CAPTAIN KANGAROO

TOMA ABC
4 OCTOBER 1973–6 SEPTEMBER 1974 *Toma* was an hour-long crime show based on the adventures of David Toma, a real-life detective for the Newark Police Department who relied on the art of disguise to apprehend his prey. The series starred Tony Musante as David Toma; Susan Strasberg as his wife, Patty Toma; Simon Oakland as Toma's supervisor, Inspector Spooner; Sean Manning as David and Patty's son, Jimmy; Michelle Livingston as their daughter, Donna; David Toma himself also appeared in several episodes, usually in disguise. Roy Huggins was the executive producer for Universal Television. Though *Toma* was renewed by ABC for a second season, Tony Musante surprised everyone by announcing his intention not to continue with the show. To fill the void,

Universal Television signed Robert Blake and developed an hour crime show for him: see *Baretta*.

TOMAHAWK   SYNDICATED

1957 Produced in Canada, this little-known western starred Jacques Godet as Pierre Radisson and Rene Caron as Medard, a pair of scouts.

TOMBSTONE TERRITORY   ABC

16 OCTOBER 1957–17 SEPTEMBER 1958; 13 MARCH 1959–9 OCTOBER 1959 Half-hour western from Ziv TV, starring Pat Conway as Sheriff Clay Hollister and Richard Eastham as Harris Claibourne, the editor of the Tombstone (Ariz. Terr.) *Epitaph*. The series' theme song ("Whistle me up a memory . . .") was composed by William M. Backer. The show ran for one season on ABC and was recalled in March of 1959 to replace *Man with a Camera*.

TOMFOOLERY   NBC

12 SEPTEMBER 1970–4 SEPTEMBER 1971 The segments on this Saturday-morning cartoon show were based on stories from children's literary classics.

TOMORROW   ABC

26 MARCH 1955–29 MAY 1956 This public affairs program was produced by Johns Hopkins University and moderated by Lynn Poole. It was originally a discussion program, but in September of 1955 it changed its title to *Tomorrow's Careers* and focused on presenting profiles of various occupations to young people.

TOMORROW   NBC

15 OCTOBER 1973– Network television's first entry into late-late-night programming on weeknights (NBC had introduced *The Midnight Special* on Fridays some months earlier), *Tomorrow* was scheduled at 1 a.m., immediately following the *Tonight* show. The hour-long talk show is hosted by Tom Snyder; it was originally broadcast from NBC studios in Burbank, but moved to New York in December 1974. In June of 1977 the show returned to Burbank. Joel Tator was the first producer and was succeeded early in 1976 by Pamela Burke and Bruce McKay.

TONI TWIN TIME   CBS

5 APRIL 1950–20 SEPTEMBER 1950 Jack Lemmon hosted this Wednesday-night talent show, which alternated with *What's My Line?* The half-hour series was sponsored by Toni home permanents; each week a pair of twins was featured, one of whom sported a Toni permanent. The show was written and produced by Sherman Marks.

TONIGHT ON BROADWAY CBS
6 APRIL 1948–23 MAY 1948; 2 OCTOBER 1949–18 DECEMBER 1949
Scenes from current Broadway plays were enacted on this half-hour anthology series. Martin Gosch hosted the show in 1948, John Mason Brown in 1949.

THE TONIGHT SHOW NBC
27 SEPTEMBER 1954– NBC's late-night talk show is television's most profitable series. Though it was not the first late-night network series (*Broadway Open House* holds that distinction), it is by far the most successful. It has never been seriously challenged in its time slot by any other late-night series, network or syndicated. The chief reason for the show's profitability is that production costs are relatively low and that revenues are high; because of its time slot, the show carries more minutes of commercials than do prime-time programs. *The Tonight Show* has remained popular with viewers because it has kept a predominantly light touch, steering a middle course between brainless burlesque and wordy tedium.

Like most of NBC's innovative programs of the 1950s, *The Tonight Show* was the brainchild of Sylvester "Pat" Weaver, the network executive who also conceived the *Today* show, *Home, Wide Wide World,* and *Your Show of Shows.* Though *Tonight*'s predecessor, *Broadway Open House,* perished after a fifteen-month run, it had demonstrated to Weaver that late-night television was a viable concept. Weaver abandoned the idea of a slapstick show in favor of a more relaxed, conversational program; his intuition proved right, as *The Tonight Show* has remained on the air for a quarter century.

The Tonight Show was based in New York from 1954 until May of 1972, when it moved to Los Angeles. It has had three principal hosts (and a host of guest hosts) over the years. The three hosts—Steve Allen, Jack Paar, and Johnny Carson—came to the series from similar backgrounds: all were born in the Midwest, all had brief but unspectacular careers in radio, and all had had considerable experience in television, hosting game shows and variety shows of their own, before taking their seat behind the desk of *The Tonight Show.* All three are quick-witted people who can keep a conversation going and who can ad-lib skillfully.

As a matter of convenience, the several eras of *The Tonight Show* (all of which have borne slightly different titles) are discussed individually.

I. Steve Allen—*Tonight!* (27 September 1954–25 January 1957)
The first host of *The Tonight Show* (which was then titled *Tonight!*), Steve Allen began his broadcasting career as a disc jockey. In 1950 he came to New York, where he hosted a number of TV series during the next three years (see *Songs for Sale; The Steve Allen Show; Talent Patrol*). On 27 July 1953, Allen began hosting a local show over WNBC-TV in

New York. Allen's show, which ran from 11:20 p.m. to midnight, Mondays through Fridays, had been developed by station executive Ted Cott to lure a potential sponsor, Ruppert Breweries, away from a late-night show on New York's Channel 7 (that show, *Talk of the Town*, was hosted by Louis Nye, who would later be featured on Steve Allen's variety shows). After a successful fourteen-month run, *The Steve Allen Show* became a network show; beginning 27 September 1954, the show (retitled *Tonight!*) was offered to NBC affiliates as far west as Omaha, and was expanded to 105 minutes nightly. Ruppert Breweries, the original sponsor, insisted on the unusual length; though few affiliates ever carried the first fifteen minutes, it was not until the late 1960s, at Johnny Carson's insistence, that the show was shortened to its present ninety-minute length.

The basic format of *The Tonight Show* was established during Allen's tenure: an opening monologue, a segment involving the studio audience (through interviews or games such as "Stump the Band"), and a simple set (a desk and chair for the host, a couch for the guests), were all trademarks of the Allen era. Allen inaugurated the out-of-town broadcast (the first was done from Miami), the one-guest show (Carl Sandburg was the first solo guest), and the one-topic show (entire programs were devoted to such subjects as narcotics, civil rights, and black music). Allen also established the practice of paying his guests only "scale," the minimum fee required by union-network contract (this practice led to a highly publicized feud between Steve Allen and Ed Sullivan, and later between Jack Paar and Ed Sullivan, as Sullivan paid top dollar for his guests).

Though Allen's *Tonight!* show closely resembled the shows of his successors, Jack Paar and Johnny Carson, it was a more musical show; Allen himself was an accomplished musician and composer (he wrote his theme, "This Could Be the Start of Something"), and he employed a nucleus of musical regulars on his show. In addition to announcer-sidekick Gene Rayburn, the show featured singers Steve Lawrence (who was only seventeen when he began singing on Allen's local show), Eydie Gormé (who subsequently married Steve Lawrence), Andy Williams (who later hosted several series of his own), and Pat Marshall (who was succeeded by Pat Kirby). Skitch Henderson led the orchestra. The show was produced by Bill Harbach and Nick Vanoff, and directed by Dwight Hemion; Harbach and Vanoff later produced *The Hollywood Palace,* and Hemion has produced and directed a number of award-winning variety series and specials.

Allen introduced audiences to several new comedians, including Mort Sahl, Lenny Bruce, and Shelley Berman. Other, more unusual guests also appeared, such as Joe Interleggi ("the human termite"), Ben Belefonte ("the rhyming inventor"), and upstate farmer John Schafer (who delivered terse film reviews). Two other people were also part of the show, though they sat in the audience: Mrs. Sterling and Miss Dorothy Miller, both of whom were frequently interviewed by Allen. Finally, there was

Allen himself, who used his wide-ranging improvisational skills. Sometimes he might dash out of the studio to stop traffic; sometimes he would deliver an extemporaneous narration to a street scene broadcast from a remote camera; sometimes he would compose a melody on the piano, using notes suggested by the audience. Above all, he kept the show moving.

In the summer of 1956 Allen began a Sunday-night variety hour, which NBC had devised to dent the ratings of *The Ed Sullivan Show* on CBS. To ease the strain on Allen (who obviously could not maintain a six-nights-a-week schedule for long), in the fall of 1956 Ernie Kovacs was brought in to host the *Tonight!* show on Mondays and Tuesdays. By the end of the year the network, intent on battling Ed Sullivan on Sundays, ordered Allen to drop his *Tonight!* show chores altogether and to concentrate instead on the Sunday variety show. On 25 January 1957, Allen hosted his last *Tonight!* show, as the series' first era came to a close.

II. The First Interregnum—*Tonight: America After Dark* (28 January 1957–26 July 1957)

Tonight: America After Dark was a disaster. An ill-conceived, diffuse program, it was more of a magazine show than a variety or talk show. There was no central figure around whom the show revolved: though Jack Lescoulie (who had been with the *Today* show) was nominally the host, the show featured a group of correspondents, from different cities, who reported nightly. The original lineup included Hy Gardner, Bob Considine, and Earl Wilson in New York; Irv Kupcinet in Chicago; and Paul Coates and Vernon Scott in Los Angeles. Music was provided by the Lou Stein Trio. Designed to resemble the *Today* show, *Tonight: America After Dark* was supposed to provide a window on American nightlife; mobile units were dispatched to cover celebrity-studded parties, motion picture premieres, nightclub shows, and other "special events" such as a tribute to the ninety-sixth anniversary of the statehood of Kansas, which was a highlight of the show's premiere broadcast. The show was also supposed to provide hard news coverage as well.

Tonight: America After Dark opened to poor reviews and low ratings, as affiliates began to drop the show in favor of more profitable local programs. NBC executives began tinkering with the show: Vernon Scott was replaced by Lee Giroux; singer Judy Johnson joined in March; the Mort Lindsey Quartet replaced the Lou Stein Trio, and was in turn replaced by the Johnny Guarnieri Quartet; in June, Al "Jazzbo" Collins became the new host, broadcasting from a set called the Purple Grotto. All of these efforts proved fruitless; when *Tonight: America After Dark* ended its run after twenty-six weeks, only five dozen NBC affiliates carried the show.

III. *The Jack Paar Tonight Show* (29 July 1957–30 March 1962)

As soon as it became apparent that no amount of tinkering could salvage *Tonight: America After Dark*, NBC executives began looking for someone to host its successor. Jack Paar was one of the first people contacted and was eager to take the job. A high school dropout, Paar had entertained servicemen during World War II (where his irreverence toward military brass made him a favorite of enlisted men), and had hosted several TV shows during the early 1950s, including *Bank on the Stars* and *Up to Paar* (both game shows), *The Morning Show* (CBS's abortive attempt to compete with *Today*), and the *Jack Paar Show* (which was first a morning variety show, and later an afternoon show).

With Paar at the helm, the new version of NBC's late-night show set sail on 29 July 1957; it was originally titled *Tonight* (without the exclamation point of Steve Allen's era), but was later officially retitled *The Jack Paar Tonight Show*. Paar's first task was to win back the network affiliates that had dropped his predecessor during the first half of 1957. He succeeded; within eighteen months, Paar's lineup grew from sixty-two stations and two sponsors to 115 stations and full sponsorship. Paar, unlike Allen or Carson, was not a standup comic who could also conduct a conversation; rather, he was a conversationalist who could also deliver a joke. To lure and retain viewers, his show relied more on conversation—and controversy—than on humor. Audiences came to expect the unexpected on Paar's shows; sparks could fly at any time between the host and his guests. A mercurial and petulant person who was surrounded by conflict and controversy (though he professed to detest it), Paar became enmeshed in a series of feuds with other show business luminaries, such as Steve Allen, Dorothy Kilgallen, Walter Winchell, and Ed Sullivan.

Paar began his show with a crew of regulars, but only two stayed with him for the entire run: announcer-sidekick Hugh Downs and bandleader José Melis, a former Army buddy. Others who came and went included Dody Goodman, "weather girl" Tedi Thurman, singer Betty Johnson, and the Bil and Cora Baird Puppets. Another group of people could be classified as semiregulars; all were good talkers who dropped by frequently to chat with the host. This group included, among others, Washington hostess Elsa Maxwell, British humorist Alexander King, French chanteuse Genevieve, writer Jack Douglas (and his Japanese wife, Reiko), Zsa Zsa Gabor, Hans Conried, Peggy Cass, Cliff (Charley Weaver) Arquette, and Mary Margaret McBride. Among the most famous guests who appeared were Robert Kennedy (then counsel to a Senate committee investigating racketeers, Kennedy appeared 22 February 1959), John Kennedy, Richard Nixon (who appeared, separately, during the 1960 Presidential campaign), and Barbra Streisand (who made her network TV debut on 5 April 1961, when Orson Bean was the guest host).

By 1960 the popularity of *The Jack Paar Tonight Show* was assured. The show was videotaped in the early evening, which enabled Paar, like most of his viewers, to watch the show in bed. Paar was able to cut his own appearances on the show back to three nights a week (Paar worked some Monday nights, but most Mondays featured either Hugh Downs or a guest host, and all Friday shows were reruns). Most importantly, from the network's point of view, the show was a huge moneymaker and was carried by 158 affiliates. Commercial success, however, did little to ease Paar's tensions. As early as 1958 Paar had talked publicly about leaving the show, and in February 1960 he made good on his promise. The incident that precipitated Paar's celebrated walkout was the "W.C. Joke." It was a shaggy-dog story about an Englishwoman who planned to travel abroad and wrote her host to inquire if her accommodations included a w.c., her abbreviation for water closet. Her host, who was not fluent in English, was baffled by the term; after some thought he concluded that w.c. stood for wayside chapel, and wrote back to the woman extolling in detail the sumptuousness of the nearby w.c., but cautioning her that it was likely to be crowded on the two days a week that it was open. By today's standards, the story would hardly raise an eyebrow, but in 1960 it was unacceptable, at least to NBC censors. The network deleted the entire story from the show, without advising Paar of its decision. The following night (11 February 1960) a furious Paar walked on stage, announced his displeasure with NBC's unilateral action and his weariness at being a constant center of controversy, and bade an emotional farewell to the audience. His sudden departure left a startled Hugh Downs to entertain the evening's guests, Orson Bean and Shelley Berman. Paar returned to his desk a month later, but the storm of controversy never abated; shortly after his return Paar reignited his feuds with Walter Winchell and Ed Sullivan (Jack Benny finally helped to mediate the Paar-Sullivan tiff).

The most serious incident occurred when Paar took himself, Peggy Cass, and a film crew to West Berlin in September of 1961, less than a month after the erection of the Berlin Wall. In one segment of the film, a detachment of American troops was deployed to stand in the background as Paar stood in the foreground near the Brandenburg Gate. The incident spurred a Defense Department inquiry and the censure of the U.S. Commander in West Berlin. Paar was excoriated in the press for the militaristic overtones of the Berlin broadcast; Paar blamed the press for the brouhaha, insisting that his visit had actually helped ease East-West tensions. Shortly afterward, however, Paar again announced that he would leave the show; this time he gave advance notice and remained firm in his decision to leave at the end of March 1962. His last first-run show was shown 29 March 1962 (the final show on 30 March was a rerun), as dozens of celebrities dropped by or sent film clips wishing him a fond farewell. Though Paar left his late-night show in March, he returned to NBC that fall to host a prime-time variety hour, which ran for three seasons (see *The Jack Paar Show*); in 1973 he again tried a late-night show, this time on ABC (see *Jack Paar Tonite*), which made no waves.

IV. The Second Interregnum (2 April 1962–28 September 1962)

Because of his previous contract, Jack Paar's successor, Johnny Carson, was unable to take over the show until October 1962. The twenty-six-week gap was filled by a succession of guest hosts, most of whom stayed for a week at a time. The parade included, among others, Mort Sahl, Soupy Sales, Art Linkletter, Groucho Marx, Merv Griffin, Jerry Lewis, and Arlene Francis (the first woman to guest-host the show). Hugh Downs stayed on as the announcer until August, when he succeeded John Chancellor as host of the *Today* show; Ed Herlihy replaced Downs on *Tonight*. Skitch Henderson led the band during the transition period. Though the six-month hiatus was uneventful, it was by no means a ratings disaster as *Tonight: America After Dark* had been.

V. *The Tonight Show Starring Johnny Carson* (1 October 1962–)

Johnny Carson had originally turned down NBC's offer to host *The Tonight Show*. Having substituted for Jack Paar, he was familiar with the job and initially felt that it would be too much of a grind (Carson told an interviewer in 1961 that the average life expectancy of a TV comic was about five years). Ultimately, Carson reconsidered and has stayed with the show to become one of the most popular entertainers in show business history. By 1979 he had been with the show for seventeen years, more than twice the combined tenure of Allen and Paar. He has hosted more total hours of network programming than anyone (only Mike Douglas, whose syndicated talk show marked its 4,000th broadcast in 1978, can challenge Carson's longevity).

Born in Corning, Iowa, and raised in Norfolk, Nebraska, Carson made a little money as a teenager doing magic tricks (as "The Great Carsoni"), and developed a ventriloquist act in the Navy. He attended the University of Nebraska, where he wrote his senior thesis on comedy. After a brief stint with radio station WOW in Omaha, he headed for Los Angeles and soon got his own local TV show, a half-hour Sunday program called *Carson's Cellar*. He later wrote for *The Red Skelton Show*, hosted a summer game show (*Earn Your Vacation*), and finally got his own prime-time variety show (*The Johnny Carson Show*), which lasted thirty-nine weeks. In 1956 he hosted a daytime variety show, and a year later he began his second game show, *Who Do You Trust?* It was on this five-day-a-week program that Carson honed his interviewing and ad-libbing skills, for the quiz portion of *Who Do You Trust?* was clearly secondary to the conversational portion. When Carson left the show five years later (executive producer Don Fedderson refused to release him from his contract before it expired in September 1962), it was TV's top-rated daytime series.

Carson brought with him his sidekick from *Who Do You Trust?*, Ed McMahon, as well as producer Art Stark, who became the producer of

The Tonight Show; Carson's brother, Dick Carson, was the director, and Skitch Henderson, who had led the band since Paar's departure, stayed on. Carson's guests on the 1962 premiere included Rudy Vallee, Joan Crawford, Mel Brooks, and Tony Bennett. The show opened to good reviews, and the ratings, which were fairly strong to start with, improved over the next few months.

Above all, Carson has sought to entertain viewers. A keen student of comedy (and of television in general), Carson has intentionally discouraged direct confrontation on his show in order to appeal to the broadest possible public. Though he has been criticized for his failure to take sides on controversial issues, he has defended the show's middle course ("It's not my job to deliver opinions," he once told an interviewer), while pointing out that the show has had its share of "serious" guests, such as Robert Kennedy, Barry Goldwater, Hubert Humphrey, and Martin Luther King, Jr.

Among the more celebrated incidents in the long history of *The Tonight Show Starring Johnny Carson* have been: Carson's "first-person adventures," a series of filmed segments showing Carson pitching to members of the New York Yankees, flying with the Navy Thunderbirds, or skydiving; Carson's escorting an incoherent and physically exhausted Peter O'Toole offstage during a commercial break on a 1963 program (a sleepless O'Toole had flown to the show directly from the set of *Lord Jim*); guest Ed Ames's demonstration of tomahawk-throwing on a 1964 show, in which he hit a cardboard dummy directly in the crotch (thereby triggering one of the longest bursts of sustained laughter in TV history); a rare TV appearance by John Lennon and Paul McCartney in the spring of 1968 (announcing the formation of Apple Records to guest host Joe Garagiola); the wedding of singer Tiny Tim to Victoria May Budinger in December of 1969; Carson's joking reference in a 1973 monologue to a possible toilet paper shortage, which led to mass hoarding of toilet tissue by American consumers; and author Alex Haley's presentation (to a surprised Carson) of the latter's genealogical charts on a 1977 show.

Carson's most serious dispute with NBC arose in 1967, when Carson honored a strike by members of AFTRA, a performers' trade union. During the strike NBC aired reruns of Carson's shows, without his consent, in apparent violation of Carson's contract. Carson rescinded his contract and refused to return to the *Tonight* show after the AFTRA strike was settled until a new contract was negotiated. From that point on Carson became more actively involved in the financial arrangements and in the production details of the show. Art Stark, Carson's first producer, left the show in 1967 and was replaced by Stan Irwin (Irwin was succeeded by Rudy Tellez, who was in turn succeeded by Fred DeCordova, who had previously worked with Jack Benny). Carson's brother and director, Dick Carson, left in 1968 and was succeeded by Bob Quinn; Dick Carson later went to work for Merv Griffin, directing the latter's talk show. In 1969 Johnny Carson formed Raritan Enterprises with business partner Sonny Werblin; Raritan took over the actual production of *The Tonight Show Starring Johnny Carson* and also served as a vehicle for other ventures, such as television specials, an abortive fast-food restaurant chain, and the successful Johnny Carson Apparel, Inc.

Skitch Henderson, the show's bandleader, left in 1966 and was succeeded briefly by Milton DeLugg. In 1967 trumpet player Carl "Doc" Severinsen took over as bandleader; Severinsen's outlandish stage clothes have inspired many a one-liner in Carson's nightly monologue. Through it all, Ed McMahon has remained with Carson. A onetime boardwalk pitchman at Atlantic City, and a former all-purpose on-camera performer at a Philadelphia TV station, McMahon hooked up with Carson on *Who Do You Trust?* and has stayed with him ever since. The two were said to have been drinking companions in New York during the late 1960s, but as Carson has virtually given up alcohol in recent years, the two see little of each other offstage. Nevertheless, McMahon's services as audience warm-up man, announcer, and commercial spokesman are fully appreciated, and he is surely television's best-known second banana. McMahon's famous introduction ("Heerre's . . . Johnny!") is intoned to the strains of "Johnny's Theme," which was composed by Paul Anka.

In 1972 the show moved from New York to Los Angeles (the show had been broadcast from the West Coast on a periodic basis before then). Later that year Carson married Joanna Holland. In 1977 Carson negotiated a new contract with NBC, which not only gave him a lot of money (the exact figure was not divulged, but was said to be well above $2 million a year), but also a lot of time off; he currently puts in about twenty-five 3-show weeks and twelve 4-show weeks, and enjoys fifteen weeks' vacation (much of which he spends headlining in Las Vegas). His new life and his easier TV schedule has made him a more relaxed person. Executives at NBC, however, found it difficult to relax when word spread of Carson's possible desire to terminate his contract before its April 1981 expiration date.

THE TONY BENNETT SHOW   NBC
11 AUGUST 1956–8 SEPTEMBER 1956 Singer Tony Bennett hosted a summer replacement for *The Perry Como Show.* An hour series, it also featured the Spellbinders. In 1959 Bennett again replaced Como for the summer: see *Perry Presents.*

TONY BROWN'S JOURNAL   SYNDICATED
1978 Tony Brown, formerly the executive producer and host of the PBS series, *Black Journal,* hosted this syndicated public affairs show which presented information aimed chiefly at black viewers.

THE TONY MARTIN SHOW NBC

26 APRIL 1954–27 FEBRUARY 1956 Singer-actor Tony Martin hosted his own fifteen-minute musical show on Monday nights before the network news; also on hand were the Interludes.

TONY ORLANDO AND DAWN CBS

3 JULY 1974–24 JULY 1974; 4 DECEMBER 1974–28 DECEMBER 1976 After a short recording career in 1961 (during which he recorded "Bless You" and "Halfway to Paradise"), Tony Orlando became a record producer and promoter. In 1970, as a favor for a friend, he added the lead vocal to a demonstration record, "Candida"; as the background vocals had already been recorded, Orlando did not meet the other singers—Telma Hopkins and Joyce Vincent Wilson, who called themselves Dawn—until after the record became a national hit. The three recorded several more hits, including "Knock Three Times" and "Tie a Yellow Ribbon," the biggest record of 1973. In 1974 they hosted a four-week summer replacement for *The Sonny and Cher Comedy Hour;* the series resurfaced later that year in the Wednesday slot previously occupied by *Sons and Daughters.* During the 1975–1976 season regulars included Alice Nunn, Lonnie Schorr, and Lynn Stuart. In the fall of 1976 the show was retitled *Tony Orlando and Dawn Rainbow Hour;* the regulars included George Carlin, Susan Lanier, Bob Holt, Edie McClurg, Adam Wade, and Nancy Steen. Saul Ilson and Ernest Chambers were the producers.

THE TONY RANDALL SHOW ABC/CBS

23 SEPTEMBER 1976–10 MARCH 1977 (ABC); 24 SEPTEMBER 1977–25 MARCH 1978 (CBS) Half-hour sitcom starring Tony Randall as Judge Walter Franklin, a widowed Superior Court judge who lived and worked in Philadelphia. Also featured were Devon Scott (1976–1977) and Penny Peyser (1977–1978) as his daughter, Roberta (Bobby); Brad Savage as his son, Oliver; Rachel Roberts as the housekeeper, Bonnie McClellan; Allyn Ann McLerie as his prim and proper secretary, Janet Reubner; Barney Martin as court stenographer Jack Terwilliger, an ex-cop; Zane Lasky as the aggressive but addled Mario Lanza, who worked as a law clerk during the first season and as a prosecutor during the second. In the fall of 1977 Hans Conried was added as Walter's father, Ryan Franklin, and Diana Muldaur was seen as Walter's romantic interest, Judge Eleanor Hooper. Tom Patchett and Jay Tarses produced the series for MTM Enterprises.

TOO YOUNG TO GO STEADY NBC

14 MAY 1959–25 JUNE 1959 Half-hour sitcom starring Brigid Bazlen as fourteen-year-old Pam Blake, boy-crazy teenager; Donald Cook as her father, attorney Tom Blake; Joan Bennett as her mother, Mary Blake; and

Martin Huston as her brother, seventeen-year-old John Blake. David Susskind was executive producer of the series, which was broadcast live from New York.

TOOTSIE HIPPODROME ABC

3 FEBRUARY 1952–30 JANUARY 1954 This half-hour children's show consisted of variety acts and games for the kids in the studio audience. John Reed King was the first host but was succeeded by Whitey Carson and His Musical Ranch Hands; Mary Reynolds also appeared as Whitey's assistant, Judy Ann. The show began on Sunday mornings and shifted to Saturdays in August of 1953.

TOP CAT ABC

27 SEPTEMBER 1961–26 SEPTEMBER 1962 First introduced as a prime-time series a year after *The Flintstones,* this cartoon series lasted a season in prime time before reverting to Saturday mornings, where reruns were shown for several years. A Hanna-Barbera production, the series' central character, Top Cat, was a scheming feline who lived in a trash can in Manhattan; Arnold Stang provided the voice of Top Cat, and Maurice Gosfield (better known as Doberman on *You'll Never Get Rich*) was heard as Benny the Ball, one of his hench cats.

TOP DOLLAR CBS

Nighttime: 29 MARCH 1958–30 AUGUST 1958; *Daytime:* 18 AUGUST 1958–23 OCTOBER 1959 Contestants played a word game similar to "ghosts" on this game show, hosted first by Toby Reed, later by Jack Narz. Home viewers who owned dollar bills with serial numbers that matched numbers announced on the show could also win cash by sending the matching bills in to the show.

TOP PRO GOLF ABC

6 APRIL 1959–28 SEPTEMBER 1959 Network television's only prime-time golf series, *Top Pro Golf* presented filmed coverage of eighteen-hole head-to-head matches.

TOP SECRET SYNDICATED

1955 Half-hour adventure series starring Paul Stewart as Professor Brand, an agent for the Bureau of Science Information.

TOP VIEWS IN SPORTS NBC

5 OCTOBER 1949–21 DECEMBER 1949 Fifteen-minute sports newsreel.

TOPPER CBS

9 OCTOBER 1953–30 SEPTEMBER 1955 This sitcom, based on Thorne Smith's novel (which was made into a film in 1937) starred Leo G. Car-

roll as Cosmo Topper, a staid banker who moved into a new home, only to discover that it was haunted by the ghosts of its previous owners. Also featured were Anne Jeffreys as Marion Kerby, "the ghostess with the mostest," and Robert Sterling as her husband, George Kerby, "that most sporting spirit"; the Kerbys had been killed in a skiing accident while celebrating their fifth anniversary, and their spirits returned to their former home together with that of Neil, the alcoholic St. Bernard who also perished trying to rescue the Kerbys (Neil was played by Buck). The three ghosts could be seen and heard only by Topper, much to the consternation of Topper's wife and his employer. Rounding out the cast were Lee Patrick as Henrietta Topper, Cosmo's wife; Thurston Hall as Topper's officious boss, Mr. Schuyler; Edna Skinner (1953–1954) as the Toppers' maid, Maggie; and Kathleen Freeman (1954–1955) as their maid, Katy. The half-hour series was produced by John W. Loveton and Bernard L. Schubert; it made effective use of trick photography by making the ghosts appear transparent in scenes in which Topper was present with other mortals.

A TOUCH OF GRACE   ABC
20 JANUARY 1973–16 JUNE 1973 Based on the British series, *For the Love of Ada,* this half-hour sitcom starred Shirley Booth as widow Grace Simpson; J. Pat O'Malley as Grace's boyfriend, gravedigger Herbert Morrison; Marian Mercer as Grace's daughter, Myra Bradley; and Warren Berlinger as Myra's husband, Walter Bradley (Grace lived with her daughter and son-in-law). The series was written and produced by Saul Turteltaub and Bernie Orenstein.

TOWARDS THE YEAR 2000   SYNDICATED
1971 Half-hour documentary series on ecology and the future.

TOWN HALL
See AMERICAN RELIGIOUS TOWN HALL

THE TRACER   SYNDICATED
1957 Jim Chandler starred in this half-hour series as Regan, the Tracer. The thirty-nine episodes were drawn from the files of the Tracers Company, an organization founded in 1924 by Dan Eisenberg to locate lost heirs and missing beneficiaries. At the end of each show, a list of those persons was broadcast, and several viewers were pleasantly surprised to find themselves on it.

TRACKDOWN   CBS
4 OCTOBER 1957–23 SEPTEMBER 1959 Half-hour western starring Robert Culp as Hoby Gilman, a Texas Ranger. Vincent Fennelly produced the series for Four Star Films; several episodes were written by Culp.

TRAFFIC COURT   ABC

18 JUNE 1958–30 MARCH 1959; 11 SEPTEMBER 1959–2 OCTOBER
1959   Traffic court cases were reenacted on this half-hour prime-time series. Edgar Allan Jones, Jr., played the judge (Jones also presided over
ABC's daytime show, *Day in Court*), Frank Chandler McClure the
bailiff, and Samuel Whitson the chief clerk.

THE TRAP   CBS

29 APRIL 1950–24 JUNE 1950   Half-hour suspense anthology series produced by Franklin Heller.

TRAPPER JOHN, M.D.   CBS

23 SEPTEMBER 1979–   On this hour medical
drama Pernell Roberts stars as Dr. John (Trapper) McIntyre, who works
at San Francisco Memorial Hospital; the character had been featured in
M*A*S*H, the sitcom set during the Korean War some twenty-seven
years earlier. Also featured are Gregory Harrison as Dr. G. Alonzo
(Gonzo) Gates, a brash young physician who had spent three years in a
Vietnam MASH unit and who had heard of the legendary Trapper John
during his tour of duty; Mary McCarty as Nurse "Starch" Willoughby;
Charles Siebert as Dr. Stanley Riverside II, chief of emergency services;
Christopher Norris as Nurse "Ripples" Brancusi; Brian Mitchell as Dr.
"Jackpot" Jackson; and Jessica Walter as Melanie McIntyre, Trapper
John's ex-wife. Frank Glicksman, the executive producer, and Don
Brinkley, the producer, developed the series.

TRASH OR TREASURE?   DUMONT

1 OCTOBER 1952–27 SEPTEMBER 1953   A panel show similar to *What's
It Worth?*, this half-hour show was hosted by Sigmund Rothschild and
Nelson Case. Each week people brought various antiques to the show for
Rothschild's expert appraisal. The show's title changed to *Treasure Hunt*
in April.

THE TRAVELS OF JAIMIE McPHEETERS   ABC

15 SEPTEMBER 1963–15 MARCH 1964   Based on the novel by Robert
Lewis Taylor, this hour-long western told the story of a twelve-year-old
boy from Kentucky who joined a wagon train with his father in 1849.
Featured were Kurt Russell as Jaimie McPheeters; Dan O'Herlihy as his
father, Doc Sardius McPheeters; Michael Witney as Coulter, the wagonmaster; Donna Anderson as Jenny; James Westerfield as Murrel; Charles
Bronson as Murdock; Mark Allen as Matt Kissel; Meg Wyllie as Mrs.
Kissel; the singing Osmond Brothers as The Kissel Boys; Sandy Kenyon
as Baggott; Hedley Mattingly as Coe; and Vernett Allen as Othello.

TREASURE
1958   Bill Burrud hosted this half-hour documentary series, presenting films about buried treasure, lost artifacts, and assorted searches for riches.

TREASURE HUNT
ABC/NBC/SYNDICATED
7 SEPTEMBER 1956–24 MAY 1957 (ABC); 12 AUGUST 1957–4 DECEMBER 1959 (NBC); 1974–1977 (SYNDICATED)   The network versions of this half-hour game show were hosted by Jan Murray. Each day two contestants competed in a question-and-answer segment; the winner then chose one of thirty numbered "treasure boxes," and took home the contents. The show began on ABC as a prime-time series before moving to NBC, where it enjoyed a two-year daytime run as well as a brief prime-time run early in 1958. In 1974 *The New Treasure Hunt* emerged, hosted by Geoff Edwards; this slow-moving and sometimes cruelly suspenseful version (a Chuck Barris Production) eliminated the quiz portion and featured two treasure-box giveaway segments, with a top prize of $25,000.

TREASURE ISLE
ABC
18 DECEMBER 1967–27 DECEMBER 1968   This elaborate daytime game show was played on a specially constructed lagoon at the Colonnades Beach Hotel in Palm Beach Shores, Florida. In the first round of the game, married couples paddled around in rafts, picking up pieces of a giant jigsaw puzzle floating off "Puzzle Isle." After putting together the puzzle, the couples deciphered the clue contained in the puzzle and proceeded to Treasure Isle, where they searched for buried treasure. John Bartholomew Tucker hosted the half-hour show, which was produced and directed by Paul Alter for John D. MacArthur, the Florida millionaire who owned the Colonnades Beach Hotel and built the lagoon.

TREASURE QUEST
ABC
24 APRIL 1949–26 AUGUST 1949   John Weigel hosted this half-hour game show on which contestants could win a trip by answering questions about geography.

TREASURY MEN IN ACTION
ABC/NBC
11 SEPTEMBER 1950–4 DECEMBER 1950 (ABC); 5 APRIL 1951–1 APRIL 1954 (NBC); 7 OCTOBER 1954–30 SEPTEMBER 1955 (ABC)   Half-hour crime show that chronicled the exploits of agents for the United States Treasury Department, starring Walter Greaza as The Chief. Everett Rosenthal produced the series, and David Pressman directed it for Prokter Television Enterprises.

TRIALS OF O'BRIEN CBS

18 SEPTEMBER 1965–27 MAY 1966   Peter Falk starred in this hour-long dramatic series as New York lawyer Daniel J. O'Brien, a shrewd defense attorney. Also featured were Joanna Barnes as O'Brien's ex-wife, Katie; Elaine Stritch as Miss G., O'Brien's secretary; Ilka Chase as Margaret, Katie's mother; Dolph Sweet as Lieutenant Garrison; David Burns as The Great McGonigle, a legendary con man who was a crony of O'Brien's. Richard Alan Simmons was executive producer of the series for Filmways. Among the guest stars who appeared were: Alan Alda ("Picture Me a Murder," 27 November), Faye Dunaway (in her first major TV role, "The 10-Foot, 6-Inch Pole," 14 January), Frank Langella ("How Do You Get to Carnegie Hall," 13 November), and Tony Roberts ("Charlie Has All the Luck," 20 November).

THE TROUBLE WITH FATHER
See THE STU ERWIN SHOW

THE TROUBLESHOOTERS NBC

11 SEPTEMBER 1959–17 JUNE 1960   Half-hour adventure series starring Keenan Wynn as Kodiak and former Olympic decathlon champion Bob Mathias as Dugan, a pair of freelance construction engineers.

TRUE STORY NBC

16 MARCH 1957–9 SEPTEMBER 1961   Kathi Norris hosted this half-hour anthology series consisting of stories ostensibly based on actual incidents. Broadcast at noon on Saturdays, the show was originally aired live and later shifted to videotape.

TRUTH OR CONSEQUENCES CBS/NBC/SYNDICATED

7 SEPTEMBER 1950–7 JUNE 1951 (CBS); 14 JANUARY 1952–16 MAY 1952 (NBC); 18 MAY 1954–28 SEPTEMBER 1956 (NBC); 31 DECEMBER 1956–24 SEPTEMBER 1965 (NBC); 1966–1974 (SYNDICATED)

THE NEW TRUTH OR CONSEQUENCES SYNDICATED

1977   One of broadcasting's most durable programs, *Truth or Consequences* ran seventeen years on radio and (with some interruptions) twenty-seven years on TV. The raucous half-hour game show was created by Ralph Edwards in 1940 and was based on a parlor game: contestants who failed to answer a question before the buzzer sounded (the buzzer, nicknamed Beulah, usually went off a fraction of a second after the question was asked) were forced to pay the consequences. Most consequences involved the performance of stunts of all description, much to the delight of the studio audiences. Edwards, who later created *This Is Your Life*, hosted the radio version for several years as well as the first TV versions of *Truth or Consequences*. The show was first seen Thursday nights on CBS for one season, and in 1952, it was a daytime entry on NBC. When the show returned to NBC's schedule in 1954, as a prime-time series, Jack Bailey was the host. Bob Barker succeeded him at the end of 1956, when the show began a nine-year daytime run on NBC (a nighttime version also popped up on NBC early in 1958, hosted by Steve Dunne); Barker continued to host the show during its eight-year syndicated run, which began in 1966. The series was revived in 1977 and was shown under the title *The New Truth or Consequences,* with Bob Hilton as host.

TUGBOAT ANNIE   SYNDICATED
1958   Half-hour sitcom starring Minerva Urecal as Annie Brennan, skipper of a tug in the Northwest; Walter Sande costarred as Captain Horatio Bullwinkle, Annie's boss.

TURN TO A FRIEND   ABC
5 OCTOBER 1953–31 DECEMBER 1953   Cast from the same mold as *Queen for a Day* and *Strike It Rich, Turn to a Friend* was a half-hour game show on which contestants related heart-breaking tales of woe and misfortune; at the end of the show, the studio audience selected the most deserving recipient, who was then showered with gifts. Dennis James hosted the half-hour show.

TURNABOUT   NBC
26 JANUARY 1979–30 MARCH 1979   Half-hour sitcom about a husband and wife who woke up one morning to find themselves occupying each other's bodies. With John Schuck as Sam Alston, a sportswriter; Sharon Gless as Penny Alston, vice-president of a cosmetics firm; Richard Stahl and Bobbi Jordan as neighbors Jack and Judy Overmeyer; James Sikking as Penny's boss, Geoffrey St. James; and Bruce Kirby as Al Brennan, Sam's boss. Executive producer: Sam Denoff for Universal TV.

TURN-ON   ABC
5 FEBRUARY 1969   Television's most notorious flop, *Turn-On* was canceled after one outing. Produced by George Schlatter and Ed Friendly, the producers of *Laugh-In,* and by Digby Wolfe, a *Laugh-In* production executive, it was a half-hour of skits and blackouts, bridged together not by a host or narrator, but by electronic music. Most of the skits were overly suggestive (at least by 1969 standards)—one featured a vending machine that dispensed birth control pills, and the longest segment consisted of the word "SEX" flashing on the screen while Tim Conway and Bonnie Boland mugged beneath. The pilot for the show had been developed in 1968; both CBS and NBC turned it down, but ABC picked it up, scheduling it to replace the Wednesday broadcast of *Peyton Place.* Before the first *Turn-On* was over, however, most ABC affiliates had been swamped with telephone calls, virtually all of them negative. By Febru-

ary 7, seventy-five affiliates had dropped the show, and by the end of the week *Turn-On* had been turned off by the network. The cast on the lone broadcast included, in addition to Tim Conway (the guest star) and Bonnie Boland, Hamilton Camp, Teresa Graves, Ken Greenwald, Maxine Greene, Debbie Macomber, Maura McGiveney, Chuck McCann, Carlos Manteca, Alma Murphy, Cecile Ozorio, Bob Staats, Mel Stuart, and Carol Wayne. Mark Warren directed the show, and Bill Melendez Associates provided the animation.

TWELVE O'CLOCK HIGH   ABC
18 SEPTEMBER 1964–13 JANUARY 1967   Another of the several World War II shows of the mid-1960s, this one told the stories of the 918th Flyer Squadron based in England. Featured were Robert Lansing (1964–1965) as Brigadier General Frank Savage, who was killed off after the first season (it was reported that Lansing was upset by the network's decision to change the show's time slot and to lessen his role); Paul Burke as Colonel Joseph Gallagher; Frank Overton as Major Harvey Stovall; Barney Phillips as Major Doc Kaiser; Chris Robinson as Sergeant Komansky; Andrew Duggan as Brigadier General Edward Britt; John Larkin as Major General Wiley Crowe; and Larry Gates as Johnny. The hour series, adapted from the 1949 film, was a Quinn Martin Production.

THE TWENTIETH CENTURY   CBS
20 OCTOBER 1957–7 SEPTEMBER 1969   Walter Cronkite hosted this Sunday-evening documentary series, which presented filmed reports on a wide variety of historical and scientific subjects. In January of 1967 the show's title was changed to *The Twenty-First Century*.

THE 20TH CENTURY-FOX HOUR   CBS
5 OCTOBER 1955–18 SEPTEMBER 1957   One of the first television ventures by 20th Century-Fox, this hour dramatic anthology series alternated on Wednesdays with *The U.S. Steel Hour* for two seasons. Peter Packer produced the series, and Joseph Cotten hosted it during the first season.

TWENTY QUESTIONS   NBC/ABC/DUMONT
26 NOVEMBER 1949–24 DECEMBER 1949 (NBC); 17 MARCH 1950–29 JUNE 1951 (ABC); 6 JULY 1951–5 APRIL 1954 (DUMONT); 6 JULY 1954–3 MAY 1955 (ABC)   A game show based on the old parlor game, *Twenty Questions* began on radio in 1946 and first came to TV three years later. The object of the game was for a celebrity panel to identify an object by asking up to twenty questions about it; the only clue given to the panel was whether the object was "animal, vegetable, or mineral." Bill Slater hosted the NBC and DuMont versions of the show, Jay Jackson

the ABC version. Regular panelists included Fred Van Deventer, Florence Rinard (Van Deventer's wife), Herb Polesie, and Johnny McPhee.

THE $20,000 PYRAMID
See THE $10,000 PYRAMID

20/20 ABC
6 JUNE 1978– An hour newsmagazine, *20/20* is ABC's answer to CBS's *60 Minutes*. Poorly organized, it got off to a rocky start—the original hosts, TV newcomers Harold Hayes and Robert Hughes, were axed after the first show, and Hugh Downs was brought in the following week. After the first show, an uneven blend of investigative reports and humorous features, interspersed with definitions of polysyllabic words, *20/20* settled down under Downs to a more straightforward presentation of investigative and background reports. The show was scheduled weekly during the summer of 1978 and switched to a monthly slot in the fall before returning to a weekly berth. Bob Shanks is the executive producer for ABC News.

THE $25,000 PYRAMID
See THE $10,000 PYRAMID

TWENTY-ONE NBC
12 SEPTEMBER 1956–16 OCTOBER 1958 One of TV's most famous big-money, prime-time game shows, *Twenty-One* was NBC's answer to CBS's *The $64,000 Question*. It was hosted by Jack Barry, who created the series with his longtime partner, Dan Enright. Each week two contestants competed; the object of the game was to score twenty-one points as quickly as possible. Each contestant was placed in an isolation booth on stage and could choose a question from an announced category; within the category the questions were rated for difficulty from one to eleven points. Thus, a contestant who correctly answered a ten-point and an eleven-point question in succession was assured of at least a tie. The money was big——Charles Van Doren, who defeated Herbert Stempel in 1957, won $129,000 in fourteen appearances (Van Doren was beaten by Vivian Nearing). The biggest winner of all was Elfreda Von Nardroff, who went home with $253,500 after twenty-one appearances. Contestant Stempel may have had the last laugh, however, as it was he who revealed that Van Doren had been given some of the answers before air time (it was reported that Stempel was an unpopular contestant). Stempel's allegations, together with charges concerning other game shows, precipitated the cancellation of *Twenty-One, Dotto, The $64,000 Challenge,* and *The $64,000 Question*—all in the fall of 1958. Jack Barry, *Twenty-One*'s host and creator, did not work again in national television for a decade.

21 BEACON STREET   NBC/ABC
2 JULY 1959–24 SEPTEMBER 1959 (NBC); 27 DECEMBER 1959–20
MARCH 1960 (ABC) Set in Boston, this half-hour crime show starred
Dennis Morgan as private eye David Chase; Joanna Barnes as Lola, his
confederate; Brian Kelly as Brian, their legman, a recent law school graduate; James Maloney as Jim, an expert machinist who worked with them.
More than most of the detective shows of the late 1950s, *21 Beacon Street*
emphasized gadgetry. The series was introduced as a summer replacement for *The Tennessee Ernie Ford Show* on NBC, and later turned up on
ABC.

TWENTY-SIX MEN   SYNDICATED
1957 Half-hour western about the Arizona Rangers, a group of law
officers whose membership was limited to twenty-six. Featured were Tris
Coffin as Captain Tom Rynning; Kelo Henderson as Ranger Clint Travis.
Russell Hayden produced the series. The force was established in 1901 by
the Arizona Territorial Legislature.

THE TWILIGHT ZONE   CBS
2 OCTOBER 1959–14 SEPTEMBER 1962; 3 JANUARY 1963–18 SEPTEMBER
1964 Television's most popular science fiction anthology series was created and hosted by Rod Serling. One of the medium's most gifted writers,
Serling had previously won Emmys for "Patterns," broadcast on *Kraft
Television Theatre* in 1955, and "Requiem for a Heavyweight," shown on
Playhouse 90 in 1956. On *The Twilight Zone,* Serling introduced his audiences to "a sixth dimension, beyond that which is known to man." The
trademarks of the series were Serling's introductions (usually given about
a minute into each episode) and surprise endings. Serling himself wrote
eighty-nine of the 151 shows; Charles Beaumont and Richard Matheson
also wrote several each, and seven were contributed by Earl Hamner, creator of *The Waltons.* All of the shows were filmed in black and white. *The
Twilight Zone* began as a half-hour series and was dropped after three
seasons; it was brought back by popular demand early in 1963, but in an
hour format. The eighteen hour episodes were not as well liked, and the
show reverted to a half hour for its final season. Among the best-known
episodes were: "Where Is Everybody?" with Earl Holliman (2 October
1959); "People Are Alike All Over," with Roddy McDowall (25 March
1960); "The Mighty Casey," with Jack Warden (17 June 1960); "The
Hitch-Hiker," with Inger Stevens (12 August 1960); "The Silence," with
Franchot Tone (25 April 1961); "Nothing in the Dark," with Gladys
Cooper and Robert Redford (5 January 1962); and "The Dummy," with
Cliff Robertson (4 May 1962).

TWO FACES WEST   SYNDICATED
1961 In this half-hour western, star Charles Bateman played two

roles—Ben January, the marshal, and Rick January, his twin brother, a doctor. Matthew Rapf produced the show, which was set in the town of Gunnison.

TWO FOR THE MONEY   NBC/CBS
30 SEPTEMBER 1952–11 AUGUST 1953 (NBC); 15 AUGUST 1953–22 SEPTEMBER 1956 (CBS); 23 MARCH 1957–7 SEPTEMBER 1957 (CBS)   This prime-time general knowledge quiz show was a Goodson-Todman Production. A pilot was made in 1952 with Fred Allen as host, but Allen became ill and was unable to assume the hosting chores when the show was picked up. Herb Shriner, the Hoosier humorist, took over as emcee and hosted the show for most of its run; Walter O'Keefe substituted for Shriner during the summer of 1954, and Dennis James and Sam Levenson later hosted the show.

240–ROBERT   ABC
28 AUGUST 1979–10 DECEMBER 1979   Hour adventure series focusing on the exploits of the Emergency Services Unit of the Los Angeles County Sheriff's Department. With Mark Harmon as Dwayne "Thib" Thibideaux; John Bennett Perry as T. R. "Trap" Applegate; Joanna Cassidy as helicopter pilot Morgan Wainwright; Lew Saunders as C. B.; JoeAl Nicassio as Roverino; Steve Tannen as Kestenbaum; and Thomas Babson as Terry. Rick Rosner created the show and was the executive producer for Rosner TV in association with Filmways TV Productions.

TWO GIRLS NAMED SMITH   ABC
20 JANUARY 1951–13 OCTOBER 1951   Broadcast Saturdays at noon, this half-hour sitcom told the story of two sisters trying to become fashion models in New York. With Peggy French as Peggy Smith; Peggy Ann Garner and Marcia Henderson as Babs Smith. Also featured were Joseph Buloff, Richard Hayes, and Nina Foch.

TWO IN LOVE   CBS
19 JUNE 1954–11 SEPTEMBER 1954   Bert Parks hosted this Saturday-night game show on which engaged couples competed. In the first round, relatives and friends of each couple were asked questions about the couple. In the second round, the couples themselves participated in a quiz segment.

THE TYCOON   ABC
15 SEPTEMBER 1964–7 SEPTEMBER 1965   A season after *The Real McCoys* left the air, Walter Brennan returned to star in this unsuccessful sitcom. Brennan played Walter Andrews, a crusty widower who was chairman of the board of Thunder Corporation, a huge California conglomerate. Also featured were Van Williams as Pat Burns, Walter's per-

sonal assistant; Jerome Cowan as Herbert Wilson, president of Thunder Corporation; Pat McNulty as Martha, Walter's granddaughter; George Lindsey as Martha's husband, Tom Keane, a naval officer; Janet Lake as Betty, Walter's secretary; Monty Margetts as Una, Walter's housekeeper; and Grace Albertson as Louise Wilson, Herbert's wife.

UFO   SYNDICATED
1972   This hour science fiction series, produced in England by Gerry and Sylvia Anderson, was set in the 1980s at SHADO (Supreme Headquarters, Alien Defense Organization), a top-secret agency which monitored an ever-increasing number of civilization-threatening UFO's. SHADO's cover operation was the Harlington-Straker Film Studios in London. One reason for the series' lack of success was that many of the shows seemed incomprehensible to American viewers. Featured were Ed Bishop as Commander Edward Straker, SHADO chief; George Sewell as Colonel Alec Freeman; Michael Billington as Colonel Paul Foster; Peter Gordeno as Captain Peter Carlin; and Gabrielle Drake as Lieutenant Gay Ellis.

U.N. CASEBOOK   CBS
19 SEPTEMBER 1948–6 MARCH 1949   Half-hour discussion show about the work of the United Nations. See also *The U.N. in Action* and *United Or Not?*

THE U.N. IN ACTION   CBS
2 OCTOBER 1955–18 DECEMBER 1955; 11 NOVEMBER 1956–2 JUNE 1957; 8 SEPTEMBER 1957–23 FEBRUARY 1958; 7 SEPTEMBER 1958–21 DECEMBER 1958; 13 SEPTEMBER 1959–27 DECEMBER 1959; 18 SEPTEMBER 1960–25 DECEMBER 1960   Larry LeSueur hosted this Sunday-morning public affairs program that examined the work of the United Nations. The half-hour series shared a time slot with *Eye on New York* during most of its run. In 1960 Stuart Novins succeeded Larry LeSueur as host.

U.S.A. CANTEEN
See JANE FROMAN'S U.S.A. CANTEEN

U.S. BORDER PATROL
See BORDER PATROL

THE U.S. MARINE BAND   NBC
9 JULY 1949–20 AUGUST 1949   Broadcast from Washington, D.C., on Saturday nights, this half-hour series featured the music of the U.S. Marine Band. The band was also seen on many local stations, as a film of the band playing the national anthem was made available to any station, free of charge, for use as its sign-off.

U.S. MARSHAL
See SHERIFF OF COCHISE

U.S. OF ARCHIE
See THE ARCHIE SHOW

U.S. ROYAL SHOWCASE NBC
13 JANUARY 1952–29 JUNE 1952 Half-hour comedy-variety show, sponsored by the United States Rubber Company. George Abbott was the first host of the Sunday-night show; Jack Carson succeeded him.

THE U.S. STEEL HOUR ABC/CBS
27 OCTOBER 1953–21 JUNE 1955 (ABC); 6 JULY 1955–12 JUNE 1963 (CBS) Another of television's high-quality dramatic anthology series, *The U.S. Steel Hour* was sponsored by United States Steel and produced under the auspices of the Theatre Guild, a group of show business people that was organized in the 1920s and which brought a radio show, *The Theatre Guild on the Air* (also sponsored by U.S. Steel), to the airwaves in 1945. The television version of the show began eight years later, in the heyday of TV's "Golden Age," and lasted ten years. Broadcast live from New York, the hour show was seen biweekly, alternating with *The Motorola TV Hour* and *The Elgin TV Hour* on ABC, and with *Armstrong Circle Theater* and *The 20th Century-Fox Hour* on CBS. A small sample of its presentations includes: "P.O.W.," with Richard Kiley, Phyllis Kirk, Gary Merrill, and Sally Forrest (27 October 1953); "No Time for Sergeants," with Andy Griffith (in his TV debut), Harry Clark, and Eddie LeRoy (15 March 1955; directed by Alex Segal, it was later a Broadway play, a motion picture, and a TV sitcom); "The Rack," with Keenan Wynn (12 April 1955); "The Outcast," with Lillian Roth (9 November 1955); "The Old Lady Shows Her Medals," with Gracie Fields (in her first dramatic role on American TV) and Alfred Lunt (23 May 1956); "Bang the Drum Slowly," with Paul Newman (26 September 1956); "A Drum Is a Woman," a musical fantasy composed and narrated by Duke Ellington, with dialogue written by Will Lorin (8 May 1957); "Beaver Patrol," a rare comedy presentation, starring Walter Slezak (9 April 1958); "Little Tin God," with Gene Hackman (in his first major TV role, 22 April 1959); "Queen of the Orange Bowl," with Anne Francis and Johnny Carson (making a rare TV dramatic appearance, 13 January 1960); "Girl in the Gold Bathtub," with Johnny Carson (in another rare TV dramatic appearance, 4 May 1960); "Brandenburg Gate," with Richard Kiley and Gene Hackman (4 October 1961).

THE UGLIEST GIRL IN TOWN ABC
26 SEPTEMBER 1968–30 JANUARY 1969 Asinine sitcom about a Hollywood talent agent who disguised himself as a hip female fashion model in

order to be closer to his girlfriend, an actress who had returned home to England; much to his chagrin, he discovered that, as a model, he was suddenly a mod sensation. With Peter Kastner as Tim Blair, the agent, and as Timmy Blair, the model; Patricia Brake as his girlfriend, Julia Renfield; Nicholas Parsons as Mr. Courtney, boss of a London modeling agency; and Gary Marshall as Tim's brother, Gene Blair, a photographer.

UKULELE IKE
See THE CLIFF EDWARDS SHOW

ULTRAMAN SYNDICATED
1966 Japanese-produced science fiction series about Iota, who came to Earth from another civilization and, as Ultraman, battled alien invaders. The live-action, half-hour series was created by Eiji Tsuburaya, who had created Godzilla for the movie of the same name.

THE UNCLE AL SHOW ABC
1 NOVEMBER 1958–19 SEPTEMBER 1959 Saturday-morning variety show for children, hosted by Al Lewis, with Wanda Lewis, Janet Greene, and puppeteer Larry Smith.

UNCLE CROC'S BLOCK ABC
6 SEPTEMBER 1975–14 FEBRUARY 1976 This Saturday-morning children's show was intended to be a spoof of Saturday-morning children's shows—its host constantly bantered with his assistant and his director and occasionally found the time to introduce a few cartoons. With Charles Nelson Reilly as Uncle Croc, the host; Alfie Wise as Mr. Rabbit Ears, his assistant; and Jonathan Harris as Mr. Bitterbottom, the director. Produced by Mack Bing and Don Christensen for Filmation Productions, the show was trimmed from sixty to thirty minutes late in October.

UNCLE JOHNNY COONS CBS/NBC
19 FEBRUARY 1955–3 DECEMBER 1955 (CBS); 3 MARCH 1956–24 NOVEMBER 1956 (NBC) On this Chicago-based Saturday show for children, ventriloquist Johnny Coons introduced silent films and traded quips with his wooden partner, George Dummy, and his invisible dog, Blackie.

UNCOMMON VALOR SYNDICATED
1955 A series of twenty-six half-hour documentaries about the United States Marines narrated by Daniel Riss and featuring General Holland M. (Howlin' Mad) Smith. Cliff Karling and William Karn produced the series.

UNDERDOG   NBC/CBS

3 OCTOBER 1964–3 SEPTEMBER 1966 (NBC); 10 SEPTEMBER 1966–1 SEP-
TEMBER 1968 (CBS); 7 SEPTEMBER 1968–5 SEPTEMBER 1970 (NBC); 9
SEPTEMBER 1972–1 SEPTEMBER 1973 (NBC) This durable weekend
cartoon series featured the voice of Wally Cox as that of Underdog, a canine superhero whose alter ego was Shoeshine Boy.

THE UNEXPECTED   SYNDICATED

1952 Half-hour suspense anthology series from Ziv TV, hosted by Herbert Marshall.

UNION PACIFIC   SYNDICATED

1958 Half-hour western, set along the right of way of the Union Pacific
Railroad. With Jeff Morrow as Bart McClelland, district supervisor;
Judd Pratt as surveyor Bill Kinkaid.

UNITED OR NOT   ABC

2 JULY 1951–27 OCTOBER 1952 Half-hour discussion series about the
United Nations, hosted by John MacVane.

THE UNITED STATES STEEL HOUR

See THE U.S. STEEL HOUR

THE UNTAMED WORLD   SYNDICATED/NBC

1968 (SYNDICATED); 11 JANUARY 1969–30 AUGUST 1969 (NBC);
Half-hour series of natural history films, narrated by Phil Carey.

THE UNTOUCHABLES   ABC

15 OCTOBER 1959–10 SEPTEMBER 1963 This hour-long crime show, set
in Chicago during the 1930s was based on the real-life exploits of Eliot
Ness and his squad of Treasury agents, nicknamed "The Untouchables."
One of TV's most consistently violent series, *The Untouchables* received
much criticism during its four-season run, especially from Italian-American civic groups, who objected to the show's repetitive use of Italian-sur-
named gangsters in its early seasons. Their efforts led to a diversification
of villains, and by 1963 virtually every ethnic group had been represented
(even Russians could not claim to have been slighted, as one hood was
named Joe Vodka). More criticism came from the U.S. Bureau of Prisons, which strongly objected to the portrayal of prison officials in certain
episodes involving Al Capone. The series was produced by Quinn Martin
for Desilu and was narrated by Walter Winchell (Martin would later use
offscreen narration in several of his hit series, such as *The Fugitive* and
The Invaders). Featured on-screen were: Robert Stack as Eliot Ness (the
part had been offered to Van Johnson and Van Heflin, but both had

turned it down); Jerry Paris (1959–1961) as Marvin Flaherty; Nicholas Georgiade as Rossi; Anthony George (1959–1960) as Allison; Abel Fernandez as Youngfellow; Paul Picerni as Hobson; and Steve London as Rossman. Guest villains included: Neville Brand as Al Capone; Bruce Gordon as Frank Nitti; and Clu Gulagher as "Mad Dog" Coll. James Caan played his first major TV role on one episode, "A Fist of Five" (4 December 1962), and Robert Redford appeared in "Snowball" (15 January 1963).

UP TO PAAR
NBC

28 JULY 1952–26 SEPTEMBER 1952 In his first national television assignment, Jack Paar hosted this current events quiz, which was also known as *I've Got News for You.* The half-hour show was seen Monday, Wednesday, and Friday evenings.

UPBEAT
CBS

5 JULY 1955–22 SEPTEMBER 1955 This fifteen-minute, twice-weekly summer musical series featured the Russ Case Orchestra, the Tommy Morton Dancers, and guests. Jerome Shaw produced and directed.

UPBEAT
SYNDICATED

1966–1971 A Cleveland-based rock music show, hosted by Don Webster. Frequent guests on the hour series included Jeff Kutash and the GTOs.

UPDATE
NBC

16 SEPTEMBER 1961–2 JUNE 1963 A weekend newsmagazine for teenagers, hosted by Robert Abernethy.

UPTOWN JUBILEE
CBS

13 SEPTEMBER 1949–20 OCTOBER 1949 This short-lived all-black variety show was hosted by Willie Bryant. Regulars included Timmie Rogers and Harry Belafonte. The show was later titled *Sugar Hill Times.*

VACATIONLAND AMERICA
NBC

29 MARCH 1953–28 JUNE 1953 Also known as *Sightseeing with Swayze,* this fifteen-minute travelogue was hosted by NBC newscaster John Cameron Swayze and members of his family.

THE VAL DOONICAN SHOW
ABC

5 JUNE 1971–14 AUGUST 1971 Hour-long musical show hosted by Irish folksinger Val Doonican.

VALENTINE'S DAY
ABC

18 SEPTEMBER 1964–10 SEPTEMBER 1965 Half-hour sitcom starring

Tony Franciosa as Valentine Farrow, a swinging New York publishing executive. Also on hand were Jack Soo as Rockwell (Rocky) Sin, Val's valet; Janet Waldo as Libby, his secretary; Mimi Dillard as Molly; Eddie Quillan as Fipple, the custodian in Val's apartment house; and Jerry Hausner as Mr. Dunstall, Val's boss.

VALENTINO
ABC

18 DECEMBER 1952–5 MARCH 1953 ABC's answer to CBS's *The Continental*, *Valentino* was a half-hour series on which singer Barry Valentino tried to woo the female viewers at home.

VALIANT LADY
CBS

12 OCTOBER 1953–16 AUGUST 1957 A daytime serial, *Valiant Lady* was created by Frank and Ann Hummert and ran on radio from 1938 to 1952. The TV version starred Nancy Coleman and Flora Campbell as Helen Emerson; Jerome Cowan as her husband, Mr. Emerson; James Kirkwood, Jr., as their son, Mickey; Anne Pearson as their daughter, Diane; and Lydia Reed (who later appeared on *The Real McCoys*) as their younger daughter. Others who appeared over the years included Sue Randall, Bonnie Sawyer, Pat Peardon, and Terry O'Sullivan. The fifteen-minute show, broadcast live from New York, was produced by Carl Green, written by Charles Elwyn, and directed by Herb Kenwith.

VALLEY OF THE DINOSAURS
CBS

7 SEPTEMBER 1974–4 SEPTEMBER 1976 Saturday-morning cartoon series from Hanna-Barbera Productions about the Butler family, who found themselves trapped in a prehistoric world. Though the show ran for two seasons, the second season consisted entirely of reruns.

VAN DYKE AND COMPANY
NBC

20 SEPTEMBER 1976–30 DECEMBER 1976 An unsuccessful variety hour hosted by Dick Van Dyke. Other regulars included Andy Kaufman, Pat Proft, Marilyn Sokol, and the Los Angeles Mime Company. Allan Blye and Bob Einstein were the producers.

VANITY FAIR
CBS

12 OCTOBER 1948–2 NOVEMBER 1951 One of CBS's first daytime shows, *Vanity Fair* began as a twice-weekly show, but by January of 1949 it was broadcast five days a week. Hosted by Robin Chandler and by Dorothy Doan, it presented features of interest to housewives. In 1949 it was produced and directed by Frances Buss, and in 1951 it was written and produced by Virginia Schone and directed by Dan Levin.

VAUDEO VARIETIES
ABC

14 JANUARY 1949–15 APRIL 1949 One of the first Chicago-based pro-

grams to be broadcast in the East following the opening of the coaxial cables between New York and Chicago, *Vaudeo Varieties* presented five acts each week. Eddie Hubbard hosted the hour show.

VAUDEVILLE   SYNDICATED

1974   A variety hour with no regulars (except Donna Jean Young, the cardholder), *Vaudeville* consisted of assorted vaudeville acts, introduced by celebrity guest hosts. Burt Rosen was the executive producer for Metromedia.

VAUDEVILLE SHOW   ABC

9 DECEMBER 1953–30 DECEMBER 1953   Five vaudeville acts were presented each week on this short-lived variety show.

THE VAUGHN MONROE SHOW   NBC

31 AUGUST 1954–30 SEPTEMBER 1954; 28 JUNE 1955–8 SEPTEMBER 1955   Bandleader-singer Vaughn Monroe twice hosted a summer replacement for *The Dinah Shore Show;* the fifteen-minute series was seen twice a week. See also *Camel Caravan.*

VEGA$ ABC

20 SEPTEMBER 1978–   A flashy hour-long crime show set in Las Vegas, starring Robert Urich as private eye Dan Tanna, with Tony Curtis as Roth, an important hotelier; Phyllis Davis as Dan's assistant, Beatrice; Bart Braverman as Dan's inept investigator, Binzer; Naomi Stevens as Sergeant Bella Archer of the Las Vegas Police, Will Sampson as Harlon Twoleaf, an American Indian who occasionally works for Dan; Judy Landers as Angie Turner, a chorus girl who sometimes takes messages for Dan; and Greg Morris as Lieutenant Nelson. Aaron Spelling and Douglas S. Cramer are the executive producers.

VEGETABLE SOUP   SYNDICATED

1975   An ambitious magazine show for children, *Vegetable Soup* featured such guest hosts as Bette Midler and James Earl Jones, who introduced live and animated segments. Yanna Kroyt Brandt was the executive producer for the New York State Department of Education. The show was seen in most areas in half-hour form, though it could be adapted into a fifteen-minute format.

THE VERDICT IS YOURS   CBS

2 SEPTEMBER 1957–28 SEPTEMBER 1962   This popular courtroom drama began as a daytime show; it also enjoyed a prime-time run on CBS during the summer of 1958. The series was done without scripts; the show's writers prepared an outline for each case, which served as the starting point for the performers. Professional actors played the litigants

and witnesses, while real attorneys played the lawyers and judges. Jim McKay, *Verdict*'s first "court reporter," was succeeded by Bill Stout in 1959. The half-hour show was produced by Eugene Burr.

VERSATILE VARIETIES   NBC/CBS/ABC
26 AUGUST 1949–19 JANUARY 1951 (NBC); 28 JANUARY 1951–22 JULY 1951 (CBS); 21 SEPTEMBER 1951–14 DECEMBER 1951 (ABC)   *Versatile Varieties* premiered as a prime-time variety revue in 1949, hosted by George Givot and Bob Russell. Produced by Charles Basch and Frances Scott, and directed by Jay Strong, it was officially titled *The Bonny Maid Versatile Variety Show;* commercials were handled by an eighteen-year-old model named Anne Francis. When the show switched networks in January 1951, it retained little else but its title, as it moved from prime time to Sunday mornings and became a children's show. Lady Iris Mountbatten was the new host, telling stories and singing songs. In the fall of 1951 *Versatile Varieties* again shifted networks.

THE VIC DAMONE SHOW   CBS/NBC
2 JULY 1956–24 SEPTEMBER 1956 (CBS); 3 JULY 1957–11 SEPTEMBER 1957 (CBS); 22 JUNE 1967–7 SEPTEMBER 1967 (NBC)   Born Vito Farinola, singer Vic Damone appeared on the radio version of Arthur Godfrey's *Talent Scouts,* and began making records in 1947. He hosted the first of his TV shows in 1956, a summer replacement for *December Bride.* In 1957 he hosted an hour series, a summer replacement for *Arthur Godfrey and His Friends,* which featured Peggy King and the Spellbinders. After hosting *The Lively Ones* for two summers (see that title), he filled in for *The Dean Martin Show* during the summer of 1967; other regulars on that series included Gail Martin (Dean's daughter) and Carol Lawrence; the latter series was rerun on NBC during the summer of 1971.

THE VICTOR BORGE SHOW   NBC
3 FEBRUARY 1951–30 JUNE 1951   A Danish pianist with a sense of humor, Victor Borge hosted his own half-hour comedy-variety series on Saturday evenings.

VICTORY AT SEA   NBC
26 OCTOBER 1952–26 APRIL 1953   A documentary series of twenty-six half hours on naval warfare during World War II, *Victory at Sea* was produced by Henry Salomon and narrated by Leonard Graves. Richard Rodgers composed a special score for the program.

VIDEO VILLAGE   CBS
Nighttime: 1 JULY 1960–16 SEPTEMBER 1960; *Daytime:* 11 JULY 1960–15 JUNE 1962   On this half-hour game show two couples competed. One spouse rolled a giant die inside a cage, after which his or her spouse ad-

vanced along a life-sized game board according to the roll of the die. Jack Narz was the first host, Monty Hall the second; they were assisted by Joanna Copeland and Eileen Barton; Merrill Heatter and Bob Quigley were the producers. See also *Video Village Junior.*

VIDEO VILLAGE JUNIOR   CBS
30 SEPTEMBER 1961–16 JUNE 1962 This Saturday-morning children's version of Video Village was hosted by Monty Hall, with assistance from Eileen Barton.

THE VIKINGS   SYNDICATED
1960 Officially titled *Tales of the Vikings,* this half-hour medieval adventure series starred Jerome Courtland as Leif Ericson, Norse explorer. Also on hand were Walter Barnes as Finn, Stefan Schnabel as Firebeard, and Buddy Baer. The show was produced by Brynapod Productions, a company owned by Kirk Douglas, and was filmed on location in Europe using sets, costumes, and ships left over from the motion picture, *The Vikings,* in which Douglas had starred.

VILLA ALEGRE   PBS
23 SEPTEMBER 1974–   Half-hour daytime series for children, presented in Spanish and English ("Villa Alegre" is Spanish for "Happy Village"), geared to Spanish-speaking preschool children. Claudio Guzman is the executive producer, and the show's regulars included Nono Arsu, Linda Dangcil, Sam Edwards, Maria Grimm, Darryl Henriquez, Julio Medina, Federico Roberto, Wilfredo H. Rodriquez, Hal Smith, Catana Tully, and Carmen Zapata.

THE VILLAGE BARN   NBC
17 MAY 1948–4 JULY 1949; 16 JANUARY 1950–29 MAY 1950 Square dancing from New York's Greenwich Village.

THE VIN SCULLY SHOW   CBS
15 JANUARY 1973–23 MARCH 1973 Short-lived half-hour daytime variety series, hosted by Vin Scully.

THE VINCENT LOPEZ SHOW   DUMONT/CBS
7 MARCH 1949–30 MARCH 1950 (DUMONT); 13 JUNE 1951–11 JULY 1951 (DUMONT); 9 FEBRUARY 1957–9 MARCH 1957 (CBS) Orchestra leader Vincent Lopez hosted three eponymous programs. The first was a fifteen-minute show, seen Mondays, Wednesdays, and Fridays. The second was a half-hour show on Wednesday nights, with Barry Valentino and Ann Warren. The third was a Saturday-evening half hour on CBS, with Judy Lynn, Johnny Amorosa, Johnny Messner, Teddy Norman, Eddie O'Connor, and the Lopezians. See also *Dinner Date.*

THE VIRGINIA GRAHAM SHOW   SYNDICATED

1970–1972   Hour-long talk show hosted by Virginia Graham, veteran of two previous talk shows (*Food for Thought* and *Girl Talk*). Phil Mayer was the producer.

THE VIRGINIAN   NBC

19 SEPTEMBER 1962–9 SEPTEMBER 1970

THE MEN FROM SHILOH   NBC

16 SEPTEMBER 1970–8 SEPTEMBER 1971   Television's first ninety-minute western series, *The Virginian* was based on Owen Wister's novel, which had been filmed at least three times. Set at the sprawling Shiloh Ranch in Medicine Bow, Wyoming, its central character was a taciturn foreman known simply as the Virginian, a man trying to come to grips with the inexorable westward advance of technology, culture, and civilization. The only members of the cast who remained with the show for its entire run were James Drury as the Virginian and Doug McClure as Trampas, the headstrong assistant foreman. Other players included: Lee J. Cobb (1962–1966) as Judge Henry Garth, first owner of the Shiloh Ranch; Roberta Shore (1962–1965) as Betsy Garth, his daughter; Pippa Scott (1962–1964) as newspaper publisher Molly Wood; Gary Clarke (1962–1964) as Steve, a ranch hand; Randy Boone (1963–1966) as Randy Garth, Judge Garth's son; L. Q. Jones (1964–1967) as Belden, a ranch hand; Harlan Warde (1964–1966) as Sheriff Brannon; Clu Gulagher (1964–1968) as Deputy Ryker; Diane Roter (1965–1966) as Jennifer, Judge Garth's niece; John Dehner (1965–1966) as Starr, a ranch hand; Charles Bickford (1966–November 1967) as John Grainger, second owner of the Shiloh Ranch; Don Quine (1966–1968) as his grandson, Stacy Grainger; Sara Lane (1966–1970) as his granddaughter, Elizabeth Grainger; Ross Elliott (1966–1970) as Sheriff Abbott; John McIntire (November 1967–1970) as his brother, Clay Grainger, who became the third owner of the ranch; Jeanette Nolan (1968–1970) as Holly Grainger, Clay's wife; David Hartman (1968–1969) as David Sutton, a ranch hand; Tim Matheson (1969–1970) as Jim Horn, a ranch hand. In the fall of 1970 the series was retitled *The Men from Shiloh,* and continued for one final season. Ownership of the Shiloh Ranch again changed hands, as Stewart Granger joined the cast as new owner Colonel Alan MacKenzie, an Englishman. James Drury and Doug McClure remained with the show, and Lee Majors signed on as hired hand Roy Tate. *The Virginian* and *The Men from Shiloh* were produced by Universal Television.

THE VISE   ABC

1 OCTOBER 1954–5 JULY 1957   Half-hour dramatic anthology series, produced in England, and hosted by Ron Randell during the first season. Some telecasts were from the series *Mark Saber* (see also that title).

VISION ON   SYNDICATED

1972   An inventive British children's series, *Vision On* was developed to
aid children with hearing problems. A total of seventy-four half-hour
programs were produced by BBC-TV, with Tony Hart as host (Hart also
designed the animated sequences).

VISIONS   PBS

21 OCTOBER 1976–   An ambitious anthology series, *Visions*
provides a showcase for young American playwrights. Funded by several
grants, it is produced by Barbara Schultz at KCET-TV, Los Angeles.

VISIT WITH THE ARMED FORCES   DUMONT

3 JULY 1950–22 JANUARY 1951   Half-hour public service series of films
about the armed forces. See also *The Armed Forces Hour*.

THE VISUAL GIRL   SYNDICATED

1971   Ron Russell hosted this half-hour series, which focused on beauty
care.

VIVA VALDEZ   ABC

31 MAY 1976–6 SEPTEMBER 1976   Half-hour sitcom about a Chicano
family living in East Los Angeles. With Carmen Zapata as Sophia Valdez; Rodolfo Hoyos as her husband, Luis Valdez, owner of a plumbing
business; Nelson D. Cuevas as Ernesto, their eldest son, a telephone company executive trainee; James Victor as Victor, the second eldest son;
Lisa Mordente as daughter Connie; Claudio Martinez as Pepe, the youngest son; Maria O'Brien as Connie's friend Inez; Jorge Cervera, Jr., as the
Valdez' cousin, Jerry Ramirez, newly arrived in the United States. The
series was created by Bernard Rothman, Stan Jacobson, and Jack Wohl,
who were also its executive producers.

VOICE OF FIRESTONE   NBC/ABC

5 SEPTEMBER 1949–7 JUNE 1954 (NBC); 14 JUNE 1954–16 JUNE 1963
(ABC)   *Voice of Firestone*, which began on radio in 1928, was a Monday-
night perennial for more than two decades before coming to television in
1949; for the next five years it was simulcast on NBC radio and television, until a dispute between the sponsor and the network over the Monday time slot led Firestone to shift the program to ABC. The half-hour
musical series presented all kinds of music, but emphasized classical and
semiclassical selections. Each week a guest celebrity was featured, and for
many years the principal guests came from the Metropolitan Opera Company. The Firestone Orchestra was conducted by Howard Barlow, and
the show was hosted by John Daly during its years on ABC; Hugh James
was the announcer. *Voice of Firestone* was seen as a series of specials from
1959 until 1962; it returned as a weekly series in the fall of 1962 for a
final season.

VOLUME ONE ABC

16 JUNE 1949–21 JULY 1949   Wyllis Cooper wrote and produced the six programs telecast on this half-hour anthology series; the programs were titled "Volume One, Number One," "Volume One, Number Two," etc. Jack Lescoulie and Nancy Sheridan starred in the premiere, a story about a couple who robbed a bank and became trapped in their hotel room.

VOYAGE TO THE BOTTOM OF THE SEA ABC

14 SEPTEMBER 1964–15 SEPTEMBER 1968   Hour-long science fiction series set aboard the *Seaview,* an American research submarine whose crew came in contact with a never-ending parade of aliens, monsters, and maniacs. Based on the film of the same name, the series featured Richard Basehart as Admiral Harriman Nelson; David Hedison as Captain Lee Crane; Bob Dowdell as Lieutenant Commander Chip Morton; Terry Becker as Chief Sharkey; Del Monroe as Kowalski; and Paul Trinka as Patterson; Irwin Allen created the series and was its executive producer. There were 110 episodes produced.

W.E.B. NBC

13 SEPTEMBER 1978–5 OCTOBER 1978   The first dramatic series concerning the television industry, *W.E.B.* was the first fatality of the 1978–1979 season, lasting only five shows. It was inspired by the movie *Network* and was set at Trans American Broadcasting, a network staffed by a motley crew of lechers and cutthroats. Featured were Pamela Bellwood as Ellen Cunningham, a twenty-nine-year-old programming executive trying to make it in the male-dominated corporate structure; Alex Cord as Jack Kiley, the venal chief of programming; Richard Basehart as news director Gus Dunlap; Andrew Prine as the alcoholic sales chief, Dan Costello; Howard Witt as Walter Matthews, director of operations; Lee Wilkof as Harvey Pearlstein, head of research; Tisch Raye as Christine Nichols; Peter Coffield as Kevin; and Stephen McNally as the Chairman of the Board. The executive producer of the hour show was Lin Bolen, former vice president in charge of daytime programming for NBC; Bolen was reported to have been the model for Faye Dunaway's character in *Network.*

WKRP IN CINCINNATI CBS

18 SEPTEMBER 1978–   Half-hour sitcom set at WKRP, a moribund radio station in Cincinnati (coincidentally or not, Cincinnati has a real-life radio station with the call letters WKRC). With Gary Sandy as Andy Travis, the new program director hired to turn the station around, and who turned it into a rock and roll station; Gordon Jump as Arthur Carlson, the station manager; Loni Anderson as Jennifer Marlowe, the secretary; Richard Sanders as Les Nessman, the station's news, weather, and agricultural department; Frank Bonner as Herb Tarlek, the

sales manager; Jan Smithers as Bailey Quarters, program assistant; Howard Hesseman as disc jockey Johnny Caravella, whose on-the-air nom de plume was Dr. Johnny Fever; Tim Reid as Venus Flytrap, a flamboyant black DJ brought in by Travis. Hugh Wilson created and produced the show for MTM Enterprises. Production of the series was ordered suspended by CBS after eight weeks, but *WKRP* returned to the network's schedule in January 1979.

THE WACKIEST SHIP IN THE ARMY   NBC

19 SEPTEMBER 1965–4 SEPTEMBER 1966   Half-hour sitcom set during World War II aboard the *Kiwi*, a decrepit schooner built in 1871 and pressed into service by Army intelligence for use in the South Pacific. With Jack Warden as Major Simon Butcher; Gary Collins as Lieutenant Rip Riddle; Mike Kellin as Chief Miller; Rudy Solari as Nagurski; Mark Slade as Hollis; Don Penny as Tyler; Fred Smoot as Trivers; Duke Hobbie as Finch; William Zuckert as General Cross; and Charles Irving as Admiral Beckett. Based on the 1960 motion picture, the series was produced by Screen Gems.

WACKO   CBS

17 SEPTEMBER 1977–3 SEPTEMBER 1978   Half-hour weekend variety series for children, featuring musical numbers, skits, and blackouts. The Sylvers and Rip Taylor were frequent guests.

WACKY RACES   CBS

14 SEPTEMBER 1968–5 SEPTEMBER 1970   Saturday-morning cartoon series about a transcontinental automobile race. Spinoffs included *Dastardly and Muttley* and *The Perils of Penelope Pitstop*.

THE WACKY WORLD OF JONATHAN WINTERS   SYNDICATED

1972   Half-hour comedy series starring improvisational comedian Jonathan Winters and featuring Marian Mercer and the Soul Sisters. See also *The Jonathan Winters Show*.

WAGON TRAIN   NBC/ABC

18 SEPTEMBER 1957–12 SEPTEMBER 1962 (NBC); 19 SEPTEMBER 1962–5 SEPTEMBER 1965 (ABC)   One of television's most popular westerns, *Wagon Train* was the number-two rated series for three seasons (1958–1959 through 1960–1961) before rising to the number-one spot in 1961–1962. It lost ground after switching networks in 1962 and an attempt to expand it from sixty to ninety minutes (emulating *The Virginian*) in the fall of 1963 was unsuccessful. *Wagon Train* was, of course, set aboard a wagon train along the trail from Missouri to California. To a greater extent than most westerns it relied on guest stars—each episode was entitled "The _____ Story," and was named after that week's guest

character. Ward Bond (who had starred in *Wagonmaster*, the 1950 film on which the series was based) starred as the wagonmaster, Major Seth Adams, from 1957 until his death late in 1960. On 15 March 1961, John McIntire was introduced as the new wagonmaster, Chris Hale; McIntire remained with the show until the end. Also featured were Robert Horton (1957–1960 and 1961–1962) as scout Flint McCullough; Frank McGrath as Charlie Wooster, the cook; Terry Wilson as Bill Hawks; Denny (Scott) Miller (spring 1961–1963) as scout Duke Shannon; Michael Burns (spring 1963–1965) as Barnaby West, a teenager; Robert Fuller (1963–1965) as Cooper, *Wagon Train's* last scout. Howard Christie produced the show for Revue Studios.

WAIT 'TIL YOUR FATHER GETS HOME SYNDICATED
1972 This Hanna-Barbera cartoon series was aimed at an adult audience and was strongly reminiscent of *All in the Family*. Voices included those of Tom Bosley as Harry Boyle, the father; Joan Gerber as wife Irma; Kristina Holland as daughter Alice; David Hayward as son Chet; Jackie Haley as son Jamie; and Jack Burns as neighbor Ralph.

WALL $TREET WEEK PBS
7 JANUARY 1972– Public affairs program, focusing on the American economy, the stock market, and personal investing. Louis Rukeyser is the host and moderator.

WALLY GATOR SYNDICATED
1963 Hanna-Barbera cartoon series about an alligator.

WALLY'S WORKSHOP SYNDICATED
1971 Half-hour home improvement show, hosted by Wally Bruner, with help from his wife, Natalie Bruner.

WALT DISNEY ABC/NBC
27 OCTOBER 1954–17 SEPTEMBER 1961 (ABC); 24 SEPTEMBER 1961– (NBC) Walt Disney is remembered chiefly for his film work, but his television series has been one of the most successful, and remarkable, in the history of broadcasting. Though it has been aired on two networks under several titles (including *Disneyland, Walt Disney Presents, Walt Disney's Wonderful World of Color, The Wonderful World of Disney*, and *Disney's Wonderful World*), it is really one continuous series, and as such is television's longest-running prime-time show. *Disneyland* was the first ABC series to crack Nielsen's Top Twenty (this was no mean achievement, because for many years ABC had far fewer affiliates than CBS or NBC). It was also the first prime-time anthology series for children, and the first to incorporate miniseries (though the term itself

755

was not used until much later). It has even survived the death of its host and creator.

Walter Elias Disney was born in Chicago in 1901, and began making cartoons in Kansas City in the 1920s. In 1926 he moved to Los Angeles and formed a production company with his older brother, Roy Disney. In 1928 Disney's most famous cartoon character, Mickey Mouse, first came to the screen (Disney himself supplied Mickey's voice). Disney also made some of the first sound cartoons that year, and in 1932 produced the first film in full technicolor. Two years later Disney's second most famous cartoon star, Donald Duck, appeared. By the end of the decade Disney had produced the first feature length animated film, *Snow White and the Seven Dwarfs*. Other features, such as *Fantasia, Dumbo,* and *Bambi* followed soon thereafter. By the end of the 1940s he had begun his famous nature documentaries, *True Life Adventures,* and had also started producing live-action (or combination live and animated) films, such as *Song of the South.*

Though Disney produced one or two television specials early in the 1950s, it was not until 1954 that he seriously pursued the idea of a weekly show. By this time he had also laid the plans for his real-life "Magic Kingdom," Disneyland, a year-round amusement park divided into four areas—Frontierland, Adventureland, Fantasyland, and Tomorrowland. The ABC network, which had merged with United Paramount Theaters in 1953, agreed to invest in the venture and to carry the proposed series. Disney was thus able to use the show, which was titled *Disneyland* from 1954 to 1958, not only to promote the park but also to publicize upcoming theatrical features from Disney Studios (a year later, ABC managed to interest two other film studios in similar promotional shows; see *M-G-M Parade* and *Warner Brothers Presents*). The series' premiere telecast, "The Disneyland Story," showed the construction of the park and whetted the curiosity of countless young viewers. Over the succeeding years, several shows were devoted to Disneyland.

In general, the mixture of programs during the first year was typical of the subsequent seasons: edited versions of previously released theatrical features, coupled with a number of original productions (teasers for forthcoming releases were also featured in later seasons). The original shows included documentaries on natural history, behind-the-scenes broadcasts from Disney Studios, and several dramatic shows. The most popular programs of the first season (and perhaps of the entire series) fell into the latter category: the three Davy Crockett segments. These shows (together with two more that were televised the following season) may properly be considered as television's first miniseries. All of them starred Fess Parker as American folk hero Davy Crockett, and they included: "Davy Crockett, Indian Fighter" (15 December 1954), "Davy Crockett Goes to Congress" (26 January 1955), "Davy Crockett at the Alamo" (23 February 1955), "Davy Crockett's Keelboat Race" (16 November 1955), and "Davy Crockett and the River Pirates" (14 December 1955). Disney later admitted that the enormous popularity of the first three segments (especially "Davy Crockett at the Alamo") caught everyone at Disney Studios by surprise; fortunately, however, Disney was quick to capitalize on the hit show by licensing the distribution and sale of all kinds of Davy Crockett paraphernalia; hundreds of thousands of "coonskin" caps and bubble gum cards were quickly bought by young fans.

The Disney people tried hard for the next several years to develop a character as popular as Davy Crockett. Several miniseries were launched hopefully between 1957 and 1960, but none of them came close to eclipsing the Crockett stories. Among the also-rans were: "The Saga of Andy Burnett," starring Jerome Courtland as Andy Burnett, a pioneer who traveled from Pittsburgh to the Rockies (the first of the six stories was introduced 2 October 1957; they were written by Tom Blackburn, and were based on the novels by Stewart Edward White); "The Nine Lives of Elfego Baca," starring Robert Loggia as Elfego Baca, a peace-loving New Mexico lawman (introduced 3 October 1958, six episodes were shown during the 1958–1959 season, and more were shown during the following season); "Tales of Texas John Slaughter," starring Tom Tryon as Texas Ranger John Slaughter (at least thirteen segments were shown, beginning 31 October 1958); "The Swamp Fox," starring Leslie Nielsen as General Francis Marion, the Revolutionary War hero of the Carolinas (six episodes were shown during the 1959–1960 season, beginning 23 October, and more were shown during the 1960–1961 season; General Marion even sported a foxtail on his three-cornered hat, but the headpiece failed to capture the public fancy as the Crockett cap had).

In the fall of 1958 the title of Disney's series was changed to *Walt Disney Presents*. Later that season a Disney experiment produced what is credited as the first stereophonic broadcast of a television program; on 30 January 1959, "The Peter Tchaikovsky Story" was telecast, and in certain cities the audio portion of the broadcast was transmitted by two radio stations—an AM station carried one channel, while an FM outlet carried the other (FM multiplex stereo was still a phenomenon of the future).

After seven seasons on ABC, Disney switched to NBC in the fall of 1961; the new network affiliation gave Disney the opportunity to broadcast in color, and the show was thus retitled *Walt Disney's Wonderful World of Color*. On the 1961 premiere (24 September), Disney introduced his first major new cartoon character in years, the highly knowledgeable Professor Ludwig von Drake, in "An Adventure in Color, Mathmagic Land." It was the first of several educational shows hosted by von Drake, who was an uncle of Donald Duck (some of the shows were cohosted by Disney himself). The first few seasons of *Wonderful World of Color* consisted mainly of new features, such as the three-part "The Prince and the Pauper," or the two-part "The Mooncussers." The miniseries idea was revived briefly in 1964, with "The Adventures of Gallagher," starring Roger Mobley as Gallagher, a nineteenth-century boy reporter. By the late 1960s, however, more and more of the programs consisted of reruns of Disney films and cartoons. In 1969, almost three years after Disney's death, the show was retitled *The Wonderful World of Disney.* In the fall of 1978 the show celebrated the beginning of its twenty-fifth year on television with a two-part retrospective. The show was retitled *Disney's Wonderful World* in the fall of 1979.

It should also be noted that Walt Disney Productions brought other series to the air. See also *The Mickey Mouse Club* and *Zorro.*

THE WALTER WINCHELL SHOW   ABC/NBC
5 OCTOBER 1952–26 JUNE 1955 (ABC); 5 OCTOBER 1956–28 DECEMBER 1956 (NBC); 2 OCTOBER 1960–6 NOVEMBER 1960 (ABC)
THE WALTER WINCHELL FILE   ABC/SYNDICATED
2 OCTOBER 1957–28 MARCH 1958 (ABC); 1958 (SYNDICATED)   Syndicated newspaper columnist Walter Winchell tried several formats on television, but none was particularly successful (Winchell, who died in 1972, is probably best remembered by TV audiences as the narrator of *The Untouchables*). His first series was a fifteen-minute Sunday-night newscast, which lasted three seasons. In 1956, and again in 1960, he was the host of a half-hour variety show; both series were dropped in midseason. In 1957 he was the host and narrator of *The Walter Winchell File,* a half-hour series of crime dramas produced by Mort Briskin. Twenty-six programs were shown on ABC during the 1957–1958 season, and an additional thirteen were added to the first twenty-six when the series went into syndication.

THE WALTONS   CBS
14 SEPTEMBER 1972–   An unpretentious, low-key dramatic series, *The Waltons* tells the story of a close-knit family living in rural Virginia during the Depression years. Its creator, Earl Hamner, Jr., based the show largely on his own experiences. One of eight children, Hamner grew up near Schuyler, Virginia, and left home in the late 1930s to become a professional writer. Hamner's first effort at dramatizing his boyhood ended up as a film, *Spencer's Mountain,* set in Wyoming, and starring Henry Fonda, Maureen O'Hara, and James MacArthur as Clay-Boy.

The genesis of the TV series was a Christmas special, "The Homecoming" (19 December 1971), written by Hamner; the telecast was not intended to be a pilot for a series, but it attracted such favorable public reaction that CBS decided to build a series around the Walton family that Hamner had created. The roles of three of the four Walton adults were recast for the series, but the roles of the seven Walton children were filled by those who had appeared in "The Homecoming": Richard Thomas as John (John-Boy) Walton, Jr., the eldest; Jon Walmsley as Jason; Judy Norton as Mary Ellen; Eric Scott as Ben; Mary Elizabeth McDonough as Erin; David W. Harper as James Robert (Jim-Bob); and Kami Cotler as Elizabeth. The adult roles on the series were played by: Michael Learned as Olivia Walton, the mother; Ralph Waite as John Walton, the father; Will Geer as Zeb Walton, the grandfather; Ellen Corby as Esther Walton, the grandmother (in "The Homecoming," those parts were played by Patricia Neal, Andrew Duggan, Edgar Bergen, and Ellen Corby).

As a series, *The Waltons* was given little chance to succeed in 1972 when CBS scheduled it on Thursdays opposite *The Flip Wilson Show* on NBC. However, the show attracted not only good reviews (and several Emmys), but also a large enough audience to warrant its renewal (it finished twentieth its first season); in its second season it toppled Flip Wilson, finishing second to *All in the Family* in the seasonal Nielsens. Its popularity has remained fairly steady through the 1970s. One reason for its endurance is that, as the show has evolved in time (between 1972 and 1980, it has moved from 1933 to 1943), its characters have been allowed to mature and develop. A second reason may be that the large Walton family is complemented by a small host of supporting characters. Principal members of the latter category would include: Joe Conley as Ike Godsey, proprietor of the general store in Walton's Mountain, the tiny Jefferson County hamlet where most of the action takes place; Helen Kleeb and Mary Jackson as sisters Mamie and Emily Baldwin, a pair of spinsters who innocently brew moonshine in their stately home; John Crawford as Sheriff Ep Bridges; Mariclare Costello (1972–1975) as Emily Hunter, the schoolteacher; John Ritter (1973–1975) as Reverend Fordwick, who married Miss Hunter; Ronnie Claire Edwards (January 1975–   ) as Olivia's distant cousin, Cora Beth, a frustrated socialite who married Ike Godsey; and Rachel Longaker (1976–   ) as Aimée, a little girl adopted by Ike and Cora Beth.

Life did not remain static for the several members of the Walton clan. John-Boy, an aspiring writer (like his creator, Earl Hamner, Jr.), graduated from high school, attended Boatwright University, started a local newspaper, finally left Walton's Mountain for New York, and later became a war correspondent in London (in real life, Richard Thomas decided to leave *The Waltons* in 1977 after five seasons, though he returned afterward for guest appearances); Jason, a musician, also finished high school and got a job playing piano in a roadhouse in order to pay for further studies; Mary Ellen became a nurse, got married (Tom Bower joined the cast in November 1976 as her husband, Dr. Curtis Willard), and had a baby, John Curtis (in real life, Judy Norton was married in 1976, and was billed as Judy Norton-Taylor afterward; John Curtis is played by Marshall and Michael Reed); Ben helped out John-Boy on the newspaper, and later worked for the family lumber business; and Erin found secretarial work.

Other changes have affected the Walton adults. Ellen Corby, who plays Grandma, suffered a stroke in the fall of 1976 and was absent from the series for a year and a half, returning at the end of the 1977–1978 season. Before production resumed for the 1978–1979 season, Will Geer (Grandpa) died. He was not replaced, and the opening show of the seventh season concerned the family's adjustment to Grandpa Walton's death. During the 1978–1979 season an episode was televised in which Mary Ellen's husband, Dr. Curtis Willard, was killed at Pearl Harbor. Later that season, Olivia Walton learned that she had tuberculosis and left Walton's Mountain for a sanitarium (in real life, Michael Learned's contract with the show's production company expired late in 1978, and she announced her intention to cease appearing as a regular). In the spring of 1979 Leslie Winston joined the cast as Cindy, Ben's wife, and in the fall of that year more changes occurred. Ellen Corby did not return to the series, but Michael Learned agreed to make a number of appearances. Three new regulars were also added: Peggy Rea as Olivia's cousin, Rose Burton, who came with her two grandchildren to take care of the Walton household; Martha Nix as Rose's granddaughter, Serena; and Keith Mitchell as her grandson, Jeffrey. Robert Wightman appeared as John-Boy in the 1979 Thanksgiving episode.

The Waltons was the first family dramatic series of the 1970s; its success led to a proliferation of similar efforts, such as *Apple's Way, Eight Is Enough, Family, The Family Holvak, The Fitzpatricks, Little House on the Prairie, Mulligan's Stew,* and *The New Land.* It was also the first series from Lorimar Productions, a company founded in 1968 by Lee Rich and Merv Adelson (*Apple's Way* and *Eight Is Enough* were also from Lorimar). Lee Rich and Earl Hamner are the executive producers of *The Waltons.*

WANTED CBS
20 OCTOBER 1955–12 JANUARY 1956 Fugitives from justice were the quarry on this half-hour documentary series hosted by Walter McGraw. Dossiers of wanted criminals were presented, along with interviews with law enforcement officials and relatives of those wanted.

WANTED—DEAD OR ALIVE CBS
6 SEPTEMBER 1958–29 MARCH 1961 Western starring Steve McQueen as bounty hunter Josh Randall, who toted a sawed-off shotgun that he called his "Mare's Laig." In the spring of 1960, Wright King was featured as Jason Nichols, a deputy sheriff who teamed up with Randall. A total of 117 half-hour episodes were filmed, with Vincent Fennelly the executive producer for Four Star Films. The pilot for the series, "The Bounty Hunter," was aired on *Trackdown* on 7 March 1958.

WAR AND PEACE   PBS
20 NOVEMBER 1973–15 JANUARY 1974   The fourteen-and-a-half-hour
adaptation of Tolstoy's novel by the BBC was shown on American television in nine parts. Principal players included: Anthony Hopkins as
Pierre; David Swift as Napoleon; Morag Hood as Natasha; Alan Dobie
as Andrei; and Anthony Jacobs as Prince Nikolai.

WARNER BROTHERS PRESENTS   ABC
13 SEPTEMBER 1955–4 SEPTEMBER 1956   This hour umbrella series,
which heralded Warner Brothers' entry into television series production,
was hosted by Gig Young. During the season three series were regularly
shown in the time slot, together with occasional hour dramas. All three
shows were based on popular Warner Brothers films: *Casablanca, Cheyenne,* and *King's Row. Cheyenne* was the only one of the trio to be renewed for a second season. See individual titles for details.

WASHINGTON: BEHIND CLOSED DOORS   ABC
6 SEPTEMBER 1977–11 SEPTEMBER 1977   Six-part miniseries adapted
from John Ehrlichman's novel, *The Company*. Principal players included:
Jason Robards as President Richard Monckton; Cliff Robertson as Wil-
liam Martin, director of the CIA; Lois Nettleton as Linda Martin; Ste-
fanie Powers as Sally Whalen; Andy Griffith as Esker Anderson,
Monckton's predecessor in office; Robert Vaughn as Frank Flaherty,
Monckton's brusque chief of staff; Barry Nelson as Bob Bailey; Harold
Gould as Carl Tessler; Tony Bill as Adam Gardiner; Nicholas Pryor as
Hank Ferris, press secretary; John Houseman as Myron Dunn; and Skip
Homeier as Lars Haglund. Stan Kallis was the executive producer for
Paramount TV; David Rintels and Eric Bercovici wrote the script.

WASHINGTON CONVERSATION   CBS
26 FEBRUARY 1961–16 SEPTEMBER 1962   Paul Niven interviewed a single guest each week on this Sunday-afternoon public affairs program.

WASHINGTON EXCLUSIVE   DUMONT
21 JUNE 1953–1 NOVEMBER 1953   Sunday-evening public affairs program, moderated by Frank McNaughton, featuring a panel of former
senators.

WASHINGTON MERRY-GO-ROUND   SYNDICATED
1956–1957   Fifteen minutes of commentary on political goings-on by
Drew Pearson, whose syndicated newspaper column bore the same title.

WASHINGTON REPORT   DUMONT
22 MAY 1951–31 AUGUST 1951   Tris Coffin hosted this twice-weekly
fifteen-minute interview series, broadcast from Washington, D.C.

WASHINGTON SPOTLIGHT   SYNDICATED
1953   Marquis Childs interviewed newsmakers on this filmed series.

WASHINGTON SQUARE   NBC
21 OCTOBER 1956–13 JUNE 1957 This hour-long musical comedy series
was scheduled approximately every other week. It was originally seen on
Sunday afternoons, but later shifted to various time slots throughout the
week. Its star, Ray Bolger, played himself, and Elaine Stritch costarred as
the operator of the Greenwich Village Inn. Other regulars included Dan-
iza Ilitsch, Jo Wilder, Kay Armen, Rusty Draper, Arnold Stang, the
Three Flames, the Martins, and the Bil and Cora Baird Puppets.

WASHINGTON WEEK IN REVIEW   NET–PBS
22 FEBRUARY 1967–   Half-hour public affairs discussion
program on current events. Regulars have included Peter Lisagor (until
his death late in 1976), Neil McNeil, and Charles Corddry.

WATCH MR. WIZARD
See MR. WIZARD

WATCH THE WORLD   NBC
23 APRIL 1950–20 AUGUST 1950 John Cameron Swayze first hosted this
Sunday-afternoon show, presenting film features of interest to children.
Frank McCall produced the half-hour show. Don Goddard succeeded
Swayze.

WATER WORLD   SYNDICATED
1972–1975 Half-hour documentary series on the oceans and marine
world, narrated first by Lloyd Bridges, later by James Franciscus.

WATERFRONT   SYNDICATED
1954–1956 Half-hour adventure series, set principally aboard the
Cheryl Ann, a tugboat in the San Pedro (Calif.) harbor. With Preston
Foster as Captain John Herrick; Lois Moran·as his wife, May Herrick;
Pinky Tomlin as Tip Hubbard; Douglas Dick as Carl, the Herricks' son,
who worked aboard the tug. Ben Fox created and produced the show,
which was filmed at Hal Roach Studios. The *Cheryl Ann* was really the
Milton S. Patrick, an honest-to-goodness tug which plied the San Pedro
harbor.

THE WAVERLY WONDERS   NBC
22 SEPTEMBER 1978–6 OCTOBER 1978 An early fatality of the 1978–
1979 season, *The Waverly Wonders* was dropped after only three airings.
The half-hour sitcom, apparently inspired by the movie *The Bad News
Bears,* starred Joe Namath as Joe Casey, the newly arrived coach of the

hapless basketball team at Waverly High School. Also on hand were Gwynne Gilford as the principal; James Staley as faculty member Alan Kerner; Ben Piazza as faculty member George Benton; Joshua Grenrock as Faguzzi; Kim Lankford as Connie Rafkin; Tierre Turner as Hasty; and Charles Bloom as Johnny Tate. The show was created by William Bickley and Michael Warren, and produced by Steve Zacharias and Bruce Kane; Lee Rich and Marc Merson were the executive producers for Lorimar Productions.

THE WAY   SYNDICATED
1955–1957   Half-hour series of religious dramas, produced under the auspices of the Methodist Church.

THE WAY IT WAS   PBS
3 OCTOBER 1974–14 MAY 1977   Curt Gowdy hosted this sports nostalgia show, on which he and guest athletes viewed film clips of famous sporting events and reminisced.

WAY OF THE WORLD   NBC
3 JANUARY 1955–7 OCTOBER 1955   Daytime dramatic series; some presentations lasted only one day, while others ran a week or two. Stories were introduced by Gloria Louis, who appeared as Linda Porter.

WAY OUT   CBS
31 MARCH 1961–14 JULY 1961   Half-hour science fiction anthology series hosted by writer Roald Dahl.

WAY OUT GAMES   CBS
11 SEPTEMBER 1976–4 SEPTEMBER 1977   CBS's answer to ABC's *Junior Almost Anything Goes, Way Out Games* was a weekend athletic contest for teams of teenagers representing the states. Produced by Jack Barry and Dan Enright, the half-hour show was hosted by Sonny Fox.

WAYNE AND SHUSTER TAKE AN AFFECTIONATE LOOK AT ...   CBS
17 JUNE 1966–29 JULY 1966   Canadian comics Johnny Wayne and Frank Shuster hosted this semidocumentary series. Each show focused on a particular aspect of comedy; one show, for example, was a tribute to Jack Benny and incorporated clips from Benny's films and TV series.

WE TAKE YOUR WORD   CBS
1 APRIL 1950–23 JANUARY 1951; 9 MARCH 1951–1 JUNE 1951   John K. M. McCaffery hosted this prime-time game show on which a celebrity panel tried to supply the definitions and derivations of words suggested by home viewers. Ilka Chase and Abe Burrows were regular panelists.

WE, THE PEOPLE   CBS/NBC
1 JUNE 1948–25 OCTOBER 1949 (CBS); 4 NOVEMBER 1949–26 SEPTEM-
BER 1952 (NBC)   This early interview series began on radio in 1936.
When it came to television in 1948, Dwight Weist was the host, but in
1949 Dan Seymour replaced him. The show combined celebrity interviews with human interest stories.

THE WEAKER (?) SEX   SYNDICATED
1968   Pamela Mason interviewed female guests on this half-hour talk
show.

THE WEB   CBS/NBC
4 JULY 1950–26 SEPTEMBER 1954 (CBS); 7 JULY 1957–6 OCTOBER 1957
(NBC); 27 MARCH 1961–11 SEPTEMBER 1961 (NBC)   A half-hour dramatic anthology series, *The Web* specialized in stories about people who
created the very crises in which they became involved. Frank Heller, and
then Vincent McConnor, produced the show for Goodson-Todman Productions. After a four-year run on CBS *The Web* surfaced twice on NBC,
first as a summer replacement for *The Loretta Young Show* and later as a
midseason replacement for *Jackpot Bowling with Milton Berle*.

THE WEBB PIERCE SHOW   SYNDICATED
1955   Webb Pierce hosted this half-hour country-and-western-music
show, broadcast from Nashville.

WEDDING PARTY   ABC
1 APRIL 1968–12 JULY 1968   Al Hamel hosted this daytime game show
on which prospective brides and grooms could win prizes if their selections matched.

THE WEDNESDAY NIGHT FIGHTS
See THE FIGHT OF THE WEEK

THE WEEK IN RELIGION   DUMONT
16 MARCH 1952–28 SEPTEMBER 1952; 28 JUNE 1953–3 OCTOBER
1953   Sunday-evening panel show with Rabbi William S. Rosenbloom,
Reverend Robbins Wolcott Barstow, Reverend Joseph N. Moody, and
guests.

THE WEEK IN REVIEW   CBS
20 JULY 1947–13 JANUARY 1951   One of television's first news shows,
The Week in Review was a fifteen-minute wrapup of the week's top news
stories.

WEEKEND   NBC

20 OCTOBER 1974–22 APRIL 1979   A monthly series, *Weekend* evolved
from two previous NBC magazine shows, *First Tuesday* and *Chronolog*.
Hosted by Lloyd Dobyns, it aimed at a younger audience than CBS's *60*
Minutes. From 1974 until 1978 it was a ninety-minute show, usually
scheduled on the first Saturday of the month; in the fall of 1978 it was
trimmed to an hour and moved to prime time (Sundays at 10 p.m., again
once a month). Linda Ellerbee joined Lloyd Dobyns as cohost that season. Reuven Frank was the executive producer.

WELCOME ABOARD   NBC

3 OCTOBER 1948–20 FEBRUARY 1949   Half-hour musical variety show,
hosted by a guest celebrity each week. The Russ Morgan Orchestra was
featured during the early weeks, the Vincent Lopez Orchestra during the
latter weeks.

WELCOME BACK, KOTTER   ABC

9 SEPTEMBER 1975–3 AUGUST 1979   Half-hour sitcom about a high
school teacher who returns to his alma mater, James Buchanan High in
Brooklyn, to teach the "sweathogs," a supposedly untrainable group of
hard-core underachievers. With Gabriel Kaplan as Gabe Kotter; Marcia
Strassman as his wife, Julie Kotter; John Travolta (who would later sky-
rocket to superstardom in *Saturday Night Fever*) as Vinnie Barbarino;
Robert Hegyes as Juan Epstein; Ron Palillo as Arnold Horshack; Lawrence Hilton-Jacobs as Freddie "Boom-Boom" Washington; John Sylvester White as Michael Woodman, the vice principal; and James Wood as
Alex Welles, another teacher. In the fall of 1977 Julie Kotter gave birth
to twin girls, and in January 1978 Melonie Haller joined the cast as Angie
Globagoski, a female sweathog. In the fall of 1978, as John Travolta's
contract permitted him to appear less frequently, a new sweathog was
added: Stephen Shortridge as Beau De Labarre, an experienced high
schooler with seven expulsions to his credit. James Komack was the executive producer of the show, and its theme song, "Welcome Back," was
sung by John Sebastian.

WELCOME TRAVELERS   NBC/CBS

8 SEPTEMBER 1952–2 JULY 1954 (NBC); 5 JULY 1954–28 OCTOBER 1955
(CBS)   Broadcast from Chicago, this daytime show was created by
Tommy Bartlett, who brought it to radio in 1947. Travelers to Chicago
were invited to come to the show, where they talked with Bartlett and
were presented with gifts. When the show came to TV, Bartlett added a
cohost, Bob Cunningham; Jack Smith and Pat Meikle later took over as
hosts. The set for the TV version was made to look like the Porterhouse
Room of the College Inn, the site of the radio version.

WE'LL GET BY CBS

14 MARCH 1975–30 MAY 1975   Alan Alda created this family sitcom, set in suburban New Jersey. With Paul Sorvino as lawyer George Platt; Mitzi Hoag as his wife, Liz Platt; Jerry Houser as son Muff; Devon Scott as daughter Andrea; and Willie Aames as son Kenny.

WELLS FARGO NBC

18 MARCH 1957–8 SEPTEMBER 1962   Officially titled *Tales of Wells Fargo,* this western starred Dale Robertson as Jim Hardie, an agent for the transport company. When the show expanded from thirty to sixty minutes in the fall of 1961, the cast was also expanded; newcomers included Jack Ging as Beau, another Wells Fargo agent; Virginia Christine as Ovie, a widow; Lory Patrick as Ovie's daughter, Tina; Mary Jane Saunders as Ovie's daughter, Mary Gee; and William Demarest as Hardie's ranch foreman, Jeb. The show was first produced by Earle Lyon for Overland Productions and Universal Television, and later by Nat Holt for Juggernaut Productions and Universal. Jack Nicholson appeared in one of his first major TV roles in one episode, "The Washburn Girl," aired 13 February 1961.

WENDY AND ME ABC

14 SEPTEMBER 1964–6 SEPTEMBER 1965   Half-hour sitcom about an airline pilot and his wife, who move into an apartment building where George Burns (who appeared as himself, and addressed the camera as he did in *The Burns and Allen Show*) was the landlord. With Ron Harper as pilot Jeff Conway; Connie Stevens as his wife, Wendy Conway; James Callahan as Jeff's friend and copilot, bachelor Danny Adams; J. Pat O'Malley as Mr. Bundy, the handyman; and Bartlett Robinson as Willard Norton, Jeff's boss.

THE WENDY BARRIE SHOW NBC/DUMONT/ABC

10 NOVEMBER 1948–2 FEBRUARY 1949 (NBC); 17 JANUARY 1949–4 MARCH 1949 (DUMONT); 7 MARCH 1949–13 JULY 1949 (DUMONT); 26 SEPTEMBER 1949–16 FEBRUARY 1950 (ABC); 21 FEBRUARY 1950–27 SEPTEMBER 1950 (NBC)   One of TV's first popular female personalities, Wendy Barrie had several shows of her own in the medium's early days. The first was a ten-minute prime-time show on NBC, titled *Picture This*; it featured guest cartoonists who drew sketches. Early in 1949, while *Picture This* was still running on NBC, she started a daytime show on Du-Mont; in March of 1949 she moved to prime time on DuMont, with a half-hour interview show sponsored by *Photoplay* magazine. That show shifted to ABC in the fall of 1949, and in February of 1950 Barrie returned to NBC with a twice-weekly fifteen-minute show. Toward the end of its run this series was titled *Through Wendy's Window.*

WESLEY CBS

8 MAY 1949–30 AUGUST 1949   Half-hour sitcom about a precocious twelve-year-old and his family. With Donald Devlin and Johnny Stewart as Wesley; Frank Thomas as his father; Mona Thomas (the real-life wife of Frank Thomas) as his mother; Joe Sweeney as his grandfather; Joy Reese as his sister; Jack Ayers as the sister's boyfriend; and Billy Nevard as Wesley's pal. The show was produced by Worthington Miner, directed by Franklin Schaffner, and written by Samuel Taylor.

WEST POINT CBS/ABC

5 OCTOBER 1956–27 SEPTEMBER 1957 (CBS); 8 OCTOBER 1957–1 JULY 1958 (ABC)   Half-hour anthology series about life at the United States Military Academy, produced by Maurice Unger for Ziv TV. The show was hosted by Donald May, who appeared as Cadet Charles C. Thompson. Among the notable guest stars who appeared were Barbara Eden ("Decision," 23 November 1956, her first major TV role), Leonard Nimoy ("His Brother's Fist," 16 November 1956, his first major TV role), and Clint Eastwood ("White Fury," 4 February 1958). The show's theme music, "West Point March," was composed by Philip Egner and Alfred Parham.

WESTERN MARSHAL

See STEVE DONOVAN, WESTERN MARSHAL

THE WESTERNER NBC

30 SEPTEMBER 1960–30 DECEMBER 1960   Short-lived half-hour western starring Brian Keith as drifter Dave Blasingame and John Dehner as his occasional companion, Burgundy Smith. Sam Peckinpah, who created, produced, and directed the show, blamed its failure on the fact that it was "too adult."

WESTINGHOUSE PLAYHOUSE NBC

6 JANUARY 1961–7 JULY 1961   Sponsored by Westinghouse, this half-hour domestic sitcom was also known as *The Nanette Fabray Show* or *Yes Yes Nanette*. It starred Nanette Fabray as Nan McGovern, an actress who married a writer with two children from a former marriage. The story line closely paralleled Fabray's life, as she married writer Ranald MacDougall and inherited three children by MacDougall's former marriage in 1957. (MacDougall created the show for Fabray.) Also featured on the series were Wendell Corey as Nan's husband, widower Dan McGovern, a Hollywood writer; Jacklyn O'Donnell as Dan's daughter, Nancy; Bobby Diamond (late of *Fury*) as Dan's son, Buddy; Doris Kemper as the housekeeper, Mrs. Harper; and Mimi Gibson as Barby.

WESTSIDE MEDICAL   ABC
15 MARCH 1977–25 AUGUST 1977   Hour-long dramatic series about three young physicians operating a medical clinic. With James Sloyan as Dr. Sam Lanagan; Linda Carlson as Dr. Janet Cottrell; Ernest Thompson as Dr. Phil Parker; and Alice Nunn as Carrie. Martin Starger was the executive producer.

WESTWIND   NBC
6 SEPTEMBER 1975–4 SEPTEMBER 1976   Live-action Saturday-morning show about a family sailing aboard the *Westwind* off the coast of Hawaii. With Van Williams as underwater photographer Steve Andrews; Niki Dantine as his wife, marine biologist Kate Andrews; Kimberly Beck as their daughter, Robin; and Steve Burns as their son, Tom. William P. D'Angelo was the executive producer.

WE'VE GOT EACH OTHER   CBS
1 OCTOBER 1977–7 JANUARY 1978   Half-hour domestic sitcom. With Oliver Clark as Stuart Hibbard, who took care of the apartment and wrote copy for the Herman Gutman Mail Order Catalog; Beverly Archer as his wife, Judy Hibbard, office manager for a photographer; Tom Poston as Damon Jerome, Judy's befuddled boss; Joan Van Ark as Dee Dee, Jerome's main model; Ren Woods as Donna, Jerome's secretary; and Martin Kove as the Hibbards' neighbor, Ken, a swimming pool contractor. The series was created by Tom Patchett and Jay Tarses, the executive producers of *The Bob Newhart Show.*

WHAT DO YOU HAVE IN COMMON   CBS
1 JULY 1954–23 SEPTEMBER 1954   Ralph Story hosted this prime-time game show on which teams of three specially selected contestants were given three minutes to figure out what they had in common.

WHAT DO YOU THINK?   ABC
17 JANUARY 1949–14 FEBRUARY 1949   Chicago-based panel-discussion series.

WHAT EVERY WOMAN WANTS TO KNOW   SYNDICATED
1972   Half-hour talk show hosted by Bess Myerson.

WHAT IN THE WORLD   CBS
7 OCTOBER 1951–2 APRIL 1955   Perhaps the most erudite game show in television history, *What in the World* was hosted for most of its run by Dr. Froelich Rainey. Each week a panel of experts tried to identify archaeological artifacts. Regular panelists included Dr. Carlton Coon and Dr. Alfred Kidder. The show was broadcast from Philadelphia, where it began as a local show.

WHAT REALLY HAPPENED TO THE CLASS OF '65?　　　NBC

8 DECEMBER 1977–27 JULY 1978　An hour anthology series, inspired by the book of the same title by Michael Medved and David Wallechinsky, two graduates of the class of 1965, Palisades High School, Los Angeles, who tracked down several members of their class eleven years later and wrote about them. The TV series was entirely fictional; set at Bret Harte High School, it was hosted by Tony Bill as Sam, a member of the class of 1965 who returned to teach at his alma mater. Richard Irving was the executive producer.

WHAT'S GOING ON?　　　ABC

28 NOVEMBER 1954–26 DECEMBER 1954　Prime-time game show from Goodson-Todman Productions, hosted by Lee Bowman. Each week six celebrity panelists were divided into groups of three, the "ins" and the "outs." By watching the monitors, the "ins," who remained in the studio, had to guess where the "outs" were headed and what they were doing.

WHAT'S HAPPENING!!　　　ABC

5 AUGUST 1976–26 AUGUST 1976; 13 NOVEMBER 1976–28 APRIL 1979　Based on the film *Cooley High*, This half-hour sitcom told the story of three black high school students in Los Angeles. Introduced for a four-week trial run in the summer of 1976, it returned to the network schedule that fall. With Ernest Thomas as Roger "Raj" Thomas; Haywood Nelson, Jr., as his friend Dwayne; Fred Berry as their rotund friend Rerun (Freddie Stubbs); Mabel King (1976–1978) as Mama, Roger's mother; Danielle Spencer as Dee, Roger's sassy sister; and Shirley Hemphill as Shirley, the surly waitress at the boys' favorite hangout. In the fall of 1978 Roger and Dwayne started college, and moved to an apartment of their own. Added to the cast were: John Welsh as their neighbor, Big Earl, a cop; David Hollander as his son, Little Earl; and Leland Smith as Roger and Dwayne's friend Snake. Bud Yorkin, Saul Turteltaub, and Bernie Orenstein were the executive producers.

WHAT'S IN A WORD　　　CBS

22 JULY 1954–9 SEPTEMBER 1954　Clifton Fadiman hosted this prime-time game show, on which a celebrity panel had to guess a pair of rhyming words from clues supplied by the host. The panel included Audrey Meadows, Faye Emerson, Mike Wallace, and Jim Moran.

WHAT'S IT ALL ABOUT, WORLD?　　　ABC

6 FEBRUARY 1969–1 MAY 1969　*What's It All About, World?* started out as an hour of satire, hosted by Dean Jones. It proved to be a feeble effort; late in March the first format was scrapped and the show became a straightforward variety series, *The Dean Jones Variety Hour*. The second attempt was as unsuccessful as the first, and the show departed after thir-

teen uneventful weeks. Other regulars included Dennis Allen, Maureen Arthur, Dick Clair and Jenna McMahon, Scoey Mitchlll, Gerri Granger, Ron Prince, and Bayn Johnson (as Happy Hollywood).

WHAT'S IT FOR? NBC
12 OCTOBER 1957–4 JANUARY 1958   Prime-time game show, hosted by Hal March, on which a celebrity panel tried to guess the purpose of new or unusual inventions. Panelists included Abe Burrows, Hans Conried, Betsy Palmer, and Cornelia Otis Skinner.

WHAT'S IT WORTH? CBS
21 MAY 1948–28 APRIL 1949   Prime-time show on which professional art restorer Sigmund Rothschild evaluated heirlooms and art objects, answered inquiries from viewers, and interviewed guest appraisers. Rothschild was assisted by Gil Fates, who later became the executive producer of *What's My Line?* See also *Trash or Treasure?*

WHAT'S MY LINE? CBS/SYNDICATED
2 FEBRUARY 1950–3 SEPTEMBER 1967 (CBS); 1968–1975 (SYNDICA-TED)   Television's longest-running prime-time game show involved a simple format—a panel of four celebrities tried to guess the occupations of the contestants. The panelists were permitted to ask yes-or-no questions, and the contestant was awarded $5 each time a "no" answer was given; if ten "no" answers were given, the game ended and the contestant won the top prize of $50. Each week a mystery guest also dropped by, and the panelists (who were blindfolded for this segment) tried to guess his or her identity. The show was a Mark Goodson–Bill Todman Production; Goodson and Todman were responsible for several other of TV's best known and most successful game shows, such as *I've Got a Secret, To Tell the Truth,* and *Match Game,* but *What's My Line?* was their first hit show. The show was hosted for its entire seventeen-year network run by John Daly (during many of those years Daly anchored the evening newscasts on ABC as well). The first panel included syndicated columnist Dorothy Kilgallen, Louis Untermeyer, Governor Harold Hoffman (of New Jersey), and psychiatrist Dr. Richard Hoffman. Phil Rizzuto of the New York Yankees was the first mystery guest. Kilgallen remained with the show until her death in 1965, but the other original panelists did not last long. Fred Allen, Hal Block, and Steve Allen (who coined the famous question, "Is it bigger than a breadbox?") were frequently featured during the early 1950s, but by the end of the decade the regular panel consisted of Kilgallen, Arlene Francis, Bennett Cerf, and a guest celebrity. (Jimmy Carter once appeared as a contestant, when he was governor of Georgia.) The syndicated version of the show was played the same way. The latter version was hosted by Wally Bruner from 1968 until 1972, when Larry Blyden took over; Blyden died in 1975 from injuries sus-

tained in a car crash in Morocco, and production was discontinued. Arlene Francis and Soupy Sales were regular panelists on the syndicated version.

WHAT'S NEW MISTER MAGOO
See MR. MAGOO

WHAT'S ON YOUR MIND? ABC
24 JULY 1951–10 MARCH 1952   Panel show, on which psychiatry was discussed in terms comprehensible to lay people. Isabel Leighton was the moderator. The show was retitled *How Did They Get That Way?*

WHAT'S THE STORY DUMONT
25 JULY 1951–23 SEPTEMBER 1955   On this prime-time game show a panel of journalists tried to identify famous events from sketches performed on stage. Walter Kiernan was the first host; John K. M. McCaffery succeeded him.

WHAT'S THIS SONG NBC
26 OCTOBER 1964–24 SEPTEMBER 1965   Wink Martindale hosted this daytime game show on which two 2-member teams (each with a celebrity and a contestant) tried to identify songs and sing their lyrics.

WHAT'S YOUR BID ABC/DUMONT
14 FEBRUARY 1953–11 APRIL 1953 (ABC); 3 MAY 1953–28 JUNE 1953 (DUMONT)   On this prime-time game show merchandise was auctioned off to members of the studio audience; all proceeds were donated to charities. The ABC version was hosted by John Reed King, the DuMont version by Robert Alda. Leonard "Liberal Bill" Rosen was the auctioneer.

WHAT'S YOUR TROUBLE SYNDICATED
1952–1953   Half-hour series on which Dr. and Mrs. Norman Vincent Peale dispensed advice on coping with life's problems.

WHEEL OF FORTUNE CBS
3 OCTOBER 1952–25 DECEMBER 1953   The first of the two series of this title was hosted by Todd Russell. It was a human interest show similar to *Mr. Citizen* and *The Girl in My Life*—persons who had done good deeds were rewarded. The half-hour show was introduced as a Friday-morning replacement for *Arthur Godfrey Time,* and a prime-time version was shown during the summer of 1953.

WHEEL OF FORTUNE NBC
6 JANUARY 1975–   The second show with this title is a daytime game show on which three contestants take turns spinning a large

wheel for the chance to guess the letters of a mystery word or phrase. Chuck Woolery is the host and is assisted by Susan Stafford. The series, a Merv Griffin Production, expanded to one hour on 1 December 1975, and contracted to thirty minutes on 19 January 1976.

WHEELIE AND THE CHOPPER BUNCH NBC
7 SEPTEMBER 1974–30 AUGUST 1975 Saturday-morning cartoon series from Hanna-Barbera Productions about a heroic Volkswagen (Wheelie) who battled a bunch of motorcycles.

WHEN HAVOC STRUCK SYNDICATED
1978 A series of twelve half-hour films on notable disasters, narrated by Glenn Ford.

WHEN THINGS WERE ROTTEN ABC
10 SEPTEMBER 1975–24 DECEMBER 1975 This half-hour sitcom was supposed to be satire on the Robin Hood legend. Featured were Dick Gautier as Robin Hood; Misty Rowe as Maid Marian; Dick Van Patten as Friar Tuck; Henry Polic II as the Sheriff of Nottingham; Ron Rifkin as Prince John; Richard Dimitri as twins Bertram and Renaldo; David Sabin as Little John; Bernie Kopell as Alan-A-Dale; and Jane Johnston as Princess Isabelle. Mel Brooks, John Boni, and Norman Stiles created the series, and Norman Steinberg produced it for Paramount Television.

WHERE THE ACTION IS ABC
27 JUNE 1965–31 MARCH 1967 Half-hour musical show for teenagers. The daytime show was hosted by Dick Clark, and the regular performers included Paul Revere and the Raiders, Steve Alaimo, and Linda Scott. Among the many guests were Sonny and Cher, who made one of their first TV appearances on 30 July 1965.

WHERE THE HEART IS CBS
8 SEPTEMBER 1969–23 MARCH 1973 This half-hour daytime serial, set in the town of Northcross, a suburb of New York City, concerned the sexual goings-on of the members of two families, the Hathaways and the Prescotts. Principal players included: James Mitchell as Julian Hathaway, a widowed English professor; Diana Walker as Mary Hathaway, Julian's second wife; Gregory Abels as Julian's son (by his first marriage), Michael Hathaway, who fell for his stepmother; Robyn Millan and Lisa Richards as Vicky Lucas, who married Mike and later divorced him; Diana van der Vlis as Julian's sister, Kate Hathaway; Laurence Luckinbill and Ron Harper as Steve Prescott, who married Kate; Zohra Lampert as Ellie Jardin, who was murdered; Michael Bersell as Ellie's mute son, Peter, who was taken in by Kate and Steve; Tracy Brooks Swope as Liz Rainey, who became Mike Hathaway's second wife; Bill Post, Jr., as

Dr. Joe Prescott; Katherine Meskill as Nancy Prescott; Ted Leplat as Terry Prescott; Peter MacLean as John Rainey; David Cryer as Dr. Hugh Jessup; Louise Shaffer as Allison Jessup; Clarice Blackburn as Amy Snowden; Rue McClanahan as Margaret Jardin; and Alice Drummond as Loretta Jardin. After a three-and-a-half-year run, *Where the Heart Is* was replaced by *The Young and the Restless*.

WHERE WAS I   DUMONT
2 SEPTEMBER 1952–6 OCTOBER 1953   Dan Seymour first hosted this prime-time game show, which went through at least two formats. In one format, a celebrity panel tried to guess where the contestant had been at a certain time, and in a second format, a celebrity panel tried to guess the nature of photographs shown to viewers, but hidden from the panelists' view. Regular panelists included Peter Donald, Nancy Guild, and David Ross. John Reed King became the host late in 1952.

WHERE'S HUDDLES   CBS
1 JULY 1970–9 SEPTEMBER 1970   A prime-time cartoon show from Hanna-Barbera Productions, *Where's Huddles* centered around a football team. Featured voices included Cliff Norton as Ed Huddles, the quarterback; Mel Blanc as Bubba McCoy, the center; Paul Lynde as Pertwee; Jean van der Pyl as Marge Huddles, Ed's wife; Herb Jeffries as Freight Train; Marie Wilson as Penny McCoy, Bubba's wife; and Alan Reed as Coach.

WHERE'S RAYMOND?
See THE RAY BOLGER SHOW

WHEW!   CBS
23 APRIL 1979–   A fast-paced daytime game show hosted by Tom Kennedy, *Whew!* involves two contestants, each of whom tries to block the other's progress along a six-level game board. Contestants are given one minute to go from the first level up to the sixth and must negotiate their way around "blocks" strategically hidden on the board by their opponents. The show was retitled *Celebrity Whew!* in November 1979.

WHIPLASH   SYNDICATED
1961   Half-hour "western," starring Peter Graves as Chris Cobb, an American who founded a stagecoach line in Australia. The series was filmed on location.

THE WHIRLYBIRDS   SYNDICATED
1957   Half-hour adventure series about a couple of helicopter pilots who worked for Whirlybird Service, an outfit based at Longwood Field. With

Kenneth Tobey as Chuck Martin; Craig Hill as P. T. Moore. The show
was produced by Desilu.

WHISPERING SMITH   NBC
15 MAY 1961–18 SEPTEMBER 1961   Half-hour western, much criticized
during its short run for its excessive violence. Set in Denver during the
1870s, it starred Guy Mitchell as Detective George Romack, Audie Murphy as Tom "Whispering" Smith, and Sam Buffington as Chief John
Richards. Richard Lewis was the producer. Filming of the twenty-six
episodes began in 1959, but the series did not find a place on NBC's
schedule until 1961.

WHISTLE STOP U.S.A.   CBS
7 SEPTEMBER 1952–2 NOVEMBER 1952   Sunday-afternoon news show
that focused on the 1952 Presidential election. Charles Collingwood was
the host.

THE WHISTLER   SYNDICATED
1954   Half-hour suspense anthology series, based on the radio program
that began in 1942. The show was narrated by an unseen voice, known
only as "The Whistler," whose distinctive musical theme preceded his
comments. Bill Forman provided the voice.

THE WHISTLING WIZARD   CBS
3 NOVEMBER 1951–20 SEPTEMBER 1952   Saturday-morning puppet
show, featuring the puppets of Bil and Cora Baird. The story line concerned a child, J.P., who was transported to a fantasy land to search for
the Whistling Wizard.

WHITE HUNTER   SYNDICATED
1959   Half-hour adventure series set in Africa, starring Rhodes Reason
as John Hunter, guide and game hunter.

THE WHITE SHADOW   CBS
27 NOVEMBER 1978–   Hour dramatic series about a basketball star who, after an injury that curtailed his professional career, accepted an offer to coach at Carver High School in Los Angeles. With Ken
Howard as coach Ken Reeves; Ed Bernard as the principal, Jim Willis,
a former college teammate of Reeves's; Joan Pringle as vice-principal
Sybil Buchanon; Robin Rose as Ken's sister, Katie Donahue; Jerry Fogel
as her husband, Bill Donahue; Kevin Hooks as Morris Thorpe; Eric Kilpatrick as Curtis Jackson; Byron Stewart as Warren Coolidge; Thomas
Carter as James Hayward; Nathan Cook as Milton Reese; Timothy Van
Patten as Mario (Salami) Petrino; Ken Michelman as Abner Goldstein;
and Ira Angustain as Ricardo Gomez. In the fall of 1979 John Mengatti

joined the squad as Nick Vitaglia, Salami's cousin, and Russell Phillip Robinson appeared as the team manager, Phil Jeffers. Bruce Paltrow is the executive producer, Mark C. Tinker the producer, for MTM Enterprises.

WHO DO YOU TRUST? CBS/ABC

3 JANUARY 1956–26 MARCH 1957 (CBS); 30 SEPTEMBER 1957–27 DECEMBER 1963 (ABC) A popular game show, this series began as a prime-time show on CBS in 1956 under the title *Do You Trust Your Wife?* Hosted by Edgar Bergen, it featured two married couples who competed in a quiz segment; the husbands could choose to answer the questions themselves, or they could "trust" their wives to answer. In the fall of 1957 the show moved to ABC, where it became a daytime show and was hosted by Johnny Carson. Carson spent more of his time interviewing the couples than asking them questions. In July of 1958 the show adopted a less chauvinistic title, *Who Do You Trust?* but continued with the same format. In the fall of 1958 Carson was teamed up for the first time with a new announcer, Ed McMahon, who commuted from Philadelphia to do the show (McMahon succeeded Bill Nimmo). It was the start of a long association, as Carson took McMahon with him when he left *Who Do You Trust?* in 1962 to host the *Tonight* show. Carson was succeeded as host of *Who Do You Trust?* (which by then was actually titled *Whom Do You Trust?* as a concession to grammatical accuracy) by Woody Woodbury. The series was produced by Don Fedderson.

WHO IN THE WORLD CBS

24 JUNE 1962–16 SEPTEMBER 1962 Prime-time half-hour talk show on which Warren Hull conversed with a single guest each week.

WHO PAYS NBC

2 JULY 1959–24 SEPTEMBER 1959 Mike Wallace hosted this prime-time game show. Each contestant was employed by a famous person, and the object of the game was for a celebrity panel to ascertain who the well-known employers were; the employers themselves then appeared and chatted with the panel. See also *Who's the Boss.*

WHO SAID THAT? NBC/ABC

9 DECEMBER 1948–18 FEBRUARY 1951 (NBC); 5 APRIL 1952–26 APRIL 1952 (NBC); 13 APRIL 1953–5 JULY 1954 (NBC); 2 FEBRUARY 1955–26 JULY 1955 (ABC) This prime-time game show began on radio in 1948 and featured a panel of celebrities who tried to identify the sources of well-known quotations. Robert Trout was the first host and was succeeded by Walter Kiernan. Frequent panelists included June Lockhart, Morey Amsterdam, and H. V. Kaltenborn.

WHO, WHAT OR WHERE NBC

29 DECEMBER 1969–4 JANUARY 1974 Art James hosted this daytime game show on which three contestants competed in a question-and-answer format. Each player was given a stake of $125 and could wager up to $50 on a single question. At the beginning of each round the name of a category was revealed; each category contained three questions—one "Who," one "What," and one "Where." Some questions were more difficult than others and were given higher odds. The player who wagered the most on a single question won the right to answer it, and the player's winnings were increased or depleted by the amount of the wager (or by the odds, if the question was worth more than even money). If two players bid the same amount on a question, an auction was conducted. At the end of the game, players could wager any amount, up to their entire winnings, on the final round.

WHODUNNIT? NBC

12 APRIL 1979–10 MAY 1979 One of the few prime-time game shows since the 1950s, *Whodunnit?* gave three contestants the chance to match wits with a trio of experts in attempting to solve a dramatized crime. Approximately halfway through the dramatization, contestants were given the opportunity to guess the culprit for the show's top prize of $10,000. Contestants who chose not to hazard a guess at that time could then wait to hear the panel of experts announce their guess as to the culprit (the experts were also permitted to interrogate the several suspects); a contestant who then chose the real culprit won either $2500 (if any of the experts had made the same choice) or $5000 (if none of the experts had chosen correctly). Ed McMahon hosted the half-hour show, which was created by Jeremy Lloyd and Lance Percival. Though *Whodunnit?* billed itself as television's first mystery game show, it was not. A similar format had been employed thirty years earlier in CBS's *Armchair Detective* and was again used in the DuMont version of *Public Prosecutor.*

WHO'S THE BOSS ABC

19 FEBRUARY 1954–20 AUGUST 1954 A prime-time game show on which a celebrity panel tried to guess the identities of the famous employers of the show's contestants. Walter Kiernan was the first host of the show and was succeeded by Mike Wallace. Wallace hosted the 1959 version of the show, which was titled *Who Pays.* See also that title.

WHO'S THERE CBS

14 JULY 1952–15 SEPTEMBER 1952 Arlene Francis hosted this prime-time game show on which a celebrity panel tried to identify guest celebrities from physical clues associated with those celebs. The format was later used in a 1953 game show, *Personality Puzzle.*

WHO'S WATCHING THE KIDS NBC

22 SEPTEMBER 1978–15 DECEMBER 1978 Set in Las Vegas, *Who's Watching the Kids* was a distant cousin of *Blansky's Beauties,* the 1977 sitcom that starred Nancy Walker; the two shared the same producers, and a few cast members, but *Who's Watching the Kids* emphasized the younger regulars rather than the chorus girls. Featured were Caren Kaye as chorus girl Stacy Turner; Lynda Goodfriend as Stacy's roommate and partner, Angie Vitola; Marcia Lewis as their landlady, Mitzi Logan, who was also the emcee at the Club Sand Pile, where Stacy and Angie performed; Scott Baio as Angie's fifteen-year-old live-in brother, Frankie Vitola, who was sent West from South Philadelphia by his folks in the hopes that he could improve his grades; Tammy Lauren as Stacy's nine-year-old live-in sister, Melissa Turner; Larry Breeding as their neighbor, newscaster Larry Parnell; Jim Belushi (brother of John Belushi of *NBC's Saturday Night Live*) as Bert Gunkle, Larry's camera operator; Lorrie Mahaffey as Memphis; Elaine Bolton as Bridget; and Shirley Kirkes as Cochise. Garry K. Marshall, Tony Marshall, and Don Silverman were the executive producers for Henderson Productions in association with Paramount TV.

WHO'S WHO CBS

4 JANUARY 1977–26 JUNE 1977 An hour-long newsmagazine with a lighter touch than *60 Minutes.* On *Who's Who* the emphasis was on people. Dan Rather was the "chief reporter," and Barbara Howar and Charles Kuralt (reporting "on the road") were regular contributors.

WHY? ABC

29 DECEMBER 1952–20 APRIL 1953 Comedy quiz show, hosted by John Reed King, on which the contestants were told the "Who, What, Where, and When" of an event and were required to supply the "Why." The prime-time show was seen on Monday nights. King cohosted the show with Bill Cullen, who also served as the show's producer.

WICHITA TOWN NBC

30 SEPTEMBER 1959–23 SEPTEMBER 1960 Half-hour western starring Joel McCrea as Marshal Mike Dunbar of Wichita, Kansas, and Jody McCrea (Joel's son) as Ben Matheson, his deputy. Also featured were Carlos Romero as Rico and George Neise as Doc. The series was based on *Wichita,* the 1955 film which had starred the elder McCrea.

WIDE COUNTRY NBC

20 SEPTEMBER 1962–12 SEPTEMBER 1963 *Wide Country* was one of a pair of 1962 series set along the professional rodeo circuit (*Stoney Burke* was the other). The hour show starred Earl Holliman as Mitch Guthrie and Andrew Prine as his younger brother, Andy Guthrie.

WIDE WIDE WORLD   NBC
16 OCTOBER 1955–8 JUNE 1958   Another manifestation of Sylvester
"Pat" Weaver's fertile imagination, *Wide Wide World* was a Sunday-
afternoon documentary series. Most of the ninety-minute shows focused
on a single topic and featured live reports from locations throughout
North America (filmed segments from other parts of the world were also
used). Dave Garroway, whom Weaver had chosen to host the *Today*
show three years before, was the "guide" of *Wide Wide World*. The show
was first introduced on 27 June 1955, as part of *Producers' Showcase,* but
regular Sunday broadcasts did not begin until the fall. On the October
1955 premiere the topic was "A Sunday in Autumn," and reports were
made from Lake Mead, the Grand Canyon, Weeki Wachee (Fla.), Dallas,
San Francisco, St. Louis, Gloucester (Mass.), Cleveland, Omaha, and
New York City. Barry Wood was the executive producer, Herbert Sussan
the producer.

WIDE WORLD OF SPORTS
See ABC'S WIDE WORLD OF SPORTS

THE WILBURN BROTHERS SHOW   SYNDICATED
1963–1969   Country-and-western music series, hosted by Ted and Doyle
Wilburn.

WILD BILL HICKOK   SYNDICATED
1951–1956   Half-hour western starring Guy Madison as U.S. Marshal
James Butler (Wild Bill) Hickok, and Andy Devine as his sidekick, Jingles B. Jones ("Wait fer me, Wild Bill!"). Devine's inimitably gravelly
voice was the result of a childhood accident, in which he fell with a stick
in his mouth. A total of 113 episodes were filmed. Madison and Devine
also played the same roles on the radio version of the series, which began
in 1951 and ran through 1956.

WILD CARGO   SYNDICATED
1963   Half-hour documentary series on capturing wild animals for zoos.
Arthur Jones was the host.

WILD KINGDOM   NBC/SYNDICATED
6 JANUARY 1963–11 APRIL 1971 (NBC); 1971–   (SYNDICA-
TED)   Perhaps the best known, and certainly the longest running of the
several documentary series about animal life, *Wild Kingdom* is sponsored
by Mutual of Omaha and has been hosted for most of its run by Marlin
Perkins (formerly the host of *Zoo Parade*). Other hosts or cohosts have
included Jim Fowler, Tom Allen, and Stan Brock.

THE WILD, WILD WEST CBS

17 SEPTEMBER 1965–19 SEPTEMBER 1969 A fantasy western, *The Wild, Wild West* combined *The Man from U.N.C.L.E.* with *Maverick.* It starred Robert Conrad as James West, a special agent assigned to the frontier by President Ulysses S. Grant. Ross Martin costarred as his associate, Artemus Gordon. The two battled the usual assortment of mad scientists and crazed outlaws, using fanciful gadgets to thwart their adversaries. Occasionally appearing were Michael Dunn as Dr. Miguelito Loveless, West's diminutive archenemy; James Gregory as President Grant; and Charles Aidman as Jeremy, who filled in for Artemus Gordon when Ross Martin was sidelined with a mild heart attack. The hour show was created by Michael Garrison for Bruce Lansbury Productions. It was rerun on CBS during the summer of 1970. On 9 May 1979 Conrad and Martin were reunited in a made-for-TV movie, "The Wild, Wild West Revisited."

WILD, WILD WORLD OF ANIMALS SYNDICATED

1973–1976 Half-hour documentary series on animal life, from Time–Life Films, narrated by William Conrad.

WILDCAT
See THE TROUBLESHOOTERS

WILL THE REAL JERRY LEWIS PLEASE SIT DOWN ABC

12 SEPTEMBER 1970–2 SEPTEMBER 1972 Half-hour Saturday-morning cartoon show created by Jerry Lewis.

WILLIAM TELL SYNDICATED

1958 Officially titled *The Adventures of William Tell,* this half-hour adventure series was filmed in Switzerland and produced by National Telefilm Associates. It starred Conrad Phillips as William Tell, the legendary Swiss freedom fighter; Jennifer Jayne as Hedda Tell; Richard Rogers as Walter Tell; and Willoughby Goddard as Gessler, Tell's nemesis.

WILLY CBS

18 SEPTEMBER 1954–7 JULY 1955 Half-hour sitcom starring June Havoc as Willa (Willy) Dodger, a lawyer in a small New England town. Other regulars included Lloyd Corrigan as Papa; Mary Treen as Willy's sister, Emily; Danny Richards, Jr., as her nephew, Franklin; and Whitfield Connor as her boyfriend, Charlie Bush. In the later episodes Hal Peary appeared as her new employer, Mr. Bannister, and Sterling Holloway played Harvey Evelyn, manager of a theatrical repertory company. Filmed at Desilu Studios, the show was produced by June Havoc's husband, Bill Spier.

WIN WITH A WINNER   NBC

24 JUNE 1958–9 SEPTEMBER 1958   Also known as *Winners Circle,* this prime-time game show was hosted by Sandy Becker and involved five players who, like horses in a race, moved along a track as they answered questions. Home viewers could also participate by sending in postcards predicting the players' exact order of finish.

WIN WITH THE STARS   SYNDICATED

1968   Allen Ludden hosted this game show on which teams made up of celebrities and contestants competed in a song-identification game.

WINDOW ON MAIN STREET   CBS

2 OCTOBER 1961–12 SEPTEMBER 1962   Robert Young, fresh from *Father Knows Best,* starred in this comedy-drama as Cameron Garrett Brooks, a widowed novelist who returned to his hometown, Millsburg, to write about the people there. Also featured were Ford Rainey as Lloyd Ramsey, editor of the town paper; Constance Moore as widow Chris Logan, who worked on the paper; Brad Berwick as Arny Logan, Chris's young son; Warner Jones as Harry McGil, desk clerk at the Majestic Hotel; James Davidson as Wally Evans, owner of the hotel; Carol Byron as Wally's wife, Peggy Evans; Marilyn Harvey as Mrs. Miller; Tim Matheson as her son, Roddy Miller; Coleen Gray as Miss Wycliffe; William Cort as Dick Aldrich; and Richard Wyler as Phil Rowan. The half-hour show was created and owned by Robert Young and Eugene R. Rodney, who had owned *Father Knows Best;* the two were given a free hand by CBS in developing this show.

WINDOW ON THE WORLD   DUMONT

27 JANUARY 1949–14 APRIL 1949   Half-hour variety show hosted by Gil Lamb.

WINDOW ON WASHINGTON   NBC

4 JANUARY 1953–12 JULY 1953   Fifteen-minute Sunday-afternoon public affairs program, hosted by Bill Henry and produced by Julian Goodman.

WINDOW SHOPPING   ABC

2 APRIL 1962–29 JUNE 1962   Bob Kennedy hosted this short-lived daytime game show, on which three contestants studied a picture for a few seconds and could then win points by recalling details about it. Professor William Wood of the Columbia University School of Journalism was the judge. The half-hour series was produced by Alan Gilbert for Wolf Productions.

WINDOWS   CBS

8 JULY 1955–26 AUGUST 1955 A live half-hour dramatic anthology series, *Windows* was produced by Mort Abrahams. Four directors shared the assignments: Jack Garfein, José Quintero, John Stix, and Leonard Valenta.

WINDY CITY JAMBOREE   DUMONT

26 MARCH 1950–18 JUNE 1950 An hour-long musical show, broadcast from the Rainbow Gardens in Chicago. Featured were Danny O'Neil, Gloria Van, Jane Brockman and Bud Tygett, Jimmy McPartland, Dick Edwards, "Woo-Woo" Stephens, Paula Raye, John Dalce, and the Julian Stockdale Orchestra.

WINGO   CBS

1 APRIL 1958–6 MAY 1958 A prime-time game show, *Wingo* pitted a champion against a challenger in a question-and-answer format. A contestant won $1,000 each time his or her opponent was defeated, plus the chance to compete for the show's top prize of $250,000. Bob Kennedy was the host.

WINKY-DINK AND YOU   CBS

10 OCTOBER 1953–27 APRIL 1957 Jack Barry hosted this popular weekend children's show, which featured skits and cartoons (Winky-Dink, a little boy, was the star of many of the cartoons). The gimmick for which the show is best remembered was the Winky-Dink Kit, which could be bought by mail; it consisted of a piece of plastic that could be placed over a television screen, some crayons, and a cloth to wipe clean the plastic. The kit enabled viewers to participate in Winky's adventures by drawing props as suggested by Jack Barry. It also enabled viewers to transcribe a secret message, which was broadcast bit by bit at the end of the day's cartoon adventures. Also featured on the half-hour show was Dayton Allen, who played Barry's inept assistant, Mr. Bungle.

WINNER TAKE ALL   CBS

15 JUNE 1948–3 OCTOBER 1950; 12 FEBRUARY 1951–20 APRIL 1951; 25 FEBRUARY 1952–5 OCTOBER 1952 One of the first game shows developed by Mark Goodson and Bill Todman, *Winner Take All* began on radio in 1946 and came to television two years later; from 1948 to 1950 it was a prime-time series, and in 1951 and 1952 it was a daytime show. The prime-time version involved a straight question-and-answer format. On the daytime version two contestants competed, answering questions about skits performed on stage by a group of players. Bud Collyer was the first host; he was succeeded by Barry Gray, and in 1952, by Bill Cullen. Gil Fates was the producer.

WINNING STREAK NBC

1 JULY 1974–3 JANUARY 1975   Daytime game show hosted by Bill Cullen on which contestants answered questions to win letters of the alphabet, which they could then use to assemble words. The show was a Bob Stewart Production.

WINSTON CHURCHILL—THE VALIANT YEARS ABC

27 NOVEMBER 1960–11 JUNE 1961   A highly acclaimed series of twenty-six half hours that focused on Churchill's leadership during World War II. The series was produced by Robert D. Graff and Ben Feiner, Jr. It was narrated by Gary Merrill, and selections from Churchill's memoirs were read by Richard Burton. The series was rerun on ABC in 1962 and 1963. Richard Rodgers composed the score.

WIRE SERVICE ABC

4 OCTOBER 1956–23 SEPTEMBER 1957   Hour-long adventure series about three reporters for the Trans Globe News Service; the three stars—Mercedes McCambridge as Kate Wells, Dane Clark as Dan Miller, and George Brent as Dean Evans—appeared on a rotating basis. Sharp-eyed viewers could have noticed Michael Landon in one episode, "High Adventure," playing his first major TV role (20 December). Don Sharpe and Warren Lewis produced the series.

WISDOM OF THE AGES DUMONT

16 DECEMBER 1952–30 JUNE 1953   On this prime-time panel show, Jack Barry combined features of two of his earlier shows, *Juvenile Jury* and *Life Begins at Eighty,* both of which he created with his longtime partner, Dan Enright. *Wisdom of the Ages* featured five panelists—one under twenty, one between twenty-one and forty, one between forty-one and sixty, one between sixty-one and eighty, and one over eighty—who dispensed advice on problems suggested by viewers.

THE WISDOM SERIES NBC

13 OCTOBER 1957–6 APRIL 1958   A Sunday-afternoon series of filmed interviews with some of the world's greatest figures, *The Wisdom Series* was produced by Robert D. Graff. Like many of NBC's highly praised programming ideas of the decade, it was conceived by Sylvester "Pat" Weaver. Though the series did not reach the air until 1957, filming had begun as early as 1952. As a rule, subjects had to be over sixty-five years of age in order to be eligible for consideration. Among those who participated in the series were Bertrand Russell, Jawaharlal Nehru, Carl Sandburg, Sean O'Casey, Herbert Hoover, Edward Steichen, Pablo Casals, Wanda Landowska, Igor Stravinsky, Edith Hamilton, and Frank Lloyd Wright. The show was rerun in 1959.

WITH THIS RING   DUMONT
21 JANUARY 1951–11 MARCH 1951   Prime-time panel show on which engaged couples discussed marriage and marital problems. Bill Slater hosted the show for the first few weeks and was succeeded by Martin Gabel.

THE WITNESS   CBS
29 SEPTEMBER 1960–26 JANUARY 1961   This unusual anthology series was cloaked in pseudo-documentary trappings. Each show was set at a Congressional hearing room, where suspected racketeers were grilled by a panel of investigators. Some of the characters who appeared were entirely fictional, while others were based on real people; Telly Savalas guest starred on the premiere as Lucky Luciano. Paul McGrath appeared as the chairman of the investigating panel, and other members of the body were played by Charles Haydon, Frank Milan, and William Smithers.

THE WIZARD OF ODDS   NBC
17 JULY 1973–28 JUNE 1974   Alex Trebek hosted this daytime game show, which replaced *Sale of the Century*. Members of the studio audience competed in a number of rounds, most of which required answering statistical questions posed by the host.

THE WOLFMAN JACK SHOW   SYNDICATED
1974   Half-hour talk show on which Wolfman Jack, legendary disc jockey of the 1950s, rapped with rock stars.

WOMAN   SYNDICATED
1971   Half-hour talk show for women, hosted by Sherrye Henry.

WOMAN   PBS
1973–1977   Half-hour public affairs program on topics of interest to women, produced and hosted by Sandra Elkin for WNED-TV, Buffalo.

A WOMAN TO REMEMBER   DUMONT
21 FEBRUARY 1949–15 JULY 1949   One of television's first serials, *A Woman to Remember* began as a daytime show and shifted to an early-evening slot after a few weeks. Its format was that of a serial within a serial, as it dealt with the interaction between the cast and crew of a mythical radio soap opera. The fifteen-minute show featured Patricia Wheel as the leading lady of the radio soap, Joan Catlin as its villain, John Raby as its director, Frank Thomas, Jr., as its sound man, and Ruth McDevitt.

WOMAN WITH A PAST   CBS
1 FEBRUARY 1954–2 JULY 1954   This daytime serial premiered on the same day as *The Secret Storm,* but lasted one-sixtieth as long. It starred Constance Ford as Lynn Sherwood, a dress designer.

WONDER WOMAN   ABC/CBS

18 DECEMBER 1976–30 JULY 1977 (ABC); 16 SEPTEMBER 1977–11 SEP-
TEMBER 1979 (CBS)   An hour adventure series based on the comic book
character created by Charles Moulton, *Wonder Woman* was first introduced to television audiences in a 1974 made-for-TV movie, which
starred Cathy Lee Crosby. The character reappeared in three specials
aired during the 1975–1976 season, all of which starred Lynda Carter—
"The New, Original Wonder Woman," "Fausta, the Nazi Wonder Woman," and "Wonder Woman Meets Baroness Von Gunter." Regularly
scheduled broadcasts began the following season, again starring Lynda
Carter in the title role. A resident of a mysterious island, the powerfully
endowed Wonder Woman helped the Americans fight the Nazis; she took
the name Diana Prince as her cover. Also featured on the ABC version of
the series were Lyle Waggoner as Major Steve Trevor, Diana's romantic
interest; Richard Eastham as General Blankenship; and Beatrice Colen as
Corporal Etta Candy. When the series moved to CBS in the fall of 1977,
it was updated to the present time; Lynda Carter continued as Diana
Prince, and Lyle Waggoner returned as Steve Trevor, Jr. (the son of the
major), a government agent. Normann Burton joined the cast as Joe Atkinson. The CBS version carried the official title of *The New Adventures
of Wonder Woman;* Douglas S. Cramer was the executive producer.

WONDERFUL JOHN ACTON   NBC

12 JULY 1953–6 OCTOBER 1953   Half-hour sitcom set in 1919 in a small
Kentucky town on the banks of the Ohio River. With Harry Holcombe
as John Acton, the court clerk and town storekeeper; Virginia Dwyer as
Julia, John's widowed daughter; Ronnie Walken as Kevin Acton, John's
twelve-year-old son; Ian Martin as Uncle Terence; Jane Rose as John's
sister, Bessie; and Pat Harrington as Peter Bodkin, Jr. Edward A. Byron
was the producer, Grey Lockwood the director. The show was seen Sundays over most NBC outlets; in New York, however, it was shown Mondays.

WONDERFUL TOWN, U.S.A.

See FAYE EMERSON'S WONDERFUL TOWN

WONDERS OF THE WORLD   SYNDICATED

1958   Travelogue, hosted and narrated by the Linker family.

THE WOODY WOODBURY SHOW   SYNDICATED

1967   Ninety-minute talk show, hosted by Woody Woodbury.

THE WOODY WOODPECKER SHOW   ABC/NBC

3 OCTOBER 1957–25 SEPTEMBER 1958 (ABC); 12 SEPTEMBER 1970–2
SEPTEMBER 1972 (NBC); 11 SEPTEMBER 1976–3 SEPTEMBER 1977

(NBC)   Woody Woodpecker, the cartoon character created in the 1930s by Walter Lantz, first came to network TV in 1957 in a half-hour series that was carried by ABC on weekday afternoons. The cartoon segments included not only Woody Woodpecker, but also Gabby Gator, Andy Panda, and others. Lantz himself hosted the series and showed viewers the basics of animation. NBC later carried the cartoons on Saturday mornings. Woody Woodpecker's voice, and his distinctive laugh, were supplied by Lantz's wife, Gracie Lantz.

WORD FOR WORD   NBC
30 SEPTEMBER 1963–23 OCTOBER 1964   Merv Griffin hosted this daytime game show on which contestants tried to make three- and four-letter words from larger ones, and then tried to unscramble words flashed on a screen.

WORDS AND MUSIC   NBC
2 AUGUST 1949–8 SEPTEMBER 1949   Fifteen-minute twice-weekly musical show, with Barbara Marshall and the Jerry Jerome Trio. Duane McKinney produced and directed.

WORDS AND MUSIC   NBC
28 SEPTEMBER 1970–12 FEBRUARY 1971   Daytime game show hosted by Wink Martindale, on which contestants tried to find word "clues" hidden in the lyrics of songs, which were sung by the show's regulars—Katie Gran, Bob Marlo, Pat Henderson, and Don Minter.

WORKING STIFFS   CBS
15 SEPTEMBER 1979–6 OCTOBER 1979   Short-lived Saturday-night sitcom starring Jim Belushi as Ernie O'Rourke and Michael Keaton as his brother, Mike O'Rourke, who worked as janitors at the O'Rourke Building in Chicago. Also featured were Val Bisoglio as Al Steckler, the building manager; Phil Rubinstein as Falzone; Alan Arbus as Mitch; and Lorna Patterson as Nikki. Arthur Silver and Bob Brunner were the executive producers for Paramount TV-Frog Productions-Huk, Inc.

WORLD   PBS
5 FEBRUARY 1978–   Umbrella title for a series of documentaries produced at home and abroad. The premiere telecast, "The Clouded Window," which examined America's TV news industry, was hosted by Daniel Schorr.

A WORLD APART   ABC
30 MARCH 1970–25 JUNE 1971   This half-hour daytime serial premiered on the same day as two other soap operas, *The Best of Everything* and *Somerset.* Written by Kathryn Phillips, the daughter of Irna Phillips, it

told the stories of a brother and sister, the adopted children of a television writer. Principal players included: Augusta Dabney and Elizabeth Lawrence as Betty Kahlman, the writer; Susan Sarandon as Patrice Kahlman, her daughter; Matthew Cowles as Chris Kahlman, her son; William Prince as Russell Barry, whom Betty eventually married; Robert Gentry as Dr. John Carr; Tom Ligon as P. D. Drinkard; Rosetta LeNoire as Matilda; James Noble as Ed Sims; Erin Connor as Becky Sims; Kathleen McGuire as Adrian Sims; William Tynan as Bill Sims; Stephen Elliott as Jack Condon; Susan Sullivan as Nancy Condon; Nicholas Surovy as Fred Turner; Carol Willard as Louise Turner; John Devlin as Dr. Nathaniel Fuller; Anna Minot as Meg Johns; Kevin Conway as Bud Whitman; Clifton Davis as Matt Hampton; Jane White as Olivia Hampton; Heather MacRae as Linda Peters; and Albert Paulsen as Dr. Neil Stevens.

THE WORLD AT WAR   SYNDICATED
1974   An hour documentary series on World War II, *The World at War* was produced in Great Britain and narrated by Sir Laurence Olivier.

THE WORLD OF GIANTS   SYNDICATED
1960   Half-hour adventure series starring Marshall Thompson as Mel Hunter, a six-inch-tall secret agent, and Arthur Franz as Bill Winters, his normal-sized partner. Hunter usually traveled by briefcase. The show was produced by William Alland for CBS Syndication.

THE WORLD OF IDEAS   CBS
18 JANUARY 1959–3 MAY 1959   Sunday-afternoon discussion series, moderated by Dr. Charles Frankel, chairman of the philosophy department at Columbia University.

THE WORLD OF LOWELL THOMAS   SYNDICATED
1966   Travelogue, hosted by veteran broadcaster Lowell Thomas.

THE WORLD OF MR. SWEENEY   NBC
30 JUNE 1954–31 DECEMBER 1955   This fifteen-minute comedy series began as a feature on *The Kate Smith Hour* before getting its own slot in the summer of 1954. Set in the small town of Mapleton, it starred Charles Ruggles as Cicero P. Sweeney, proprietor of the general store and teller of tales. Also featured were Helen Wagner as Marge, his daughter; Glenn Walker as Kippie, his young grandson; Harrison Dowd as Harvey; and Nell Harris as Hannah.

THE WORLD OF SPORTS ILLUSTRATED   SYNDICATED/CBS
1971–1972 (SYNDICATED); 28 JANUARY 1973–9 SEPTEMBER 1973 (CBS)   This half-hour sports magazine began as a syndicated effort;

when it was picked up by CBS in 1973, its title was changed to *CBS Sports Illustrated;* Jack Whitaker was the host.

THE WORLD OF SURVIVAL   SYNDICATED
1971–1977   Half-hour documentary series on animal life, narrated by John Forsythe. Aubrey Buxton was the executive producer for Anglia, Ltd., in association with the World Wildlife Fund.

WORLD OF TALENT
See DICK CLARK'S WORLD OF TALENT

WORLD WAR ONE   CBS
22 SEPTEMBER 1964–5 SEPTEMBER 1965   A prime-time half-hour documentary series on World War I, narrated by Robert Ryan.

WORLD WAR II: G.I. DIARY   SYNDICATED
1978   Narrated by Lloyd Bridges, this series of twenty-five half-hour documentaries looked at World War II from the point of view of the American soldier. Arthur Holch was the executive producer for Time–Life TV.

WORLD WIDE 60   NBC
23 JANUARY 1960–10 SEPTEMBER 1960   A prime-time hour-long documentary series on current events, *World Wide 60* was hosted by NBC newsmen Chet Huntley and Frank McGee.

THE WORLD'S GREATEST SUPERFRIENDS
See SUPER FRIENDS

WRANGLER   NBC
7 JULY 1960–15 SEPTEMBER 1960   A summer replacement for *The Tennessee Ernie Ford Show, Wrangler* was a half-hour western starring Jason Evers as Pitcairn, an occasionally philosophical cowboy who roamed the West.

THE WREN'S NEST   ABC
13 JANUARY 1949–30 APRIL 1949   A thrice-weekly, fifteen-minute comedy serial about a New York City family, *The Wren's Nest* starred Virginia Sale and Sam Wren (who were married in real life) and their twelve-year-old twins. Tom DeHuff directed.

WYATT EARP   ABC
6 SEPTEMBER 1955–26 SEPTEMBER 1961   Officially titled *The Life and Legend of Wyatt Earp,* this half-hour series, together with *Gunsmoke* and

Cheyenne, marked the beginning of the so-called "adult western." The concept gained popularity over the next few seasons, and by the fall of 1959 there were no fewer than twenty-seven westerns scheduled in prime time. This one was based loosely on fact and starred Hugh O'Brian as Wyatt Earp; for the show's first four seasons Earp was the marshal of Dodge City, Kansas (*Gunsmoke*'s Matt Dillon was also the marshal of Dodge City, but the two lawmen never met, as their shows were on different networks). Also featured were Douglas Fowley and Myron Healey as Doc Holliday and Morgan Woodward as Shotgun Gibbs, Earp's deputy. In the fall of 1959 the show shifted its locale to Tombstone, Arizona (the real Earp had done the same thing), and Earp became the marshal there. Joining the cast were Randy Stuart as hotelkeeper Carol Thurston; Damian O'Flynn as Goodfellow; Steve Brodie as John Behan, Earp's chief enemy; and Trevor Bardette as Clanton, one of Behan's lackeys. Robert F. Sisk produced the series.

THE XAVIER CUGAT SHOW   NBC
27 FEBRUARY 1957–24 MAY 1957   A twice-weekly, fifteen-minute musical series, *The Xavier Cugat Show* replaced Eddie Fisher's *Coke Time* on Wednesdays and Fridays. Bandleader Xavier Cugat and his orchestra supplied the music, and vocals were performed by Abbe Lane, Cugat's then wife.

YANCY DERRINGER   CBS
2 OCTOBER 1958–24 SEPTEMBER 1959   Half-hour western set in New Orleans after the Civil War. With Jock Mahoney as Yancy Derringer, a suave and stylishly dressed bon vivant who carried the pistol for which he was known in his hat; X Brands as Pahoo, Yancy's silent and unsmiling Indian companion, who always kept a knife in his headdress (Pahoo's full name, Pahoo Ka-Ta-Wah, was Pawnee for "Wolf who stand in water"); Kevin Hagen as John Colton, the beleaguered city administrator of New Orleans; Frances Bergen as Madame Francine, one of Yancy's female friends. The series was created by Mary Loos and Richard Sale, who owned the show together with executive producers Warren Lewis and Don Sharpe.

A YEAR AT THE TOP   CBS
5 AUGUST 1977–4 SEPTEMBER 1977   Comedy-fantasy about a pair of songwriters who sold their souls to the devil for a year at the top of their profession. With Greg Evigan as Greg; Paul Shaffer as his partner, Paul Durban; Gabe Dell as their agent, Frederick Hanover, the son of the devil; Nedra Volz as Belle, Paul's grandmother; Priscilla Morrill as Miss Worley, Hanover's secretary; and Julie Cobb as Trish. The pilot for the series, "Hereafter," was shown on NBC 27 November 1975. The series

was created by Woody Kling, and developed by Don Kirshner in association with Norman Lear. Darryl Hickman was the producer.

YOGI BEAR SYNDICATED
1958–1961

YOGI'S GANG ABC
8 SEPTEMBER 1973–30 AUGUST 1975

YOGI'S SPACE RACE NBC
9 SEPTEMBER 1978–3 MARCH 1979 *Yogi Bear,* one of the most famous cartoon creations from Hanna-Barbera Productions, first appeared in 1958 as the star of his own half-hour series. At that time he was a resident of Jellystone National Park, where he spent his days devising ways of pilfering picnic baskets, together with his diminutive companion, Boo Boo. Daws Butler provided the voice of Yogi, while Boo Boo's was supplied by Don Messick. By the 1970s, however, Yogi and his pals had long since left Jellystone Park. In *Yogi's Gang,* an hour show, they battled environmental enemies like Mr. Pollution. The "Gang" included many other Hanna-Barbera characters, such as Huckleberry Hound, Wally Gator, and Magilla Gorilla, among others. In the fall of 1978 Yogi and his friends left the planet to star in a ninety-minute show, *Yogi's Space Race.* This series consisted of several segments: "Space Race," in which characters such as Yogi, Huckleberry Hound, Jabberjaw, the Phantom Phink, and Rita and Wendy piloted their respective vehicles through the solar system; "The Buford Files," starring a slow-witted bloodhound who lived in a swamp; "Galaxy Goof-Ups," starring Yogi, Huck, and others; and "The Galloping Ghost," the adventures of a fast-moving spirit. In November of 1978 *Yogi's Space Race* was trimmed to sixty minutes, and *The Galaxy Goof-Ups* became a separate half-hour series. Early in 1979 the show was trimmed to thirty minutes, as *Buford* became a separate series.

YOU ARE AN ARTIST NBC
1 NOVEMBER 1946–17 JANUARY 1950 One of television's earliest instructional shows, *You Are an Artist* was hosted by Jon Gnagy, who showed viewers how to draw.

YOU ARE THERE CBS
1 FEBRUARY 1953–13 OCTOBER 1957; 11 SEPTEMBER 1971–2 SEPTEMBER 1972 An unusual public affairs series, *You Are There* began in 1947 as a radio show (it was originally titled *CBS Was There*). Each week a well-known historical event was recreated, and the leading figures in each drama were interviewed by CBS news correspondents (the correspondents always appeared in modern-day dress, regardless of the setting of the story). The television version ran from 1953 to 1957 on Sunday afternoons, and was revived in 1971 as a Saturday-afternoon show, aimed

principally at children. Walter Cronkite was the chief correspondent on both TV versions. Paul Newman guest-starred on one program, as Nathan Hale (30 August 1953); and the 1971 premiere, "The Mystery of Amelia Earhart," featured Geraldine Brooks and Richard Dreyfuss.

YOU ASKED FOR IT   DUMONT/ABC/SYNDICATED
29 DECEMBER 1950–7 DECEMBER 1951 (DUMONT); 10 DECEMBER 1951–27 SEPTEMBER 1959 (ABC); 1972 (SYNDICATED)   A half-hour human-interest series, *You Asked for It* answered viewers' requests for unusual acrobatic or magic acts, trained animals, good Samaritans, or whatever. On the network versions of the show, the viewer's letter was read before the act or feature was introduced, while a picture of the viewer was superimposed on a jar of the sponsor's product, Skippy Peanut Butter. Kindly Art Baker hosted the show from 1950 until early 1958, when Jack Smith took over; Smith also hosted the 1972 syndicated version.

YOU BET YOUR LIFE   NBC
5 OCTOBER 1950–21 SEPTEMBER 1961   Television's funniest game show was emceed by "The One, the Only"—Groucho Marx. The game was simple enough—a pair of players tried to answer a few questions in a category of their choice (the exact procedure varied somewhat from year to year)—but it took a back seat to the freewheeling interviews conducted by Groucho. The show's production staff was constantly on the lookout for unusual guests and managed to find quite a few. Some stood on their heads, some danced, and some had funny stories to tell, but all provided targets for Groucho's verbal salvos. Most guests were nonprofessionals, but a few—like Richard Rodgers and Oscar Hammerstein—were well known; others, such as Phyllis Diller, Candice Bergen (who appeared with her father, Edgar Bergen), and William Peter Blatty (who wrote *The Exorcist*), later became celebrities. Contestants could win money not only by answering questions, but also if they managed "to say the secret word"—at the outset of each show, an everyday word was selected, then attached to a toy duck that was raised above the stage. If one of the contestants uttered the preselected word, the duck dropped down, and the couple split an extra $50; occasionally, model Marilyn Burtis came down instead of the duck, and on one show Groucho's brother, Harpo Marx, descended. Groucho's longtime sidekick was George Fenneman, who did the announcing, carried in the questions, and kept score; the two began working together when *You Bet Your Life* began on radio in 1947. The television version was produced by John Guedel and was one of the few game shows to be filmed (because the interviews with the contestants ran overtime and had to be edited).

YOU DON'T SAY NBC/ABC/SYNDICATED

1 APRIL 1963–26 SEPTEMBER 1969 (NBC); 7 JULY 1975–26 NOVEMBER
1975 (ABC); 1978 (SYNDICATED)   This durable game show involved
both contestants and celebrities, who tried to get each other to say the
name of a famous person or place by suggesting sentences with blanks in
them. Tom Kennedy hosted the show. The NBC version enjoyed a six-
year daytime run and also popped up on the prime-time schedule early in
1964. The ABC version was seen only as a daytime program. The half-
hour show was a Ralph Andrews Production.

YOU'LL NEVER GET RICH CBS

20 SEPTEMBER 1955–11 SEPTEMBER 1959   One of the favorite sitcoms
of the 1950s, *You'll Never Get Rich* was created by Nat Hiken and starred
Phil Silvers as Master Sergeant Ernie Bilko, a conniving con man with a
heart of gold, whose unceasing efforts to raise money almost never paid
off. By the end of its four-year network run the half-hour series was titled
The Phil Silvers Show and, in syndication, the reruns were titled *Sergeant
Bilko*. The show was set at Camp Fremont, which was apparently part of
sprawling Fort Baxter, located near Roseville, Kansas. Over the years a
large number of regulars appeared, but the long-term supporting cast included: Harvey Lembeck and Allan Melvin as Bilko's two main henchmen, Corporal Rocco Barbella and Corporal Henshaw; Paul Ford as
Bilko's short-tempered commanding officer, Colonel John Hall; Elisabeth
Fraser as Bilko's occasional girlfriend, Sergeant Joan Hogan; Maurice
Gosfield as Private Duane Doberman, the fattest and most hapless member of Bilko's motley platoon; Herbie Faye as Private Sam Fender; Billy
Sands as Private Dino Paparelli; Mickey Freeman as Private Zimmer-
man; Hope Sansberry as the colonel's wife, Nell Hall, an easy mark for
Bilko's flattery; Joe E. Ross as Sergeant Rupert Ridzik; Jimmy Little as
Sergeant Francis Grover (also known, inexplicably, as Steve Grover); Be-
atrice Pons as Ridzik's nagging wife, Emma Ridzik; and Nicholas
Saunders as Colonel Hall's adjutant, Captain Barker. Others who came
and went included Tige Andrews as Private Gander; P. Jay Sidney as Private Palmer; Walter Cartier as Private Dillingham; Jack Healy as Private
Mullen; Bernie Fein as Private Gomez; Maurice Brenner as Private
Fleishman; Ned Glass as Sergeant Andy Pendleton; and Gary Clarke as
Sergeant Stanley Zewicki. *You'll Never Get Rich* was one of the few
shows of the 1950s to feature black performers—Bilko's platoon almost
always included at least one black. Among those who made guest appearances on the show were Fred Gwynne ("The Eating Contest," 15 November 1955), Dody Goodman ("The Rich Kid," 27 December 1955),
Margaret Hamilton ("The Merry Widow," 17 September 1957), Dick
Van Dyke ("Bilko's Cousin," 28 January 1958), Alan Alda (in his first
major TV role, "Bilko, the Art Lover," 7 March 1958), and Dick Cavett,

in an uncredited appearance as an extra sometime in 1959. Two of the show's regulars, Joe E. Ross and Beatrice Pons, later appeared on Nat Hiken's next show, *Car 54, Where Are You?*

YOUNG AND GAY CBS

1 JANUARY 1950–26 MARCH 1950   Also knows as *The Girls,* this half-hour sitcom was based loosely on two real characters, Cornelia Otis Skinner and Emily Kimbrough. It starred Bethel Leslie as Beth Skinner; Mary Malone as Mary Kimbrough; and Kenneth Forbes as Tod Hunter. Others in the cast included Harry Bannister, John Campbell, Audrey Christie, Alexander Ivo, and Agnes Young. Carol Irwin was the producer, David Rich the director.

THE YOUNG AND THE RESTLESS CBS

26 MARCH 1973–   A stylish half-hour daytime serial, *The Young and the Restless* replaced *Where the Heart Is* in 1973; specifically aimed at a younger audience than most other soaps, the series is generally considered to be television's most artistic serial. It was created by William Bell (who has remained its head writer) and Lee Phillip Bell. John Conboy is the executive producer. Set in the medium-sized town of Genoa City, its story revolves around the several members of the Brooks family—Stuart, Jennifer, and their four daughters. The cast has included: Robert Colbert as Stuart Brooks, owner of the Genoa City Chronicle; Dorothy Green as his wife, Jennifer Brooks; Trish Stewart as daughter Chris; Janice Lynde (1973–1977) and Victoria Mallory (1977–   ) as daughter Leslie; Jaime Lyn Bauer as daughter Lauralee (Lauri); Pamela (Peters) Solow as daughter Peggy; Julianna McCarthy as Liz Foster; James Houghton (1973–1976), Brian Kerwin (1976–1977), and Wings Hauser (1977–   ) as Liz's son, Greg Foster, a lawyer; William Gray Espy (1973–1975) and David Hasselhoff (1975–   ) as Liz's son, Bill "Snapper" Foster, who married Chris Brooks while he was in medical school (Chris had been raped shortly before her marriage, and was fearful that she would be unable to respond sexually to her husband; Snapper's patience and gentleness helped resolve the problem); Brenda Dickson as Liz's daughter, Jill Foster, a hairdresser who was hired as personal assistant to a wealthy matron; Lee Crawford as Sally McGuire, who had a brief affair with Snapper before his marriage; Tom Hallick as Brad Eliot, a former surgeon who married Leslie Brooks; Robert Clary as Pierre Rouland, a nightclub owner who married Sally and was later murdered; Lilyan Chauvin as Pierre's sister, Marianna Rouland; Jeanne Cooper as Kay Chancellor, the woman who hired Jill Foster; Donnelly Rhodes as Kay's husband, Philip Chancellor, who fell for Jill and married her just before his death; Paul Stevens as Dr. Bruce Henderson, an old boyfriend of Jennifer's who fell for her again; Steve Carlson as Bruce's son, Mark Henderson, who fell for Peggy Brooks (Peggy's mother, Jennifer, eventu-

ally confessed to her that her real father was not Stuart Brooks, but rather Bruce Henderson, Mark's father); Beau Kayzer as Brock Reynolds, son of Kay Chancellor; Anthony Herrera (1976–1977) as Jack Curtis (or Curtzynski), a college teacher who fell for Peggy; Kay Heberle (1976–1977) as Jack's wife, Joann Curtis; John McCook as Lance Prentiss, who fell for Lauri; Deidre Hall as Barbara Anderson; Jennifer Leak as Gwen Sherman; Charles Gray as Bill Foster, Sr.; Barry Cahill as Sam Powers; Tom Sellick as Jed Andrews; Jordeann Russo as Regina Henderson; Cathy Carricaburu as Nancy Becker; Dick DeCoit as Ron Becker; K. T. Stevens as Vanessa Prentiss; Joe LaDue as Derek Thurston; Tom Ligon as Lucas Prentiss; Brandi Tucker as Karen Becker; Cynthia Harris as Heather Lowe; Karl Bruck as Maestro Fausch; Gary Giem as Larry Larkin; Susan Walden as Linda Larkin; Erica Hope as Nikki Reed; Carol Jones as Patty Minter; and Roberta Leighton as Dr. Casey Reed.

YOUNG DAN'L BOONE
CBS

12 SEPTEMBER 1977–4 OCTOBER 1977   The first casualty of the 1977–1978 season, *Young Dan'l Boone* vanished after four episodes. Not to be confused with *Daniel Boone,* a popular show which lasted six seasons, this one starred Rick Moses as Dan'l Boone, who seemed to be in his mid-twenties; Devon Ericson as his intended, Rebecca Bryan; Ji-Tu Cumbuka as his friend, Hawk, a former slave; John Joseph Thomas as Peter, a twelve-year-old companion of Boone's. Ernie Frankel was the executive producer, and Jimmy Sangster the producer, of the hour show.

YOUNG DR. KILDARE
SYNDICATED

1972   A remake of *Dr. Kildare,* the popular medical show of the early 1960s, *Young Dr. Kildare* starred Mark Jenkins as the intern, Dr. James Kildare, and Gary Merrill as his guiding light, Dr. Leonard Gillespie. The half-hour series was videotaped; Joseph Gantman was the executive producer.

YOUNG DR. MALONE
NBC

29 DECEMBER 1958–29 MARCH 1963   A daytime serial, *Young Dr. Malone* enjoyed a lengthy radio run (from 1939 to 1960) as well as a moderately successful television run. The TV version replaced another serial, *Today Is Ours,* and six characters from that show were worked into the story lines of the new soap opera. Set at Valley Hospital in the town of Three Oaks, *Young Dr. Malone* involved two generations of the Malone family. The cast included: William Prince as Dr. Jerry Malone, chief of staff at the hospital; Augusta Dabney and Diana Hyland as Jerry's wife, Tracey Malone (William Prince and Augusta Dabney later married in real life); John Connell as their adopted son, Dr. David Malone, a young physician; Freda Holloway and Sarah Hardy as Tracey and Jerry's daughter, Jill Malone; Emily McLaughlin as David's romantic interest,

Dr. Eileen Seaton; Peter Brandon as Dr. Tad Powell; and Lesley Woods as Clare.

THE YOUNG LAWYERS   ABC
21 SEPTEMBER 1970–5 MAY 1971   An hour-long dramatic series set at the Neighborhood Law Office in Boston, where law students handled cases under the supervision of a senior attorney. With Lee J. Cobb as David Barrett, a private practitioner who oversaw the operation; Zalman King as law student Aaron Silverman; Judy Pace as law student Pat Walters; and Phillip Clark (January 1971–May 1971) as law student Chris Blake. Matthew Rapf produced the show for Paramount TV.

THE YOUNG MARRIEDS   ABC
5 OCTOBER 1964–25 MARCH 1966   A late-afternoon serial aimed at a younger audience than most soaps, *The Young Marrieds* told the stories of several young couples who lived in a suburban town. The cast included: Paul Picerni as Dr. Dan Garrett; Peggy McCay as Susan Garrett; Mike Mikler as Walter Reynolds; Susan Brown as Ann Reynolds; Floy Dean as Liz Forsythe; Constance Moore as Liz's mother, Irene Forsythe; Norma Connolly as Lena Karr Gilroy; Barry Russo as Roy Gilroy; Betty Connor and Brenda Benet as model Jill McComb; Scott Graham and Charles Grodin as Matt Crane; Les Brown, Jr., as Buzz Korman; Frank Maxwell as Mr. Korman; Maxine Stuart as Mrs. Korman; Pat Rossen as Jerry; Irene Tedrow as Aunt Alex; Frank Marvel as Mr. Coleman; Ken Metcalfe as Jimmy; Michael Stefani as Paul; Maria Palmer as Mady; Don Randolph as Theo; Robert Hogan as Gillespie; Ben Astar as Mr. Killeran; and Susan Seaforth as Carol West.

YOUNG MAVERICK   CBS
28 NOVEMBER 1979–16 JANUARY 1980   A sequel to *Maverick,* one of TV's more popular westerns, *Young Maverick* starred Charles Frank as Harvard-educated Ben Maverick, a younger cousin of Bart and Bret, who shared the family's version to violence. Also featured were Susan Blanchard as Ben's friend, Nell McGarrahan, and John Dehner as grim Marshal Edge Troy, the Idaho Territory lawman who tried to keep a watchful eye on young Maverick. Executive producer: Robert Van Scoyk for Warner Brothers TV.

YOUNG MR. BOBBIN   NBC
26 AUGUST 1951–18 MAY 1952   Half-hour sitcom starring Jackie Kelk as Alexander Bobbin, a young man working at his first job, and Jane Seymour and Nydia Westman as his two spinster aunts.

THE YOUNG REBELS   ABC
20 SEPTEMBER 1970–3 JANUARY 1971   A historical adventure series,

The Young Rebels was set in Chester, Pennsylvania, in 1777, and chronicled the exploits of the members of the Yankee Doodle Society, a group of young guerilla fighters. With Rick Ely as Jeremy Larkin, son of the mayor; Lou Gossett as Isak Poole, a blacksmith and freeman; Alex Henteloff as the scientifically inclined Henry Abington, a young Ben Franklin; Hilarie Thompson as Elizabeth Coates; and Philippe Fourquet as the young General Lafayette, one of the few outsiders who knew this group's identities. The hour series was a Screen Gems production.

THE YOUNG SENTINELS   NBC
10 SEPTEMBER 1977–2 SEPTEMBER 1978   This Saturday-morning cartoon show was set in outer space and changed its name to *Space Sentinels* in midseason.

THE YOUNG SET   ABC
6 SEPTEMBER 1965–17 DECEMBER 1965   An hour daytime talk show, hosted by Phyllis Kirk and a weekly celebrity cohost.

YOUR ALL-AMERICAN COLLEGE SHOW   SYNDICATED
1968–1970   Half-hour talent show featuring college-age acts, hosted first by Dennis James and later by Rich Little and Arthur Godfrey.

YOUR BIG MOMENT   DUMONT
19 MAY 1953–2 JUNE 1953   Melvyn Douglas hosted this prime-time program, on which viewers who had written to the show requesting blind dates had the chance to meet the person of their dreams. Ken Roberts and the Ray Bloch Orchestra were also featured on the half-hour series, which was retitled *Blind Date* when Jan Murray succeeded Douglas on 9 June (see also that title).

YOUR FIRST IMPRESSION   NBC
2 JANUARY 1962–26 JUNE 1964   On this daytime game show a panel of three celebrities tried to guess the identity of mystery guests from clues supplied by the host. Dennis James was the first emcee and was succeeded by Bill Leyden. Monty Hall was the executive producer.

YOUR FUNNY, FUNNY FILMS   ABC
8 JULY 1963–9 SEPTEMBER 1963   Amateur filmmakers had a rare chance to show their stuff on network television on this half-hour show, hosted by George Fenneman. The accent was on comedy rather than artistry.

YOUR HIT PARADE   NBC/CBS
7 OCTOBER 1950–7 JUNE 1958 (NBC); 10 OCTOBER 1958–24 APRIL 1959 (CBS); 2 AUGUST 1974–30 AUGUST 1974 (CBS)   *Your Hit Parade* began

on radio in 1935 and came to television fifteen years later (four trial tele-casts were aired during the summer of 1950, though regular broadcasts did not begin until the fall). For its first eight years on TV, the show was a Saturday-night fixture on NBC; on each show the top musical hits of the week were performed by the show's regulars. Because some songs re-mained popular week after week, imaginative production sequences were designed to help sustain viewer interest; some of the medium's best-known choreographers—such as Tony Charmoli, Ernie Flatt, and Peter Gennaro—started out on *Your Hit Parade,* and one of its featured danc-ers was Bob Fosse, who later directed *Cabaret.* The show's early regulars included Dorothy Collins, Eileen Wilson, Snooky Lanson, and Sue Ben-nett; Russell Arms, June Valli, and bandleader Ray Scott were all aboard by 1952, though June Valli was succeeded by Gisele MacKenzie in 1953. In the fall of 1957 (the series' last season on NBC) the show was over-hauled completely, and four new regulars were brought in: Tommy Leon-etti, Jill Corey, Alan Copeland, and Virginia Gibson. A year later *Your Hit Parade* switched to CBS and was again overhauled, but the show failed to generate much interest; Dorothy Collins returned to costar with Johnny Desmond for one season. The show was moved to a Tuesday spot, and later to Fridays, before leaving the air in April 1959. *Your Hit Parade* was revived in the summer of 1974, but again failed to catch hold; the regulars at that time included Chuck Woolery, Kelly Garrett, and Sheralee.

YOUR LUCKY CLUE CBS
13 JULY 1952–31 AUGUST 1952 A summer replacement for *This Is Show Business,* this half-hour game show was hosted by Basil Rathbone. Four contestants competed as two twosomes, and tried to solve criminal cases enacted before them by a group of regular performers.

YOUR PET PARADE ABC
18 MARCH 1951–2 SEPTEMBER 1951 A Sunday-afternoon show on pets and pet care, *Your Pet Parade* was hosted by Jack Gregson; Billy Barty was featured as Billy Bitesize, the commercial spokesman for the sponsor, Ralston Purina. Music was supplied by Ivan Ditmars, and the half-hour show was produced by John Nelson.

YOUR PLAY TIME CBS/NBC
14 JUNE 1953–6 SEPTEMBER 1953 (CBS); 13 JUNE 1954–5 SEPTEMBER 1954 (CBS); 18 JUNE 1955–3 SEPTEMBER 1955 (NBC) A half-hour dra-matic anthology series of little note, *Your Play Time* popped up three times as a summer replacement series.

YOUR PRIZE STORY NBC
2 APRIL 1952–28 MAY 1952 The stories on this half-hour dramatic an-

thology series were submitted by viewers. Any aspiring author whose script was accepted for adaptation by story editor Margaret Sangster won $1,000.

YOUR SHOW OF SHOWS NBC

25 FEBRUARY 1950–5 JUNE 1954   A ninety-minute variety series, *Your Show of Shows* was a Saturday-night fixture for four years. It was a showcase not for guest stars, but for the comedic talents of its star, Sid Caesar, and his costar, Imogene Coca, who were backed up by two talented supporting players, Carl Reiner and Howard Morris. Most shows followed the same pattern: Sid Caesar introduced the evening's guest host (who usually played a comparatively minor role on the show), then appeared in a sketch with Imogene Coca. After a couple of production numbers and another sketch or two came the main segment—a satire of a popular film. After that, Caesar did a monologue or pantomime, and the entire company then participated in the final production number.

Your Show of Shows was produced by Max Liebman, who had worked with Caesar and Coca previously in theatrical revues he had staged in the Catskills and in Florida. Liebman first brought the revue idea to television in 1949 on *The Admiral Broadway Revue* (see also that title), an hour show that lasted seventeen weeks. In 1950, at the request of NBC programming chief Sylvester "Pat" Weaver, Liebman agreed to do a ninety-minute revue on Saturday nights; he brought with him most of the people who had been featured on *The Admiral Broadway Revue:* Caesar, Coca, Howard Morris, writers Mel Tolkin and Lucille Kallen, choreographer James Starbuck, set designer Frederick Fox, and conductor Charles Sanford. Other regulars on the first season of *Your Show of Shows* included Tom Avera, dancers Mata and Hari, Nelle Fisher and Jerry Ross, the Hamilton Trio, operatic singers Marguerite Piazza and Robert Merrill, pop singers Bill Hayes and Jack Russell, and the Billy Williams Quartet. Tom Avera left after the first season and was replaced by Carl Reiner. Jack Russell also left the show after a short time, and Judy Johnson became Bill Hayes's singing partner. Dancers Fisher and Ross left after the 1951–1952 season and were succeeded by Bambi Linn and Rod Alexander.

In addition to writers Mel Tolkin and Lucille Kallen, several other talented comedy writers worked for the show, including Mel Brooks, Larry Gelbart (*M*A*S*H*), Bill Persky, and Sam Denoff (who later worked with Carl Reiner on *The Dick Van Dyke Show*), Neil Simon, and Woody Allen.

A melancholy man offstage, Sid Caesar brought his own unique style to the show; notorious for his deviations from the scripts, Caesar was a skilled mime, a gifted dialectician, an inimitable monologist, and a superb comic actor, especially when he was paired with Imogene Coca. Coca, who was born into a showbiz family, was a talented singer and dancer as well as a natural comedienne, who brought several years of professional experience to the show. The most famous characters that they portrayed on the show were Charlie and Doris Hickenlooper, a hopelessly mismatched married couple. In the solo spots, Caesar played hundreds of characters, but the best known include jazz musicians Progress Hornsby and Cool Cees (in real life, Caesar played the saxophone and had been in several bands), storyteller Somerset Winterset, and Italian film authority Giuseppe Marinara. Among the dozens of motion pictures that were lampooned were *From Here to Eternity* (which came out as "From Here to Obscurity") and *Shane* ("Strange").

Your Show of Shows was seen every Saturday night (with a hiatus each summer) from 1950 until the spring of 1953. In its last season it was seen three of every four weeks and left the air in June of 1954, after some 160 telecasts—all of them live. In the fall of 1954 Caesar and Coca went their separate ways; Caesar to *Caesar's Hour,* a comedy-variety show which lasted three seasons, and Coca to *The Imogene Coca Show,* a half-hour effort that lasted one season. The two were reunited in 1958 on *Sid Caesar Invites You,* but the magic had gone. In 1973 Max Liebman packaged a number of outstanding segments from *Your Show of Shows* into a theatrical release, *Ten From Your Show of Shows.*

YOUR SHOW TIME NBC
21 JANUARY 1949–15 JULY 1949   This filmed dramatic anthology series was hosted by Arthur Shields. The half-hour show was a Marshall Grant–Realm Production.

YOUR SURPRISE PACKAGE CBS
13 MARCH 1961–23 FEBRUARY 1962   A daytime game show hosted by George Fenneman (formerly the assistant on *You Bet Your Life*) on which contestants competed in a quiz segment for the chance to identify and win a "surprise package" of merchandise.

YOUR SURPRISE STORE CBS
12 MAY 1952–27 JUNE 1952   Lew Parker and Jacqueline Susann cohosted this daytime merchandise giveaway show.

YOUR WITNESS ABC
17 OCTOBER 1949–26 SEPTEMBER 1950   Another of TV's early courtroom drama shows, *Your Witness* should not be confused with its contemporaries, such as *Famous Jury Trials* and *They Stand Accused,* or with its successors, such as *Day in Court, Divorce Court, Traffic Court,* or *The Verdict Is Yours.*

YOU'RE IN THE PICTURE CBS
20 JANUARY 1961–27 JANUARY 1961   One of TV's biggest flops, *You're

in the Picture was a prime-time game show hosted by Jackie Gleason. Celebrities would drop by and stick their heads through holes in life-sized tableaux. From clues supplied by Gleason, the celebs (who could not see the scene of which they were part) tried to guess what picture they were in. Gleason abandoned the game show format after one week; on the second show he appeared alone, apologizing to viewers for "that bomb" and turned the show into a half-hour talk show for the remaining weeks (its title was then changed to *The Jackie Gleason Show*).

YOU'RE ON YOUR OWN   CBS
22 DECEMBER 1956–16 MARCH 1957   A prime-time game show hosted by Steve Dunne, *You're On Your Own* began as a quiz show on which contestants were given time to answer the questions (they were free to use any reference source to obtain the answers). By the end of its short run, however, it had devolved into a stunt show, on which contestants who gave incorrect answers to general knowledge questions had to pay the consequences.

YOU'RE PUTTING ME ON   NBC
30 MAY 1969–26 DECEMBER 1969   This daytime game show involved six celebrities, divided into three teams. One member of each team assumed the identity of a famous person (real or fictional), and the other member tried to guess who was being depicted. Bill Leyden hosted the show until late September, when Larry Blyden succeeded him.

YOURS FOR A SONG   ABC
Nighttime: 14 NOVEMBER 1961–18 SEPTEMBER 1962; *Daytime:* 4 DECEMBER 1961–29 MARCH 1963   Bert Parks hosted this half-hour game show, on which contestants won money by supplying the missing words in lyrics sung to them. Bob Russell created the show.

YOUTH ON THE MARCH   ABC/DUMONT
9 OCTOBER 1949–25 MAY 1952 (ABC); 5 OCTOBER 1952–7 JUNE 1953 (DUMONT)   Sunday-evening religious show with the Reverend Percy Crawford and his Glee Club.

YOUTH TAKES A STAND   CBS
18 AUGUST 1953–28 MARCH 1954   One of several Sunday-afternoon public affairs programs on which a group of young people questioned a newsmaker, *Youth Takes a Stand* was moderated by Marc Cramer.

YOUTH WANTS TO KNOW   NBC
8 SEPTEMBER 1951–1 JUNE 1958   Like *Youth Takes a Stand, Youth Wants to Know* was a Sunday show on which a team of youngsters interviewed newsmakers.

799

ZANE GREY THEATER CBS

5 OCTOBER 1956–20 SEPTEMBER 1962 Like *Death Valley Days* and *Frontier, Zane Grey Theater* was a western anthology series. It was hosted by Dick Powell and was officially titled *Dick Powell's Zane Grey Theater;* Powell occasionally starred in an episode. Some of the stories were based on those written by Zane Grey, but most were original teleplays. Among the guest stars who appeared were Hedy Lamarr (in her only TV dramatic appearance, "Proud Woman," 25 October 1957), Jack Lemmon ("The Three Graves," 4 January 1957), Ginger Rogers (in a rare TV appearance, "Never Too Late," 4 February 1960), Claudette Colbert (in her last TV dramatic appearance to date, "So Young the Savage Land," 10 November 1960), and Esther Williams (in her last TV dramatic appearance to date, "The Black Wagon," 1 December 1960). Hal Hudson was the first producer of the half-hour show, which was supplied by Four Star Films, Zane Grey, and Pamric Productions.

THE ZOO GANG NBC

16 JULY 1975–6 AUGUST 1975 A three-hour miniseries, *The Zoo Gang* was shown in six parts by NBC during the summer of 1975. It told the story of four freedom fighters who worked together during World War II and reunited almost thirty years later to continue their adventures. With Brian Keith as Stephen Halliday (The Fox); John Mills as Captain Tommy Devon (The Elephant); Lilli Palmer as Manouche Roget (The Leopard); and Barry Morse as Alec Marlowe (The Tiger). Filmed in Europe, the series was developed by Reginald Rose and produced by Herbert Hirschman for ATV–ITC Productions. Theme music was composed by Paul and Linda McCartney.

ZOO PARADE NBC

28 MAY 1950–1 SEPTEMBER 1957 This half-hour Sunday-afternoon series on animals and animal behavior was cohosted by Marlin Perkins and Jim Hurlbut. It was broadcast from Chicago's Lincoln Park Zoo until 1955; for the show's last two seasons, Perkins and Hurlbut traveled to zoos throughout the country.

ZOOM PBS

9 JANUARY 1972–1979 A half-hour potpourri of features for children, *Zoom* was hosted by a group of seven children, whose membership changed periodically. Many of the presentations were games, stunts, or filmed segments suggested by the show's legions of young viewers. The show was produced at WGBH-TV, Boston.

ZOORAMA CBS

25 APRIL 1965–26 SEPTEMBER 1965 Not to be confused with *Zoo Parade,* this half-hour animalogue was hosted by Bob Dale at the San Diego Zoo.

ZORRO

10 OCTOBER 1957–24 SEPTEMBER 1959 *Zorro,* the masked Spanish swordsman of California, first appeared in a comic strip drawn by Johnston McCulley in 1919, and was the hero of several motion pictures before this Walt Disney TV series came to the air in 1957. The character was essentially the Batman of the 1820s (*Zorro* is the Spanish word for "fox"); his real identity was Don Diego de la Vega, a young Spanish nobleman who was summoned to California by his father to help fight the region's despotic commandant. On his way to North America Don Diego decided that he would purport to be a timid fop, so that no one would believe him to be the real "Zorro," defender of the people. The half-hour TV series starred Guy Williams as Don Diego/Zorro; George J. Lewis as his father, Don Alejandro de la Vega; Gene Sheldon as Bernardo, Don Diego's mute manservant, the only person who knew of his dual identity; Henry Calvin as portly Sergeant Garcia, Zorro's hapless pursuer; Britt Lomond as Garcia's superior, Captain Monastario; Don Diamond as Corporal Rey, Garcia's lackey; and Jolene Brand (1958–1959) as Anna Maria, Don Diego's sometime girlfriend. Walt Disney was executive producer of the series, William H. Anderson producer. In 1974 the character reappeared in a made-for-TV movie, *The Mark of Zorro,* starring Frank Langella (29 October 1974).

SPECIAL OCCASIONS

1948

2 NOVEMBER	Election coverage (all four networks)
29 NOVEMBER	Live coverage at the New York Metropolitan Opera (ABC)

1949

11 JANUARY	East-to-Midwest coaxial cable opening (all four networks)
20 JANUARY	Inauguration of President Truman (all four networks)
4 MARCH	Golden Gloves boxing championship (CBS)
26 MARCH	"The NBC Symphony" (NBC)—classical music, conducted by Arturo Toscanini
4 APRIL	Signing of the NATO Pact by President Truman (all four networks)
9 APRIL	"Damon Runyon Memorial Fund" (NBC)—Milton Berle anchors the first telethon for charity
14 MAY	The Preakness (CBS)—live coverage of the horse race from Pimlico

1950

29 APRIL	"Damon Runyon Memorial Fund" (NBC)—second annual telethon, hosted by Milton Berle
11 MAY	The Four Freedoms Award (CBS)—presentations by Eleanor Roosevelt
3 SEPTEMBER	"Miss Television U.S.A. Contest" (DUMONT)—beauty pageant, won by Edie Adams
28 OCTOBER	"The Jack Benny Show" (CBS)—Jack Benny's first TV program, with guest Ken Murray
6 NOVEMBER	Opening night at the Metropolitan Opera (ABC)—Verdi's *Don Carlo*, with Robert Merrill
25 DECEMBER	"One Hour in Wonderland" (NBC)—Walt Disney's first TV production, with Edgar Bergen and Charlie McCarthy, and previews of the new Disney film, *Alice in Wonderland*

1951

28 JANUARY	"The Jack Benny Show" (CBS)—comedy with Jack Benny and guests Frank Sinatra and Faye Emerson
4 MARCH	"Richard Rodgers' Jubilee Show" (NBC)—tribute to composer Richard Rodgers, with Mary Martin, Celeste Holm, and Patrice Munsel
14 MAY et seq.	Kefauver Crime Commission Hearings (live coverage by CBS and NBC)
25 JUNE	First regularly scheduled intercity colorcasting (CBS, for its East Coast affiliates)
4 SEPTEMBER	First regular coast-to-coast telecast: President Truman's address at the opening of the Japanese Peace Treaty Conference in San Francisco (live coverage by all four networks)
12 SEPTEMBER	"Irving Berlin: Salute to America" (NBC)—music with Irving Berlin and guests Tony Martin, Dinah Shore, and Margaret Truman
23 DECEMBER	National Football League Championship Game (DUMONT)—first network coverage of an NFL championship game
24 DECEMBER	"Amahl and the Night Visitors" (NBC)—first production of Gian Carlo Menotti's Christmas opera

1952

27 JANUARY	Address by former President Herbert Hoover (CBS)
27 JANUARY	"The Jack Benny Show" (CBS)—comedy with Jack Benny and guest Barbara Stanwyck (in her TV debut)
3 MAY	Kentucky Derby (CBS)—first live coverage of the horse race
11 MAY	"President Truman: Tour of the White House" (CBS)—a filmed tour of the newly refurbished White House conducted by President Truman
22 JUNE	Telethon for the United States Olympic Team (NBC)—hosted by Bob Hope and Bing Crosby
7–11 JULY	Republican National Convention (live coverage by all four networks)
21–24 JULY	Democratic National Convention (live coverage by all four networks)

23 SEPTEMBER	Richard Nixon's "Checkers" speech (CBS and NBC)
19 OCTOBER	"Billy Budd," *NBC Opera Theatre* (NBC)—first of several opera specials, with Theodor Uppman starring in Benjamin Britten's opera
16 NOVEMBER	"Trouble in Tahiti," *NBC Opera Theatre* (NBC)—opera by Leonard Bernstein, with Beverly Wolff and David Atkinson

1953

8 FEBRUARY	"A Visit with Carl Sandburg" (NBC)—Sunday-afternoon interview
1 MARCH	"Answer the Call" (ABC and CBS)— special appeal by the American Red Cross, with President Eisenhower and several celebrity guests
19 MARCH	The Academy Awards (NBC)—first coast-to-coast Oscar telecast, with host Bob Hope
19 APRIL	"And It Came to Pass" (NBC)—a tribute to the fifth anniversary of Israel, with Ezio Pinza, Melvyn Douglas, and Jennie Tourel
17 MAY	"A Conversation with Frank Lloyd Wright" (NBC)—Sunday afternoon interview with the architect
2 JUNE	Coronation of Queen Elizabeth II (CBS and NBC)—filmed coverage
15 JUNE	"The Ford Fiftieth Anniversary Show" (CBS and NBC)—variety tribute, highlighted by the duet of Mary Martin and Ethel Merman, with appearances by Marian Anderson, Oscar Hammerstein II, Eddie Fisher, Frank Sinatra, Lowell Thomas, and Rudy Vallee (produced by Leland Hayward)
23 AUGUST	Arrival of POWs from Korea at San Francisco (NBC)
25 OCTOBER	"Wanda Landowska at Home" (NBC)—Sunday afternoon interview with the harpsichordist
15 NOVEMBER	"Television City" (CBS)—a tour of CBS's new West Coast production facility with Edward R. Murrow

1954

3 JANUARY	"The Bing Crosby Show" (CBS)—Bing Crosby's first variety special, with guest Jack Benny
10 JANUARY	"Resources of Freedom" (CBS)—Edward R. Murrow and a panel of experts discuss a Presidential commission report on technological resources
7 FEBRUARY	"Back to God" (CBS)—interdenominational religious program with President Eisenhower and American religious leaders
14 FEBRUARY	"Guatemala" (NBC)—documentary on Communist influence in Guatemala with Marshall Bannell
28 MARCH	"The General Foods Anniversary Show" (all four networks)—variety, with Richard Rodgers and Oscar Hammerstein II, Mary Martin, Jack Benny, Ezio Pinza, Groucho Marx, John Raitt, Tony Martin, Rosemary Clooney, Ed Sullivan, Yul Brynner, and Gordon MacRae
22 APRIL et seq.	The Army-McCarthy Hearings (live coverage by ABC and DuMont)
25 APRIL	"230,000 Will Die" (NBC)—documentary on cancer, narrated by Dr. Charles Cameron of the American Cancer Society
9 MAY	First of three filmed lectures by Bernard Baruch (NBC)
27 JUNE	"The Road to Spandau" (NBC)—documentary on seven convicted Nazi war criminals, narrated by Joseph C. Harsch
11 SEPTEMBER	Miss America Beauty Pageant (ABC)—first coast-to-coast telecast
12 SEPTEMBER	"Satins and Spurs," *Max Liebman Presents* (NBC)—lavish color musical, with Betty Hutton (in her TV debut), Kevin McCarthy, and Genevieve
13 SEPTEMBER	"Three Two One Zero" (NBC)—documentary on atomic power, produced by Henry Salomon
10 OCTOBER	"Sunday in Town" (NBC)—revue with Judy Holliday, Steve Allen, and Dick Shawn
24 OCTOBER	"Light's Diamond Jubilee" (all four networks)—commemoration of the seventy-fifth anniversary of electric light, with appearances by Helen Hayes, George Gobel, and Kim Novak

5 DECEMBER	"Spotlight" (NBC)—revue on ice, with Sonja Henie, Jimmy Durante, Jack Buchanan, Jeannie Carson, and Pat Carroll
18 DECEMBER	"Babes in Toyland" (NBC)—musical with Wally Cox, Jack E. Leonard, and Dave Garroway

1955

7 MARCH	Seventh annual Emmy Awards (NBC)—first coast-to-coast telecast, hosted by Steve Allen
12 MARCH	"A Connecticut Yankee," *Max Liebman Presents* (NBC)—musical with Eddie Albert, Janet Blair, Boris Karloff, and Gale Sherwood
9 APRIL	"The Merry Widow," *Max Liebman Presents* (NBC)—operetta with Anne Jeffreys, John Conte, Brian Sullivan, and Edward Everett Horton
4 JUNE	"The Chocolate Soldier," *Max Liebman Presents* (NBC)—musical adaptation of Shaw's *Arms and the Man*, with Rise Stevens, Eddie Albert, and Akim Tamiroff
7 JUNE	Address by President Eisenhower to the graduates of West Point (NBC)—first colorcast of Eisenhower
22 JUNE	"Three for Tonight" (CBS)—revue with Marge and Gower Champion and Harry Belafonte
30 JULY	"Svengali and the Blonde" (NBC)—musical with Carol Channing and Basil Rathbone
27 AUGUST	"One Touch of Venus" (NBC)—musical with Janet Blair and Russell Nype (broadcast live from Dallas)
11 SEPTEMBER	"The Skin of Our Teeth," *Color Spread* (NBC)—Thornton Wilder's comedy, with Helen Hayes, Mary Martin, and George Abbott
1 OCTOBER	"Heidi" (NBC)—children's drama, with Natalie Wood, Wally Cox, and Jeannie Carson
5 NOVEMBER	"The Great Waltz" (NBC)—musical with Bert Lahr
26 NOVEMBER	"Dearest Enemy" (NBC)—drama with Cornelia Otis Skinner and Robert Sterling
4 DECEMBER	"The Maurice Chevalier Show" (NBC)—variety with Maurice Chevalier, Marcel Marceau, Jeannie Carson, and Pat Carroll

1956

21 JANUARY	"Paris in the Springtime," *Max Liebman Presents* (NBC)—musical with Dan Dailey, Gale Sherwood, and Helen Gallagher
14 MARCH	"The Twisted Cross," *Project 20* (NBC)—documentary on the rise and fall of Adolf Hitler, narrated by Alexander Scourby
14 APRIL	"Marco Polo" (NBC)—musical (cowritten by Neil Simon) with Alfred Drake, Doretta Morrow, and Beatrice Kraft
27 MAY	"Antarctica—the Third World" (NBC)—documentary on Operation Deepfreeze, narrated by Bill Hartigan
9 JUNE	"Holiday" (NBC)—musical with Kitty Carlisle and Tammy Grimes
15 JULY	"The Bachelor," *Sunday Spectacular* (NBC)—musical (with songs by Steve Allen) with Hal March, Jayne Mansfield, and Carol Haney
27 OCTOBER	"Manhattan Tower," *Saturday Spectacular* (NBC)—musical with Peter Marshall, Helen O'Connell, Phil Harris, Ethel Waters, and Edward Everett Horton
19 NOVEMBER	"Our Mr. Sun," *Bell Science Series* (CBS)—first of a series of science documentaries hosted by Dr. Frank Baxter ("Our Mr. Sun" was produced and directed by Frank Capra)
24 NOVEMBER	"High Button Shoes" (NBC)—musical with Nanette Fabray, Hal March, and Don Ameche
30 NOVEMBER	First videotaped news broadcast (CBS to its West Coast outlets)
6 DECEMBER	"The Jazz Age," *Project 20* (NBC)—documentary on American life during the 1920s, narrated by Fred Allen
11 DECEMBER	"The Victor Borge Show" (CBS)—one-man show by the Danish pianist
22 DECEMBER	"Holiday on Ice," *Saturday Spectacular* (NBC)—revue with Sonja Henie, Hayes Alan Jenkins, Julius LaRosa, Ernie Kovacs, and Jaye P. Morgan

1957

19 JANUARY	"The Jerry Lewis Show" (NBC)—Jerry Lewis's

	first variety special since splitting up with Dean Martin
19 JANUARY	"The Ernie Kovacs Show" (NBC)—Ernie Kovacs in a half-hour comedy special without words
6 MARCH	"Maurice Chevalier's Paris" (NBC)—documentary on modern Paris hosted by Maurice Chevalier
20 MARCH	"Hemo the Magnificent," *Bell Science Series* (NBC)—documentary on blood, with Dr. Frank Baxter (as Dr. Research) and Richard Carlson (produced and directed by Frank Capra)
24 MARCH	"The Black Star Rises" (CBS)—documentary on Vice President Nixon's trip to Africa
31 MARCH	"Cinderella" (CBS)—original musical by Rodgers and Hammerstein, with Julie Andrews, Jon Cypher, Howard Lindsay, and Ilka Chase
13 APRIL	"Salute to Baseball" (NBC)—variety special hosted by Gene Kelly with Paul Winchell, Tony Bennett, Robert Alda, Mickey Mantle, Stan Musial, and Ted Williams
4 and 11 MAY	"Rock 'n' Roll Show" (ABC)—first prime-time network special devoted to rock music, hosted by Alan Freed, with Sal Mineo, Guy Mitchell, June Valli, Martha Carson, the Clovers, Screamin' Jay Hawkins, and the Del-Vikings
11 MAY	"Mr. Broadway" (NBC)—musical with Mickey Rooney (as George M. Cohan), Gloria DeHaven, June Havoc, and Garry Moore
19 MAY	"This Is Defense" (CBS)—one-hour demonstration of American military might from Andrews Air Force Base
19 MAY	"The Rebels of Sierra Maestra—Cuba's Jungle Fighters" (CBS)—news documentary on Cuban guerillas, with an interview of leader Fidel Castro
8 JUNE	"The Jerry Lewis Show" (NBC)—Jerry Lewis's second variety special, with guests Eydie Gormé and Dan Rowan and Dick Martin
4 AUGUST	"As Others See Us" (NBC)—documentary exploring perceptions of America by foreigners
5 SEPTEMBER	"The Dean Martin Show" (NBC)—Dean Martin's first variety special since splitting up with Jerry Lewis, with guests James Mason, Louis Prima, and Keely Smith

811

13 OCTOBER	"Pinocchio" (NBC)—musical with Mickey Rooney and Fran Allison (simulcast on radio and television)
12 NOVEMBER	"High Adventure" (CBS)—first of a series of travel documentaries hosted by Lowell Thomas
16 NOVEMBER	"Holiday in Las Vegas" (NBC)—variety show from Las Vegas, with Ann Sothern, Jayne Mansfield, Mickey Hargitay, Sammy Davis, Jr., Tony Randall, and Vic Damone
17 NOVEMBER	"General Motors Fiftieth Anniversary Show" (NBC)—variety tribute hosted by Kirk Douglas, with appearances by Ernest Borgnine, Cyril Ritchard, Claudette Colbert, Helen Hayes, Pat Boone, Dean Martin, Carol Burnett, June Allyson, and Steve Lawrence
26 NOVEMBER	"The Pied Piper of Hamelin" (NBC)—musical with Van Johnson, Claude Rains, and Kay Starr
27 NOVEMBER	"Annie Get Your Gun" (NBC)—musical with Mary Martin, John Raitt, and William O'Neal
8 DECEMBER	"A Day Called X" (CBS)—documentary examining the civil defense system of Portland, Oregon, in response to a simulated nuclear attack
30 DECEMBER	"All Star Jazz" (NBC)—musical program hosted by Steve Allen, with Louis Armstrong, Dave Brubeck, Paul Desmond, Duke Ellington, Woody Herman, Gene Krupa, Carmen McRae, and Charlie Ventura
30 DECEMBER	"The Lady from Philadelphia: Through Asia with Marian Anderson," *See It Now* (CBS)—documentary on Marian Anderson's goodwill tour of Asia sponsored by the U.S. State Department

1958

1 FEBRUARY	"Young People's Concert" (CBS)—second musical special hosted by Leonard Bernstein, with guest Aaron Copland
1 FEBRUARY	"The Dean Martin Show" (NBC)—variety, with Dean Martin and guests Frank Sinatra, Danny Thomas, and Barbara Perry
23 FEBRUARY	"Education for What?" *The Great Challenge* (CBS)—first of a series of symposiums on con-

temporary issues, moderated by Howard K. Smith

2 MARCH   "Statehood for Alaska and Hawaii?" *See It Now* (CBS)—news documentary hosted by Edward R. Murrow

30 MARCH   "Radiation and Fallout," *See It Now* (CBS)—investigative documentary narrated by Edward R. Murrow

15 APRIL   "The Jerry Lewis Show" (NBC)—variety with Jerry Lewis and guests Everett Sloane and Helen Traubel

27 APRIL   "Hansel and Gretel" (NBC)—musical with Red Buttons, Barbara Cook, Rise Stevens, and Rudy Vallee

19 SEPTEMBER   "Roberta" (NBC)—musical with Bob Hope, Anna Maria Alberghetti, Howard Keel, and Janis Paige

10 OCTOBER   "The Bing Crosby Show" (ABC)— variety with Bing Crosby and guests Patti Page, Dean Martin, and Mahalia Jackson

12 OCTOBER   "Swiss Family Robinson" (NBC)—adventure with Walter Pidgeon and Laraine Day

15 OCTOBER   "Dead of Noon" (CBS)—drama with Richard Boone as western outlaw John Wesley Hardin

15 OCTOBER   "Ginger Rogers" (CBS)—variety with Ginger Rogers and guests Ray Bolger and the Ritz Brothers

16 OCTOBER   "Little Women" (NBC)—drama with Zina Bethune, Jeannie Carson, Florence Henderson, Margaret O'Brien, Rise Stevens, and Joel Grey

17 OCTOBER   "An Evening with Fred Astaire" (NBC)—Fred Astaire's first variety special, with Barrie Chase (produced by Bud Yorkin and choreographed by Hermes Pan)

26 OCTOBER   "United Nations Day Concert," *The U.N. in Action* (CBS)—concert by cellist Pablo Casals

10 NOVEMBER   "All-Star Jazz" (CBS)—music with Louis Armstrong, Gene Krupa, Lionel Hampton, Les Brown, Bob Crosby's Bobcats, and Jane Morgan

30 NOVEMBER   "Wonderful Town" (CBS)—musical with Rosalind Russell, Jacquelyn McKeever, and Sydney Chaplin

30 NOVEMBER   "Art Carney Meets Peter and the Wolf" (ABC)—musical with Art Carney and the puppets of Bil and Cora Baird

| 9 DECEMBER | "The Gift of the Magi" (CBS)—musical adaptation of O. Henry's story, with Gordon MacRae, Sally Ann Howes, and Bea Arthur |
| 28 DECEMBER | "The Face of Red China" (CBS)—documentary using film shot by a German journalist |

1959

7 JANUARY	"The Golden Age of Jazz" (CBS)—musical hour hosted by Jackie Gleason, with guests Louis Armstrong, Duke Ellington, Dizzy Gillespie, Gene Krupa, and George Shearing
18 JANUARY	"Ten Little Indians" (NBC)—Agatha Christie mystery, with Nina Foch, Kenneth Haigh, and Barry Jones
21 JANUARY	"The Lost Class of '59" (CBS)—news documentary hosted by Edward R. Murrow on the closing of six Norfolk high schools to forestall federally ordered desegregation
26 JANUARY	"The Alphabet Conspiracy," *Bell Science Series* (NBC)—fantasy on language, with Dr. Frank Baxter (as Dr. Linguistics) and Hans Conried
11 FEBRUARY	"Meet Mr. Lincoln," *Project 20* (NBC)—photographs and drawings of Abraham Lincoln with narration by Alexander Scourby
28 FEBRUARY	"Accent on Love" (NBC)—musical revue with Ginger Rogers, Louis Jourdan, Mike Nichols and Elaine May, Marge and Gower Champion, and Jaye P. Morgan
29 MARCH	"Magic with Mary Martin" and "Music with Mary Martin" (NBC)—two Easter Sunday programs (one afternoon, one evening) with Mary Martin
24 APRIL	"The Gene Kelly Show" (CBS)—variety with Gene Kelly and guests Liza Minnelli (then age thirteen) and Carl Sandburg
26 APRIL	"Meet Me in St. Louis" (CBS)—musical with Jane Powell, Tab Hunter, Myrna Loy, Walter Pidgeon, Ed Wynn, and Patty Duke
8 MAY	"Why Berlin?" (NBC)—news documentary narrated by Chet Huntley
28 JUNE	"The Record Years" (ABC)—tribute to the recording industry hosted by Dick Clark, with guests Johnny Mathis, Fabian, the McGuire Sis-

	ters, Les Paul and Mary Ford, Fats Domino, and Stan Freberg
20 SEPTEMBER	"People Kill People Sometimes," *Sunday Showcase* (NBC)—drama with George C. Scott, Geraldine Page, and Jason Robards, Jr.
27 SEPTEMBER and 4 OCTOBER	"What Makes Sammy Run?" *Sunday Showcase* (NBC)—drama with Larry Blyden, Barbara Rush, and John Forsythe
27 OCTOBER	"The Bells of St. Mary's" (CBS)—musical with Claudette Colbert (in a rare TV appearance) and Robert Preston
30 OCTOBER	"The Moon and Sixpence" (NBC)—drama adapted by S. Lee Pogostin and directed by Robert Mulligan, with Laurence Olivier (in his American TV debut), Judith Anderson, Hume Cronyn, Jessica Tandy, and Geraldine Fitzgerald
7 DECEMBER	"The Philadelphia Story" (NBC)—drama with Christopher Plummer and Gig Young
10 DECEMBER	"Tonight with Belafonte" (CBS)—music with Harry Belafonte
18 DECEMBER	"Iran: Brittle Ally," *CBS Reports* (CBS)—news documentary narrated by Edward R. Murrow and Winston Burdett

1960

7 JANUARY	"Mrs. Miniver" (CBS)—drama with Maureen O'Hara, Leo Genn, and Cathleen Nesbitt
29 JANUARY	"The Fifth Column" (CBS)—drama with Richard Burton
31 JANUARY	"The Fabulous Fifties" (CBS)—retrospective, produced by Leland Hayward, hosted by Henry Fonda, with appearances by Rex Harrison, Julie Andrews, Dick Van Dyke, Mike Nichols and Elaine May, Betty Comden and Adolph Green, Shelley Berman, Suzy Parker, Jackie Gleason, and Eric Sevareid
14 FEBRUARY	"The Devil and Daniel Webster" (NBC)—drama with Edward G. Robinson and David Wayne
24 FEBRUARY	"Four for Tonight," *Star Parade* (NBC)—live and taped variety, with Cyril Ritchard, Beatrice Lillie, Tony Randall, and Tammy Grimes
25 MARCH	"The Snows of Kilimanjaro" (CBS)—adaptation

	of Hemingway's story, with Robert Ryan, Janice Rule, and Ann Todd
31 MARCH	"The Bat," *The Dow Hour of Great Mysteries* (NBC)—drama with Helen Hayes, Jason Robards, Jr., and Margaret Hamilton (first of a series of specials, hosted by Joseph N. Welch)
20 APRIL	"Ninotchka," *Special Tonight* (ABC)—comedy, with Maria Schell, Gig Young, Zsa Zsa Gabor, and Anne Meara
7 MAY	"The Slowest Gun in the West" (CBS)—comedy western with Jack Benny and Phil Silvers
3 and 10 JUNE	"The Sacco-Vanzetti Story" (NBC)—docudrama written by Reginald Rose and directed by Sidney Lumet, with Martin Balsam (as Sacco), Steven Hill (Vanzetti), E. G. Marshall, and Peter Falk
7 JULY	"Lippmann on Leadership," *CBS Reports* (CBS)—political observer Walter Lippmann interviewed by Howard K. Smith
26 AUGUST–12 SEPTEMBER	Summer Olympics from Rome (coverage by CBS)
26 SEPTEMBER	First of the Kennedy–Nixon Debates (coverage by all three networks)
28 SEPTEMBER	"Astaire Time" (NBC)—variety, with Fred Astaire and Barrie Chase
25 OCTOBER	"John Brown's Raid" (NBC)—drama with James Mason, Robert Duvall, and Ossie Davis
30 OCTOBER	"Danny Kaye" (CBS)—Danny Kaye's first variety special, with guest Louis Armstrong
1 NOVEMBER	"Dean Martin" (NBC)—variety with Dean Martin and guests Frank Sinatra, Dorothy Provine, and Don Knotts
14 NOVEMBER	"The Spirit of the Alamo" (ABC)—tour of the Alamo and promotion of the film *The Alamo,* hosted by John Wayne
30 NOVEMBER	"The Three Musketeers," *Family Classics* (CBS)—adventure with Maximillian Schell, John Colicos, Barry Morse, Tim O'Connor, and Vincent Price
8 DECEMBER	"Peter Pan" (NBC)—restaged version, with Mary Martin, Cyril Ritchard, and Maureen Bailey
20 DECEMBER	"Sit-In," *NBC White Paper* (NBC)—documentary on desegregation in Nashville

| 21 DECEMBER | "The Coming of Christ," *Project 20* (NBC)—art documentary narrated by Alexander Scourby |

1961

15 JANUARY	"The Gershwin Years" (CBS)—music, with Ethel Merman
22 JANUARY	"The Red and the Black," *Closeup* (ABC)—documentary produced by Helen Jean Rogers on Soviet influence in Africa
25 JANUARY	President Kennedy's first press conference (coverage by all three networks; first live telecast of a Presidential news conference)
7 FEBRUARY	"A String of Beads" (NBC)—drama with Jane Fonda (her only dramatic appearance on American TV)
12 FEBRUARY	"Aaron Copland's Birthday Party," *Young People's Concert* (CBS)—music with Leonard Bernstein and the New York Philharmonic
13 FEBRUARY	"The Heiress," *Family Classics* (CBS)—adaptation of the play based on Henry James's *Washington Square,* with Julie Harris, Farley Granger, and Barry Morse
14 FEBRUARY	"Panama—Danger Zone," *NBC White Paper* (NBC)—documentary on the Canal Zone and Panamanian nationalism, narrated by Chet Huntley
5 MARCH	"Fierce, Funny and Far Out," *Omnibus* (NBC)—a look at contemporary drama with William Saroyan and scenes from four recent plays
9 MARCH	"Mother and Daughter," *Purex Special for Women* (NBC)—daytime drama with Patricia Neal, Lynn Loring, and Arthur Hill
20 MARCH	"Twenty-Four Hours in a Woman's Life" (CBS)—drama with Ingrid Bergman and Rip Torn
29 MARCH	"The Real West," *Project 20* (NBC)—cultural documentary narrated by Gary Cooper
18 APRIL	"90 Miles to Communism," *Closeup* (ABC)—documentary on Cuba's political climate
27 APRIL	"Jane Eyre," *Family Classics* (CBS)—live dra-

ma, with Sally Ann Howes, Zachary Scott, and Fritz Weaver

9 AUGUST "The Jimmy Durante Show" (NBC)—comedy on the modern American husband, with Jimmy Durante and guests Bob Hope, Garry Moore, and Janice Rule

23 and 30 SEPTEMBER "The Assassination Plot at Teheran" (ABC)—two-part drama on a supposed German plot to kill Stalin, Churchill, and Roosevelt, with John Larch, Oscar Homolka, and Hermione Gingold

4 OCTOBER "The Spiral Staircase," *Theatre 62* (NBC)—live drama with Gig Young, Elizabeth Montgomery, and Eddie Albert

12 OCTOBER "Eisenhower on the Presidency" (CBS)—first of three interviews conducted by Walter Cronkite

29 OCTOBER "The Power and the Glory" (CBS)—drama with George C. Scott, Laurence Olivier, Patty Duke, and Keenan Wynn

16 NOVEMBER "The Glamor Trap," *Purex Special for Women* (NBC)—daytime documentary on the beauty and cosmetics industries

17 NOVEMBER "Vincent Van Gogh: A Self-Portrait" (NBC)—art documentary narrated by Martin Gabel, with Lee J. Cobb reading from Van Gogh's letters

23 DECEMBER "The Enchanted Nutcracker," *Westinghouse Presents* (ABC)—adaptation of the Tchaikovsky ballet, with Carol Lawrence, Robert Goulet, and Linda Canby

26 DECEMBER "Khrushchev and Berlin," *NBC White Paper* (NBC)—news documentary (first NBC documentary produced by Fred Freed)

1962

14 JANUARY "John Brown's Body" (CBS)—adaptation of Benet's poem, narrated by Richard Boone

14 JANUARY "The Farmer's Daughter," *Theater 62* (NBC)—live comedy, with Lee Remick, Peter Lawford, Charles Bickford, and Cornelia Otis Skinner

28 JANUARY "The Battle of Newburgh," *NBC White Paper* (NBC)—investigative documentary on the effect of a tightening of the welfare code in Newburgh, New York

18 FEBRUARY "A Tour of the White House with Mrs. John F.

	Kennedy" (CBS and NBC)—deftly directed by Franklin Schaffner
20 FEBRUARY	Orbital space flight of Lieutenant Colonel John Glenn (coverage by all three networks)
9 MARCH	"The Milton Berle Show" (NBC)—variety, with Milton Berle and guests Jack Benny, Lena Horne, Janis Paige, and Laurence Harvey
24 MARCH	"Tonight in Samarkand," *Breck Golden Showcase* (CBS)—drama with Janice Rule and James Mason
29 MARCH	"U.S. Route #1: An American Profile" (NBC)—a trip down the East Coast, narrated by Van Heflin
1 APRIL	"Jacqueline Kennedy's Journey" (NBC)—coverage of the First Lady's trip to India and Pakistan
6 APRIL	"The Vanishing 400" (NBC)—a look at high society, narrated by Walter Pidgeon with commentary by Cleveland Amory
25 MAY	"Robert Ruark's Africa" (NBC)—documentary filmed in Kenya, with Robert Ruark defending colonialism
10 JULY	First transmission from the Telstar satellite (coverage by all three networks)
27 JULY	"The World of Sophia Loren" (NBC)—profile of the Italian actress, with appearances by Vittorio DeSica, Anatole Litvak, Anthony Perkins, and Art Buchwald
14 AUGUST	"Shelley Berman: A Personal Appearance" (ABC)—one-man show
16 AUGUST	"Americans: A Portrait in Verses" (CBS)—a series of sketches set to poems by Poe, Emerson, cummings, and Ginsberg, with Alexander Scourby, Peggy Wood, Kim Hunter, and James Whitmore
11 SEPTEMBER	"Julie and Carol at Carnegie Hall" (CBS)—music and comedy with Julie Andrews and Carol Burnett
28 SEPTEMBER	"Meet Comrade Student" (ABC)—investigative documentary on the Soviet educational system
28 OCTOBER	"The River Nile" (NBC)—documentary narrated by James Mason
11 NOVEMBER	"The Danny Kaye Show" (NBC)—variety with Danny Kaye and guest Lucille Ball
10 DECEMBER	"The Tunnel" (NBC)—documentary on the

construction of a tunnel underneath the Berlin Wall by a group of West Germans, narrated by Piers Anderton (who cowrote the show with Reuven Frank)

21 DECEMBER — "What Is a Melody?" *Young People's Concert* (CBS)—musical education with Leonard Bernstein and the New York Philharmonic

1963

24 JANUARY — "The World of Benny Goodman" (NBC)— profile of the jazz clarinetist, narrated by Alexander Scourby

3 FEBRUARY — "The Rise of Khrushchev," *NBC White Paper* (NBC)—documentary produced by Fred Freed and narrated by Chet Huntley

11 FEBRUARY — "Eisenhower on Lincoln" (NBC)—Ike talks with Bruce Catton

17 FEBRUARY — "A Look at Monaco" (CBS)—a guided tour with Princess Grace (CBS's only colorcast of the 1962–1963 season)

22 FEBRUARY — "World of Chevalier" (NBC)—portrait of Maurice Chevalier

19 MARCH — "Judy Garland" (CBS)—variety with Judy Garland and guests Phil Silvers and Robert Goulet

21 MAY — "The Kremlin" (NBC)—a tour with Frank Bourgholtzer

6 AUGUST — "Picture of a Cuban," *Focus on America* (ABC)—documentary about a Cuban family that relocated in Miami

11 AUGUST — "The Crucial Summer" (ABC)—first of five half-hour reports on civil rights

22 AUGUST — "The Voice of the Desert," *Summer Special* (NBC)—documentary on Arizona's Sonora Desert with naturalist Joseph Wood Krutch

28 AUGUST — Civil Rights March on Washington (live coverage by NBC)

2 SEPTEMBER — "The American Revolution of '63" (NBC)— three-hour documentary on the struggle for civil rights

9 SEPTEMBER — "What Happened to Royalty?" (ABC)—profiles of Europe's remaining monarchs, produced by Warren Wallace

11 SEPTEMBER — "Athens, Where the Theater Began," *The Roots*

	of Freedom (CBS)—cultural documentary with Alfred Lunt and Lynn Fontanne
20 SEPTEMBER	"Hedda Gabler" (CBS)—drama, with Ingrid Bergman (in a rare TV appearance), Trevor Howard, Ralph Richardson, and Michael Redgrave
6 OCTOBER	"Elizabeth Taylor in London" (CBS)—cultural documentary hosted by Elizabeth Taylor (in a rare TV appearance)
6 OCTOBER	"A Man Named Mays" (NBC)—profile of baseball great Willie Mays, written and narrated by Charles Einstein
21 OCTOBER	"Crisis—Behind a Presidential Commitment" (ABC)—documentary on the June 1963 integration crisis at the University of Alabama
25 OCTOBER	"The World's Girls" (ABC)—documentary on feminism, with appearances by Simone de Beauvoir, Simone Signoret, and Betty Friedan
10 NOVEMBER	"That Was the Week That Was" (NBC)—satire, with Henry Morgan, Charlie Manna, and Nancy Ames (later a series)
22–25 NOVEMBER	Coverage by all three networks of the events following the assassination of President John F. Kennedy
1 DECEMBER	"The Greatest Showman" (NBC)—profile of Cecil B. DeMille, with appearances by Bob Hope, Charlton Heston, Gloria Swanson, Yul Brynner, Betty Hutton, and Billy Graham
10 DECEMBER	"The Soviet Woman" (ABC)—documentary hosted by John Secondari
25 DECEMBER	"Amahl and the Night Visitors" (NBC)—new version of the Menotti opera, with Kurt Yaghjian and Martha King
29 DECEMBER	"The Making of the President 1960" (ABC)—documentary on the Nixon–Kennedy campaign, narrated by Martin Gabel with commentary by author Theodore H. White

1964

7 JANUARY	"The Orient Express" (NBC)—documentary with Edwin Newman aboard
12 JANUARY	"Birth Control: How?" (NBC)—documentary hosted by David Brinkley

24 JANUARY	"The Restless Sea," *Bell Science Series* (NBC)—documentary from Disney Studios on marine life
4 and 9 FEBRUARY	*NBC White Paper* (NBC)—two-part examination of Cuba (I—"The Bay of Pigs;" II—"The Missile Crisis")
15 FEBRUARY	"Robin Hood," *NBC Children's Theatre* (NBC)—adventure with Dan Ferrone, Lynda Day, and Sorrell Booke
1 APRIL	"Vietnam: The Deadly Decision" (CBS)—examination of America's increasing involvement, anchored by Charles Collingwood
28 APRIL	"Boxing's Last Round" (NBC)—documentary on the decline in boxing's popularity, hosted by David Brinkley
29 APRIL and 6 MAY	"DeGaulle: Roots of Power," *CBS Reports* (CBS)—biography
27 MAY	"Town Meeting of the World" (CBS)—one of several such broadcasts made possible by satellite technology, this one featured Richard Nixon, J. William Fulbright, Harold Wilson, and Maurice Schumann, with host Eric Sevareid
3 JUNE	"Once upon a Mattress" (CBS)—musical, with Carol Burnett
5 JUNE	"D-Day Plus 20 Years: Eisenhower Returns to Normandy," *CBS Reports* (CBS)—retrospective, with Ike and Walter Cronkite
29 AUGUST	"The King Family" (ABC)—their first TV special
1 SEPTEMBER	"Civil War Portraits" (NBC)—profiles of U. S. Grant and Robert E. Lee, introduced by Hugh Downs
10 SEPTEMBER	"Letters from Viet Nam" (ABC)—profile of an American helicopter squadron, produced by Gregory Shuker
16 OCTOBER	"Have Girls—Will Travel" (NBC)—comedy, with Bob Hope, Rhonda Fleming, Jill St. John, and Marilyn Maxwell
12 NOVEMBER	"Sophia Loren in Rome" (ABC)—tour of Rome with Sophia Loren and her guest, Marcello Mastroianni
15 NOVEMBER	"Around the Beatles" (ABC)—musical special, taped in London in May 1964, with the Beatles and guests Cilla Black, P. J. Proby, and Millie Small

17 NOVEMBER	"The Louvre" (NBC)—cultural documentary produced by Lucy Jarvis and narrated by Charles Boyer
16 DECEMBER	"Casals at Eighty-eight" (CBS)—profile of cellist Pablo Casals
28 DECEMBER	"Carol for Another Christmas" (ABC)—drama, with Peter Sellers (in his American TV dramatic debut), Ben Gazzara, Sterling Hayden, Steve Lawrence, and Eva Marie Saint

1965

25 JANUARY	"The Stately Ghosts of England" (NBC)—light-hearted documentary hosted by Margaret Rutherford
15 FEBRUARY	"Dinah Shore" (ABC)—a tribute to the Peace Corps, with guests Harry Belafonte and Sargent Shriver
22 FEBRUARY	"Cinderella" (CBS)—restaged version of the Rodgers and Hammerstein musical, with Lesley Ann Warren, Stuart Damon, Ginger Rogers, Jo Van Fleet, Walter Pidgeon, and Celeste Holm
23 FEBRUARY	"I, Leonardo da Vinci," *Saga of Western Man* (ABC)—historical documentary produced by John Secondari and Helen Jean Rogers
23 FEBRUARY	"The Journals of Lewis and Clark," *NBC News Special* (NBC)—historical documentary, narrated by Lorne Greene
1 MARCH	"T-Minus 4 Years, 9 Months and 30 Days" (CBS)—documentary examining whether the United States will reach its goal of landing a man on the moon by 1970
28 APRIL	"My Name is Barbra" (CBS)—Barbra Streisand's first TV special
24 MAY	"The National Driver's Test," *CBS News Special* (CBS)—an audience-participation special hosted by Mike Wallace
1 JUNE	"A Journey with Joseph Wood Krutch" (NBC)—a trip through the Grand Canyon with naturalist Joseph Wood Krutch
18 JUNE	"Everybody's Got a System" (ABC)—Terry-Thomas takes a look at gambling
25 AUGUST	"The Agony of Vietnam" (ABC)—documentary

focusing on the impact of the war on the Vietnamese people

7 SEPTEMBER	"American White Paper: United States Foreign Policy" (NBC)—three-and-a-half-hour examination of American foreign policy (longest public service documentary to date)
10 SEPTEMBER	"Americans on Everest," *National Geographic Special* (CBS)—chronicle of the 1963 U.S. expedition, narrated by Orson Welles (first of the *National Geographic Specials*)
29 SEPTEMBER	"Bob Hope" (NBC)—variety with Bob Hope and guests Beatrice Lillie, Douglas Fairbanks, Jr., Dinah Shore, and Andy Williams
5 OCTOBER	"Henry Moore: Man of Form," *CBS News Special* (CBS)—profile of the sculptor
24 NOVEMBER	"Frank Sinatra: A Man and His Music" (NBC)—a one-man show, produced by Dwight Hemion
28 NOVEMBER	"The Dangerous Christmas of Red Riding Hood" (ABC)—musical with Liza Minnelli (as Lillian Hood), Cyril Ritchard (as Lone T. Wolf), Vic Damone, and the Animals
9 DECEMBER	"A Charlie Brown Christmas" (CBS)—the first of the *Peanuts* specials, based on Charles Schulz's comic strip
20 DECEMBER	"Vietnam: December, 1965," *NBC News Special* (NBC)—documentary produced by Chet Hagan, hosted by Chet Huntley and Frank McGee
21 DECEMBER	"The Nutcracker" (CBS)—ballet with Edward Villella, Patricia McBride, and the New York City Ballet

1966

23 and 30 JANUARY	"The Ages of Man" (CBS)—readings from Shakespeare by John Gielgud
18 FEBRUARY	"An Evening with Carol Channing" (CBS)—Carol Channing's first variety special, with guests George Burns and David McCallum
30 MARCH	"Alice in Wonderland, or What's a Nice Girl Like You Doing in a Place Like This?" (ABC)—cartoon, with the voices of Sammy Davis, Jr., Hedda Hopper, Zsa Zsa Gabor, and Harvey Korman
30 MARCH	"Color Me Barbra" (CBS)—Barbra Streisand's

	second TV special, a one-woman show directed by Dwight Hemion
17 APRIL	"Countdown to Zero," *NBC White Paper* (NBC)—news documentary on the proliferation of nuclear weapons, produced by Fred Freed
22 APRIL	"The Poppy Is Also a Flower" (ABC)—one of a series of dramas depicting some of the work of the United Nations; introduced by Princess Grace of Monaco, with a star-studded cast including E. G. Marshall, Trevor Howard, Angie Dickinson, Eli Wallach, Yul Brynner, Stephen Boyd, Rita Hayworth (in her only TV dramatic appearance), Jack Hawkins, Marcello Mastroianni, and Omar Sharif
1 MAY	"Mississippi: A Self-Portrait," *NBC News Special* (NBC)—documentary produced and directed by Frank DeFelitta
3 MAY	"Stravinsky," *CBS News Special* (CBS)—profile, narrated by Charles Kuralt
8 MAY	"Death of a Salesman" (CBS)—new version of Arthur Miller's play, with Lee J. Cobb, Mildred Dunnock, George Segal, and James Farentino (directed by Alex Segal)
9 MAY	"LBJ's Texas" (NBC)—a tour of the hill country with President Johnson, accompanied by Ray Scherer
12 JUNE	"Politics: The Outer Fringe," *NBC News Special* (NBC)—documentary on the John Birch Society, the Minute Men, the American Nazi Party, and the Ku Klux Klan
15 JUNE	"The Undeclared War," *NBC News Special* (NBC)—documentary on guerilla activities in Guatemala
16 JUNE	"The Baffling World of ESP" (ABC)—documentary narrated by Basil Rathbone
20 JULY	"Siberia: A Day in Irkutsk," *NBC News Special* (NBC)—documentary narrated by Kenneth Bernstein
6 AUGUST	Wedding of Luci Baines Johnson and Patrick J. Nugent at the White House (coverage by all three networks)
16 AUGUST	"The Angry Voices of Watts," *NBC News Special* (NBC)—black writers and poets present their works at the writers' workshop established in Watts by Budd Schulberg

25 AUGUST	"American White Paper: Organized Crime in America" (NBC)—three-and-a-half-hour examination of organized crime, narrated by Frank McGee
15 OCTOBER	"Brigadoon" (ABC)—musical, with Robert Goulet, Sally Ann Howes, Edward Villella, and Peter Falk
6 NOVEMBER	"Alice Through the Looking Glass" (NBC)—musical, with Judi Robin (as Alice), Nanette Fabray, Jimmy Durante, Tom and Dick Smothers, Agnes Moorehead, Jack Palance, Ricardo Montalban, and Richard Denning
22 NOVEMBER	"Inside Red China," CBS Reports (CBS)—film shot by a German camera crew hired by CBS News
24 NOVEMBER	"Smokey the Bear" (NBC)—children's musical with animated puppets, narrated by James Cagney
6 DECEMBER	"The Legacy of Rome," Saga of Western Man (ABC)—historical documentary narrated by Fredric March
7 DECEMBER	"Frank Sinatra: A Man and His Music—Part II" (CBS)—a sequel to Sinatra's 1965 special
8 DECEMBER	"The Glass Menagerie" (CBS)—new version of Tennessee Williams's play, with Shirley Booth, Barbara Loden, Pat Hingle, and Hal Holbrook
13 DECEMBER	"The Long Childhood of Timmy" (ABC)—profile of a retarded child, narrated by E. G. Marshall
18 DECEMBER	"How the Grinch Stole Christmas" (CBS)—cartoon, based on the Dr. Seuss story, narrated by Boris Karloff (animation by Chuck Jones)
27 DECEMBER	CBS News Special (CBS)—Charles Collingwood and Morley Safer interview General William Westmoreland in Saigon

1967

10 JANUARY	"The Beatles at Shea Stadium" (ABC)—film of the Beatles' 1965 New York concert

15 JANUARY	Super Bowl I (CBS and NBC)—Green Bay versus Kansas City
26 FEBRUARY	"Jack and the Beanstalk" (NBC)—fantasy, produced by Hanna-Barbera, hosted by Gene Kelly (first TV special to combine live action with animation)
5 MARCH	"Good Day," *Experiment in Television* (NBC)—drama with Jo Van Fleet and Frank Langella
6 MARCH	"Mark Twain Tonight!" (CBS)—one-man show with Hal Holbrook
19 MARCH	"The Medium Is the Message," *Experiment in Television* (NBC)—documentary on Marshall McLuhan
19 MARCH	"Annie Get Your Gun" (NBC)—musical with Ethel Merman
4 MAY	"The Crucible" (CBS)—drama by Arthur Miller, with George C. Scott, Colleen Dewhurst, Fritz Weaver, and Tuesday Weld
7 MAY	"Carousel" (ABC)—musical with Robert Goulet and Mary Grover
30 MAY	"Ivanov" (CBS)—drama by Chekhov, with Claire Bloom and John Gielgud
6 JUNE	"Gauguin in Tahiti: The Search for Paradise," *CBS News Special* (CBS)—documentary, with Michael Redgrave reading from Gauguin's journals
25 JUNE	"Our World" (NET)—first live worldwide broadcast, transmitted by four satellites to thirty countries, with appearances by Franco Zeffirelli, Joan Miro, Marc Chagall, Van Cliburn, and the Beatles
11 JULY	"Khrushchev in Exile," *NBC News Special* (NBC)—documentary produced by Lucy Jarvis and narrated by Edwin Newman
9 SEPTEMBER	"Rowan and Martin's Laugh-In Special" (NBC)—comedy with Dan Rowan and Dick Martin (later a series)
10 SEPTEMBER	"Africa" (ABC)—four-hour news and cultural special on Africa, hosted by Gregory Peck
15 SEPTEMBER	"Summer '67: What We Learned," *NBC News Special* (NBC)—news documentary
11 OCTOBER	"Belle of 14th Street" (CBS)—musical with Barbra Streisand, Jason Robards, and John Bubbles

17 OCTOBER	"Do Not Go Gentle into That Good Night," *CBS Playhouse* (CBS)—drama with Melvyn Douglas, Shirley Booth, and Claudia McNeil
24 OCTOBER	"Kismet" (ABC)—musical with Anna Maria Alberghetti, George Chakiris, and José Ferrer
13 NOVEMBER	"Frank Sinatra" (NBC)—music with Frank Sinatra and guests Ella Fitzgerald and Antonio Carlos Jobim
15 NOVEMBER	"Dial M for Murder" (ABC)—drama with Laurence Harvey, Hugh O'Brian, and Diane Cilento
15 NOVEMBER	"Androcles and the Lion" (NBC)—musical with Noel Coward and Norman Wisdom
26 NOVEMBER	"The Diary of Anne Frank" (ABC)—drama with Diane Davila (as Anne Frank), Peter Beiger, Viveca Lindfors, Theodore Bikel, Donald Pleasance, Marisa Pavan, and Max von Sydow
1 DECEMBER	"Ten Days That Shook the World" (NBC)—documentary on the Russian Revolution, narrated by Orson Welles
17 DECEMBER	"Among the Paths to Eden" (ABC)—drama by Truman Capote, with Maureen Stapleton and Martin Balsam

1968

7 JANUARY	"Dr. Jekyll and Mr. Hyde" (ABC)—new version, with Jack Palance
8 JANUARY	"Sharks," *The Undersea World of Jacques Cousteau* (ABC)—first of the Cousteau specials for ABC
24 JANUARY	"Laura" (ABC)—drama with Lee Bouvier and Farley Granger
26 JANUARY	"Flesh and Blood" (NBC)—drama with Edmond O'Brien, Kim Stanley, E. G. Marshall, Suzanne Pleshette, Kim Darby, and Robert Duvall
31 JANUARY	"Of Mice and Men" (ABC)—adaptation of Steinbeck's novel, with Will Geer, Joey Heatherton, and Nicol Williamson
7 FEBRUARY	"The Fred Astaire Show" (NBC)—variety with Fred Astaire and guests Barrie Chase and Simon and Garfunkel
11 FEBRUARY	"A Case of Libel" (ABC)—adaptation of the

	Broadway play, with Lloyd Bridges, Van Heflin, and Angie Dickinson
18 FEBRUARY	"The Legend of Robin Hood" (NBC)—adventure with David Watson (as Robin Hood), Victor Buono, Walter Slezak, and Noel Harrison
27 FEBRUARY	"Walter Cronkite in Vietnam," *CBS News Special* (CBS)—first-hand reporting by Walter Cronkite
3 MARCH	"A Hatful of Rain" (ABC)—adaptation of the Broadway play, with Sandy Dennis, Peter Falk, Michael Parks, and Don Stroud
6 MARCH	"Tour of Monaco" (ABC)—documentary hosted by Princess Grace (the former Grace Kelly), with appearances by Terry-Thomas and Françoise Hardy
6, 8, and 9 MARCH	"The Rise and Fall of the Third Reich" (ABC)—historical documentary narrated by Richard Basehart
17 MARCH	"Travels with Charley" (NBC)—adaptation of Steinbeck's book, narrated by Henry Fonda
18 MARCH	"The Bill Cosby Special" (NBC)—his first variety show
25 MARCH	"Kiss Me Kate" (ABC)—musical, with Robert Goulet, Carol Lawrence, and Jessica Walter
4 and 9 APRIL	Special coverage of the Martin Luther King, Jr., assassination and aftermath (CBS)
27 JUNE	"Bias and the Media" (ABC)—first of six hourlong specials on racism
26–29 AUGUST	Coverage of the Democratic National Convention in Chicago (all three commercial networks)
8 SEPTEMBER	"Around the World of Mike Todd" (ABC)—retrospective narrated by Orson Welles, with appearances by Elizabeth Taylor, Gypsy Rose Lee, and Ethel Merman
12 SEPTEMBER	"Certain Honorable Men," *Prudential's On Stage* (NBC)—drama by Rod Serling, with Van Heflin and Peter Fonda
15 OCTOBER	"The People Next Door," *CBS Playhouse* (CBS)—drama by J. P. Miller, with Lloyd Bridges, Kim Hunter, and Deborah Winters
23 OCTOBER	"Sophia" (ABC)—profile of Sophia Loren
17 NOVEMBER	"Heidi" (NBC)—adapted for television by Earl Hamner, with Jennifer Edwards (as Heidi), Michael Redgrave, Jean Simmons, and Walter Slezak (NBC incurred the wrath of many viewers

	by interrupting the end of a pro football game to start the broadcast of "Heidi" on time)
3 DECEMBER	"Brigitte Bardot" (NBC)—a partially censored variety hour
3 DECEMBER	"Elvis" (NBC)—Elvis Presley's first major TV appearance in several years
3 DECEMBER	"Justice Black and the Bill of Rights," *CBS News Special* (CBS)—the eighty-two-year-old Supreme Court Justice reminisces
5 DECEMBER	"The Secret of Michelangelo: Every Man's Dream" (ABC)—art documentary, narrated by Christopher Plummer and Zoe Caldwell

1969

3 JANUARY	"Male of the Species," *Prudential's On Stage* (NBC)—dramatic vignettes, with host and narrator Laurence Olivier; guest appearances by Sean Connery, Paul Scofield, and Michael Caine
13 JANUARY	"To Love a Child," *ABC News Special* (ABC)—a report on a couple adopting a child
13 JANUARY	"Jean-Claude Killy" (ABC)—a profile of the skier
7 FEBRUARY	"This Is Sholom Aleichem," *Experiment in Television* (NBC)—biographical profile written by David Steinberg, with Jack Gilford (as Aleichem)
9 FEBRUARY	"A Midsummer Night's Dream" (CBS)—filmed performance by the Royal Shakespeare Company
2 APRIL	"Arsenic and Old Lace" (ABC)—new version, with Lillian Gish, Helen Hayes, Fred Gwynne, Sue Lyon, and Bob Crane
11 APRIL	"Fellini: A Director's Notebook," *Experiment in Television* (NBC)—profile, narrated in part by Federico Fellini
21 APRIL	"Francis Albert Sinatra Does His Thing" (CBS)—music with Frank Sinatra, Diahann Carroll, and the 5th Dimension (satisfied with the dress rehearsal tape, Sinatra elected not to do a final taping)
18 MAY	"Pogo" (NBC)—musical cartoon based on Walt Kelly's comic strip (animation by Chuck Jones)

5 JUNE	"Abortion," *Summer Focus* (ABC)—investigative report narrated by Frank Reynolds
1 JULY	Investiture of the Prince of Wales (satellite coverage carried by all three commercial networks)
20–21 JULY	Landing of Apollo 11 on the moon (coverage by all three commercial networks)
25 JULY	Senator Ted Kennedy obtains air time to explain the Chappaquiddick incident (ABC/NBC/CBS)
9 SEPTEMBER	"The Making of the President: 1968," *CBS News Special* (CBS)—documentary narrated by Joseph Campanella, with commentary by author Theodore H. White
12 SEPTEMBER	"Who Killed Lake Erie?" *NBC News Special* (NBC)—documentary on pollution, produced by Fred Freed
21 SEPTEMBER	"Woody Allen" (CBS)—comedy with Woody Allen and guests Candice Bergen and Billy Graham
7 OCTOBER	"From Here to the Seventies," *NBC News Special* (NBC)—two-and-a-half-hour special hosted by Paul Newman, with essays by twelve NBC correspondents
28 OCTOBER	"The Desert Whales," *The Undersea World of Jacques Cousteau* (ABC)—documentary
5 NOVEMBER	"Sinatra" (CBS)—a one-man musical show
9 NOVEMBER	"An Evening with Julie Andrews and Harry Belafonte" (NBC)—music
12 NOVEMBER	"Johnny Carson's Repertory Company" (NBC)—comedy with Johnny Carson, George C. Scott, Maureen Stapleton, and Marian Mercer
12 NOVEMBER	"Hey, Hey, Hey—It's Fat Albert" (NBC)—animated feature based on Bill Cosby's stories
13 NOVEMBER	Coverage by all networks of Vice President Agnew's Iowa speech attacking news commentaries
30 NOVEMBER	"Songs of America" (CBS)—music with Simon and Garfunkel
13 DECEMBER	"J. T.," *CBS Children's Hour* (CBS)—drama set in Harlem with Kevin Hooks and Ja'Net DuBois (later repeated in prime time)

1970

20 JANUARY	"My Sweet Charlie" (NBC)—drama with Patty Duke and Al Freeman, Jr.

18 FEBRUARY	"Annie, the Women in the Life of a Man" (CBS)—Anne Bancroft in a series of vignettes
15 MARCH	"David Copperfield" (NBC)—new version, produced in England, with Alastair Mackenzie and Robin Phillips (as David Copperfield), Laurence Olivier, Michael Redgrave, and Ralph Richardson
22 MARCH	"Harry and Lena" (ABC)—music with Harry Belafonte and Lena Horne
28 MARCH	"The Water Planet," *The Undersea World of Jacques Cousteau* (ABC)—Cousteau expounds on his philosophy
6 APRIL	"This Land Is Mine," *ABC News Special* (ABC)—a look at the American landscape, narrated by Robert Culp, featuring Kim Novak (in a rare TV appearance)
10 APRIL	"Tales from Muppetland" (ABC)—fantasy directed by Jim Henson, with Belinda Montgomery and Robin Ward
26 APRIL	"Raquel" (NBC)—variety with Raquel Welch and guests Bob Hope, John Wayne, and Tom Jones
5 MAY	"Once Before I Die" (NBC)—documentary on mountain climbing in Afghanistan filmed by Michael ("Woodstock") Wadleigh
5 MAY	"California Impressions by Henri Cartier-Bresson," *CBS News Special* (CBS)—Cartier-Bresson's filmed impressions of life in the U. S.
8 SEPTEMBER	"A Day in the Life of the United States," *CBS News Special* (CBS)—a look at what was happening on 20 July 1969, the day of the moon landing
12 SEPTEMBER	"George M!" (NBC)—musical with Joel Grey (as George M. Cohan), Bernadette Peters and Red Buttons
13 OCTOBER	"The Old Man Who Cried Wolf," *ABC Movie of the Week* (ABC)—drama with Edward G. Robinson, Martin Balsam, and Diane Baker
29 NOVEMBER	"Swing Out, Sweet Land" (NBC)—a look at American history, with John Wayne and two dozen guest stars
18 DECEMBER	"The Smokey Robinson Show" (ABC)—music from Motown, with Smokey Robinson and the Miracles, the Temptations, the Supremes, Stevie Wonder, and Fran Jeffries

| 22 DECEMBER | "A World of Love" (CBS)—a salute to children, produced in conjunction with UNICEF, hosted by Bill Cosby and Shirley MacLaine, with guests Julie Andrews, Richard Burton, Audrey Hepburn, Barbra Streisand, and Harry Belafonte |
| 31 DECEMBER | "Courts, Warts and All" (PBS)—Walter Cronkite, interviewed by Kevin O'Donnell, speaks on TV coverage of trials |

1971

2 FEBRUARY	"The Point," *ABC Tuesday Movie of the Week* (ABC)—animated film (by Fred Wolf) based on Harry Nilsson's story, narrated by Dustin Hoffman
15 FEBRUARY	"Goldie Hawn" (NBC)—variety, with Goldie Hawn and guests Ruth Buzzi, Bob Dishy and Kermit the Frog
23 FEBRUARY	"The Selling of the Pentagon," *CBS Reports* (CBS)—investigative documentary
8–9 MARCH	"Vanished" (NBC)—drama with Arthur Hill, Richard Widmark, and Eleanor Parker
24 MARCH	"Jane Eyre" (NBC)—new version, directed by Delbert Mann, with Susannah York, George C. Scott, Nyree Dawn Porter, and Jack Hawkins
27 MARCH	"Bill Cosby Talks with Children About Drugs," *NBC Children's Theatre*—informational special
6 APRIL	"The American Revolution: 1770–1783—A Conversation with Lord North," *CBS News Special* (CBS)—"interview" by Eric Sevareid of Lord North (played by Peter Ustinov)
18 APRIL	"Once Upon a Wheel" (ABC)—documentary on auto racing, narrated by Paul Newman
18 APRIL	"Diana!" (ABC)—music with Diana Ross and guests Bill Cosby, Danny Thomas, and the Jackson 5
2 MAY	"NBC White Paper: This Child Is Rated X" (NBC)—documentary on the criminal justice system and juveniles
21 MAY	"Venice Be Damned!" *NBC News Special* (NBC)—documentary on modern-day Venice narrated by José Ferrer

23 JUNE	Walter Cronkite interviews Daniel Ellsberg about the Pentagon Papers, *CBS News Special* (CBS)
30 JUNE	"June 30, 1971, a Day for History: The Supreme Court and the Pentagon Papers" (NBC)—news documentary
21 AUGUST	"Heroes and Heroin," *ABC News Special* (ABC)—investigative documentary on drug use among U.S. servicemen
11 OCTOBER	"Hogan's Goat" (PBS)—drama with Faye Dunaway (repeating her stage role) and Robert Foxworth
13 OCTOBER	First World Series night game (NBC)—record audience for a World Series telecast
15 OCTOBER	"Marriage: Year One" (NBC)—drama with Sally Field, Robert Pratt, William Windom, and Cicely Tyson
22 OCTOBER	"Good-bye, Raggedy Ann" (CBS)—drama with Mia Farrow and Hal Holbrook
31 OCTOBER	"Aesop's Fables" (CBS)—live-and-animated fantasy written by Earl Hamner, with Bill Cosby as Aesop
13 NOVEMBER	"Duel," *ABC Movie of the Weekend* (ABC)—drama, directed by Steven Spielberg, with Dennis Weaver
29 NOVEMBER	"Home" (PBS)—abridged version of the play, with John Gielgud and Ralph Richardson
30 NOVEMBER	"Brian's Song," *ABC Movie of the Week* (ABC)—biographical drama (later released theatrically) with James Caan (as Chicago Bears halfback and cancer victim Brian Piccolo) and Billy Dee Williams (Gale Sayers)
5 DECEMBER	"The American West of John Ford" (CBS)—a nostalgic look at the West and westerns, with John Wayne, Henry Fonda, and James Stewart
7 DECEMBER	"Julie and Carol at Lincoln Center" (CBS)—musical variety with Julie Andrews and Carol Burnett
19 DECEMBER	"The Homecoming" (CBS)—Christmas drama, written by Earl Hamner, with Patricia Neal, William Windom, and Ellen Corby

1972

17 JANUARY	"Jack Lemmon in 'S Wonderful, 'S Marvelous, 'S Gershwin" (NBC)—a salute to George and Ira Gershwin, hosted by Jack Lemmon, with guests Fred Astaire, Ethel Merman, and Leslie Uggams
27 JANUARY	"LBJ: Lyndon Johnson Talks Politics" (CBS)—interview with Walter Cronkite
12 FEBRUARY	"The Hound of the Baskervilles" (ABC)—new version, with Stewart Granger (as Sherlock Holmes) and Bernard Fox (Watson)
14 FEBRUARY	"The Trial of Mary Lincoln," *NET Opera Theater* (PBS)—original opera by composer Thomas Pasatieri and librettist Anne Howard Bailey
17 FEBRUARY et seq.	Coverage of President Nixon's trip to China (all networks)
21 FEBRUARY	"The Politics—and Comedy—of Woody Allen" (PBS)—Woody Allen in an original work followed by an interview
31 MARCH	"The Crucifixion of Jesus," *Appointment with Destiny* (CBS)—docu-drama filmed on location, narrated by John Huston, with Ron Greenblatt as Jesus (the print of the film was tinted gold)
16 APRIL et seq.	Coverage of the Apollo 16 voyage to the moon (all networks)
24 JULY	"The American Indian: This Was His Land," *ABC News Inquiry* (ABC)—documentary, narrated by Frank Reynolds
12–15 AUGUST	*War and Peace* (ABC)—the six-and-a-half-hour Russian film was shown in four parts
26 AUGUST –10 SEPTEMBER	Coverage of the Olympic Games from Munich (ABC)
10 SEPTEMBER	"Singer Presents Liza with a 'Z' " (NBC)—variety special with Liza Minnelli
10 SEPTEMBER	"The Cave People of the Philippines," *NBC Reports* (NBC)—documentary on the gentle Tasaday people
24 OCTOBER	"Of Thee I Sing" (CBS)—adaptation of George S. Kaufman's comedy, with Carroll O'Connor and Cloris Leachman
1 NOVEMBER	"That Certain Summer" (ABC)—drama about a homosexual father and his son, with Hal Holbrook, Martin Sheen, and Scott Jacoby

12 NOVEMBER	"The Trouble with People" (NBC)—five sketches written by Neil Simon, with George C. Scott, Gene Wilder, Renée Taylor, Alan Arkin, and Valerie Harper
24 NOVEMBER	"In Concert" (ABC)—the first of ABC's late night rock music specials; Alice Cooper's act causes ABC's Cincinnati affiliate to drop the show in midperformance
3 DECEMBER	"The House Without a Christmas Tree" (CBS)—drama with Mildred Natwick, Jason Robards, and Lisa Lucas
12 DECEMBER	"Once upon a Mattress" (CBS)—restaged version of the musical comedy, with Carol Burnett, Ken Berry, Jack Gilford, and Wally Cox
15 DECEMBER	"John Lennon and Yoko Ono: In Concert" (ABC)—benefit performance for the Willowbrook Home for Retarded Children
17 DECEMBER	"Portrait: The Woman I Love" (NBC)—biographical drama with Richard Chamberlain (as Edward VIII) and Faye Dunaway (as Wallis Warfield)
17 DECEMBER	"Sleeping Beauty" (PBS)—ballet, with Rudolf Nureyev, Veronica Tennant, and the National Ballet of Canada

1973

23 JANUARY	"The Incredible Flight of the Snow Geese" (NBC)—nature documentary filmed by Des and Jan Bartlett, narrated by Glen Campbell
1 FEBRUARY	"The Last King of America" (CBS)—drama with Peter Ustinov as King George III, interviewed by Eric Sevareid
11 FEBRUARY	"Duke Ellington ... We Love You Madly" (CBS)—an all-star tribute to Duke Ellington, with guests Count Basie, Ray Charles, Roberta Flack, Sammy Davis, Jr., Peggy Lee, and Sarah Vaughan
20 FEBRUARY	"A Brand New Life," *Tuesday Movie of the Week* (ABC)—drama with Cloris Leachman and Martin Balsam as a couple who have their first child after eighteen years of marriage
7 MARCH	"Dr. Jekyll and Mr. Hyde" (NBC)—musical version, with Kirk Douglas (in a rare TV ap-

	pearance), Susan Hampshire, Michael Redgrave, Susan George, and Donald Pleasance
8 MARCH	"The Marcus-Nelson Murders" (CBS)—the pilot for *Kojak*
10 MARCH	"Long Day's Journey into Night" (ABC)—drama with Laurence Olivier and Constance Cummings
15 MARCH	"Applause" (CBS)—adaptation of the Broadway hit, with Lauren Bacall
16 MARCH	"Acts of Love—and Other Comedies" (ABC)—short sketches written by Renée Taylor and Joseph Bologna, with Marlo Thomas, Art Garfunkel, and Gene Wilder
16 MARCH	"Lily Tomlin" (CBS)—comedy with Lily Tomlin and guests Richard Crenna and Richard Pryor
29 MARCH	"Pueblo," *ABC Theatre* (ABC)—docu-drama with Hal Holbrook
4 APRIL	"Elvis: Aloha from Hawaii" (NBC)—musical special taped in Honolulu with Elvis Presley
22 APRIL	"Portrait: A Man Whose Name Was John" (ABC)—biographical drama with Raymond Burr (as Pope John XXIII)
23 APRIL	"Adventures of Don Quixote" (CBS)—drama with Rex Harrison
24 APRIL	"The Lie," *Playhouse 90* (CBS)—drama written by Ingmar Bergman, with George Segal and Shirley Knight Hopkins
17 MAY– 15 NOVEMBER	Watergate coverage; the three commercial networks form a pool, with one network broadcasting live coverage of the hearings of the Senate Select Committee, and PBS broadcasting taped highlights each evening
5 JULY	"The First and Essential Freedom," *ABC News Special* (ABC)—documentary on the First Amendment and a free press
27 JULY	"POWs: The Black Homecoming," *ABC News Special* (ABC)—documentary on the adjustment of black POWs returned to the United States
17 AUGUST	"Sticks and Bones" (CBS)—controversial drama about a blinded Vietnam veteran, originally scheduled for March, with Cliff DeYoung, Tom Aldredge, Asa Gim, and Anne Jackson
20 SEPTEMBER	Tennis—Billie Jean King versus Bobby Riggs (ABC)—live

12 OCTOBER	"Dracula" (CBS)—drama with Jack Palance
2 NOVEMBER	"Barbra Streisand . . . and Other Musical Instruments" (CBS)—music with Barbra Streisand and guest Ray Charles
29 NOVEMBER	"Catholics," *Playhouse 90* (CBS)—drama with Trevor Howard and Martin Sheen
30 NOVEMBER–1 DECEMBER	"Frankenstein: The True Story" (NBC)—drama with Michael Sarrazin (as the creature), Leonard Whiting, and James Mason
16 DECEMBER	"A Child's Christmas in Wales" (CBS)—with narrator Michael Redgrave and the National Theatre of the Deaf
16 DECEMBER	"The Glass Menagerie" (ABC)—drama with Katharine Hepburn (in her TV dramatic debut) and Joanna Miles

1974

31 JANUARY	"The Autobiography of Miss Jane Pittman" (CBS)—biographical drama with Cicely Tyson
11 MARCH	"Marlo Thomas and Friends in Free to Be . . . You and Me" (ABC)—consciousness-raising special for adults and children
13 MARCH	"The Execution of Private Slovik," *NBC Wednesday Night at the Movies* (NBC)—docudrama with Martin Sheen
17 MARCH	"6 Rms Riv Vu" (CBS)—drama with Alan Alda and Carol Burnett
29–30 APRIL	"QB VII," *ABC Theatre* (ABC)—adaptation of Leon Uris's book, with Ben Gazzara, Anthony Hopkins, Leslie Caron, Lee Remick, and Jack Hawkins
24 JUNE	"Solzhenitsyn," *CBS News Special* (CBS)—interview
24–30 JULY	Coverage by all networks of the House Judiciary Committee debate on the impeachment of President Nixon
8 AUGUST	Nixon's resignation speech (all networks)
4 SEPTEMBER	"IBM Presents Clarence Darrow" (NBC)—drama with Henry Fonda
6 SEPTEMBER	"Mrs. Lincoln's Husband" (NBC)—first of the six-part *Sandburg's Lincoln* series, with Hal Holbrook and Sada Thompson

17 OCTOBER	"Rubinstein," *Great Performances* (PBS)—musical special
22 OCTOBER	"The Law," *NBC World Premiere Movie* (NBC)—drama with Judd Hirsch as a New York public defender (later a three-part mini-series)
29 OCTOBER	"The Mark of Zorro," *The ABC Tuesday Movie of the Week* (ABC)—drama with Frank Langella and Ricardo Montalban
28 NOVEMBER	"Shirley MacLaine: If They Could See Me Now" (CBS)—music and variety with Shirley MacLaine and guest Carol Burnett
18 DECEMBER	"The Missiles of October," *ABC Theatre* (ABC)—docu-drama with William Devane (as John Kennedy), Martin Sheen (Robert Kennedy), Howard Da Silva (Nikita Khrushchev), and Ralph Bellamy (Adlai Stevenson)

1975

12 JANUARY	"Judgment: The Court-Martial of Lieutenant William Calley," *ABC Theatre* (ABC)—docu-drama with Tony Musante (as Calley), Richard Basehart, and Bo Hopkins
14 JANUARY	"Satan's Triangle," *Tuesday Movie of the Week* (ABC)—drama with Kim Novak (in a rare TV appearance) and Doug McClure
10 FEBRUARY	"The Legend of Lizzie Borden," *ABC Monday Night Movie* (ABC)—drama, with Elizabeth Montgomery
11 FEBRUARY	"Sara T.—Portrait of a Teenage Alcoholic," *NBC World Premiere Movie* (NBC)—drama with Linda Blair
12 FEBRUARY	"Sad Figure, Laughing" (NBC)—second in the *Sandburg's Lincoln* series
13 FEBRUARY	"Queen of the Stardust Ballroom" (CBS)—drama with Maureen Stapleton and Charles Durning
22 FEBRUARY	"Hustling," *The ABC Saturday Night Movie* (ABC)—drama with Lee Remick and Jill Clayburgh
27 FEBRUARY	"In This House of Brede," *General Electric Theater* (CBS)—drama with Diana Rigg

6 MARCH	"Love among the Ruins," *ABC Theatre* (ABC)—drama with Laurence Olivier and Katharine Hepburn
7 APRIL	"Prairie Lawyer"—third of the *Sandburg's Lincoln* series
14 APRIL	"I Will Fight No More Forever," *ABC Theatre* (ABC)—drama about the Nez Perce Indians, with James Whitmore and Ned Romero
29 APRIL	"7,382 Days in Vietnam," *NBC News Special* (NBC)—retrospective
27 MAY	"A Moon for the Misbegotten," *ABC Theatre* (ABC)—adaptation of Eugene O'Neill's play, with Jason Robards and Colleen Dewhurst
25 JULY	"Lily Tomlin" (ABC)—comedy special
3 SEPTEMBER	"The Unwilling Warrior" (NBC)—fourth of the *Sandburg's Lincoln* series
2 OCTOBER	"Fear on Trial" (CBS)—biographical drama with William Devane (as blacklisted broadcaster John Henry Faulk) and George C. Scott (as attorney Louis Nizer)
23 OCTOBER	"Babe" (CBS)—biographical drama with Susan Clark (as athlete Mildred Zaharias) and Alex Karras
28 OCTOBER	"The Incredible Machine" (PBS)—special about the human body, narrated by E. G. Marshall

1976

11–12 JANUARY	"Eleanor and Franklin," *ABC Theatre* (ABC)—biographical drama with Jane Alexander and Edward Herrman as Eleanor and Franklin Roosevelt (a sequel aired in 1977)
12 JANUARY	"Crossing Fox River" (NBC)—fifth in the *Sandburg's Lincoln* series
26 FEBRUARY	"The Lindbergh Kidnapping Case," *NBC Thursday Night at the Movies* (NBC)—docudrama with Cliff DeYoung (as Charles Lindbergh), Anthony Hopkins (Bruno Hauptmann), Joseph Cotten, and Walter Pidgeon
10 MARCH	"The Entertainer" (NBC)—drama with music, with Jack Lemmon, Ray Bolger, and Sada Thompson
1–2 APRIL	"Helter Skelter" (CBS)—four-hour adaptation of prosecutor Vincent Bugliosi's book about the

Charles Manson case, with George DiCenzo (Bugliosi) and Steve Railsback (Manson)

14 APRIL   "The Last Days" (NBC)—sixth and final telecast of the *Sandburg's Lincoln* series

22 APRIL   "Judge Horton and the Scottsboro Boys," *NBC World Premiere Movie* (NBC)—drama based on a 1931 rape trial, with Arthur Hill and Vera Miles

4 JULY   "In Celebration of US" (CBS)—sixteen-hour coverage of America's bicentennial celebrations, plus satellite transmission from England (with Alistair Cooke)

23 SEPTEMBER   The Ford-Carter Debate (all networks)—the first of three debates, broadcast live from Philadelphia

25 OCTOBER   "Amelia Earhart," *NBC Monday Night at the Movies* (NBC)—biographical drama, with Susan Clark

7–8 NOVEMBER   "Gone with the Wind" (NBC)—first television broadcast of the movie (highest-rated movie in TV history)

12 NOVEMBER   "The Boy in the Plastic Bubble," *The ABC Friday Night Movie* (ABC)—drama, with John Travolta, Diana Hyland, and Glynnis O'Connor

14–15 NOVEMBER   "Sybil," *The Big Event* (NBC)—drama based on a true case history of a multiple personality, with Sally Field (as Sybil) and Joanne Woodward

25 NOVEMBER   "Sills and Burnett at the Met" (CBS)—music, with Beverly Sills and Carol Burnett

6 DECEMBER   "Cat on a Hot Tin Roof," *NBC Monday Night at the Movies* (NBC)—new production, with Laurence Olivier, Natalie Wood, Robert Wagner, and Maureen Stapleton

9 DECEMBER   "America Salutes Richard Rodgers: The Sound of His Music" (CBS)—musical variety hosted by Gene Kelly (as Oscar Hammerstein II) and Henry Winkler (Lorenz Hart)

13 DECEMBER   "Victory at Entebbe" (ABC)—three-hour special based on the rescue of a hijacked airliner by Israeli commandos, with Burt Lancaster, Anthony Hopkins, Helen Hayes, Elizabeth Taylor, Linda Blair, Kirk Douglas, and Richard Dreyfuss

29 DECEMBER   "The Belle of Amherst" (PBS)—one-woman show by Julie Harris (as Emily Dickinson)

1977

9 JANUARY — "Raid on Entebbe," *The Big Event* (NBC)—dramatization of the raid by Israeli commandos on a hijacked airliner, with Charles Bronson, Peter Finch, and Yaphet Kotto

16 JANUARY — "Little Ladies of the Night," *The ABC Sunday Night Movie* (ABC)—drama on teenage prostitution (one of the highest-rated made-for-TV movies in history), with David Soul, Lou Gossett, and Linda Purl

19 JANUARY — "Inaugural Eve Gala Performance" (CBS)—variety from Washington, D.C., with an all-star cast (including Freddie Prinze, who died ten days later)

6 FEBRUARY — "Tail Gunner Joe," *The Big Event* (NBC)—biographical drama with Peter Boyle (as Senator Joseph McCarthy), Burgess Meredith, and Patricia Neal

13 MARCH — "Eleanor and Franklin: The White House Years," *ABC Theatre* (ABC)—sequel to "Eleanor and Franklin," with Jane Alexander and Edward Herrmann

22 MARCH — "The Fire Next Door," *CBS Reports* (CBS)—documentary on arson in the South Bronx, with Bill Moyers

13–14 APRIL — "The Amazing Howard Hughes" (CBS)—biographical drama with Tommy Lee Jones, Ed Flanders, and Tovah Feldshuh

21 APRIL — "Sinatra and Friends" (ABC)—music, with Frank Sinatra, Tony Bennett, Natalie Cole, and John Denver

5 MAY — "The Richard Pryor Special?" (NBC)—Richard Pryor's first comedy special, with guests John Belushi, Maya Angelou, and Mike Evans

26 SEPTEMBER — "In the Matter of Karen Ann Quinlan," *NBC World Premiere Movie* (NBC)—docu-drama with Brian Keith and Piper Laurie

30 SEPTEMBER and 2 OCTOBER — "The Trial of Lee Harvey Oswald" (ABC)—drama speculating on what might have happened if Lee Harvey Oswald had lived, with John Pleshette (as Oswald), Ben Gazzara, and Lorne Greene

19 NOVEMBER	"Contract on Cherry Street," *Saturday Night at the Movies* (NBC)—drama with Frank Sinatra as a vigilante cop
24 NOVEMBER	"The Happy World of Hanna-Barbera" (CBS)—prime-time retrospective of Hanna-Barbera Studios, one of TV's major suppliers of animated features
25 NOVEMBER	"Rolling Stone: The Tenth Anniversary" (CBS)—celebrating a decade of *Rolling Stone* magazine, with guests such as Bette Midler, Steve Martin, Sissy Spacek, and Martin Sheen
27 NOVEMBER	"Doonesbury" (NBC)—animated special based on the Pulitzer-Prize-winning comic strip drawn by Garry Trudeau (animation for TV done by Faith and John Hubley)
7 DECEMBER	"Bette Midler" (NBC)—music with Bette Midler and guests Dustin Hoffman and Emmett Kelly
20 DECEMBER	"Greenpeace: Voyages to Save the Whale" (PBS)—documentary on the conservation efforts of the Greenpeace Foundation

1978

1 FEBRUARY	"See How She Runs," *General Electric Theater* (CBS)—drama with Joanne Woodward as a forty-year-old marathoner
5 FEBRUARY	"ABC's Silver Anniversary Celebration" (ABC)—a retrospective
12–13–14 FEBRUARY	"King" (NBC)—biographical drama with Paul Winfield (as Martin Luther King, Jr.) and Cicely Tyson (as Coretta King)
2 MARCH	"Ben Vereen: Showcase for a Man of Many Talents" (ABC)—variety with Ben Vereen and guests Cheryl Ladd and Louis Gossett, Jr.
5 MARCH	"TV: The Fabulous Fifties" (NBC)—another retrospective
6 MARCH	"The Body Human" (CBS)—science documentary
13 MARCH	"Gene Kelly: An American in Pasadena" (CBS)—variety with Gene Kelly and guests Frank Sinatra, Cyd Charisse, Cindy Williams, Lucille Ball, and Liza Minnelli

26 MARCH– 1 APRIL	"CBS: On the Air" (CBS)—a nine-and-one-half-hour retrospective spread out over seven nights
26 MARCH	"Tribute to 'Mr. Television,' Milton Berle" (NBC)—clips of Berle's shows, plus appearances by Frank Sinatra, Johnny Carson, Bob Hope, and Lucille Ball
9 APRIL	"A Family Upside Down" (NBC)—drama with Fred Astaire, Helen Hayes, and Patty Duke Astin
MAY	"The Bastard" or "The Kent Family Chronicles" (SYNDICATED)—a two-part adaptation of John Jakes's novel, with Andrew Stevens and Buddy Ebsen
21 MAY	"Ziegfeld: The Man and His Women" (NBC)—biographical drama with Paul Shenar, Samantha Eggar, Barbara Parkins, Valerie Perrine, and Pamela Peadon
25 JUNE	"The Last Tenant," *ABC Theatre* (ABC)—drama, with Lee Strasberg (in a rare TV appearance) and Tony LoBianco
28 JUNE	"Youth Terror: The View from Behind the Gun," *ABC News Closeup* (ABC)—a cinema-verité look at urban street gangs
14 JULY	"Evening of French Television" (PBS)—a three-hour sampler
22 AUGUST	"Steve and Eydie Celebrate Irving Berlin" (NBC)—a tribute to Irving Berlin on his ninetieth birthday, with Steve Lawrence, Eydie Gormé, Carol Burnett, and Sammy Davis, Jr.
24 SEPTEMBER	"Horowitz—Live!" (NBC)—Vladimir Horowitz and the New York Philharmonic from Lincoln Center
26 SEPTEMBER	"One in a Million: The Ron LeFlore Story" (CBS)—biographical drama with LeVar Burton (as Ron LeFlore, who went from prison to professional baseball), Paul Benjamin, Larry B. Scott, and Billy Martin (as himself)
8 NOVEMBER	"First You Cry" (CBS)—biographical drama with Mary Tyler Moore (as breast cancer victim Betty Rollin), Anthony Perkins, and Richard Crenna
11–12 DECEMBER	"A Woman Called Moses," *NBC World Premiere Movie* (NBC)—biographical drama with Cicely Tyson (as ex-slave Harriet Tubman)

| 14 DECEMBER | "Rockette: A Holiday Tribute to the Radio City Music Hall" (NBC)—variety-drama, with host Gregory Peck (in a rare TV appearance), Ann-Margret, and Ben Vereen |

1979

10 JANUARY	"A Gift of Song" (NBC)—a musical benefit for UNICEF, hosted by David Frost, with the Bee Gees, John Denver, Elton John, and Rod Stewart
28 JANUARY	". . . And Your Name Is Jonah" (CBS)—drama starring Sally Struthers and James Woods as parents and Jeffrey Bravin as their deaf son
29 JANUARY	"The Corn Is Green" (CBS)—drama starring Katharine Hepburn as a Welsh schoolteacher
9 FEBRUARY	"Heroes of Rock 'n' Roll" (ABC)—musical retrospective hosted by Jeff Bridges
11 FEBRUARY	"Elvis" (ABC)—three-hour biographical drama starring Kurt Russell as Elvis Presley
14 FEBRUARY	"Dolly and Carol in Nashville" (CBS)—variety, with Dolly Parton and Carol Burnett
3 MARCH	"Live from the Grand Ole Opry" (PBS)—six-hour fund raiser, with a host of country and western music stars
4 MARCH	"The Ordeal of Patty Hearst" (ABC)—docudrama starring Lisa Eilbacher as kidnap victim Patty Hearst
12 MARCH	"The American Film Institute Salute to Alfred Hitchcock" (CBS)—tribute to director Alfred Hitchcock, hosted by Ingrid Bergman
13 MARCH	"Einstein's Universe" (PBS)—two-hour documentary hosted by Peter Ustinov (televised on the eve of the one-hundredth anniversary of Einstein's birth)
1, 2, 3, 8 APRIL	"Jesus of Nazareth" (NBC)—an expanded version of Franco Zeffirelli's film, previously shown in 1977
15 APRIL	"Baryshnikov at the White House" (PBS)—excerpts from ballet dancer Mikhail Baryshnikov's February recital at the White House
22 APRIL	"Friendly Fire," *ABC Theatre* (ABC)—an adaptation of C. D. B. Bryan's book about the efforts

of an Iowa couple to learn the truth of their son's death in Vietnam, starring Carol Burnett and Ned Beatty as Peg and Gene Mullen

28 APRIL — "I Know Why the Caged Bird Sings" (CBS)—an adaptation of Maya Angelou's book about growing up in Arkansas, starring Constance Good and Esther Rolle

14 MAY — "The Television Annual 1978/79" (ABC)—a two-hour retrospective of the 1978–1979 TV season

22 MAY — "The Helen Reddy Special" (ABC)—variety, with Helen Reddy and guests Jane Fonda and Elliott Gould (the special had originally been sold to NBC, but was bought back from that network by the producers following a dispute over the air date)

8 JUNE — "The Shooting of Big Man: Anatomy of a Criminal Case," *ABC News Closeup* (ABC)—documentary detailing the investigation and trial of a criminal case in Seattle

24 and 25 JULY — "Blacks in America: With All Deliberate Speed?" *CBS Reports* (CBS)—an examination of 25 years of desegregation, hosted by Ed Bradley

11 SEPTEMBER — "Can You Hear the Laughter? The Story of Freddie Prinze" (CBS)—biographical drama starring Ira Angustain as the late comedian

16 SEPTEMBER — "The Road to China" (NBC)—three-hour variety special starring Bob Hope, produced on location in China

1 OCTOBER et seq. — Coverage by all three commercial networks of the visit of Pope John Paul II to the United States

1 OCTOBER — "The Tonight Show Starring Johnny Carson" (NBC)—the seventeenth-anniversary show, broadcast live in prime time

8 OCTOBER — "Paul Robeson" (PBS)—one-man show starring James Earl Jones

8 OCTOBER — "When Hell Was in Session," *NBC Theatre* (NBC)—docu-drama starring Hal Holbrook as Admiral Jeremiah Denton, an American POW in North Vietnam

14 OCTOBER — "The Miracle Worker," *NBC Theatre* (NBC)—drama with Patty Duke Astin (who had played Helen Keller in the Broadway and film versions

	twenty years earlier) as Annie Sullivan and Melissa Gilbert as Helen Keller
29 and 31 OCTOBER	"Freedom Road" (NBC)—four-hour historical drama starring Muhammad Ali as Gideon Jackson, a former slave who became a U.S. senator
12 NOVEMBER	"Jane Fonda" (PBS)—biography of the activist actress, filmed by the BBC in 1977
17 NOVEMBER	"Puff the Magic Dragon" (CBS)—animated fantasy for children, narrated by Burgess Meredith
7 DECEMBER	"Valentine" (ABC)—made-for-TV movie starring Mary Martin (in a rare TV dramatic role) and Jack Albertson as septuagenarians who fall in love
16 DECEMBER	"An American Christmas Carol" (ABC)—an updated version of the Dickens story, starring Henry Winkler as Benedict Slade
18 DECEMBER	"Homosexuals," *ABC News Closeup* (ABC)—cinema verité study of urban homosexual lifestyles
28 and 29 DECEMBER	"American Dream, American Nightmare" (CBS)—retrospective of the 1970s

1980

9 JANUARY	"The Lathe of Heaven" (PBS)—science-fiction drama starring Bruce Davison and Kevin Conway
9 JANUARY	"Live from Studio 8H" (NBC)—first of a series of cultural specials, featuring a tribute to conductor Arturo Toscanini
27–28–29 JANUARY	"The Martian Chronicles" (NBC)—six-hour adaptation of Ray Bradbury's science-fiction story, with Rock Hudson, Gayle Hunnicutt, and Darren McGavin

PART III

PRIME TIMES

Explanatory notes: The following charts show the prime-time fall schedules for each of the three surviving commercial networks. The times shown are the times when the network broadcast the program (eastern standard time), rather than when a local affiliate broadcast it; in most cases, however, the New York City network affiliates (particularly those of CBS and NBC) carried network programs at the same time as the network.

Series that appear in boldface are new for that season; a series is considered "new" if it premiered after 1 June in a given year. Series that are shaded are those which were canceled that season. A series is deemed canceled if it did not appear on a regularly scheduled first-run basis on a network schedule for the following fall season. Examples: *Father Knows Best* is deemed canceled during the 1960–1961 season, though it was rerun in prime time the following season. *The Twilight Zone* is deemed canceled during the 1961–1962 season, though it returned the following midseason. *Police Story* is deemed canceled during the 1976–1977 season, though a few *Police Story* specials were broadcast during the following season. The chart for the 1979–1980 season does not indicate which shows were canceled during that period because full information on the 1980–1981 network schedules was not available at the time the book went to press.

The numbers that appear at the right of the boxes indicate the age of the series in seasons.

Motion pictures are not considered "series" for the purposes of renewal or cancellation. The titles of some series have been abbreviated as a matter of convenience.

KEY TO NETWORK-SCHEDULE CHARTS	
*	New network affiliation
†	Reruns
‡	Once a month
§	Every fourth week
‖	Alternating every fourth week
#	Concurrently running on two networks
**	From 6:30 p.m.
††	To 11:30 p.m.
‡‡	From late afternoon

1948–1949

Prime-time network television schedule grid (times shown across the top; networks at right).

Day	Net	7:00	7:30	8:00	8:30	9:00	9:30	10:00	10:30	11:00
SUN	ABC	LOCAL		HOLLYWOOD SCREEN TEST	ACTORS' STUDIO	LOCAL				
	CBS	WEEK IN REVIEW / FILM [2]	FORD THEATER / STUDIO ONE			THE ED SULLIVAN SHOW		NEWS-REEL		
	NBC	MARY KAY & JOHNNY / NEWS	WELCOME ABOARD	PAULINE FREDERICK		PHILCO TELEVISION PLAYHOUSE				
MON	ABC		KIERNAN'S CORNER	QUIZZING THE NEWS	RIDDLE ME THIS	LOCAL				
	CBS		NEWS / FACE THE MUSIC [2]	PRIZE PARTY	TALENT SCOUTS					
	NBC		AUTHOR MEETS THE CRITICS [2] / NEWS	TELE-THEATRE	MEET THE PRESS [2]	SPORTING EVENT				
TUE	ABC		CHILD'S WORLD	FILM	AMERICA'S TOWN MEETING					
	CBS		NEWS / FACE THE MUSIC [2]	FILM	BEN GRAUER'S AMERICANA [2]	WE THE PEOPLE	PEOPLE'S PLATFORM	NEWS-REEL		
	NBC		AMERICAN SONG [2] / NEWS	THE MILTON BERLE SHOW		M.M. McBRIDE	WRESTLING			
WED	ABC		BUZZY WUZZY	CLUB SEVEN	QUIZZING THE NEWS	WRESTLING				
	CBS		NEWS / FACE THE MUSIC [2]	KOBB'S KORNER	WINNER TAKE ALL	BOXING (PABST BLUE RIBBON BOUTS)				
	NBC		YOU ARE AN ARTIST [3] / NEWS	GIRL ABOUT TOWN / FILM	RICHARD HARKNESS [2]	KRAFT TELEVISION THEATER		NEWS-REEL	THE VILLAGE BARN [2]	
THU	ABC		LOCAL	FASHION STORY	CRITIC AT LARGE	LOCAL				
	CBS		NEWS	DIONE LUCAS COOKING SHOW [2]	FILMS			NEWS-REEL		
	NBC		NEWS	LANNY ROSS [2]	NATURE OF THGS. [2]					
FRI	ABC		RED CABOOSE	FILM	GAY NINETIES REVUE	GULF ROAD SHOW	BIGELOW SHOW			
	CBS		NEWS / FACE THE MUSIC [2]	CANDID MICROPHONE	WHAT'S IT WORTH? [2]	BREAK THE BANK	LOCAL			
	NBC		MUSICAL MERRYGRD. [2] / NEWS	CAPT. BILLY'S MUSIC HALL	STOP ME IF YOU HEARD THIS ONE [2]	I'D LIKE TO SEE	BOXING (GILLETTE CAVALCADE OF SPORTS)			
SAT	ABC		ABC SPORTS		SPORTING EVENT	LOCAL				
	CBS	FILMS	FILM	LOCAL		LOCAL				
	NBC		FILMS	PROGRAM PREVIEW	TV SCREEN MAGAZINE [3]	FILMS [3]				

NOTES: [1]Girl of the Week (7:45) [2]Sportsmen's Quiz (8:00)

1949–1950

Day	Net	7	7:30	8	8:30	9	9:30	10	10:30	11 PM
SUN	ABC	PAUL WHITEMAN REVUE	PENTHOUSE PLAYERS [2]	THINK FAST [2]	LITTLE REVUE [2]	LET THERE BE STARS		CELEBRITY TIME	YOUTH ON THE MARCH [2]	
	CBS	TONIGHT ON BROADWAY [2]	THIS IS SHOW BUSINESS	THE ED SULLIVAN SHOW			THE FRED WARING SHOW [2]	WEEK IN REVIEW [3]		
	NBC	LEAVE IT TO THE GIRLS [2]	ALDRICH FAMILY		COLGATE THEATRE [2]	PHILCO TELEVISION PLAYHOUSE [2]		GARROWAY AT LARGE [2]	LOCAL	
MON	ABC	LOCAL		LOCAL	AUTHOR MEETS THE CRITICS [3]	MR. BLACK	WRESTLING			
	CBS	NEWS	SONNY KENDIS [2]	SILVER THEATER	TALENT SCOUTS	CANDID CAMERA [2]	GOLDBERGS [2]	STUDIO ONE [2]		
	NBC	NEWS	MORTON DOWNEY [2]	TELE-THEATRE [2]	VOICE OF FIRESTONE [2]	LIGHTS OUT	BAND OF AMERICA	QUIZ KIDS		
TUE	ABC	LOCAL		FILM			ON TRIAL		PANTOMIME QUIZ [*3]	
	CBS	NEWS	SONNY KENDIS [2]			ACTORS' STUDIO [2]	SUSPENSE [2]	THIS WK. IN SPTS. [2]	BLUES BY BARGY	
	NBC	NEWS	ROBERTA QUINLAN [2]	THE MILTON BERLE SHOW		FIRESIDE THEATRE [2]	LIFE OF RILEY [2]	TED MACK'S AMATEUR HOUR [*3]		
WED	ABC	LOCAL		PHOTOPLAY TIME	PHOTOCRIME	FILM	WRESTLING		LOCAL [*2]	
	CBS	NEWS	MASLAND AT HOME	ARTHUR GODFREY & HIS FRIENDS		BIGELOW SHOW [2]	BOXING (PABST BLUE RIBBON BOUTS) [4]			
	NBC	NEWS	MORTON DOWNEY [2]	CRISIS	THE CLOCK	KRAFT TELEVISION THEATER		BREAK THE BANK [*2]	TOP VIEW IN SPORT	
THU	ABC		LONE RANGER	STOP THE MUSIC		CRUSADE IN EUROPE [2]	STARRING BORIS KARLOFF [2]	ROLLER DERBY		
	CBS	NEWS	SONNY KENDIS [2]	THE FRONT PAGE	INSIDE U.S.A. / ROMANCE	ED WYNN SHOW	FILM		BLUES BY BARGY [2] / NEWS-REEL	
	NBC	NEWS	ROBERTA QUINLAN [2]	SPECIALS	MARY KAY & JOHNNY	FIREBALL FUN FOR ALL		MARTIN KANE	LOCAL	
FRI	ABC	FILM		MAJORITY RULES	BLIND DATE	AUCTION-AIRE [2]	FUN FOR THE MONEY	ROLLER DERBY		
	CBS	NEWS	AMAZING POLGAR [1]	MAMA	MAN AGAINST CRIME	FORD THEATER / 54TH ST. REVUE [2] / THEATER HOUR		PEOPLE'S PLATFORM [2]	CAPITOL CLOAKROOM [2]	
	NBC		MORTON DOWNEY [2]	ONE MAN'S FAMILY	WE THE PEOPLE [*2]	VERSATILE VARIETIES	BIG STORY	BOXING (GILLETTE CAVALCADE OF SPORTS) [2]		
SAT	ABC	HOLLYWOOD SCREEN TEST		TV TEEN CLUB		FILM				
	CBS	IN THE 1ST POSITION [2]	BLUES BY BARGY [2]	WINNER TAKE ALL	FILMS					
	NBC	NATURE OF THINGS [2]	NEWS [2]	MEET YOUR CONGRESS	MIXED DOUBLES	WHO SAID THAT [2]	MEET THE PRESS [2]	FILM [3]		

NOTE: [1] *Ruthie on the Telephone* (7:55 p.m.)

1950–1951

Day	Net	7:00	7:30	8:00	8:30	9:00	9:30	10:00	10:30	11 PM
SUN	ABC	Paul Whiteman Revue	Showtime USA	Hollywood Theater Time	Sit or Miss	Marshall Plan in Action	Local	Old Fashioned Meeting	Youth on the March	ABC
	CBS	Gene Autry	This Is Show Business	The Ed Sullivan Show		The Fred Waring Show		Celebrity Time	What's My Line	CBS
	NBC	Leave It to the Girls		The Colgate Comedy Hour		Philco Television Playhouse		Garroway at Large	Take a Chance	NBC
MON	ABC		Hollywood Screen Test	Treasury Men in Action		College Bowl (Chico Marx)	On Trial	Film		ABC
	CBS		News / Perry Como	Lux Video Theatre		Horace Heidt	Goldbergs	Studio One		CBS
	NBC		News / Roberta Quinlan	Paul Winchell	Voice of Firestone	Lights Out	Robert Montgomery Presents / Musical Comedy Time		Talent Search	NBC
TUE	ABC			Beulah	Buck Rogers	Billy Rose's Playbill	Can You Top This	Life Begins at Eighty	Roller Derby	ABC
	CBS		News — Faye Emerson	Sure as Fate / Prudential Family Theater		Camel Caravan	Suspense	Danger	We Take Your Word	CBS
	NBC		Little Show / News	The Milton Berle Show		Fireside Theater	Armstrong Circle Th.	Ted Mack's Amateur Hour		NBC
WED	ABC		Chance of a Lifetime	Film		Don McNeill's TV Club		Wrestling		ABC
	CBS		News / Perry Como	Arthur Godfrey & His Friends		Somerset Maugham Theater	The Web	Pabst Blue Ribbon Bouts		CBS
	NBC		News / Roberta Quinlan	Four Star Revue		Kraft Television Theater		Break the Bank	Stars Over Hollywood	NBC
THU	ABC		Lone Ranger	Stop the Music		Holiday Hotel	Blind Date	I Cover Times Square	Roller Derby	ABC
	CBS		News — Faye Emerson	Starlight Th. / Burns & Allen	The Show Goes On	Alan Young Show	Big Town	Truth or Consequences	Airflyte Theatre	CBS
	NBC		Little Show / News	You Bet Your Life	Peter Lind Hayes Show	College of Musical Knowledge		Martin Kane	Quick on the Draw	NBC
FRI	ABC		Life with Linkletter	Soap Box Theater	Pro Football Highlights	Pulitzer Prize Playhouse		Penthouse Party	Studs' Place	ABC
	CBS		News / Perry Como	Mama	Man Against Crime	Ford Theater		Star of the Family	Beat the Clock	CBS
	NBC		News / Roberta Quinlan	Quiz Kids	We the People	Magnavox Theater / Versatile Varieties	The Clock / Big Story	Gillette Cavalcade of Sports		NBC
SAT	ABC		Stu Erwin Show	TV Teen Club		Roller Derby				ABC
	CBS		Week in Review / Faye Emerson	The Ken Murray Show		The Frank Sinatra Show		Sing It Again		CBS
	NBC		One Man's Family	All-Star Revue		Your Show of Shows			Your Hit Parade	NBC

1951–1952

Day	Net	7	7:30	8	8:30	9	9:30	10	10:30	11 PM
SUN	ABC	PAUL WHITEMAN REVUE 3	BY-LINE 3	MOVIE		THE FRED WARING SHOW	LOCAL	BILLY GRAHAM	YOUTH ON THE MARCH	3
SUN	CBS	GENE AUTRY	THIS IS SHOW BUSINESS 3	THE ED SULLIVAN SHOW				CELEBRITY TIME 4	WHAT'S MY LINE 4	3
SUN	NBC	SOUND-OFF TIME	YOUNG MR. BOBBIN	THE COLGATE COMEDY HOUR		PHILCO TELEVISION PLAYHOUSE 4 / GOODYEAR TELEVISION PLAYHOUSE 4		RED SKELTON 4	LEAVE IT TO THE GIRLS 4	4
MON	ABC		HOLLYWOOD SCREEN TEST 3	THE AMAZING MR. MALONE 3	LIFE BEGINS AT EIGHTY	FILM 3		BILL GWINN SHOW 2	STUDS' PLACE 3	3
MON	CBS		NEWS / PERRY COMO 4	LUX VIDEO THEATRE 4	TALENT SCOUTS 2	I LOVE LUCY 4	IT'S NEWS TO ME 2	STUDIO ONE 2		4
MON	NBC		THOSE TWO / NEWS	PAUL WINCHELL 2	VOICE OF FIRESTONE 2	LIGHTS OUT 4	ROBERT MONTGOMERY PRESENTS 3 / SOMERSET MAUGHAM THEATRE		LOCAL *2 3	
TUE	ABC		BEULAH 2	CHARLIE WILD 2	HOW DID THEY GET THAT WAY *2 2	UNITED OR NOT 4	ON TRIAL 4	LOCAL 4	ACTORS HOTEL	
TUE	CBS		NEWS / STORK CLUB 2	THE FRANK SINATRA SHOW 2		CRIME SYNDICATED 2	SUSPENSE 4	DANGER 2	LOCAL 2	
TUE	NBC		DINAH SHORE / NEWS 2	THE MILTON BERLE SHOW 4		FIRESIDE THEATER 4	ARMSTRONG CIRCLE TH. 4	TED MACK'S AMATEUR HOUR 3		5
WED	ABC		CHANCE OF A LIFETIME 2	THE PAUL DIXON SHOW 2		A. MURRAY / DON McNEILL 2	THE CLOCK 2	CELANESE THEATER / KING'S CROSSROADS *4 4		
WED	CBS		NEWS / PERRY COMO 4	ARTHUR GODFREY & HIS FRIENDS 4		STRIKE IT RICH 4	THE WEB 2	PABST BLUE RIBBON BOUTS 4		4
WED	NBC		THOSE TWO / NEWS	THE KATE SMITH EVENING HOUR		KRAFT TELEVISION THEATER		BREAK THE BANK 6	FREDDY MARTIN 4	
THU	ABC		LONE RANGER 3	STOP THE MUSIC		HERB SHRINER 4	GRUEN GUILD PLAYHOUSE	PAUL DIXON SHOW	MASLAND AT HOME / CARMEL MYERS	
THU	CBS		NEWS / STORK CLUB 3	BURNS & ALLEN 2 / STAR OF FAMILY 2	AMOS & ANDY 2	ALAN YOUNG 3	BIG TOWN 3	RACKET SQUAD 2	CRIME PHOTOG.	2
THU	NBC		DINAH SHORE / NEWS	YOU BET YOUR LIFE 2	TREASURY MEN IN ACTION *2 2	FORD FESTIVAL *2 2		MARTIN KANE 2	LOCAL *3 3	
FRI	ABC		LIFE W/LINK/'R / SAY IT W/ACT *2 2	MARK SABER *2 2		CRIME WITH FATHER 2	VERSATILE VAR / TALES OF TOMORROW	LIVE LIKE A MILLIONAIRE *3 2	HOLLYWOOD OPENING NIGHT 2	
FRI	CBS		NEWS / PERRY COMO 4	MAMA 4	MAN AGAINST CRIME 3	SCHLITZ PLAYHOUSE OF STARS 3		LOCAL	LOCAL	
FRI	NBC		THOSE TWO / NEWS	RCA VICTOR SHOW (EZIO PINZA) 4	WE THE PEOPLE 2	BIG STORY 4	ALDRICH FAMILY 3	GILLETTE CAVALCADE OF SPORTS 3		4
SAT	ABC		LOCAL	TV TEEN CLUB		LOCAL		LOCAL		
SAT	CBS		BEAT THE CLOCK	THE KEN MURRAY SHOW 3		FAYE EMERSON'S WONDERFUL TOWN 3	THE SHOW GOES ON 3	SONGS FOR SALE 3		2
SAT	NBC		ONE MAN'S FAMILY	ALL-STAR REVUE 3		YOUR SHOW OF SHOWS 3			YOUR HIT PARADE 3	2

1952–1953

Day	Net	7:00	7:30	8:00	8:30	9:00	9:30	10:00	10:30	11 PM
SUN	ABC	YOU ASKED FOR IT *3	LOCAL	ALL-STAR NEWS		FILM	THIS IS THE LIFE	BILLY GRAHAM 2 / LOCAL	ANYWHERE USA	ABC
SUN	CBS	GENE AUTRY 3	THIS IS SHOWBIZ 3 / JACK BENNY 4	THE ED SULLIVAN SHOW 4		THE FRED WARING SHOW 5	BREAK THE BANK 5	THE WEB *5	WHAT'S MY LINE 3	CBS 4
SUN	NBC	RED SKELTON 2	DOC CORKLE 2	THE COLGATE COMEDY HOUR		PHILCO TELEVISION PLAYHOUSE 5 / GOODYEAR TELEVISION PLAYHOUSE 2		THE DOCTOR	LOCAL	NBC 5
MON	ABC			HOLLYWOOD SCREEN TEST 5	MARK SABER 2	THE HOT SEAT 2		LOCAL	LOCAL	ABC
MON	CBS		NEWS / PERRY COMO 5	LUX VIDEO THEATRE 3	TALENT SCOUTS 3	I LOVE LUCY 5	LIFE WITH LUIGI 2	STUDIO ONE		CBS 5
MON	NBC		THOSE TWO 2 / NEWS	PAUL WINCHELL 3	VOICE OF FIRESTONE 3	HOLLYWOOD OPEN. NIGHT 4	ROBERT MONTGOMERY PRESENTS *2		WHO SAID THAT? 4	NBC 5
TUE	ABC		BEULAH 3	LOCAL	LEAVE IT TO LARRY			LOCAL	LOCAL	ABC
TUE	CBS		NEWS / HEAVEN FOR BETSY 5		RED BUTTONS	CRIME SYND. / CITY HOSPITAL 2	SUSPENSE 2	DANGER 5	LOCAL	CBS
TUE	NBC		DINAH SHORE 2 / NEWS	THE MILTON BERLE SHOW	THE BUICK CIRCUS HOUR	FIRESIDE THEATER 5	ARMSTRONG CIRCLE TH. 4	TWO FOR THE MONEY 4	BOB & RAY / BOB CONSIDINE 3	NBC
WED	ABC		THE NAME'S THE SAME 2	ALL-STAR NEWS 2		ELLERY QUEEN *2	MARCH OF TIME 2	WRESTLING 2		ABC
WED	CBS		PERRY COMO 5 / NEWS	ARTHUR GODFREY & HIS FRIENDS		STRIKE IT RICH 5	MAN AGAINST CRIME 2	PABST BLUE RIBBON BOUTS 5		CBS 5
WED	NBC		THOSE TWO 2 / NEWS	I MARRIED JOAN 5	CAVALCADE OF AMERICA / SCOTT MUSIC HALL	KRAFT TELEVISION THEATER				NBC
THU	ABC		LONE RANGER 4	ALL-STAR NEWS 4		PERSPECTIVE 3	ON GUARD 2	LOCAL	LOCAL	ABC
THU	CBS		NEWS / HEAVEN FOR BETSY 5	BURNS & ALLEN	AMOS & ANDY / FOUR STAR PLAYHOUSE	BIFF BAKER USA 2	BIG TOWN 2	RACKET SQUAD 3	I'VE GOT A SECRET 2	CBS
THU	NBC		DINAH SHORE 2 / NEWS	YOU BET YOUR LIFE 3	TREASURY MEN IN ACTION 3	DRAGNET 2	GANGBUSTERS 3	MARTIN KANE *4	LOCAL	NBC
FRI	ABC		STU ERWIN SHOW 3	OZZIE & HARRIET 3	ALL-STAR NEWS 3	TALES OF TOMORROW 2		LOCAL	LOCAL	ABC
FRI	CBS		NEWS / PERRY COMO 5	MAMA 4	MY FRIEND IRMA 4	SCHLITZ PLAYHOUSE 2	OUR MISS BROOKS 2	MR. & MRS. NORTH 2	LOCAL	CBS
FRI	NBC		THOSE TWO 2 / NEWS	RCA VICTOR SHOW (DENNIS DAY) 5	GULF PLAYHOUSE 2	BIG STORY 4	ALDRICH FAMILY 4	GILLETTE CAVALCADE OF SPORTS 4		NBC 5
SAT	ABC		LIVE LIKE A MILLIONAIRE *3	FILM		LOCAL		LOCAL		ABC
SAT	CBS		BEAT THE CLOCK 4	THE JACKIE GLEASON SHOW		JANE FROMAN'S USA CANTEEN 4	MEET MILLIE	BALANCE YOUR BUDGET	BATTLE OF THE AGES *2	CBS
SAT	NBC		MY HERO 3	ALL-STAR REVUE		YOUR SHOW OF SHOWS			YOUR HIT PARADE 4	NBC 3

1953–1954

Day	Net	7	7:30	8	8:30	9	9:30	10	10:30	11 PM
SUN	ABC	YOU ASKED FOR IT 4				WALTER WINCHELL 2 / ORCHID AWARD 2			BILLY GRAHAM 3 / LOCAL	ABC
SUN	CBS	LIFE WITH FATHER	FRANK LEAHY 4 — NOTRE DAME FOOTBALL	JACK BENNY 2	THE ED SULLIVAN SHOW 2	FRED WARING 6	G.E. THEATER 2	THE WEB	WHAT'S MY LINE 5	CBS
SUN	NBC	PAUL WINCHELL 4	PRIVATE SECY. 2	THE COLGATE COMEDY HOUR 2		THE MAN BEHIND 6 / THE BADGE 3		LORETTA YOUNG 6 (A LETTER TO…) 3	MAN AGAINST CRIME * 5	NBC
MON	ABC			JAMIE †	OF MANY THINGS	JUNIOR PRESS CONFERENCE 2		RACKET SQUAD 3 / LOCAL †		ABC
MON	CBS		NEWS / PERRY COMO 6	BURNS & ALLEN 4	TALENT SCOUTS 4	I LOVE LUCY 6	RED BUTTONS 3	STUDIO ONE 3	LOCAL	CBS 6
MON	NBC		ARTHUR MURRAY 4 / NEWS	NAME THAT TUNE 5	VOICE OF FIRESTONE	DENNIS DAY 5	ROBERT MONTGOMERY PRESENTS 3		WHO SAID THAT 5	NBC
TUE	ABC		CAVALCADE OF AMERICA * 2	LOCAL * 2	LOCAL	MAKE ROOM FOR DADDY	THE U.S. STEEL HOUR 2		THE NAME'S THE SAME 3	ABC
TUE	CBS		NEWS / JANE FROMAN 2	GENE AUTRY 4	RED SKELTON 4	THIS IS SHOW BUSINESS * 3	SUSPENSE 5	DANGER 6	SEE IT NOW 3	CBS
TUE	NBC		DINAH SHORE 3 / NEWS	THE MILTON BERLE SHOW 2 — THE BOB HOPE SHOW §		FIRESIDE THEATER 6	ARMSTRONG CIRCLE TH. 6	JUDGE FOR YOURSELF 5	BOB CONSIDINE 4 / 'I.H.I.S.'	NBC
WED	ABC		MARK SABER 3	AT ISSUE 3	THRU THE CURTAIN — ANSWERS FOR AMERICANS	JEAN CARROLL 2		WRESTLING		ABC
WED	CBS		NEWS / PERRY COMO 6	ARTHUR GODFREY & HIS FRIENDS 6		STRIKE IT RICH 3	I'VE GOT A SECRET 2	PABST BLUE RIBBON BOUTS 2	6	CBS
WED	NBC		COKE TIME 2 / NEWS	I MARRIED JOAN 6	MY LITTLE MARGIE 2	KRAFT TELEVISION THEATER * 2		THIS IS YOUR LIFE # 8	LOCAL 2	NBC
THU	ABC		LONE RANGER 2		RAY BOLGER 2	BACK THAT FACT 2		KRAFT TELEVISION THEATER	LOCAL # 8	ABC
THU	CBS		NEWS / JANE FROMAN 5	RAY MILLAND 2	FOUR STAR PLAYHOUSE 2	LUX VIDEO THEATRE 2	BIG TOWN 4	PHILIP MORRIS PLAYHOUSE 4	PLACE THE FACE	CBS
THU	NBC		DINAH SHORE 3 / NEWS	YOU BET YOUR LIFE 2	TREASURY MEN IN ACTION 4	DRAGNET 4	FORD THEATER 3	MARTIN KANE 4	LOCAL 5	NBC
FRI	ABC		STU ERWIN SHOW 4	OZZIE AND HARRIET 4	PEPSI-COLA PLAYHOUSE 2	PRIDE OF THE FAMILY 2	COMEBACK STORY 2	CHEVROLET SHOWROOM	PERSON TO PERSON 3	ABC
FRI	CBS		NEWS / PERRY COMO 6	MAMA 6	TOPPER 5	SCHLITZ PLAYHOUSE 3	OUR MISS BROOKS 3	MY FRIEND IRMA 2		CBS
FRI	NBC		COKE TIME 2 / NEWS	DAVE GARROWAY 5	LIFE OF RILEY 5	BIG STORY 2	TV SOUNDSTAGE 5	GILLETTE CAVALCADE OF SPORTS	6	NBC
SAT	ABC		LEAVE IT TO THE GIRLS * 5	TALENT PATROL * 5	MUSIC FROM MEADOWBRK. 2	SATURDAY NIGHT FIGHTS 2		LOCAL 2	LOCAL	ABC
SAT	CBS		BEAT THE CLOCK 5	THE JACKIE GLEASON SHOW 5		TWO FOR THE MONEY 2	MY FAVORITE HUSBAND 2	MEDALLION THEATER 2	MIRROR THEATER *	CBS
SAT	NBC		ETHEL AND ALBERT 2	BONINO 2	TED MACK'S AMATEUR HOUR 7	YOUR SHOW OF SHOWS — ALL-STAR REVUE			YOUR HIT PARADE §5	NBC

NOTE: *It Happened in Sports (Tues. 10:45)

1954–1955

SUNDAY

Net	7	7:30	8	8:30	9	9:30	10	10:30	11 PM
ABC	YOU ASKED FOR IT	PEPSI-COLA PLAYHOUSE 5	FLIGHT NO. 7 2	BIG PICTURE	WALTER WINCHELL 4 / PACKARD SHOWRM. 3	WHAT'S GOING ON 2	BREAK THE BANK	LOCAL *7	ABC
CBS	LASSIE	JACK BENNY 3 / PRIVATE SECY. 3	THE ED SULLIVAN SHOW 7		G.E. THEATER 7	HONESTLY, CELESTE!	FATHER KNOWS BEST	WHAT'S MY LINE	CBS 6
NBC	PEOPLE ARE FUNNY	MR. PEEPERS 3	THE COLGATE COMEDY HOUR 3	PHILCO TELEVISION PLAYHOUSE 5 / GOODYEAR TELEVISION PLAYHOUSE 5			LORETTA YOUNG 7	THE HUNTER 2	NBC *2

MONDAY

Net	7	7:30	8	8:30	9	9:30	10	10:30	11 PM
ABC		THE NAME'S THE SAME 4	COME CLOSER 4	VOICE OF FIRESTONE	COLLEGE PRESS CONFERENCE *6				ABC
CBS		NEWS / PERRY COMO 7	BURNS & ALLEN 7	TALENT SCOUTS 5	I LOVE LUCY 7	DECEMBER BRIDE 4	STUDIO ONE		CBS 7
NBC		TONY MARTIN 2 / NEWS	CAESAR'S HOUR		ROBERT MONTGOMERY PRESENTS			LOCAL 6	NBC

TUESDAY

Net	7	7:30	8	8:30	9	9:30	10	10:30	11 PM
ABC		CAVALCADE OF AMERICA 3	LOCAL	TWENTY QUESTIONS	MAKE ROOM FOR DADDY *5	THE U.S. STEEL HOUR		STOP THE MUSIC 2	ABC 5
CBS		NEWS 3 / JO STAFFORD 2	RED SKELTON 4	HALLS OF IVY 4	MEET MILLIE 3	DANGER 3	LIFE WITH FATHER 5	SEE IT NOW 2	CBS 4
NBC		DINAH SHORE 4 / NEWS	THE MILTON BERLE SHOW		FIRESIDE THEATER §7	ARMSTRONG CIRCLE THEATER 7	TRUTH OR CONSEQUENCES 6	IT'S A GREAT LIFE *4	NBC

WEDNESDAY

Net	7	7:30	8	8:30	9	9:30	10	10:30	11 PM
ABC		DISNEYLAND			MASQUERADE PARTY 5	ENTERPRISE USA *3	LOCAL	LOCAL	ABC
CBS		NEWS / PERRY COMO 7	ARTHUR GODFREY & HIS FRIENDS 7		STRIKE IT RICH 7	I'VE GOT A SECRET 3	PABST BLUE RIBBON BOUTS 3	THE BEST OF BROADWAY 6	CBS 7 / 6
NBC		COKE TIME 3 / NEWS 3	I MARRIED JOAN 3	MY LITTLE MARGIE 3	KRAFT TELEVISION THEATER 3		THIS IS YOUR LIFE #9	BIG TOWN 3	NBC *5

THURSDAY

Net	7	7:30	8	8:30	9	9:30	10	10:30	11 PM
ABC		LONE RANGER 6	TREASURY MEN IN ACTION		SO YOU WANT TO LEAD A BAND *5	KRAFT TELEVISION THEATER	PUBLIC DEFENDER 3	LOCAL #9	ABC
CBS		NEWS / JANE FROMAN	RAY MILLAND 2	CLIMAX! 2 / SHOWER OF STARS	FOUR STAR PLAYHOUSE §		PUBLIC DEFENDER 3	NAME THAT TUNE 2	CBS *2
NBC		DINAH SHORE 4 / NEWS	YOU BET YOUR LIFE 2	JUSTICE 5	DRAGNET 2	FORD THEATER 4	LUX VIDEO THEATER 5		NBC *5

FRIDAY

Net	7	7:30	8	8:30	9	9:30	10	10:30	11 PM
ABC		RIN TIN TIN	OZZIE AND HARRIET 3	RAY BOLGER 3	DOLLAR A SECOND 2	THE VISE *2	LOCAL	LOCAL	ABC
CBS		NEWS / PERRY COMO 7	MAMA 6	TOPPER 6	SCHLITZ PLAYHOUSE 2	OUR MISS BROOKS 4	THE LINEUP 3	PERSON TO PERSON 2	CBS 2
NBC		COKE TIME 3 / NEWS 3	RED BUTTONS *3 / JACK CARSON §	LIFE OF RILEY 3	BIG STORY 3	DEAR PHOEBE 6	GILLETTE CAVALCADE OF SPORTS		NBC 7

SATURDAY

Net	7	7:30	8	8:30	9	9:30	10	10:30	11 PM
ABC		COMPASS	THE DOTTY MACK SHOW				STORK CLUB 3	LOCAL *4	ABC
CBS		BEAT THE CLOCK 6	THE JACKIE GLEASON SHOW		TWO FOR THE MONEY 3	MY FAVORITE HUSBAND 2	THAT'S MY BOY 2	WILLY	CBS 2
NBC		ETHEL AND ALBERT 3	MICKEY ROONEY 3	PLACE THE FACE 3	IMOGENE COCA *2	JIMMY DURANTE / DONALD O'CONNOR	GEORGE GOBEL	YOUR HIT PARADE	NBC 5

1955–1956

Day	Net	7	7:30	8	8:30	9	9:30	10	10:30	11 PM
SUN	ABC	YOU ASKED FOR IT [6]	MOVIE [6]			CHANGE OF A LIFETIME		LIFE BEGINS AT EIGHTY [*9]	LOCAL [*6]	
SUN	CBS	LASSIE [2]	JACK BENNY / PRIVATE SECY. [4]	THE ED SULLIVAN SHOW [4]		TED MACK'S AMATEUR HR. [*6]	G.E. THEATER [8]	APPT. WITH ADVENTURE	WHAT'S MY LINE [2]	[7]
SUN	NBC	IT'S A GREAT LIFE [2]	FRONTIER [2]	THE COLGATE VARIETY HOUR		GOODYEAR PLAYHOUSE / THE ALCOA HOUR [6]		LORETTA YOUNG [5]	JUSTICE [3]	[3]
MON	ABC		TOPPER [†]	TV READERS' DIGEST [†]	VOICE OF FIRESTONE [2]	DOTTY MACK [7]	MEDICAL HORIZONS [3]	BIG PICTURE	LOCAL [5]	
MON	CBS		ROBIN HOOD	BURNS & ALLEN [6]	TALENT SCOUTS	I LOVE LUCY [8]	DECEMBER BRIDE [5]	STUDIO ONE [2]	LOCAL	[8]
MON	NBC		TONY MARTIN [3] / NEWS	CAESAR'S HOUR		MEDIC [2]	ROBERT MONTGOMERY PRESENTS [2]		LOCAL [7]	
TUE	ABC		WARNER BROTHERS PRESENTS		WYATT EARP	MAKE ROOM FOR DADDY	CAVALCADE THEATER [3]	TALENT VARIETIES [4]	LOCAL	
TUE	CBS		NAME THAT TUNE [3]		YOU'LL NEVER GET RICH	MEET MILLIE	RED SKELTON [4]	THE $64,000 QUESTION [5]	MY FAVORITE HUSBAND	[3]
TUE	NBC		DINAH SHORE [5] / NEWS	MILTON BERLE / BOB HOPE / MARTHA RAYE / GUEST HOSTS [‖8]		JANE WYMAN PRESENTS [‖8]	ARMSTRONG CIRCLE THEATER / PLAYWRIGHTS '56		BIG TOWN [7]	[6]
WED	ABC		DISNEYLAND		M-G-M PARADE [2]	MASQUERADE PARTY	BREAK THE BANK [4]	WEDNESDAY NIGHT FIGHTS [8]		
WED	CBS		BRAVE EAGLE	ARTHUR GODFREY & HIS FRIENDS [8]		THE MILLIONAIRE	I'VE GOT A SECRET [4]	THE U.S. STEEL HOUR / 20TH CENTURY-FOX HOUR [4]		[*3]
WED	NBC		COKE TIME [4] / NEWS	SCREEN DIRECTORS PLAYHOUSE	FATHER KNOWS BEST [*2]	KRAFT TELEVISION THEATER [2]		THIS IS YOUR LIFE [10]	MIDWEST HAYRIDE	[5]
THU	ABC		LONE RANGER [7]		STOP THE MUSIC [*4]	STAR TONIGHT [6]	DOWN YOU GO [*6]	OUTSIDE U.S.A. [*6]	LOCAL [4]	
THU	CBS		SGT. PRESTON	BOB CUMMINGS (LOVE THAT BOB) [2]	CLIMAX! / SHOWER OF STARS [§2]		FOUR STAR PLAYHOUSE [§2]	JOHNNY CARSON [4]	WANTED	[3]
THU	NBC		DINAH SHORE [5] / NEWS	YOU BET YOUR LIFE	PEOPLES' CHOICE [6]	DRAGNET	FORD THEATER [5]	LUX VIDEO THEATRE [6]		[6]
FRI	ABC		RIN TIN TIN	OZZIE AND HARRIET [2]	CROSSROADS [4]	DOLLAR A SECOND	THE VISE [3]	ETHEL AND ALBERT [2]	LOCAL [*4]	
FRI	CBS		ADVENTURES OF CHAMPION	MAMA [7]	OUR MISS BROOKS	THE CRUSADER [4]	SCHLITZ PLAYHOUSE	THE LINEUP [5]	PERSON TO PERSON [2]	[3]
FRI	NBC		COKE TIME [4] / NEWS	TRUTH OR CONSEQUENCES	LIFE OF RILEY [5]	BIG STORY [4]	STAR STAGE [7]	GILLETTE CAVALCADE OF SPORTS		[8]
SAT	ABC	OZARK JUBILEE / GRAND OLE OPRY				THE LAWRENCE WELK SHOW [§2]		TOMORROW	LOCAL [2]	
SAT	CBS		BEAT THE CLOCK [7]	STAGE SHOW [2]	HONEYMOONERS (J. GLEASON) [2]	TWO FOR THE MONEY [4]	IT'S ALWAYS JAN [3]	GUNSMOKE [4]	DAMON RUNYON THEATER	[2]
SAT	NBC		BIG SURPRISE	THE PERRY COMO SHOW		PEOPLE ARE FUNNY [2]	JIMMY DURANTE [2]	GEORGE GOBEL [2]	YOUR HIT PARADE	[6]

1956–1957

Day	Net	7	7:30	8	8:30	9	9:30	10	10:30	11 PM
S U N	ABC		YOU ASKED FOR IT 7	TED MACK'S AMATEUR HOUR	PRESS CONFERENCE 10	OMNIBUS			LOCAL *5	ABC
	CBS		LASSIE 3	JACK BENNY 5 / PRIVATE SECY. 5	THE ED SULLIVAN SHOW	G.E. THEATER 9	ALFRED HITCHCOCK 5	THE $64,000 CHALLENGE	WHAT'S MY LINE 2	CBS 8
	NBC	77TH BENGAL LANCERS	CIRCUS BOY	THE STEVE ALLEN SHOW		GOODYEAR PLAYHOUSE / THE ALCOA HOUR 6		LORETTA YOUNG 6	NATIONAL BOWLING CHAMPS 4	NBC 2
M O N	ABC		BOLD JOURNEY	MAKE ROOM FOR DADDY 4	VOICE OF FIRESTONE 7	LAWRENCE WELK'S TOP TUNES AND NEW TALENT 8			LOCAL	ABC
	CBS		ROBIN HOOD 2	BURNS & ALLEN 2	TALENT SCOUTS 7	I LOVE LUCY 9	DECEMBER BRIDE 6	STUDIO ONE 3		CBS 9
	NBC		NAT KING COLE / NEWS 5	SIR LANCELOT 9	STANLEY	MEDIC 3	ROBERT MONTGOMERY PRESENTS 3		LOCAL 8	NBC
T U E	ABC		CHEYENNE / CONFLICT	WYATT EARP 2	BROKEN ARROW 2	CAVALCADE THEATER 3	IT'S POLKA TIME 5		LOCAL	ABC
	CBS		NAME THAT TUNE 4	YOU'LL NEVER GET RICH	THE BROTHERS 2	HERB SHRINER 5	RED SKELTON 6	THE $64,000 QUESTION 2	DO YOU TRUST YOUR WIFE? 2	CBS
	NBC		JONATHAN WINTERS / NEWS	BIG SURPRISE 2	NOAH'S ARK 2	JANE WYMAN THEATER 2	ARMSTRONG CIRCLE THEATER 2	KAISER ALUMINUM HOUR	BREAK THE $250,000 BANK 8	NBC *9
W E D	ABC		DISNEYLAND		NAVY LOG 3	OZZIE AND HARRIET *6	FORD THEATER *7	WEDNESDAY NIGHT FIGHTS *7		ABC 2
	CBS		GIANT STEP	THE ARTHUR GODFREY SHOW		MILLIONAIRE 9	I'VE GOT A SECRET 3	THE U.S. STEEL HOUR / 20TH CENTURY-FOX HOUR 5		CBS 4 / 2
	NBC		COKE TIME / NEWS 5	HIRAM HOLLIDAY	FATHER KNOWS BEST	KRAFT TELEVISION THEATER 3		THIS IS YOUR LIFE 11	TWENTY-ONE 5	NBC
T H U	ABC		LONE RANGER	CIRCUS TIME 8		WIRE SERVICE 3		OZARK JUBILEE		ABC 3
	CBS		SGT. PRESTON 2	LOVE THAT BOB 2	CLIMAX! 3 / SHOWER OF STARS 3	PLAYHOUSE 90 3 §3				CBS
	NBC		DINAH SHORE 6 / NEWS	YOU BET YOUR LIFE 7	DRAGNET 7	PEOPLES' CHOICE 6	TENNESSEE ERNIE FORD 2	LUX VIDEO THEATRE		NBC 7
F R I	ABC		RIN TIN TIN 3	JIM BOWIE 3	CROSSROADS 2	TREASURE HUNT 2	THE VISE	RAY ANTHONY 3		ABC
	CBS		MY FRIEND FLICKA 2 / COKE TIME NEWS 5	WEST POINT 2	ZANE GREY THEATER	THE CRUSADER	SCHLITZ PLAYHOUSE 6	THE LINEUP	PERSON TO PERSON 3	CBS 4
	NBC		LIFE OF RILEY 5	WALTER WINCHELL 5		ON TRIAL	BIG STORY	GILLETTE CAVALCADE OF SPORTS 8		NBC 9
S A T	ABC		MOVIE			THE LAWRENCE WELK SHOW		MASQUERADE PARTY 2	LOCAL 5	ABC
	CBS		THE BUCCANEERS	THE JACKIE GLEASON SHOW		OH! SUSANNA 5	HEY JEANNIE	GUNSMOKE	HIGH FINANCE 2	CBS
	NBC		PEOPLE ARE FUNNY	THE PERRY COMO SHOW 3		CAESAR'S HOUR 2		GEORGE GOBEL 3	YOUR HIT PARADE 3	NBC 7

NOTE: *Formerly one segment of Warner Brothers Presents*

1957–1958

Day	Network	7	7:30	8	8:30	9	9:30	10	10:30	11 PM
SUN	ABC	YOU ASKED FOR IT	MAVERICK		BOWLING STARS	OPEN HEARING	FOOTBALL FILMS	SCOTLAND YARD	LOCAL	ABC
	CBS	LASSIE	JACK BENNY / BACHELOR FATHER	THE ED SULLIVAN SHOW		G.E. THEATER	ALFRED HITCHCOCK	THE $64,000 CHALLENGE	WHAT'S MY LINE	CBS
	NBC	TED MACK'S AMATEUR HR.	SALLY	THE STEVE ALLEN SHOW		THE DINAH SHORE CHEVY SHOW		LORETTA YOUNG	LOCAL	NBC
MON	ABC		AMERICAN BANDSTAND	GUY MITCHELL	BOLD JOURNEY	VOICE OF FIRESTONE	LAWRENCE WELK'S TOP TUNES AND NEW TALENT		LOCAL	ABC
	CBS		ROBIN HOOD	BURNS & ALLEN	TALENT SCOUTS	DANNY THOMAS'	DECEMBER BRIDE	STUDIO ONE		CBS
	NBC		PRICE IS RIGHT	RESTLESS GUN	WELLS FARGO	TWENTY-ONE	GOODYEAR TH. / ALCOA TH.	SUSPICION		NBC
TUE	ABC		CHEYENNE SUGARFOOT		WYATT EARP	BROKEN ARROW	TELEPHONE TIME	WEST POINT	LOCAL	ABC
	CBS		NAME THAT TUNE	YOU'LL NEVER GET RICH	EVE ARDEN SHOW	TO TELL THE TRUTH	RED SKELTON	THE $64,000 QUESTION	ASSIGNMENT: FOREIGN LEGION	CBS
	NBC		NAT KING COLE	THE GEORGE GOBEL SHOW / THE EDDIE FISHER SHOW		MEET McGRAW	LOVE THAT BOB	CALIFORNIANS	LOCAL	NBC
WED	ABC		DISNEYLAND		TOMBSTONE TERRITORY	OZZIE AND HARRIET	WALTER WINCHELL FILE	WEDNESDAY NIGHT FIGHTS	LOCAL	ABC
	CBS		I LOVE LUCY	THE BIG RECORD		MILLIONAIRE	I'VE GOT A SECRET	ARMSTRONG CIRCLE THEATER / THE U.S. STEEL HOUR		CBS
	NBC		WAGON TRAIN		FATHER KNOWS BEST	KRAFT TELEVISION THEATER		THIS IS YOUR LIFE	LOCAL	NBC
THU	ABC		CIRCUS BOY	ZORRO		PAT BOONE SHOW		NAVY LOG	LOCAL	ABC
	CBS		SGT. PRESTON	HARBOURMASTER	CLIMAX! / SHOWER OF STARS		PLAYHOUSE 90		LOCAL	CBS
	NBC		TIC TAC DOUGH	YOU BET YOUR LIFE	DRAGNET	PEOPLES' CHOICE	TENNESSEE ERNIE FORD	THE LUX SHOW (R. CLOONEY)	JANE WYMAN THEATER	NBC
FRI	ABC		RIN TIN TIN	JIM BOWIE	PATRICE MUNSEL	FRANK SINATRA	DATE WITH THE ANGELS	COLT .45	LOCAL	ABC
	CBS		LEAVE IT TO BEAVER	TRACKDOWN	ZANE GREY THEATER	MR. ADAMS AND EVE	SCHLITZ PLAYHOUSE	THE LINEUP	PERSON TO PERSON	CBS
	NBC		SABER OF LONDON	COURT OF LAST RESORT	LIFE OF RILEY	M SQUAD	THE THIN MAN	GILLETTE CAVALCADE OF SPORTS		NBC
SAT	ABC		KEEP IT IN THE FAMILY	OZARK (COUNTRY MUSIC); JUBILEE		THE LAWRENCE WELK SHOW		MIKE WALLACE INTERVIEW	LOCAL	ABC
	CBS		PERRY MASON		DICK AND THE DUCHESS	OH! SUSANNA	HAVE GUN WILL TRAVEL	GUNSMOKE	LOCAL	CBS
	NBC		PEOPLE ARE FUNNY	THE PERRY COMO SHOW		POLLY BERGEN / CLUB OASIS	GISELE MacKENZIE	WHAT'S IT FOR	YOUR HIT PARADE	NBC

NOTE: *Formerly Make Room for Daddy*

1958–1959

Day	Net	7	7:30	8	8:30	9	9:30	10	10:30	11 PM
SUN	ABC	YOU ASKED FOR IT	MAVERICK		THE LAWMAN	COLT .45	ENCOUNTER		LOCAL	
SUN	CBS	LASSIE	JACK BENNY / BACHELOR FATHER	THE ED SULLIVAN SHOW		G.E. THEATER	ALFRED HITCHCOCK	THE $64,000 QUESTION	WHAT'S MY LINE	
SUN	NBC	SABER OF LONDON	NORTHWEST PASSAGE	THE STEVE ALLEN SHOW		THE DINAH SHORE CHEVY SHOW		LORETTA YOUNG	LOCAL	
MON	ABC		POLKA-GO-ROUND		BOLD JOURNEY	VOICE OF FIRESTONE	ANYBODY CAN PLAY	THIS IS MUSIC	NEWS	
MON	CBS		NAME THAT TUNE		FATHER KNOWS BEST	DANNY THOMAS	ANN SOTHERN	DESILU PLAYHOUSE		
MON	NBC		TIC TAC DOUGH	RESTLESS GUN	WELLS FARGO	PETER GUNN	GOODYEAR TH. / ALCOA TH.	ARTHUR MURRAY	LOCAL	
TUE	ABC		CHEYENNE¹ / SUGARFOOT		WYATT EARP	THE RIFLEMAN	NAKED CITY	CONFESSION	NEWS	
TUE	CBS		BURNS & ALLEN	KEEP TALKING	TO TELL THE TRUTH	ARTHUR GODFREY	RED SKELTON	THE GARRY MOORE SHOW		
TUE	NBC		DRAGNET	THE GEORGE GOBEL SHOW / THE EDDIE FISHER SHOW		GEORGE BURNS	BOB CUMMINGS	CALIFORNIANS	LOCAL	
WED	ABC		LAWRENCE WELK'S LITTLE BAND		OZZIE AND HARRIET	DONNA REED SHOW	PATTI PAGE (OLDSMOBILE)	WEDNESDAY NIGHT FIGHTS	LOCAL	
WED	CBS		TWILIGHT THEATER	PURSUIT		MILLIONAIRE	I'VE GOT A SECRET	ARMSTRONG CIRCLE THEATER / THE U.S. STEEL HOUR	LOCAL	
WED	NBC		WAGON TRAIN		PRICE IS RIGHT	MILTON BERLE (KRAFT MUSIC H.)	BAT MASTERSON	THIS IS YOUR LIFE	LOCAL	
THU	ABC		LEAVE IT TO BEAVER	ZORRO	REAL McCOYS	PAT BOONE	ROUGH RIDERS	TRAFFIC COURT	NEWS	
THU	CBS		I LOVE LUCY	DECEMBER BRIDE	YANCY DERRINGER	ZANE GREY THEATER	PLAYHOUSE 90	DUPONT SHOW OF THE MONTH		
THU	NBC		JEFFERSON DRUM	ED WYNN SHOW	TWENTY-ONE	BEHIND CLOSED DOORS	TENNESSEE ERNIE FORD	YOU BET YOUR LIFE	MASQUERADE PARTY	
FRI	ABC		RIN TIN TIN	WALT DISNEY PRESENTS²		MAN WITH A CAMERA	77 SUNSET STRIP		NEWS	
FRI	CBS		YOUR HIT PARADE	TRACKDOWN	JACKIE GLEASON	YOU'LL NEVER GET RICH	SCHLITZ PLAYH. / LUX PLAYHOUSE	THE LINEUP	PERSON TO PERSON	
FRI	NBC		BUCKSKIN	ELLERY QUEEN		M SQUAD	THE THIN MAN	GILLETTE CAVALCADE OF SPORTS	LOCAL	
SAT	ABC		DICK CLARK	JUBILEE U.S.A.³		LAWRENCE WELK		SAMMY KAYE'S MUSIC	LOCAL	
SAT	CBS		PERRY MASON		WANTED: DEAD OR ALIVE	OH! SUSANNA	HAVE GUN WILL TRAVEL	GUNSMOKE	LOCAL	
SAT	NBC		PEOPLE ARE FUNNY	THE PERRY COMO SHOW		STEVE CANYON	CIMARRON CITY		BRAINS AND BRAWN	

NOTES: ¹Bronco episodes shown under Cheyenne title during 1958-1959 season ²Formerly Disneyland ³Formerly Ozark Jubilee

1959–1960

Day	Network	7	7:30	8	8:30	9	9:30	10	10:30	11 PM
SUN	ABC	COLT .45	MAVERICK		THE LAWMAN	THE REBEL	THE ALASKANS		DICK CLARK'S WORLD OF TALENT	
SUN	CBS	LASSIE	DENNIS THE MENACE	THE ED SULLIVAN SHOW		G.E. THEATER	ALFRED HITCHCOCK	JACK BENNY / GEO. GOBEL	WHAT'S MY LINE	
SUN	NBC	RIVERBOAT		SPECIALS	THE CHEVY SHOW (DINAH SHORE AND GUEST HOSTS)			LORETTA YOUNG	LOCAL	
MON	ABC		CHEYENNE	BOURBON STREET BEAT		ADVENTURES IN PARADISE		MAN WITH A CAMERA		
MON	CBS		MASQUERADE PARTY	THE TEXAN	FATHER KNOWS BEST	DANNY THOMAS	ANN SOTHERN	HENNESEY	JUNE ALLYSON	
MON	NBC		RICHARD DIAMOND	LOVE & MARRIAGE	WELLS FARGO	PETER GUNN	GOODYEAR TH. / ALCOA TH.	THE STEVE ALLEN SHOW		
TUE	ABC		SUGARFOOT / BRONCO		WYATT EARP	THE RIFLEMAN	PHILIP MARLOWE	ONE STEP BEYOND	KEEP TALKING	
TUE	CBS		LOCAL	DENNIS O'KEEFE	DOBIE GILLIS	TIGHTROPE!	RED SKELTON	THE GARRY MOORE SHOW		
TUE	NBC		LARAMIE			FIBBER McGEE AND MOLLY	FORD STARTIME		LOCAL	
WED	ABC		COURT OF LAST RESORT	CHARLEY WEAVER'S HOBBY LOBBY	OZZIE AND HARRIET	HAWAIIAN EYE		WEDNESDAY NIGHT FIGHTS		
WED	CBS		THE LINEUP	MEN INTO SPACE		MILLIONAIRE	I'VE GOT A SECRET	ARMSTRONG CIRCLE THEATER / THE U.S. STEEL HOUR		
WED	NBC		WAGON TRAIN	PRICE IS RIGHT		THE PERRY COMO SHOW (THE KRAFT MUSIC HALL)		THIS IS YOUR LIFE	WICHITA TOWN	
THU	ABC		GALE STORM (OH! SUSANNA)	DONNA REED	REAL McCOYS	PAT BOONE	THE UNTOUCHABLES		TAKE A GOOD LOOK	
THU	CBS		TO TELL THE TRUTH	BETTY HUTTON	JOHNNY RINGO	ZANE GREY THEATER	PLAYHOUSE 90 / THE BIG PARTY			
THU	NBC		LAW OF THE PLAINSMAN	BAT MASTERSON	STACCATO	BACHELOR FATHER	TENNESSEE ERNIE FORD	YOU BET YOUR LIFE	LAWLESS YEARS	
FRI	ABC		WALT DISNEY PRESENTS	MAN FROM BLACKHAWK		77 SUNSET STRIP		THE DETECTIVES	BLACK SADDLE	
FRI	CBS		RAWHIDE		HOTEL DE PAREE	DESILU PLAYHOUSE		TWILIGHT ZONE	PERSON TO PERSON	
FRI	NBC		PEOPLE ARE FUNNY	TROUBLE-SHOOTERS	BELL TELEPHONE HOUR SPECIALS		M SQUAD	GILLETTE CAVALCADE OF SPORTS		
SAT	ABC		DICK CLARK	HIGH ROAD	LEAVE IT TO BEAVER	THE LAWRENCE WELK SHOW		JUBILEE U.S.A.		
SAT	CBS		PERRY MASON		WANTED: DEAD OR ALIVE	MR. LUCKY	HAVE GUN WILL TRAVEL	GUNSMOKE	MARKHAM	
SAT	NBC		BONANZA		THE MAN AND THE CHALLENGE	THE DEPUTY	FIVE FINGERS		IT COULD BE YOU	

1960–1961

Day	Net	7:00	7:30	8:00	8:30	9:00	9:30	10:00	10:30	11 PM
SUN	ABC	WALT DISNEY PRESENTS **7	MAVERICK		THE LAWMAN 4	THE REBEL 3	THE ISLANDERS 2		THE WALTER WINCHELL SHOW	ABC
	CBS	LASSIE 7	DENNIS THE MENACE 7	THE ED SULLIVAN SHOW		G.E. THEATER 13	JACK BENNY 9	CANDID CAMERA 9	WHAT'S MY LINE 12	CBS
	NBC	SHIRLEY TEMPLE THEATRE		NATIONAL VELVET	THE TAB HUNTER SHOW	THE DINAH SHORE CHEVY SHOW		LORETTA YOUNG 4	THIS IS YOUR LIFE 8	NBC 9
MON	ABC		CHEYENNE![1] 6		SURFSIDE 6 6		ADVENTURES IN PARADISE		PETER GUNN 2 *3	ABC
	CBS		TO TELL THE TRUTH 5	PETE & GLADYS 5	BRINGING UP BUDDY	DANNY THOMAS 8	ANDY GRIFFITH 8	HENNESEY 2	FACE THE NATION 2	CBS 7
	NBC		RIVERBOAT		WELLS FARGO 2	KLONDIKE 5	DANTE	BARBARA STANWYCK SHOW	JACKPOT BOWLING (MILTON BERLE)	NBC
TUE	ABC		BUGS BUNNY	THE RIFLEMAN	WYATT EARP 3	STAGECOACH WEST 6		ONE STEP BEYOND	LOCAL 3	ABC
	CBS		LOCAL	FATHER KNOWS BEST	DOBIE GILLIS 7	TOM EWELL SHOW 2	RED SKELTON	THE GARRY MOORE SHOW 10		CBS 3
	NBC		LARAMIE		ALFRED HITCHCOCK 2	THRILLER *6		SPECIALS[2]	LOCAL 3	NBC
WED	ABC		HONG KONG 9		OZZIE AND HARRIET 9	HAWAIIAN EYE		NAKED CITY 2		ABC 2
	CBS		THE AQUANAUTS		WANTED: DEAD OR ALIVE 3	MY SISTER EILEEN 3	I'VE GOT A SECRET	ARMSTRONG CIRCLE THEATER / THE U.S. STEEL HOUR 9		CBS 12 8
	NBC		WAGON TRAIN		PRICE IS RIGHT 4	THE PERRY COMO SHOW (THE KRAFT MUSIC HALL) 4		PETER LOVES MARY 6	LOCAL	NBC
THU	ABC		GUESTWARD HO!	DONNA REED 3	REAL McCOYS 3	MY THREE SONS 4	THE UNTOUCHABLES		TAKE A GOOD LOOK 2	ABC 2
	CBS		THE WITNESS		ZANE GREY THEATER 5	ANGEL 5	ANN SOTHERN	PERSON TO PERSON 3	JUNE ALLYSON 8	CBS 2
	NBC		THE OUTLAWS		BAT MASTERSON 3	BACHELOR FATHER 3	TENNESSEE ERNIE FORD 4	YOU BET YOUR LIFE 5	LOCAL 11	NBC
FRI	ABC		MATTY'S FUNDAY FUNNIES 2	HARRIGAN & SON 2	FLINTSTONES	77 SUNSET STRIP		THE DETECTIVES 3	THE LAW AND MR. JONES 2	ABC
	CBS		RAWHIDE 3		ROUTE 66 3		MR. GARLUND	TWILIGHT ZONE 3	EYEWITNESS TO HISTORY 2	CBS
	NBC		DAN RAVEN		THE WESTERNER	THE BELL TELEPHONE HOUR SPECIALS		MICHAEL SHAYNE 3		NBC
SAT	ABC		THE ROARING TWENTIES		LEAVE IT TO BEAVER 4	THE LAWRENCE WELK SHOW		THE FIGHT OF THE WEEK[3] 6		ABC
	CBS		PERRY MASON		CHECKMATE 4		HAVE GUN WILL TRAVEL	GUNSMOKE 4	LOCAL 6	CBS
	NBC		BONANZA		THE TALL MAN 2	THE DEPUTY	THE NATION'S FUTURE 2		LOCAL	NBC

NOTES: [1]Including episodes of *Bronco* and *Sugarfoot* [2]Including *The Dow Hour of Great Mysteries* and NBC news specials [3]Followed by *Make That Spare*

1961–1962

Day	Network	7	7:30	8	8:30	9	9:30	10	10:30	11 PM
SUN	ABC	*** 5 MAVERICK	FOLLOW THE SUN		4 THE LAWMAN	4 BUS STOP		ADVENTURES IN PARADISE		3
SUN	CBS		8 LASSIE / DENNIS THE MENACE 3	3 THE ED SULLIVAN SHOW		14 G.E. THEATER	10 JACK BENNY		10 CANDID CAMERA / WHAT'S MY LINE 2	13
SUN	NBC	BULLWINKLE SHOW	WALT DISNEY'S WONDERFUL WORLD OF COLOR[1] * 8		CAR 54, WHERE ARE YOU	BONANZA		3 THE DUPONT SHOW OF THE WEEK		2
MON	ABC		CHEYENNE[2] 7		THE RIFLEMAN 4	SURFSIDE 6 4		BEN CASEY 2		3
MON	CBS		TO TELL THE TRUTH 6	PETE & GLADYS 2	WINDOW ON MAIN STREET 9	DANNY THOMAS	ANDY GRIFFITH 2	HENNESEY 3	I'VE GOT A SECRET 3	10
MON	NBC		LOCAL	NATIONAL VELVET 2	PRICE IS RIGHT 5	87TH PRECINCT		THRILLER		2
TUE	ABC		BUGS BUNNY 2	BACHELOR FATHER * 5	CALVIN AND THE COLONEL	THE NEW BREED		ALCOA PREMIERE		3
TUE	CBS		MARSHAL DILLON †	DICK VAN DYKE †	DOBIE GILLIS 3	RED SKELTON	ICHABOD AND ME 11	THE GARRY MOORE SHOW		4
TUE	NBC		LARAMIE		ALFRED HITCHCOCK 3	THE DICK POWELL SHOW 7		CAIN'S HUNDRED		2
WED	ABC		THE NEW STEVE ALLEN SHOW		TOP CAT 3	HAWAIIAN EYE		NAKED CITY 3		3
WED	CBS		THE ALVIN SHOW / FATHER KNOWS BEST		CHECKMATE †		MRS. G. GOES TO COLLEGE 2	ARMSTRONG CIRCLE THEATER 13 / THE U.S. STEEL HOUR 9		
WED	NBC		WAGON TRAIN		JOEY BISHOP 5	THE PERRY COMO SHOW (THE KRAFT MUSIC HALL)		BOB NEWHART 7	DAVID BRINK-LEY'S JOURNAL	
THU	ABC		OZZIE AND HARRIET 10		REAL McCOY'S 4	MY THREE SONS 5	MARGIE 2	THE UNTOUCHABLES		3
THU	CBS		FRONTIER CIRCUS	DONNA REED	BOB CUMMINGS	THE INVESTIGATORS		CBS REPORTS		3
THU	NBC		THE OUTLAWS		DOCTOR KILDARE 2		HAZEL	SING ALONG WITH MITCH		2
FRI	ABC		STRAIGHTAWAY	THE HATHAWAYS	FLINTSTONES 2	77 SUNSET STRIP 2		4 TARGET: THE CORRUPTORS		3
FRI	CBS		RAWHIDE		ROUTE 66 4		FATHER OF THE BRIDE 2	TWILIGHT ZONE 2	EYEWITNESS TO HISTORY 3	2
FRI	NBC		INTERNATIONAL SHOWTIME		ROBERT TAYLOR'S DETECTIVES[3]	THE DINAH SHORE SHOW * 3 / THE BELL TELEPHONE HOUR		FRANK McGEE: HERE AND NOW 5 / 4	
SAT	ABC		THE ROARING TWENTIES		LEAVE IT TO BEAVER 2	THE LAWRENCE WELK SHOW 5		THE FIGHT OF THE WEEK* 7		2
SAT	CBS		PERRY MASON		THE DEFENDERS 5	HAVE GUN WILL TRAVEL		GUNSMOKE 5		7
SAT	NBC		WELLS FARGO		THE TALL MAN 6	MOVIE 2				

NOTES: [1]Formerly Walt Disney Presents [2]Including episodes of Bronco [3]Formerly The Detectives [4]Followed by Make That Spare

1962–1963

Day	Net	7	7:30	8	8:30	9	9:30	10	10:30	11 PM
SUN	ABC	FATHER KNOWS BEST	THE JETSONS *1	MOVIE				VOICE OF FIRESTONE	HOWARD K. SMITH 14	ABC 2
SUN	CBS	LASSIE 9	DENNIS THE MENACE	THE ED SULLIVAN SHOW 4		REAL McCOYS 15	G.E. TRUE *6	CANDID CAMERA	WHAT'S MY LINE 3	CBS 14
SUN	NBC	ENSIGN O'TOOLE	WALT DISNEY'S WONDERFUL WORLD OF COLOR		CAR 54, WHERE ARE YOU 9	BONANZA 2		THE DUPONT SHOW OF THE WEEK 4		NBC 2
MON	ABC		CHEYENNE	THE RIFLEMAN 8		STONEY BURKE 5		BEN CASEY 4		ABC 2
MON	CBS		TO TELL THE TRUTH 7	I'VE GOT A SECRET 11	THE LUCY SHOW	DANNY THOMAS	ANDY GRIFFITH 10	THE NEW LORETTA YOUNG SHOW 3	STUMP THE STARS	CBS
MON	NBC		IT'S A MAN'S WORLD		SAINTS AND SINNERS 11		PRICE IS RIGHT	DAVID BRINKLEY'S JOURNAL 6	LOCAL 2	NBC
TUE	ABC		COMBAT		HAWAIIAN EYE 4		THE UNTOUCHABLES		SPECIALS² 4	ABC 5
TUE	CBS		MARSHAL DILLON¹	LLOYD BRIDGES	THE RED SKELTON SHOW		JACK BENNY 12	THE GARRY MOORE SHOW 11		CBS 5
TUE	NBC		LARAMIE		EMPIRE 4		THE DICK POWELL SHOW		CHET HUNTLEY REPORTING 2	NBC 5
WED	ABC		WAGON TRAIN		GOING MY WAY *6		OUR MAN HIGGINS	NAKED CITY		ABC 4
WED	CBS		CBS REPORTS		DOBIE GILLIS 4	THE BEVERLY HILLBILLIES	DICK VAN DYKE	ARMSTRONG CIRCLE THEATER 2	THE U.S. STEEL HOUR	CBS 14 / 10
WED	NBC		THE VIRGINIAN			THE PERRY COMO SHOW (THE KRAFT MUSIC HALL)		THE ELEVENTH HOUR 8		NBC
THU	ABC		OZZIE AND HARRIET	DONNA REED 11	LEAVE IT TO BEAVER 5	MY THREE SONS 6	McHALE'S NAVY 3	ALCOA PREMIERE		ABC 2
THU	CBS		MISTER ED³	PERRY MASON 3		THE NURSES		ALFRED HITCHCOCK		CBS *8
THU	NBC		WIDE COUNTRY		DOCTOR KILDARE		HAZEL 2	THE ANDY WILLIAMS SHOW 2		NBC
FRI	ABC		THE GALLANT MEN		FLINTSTONES	I'M DICKENS, HE'S FENSTER 3	77 SUNSET STRIP		LOCAL 5	ABC
FRI	CBS		RAWHIDE		ROUTE 66 5		FAIR EXCHANGE 3		EYEWITNESS 3	CBS
FRI	NBC		INTERNATIONAL SHOWTIME		SING ALONG WITH MITCH 2		DON'T CALL ME CHARLIE 3	THE JACK PAAR PROGRAM		NBC 3
SAT	ABC		ROY ROGERS & DALE EVANS SHOW		MR. SMITH GOES TO WASHINGTON	THE LAWRENCE WELK SHOW		THE FIGHT OF THE WEEK⁴ 8		ABC 3
SAT	CBS		JACKIE GLEASON'S AMERICAN SCENE MAGAZINE		THE DEFENDERS 3		HAVE GUN WILL TRAVEL 2	GUNSMOKE 6		CBS 8
SAT	NBC		SAM BENEDICT		JOEY BISHOP	MOVIE 2				NBC

NOTES: ¹Reruns of Gunsmoke. ²Including Close-Up, Here's Edie and As Caesar Sees It. ³Including one season in syndication. ⁴Followed by Make That Spare

1963–1964

Day	Net	7	7:30	8	8:30	9	9:30	10	10:30	11 PM
SUN	ABC	LOCAL	TRAVELS OF JAIMIE McPHEETERS		ARREST AND TRIAL			100 GRAND	ABC NEWS REPORT	ABC
SUN	CBS	LASSIE 10	MY FAVORITE MARTIAN	THE ED SULLIVAN SHOW		THE JUDY GARLAND SHOW 16		CANDID CAMERA 4	WHAT'S MY LINE 15	CBS
SUN	NBC	BILL DANA SHOW	WALT DISNEY'S WONDERFUL WORLD OF COLOR 10		GRINDL	BONANZA		THE DUPONT SHOW OF THE WEEK 5		NBC 3
MON	ABC		THE OUTER LIMITS		WAGON TRAIN			BREAKING POINT 7		ABC
MON	CBS		TO TELL THE TRUTH 8	I'VE GOT A SECRET 12	THE LUCY SHOW	DANNY THOMAS 2	ANDY GRIFFITH 11	EAST SIDE, WEST SIDE 4		CBS
MON	NBC		MOVIE				HOLLYWOOD AND THE STARS	SING ALONG WITH MITCH		NBC 4
TUE	ABC		COMBAT		McHALE'S NAVY 2	THE GREATEST SHOW ON EARTH 2		THE FUGITIVE		ABC
TUE	CBS		MARSHAL DILLON[1]	THE RED SKELTON SHOW		PETTICOAT JUNCTION 13	JACK BENNY	THE GARRY MOORE SHOW 6		CBS
TUE	NBC		MR. NOVAK		REDIGO[2]	THE RICHARD BOONE SHOW		THE BELL TELEPHONE HOUR / THE ANDY WILLIAMS SHOW		NBC 2
WED	ABC		OZZIE AND HARRIET	PATTY DUKE SHOW 12	PRICE IS RIGHT *7	BEN CASEY		CHANNING 3		ABC
WED	CBS		CBS REPORTS / CHRONICLE	GLYNIS 5		THE BEVERLY HILLBILLIES 2	DICK VAN DYKE 2	THE DANNY KAYE SHOW 3		CBS
WED	NBC		THE VIRGINIAN			ESPIONAGE 2		THE ELEVENTH HOUR		NBC 2
THU	ABC		FLINTSTONES 4	DONNA REED	MY THREE SONS 6	THE JIMMY DEAN SHOW 4		SID CAESAR / HERE'S EDIE	LOCAL	ABC
THU	CBS		PASSWORD 3	RAWHIDE		PERRY MASON 6		THE NURSES 7		CBS 2
THU	NBC		TEMPLE HOUSTON		DOCTOR KILDARE		HAZEL 3	KRAFT SUSPENSE THEATRE[3]		NBC 3
FRI	ABC		77 SUNSET STRIP		BURKE'S LAW 6		THE FARMER'S DAUGHTER	THE FIGHT OF THE WEEK[4]		ABC 4
FRI	CBS		THE GREAT ADVENTURE		ROUTE 66		TWILIGHT ZONE 4	ALFRED HITCHCOCK 5		CBS 9
FRI	NBC		INTERNATIONAL SHOWTIME		BOB HOPE PRESENTS THE CHRYSLER THEATER 3		HARRY'S GIRLS	THE JACK PAAR PROGRAM		NBC 2
SAT	ABC		HOOTENANNY		THE LAWRENCE WELK SHOW 2		THE JERRY LEWIS SHOW 9			ABC ††
SAT	CBS		JACKIE GLEASON'S AMERICAN SCENE MAGAZINE		THE NEW PHIL SILVERS SHOW 2	THE DEFENDERS		GUNSMOKE 3		CBS 9
SAT	NBC		THE LIEUTENANT		JOEY BISHOP	MOVIE 3				NBC

NOTES: [1]Reruns of Gunsmoke [2]Formerly Empire [3]Kraft Music Hall (Perry Como) every fourth week [4]Followed by Make That Spare

1964–1965

Day	Net	7	7:30	8	8:30	9	9:30	10	10:30	11 PM
SUN	ABC	LOCAL	WAGON TRAIN			MOVIE				ABC
SUN	CBS	LASSIE (11)	MY FAVORITE MARTIAN	THE ED SULLIVAN SHOW (2)	BROADSIDE (8)	MY LIVING DOLL (17)	JOEY BISHOP	CANDID CAMERA (*4)	WHAT'S MY LINE (5)	CBS (16)
SUN	NBC	PROFILES IN COURAGE	WALT DISNEY'S WONDERFUL WORLD OF COLOR (**)		BILL DANA SHOW (11)	BONANZA (2)		THE ROGUES (6)		NBC
MON	ABC		VOYAGE TO THE BOTTOM OF THE SEA		NO TIME FOR SERGEANTS (11)	WENDY AND ME	BING CROSBY	BEN CASEY (4)		ABC
MON	CBS		TO TELL THE TRUTH (9)	I'VE GOT A SECRET (13)	ANDY GRIFFITH (5)	THE LUCY SHOW	MANY HAPPY RETURNS (3)	SLATTERY'S PEOPLE		CBS
MON	NBC		90 BRISTOL COURT (KAREN; HARRIS AGAINST THE WORLD; TOM, DICK & MARY)			THE ANDY WILLIAMS SHOW[2] (3)		ALFRED HITCHCOCK (3)		NBC (*10)
TUE	ABC		COMBAT		McHALE'S NAVY (3)	THE TYCOON (3)	PEYTON PLACE (I)	THE FUGITIVE (2)		ABC (2)
TUE	CBS		MARSHAL DILLON	WORLD WAR ONE	THE RED SKELTON SHOW (14)		PETTICOAT JUNCTION (2)	THE DOCTORS AND THE NURSES[1] (3)		CBS (3)
TUE	NBC		MR. NOVAK		THE MAN FROM U.N.C.L.E.		THAT WAS THE WK. THAT WAS (2)	THE BELL TELEPHONE HOUR / SPECIALS (2)		NBC (7)
WED	ABC		OZZIE AND HARRIET	PATTY DUKE SHOW (13)	SHINDIG (2)	MICKEY (2)	BURKE'S LAW (4)		ABC SCOPE (2)	ABC
WED	CBS		CBS REPORTS		THE BEVERLY HILLBILLIES (6)	DICK VAN DYKE (3)	CARA WILLIAMS (4)	THE DANNY KAYE SHOW (2)		CBS (2)
WED	NBC		THE VIRGINIAN			MOVIE				NBC
THU	ABC		FLINTSTONES	DONNA REED (5)	MY THREE SONS (7)	BEWITCHED (5)	PEYTON PLACE (II)	THE JIMMY DEAN SHOW (2)		ABC (2)
THU	CBS		THE MUNSTERS	PERRY MASON		PASSWORD (8)	THE BAILEYS OF BALBOA (4)	THE DEFENDERS (4)		CBS (4)
THU	NBC		DANIEL BOONE		DOCTOR KILDARE		HAZEL (4)	KRAFT SUSPENSE THEATRE[3] (4)		NBC (2)
FRI	ABC		JONNY QUEST	THE FARMER'S DAUGHTER (2)	ADDAMS FAMILY (2)	VALENTINE'S DAY	TWELVE O'CLOCK HIGH (4)		LOCAL	ABC
FRI	CBS		RAWHIDE		THE ENTERTAINERS (7)		GOMER PYLE (10)	THE REPORTER		CBS
FRI	NBC		INTERNATIONAL SHOWTIME		BOB HOPE PRESENTS THE CHRYSLER THEATER (4)		JACK BENNY (*13)	THE JACK PAAR PROGRAM		NBC (3)
SAT	ABC		THE OUTER LIMITS		THE LAWRENCE WELK SHOW (2)		THE HOLLYWOOD PALACE (10)		LOCAL (2)	ABC
SAT	CBS		JACKIE GLEASON'S AMERICAN SCENE MAGAZINE		GILLIGAN'S ISLAND (3)	MR. BROADWAY		GUNSMOKE (10)		CBS
SAT	NBC	MR. MAGOO	FLIPPER		KENTUCKY JONES (3)	MOVIE				NBC

NOTES: [1]Formerly *The Nurses* [2]Jonathan Winters specials once a month [3]*Kraft Music Hall* (Perry Como) every fourth week [4]Reruns of *Gunsmoke*

1965–1966

Day	Net	7	7:30	8	8:30	9	9:30	10	10:30	11 PM
SUN	ABC	VOYAGE TO THE BOTTOM OF THE SEA		THE F.B.I. [2]		MOVIE				ABC
	CBS	LASSIE [12]	MY FAVORITE MARTIAN	THE ED SULLIVAN SHOW [3]		PERRY MASON [18]		CANDID CAMERA [9]	WHAT'S MY LINE [6]	CBS — 17
	NBC	BELL TEL. HR. **[8] / SPECIALS	WALT DISNEY'S WONDERFUL WORLD OF COLOR		BRANDED [12]	BONANZA [2]		THE WACKIEST SHIP IN THE ARMY [7]		NBC
MON	ABC		TWELVE O'CLOCK HIGH		THE LEGEND OF JESSE JAMES [2]	A MAN CALLED SHENANDOAH	THE FARMER'S DAUGHTER	BEN CASEY [3]		ABC — 5
	CBS		TO TELL THE TRUTH [10]	I'VE GOT A SECRET [14]	THE LUCY SHOW [4]	ANDY GRIFFITH [6]	HAZEL	THE STEVE LAWRENCE SHOW *[5]		CBS — 5
	NBC		HULLABALOO [4]	JOHN FORSYTHE [2]	DR. KILDARE (I) [5]	THE ANDY WILLIAMS SHOW' [4]		RUN FOR YOUR LIFE		NBC
TUE	ABC		COMBAT		McHALE'S NAVY [4]	F TROOP [4]	PEYTON PLACE (I) [2]	THE FUGITIVE [2]		ABC — 3
	CBS		RAWHIDE		THE RED SKELTON SHOW [8]		PETTICOAT JUNCTION [15]	CBS REPORTS		CBS — 7
	NBC		MY MOTHER THE CAR	PLEASE DON'T EAT THE DAISIES	DR. KILDARE (II)	MOVIE [5]		SPECIALS [3]		NBC
WED	ABC		OZZIE AND HARRIET	PATTY DUKE SHOW [14]	GIDGET [3]	THE BIG VALLEY [5]		AMOS BURKE, SECRET AGENT [2] [3]		ABC — 3
	CBS		LOST IN SPACE		THE BEVERLY HILLBILLIES [4]	GREEN ACRES	DICK VAN DYKE [5]	THE DANNY KAYE SHOW [3]		CBS — 3
	NBC		THE VIRGINIAN			BOB HOPE PRESENTS THE CHRYSLER THEATER [4]		I SPY [3]		NBC
THU	ABC		SHINDIG (I) [2]		O.K. CRACKERBY [8]	BEWITCHED [2]	PEYTON PLACE (II) [2]	THE LONG HOT SUMMER [2]		ABC
	CBS		THE MUNSTERS [2]	GILLIGAN'S ISLAND [2]	MY THREE SONS [2]	MOVIE *[6]				CBS
	NBC		DANIEL BOONE		LAREDO [2]		MONA McCLUSKEY	THE DEAN MARTIN SHOW		NBC
FRI	ABC		FLINTSTONES [2]	TAMMY [6]	ADDAMS FAMILY [2]	HONEY WEST [2]	PEYTON PLACE (III) [2]	THE JIMMY DEAN SHOW [2]		ABC — 3
	CBS		THE WILD, WILD WEST		HOGAN'S HEROES [2]	GOMER PYLE [2]	THE SMOTHERS BROTHERS SHOW	SLATTERY'S PEOPLE		CBS — 2
	NBC		CAMP RUNAMUCK	HANK	CONVOY [2]		MR. ROBERTS	THE MAN FROM U.N.C.L.E. [2]		NBC — 2
SAT	ABC		SHINDIG (II) [2]	KING FAMILY [2]		THE LAWRENCE WELK SHOW [2]	THE HOLLYWOOD PALACE [11]		ABC SCOPE [3]	ABC — 2
	CBS		THE JACKIE GLEASON SHOW		TRIALS OF O'BRIEN [4]		THE LONER	GUNSMOKE		CBS — 11
	NBC		FLIPPER	I DREAM OF JEANNIE	GET SMART	MOVIE				NBC

NOTES: [1] Perry Como special every fourth week. [2] Formerly *Burke's Law*

1966–1967

Day	Net	7	7:30	8	8:30	9	9:30	10	10:30	11 PM
SUN	ABC	VOYAGE TO THE BOTTOM OF THE SEA		THE F.B.I. [3]		MOVIE [2]				
	CBS	LASSIE [13]	IT'S ABOUT TIME	THE ED SULLIVAN SHOW		THE GARRY MOORE SHOW [19]		CANDID CAMERA	WHAT'S MY LINE [7]	[18]
	NBC	BELL TEL. HR. **9 / SPECIALS	WALT DISNEY'S WONDERFUL WORLD OF COLOR		HEY LANDLORD [13]	BONANZA		THE ANDY WILLIAMS SHOW [8]		[5]
MON	ABC		IRON HORSE		RAT PATROL	FELONY SQUAD	PEYTON PLACE (I) [3]	THE BIG VALLEY		[2]
	CBS		GILLIGAN'S ISLAND	RUN BUDDY RUN [3]	THE LUCY SHOW	ANDY GRIFFITH [5]	FAMILY AFFAIR [7]	JEAN ARTHUR	I'VE GOT A SECRET	[15]
	NBC		THE MONKEES	I DREAM OF JEANNIE	ROGER MILLER	THE ROAD WEST		RUN FOR YOUR LIFE		[2]
TUE	ABC		COMBAT		THE ROUNDERS [5]	THE PRUITTS OF SOUTHAMPTON	LOVE ON A ROOFTOP	THE FUGITIVE		[4]
	CBS		DAKTARI		THE RED SKELTON SHOW [2]		PETTICOAT JUNCTION [16]	CBS REPORTS / SPECIALS [4]		[8]
	NBC		THE GIRL FROM U.N.C.L.E.		OCCASIONAL WIFE	MOVIE				
WED	ABC		BATMAN (I)	THE MONROES [2]		THE MAN WHO NEVER WAS	PEYTON PLACE (II)	ABC STAGE '67 [3]		[4]
	CBS		LOST IN SPACE		THE BEVERLY HILLBILLIES [2]	GREEN ACRES [5]	GOMER PYLE [2]	THE DANNY KAYE SHOW [3]		[4]
	NBC		THE VIRGINIAN			BOB HOPE PRESENTS THE CHRYSLER THEATER [5]		I SPY [4]		[2]
THU	ABC		BATMAN (II)	F TROOP [2]	TAMMY GRIMES	BEWITCHED	THAT GIRL [3]	HAWK		[4]
	CBS		JERICHO	MY THREE SONS		MOVIE [7]				[2]
	NBC		DANIEL BOONE		STAR TREK [3]		THE HERO	THE DEAN MARTIN SHOW		[2]
FRI	ABC		GREEN HORNET	THE TIME TUNNEL		THE MILTON BERLE SHOW		TWELVE O'CLOCK HIGH		[3]
	CBS		THE WILD, WILD WEST		HOGAN'S HEROES	MOVIE [2]				
	NBC		TARZAN		THE MAN FROM U.N.C.L.E. [2]		T.H.E. CAT [3]	LAREDO		[2]
SAT	ABC		SHANE		THE LAWRENCE WELK SHOW		THE HOLLYWOOD PALACE [12]		ABC SCOPE [4]	[3]
	CBS		THE JACKIE GLEASON SHOW		PISTOLS 'N' PETTICOATS [5]	MISSION: IMPOSSIBLE		GUNSMOKE		[12]
	NBC		FLIPPER	PLS. DON'T EAT THE DAISIES [3]	GET SMART [2]	MOVIE [2]				

1967–1968

Day	Network	7	7:30	8	8:30	9	9:30	10	10:30	11 PM
SUN	ABC	VOYAGE TO THE BOTTOM OF THE SEA		THE F.B.I. 4		MOVIE 3				ABC
SUN	CBS	LASSIE 14	GENTLE BEN	THE ED SULLIVAN SHOW		THE SMOTHERS BROTHERS		MISSION: IMPOSSIBLE 2		CBS 2
SUN	NBC	AFL FOOTBALL 11	WALT DISNEY'S WONDERFUL WORLD OF COLOR 14		MOTHERS-IN-LAW	BONANZA 20		THE HIGH CHAPARRAL 9		NBC 3
MON	ABC		COWBOY IN AFRICA		RAT PATROL 2	FELONY SQUAD 2	PEYTON PLACE (I) 2	THE BIG VALLEY 4		ABC 3
MON	CBS		GUNSMOKE	THE LUCY SHOW 13	ANDY GRIFFITH 6	FAMILY AFFAIR 8		THE CAROL BURNETT SHOW 2		CBS
MON	NBC		THE MONKEES 2	THE MAN FROM U.N.C.L.E.		THE DANNY THOMAS HOUR 4		I SPY		NBC 3
TUE	ABC		GARRISON'S GORILLAS		THE INVADERS		N.Y.P.D. 2	THE HOLLYWOOD PALACE		ABC 5
TUE	CBS		DAKTARI 3		THE RED SKELTON SHOW		GOOD MORNING WORLD 17	CBS REPORTS SPECIALS		CBS 9
TUE	NBC		I DREAM OF JEANNIE	THE JERRY LEWIS SHOW 3		MOVIE				NBC
WED	ABC		CUSTER		THE SECOND HUNDRED YEARS	MOVIE				ABC
WED	CBS		LOST IN SPACE 3		THE BEVERLY HILLBILLIES 6	GREEN ACRES 3	HE & SHE 3	DUNDEE AND THE CULHANE		CBS
WED	NBC		THE VIRGINIAN			THE KRAFT MUSIC HALL 6		RUN FOR YOUR LIFE		NBC 3
THU	ABC		BATMAN 3	THE FLYING NUN 3	BEWITCHED 4	THAT GIRL 2	PEYTON PLACE (II) 2	GOOD COMPANY 4	LOCAL	ABC
THU	CBS		CIMARRON STRIP			MOVIE				CBS
THU	NBC		DANIEL BOONE 4		IRONSIDE		DRAGNET 2	THE DEAN MARTIN SHOW 2		NBC 3
FRI	ABC		OFF TO SEE THE WIZARD		HONDO		THE GUNS OF WILL SONNETT	JUDD FOR THE DEFENSE		ABC
FRI	CBS		THE WILD WILD WEST		GOMER PYLE 3	MOVIE 4				CBS
FRI	NBC		TARZAN		STAR TREK 2		ACCIDENTAL FAMILY 2	THE BELL TELEPHONE HOUR SPECIALS		NBC 10
SAT	ABC		DATING GAME 2	NEWLYWED GAME 2	THE LAWRENCE WELK SHOW 2		IRON HORSE 13		ABC SCOPE 2	ABC 4
SAT	CBS		THE JACKIE GLEASON SHOW		MY THREE SONS 6	HOGAN'S HEROES 8	PETTICOAT JUNCTION 3	MANNIX 5		CBS
SAT	NBC		MAYA		GET SMART 3	MOVIE 3				NBC

1968–1969

Day	Net	7:00	7:30	8:00	8:30	9:00	9:30	10:00	10:30	11 PM
SUN	ABC	LAND OF THE GIANTS		THE F.B.I.		MOVIE				
SUN	CBS	LASSIE 15	GENTLE BEN	THE ED SULLIVAN SHOW 2		THE SMOTHERS BROTHERS 21		MISSION: IMPOSSIBLE 3		
SUN	NBC	NEW ADVENTURES OF HUCK FINN	WALT DISNEY'S WONDERFUL WORLD OF COLOR	MOTHERS-IN-LAW 15		BONANZA 2		BEAUTIFUL PHYLLIS DILLER SHOW 10		
MON	ABC		THE AVENGERS	PEYTON PLACE (I) 4		THE OUTCASTS 5		THE BIG VALLEY		
MON	CBS		GUNSMOKE		HERE'S LUCY 14	MAYBERRY RFD	FAMILY AFFAIR 3	THE CAROL BURNETT SHOW		
MON	NBC		I DREAM OF JEANNIE	LAUGH-IN 4		MOVIE 2				
TUE	ABC		THE MOD SQUAD	IT TAKES A THIEF			N.Y.P.D. 2	THAT'S LIFE 2		
TUE	CBS		LANCER	THE RED SKELTON SHOW			DORIS DAY SHOW 18	60 MINUTES / SPECIALS		
TUE	NBC		THE JERRY LEWIS SHOW	JULIA 2		MOVIE 5				
WED	ABC		HERE COME THE BRIDES	PEYTON PLACE (II)		MOVIE 5				
WED	CBS		DAKTARI	THE GOOD GUYS 4		THE BEVERLY HILLBILLIES	GREEN ACRES 4	THE JONATHAN WINTERS SHOW 2		
WED	NBC		THE VIRGINIAN			THE KRAFT MUSIC HALL 7		THE OUTSIDER 2		
THU	ABC		THE UGLIEST GIRL IN TOWN	THE FLYING NUN	BEWITCHED 2	THAT GIRL 5	JOURNEY TO THE UNKNOWN 3		LOCAL	
THU	CBS		BLONDIE	HAWAII FIVE-0		MOVIE				
THU	NBC		DANIEL BOONE		IRONSIDE 5		DRAGNET 2	THE DEAN MARTIN SHOW 3		
FRI	ABC		OPERATION: ENTERTAINMENT		FELONY SQUAD 2	DON RICKLES 3	THE GUNS OF WILL SONNETT	JUDD FOR THE DEFENSE 2		
FRI	CBS		THE WILD WILD WEST		GOMER PYLE 4	MOVIE 5				
FRI	NBC		THE HIGH CHAPARRAL		THE NAME OF THE GAME 2			STAR TREK 3		
SAT	ABC		DATING GAME 3	NEWLYWED GAME 3	THE LAWRENCE WELK SHOW 3		THE HOLLYWOOD PALACE 14		LOCAL 6	
SAT	CBS		THE JACKIE GLEASON SHOW		MY THREE SONS 7	HOGAN'S HEROES 9	PETTICOAT JUNCTION 4	MANNIX 6		
SAT	NBC		ADAM-12	GET SMART	THE GHOST & MRS. MUIR 4	MOVIE				

1969–1970

Day	Network	7:00	7:30	8:00	8:30	9:00	9:30	10:00	10:30	11 PM
SUN	ABC	LAND OF THE GIANTS		THE F.B.I.		MOVIE				
SUN	CBS	LASSIE	TO ROME WITH LOVE	THE ED SULLIVAN SHOW		THE LESLIE UGGAMS SHOW		MISSION: IMPOSSIBLE		4
SUN	NBC	WILD KINGDOM	THE WONDERFUL WORLD OF DISNEY¹			BONANZA		THE BOLD ONES		
MON	ABC		THE MUSIC SCENE	THE NEW PEOPLE				LOVE, AMERICAN STYLE		
MON	CBS		GUNSMOKE		HERE'S LUCY	MAYBERRY RFD	DORIS DAY SHOW	THE CAROL BURNETT SHOW		3
MON	NBC		MY WORLD AND WELCOME TO IT	LAUGH-IN		MOVIE				
TUE	ABC		THE MOD SQUAD		MOVIE			MARCUS WELBY, M.D.		
TUE	CBS		LANCER		THE RED SKELTON SHOW		THE GOVERNOR AND J.J.	60 MINUTES / SPECIALS		2
TUE	NBC		I DREAM OF JEANNIE	THE DEBBIE REYNOLDS SHOW	JULIA	MOVIE / FIRST TUESDAY				‡2
WED	ABC		THE FLYING NUN	THE COURTSHIP OF EDDIE'S FATHER	ROOM 222	MOVIE				
WED	CBS		THE GLEN CAMPBELL GOODTIME HOUR		THE BEVERLY HILLBILLIES	MEDICAL CENTER		HAWAII FIVE-O		2
WED	NBC		THE VIRGINIAN			THE KRAFT MUSIC HALL		THEN CAME BRONSON		
THU	ABC		THE GHOST & MRS. MUIR	THAT GIRL	BEWITCHED			IT TAKES A THIEF		3
THU	CBS		FAMILY AFFAIR	THE JIM NABORS HOUR		THIS IS TOM JONES		MOVIE		
THU	NBC		DANIEL BOONE		IRONSIDE		DRAGNET	THE DEAN MARTIN SHOW		5
FRI	ABC		LET'S MAKE A DEAL	THE BRADY BUNCH	MR. DEEDS GOES TO TOWN	HERE COME THE BRIDES		JIMMY DURANTE PRESENTS THE LENNON SISTERS HOUR		
FRI	CBS		GET SMART	THE GOOD GUYS	HOGAN'S HEROES	MOVIE				
FRI	NBC		THE HIGH CHAPARRAL		THE NAME OF THE GAME			BRACKEN'S WORLD		
SAT	ABC		DATING GAME	NEWLYWED GAME	THE LAWRENCE WELK SHOW			THE HOLLYWOOD PALACE	LOCAL	
SAT	CBS		THE JACKIE GLEASON SHOW		MY THREE SONS	GREEN ACRES	PETTICOAT JUNCTION	MANNIX		3
SAT	NBC		THE ANDY WILLIAMS SHOW		ADAM-12	MOVIE				

NOTE: ¹Formerly *Walt Disney's Wonderful World of Color*

1970–1971

Prime-time network television schedule (7:00 PM – 11:00 PM)

Day	Net	7:00	7:30	8:00	8:30	9:00	9:30	10:00	10:30	11:00 PM
SUN	ABC	THE YOUNG REBELS	THE F.B.I.			6 MOVIE				ABC
SUN	CBS	17 LASSIE	6 HOGAN'S HEROES	THE ED SULLIVAN SHOW		23 GLEN CAMPBELL GOODTIME HOUR			2 THE TIM CONWAY COMEDY HOUR	CBS
SUN	NBC	9 WILD KINGDOM	THE WONDERFUL WORLD OF DISNEY		17 BILL COSBY	2 BONANZA		12 THE BOLD ONES		2 NBC
MON	ABC		THE YOUNG LAWYERS		SILENT FORCE	NFL MONDAY NIGHT FOOTBALL				ABC
MON	CBS			GUNSMOKE	16 HERE'S LUCY	3 MAYBERRY RFD	3 DORIS DAY SHOW	3 THE CAROL BURNETT SHOW		CBS
MON	NBC			RED SKELTON *20	LAUGH-IN	4 MOVIE				NBC
TUE	ABC		THE MOD SQUAD		3 MOVIE			MARCUS WELBY, M.D.		2 ABC
TUE	CBS		9 THE BEVERLY HILLBILLIES	6 GREEN ACRES	HEE HAW		2 TO ROME WITH LOVE	60 MINUTES	2 SPECIALS	3 CBS
TUE	NBC		THE DON KNOTTS SHOW		JULIA	3 MOVIE	FIRST TUESDAY			13 NBC
WED	ABC			2 THE COURTSHIP OF EDDIE'S FATHER	2 MAKE ROOM FOR GRANDDADDY	2 ROOM 222		2 DAN AUGUST		ABC
WED	CBS			THE STOREFRONT LAWYERS	2 THE GOVERNOR AND J.J.	2 MEDICAL CENTER		3 HAWAII FIVE-O		3 CBS
WED	NBC			9 THE MEN FROM SHILOH		9 THE KRAFT MUSIC HALL		4 FOUR-IN-ONE (McCLOUD / NIGHT GALLERY / PSYCHIATRIST / S.F. AIRPORT)		NBC
THU	ABC			MATT LINCOLN	7 BEWITCHED	7 BAREFOOT IN THE PARK	THE ODD COUPLE	THE IMMORTAL		ABC
THU	CBS			5 FAMILY AFFAIR	5 THE JIM NABORS HOUR	2 MOVIE				CBS
THU	NBC		THE FLIP WILSON SHOW		IRONSIDE		4 NANCY	THE DEAN MARTIN SHOW		6 NBC
FRI	ABC		2 THE BRADY BUNCH	2 NANNY AND THE PROFESSOR	THE PARTRIDGE FAMILY	THAT GIRL	5 LOVE, AMERICAN STYLE	2 THIS IS TOM JONES		3 ABC
FRI	CBS			THE INTERNS	HEADMASTER	MOVIE				CBS
FRI	NBC		4 THE HIGH CHAPARRAL		THE NAME OF THE GAME			3 BRACKEN'S WORLD		3 NBC
SAT	ABC		4 LET'S MAKE A DEAL	NEWLYWED GAME	THE LAWRENCE WELK SHOW		16 THE MOST DEADLY GAME		LOCAL	ABC
SAT	CBS		MISSION: IMPOSSIBLE	5 MY THREE SONS	11 ARNIE		THE MARY TYLER MOORE SHOW	MANNIX		4 CBS
SAT	NBC		THE ANDY WILLIAMS SHOW		2 ADAM-12	3 MOVIE				NBC

NOTE: *Formerly *The Virginian*

Day / Net	7	7:30	8	8:30	9	9:30	10	10:30	11 PM
SUN ABC	LOCAL	LOCAL	THE F.B.I.		7 MOVIE				ABC
SUN CBS	LOCAL	MOVIE				CADE'S COUNTY		LOCAL	CBS
SUN NBC	LOCAL	THE WONDERFUL WORLD OF DISNEY		18 THE JIMMY STEWART SHOW	BONANZA		13 THE BOLD ONES		3 NBC
MON ABC	LOCAL		NANNY AND THE PROFESSOR	3 LOCAL	NFL MONDAY NIGHT FOOTBALL				2 ABC
MON CBS		LOCAL	GUNSMOKE		17 HERE'S LUCY	4 DORIS DAY SHOW	4 MY THREE SONS	12 ARNIE	2 CBS
MON NBC		LOCAL	LAUGH-IN		5 MOVIE				NBC
TUE ABC		LOCAL	THE MOD SQUAD	4 MOVIE			MARCUS WELBY, M.D.		3 ABC
TUE CBS		LOCAL	GLEN CAMPBELL GOODTIME HOUR	3 HAWAII FIVE-0		4 CANNON		LOCAL	CBS
TUE NBC		LOCAL	IRONSIDE	5 SARGE		THE FUNNY SIDE		LOCAL	NBC
WED ABC		LOCAL	8 BEWITCHED	THE COURTSHIP OF EDDIE'S FATHER	3 SMITH FAMILY	2 SHIRLEY'S WORLD	THE MAN AND THE CITY		ABC
WED CBS		LOCAL	THE CAROL BURNETT SHOW		5 MEDICAL CENTER		3 MANNIX		5 CBS
WED NBC		LOCAL	4 ADAM-12		THE NBC MYSTERY MOVIE (McCLOUD [2]; COLUMBO; McMILLAN AND WIFE)		NIGHT GALLERY†		2 NBC
THU ABC		LOCAL	ALIAS SMITH AND JONES		2 LONGSTREET		OWEN MARSHALL: COUNSELOR AT LAW		ABC
THU CBS		LOCAL	BEARCATS!		MOVIE / † CBS REPORTS				† CBS
THU NBC		LOCAL	THE FLIP WILSON SHOW		2 NICHOLS		THE DEAN MARTIN SHOW		7 NBC
FRI ABC		LOCAL	3 BRADY BUNCH	THE PARTRIDGE FAMILY	2 ROOM 222	3 THE ODD COUPLE	2 LOVE, AMERICAN STYLE		3 ABC
FRI CBS		LOCAL	THE CHICAGO TEDDY BEARS	O'HARA, UNITED STATES TREASURY	MOVIE				CBS
FRI NBC		LOCAL	THE D.A.	MOVIE / CHRONOLOG				LOCAL	NBC
SAT ABC		LOCAL	GETTING TOGETHER	MOVIE			THE PERSUADERS		ABC
SAT CBS		LOCAL	2 ALL IN THE FAMILY	2 FUNNY FACE	THE NEW DICK VAN DYKE SHOW	THE MARY TYLER MOORE SHOW	2 MISSION: IMPOSSIBLE		6 CBS
SAT NBC		LOCAL	THE PARTNERS	THE GOOD LIFE	MOVIE				NBC

NOTE: †Formerly one segment of *Four-In-One*

1972–1973

Day	Net	7:00	7:30	8:00	8:30	9:00	9:30	10:00	10:30	11 PM
SUN	ABC	LOCAL	LOCAL	THE F.B.I.		MOVIE (8)				ABC (3)
	CBS	LOCAL	ANNA & THE KING	M*A*S*H	SANDY DUNCAN	THE NEW DICK VAN DYKE SHOW	MANNIX (2)		LOCAL (6)	CBS
	NBC	LOCAL	THE WONDERFUL WORLD OF DISNEY	THE NBC SUNDAY MYSTERY MOVIE (McCLOUD [3]; COLUMBO [2]; McMILLAN AND WIFE [2] & HEC RAMSEY) (19)					NIGHT GALLERY / LOCAL (3)	NBC
MON	ABC			THE ROOKIES		NFL MONDAY NIGHT FOOTBALL				ABC (3)
	CBS			GUNSMOKE (18)		HERE'S LUCY (5)	DORIS DAY SHOW	THE NEW BILL COSBY SHOW (5)		CBS
	NBC			LAUGH-IN (6)		MOVIE				NBC
TUE	ABC			TEMPERATURES RISING	MOVIE			MARCUS WELBY, M.D.		ABC (4)
	CBS			MAUDE	HAWAII FIVE-O		MOVIE (5)			CBS
	NBC			BONANZA		THE BOLD ONES (14)		NBC REPORTS[1] (4) / AMERICA		NBC
WED	ABC			PAUL LYNDE SHOW	MOVIE			THE JULIE ANDREWS HOUR		ABC
	CBS			THE CAROL BURNETT SHOW		MEDICAL CENTER (6)		CANNON (4)		CBS (2)
	NBC			ADAM-12	THE NBC WEDNESDAY MYSTERY MOVIE (BANACEK; COOL MILLION; MADIGAN) (5)			SEARCH		NBC
THU	ABC			THE MOD SQUAD		THE MEN (ASSIGNMENT: VIENNA; THE DELPHI BUREAU; JIGSAW) (5)		OWEN MARSHALL: COUNSELOR AT LAW		ABC (2)
	CBS			THE WALTONS		MOVIE				CBS
	NBC			THE FLIP WILSON SHOW		IRONSIDE (3)		THE DEAN MARTIN SHOW (6)		NBC (8)
FRI	ABC			BRADY BUNCH (4)	THE PARTRIDGE FAMILY	ROOM 222 (3)	THE ODD COUPLE (4)	LOVE, AMERICAN STYLE (3)		ABC (4)
	CBS			THE SONNY AND CHER COMEDY HOUR		MOVIE (2)				CBS
	NBC			SANFORD & SON (2)	THE LITTLE PEOPLE	GHOST STORY (3)		BANYON		NBC
SAT	ABC			ALIAS SMITH AND JONES / KUNG FU		THE STREETS OF SAN FRANCISCO (3)		THE SIXTH SENSE		ABC (2)
	CBS			ALL IN THE FAMILY	BRIDGET LOVES BERNIE (3)	THE MARY TYLER MOORE SHOW	BOB NEWHART (3)	MISSION: IMPOSSIBLE		CBS (7)
	NBC			EMERGENCY!		MOVIE (2)				NBC

NOTE: [1]First Tuesday once a month

1973–1974

		7	7:30	8	8:30	9	9:30	10	10:30	11 PM	
SUN		LOCAL	THE F.B.I.		9 MOVIE				LOCAL		ABC
		LOCAL	THE NEW PERRY MASON		MANNIX		7 BARNABY JONES			2 LOCAL	CBS
		LOCAL	THE WONDERFUL WORLD OF DISNEY		THE NBC SUNDAY MYSTERY MOVIE 20 (McCLOUD [4]; COLUMBO [3]; McMILLAN AND WIFE [3]; HEC RAMSEY [2])				LOCAL		NBC
MON				THE ROOKIES		2 NFL MONDAY NIGHT FOOTBALL				4	ABC
				GUNSMOKE		19 HERE'S LUCY	6 THE NEW DICK VAN DYKE SHOW	3 MEDICAL CENTER		5	CBS
				LOTSA LUCK	DIANA	MOVIE					NBC
TUE				THE NEW TEMPERATURES RISING[1]	MOVIE			MARCUS WELBY, M.D.		5	ABC
				MAUDE	2 HAWAII FIVE-0		6 MOVIE / HAWKINS/SHAFT				CBS
				CHASE		THE MAGICIAN		POLICE STORY		2	NBC
WED				BOB & CAROL & TED & ALICE	MOVIE			OWEN MARSHALL, COUNSELOR AT LAW / DOC ELLIOT		3 / 1	ABC
				THE SONNY AND CHER COMEDY HOUR		3 CANNON		3 KOJAK			CBS
				ADAM-12	6 THE NBC WEDNESDAY MYSTERY MOVIE (BANACEK [2]; FARADAY AND CO.; THE SNOOP SISTERS; TENAFLY)			LOVE STORY			NBC
THU				TOMA		2 KUNG FU		2 THE STREETS OF SAN FRANCISCO		2	ABC
				THE WALTONS		MOVIE					CBS
				THE FLIP WILSON SHOW		4 IRONSIDE		7 NBC FOLLIES			NBC
FRI				BRADY BUNCH	5 THE ODD COUPLE	4 ROOM 222	5 ADAM'S RIB	5 LOVE, AMERICAN STYLE		5	ABC
				CALUCCI'S DEPT.	ROLL OUT!	MOVIE					CBS
				SANFORD & SON	3 THE GIRL WITH SOMETHING EXTRA	NEEDLES AND PINS	BRIAN KEITH[2]	2 THE DEAN MARTIN COMEDY HOUR		9	NBC
SAT				THE PARTRIDGE FAMILY	MOVIE			THE SIX MILLION DOLLAR MAN		4	ABC
				ALL IN THE FAMILY	4 M*A*S*H	2 THE MARY TYLER MOORE SHOW	2 BOB NEWHART	4 THE CAROL BURNETT SHOW		7	CBS
				EMERGENCY!		3 MOVIE					NBC

NOTES: [1]Formerly *Temperatures Rising* [2]Formerly *The Little People*

1974–1975

Day	Net	7	7:30	8	8:30	9	9:30	10	10:30	11 PM
SUN	ABC	LOCAL	LOCAL	THE SONNY COMEDY REVUE		MOVIE				ABC
	CBS	LOCAL	APPLE'S WAY		KOJAK (2)		MANNIX (2)		LOCAL (8)	CBS
	NBC	LOCAL	THE WONDERFUL WORLD OF DISNEY		THE NBC SUNDAY MYSTERY MOVIE (McCLOUD [5]; COLUMBO [4]; McMILLAN AND WIFE [4]; AMY PRENTISS) (21)				LOCAL	NBC
MON	ABC			THE ROOKIES		NFL MONDAY NIGHT FOOTBALL (3)				ABC (5)
	CBS			GUNSMOKE		MAUDE (20)	RHODA (3)	MEDICAL CENTER		CBS (6)
	NBC			BORN FREE		MOVIE				NBC
TUE	ABC			HAPPY DAYS	MOVIE (2)			MARCUS WELBY, M.D.		ABC (6)
	CBS			GOOD TIMES	M*A*S*H (2)	HAWAII FIVE-O (3)		BARNABY JONES (7)		CBS (3)
	NBC			ADAM-12	MOVIE (7)			POLICE STORY		NBC (2)
WED	ABC			THAT'S MY MAMA	MOVIE			GET CHRISTIE LOVE!		ABC
	CBS			SONS AND DAUGHTERS		CANNON		THE MANHUNTER (4)		CBS
	NBC			LITTLE HOUSE ON THE PRAIRIE		LUCAS TANNER		PETROCELLI		NBC
THU	ABC			THE ODD COUPLE	PAPER MOON (5)	THE STREETS OF SAN FRANCISCO		HARRY O (3)		ABC
	CBS			THE WALTONS		MOVIE (3)				CBS
	NBC			SIERRA		IRONSIDE		MOVIN' ON (8)		NBC
FRI	ABC			KODIAK	THE SIX MILLION DOLLAR MAN		TEXAS WHEELERS (2)	THE NIGHT STALKER		ABC
	CBS			PLANET OF THE APES		MOVIE				CBS
	NBC			SANFORD & SON	CHICO & THE MAN (4)	THE ROCKFORD FILES		POLICE WOMAN		NBC
SAT	ABC			THE NEW LAND		KUNG FU		NAKIA (3)		ABC
	CBS			ALL IN THE FAMILY	FRIENDS AND LOVERS (5)	THE MARY TYLER MOORE SHOW	BOB NEWHART (5)	THE CAROL BURNETT SHOW (3)		CBS (8)
	NBC			EMERGENCY!		MOVIE (4)				NBC

1975–1976

Day	Network	7:30	8	8:30	9	9:30	10	10:30	11 PM
SUN	ABC	SWISS FAMILY ROBINSON	THE SIX MILLION DOLLAR MAN		3 MOVIE				6
	CBS	THREE FOR THE ROAD	CHER		2 KOJAK		2 BRONK		
	NBC	THE WONDERFUL WORLD OF DISNEY	22 THE FAMILY HOLVAK		THE NBC SUNDAY MYSTERY MOVIE (McCLOUD [6]; COLUMBO [5]; McMILLAN AND WIFE [5]; McCOY)				
MON	ABC		BARBARY COAST		NFL MONDAY NIGHT FOOTBALL				6
	CBS		RHODA	2 PHYLLIS	ALL IN THE FAMILY	6 MAUDE	4 MEDICAL CENTER		7
	NBC		THE INVISIBLE MAN		MOVIE				
TUE	ABC		HAPPY DAYS	3 WELCOME BACK, KOTTER	THE ROOKIES		4 MARCUS WELBY, M.D.		7
	CBS		GOOD TIMES	3 JOE AND SONS	SWITCH		BEACON HILL		
	NBC		MOVIN' ON		2 POLICE STORY		3 JOE FORRESTER		
WED	ABC		WHEN THINGS WERE ROTTEN	THAT'S MY MAMA	2 BARETTA		2 STARSKY AND HUTCH		
	CBS		TONY ORLANDO AND DAWN		2 CANNON		5 KATE McSHANE		
	NBC		LITTLE HOUSE ON THE PRAIRIE		2 DOCTORS HOSPITAL		PETROCELLI		2
THU	ABC		BARNEY MILLER	2 ON THE ROCKS	THE STREETS OF SAN FRANCISCO		4 HARRY O		2
	CBS		THE WALTONS		4 MOVIE				
	NBC		THE MONTEFUSCOS	FAY	ELLERY QUEEN		MEDICAL STORY		
FRI	ABC		MOBILE ONE		MOVIE				
	CBS		BIG EDDIE	M*A*S*H	4 HAWAII FIVE-O		8 BARNABY JONES		4
	NBC		SANFORD & SON	5 CHICO & THE MAN	2 THE ROCKFORD FILES		2 POLICE WOMAN		2
SAT	ABC		SATURDAY NIGHT LIVE		S.W.A.T.		2 MATT HELM		
	CBS		THE JEFFERSONS	2 DOC	THE MARY TYLER MOORE SHOW	6 BOB NEWHART	4 THE CAROL BURNETT SHOW		9
	NBC		EMERGENCY!		5 MOVIE				

1976–1977

Day	Net	7	7:30	8	8:30	9	9:30	10	10:30	11 PM
SUN	ABC	COS		THE SIX MILLION DOLLAR MAN		MOVIE 4				ABC
	CBS	60 MINUTES		THE SONNY AND CHER SHOW 9		KOJAK 2		DELVECCHIO 3		CBS
	NBC	THE WONDERFUL WORLD OF DISNEY		THE NBC SUNDAY MYSTERY MOVIE (McCLOUD [7]; COLUMBO [6]; McMILLAN* [6]; QUINCY) 23		THE BIG EVENT				NBC
MON	ABC			THE CAPTAIN & TENNILLE		NFL MONDAY NIGHT FOOTBALL				7 ABC
	CBS			RHODA 3	PHYLLIS	MAUDE 2	ALL'S FAIR 5	EXECUTIVE SUITE		CBS
	NBC			LITTLE HOUSE ON THE PRAIRIE		MOVIE 3				NBC
TUE	ABC			HAPPY DAYS 4	LAVERNE AND SHIRLEY	RICH MAN, POOR MAN—BOOK II 2		FAMILY 2		2 ABC
	CBS			TONY ORLANDO AND DAWN RAINBOW HOUR		M*A*S*H 3	ONE DAY AT A TIME 5	SWITCH 2		2 CBS
	NBC			BAA BAA BLACK SHEEP		POLICE WOMAN 3		POLICE STORY 3		4 NBC
WED	ABC			THE BIONIC WOMAN		BARETTA 2		CHARLIE'S ANGELS 3		ABC
	CBS			GOOD TIMES 4	BALL FOUR	ALL IN THE FAMILY	ALICE 7	THE BLUE KNIGHT		CBS
	NBC			THE PRACTICE 2	MOVIE 2			THE QUEST		NBC
THU	ABC			WELCOME BACK, KOTTER	BARNEY MILLER 2	TONY RANDALL 3	NANCY WALKER	THE STREETS OF SAN FRANCISCO 5		5 ABC
	CBS			THE WALTONS		HAWAII FIVE-O 5		BARNABY JONES 9		5 CBS
	NBC			GEMINI MAN		BEST SELLERS		VAN DYKE AND COMPANY		NBC
FRI	ABC			DONNY AND MARIE		MOVIE 2				ABC
	CBS			SPENCER'S PILOTS		MOVIE				CBS
	NBC			SANFORD & SON	CHICO & THE MAN 6	THE ROCKFORD FILES 3		SERPICO 3		NBC
SAT	ABC			HOLMES & YOYO	MR. T AND TINA	STARSKY AND HUTCH		MOST WANTED 2		2 ABC
	CBS			THE JEFFERSONS 3	DOC	THE MARY TYLER MOORE SHOW 2	BOB NEWHART 7	THE CAROL BURNETT SHOW 5		10 CBS
	NBC			EMERGENCY!		MOVIE 6				NBC

NOTE: *Formerly McMillan and Wife

1977–1978

		7	7:30	8	8:30	9	9:30	10	10:30	11 PM
SUN	ABC		THE HARDY BOYS/ NANCY DREW MYSTERIES	2 THE SIX MILLION DOLLAR MAN		5 MOVIE				ABC
	CBS	60 MINUTES		10 RHODA	4 ON OUR OWN	ALL IN THE FAMILY	8 ALICE	2 KOJAK		4 CBS
	NBC	THE WONDERFUL WORLD OF DISNEY				24 THE BIG EVENT				2 NBC
MON	ABC			THE SAN PEDRO BEACH BUMS		NFL MONDAY NIGHT FOOTBALL				8 ABC
	CBS			YOUNG DAN'L BOONE		BETTY WHITE	6 MAUDE	6 RAFFERTY		CBS
	NBC			LITTLE HOUSE ON THE PRAIRIE		4 MOVIE				NBC
TUE	ABC			HAPPY DAYS	5 LAVERNE AND SHIRLEY	3 THREE'S COMPANY	2 SOAP	FAMILY		3 ABC
	CBS			THE FITZPATRICKS		M*A*S*H	6 ONE DAY AT A TIME	3 LOU GRANT		CBS
	NBC			THE RICHARD PRYOR SHOW		MULLIGAN'S STEW		POLICE WOMAN		4 NBC
WED	ABC			EIGHT IS ENOUGH		2 CHARLIE'S ANGELS		2 BARETTA		4 ABC
	CBS			GOOD TIMES	5 BUSTING LOOSE	2 MOVIE				CBS
	NBC			THE LIFE AND TIMES OF GRIZZLY ADAMS		2 THE OREGON TRAIL		BIG HAWAII		NBC
THU	ABC			WELCOME BACK, KOTTER	3 WHAT'S HAPPENING!!	2 BARNEY MILLER	4 CARTER COUNTRY	THE REDD FOXX COMEDY HOUR		ABC
	CBS			THE WALTONS		6 HAWAII FIVE-O		10 BARNABY JONES		6 CBS
	NBC			CHIPS		THE MAN FROM ATLANTIS		ROSETTI AND RYAN		NBC
FRI	ABC			DONNY AND MARIE		3 MOVIE				ABC
	CBS			WONDER WOMAN		* 2 LOGAN'S RUN		SWITCH		3 CBS
	NBC			SANFORD ARMS	CHICO & THE MAN	4 THE ROCKFORD FILES		4 QUINCY		2 NBC
SAT	ABC			FISH	2 OPERATION PETTICOAT	STARSKY AND HUTCH		3 THE LOVE BOAT		ABC
	CBS			BOB NEWHART	6 WE'VE GOT EACH OTHER	THE JEFFERSONS	4 TONY RANDALL	* 2 THE CAROL BURNETT SHOW		11 CBS
	NBC			THE BIONIC WOMAN		* 3 MOVIE				NBC

1978–1979

Day	Network	7	7:30	8	8:30	9	9:30	10	10:30	11 PM
SUN	ABC		THE HARDY BOYS MYSTERIES	3 BATTLESTAR GALACTICA		MOVIE				9
SUN	CBS	60 MINUTES		11 MARY		ALL IN THE FAMILY	9 ALICE	3 KAZ		
SUN	NBC	THE WONDERFUL WORLD OF DISNEY		25 THE BIG EVENT (I)				2 LIFELINE		
MON	ABC			WELCOME BACK, KOTTER	4 OPERATION PETTICOAT	2 NFL MONDAY NIGHT FOOTBALL				9
MON	CBS			WKRP IN CINCINNATI	4 PEOPLE	M*A*S*H	7 ONE DAY AT A TIME	4 LOU GRANT		2
MON	NBC			LITTLE HOUSE ON THE PRAIRIE		5 MOVIE				
TUE	ABC			HAPPY DAYS	6 LAVERNE AND SHIRLEY	4 THREE'S COMPANY	3 TAXI	STARSKY AND HUTCH		4
TUE	CBS			THE PAPER CHASE		MOVIE				
TUE	NBC			GRANDPA GOES TO WASHINGTON		THE BIG EVENT (II)				2
WED	ABC			EIGHT IS ENOUGH		3 CHARLIE'S ANGELS		3 VEGAS		
WED	CBS			THE JEFFERSONS	5 IN THE BEGINNING	MOVIE				
WED	NBC			DICK CLARK'S LIVE WEDNESDAY		MOVIE				
THU	ABC			MORK & MINDY	WHAT'S HAPPENING!!	3 BARNEY MILLER	5 SOAP	2 FAMILY		4
THU	CBS			THE WALTONS		7 HAWAII FIVE-O		11 BARNABY JONES		7
THU	NBC			PROJECT U.F.O.		2 QUINCY		3 W.E.B.		
FRI	ABC			DONNY AND MARIE		4 MOVIE				
FRI	CBS			WONDER WOMAN		3 THE INCREDIBLE HULK		2 FLYING HIGH		
FRI	NBC			THE WAVERLY WONDERS	WHO'S WATCHING THE KIDS	THE ROCKFORD FILES		5 THE EDDIE CAPRA MYSTERIES		
SAT	ABC			CARTER COUNTRY	2 APPLE PIE	THE LOVE BOAT		2 FANTASY ISLAND		2
SAT	CBS			RHODA	5 GOOD TIMES	6 THE AMERICAN GIRLS		DALLAS		2
SAT	NBC			CHIPS		2 SPECIALS		SWORD OF JUSTICE		

1979–1980

Day	Network	7	7:30	8	8:30	9	9:30	10	10:30	11 PM
SUN	ABC	OUT OF THE BLUE	A NEW KIND OF FAMILY	MORK & MINDY	2 THE ASSOCIATES	MOVIE		6 TRAPPER JOHN, M.D.		ABC
SUN	CBS	60 MINUTES		12 ARCHIE BUNKER'S PLACE¹	10 ONE DAY AT A TIME	5 ALICE	4 THE JEFFERSONS			CBS
SUN	NBC		DISNEY'S WONDERFUL WORLD	26 THE BIG EVENT				3 PRIME TIME SUNDAY		NBC
MON	ABC			240-ROBERT		NFL MONDAY NIGHT FOOTBALL				10 ABC
MON	CBS			THE WHITE SHADOW		2 M*A*S*H	8 WKRP IN CINCINNATI	2 LOU GRANT		3 CBS
MON	NBC			LITTLE HOUSE ON THE PRAIRIE		6 MOVIE				NBC
TUE	ABC			7 HAPPY DAYS	ANGIE	2 THREE'S COMPANY	4 TAXI	2 THE LAZARUS SYNDROME		ABC
TUE	CBS			CALIFORNIA FEVER		MOVIE				CBS
TUE	NBC			THE MISADVENTURES OF SHERIFF LOBO		MOVIE				NBC
WED	ABC			EIGHT IS ENOUGH		4 CHARLIE'S ANGELS		4 VEGA$		2 ABC
WED	CBS			THE LAST RESORT	STRUCK BY LIGHTNING	MOVIE				CBS
WED	NBC			REAL PEOPLE		2 DIFF'RENT STROKES	2 HELLO, LARRY	2 THE BEST OF SATURDAY NIGHT LIVE²		NBC
THU	ABC			LAVERNE AND SHIRLEY	5 BENSON	6 BARNEY MILLER	2 SOAP	3 20/20		2 ABC
THU	CBS			THE WALTONS		8 HAWAII FIVE-O		12 BARNABY JONES		8 CBS
THU	NBC			BUCK ROGERS IN THE 25TH CENTURY		8 QUINCY		4 KATE LOVES A MYSTERY		NBC
FRI	ABC			FANTASY ISLAND		3 MOVIE				ABC
FRI	CBS			THE INCREDIBLE HULK		3 THE DUKES OF HAZZARD		2 DALLAS		3 CBS
FRI	NBC			SHIRLEY		THE ROCKFORD FILES		6 EISCHIED		NBC
SAT	ABC			THE ROPERS	2 DETECTIVE SCHOOL	THE LOVE BOAT		3 HART TO HART		ABC
SAT	CBS			WORKING STIFFS	THE BAD NEWS BEARS	BIG SHAMUS, LITTLE SHAMUS		PARIS		CBS
SAT	NBC			CHIPS		3 BJ AND THE BEAR		2 A MAN CALLED SLOANE		NBC

NOTES: ¹Formerly *All in the Family* ²Reruns of *NBC's Saturday Night Live*

PART IV

THE ENVELOPES, PLEASE

EMMY AWARDS

Television's best-known awards, the Emmys were first presented in January 1949 in Hollywood by the newly formed Academy of Television Arts and Sciences. The awards bore a distinctly local flavor for the first few years, but by 1955 (the year of the first coast-to-coast Emmy telecast, honoring achievements for 1954) they had acquired a truly national character. In 1957 the National Academy of Television Arts and Sciences was formed, which administered the awards exclusively from that year through 1976. In 1977 tension between the Hollywood and New York chapters of the National Academy led to the secession of the Hollywood group, which was reborn as the Academy of Television Arts and Sciences. Lawsuits and countersuits concerning the right to confer the Emmy statuette ensued; eventually a compromise was struck, permitting the Hollywood-based Academy of Television Arts and Sciences to administer the Emmys for prime-time entertainment programs and the New York-based National Academy of Television Arts and Sciences to award Emmys for daytime, sports, and local shows (the National Academy was also authorized to present awards for news programs, but the news divisions of the three commercial networks had for several years declined to participate in the Emmys).

Despite a troubled history of internecine warfare, boycotts and frequently boring awards telecasts, the Emmys remain popular. Presented here are all the winners of Emmy awards from 1948 through 1953; from 1954 on, as the number of award categories began to proliferate, the list has been edited. Included are all awards given to series and individual programs, all awards given to actors, performers, directors, writers, and any noteworthy engineering and special awards. Not included are awards in the technical craft areas (such as cinematography, film and tape editing, sound mixing and editing, lighting, costume design, makeup, choreography, and musical direction). The awards for each year are not listed in the order in which they were presented, but rather have been grouped together insofar as practicable so that awards to programs are listed first, awards to actors and performers second, and awards for directing, writing and other achievements third. The titles of some award categories have been abridged slightly. Though separate awards for daytime shows were first presented in 1974, the daytime Emmys have been integrated with the prime-time Emmys through 1975–1976. Beginning with the 1976–1977 awards—the first to be separately administered by the two Television Academies—the daytime Emmys are listed separately. It should also be noted that for the years 1948 through 1957 the Emmys were presented on a calendar year basis. Beginning in 1958, however, the awards were given on a seasonal basis; the 1958–1959 Emmy season covers a fourteen-month period, and later awards cover a twelve-to-thirteen-month period which usually runs from March to March or April to April. The term "Emmy" is derived from "Immy," a nickname for the image orthicon camera tube developed during the late 1940s.

1948

MOST POPULAR TELEVISION PROGRAM: *Pantomime Quiz Time*, KTLA
BEST FILM MADE FOR TELEVISION: "The Necklace," *Your Show Time*
MOST OUTSTANDING TELEVISION PERSONALITY: Shirley Dinsdale and her puppet, Judy Splinters, KTLA
TECHNICAL AWARD: Charles Mesak, Don Lee Television, for the phase-finder
STATION AWARD: KTLA, Los Angeles
SPECIAL AWARD: Louis McManus, "for his original design of the Emmy"

1949

BEST LIVE SHOW: *The Ed Wynn Show*, KTTV (CBS)
BEST KINESCOPE SHOW: *The Texaco Star Theater*, KNBH (NBC)
BEST FILM MADE FOR, AND VIEWED ON TELEVISION: *The Life of Riley*, KNBH (NBC)
BEST PUBLIC SERVICE, CULTURAL, OR EDUCATIONAL PROGRAM: *Crusade in Europe*, KECA-TV and KTTV (ABC)
BEST CHILDREN'S SHOW: *Time for Beany*, KTLA
MOST OUTSTANDING LIVE PERSONALITY: Ed Wynn
MOST OUTSTANDING KINESCOPE PERSONALITY: Milton Berle
BEST SPORTS COVERAGE: Wrestling, KTLA
STATION ACHIEVEMENT: KTLA, Los Angeles (Honorable mention: KECA-TV)
BEST COMMERCIAL MADE FOR TELEVISION: Lucky Strike, N. W. Ayer & Son, Inc., for the American Tobacco Company
TECHNICAL AWARD: Harold W. Jury, KTSL, Los Angeles, for the synchronizing coordinator

1950

BEST VARIETY SHOW: *The Alan Young Show*, KTTV (CBS)
BEST DRAMATIC SHOW: *Pulitzer Prize Playhouse*, KECA-TV (ABC)

BEST GAME AND AUDIENCE PARTICIPATION SHOW: *Truth or Consequences*, KTTV (CBS)

BEST CHILDREN'S SHOW: *Time for Beany*, KTLA

BEST EDUCATIONAL SHOW: *KFI University*, KFI-TV

BEST CULTURAL SHOW: *Campus Chorus and Orchestra*, KTSL

BEST PUBLIC SERVICE: *City at Night*, KTLA

BEST SPORTS COVERAGE: *Rams Football*, KNBH

BEST NEWS PROGRAM: *KTLA Newsreel*, KTLA

SPECIAL EVENTS: "Departure of Marines for Korea," KFMB-TV and KTLA

MOST OUTSTANDING PERSONALITY: Groucho Marx, KNBH (NBC)

BEST ACTOR: Alan Young, KTTV (CBS)

BEST ACTRESS: Gertrude Berg, KTTV (CBS)

STATION ACHIEVEMENT: KTLA, Los Angeles

TECHNICAL ACHIEVEMENT: KNBH (NBC), for the Orthogram TV Amplifier

1951

BEST VARIETY SHOW: *Your Show of Shows* (NBC)

BEST COMEDY SHOW: *The Red Skelton Show* (NBC)

BEST DRAMATIC SHOW: *Studio One* (CBS)

BEST ACTOR: Sid Caesar (NBC)

BEST ACTRESS: Imogene Coca (NBC)

BEST COMEDIAN OR COMEDIENNE: Red Skelton (NBC)

SPECIAL ACHIEVEMENT AWARD: Senator Estes Kefauver, "for outstanding public service on television"

1952

BEST VARIETY PROGRAM: *Your Show of Shows* (NBC)

BEST SITUATION COMEDY: *I Love Lucy* (CBS)

BEST DRAMATIC PROGRAM: *Robert Montgomery Presents* (NBC)

BEST MYSTERY, ACTION, OR ADVENTURE PROGRAM: *Dragnet* (NBC)

BEST PUBLIC AFFAIRS PROGRAM: *See It Now* (CBS)

BEST AUDIENCE PARTICIPATION, QUIZ, OR PANEL PROGRAM: *What's My Line?* (CBS)

BEST CHILDREN'S PROGRAM: *Time for Beany* (SYNDICATED)

MOST OUTSTANDING PERSONALITY: Bishop Fulton J. Sheen (DUMONT)

BEST ACTOR: Thomas Mitchell

BEST ACTRESS: Helen Hayes

BEST COMEDIAN: Jimmy Durante (NBC)
BEST COMEDIENNE: Lucille Ball (CBS)

1953

BEST NEW PROGRAMS: *Make Room for Daddy* (ABC); *The U.S. Steel Hour* (ABC)
BEST VARIETY PROGRAM: *Omnibus* (CBS)
BEST SITUATION COMEDY: *I Love Lucy* (CBS)
BEST DRAMATIC PROGRAM: *The U.S. Steel Hour* (ABC)
BEST MYSTERY, ACTION, OR ADVENTURE PROGRAM: *Dragnet* (NBC)
BEST PUBLIC AFFAIRS PROGRAM: *Victory at Sea* (NBC)
BEST PROGRAM OF NEWS OR SPORTS: *See It Now* (CBS)
BEST AUDIENCE PARTICIPATION, QUIZ, OR PANEL PROGRAMS: *This Is Your Life* (NBC); *What's My Line?* (CBS)
BEST CHILDREN'S PROGRAM: *Kukla, Fran and Ollie* (NBC)
MOST OUTSTANDING PERSONALITY: Edward R. Murrow (CBS)
BEST MALE STAR OF REGULAR SERIES: Donald O'Connor, *The Colgate Comedy Hour* (NBC)
BEST FEMALE STAR OF REGULAR SERIES: Eve Arden, *Our Miss Brooks* (CBS)
BEST SERIES SUPPORTING ACTOR: Art Carney, *The Jackie Gleason Show* (CBS)
BEST SERIES SUPPORTING ACTRESS: Vivian Vance, *I Love Lucy* (CBS)

1954

BEST VARIETY SERIES, INCLUDING MUSICAL VARIETIES: *Disneyland* (ABC)
BEST SITUATION COMEDY SERIES: *Make Room for Daddy* (ABC)
BEST DRAMATIC SERIES: *The U.S. Steel Hour* (ABC)
BEST MYSTERY OR INTRIGUE SERIES: *Dragnet* (NBC)
BEST WESTERN OR ADVENTURE SERIES: *Stories of the Century* (SYNDICATED)
BEST CULTURAL, RELIGIOUS, OR EDUCATIONAL PROGRAM: *Omnibus* (CBS)
BEST SPORTS PROGRAM: *Gillette Cavalcade of Sports* (NBC)
BEST AUDIENCE, GUEST PARTICIPATION, OR PANEL PROGRAM: *This Is Your Life* (NBC)
BEST DAYTIME PROGRAM: *Art Linkletter's House Party* (CBS)
BEST CHILDREN'S PROGRAM: *Lassie* (CBS)
BEST INDIVIDUAL PROGRAM OF THE YEAR: "Operation Undersea," *Disneyland* (ABC)

MOST OUTSTANDING NEW PERSONALITY: George Gobel (NBC)

BEST ACTOR STARRING IN A REGULAR SERIES: Danny Thomas, *Make Room for Daddy* (ABC)

BEST ACTRESS STARRING IN A REGULAR SERIES: Loretta Young, *The Loretta Young Show* (NBC)

BEST ACTOR IN A SINGLE PERFORMANCE: Robert Cummings, "Twelve Angry Men," *Studio One* (CBS)

BEST ACTRESS IN A SINGLE PERFORMANCE: Judith Anderson, "Macbeth," *Hallmark Hall of Fame* (NBC)

BEST SUPPORTING ACTOR IN A REGULAR SERIES: Art Carney, *The Jackie Gleason Show* (CBS)

BEST SUPPORTING ACTRESS IN A REGULAR SERIES: Audrey Meadows, *The Jackie Gleason Show* (CBS)

BEST MALE SINGER: Perry Como (CBS)

BEST FEMALE SINGER: Dinah Shore (NBC)

BEST NEWS REPORTER OR COMMENTATOR: John Daly (ABC)

BEST DIRECTION: Franklin Schaffner, "Twelve Angry Men," *Studio One* (CBS)

BEST WRITTEN DRAMATIC MATERIAL: Reginald Rose, "Twelve Angry Men," *Studio One* (CBS)

BEST WRITTEN COMEDY MATERIAL: James Allardice, Jack Douglas, Hal Kanter, Harry Winkler, *The George Gobel Show* (NBC)

BEST TECHNICAL ACHIEVEMENT: John West, Color TV Policy and Burbank Color (NBC)

1955

BEST VARIETY SERIES: *The Ed Sullivan Show* (CBS)

BEST COMEDY SERIES: *You'll Never Get Rich* (CBS)

BEST DRAMATIC SERIES: *Producers' Showcase* (NBC)

BEST ACTION OR ADVENTURE SERIES: *Disneyland* (ABC)

BEST MUSIC SERIES: *Your Hit Parade* (NBC)

BEST DOCUMENTARY (RELIGIOUS, EDUCATIONAL OR INTERVIEW PROGRAM): *Omnibus* (CBS)

BEST AUDIENCE PARTICIPATION SERIES: *The $64,000 Question* (CBS)

BEST CONTRIBUTION TO DAYTIME PROGRAMMING: *Matinee Theater* (NBC)

BEST CHILDREN'S SERIES: *Lassie* (CBS)

BEST SINGLE PROGRAM OF THE YEAR: "Peter Pan," *Producers' Showcase* (NBC)

BEST SPECIAL EVENT OR NEWS PROGRAM: A-Bomb Coverage (CBS)

BEST ACTOR IN A CONTINUING PERFORMANCE: Phil Silvers, *You'll Never Get Rich* (CBS)

BEST ACTRESS IN A CONTINUING PERFORMANCE: Lucille Ball, *I Love Lucy* (CBS)

BEST ACTOR IN A SINGLE PERFORMANCE: Lloyd Nolan, "The Caine Mutiny Court Martial," *Ford Star Jubilee* (CBS)

BEST ACTRESS IN A SINGLE PERFORMANCE: Mary Martin, "Peter Pan," *Producers' Showcase* (NBC)

BEST ACTOR IN A SUPPORTING ROLE: Art Carney, *The Honeymooners* (CBS)

BEST ACTRESS IN A SUPPORTING ROLE: Nanette Fabray, *Caesar's Hour* (NBC)

BEST EMCEE OR PROGRAM HOST: Perry Como (NBC)

BEST COMEDIAN: Phil Silvers (CBS)

BEST COMEDIENNE: Nanette Fabray (NBC)

BEST MALE SINGER: Perry Como (NBC)

BEST FEMALE SINGER: Dinah Shore (NBC)

BEST NEWS COMMENTATOR OR REPORTER: Edward R. Murrow (CBS)

BEST SPECIALTY ACT: Marcel Marceau (NBC)

BEST PRODUCER (LIVE SERIES): Fred Coe, *Producers' Showcase* (NBC)

BEST PRODUCER (FILM SERIES): Walt Disney, *Disneyland* (ABC)

BEST DIRECTOR (LIVE SERIES): Franklin Schaffner, "The Caine Mutiny Court Martial," *Ford Star Jubilee* (CBS)

BEST DIRECTOR (FILM SERIES): Nat Hiken, *You'll Never Get Rich* (CBS)

BEST ORIGINAL TELEPLAY WRITING: Rod Serling, "Patterns," *Kraft Television Theatre* (NBC)

BEST TELEVISION ADAPTATION: Paul Gregory and Franklin Schaffner, "The Caine Mutiny Court Martial," *Ford Star Jubilee* (CBS)

BEST COMEDY WRITING: Nat Hiken, Barry Blitser, Arnold Auerbach, Harvey Orkin, Vincent Bogert, Arnie Rosen, Coleman Jacoby, Tony Webster, and Harry Ryan, *You'll Never Get Rich* (CBS)

1956

BEST SERIES (HALF HOUR OR LESS): *You'll Never Get Rich* (CBS)

BEST SERIES (ONE HOUR OR MORE): *Caesar's Hour* (NBC)

BEST NEW PROGRAM SERIES: *Playhouse 90* (CBS)

BEST PUBLIC SERVICE SERIES: *See It Now* (CBS)

BEST SINGLE PROGRAM OF THE YEAR: "Requiem for a Heavyweight," *Playhouse 90* (CBS)

BEST COVERAGE OF A NEWSWORTHY EVENT: "Years of Crisis," Edward R. Murrow and correspondents (CBS)

BEST CONTINUING PERFORMANCE IN A DRAMATIC SERIES (ACTOR): Robert Young, *Father Knows Best* (NBC)

BEST CONTINUING PERFORMANCE IN A DRAMATIC SERIES (ACTRESS): Loretta Young, *The Loretta Young Show* (NBC)

BEST SINGLE PERFORMANCE (ACTOR): Jack Palance, "Requiem for a Heavyweight," *Playhouse 90* (CBS)

BEST SINGLE PERFORMANCE (ACTRESS): Claire Trevor, "Dodsworth," *Producers' Showcase* (NBC)

BEST MALE PERSONALITY (CONTINUING PERFORMANCE): Perry Como (NBC)

BEST FEMALE PERSONALITY (CONTINUING PERFORMANCE): Dinah Shore (NBC)

BEST CONTINUING PERFORMANCE BY A COMEDIAN IN A SERIES: Sid Caesar, *Caesar's Hour* (NBC)

BEST CONTINUING PERFORMANCE BY A COMEDIENNE IN A SERIES: Nanette Fabray, *Caesar's Hour* (NBC)

BEST SUPPORTING PERFORMANCE (ACTOR): Carl Reiner, *Caesar's Hour* (NBC)

BEST SUPPORTING PERFORMANCE (ACTRESS): Pat Carroll, *Caesar's Hour* (NBC)

BEST NEWS COMMENTATOR: Edward R. Murrow (CBS)

BEST DIRECTION (HALF HOUR OR LESS): Sheldon Leonard, "Danny's Comeback," *The Danny Thomas Show* (ABC)

BEST DIRECTION (ONE HOUR OR MORE): Ralph Nelson, "Requiem for a Heavyweight," *Playhouse 90* (CBS)

BEST TELEPLAY WRITING (HALF HOUR OR LESS): James P. Cavanaugh, "Fog Closing in," *Alfred Hitchcock Presents* (CBS)

BEST TELEPLAY WRITING (ONE HOUR OR MORE): Rod Serling, "Requiem for a Heavyweight," *Playhouse 90* (CBS)

BEST COMEDY WRITING: *You'll Never Get Rich* (CBS)

BEST ENGINEERING OR TECHNICAL ACHIEVEMENT: Ampex and CBS, for videotape development

1957

BEST MUSICAL, VARIETY, AUDIENCE PARTICIPATION, OR QUIZ SERIES: *The Dinah Shore Show* (NBC)

BEST COMEDY SERIES: *The Phil Silvers Show (You'll Never Get Rich)* (CBS)

BEST DRAMATIC SERIES WITH CONTINUING CHARACTERS: *Gunsmoke* (CBS)

BEST DRAMATIC ANTHOLOLGY SERIES: *Playhouse 90* (CBS)

BEST NEW PROGRAM SERIES: *The Seven Lively Arts* (CBS)

BEST PUBLIC SERVICE PROGRAM OR SERIES: *Omnibus* (ABC and NBC)

BEST SINGLE PROGRAM OF THE YEAR: "The Comedian," *Playhouse 90* (CBS)

BEST CONTINUING PERFORMANCE BY AN ACTOR IN A LEADING ROLE IN A DRAMATIC OR COMEDY SERIES: Robert Young, *Father Knows Best* (NBC)

BEST CONTINUING PERFORMANCE BY AN ACTRESS IN A LEADING ROLE IN A DRAMATIC OR COMEDY SERIES: Jane Wyatt, *Father Knows Best* (NBC)

BEST SINGLE PERFORMANCE BY AN ACTOR: Peter Ustinov, "Life of Samuel Johnson," *Omnibus* (NBC)

BEST SINGLE PERFORMANCE BY AN ACTRESS: Polly Bergen, "The Helen Morgan Story," *Playhouse 90* (CBS)

BEST CONTINUING PERFORMANCE BY A MALE WHO PLAYS HIMSELF: Jack Benny, *The Jack Benny Show* (CBS)

BEST CONTINUING PERFORMANCE BY A FEMALE WHO PLAYS HERSELF: Dinah Shore, *The Dinah Shore Show* (NBC)

BEST CONTINUING SUPPORTING PERFORMANCE BY AN ACTOR IN A DRAMATIC OR COMEDY SERIES: Carl Reiner, *Caesar's Hour* (NBC)

BEST CONTINUING SUPPORTING PERFORMANCE BY AN ACTRESS IN A DRAMATIC OR COMEDY SERIES: Ann B. Davis, *The Bob Cummings Show* (CBS and NBC)

BEST NEWS COMMENTARY: Edward R. Murrow, *See It Now* (CBS)

BEST DIRECTION (HALF HOUR OR LESS): Robert Stevens, "The Glass Eye," *Alfred Hitchcock Presents* (CBS)

BEST DIRECTION (ONE HOUR OR MORE): Bob Banner, *The Dinah Shore Show* (NBC)

BEST TELEPLAY WRITING (HALF HOUR OR LESS): Paul Monash, "The Lonely Wizard," *Schlitz Playhouse of Stars* (CBS)

BEST TELEPLAY WRITING (HOUR OR MORE): Rod Serling, "The Comedian," *Playhouse 90* (CBS)

BEST COMEDY WRITING: Nat Hiken, Billy Friedberg, Phil Sharp, Terry Ryan, Coleman Jacoby, Arnold Rosen, Sidney Zelinka, A. J. Russell, and Tony Webster, *The Phil Silvers Show* (*You'll Never Get Rich*) (CBS)

BEST ENGINEERING OR TECHNICAL ACHIEVEMENT: *Wide, Wide World* (NBC)

1958–1959   (1 JANUARY 1958–28 FEBRUARY 1959)

BEST MUSICAL OR VARIETY SERIES: *The Dinah Shore Chevy Show* (NBC)

BEST COMEDY SERIES: *The Jack Benny Show* (CBS)

BEST DRAMATIC SERIES (LESS THAN ONE HOUR): *Alcoa-Goodyear Theatre* (NBC)

BEST DRAMATIC SERIES (ONE HOUR OR LONGER): *Playhouse 90* (CBS)

BEST WESTERN SERIES: *Maverick* (ABC)

BEST NEWS REPORTING SERIES: *The Huntley-Brinkley Report* (NBC)

BEST PUBLIC SERVICE PROGRAM OR SERIES: *Omnibus* (NBC)

BEST PANEL, QUIZ, OR AUDIENCE PARTICIPATION SERIES: *What's My Line?* (CBS)

MOST OUTSTANDING SINGLE PROGRAM OF THE YEAR: "An Evening with Fred Astaire" (NBC)

BEST SPECIAL MUSICAL OR VARIETY PROGRAM: "An Evening with Fred Astaire" (NBC)

BEST SPECIAL DRAMATIC PROGRAM: "Little Moon of Alban," *Hallmark Hall of Fame* (NBC)

BEST SPECIAL NEWS PROGRAM: "Face of Red China" (CBS)

BEST ACTOR IN A LEADING ROLE IN A DRAMATIC SERIES: Raymond Burr, *Perry Mason* (CBS)

BEST ACTRESS IN A LEADING ROLE IN A DRAMATIC SERIES: Loretta Young, *The Loretta Young Show* (NBC)

BEST ACTOR IN A LEADING ROLE IN A COMEDY SERIES: Jack Benny, *The Jack Benny Show* (CBS)

BEST ACTRESS IN A LEADING ROLE IN A COMEDY SERIES: Jane Wyatt, *Father Knows Best* (NBC and CBS)

BEST PERFORMANCE BY AN ACTOR IN A MUSICAL OR VARIETY SERIES: Perry Como, *The Perry Como Show* (NBC)

BEST PERFORMANCE BY AN ACTRESS IN A MUSICAL OR VARIETY SERIES: Dinah Shore, *The Dinah Shore Chevy Show* (NBC)

BEST SINGLE PERFORMANCE BY AN ACTOR: Fred Astaire, "An Evening with Fred Astaire," (NBC)

BEST SINGLE PERFORMANCE BY AN ACTRESS: Julie Harris, "Little Moon of Alban," *Hallmark Hall of Fame* (NBC)

BEST SUPPORTING ACTOR IN A DRAMATIC SERIES: Dennis Weaver, *Gunsmoke* (CBS)

BEST SUPPORTING ACTRESS IN A DRAMATIC SERIES: Barbara Hale, *Perry Mason* (CBS)

BEST SUPPORTING ACTOR IN A COMEDY SERIES: Tom Poston, *The Steve Allen Show* (NBC)

BEST SUPPORTING ACTRESS IN A COMEDY SERIES: Ann B. Davis, *The Bob Cummings Show* (NBC)

BEST NEWS COMMENTATOR OR ANALYST: Edward R. Murrow (CBS)

BEST DIRECTION OF A SINGLE PROGRAM OF A DRAMATIC SERIES (LESS THAN ONE HOUR): Jack Smight, "Eddie," *Alcoa-Goodyear Theatre* (NBC)

BEST DIRECTION OF A SINGLE PROGRAM OF A DRAMATIC SERIES (ONE HOUR OR LONGER): George Schaefer, "Little Moon of Alban," *Hallmark Hall of Fame* (NBC)

BEST DIRECTION OF A SINGLE MUSICAL OR VARIETY PROGRAM: Bud Yorkin, "An Evening with Fred Astaire" (NBC)

BEST DIRECTION OF A SINGLE PROGRAM OF A COMEDY SERIES: Peter Tewksbury, "A Medal for Margaret," *Father Knows Best* (CBS)

BEST WRITING OF A SINGLE PROGRAM OF A DRAMATIC SERIES (LESS THAN ONE HOUR): Alfred Brenner and Ken Hughes, "Eddie," *Alcoa-Goodyear Theatre* (NBC)

BEST WRITING OF A SINGLE PROGRAM OF A DRAMATIC SERIES (ONE HOUR OR LONGER): James Costigan, "Little Moon of Alban," *Hallmark Hall of Fame* (NBC)

BEST WRITING OF A SINGLE MUSICAL OR VARIETY PROGRAM: Bud Yorkin and Herbert Baker, "An Evening with Fred Astaire" (NBC)

BEST WRITING OF A SINGLE PROGRAM OF A COMEDY SERIES: Sam Perrin, George Balzer, Hal Goodman, and Al Gordon, "The Jack Benny Show with Ernie Kovacs," *The Jack Benny Show* (CBS)

BEST ON-THE-SPOT COVERAGE OF A NEWS EVENT: CBS, for coverage of the Cuban Revolution

BEST ENGINEERING OR TECHNICAL ACHIEVEMENT: "Industry-wide improvement of editing videotape as exemplified by ABC, CBS, NBC"

TRUSTEES' AWARD: Bob Hope

1959–1960   (1 MARCH 1959–31 MARCH 1960)

OUTSTANDING PROGRAM ACHIEVEMENT IN THE FIELD OF VARIETY: "The Fabulous Fifties" (CBS)

OUTSTANDING PROGRAM ACHIEVEMENT IN THE FIELD OF HUMOR: "Art Carney Special" ("Very Important People") (NBC)

OUTSTANDING PROGRAM ACHIEVEMENT IN THE FIELD OF DRAMA: *Playhouse 90* (CBS)

OUTSTANDING ACHIEVEMENT IN THE FIELD OF MUSIC: "Leonard Bernstein and the New York Philharmonic" (CBS)

OUTSTANDING PROGRAM ACHIEVEMENT IN THE FIELD OF NEWS: *The Huntley-Brinkley Report* (NBC)

OUTSTANDING PROGRAM ACHIEVEMENT IN THE FIELD OF PUBLIC AFFAIRS AND EDUCATION: *The Twentieth Century* (CBS)

OUTSTANDING PROGRAM ACHIEVEMENT IN THE FIELD OF CHILDREN'S PROGRAMMING: *Huckleberry Hound* (SYNDICATED)

OUTSTANDING PERFORMANCE BY AN ACTOR IN A SERIES: Robert Stack, *The Untouchables* (ABC)

OUTSTANDING PERFORMANCE BY AN ACTRESS IN A SERIES: Jane Wyatt, *Father Knows Best* (CBS)

OUTSTANDING SINGLE PERFORMANCE BY AN ACTOR: Laurence Olivier, "The Moon and Sixpence" (NBC)

OUTSTANDING SINGLE PERFORMANCE BY AN ACTRESS: Ingrid Bergman, "The Turn of the Screw," *Ford Startime* (NBC)

OUTSTANDING PERFORMANCE IN A VARIETY OR MUSICAL PROGRAM OR SERIES: Harry Belafonte, "Tonight with Belafonte," *The Revlon Revue* (CBS)

OUTSTANDING DIRECTORIAL ACHIEVEMENT IN DRAMA: Robert Mulligan, "The Moon and Sixpence" (NBC)

OUTSTANDING DIRECTORIAL ACHIEVEMENT IN COMEDY: Ralph Levy, for the Jack Benny hour specials (CBS)

OUTSTANDING WRITING ACHIEVEMENT IN DRAMA: Rod Serling, *The Twilight Zone* (CBS)

OUTSTANDING WRITING ACHIEVEMENT IN COMEDY: Al Gordon and Hal Goldman, *The Jack Benny Show* (CBS)

OUTSTANDING WRITING ACHIEVEMENT IN THE DOCUMENTARY FIELD: Howard K. Smith and Av Westin, "The Population Explosion" (CBS)

TRUSTEES' AWARD: Dr. Frank Stanton, president of CBS, Inc., "for outstanding service to television"

1960–1961   (1 APRIL 1960–15 APRIL 1961)

OUTSTANDING PROGRAM ACHIEVEMENT IN THE FIELD OF VARIETY: "Astaire Time" (NBC)

OUTSTANDING PROGRAM ACHIEVEMENT IN THE FIELD OF HUMOR: *The Jack Benny Show* (CBS)

OUTSTANDING PROGRAM ACHIEVEMENT IN THE FIELD OF DRAMA: "Macbeth," *Hallmark Hall of Fame* (NBC)

OUTSTANDING PROGRAM ACHIEVEMENT IN THE FIELD OF NEWS: *The Huntley-Brinkley Report* (NBC)

OUTSTANDING PROGRAM ACHIEVEMENT IN THE FIELD OF PUBLIC AFFAIRS AND EDUCATION: *The Twentieth Century* (CBS)

OUTSTANDING ACHIEVEMENT IN THE FIELD OF CHILDREN'S PROGRAMMING: "Aaron Copland's Birthday Party," *Young People's Concert* (CBS)

OUTSTANDING ACHIEVEMENT IN THE FIELD OF MUSIC FOR TELEVISION: "Leonard Bernstein and the New York Philharmonic" (CBS)

PROGRAM OF THE YEAR: "Macbeth," *Hallmark Hall of Fame* (NBC)

OUTSTANDING PERFORMANCE BY AN ACTOR IN A SERIES: Raymond Burr, *Perry Mason* (CBS)

OUTSTANDING PERFORMANCE BY AN ACTRESS IN A SERIES: Barbara Stanwyck, *The Barbara Stanwyck Show* (NBC)

OUTSTANDING SINGLE PERFORMANCE BY AN ACTOR IN A LEADING ROLE: Maurice Evans, "Macbeth," *Hallmark Hall of Fame* (NBC)

OUTSTANDING SINGLE PERFORMANCE BY AN ACTRESS IN A LEADING ROLE: Judith Anderson, "Macbeth," *Hallmark Hall of Fame* (NBC)

OUTSTANDING PERFORMANCE IN A VARIETY OR MUSICAL PROGRAM OR SERIES: Fred Astaire, "Astaire Time" (NBC)

OUTSTANDING PERFORMANCE IN A SUPPORTING ROLE BY AN ACTOR OR ACTRESS IN A SERIES: Don Knotts, *The Andy Griffith Show* (CBS)

OUTSTANDING PERFORMANCE IN A SUPPORTING ROLE BY AN ACTOR OR ACTRESS IN A SINGLE PROGRAM: Roddy McDowall, "Not Without Honor," *Our American Heritage* (NBC)

OUTSTANDING DIRECTORIAL ACHIEVEMENT IN DRAMA: George Schaefer, "Macbeth," *Hallmark Hall of Fame* (NBC)

OUTSTANDING DIRECTORIAL ACHIEVEMENT IN COMEDY: Sheldon Leonard, *The Danny Thomas Show* (CBS)

OUTSTANDING WRITING ACHIEVEMENT IN DRAMA: Rod Serling, *The Twilight Zone* (CBS)

OUTSTANDING WRITING ACHIEVEMENT IN COMEDY: Sherwood Schwartz, Dave O'Brien, Al Schwartz, Martin Ragaway, and Red Skelton, *The Red Skelton Show* (CBS)

OUTSTANDING WRITING ACHIEVEMENT IN THE DOCUMENTARY FIELD: Victor Wolfson, *Winston Churchill—The Valiant Years* (ABC)

TRUSTEES' AWARDS: (1) National Educational Television and Radio Center and its affiliated stations; and (2) Joyce C. Hall, president of Hallmark Cards, Inc. (sponsor of *Hallmark Hall of Fame*)

1961–1962   (16 APRIL 1961–14 APRIL 1962)

OUTSTANDING PROGRAM ACHIEVEMENT IN THE FIELD OF VARIETY: *The Garry Moore Show* (CBS)

OUTSTANDING PROGRAM ACHIEVEMENT IN THE FIELD OF HUMOR: *The Bob Newhart Show* (NBC)

OUTSTANDING PROGRAM ACHIEVEMENT IN THE FIELD OF DRAMA: *The Defenders* (CBS)

OUTSTANDING PROGRAM ACHIEVEMENT IN THE FIELD OF MUSIC: "Leonard Bernstein and the New York Philharmonic in Japan" (CBS)

OUTSTANDING PROGRAM ACHIEVEMENT IN THE FIELD OF NEWS: *The Huntley-Brinkley Report* (NBC)

OUTSTANDING PROGRAM ACHIEVEMENT IN THE FIELDS OF EDUCATIONAL AND PUBLIC AFFAIRS PROGRAMMING: *David Brinkley's Journal* (NBC)

OUTSTANDING PROGRAM ACHIEVEMENT IN THE FIELD OF CHILDREN'S PROGRAMMING: "New York Philharmonic Young People's Concert with Leonard Bernstein" (CBS)

OUTSTANDING DAYTIME PROGRAM: "Purex Specials for Women" (NBC)

PROGRAM OF THE YEAR: "Victoria Regina," *Hallmark Hall of Fame* (NBC)

OUTSTANDING CONTINUED PERFORMANCE BY AN ACTOR IN A SERIES: E. G. Marshall, *The Defenders* (CBS)

OUTSTANDING CONTINUED PERFORMANCE BY AN ACTRESS IN A SERIES: Shirley Booth, *Hazel* (NBC)

OUTSTANDING SINGLE PERFORMANCE BY AN ACTOR IN A LEADING ROLE: Peter Falk, "Price of Tomatoes," *Dick Powell Theatre* (NBC)

OUTSTANDING SINGLE PERFORMANCE BY AN ACTRESS IN A LEADING ROLE: Julie Harris, "Victoria Regina," *Hallmark Hall of Fame* (NBC)

OUTSTANDING PERFORMANCE IN A VARIETY OR MUSICAL PROGRAM OR SERIES: Carol Burnett, *The Garry Moore Show* (CBS)

OUTSTANDING PERFORMANCE IN A SUPPORTING ROLE BY AN ACTOR: Don Knotts, *The Andy Griffith Show* (CBS)

OUTSTANDING PERFORMANCE IN A SUPPORTING ROLE BY AN ACTRESS: Pamela Brown, "Victoria Regina," *Hallmark Hall of Fame* (NBC)

OUTSTANDING DIRECTORIAL ACHIEVEMENT IN DRAMA: Franklin Schaffner, *The Defenders* (various episodes) (CBS)

OUTSTANDING DIRECTORIAL ACHIEVEMENT IN COMEDY: Nat Hiken, *Car 54, Where Are You?* (NBC)

OUTSTANDING WRITING ACHIEVEMENT IN DRAMA: Reginald Rose, *The Defenders* (various episodes) (CBS)

OUTSTANDING WRITING ACHIEVEMENT IN COMEDY: Carl Reiner, *The Dick Van Dyke Show* (CBS)

OUTSTANDING WRITING ACHIEVEMENT IN THE DOCUMENTARY FIELD: Lou Hazam, "Vincent Van Gogh: A Self-Portrait" (NBC)

SPECIAL TRUSTEE AWARDS: (1) CBS, "A Tour of the White House with Mrs. Jacqueline Kennedy"; (2) Mrs. Jacqueline Kennedy; (3) The news departments of ABC, CBS, and NBC for coverage of Colonel John Glenn's orbital flight; and (4) Brigadier General David Sarnoff, chairman of the board, RCA

1962–1963   (15 APRIL 1962–14 APRIL 1963)

OUTSTANDING ACHIEVEMENT IN THE FIELD OF VARIETY: *The Andy Williams Show* (NBC)

OUTSTANDING PROGRAM ACHIEVEMENT IN THE FIELD OF HUMOR: *The Dick Van Dyke Show* (CBS)

OUTSTANDING PROGRAM ACHIEVEMENT IN THE FIELD OF DRAMA: *The Defenders* (CBS)

OUTSTANDING ACHIEVEMENT IN THE FIELD OF NEWS: *The Huntley-Brinkley Report* (NBC)

OUTSTANDING PROGRAM ACHIEVEMENT IN THE FIELD OF NEWS COMMENTARY OR PUBLIC AFFAIRS: *David Brinkley's Journal* (NBC)

OUTSTANDING ACHIEVEMENT IN THE FIELD OF DOCUMENTARY PROGRAMS: "The Tunnel," Reuven Frank, producer (NBC)

OUTSTANDING PROGRAM ACHIEVEMENT IN THE FIELD OF PANEL, QUIZ, OR AUDIENCE PARTICIPATION: *G-E College Bowl* (CBS)

OUTSTANDING PROGRAM ACHIEVEMENT IN THE FIELD OF MUSIC: "Julie and Carol at Carnegie Hall" (CBS)

OUTSTANDING PROGRAM ACHIEVEMENT IN THE FIELD OF CHILDREN'S PROGRAMMING: *Walt Disney's Wonderful World of Color* (NBC)

PROGRAM OF THE YEAR: "The Tunnel" (NBC)

OUTSTANDING CONTINUED PERFORMANCE BY AN ACTOR IN A SERIES: E. G. Marshall, *The Defenders* (CBS)

OUTSTANDING CONTINUED PERFORMANCE BY AN ACTRESS IN A SERIES: Shirley Booth, *Hazel* (NBC)

OUTSTANDING PERFORMANCE IN A VARIETY OR MUSICAL PROGRAM OR SERIES: Carol Burnett, "Julie and Carol at Carnegie Hall" and "Carol and Company" (CBS)

OUTSTANDING SINGLE PERFORMANCE BY AN ACTOR IN A LEADING ROLE: Trevor Howard, "The Invincible Mr. Disraeli," *Hallmark Hall of Fame* (NBC)

OUTSTANDING SINGLE PERFORMANCE BY AN ACTRESS IN A LEADING ROLE: Kim Stanley, "A Cardinal Act of Mercy," *Ben Casey* (ABC)

OUTSTANDING PERFORMANCE IN A SUPPORTING ROLE BY AN ACTOR: Don Knotts, *The Andy Griffith Show* (CBS)

OUTSTANDING PERFORMANCE IN A SUPPORTING ROLE BY AN ACTRESS: Glenda Farrell, "A Cardinal Act of Mercy," *Ben Casey* (ABC)

OUTSTANDING ACHIEVEMENT IN INTERNATIONAL REPORTING OR COMMENTARY: Piers Anderton, "The Tunnel" (NBC)

OUTSTANDING DIRECTORIAL ACHIEVEMENT IN DRAMA: Stuart Rosenberg, "The Madman," *The Defenders* (CBS)

OUTSTANDING DIRECTORIAL ACHIEVEMENT IN COMEDY: John Rich, *The Dick Van Dyke Show* (CBS)

OUTSTANDING WRITING ACHIEVEMENT IN DRAMA: Robert Thom and Reginald Rose, "The Madman," *The Defenders* (CBS)

OUTSTANDING WRITING ACHIEVEMENT IN COMEDY: Carl Reiner, *The Dick Van Dyke Show* (CBS)

TRUSTEES' AWARDS: (1) American Telephone and Telegraph Company (for Telstar I and II); (2) Dick Powell (in memoriam)

TRUSTEES' CITATION: To the President of the United States

1963–1964   (15 APRIL 1963–12 APRIL 1964)

OUTSTANDING PROGRAM ACHIEVEMENT IN THE FIELD OF VARIETY: *The Danny Kaye Show* (CBS)

OUTSTANDING PROGRAM ACHIEVEMENT IN THE FIELD OF COMEDY: *The Dick Van Dyke Show* (CBS)

OUTSTANDING PROGRAM ACHIEVEMENT IN THE FIELD OF DRAMA: *The Defenders* (CBS)

OUTSTANDING PROGRAM ACHIEVEMENT IN THE FIELD OF NEWS RE-PORTS: *The Huntley-Brinkley Report* (NBC)

OUTSTANDING PROGRAM ACHIEVEMENT IN THE FIELD OF NEWS COM-MENTARY OR PUBLIC AFFAIRS: "Cuba: Parts I and II—The Bay of Pigs and the Missile Crisis," *NBC White Paper* (NBC)

OUTSTANDING ACHIEVEMENT IN THE FIELD OF DOCUMENTARY PRO-GRAMS: "The Making of the President 1960" (ABC)

OUTSTANDING PROGRAM ACHIEVEMENT IN THE FIELD OF MUSIC: *The Bell Telephone Hour* (NBC)

OUTSTANDING PROGRAM ACHIEVEMENT IN THE FIELD OF CHILDREN'S PROGRAMMING: *Discovery '63–'64* (ABC)

PROGRAM OF THE YEAR: "The Making of the President 1960" (ABC)

OUTSTANDING CONTINUED PERFORMANCE BY AN ACTOR IN A SERIES: Dick Van Dyke, *The Dick Van Dyke Show* (CBS)

OUTSTANDING CONTINUED PERFORMANCE BY AN ACTRESS IN A SERIES: Mary Tyler Moore, *The Dick Van Dyke Show* (CBS)

OUTSTANDING SINGLE PERFORMANCE BY AN ACTOR IN A LEADING ROLE: Jack Klugman, "Blacklist," *The Defenders* (CBS)

OUTSTANDING SINGLE PERFORMANCE BY AN ACTRESS IN A LEADING ROLE: Shelley Winters, "Two Is the Number," *Bob Hope Presents the Chrysler Theatre* (NBC)

OUTSTANDING PERFORMANCE IN A VARIETY PROGRAM OR SERIES: Dan-ny Kaye, *The Danny Kaye Show* (CBS)

OUTSTANDING PERFORMANCE IN A SUPPORTING ROLE BY AN ACTOR: Albert Paulsen, "One Day in the Life of Ivan Denisovich," *Bob Hope Presents the Chrysler Theatre* (NBC)

OUTSTANDING PERFORMANCE IN A SUPPORTING ROLE BY AN ACTRESS: Ruth White, "Little Moon of Alban," *Hallmark Hall of Fame* (NBC)

OUTSTANDING DIRECTORIAL ACHIEVEMENT IN DRAMA: Tom Gries, "Who Do You Kill?" *East Side, West Side* (CBS)

OUTSTANDING DIRECTORIAL ACHIEVEMENT IN COMEDY: Jerry Paris, *The Dick Van Dyke Show* (CBS)

OUTSTANDING DIRECTORIAL ACHIEVEMENT IN VARIETY OR MUSIC: Robert Scherer, *The Danny Kaye Show* (CBS)

OUTSTANDING WRITING ACHIEVEMENT IN DRAMA (ORIGINAL WORK): Ernest Kinoy, "Blacklist," *The Defenders* (CBS)

OUTSTANDING WRITING ACHIEVEMENT IN DRAMA (ADAPTATION): Rod Serling, "It's Mental Work," *Bob Hope Presents the Chrysler Theatre* (NBC)

OUTSTANDING WRITING ACHIEVEMENT IN COMEDY OR VARIETY: Carl Reiner, Sam Denoff, and Bill Persky, *The Dick Van Dyke Show* (CBS)

OUTSTANDING PROGRAM ACHIEVEMENTS IN ENTERTAINMENT: (1) *The Dick Van Dyke Show* (CBS); Carl Reiner, producer; (2) "The Magnificent Yankee," *Hallmark Hall of Fame* (NBC); George Schaefer, producer; (3) "My Name Is Barbra" (CBS); Richard Lewine, producer; and (4) "What Is Sonata Form?" *New York Philharmonic Young People's Concerts with Leonard Bernstein* (CBS); Roger Englander, producer

OUTSTANDING PROGRAM ACHIEVEMENTS IN NEWS, DOCUMENTARIES, INFORMATION, AND SPORTS: (1) "I, Leonardo da Vinci," *Saga of Western Man* (ABC); John H. Secondari and Helen Jean Rogers, producers; and (2) "The Louvre" (NBC); Lucy Jarvis, producer; John J. Sughrue, coproducer

OUTSTANDING INDIVIDUAL ACHIEVEMENTS IN ENTERTAINMENT (ACTORS AND PERFORMERS): (1) Dick Van Dyke, *The Dick Van Dyke Show* (CBS); (2) Alfred Lunt, "The Magnificent Yankee," *Hallmark Hall of Fame* (NBC); (3) Lynn Fontanne, "The Magnificent Yankee," *Hallmark Hall of Fame* (NBC); (4) Barbra Streisand, "My Name is Barbra" (CBS); and (5) Leonard Bernstein, *New York Philharmonic Young People's Concerts with Leonard Bernstein* (CBS)

OUTSTANDING INDIVIDUAL ACHIEVEMENTS IN ENTERTAINMENT (DIRECTORS AND WRITERS): (1) Paul Bogart (director), "The 700-Year-Old Gang," *The Defenders* (CBS); (2) David Karp (writer), "The 700-Year-Old Gang," *The Defenders* (CBS)

OUTSTANDING INDIVIDUAL ACHIEVEMENTS IN NEWS, DOCUMENTARIES, INFORMATION, AND SPORTS: (1) John J. Sughrue (director), "The Louvre" (NBC); and (2) Sidney Carroll (writer), "The Louvre" (NBC)

OUTSTANDING VARIETY SERIES: *The Andy Williams Show* (NBC); Bob Finkel, producer

OUTSTANDING COMEDY SERIES: *The Dick Van Dyke Show* (CBS); Carl Reiner, producer

OUTSTANDING DRAMATIC SERIES: *The Fugitive* (ABC); Alan Armer, producer

OUTSTANDING VARIETY SPECIAL: "Chrysler Presents the Bob Hope Christmas Special" (NBC); Bob Hope, executive producer

OUTSTANDING DRAMATIC PROGRAM: "Ages of Man" (CBS); David Susskind and Daniel Melnick, producers

OUTSTANDING MUSICAL PROGRAM: "Frank Sinatra: A Man and His Music" (NBC); Dwight Hemion, producer

OUTSTANDING CHILDREN'S PROGRAM: "A Charlie Brown Christmas" (CBS); Lee Mendelson and Bill Melendez, producers

ACHIEVEMENTS IN NEWS AND DOCUMENTARIES—PROGRAMS: (1) "American White Paper: United States Foreign Policy" (NBC); Fred Freed, producer; (2) "KKK—The Invisible Empire," *CBS Reports* (CBS); David Lowe, producer; (3) "Senate Hearings on Vietnam" (NBC); Chet Hagan, producer

ACHIEVEMENTS IN DAYTIME PROGRAMMING: (1) *Camera Three* (CBS); Dan Gallagher, producer; and (2) *Mutual of Omaha's Wild Kingdom* (NBC); Don Meier, producer

ACHIEVEMENTS IN SPORTS (PROGRAMS): (1) *ABC's Wide World of Sports* (ABC); Roone Arledge, executive producer; (2) "CBS Golf Classic" (CBS); Frank Chirkinian, producer; and (3) *Shell's Wonderful World of Golf* (NBC); Fred Raphael, producer

OUTSTANDING CONTINUED PERFORMANCE BY AN ACTOR IN A LEADING ROLE IN A DRAMATIC SERIES: Bill Cosby, *I Spy* (NBC)

OUTSTANDING CONTINUED PERFORMANCE BY AN ACTRESS IN A LEADING ROLE IN A DRAMATIC SERIES: Barbara Stanwyck, *The Big Valley* (ABC)

OUTSTANDING CONTINUED PERFORMANCE BY AN ACTOR IN A LEADING ROLE IN A COMEDY SERIES: Dick Van Dyke, *The Dick Van Dyke Show* (CBS)

OUTSTANDING CONTINUED PERFORMANCE BY AN ACTRESS IN A LEADING ROLE IN A COMEDY SERIES: Mary Tyler Moore, *The Dick Van Dyke Show* (CBS)

OUTSTANDING SINGLE PERFORMANCE BY AN ACTOR IN A LEADING ROLE IN A DRAMA: Cliff Robertson, "The Game," *Bob Hope Presents the Chrysler Theatre* (NBC)

OUTSTANDING SINGLE PERFORMANCE BY AN ACTRESS IN A LEADING ROLE IN A DRAMA: Simone Signoret, "A Small Rebellion," *Bob Hope Presents the Chrysler Theatre* (NBC)

OUTSTANDING PERFORMANCE BY AN ACTOR IN A SUPPORTING ROLE IN A DRAMA: James Daly, "Eagle in a Cage," *Hallmark Hall of Fame* (NBC)

OUTSTANDING PERFORMANCE BY AN ACTRESS IN A SUPPORTING ROLE IN A DRAMA: Lee Grant, *Peyton Place* (ABC)

OUTSTANDING PERFORMANCE BY AN ACTOR IN A SUPPORTING ROLE IN A COMEDY: Don Knotts, "The Return of Barney Fife," *The Andy Griffith Show* (CBS)

OUTSTANDING PERFORMANCE BY AN ACTRESS IN A SUPPORTING ROLE IN A COMEDY: Alice Pearce, *Bewitched* (ABC)

ACHIEVEMENT IN EDUCATIONAL TELEVISION (INDIVIDUAL): Julia Child, *The French Chef* (NET)

OUTSTANDING DIRECTORIAL ACHIEVEMENT IN DRAMA: Sidney Pollack, "The Game," *Bob Hope Presents the Chrysler Theatre* (NBC)

OUTSTANDING DIRECTORIAL ACHIEVEMENT IN COMEDY: William Asher, *Bewitched* (ABC)

OUTSTANDING DIRECTORIAL ACHIEVEMENT IN VARIETY OR MUSIC: Alan Handley, "The Julie Andrews Show" (NBC)

OUTSTANDING WRITING ACHIEVEMENT IN DRAMA: Millard Lampell, "Eagle in a Cage," *Hallmark Hall of Fame* (NBC)

OUTSTANDING WRITING ACHIEVEMENT IN COMEDY: Bill Persky and Sam Denoff, "Coast to Coast Big Mouth," *The Dick Van Dyke Show* (CBS)

OUTSTANDING WRITING ACHIEVEMENT IN VARIETY: Al Gordon, Hal Goldman, and Sheldon Keller, "An Evening with Carol Channing" (CBS)

SPECIAL CLASSIFICATIONS OF INDIVIDUAL ACHIEVEMENTS: Burr Tillstrom, *That Was the Week That Was* (NBC), "for his 'Berlin Wall' hand ballet"

TRUSTEES' AWARDS: (1) Edward R. Murrow; and (2) Xerox Corporation

1966–1967   (25 MARCH 1966–16 APRIL 1967)

OUTSTANDING VARIETY SERIES: *The Andy Williams Show* (NBC); Edward Stephenson and Bob Finkel, producers

OUTSTANDING COMEDY SERIES: *The Monkees* (NBC); Bert Schneider and Bob Rafelson, producers

OUTSTANDING DRAMATIC SERIES: *Mission: Impossible* (CBS); Joseph Gantman and Bruce Geller, producers

OUTSTANDING VARIETY SPECIAL: "The Sid Caesar, Imogene Coca, Carl Reiner, Howard Morris Special" (CBS); Jack Arnold, producer

OUTSTANDING DRAMATIC PROGRAM: "Death of a Salesman" (CBS); David Susskind and Daniel Melnick, producers

OUTSTANDING MUSICAL PROGRAM: "Brigadoon" (ABC); Fielder Cook, producer

OUTSTANDING CHILDREN'S PROGRAM: "Jack and the Beanstalk" (NBC); Gene Kelly, producer

ACHIEVEMENTS IN NEWS AND DOCUMENTARIES—PROGRAMS: (1) "China: The Roots of Madness" (SYNDICATED); Mel Stuart, producer; (2) "Hall of Kings" (ABC); Harry Rasky, producer; and (3) "The Italians" (CBS); Bernard Birnbaum, producer

ACHIEVEMENTS IN NEWS AND DOCUMENTARIES—INDIVIDUAL: Theodore H. White, writer of "China: The Roots of Madness" (SYNDICATED)

ACHIEVEMENTS IN DAYTIME PROGRAMMING—PROGRAMS: *Mutual of Omaha's Wild Kingdom* (NBC); Don Meier, producer

ACHIEVEMENTS IN DAYTIME PROGRAMMING—INDIVIDUAL: Mike Douglas, *The Mike Douglas Show* (SYNDICATED)

ACHIEVEMENTS IN SPORTS—PROGRAMS: *ABC's Wide World of Sports* (ABC); Roone Arledge, executive producer

OUTSTANDING CONTINUED PERFORMANCE BY AN ACTOR IN A LEADING ROLE IN A DRAMATIC SERIES: Bill Cosby, *I Spy* (NBC)

OUTSTANDING CONTINUED PERFORMANCE BY AN ACTRESS IN A LEADING ROLE IN A DRAMATIC SERIES: Barbara Bain, *Mission: Impossible* (CBS)

OUTSTANDING CONTINUED PERFORMANCE BY AN ACTOR IN A LEADING ROLE IN A COMEDY SERIES: Don Adams, *Get Smart* (NBC)

OUTSTANDING CONTINUED PERFORMANCE BY AN ACTRESS IN A LEADING ROLE IN A COMEDY SERIES: Lucille Ball, *The Lucy Show* (CBS)

OUTSTANDING SINGLE PERFORMANCE BY AN ACTOR IN A LEADING ROLE IN A DRAMA: Peter Ustinov, "Barefoot in Athens," *Hallmark Hall of Fame* (NBC)

OUTSTANDING SINGLE PERFORMANCE BY AN ACTRESS IN A LEADING ROLE IN A DRAMA: Geraldine Page, "A Christmas Memory," *ABC Stage 67* (ABC)

OUTSTANDING PERFORMANCE BY AN ACTOR IN A SUPPORTING ROLE IN A DRAMA: Eli Wallach, "The Poppy Is also a Flower" (ABC)

OUTSTANDING PERFORMANCE BY AN ACTRESS IN A SUPPORTING ROLE IN A DRAMA: Agnes Moorehead, "Night of the Vicious Valentine," *The Wild, Wild West* (CBS)

OUTSTANDING PERFORMANCE BY AN ACTOR IN A SUPPORTING ROLE IN A COMEDY: Don Knotts, "Barney Comes to Mayberry," *The Andy Griffith Show* (CBS)

OUTSTANDING PERFORANCE BY AN ACTRESS IN A SUPPORTING ROLE IN A COMEDY: Frances Bavier, *The Andy Griffith Show* (CBS)

OUTSTANDING DIRECTORIAL ACHIEVEMENT IN DRAMA: Alex Segal, "Death of a Salesman" (CBS)

OUTSTANDING DIRECTORIAL ACHIEVEMENT IN COMEDY: James Frawley, "Royal Flush," *The Monkees* (NBC)

OUTSTANDING DIRECTORIAL ACHIEVEMENT IN VARIETY OR MUSIC: Fielder Cook, "Brigadoon" (ABC)

OUTSTANDING WRITING ACHIEVEMENT IN DRAMA: Bruce Geller, *Mission: Impossible* (CBS)

OUTSTANDING WRITING ACHIEVEMENT IN COMEDY: Buck Henry and Leonard Stern, "Ship of Spies," *Get Smart* (NBC)

OUTSTANDING WRITING ACHIEVEMENT IN VARIETY: Mel Brooks, Sam Denoff, Bill Persky, Carl Reiner, and Mel Tolkin, "The Sid Caesar, Imogene Coca, Carl Reiner, Howard Morris Special" (CBS)

SPECIAL CLASSIFICATIONS OF INDIVIDUAL ACHIEVEMENTS: (1) Art Carney, *The Jackie Gleason Show* (CBS); (2) Truman Capote and Eleanor Perry, for the adaptation of "A Christmas Memory," *ABC Stage 67*

(ABC); and (3) Arthur Miller, for the adaptation of "Death of a Salesman" (CBS)

TRUSTEES' AWARD: Sylvester L. "Pat" Weaver, Jr.

1967–1968 (27 MARCH 1967–6 MARCH 1968)

OUTSTANDING MUSICAL OR VARIETY SERIES: *Rowan and Martin's Laugh-In* (NBC); George Schlatter, producer

OUTSTANDING COMEDY SERIES: *Get Smart* (NBC); Burt Nodella, producer

OUTSTANDING DRAMATIC SERIES: *Mission: Impossible* (CBS); Joseph E. Gantman, producer

OUTSTANDING MUSICAL OR VARIETY PROGRAM: "Rowan and Martin's Laugh-In Special" (NBC); George Schlatter, producer

OUTSTANDING DRAMATIC PROGRAM: "Elizabeth the Queen," *Hallmark Hall of Fame* (NBC); George Schaefer, producer

OUTSTANDING ACHIEVEMENT IN CULTURAL DOCUMENTARIES: (1) "Eric Hoffer, the Passionate State of Mind," Jack Beck, producer, *The CBS News Hour* (CBS); (2) "Gauguin in Tahiti: The Search for Paradise," Martin Carr, producer, *The CBS News Hour* (CBS); (3) "John Steinbeck's 'America and Americans' " (NBC); Lee Mendelson, producer; (4) "Dylan Thomas: The World I Breathe," Perry Miller Adato, producer, *NET Festival* (NET); (5) Nathaniel Dorsky, art photographer, "Gauguin in Tahiti: The Search for Paradise," *The CBS News Hour* (CBS); (6) Harry Morgan, writer, "The Wyeth Phenomenon, on Who, What, When, Where, Why with Harry Reasoner," *The CBS News Hour* (CBS); and (7) Thomas A. Priestley, director of photography, and Robert Loweree, film editor, "John Steinbeck's 'America and Americans' " (NBC)

OUTSTANDING ACHIEVEMENT IN NEWS DOCUMENTARIES: (1) "Africa" (ABC); James Fleming, executive producer; (2) "Summer '67: What We Learned" (NBC); Fred Freed, producer; (3) "CBS Reports: What About Ronald Reagan?" *The CBS News Hour* (CBS); Harry Reasoner, writer; and (4) "Same Mud, Same Blood" (NBC); Vo Huynh, cameraman

OUTSTANDING ACHIEVEMENT WITHIN REGULARLY SCHEDULED NEWS PROGRAMS: (1) "1st Cavalry, Con Thien" and other segments, *The CBS Evening News with Walter Cronkite* (CBS); John Laurence, correspondent; Keith Kay, cameraman; and (2) "Crisis in the Cities," *PBL* (NET); Av Westin, executive producer

OUTSTANDING ACHIEVEMENT IN COVERAGE OF SPECIAL EVENTS (NEWS ANALYSIS): (1) "State of the Union/68" (NET); Jim Karayn, executive producer; and (2) Satellite coverage of Adenauer's funeral (NBC); Frank McGee, commentator

OTHER OUTSTANDING NEWS AND DOCUMENTARY ACHIEVEMENTS: (1) *The Twenty-First Century* (CBS); Isaac Kleinerman, producer; (2) "Science and Religion: Who Will Play God?" *CBS News Special* (CBS); Ben Flynn, producer; and (3) George Delerue, composer, "Our World" (NET)

OUTSTANDING ACHIEVEMENT IN DAYTIME PROGRAMMING: *Today* (NBC); Al Morgan, producer.

OUTSTANDING ACHIEVEMENTS IN SPORTS PROGRAMMING: (1) *ABC's Wide World of Sports* (ABC); Roone Arledge, executive producer; and (2) Jim McKay, commentator, *ABC's Wide World of Sports* (ABC)

OUTSTANDING CONTINUED PERFORMANCE BY AN ACTOR IN A LEADING ROLE IN A DRAMATIC SERIES: Bill Cosby, *I Spy* (NBC)

OUTSTANDING CONTINUED PERFORMANCE BY AN ACTRESS IN A LEADING ROLE IN A DRAMATIC SERIES: Barbara Bain, *Mission: Impossible* (CBS)

OUTSTANDING CONTINUED PERFORMANCE BY AN ACTOR IN A LEADING ROLE IN A COMEDY SERIES: Don Adams, *Get Smart* (NBC)

OUTSTANDING CONTINUED PERFORMANCE BY AN ACTRESS IN A LEADING ROLE IN A COMEDY SERIES: Lucille Ball, *The Lucy Show* (CBS)

OUTSTANDING SINGLE PERFORMANCE BY AN ACTOR IN A LEADING ROLE IN A DRAMA: Melvyn Douglas, "Do Not Go Gentle into That Good Night," *CBS Playhouse* (CBS)

OUTSTANDING SINGLE PERFORMANCE BY AN ACTRESS IN A LEADING ROLE IN A DRAMA: Maureen Stapleton, "Among the Paths to Eden," *Xerox Special Event* (ABC)

OUTSTANDING PERFORMANCE BY AN ACTOR IN A SUPPORTING ROLE IN A DRAMA: Milburn Stone, *Gunsmoke* (CBS)

OUTSTANDING PERFORMANCE BY AN ACTRESS IN A SUPPORTING ROLE IN A DRAMA: Barbara Anderson, *Ironside* (NBC)

OUTSTANDING PERFORMANCE BY AN ACTOR IN A SUPPORTING ROLE IN A COMEDY: Werner Klemperer, *Hogan's Heroes* (CBS)

OUTSTANDING PERFORMANCE BY AN ACTRESS IN A SUPPORTING ROLE IN A COMEDY: Marion Lorne, *Bewitched* (ABC)

SPECIAL CLASSIFICATIONS OF OUTSTANDING INDIVIDUAL ACHIEVEMENT: (1) Art Carney, *The Jackie Gleason Show* (CBS); and (2) Pat Paulsen, *The Smothers Brothers Comedy Hour* (CBS)

OUTSTANDING DIRECTORIAL ACHIEVEMENT IN DRAMA: Paul Bogart, "Dear Friends," *CBS Playhouse* (CBS)

OUTSTANDING DIRECTORIAL ACHIEVEMENT IN COMEDY: Bruce Bilson, "Maxwell Smart, Private Eye," *Get Smart* (NBC)

OUTSTANDING DIRECTORIAL ACHIEVEMENT IN MUSIC OR VARIETY: Jack Haley, Jr., "Movin' with Nancy" (NBC)

OUTSTANDING WRITING ACHIEVEMENT IN DRAMA: Loring Mandel, "Do Not Go Gentle into That Good Night," *CBS Playhouse* (CBS)

OUTSTANDING WRITING ACHIEVEMENT IN COMEDY: Alan Burns and Chris Hayward, "The Coming-Out Party," *He & She* (CBS)

OUTSTANDING WRITING ACHIEVEMENT IN MUSIC OR VARIETY: Paul Keyes, Hugh Wedlock, Allan Manings, Chris Bearde, David Panich, Phil Hahn, Jack Hanrahan, Coslough Johnson, Marc London, and Digby Wolfe, *Rowan and Martin's Laugh-In* (NBC)

TRUSTEES' AWARD: Donald H. McGannon, president and chairman of the board of directors of Group W (Westinghouse Broadcasting Company)

1968–1969   (7 MARCH 1968–16 MARCH 1969)

OUTSTANDING MUSICAL OR VARIETY SERIES: *Rowan and Martin's Laugh-In* (NBC); George Schlatter, executive producer; Paul W. Keyes and Carolyn Raskin, producers; Dan Rowan and Dick Martin, stars

OUTSTANDING COMEDY SERIES: *Get Smart* (NBC); Arne Sultan, executive producer; Burt Nodella, producer

OUTSTANDING DRAMATIC SERIES: *NET Playhouse* (NET); Curtis Davis, executive producer

OUTSTANDING VARIETY OR MUSICAL PROGRAM: "The Bill Cosby Special" (NBC); Roy Silver, executive producer; Bill Hobin, Bill Persky, and Sam Denoff, producers; Bill Cosby, star

OUTSTANDING DRAMATIC PROGRAM: "Teacher, Teacher," *Hallmark Hall of Fame* (NBC); Henry Jaffe, executive producer; George Lefferts, producer

OUTSTANDING CULTURAL DOCUMENTARY AND MAGAZINE-TYPE PROGRAM OR SERIES ACHIEVEMENT (PROGRAMS AND INDIVIDUALS): (1) "Don't Count the Candles," William K. McClure, producer, *The CBS News Hour* (CBS); (2) "Justice Black and the Bill of Rights," Burton Benjamin, producer, *CBS News Special* (CBS); (3) "Man Who Dances: Edward Villella," Robert Drew and Mike Jackson, producers, *The Bell Telephone Hour* (NBC); and (4) "The Great American Novel," Arthur Barron, producer, *The CBS News Hour* (CBS); (5) Walter Dombrow and Jerry Sims, cinematographers, "The Great American Novel," *The CBS News Hour* (CBS); (6) Tom Pettit, producer, "CBW: The Secrets of Secrecy," *First Tuesday* (NBC); and (7) Lord Snowdon, cinematographer, "Don't Count the Candles," *The CBS News Hour* (CBS)

OUTSTANDING NEWS DOCUMENTARY PROGRAM ACHIEVEMENT (programs and individuals): (1) "Hunger in America," Martin Carr, producer, *The CBS News Hour* (CBS); (2) "Law and Order," Frederick Wiseman, producer, *PBL* (NET); and (3) Perry Wolff and Andrew A. Rooney, writers, "Black History: Lost, Stolen or Strayed—Of Black America," *The CBS News Hour* (CBS)

OUTSTANDING ACHIEVEMENT WITHIN REGULARLY SCHEDULED NEWS PROGRAMS: (1) Coverage of hunger in the United States, Wallace Westfeldt, executive producer, *The Huntley-Brinkley Report* (NBC); (2) "On the Road," *The CBS Evening News with Walter Cronkite* (CBS); Charles Kuralt, correspondent; James Wilson, cameraman; Robert Funk, soundman; and (3) "Police after Chicago," *The CBS Evening News with Walker Cronkite* (CBS); John Laurence, correspondent

OUTSTANDING ACHIEVEMENT IN COVERAGE OF SPECIAL EVENTS: "Coverage of Martin Luther King Assassination and Aftermath," *CBS News Special Reports and Special Broadcasts* (CBS); Robert Wussler, Ernest Leiser, Don Hewitt, and Burton Benjamin, executive producers

OUTSTANDING ACHIEVEMENT IN DAYTIME PROGRAMMING: *The Dick Cavett Show* (ABC); Don Silverman, producer

OUTSTANDING ACHIEVEMENT IN SPORTS PROGRAMMING: "19th Summer Olympic Games" (ABC); Roone P. Arledge, executive producer; Bill Bennington, Mike Freedman, Mac Hemion, Robert Riger, Marv Schlenker, Andy Sidaris, Lou Volpicelli and Doug Wilson, directors

OUTSTANDING PROGRAM ACHIEVEMENT, SPECIAL CLASSIFICATION: (1) *Firing Line with William F. Buckley, Jr.* (SYNDICATED); Warren Steibel, producer; and (2) *Mutual of Omaha's Wild Kingdom* (NBC); Don Meier, producer

OUTSTANDING CONTINUED PERFORMANCE BY AN ACTOR IN A LEADING ROLE IN A DRAMATIC SERIES: Carl Betz, *Judd for the Defense* (ABC)

OUTSTANDING CONTINUED PERFORMANCE BY AN ACTRESS IN A LEADING ROLE IN A DRAMATIC SERIES: Barbara Bain, *Mission: Impossible* (CBS)

OUTSTANDING CONTINUED PERFORMANCE BY AN ACTOR IN A LEADING ROLE IN A COMEDY SERIES: Don Adams, *Get Smart* (NBC)

OUTSTANDING CONTINUED PERFORMANCE BY AN ACTRESS IN A LEADING ROLE IN A COMEDY SERIES: Hope Lange, *The Ghost and Mrs. Muir* (NBC)

OUTSTANDING SINGLE PERFORMANCE BY AN ACTOR IN A LEADING ROLE: Paul Scofield, "Male of the Species," *Prudential's On Stage* (NBC)

OUTSTANDING SINGLE PERFORMANCE BY AN ACTRESS IN A LEADING ROLE: Geraldine Page, "The Thanksgiving Visitor" (ABC)

OUTSTANDING CONTINUED PERFORMANCE BY AN ACTOR IN A SUPPORTING ROLE IN A SERIES: Werner Klemperer, *Hogan's Heroes* (CBS)

OUTSTANDING CONTINUED PERFORMANCE BY AN ACTRESS IN A SUPPORTING ROLE IN A SERIES: Susan Saint James, *The Name of the Game* (NBC)

OUTSTANDING SINGLE PERFORMANCE BY AN ACTRESS IN A SUPPORTING ROLE: Anna Calder-Marshall, "Male of the Species," *Prudential's On Stage* (NBC)

OUTSTANDING INDIVIDUAL ACHIEVEMENT, SPECIAL CLASSIFICATION: (1) Arte Johnson, *Rowan and Martin's Laugh-In* (NBC); and (2) Harvey Korman, *The Carol Burnett Show* (CBS)

OUTSTANDING DIRECTORIAL ACHIEVEMENT IN DRAMA: David Greene, "The People Next Door," *CBS Playhouse* (CBS)

OUTSTANDING WRITING ACHIEVEMENT IN DRAMA: J. P. Miller, "The People Next Door," *CBS Playhouse* (CBS)

OUTSTANDING WRITING ACHIEVEMENT IN COMEDY, VARIETY, OR MUSIC: Allan Blye, Bob Einstein, Murray Roman, Carl Gottlieb, Jerry Music, Steve Martin, Cecil Tuck, Paul Wayne, Cy Howard, and Mason Williams, *The Smothers Brothers Comedy Hour* (CBS)

TRUSTEES' AWARDS: (1) William R. McAndrew, NBC News; and (2) Apollo VII, VIII, IX and X Space Missions; Apollo VII astronauts Walter Schirra, Don Eisele, and Walter Cunningham; Apollo VIII astronauts Frank Borman, James A. Lovell, Jr., and William A. Anders; Apollo IX astronauts James A. McDivitt, David R. Scott, and Russell L. Schweickart; Apollo X astronauts Thomas B. Stafford, Eugene A. Cernan, and John W. Young.

1969–1970   (17 MARCH 1969–15 MARCH 1970)

OUTSTANDING VARIETY OR MUSICAL SERIES: *The David Frost Show* (SYNDICATED); Peter Baker, producer; David Frost, star

OUTSTANDING COMEDY SERIES: *My World and Welcome to It* (NBC); Sheldon Leonard, executive producer; Danny Arnold, producer

OUTSTANDING DRAMATIC SERIES: *Marcus Welby, M.D.* (ABC); David Victor, executive producer; David J. O'Connell, producer

OUTSTANDING NEW SERIES: *Room 222* (ABC); Gene Reynolds, producer

OUTSTANDING DRAMATIC PROGRAM: "A Storm in Summer," *Hallmark Hall of Fame* (NBC); M. J. Rifkin, executive producer; Alan Landsburg, producer

OUTSTANDING VARIETY OR MUSICAL PROGRAMS: (1) (Classical music) "Cinderella" (National Ballet of Canada), *NET Festival* (NET); John Barnes and Curtis Davis, executive producers; Norman Campbell, producer; and (2) (Variety and popular music) "Annie, the Women in the Life of a Man" (CBS); Joseph Cates, executive producer; Martin Charnin, producer; Anne Bancroft, star

OUTSTANDING ACHIEVEMENT IN CHILDREN'S PROGRAMMING: *Sesame Street* (NET); David D. Connell, executive producer; Sam Gibson, Jon Stone, and Lutrelle Horne, producers; Jon Stone, Jeffrey Moss, Ray Sipherd, Jerry Juhl, Dan Wilcox, Dave Connell, Bruce Hart, Carole Hart, and Virginia Schone, writers, for "Sally Sees Sesame Street"

OUTSTANDING ACHIEVEMENT IN DAYTIME PROGRAMMING: *Today* (NBC); Stuart Schulberg, producer

OUTSTANDING ACHIEVEMENT IN SPORTS PROGRAMMING: (1) *ABC's Wide World of Sports* (ABC); Roone P. Arledge, executive producer; and (2) *The NFL Games* (CBS); William Fitts, executive producer

SPECIAL CLASSIFICATION OF OUTSTANDING PROGRAM AND INDIVIDUAL ACHIEVEMENT: *Mutual of Omaha's Wild Kingdom* (NBC); Don Meier, producer

OUTSTANDING ACHIEVEMENT IN "MAGAZINE TYPE" PROGRAMMING: (1) *Black Journal* (NET); William Greaves, executive producer; and (2) Tom Pettit, reporter and writer, "Some Footnotes to 25 Nuclear Years," *First Tuesday* (NBC)

OUTSTANDING ACHIEVEMENT IN NEWS DOCUMENTARY PROGRAMMING: (1) "Hospital," Frederick Wiseman, producer, *NET Journal* (NET); and (2) "The Making of the President, 1968" (CBS); M. J. Rifkin, executive producer; Mel Stuart, producer

OUTSTANDING ACHIEVEMENT WITHIN REGULARLY SCHEDULED NEWS PROGRAMS: (1) "An Investigation of Teenage Drug Addiction—Odyssey House," Wallace Westfeldt, executive producer, Les Crystal, producer, *The Huntley-Brinkley Report* (NBC); and (2) "Can the World Be Saved?" Ronald Bonn, producer, *The CBS Evening News with Walter Cronkite* (CBS)

OUTSTANDING ACHIEVEMENT IN CULTURAL DOCUMENTARY PROGRAMMING: (1) "Artur Rubinstein" (NBC); George A. Vicas, producer; (2) Artur Rubinstein, commentator, "Artur Rubinstein" (NBC); (3) "Fathers and Sons," Ernest Leiser, executive producer, Harry Morgan, producer, *The CBS News Hour* (CBS); (4) "The Japanese," Perry Wolff, executive producer, Igor Oganesoff, producer, *The CBS News Hour* (CBS); and (5) Edwin O. Reischauer, commentator, "The Japanese," *The CBS News Hour* (CBS)

OUTSTANDING ACHIEVEMENT IN COVERAGE OF SPECIAL EVENTS: (1) "Apollo: A Journey to the Moon (Apollo X, XI, XII)" (NBC); James W. Kitchell, executive producer; (2) "Solar Eclipse: A Darkness at Noon" (NBC); Robert Northshield, executive producer; Walter Kravetz, producer; and (3) Walter Cronkite, reporter, "Man on the Moon: The Epic Journey of Apollo XI" (CBS)

OUTSTANDING CONTINUED PERFORMANCE BY AN ACTOR IN A LEADING ROLE IN A DRAMATIC SERIES: Robert Young, *Marcus Welby, M.D.* (ABC)

OUTSTANDING CONTINUED PERFORMANCE BY AN ACTRESS IN A LEADING ROLE IN A DRAMATIC SERIES: Susan Hampshire, *The Forsyte Saga* (NET)

OUTSTANDING CONTINUED PERFORMANCE BY AN ACTOR IN A LEADING ROLE IN A COMEDY SERIES: William Windom, *My World and Welcome to It* (NBC)

OUTSTANDING CONTINUED PERFORMANCE BY AN ACTRESS IN A LEAD-ING ROLE IN A COMEDY SERIES: Hope Lange, *The Ghost and Mrs. Muir* (ABC)

OUTSTANDING SINGLE PERFORMANCE BY AN ACTOR IN A LEADING ROLE: Peter Ustinov, "A Storm in Summer," *Hallmark Hall of Fame* (NBC)

OUTSTANDING SINGLE PERFORMANCE BY AN ACTRESS IN A LEADING ROLE: Patty Duke, "My Sweet Charlie" (NBC)

OUTSTANDING PERFORMANCE BY AN ACTOR IN A SUPPORTING ROLE IN A DRAMA: James Brolin, *Marcus Welby, M.D.* (ABC)

OUTSTANDING PERFORMANCE BY AN ACTRESS IN A SUPPORTING ROLE IN A DRAMA: Gail Fisher, *Mannix* (CBS)

OUTSTANDING PERFORMANCE BY AN ACTOR IN A SUPPORTING ROLE IN A COMEDY: Michael Constantine, *Room 222* (ABC)

OUTSTANDING PERFORMANCE BY AN ACTRESS IN A SUPPORTING ROLE IN A COMEDY: Karen Valentine, *Room 222* (ABC)

OUTSTANDING DIRECTORIAL ACHIEVEMENT IN DRAMA: Paul Bogart, "Shadow Game," *CBS Playhouse* (CBS)

OUTSTANDING DIRECTORIAL ACHIEVEMENT IN COMEDY, VARIETY, OR MUSIC: Dwight A. Hemion, "The Sound of Burt Bacharach," *Kraft Music Hall* (NBC)

OUTSTANDING WRITING ACHIEVEMENT IN DRAMA: Richard Levinson and William Link, "My Sweet Charlie" (NBC)

OUTSTANDING WRITING ACHIEVEMENT IN COMEDY, VARIETY, OR MUSIC: Gary Belkin, Peter Bellwood, Herb Sargent, Thomas Meehan, and Judith Viorst, "Annie, the Women in the Life of a Man" (CBS)

OUTSTANDING ACHIEVEMENT IN ENGINEERING DEVELOPMENT: "Apollo Color Television from Space"—Video Communications Division of NASA; Westinghouse Electric Corporation, and Ampex Corporation

TRUSTEES' AWARDS: (1) To the Presidents of the network News Divisions, for "safeguarding the public's right to full information, at a time when the constitutional right of freedom of the press is under its strongest attack"; (2) "To the hundreds of men comprising the Staff of NASA for television coverage of the Apollo XI moon landing"; and (3) To the 3M Company, for "having presented some of the finest art, cultural, scientific, and entertainment programs in the public interest"

1970–1971

OUTSTANDING COMEDY SERIES: *All in the Family* (CBS); Norman Lear, producer

OUTSTANDING DRAMATIC SERIES: *The Senator* (segment), *The Bold Ones* (NBC); David Levinson, producer

OUTSTANDING VARIETY MUSICAL SERIES: *The Flip Wilson Show* (NBC); Monte Kay, executive producer; Bob Henry, producer; Flip Wilson, star

OUTSTANDING VARIETY SERIES—TALK: *The David Frost Show* (SYNDI-CATED); Peter Baker, producer; David Frost, star

OUTSTANDING NEW SERIES: *All in the Family* (CBS); Norman Lear, producer

OUTSTANDING SINGLE PROGRAM: "The Andersonville Trial," *Hollywood Television Theatre* (PBS); Lewis Freedman, producer

OUTSTANDING VARIETY OR MUSICAL PROGRAMS: (1) (Classical music) "Leopold Stokowski," *NET Festival* (PBS); Curtis W. Davis, executive producer; Thomas Slevin, producer; Leopold Stokowski, star; and (2) (Variety and popular music) "Singer Presents Burt Bacharach" (NBC); Gary Smith and Dwight Hemion, producers; Burt Bacharach, star

OUTSTANDING ACHIEVEMENT IN CHILDREN'S PROGRAMMING: (1) Burr Tillstrom, *Kukla, Fran and Ollie* (PBS); and (2) *Sesame Street* (PBS); David Connell, executive producer; Jon Stone and Lutrelle Horn, producers; Jeffrey Moss, Ray Sipherd, Jerry Juhl, Dan Wilcox, Dave Connell, Bruce Hart, Carole Hart, and Virginia Schone, writers

OUTSTANDING ACHIEVEMENT IN DAYTIME PROGRAMMING: *Today* (NBC); Stuart Schulberg, producer

OUTSTANDING ACHIEVEMENT IN SPORTS PROGRAMMING: (1) *ABC's Wide World of Sports* (ABC); Roone P. Arledge, executive producer; (2) Jim McKay, commentator, *ABC's Wide World of Sports* (ABC); and (3) Don Meredith, commentator, *NFL Monday Night Football* (ABC)

OUTSTANDING ACHIEVEMENT IN MAGAZINE-TYPE PROGRAMMING: (1) Gulf of Tonkin segment, Joseph Wershba, producer, *60 Minutes* (CBS); and (2) *The Great American Dream Machine* (PBS); A. H. Perlmutter and Jack Willis, executive producers

OUTSTANDING ACHIEVEMENT IN CULTURAL DOCUMENTARY PROGRAMMING: (1) "The Everglades" (NBC); Craig Fisher, producer; (2) "The Making of Butch Cassidy and the Sundance Kid" (NBC); Ronald Reissman, producer; and (3) "Arthur Penn, 1922–   : Themes and Variants" (PBS); Robert Hughes, producer

OUTSTANDING ACHIEVEMENT IN NEWS DOCUMENTARY PROGRAMMING: (1) "The Selling of the Pentagon" (CBS); Perry Wolff, executive producer; Peter Davis, producer; (2) "The World of Charlie Company" (CBS); Ernest Leiser, executive producer; Russ Bensley, producer; and (3) "NBC White Paper: Pollution Is a Matter of Choice" (NBC); Fred Freed, producer

OUTSTANDING ACHIEVEMENT WITHIN REGULARLY SCHEDULED NEWS PROGRAMS: (1) Five-part investigation of welfare, Wallace Westfeldt, executive producer, *The Huntley-Brinkley Report* (NBC); and (2) Bruce Morton, correspondent, reporting from the trial of Lieutenant Calley, *The CBS Evening News with Walter Cronkite* (CBS)

OUTSTANDING ACHIEVEMENT IN COVERAGE OF SPECIAL EVENTS: CBS News, for its space coverage in 1970–1971

OUTSTANDING CONTINUED PERFORMANCE BY AN ACTOR IN A LEADING ROLE IN A DRAMATIC SERIES: Hal Holbrook, *The Senator* (segment), *The Bold Ones* (NBC)

OUTSTANDING CONTINUED PERFORMANCE BY AN ACTRESS IN A LEADING ROLE IN A DRAMATIC SERIES: Susan Hampshire, *The First Churchills* (PBS)

OUTSTANDING CONTINUED PERFORMANCE BY AN ACTOR IN A LEADING ROLE IN A COMEDY SERIES: Jack Klugman, *The Odd Couple* (ABC)

OUTSTANDING CONTINUED PERFORMANCE BY AN ACTRESS IN A LEADING ROLE IN A COMEDY SERIES: Jean Stapleton, *All in the Family* (CBS)

OUTSTANDING SINGLE PERFORMANCE BY AN ACTOR IN A LEADING ROLE: George C. Scott, "The Price," *Hallmark Hall of Fame* (NBC)

OUTSTANDING SINGLE PERFORMANCE BY AN ACTRESS IN A LEADING ROLE: Lee Grant, "The Neon Ceiling," *NBC Monday Night at the Movies* (NBC)

OUTSTANDING PERFORMANCE BY AN ACTOR IN A SUPPORTING ROLE IN A DRAMA: David Burns, "The Price," *Hallmark Hall of Fame* (NBC)

OUTSTANDING PERFORMANCE BY AN ACTRESS IN A SUPPORTING ROLE IN A DRAMA: Margaret Leighton, "Hamlet," *Hallmark Hall of Fame* (NBC)

OUTSTANDING PERFORMANCE BY AN ACTOR IN A SUPPORTING ROLE IN A COMEDY: Edward Asner, *The Mary Tyler Moore Show* (CBS)

OUTSTANDING PERFORMANCE BY AN ACTRESS IN A SUPPORTING ROLE IN A COMEDY: Valerie Harper, *The Mary Tyler Moore Show* (CBS)

OUTSTANDING PROGRAM AND INDIVIDUAL ACHIEVEMENT, SPECIAL CLASSIFICATION: Harvey Korman, *The Carol Burnett Show* (CBS)

OUTSTANDING DIRECTORIAL ACHIEVEMENT IN DRAMA, SINGLE PROGRAM OF CONTINUING SERIES: Daryl Duke, "The Day the Lion Died," *The Senator* (segment), *The Bold Ones* (NBC)

OUTSTANDING DIRECTORIAL ACHIEVEMENT IN DRAMA, SINGLE PROGRAM: Fielder Cook, "The Price," *Hallmark Hall of Fame* (NBC)

OUTSTANDING DIRECTORIAL ACHIEVEMENT IN COMEDY, SINGLE PROGRAM OF CONTINUING SERIES: Jay Sandrich, "Toulouse Lautrec Is One of My Favorite Artists," *The Mary Tyler Moore Show* (CBS)

OUTSTANDING DIRECTORIAL ACHIEVEMENT IN VARIETY OR MUSIC, SINGLE PROGRAM OF A SERIES: Mark Warren, *Rowan and Martin's Laugh-In* (NBC)

OUTSTANDING DIRECTORIAL ACHIEVEMENT IN COMEDY, VARIETY, OR

MUSIC, SPECIAL PROGRAM: Sterling Johnson, "Timex Presents Peggy Fleming at Sun Valley" (NBC)

OUTSTANDING WRITING ACHIEVEMENT IN DRAMA, SINGLE PROGRAM OF CONTINUING SERIES: Joel Oliansky, "To Taste of Death but Once," *The Senator* (segment), *The Bold Ones* (NBC)

OUTSTANDING WRITING ACHIEVEMENT IN DRAMA, ORIGINAL TELE-PLAY, SINGLE PROGRAM: Tracy Keenan Wynn and Marvin Schwartz, "Tribes," *ABC Movie of the Week* (ABC)

OUTSTANDING WRITING ACHIEVEMENT IN DRAMA, ADAPTATION, SIN-GLE PROGRAM: Saul Levitt, "The Andersonville Trial," *Hollywood Television Theatre* (PBS)

OUTSTANDING WRITING ACHIEVEMENT IN COMEDY, SINGLE PROGRAM OF CONTINUING SERIES: James L. Brooks and Allan Burns, "Support Your Local Mother," *The Mary Tyler Moore Show* (CBS)

OUTSTANDING WRITING ACHIEVEMENT IN VARIETY OR MUSIC, SINGLE PROGRAM OF A SERIES: Herbert Baker, Hal Goodman, Larry Klein, Bob Weiskopf, Bob Schiller, Norman Steinberg, and Flip Wilson, *The Flip Wilson Show* (NBC)

OUTSTANDING WRITING ACHIEVEMENT IN COMEDY, VARIETY, OR MU-SIC, SPECIAL PROGRAM: Bob Ellison and Marty Farrell, "Singer Presents Burt Bacharach" (NBC)

TRUSTEES' AWARD: Ed Sullivan

1971–1972

OUTSTANDING COMEDY SERIES: *All in the Family* (CBS); Norman Lear, producer

OUTSTANDING DRAMATIC SERIES: "Elizabeth R.," *Masterpiece Theatre* (PBS); Christopher Sarson, executive producer; Roderick Graham, producer

OUTSTANDING VARIETY MUSICAL SERIES: *The Carol Burnett Show* (CBS); Joe Hamilton, executive producer; Arnie Rosen, producer; Carol Burnett, star

OUTSTANDING VARIETY SERIES—TALK: *The Dick Cavett Show* (ABC); John Gilroy, producer; Dick Cavett, star

OUTSTANDING NEW SERIES: "Elizabeth R.," *Masterpiece Theatre* (PBS); Christopher Sarson, executive producer; Roderick Graham, producer

OUTSTANDING SINGLE PROGRAM: "Brian's Song," Paul Younger Witt, producer, *ABC Movie of the Week* (ABC)

OUTSTANDING VARIETY OR MUSICAL PROGRAM: (1) (Classical music) "Beethoven's Birthday: A Celebration in Vienna with Leonard Bernstein" (CBS); James Krayer, executive producer; Humphrey Burton, producer; Leonard Bernstein, star; and (2) (Variety and popular music)

"Jack Lemmon in 'S Wonderful, 'S Marvelous, 'S Gershwin," *Bell System Family Theatre* (NBC); Joseph Cates, executive producer; Martin Charnin, producer; Jack Lemmon, star

OUTSTANDING ACHIEVEMENT IN CHILDREN'S PROGRAMMING: *Sesame Street* (PBS); David D. Connell, executive producer; Jon Stone, producer

OUTSTANDING ACHIEVEMENT IN DAYTIME PROGRAMMING: *The Doctors* (NBC); Allen Potter, producer

OUTSTANDING ACHIEVEMENT IN SPORTS PROGRAMMING: (1) *ABC's Wide World of Sports* (ABC); Roone Arledge, executive producer; and (2) "AFC Championship Game" (NBC); William P. Kelley, technical director

OUTSTANDING ACHIEVEMENT IN MAGAZINE-TYPE PROGRAMMING: (1) *Chronolog* (NBC); Eliot Frankel, executive producer; (2) *The Great American Dream Machine* (PBS); A. H. Perlmutter, executive producer; (3) Mike Wallace, correspondent, *60 Minutes* (CBS)

OUTSTANDING ACHIEVEMENT IN CULTURAL DOCUMENTARY PROGRAMMING: (1) "Hollywood: The Dream Factory" (ABC); Nicholas Noxon, executive producer; Irwin Rosten and Bud Friedgen, producers; and (2) "A Sound of Dolphins," *The Undersea World of Jacques Cousteau* (ABC); Jacques Cousteau and Marshall Flaum, executive producers; Andy White, producer; (3) "The Unsinkable Sea Otter," *The Undersea World of Jacques Cousteau* (ABC); Jacques Cousteau and Marshall Flaum, executive producers; Andy White, producer; (4) Louis J. Hazam, writer, "Venice Be Damned!" (NBC); and (5) Robert Northshield, writer, "Suffer the Little Children—An NBC News White Paper on Northern Ireland" (NBC)

OUTSTANDING ACHIEVEMENT IN NEWS DOCUMENTARY PROGRAMMING: (1) "A Night in Jail, a Day in Court," Burton Benjamin, executive producer, John Sharnik, producer, *CBS Reports* (CBS); and (2) "This Child Is Rated X: An NBC White Paper on Juvenile Justice" (NBC); Martin Carr, producer

OUTSTANDING ACHIEVEMENT WITHIN REGULARLY SCHEDULED NEWS PROGRAMS: (1) Defeat of Dacca, Wallace Westfeldt, executive producer, Robert Mulholland and David Teitelbaum, producers, *The NBC Nightly News* (NBC); (2) Phil Brady, reporter, Defeat of Dacca, *The NBC Nightly News* (NBC); and (3) Bob Schieffer, Phil Jones, Don Webster, and Bill Plante, correspondents, covering "The Air War," *CBS Evening News* (CBS)

OUTSTANDING ACHIEVEMENT IN COVERAGE OF SPECIAL EVENTS: (1) "The China Trip" (ABC); Av Westin and Wally Pfister, executive producers; Bill Lord, producer; (2) "June 30, 1971, A Day for History: The Supreme Court and the Pentagon Papers" (NBC); Lawrence E. Spivak, executive producer; and (3) "A Ride on the Moon: The Flight of Apollo 15" (CBS); Robert Wussler, executive producer; Joan Richman, producer

SPECIAL CLASSIFICATIONS OF OUTSTANDING PROGRAM AND INDIVIDUAL ACHIEVEMENT: (1) (general programming) "The Pentagon Papers: PBS Special" (PBS); David Prowitt, executive producer; Martin Clancy, producer; (2) (docu-drama) *The Search for the Nile* (parts I–VI) (NBC); Christopher Ralling, producer; and (3) (individuals) Michael Hastings and Derek Marlowe, writers, *The Search for the Nile* (parts I–VI) (NBC)

OUTSTANDING CONTINUED PERFORMANCE BY AN ACTOR IN A LEADING ROLE IN A DRAMATIC SERIES: Peter Falk, *Columbo* (NBC)

OUTSTANDING CONTINUED PERFORMANCE BY AN ACTRESS IN A LEADING ROLE IN A DRAMATIC SERIES: Glenda Jackson, "Elizabeth R.," *Masterpiece Theatre* (PBS)

OUTSTANDING CONTINUED PERFORMANCE BY AN ACTOR IN A LEADING ROLE IN A COMEDY SERIES: Carroll O'Connor, *All in the Family* (CBS)

OUTSTANDING CONTINUED PERFORMANCE BY AN ACTRESS IN A LEADING ROLE IN A COMEDY SERIES: Jean Stapleton, *All in the Family* (CBS)

OUTSTANDING ACHIEVEMENT BY A PERFORMER IN MUSIC OR VARIETY: Harvey Korman, *The Carol Burnett Show* (CBS)

OUTSTANDING SINGLE PERFORMANCE BY AN ACTOR IN A LEADING ROLE: Keith Michell, "Catherine Howard," *The Six Wives of Henry VIII* (CBS)

OUTSTANDING SINGLE PERFORMANCE BY AN ACTRESS IN A LEADING ROLE: Glenda Jackson, "Shadow in the Sun," "Elizabeth R.," *Masterpiece Theatre* (PBS)

OUTSTANDING PERFORMANCE BY AN ACTOR IN A SUPPORTING ROLE IN A DRAMA: Jack Warden, "Brian's Song," *ABC Movie of the Week* (ABC)

OUTSTANDING PERFORMANCE BY AN ACTRESS IN A SUPPORTING ROLE IN A DRAMA: Jenny Agutter, "The Snow Goose," *Hallmark Hall of Fame* (NBC)

OUTSTANDING PERFORMANCE BY AN ACTOR IN A SUPPORTING ROLE IN A COMEDY: Edward Asner, *The Mary Tyler Moore Show* (CBS)

OUTSTANDING PERFORMANCE BY AN ACTRESS IN A SUPPORTING ROLE IN A COMEDY: (1) Valerie Harper, *The Mary Tyler Moore Show* (CBS); and (2) Sally Struthers, *All in the Family* (CBS)

OUTSTANDING DIRECTORIAL ACHIEVEMENT IN DRAMA, SINGLE PROGRAM OF CONTINUING SERIES: Alexander Singer, "The Invasion of Kevin Ireland," *The Lawyers* (*The Bold Ones*) (NBC)

OUTSTANDING DIRECTORIAL ACHIEVEMENT IN DRAMA, SINGLE PROGRAM: Tom Gries, "The Glass House," *The New CBS Friday Night Movies* (CBS)

OUTSTANDING DIRECTORIAL ACHIEVEMENT IN COMEDY, SINGLE PROGRAM OF CONTINUING SERIES: John Rich, "Sammy's Visit," *All in the Family* (CBS)

OUTSTANDING DIRECTORIAL ACHIEVEMENT IN VARIETY OR MUSIC, SINGLE PROGRAM OF A SERIES: Art Fisher, *The Sonny and Cher Comedy Hour* (program of 31 January 1972, with guest star Tony Randall) (CBS)

OUTSTANDING DIRECTORIAL ACHIEVEMENT IN COMEDY, VARIETY, OR MUSIC, SPECIAL PROGRAM: Walter C. Miller and Martin Charnin, "Jack Lemmon in 'S Wonderful, 'S Marvelous, 'S Gershwin," *Bell System Family Theatre* (NBC)

OUTSTANDING WRITING ACHIEVEMENT IN DRAMA, SINGLE PROGRAM OF CONTINUING SERIES: Richard L. Levinson and William Link, "Death Lends a Hand," *Columbo* (NBC)

OUTSTANDING WRITING ACHIEVEMENT IN DRAMA, ORIGINAL TELEPLAY, SINGLE PROGRAM: Allan Sloane, "To All My Friends on Shore" (CBS)

OUTSTANDING WRITING ACHIEVEMENT IN DRAMA, ADAPTATION, SINGLE PROGRAM: William Blinn, "Brian's Song," *ABC Movie of the Week* (ABC)

OUTSTANDING WRITING ACHIEVEMENT IN COMEDY, SINGLE PROGRAM OF CONTINUING SERIES: Burt Styler, "Edith's Problem," *All in the Family* (CBS)

OUTSTANDING WRITING ACHIEVEMENT IN VARIETY OR MUSIC, SINGLE PROGRAM OF SERIES: Don Hinkley, Stan Hart, Larry Siegel, Woody Kling, Roger Beatty, Art Baer, Ben Joelson, Stan Burns, Mike Marmer, and Arnie Rosen, *The Carol Burnett Show* (program of 26 January 1972, with guests Tim Conway and Ray Charles) (CBS)

OUTSTANDING WRITING ACHIEVEMENT IN COMEDY, VARIETY, OR MUSIC, SPECIAL PROGRAM: Anne Howard Bailey, "The Trial of Mary Lincoln," *NET Opera Theatre* (PBS)

TRUSTEES' AWARDS: (1) Bill Lawrence; and (2) Dr. Frank Stanton

1972–1973

OUTSTANDING COMEDY SERIES: *All in the Family* (CBS); Norman Lear, executive producer; John Rich, producer

OUTSTANDING DRAMA SERIES (CONTINUING): *The Waltons* (CBS); Lee Rich, executive producer; Robert L. Jacks, producer

OUTSTANDING DRAMA OR COMEDY (LIMITED EPISODES): "Tom Brown's Schooldays" (*Masterpiece Theatre*) (PBS); John McRae, producer

OUTSTANDING VARIETY MUSICAL SERIES: *The Julie Andrews Hour* (ABC); Nick Vanoff, producer; Julie Andrews, star

OUTSTANDING NEW SERIES: *America* (NBC); Michael Gill, producer

OUTSTANDING SINGLE PROGRAM, DRAMA OR COMEDY: "A War of Children," Roger Gimbel, executive producer, George Schaefer, producer, *The New CBS Tuesday Night Movies* (CBS)

OUTSTANDING SINGLE PROGRAM, CLASSICAL MUSIC: "The Sleeping Beauty" (PBS); J. W. Barnes and Robert Kotlowitz, executive producers; Norman Campbell, producer

OUTSTANDING SINGLE PROGRAM, VARIETY OR MUSICAL: "Singer Presents Liza with a 'Z' " (NBC); Bob Fosse and Fred Ebb, producers; Liza Minnelli, star

OUTSTANDING ACHIEVEMENT IN CHILDREN'S PROGRAMMING (PROGRAMS AND INDIVIDUAL ACHIEVEMENTS): Entertainment and fictional—(1) *Sesame Street* (PBS); Jon Stone, executive producer; Bob Cuniff, producer; (2) *Zoom* (PBS); Christopher Sarson, producer; and (3) Tom Whedon, John Boni, Sara Compton, Tom Dunsmuir, Thad Mumford, Jeremy Stevens, and Jim Thurman, writers, *The Electric Company* (PBS). Information and factual—(1) "Last of the Curlews," William Hanna and Joseph Barbera, producers, *The ABC Afterschool Special* (ABC); and (2) Shari Lewis, performer, "A Picture of Us," *NBC Children's Theatre* (NBC)

OUTSTANDING ACHIEVEMENT IN SPORTS PROGRAMMING: (1) *ABC's Wide World of Sports* (ABC); Roone Arledge, executive producer; (2) "1972 Summer Olympic Games" (ABC); Roone Arledge, executive producer; (3) Jim McKay, commentator, "1972 Summer Olympic Games" (ABC); and (4) John Croak, Charles Gardner, Jakob Hierl, Conrad Kraus, Edward McCarthy, Nick Mazur, Alex Moskovic, James Parker, Louis Rende, Ross Skipper, Robert Steinback, John DeLisa, George Boettcher, Merrit Roesser, Leo Scharf, Randy Cohen, Vito Gerardi, Harold Byers, Winfield Gross, Paul Scoskie, Peter Fritz, Leo Stephan, Gerber McBeath, Louis Torino, Michael Wenig, Tom Wight, and James Kelley, videotape editors, "1972 Summer Olympic Games" (ABC)

OUTSTANDING PROGRAM ACHIEVEMENT IN DAYTIME: *Dinah's Place* (NBC); Henry Jaffe, executive producer; Fred Tatashore, producer; Dinah Shore, star

OUTSTANDING PROGRAM ACHIEVEMENT IN DAYTIME DRAMA: *The Edge of Night* (CBS); Erwin Nicholson, producer

OUTSTANDING ACHIEVEMENT FOR REGULARLY SCHEDULED MAGAZINE-TYPE PROGRAMS (PROGRAMS AND INDIVIDUALS): (1) "Poppy Fields of Turkey—The Heroin Labs of Marseilles—The New York Connection," Don Hewitt, executive producer, William McClure, John Tiffin, and Philip Scheffler, producers, *60 Minutes* (CBS); (2) "The Selling of Colonel Herbert," Don Hewitt, executive producer, Barry Lando, producer, *60 Minutes* (CBS); (3) *60 Minutes* (CBS); Don

Hewitt, executive producer; (4) Mike Wallace, correspondent, "The Selling of Colonel Herbert," *60 Minutes* (CBS); (5) Mike Wallace, correspondent, *60 Minutes* (CBS)

OUTSTANDING DOCUMENTARY PROGRAM ACHIEVEMENT—CULTURAL (PROGRAMS AND INDIVIDUALS): (1) *America* (NBC); Michael Gill, executive producer; (2) "Jane Goodall and the World of Animal Behavior—The Wild Dogs of Africa" (ABC); Marshall Flaum, executive producer; Hugo Van Lawick, Bill Travers, and James Hill, producers; (3) Alistair Cooke, narrator, *America* (NBC); (4) Alistair Cooke, writer, "A Fireball in the Night," *America* (NBC); (5) Hugo Van Lawick, director, "Jane Goodall and the World of Animal Behavior—The Wild Dogs of Africa" (ABC)

OUTSTANDING DOCUMENTARY PROGRAM ACHIEVEMENT—CURRENT EVENTS: (1) "The Blue Collar Trap," Fred Freed, producer, *NBC News White Paper* (NBC); (2) "The Mexican Connection," Burton Benjamin, executive producer, Jay McMullen, producer, *CBS Reports* (CBS); (3) "One Billion Dollar Weapon and Now the War is Over—The American Military in the 1970s," Fred Freed, executive producer, Al Davis, producer, *NBC Reports* (NBC)

OUTSTANDING ACHIEVEMENT WITHIN REGULARLY SCHEDULED NEWS PROGRAMS (PROGRAMS AND INDIVIDUALS): (1) "The U.S./Soviet Wheat Deal: Is There a Scandal?" Paul Greenberg and Russ Bensley, executive producers, Stanhope Gould and Linda Mason, producers, *The CBS Evening News with Walter Cronkite* (CBS); (2) Walter Cronkite, Dan Rather, Daniel Schorr, and Joel Blocker, correspondents, "The Watergate Affair," *The CBS Evening News with Walter Cronkite* (CBS); (3) David Dick, Dan Rather, Roger Mudd, and Walter Cronkite, correspondents, "Coverage of the Shooting of Governor Wallace," *The CBS Evening News with Walter Cronkite* (CBS); (4) Eric Sevareid, correspondent, "LBJ—The Man and the President," *The CBS Evening News with Walter Cronkite* (CBS)

SPECIAL CLASSIFICATION OF OUTSTANDING PROGRAM AND INDIVIDUAL ACHIEVEMENT: (1) *The Advocates* (PBS); Greg Harney, executive producer; Tom Burrows, Russ Morash, and Peter McGhee, producers; (2) "VD Blues," *The Special of the Week* (PBS), Don Fouser, producer

OUTSTANDING PERFORMANCE BY AN ACTOR IN A LEADING ROLE IN A DRAMA SERIES (CONTINUING): Richard Thomas, *The Waltons* (CBS)

OUTSTANDING PERFORMANCE BY AN ACTRESS IN A LEADING ROLE IN A DRAMA SERIES (CONTINUING): Michael Learned, *The Waltons* (CBS)

OUTSTANDING PERFORMANCE BY AN ACTOR IN A LEADING ROLE IN A DRAMA OR COMEDY (LIMITED EPISODES): Anthony Murphy, "Tom Brown's Schooldays," (*Masterpiece Theater*) (PBS)

OUTSTANDING PERFORMANCE BY AN ACTRESS IN A LEADING ROLE IN A DRAMA OR COMEDY (LIMITED EPISODES): Susan Hampshire, "Vanity Fair," *Masterpiece Theatre* (PBS)

OUTSTANDING CONTINUED PERFORMANCE BY AN ACTOR IN A LEADING ROLE IN A COMEDY SERIES: Jack Klugman, *The Odd Couple* (ABC)

OUTSTANDING CONTINUED PERFORMANCE BY AN ACTRESS IN A LEADING ROLE IN A COMEDY SERIES: Mary Tyler Moore, *The Mary Tyler Moore Show* (CBS)

OUTSTANDING SINGLE PERFORMANCE BY AN ACTOR IN A LEADING ROLE: Laurence Olivier, "Long Day's Journey into Night" (ABC)

OUTSTANDING SINGLE PERFORMANCE BY AN ACTRESS IN A LEADING ROLE: Cloris Leachman, "A Brand New Life," *Tuesday Movie of the Week* (ABC)

OUTSTANDING PERFORMANCE BY AN ACTOR IN A SUPPORTING ROLE IN DRAMA, A CONTINUING OR ONE-TIME APPEARANCE IN A SERIES, OR FOR A SPECIAL PROGRAM: Scott Jacoby, "That Certain Summer," *Wednesday Movie of the Week* (ABC)

OUTSTANDING PERFORMANCE BY AN ACTRESS IN A SUPPORTING ROLE IN DRAMA, A CONTINUING OR ONE-TIME APPEARANCE IN A SERIES, OR FOR A SPECIAL PROGRAM: Ellen Corby, *The Waltons* (CBS)

OUTSTANDING PERFORMANCE BY AN ACTOR IN A SUPPORTING ROLE IN COMEDY, A CONTINUING OR ONE-TIME APPEARANCE IN A SERIES, OR FOR A SPECIAL PROGRAM: Ted Knight, *The Mary Tyler Moore Show* (CBS)

OUTSTANDING PERFORMANCE BY AN ACTRESS IN A SUPPORTING ROLE IN COMEDY, A CONTINUING OR ONE-TIME APPEARANCE IN A SERIES, OR FOR A SPECIAL PROGRAM: Valerie Harper, *The Mary Tyler Moore Show* (CBS)

OUTSTANDING ACHIEVEMENT BY A SUPPORTING PERFORMER IN MUSIC OR VARIETY, A CONTINUING OR ONE-TIME APPEARANCE IN A SERIES, OR FOR A SPECIAL PROGRAM: Tim Conway, *The Carol Burnett Show* (program of 17 February 1973) (CBS)

OUTSTANDING ACHIEVEMENT BY AN INDIVIDUAL IN DAYTIME DRAMA: Mary Fickett, *All My Children* (ABC)

OUTSTANDING DIRECTORIAL ACHIEVEMENT IN DRAMA, A SINGLE PROGRAM OF A SERIES WITH CONTINUING CHARACTERS AND/OR THEME: Jerry Thorpe, "An Eye for an Eye," *Kung Fu* (ABC)

OUTSTANDING DIRECTORIAL ACHIEVEMENT IN DRAMA, A SINGLE PROGRAM: Joseph Sargent, "The Marcus–Nelson Murders," *The CBS Thursday Night Movies* (CBS)

OUTSTANDING DIRECTORIAL ACHIEVEMENT IN COMEDY, A SINGLE PROGRAM OF A SERIES WITH CONTINUING CHARACTERS AND/OR THEME: Jay Sandrich, "It's Whether You Win or Lose," *The Mary Tyler Moore Show* (CBS)

OUTSTANDING DIRECTORIAL ACHIEVEMENT IN VARIETY OR MUSIC, A SINGLE PROGRAM OF A SERIES: Bill Davis, *The Julie Andrews Hour* (program of 13 September 1972) (ABC)

OUTSTANDING DIRECTORIAL ACHIEVEMENT IN COMEDY, VARIETY, OR MUSIC, A SPECIAL PROGRAM: Bob Fosse, "Singer Presents Liza with a 'Z' " (NBC)

OUTSTANDING WRITING ACHIEVEMENT IN DRAMA, A SINGLE PROGRAM OF A SERIES WITH CONTINUING CHARACTERS AND/OR THEME: John McGreevey, "The Scholar," *The Waltons* (CBS)

OUTSTANDING WRITING ACHIEVEMENT IN DRAMA, ORIGNAL TELEPLAY, A SINGLE PROGRAM: Abby Mann, "The Marcus–Nelson Murders," *The CBS Thursday Night Movies* (CBS)

OUTSTANDING WRITING ACHIEVEMENT IN DRAMA, ADAPTATION, A SINGLE PROGRAM: Eleanor Perry, "The House without a Christmas Tree" (CBS)

OUTSTANDING WRITING ACHIEVEMENT IN COMEDY, A SINGLE PROGRAM OF A SERIES WITH CONTINUING CHARACTERS AND/OR THEME: Michael Ross, Bernie West, and Lee Kalcheim, "The Bunkers and the Swingers," *All in the Family* (CBS)

OUTSTANDING WRITING ACHIEVEMENT IN VARIETY OR MUSIC, A SINGLE PROGRAM OF A SERIES: Stan Hart, Larry Siegel, Gail Parent, Woody Kling, Roger Beatty, Tom Patchett, Jay Tarses, Robert Hillard, Arnie Kogen, Bill Angelos, and Buz Kohan, *The Carol Burnett Show* (program of 8 November 1972) (CBS)

OUTSTANDING WRITING ACHIEVEMENT IN COMEDY, VARIETY, OR MUSIC, A SPECIAL PROGRAM: Renee Taylor and Joseph Bologna, "Acts of Love—and Other Comedies" (ABC)

1973–1974

OUTSTANDING COMEDY SERIES: *M*A*S*H* (CBS); Gene Reynolds and Larry Gelbart, producers

OUTSTANDING DRAMA SERIES: "Upstairs, Downstairs," *Masterpiece Theatre* (PBS); Rex Firkin, executive producer; John Hawkesworth, producer

OUTSTANDING LIMITED SERIES: *Columbo* (NBC); Dean Hargrove and Roland Kibbee, executive producers; Douglas Benton, Robert F. O'Neil, and Edward K. Dodds, producers

OUTSTANDING MUSIC-VARIETY SERIES: *The Carol Burnett Show* (CBS); Joe Hamilton, executive producer; Ed Simmons, producer; Carol Burnett, star

OUTSTANDING SPECIAL, COMEDY, OR DRAMA: "The Autobiography of Miss Jane Pittman" (CBS); Robert Christiansen and Rick Rosenberg, producers

OUTSTANDING COMEDY-VARIETY, VARIETY OR MUSIC SPECIAL: "Lily" (CBS); Irene Pinn, executive producer; Herb Sargent and Jerry McPhie, producers; Lily Tomlin, star

OUTSTANDING CHILDREN'S SPECIAL (BROADCAST DURING THE EVE-NING): "Marlo Thomas and Friends in Free to Be . . . You and Me" (ABC); Marlo Thomas and Carole Hart, producers; Marlo Thomas, star

OUTSTANDING ACHIEVEMENT IN SPORTS PROGRAMMING: (1) *ABC's Wide World of Sports* (ABC); Roone Arledge, executive producer; Dennis Lewin, producer; and (2) Jim McKay, host, *ABC's Wide World of Sports* (ABC)

OUTSTANDING DRAMA SERIES (DAYTIME): *The Doctors* (NBC); Joseph Stuart, producer

OUTSTANDING TALK, SERVICE OR VARIETY SERIES (DAYTIME): *The Merv Griffin Show* (SYNDICATED); Bob Murphy, producer

OUTSTANDING GAME SHOW (DAYTIME): *Password* (ABC); Frank Wayne, executive producer; Howard Felsher, producer

OUTSTANDING DRAMA SPECIAL (DAYTIME): "The Other Woman," *ABC Matinee Today* (ABC); John Conboy, producer

OUTSTANDING ENTERTAINMENT CHILDREN'S SERIES (DAYTIME): *Zoom* (PBS); Jim Crum and Christopher Sarson, producers

OUTSTANDING INFORMATIONAL CHILDREN'S SERIES: *Make a Wish* (ABC); Lester Cooper, executive producer; Tom Bywaters, producer

OUTSTANDING INSTRUCTIONAL CHILDREN'S PROGRAMMING: *Inside/Out* (SYNDICATED); Larry Walcoff, executive producer

OUTSTANDING ENTERTAINMENT CHILDREN'S SPECIAL (DAYTIME): "Rookie of the Year," Dan Wilson, producer, *The ABC Afterschool Special* (ABC)

OUTSTANDING INFORMATIONAL CHILDREN'S SPECIAL: "The Runaways" (ABC); Joseph Barbera and William Hanna, executive producers; Bill Schwartz, producer

OUTSTANDING DOCUMENTARY PROGRAM ACHIEVEMENTS, PROGRAMS DEALING WITH EVENTS OR MATTERS OF CURRENT SIGNIFICANCE: (1) "Fire!" *ABC News Close-Up* (ABC); Pamela Hill, producer; Jules Bergman, correspondent/narrator; and (2) "CBS News Special Report: The Senate and the Watergate Affair" (CBS); Leslie Midgley, executive producer; Hal Haley, Bernard Birnbaum and David Browning, producers; Dan Rather, Roger Mudd, Daniel Schorr and Fred Graham, correspondents

OUTSTANDING DOCUMENTARY PROGRAM ACHIEVEMENTS, PROGRAMS DEALING WITH ARTISTIC, HISTORICAL OR CULTURAL SUBJECTS: (1) "Journey to the Outer Limits," *National Geographic Society Specials* (ABC); Nicholas Clapp and Dennis Kane, executive producers; Alex Grasshoff, producer; (2) *The World at War* (SYNDICATED); Jeremy Isaacs, producer; and (3) "CBS Reports: The Rockefellers" (CBS); Burton Benjamin, executive producer; Howard Stringer, producer; Walter Cronkite, correspondent

OUTSTANDING ACHIEVEMENT FOR REGULARLY SCHEDULED MAGA-ZINE-TYPE PROGRAMS (FOR PROGRAM SEGMENTS): (1) "America's Nerve Gas Arsenal," Eliot Frankel, executive producer, William B. Hill and Anthony Potter, producers, Tom Pettit, correspondent, *First Tuesday* (NBC); (2) "The Adversaries," Carey Winfrey, executive producer, Peter Forbath, producer/reporter, Brendan Gill, host/moderator, *Behind the Lines* (PBS); and (3) "A Question of Impeachment," Jerome Toobin, executive producer, Martin Clancy, producer, Bill Moyers, broadcaster, *Bill Moyers' Journal* (PBS)

OUTSTANDING INTERVIEW PROGRAM (PUBLIC AFFAIRS, SINGLE PRO-GRAM): (1) "Solzhenitsyn," *CBS News Special* (CBS); Burton Benjamin, producer; Walter Cronkite, correspondent; and (2) "Henry Steele Commager," Jerome Toobin, executive producer, Jack Sameth, producer, Bill Moyers, broadcaster, *Bill Moyers' Journal* (PBS)

OUTSTANDING ACHIEVEMENT WITHIN REGULARLY SCHEDULED NEWS PROGRAMS: (1) Coverage of the October War from Israel's Northern Front, *CBS Evening News with Walter Cronkite* (CBS); John Laurence, correspondent; (2) The Agnew Resignation, *CBS Evening News with Walter Cronkite* (CBS); Paul Greenberg, executive producer; Ron Bonn, Ed Fouhy, John Lane, Don Bowers, John Armstrong and Robert Mead, producers; Walter Cronkite, Robert Schakne, Fred Graham, Robert Pierpoint, Roger Mudd, Dan Rather, John Hart, and Eric Sevareid, correspondents; (3) The Key Biscayne Bank Charter Struggle, *CBS Evening News with Walter Cronkite* (CBS); Ed Fouhy, producer; Robert Pierpoint, correspondent; and (4) Reports on World Hunger, *The NBC Nightly News* (NBC); Lester M. Crystal, executive producer; Richard Fischer, Joseph Angotti and Fred Flamenhaft, producers; Tom Streithorst, Phil Brady, John Palmer and Liz Trotta, correspondents

OUTSTANDING ACHIEVEMENT IN COVERAGE OF SPECIAL EVENTS: (1) "Watergate: The White House Transcripts" (CBS); Russ Bensley, executive producer; Sylvia Westerman, Barry Jagoda, Mark Harrington and Jack Kelly, producers; Walter Cronkite, Dan Rather, Barry Serafin, Bob Schieffer, Daniel Schorr, Nelson Benton, Bruce Morton, Roger Mudd and Fred Graham, correspondents; and (2) Watergate Coverage (17 May through 15 November 1973) (PBS); Martin Clancy, executive producer; the NPACT Staff, producers; Jim Lehrer, Peter Kaye and Robert MacNeil, reporters

SPECIAL CLASSIFICATION OF OUTSTANDING PROGRAM AND INDIVIDUAL ACHIEVEMENT: (1) *The Dick Cavett Show* (ABC); John Gilroy, producer; Dick Cavett, star; and (2) Tom Snyder, host, *Tomorrow* (NBC)

ACTOR OF THE YEAR (SERIES): Alan Alda, *M*A*S*H* (CBS)

ACTRESS OF THE YEAR (SERIES): Mary Tyler Moore, *The Mary Tyler Moore Show* (CBS)

ACTOR OF THE YEAR (SPECIAL): Hal Holbrook, "Pueblo," *ABC Theatre* (ABC)

ACTRESS OF THE YEAR (SPECIAL): Cicely Tyson, "The Autobiography of Miss Jane Pittman" (CBS)

SUPPORTING ACTOR OF THE YEAR: Michael Moriarty, "The Glass Menagerie" (ABC)

SUPPORTING ACTRESS OF THE YEAR: Joanna Miles, "The Glass Menagerie" (ABC)

BEST LEAD ACTOR IN A DRAMA SERIES: Telly Savalas, *Kojak* (CBS)

BEST LEAD ACTRESS IN A DRAMA SERIES: Michael Learned, *The Waltons* (CBS)

BEST LEAD ACTOR IN A LIMITED SERIES: William Holden, *The Blue Knight* (NBC)

BEST LEAD ACTRESS IN A LIMITED SERIES: Mildred Natwick, *The Snoop Sisters* (NBC)

BEST LEAD ACTOR IN A COMEDY SERIES: Alan Alda, *M*A*S*H* (CBS)

BEST LEAD ACTRESS IN A COMEDY SERIES: Mary Tyler Moore, *The Mary Tyler Moore Show* (CBS)

BEST LEAD ACTOR IN A DRAMA (SPECIAL PROGRAM OR SINGLE APPEARANCE IN A DRAMA OR COMEDY SERIES): Hal Holbrook, "Pueblo," *ABC Theatre* (ABC)

BEST LEAD ACTRESS IN A DRAMA (SPECIAL PROGRAM OR SINGLE APPEARANCE IN A DRAMA OR COMEDY SERIES): Cicely Tyson, "The Autobiography of Miss Jane Pittman" (CBS)

BEST SUPPORTING ACTOR IN DRAMA (SPECIAL PROGRAM, ONE-TIME APPEARANCE, OR CONTINUING ROLE): Michael Moriarty, "The Glass Menagerie" (ABC)

BEST SUPPORTING ACTRESS IN DRAMA (SPECIAL PROGRAM, ONE-TIME APPEARANCE, OR CONTINUING ROLE): Joanna Miles, "The Glass Menagerie" (ABC)

BEST SUPPORTING ACTOR IN COMEDY (SPECIAL PROGRAM, ONE-TIME APPEARANCE, OR CONTINUING ROLE): Rob Reiner, *All in the Family* (CBS)

BEST SUPPORTING ACTRESS IN COMEDY (SPECIAL PROGRAM, ONE-TIME APPEARANCE, OR CONTINUING ROLE): Cloris Leachman, "The Lars Affair," *The Mary Tyler Moore Show* (CBS)

BEST SUPPORTING ACTOR IN COMEDY-VARIETY, VARIETY OR MUSIC (SPECIAL PROGRAM, ONE-TIME APPEARANCE, OR CONTINUING ROLE): Harvey Korman, *The Carol Burnett Show* (CBS)

BEST SUPPORTING ACTRESS IN COMEDY-VARIETY, VARIETY OR MUSIC (SPECIAL PROGRAM, ONE-TIME APPEARANCE, OR CONTINUING ROLE): Brenda Vaccaro, "The Shape of Things" (CBS)

DAYTIME ACTOR OF THE YEAR: Pat O'Brien, "The Other Woman," *ABC Matinee Today* (ABC)

DAYTIME ACTRESS OF THE YEAR: Cathleen Nesbitt, "The Mask of Love," *ABC Matinee Today* (ABC)

DAYTIME HOST OF THE YEAR: Peter Marshall, *The Hollywood Squares* (NBC)

BEST ACTOR IN DAYTIME DRAMA (SERIES): Macdonald Carey, *Days of Our Lives* (NBC)

BEST ACTRESS IN DAYTIME DRAMA (SERIES): Elizabeth Hubbard, *The Doctors* (NBC)

BEST ACTOR IN DAYTIME DRAMA (SPECIAL PROGRAM): Pat O'Brien, "The Other Woman," *ABC Matinee Today* (ABC)

BEST ACTRESS IN DAYTIME DRAMA (SPECIAL PROGRAM): Cathleen Nesbitt, "The Mask of Love," *ABC Matinee Today* (ABC)

BEST HOST OR HOSTESS IN A GAME SHOW (DAYTIME): Peter Marshall, *The Hollywood Squares* (NBC)

BEST HOST OR HOSTESS IN A TALK, SERVICE, OR VARIETY SERIES (DAYTIME): Dinah Shore, *Dinah's Place* (NBC)

OUTSTANDING TELEVISION NEWS BROADCASTER: (1) Harry Reasoner, *ABC News* (ABC); and (2) Bill Moyers, "Essay on Watergate," *Bill Moyers' Journal* (PBS)

DIRECTOR OF THE YEAR (SERIES): Robert Butler, *The Blue Knight* (part III) (NBC)

DIRECTOR OF THE YEAR (SPECIAL): Dwight Hemion, "Barbra Streisand . . . And Other Musical Instruments" (CBS)

WRITER OF THE YEAR (SERIES): Treva Silverman, "The Lou and Edie Story," *The Mary Tyler Moore Show* (CBS)

WRITER OF THE YEAR (SPECIAL): Fay Kanin, "Tell Me Where It Hurts," *G-E Theater* (CBS)

BEST DIRECTING IN DRAMA, SINGLE PROGRAM OF A SERIES WITH CONTINUING CHARACTERS AND/OR THEME: Robert Butler, *The Blue Knight* (part III) (NBC)

BEST DIRECTING IN DRAMA, SINGLE PROGRAM, COMEDY, OR DRAMA: John Korty, "The Autobiography of Miss Jane Pittman" (CBS)

BEST DIRECTING IN COMEDY, SINGLE PROGRAM OF A SERIES WITH CONTINUING CHARACTERS AND/OR THEME: Jackie Cooper, "Carry On, Hawkeye," *M*A*S*H* (CBS)

BEST DIRECTING IN VARIETY OR MUSIC, SINGLE PROGRAM OF A SERIES: Dave Powers, "The Australia Show," *The Carol Burnett Show* (CBS)

BEST DIRECTING IN COMEDY-VARIETY, VARIETY OR MUSIC, A SPECIAL PROGRAM: Dwight Hemion, "Barbra Streisand . . . And Other Musical Instruments" (CBS)

DAYTIME DIRECTOR OF THE YEAR: H. Wesley Kenney, "Miss Kline, We Love You," *ABC Afternoon Playbreak* (ABC)

BEST INDIVIDUAL DIRECTOR FOR A DRAMA SERIES (DAYTIME): H. Wesley Kenney, *Days of Our Lives* (NBC)

BEST INDIVIDUAL DIRECTOR FOR A SPECIAL PROGRAM (DAYTIME): H. Wesley Kenney, "Miss Kline, We Love You," *ABC Afternoon Playbreak* (ABC)

BEST INDIVIDUAL DIRECTOR FOR A TALK, SERVICE, OR VARIETY PRO-GRAM (DAYTIME): Dick Carson, *The Merv Griffin Show* (program with guests Rosemary Clooney, Helen O'Connell, Fran Warren, and Kay Starr) (SYNDICATED)

BEST INDIVIDUAL DIRECTOR FOR A GAME SHOW (DAYTIME): Mike Gargiulo, *Jackpot!* (NBC)

OUTSTANDING ACHIEVEMENT IN NEWS AND DOCUMENTARY DIRECT-ING: Pamela Hill, "Fire!" *ABC News Close-Up* (ABC)

BEST WRITING IN DRAMA, SINGLE PROGRAM OF A SERIES WITH CON-TINUING CHARACTERS AND/OR THEME: Joanna Lee, "The Thanksgiving Story," *The Waltons* (CBS)

BEST WRITING IN DRAMA, ORIGINAL TELEPLAY (SINGLE PROGRAM, COMEDY OR DRAMA): Fay Kanin, "Tell Me Where It Hurts," *G-E Theater* (CBS)

BEST WRITING IN DRAMA, ADAPTATION (SINGLE PROGRAM, COMEDY OR DRAMA): Tracy Keenan Wynn, "The Autobiography of Miss Jane Pittman" (CBS)

BEST WRITING IN COMEDY, SINGLE PROGRAM OF A SERIES WITH CON-TINUING CHARACTERS AND/OR THEME: Treva Silverman, "The Lou and Edie Story," *The Mary Tyler Moore Show* (CBS)

BEST WRITING IN VARIETY OR MUSIC, SINGLE PROGRAM OF A SERIES: Ed Simmons, Gary Belkin, Roger Beatty, Arnie Kogen, Bill Richmond, Gene Perret, Rudy DeLuca, Barry Levinson, Dick Clair, Jenna McMahon and Barry Harman, *The Carol Burnett Show* (program of 16 February 1974) (CBS)

BEST WRITING IN COMEDY-VARIETY, VARIETY OR MUSIC, SPECIAL PRO-GRAM: Herb Sargent, Rosalyn Drexler, Lorne Michaels, Richard Pryor, Jim Rusk, James R. Stein, Robert Illes, Lily Tomlin, George Yanok, Jane Wagner, Rod Warren, Ann Elder and Karyl Geld, "Lily" (CBS)

DAYTIME WRITER OF THE YEAR: Lila Garrett and Sandy Krinski, "Mother of the Bride," *ABC Afternoon Playbreak* (ABC)

BEST WRITING FOR A DRAMA SERIES (DAYTIME): Henry Slesar, *The Edge of Night* (CBS)

BEST WRITING FOR A SPECIAL PROGRAM (DAYTIME): Lila Garrett and Sandy Krinski, "Mother of the Bride," *ABC Afternoon Playbreak* (ABC)

BEST WRITING FOR A TALK, SERVICE OR VARIETY PROGRAM (DAY-TIME): Tony Garafalo, Bob Murphy and Merv Griffin, *The Merv Griffin Show* (program with guests Billie Jean King, Mark Spitz, Hank Aaron, and Johnny Unitas) (SYNDICATED)

BEST WRITING FOR A GAME SHOW (DAYTIME): Jay Redack, Harry Friedman, Harold Schneider, Gary Johnson, Steve Levitch, Rick Kellard, and Rowby Goren, *The Hollywood Squares* (NBC)

OUTSTANDING INDIVIDUAL ACHIEVEMENTS IN CHILDREN'S PROGRAM-
MING: (1) Charles M. Schulz, writer, "A Charlie Brown Thanksgiving" (CBS); (2) William Zaharuk, art director; Peter Razmofski, set
decorator, "The Borrowers," *Hallmark Hall of Fame* (NBC); (3) Ronald Baldwin, art director; Nat Mongioli, set director, *The Electric
Company* (program of 19 February 1974) (PBS); (4) The Muppets, *Sesame Street* (PBS); Jim Henson, Frank Oz, Carroll Spinney, Jerry Nelson, Richard Hunt, and Fran Brill, performers; and (5) Jon Stone,
Joseph A. Bailey, Jerry Juhl, Emily Perl Kingsley, Jeffrey Moss, Ray
Sipherd, and Norman Stiles, writers, *Sesame Street* (program of 19 November 1973)

1974–1975

OUTSTANDING COMEDY SERIES: *The Mary Tyler Moore Show* (CBS);
James L. Brooks and Allan Burns, executive producers; Ed. Weinberger and Stan Daniels, producers

OUTSTANDING DRAMA SERIES: "Upstairs, Downstairs," *Masterpiece
Theatre* (PBS); Rex Firkin, executive producer; John Hawkesworth,
producer

OUTSTANDING LIMITED SERIES: "Benjamin Franklin" (CBS); Lewis
Freedman, executive producer; George Lefferts and Glenn Jordan,
producers

OUTSTANDING COMEDY-VARIETY OR MUSIC SERIES: *The Carol Burnett
Show* (CBS); Joe Hamilton, executive producer; Ed Simmons, producer; Carol Burnett, star

OUTSTANDING SPECIAL, DRAMA OR COMEDY: "The Law," *NBC World
Premiere Movie* (NBC); William Sackheim, producer

OUTSTANDING SPECIAL, COMEDY-VARIETY OR MUSIC: "An Evening
with John Denver" (ABC); Jerry Weintraub, executive producer; Al
Rogers and Rich Eustis, producers; John Denver, star

OUTSTANDING CLASSICAL MUSIC PROGRAM: "Profile in Music: Beverly
Sills" (PBS); Patricia Foy, producer; Beverly Sills, star

OUTSTANDING CHILDREN'S SPECIAL (BROADCAST DURING THE EVE-
NING): "Yes, Virginia, There Is a Santa Claus" (ABC); Burt Rosen, executive producer; Bill Melendez and Mort Green, producers

OUTSTANDING SPORTS PROGRAM (PROGRAM CONTAINING EDITED SEG-
MENTS): *ABC's Wide World of Sports* (program of 14 April 1974)
(ABC); Roone Arledge, executive producer; Doug Wilson, Ned
Steckel, Dennis Lewin, John Martin and Chet Forte, producers

OUTSTANDING SPORTS EVENT (BROADCAST UNEDITED): "Jimmy Connors vs. Rod Laver Tennis Challenge" (CBS); Frank Chirkinian, executive producer

OUTSTANDING DAYTIME DRAMA SERIES: *The Young and the Restless* (CBS); John J. Conboy, producer; William J. Bell and Lee Phillip Bell, creators

OUTSTANDING TALK, SERVICE, OR VARIETY SERIES (DAYTIME): *Dinah!* (SYNDICATED); Henry Jaffe and Carolyn Raskin, executive producers; Fred Tatashore, producer

OUTSTANDING GAME OR AUDIENCE PARTICIPATION SHOW (DAYTIME): *The Hollywood Squares* (NBC); Merrill Heatter and Bob Quigley, executive producers; Jay Redack, producer

OUTSTANDING DAYTIME DRAMA SPECIAL: "The Girl Who Couldn't Lose," *ABC Afternoon Playbreak* (ABC); Ira Barmak, executive producer; Lila Garrett, producer

OUTSTANDING ENTERTAINMENT CHILDREN'S SERIES (DAYTIME): *Star Trek* (NBC); Lou Scheimer and Norm Prescott, producers

OUTSTANDING ENTERTAINMENT CHILDREN'S SPECIAL (DAYTIME): "Harlequin," *The CBS Festival of Lively Arts for Young People* (CBS); Edward Villella, executive producer; Gardner Compton, producer

SPECIAL CLASSIFICATION OF OUTSTANDING PROGRAM AND INDIVIDUAL ACHIEVEMENT: (1) "The American Film Institute Salute to James Cagney" (CBS); George Stevens, Jr., executive producer; Paul W. Keyes, producer; and (2) Alistair Cooke, host, *Masterpiece Theatre* (PBS)

OUTSTANDING LEAD ACTOR IN A DRAMA SERIES: Robert Blake, *Baretta* (ABC)

OUTSTANDING LEAD ACTRESS IN A DRAMA SERIES: Jean Marsh, "Upstairs, Downstairs," *Masterpiece Theatre* (PBS)

OUTSTANDING LEAD ACTOR IN A LIMITED SERIES: Peter Falk, *Columbo* (NBC)

OUTSTANDING LEAD ACTRESS IN A LIMITED SERIES: Jessica Walter, *Amy Prentiss* (NBC)

OUTSTANDING LEAD ACTOR IN A COMEDY SERIES: Tony Randall, *The Odd Couple* (ABC)

OUTSTANDING LEAD ACTRESS IN A COMEDY SERIES: Valerie Harper, *Rhoda* (CBS)

OUTSTANDING LEAD ACTOR IN A SPECIAL PROGRAM (DRAMA OR COMEDY): Laurence Olivier, "Love Among the Ruins," *ABC Theatre* (ABC)

OUTSTANDING LEAD ACTRESS IN A SPECIAL PROGRAM (DRAMA OR COMEDY): Katharine Hepburn, "Love Among the Ruins," *ABC Theatre* (ABC)

OUTSTANDING CONTINUING PERFORMANCE BY A SUPPORTING ACTOR IN A DRAMA SERIES: Will Geer, *The Waltons* (CBS)

OUTSTANDING CONTINUING PERFORMANCE BY A SUPPORTING ACTRESS IN A DRAMA SERIES: Ellen Corby, *The Waltons* (CBS)

OUTSTANDING CONTINUING PERFORMANCE BY A SUPPORTING ACTOR IN A COMEDY SERIES: Ed Asner, *The Mary Tyler Moore Show* (CBS)

OUTSTANDING CONTINUING PERFORMANCE BY A SUPPORTING ACTRESS IN A COMEDY SERIES: Betty White, *The Mary Tyler Moore Show* (CBS)

OUTSTANDING CONTINUING OR SINGLE PERFORMANCE BY A SUPPORTING ACTOR IN VARIETY OR MUSIC: Jack Albertson, *Cher* (program of 2 March 1975) (CBS)

OUTSTANDING CONTINUING OR SINGLE PERFORMANCE BY A SUPPORTING ACTRESS IN VARIETY OR MUSIC: Cloris Leachman, *Cher* (program of 2 March 1975) (CBS)

OUTSTANDING SINGLE PERFORMANCE BY A SUPPORTING ACTOR IN A COMEDY OR DRAMA SERIES: Patrick McGoohan, "By Dawn's Early Light," *Columbo* (NBC)

OUTSTANDING SINGLE PERFORMANCE BY A SUPPORTING ACTRESS IN A COMEDY OR DRAMA SERIES: Cloris Leachman, "Phyllis Whips Inflation," *The Mary Tyler Moore Show* (CBS)

OUTSTANDING SINGLE PERFORMANCE BY A SUPPORTING ACTOR IN A COMEDY OR DRAMA SPECIAL: Anthony Quayle, "QB VII" (parts 1 and 2), *ABC Movie Special* (ABC)

OUTSTANDING SINGLE PERFORMANCE BY A SUPPORTING ACTRESS IN A COMEDY OR DRAMA SPECIAL: Juliet Mills, "QB VII" (parts 1 and 2), *ABC Movie Special* (ABC)

OUTSTANDING SPORTS BROADCASTER: Jim McKay, *ABC's Wide World of Sports* (ABC)

OUTSTANDING ACTOR IN A DAYTIME DRAMA SERIES: Macdonald Carey, *Days of Our Lives* (NBC)

OUTSTANDING ACTRESS IN A DAYTIME DRAMA SERIES: Susan Flannery, *Days of Our Lives* (NBC)

OUTSTANDING ACTOR IN A DAYTIME DRAMA SPECIAL: Bradford Dillman, "The Last Bride of Salem," *ABC Afternoon Playbreak* (ABC)

OUTSTANDING ACTRESS IN A DAYTIME DRAMA SPECIAL: Kay Lenz, "Heart in Hiding," *ABC Afternoon Playbreak* (ABC)

OUTSTANDING HOST OR HOSTESS IN A TALK, SERVICE, OR VARIETY SERIES (DAYTIME): Barbara Walters, *Today* (NBC)

OUTSTANDING HOST IN A GAME OR AUDIENCE PARTICIPATION SHOW (DAYTIME): Peter Marshall, *The Hollywood Squares* (NBC)

OUTSTANDING INDIVIDUAL ACHIEVEMENT IN DAYTIME PROGRAMMING: Paul Lynde, performer, *The Hollywood Squares* (NBC)

OUTSTANDING DIRECTING IN A DRAMA SERIES (SINGLE EPISODE): Bill Bain, "A Sudden Storm," "Upstairs, Downstairs," *Masterpiece Theatre* (PBS)

OUTSTANDING DIRECTING IN A COMEDY SERIES (SINGLE EPISODE): Gene Reynolds, "O.R.," *M*A*S*H* (CBS)

OUTSTANDING DIRECTING IN A SPECIAL PROGRAM, DRAMA OR COMEDY: George Cukor, "Love Among the Ruins," *ABC Theatre* (ABC)

OUTSTANDING DIRECTING IN A COMEDY-VARIETY OR MUSIC SERIES (SINGLE EPISODE): Dave Powers, *The Carol Burnett Show* (program of 21 December 1974) (CBS)

OUTSTANDING DIRECTING IN A COMEDY-VARIETY OR MUSIC SPECIAL: Bill Davis, "An Evening with John Denver" (ABC)

OUTSTANDING INDIVIDUAL DIRECTOR FOR A DAYTIME DRAMA SERIES (SINGLE EPISODE): Richard Dunlap, *The Young and the Restless* (program of 25 November 1974) (CBS)

OUTSTANDING INDIVIDUAL DIRECTOR FOR A DAYTIME SPECIAL PROGRAM: Mort Lachman, "The Girl Who Couldn't Lose," *ABC Afternoon Playbreak* (ABC)

OUTSTANDING INDIVIDUAL DIRECTOR FOR A DAYTIME VARIETY PROGRAM (SINGLE EPISODE): Glen Swanson, "Dinah Salutes Broadway," *Dinah!* (SYNDICATED)

OUTSTANDING INDIVIDUAL DIRECTOR FOR A GAME OR AUDIENCE PARTICIPATION SHOW (SINGLE EPISODE): Jerome Shaw, *The Hollywood Squares* (program of 28 October 1974) (NBC)

OUTSTANDING WRITING IN A DRAMA SERIES (SINGLE EPISODE): Howard Fast, "The Ambassador," "Benjamin Franklin" (CBS)

OUTSTANDING WRITING IN A SPECIAL PROGRAM (ORIGINAL TELEPLAY, DRAMA OR COMEDY): James Costigan, "Love Among the Ruins," *ABC Theatre* (ABC)

OUTSTANDING WRITING IN A SPECIAL PROGRAM (ADAPTATION, DRAMA, OR COMEDY): David W. Rintels, "IBM Presents Clarence Darrow" (NBC)

OUTSTANDING WRITING IN A COMEDY SERIES (SINGLE EPISODE): Ed. Weinberger and Stan Daniels, "Mary Richards Goes to Jail," *The Mary Tyler Moore Show* (CBS)

OUTSTANDING WRITING IN A COMEDY-VARIETY OR MUSIC SERIES (SINGLE EPISODE): Ed Simmons, Gary Belkin, Roger Beatty, Arnie Kogen, Bill Richmond, Gene Perret, Rudy DeLuca, Barry Levinson, Dick Clair and Jenna McMahon, *The Carol Burnett Show* (program of 21 December 1974) (CBS)

OUTSTANDING WRITING IN A COMEDY-VARIETY OR MUSICAL SPECIAL: Bob Wells, John Bradford and Cy Coleman, "Shirley MacLaine: If They Could See Me Now" (CBS)

OUTSTANDING WRITING FOR A DAYTIME DRAMA SERIES: Harding Lemay, Tom King, Charles Kozloff, Jan Merlin, and Douglas Marland, *Another World* (NBC)

OUTSTANDING WRITING FOR A DAYTIME SPECIAL PROGRAM: Audrey Davis Levin, "Heart in Hiding," *ABC Afternoon Playbreak* (ABC)

TRUSTEES' AWARDS: (1) Elmer Lower, vice president, corporate affairs, American Broadcasting Companies, Inc.; and (2) Dr. Peter Goldmark, president, Goldmark Laboratories

OUTSTANDING COMEDY SERIES: *The Mary Tyler Moore Show* (CBS); James L. Brooks and Allan Burns, executive producers; Ed. Weinberger and Stan Daniels, producers

OUTSTANDING DRAMA SERIES: *Police Story* (NBC); David Gerber and Stanley Kallis, executive producers; Liam O'Brien and Carl Pingitore, producers

OUTSTANDING LIMITED SERIES: "Upstairs, Downstairs," *Masterpiece Theatre* (PBS); Rex Firkin, executive producer; John Hawkesworth, producer

OUTSTANDING COMEDY-VARIETY OR MUSIC SERIES: *NBC's Saturday Night* (NBC); Lorne Michaels, producer

OUTSTANDING SPECIAL, DRAMA OR COMEDY: "Eleanor and Franklin," *ABC Theatre* (ABC); David Susskind, executive producer; Harry Sherman and Audrey Maas, producers

OUTSTANDING SPECIAL, COMEDY-VARIETY OR MUSIC: "Gypsy in My Soul" (CBS); William O. Harbach, executive producer; Cy Coleman and Fred Ebb, producers; Shirley MacLaine, star

OUTSTANDING CLASSICAL MUSIC PROGRAM: "Bernstein and the New York Philharmonic, Great Performances" (PBS); Klaus Hallig and Harry Kraut, executive producers; David Griffiths, producer; Leonard Bernstein, star

OUTSTANDING CHILDREN'S SPECIAL (BROADCAST DURING THE EVENING): (1) "You're a Good Sport, Charlie Brown" (CBS); Lee Mendelson, executive producer; Bill Melendez, producer; and (2) "Huckleberry Finn" (ABC); Steven North, producer

OUTSTANDING EDITED SPORTS SERIES: *ABC's Wide World of Sports* (ABC); Roone Arledge, executive producer; Doug Wilson, Chet Forte, Ned Steckel, Brice Weisman, Terry Jastrow, Bob Goodrich, John Martin, Dennis Lewin and Don Ohlmeyer, producers

OUTSTANDING LIVE SPORTS SERIES: *NFL Monday Night Football* (ABC); Roone Arledge, executive producer; Don Ohlmeyer, producer

OUTSTANDING EDITED SPORTS SPECIAL: (1) "XII Winter Olympic Games" (ABC); Roone Arledge, executive producer; Chuck Howard, Don Ohlmeyer, Geoff Mason, Chet Forte, Bob Goodrich, Ellie Riger, Brice Weisman, Doug Wilson, and Bob Wilcox, producers; (2) "Triumph and Tragedy . . . The Olympic Experience" (ABC); Roone Arledge, executive producer; Don Ohlmeyer, producer

OUTSTANDING LIVE SPORTS SPECIAL: "1975 World Series" (NBC); Scotty Connal, executive producer; Roy Hammerman, producer

OUTSTANDING DRAMA SERIES (DAYTIME): *Another World* (NBC); Paul Rauch, executive producer; Joe Rothenberger and Mary S. Bonner, producers

OUTSTANDING TALK, SERVICE OR VARIETY SERIES (DAYTIME): *Dinah!* (SYNDICATED); Henry Jaffe and Carolyn Raskin, executive producers; Fred Tatashore, producer

OUTSTANDING GAME OR AUDIENCE PARTICIPATION SHOW (DAYTIME): *The $20,000 Pyramid* (ABC); Bob Stewart, executive producer; Anne Marie Schmitt, producer

OUTSTANDING DRAMA SPECIAL (DAYTIME): "First Ladies' Diaries: Edith Wilson" (NBC); Jeff Young, producer

OUTSTANDING ENTERTAINMENT CHILDREN'S SERIES (DAYTIME): *Big Blue Marble* (SYNDICATED); Henry Fownes, producer

OUTSTANDING INFORMATIONAL CHILDREN'S SERIES (FOR THE PERIOD 1 JULY 1974 TO 15 MARCH 1976): *Go* (NBC); George A. Heinemann, executive producer; Rift Fournier, J. Phillip Miller, William W. Lewis and Joan Bender, producers

OUTSTANDING INSTRUCTIONAL CHILDREN'S PROGRAMMING (SERIES AND SPECIALS): "Grammar Rock" (ABC); Thomas G. Yohe, executive producer; Radford Stone, producer

OUTSTANDING ENTERTAINMENT CHILDREN'S SPECIAL (DAYTIME): "Danny Kaye's Look-In at the Metropolitan Opera," *The CBS Festival of Lively Arts for Young People* (CBS); Sylvia Fine, executive producer; Bernard Rothman, Herbert Bones and Jack Wohl, producers

OUTSTANDING INFORMATIONAL CHILDREN'S SPECIAL (FOR THE PERIOD 1 JULY 1974 TO 15 MARCH 1976): "Happy Anniversary, Charlie Brown" (CBS); Lee Mendelson and Warren Lockhart, producers

SPECIAL CLASSIFICATION OF OUTSTANDING PROGRAM AND INDIVIDUAL ACHIEVEMENT: (1) "Bicentennial Minutes" (CBS); Bob Markel, executive producer; Gareth Davies and Paul Waigner, producers; (2) *The Tonight Show Starring Johnny Carson* (NBC); Fred DeCordova, producer; Johnny Carson, star; (3) Ann Marcus, Jerry Adelman and Daniel Gregory Browne, writers, *Mary Hartman, Mary Hartman* (pilot episode) (SYNDICATED)

OUTSTANDING LEAD ACTOR IN A DRAMA SERIES: Peter Falk, *Columbo* (NBC)

OUTSTANDING LEAD ACTRESS IN A DRAMA SERIES: Michael Learned, *The Waltons* (CBS)

OUTSTANDING LEAD ACTOR IN A LIMITED SERIES: Hal Holbrook, "Sandburg's Lincoln" (NBC)

OUTSTANDING LEAD ACTRESS IN A LIMITED SERIES: Rosemary Harris, "Notorious Woman," *Masterpiece Theatre* (PBS)

OUTSTANDING LEAD ACTOR IN A COMEDY SERIES: Jack Albertson, *Chico and the Man* (NBC)

OUTSTANDING LEAD ACTRESS IN A COMEDY SERIES: Mary Tyler Moore, *The Mary Tyler Moore Show* (CBS)

OUTSTANDING LEAD ACTOR (SINGLE APPEARANCE, DRAMA OR COMEDY SERIES): Edward Asner, *Rich Man, Poor Man* (program of 1 February 1976) (ABC)

OUTSTANDING LEAD ACTRESS (SINGLE APPEARANCE, DRAMA OR COMEDY SERIES): Kathryn Walker, "John Adams, Lawyer," *The Adams Chronicles* (PBS)

OUTSTANDING LEAD ACTOR IN A DRAMA OR COMEDY SPECIAL: Anthony Hopkins, "The Lindbergh Kidnapping Case," *NBC World Premiere Movie* (NBC)

OUTSTANDING LEAD ACTRESS IN A DRAMA OR COMEDY SPECIAL: Susan Clark, "Babe" (CBS)

OUTSTANDING CONTINUING PERFORMANCE BY A SUPPORTING ACTOR IN A DRAMA SERIES (REGULAR OR LIMITED): Anthony Zerbe, *Harry O* (ABC)

OUTSTANDING CONTINUING PERFORMANCE BY A SUPPORTING ACTRESS IN A DRAMA SERIES (REGULAR OR LIMITED): Ellen Corby, *The Waltons* (CBS)

OUTSTANDING CONTINUING PERFORMANCE BY A SUPPORTING ACTOR IN A COMEDY SERIES (REGULAR OR LIMITED): Ted Knight, *The Mary Tyler Moore Show* (CBS)

OUTSTANDING CONTINUING PERFORMANCE BY A SUPPORTING ACTRESS IN A COMEDY SERIES (REGULAR OR LIMITED): Betty White, *The Mary Tyler Moore Show* (CBS)

OUTSTANDING CONTINUING OR SINGLE PERFORMANCE BY A SUPPORTING ACTOR IN VARIETY OR MUSIC (CONTINUING ROLE, ONE-TIME APPEARANCE, OR SPECIAL): Chevy Chase, *NBC's Saturday Night* (program of 17 January 1976) (NBC)

OUTSTANDING CONTINUING OR SINGLE PERFORMANCE BY A SUPPORTING ACTRESS IN VARIETY OR MUSIC (CONTINUING ROLE, ONE-TIME APPEARANCE, OR SPECIAL): Vicki Lawrence, *The Carol Burnett Show* (program of 7 February 1976) (CBS)

OUTSTANDING SINGLE PERFORMANCE BY A SUPPORTING ACTOR IN A COMEDY OR DRAMA SERIES: Gordon Jackson, "The Beastly Hun," "Upstairs, Downstairs," *Masterpiece Theatre* (PBS)

OUTSTANDING SINGLE PERFORMANCE BY A SUPPORTING ACTRESS IN A COMEDY OR DRAMA SERIES: Fionnuala Flanagan, *Rich Man, Poor Man* (program of 2 February 1976) (ABC)

OUTSTANDING SINGLE PERFORMANCE BY A SUPPORTING ACTOR IN A COMEDY OR DRAMA SPECIAL: Ed Flanders, "A Moon for the Misbegotten," *ABC Theatre* (ABC)

OUTSTANDING SINGLE PERFORMANCE BY A SUPPORTING ACTRESS IN A COMEDY OR DRAMA SPECIAL: Rosemary Murphy, "Eleanor and Franklin," *ABC Theatre* (ABC)

OUTSTANDING SPORTS PERSONALITY: Jim McKay, *ABC's Wide World of Sports* and *ABC's XII Winter Olympics* (ABC)

OUTSTANDING ACTOR IN A DAYTIME DRAMA SERIES: Larry Haines, *Search for Tomorrow* (CBS)

OUTSTANDING ACTRESS IN A DAYTIME DRAMA SERIES: Helen Gallagher, *Ryan's Hope* (ABC)

OUTSTANDING ACTOR IN A DAYTIME DRAMA SPECIAL: (1) Gerald Gordon, "First Ladies' Diaries: Rachel Jackson" (NBC); (2) James Luisi, "First Ladies' Diaries: Martha Washington" (NBC)

OUTSTANDING ACTRESS IN A DAYTIME DRAMA SPECIAL: Elizabeth Hubbard, "First Ladies' Diaries: Edith Wilson" (NBC)

OUTSTANDING HOST OR HOSTESS IN A TALK, SERVICE OR VARIETY SERIES (DAYTIME): Dinah Shore, *Dinah!* (SYNDICATED)

OUTSTANDING HOST OR HOSTESS IN A GAME OR AUDIENCE PARTICIPATION SHOW: Allen Ludden, *Password* (ABC)

OUTSTANDING INDIVIDUAL ACHIEVEMENT IN CHILDREN'S PROGRAMMING (SINGLE EPISODE OF A SERIES OR SPECIAL PROGRAM): The Muppets, *Sesame Street* (program of 25 April 1975) (PBS); Jim Henson, Frank Oz, Jerry Nelson, Carroll Spinney and Richard Hunt, performers

OUTSTANDING DIRECTING IN A DRAMA SERIES (SINGLE EPISODE): David Greene, *Rich Man, Poor Man* (program of 15 March 1976) (ABC)

OUTSTANDING DIRECTING IN A COMEDY SERIES (SINGLE EPISODE): Gene Reynolds, "Welcome to Korea," *M*A*S*H* (CBS)

OUTSTANDING DIRECTING IN A COMEDY-VARIETY OR MUSIC SERIES (SINGLE EPISODE): Dave Wilson, *NBC's Saturday Night* (program of 18 October 1975, with host Paul Simon) (NBC)

OUTSTANDING DIRECTING IN A SPECIAL PROGRAM, DRAMA OR COMEDY: Daniel Petrie, "Eleanor and Franklin," *ABC Theatre* (ABC)

OUTSTANDING DIRECTING IN A COMEDY-VARIETY OR MUSIC SPECIAL: Dwight Hemion, "Steve and Eydie: 'Our Love Is Here to Stay' " (CBS)

OUTSTANDING INDIVIDUAL DIRECTOR FOR A DRAMA SERIES (SINGLE EPISODE, DAYTIME SERIES): David Pressman, *One Life to Live* (program of 26 January 1976) (ABC)

OUTSTANDING INDIVIDUAL DIRECTOR FOR A SPECIAL PROGRAM (DAYTIME): Nicholas Havinga, "First Ladies' Diaries: Edith Wilson" (NBC)

OUTSTANDING INDIVIDUAL DIRECTOR FOR A VARIETY PROGRAM (SINGLE EPISODE, DAYTIME SERIES): Glen Swanson, "Dinah Salutes Tony Orlando and Dawn on Their Fifth Anniversary," *Dinah!* (SYNDICATED)

OUTSTANDING INDIVIDUAL DIRECTOR FOR A GAME OR AUDIENCE PARTICIPATION SHOW (SINGLE EPISODE, DAYTIME SERIES): Mike Gargiulo, *The $20,000 Pyramid* (program of 18 February 1976) (ABC)

OUTSTANDING WRITING IN A DRAMA SERIES (SINGLE EPISODE): Sherman Yellen, "John Adams, Lawyer," *The Adams Chronicles* (PBS)

OUTSTANDING WRITING IN A SPECIAL PROGRAM (ORIGINAL TELEPLAY, DRAMA OR COMEDY): James Costigan, "Eleanor and Franklin," *ABC Theatre* (ABC)

OUTSTANDING WRITING IN A SPECIAL PROGRAM (ADAPTATION, DRAMA, OR COMEDY): David W. Rintels, "Fear on Trial" (CBS)

OUTSTANDING WRITING IN A COMEDY SERIES (SINGLE EPISODE): David Lloyd, "Chuckles Bites the Dust," *The Mary Tyler Moore Show* (CBS)

OUTSTANDING WRITING IN A COMEDY-VARIETY OR MUSIC SERIES (SINGLE EPISODE): Anne Beatts, Chevy Chase, Al Franken, Tom Davis, Lorne Michaels, Marilyn Suzanne Miller, Michael O'Donoghue, Herb Sargent, Tom Schiller, Rosie Shuster and Alan Zweibel, *NBC's Saturday Night* (program of 10 January 1976, with host Elliott Gould) (NBC)

OUTSTANDING WRITING IN A COMEDY-VARIETY OR MUSIC SPECIAL: Jane Wagner, Lorne Michaels, Ann Elder, Christopher Guest, Earl Pomerantz, Jim Rusk, Lily Tomlin, Rod Warren and George Yanok, "Lily Tomlin" (ABC)

OUTSTANDING WRITING FOR A DRAMA SERIES (DAYTIME): William J. Bell, Kay Lenard, Pat Falken Smith, Bill Rega, Margaret Stewart, Sheri Anderson, and Wanda Coleman, *Days of Our Lives* (NBC)

OUTSTANDING WRITING FOR A SPECIAL PROGRAM (DAYTIME): Audrey Davis Levin, "First Ladies' Diaries: Edith Wilson" (NBC)

1976–1977

I. PRIME-TIME AWARDS (administered by the Academy of Television Arts and Sciences)

OUTSTANDING COMEDY SERIES: *The Mary Tyler Moore Show* (CBS); Allan Burns and James L. Brooks, executive producers; Ed. Weinberger and Stan Daniels, producers

OUTSTANDING DRAMA SERIES: "Upstairs, Downstairs," *Masterpiece Theatre* (PBS); John Hawkesworth and Joan Sullivan, producers

OUTSTANDING LIMITED SERIES: *Roots* (ABC); David L. Wolper, executive producer; Stan Margulies, producer

OUTSTANDING COMEDY-VARIETY OR MUSIC SERIES: *Van Dyke and Company* (NBC); Byron Paul, executive producer; Allan Blye and Bob Einstein, producers; Dick Van Dyke, star

OUTSTANDING SPECIAL, DRAMA OR COMEDY: (1) "Eleanor and Franklin: The White House Years," *ABC Theatre* (ABC); David Susskind, executive producer; Harry R. Sherman, producer; and (2) "Sybil," *The Big Event* (NBC); Philip Capice and Peter Dunne, executive producers; Jacqueline Babbin, producer

OUTSTANDING SPECIAL, COMEDY-VARIETY OR MUSIC: "The Barry Manilow Special" (ABC); Miles Lourie, executive producer; Steve Binder, producer; Barry Manilow, star

OUTSTANDING CLASSICAL PROGRAM IN THE PERFORMING ARTS (SERIES OR SPECIAL): "American Ballet Theatre: Swan Lake Live from Lincoln Center," *Great Performances* (PBS); John Goberman, producer

OUTSTANDING CHILDREN'S SPECIAL (BROADCAST DURING THE EVENING): "Ballet Shoes" (parts 1 and 2), *Piccadilly Circus* (PBS); John McRae and Joan Sullivan, producers

SPECIAL CLASSIFICATION OF OUTSTANDING PROGRAMMING ACHIEVEMENT: *The Tonight Show Starring Johnny Carson* (NBC); Fred DeCordova, producer; Johnny Carson, star

OUTSTANDING LEAD ACTOR IN A DRAMA SERIES: James Garner, *The Rockford Files* (NBC)

OUTSTANDING LEAD ACTRESS IN A DRAMA SERIES: Lindsay Wagner, *The Bionic Woman* (ABC)

OUTSTANDING LEAD ACTOR IN A LIMITED SERIES: Christopher Plummer, "The Moneychangers," *The Big Event* (NBC)

OUTSTANDING LEAD ACTRESS IN A LIMITED SERIES: Patty Duke Astin, "Captains and the Kings," *Best Sellers* (NBC)

OUTSTANDING LEAD ACTOR IN A COMEDY SERIES: Carroll O'Connor, *All in the Family* (CBS)

OUTSTANDING LEAD ACTRESS IN A COMEDY SERIES: Beatrice Arthur, *Maude* (CBS)

OUTSTANDING LEAD ACTOR FOR A SINGLE APPEARANCE IN A DRAMA OR COMEDY SERIES: Louis Gossett, Jr., *Roots* (part 2) (ABC)

OUTSTANDING LEAD ACTRESS FOR A SINGLE APPEARANCE IN A DRAMA OR COMEDY SERIES: Beulah Bondi, "The Pony Cart," *The Waltons* (CBS)

OUTSTANDING LEAD ACTOR IN A DRAMA OR COMEDY SPECIAL: Ed Flanders, "Harry S Truman: Plain Speaking" (PBS)

OUTSTANDING LEAD ACTRESS IN A DRAMA OR COMEDY SPECIAL: Sally Field, "Sybil," *The Big Event* (NBC)

OUTSTANDING CONTINUING PERFORMANCE BY A SUPPORTING ACTOR IN A DRAMA SERIES: Gary Frank, *Family* (ABC)

OUTSTANDING CONTINUING PERFORMANCE BY A SUPPORTING ACTRESS IN A DRAMA SERIES: Kristy McNichol, *Family* (ABC)

OUTSTANDING CONTINUING PERFORMANCE BY A SUPPORTING ACTOR IN A COMEDY SERIES: Gary Burghoff, *M*A*S*H* (CBS)

OUTSTANDING CONTINUING PERFORMANCE BY A SUPPORTING ACTRESS IN A COMEDY SERIES: Mary Kay Place, *Mary Hartman, Mary Hartman* (SYNDICATED)

OUTSTANDING CONTINUING OR SINGLE PERFORMANCE BY A SUPPORTING ACTOR IN VARIETY OR MUSIC: Tim Conway, *The Carol Burnett Show* (CBS)

OUTSTANDING CONTINUING OR SINGLE PERFORMANCE BY A SUPPORTING ACTRESS IN VARIETY OR MUSIC: Rita Moreno, *The Muppet Show* (SYNDICATED)

OUTSTANDING SINGLE PERFORMANCE BY A SUPPORTING ACTOR IN A COMEDY OR DRAMA SERIES: Edward Asner, *Roots* (part 1) (ABC)

OUTSTANDING SINGLE PERFORMANCE BY A SUPPORTING ACTRESS IN A COMEDY OR DRAMA SERIES: Olivia Cole, *Roots* (part 8) (ABC)

OUTSTANDING PERFORMANCE BY A SUPPORTING ACTOR IN A COMEDY OR DRAMA SPECIAL: Burgess Meredith, "Tail Gunner Joe," *The Big Event* (NBC)

OUTSTANDING PERFORMANCE BY A SUPPORTING ACTRESS IN A COMEDY OR DRAMA SPECIAL: Diana Hyland, "The Boy in the Plastic Bubble," *The ABC Friday Night Movie* (ABC)

OUTSTANDING DIRECTING IN A DRAMA SERIES (SINGLE EPISODE): David Greene, *Roots* (part 1) (ABC)

OUTSTANDING DIRECTING IN A COMEDY SERIES (SINGLE EPISODE): Alan Alda, "Dear Sigmund," *M*A*S*H* (CBS)

OUTSTANDING DIRECTING IN A COMEDY-VARIETY OR MUSIC SERIES (SINGLE EPISODE): Dave Powers, *The Carol Burnett Show* (program of 12 February 1977) (CBS)

OUTSTANDING DIRECTING IN A SPECIAL PROGRAM, DRAMA OR COMEDY: Daniel Petrie, "Eleanor and Franklin: The White House Years," *ABC Theatre* (ABC)

OUTSTANDING DIRECTING IN A COMEDY-VARIETY OR MUSIC SPECIAL: Dwight Hemion, "America Salutes Richard Rodgers: The Sound of His Music" (CBS)

OUTSTANDING WRITING IN A DRAMA SERIES (SINGLE EPISODE): Ernest Kinoy and William Blinn, *Roots* (part 2) (ABC)

OUTSTANDING WRITING IN A SPECIAL PROGRAM (ORIGINAL TELEPLAY, DRAMA OR COMEDY): Lane Slate, "Tail Gunner Joe," *The Big Event* (NBC)

OUTSTANDING WRITING IN A SPECIAL PROGRAM (ADAPTATION, DRAMA OR COMEDY): Stewart Stern, "Sybil," *The Big Event* (NBC)

OUTSTANDING WRITING IN A COMEDY SERIES (SINGLE EPISODE): Allan Burns, James L. Brooks, Ed. Weinberger, Stan Daniels, David Lloyd and Bob Ellison, "The Last Show," *The Mary Tyler Moore Show* (CBS)

OUTSTANDING WRITING IN A COMEDY-VARIETY OR MUSIC SERIES (SINGLE EPISODE): Anne Beatts, Dan Aykroyd, Al Franken, Tom Davis, James Downey, Lorne Michaels, Marilyn Suzanne Miller, Michael O'Donoghue, Herb Sargent, Tom Schiller, Rosie Shuster, Alan Zweibel, John Belushi and Bill Murray, *NBC's Saturday Night* (program of 12 March 1977, with host Sissy Spacek) (NBC)

OUTSTANDING WRITING IN A COMEDY–VARIETY OR MUSICAL SPECIAL: Alan Buz Kohan and Ted Strauss, "America Salutes Richard Rodgers: The Sound of His Music" (CBS)

II. DAYTIME AWARDS (administered by the National Academy of Television Arts and Sciences)

OUTSTANDING DAYTIME DRAMA SERIES: *Ryan's Hope* (ABC); Paul Avila Mayer and Claire Labine, executive produers; Robert Costello, producer

OUTSTANDING DAYTIME TALK, SERVICE OR VARIETY SERIES: *The Merv Griffin Show* (SYNDICATED); Bob Murphy, producer

OUTSTANDING GAME OR AUDIENCE PARTICIPATION SHOW: *The Family Feud* (ABC); Howard Felsher, producer

OUTSTANDING ENTERTAINMENT CHILDREN'S SERIES: *Zoom* (PBS); Cheryl Susheel Biggs, executive producer; Monia Joblin and Mary Benjamin Blau, producers

OUTSTANDING INFORMATIONAL CHILDREN'S SERIES: *The Electric Company* (PBS); Samuel Y. Gibbon, Jr., executive producer

OUTSTANDING INSTRUCTIONAL CHILDREN'S PROGRAMMING (SERIES AND SPECIALS): *Sesame Street* (PBS); Jon Stone, executive producer; Dulcy Singer, producer

OUTSTANDING ENTERTAINMENT CHILDREN'S SPECIAL: "Big Henry and the Polka Dot Kid," *Special Treat* (NBC); Linda Gottlieb, producer

OUTSTANDING INFORMATIONAL CHILDREN'S SPECIAL: "My Mom's Having a Baby," *ABC Afterschool Specials* (ABC); David H. DePatie and Friz Freleng, executive producers; Bob Chenault, producer

OUTSTANDING PROGRAM AND INDIVIDUAL ACHIEVEMENT IN DAYTIME DRAMA SPECIALS: (1) "The American Woman: Portraits of Courage" (ABC); Gaby Monet, producer; (2) Lois Nettleton, performer, "The American Woman: Portraits of Courage" (ABC); and (3) Gaby Monet and Anne Grant, writers, "The American Woman: Portraits of Courage" (ABC)

OUTSTANDING ACTOR IN A DAYTIME DRAMA SERIES: Val Dufour, *Search for Tomorrow* (CBS)

OUTSTANDING ACTRESS IN A DAYTIME DRAMA SERIES: Helen Gallagher, *Ryan's Hope* (ABC)

OUTSTANDING HOST OR HOSTESS IN A TALK, SERVICE OR VARIETY SERIES: Phil Donahue, *Donahue* (SYNDICATED)

OUTSTANDING HOST OR HOSTESS IN A GAME OR AUDIENCE PARTICIPATION SHOW: Bert Convy, *Tattletales* (CBS)

OUTSTANDING INDIVIDUAL DIRECTOR FOR A DAYTIME DRAMA SERIES: Lela Swift, *Ryan's Hope* (program of 8 February 1977) (ABC)

OUTSTANDING INDIVIDUAL DIRECTOR FOR A DAYTIME VARIETY PROGRAM (SINGLE EPISODE): Donald R. King, "Mike in Hollywood with

Ray Charles and Michel Legrand," *The Mike Douglas Show* (SYNDI-CATED)

OUTSTANDING INDIVIDUAL DIRECTOR FOR A GAME OR AUDIENCE PAR-TICIPATION SHOW (SINGLE EPISODE): Mike Gargiulo, *The $20,000 Pyramid* (program of 10 August 1976) (ABC)

OUTSTANDING WRITING FOR A DAYTIME DRAMA SERIES (SINGLE EPI-SODE OR ENTIRE SERIES): Claire Labine, Paul Avila Mayer and Mary Munisteri, *Ryan's Hope* (ABC)

1977–1978
I. PRIME-TIME AWARDS (administered by the Academy of Television Arts and Sciences)

OUTSTANDING COMEDY SERIES: *All in the Family* (CBS); Mort Lachman, executive producer; Milt Josefsberg, producer

OUTSTANDING DRAMA SERIES: *The Rockford Files* (NBC); Meta Rosen-berg, executive producer; Stephen J. Cannell, supervising producer; David Chase and Charles F. Johnson, producers

OUTSTANDING LIMITED SERIES: *Holocaust* (NBC); Herbert Brodkin, ex-ecutive producer; Robert Berger, producer

OUTSTANDING COMEDY-VARIETY OR MUSIC SERIES: *The Muppet Show* (SYNDICATED); David Lazer, executive producer; Jim Henson, pro-ducer; The Muppets—Frank Oz, Jerry Nelson, Richard Hunt, Dave Goelz and Jim Henson, stars

OUTSTANDING INFORMATIONAL SERIES: *The Body Human* (CBS); Thomas W. Moore, executive producer; Alfred R. Kelman, producer

OUTSTANDING SPECIAL, DRAMA OR COMEDY: "The Gathering" (ABC); Joseph Barbera, executive producer; Harry R. Sherman, producer

OUTSTANDING SPECIAL, COMEDY-VARIETY OR MUSIC: "Bette Midler—Ol' Red Hair Is Back" (NBC); Aaron Russo, executive producer; Gary Smith and Dwight Hemion, producers; Bette Midler, star

OUTSTANDING CLASSICAL PROGRAM IN THE PERFORMING ARTS: Ameri-can Ballet Theatre's "Giselle," *Live from Lincoln Center* (PBS); John Goberman, producer

OUTSTANDING INFORMATIONAL SPECIAL: "The Great Whales," *Nation-al Geographic Specials* (PBS); Thomas Skinner and Dennis B. Kane, executive producers; Nicolas Noxon, producer

OUTSTANDING CHILDREN'S SPECIAL (BROADCAST DURING THE EVE-NING): "Halloween Is Grinch Night" (ABC); David H. DePatie and Friz Freleng, executive producers; Ted Geisel, producer

SPECIAL CLASSIFICATION OF OUTSTANDING PROGRAM ACHIEVEMENT: *The Tonight Show Starring Johnny Carson* (NBC); Fred De Cordova, producer; Johnny Carson, star

OUTSTANDING LEAD ACTOR IN A DRAMA SERIES: Edward Asner, *Lou Grant* (CBS)

OUTSTANDING LEAD ACTRESS IN A DRAMA SERIES: Sada Thompson, *Family* (ABC)

OUTSTANDING LEAD ACTOR IN A LIMITED SERIES: Michael Moriarty, *Holocaust* (NBC)

OUTSTANDING LEAD ACTRESS IN A LIMITED SERIES: Meryl Streep, *Holocaust* (NBC)

OUTSTANDING LEAD ACTOR IN A COMEDY SERIES: Carroll O'Connor, *All in the Family* (CBS)

OUTSTANDING LEAD ACTRESS IN A COMEDY SERIES: Jean Stapleton, *All in the Family* (CBS)

OUTSTANDING LEAD ACTOR FOR A SINGLE APPEARANCE IN A DRAMA OR COMEDY SERIES: Barnard Hughes, "Judge," *Lou Grant* (CBS)

OUTSTANDING LEAD ACTRESS FOR A SINGLE APPEARANCE IN A DRAMA OR COMEDY SERIES: Rita Moreno, "The Paper Palace," *The Rockford Files* (NBC)

OUTSTANDING LEAD ACTOR IN A DRAMA OR COMEDY SPECIAL: Fred Astaire, "A Family Upside Down" (NBC)

OUTSTANDING LEAD ACTRESS IN A DRAMA OR COMEDY SPECIAL: Joanne Woodward, "See How She Runs," *G.E. Theater* (CBS)

OUTSTANDING CONTINUING PERFORMANCE BY A SUPPORTING ACTOR IN A DRAMA SERIES: Robert Vaughn, *Washington: Behind Closed Doors* (ABC)

OUTSTANDING CONTINUING PERFORMANCE BY A SUPPORTING ACTRESS IN A DRAMA SERIES: Nancy Marchand, *Lou Grant* (CBS)

OUTSTANDING CONTINUING PERFORMANCE BY A SUPPORTING ACTOR IN A COMEDY SERIES: Rob Reiner, *All in the Family* (CBS)

OUTSTANDING CONTINUING PERFORMANCE BY A SUPPORTING ACTRESS IN A COMEDY SERIES: Julie Kavner, *Rhoda* (CBS)

OUTSTANDING CONTINUING OR SINGLE PERFORMANCE BY A SUPPORTING ACTOR IN VARIETY OR MUSIC: Tim Conway, *The Carol Burnett Show* (CBS)

OUTSTANDING CONTINUING OR SINGLE PERFORMANCE BY A SUPPORTING ACTRESS IN VARIETY OR MUSIC: Gilda Radner, *NBC's Saturday Night Live* (NBC)

OUTSTANDING SINGLE PERFORMANCE BY A SUPPORTING ACTOR IN A COMEDY OR DRAMA SERIES: Ricardo Montalban, *How the West Was Won* (Part II) ABC

OUTSTANDING SINGLE PERFORMANCE BY A SUPPORTING ACTRESS IN A COMEDY OR DRAMA SERIES: Blanche Baker, *Holocaust* (Part I) (NBC)

OUTSTANDING PERFORMANCE BY A SUPPORTING ACTOR IN A COMEDY OR DRAMA SPECIAL: Howard Da Silva, "Verna: USO Girl," *Great Performances* (PBS)

OUTSTANDING PERFORMANCE BY A SUPPORTING ACTRESS IN A COMEDY OR DRAMA SPECIAL: Eva La Gallienne, "The Royal Family" (PBS)

OUTSTANDING DIRECTING IN A DRAMA SERIES: Marvin J. Chomsky, *Holocaust* (NBC)

OUTSTANDING DIRECTING IN A COMEDY SERIES: Paul Bogart, "Edith's 50th Birthday," *All in the Family* (CBS)

OUTSTANDING DIRECTING IN A COMEDY-VARIETY OR MUSIC SERIES: Dave Powers, *The Carol Burnett Show* (program of 5 March 1978, with guests Steve Martin and Betty White) (CBS)

OUTSTANDING DIRECTING IN A SPECIAL PROGRAM, DRAMA OR COMEDY: David Lowell Rich, "The Defection of Simas Kudirka" (CBS)

OUTSTANDING DIRECTING IN A COMEDY-VARIETY OR MUSIC SPECIAL: Dwight Hemion, "The Sentry Collection Presents Ben Vereen—His Roots" (ABC)

OUTSTANDING WRITING IN A DRAMA SERIES: Gerald Green, *Holocaust* (NBC)

OUTSTANDING WRITING IN A SPECIAL PROGRAM, DRAMA OR COMEDY (ORIGINAL TELEPLAY): George Rubino, "The Last Tenant" (ABC)

OUTSTANDING WRITING IN A SPECIAL PROGRAM, DRAMA OR COMEDY (ADAPTATION): Caryl Lender, "Mary White" (ABC)

OUTSTANDING WRITING IN A COMEDY SERIES: Bob Weiskopf and Bob Schiller (teleplay), Barry Harman and Harve Brosten (story), "Cousin Liz," *All in the Family* (CBS)

OUTSTANDING WRITING IN A COMEDY-VARIETY OR MUSIC SERIES: Ed Simmons, Roger Beatty, Rick Hawkins, Liz Sage, Robert Illes, James Stein, Franelle Silver, Larry Siegel, Tim Conway, Bill Richmond, Gene Perrett, Dick Clair and Jenna McMahon, *The Carol Burnett Show* (program of 5 March 1978, with guests Steve Martin and Betty White) (CBS)

FIRST ANNUAL ATAS GOVERNOR'S AWARD: William S. Paley, Chairman of the Board, CBS

II. DAYTIME AWARDS (administered by the National Academy of Television Arts and Sciences)

OUTSTANDING DAYTIME DRAMA SERIES: *Days of Our Lives* (NBC); Betty Corday and Wesley Kenney, executive producers; Jack Herzberg, producer

OUTSTANDING DAYTIME TALK, SERVICE OR VARIETY SERIES: *Donahue* (SYNDICATED); Richard Mincer, executive producer; Patricia McMillen, producer

OUTSTANDING GAME OR AUDIENCE PARTICIPATION SHOW: *The Hollywood Squares* (NBC); Merrill Heatter and Bob Quigley, executive producers; Jay Redack, producer

OUTSTANDING CHILDREN'S ENTERTAINMENT SERIES: *Captain Kangaroo* (CBS); Jim Hirschfeld, producer

OUTSTANDING CHILDREN'S INFORMATION SERIES: *Animals Animals Animals* (ABC); Lester Cooper, executive producer; Peter Weinberg, producer

OUTSTANDING CHILDREN'S INSTRUCTIONAL SERIES: *Schoolhouse Rock* (ABC); Tom Yohe, executive producer; Radford Stone and George Newall, producers

OUTSTANDING CHILDREN'S ENTERTAINMENT SPECIAL: "Hewitt's Just Different," *ABC Afterschool Special* (ABC); Daniel Wilson, executive producer; Fran Sears, producer

OUTSTANDING CHILDREN'S INFORMATION SPECIAL: "Very Good Friends," *ABC Afterschool Special* (ABC); Martin Tahse, producer

OUTSTANDING ACTOR IN A DAYTIME DRAMA SERIES: James Pritchett, *The Doctors* (NBC)

OUTSTANDING ACTRESS IN A DAYTIME DRAMA SERIES: Laurie Heineman, *Another World* (NBC)

OUTSTANDING HOST OR HOSTESS IN A TALK, SERVICE OR VARIETY SERIES: Phil Donahue, *Donahue* (SYNDICATED)

OUTSTANDING HOST OR HOSTESS IN A GAME OR AUDIENCE PARTICIPATION SHOW: Richard Dawson, *The Family Feud* (ABC)

OUTSTANDING INDIVIDUAL DIRECTOR FOR A DAYTIME DRAMA SERIES FOR A SINGLE EPISODE: Richard Dunlap, *The Young and the Restless* (program of 3 March 1978) (CBS)

OUTSTANDING INDIVIDUAL DIRECTOR FOR A VARIETY PROGRAM FOR A SINGLE EPISODE: Martin Haig Mackey, *Over Easy* (program of 20 March 1978) (PBS)

OUTSTANDING INDIVIDUAL DIRECTOR FOR A DAYTIME GAME OR AUDIENCE PARTICIPATION SHOW: Mike Gargiulo, *The $20,000 Pyramid* (program of 20 June 1977) (ABC)

OUTSTANDING WRITING FOR A DAYTIME DRAMA SERIES (SINGLE EPISODE OR ENTIRE SERIES): Claire Labine, Paul Avila Mayer, Mary Munisteri, Allan Leicht and Judith Pinsker, *Ryan's Hope* (ABC)

1978–1979

I. PRIME-TIME AWARDS (administered by the Academy of Television Arts and Sciences)

OUTSTANDING COMEDY SERIES: *Taxi* (ABC); James L. Brooks, Stan Daniels, David Davis, and Ed. Weinberger, executive producers; Glen Charles and Les Charles, producers

OUTSTANDING DRAMA SERIES: *Lou Grant* (CBS); Gene Reynolds, executive producer; Seth Freeman and Gary David Goldberg, producers

OUTSTANDING LIMITED SERIES: *Roots: The Next Generations* (ABC); David L. Wolper, executive producer; Stan Margulies, producer

OUTSTANDING COMEDY-VARIETY OR MUSIC PROGRAM (SPECIAL OR SERIES): "Steve and Eydie Celebrate Irving Berlin" (NBC); Steve Lawrence and Gary Smith, executive producers; Gary Smith and Dwight Hemion, producers; Steve Lawrence and Eydie Gormé, stars

OUTSTANDING INFORMATIONAL PROGRAM (SPECIAL OR SERIES): "Scared Straight!" (SYNDICATED); Arnold Shapiro, producer

OUTSTANDING CLASSICAL PROGRAM IN THE PERFORMING ARTS (SPECIAL OR SERIES): "Balanchine IV," *Great Performances* (PBS); Jac Venza, executive producer; Merrill Brockway, series producer; Emile Ardolino, series co-ordinating producer; Judy Kinberg, producer

OUTSTANDING CHILDREN'S PROGRAM (SPECIAL OR SERIES): "Christmas Eve on Sesame Street" (PBS); Jon Stone, executive producer; Dulcy Singer, producer

OUTSTANDING ANIMATED PROGRAM (SPECIAL OR SERIES): "The Lion, the Witch and the Wardrobe" (CBS); David Connell, executive producer; Steve Melendez, producer

OUTSTANDING DRAMA OR COMEDY SPECIAL: "Friendly Fire" (ABC); Martin Starger, executive producer; Philip Barry, producer; Fay Kanin, coproducer

OUTSTANDING PROGRAM ACHIEVEMENT—SPECIAL CLASS: (1) *The Tonight Show Starring Johnny Carson* (NBC); Fred De Cordova, producer; Johnny Carson, star; (2) *Lifeline* (NBC); Thomas W. Moore and Robert E. Fuisz, M.D., executive producers; Alfred Kelman, producer; Geof Bartz, coproducer

OUTSTANDING PROGRAM ACHIEVEMENT—SPECIAL EVENTS: (1) "51st Annual Awards Presentation of the Academy of Motion Picture Arts and Sciences" (ABC); Jack Haley, Jr., producer (2) "Baryshnikov at the White House" (PBS); Gerald Slater, executive producer; Hal Hutkoff, producer

OUTSTANDING LEAD ACTOR IN A DRAMA SERIES (CONTINUING OR SINGLE PERFORMANCE): Ron Leibman, *Kaz* (CBS)

OUTSTANDING LEAD ACTRESS IN A DRAMA SERIES (CONTINUING OR SINGLE PERFORMANCE): Mariette Hartley, "Married," *The Incredible Hulk* (CBS)

OUTSTANDING LEAD ACTOR IN A COMEDY SERIES (CONTINUING OR SINGLE PERFORMANCE): Carroll O'Connor, *All in the Family* (CBS)

OUTSTANDING LEAD ACTRESS IN A COMEDY SERIES (CONTINUING OR SINGLE PERFORMANCE): Ruth Gordon, "Sugar Mama," *Taxi* (ABC)

OUTSTANDING LEAD ACTOR IN A LIMITED SERIES OR A SPECIAL (CONTINUING OR SINGLE APPEARANCE): Peter Strauss, "The Jericho Mile" (ABC)

OUTSTANDING LEAD ACTRESS IN A LIMITED SERIES OR A SPECIAL (CONTINUING OR SINGLE APPEARANCE): Bette Davis, "Strangers: The Story of a Mother and Daughter" (CBS)

OUTSTANDING SUPPORTING ACTOR IN A DRAMA SERIES (CONTINUING OR SINGLE PERFORMANCE): Stuart Margolin, *The Rockford Files* (NBC)

OUTSTANDING SUPPORTING ACTRESS IN A DRAMA SERIES (CONTINUING OR SINGLE PERFORMANCE): Kristy McNichol, *Family* (ABC)

OUTSTANDING SUPPORTING ACTOR IN A COMEDY, COMEDY-VARIETY OR MUSIC SERIES (CONTINUING OR SINGLE PERFORMANCE): Robert Guillaume, *Soap* (ABC)

OUTSTANDING SUPPORTING ACTRESS IN A COMEDY, COMEDY-VARIETY OR MUSIC SERIES (CONTINUING OR SINGLE PERFORMANCE): Sally Struthers, "California Here We Are," *All in the Family* (CBS)

OUTSTANDING SUPPORTING ACTOR IN A LIMITED SERIES OR A SPECIAL (CONTINUING OR SINGLE APPEARANCE): Marlon Brando, *Roots: The Next Generations,* episode seven (ABC)

OUTSTANDING SUPPORTING ACTRESS IN A LIMITED SERIES OR A SPECIAL (CONTINUING OR SINGLE APPEARANCE): Esther Rolle, "Summer of My German Soldier" (NBC)

OUTSTANDING INDIVIDUAL ACHIEVEMENT—SPECIAL EVENTS: Mikhail Baryshnikov (as himself), "Baryshnikov at the White House" (PBS)

OUTSTANDING DIRECTING IN A DRAMA SERIES (SINGLE EPISODE): Jackie Cooper, *The White Shadow,* pilot episode (CBS)

OUTSTANDING DIRECTING IN A COMEDY OR COMEDY-VARIETY OR MUSIC SERIES (SINGLE EPISODE): Noam Pitlik, "The Harris Incident," *Barney Miller* (ABC)

OUTSTANDING DIRECTING IN A LIMITED SERIES (SINGLE EPISODE) OR A SPECIAL: David Greene, "Friendly Fire" (ABC)

OUTSTANDING INDIVIDUAL ACHIEVEMENT—INFORMATIONAL PROGRAM: John Korty, director, "Who Are the DeBolts . . . and Where Did They Get 19 Kids?" (ABC)

OUTSTANDING WRITING IN A DRAMA SERIES (SINGLE EPISODE): Michele Gallery, "Dying," *Lou Grant* (CBS)

OUTSTANDING WRITING IN A COMEDY OR COMEDY-VARIETY OR MUSIC SERIES (SINGLE EPISODE): Alan Alda, "Inga," *M*A*S*H* (CBS)

OUTSTANDING WRITING IN A LIMITED SERIES (SINGLE EPISODE) OR A SPECIAL (ORIGINAL TELEPLAY OR ADAPTATION): Patrick Nolan and Michael Mann, "The Jericho Mile" (ABC)

SECOND ANNUAL ATAS GOVERNORS' AWARD: Walter Cronkite, CBS News

SPECIAL PRESENTATION: Milton Berle, "Mr. Television"

II. DAYTIME AWARDS (administered by the National Academy of Television Arts and Sciences)

OUTSTANDING DAYTIME DRAMA SERIES: *Ryan's Hope* (ABC); Claire Labine and Paul Avila Mayer, executive producers; Ellen Barrett and Robert Costello, producers

OUTSTANDING TALK, SERVICE OR VARIETY SERIES: *Donahue* (SYNDICATED); Richard Mincer, executive producer; Patricia McMillen, producer

OUTSTANDING GAME OR AUDIENCE PARTICIPATION SHOW: *The Hollywood Squares* (NBC); Merrill Heatter and Bob Quigley, executive producers; Jay Redack, producer

OUTSTANDING CHILDREN'S ENTERTAINMENT SERIES: *Kids Are People Too* (ABC); Lawrence Einhorn, executive producer; Noreen Conlin, coproducer; Laura Shrock, producer

OUTSTANDING CHILDREN'S INFORMATIONAL SERIES: *Big Blue Marble* (SYNDICATED); Robert Wiemer, executive producer; Richard Berman, producer

OUTSTANDING CHILDREN'S INSTRUCTIONAL SERIES: *Science Rock* (ABC); Tom Yohe, executive producer; George Newall and Radford Stone, producers

OUTSTANDING CHILDREN'S ENTERTAINMENT SPECIAL: "The Tap Dance Kid" (NBC); Linda Gottlieb, executive producer; Evelyn Barron, producer

OUTSTANDING CHILDREN'S INFORMATIONAL SPECIAL: *Razzmatazz* (program of 1 February 1979) (CBS); Joel Heller, executive producer; Vern Diamond, producer

SPECIAL CLASSIFICATION OF OUTSTANDING PROGRAM ACHIEVEMENT: *Camera Three* (CBS); John Musilli, executive producer; Roger Englander, producer

OUTSTANDING ACHIEVEMENT IN RELIGIOUS PROGRAMMING—SPECIAL: *Marshall Efron's Illustrated, Simplified and Painless Sunday School* (CBS); Pamela Ilott, executive producer; Ted Holmes, producer

OUTSTANDING ACHIEVEMENT IN COVERAGE OF SPECIAL EVENTS—PROGRAMS: (1) "Horowitz: Live!" (NBC); Herbert Kloiber, executive producer; John Goberman, producer (2) "Leontyne Price at the White House" (PBS); Hal Hutkoff, producer

OUTSTANDING ACTOR IN A DAYTIME DRAMA SERIES: Al Freeman, Jr., *One Life to Live* (ABC)

OUTSTANDING ACTRESS IN A DAYTIME DRAMA SERIES: Irene Dailey, *Another World* (NBC)

OUTSTANDING SUPPORTING ACTOR IN A DAYTIME DRAMA SERIES: Peter Hansen, *General Hospital* (ABC)

OUTSTANDING SUPPORTING ACTRESS IN A DAYTIME DRAMA SERIES: Suzanne Rogers, *Days of Our Lives* (NBC)

OUTSTANDING HOST OR HOSTESS IN A TALK, SERVICE OR VARIETY SERIES: Phil Donahue, *Donahue* (SYNDICATED)

OUTSTANDING HOST IN A GAME OR AUDIENCE PARTICIPATION SHOW: Dick Clark, *The $20,000 Pyramid* (ABC)

OUTSTANDING INDIVIDUAL ACHIEVEMENT IN CHILDREN'S PROGRAMMING (PERFORMERS): (1) Geraldine Fitzgerald, "Rodeo Red and the Runaway," *NBC Special Treat* (NBC); (2) Jack Gilford, "Hello in There," *Big Blue Marble* (SYNDICATED); (3) Jim Henson, Frank Oz, Carroll Spinney, Jerry Nelson, and Richard Hunt, "The Muppets of Sesame Street," *Sesame Street* (PBS)

OUTSTANDING INDIVIDUAL ACHIEVEMENT IN RELIGIOUS PROGRAMMING: (1) Rolanda Mendels (performer), "Interrogation in Budapest" (NBC); (2) Martin Hoade (director), "Interrogation in Budapest" (NBC)

OUTSTANDING ACHIEVEMENT IN COVERAGE IF SPECIAL EVENTS—PERFORMERS: (1) Vladimir Horowitz, "Horowitz: Live!" (NBC); (2) Leontyne Price, "Leontyne Price at the White House" (PBS)

SPECIAL CLASSIFICATION OF OUTSTANDING INDIVIDUAL ACHIEVEMENT: (1) Paul Lynde (panelist), *The Hollywood Squares* (program of 18 May 1978) (NBC); (2) Bill Walker, Jay Burton, Tom Perew, Mark Davidson, and Fred Tatashore (writers), *Dinah!* (SYNDICATED)

OUTSTANDING DIRECTION FOR A DAYTIME DRAMA SERIES: Jerry Evans and Lela Swift, *Ryan's Hope* (ABC)

OUTSTANDING INDIVIDUAL DIRECTION FOR A VARIETY PROGRAM: Ron Wiener, "Nazis and the Klan," *Donahue* (SYNDICATED)

OUTSTANDING INDIVIDUAL DIRECTION FOR A GAME OR AUDIENCE PARTICIPATION SHOW: Jerome Shaw, *The Hollywood Squares* (program of 20 June 1978) (NBC)

OUTSTANDING INDIVIDUAL ACHIEVEMENT IN CHILDREN'S PROGRAMMING (DIRECTOR): Larry Elikann, "Mom & Dad Can't Hear Me," *ABC Afterschool Special* (ABC)

OUTSTANDING WRITING FOR A DAYTIME DRAMA SERIES: Claire Labine, Paul Avila Mayer, Mary Munisteri, Judith Pinsker, and Jeffrey Lane, *Ryan's Hope* (ABC)

PEABODY AWARDS

The George Foster Peabody Broadcasting Awards were established in 1940, and are administered by the Henry W. Grady School of Journalism at the University of Georgia. Awards are given in radio, television and related fields, but only those pertaining to television are listed here. The award categories have varied from year to year, and in recent years the categories themselves have been abolished.

1948

OUTSTANDING CONTRIBUTION TO THE ART OF TELEVISION: *Actors' Studio* (ABC)
OUTSTANDING CHILDREN'S PROGRAM: *Howdy Doody* (NBC)

1949

ENTERTAINMENT: *The Ed Wynn Show* (CBS)
EDUCATION: *Crusade in Europe* (ABC)
REPORTING AND INTERPRETATION OF THE NEWS: *The United Nations in Action* (CBS)
OUTSTANDING CHILDREN'S PROGRAM: *Kukla, Fran and Ollie* (NBC)

1950

ENTERTAINMENT: Jimmy Durante (NBC)
CHILDREN'S PROGRAMS: (1) *Saturday at the Zoo* (ABC); and (2) *Zoo Parade* (NBC)
SPECIAL AWARD: To ABC (Robert E. Kintner, president, and associates Robert Saudek and Joseph McDonald) "for their courageous stand in resisting organized pressures and their reaffirmation of basic American principles."

1951

ENTERTAINMENT (NONMUSICAL): *Celanese Theatre* (ABC)
ENTERTAINMENT (MUSICAL): Gian Carlo Menotti, "Amahl and the Night Visitors" (NBC)

EDUCATION: *What in the World* (WCAU-TV, Philadelphia)

NEWS AND INTERPRETATION: Edward R. Murrow and *See It Now* (CBS)

MERITORIOUS REGIONAL PUBLIC SERVICE BY RADIO AND TELEVISION: WSB, Atlanta, for *The Pastor's Study* and *Our World Today*

1952

ENTERTAINMENT: (1) *Mr. Peepers* (NBC); and (2) *Your Hit Parade* (NBC)

EDUCATION: *The Johns Hopkins Science Review* (DUMONT)

NEWS: *Meet the Press* (NBC)

YOUTH AND CHILDREN'S PROGRAMS: *Ding Dong School* (NBC)

SPECIAL AWARD: *Victory at Sea* (NBC)

LOCAL PUBLIC SERVICE: WEWS-TV, Cleveland

1953

ENTERTAINMENT: (1) (*Philco*) *Television Playhouse* (NBC); and (2) Imogene Coca (*Your Show of Shows*) (NBC)

MUSIC: *NBC Television Opera Theatre* (NBC)

EDUCATION: (1) *Cavalcade of Books* (KNXT-TV, Los Angeles); and (2) *Camera Three* (WCBS-TV, New York)

NEWS: Gerald W. Johnson, WAAM-TV, Baltimore

YOUTH AND CHILDREN'S PROGRAMS: *Mr. Wizard* (NBC)

SPECIAL AWARD: Edward R. Murrow (CBS)

PROMOTION OF INTERNATIONAL UNDERSTANDING THROUGH TELEVISION: British Broadcasting Corporation for coverage of the coronation

1954

ENTERTAINMENT: George Gobel (NBC)

EDUCATION: *Adventure* (CBS)

NEWS (RADIO AND TELEVISION): John Daly (ABC)

YOUTH AND CHILDREN'S PROGRAMS: *Disneyland* (ABC)

SPECIAL AWARDS: (1) *Omnibus* (CBS); and (2) *The Search* (CBS)

NATIONAL PUBLIC SERVICE: *Industry on Parade* (National Association of Manufacturers)

REGIONAL PUBLIC SERVICE: WJAR-TV, Providence (for hurricane coverage)

1955

ENTERTAINMENT: (1) Jackie Gleason (CBS); and (2) Perry Como (NBC)
DRAMATIC ENTERTAINMENT: *Producers' Showcase* (NBC)
MUSIC (RADIO AND TELEVISION): *Voice of Firestone* (ABC)
EDUCATION: Dr. Frank Baxter (KNXT-TV, Los Angeles)
NEWS: Douglas Edwards (CBS)
YOUTH AND CHILDREN'S PROGRAMS: *Lassie* (CBS)
PUBLIC SERVICE (RADIO AND TELEVISION): Sylvester L. Weaver, Jr., NBC, "for pioneering program concepts"
PROMOTION OF INTERNATIONAL UNDERSTANDING (RADIO AND TELEVISION): Quincy Howe (ABC)

1956

ENTERTAINMENT: *The Ed Sullivan Show* (CBS)
EDUCATION: *You Are There* (CBS)
NEWS: ABC, John Daly and associates (for convention coverage)
YOUTH AND CHILDREN'S PROGRAMS: *Youth Wants to Know* (NBC)
PUBLIC SERVICE: "World in Crisis" (CBS)
LOCAL AND REGIONAL PUBLIC SERVICE (RADIO AND TELEVISION): "Regimented Raindrops" (WOW, Omaha)
WRITING: Rod Serling
PROMOTION OF INTERNATIONAL UNDERSTANDING: "The Secret Life of Danny Kaye" (UNICEF)
PROMOTION OF INTERNATIONAL UNDERSTANDING (SPECIAL AWARD): United Nations Radio and Television
SPECIAL AWARD: Jack Gould of *The New York Times* (for his writings on radio and television)

1957

ENTERTAINMENT (NONMUSICAL): *Hallmark Hall of Fame* (NBC)
ENTERTAINMENT (MUSICAL): *The Dinah Shore Chevy Show* (NBC)
EDUCATION: *The Heritage Series* (WQED-TV, Pittsburgh)
NEWS: ABC, for " 'Prologue '58' and other significant news coverage"
NEWS (RADIO AND TELEVISION): CBS, "for depth and range"
LOCAL NEWS (RADIO AND TELEVISION): Louis M. Lyons (WGBH, Boston)
YOUTH AND CHILDREN'S PROGRAMS: *Captain Kangaroo* (CBS)
LOCAL YOUTH AND CHILDREN'S PROGRAMS: *Wunda Wunda* (KING-TV, Seattle)
PUBLIC SERVICE: *The Last Word* (CBS)

LOCAL PUBLIC SERVICE: *Panorama* (KLZ-TV, Denver)

CONTRIBUTION TO INTERNATIONAL UNDERSTANDING: Bob Hope (NBC)

SPECIAL AWARDS: (1) NBC, for "outstanding contribution to education"; and (2) Westinghouse Broadcasting Company, Inc., for "its Boston Conference and the high quality of its public service broadcasting"

1958

DRAMATIC ENTERTAINMENT: *Playhouse 90* (CBS)

ENTERTAINMENT WITH HUMOR: *The Steve Allen Show* (NBC)

MUSICAL ENTERTAINMENT: "Lincoln Presents Leonard Bernstein and the New York Philharmonic" (CBS)

EDUCATION: *Continental Classroom* (NBC)

NEWS: *The Huntley-Brinkley Report* (NBC)

PROGRAMS FOR YOUTH: *College News Conference* (ABC)

PROGRAMS FOR CHILDREN: *The Blue Fairy* (WGN-TV, Chicago)

PUBLIC SERVICE: CBS

WRITING: James Costigan, for "Little Moon of Alban," *Hallmark Hall of Fame* (NBC)

CONTRIBUTION TO INTERNATIONAL UNDERSTANDING: "M.D. International" (NBC)

SPECIAL AWARDS: (1) "An Evening with Fred Astaire" (NBC); and (2) Orson Welles, "Fountain of Youth," *Colgate Theatre* (NBC)

1959

ENTERTAINMENT (NONMUSICAL): (1) *The Play of the Week* (WNTA-TV), Newark); and (2) David Susskind, executive producer, "The Moon and Sixpence" (NBC)

ENTERTAINMENT (MUSICAL): (1) *The Bell Telephone Hour* (NBC); and (2) *Great Music from Chicago* (WGN-TV, Chicago)

EDUCATION: (1) "Decisions" (WGBH-TV, Boston, and the World Affairs Council); and (2) "The Population Explosion" (CBS)

NEWS: "Khrushchev Abroad" (ABC)

LOCAL PUBLIC SERVICE: WDSU-TV, New Orleans

CONTRIBUTION TO INTERNATIONAL UNDERSTANDING: (1) *The Ed Sullivan Show* (CBS); and (2) *Small World* (CBS)

SPECIAL AWARDS: (1) Dr. Frank Stanton (CBS); and (2) "The Lost Class of '59" (CBS)

1960

ENTERTAINMENT: "The Fabulous Fifties" (CBS)
EDUCATION: *White Paper* series (NBC)
NEWS: *The Texaco Huntley-Brinkley Report* (NBC)
PROGRAMS FOR YOUTH: *G-E College Bowl* (CBS)
PROGRAMS FOR CHILDREN: *The Shari Lewis Show* (NBC)
PUBLIC SERVICE: *CBS Reports* (CBS)
CONTRIBUTION TO INTERNATIONAL UNDERSTANDING: CBS (for its Olympics coverage)
EDUCATION (RADIO AND TELEVISION): Broadcasting and Film Commission, National Council of Churches of Christ in the U.S.A.
LOCALLY PRODUCED PROGRAMS (RADIO AND TELEVISION): (1) WOOD and WOOD-TV, Grand Rapids; (2) WCKT-TV, Miami; (3) WCCO-TV, Minneapolis; and (4) KPFK-FM, Los Angeles
SPECIAL AWARD: Dr. Frank Stanton (CBS)

1961

ENTERTAINMENT: *The Bob Newhart Show* (NBC)
EDUCATION: (1) *An Age of Kings* (BBC); and (2) "Vincent Van Gogh: A Self-Portrait" (NBC)
NEWS: *David Brinkley's Journal* (NBC)
YOUTH AND CHILDREN'S PROGRAMS: *Expedition!* (ABC)
PUBLIC SERVICE: *Let Freedom Ring* (KSL-TV, Salt Lake City)
CONTRIBUTION TO INTERNATIONAL UNDERSTANDING: Walter Lippmann and CBS
SPECIAL AWARDS: (1) Fred W. Friendly, CBS; (2) Newton N. Minow, chairman, Federal Communications Commission; and (3) Capital Cities Broadcasting Corporation, for "Verdict for Tomorrow: The Eichmann Trial on Television"

1962

ENTERTAINMENT: (1) Carol Burnett (CBS); and (2) *The Dupont Show of the Week* (NBC)
EDUCATION: *Biography* (Official Films, Inc.)
NEWS: Walter Cronkite (CBS)
YOUTH AND CHILDREN'S PROGRAMS: (1) *Exploring* (NBC); and (2) *Walt Disney's Wonderful World of Color* (NBC)
PUBLIC SERVICE: "A Tour of the White House with Mrs. John F. Kennedy" (CBS)

CONTRIBUTION TO INTERNATIONAL UNDERSTANDING: *Adlai Stevenson Reports* (ABC)

LOCALLY PRODUCED PROGRAMS: (1) *Books for Our Time* (WNDT-TV, New York); (2) *Elliott Norton Reviews* (WGBH-TV, Boston); and (3) *San Francisco Pageant* (KPIX-TV, San Francisco)

SPECIAL AWARDS: (1) William R. McAndrew and NBC News; and (2) Television Information Office of the National Association of Broadcasters (for a study on local children's programming)

1963

ENTERTAINMENT: (1) *The Danny Kaye Show* (CBS); and (2) *Mr. Novak* (NBC)

EDUCATION: (1) "American Revolution '63" (NBC); and (2) "Saga of Western Man" (ABC)

NEWS: Eric Sevareid (CBS)

PROGRAMS FOR YOUTH: *The Dorothy Gordon Forum* (WNBC-TV, New York)

PROGRAMS FOR CHILDREN: *Treetop House* (WGN-TV, Chicago)

PUBLIC SERVICE: "Storm over the Supreme Court," *CBS Reports* (CBS)

CONTRIBUTION TO INTERNATIONAL UNDERSTANDING: "Town Meeting of the World" CBS, and Dr. Frank Stanton, president

SPECIAL AWARD: To the broadcasting industry of the United States for its coverage of President John F. Kennedy and related events

1964

AWARDS NOT GIVEN IN SPECIFIC CATEGORIES

(1) Joyce Hall (president, Hallmark Cards, Inc., sponsor of *Hallmark Hall of Fame*); (2) *Profiles in Courage* (NBC); (3) *CBS Reports* (CBS); (4) William H. Lawrence, ABC News; (5) "The Louvre" (NBC); (6) Julia Child, *The French Chef* (WGBH-TV, Boston, and NET); (7) Intertel (International Television Federation); (8) Burr Tillstrom; and (9) The networks and the broadcasting industry, "for inescapably confronting the American public with the realities of racial discontent"

1965

ENTERTAINMENT: (1) "Frank Sinatra—a Man and His Music" (NBC); (2) "The Julie Andrews Show" (NBC); and (3) "My Name is Barbra" (CBS)

EDUCATION: National Educational Television

NEWS: (1) Frank McGee (NBC); (2) Morley Safer (CBS); and (3) KTLA-TV, Los Angeles

YOUTH AND CHILDREN'S PROGRAMS: "A Charlie Brown Christmas" (CBS)

PUBLIC SERVICE: "KKK—The Invisible Empire," *CBS Reports* (CBS)

CONTRIBUTION TO INTERNATIONAL UNDERSTANDING: Xerox Corporation

INNOVATION: "The National Driver's Test" (CBS)

MOST INVENTIVE ART DOCUMENTARY: "The Mystery of Stonehenge" (CBS)

SPECIAL AWARD: "A Visit to Washington with Mrs. Lyndon B. Johnson—On Behalf of a More Beautiful America" (ABC)

1966

ENTERTAINMENT: "A Christmas Memory," *ABC Stage 67* (ABC)

EDUCATION: (1) "American White Paper: Organized Crime in the United States" (NBC); and (2) *National Geographic Specials* (CBS)

NEWS: Harry Reasoner (CBS)

YOUTH AND CHILDREN'S PROGRAMS: "The World of Stuart Little" (NBC)

PUBLIC SERVICE (RADIO AND TELEVISION): "Youth and Narcotics—Who Has the Answer?" *Dorothy Gordon Youth Forum* (WNBC-TV, New York and NBC Radio)

PROMOTION OF INTERNATIONAL UNDERSTANDING: (1) *ABC's Wide World of Sports* (ABC); and (2) "Siberia: A Day in Irkutsk" (NBC)

LOCAL NEWS AND ENTERTAINMENT: *Kup's Show* (WBKB-TV, Chicago)

LOCAL MUSICAL PROGRAMS: (1) *Artists' Showcase* (WGN-TV, Chicago); and (2) "A Polish Millenium Concert" (WTMJ-TV, Milwaukee)

LOCAL PUBLIC SERVICE: *Assignment Four* (KRON-TV, San Francisco)

SPECIAL AWARDS: (1) *The Bell Telephone Hour* (NBC); (2) Tom John (CBS) (for art direction in "Death of a Salesman," "The Strollin' Twenties," and "Color Me Barbra"); (3) National Educational Television; and (4) "The Poisoned Air," *CBS Reports* (CBS)

1967

ENTERTAINMENT: (1) *CBS Playhouse* (CBS); and (2) "An Evening at Tanglewood" (NBC)

NEWS ANALYSIS AND COMMENTARY (RADIO AND TELEVISION): Eric Sevareid (CBS)

YOUTH OR CHILDREN'S PROGRAMS: (1) *CBS Children's Film Festival* (CBS); and (2) *Mr. Knozit* (WIS-TV, Columbia, S.C.)

PUBLIC SERVICE: *The Opportunity Line* (WBBM-TV, Chicago)

PROMOTION OF INTERNATIONAL UNDERSTANDING: "Africa" (ABC)

SPECIAL AWARDS: (1) *The Ed Sullivan Show* (CBS); (2) Bob Hope (NBC Radio and Television); and (3) Dr. James R. Killian, Jr., Massachusetts Institute of Technology (broadcasting education); and (4) *Meet the Press* (NBC Radio and Television)

1968

ENTERTAINMENT: *Playhouse* (NET)

EDUCATION: (1) Robert Cromie and *Book Beat* (WTTW-TV, Chicago); and (2) ABC, "for its creative 1968 documentaries"

NEWS: Charles Kuralt and "On the Road" (CBS)

YOUTH OR CHILDREN'S PROGRAMS: *Misterogers' Neighborhood* (NET)

PUBLIC SERVICE: Westinghouse Broadcasting Company, for "One Nation Indivisible"

PROMOTION OF INTERNATIONAL UNDERSTANDING: ABC, for its coverage of the 1968 Olympic Games

SPECIAL AWARD: "Hunger in America," *CBS Reports* (CBS)

1969

ENTERTAINMENT: (1) "Experiment in Television" (NBC); and (2) Curt Gowdy, sportscaster

EDUCATION: (1) *The Advocates* (WGBH-TV, Boston, and KCET-TV, Los Angeles); and (2) "Who Killed Lake Erie?" (NBC)

NEWS: (1) *Newsroom* (KQED-TV, San Francisco); and (2) Frank Reynolds (ABC)

YOUTH OR CHILDREN'S PROGRAMS: *Sesame Street* (Children's Television Workshop)

PUBLIC SERVICE: Tom Pettit (NBC)

PROMOTION OF INTERNATIONAL UNDERSTANDING: "The Japanese" (CBS)

LOCAL PUBLIC SERVICE: "The Negro in Indianapolis" (WFBM-TV, Indianapolis)

SPECIAL AWARDS: (1) Bing Crosby (outstanding service to television); (2) Chet Huntley (contributions to television news); and (3) "J. T.," *CBS Children's Hour* (CBS)

1970

ENTERTAINMENT: (1) "The Andersonville Trial" (PBS and KCET-TV, Los Angeles); (2) *Evening at Pops* (PBS); and (3) *The Flip Wilson Show* (NBC)

EDUCATION: "Eye of the Storm" (ABC)

NEWS: (1) *60 Minutes* (CBS); and (2) "Politithon '70" (WPBT-TV, Miami)

YOUTH OR CHILDREN'S PROGRAMS: (1) The "Dr. Seuss" programs (NBC); and (2) *Hot Dog* (NBC)

PUBLIC SERVICE: (1) "Peace ... On Our Time: KMEX-TV and the Death of Ruben Salazar" (KMEX-TV, Los Angeles); and (2) "Migrant: An NBC White Paper" (NBC)

PROMOTION OF INTERNATIONAL UNDERSTANDING: (1) *Civilisation* (BBC); and (2) "This New Frontier" (WWL-TV, New Orleans)

SPECIAL AWARD: "The Selling of the Pentagon" (CBS)

1971

ENTERTAINMENT: (1) "The American Revolution: 1770–1783, A Conversation with Lord North" (CBS); (2) "Brian's Song" (ABC and William Blinn); and (3) NBC, for its dramatic programming

EDUCATION: "The Turned On Crisis" (WQED-TV, Pittsburgh)

NEWS: John Rich (NBC Radio and Television)

YOUTH OR CHILDREN'S PROGRAMS: *Make a Wish* (ABC)

PUBLIC SERVICE: "This Child Is Rated X" (NBC)

PROMOTION OF INTERNATIONAL UNDERSTANDING: "United Nations Day Concert with Pablo Casals" (United Nations Television)

SPECIAL AWARDS: (1) George Heinemann of NBC (for contributions to children's programming); (2) Mississippi Authority for Educational Television and William Smith, executive director; and (3) Dr. Frank Stanton, president, CBS, Inc.

1972

AWARDS NOT GIVEN IN SPECIFIC CATEGORIES

(1) CBS, for *The Waltons* ("A sensitive dramatic interpretation of life during the Depression"); (2) NBC, for "Jack Lemmon in 'S Wonderful, 'S Marvelous, 'S Gershwin," "Singer Presents Liza with a 'Z'," and "The Timex All-Star Swing Festival" ("three special programs devoted to Twentieth Century American music"); (3) BBC and NBC, for *The Search for the Nile* ("outstanding series of documentaries"); (4) NBC, for

"Pensions: The Broken Promise" (investigative documentary); (5) Bill Monroe, NBC-TV, Washington editor of *Today* ("excellence in news reporting"); (6) Alistair Cooke ("for a meaningful perspective look at America"); (7) ABC, for *ABC Afterschool Specials* ("an innovative series for young people"); (8) CBS, for *Captain Kangaroo* ("a long-running show for young children"); (9) WHRO-TV, Norfolk ("for its overall classroom programming"); (10) WNET, New York, and BBC, for "The Restless Earth" (promotion of international understanding); (11) WWL-TV, New Orleans, for "China '72: A Hole in the Bamboo Curtain" (locally produced documentary); (12) WABC-TV, New York, for "Willowbrook: The Last Great Disgrace" (locally produced documentary); and (13) ABC for "XX Olympiad" (sports coverage)

1973

ENTERTAINMENT: (1) "Myshkin" (WTIU-TV, Bloomington, Ind.); and (2) NBC, ABC, and CBS (joint award for "outstanding contributions to television drama as evidenced by 'The Red Pony' [NBC], 'Pueblo' and 'The Glass Menagerie' [ABC], and 'CBS Playhouse 90: The Catholics' [CBS]")

EDUCATION: (1) ABC ("as evidenced by 'The First and Essential Freedom' and 'Learning Can Be Fun'"); and (2) *Dusty's Treehouse* (KNXT-TV, Los Angeles)

NEWS: *Close-Up* (ABC)

YOUTH AND CHILDREN'S PROGRAMS: (1) "The Borrowers," *Hallmark Hall of Fame* (NBC); and (2) "Street of the Flower Boxes," *NBC Children's Theatre* (NBC)

PUBLIC SERVICE: (1) "Home Rule Campaign" (WRC-TV, Washington, D.C.); and (2) Pamela Ilott (CBS) (executive producer of *Lamp unto My Feet* and *Look Up and Live*)

PROMOTION OF INTERNATIONAL UNDERSTANDING: "Overture to Friendship: The Philadelphia Orchestra in China" (WCAU-TV, Philadelphia)

SPECIAL AWARDS: (1) "The Energy Crisis . . . An American White Paper" (NBC); (2) Joe Garagiola, for *The Baseball World of Joe Garagiola* (NBC); and (3) Peter Lisagor, *Chicago Daily News* (for contributions to broadcast news)

1974

AWARDS NOT GIVEN IN SPECIFIC CATEGORIES

(1) NBC, for "distinguished . . . dramatic programs, as evidenced by 'The

Execution of Private Slovik,' 'The Law' and 'IBM Presents Clarence Darrow' "; (2) CBS, for the "four-part series of dramatic specials based on the life of Benjamin Franklin"; (3) WNET, New York, and PBS, for *Theatre in America*; (4) WGBH-TV, Boston, for *Nova*; (5) Carl Stern of NBC News, for "exceptional journalistic enterprise during a time of national crisis"; (6) Fred Graham of CBS News, for "thoroughly professional and consistently penetrating reporting during a time of national crisis"; (7) ABC, for "Free to Be . . . You and Me" (excellence in programming for young people); (8) NBC, for *Go!* (excellence in children's programming); (9) ABC, for "Sadat: Action Biography" (news documentary); (10) NBC, for "Tornado! 4:40 p.m., Xenia, Ohio" (news documentary); (11) WCCO-TV, Minneapolis, for "From Belfast with Love" (locally produced documentary); (12) KPRC-TV, Houston, for "The Right Man" (locally produced documentary); (13) WCKT-TV, Miami, for local investigative reporting; (14) Marilyn Baker, KQED-TV, San Francisco (local investigative reporting); (15) KING-TV, Seattle, for *How Come?* (locally produced children's program); (16) The National Public Affairs Center for Television (NPACT), for "outstanding overall effort to bring meaningful public affairs programming to the nation"; and (17) Julian Goodman, chairman of the board of NBC, for "outstanding work in the area of first amendment rights and privileges for broadcasting"

1975

AWARDS NOT GIVEN IN SPECIFIC CATEGORIES

(1) CBS, for *M*A*S*H* ("a creative entertainment effort . . . with first-rate humor"); (2) ABC, for *ABC Theatre*: "Love Among the Ruins" ("entertainment programming of the highest order"); (3) CBS News, for "Mr. Rooney Goes to Washington" ("outstanding and meritorious service"); (4) CBS News, for "The American Assassins" (news documentary); (5) NBC, for *Weekend* ("a new and refreshing approach to television programming"); (6) Charles Kuralt, CBS News, for "On the Road to '76" ("a first-rate effort"); (7) ABC, for *The ABC Afterschool Specials* (outstanding children's programming); (8) Group W, for *Call It Macaroni* (outstanding children's programming); (9) Alphaventure, for *Big Blue Marble* (outstanding children's programming); (10) Kaiser Broadcasting, for *Snipets* ("an excellent way in which children can learn from television"); (11) WCVB, Boston, for excellence in "viewer-oriented" programming; (12) WTOP-TV, Washington, D.C., for "overall public service effort"; (13) WCKT-TV, Miami, for "outstanding investigative reporting"; (14) KABC-TV, Los Angeles, for "The Dale Car: A Dream

or a Nightmare" (locally produced news documentary); (15) WWL-TV, New Orleans, for *A Sunday Journal* (locally produced magazine program); (16) WAPA-TV, San Juan, for "Las Rosas Blancas" (locally produced dramatic program); (17) Dr. James Killian, Boston, for "outstanding contributions to educational television"

1976

AWARDS NOT GIVEN IN SPECIFIC CATEGORIES

(1) NBC, for "Sybil" (outstanding dramatic program); (2) ABC, for "Eleanor and Franklin" (outstanding historical drama); (3) KCET/28, Los Angeles, for *Visions* ("for giving extensive new opportunities to writers and independent filmmakers"); (4) WETA-TV, Washington, D.C., for *In Performance at Wolf Trap* ("a superb example of the use of television to expand exponentially the audience for great cultural events"); (5) Perry Como ("with especial reference to .. 'Perry Como's Christmas in Austria' " [NBC]); (6) Tomorrow Entertainment, Inc., for "Judge Horton and the Scottsboro Boys" ("a program representative of the excellence one has come to expect from Thomas W. Moore and his associates"); (7) CBS News for *60 Minutes* (broadcast journalism); (8) WNET/13, New York, for *The Adams Chronicles* ("an impressive endeavor"); (9) ABC News, for "Suddenly an Eagle" (historical documentary); (10) ABC News, for *Animals Animals Animals* (documentary series); (11) Hughes Rudd and Bruce Morton of *The CBS Morning News* ("for their inventive and creative writing coupled with their reporting of significant and insignificant events"); (12) Sy Pearlman, producer of *Weekend*'s "Sawyer Brothers" segment (NBC) ("an outstanding example of the power of television to investigate and uncover new facts resulting in a reexamination of criminal justice in this case"); (13) CBS News, for "In Celebration of US" (coverage of July 4, 1976); (14) Jim Karayn and the League of Women Voters for " '76 Presidential Debates" ("for persistence against formidable obstacles which resulted in a series of joint appearances"); (15) WETA-TV, Washington, D.C., and WNET/13, New York, for "A Conversation with Jimmy Carter" (demonstrating "the tremendous impact through which television brought Candidate Jimmy Carter to the attention of the American people"); (16) CBS News for *In the News* (enabling "children to better understand events, people and concepts"); (17) ABC Sports, for its Olympics coverage; (18) WLBT-TV, Jackson, for "Power Politics in Mississippi" (locally produced "documentary reporting in an area seemingly untouched in the recent past"); (19) KERA-TV, Dallas, for "A Thirst in the Garden" (locally produced documentary); (20) Franklin McMahon, WBBM-TV, Chicago, for "Pri-

mary Colors, an Artist on the Campaign Trail" ("lending a new dimension to political reporting"); and (21) Charles Barthold, WHO-TV, Des Moines, "for his filming of a powerful and destructive tornado in action"

1977

AWARDS NOT GIVEN IN SPECIFIC CATEGORIES

(1) David Wolper and ABC-TV, for *Roots* ("for dramatically exposing us to an aspect of our history"); (2) Norman Lear, for *All in the Family* ("for establishing the right to express social comment in a social comedy, for devising the technique of humor as the bridge to better understanding of national issues, for presenting an excellent production in every way, for providing the public with that greatest of all healers, humor"); (3) London Weekend Television, for *Upstairs, Downstairs* ("it has no equal in the level of its intelligence, its humanity, and its performances . . . a model of civilized entertainment"); (4) MTM Productions, for *The Mary Tyler Moore Show* ("for maintaining a consistent high level of characterization and writing . . . and for presenting an affectionate and sympathetic portrayal of the career woman in today's changing society"); (5) WNET/13, New York, and WETA, Arlington, Virginia, for *The MacNeil-Lehrer Report* ("an example of broadcast journalism of the highest order"); (6) WCBS-TV (New York), for *Camera Three* ("its consistently high quality fare has won a remarkably loyal audience"); (7) Steve Allen, for *Meeting of Minds* (an "ingenious re-creation of the essence of historical personages who come alive in a theatrical form rich in philosophical fireworks and engaging wit"); (8) Lorimar Productions, for "Green Eyes" ("a touching, moving treatment of an excellent script—the story of a young, black veteran of the war in Vietnam . . . desperately searching for the child he fathered but left behind"); (9) NBC-TV, Arthur Rankin and Jules Bass, for "The Hobbit" ("a vividly original animated version of J.R.R. Tolkien's classic"); (10) NBC-TV, for "Tut: The Boy King" ("exceptional accomplishment in bringing outstanding cultural treasures to a widespread public with dramatic force"); (11) Metropolitan Opera Association, for "Live from the Met" (for "building an extraordinarily successful bridge between a necessarily limited audience within the Metropolitan Opera House and the vast audience viewing the performance on television"); (12) WNBC-TV, New York, for "F.I.N.D. Investigative Reports" ("impressive use of the resources of a great metropolitan television station to effect something for the common good"); (13) WNBC-TV, New York, for "Buyline: Betty Furness" ("the guardian angel of the consumer"); (14) WNET/13, New York, for "A Good Dissonance Like a Man" ("an informative, entertaining, and inspiring presentation" on the life of composer Charles Ives); (15)

WNET/13, New York, for "Police Tapes" (a documentary dealing "sensitively but searingly with the unglamorous front-line in a ghetto"); (16) WPIX, New York, for "The Lifers' Group—I Am My Brother's Keeper" (a "forcibly impressive" documentary, which "cut a raw slice of life out of the blackness of a major prison"); (17) KABC-TV, Los Angeles, for "Police Accountability" ("a first-rate example of persistent inquiry into the practices of the Los Angeles Police Department in a case involving shooting of civilians by its officers"); (18) KCMO-TV, Fairway, Kansas, for "Where Have All the Flood Cars Gone?" ("a brilliant effort in electronic journalism"); (19) WBTV, Charlotte, North Carolina, for "The Rowe String Quartet Plays on Your Imagination" (an "imaginative product of a local television station" in showcasing two professional musical and dance gorups); (20) Multimedia Program Productions, for "Joshua's Confusion" (a locally produced drama about an Amish youngster, "done in exemplary fashion . . . [which] gave the viewer an opportunity for introspection rarely found")

1978

AWARDS NOT GIVEN IN SPECIFIC CATEGORIES

(1) MTM Enterprises and the CBS Television Network, for *Lou Grant* ("an entertaining yet realistic look at the problems and issues which face those involved in the 'Fourth Estate' "); (2) Four D Productions/Trisene Corporation and the ABC Television Network, for *Barney Miller* ("a prime example of excellence in scripting, the use of humor with a message, and a program which provides Americans with entertainment of value"); (3) CBS News, for *30 Minutes* ("the excellent television magazine for teenagers"); (4) Newsweek Broadcasting, for "Cartoon-A-Torial" ("for successfully translating the editorial cartoon from the newspaper page to the television screen"); (5) KQED-TV, San Francisco, for *Over Easy* (a series which shows how "those of various ages and ethnic backgrounds cope with growing older by living meaningful and rewarding lives"); (6) Titus Productions and NBC Television, for *Holocaust* ("this series has won international acclaim, despite the controversial nature of its subject in some countries of the world"); (7) CBS News, for "The Battle for South Africa" ("an in-depth look at the terrorist war being ravaged against the government in that country"); (8) Survival Anglia Limited/World Wildlife Fund and NBC Television, for "Mysterious Castles of Clay" (a "fascinating story of the life cycle of the energetic African termite"); (9) WQED-TV, Pittsburgh, for "A Connecticut Yankee in King Arthur's Court," from *Once upon a Classic* [PBS] ("the first fully American production in the *Classic* series," it was done with a "high level of quality"); (10) Tomorrow Entertainment/Medcom Company and the

CBS Television Network, for "The Body Human: The Vital Connection" (a "marvelous and absorbing production," which took "an excursion into the workings of the human brain"); (11) Bob Keeshan, "known to millions as 'Captain Kangaroo' " ("he has not only brought superior entertainment to children of all ages but" has also "promoted quality children's programs on American television"); (12) Richard S. Salant ("in recognition of his leadership at CBS News and also in recognition of his staunch defense of the First Amendment guarantee of a free press"); (13) The Muppets ("for gentle satire, clever characters, genuine good humor and for high standards in family viewing"); (14) WDVM-TV, Washington, D.C., for "Race War in Rhodesia" ("a powerful look at the political tensions in Rhodesia and neighboring African nations"); (15) WDVM-TV, Washington, D.C., for "Your Health and Your Wallet" ("a mini-series focusing on rising medical costs and what can be done about them"); (16) The Baptist Radio-TV Commission of Fort Worth, Texas, for "A River to the Sea" ("a fascinating look at English history from the early Roman occupation of Britain to modern times"); (17) WENH-TV, Durham, New Hampshire, for "Arts in New Hampshire" (a 48-part effort which "proved that limited facilities and limited funds do not necessarily prevent entertaining and meaningful reports from being made available to the public"); (18) KGO-TV, San Francisco, for "Old Age: Do Not Go Gentle" ("a direct but sensitive portrayal of the treatment of the elderly in this country"); (19) KHET, Honolulu, for "Damien" ("the moving story of the life of the leper priest of Molokai, Joseph deVeuster"); (20) WAVE-TV, Louisville, for "Whose Child Is This?" ("a highly realistic look at the problem of child abuse from the perspective of a second grade teacher")

1979

AWARDS NOT GIVEN IN SPECIFIC CATEGORIES

(1) CBS NEWS, for *CBS News Sunday Morning*, hosted by Charles Kuralt; (2) Sylvia Fine Kaye, for "Musical Comedy Tonight" ("an entertaining look at American musical comedy through four significant eras"); (3) ABC-TV, for "Valentine" ("a sensitive and sentimental love story of two people in their declining years"); (4) ABC-TV, for "Friendly Fire" ("a powerful dramatization of the human tragedy of an American family's involvement in the Vietnam War"); (5) NBC-TV, for "When Hell Was in Session" ("detailing the true story of Navy Commander Jeremiah Denton, a Vietnam prisoner of war for $7\frac{1}{2}$ years"); (6) NBC-TV, for "Dummy" ("the story of an illiterate black deaf youth, who suffered injustice after his arrest as a murder suspect because of his handicap"); (7) NBC and the BBC, for "Treasures of the British Crown" ("an intriguing look at the priceless paintings and crown jewels of the Royal Collection in Britain, as described by members of the Royal Family"); (8) ABC-TV,

for "A Special Gift," *ABC Afterschool Special* ("the fascinating story of a young boy with two talents: ballet and basketball"); (9) Roger Mudd, CBS News, "for his searching questions of Senator Edward Kennedy in the *CBS Reports* program "Teddy"; (10) CBS NEWS, for "The Boston Goes to China" ("coverage of the Boston Symphony Orchestra's trip and the combined concert presented by the Symphony and the Peking Philharmonic"); (11) Robert Trout of ABC News ("for his nearly 50 years of service as a thoroughly knowledgeable and articulate commentator on national and international affairs"); (12) WGBH-TV, Boston, for *World* ("a series of international documentaries on diverse topics"); (13) KTVI, St. Louis, for "The Adventures of Whistling Sam" ("locally produced cartoon comments on issues of importance produced with great humor, sharp satire, and sound common sense"); (14) WMAQ-TV, Chicago, for "Strip and Search" (an investigative report "which exposed the practice by Chicago police of routinely strip-searching women brought in on minor charges"); (15) KOOL Television, Phoenix, for "The Long Eyes of Kitt Peak" ("a look at what has been called 'the largest and most complex astronomical research facility on earth'"); (16) KRON-TV, San Francisco, for "Politics of Poison" ("which exposed public health problems caused by herbicide sprayings in Northern California"); (17) WTTW-TV, Chicago, for "Miles to Go Before We Sleep" ("a documentary about age discrimination growing out of mandatory retirement"); (18) WTTW-TV, Chicago, for "Little Rock Central High School" ("a moving story looking at the year since the desegration crisis which shook that campus"); (19) KNXT, Hollywood, for "Down at the Dunbar" ("which recalls the jazz greats who made the Dunbar Hotel famous").

PART V

THE HIT PARADE

Explanatory note: The following lists of top-rated series for each season are based on the rating reports compiled by the A. C. Nielsen Company. The list for the 1949–1950 season is for the month of October 1949, and was supplied by *Variety*. The lists for the 1950–1951 through 1976–1977 seasons and the 1978–1979 season were supplied by CBS Research, and are based on October-through-April averages. The list for the 1977–1978 season appeared in *TV Guide*.

1949–1950

(1)	Texaco Star Theater	NBC
(2)	Toast of the Town (Ed Sullivan)	CBS
(3)	Arthur Godfrey's Talent Scouts	CBS
(4)	Fireball Fun for All	NBC
(5)	Philco Television Playhouse	NBC
(6)	Fireside Theatre	NBC
(7)	The Goldbergs	CBS
(8)	Suspense	CBS
(9)	Ford Theater	CBS
(10)	Cavalcade of Stars	DUMONT

1950–1951

(1)	Texaco Star Theater	NBC
(2)	Fireside Theatre	NBC
(3)	Your Show of Shows	NBC
(4)	Philco Television Playhouse	NBC
(5)	The Colgate Comedy Hour	NBC
(6)	Gillette Cavalcade of Sports	NBC
(7)	Arthur Godfrey's Talent Scouts	CBS
(8)	Mama	CBS
(9)	Robert Montgomery Presents	NBC
(10)	Martin Kane, Private Eye	NBC
(11)	Man Against Crime	CBS
(12)	Somerset Maugham Theatre	CBS
(13)	Kraft Television Theatre	NBC
(14)	Toast of the Town (Ed Sullivan)	CBS
(15)	The Aldrich Family	NBC

(16)	You Bet Your Life	NBC
(17)	Armstrong Circle Theater	NBC
(18)	Big Town	CBS
(19)	Lights Out	NBC
(20)	The Alan Young Show	CBS

1951–1952

(1)	Arthur Godfrey's Talent Scouts	CBS
(2)	Texaco Star Theater	NBC
(3)	I Love Lucy	CBS
(4)	The Red Skelton Show	NBC
(5)	The Colgate Comedy Hour	NBC
(6)	Fireside Theatre	NBC
(7)	The Jack Benny Program	CBS
(8)	Your Show of Shows	NBC
(9)	You Bet Your Life	NBC
(10)	Arthur Godfrey and His Friends	CBS
(11)	Mama	CBS
(12)	Philco Television Playhouse	NBC
(13)	Amos 'n' Andy	CBS
(14)	Big Town	CBS
(15)	Pabst Blue Ribbon Bouts	CBS
(16)	Gillette Cavalcade of Sports	NBC
(17)	The Alan Young Show	CBS
(18)	All-Star Revue	NBC
(19)	Dragnet	NBC
(20)	Kraft Television Theatre	NBC

1952–1953

(1)	I Love Lucy	CBS
(2)	Arthur Godfrey's Talent Scouts	CBS
(3)	Arthur Godfrey and His Friends	CBS
(4)	Dragnet	NBC
(5)	Texaco Star Theater	NBC
(6)	The Buick Circus Hour	NBC
(7)	The Colgate Comedy Hour	NBC
(8)	Gangbusters	NBC
(9)	You Bet Your Life	NBC
(10)	Fireside Theatre	NBC
(11)	The Red Buttons Show	CBS
(12)	The Jack Benny Program	CBS

(13)	Life with Luigi	CBS
(14)	Pabst Blue Ribbon Bouts	CBS
(15)	Goodyear Television Playhouse	NBC
(16)	The Life of Riley	NBC
(17)	Mama	CBS
(18)	Your Show of Shows	NBC
(19)	What's My Line?	CBS
(20)	Strike It Rich	CBS

1953–1954

(1)	I Love Lucy	CBS
(2)	Dragnet	NBC
(3)	Arthur Godfrey's Talent Scouts	CBS
(4)	You Bet Your Life	NBC
(5)	The Bob Hope Show	NBC
(6)	The Buick–Berle Show	NBC
(7)	Arthur Godfrey and His Friends	CBS
(8)	Ford Theater	NBC
(9)	The Jackie Gleason Show	CBS
(10)	Fireside Theatre	NBC
(11)	The Colgate Comedy Hour	NBC
(12)	This Is Your Life	NBC
(13)	The Red Buttons Show	CBS
(14)	The Life of Riley	NBC
(15)	Our Miss Brooks	CBS
(16)	Treasury Men in Action	NBC
(17)	All-Star Revue (Martha Raye)	NBC
(18)	The Jack Benny Program	CBS
(19)	Gillette Cavalcade of Sports	NBC
(20)	Philco Television Playhouse	NBC

1954–1955

(1)	I Love Lucy	CBS
(2)	The Jackie Gleason Show	CBS
(3)	Dragnet	NBC
(4)	You Bet Your Life	NBC
(5)	Toast of the Town (Ed Sullivan)	CBS
(6)	Disneyland	ABC
(7)	The Bob Hope Show	NBC
(8)	The Jack Benny Program	CBS
(9)	The Martha Raye Show	NBC

(10)	The George Gobel Show	NBC
(11)	Ford Theater	NBC
(12)	December Bride	CBS
(13)	The Buick-Berle Show	NBC
(14)	This Is Your Life	NBC
(15)	I've Got a Secret	CBS
(16)	Two for the Money	CBS
(17)	Your Hit Parade	NBC
(18)	The Millionaire	CBS
(19)	General Electric Theater	CBS
(20)	Arthur Godfrey's Talent Scouts	CBS

1955–1956

(1)	The $64,000 Question	CBS
(2)	I Love Lucy	CBS
(3)	The Ed Sullivan Show	CBS
(4)	Disneyland	ABC
(5)	The Jack Benny Program	CBS
(6)	December Bride	CBS
(7)	You Bet Your Life	NBC
(8)	Dragnet	NBC
(9)	I've Got a Secret	CBS
(10)	General Electric Theater	CBS
(11)	Private Secretary	CBS
(12)	Ford Theater	NBC
(13)	The Red Skelton Show	CBS
(14)	The George Gobel Show	NBC
(15)	The $64,000 Challenge	CBS
(16)	Arthur Godfrey's Talent Scouts	CBS
(17)	The Lineup	CBS
(18)	Shower of Stars	CBS
(19)	The Perry Como Show	NBC
(20)	The Honeymooners (Jackie Gleason)	CBS

1956–1957

(1)	I Love Lucy	CBS
(2)	The Ed Sullivan Show	CBS
(3)	General Electric Theater	CBS
(4)	The $64,000 Question	CBS
(5)	December Bride	CBS
(6)	Alfred Hitchcock Presents	CBS

(7)	I've Got a Secret	CBS
(8)	Gunsmoke	CBS
(9)	The Perry Como Show	NBC
(10)	The Jack Benny Program	CBS
(11)	Dragnet	NBC
(12)	Arthur Godfrey's Talent Scouts	CBS
(13)	The Millionaire	CBS
(14)	Disneyland	ABC
(15)	Shower of Stars	CBS
(16)	The Lineup	CBS
(17)	The Red Skelton Show	CBS
(18)	You Bet Your Life	NBC
(19)	Wyatt Earp	ABC
(20)	Private Secretary	CBS

1957–1958

(1)	Gunsmoke	CBS
(2)	The Danny Thomas Show	CBS
(3)	Tales of Wells Fargo	NBC
(4)	Have Gun, Will Travel	CBS
(5)	I've Got a Secret	CBS
(6)	Wyatt Earp	ABC
(7)	General Electric Theater	CBS
(8)	The Restless Gun	NBC
(9)	December Bride	CBS
(10)	You Bet Your Life	NBC
(11)	Alfred Hitchcock Presents	CBS
(12)	Cheyenne	ABC
(13)	The Tennessee Ernie Ford Show	NBC
(14)	The Red Skelton Show	CBS
(15)	Wagon Train	NBC
(16)	Sugarfoot	ABC
(17)	Father Knows Best	NBC
(18)	Twenty-One	NBC
(19)	The Ed Sullivan Show	CBS
(20)	The Jack Benny Program	CBS

1958–1959

(1)	Gunsmoke	CBS
(2)	Wagon Train	NBC
(3)	Have Gun, Will Travel	CBS

(4)	The Rifleman	ABC
(5)	The Danny Thomas Show	CBS
(6)	Maverick	ABC
(7)	Tales of Wells Fargo	NBC
(8)	The Real McCoys	ABC
(9)	I've Got a Secret	CBS
(10)	Wyatt Earp	ABC
(11)	The Price Is Right	NBC
(12)	The Red Skelton Show	CBS
(13)	Zane Grey Theater	CBS
(14)	Father Knows Best	CBS
(15)	The Texan	CBS
(16)	Wanted: Dead or Alive	CBS
(17)	Peter Gunn	NBC
(18)	Cheyenne	ABC
(19)	Perry Mason	CBS
(20)	The Tennessee Ernie Ford Show	NBC

1959–1960

(1)	Gunsmoke	CBS
(2)	Wagon Train	NBC
(3)	Have Gun, Will Travel	NBC
(4)	The Danny Thomas Show	CBS
(5)	The Red Skelton Show	CBS
(6)	Father Knows Best	CBS
(7)	77 Sunset Strip	ABC
(8)	The Price Is Right	NBC
(9)	Wanted: Dead or Alive	CBS
(10)	Perry Mason	CBS
(11)	The Real McCoys	ABC
(12)	The Ed Sullivan Show	CBS
(13)	Bing Crosby (specials)	ABC
(14)	The Rifleman	ABC
(15)	The Tennessee Ernie Ford Show	NBC
(16)	The Lawman	ABC
(17)	Dennis the Menace	CBS
(18)	Cheyenne	ABC
(19)	Rawhide	CBS
(20)	Maverick	ABC

1960–1961

(1)	Gunsmoke	CBS
(2)	Wagon Train	NBC
(3)	Have Gun, Will Travel	CBS
(4)	The Andy Griffith Show	CBS
(5)	The Real McCoys	ABC
(6)	Rawhide	CBS
(7)	Candid Camera	CBS
(8)	The Untouchables	ABC
(9)	The Price Is Right	NBC
(10)	The Jack Benny Program	CBS
(11)	Dennis the Menace	CBS
(12)	The Danny Thomas Show	CBS
(13)	My Three Sons	ABC
(14)	77 Sunset Strip	ABC
(15)	The Ed Sullivan Show	CBS
(16)	Perry Mason	CBS
(17)	Bonanza	NBC
(18)	The Flintstones	ABC
(19)	The Red Skelton Show	CBS
(20)	Alfred Hitchcock Presents	NBC

1961–1962

(1)	Wagon Train	NBC
(2)	Bonanza	NBC
(3)	Gunsmoke	CBS
(4)	Hazel	NBC
(5)	Perry Mason	CBS
(6)	The Red Skelton Show	CBS
(7)	The Andy Griffith Show	CBS
(8)	The Danny Thomas Show	CBS
(9)	Dr. Kildare	NBC
(10)	Candid Camera	CBS
(11)	My Three Sons	ABC
(12)	The Garry Moore Show	CBS
(13)	Rawhide	CBS
(14)	The Real McCoys	ABC
(15)	Lassie	CBS
(16)	Sing Along with Mitch	NBC
(17)	Dennis the Menace	CBS
(18)	Marshal Dillon (Gunsmoke *reruns*)	CBS

| (19) | Ben Casey | ABC |
| (20) | The Ed Sullivan Show | CBS |

1962–1963

(1)	The Beverly Hillbillies	CBS
(2)	Candid Camera	CBS
(3)	The Red Skelton Show	CBS
(4)	Bonanza	NBC
(5)	The Lucy Show	CBS
(6)	The Andy Griffith Show	CBS
(7)	Ben Casey	ABC
(8)	The Danny Thomas Show	CBS
(9)	The Dick Van Dyke Show	CBS
(10)	Gunsmoke	CBS
(11)	Dr. Kildare	NBC
(12)	The Jack Benny Program	CBS
(13)	What's My Line?	CBS
(14)	The Ed Sullivan Show	CBS
(15)	Hazel	NBC
(16)	I've Got a Secret	CBS
(17)	The Jackie Gleason Show	CBS
(18)	The Defenders	CBS
(19)	The Garry Moore Show	CBS
(20)	(tie) Lassie	CBS
(20)	(tie) To Tell the Truth	CBS

1963–1964

(1)	The Beverly Hillbillies	CBS
(2)	Bonanza	NBC
(3)	The Dick Van Dyke Show	CBS
(4)	Petticoat Junction	CBS
(5)	The Andy Griffith Show	CBS
(6)	The Lucy Show	CBS
(7)	Candid Camera	CBS
(8)	The Ed Sullivan Show	CBS
(9)	The Danny Thomas Show	CBS
(10)	My Favorite Martian	CBS
(11)	The Red Skelton Show	CBS
(12)	I've Got a Secret	CBS
(13)	Lassie	CBS
(14)	The Jack Benny Program	CBS

(15)	The Jackie Gleason Show	CBS
(16)	The Donna Reed Show	ABC
(17)	The Virginian	NBC
(18)	The Patty Duke Show	ABC
(19)	Dr. Kildare	NBC
(20)	Gunsmoke	CBS

1964–1965

(1)	Bonanza	NBC
(2)	Bewitched	ABC
(3)	Gomer Pyle, U.S.M.C.	CBS
(4)	The Andy Griffith Show	CBS
(5)	The Fugitive	ABC
(6)	The Red Skelton Hour	CBS
(7)	The Dick Van Dyke Show	CBS
(8)	The Lucy Show	CBS
(9)	Peyton Place (II)	ABC
(10)	Combat	ABC
(11)	Walt Disney's Wonderful World	NBC
(12)	The Beverly Hillbillies	CBS
(13)	My Three Sons	ABC
(14)	Branded	NBC
(15)	Petticoat Junction	CBS
(16)	The Ed Sullivan Show	CBS
(17)	Lassie	CBS
(18)	The Munsters	CBS
(19)	Gilligan's Island	CBS
(20)	Peyton Place (I)	ABC

1965–1966

(1)	Bonanza	NBC
(2)	Gomer Pyle, U.S.M.C.	CBS
(3)	The Lucy Show	CBS
(4)	The Red Skelton Hour	CBS
(5)	Batman (II)	ABC
(6)	The Andy Griffith Show	CBS
(7)	Bewitched	ABC
(8)	The Beverly Hillbillies	CBS
(9)	Hogan's Heroes	CBS
(10)	Batman (I)	ABC
(11)	Green Acres	CBS

(12)	Get Smart	NBC
(13)	The Man from U.N.C.L.E.	NBC
(14)	Daktari	CBS
(15)	My Three Sons	CBS
(16)	The Dick Van Dyke Show	CBS
(17)	Walt Disney's Wonderful World	NBC
(18)	The Ed Sullivan Show	CBS
(19)	The Lawrence Welk Show	ABC
(20)	I've Got a Secret	CBS

1966–1967

(1)	Bonanza	NBC
(2)	The Red Skelton Hour	CBS
(3)	The Andy Griffith Show	CBS
(4)	The Lucy Show	CBS
(5)	The Jackie Gleason Show	CBS
(6)	Green Acres	CBS
(7)	Daktari	CBS
(8)	Bewitched	ABC
(9)	The Beverly Hillbillies	CBS
(10)	Gomer Pyle, U.S.M.C.	CBS
(11)	The Virginian	NBC
(12)	The Lawrence Welk Show	ABC
(13)	The Ed Sullivan Show	CBS
(14)	The Dean Martin Show	NBC
(15)	Family Affair	CBS
(16)	Smothers Brothers Comedy Hour	CBS
(17)	CBS Friday Night Movies	CBS
(18)	Hogan's Heroes	CBS
(19)	Walt Disney's Wonderful World	NBC
(20)	Saturday Night at the Movies	NBC

1967–1968

(1)	The Andy Griffith Show	CBS
(2)	The Lucy Show	CBS
(3)	Gomer Pyle, U.S.M.C.	CBS
(4)	Gunsmoke	CBS
(5)	Family Affair	CBS
(6)	Bonanza	NBC
(7)	The Red Skelton Hour	CBS

(8)	The Dean Martin Show	NBC
(9)	The Jackie Gleason Show	CBS
(10)	Saturday Night at the Movies	NBC
(11)	Bewitched	ABC
(12)	The Beverly Hillbillies	CBS
(13)	The Ed Sullivan Show	CBS
(14)	The Virginian	NBC
(15)	The CBS Friday Night Movie	CBS
(16)	Green Acres	CBS
(17)	The Lawrence Welk Show	ABC
(18)	Smothers Brothers Comedy Hour	CBS
(19)	Gentle Ben	CBS
(20)	Tuesday Night at the Movies	NBC

1968–1969

(1)	Rowan and Martin's Laugh-In	NBC
(2)	Gomer Pyle, U.S.M.C.	CBS
(3)	Bonanza	NBC
(4)	Mayberry R.F.D.	CBS
(5)	Family Affair	CBS
(6)	Gunsmoke	CBS
(7)	Julia	NBC
(8)	The Dean Martin Show	NBC
(9)	Here's Lucy	CBS
(10)	The Beverly Hillbillies	CBS
(11)	Mission: Impossible	CBS
(12)	Bewitched	ABC
(13)	The Red Skelton Hour	CBS
(14)	My Three Sons	CBS
(15)	The Glen Campbell Goodtime Hour	CBS
(16)	Ironside	NBC
(17)	The Virginian	NBC
(18)	The F.B.I.	ABC
(19)	Green Acres	CBS
(20)	Dragnet	NBC

1969–1970

(1)	Rowan and Martin's Laugh-In	NBC
(2)	Gunsmoke	CBS
(3)	Bonanza	NBC

(4)	Mayberry R.F.D.	CBS
(5)	Family Affair	CBS
(6)	Here's Lucy	CBS
(7)	The Red Skelton Hour	CBS
(8)	Marcus Welby, M.D.	ABC
(9)	The Wonderful World of Disney	NBC
(10)	The Doris Day Show	CBS
(11)	The Bill Cosby Show	NBC
(12)	The Jim Nabors Hour	CBS
(13)	The Carol Burnett Show	CBS
(14)	The Dean Martin Show	NBC
(15)	My Three Sons	CBS
(16)	Ironside	NBC
(17)	The Johnny Cash Show	ABC
(18)	The Beverly Hillbillies	CBS
(19)	Hawaii Five-O	CBS
(20)	(tie) Glen Campbell Goodtime Hour	CBS
(20)	(tie) Hee Haw	CBS

1970–1971

(1)	Marcus Welby, M.D.	ABC
(2)	The Flip Wilson Show	NBC
(3)	Here's Lucy	CBS
(4)	Ironside	NBC
(5)	Gunsmoke	CBS
(6)	ABC Movie of the Week	ABC
(7)	Hawaii Five-O	CBS
(8)	Medical Center	CBS
(9)	Bonanza	NBC
(10)	The F.B.I.	ABC
(11)	The Mod Squad	ABC
(12)	Adam-12	NBC
(13)	Rowan and Martin's Laugh-In	NBC
(14)	The Wonderful World of Disney	NBC
(15)	Mayberry R.F.D.	CBS
(16)	Hee Haw	CBS
(17)	Mannix	CBS
(18)	The Men from Shiloh	NBC
(19)	My Three Sons	CBS
(20)	The Doris Day Show	CBS

1971–1972

(1)	All in the Family	CBS
(2)	The Flip Wilson Show	NBC
(3)	Marcus Welby, M.D.	ABC
(4)	Gunsmoke	CBS
(5)	The ABC Movie of the Week	ABC
(6)	Sanford and Son	NBC
(7)	Mannix	CBS
(8)	Funny Face	CBS
(9)	Adam-12	NBC
(10)	The Mary Tyler Moore Show	CBS
(11)	Here's Lucy	CBS
(12)	Hawaii Five-O	CBS
(13)	Medical Center	CBS
(14)	The NBC Mystery Movie	NBC
(15)	Ironside	NBC
(16)	The Partridge Family	ABC
(17)	The F.B.I.	ABC
(18)	The New Dick Van Dyke Show	CBS
(19)	The Wonderful World of Disney	NBC
(20)	Bonanza	NBC

1972–1973

(1)	All in the Family	CBS
(2)	Sanford and Son	NBC
(3)	Hawaii Five-O	CBS
(4)	Maude	CBS
(5)	Bridget Loves Bernie	CBS
(6)	The NBC Sunday Mystery Movie	NBC
(7)	The Mary Tyler Moore Show	CBS
(8)	Gunsmoke	CBS
(9)	The Wonderful World of Disney	NBC
(10)	Ironside	NBC
(11)	Adam-12	NBC
(12)	The Flip Wilson Show	NBC
(13)	Marcus Welby, M.D.	ABC
(14)	Cannon	CBS
(15)	Here's Lucy	CBS
(16)	The Bob Newhart Show	CBS
(17)	ABC Tuesday Movie of the Week	ABC
(18)	NFL Monday Night Football	ABC

| (19) | (tie) The Partridge Family | ABC |
| (19) | (tie) The Waltons | CBS |

1973-1974

(1)	All in the Family	CBS
(2)	The Waltons	CBS
(3)	Sanford and Son	NBC
(4)	M*A*S*H	CBS
(5)	Hawaii Five-O	CBS
(6)	Maude	CBS
(7)	Kojak	CBS
(8)	The Sonny and Cher Comedy Hour	CBS
(9)	The Mary Tyler Moore Show	CBS
(10)	Cannon	CBS
(11)	The Six Million Dollar Man	ABC
(12)	The Bob Newhart Show	CBS
(13)	The Wonderful World of Disney	NBC
(14)	The NBC Sunday Mystery Movie	NBC
(15)	Gunsmoke	CBS
(16)	Happy Days	ABC
(17)	Good Times	CBS
(18)	Barnaby Jones	CBS
(19)	(tie) NFL Monday Night Football	ABC
(19)	(tie) The CBS Friday Night Movie	CBS

1974-1975

(1)	All in the Family	CBS
(2)	Sanford and Son	NBC
(3)	Chico and the Man	NBC
(4)	The Jeffersons	CBS
(5)	M*A*S*H	CBS
(6)	Rhoda	CBS
(7)	The Waltons	CBS
(8)	Good Times	CBS
(9)	Maude	CBS
(10)	Hawaii Five-O	CBS
(11)	The Mary Tyler Moore Show	CBS
(12)	The Rockford Files	NBC
(13)	Kojak	CBS
(14)	Little House on the Prairie	NBC
(15)	Police Woman	NBC

(16)	S.W.A.T.	ABC
(17)	The Bob Newhart Show	CBS
(18)	The Wonderful World of Disney	NBC
(19)	Mannix	CBS
(20)	(tie) Cannon	CBS
(20)	(tie) The Rookies	ABC
(20)	(tie) The NBC Sunday Mystery Movie	NBC

1975–1976

(1)	All in the Family	CBS
(2)	Laverne and Shirley	ABC
(3)	Rich Man, Poor Man	ABC
(4)	Maude	CBS
(5)	The Bionic Woman	ABC
(6)	Phyllis	CBS
(7)	The Six Million Dollar Man	ABC
(8)	Sanford and Son	NBC
(9)	Rhoda	CBS
(10)	Happy Days	ABC
(11)	The ABC Monday Movie	ABC
(12)	M*A*S*H	CBS
(13)	One Day at a Time	CBS
(14)	The Waltons	CBS
(15)	Starsky and Hutch	ABC
(16)	Good Heavens	ABC
(17)	Welcome Back, Kotter	ABC
(18)	Kojak	CBS
(19)	The Mary Tyler Moore Show	CBS
(20)	The ABC Sunday Movie	ABC

1976–1977

(1)	Happy Days	ABC
(2)	Laverne and Shirley	ABC
(3)	The ABC Monday Night Movie	ABC
(4)	M*A*S*H	CBS
(5)	Charlie's Angels	ABC
(6)	The Big Event	NBC
(7)	The Six Million Dollar Man	ABC
(8)	The ABC Sunday Night Movie	ABC
(9)	Baretta	ABC
(10)	One Day at a Time	CBS

(11)	Three's Company	ABC
(12)	All in the Family	CBS
(13)	Welcome Back, Kotter	ABC
(14)	The Bionic Woman	ABC
(15)	The Waltons	CBS
(16)	Little House on the Prairie	NBC
(17)	Barney Miller	ABC
(18)	60 Minutes	CBS
(19)	Hawaii Five-O	CBS
(20)	NBC Monday Night at the Movies	NBC

(Note: *Roots* was not considered a regularly scheduled series for ratings purposes.)

1977–1978

(1)	Laverne and Shirley	ABC
(2)	Happy Days	ABC
(3)	Three's Company	ABC
(4)	Charlie's Angels	ABC
(5)	All in the Family	CBS
(6)	(tie) Little House on the Prairie	NBC
(6)	(tie) 60 Minutes	CBS
(8)	(tie) M*A*S*H	CBS
(8)	(tie) One Day at a Time	CBS
(10)	Alice	CBS
(11)	Soap	ABC
(12)	How the West Was Won	ABC
(13)	(tie) Monday Night at the Movies	NBC
(13)	(tie) Eight Is Enough	ABC
(13)	(tie) NFL Monday Night Football	ABC
(13)	(tie) The Love Boat	ABC
(17)	Barney Miller	ABC
(18)	The ABC Sunday Night Movie	ABC
(19)	(tie) Fantasy Island	ABC
(19)	(tie) Project U.F.O.	NBC

1978–1979

(1)	Three's Company	ABC
(2)	Laverne and Shirley	ABC
(3)	Mork & Mindy	ABC

(4)	Happy Days	ABC
(5)	Angie	ABC
(6)	(tie) 60 Minutes	CBS
(6)	(tie) M*A*S*H	CBS
(8)	The Ropers	ABC
(9)	Charlie's Angels	ABC
(10)	(tie) All in the Family	CBS
(10)	(tie) Taxi	ABC
(12)	Eight Is Enough	ABC
(13)	Alice	CBS
(14)	Little House on the Prairie	NBC
(15)	Barney Miller	ABC
(16)	(tie) The ABC Sunday Night Movie	ABC
(16)	(tie) The Love Boat	ABC
(16)	The MacKenzies of Paradise Cove	ABC
(19)	(tie) One Day at a Time	CBS
(19)	(tie) Soap	ABC

APPENDIX

APPENDIX

B.A.D. CATS
CBS

4 JANUARY 1980–8 FEBRUARY 1980   An hour of car chases with the
Burglary Auto Detail of the Los Angeles Police Department. With Asher
Brauner as Nick Donovan; Steve Hanks as his partner and roommate,
Ocee James; Michelle Pfeiffer as their associate, Samantha; LaWanda
Page as Ma, owner of a local rib joint; Vic Morrow as Captain Nathan;
and Jimmie Walker as Rodney Washington, a good-natured car thief.

BEYOND WESTWORLD
CBS

5 MARCH 1980–   Hour fantasy series about a mad scientist
hoping to take over the world with his crew of remarkably humanlike robots, and the security agent assigned to thwart him. With Jim McMullan
as John Moore, security agent for the Delos Corporation; James Wainwright as Simon Quaid, the mad scientist; Judith Chapman as Laura
Garvey, Moore's partner; William Jordan as Professor Joseph Oppenheimer, who created the robots, only to have them fall into Quaid's evil
clutches; Stewart Moss and Severn Darden as Foley, one of Quaid's assistants; Ann McCurry as Roberta, another of Quaid's assistants; and Connie Sellecca as Pam. The series is based on Michael Crichton's novel
Westworld, and was developed for television by Lou Shaw. John Meredyth Lucas is the producer.

THE BIG SHOW
NBC

4 MARCH 1980–   Ninety-minute variety series, with regulars
Graham Chapman, Mimi Kennedy, Charlie Hill, Owen Sullivan, Edie
McClurg, Paul Grimm, Joe Baker, and a dancing group known as
Shabba-Doo.

CHAIN REACTION
NBC

14 JANUARY 1980–   Half-hour daytime game show hosted by
Bill Cullen, on which two teams of three players (each with two celebrities and a contestant) compete. The teams are shown the first and last
words in a "chain" of eight words, and try to win points by guessing the
six missing words.

THE CHISHOLMS
CBS

19 JANUARY 1980–   This western returned to CBS's schedule
with a few cast changes: Robert Preston returned as Hadley Chisholm,
but soon exited, as Hadley died after a few episodes; Rosemary Harris,
Ben Murphy, and James Van Patten repeated their roles as wife Minerva,

son Will, and son Bo; Brett Cullen replaced Brian Kerwin as son Gideon; Delta Burke replaced Stacey Nelkin as daughter Bonnie Sue; Reid Smith succeeded Charles Frank as guide Lester Hackett; and Susan Swift, who had played Annabel, the daughter who died, returned as Mercy, a young woman who joined up with the Chisholms. Other new cast members included Mitchell Ryan as wagonmaster Cooper Hawkins, and Victoria Racimo as Kewedinok, Will's Indian wife. See also *The Chisholms* in Part I.

EDWARD & MRS. SIMPSON   SYNDICATED
1980   Six-part historical drama about England's King Edward VIII. The king, known as David to his family and friends, abdicated after a brief reign to marry "the woman I love." With Edward Fox as Edward; Cynthia Harris as Wallis Warfield Simpson, the American socialite whom Edward married in 1937; Marius Goring as Edward's father, King George V; and Peggy Ashcroft as Edward's mother, Queen Mary. The series was produced in England by Thames Television, and was hosted by Robert MacNeil.

FACE THE MUSIC   SYNDICATED
1980   Half-hour game show hosted by Ron Ely (formerly the star of the TV *Tarzan*) on which three contestants tried to identify song titles and associate them with photographs of celebrities.

FREE TO CHOOSE   PBS
11 JANUARY 1980–   Ten-part series on capitalism and free enterprise, hosted by economist Milton Friedman.

FROM HERE TO ETERNITY   NBC
10 MARCH 1980–   A prime-time serial set in wartime Hawaii following the attack on Pearl Harbor, *From Here to Eternity* picks up where James Jones's novel left off. Principal players include William Devane as Seargeant Milt Warden; Barbara Hershey as Karen Holmes, who has an affair with Warden; Roy Thinnes as Major Dana Holmes, her husband; Don Johnson as Jeff Prewitt; Kim Basinger as prostitute Lorene Rogers; Lacey Neuhaus as Emily Austin; and Daniel Spielberg as Captain Ross. The hour series was introduced on *NBC Movies for Television* in 1979, and had been slated to reappear during NBC's fall 1979 season.

GOODTIME GIRLS   ABC
22 JANUARY 1980–   Half-hour sitcom set in 1942 in Washington, D.C., in which four young women share an attic room in a boardinghouse. With Annie Potts as Edith Bedelmyer; Lorna Patterson as Betty Crandall; Georgia Engel as war bride Loretta Smoot; Francine

Tacker as photographer Camille Rittenhouse; Marcia Lewis as Irma Coolidge, the landlady; Merwin Goldsmith as George Coolidge, her husband, the landlord; and Adrian Zmed as cabbie Frankie Malardo, who also resides in the rooming house. Leonora Thuna, Thomas L. Miller, and Robert Boyett created the show.

HAGEN
CBS

1 MARCH 1980–   Hour crime show starring Chad Everett as Paul Hagen, an expert animal tracker who became an investigator for a San Francisco attorney. With Arthur Hill as lawyer Carl Palmer, and Carmen Zapata as Palmer's housekeeper, Mrs. Chavez. Frank Glicksman, the executive producer, created the series with Charles Larson.

HERE'S BOOMER
NBC

14 MARCH 1980–   A remake of *The Littlest Hobo,* this half-hour comedy-drama tells the story of Boomer, a lovable mutt who helps out people in distress. The series was developed by Dan Bulluck and A. C. Lyles. Boomer is owned and trained by Ray Berwick.

HOUSE CALLS
CBS

17 DECEMBER 1979–   Half-hour sitcom based on the movie of the same title, set at Kensington General Hospital. With Wayne Rogers as surgeon Charley Michaels; Lynn Redgrave as hospital administrator Ann Anderson; David Wayne as senile chief of surgery Amos Wetherby; and Ray Buktenica as Dr. Norman Solomon. Max Shulman and Julius J. Epstein created the series.

KNOTS LANDING
CBS

27 DECEMBER 1979–   Spun-off from *Dallas,* this hour prime-time serial tells the stories of four couples living on a cul-de-sac in Knots Landing, a Southern California community. With Ted Shackelford as Gary Ewing (son of the *Dallas* Ewings); Joan Van Ark as Valene Ewing, who had remarried Gary as the series got underway; James Houghton as Kenny Ward, a recording executive; Kim Lankford as his wife, Ginger Ward; Don Murray as Sid Fairgate, owner of Knots Landing Motors; Michele Lee as his wife, Karen Fairgate; John Pleshette as Richard Avery, an attorney; and Constance McCashin as his wife, Laura Avery. David Jacobs created and produces the series.

LIFE AND TIMES OF EDDIE ROBERTS
SYNDICATED

1980 Half-hour comedy serial in the *Mary Hartman, Mary Hartman* vein. With Renny Temple as Eddie Roberts, a professor scrambling for tenure at Cranepool University; Udana Power as his wife, Dolores, an aspiring major-league ball player; Allison Balson as their young daughter, Chrissy; Stephen Parr as faculty colleague Tony Cranepool; Allen Case as Dean Knitzer; Joan Hotchkis as Lydia; Loyita Chapel as Vivian Blankett; Jon Lormer as Boggs; and Daryl Roach as Turner Lequatro. Ann and Ellis Marcus created and wrote the series.

MYSTERY! PBS
5 FEBRUARY 1980–   Fifteen-week hour mystery anthology series.

ONE IN A MILLION ABC
8 JANUARY 1980–   Half-hour sitcom about a Los Angeles cabbie who inherits the chairmanship and controlling financial interest in Grayson Enterprises, a huge conglomerate. With Shirley Hemphill as cabbie-cum-chairperson Shirley Simmons; Richard Paul as Mr. Stone, another Grayson executive; Carl Ballantine as Max, proprietor of Shirley's favorite restaurant; Dorothy Fielding as Nancy, Shirley's secretary; Ralph Wilcox, as Duke, a neighborhood street vendor; Keene Curtis as Mr. Cushing, Grayson's vice chairman and Shirley's chief rival; Mel Stewart as Raymond Simmons, Shirley's father; and Ann Weldon as Edna Simmons, Shirley's stepmother. Alan W. Livingston created the show, and Saul Turteltaub and Bernie Orenstein developed it.

PINK LADY NBC
1 MARCH 1980–   Hour variety series starring Japan's popular rock-and-roll duo Pink Lady—Mitsuyo (Mie) Nemoto and Keko (Kei) Masuda—and American comedian Jeff Altman.

PLAY THE PERCENTAGES SYNDICATED
1980   Geoff Edwards hosts this game show, on which two married couples compete. Each couple tries to predict what percentage of persons previously surveyed had provided the correct answer to a given question. The couple with the more accurate prediction wins points, and can win additional points by providing the correct answer to the question. The first couple to score 300 points wins the game and a chance at the bonus round for a possible jackpot of $25,000 or more. The half-hour show is a Jack Barry & Dan Enright Production.

SANFORD NBC
15 MARCH 1980–   In this sequel to *Sanford and Son,* Redd Foxx returns as junk dealer Fred Sanford. With Dennis Burkley as Cal Tenny, his new partner; Marguerite Ray as Beverly Hills widow Evelyn Lewis, Fred's romantic interest; Nathaniel Taylor as Raoul; Suzanne Stone as Sissy, Evelyn's daughter; Cathy Cooper as Clara, Evelyn's maid; and Percy Rodriguez as Winston, Evelyn's stuffy brother.

SKAG   NBC
6 JANUARY 1980–21 FEBRUARY 1980   Hour family drama starring Karl
Malden as Pete "Skag" Skagska, a foreman at a Pittsburgh steel mill.
With Piper Laurie as wife Jo; Craig Wasson as son David; Peter Gal-
lagher as son John; Leslie Ackerman as daughter Barbara; and Kitty
Holcomb as daughter Patricia. Abby Mann created the series.

STONE   ABC
14 JANUARY 1980–   Hour crime show starring Dennis Weaver
as Sergeant Daniel Ellis Stone, a cop and a writer, with Bobby Weaver
(his real-life son) as his young partner, Buck Rogers.

TENSPEED AND BROWN SHOE   ABC
27 JANUARY 1980–   Hour adventure series about a black con
artist and a white stockbroker who team up as private investigators. With
Ben Vereen as E. L. "Tenspeed" Turner and Jeff Goldblum as Lionel
"Brown Shoe" Whitney.

THAT'S INCREDIBLE!   ABC
3 MARCH 1980–   ABC's answer to NBC's *Real People, That's
Incredible!* is an hour human-interest series featuring unusual folks. John
Davidson, Cathy Lee Crosby, and Fran Tarkenton serve as hosts.

3-2-1 CONTACT   PBS
14 JANUARY 1980–   A science series for children, featuring Liz
Moses, Ginny Ortiz, and Leon W. Grant, produced by Kathy Mendoza
for the Children's Television Workshop.

UNITED STATES   NBC
11 MARCH 1980–   A contemporary look at marriage, starring
Beau Bridges and Helen Shaver as Richard and Libby Chapin, with
Rossie Harris and Justin Dana as their children, Dylan and Nicky. Larry
Gelbart (cocreator of the *M*A*S*H* TV series) created the half-hour
series.

WHEN THE WHISTLE BLOWS   ABC
14 MARCH 1980–   Construction workers are the central characters of this sitcom. With Dolph Sweet as Norm Jenkins; Doug Barr as
Buzz Dillard; Susan Buckner as Lucy; Philip Brown as Randy; Tim Ros-
sovich as Hunk; Sue Ane Langdon as Darlene; Gary Allen as Hanrahan;
Alice Hirson as Dottie Jenkins, Norm's wife; and Noble Willingham as
Bulldog. Chuck Gordon and Tom Kardozian created the show.

INDEX OF NAMES

Alda, Robert, 119, 126, 419, 552, 622, 682, 736, 771, 811
Alden, Norman, 240, 391, 513, 579
Alderson, John, 106
Aldredge, Tom, 294, 837
Aleman, Jose, 606
Aletter, Frank, 112, 132, 350
Alexander, Ben, 19, 31, 207, 241, 541, 689
Alexander, Denise, 150, 177, 270
Alexander, Jane, 840, 842
Alexander, Millette, 62, 217, 218, 259, 293
Alexander, Rod, 667, 797
Alexander, Shana, 641
Alexander, Terry, 52
Alexander, Van, 298
Alford, Bobby, 61
Ali, Muhammad, 333, 847
Allan, Jed, 136, 177, 623
Alland, William, 786
Allardice, James, 889
Allbritton, Louise, 157, 661
Allegretti, Cosmo, 129
Allen, Byron, 582
Allen, Chet, 105
Allen, Craig G., 665
Allen, Dayton, 331, 667–668, 781
Allen, Debbie (Deborah), 365, 601, 708
Allen, Dennis, 398, 770
Allen, Ed, 213
Allen, Elizabeth, 107, 123, 544
Allen, Fred, 152, 374, 655, 741, 770, 810
Allen, Gary, 989
Allen, George, 254
Allen, Gracie, 117, 271
Allen, Grover J., 201
Allen, Herb, 298
Allen, Irwin, 394, 416, 685, 713, 753
Allen, Jay Presson, 234
Allen, Joe, Jr. (Joseph Jr.), 419, 473
Allen, Mark, 734
Allen, Michael, 292
Allen, Patrick, 279
Allen, Philip R., 69
Allen, Raymond, 611
Allen, Rex, 246, 260
Allen, Roy, 677
Allen, Sherry, 464
Allen, Steve, 146, 170, 225, 352, 354, 459, 585, 653, 666–668, 690, 723–725, 726, 770, 808, 809, 810, 812, 958
Allen, Tom, 778
Allen, Vera, 50, 259, 527, 620
Allen, Vernett, 734
Allen, Woody, 318, 325, 461, 797, 831, 835
Allenby, Peggy, 217
Allinson, Michael, 421
Allison, Allegra, 591
Allison, Betsi, 708
Allison, Fran, 119, 201, 391, 812
Allison, Jone, 61, 292

Allison, Patricia, 530
Allman, Elvia, 555
Allman, Sheldon, 304
Allport, Chris, 51
Allrud, Romola Robb, 420
Allyn, William, 150
Allyson, June, 376, 812
Alt, Joan, 703
Altay, Derin, 77
Alter, Paul, 735
Altman, Frieda, 619
Altman, Jeff, 161, 665, 988
Altman, Robert, 29, 425
Alyn, Kirk, 680
Amateau, Rod, 193, 492
Ameche, Don, 200, 256, 319, 344, 663, 689, 810
Ameche, Jim, 242
American Breed, 636
American Nazi Party, 369, 825
Ames, Ed, 44, 171, 729
Ames, Florenz, 98, 222, 464
Ames, Gene, 44
Ames, Joe, 44
Ames, Leon, 239, 260, 407, 474
Ames, Nancy, 701, 821
Ames, Rachel, 269, 409
Ames, Teal, 217
Ames, Trudi, 379
Ames, Vic, 44
Amorosa, Johnny, 750
Amory, Cleveland, 515, 819
Amos, John, 263, 284, 446, 451, 600
Amour, John, 177
Amsterdam, Morey, 76, 112, 127, 189, 382, 482, 669, 775
Amundsen, Roald, 698
Anders, Laurie, 383
Anders, Merry, 329, 350, 383, 674
Anders, William A., 908
Anderson, Alexander, 166
Anderson, Barbara, 346, 472, 905
Anderson, Bill, 84, 93
Anderson, Daryl, 416
Anderson, David, 291
Anderson, Donna, 734
Anderson, Eddie (Rochester), 353
Anderson, Ernie, 711
Anderson, George B., 429
Anderson, Gerry, 130, 244, 657, 669, 678, 711, 742
Anderson, Herbert, 183
Anderson, Jack, 18, 284
Anderson, Joan, 62
Anderson, John, 590
Anderson, Judith, 299, 574, 815, 889, 895
Anderson, Larry, 114
Anderson, Lew, 330
Anderson, Loni, 753
Anderson, Marian, 807, 812

Arsu, Nono, 750
Arthur, Beatrice, 34, 451–452, 814, 935
Arthur, Carole, 200
Arthur, Indus, 269
Arthur, Jean, 360
Arthur, Maureen, 319, 770
Arutt, Amy, 620
Arvan, Jan, 585
Ash, Glen, 505
Ashcroft, Peggy, 986
Asher, William, 87, 337, 360, 544, 634, 698, 902
Ashley, John, 671
Ashley, Paul, 600
Asner, Edward, 416, 445, 589, 600, 644, 912, 915, 928, 932, 936, 939
Assante, Armand, 197, 329
Astaire, Fred, 28, 214, 268, 321, 348, 813, 816, 828, 835, 844, 893, 895, 939
Astar, Ben, 794
Astin, John, 22, 202, 340, 528, 573
Astin, Patty Duke. *See* Duke, Patty
Astor, Mary, 82, 260, 389
Atkins, Chet, 216
Atkins, Eileen, 448
Atkins, Tom, 627
Atkinson, David, 807
Atlas, Barbara, 509
Atterbury, Malcolm, 53, 703
Attmore, Pop, 464
Atwater, Barry, 269
Atwater, Edith, 303, 381, 421
Aubrey, James T., 46, 86
Aubuchon, Jacques, 124, 454, 540
Auderson, Michael, 314
Auerbach, Arnold, 890
Auerbach, Larry, 418
Aumont, Jean-Pierre, 519
Aurthur, Robert Alan, 557
Ausbie, Geese, 304
Austin, Al, 345
Austin, Carol, 448
Austin, Nancy, 365
Austin, Ronald, 364
Austin, Stephen, 525
Autry, Gene, 24, 49, 115, 180, 268
Avalon, Frankie, 42, 212
Avalos, Luis, 221, 317
Avedon, Doe, 92
Avera, Tom, 23, 797
Averback, Hy, 201, 224, 231, 353, 478, 504
Avery, Phyllis, 150, 272, 476, 580
Avery, Tol, 644
Avramo, Peter, 173
Avruch, Frank, 107
Axelrod, George, 242
Ayers, Ted, 77
Aykroyd, Dan, 497, 936
Aylesworth, John, 304, 311, 382, 633
Ayres, Jerry, 270

Ayres, Lew, 261, 321
Ayres, Mitchell, 370, 549, 551, 688
Ayres, Robert, 142
Azzara, Candy, 125

Babbin, Jacqueline, 78, 934
Babbitt, Harry, 278
Babson, Thomas, 741
Bacall, Lauren, 101, 252, 329, 473, 571, 837
Bacalla, Donna, 271, 508, 684
Bach, Catherine, 209
Bach, Robert L., 23
Bacharach, Burt, 911
Backer, William M., 722
Backes, Alice, 68
Backus, Henny, 99
Backus, Jim, 99, 159, 276, 320, 338, 364, 475, 505, 690
Backus, Richard, 251, 423
Bacon, Cathy, 420
Baddeley, Angela, 448
Baddeley, Hermione, 126, 283, 451
Badel, Sarah, 448
Badler, Jane, 525
Baer, Art, 160, 431, 916
Baer, Buddy, 750
Baer, John, 699
Baer, Max, Jr., 86
Baer, Norman, 304
Baer, Parley, 206, 535
Baer, Richard, 704
Baer, Williams Rush, 530
Baez, Joan, 123, 325, 647
Bagdasarian, Ross. *See* Seville, David
Baggetta, Vincent, 216, 418
Bagot, Megan, 621
Bailey, Ann Howard, 329, 835, 916
Bailey, Bill, 519
Bailey, David, 50
Bailey, F. Lee, 283
Bailey, Gillian, 314
Bailey, Jack, 575, 737
Bailey, John Anthony, 391
Bailey, Jonathan, 464
Bailey, Joseph A., 926
Bailey, Maureen, 816
Bailey, Pearl, 129, 468, 546
Bailey, Raymond, 86, 492
Bailey, Wanda, 281
Bain, Barbara, 472, 590, 657, 903, 905, 907
Bain, Bill, 928
Bain, Conrad, 189, 451
Bain, Robbin, 717
Baio, Jimmy, 367, 650
Baio, Joey, 315
Baio, Scott, 97, 302, 777
Baird, Bil, 93, 483, 649, 726, 762, 774, 813
Baird, Cora, 93, 483, 649, 726, 762, 774, 813
Baird, Jimmy, 263

Baird, Sharon, 394, 463, 510
Bakal, Sid, 518
Bakalyan, Dick, 103
Baker, Ann, 457
Baker, Art, 790
Baker, Blanche, 88, 939
Baker, Carroll, 170
Baker, Cathy, 311
Baker, Colin, 448
Baker, Diane, 211, 314, 832
Baker, Elsie, 585
Baker, Herbert, 894, 913
Baker, Joby, 284
Baker, Joe, 15, 589, 985
Baker, Joe Don, 220
Baker, Lenny, 630
Baker, Peter, 908, 911
Baker, Robert S., 552
Baker, Stanley, 449
Baker, Tara, 198
Baker, Tom, 196
Bakker, James, 537
Bal, Jeanne, 417, 476
Baldavin, Barbara, 456
Balding, Rebecca, 416, 433
Baldwin, Faith, 233
Baldwin, Ronald, 926
Baldwin, Stacy, 270
Balfour, Michael, 441
Ball, Deedie, 342
Ball, Lucille, 315, 334–338, 424,
    489, 819, 843, 844, 888, 890,
    903, 905
Ballanger, Bill, 473
Ballantine, Carl, 454, 575, 988
Ballantine, Eddie, 201
Ballantine, Sara, 370
Ballard, Kaye, 204, 266, 313, 460, 485
Balsam, Martin, 34, 299, 421, 556, 816,
    828, 832, 836
Balson, Allison, 988
Balter, Allan, 631
Balzer, George, 353, 894
Banas, Bob, 434
Bancroft, Anne, 389, 832, 908
Bancroft, Griffing, 128
Banfield, Bever-Leigh, 601
Bangert, Johnny, 440
Bank, Frank, 401
Bankhead, Tallulah, 37, 75, 90
Banks, Emily, 712
Banks, Henry, 534
Banks, Joan, 570
Bannell, Marshall, 808
Banner, Bob, 38, 258, 267, 318, 563, 892
Banner, John, 144
Bannister, Harry, 792
Bannon, Jack, 416
Bannon, Jim, 24
Bara, Nina, 657

Baragrey, John, 64, 389, 623
Barasch, Norman, 193, 245
Barash, Olivia, 342
Barbeau, Adrienne, 451
Barber, Bill, 18
Barber, Ellen, 624, 652
Barber, Red, 583
Barbera, Joseph, 248, 301, 332, 603, 720,
    917, 921, 938
Barbour, John, 582
Barbour, William P., 567
Barbutti, Pete, 267, 370
Barcroft, Judith, 34, 51
Barcroft, Roy, 464
Bard, Katharine, 401
Bardette, Trevor, 788
Bardot, Brigitte, 830
Bare, Dick (Richard), 194, 649
Bargy, Jeane, 99
Bari, Lenny, 245
Bari, Lynn, 106, 185
Barker, Bob, 223, 235, 569, 737
Barker, Margaret, 423
Barkin, Marcie, 563
Barkley, Alben W., 437, 459
Barkley, Roger, 500
Barlow, Howard, 752
Barmak, Ira, 927
Barnard, Henry, 289
Barnes, Ann, 98
Barnes, Joanna, 173, 736, 739
Barnes, John, 908
Barnes, J. W., 917
Barnes, Marjorie, 241
Barnes, Paul, 320
Barnes, Priscilla, 43
Barnes, Walter, 750
Barnett, Eileen, 178
Barnouw, Erik, 627
Barnstable, Cyb, 575
Barnstable, Tricia, 575
Barnum, Pete, 229
Baron, Sandy, 315
Barr, Doug, 989
Barr, Julia, 35, 606
Barr, Leonard, 686
Barratt, Maxine, 45
Barrera, Aida, 134
Barrett, Ellen, 943
Barrett, Karen League, 191
Barrett, Laurinda, 251
Barrett, Lynne, 460
Barrett, Majel, 664
Barrett, Nancy, 198, 606
Barrett, Rona, 284
Barri, Steve, 622
Barrie, Barbara, 69, 74, 186
Barrie, Wendy, 665, 766
Barris, Chuck, 147, 173, 199, 282, 331, 510,
    527, 709, 735

Barris, Marty, 156, 398
Barron, Arthur, 906
Barron, Evelyn, 944
Barrow, Bernard (Bernie), 623
Barry, Donald, 476, 683
Barry, Gene, 23, 74, 117, 500, 531
Barry, Ivor, 474, 480
Barry, J. J., 160
Barry, Jac, 68, 91, 97, 109, 157, 158, 271,
   317, 372, 378, 406, 585, 711, 739, 763,
   781, 782, 988
Barry, Jeff, 522
Barry, Matthew, 352
Barry, Nancy, 522
Barry, Patricia, 177, 245, 251, 304
Barry, Philip, 942
Barry, Robert, 29
Barrymore, Ethel, 226, 320, 562
Barrymore, John, 226
Barrymore, Lionel, 226
Barstow, Robbins Walcott, 764
Bartelme, Joe, 719
Barth, Ed (Eddie), 333, 630
Barthold, Charles, 958
Bartlett, Bonnie, 410, 419
Bartlett, Des, 836
Bartlett, Jan, 836
Bartlett, Richard, 147
Bartlett, Tommy, 765
Barton, Dan, 169
Barton, Eileen, 94, 750
Barton, Joan, 162
Barton, Peter, 634
Bartram, Laurie, 52
Barty, Billy, 77, 391, 585, 637, 796
Bartz, Geof, 942
Baruch, Andre, 450
Baruch, Bernard, 808
Baryshnikov, Mikhail, 845, 943
Barzyk, Fred, 361
Basch, Charles, 749
Basehart, Richard, 562, 753, 829, 839
Basie, Count, 836
Basile, Louis, 678
Basinger, Kim, 199, 496, 986
Bass, Jules, 958
Bass, Todd, 398
Bassett, William H., 178, 501
Bassler, Robert, 125
Bastedo, Alexandra, 139
Batanides, Arthur, 372
Bateman, Charles, 251, 740
Bates, Alan, 449
Bates, H. E., 448
Bates, Jeanne, 81, 177
Bates, Rhonda, 97, 382, 598
Batten, Tony, 344
Battista, Lloyd, 421
Baudo, Tommy, 63
Bauer, Charita, 292

Bauer, Jaime Lyn, 792
Bauman, Jon, 630
Baumann, Kathrine, 382
Baumgartner, Leona, 323
Baur, Elizabeth, 346, 394
Bavaar, Tony, 151
Bavier, Frances, 46, 227, 349, 453, 903
Baxley, Barbara, 29, 37, 556
Baxter, Anne, 268
Baxter, Billy, 348
Baxter, Carol, 150
Baxter, Charles, 51, 62, 420
Baxter, Frank, 514, 631, 696, 810, 811, 814,
   948
Baxter, Meredith. *See* Birney, Meredith
   Baxter
Bayer, Jimmy, 419
Bazlen, Brigid, 731
Beach Boys, 128, 278
Beaird, Barbara, 242
Beaird, Betty, 376
Beal, John, 21, 50, 258, 593, 675
Bean, Orson, 82, 99, 254, 398, 715, 726,
   727
Beanblossom, Billie Jean, 463
Beard, Dita, 641
Beard, James, 359
Bearde, Chris, 103, 142, 161, 282, 332, 383,
   654, 906
Beatles, 79, 214, 228, 332, 355, 480, 517,
   634, 822, 826, 827
Beaton, Alex, 392
Beattie, Bob, 17
Beatts, Anne, 498, 934, 936
Beatty, Morgan, 547
Beatty, Ned, 686, 846
Beatty, Robert, 186
Beatty, Roger, 916, 920, 925, 929, 940
Beatty, Warren, 193, 390, 421, 675
Beauchamp, Richard, 123
Beaudine, Deka, 539
Beaudine, William, 293, 592, 687
Beaumont, Charles, 740
Beaumont, Chris, 314
Beaumont, Hugh, 401
Beauvoir, Simone de, 821
Beavers, Louise, 86, 663
Beck, Jack, 904
Beck, Jackson, 408
Beck, John, 511
Beck, Kimberley, 270, 768
Becker, Barbara, 593
Becker, Fred, 540
Becker, George, 190
Becker, Sandy, 780
Becker, Terry, 753
Becker, Tony, 529
Becker, Vernon, 363
Beckering, Raymond, 327
Becket, Scotty, 597

Beckman, Henry, 114, 262, 313, 340, 405, 454
Bedard, Rolland, 254
Bedelia, Bonnie, 420, 507
Bedford, Brian, 161
Bee, Molly, 366, 685, 699
Bee Gees, 309, 845
Beeny, Christopher, 448
Beer, Jacqueline, 629
Beers, Francine, 218
Beery, Noah (Noah Jr.), 148, 194, 323, 593, 596
Begley, Ed, 401, 594
Begley, Ed, Jr., 598
Beir, Fred, 178
Belack, Doris, 51, 524
Belafonte, Harry, 268, 647, 746, 809, 815, 823, 831, 832, 833, 894
Belanger, Paul, 710
Belasco, Leon, 363, 492
Belefonte, Ben, 724
Belenda, Carla, 465
Belford, Christine, 71, 442
Belgard, Madeline, 526
Bel Geddes, Barbara, 30, 169, 594
Belkin, Gary, 910, 925, 929
Bell, Keith, 447
Bell, Lee Phillip, 792, 927
Bell, Steven, 196
Bell, William, 792, 927, 934
Bellamy, Ralph, 182, 221, 333, 434, 484, 675, 683, 839
Belland, Bruce, 711
Bellaran, Ray, 619
Bellaver, Harry, 50, 499
Beller, Kathy, 619
Beller, Mary Linn, 111, 172
Bellflower, Nellie, 383
Bellini, Cal, 185
Bellson, Louis, 546
Bellwood, Pamela, 753
Bellwood, Peter, 910
Beloin, Ed, 649
Belushi, Jim, 777, 785
Belushi, John, 182, 497, 842, 936
Benaderet, Bea, 117, 248, 272, 335, 353, 554–555
Bench, Johnny, 427
Benchley, Robert, 494
Bender, Jim, 236
Bender, Joan, 931
Bendick, Bob, 719
Bendix, William, 117, 355, 407, 409, 534
Benedict, Dirk, 77, 146
Benedict, Greg, 512
Benedict, Nick, 34
Benedict, Paul, 362
Benesch, Lynn, 524
Benet, Brenda, 794
Beniades, Ted, 46

Benjamin, Burton, 906, 907, 914, 918, 921, 922
Benjamin, Julia, 308
Benjamin, Richard, 309, 575, 844
Benjamin, Susan, 19
Bennett, Al, 38
Bennett, Bern, 667
Bennett, Donn, 89
Bennett, Harve, 43, 96, 267, 346, 590, 609, 640
Bennett, Joan, 27, 82, 172, 652, 731
Bennett, Marjorie, 115, 364, 422
Bennett, Meg, 619
Bennett, Sue, 796
Bennett, Tony, 551, 729, 730, 811, 842
Bennington, Bill, 907
Benny, Jack, 183, 277, 353, 636, 643, 727, 729, 763, 805, 806, 808, 816, 819, 892, 893
Benoff, Mac, 408
Benoit, Patricia, 61, 476, 719
Bensfield, Dick, 312, 522
Bensley, Russ, 911, 918, 922
Benson, Barbara, 649
Benson, Court, 197
Benson, Hugh, 533
Benson, Irving, 469
Benson, Jay, 423
Benson, Leon, 592
Benson, Lucille, 502
Benson, Martin, 686
Benson, Pat, 368
Benson, Ray, 373
Benson, Red, 500
Benti, Joseph, 121
Bentley, John, 26
Benton, Barbi, 311, 676
Benton, Douglas, 277, 310, 564, 920
Benton, Eddie, 199
Benton, Nelson, 922
Bentzen, Jayne, 218
Beradino, John, 269, 506, 525, 681
Bercovici, Eric, 761
Berdis, Bert, 41
Berenger, Tom, 524
Berg, Gertrude, 280, 478
Bergen, Candice, 161, 790, 831
Bergen, Edgar, 390, 759, 775, 790, 805
Bergen, Frances, 788
Bergen, Jerry, 119
Bergen, Polly, 27, 99, 514, 548, 565, 714, 892
Berger, Ian, 713
Berger, Marilyn, 26
Berger, Robert, 938
Bergere, Lee, 326, 387
Bergerson, Bev, 429
Bergman, Alan, 285, 384, 452
Bergman, David, 650
Bergman, Ingmar, 837

Bergman, Ingrid, 17, 134, 253, 817, 821, 845, 894
Bergman, Jules, 921
Bergman, Marilyn, 285, 452
Bergman, Peter, 665
Bergmann, Ted, 471
Berjer, Barbara, 61, 259, 293
Berle, Milton, 75, 102, 116, 156, 162, 212, 216, 225, 243, 355, 357, 388, 401, 406, 467–470, 549, 573, 805, 819, 844, 886, 943
Berlin, Irving, 214, 806, 844
Berlinger, Warren, 263, 369, 528, 622, 733
Berman, Richard, 944
Berman, Shelley, 155, 254, 398, 701, 724, 727, 815, 819
Bernard, Alan, 128, 370
Bernard, Dorothy, 408
Bernard, Ed, 564, 774
Bernard, Gene, 40
Bernard, George, 40
Bernard, Glen, 457
Bernard, Susan, 270
Bernardi, Herschel, 56, 83, 553
Bernau, Chris, 294
Berner, Sara, 301
Bernhart, Sandra, 591
Bernie, Al, 243
Bernie, Helen, 308
Bernier, Daisy, 257
Berns, Larry, 329, 531
Bernstein, Kenneth, 825
Bernstein, Leonard, 519, 807, 812, 817, 820, 900, 913, 930
Berridge, Robbie, 294
Berry, Chuck, 298
Berry, Fred, 769
Berry, Ken, 46, 49, 231, 383, 452, 570, 836
Bersell, Michael, 772
Berthrong, Deirdre, 359
Bertinelli, Valerie, 522
Berwick, Brad, 780
Berwick, Ray, 987
Besch, Bibi, 218, 418, 623, 652
Bessell, Ted, 282, 349, 455, 700
Besser, Joe, 18, 369
Bessler, Brian, 398
Best, Edna, 252
Best, James, 209
Best, Willie, 491, 674
Bethune, Zina, 293, 419, 480, 515, 813
Bettger, Lyle, 162, 286
Betts, Frank, 142
Betz, Carl, 202, 374, 420, 907
Beutel, Bill, 18
Beutel, Jack, 374
Bexley, Don, 611, 612
Beyers, Bill, 368
Bibbs, Cheryl Susheel, 937
Biberman, Abner, 387

Bice, Robert, 494
Bickford, Charles, 435, 562, 751, 818
Bickley, William, 763
Bidmead, Stephanie, 411
Biehn, Michael, 605
Biener, Tom, 365
Bieri, Ramon, 613
Bigelow, Donald, 627
Bigelow, Joe, 320
Biggers, Earl Derr, 140
Bikel, Theodore, 828
Bill, Tony, 761, 769
Billet, Stu, 659
Billingsley, Barbara, 114, 401, 572
Billingsley, Jennifer, 269
Billingsley, Neil, 621
Billingsley, Sherman, 670
Billington, Michael, 742
Bilson, Bruce, 905
Binder, Steve, 427, 633, 935
Bing, Mack, 744
Binkley, Lane, 620
Binns, Edward, 110, 515, 547
Birch, Paul, 128, 162
Birch, Peter, 130
Birch, Sammy, 583
Birman, Len, 196
Birnbaum, Bernard, 902, 921
Birney, David, 21, 110, 418, 627
Birney, Meredith Baxter (Meredith Baxter), 110, 234
Biscailuz, Eugene W., 152
Bishop, Ed, 742
Bishop, Jim, 76
Bishop, Joey, 137, 187, 369, 382, 585
Bishop, Julie, 491
Bishop, Mel, 589
Bishop, William, 349
Bisoglio, Val, 587, 598, 785
Bissell, Whit, 68, 713
Bixby, Bill, 163, 342, 429, 447, 490, 589
Black, Cilla, 822
Black, Daniel, 270
Black, Fischer, 84
Black, Karen, 622
Black, Marianne, 676
Blackburn, Clarice, 63, 773
Blackburn, Dorothy, 52, 62, 197
Blackburn, Tom, 757
Blackman, Honor, 66
Blackwell, Chuck, 634
Blades, 488
Blaine, Jimmy, 94, 545, 604, 670
Blaine, Vivian, 268, 707
Blair, Frank, 677, 716–719
Blair, Janet, 97, 123, 645, 809
Blair, June, 536
Blair, Leonard, 111
Blair, Lionel, 660
Blair, Linda, 839, 841

Blair, Pat, 171, 592
Blake, Amanda, 296, 615
Blake, Jean, 170
Blake, Madge, 75, 369, 401, 582
Blake, Oliver, 114
Blake, Robert, 73, 590, 722, 927
Blake, Robin, 269
Blake, Whitney, 308, 522
Blakely, Don, 78
Blakely, Gene, 709
Blakely, Susan, 589
Blakeney, Olive, 195
Blanc, Mel, 116, 248, 353, 489, 658, 686, 773
Blanc, Shirley, 420
Blanchard, Jeri, 327
Blanchard, Keith, 197
Blanchard, Mari, 387
Blanchard, Susan, 35, 78, 477, 794
Blass, Lucille, 166
Blasucci, Dick, 262
Blattner, Buddy, 74
Blatty, William Peter, 790
Blau, Mary Benjamin, 937
Blavat, Jerry, 191
Blazo, John, 606
Blees, Robert, 317
Blessed, Brian, 449
Bleyer, Archie, 59
Bleyer, Bob, 653
Blinn, William, 333, 400, 427, 507, 600, 666 916, 936, 954
Blitser, Barry, 890
Bloch, Ray, 213, 794
Block, Hal, 688, 770
Block, Martin, 443
Blocker, Dan, 67, 105, 586
Blocker, Dirk, 67
Blocker, Joel, 918
Blodgett, Michael, 504
Blondell, Gloria, 407
Blondell, Joan, 72, 313
Bloom, Anne, 228
Bloom, Charles, 763
Bloom, Claire, 69, 562, 827
Bloom, John, 633
Blossom, Roberts, 52
Blossoms, 633
Bloudeau, Jean-Pierre, 199
Blue, Ben, 19, 256, 613
Bluel, Richard, 290
Bly, Alan, 480, 934
Blyden, Larry, 304, 367, 485, 552, 636, 770, 799, 815
Blye, Allan, 103, 333, 369, 383, 585, 647, 648, 654, 747, 908
Blye, Maggie, 388
Boardman, Nan, 706
Bobo, Willie, 161
Bochco, Steven, 540, 591

Bochner, Lloyd, 324, 590
Boda, Harry, 36
Bodwell, Phil, 164
Boettcher, George, 917
Bogarde, Dirk, 299
Bogart, Humphrey, 134, 353, 571
Bogart, Paul, 161, 900, 905, 910, 940
Bogdanovich, Peter, 539
Bogert, Vinnie (Vincent), 267, 890
Bogert, William, 471
Boggs, Bill, 38
Bogner, Norman, 83
Bogue, Mervyn, 153
Bohem, Endre, 580
Bokeno, Chris, 488
Boland, Bonnie, 145, 711, 737
Boland, Mary, 82, 556
Bolen, Lin, 329, 676
Boles, Jim, 526
Bolger, Ray, 580, 762, 813, 840
Bolling, Tiffany, 508
Bollinger, Henri, 341
Bologna, Joseph, 125, 837, 920
Bolster, Steven, 51, 525, 622
Bolton, Elaine, 777
Bombeck, Erma, 284
Bonaduce, Danny, 283, 541
Bonar, Ivan, 270, 536
Bon Bon, 606
Bond, James, 584
Bond, Julian, 497
Bond, Sudie, 698
Bond, Tony, 259
Bond, Ward, 638, 755
Bondi, Beulah, 935
Bonerz, Peter, 102, 671
Bones, Herbert, 931
Boni, John, 69, 772, 917
Bonino, Steve, 384
Bonn, Ronald (Ron), 909, 922
Bonne, Shirley, 492
Bonner, Frank, 753
Bonner, Mary S., 930
Bono, Chastity, 654
Bono, Cher, 142, 271, 653–654. See also Sonny and Cher
Bono, Sonny, 142, 653–654. See also Sonny and Cher
Booke, Sorrell, 209, 572, 589, 822
Boomer, Linwood, 410
Boone, Brendon, 265
Boone, Pat, 58, 186, 542, 690, 812
Boone, Randy, 147, 349, 751
Boone, Richard, 305, 310, 456, 590, 813, 818
Booth, Billy, 183
Booth, Shirley, 308, 733, 826, 828, 896, 898
Borden, Alice, 700
Borden, Gail, 246
Borden, Lynn, 308

Brewster, Ralph, 152
Brian, David, 341, 474
Brian, Mary, 457
Brickell, Beth, 271
Bricken, Jules, 253
Bridges, Beau, 224, 412, 989
Bridges, James, 539
Bridges, Jeff, 412, 845
Bridges, Lloyd, 92, 368, 412, 414, 600, 610, 617, 762, 787, 829
Bridges, Todd, 189, 245
Bridges, William, 677
Bright, Patricia, 350
Briles, Charles, 92
Brill, Charlie, 682
Brill, Fran, 329, 926
Brill, Leighton, 403
Brill, Marty, 506
Brinegar, Paul, 394, 579
Brinkley, David, 16, 174, 495, 821, 822
Brinkley, Don, 229, 734
Brisebois, Danielle, 33
Briskin, Jerry, 631
Briskin, Mort, 633, 758
Britt, May, 171
Britten, Benjamin, 807
Britton, Barbara
   (Barbara Monte-Britton),
   473, 620
Britton, Pamela, 98, 490
Brock, Stan, 778
Brockett, Don, 477
Brockhausen, Maurice, 528
Brockman, Jane, 781
Brockway, Merrill, 942
Broder, Dick, 441
Broderick, James, 110, 234
Broderick, Malcolm, 258, 442
Broderick, Peter, 619
Brodie, Steve, 317, 788
Brodkin, Herbert, 141, 161, 182, 226, 252, 514, 631, 674, 938
Brogan, Jimmy, 532
Brogna, Johnny, 584
Brokaw, Tom, 719
Brokenshire, Norman, 76, 255, 300
Brolin, James, 440, 910
Bromfield, John, 633
Bromilow, Peter, 459
Bromley, Sheila, 338, 484
Bronowski, Jacob, 63
Bronson, Charles, 194, 223, 437, 842
Brook, Lyndon, 448
Brook, M. C., 131
Brook, Pamela, 52
Brooke, Hillary, 18, 491
Brooke, Walter, 290, 526, 539, 709
Brooks, Albert, 281
Brooks, Elizabeth, 178
Brooks, Foster, 505

Brooks, Geraldine, 210, 237, 421, 790
Brooks, Jacqueline, 51, 623
Brooks, James L. (Jim), 64, 259, 416, 446, 588, 600, 694, 913, 926, 930, 934, 936, 941
Brooks, Martin (Martin E.), 95–96, 619, 620, 640
Brooks, Mel, 274, 729, 772, 797, 903
Brooks, Ned, 458
Brooks, Rand, 592
Brooks, Randy, 114
Brooks, Roxanne, 590
Brooks, Steven, 231, 344, 515
Brookshier, Tom, 136
Brooksmith, Jane, 703
Brophy, Kevin, 423
Brophy, Sallie, 115, 250
Brosten, Harve, 940
Brothers, Joyce, 195, 525, 642
Broun, Heywood Hale, 198
Brouwer, Peter, 421
Brown, Bill, 461, 473
Brown, Bob, 615
Brown, Candy Ann, 598
Brown, Charlotte, 589
Brown, Chelsea, 398, 439, 451
Brown, Cheryl Lynn, 294
Brown, Christopher J., 51, 528
Brown, Coral, 712
Brown, Dave, 357
Brown, Donna, 153
Brown, Doris, 424
Brown, Earl, 171, 190
Brown, Gail, 51
Brown, Georg Stanford, 599, 600, 601
Brown, Georgia, 449
Brown, Graham, 178
Brown, Helen Gurley, 284, 533
Brown, James Bowen, 602
Brown, James H., 368, 576
Brown, Jerry, 636
Brown, Jim L., 592
Brown, Jimmy, 559
Brown, Joe E., 116
Brown, Joe, Jr., 709
Brown, John, 117, 407
Brown, John Mason, 165, 397, 723
Brown, Johnny, 273, 284, 398, 402
Brown, Les, 179, 281, 603, 813
Brown, Les, Jr., 70, 794
Brown, Mitch, 164
Brown, Nate, 304
Brown, Oscar, Jr., 360
Brown, Pamela, 897
Brown, Pepe, 542
Brown, Peter, 177, 395, 400
Brown, Philip, 204, 989
Brown, R. G., 370, 589
Brown, Robert, 313, 569
Brown, Susan, 111, 270, 587, 794

Brown, Ted, 20, 289, 331, 669
Brown, Timothy (Tim), 426
Brown, Tom, 178, 270, 297
Brown, Tony, 96, 730
Brown, Vanessa, 37, 490
Brown, Wally, 338
Brown, Walter, 25
Brown, William, 90
Brown, William H., Jr., 634
Browne, Daniel Gregory, 445, 931
Browne, Kathie, 323, 644
Browne, Roscoe Lee, 453, 471, 650
Browning, David, 921
Browning, Rod, 525
Browning, Susan, 418
Brownlee, Brian, 420
Brubaker, Robert, 177
Brubeck, Dave, 473, 812
Bruce, Carol, 167
Bruce, Kitty, 145
Bruce, Lenny, 145, 724
Bruce, Lydia, 197
Bruce, Nigel, 255
Bruck, Karl, 793
Bruder, Pat, 61
Bruner, Natalie, 755
Bruner, Wally, 755, 770
Brunner, Bob, 69, 98, 114, 785
Bruns, Mona 111
Bruns, Philip, 254, 444, 624
Bruton, Carl, 90
Bry, Ellen, 40
Bryan, Arthur Q., 301, 485, 572
Bryan, C. D. B., 845
Bryant, Anita, 58, 272, 553
Bryant, Jeff, 246
Bryant, Nana, 432, 531
Bryant, Reginald, 96
Bryant, William, 270, 685
Bryant, Willie, 746
Bryar, Claudia, 439
Bryar, Paul, 414
Bryce, Ed (Edward), 292, 623, 720
Brydon, W. B., 21,
Bryggman, Larry, 62
Brynner, Yul, 49, 649, 674, 808, 821, 825
Bua, Gene, 420, 652
Bubbles, John, 827
Buchanan, Edgar, 123, 374, 555
Buchanan, Jack, 809
Buchanan, James, 364
Buchholz, Horst, 171
Buchwald, Art, 224, 819
Buck, Jack, 287, 571
Buck, Lisa, 621
Buckley, Betty, 220
Buckley, Hal, 515
Buckley, Keith, 618
Buckley, William F., Jr., 244
Buckner, Susan, 989

Buckridge, Kenneth, 471
Budd, Julie, 636
Budinger, Victoria May, 729
Budkin, Celia, 527
Bueno, Delora, 247
Bufano, Vincent, 247
Buffano, Jules, 220, 366
Buffington, Sam, 774
Buffum, Ray, 494
Bugliosi, Vincent, 840
Bujold, Genevieve, 299
Buktenica, Ray, 588, 987
Bulifant, Joyce, 89, 93, 422, 721
Bull, Richard, 410
Bull, Toni, 420
Bullock, Harvey, 454
Bulluck, Dan, 987
Buloff, John, 293
Buloff, Joseph 741
Bunce, Alan, 226
Bundy, Brooke, 178, 270
Bunetta, Frank, 172, 349, 357, 406, 672
Bunim, Mary-Ellis, 618
Bunin, Hope, 250, 424
Bunin, Morey, 250, 424
Buntrock, Bobby, 308
Buono, Victor, 69, 75, 436, 829
Burbank Quickies, 398
Burch, William, 699
Burdett, Winston 815
Burdick, Hal 511
Burgess, Bobby, 400, 463
Burghardt, Arthur, 525
Burghoff, Gary, 200, 425, 935
Burgundy Street Singers, 365, 585
Burke, Alan, 27
Burke, Billie, 193
Burke, Delta, 986
Burke, James, 158, 441
Burke, Jerry, 400
Burke, Pamela, 722
Burke, Paul, 246, 302, 499, 513, 681, 738
Burkley, Dennis, 254, 300, 700, 988
Burleigh, Stephen, 251, 620
Burnell, Peter, 197
Burnett, Carol, 36, 133, 224, 266–267, 538, 545, 662, 812, 819, 822, 834, 836, 838, 839, 841, 844, 845, 846, 897, 898, 913, 920, 926, 950
Burnett, Don, 513
Burnett, Ramona, 705
Burnett, W. R., 63
Burnette, Smiley, 534, 555, 579
Burnier, Jeannine, 382
Burns, Allan, 259, 416, 446, 492, 588, 906, 913, 926, 930, 934, 936
Burns, Bart, 675
Burns, Bob, 275
Burns, Cathy, 524

Cirino, Bruno, 406
City Slickers, 659
Clair, Dick, 263, 770, 925, 929, 940
Claire, Dorothy, 545
Claman, Julian, 64, 359
Clampett, Bob, 712
Clancy, Martin, 915, 922
Clanton, Ralph, 620, 651
Clapp, Nicholas, 921
Clare, Diene, 162
Clark, Bobby, 135
Clark, Cliff, 155
Clark, Dane, 104, 178, 378, 508, 667, 782
Clark, Dave, 687
Clark, Dick, 17, 41, 128, 161, 187, 188,
    212, 370, 471, 516, 698, 772, 814, 944
Clark, Dorothy Engel, 351
Clark, Ernest, 195, 345
Clark, Fred, 117, 205, 390, 469
Clark, Harry, 743
Clark, Jack, 166, 178, 523
Clark, Judy, 687
Clark, Marlene, 611
Clark, Marsha, 294
Clark, Matt, 199
Clark, Oliver, 379, 768
Clark, Patty, 279
Clark, Paulle, 539
Clark, Philip, 794
Clark, Ron, 326
Clark, Roy, 272, 311, 685
Clark, Susan, 101, 158, 840, 841, 932
Clarke, Brian Patrick, 182, 220
Clarke, Don, 270
Clarke, Gary, 323, 462, 751
Clarke, John, 177, 506
Clarke, Jordan, 294
Clarke, Richard, 218
Clarke, William Kendal, 471
Clary, Robert, 178, 318, 538, 792
Claster, Bert, 599
Claster, Nancy, 599
Claver, Bob, 277, 541, 622
Clawson, Cynthia, 510
Clay, Jeffrey, 649
Clay, Juanin, 218
Clayburgh, Jill, 620, 839
Clayton, Bob, 157, 431
Clayton, Jan, 396
Clayton, Lou, 366
Cleary, Jack, 153
Cleese, John, 482
Clemens, Brian, 66
Clement, Dick, 521
Clemmons, Francois, 477
Clerk, Clive, 177, 508
Cleveland, George, 396
Cleveland, Odessa, 426
Clews, Colin, 558
Cliburn, Van, 827

Clinger, Debra (Debbie), 43, 390
Clooney, Betty, 483, 595
Clooney, Nick, 480
Clooney, Rosemary, 371, 425, 529, 601,
    808, 925
Clovers, 811
Clyde, Andy, 396, 512, 582
Coates, Paul, 157, 725
Coates, Phyllis, 209, 572, 680, 705
Cobb, Buff, 466
Cobb, Julie, 167, 788
Cobb, Lee J., 211, 571, 652, 751, 794, 818,
    825
Cobb, Mel, 210
Coburn, James, 19, 387, 586
Coca, Imogene, 23, 129, 290, 341, 350, 637,
    797, 887, 947
Cochran, Ron, 15, 56
Coco, James, 125, 210
Coe, Barry, 250
Coe, Fred, 285, 476, 556, 563, 571, 890
Coe, George, 198, 651
Coffield, Peter, 753
Coffin, Tris, 740, 761
Cogan, Shaye, 232
Cohan, Martin, 101, 676, 695
Cohen, Evan, 601
Cohen, Harold, 366
Cohen, Larry, 345
Cohen, Marty, 358
Cohen, Randy, 917
Cohn, Mindy, 233
Cohoon, Patti, 53, 313, 605
Colarusso, Charles, 365
Colbert, Claudette, 82, 219, 353, 800, 812,
    815
Colbert, Robert, 452, 713, 792
Colbert, Stanley, 289
Colbin, Rod, 62
Colby, Anita, 548, 717
Colby, Barbara, 557
Colby, Carroll ("Kib"), 94
Colby, Marion, 312
Cole, Bobby, 375
Cole, Carol, 286
Cole, Dennis, 72, 79, 108, 241, 539
Cole, Eddie, 107
Cole, Harry, 311
Cole, Michael, 479
Cole, Natalie, 323, 842
Cole, Nat King, 502
Cole, Olivia, 69, 293, 686, 936
Cole, Rocky, 543
Cole, Tina, 385, 493
Cole, Tommy, 463
Coleman, Barbara, 314
Coleman, Carole, 431
Coleman, Cy, 665, 929, 930
Coleman, Dabney, 53, 111, 255, 444, 700
Coleman, Gary, 189

Coleman, James, 607
Coleman, Kathy, 394
Coleman, Nancy, 572, 747
Coleman, Wanda, 934
Coleman, William T., 573
Colen, Beatrice, 784
Colenback, John, 61
Coles, Zeida, 197
Colicos, John, 816
Colla, Dick, 177
Colleary, Bob, 130
Collier, Don, 533
Collier, Lois, 106
Collier, Marian, 476
Collier, Richard, 439
Colligan, Jim, 404
Collin, Kathy, 363
Collinge, Pat, 29
Collings, Anne, 270, 480
Collingwood, Charles, 23, 90, 483, 517, 548, 551, 567, 774, 822, 826
Collins, Al ("Jazzbo"), 725
Collins, Dorothy, 796
Collins, Gary, 106, 346, 641, 754
Collins, Jack, 516
Collins, Johnnie, III, 454, 712
Collins, Patricia, 671
Collins, Patrick, 682
Collins, Ray, 300, 550
Collins, Richard, 529, 612
Collins, Russell, 439
Collins, Stephen, 83
Collins, Ted, 380
Collins, Wilkie, 448
Collyer, Bud, 79, 109, 241, 447, 472, 514, 522, 680, 690, 715, 781
Collyer, June, 674
Colman, Booth, 560
Colman, Henry, 417
Colman, Ronald, 255, 300
Colomby, Scott, 654, 686
Colonna, Jerry, 246, 362, 678
Colpitts, Cissy, 695
Colson, C. David, 62
Colvin, Jack, 343
Combs, George Hamilton, 710
Comden, Betty, 18, 815
Comfort, David, 271
Como, Perry, 376, 549, 889, 890, 891, 893, 948, 957
Compton, Fay, 255
Compton, Forrest, 217, 282
Compton, Gardner, 927
Compton, Gail, 552
Compton, Gay, 552
Compton, John, 168
Compton, Sara, 917
Comstock, Frank, 365
Conaway, Jeff, 694
Conaway, Michelle, 270

Conboy, John (John J.), 792, 921, 927
Condon, Eddie, 249
Congdon, James, 652
Conger, Eric, 52
Coniff, Frank, 55
Conklin, Chester, 193
Conklin, Hal, 131
Conley, Corinne, 177
Conley, Joe, 759
Conlin, Noreen, 944
Conn, Didi, 382, 567
Connal, Scotty, 930
Connell, David D. (Dave), 908, 911, 914, 942
Connell, Jane, 210, 475
Connell, Jim, 203, 604
Connell, John, 793
Connelly, Chris, 539, 555
Connelly, Joe, 339, 401, 487, 560, 581
Connelly, Marc, 208
Connelly, Peggy, 689
Connery, Sean, 830
Connolly, Norma, 794
Connolly, Pat, 504
Connolly, Thomas, 198
Connor, Betty, 276, 794
Connor, Erin, 786
Connor, Lynn, 71
Connor, Whit (Whitfield), 291, 779
Connors, Chuck, 57, 108, 163, 592, 600, 681, 710
Connors, Dorsey, 323
Connors, Jimmy, 926
Connors, Mike, 253, 439, 550, 711
Conrad, Joseph, 562
Conrad, Michael, 183
Conrad, Nancy, 67
Conrad, Robert, 64, 67, 88, 167, 209, 307, 435, 779
Conrad, Sid, 178
Conrad, William, 74, 115, 116, 127, 226, 261, 295, 387, 630, 691, 707, 779
Conried, Hans, 256, 432, 538, 689, 726, 731, 770, 814
Considine, Bob, 100, 725
Considine, John (John Jr.), 51
Considine, Tim, 464, 493
Constantine, Michael, 315, 599, 640, 910
Contardo, Johnny, 630
Conte, John, 411, 450, 653, 809
Conte, Richard, 255, 360
Conteras, Roberto, 316
Conti, Tom, 449
Conti, Vince, 388
Converse, Frank, 160, 486, 499
Converse, Melissa, 710
Convy, Bert, 14, 398, 421, 564, 649, 694, 937
Conway, Gary, 117, 394
Conway, Kevin, 615, 786, 847

Ellis, Don, 287
Ellis, Herb, 494, 513
Ellis, Kathleen, 476
Ellis, Larry, 610
Ellis, Peggy Ann, 162
Ellis, Ray, 719
Ellis, Robin, 448, 449
Ellison, Bob, 48, 85, 427, 913, 936
Ellison, Harlan, 665
Ellsberg, Daniel, 834
Ellsworth, Whitney, 680
Elman, Dave, 174
Elmore, Steve, 329
Elnicky, Bob, 326
Elphick, Michael, 448
Elson, Bob, 340
Elward, Jim, 328
Elwyn, Charles, 747
Ely, Rick, 795
Ely, Ron, 54, 433, 693, 986
Emberg, Dick. See Enberg, Dick
Emerson, Faye, 240, 517, 540, 769
Emerson, Hope, 183, 193, 387, 553
Emery, Bob, 645
Emery, Ralph, 565
Emhardt, Robert, 51
Emmett, Robert, 701
Enberg, Dick (Dick Emberg), 70, 548, 660, 708
Endersby, Ralph, 254
Endo, Harry, 306
Engel, Georgia, 85, 446, 986
Engel, Peter, 640
Englander, Roger, 900, 944
English, Philip, 198
English, Raina, 400
Englund, Pat, 251, 423, 701
Enright, Dan, 68, 109, 373, 378, 739, 763, 782, 988
Enten, Boni, 156
Epstein, Brian, 332
Epstein, David, 247
Epstein, Jon, 533, 590, 685
Epstein, Julius, J., 987
Erdman, Richard, 580, 608, 688
Eric, Elspeth, 593
Erickson, Leif, 316
Erickson, Rod, 57
Ericson, Devon, 793
Ericson, John, 324
Ericson, June, 102
Erman, John, 600
Errickson, Krista, 312
Errol, Leon, 215
Erskine, Chester, 687
Erskine, Marilyn, 721
Ervin, Sam, 18
Erwin, Bill, 673
Erwin, Stu, 289, 674

Espinosa, Mary, 463
Espy, William Gray, 792
Estrada, Erik, 123
Estrin, Patricia, 52, 422
Eubanks, Bob, 37, 186, 510, 589
Eure, Wesley, 177, 394
Eustis, Rich, 365, 686, 926
Evans, Andrea, 525
Evans, Barry, 195
Evans, Bergen, 206, 349, 397, 517, 642, 678
Evans, Dale, 603
Evans, Damon, 361, 421, 601
Evans, Denny, 554
Evans, Edith, 448
Evans, Gene, 450, 490, 658
Evans, Jerry, 418, 606, 945
Evans, Linda, 92, 333
Evans, Maurice, 87, 299, 895
Evans, Mike, 33, 285, 361–362, 567, 842
Evans, Monica, 516
Evans, Nancy, 411
Evans, Rowland, 227
Evans, Samuel H., 104
Evelyn, Judith, 14, 288, 572, 674
Everett, Chad, 88, 168, 307, 456, 987
Everhart, Tex, 241
Everly Brothers, 227, 341, 634
Everly, Don, 227. See also the Everly Brothers
Everly, Phil, 227, 341. See also the Everly Brothers
Evers, Jason, 140, 299, 787
Evigan, Greg, 67, 788
Ewald, Yvonne, 585
Ewell, Tom, 21, 73, 620, 721
Ewing, Barbara, 448
Ewing, Bill, 388
Ewing, Roger, 296
Eyer, Richard, 491, 662

Fabares, Shelley, 49, 202, 254, 317, 410, 567
Fabian, 42, 118, 814
Fabray, Nanette, 123, 519, 767, 810, 826, 890, 891
Factor, Alan J., 510
Fadiman, Clifton, 209, 343, 501, 705, 769
Fafara, Stanley, 401
Fafara, Tiger, 401
Fahey, Myrna, 239
Fahrenholz, Elina, 164
Faichney, Jim, 26
Fairbairn, Bruce, 599
Fairbanks, Douglas, Jr., 206, 824
Fairbanks, Jerry, 260, 574
Fairchild, Morgan, 620
Fairfax, James, 518, 578
Fairman, Michael, 420, 606
Faison, Sandy, 191

Falana, Avelio, 189
Falana, Lola, 81, 505
Falis, Terry, 623
Falk, Peter, 154, 188, 380, 421, 594, 675, 736, 816, 826, 829, 897, 915, 927, 931
Falk, Rick, 269
Falkenburg, Jinx, 568
Falwell, Jerry, 363
Fanning, Bill, 365
Fanning, Gene, 620, 651
Fant, Lou, 704
Fantini, Dino, 587
Faracy, Stephanie, 397
Faraghan, J. E., 489
Farago, Ladislas, 435
Farber, Burt, 78
Farentino, James, 104, 160, 182, 825
Fargas, Antonio, 666
Fargé, Annie, 48
Fargo, Donna, 202
Farleigh, Lynn, 672
Farley, Duke, 132
Farley, Elizabeth, 218
Farley, James A., 326
Farnum, Marina, 702
Farr, Gordon, 417
Farr, Jamie, 144, 282, 425
Farr, Lee, 185
Farr, Lynne, 417
Farrell, Brian, 420
Farrell, Charles, 491
Farrell, Glenda, 573, 898
Farrell, James T., 496
Farrell, Marty, 913
Farrell, Mike, 177, 344, 426, 435
Farrell, Sharon, 306
Farrell, Skip, 643
Farrell, Tom (Tommy), 266, 705
Farrow, Mia, 555, 587, 834
Fasciano, Richard, 421
Faso, Laurie, 441
Fast, Howard, 929
Fates, Gil, 319, 770, 781
Faulk, John Henry, 483
Faulkner, Eric, 77
Faulkner, William, 414
Faust, Frederick Schiller, See Brand, Max
Fawcett, William, 263
Fawcett-Majors, Farrah (Farrah Fawcett), 141, 334
Fax, Jesslyn, 439
Faye, Herbie, 193, 508, 791
Faye, Janina, 411
Faylen, Carol, 95
Faylen, Frank, 192, 700
Fedderson, Don, 173, 235, 407, 467, 493, 645, 714, 728, 775
Fedderson, Gregg, 235
Fedderson, Tido, 467

Fee, Melinda, 293, 346
Feeney, Joe, 400
Feigel, Sylvia, 671
Fein, Bernie, 791
Feiner, Ben, Jr., 215, 231, 782
Feinstein, Alan, 218, 364, 605
Feist, Felix, 125
Felder, Sarah, 606
Feldkamp, Fred, 440
Feldman, Chester, 132, 318
Feldman, Corey, 69
Feldman, Ed (Edward H.), 658
Feldman, Marty, 281, 443
Feldman, Mindy, 464
Feldon, Barbara, 156, 274, 643, 658
Feldshuh, Tovah, 842
Fell, Norman, 169, 220, 504, 601, 709
Fellig, Arthur H., 499
Fellini, Federico, 830
Fellows, Arthur, 673
Felsher, Howard, 921, 937
Felton, Happy, 302, 349
Felton, Norman, 196, 221, 229, 362, 405, 436, 546, 614, 703
Felton, Verna, 187, 553
Femia, John, 312
Fenady, Andrew, 323
Fennell, Albert, 66
Fennelly, Parker, 309
Fennelly, Vincent, 175, 580, 733, 760
Fenneman, George, 52, 207, 697, 790, 795, 798
Fenwick, Millicent, 687
Ferber, Mel, 137
Ferdin, Pamelyn, 98, 167, 544
Ferguson, Frank, 490, 555, 587
Ferguson, Jason, 63
Fernandez, Abel, 668, 746
Ferrar, Catherine (Cathy), 177, 641
Ferrell, Conchata, 67, 326
Ferrell, Roy, 546
Ferrell, Todd, 396
Ferrer, Jose, 14, 83, 828, 833
Ferrer, Mel, 572
Ferrigno, Lou, 342
Ferrin, Frank, 645
Ferris, Barbara, 672
Ferris, Jack, 235
Ferris, Paul, 74
Ferrone, Dan, 822
Fickett, Mary, 34, 515, 919
Fiedler, Arthur, 227
Fiedler, John, 102, 511
Field, Betty, 447
Field, Frank, 514
Field, Sally, 88, 249, 275, 277, 834, 841, 935
Field, Sylvia, 183, 476

George, Chris, 340, 579, 638
George, Karl (Karl Kindberg), 535
George, Lynda Day (Lynda Day), 472, 600, 638, 822
George, Phyllis, 127, 138, 547
George, Susan, 837
George Tony (Anthony), 142, 525, 620, 746
Georgiade, Nick, 604, 746
Gerard, Gil, 115, 197
Gerard, Merwin, 510, 526
Gerardi, Vito, 917
Gerber, Bill, 240
Gerber, David, 106, 174, 199, 221, 271, 275, 368, 504, 564, 575, 576, 930
Gerber, Joan, 755
Gering, Dick, 440
Gerlach, Ginger, 197
Germain, Stuart, 525
Gernhard, Phil, 365
Gerritsen, Lisa, 446, 494, 557
Gerrity, Patty Ann, 705
Gerry, Roger, 630, 661, 672
Gershman, Ben, 535
Gerstad, Harry, 681
Gerussi, Bruno, 137
Getchell, Robert, 30
Gethers, Steven, 95, 378, 419
Getz, John, 51, 578
Ghostley, Alice, 87, 130, 258, 281, 373, 376, 453, 698
Giamalva, Joe, 394
Gibbon, Samuel Y., Jr., 937
Gibbons, Lewis Grassic, 449
Gibbons, Rob, 52
Gibbs, Georgia, 273
Gibbs, Marla, 362
Gibbs, Terry, 527, 668
Gibney, Hal, 207
Gibney, Jack, 678
Gibson, Amy, 421
Gibson, Don, 81
Gibson, Henry, 273, 398
Gibson, Hoot, 338
Gibson, John, 165, 172, 217, 595
Gibson, Judy, 228
Gibson, Julie, 540
Gibson, Mimi, 767
Gibson, Robert, 52
Gibson, Sam, 908
Gibson, Stella, 448
Gibson, Virginia, 191, 371, 649, 796
Gibson, William, 562
Gideon, Bond, 97, 528
Gielgud, John, 17, 211, 219, 537, 824, 827, 834
Giem, Gary, 793
Gierasch, Stefan, 17
Gifford, Alan, 218, 651
Gifford, Frank, 17, 498, 682

Giftos, Elaine, 344
Gilbert, Alan, 780
Gilbert, Carolyn, 133
Gilbert, Craig, 42
Gilbert, Edmund, 303
Gilbert, Janice, 109, 527
Gilbert, Jody, 408
Gilbert, Johnny, 238, 487
Gilbert, Jonathan, 410
Gilbert, Lauren, 218, 233, 419
Gilbert, Melissa, 410, 847
Gilbert, Nancy, 115
Gilbert, Paul, 209
Gilbert, Ruth, 469, 605
Gilchrist, Connie, 414
Giles, David, 255
Gilfillan, Sue Ann, 624
Gilford, Gwynne, 507, 763
Gilford, Jack, 53, 83, 175, 830, 836, 945
Gill, Brendan, 922
Gill, Michael, 40, 917, 918
Gillespie, Darlene, 463, 464
Gillespie, Dizzy, 814
Gillespie, Gina, 379, 399
Gillette, Anita, 37, 77, 100, 455
Gilliam, Byron, 398
Gilliam, Stu, 281, 598
Gilliam, Terry, 443, 482
Gilligan, Maura, 62
Gilliland, Richard, 411, 455, 528
Gilman, Kenneth, 204, 423
Gilman, Sam, 631
Gilman, Toni, 206
Gilmore, Art, 318
Gilmore, Virginia, 619
Gilpatric, Guy, 279
Gilroy, John, 913, 922
Gim, Asa, 837
Gimbel, Roger, 917
Ging, Jack (Jack L.), 179, 766
Gingold, Hermione, 818
Ginty, Robert, 67, 539
Girard, Henry, 28
Girardin, Ray, 269
Giroux, Fernande, 480
Giroux, Lee, 725
Gish, Dorothy, 221, 556, 594
Gish, Lillian, 252, 556, 830
Gist, Rod, 554, 598
Gitlin, Irv (Irving), 228, 503, 517, 526, 617
Givot, George, 749
Gladke, Peter, 460
Glamourlovelies, 383
Glaser, Paul Michael (Michael), 420, 666
Glass, Kathy (Katherine), 198, 524, 587
Glass, Ned, 110, 376, 791
Glass, Ron, 74
Glauberg, Joe, 483
Glavan, Gene, 433

Hart, Ralph, 424
Hart, Richard, 222
Hart, Stan, 916, 920
Hart, Tony, 752
Hart, Trisha (Patricia Harty), 98, 100, 516, 619
Hartford, John, 278, 648, 652
Hartigan, Bill, 810
Hartley, Mariette, 556, 942
Hartley, Michael Carr, 377
Hartley, Ted, 146
Hartline, Mary, 444, 678
Hartman, David, 104, 284, 423, 751
Hartman, Ena, 169
Hartman, Grace, 305
Hartman, Lisa, 688
Hartman, Paul, 29, 46, 305, 453, 569, 675
Hartmann, Edmund, 227
Harty, Patricia. See Hart, Trisha
Hartz, Jim, 718
Hartzell, Clarence, 707
Harvey, Harry (Harry Sr.), 349
Harvey, Jane, 112
Harvey, Jerry, 81
Harvey, Joan, 217
Harvey, Ken, 620
Harvey, Laurence, 28, 819, 828
Harvey, Marilyn, 780
Hasel, Joe, 16, 571
Hasely, Ruth, 614
Haskell, David, 37
Haskell, Jack, 174, 265, 354, 517
Haskell, Peter, 107, 590
Haslam, Lu Ann, 505
Hasselhoff, David, 792
Hasso, Signe, 390
Hastings, Bob, 65, 178, 271, 454
Hastings, Christopher, 63
Hastings, Don, 61, 131, 217
Hastings, Michael, 915
Hatch, Richard, 34, 77, 254, 673
Hatfield, Bob, 633
Hatfield, Hurd, 211, 321
Hathaway, Donny, 452
Hathaway, Noah, 77
Hatos, Stefan, 348, 350, 403, 447, 659, 708
Hatrak, Eddie, 225
Hauck, Charlie, 53, 64, 452
Hauser, Gayelord, 267
Hauser, Rick 615
Hauser, Tim, 438
Hauser, Wings, 792
Hausner, Jerry, 337, 747
Havinga, Nicholas, 933
Havoc, June, 136, 377, 519, 652, 779, 811
Hawkesworth, John, 920, 926, 930, 934
Hawkins, Jack, 255, 825, 833, 838
Hawkins, Jimmy, 49, 202
Hawkins, Michael, 61, 418, 606

Hawkins, Rick, 940
Hawkins, Screamin' Jay, 811
Hawkins, Tricia P. (Tricia Pursley), 35
Hawkins, Trish, 52
Hawley, Adelaide, 84, 238
Hawley, Cameron, 229
Hawn, Goldie, 284, 398, 833
Haworth, Susanne, 25
Hawthorne, Nathaniel, 614
Hayakawa, Sessue, 390
Hayden, Don, 491
Hayden, Mary, 218
Hayden, Russell, 163, 374, 442, 740
Hayden, Sterling, 211, 823
Haydn, Lili, 380
Haydon, Charles, 783
Hayes, Adrienne, 269
Hayes, Allyson, 19, 269
Hayes, Ben, 62, 293
Hayes, Beverly, 713
Hayes, Bill, 177, 244, 519, 797
Hayes, Billie, 77, 298, 405
Hayes, George ("Gabby"), 264
Hayes, Harold, 740
Hayes, Helen, 82, 573, 574, 594, 615, 649, 808, 809, 812, 816, 830, 841, 844, 887
Hayes, Margaret (Maggie), 92, 713
Hayes, Melvyn, 314
Hayes, Peter Lind, 38, 344, 553, 554, 663, 670
Hayes, Richard, 31, 67, 354, 501, 561, 650, 741
Hayes, Ron, 227, 602
Hayes, Susan Seaforth (Susan Seaforth), 795
Hayling, Patricia, 198
Hayman, Lillian, 402, 524
Haymes, Bob, 348
Haymes, Dick, 572
Haynes, Lloyd, 599
Haynes, Marques, 304
Hays, Kathryn, 62, 593
Hays, Robert, 48
Hayward, Chris, 18, 74, 492, 700, 906
Hayward, David, 755
Hayward, Leland, 701, 807, 815
Hayward, Louis, 413, 684
Hayward, Robert, 369
Hayworth, Rita, 825
Hazam, Lou, 897, 914
Healey, Myron, 788
Healy, Bill, 38
Healy, Jack, 791
Healy, Mary, 344, 553, 554, 663, 670
Heard, Daphne, 448
Heard, John, 615
Hearn, Chick, 357
Hearn, Connie Ann, 507
Hearst, Patty, 283

Heyes, Douglas, 72
Hiatt, Shelby, 269
Hibbs, Albert R., 229
Hickey, Bill, 614
Hickman, Darryl, 44, 193, 381, 418, 420, 789
Hickman, Dwayne, 192, 418, 422
Hickman, Herman, 315
Hickox, Harry, 512
Hicks, Catherine, 69, 606
Hicks, Hilly, 598, 600
Hicks, Russell, 623
Hierl, Jakob, 917
Higgins, Dennis Jay, 606
Higgins, Joe, 228
Higgins, Joel, 608
Higgs, Richard, 197
Hiken, Nat, 131, 468, 791, 890, 892, 897
Hill, Arthur, 534, 817, 833, 841, 987
Hill, Charlie, 985
Hill, Graig, 774
Hill, George Roy, 378, 389, 674
Hill, James, 918
Hill, Pamela, 921, 925
Hill, Phyllis, 269, 709
Hill, Sandy, 284
Hill, Steven, 471, 629, 816
Hill, Walter, 199
Hill, William B., 922
Hillaire, Marcel, 24
Hillard, Robert, 920
Hillerman, John, 85, 222
Hilliard, Harriet. See Nelson, Harriet
Hi-Los, 601
Hilton, Bob, 737
Hilton, Hilary, 682
Hilton, Joy, 258
Hilton-Jacobs, Lawrence, 765
Hinderstein, Howard, 398
Hindle, Art, 386
Hindman, Earl 606
Hindy, Joe, 52
Hines, Connie, 474
Hines, Janear, 376
Hingart, Maureen, 128
Hingle, Pat, 826
Hinkley, Don, 667, 916
Hinn, Michael, 106
Hinnant, Skip, 221, 544
Hinton, Darby, 171
Hirsch, Elroy, 660
Hirsch, Judd, 183, 694, 839
Hirschfeld, Jim, 130, 940
Hirschman, Herbert, 560, 615
Hirson, Alice, 218, 524, 651, 989
Hirt, Al, 236, 433
Hitchcock, Alfred, 29, 845
Hitler, Adolf, 810
Hitzig, Rupert, 613
Ho, Don, 200, 389

Hoade, Martin, 945
Hoag, Mitzi, 313, 766
Hoagland, Everett, 539
Hobbie, Duke, 754
Hobbs, Peter, 623
Hobin, Bill, 639, 906
Hodge, Al, 131
Hodges, Russ, 537, 605
Hodgins, Earle, 291
Hoff, Carl, 101
Hoffman, Abbie, 462
Hoffman, Bernie (Bern), 137, 430
Hoffman, Dustin, 182, 515, 833, 843
Hoffman, Elwood, 235
Hoffman, Gertrude, 491
Hoffman, Harold, 700, 770
Hoffman, Richard, 770
Hoffman, Wendy, 433
Hogan, Jack, 155, 637
Hogan, Jonathan, 198
Hogan, Robert, 171, 201, 269, 439, 528, 591, 794
Holbrook, Hal, 104, 111, 161, 826, 827, 834, 835, 837, 838, 846, 912, 922, 923, 931
Holch, Arthur, 787
Holchak, Victor, 177
Holcomb, Kathryn (Kitty), 328, 989
Holcombe, Harry, 73, 593, 619, 784
Holcum, Tim, 51
Holden, James, 24
Holden, William, 99, 337, 417, 923
Holder, Geoffrey, 643
Holdren, Judd, 156
Holdridge, Cheryl, 464
Holiday, Billie, 629
Holland, Joanna, 730
Holland, Kristina, 163, 755
Holland, Neail, 525
Holland, Richard, 60
Holland, Steve, 247
Hollander, Al, 509
Hollander, David, 455, 507, 769
Hollen, Rebecca, 63
Holliday, Fred, 277
Holliday, Judy, 253, 285, 808
Holliday, Kene, 134
Holliday, Mary, 342
Holliday, Polly, 30
Holliman, Earl, 327, 390, 562, 564, 740, 777
Holliman, Valerie, 448
Hollis, Jeff, 123
Holloway, Freda, 793
Holloway, Stanley, 531
Holloway, Sterling, 70, 407, 779
Holly, Ellen, 524
Holm, Celeste, 69, 83, 322, 501, 572, 806, 823
Holmes, Burton, 118

Jarrin, Mauricio, 161
Jarvis, Graham, 98, 254, 294, 444
Jarvis, Lucy, 823, 827, 900
Jarvis, Martin, 255, 448
Jason, Harvey, 83
Jason, Rick, 155, 170
Jastrow, Terry, 930
Jay, Oren, 420
Jayne, Jennifer, 779
Jefferson, Herb, Jr., 77
Jeffreys, Anne, 182, 422, 733, 809
Jeffries, Fran, 832
Jeffries, Herb, 773
Jeffries, Lang, 586
Jeffries, Vance, 525
Jellinek, Tristam, 448
Jenkins, Allen, 209, 315
Jenkins, Carol Mayo, 52
Jenkins, Hayes Alan, 810
Jenkins, Leroy, 587
Jenkins, Mark, 793
Jenks, Frank, 154
Jenner, Barry, 52, 651
Jenner, Bruce, 41, 284, 682
Jenner, Chrystie, 284
Jennings, Peter, 15
Jennings, Waylon, 209
Jensen, Karen, 108
Jensen, Maren, 77
Jerome, Ed, 419
Jerome, Jerry, 785
Jessel, George, 37, 155, 272
Jessup, Hubert, 77
Jewison, Norman, 375
Jillian, Ann, 308
Jillson, Joyce, 556, 609
Jo, Damita, 585
Jobim, Antonio Carlos, 828
Joblin, Monia, 937
Joel, Dennis, 84
Joelson, Ben, 160, 916
Johann, John Lee, 463
John Birch Society, 825
John, Elton, 142, 845
John, Tom, 952
John Paul II, 846
Johns, Glynis, 279
Johnson, Arch, 63, 395
Johnson, Arte, 70, 81, 203, 273, 282, 350, 387, 398, 439, 608, 908
Johnson, Bayn, 770
Johnson, Ben, 481
Johnson, Bess, 619
Johnson, Betty, 216, 726
Johnson, Brad, 49
Johnson, Bruce, 410, 575, 637
Johnson, Cathie Lee, 311, 501
Johnson, Charles F., 938
Johnson, Chic, 243
Johnson, Coslough, 369, 906

Johnson, Don, 986
Johnson, Gail, 178, 705
Johnson, Gary, 925
Johnson, Georgiann (Georgann), 63, 207, 476, 651
Johnson, Gerald W., 947
Johnson, Gerry, 248
Johnson, Janet Louise, 67, 303
Johnson, Jarrod, 258, 416, 686
Johnson, Jay, 137, 650
Johnson, Judy, 725, 797
Johnson, June, 244
Johnson, Kenneth, 96, 150, 343
Johnson, Luci Baines, 825
Johnson, Lyndon B., 121, 825, 835
Johnson, Mrs. Lyndon B. (Lady Bird), 952
Johnson, Michael, 332
Johnson, Nicholas, 647
Johnson, Ray, 535
Johnson, Russell, 96, 276, 505
Johnson, Stephen, 150
Johnson, Sterling, 913
Johnson, Tania, 69
Johnson, Timothy, 18, 284
Johnson, Van, 745, 812
Johnson, Virginia, 41
Johnston, Amy, 114
Johnston, Audre, 624
Johnston, Charles, 703
Johnston, Jane, 772
Johnston, John Dennis, 179
Johnston, Johnny, 323, 371, 383, 433
Johnston, Lionel, 51, 655
Johnstone, William, 62
Joliffe, David, 600
Joliffe, Dorothy, 583
Jolley, Norman, 147, 657
Jones, Amanda, 178
Jones, Anissa, 234
Jones, Archdale, 383
Jones, Arthur, 778
Jones, Arthur E., 52
Jones, Barry, 814
Jones, Candy, 663
Jones, Carol, 793
Jones, Carolyn, 22
Jones, Charlie, 38
Jones, Chris, 402
Jones, Christine, 51, 251, 423, 525
Jones, Chuck, 167, 826, 830
Jones, Clifton, 149, 657
Jones, Davy, 480
Jones, Dean, 144, 223, 769
Jones, Dick, 115, 579
Jones, Edgar Allan, Jr., 19, 176, 734
Jones, Gemma, 449
Jones, Ginger, 86
Jones, Gordon, 18, 581, 649
Jones, Henry, 21, 29, 140, 380, 557
Jones, James, 496, 986

Kirkwood, Jack, 523
Kirkwood, James, Jr., 747
Kirkwood, Joe, Jr., 368
Kirshner, Don, 200, 381, 384, 480, 789
Kiser, Terry, 197, 598, 624
Kitchell, James W., 909
Kitt, Eartha, 75, 562
Klee, Larry, 434
Kleeb, Helen, 304, 553, 759
Klein, Larry, 913
Klein, Robert, 156
Kleinerman, Isaac, 905
Klemperer, Werner, 318, 905, 907
Klenck, Margaret, 525
Klick, Mary, 272, 365
Kline, Kevin, 620
Kline, Richard, 709
Kling, Woody, 381, 468, 612, 789, 916, 920
Kloiber, Herbert, 944
Kloss, Bud, 36
Klous, Pat, 249
Kluge, George, 703
Klugman, Jack, 131, 289, 304, 516, 571, 577, 899, 912, 919
Knapp, David, 251, 422
Knapp, Robert, 99, 177
Kneeland, Ted, 395
Knight, Al ("Fuzzy"), 129
Knight, Christopher, 108
Knight, Don, 341
Knight, Evelyn, 468
Knight, Gladys, 278
Knight, Jack, 416, 567
Knight, Merald ("Bubba"), 278
Knight, Shirley. See Hopkins, Shirley Knight
Knight, Ted, 150, 445, 694, 919, 932
Knight, Viva, 37
Knotts, Don, 46, 200, 266, 299, 619, 667, 668, 709, 816, 895, 897, 898, 901, 903
Knox, Harold, 170
Knudsen, Albert T., 256
Knudsen, Peggy, 649
Kobe, Gail, 111
Kochheim, Lory, 486
Koenig, Walter, 664
Kogen, Arnie, 920, 925, 929
Kohan, Alan Buz (Buz), 531, 920, 937
Kolb, Clarence, 491
Kolden, Scott, 455, 637
Kollmar, Dick, 291, 635
Komack, James, 49, 145, 163, 312, 476, 477, 598, 676, 765
Kominsky, Sherry, 136
Konrad, Dorothy, 397
Koock, Guich, 134
Koontz, Mel, 559
Kopell, Bernie, 204, 417, 504, 700, 772
Koplin, Mert, 441

Korman, Harvey, 133, 171, 305, 824, 908, 912, 915, 923
Kortner, Peter, 370
Korty, John, 924, 943
Korvin, Charles, 344, 638
Koslo, Paul, 601
Koss, Alan, 198
Kotlowitz, Robert, 917
Kotto, Yaphet, 842
Kovacs, Ernie, 224–225, 265, 298, 314, 338, 638, 689, 713 725, 810, 811
Kove, Marty (Martin Cove), 151, 768
Kowalski, Bernard (Bernard L.), 73, 580
Kozloff, Charles, 929
Kraft, Beatrice, 810
Kramer, Bert, 246, 612
Kramer, Jeffrey, 673
Kramer, Mandel, 217
Kramer, Stepfanie, 442
Krantz, Steve, 569
Kraus, Conrad, 917
Kraut, Harry, 930
Krayer, James, 913
Kreskin, 40
Krinski, Sandy, 68, 925
Kristen, Ilene, 606
Kristen, Martha, 415
Kroeger, Barry, 661
Krofft, Marty, 116, 203, 237, 298, 391, 394, 405, 416, 637
Krofft, Sid, 116, 203, 237, 298, 391, 394, 405, 416, 637
Krolik, Dick, 440
Krolik, Jeffrey, 619
Kronman, Harry, 572
Kruger, Otto, 425
Krumholz, Chester, 564
Krupa, Gene, 812, 813, 814
Kruschen, Jack, 118, 324
Krutch, Joseph Wood, 820, 823
Kubec, Russell, 651
Kuda Bux, 391
Kugel, Frederick, 351
Kuhlman, Kathryn, 334
Ku Klux Klan, 825
Kukoff, Bernie, 185, 189, 366, 367, 528
Kulky, Henry, 312, 407
Kulp, Nancy, 86, 410, 422
Kuluva, Will, 569
Kunner, Eloise, 703
Kupcinet, Irv, 392, 725
Kupcinet, Karyn, 478
Kuralt, Charles, 122, 230, 777, 825, 907, 953, 956
Kurty, Lee, 196
Kurtz, Swoosie, 444
Kutash, Jeff, 746
Kwartin, Leslie, 292

Larch, John, 57, 818
Larken, Sheila, 670
Larkin, Dick, 411
Larkin, John, 159, 217, 608, 738
LaRoche, Mary, 379
LaRosa, Julius, 58–59, 376, 688, 810
Larrain, Mike, 451
Larroquette, John, 67
Larsen, Keith, 54, 109, 333, 513
Larsen, Larry, 464
Larson, Charles, 500, 987
Larson, Dennis, 366
Larson, Glen (Glen A.), 67, 77, 273, 303, 453, 470, 577, 685, 686
Larson, Jack, 680
LaRue, Jack, 409
LaRue, Lash, 396
LaRussa, Adrienne, 177
Laryea, Wayne, 116
Lasky, Zane, 397, 731
Lassen, Leigh, 619
Lasser, Louise, 256, 444
LaStarza, Roland, 264
Latessa, Dick, 218
Latham, Louise, 612
Latham, Philip, 537
Latimore, Frank, 294, 606
Lau, Wesley, 550, 713
Laughlin, Lisa, 642
Laughlin, Tom, 150
Laughton, Charles, 142, 215, 563, 705
Lauher, Bobby, 689
Laurel, Stan, 706
Lauren, Tammy, 48, 532, 777
Laurence, John, 904, 907, 922
Lauret, Laryssa, 197, 294
Laurie, Kimetha, 419
Laurie, Piper, 299, 562, 629, 842, 989
Lauson, Michael, 527
Lauter, Harry, 691
Lavalle, Paul, 71
Laven, Arnold, 592
Laver, Rod, 926
Lavery, Emmet G., 627
Lavin, Linda, 30
Lawford, Peter, 180, 204, 253, 704, 818
Lawlor, John, 233, 558
Lawrence, Anthony, 388
Lawrence, Bill (William H.), 58, 916, 951
Lawrence, Carol, 749, 818, 829
Lawrence, David, 87
Lawrence, Elliott, 460, 512, 583
Lawrence, Elizabeth, 198, 593, 786
Lawrence, Greg, 87
Lawrence, Mark, 30
Lawrence, Mary, 135, 422
Lawrence, Mort, 90
Lawrence, Steve, 15, 47, 666, 669, 724, 812, 823, 844, 942
Lawrence, Susan, 391

Lawrence, Taula, 610
Lawrence, Vicki, 133, 932
Laws, Sam, 567
Lawson, Lee, 419, 524
Lawson, Linda, 24, 203
Layton, George, 195
Layton, Jerry, 167
Lazar, Peter, 619, 719
Lazarus, Bill, 125
Lazer, David, 938
Leace, Donal, 635
Leach, Britt, 658
Leachman, Cloris, 29, 69, 100, 141, 319, 396, 446, 556, 557, 692, 835, 836, 919, 923, 928
Leacock, Philip, 297, 306, 507
Leahy, Frank, 256, 580
Leak, Jennifer, 52, 793
Leal, Agapito, 134
Lear, Joyce, 720
Lear, Norman, 31, 37, 53, 77, 209, 241, 285, 300, 312, 324, 326, 342, 362, 381, 444, 451, 452, 522, 611, 650, 699, 789, 910, 911, 913, 916, 958
Learned, Michael, 759, 918, 923, 931
Leary, Brianne, 67, 123
Leblanc, Diana, 685
LeCornec, Bill, 331
Leder, Herb, 393
Lederer, Suzanne, 220
Lee, Anna, 172, 271
Lee, Bonnie, 429
Lee, Brenda, 534
Lee, Bruce, 290
Lee, Cherylene, 383
Lee, Christopher, 66, 206
Lee, Costee, 671
Lee, Diana, 179
Lee, Dick, 695
Lee, Georgia, 662
Lee, Gypsy Rose, 298, 377, 573, 704, 829
Lee, Helen, 677
Lee, Irving, 219, 679
Lee, James, 526, 578
Lee, Joanna, 486, 925
Lee, Mrs. John G., 567
Lee, Johnny, 45
Lee, Manfred, 221
Lee, Michele, 282, 987
Lee, Patsy, 201
Lee, Peggy, 667, 688, 836
Lee, Pinky, 295, 463, 559, 707
Lee, Robert E., 822
Lee, Ruta, 317, 538
Lee, Stuart, 177
Lee, Sunshine, 486
Lee, Theodis, 304
Lee, Virginia Ann, 270
Lee, Will, 628
Leech, Richard, 449

Melvin, Allan, 33, 282, 791
Melvin, Donny, 623
Memmoli, George, 312
Mendels, Rolanda, 52, 945
Mendelson, Lee, 326, 901, 904, 930, 931
Mendenhall, Francie, 281
Mendoza, Kathy, 989
Menella, Buddy, 716
Mengatti, John, 775
Menges, Joyce, 714
Menjou, Adolphe, 490, 693
Menken, Shepard, 39
Menkin, Lawrence, 300, 597
Menotti, Gian Carlo, 299, 806, 946
Menzies, Heather, 412
Merande, Doro, 112, 701
Mercer, Johnny, 457, 489
Mercer, Marian, 179, 200, 254, 444, 611,
    733, 754
Merchant, Larry, 287
Meredith, Burgess, 75, 91, 239, 388, 476,
    617, 842, 847, 936
Meredith, Charles, 597
Meredith, Cheerio, 523
Meredith, Don, 498, 911
Meredith, Judi, 327
Meriwether, Lee (Lee Ann), 73, 75, 150,
    447, 505, 713, 717
Merlin, Jan, 602, 720, 929
Merman, Ethel, 75, 375, 807, 817, 827, 829,
    835
Merrill, Carol, 403
Merrill, Gary, 29, 378, 446, 586, 743, 782,
    793
Merrill, Robert, 797, 805
Merriman, Randy, 90
Merritt, Theresa, 702
Merson, Marc, 381, 763
Merton, Zienia, 657
Mesak, Charles, 886
Meshekoff, Michael, 668
Meskill, Katherine, 197, 619, 773
Messick, Don, 364, 789
Messner, Johnny, 750
Mesta, Perle, 238
Meston, John, 295
Metalious, Grace, 555
Metcalfe, Burt, 239, 301, 426
Metcalfe, Ken, 794
Mettey, Lynnette, 577
Metrano, Art, 45, 144, 423, 486, 711
Metz, Robert, 59
Metzinger, Kraig, 451, 612
Meyer, Anton, 83
Meyerink, Victoria, 171
Michael, George, 462
Michael, Marjorie, 462
Michael, Paul, 486
Michael, Ralph, 195

Michaelis, Arnold, 22
Michaels, Al, 682
Michaels, Corinne, 178
Michaels, Frankie, 62
Michaels, Lorne, 498, 930, 934, 936
Michaels, Marilyn, 15
Michaels, Ray, 610
Michaux, Solomon Lightfoot, 221
Michel, Franny, 53
Michell, Keith, 640, 915
Michelman, Ken, 774
Michenaud, Gerald, 714
Michener, James, 24, 65, 88
Mickey, Patricia, 281
Middleton, Tom, 595
Midgley, Leslie, 921
Midler, Bette, 142, 748, 843, 938
Mikler, Mike, 794
Milan, Frank, 783
Milano, Frank, 600
Miles, Hank, 267
Miles, Joanna, 34, 713, 838, 923
Miles, Richard, 84
Miles, Sherry, 311, 542
Miles, Vera, 841
Milford, John, 405
Milgrim, Lynn, 52
Milkis, Edward K., 98, 302, 399, 554
Millan, Robyn, 772
Milland, Ray, 83, 441, 580, 589
Millar, Marjie, 580
Miller, Alan, 87
Miller, Allan, 17, 329, 524
Miller, Arthur, 825, 827, 904
Miller, Barry, 367, 686
Miller, Cheryl, 168
Miller, Cory, 33
Miller, Dean, 146, 181, 314
Miller, Denise, 245, 433
Miller, Denny, 480, 755
Miller, Dorothy, 724
Miller, Gary, 370
Miller, Glenn, 279
Miller, Harvey, 640
Miller, Herman, 392, 436
Miller, Howard, 26, 151, 329 378
Miller, Jack, 54
Miller, James M., 478
Miller, J. P., 829, 908
Miller, J. Phillip, 931
Miller, J. R., 584
Miller, Kathleen, 640
Miller, Kristine, 670
Miller, Lee, 142, 550
Miller, Marilyn Suzanne, 498, 934, 936
Miller, Mark, 111, 178, 270, 299, 500, 563
Miller, Marvin, 467
Miller, Mitch, 253, 638
Miller, Pamela, 620

Neal, Patricia, 759, 817, 834, 842
Nearing, Vivian, 739
Nedwell, Robin, 195
Negri, Joe, 477
Negron, Taylor, 185
Neher, Susan, 274, 714
Nehru, Jawaharlal, 645, 782
Neil, Gloria, 412
Neill, Noel, 681
Neise, George, 777
Nelkin, Stacey, 146, 986
Nelson, Barry, 333, 489, 761
Nelson, Bek, 400
Nelson, Christine, 580
Nelson, Christopher (Christopher Stafford), 152, 271, 655
Nelson, Craig Richard, 133, 259
Nelson, Dave, 535, 536
Nelson, Don, 535
Nelson, Ed, 199, 213, 555, 587, 638
Nelson, Frank, 301, 337, 353
Nelson, Harriet (Harriet Hilliard), 535, 536
Nelson, Haywood, 284, 769
Nelson, Herb, 111, 177, 292
Nelson, Jane, 262, 504
Nelson, Jerry, 926, 933, 938, 945
Nelson, Jimmy, 155, 469
Nelson, John, 110, 411, 796
Nelson, Kenneth, 28
Nelson, Kris, 536
Nelson, Lori, 329
Nelson, Mervyn, 401
Nelson, Nan-Lynn, 326
Nelson, Ozzie, 535, 536
Nelson, Ralph, 434, 562, 891
Nelson, Rick, 21, 41, 434, 535, 536
Nemoto, Mitsuyo, 988
Nesbitt, Cathleen, 238, 815, 923, 924
Nesbitt, Joun, 696
Nesmith, Mike, 480
Ness, Eliot, 745
Nessen, Ron, 497
Nettleton, Lois, 14, 19, 37, 111, 761, 937
Neuchateau, Corinne, 421
Neufeld, Mace, 128, 575
Neuhaus, Lacey, 986
Neuman, Alan, 233
Neuman, E. Jack, 380, 435, 476, 500
Neun, Mike, 189
Nevard, Billy, 767
Nevil, Steve, 455
Neville, John, 447
Nevins, Allan, 572
Nevins, Claudette, 309, 333, 442
New Christy Minstrels, 47, 506
New Doodletown Pipers, 433
New Seekers, 383
New York City Ballet, 824
New Yorkers, 371

Newall, George, 941, 944
Newark, Derek, 448
Newell, Dave (David), 246, 477
Newell, Patrick, 66
Newhart, Bob, 102, 224, 321
Newlan, Paul, 427
Newland, John, 415, 437, 510, 526, 594, 595
Newman, Barry, 218, 554
Newman, Edwin, 156, 219, 503, 717, 719, 821, 827
Newman, Jolie, 584
Newman, Laraine, 497
Newman, Paul, 29, 170, 285, 378, 446, 563, 571, 743, 831, 833
Newman, Phyllis, 185, 701, 715, 790
Newman, Roger, 293
Newmar, Julie, 75, 492
Newton, Connie, 220
Newton, John, 198
Newton, Richard, 306
Newton, Robert, 414
Newton, Wayne, 357
Nicassio, JoeAl, 741
Nicholas, Denise, 68, 599
Nicholl, Don, 210, 362, 601, 709
Nichols, Anthony, 139
Nichols, Barbara, 422, 637
Nichols, Josephine, 713
Nichols, Mike, 210, 234, 398, 563, 814, 815
Nichols, Nichelle, 664
Nicholson, Bobby, 295, 330
Nicholson, Carol, 599
Nicholson, Erwin, 217, 917
Nicholson, Jack, 307, 766
Nicholson, Nick, 659
Nickell, Paul, 674
Nickerson, Dawn, 304
Nickerson, Denise, 619
Nickerson, Shane, 294
Nielsen, Leslie, 69, 104, 108, 285, 506, 692, 757
Nigh, Jane, 92
Nigro, Giovanna, 689
Niles, Wendell, 347
Nilsson, Harry, 883
Nimmo, Bill, 251, 382, 537, 775
Nimoy, Leonard, 160, 341, 472, 664, 767
Nisbet, Steve, 620
Nite, Norm, 38
Niven, David, 28, 175, 255, 597
Niven, Paul, 761
Nix, Martha, 178, 760
Nixon, Agnes, 34, 50, 292, 523, 618
Nixon, Richard, 175, 398, 726, 807, 811, 822, 835, 838
Noah, Robert, 327, 430
Noble, Jim (James), 60, 81, 111, 786
Noble, Trisha, 229
Nodella, Burt, 904, 906

Paul, Les, 815
Paul, Norman, 522
Paul, Richard, 134, 988
Pauley, Jane, 719
Paulsen, Albert, 199, 786, 899
Paulsen, Pat, 278, 369, 542, 648, 905
Pavan, Marisa, 378, 828
Pawluk, Mira, 479
Payne, Benny, 94
Payne, John, 82, 586, 615
Peabody, Dick, 155
Peadon, Pamela, 844
Peaker, E. J., 701
Peale, Norman Vincent, 771
Peal, Mrs. Norman Vincent, 771
Pearce, Al, 27
Pearce, Alice, 30, 87, 361, 901
Pearcy, Patricia, 525
Peardon, Pat, 372, 747
Pearl, Barry, 123
Pearl, Minnie, 311
Pearlman, Rodney, 25
Pearlman, Stephen, 333
Pearlman, Sy, 957
Pearson, Ann, 619, 747
Pearson, Billy, 642, 643
Pearson, Drew, 208, 761
Pearson, Leon, 495
Pearson, Lester B., 552
Peary, Hal, 98, 242, 288, 779
Peck, Ed, 430, 678
Peck, Gregory, 827, 845
Peck, Jim, 91, 324, 621, 629, 709
Peckinpah, Sam, 592, 767
Peden, Emily, 510
Pedi, Tom, 56, 661, 662
Peeples, Samuel, 167, 394, 692
Peerce, Jan, 527
Peigelbeck, Will, 323
Peine, Josh, 203
Pelikan, Lisa, 78, 497
Pelletier, Gilles, 578
Pelligrini, Gene, 419
Peluce, Meeno, 69
Peluso, Lisa, 620
Penberthy, Beverly, 50
Pence, Denise, 294
Pendleton, David, 36, 293
Pendleton, Karen, 463
Pendleton, Wyman, 219
Penn, Arthur, 562
Penn, Leo, 478
Penn, Leonard, 597
Pennell, Larry, 592
Pennell, Nicholas, 254
Penney, Hannibal, Jr., 606
Pennington, Marla, 270
Pennock, Chris, 271, 651
Penny, Don, 405, 754
Pentecost, George, 97

Peppard, George, 71, 198, 299, 390
Pepper, Cynthia, 440
Peppiatt, Frank, 304, 382, 633, 654
Pera, Radames, 392
Perault, Robert, 35
Percival, Lance, 776
Perelman, S. J., 629
Peretz, Susan, 17
Perew, Tom, 945
Perez, Anthony, 566, 819
Perez, José, 125, 521
Perez, Raul, 510
Perkins, Anthony (Tony), 389, 844
Perkins, Carl, 371
Perkins, David, 62
Perkins, Gay, 510
Perkins, Jack, 569
Perkins, John, 578, 606
Perkins, Marlin, 778, 800
Perkins, Voltaire, 192
Perlmutter, A. H., 288, 911, 914
Peropat, Gloria, 689
Perreau, Gigi, 84, 250
Perret, Gene, 925, 929, 940
Perrin, Nat, 22, 491
Perrin, Sam, 353, 894
Perrine, Valerie, 844
Perrito, Jennifer, 433
Perry, Barbara, 812
Perry, Dick, 544
Perry, Eleanor, 903, 920
Perry, Elizabeth, 484
Perry, Felton, 451
Perry, Jim, 132
Perry, John Bennett, 228, 741
Perry, Joseph, 93
Perry, Rod, 607
Perry, Roger, 57, 304
Perschy, Maria, 271
Persky, Bill, 88, 189, 263, 284, 416, 481, 700, 797, 899, 902, 903, 906
Persoff, Nehemiah, 562, 571, 572
Pertwee, Jon, 196
Pescow, Donna, 48
Petal, Erica, 100
Peters, Audrey, 419
Peters, Bernadette, 37, 832
Peters, Holly, 198
Peters, Jennifer, 270
Peters, Ken, 408
Peters, Pamela. *See* Solow, Pamela
Peters, Scott, 273
Peters, Susan, 471
Petersen, Chris, 77
Petersen, Patrick J., 379
Petersen, Patty, 202
Petersen, Paul, 202, 208, 464
Peterson, Arthur, 165, 650, 702
Peterson, Gene, 419
Peterson, Houston, 702

Peterson, James A., 251
Peterson, Lenka, 105, 620, 621, 713
Peterson, Maggie, 93
Peterson, Renny, 431
Peterson, Virgilia, 65
Petrie, Dan (Daniel), 229, 470, 675, 933, 936
Petrie, Doris, 316
Petrie, George, 61, 619
Pettet, Joanna, 83
Pettit, Tom, 906, 909, 922, 953
Pettus, Ken, 450
Petty, Ross, 35
Pewowar, Jules, 478
Peyser, John, 165, 583, 665
Peyser, Penny, 590, 731
Pfander, Carol, 198
Pfeiffer, Michele, 182, 985
Pfister, Wally, 914
Pfizer, Beryl, 717
Pflug, Jo Ann, 127, 528
Phares, Frank, 499
Phelps, Eleanor, 623
Phelps, Robert, 620
Phelps, Stuart, 408
Philbin, Jack, 357
Philbin, Regis, 370, 504, 585
Philbrick, Herbert A., 334
Philbrook, James, 345, 347, 507
Philipp, Karen, 423, 426
Philips, Lee, 222, 675
Phillips, Anton, 657
Phillips, Barney, 85, 207, 241, 372, 738
Phillips, Carmen, 405
Phillips, Conrad, 448, 779
Phillips, Irna, 50, 56, 111, 176, 292, 417, 523, 593, 703, 785
Phillips, Kathryn, 785
Phillips, Mackenzie, 522
Phillips, Nancie, 398
Phillips, Robin, 832
Phillips, Sian, 449
Phillips, Tacey, 152
Phillips, Wendy, 216, 229
Phillips, William F., 149
Philpott, John, 116
Phipps, William, (William Edward), 612, 712
Piazza, Ben, 123, 763
Piazza, Marguerite, 420, 797
Picard, Paul R., 209
Picerni, Paul, 746, 794
Pick and Pat, 558
Pickard, Jack (John), 106, 295
Pickard Family, 677
Pickens, Jane, 359
Pickens, Slim, 67, 167, 533
Pickering, Bob, 292
Pickett, Cindy, 294
Pickles, Christina, 52, 293

Picon, Molly, 479, 652
Pidgeon, Walter, 550, 813, 814, 819, 823, 840
Piekarski, Julie, 233, 464
Pierce, Barbara, 479
Pierce, Maggie, 492
Pierce, Verna, 621
Pierce, Webb, 534, 764
Pierpoint, Robert, 922
Pierson, Lin, 293
Pike, James A., 43
Pillar, Gary, 50, 292
Pinassi, Dominique, 481
Pincus, Irving, 222, 475, 582
Pincus, Norman, 222, 475
Pine, Robert, 82, 123, 566
Pine, Tina, 566
Pines, Gayle, 620
Pingitore, Carl 564, 930
Pinkard, Ron, 222
Pinkerton, Nancy, 524, 652
Pinkham, Dick, 719
Pinn, Irene, 920
Pinset, Gordon, 254
Pinsker, Judith, 941, 945
Pinza, Ezio, 37, 105, 230, 807, 808
Pisani, Remo, 586
Pithey, Winsley, 607
Pitlik, Noam, 102, 340, 943
Pitt, Norman, 607
Pittman, Frank, 75
Pitts, ZaSu, 117, 518
Place, Lou, 194
Place, Mary Kay, 254, 444, 935
Plank, Melinda, 515, 619, 652
Plante, Bill, 914
Plantt-Winston, Susan, 35
Plato, Dana, 189
Platt, Ed, 269, 274
Platt, Howard, 249, 611
Platt, Louise, 299
Platts, Alma, 703
Playdon, Paul, 512
Player, Gary, 138
Playten, Alice, 416
Pleasance, Donald, 596, 828, 837
Pleasence, Angela, 640
Pleshette, John, 842, 987
Pleshette, Suzanne, 102, 303, 828
Plowman, Melinda, 536
Plumb, Eve, 108, 411
Plumb, Flora, 251, 423
Plummer, Christopher, 299, 519, 815, 830, 935
Podell, Art, 506
Pogostin, S. Lee, 815
Pohle, Robin, 178
Pohlman, Ray, 634
Poindexter, Ron, 279
Poitier, Sidney, 557, 565

Reid, Tim, 591, 754
Reiko, 726
Reilly, Charles Nelson, 56, 275, 281, 348, 405, 669, 744
Reilly, David, 525
Reilly, Hugh, 149, 218, 396, 687
Reilly, Jack, 466
Reilly, John, 61
Reilly, Mike, 162
Reilly, Susan, 417
Reiner, Carl, 33, 123, 137, 189, 208, 238, 243, 283, 284, 382, 409, 416, 506, 637, 689, 797, 891, 892, 897, 898, 899, 900, 903
Reiner, Rob, 33, 258, 678, 923, 939
Reinholt, George, 51, 525
Reis, Vivian, 316
Reischauer, Edwin O., 909
Reischl, Geri, 108
Reisner, Allen, 401
Reissman, Ronald, 911
Reitman, Ivan, 182
Remes, Jorie, 460
Remey, Ethel, 62
Remick, Lee, 288, 299, 389, 390, 818, 838, 839
Remsen, Bert, 275
Renaldo, Duncan, 148
Rende, Louis, 917
Renella, Pat, 508
Renier, Yves, 23
Rennick, Nancy, 383
Rennie, Michael, 704
Renzi, Eva, 569
Reo, Don, 142
Repp, Stafford, 75, 508
Rescher, Dee Dee, 189
Resin, Dan, 520
Rettig, Tommy, 396–397, 504
Revere, Ann, 620
Revere, Paul, and the Raiders, 301, 351, 772
Rey Alejandro, 250, 644
Reynolds, Burt, 169, 307, 427, 562, 593
Reynolds, Debbie, 15, 152, 180, 216
Reynolds, Frank, 16, 831, 835, 953
Reynolds, Gene, 379, 416, 426, 600, 908, 920, 928, 933, 941
Reynolds, James, 712
Reynolds, Jay, 615
Reynolds, Katherine, 650
Reynolds, Marjorie, 407
Reynolds, Mary, 732
Reynolds, Michael J., 618
Reynolds, Quentin, 529
Reynolds, Sheldon, 253, 633
Reynolds, William, 231, 264, 347, 553
Rhilo, 382
Rhoades, Barbara, 99, 118, 137, 300
Rhodes, Donnelly, 792

Rhodes, Elise, 695
Rhodes, George, 610
Rhodes, Hari, 104, 168
Rhodes, Michael, 222, 528
Rhue, Madlyn, 107, 229
Rice, Allan, 703
Rice, Howard, 599
Rice, Rosemary, 434
Rich, Adam, 220
Rich, Buddy, 66, 440
Rich, David, 564, 792
Rich, David Lowell, 940
Rich, John, 227, 521, 898, 916, 954
Rich, Lee, 53, 91, 99, 169, 220, 315, 579, 760, 763, 916
Richard, Cliff, 517
Richard, Darryl, 202
Richards, Addison, 81, 242, 547
Richards, Beah, 93, 601
Richards, Cully, 203
Richards, Danny, Jr., 779
Richards, Grant, 203, 250
Richards, Jeff, 361
Richards, Kim, 312, 314, 502
Richards, Lisa, 525, 772
Richards, Mark, 275
Richards, Paul, 110
Richards, Stan, 683
Richardson, Chuck, 274
Richardson, James, 637
Richardson, Lee, 294
Richardson, Michael, 141
Richardson, Ralph, 821, 832, 834
Richardson, Susan, 220
Richman, Harry, 468
Richman, Joan, 915
Richman, (Peter) Mark, 124, 414
Richmond, Bill, 925, 929, 940
Rickey, Fred, 520
Rickles, Don, 123, 201, 661
Rickover, Hyman, 645
Riddle, Hal, 178
Riddle, Nelson, 278, 502, 602
Riddle, Sam, 274, 319
Ridgely, Robert, 264
Ridgeway, Agnes, 233
Rifkin, M. J., 908, 909
Rifkin, Ron, 21, 333, 445, 772
Riger, Ellie, 930
Riger, Robert, 907
Rigg, Diana, 66, 186, 839
Riggs, Bobby, 138, 837
Righteous Brothers, 633
Rigsby, Gordon, 294, 624
Riha, Bobby, 180
Riley, Jack, 102, 382
Riley, Jeannine, 211, 311, 555
Rinard, Florence, 739
Ring, Bill, 691
Ringwold, Molly, 233

Roter, Diane, 751
Rotfeld, Bert, 289
Roth, Audrey, 477
Roth, Jack, 366
Roth, Leon, 238
Roth, Lillian, 562, 743
Roth, Paul, 155
Rothenberger, Joe, 930
Rothman, Bernard, 630, 752, 931
Rothman, Mark, 118, 433, 695
Rothschild, Harry S., 578
Rothschild, Sigmund, 734, 770
Rounds, David, 78, 420
Roundtree, Richard, 600, 630
Rounseville, Robert, 460
Rountree, Martha, 382, 401, 458, 568
Rouse, Russell, 711
Rousseau, Diane, 420
Roux, Carol, 50, 651
Rowan, Dan, 398, 603, 648, 811, 827, 906
Rowan, Gay, 665
Rowbottom, Jo, 411
Rowe, Misty, 302, 311, 772
Rowe, Red, 232, 584, 697
Rowland, Jada, 197, 623
Rowland, Jeff, 61
Rowlands, Gena, 29, 220, 594
Rowles, Polly, 181, 359, 420, 515, 652
Roxanne (Dolores Rosedale), 79
Roy, Renee, 420
Royal Shakespeare Company, 830
Royal Teens, 188
Royce, Roberta, 624
Ruark, Robert, 819
Ruben, Aaron, 123, 267, 282, 309, 468, 612
Ruben, Tom, 123
Rubin, Benny, 81, 353, 669
Rubin, Ron, 359
Rubin, Stanley, 229, 546
Rubin, Theodore Isaac, 157
Rubino, George, 940
Rubinstein, Artur, 909
Rubinstein, John, 234
Rubinstein, Phil, 785
Ruby, Joe, 236
Rucker, Barbara, 62
Rucker, Dennis, 275
Rudd, Hughes, 121, 957
Rudd, Paul, 78
Rudie, Evelyn, 562
Rudley, Herb, 462, 480, 485
Rudolph, Oscar, 333
Rudy, Martin, 62
Rugg, John, 664
Ruggles, Charles, 604, 786
Ruick, Barbara, 62
Ruick, Melville, 149, 203
Ruiz, Isaac, 145
Rukeyser, Louis, 755

Rule, Janice, 816, 818, 819
Ruman, Sig, 408
Rundle, Robbie, 152
Runyon, Damon, 169
Rush, Barbara, 425, 507, 562, 608, 815
Rusher, William, 26
Rushmore, Karen, 704
Rusk, Dean, 552
Rusk, Jim, 925, 934
Ruskin, Jeannie, 218
Ruskin, Shimen, 160
Russ, Debbie, 314
Russ, William, 52
Russel, Del, 56
Russell, A. J., 892
Russell, Bertrand, 782
Russell, Bob, 662, 749, 799
Russell, Clive, 631
Russell, Connie, 265, 469
Russell, Don, 666
Russell, Ellie, 363
Russell, Gordon, 524
Russell, Jack, 797
Russell, Jeannie, 184
Russell, Jimmy, 265
Russell, John, 360, 400, 651
Russell, Kurt, 507, 576, 734, 845
Russell, Lee, 190
Russell, Leon, 634
Russell, Marion, 289
Russell, Mark, 388, 665
Russell, Nipsey, 73, 132, 156, 179, 447, 512
Russell, Ron, 587, 752
Russell, Rosalind, 255, 268, 615, 813
Russell, Theresa, 98
Russell, Todd, 600, 771
Russell, William, 215, 639
Russo, Aaron, 938
Russo, Barry, 794
Russo, Jordeann, 793
Russom, Leon, 51, 418
Rust, Richard, 609
Rutherford, Angelo, 271
Rutherford, Lori Ann, 505
Rutherford, Margaret, 823
Ruymen, Ayn, 455
Ryan, Bill, 646
Ryan, Bob, 719
Ryan, Chico, 630
Ryan, Fran, 178, 204, 637
Ryan, Harry, 890
Ryan, Helen, 219
Ryan, Irene, 86
Ryan, John P., 54
Ryan, Michael, 50, 81
Ryan, Mitchell, 141, 229, 306, 986
Ryan, Natasha, 177
Ryan, Peggy, 306
Ryan, Robert, 28, 617, 787, 816

Shaw, Stan, 601
Shaw, Susan, 526
Shaw, Victoria, 270
Shawlee, Joan, 18, 85, 189, 241
Shawn, Dick, 129, 444, 587, 808
Shayne, Robert, 680
Shea, Christopher, 631
Shea, Eric, 49
Shea, Michael, 505, 506
Sheafe, Alex, 198
Shear, Barry, 292, 366, 373, 412
Shear, Pearl, 102
Shearer, Harry, 242
Shearin, John, 197
Shearing, George, 814
Sheehan, David, 41
Sheehan, Tony, 18
Sheen, Fulton J., 406, 887
Sheen, Martin, 98, 181, 835, 838, 839, 843
Sheffield, Jay, 693
Sheffield, Jeanne, 365
Sheffield, Sally, 245
Sheiner, David, 186, 476
Sheldon, Gene, 801
Sheldon, Herb, 669
Sheldon, Jack, 132, 277, 604
Sheldon, Sidney, 501
Shelley, Carole, 516
Shelley, Joshua, 67
Shelly, Freeman, 457
Shelton, George, 348
Shelton, Sloane, 245
Shenar, Paul, 844
Shepherd, Jean, 361
Shepodd, Jon, 396
Sheppard, Sam, 283
Sher, Jack, 322
Shera, Mark, 73, 607
Sheralee, 796
Sheridan, Ann, 51, 253, 559
Sheridan, Ardell, 678
Sheridan, Nancy, 250, 753
Sheridan, Tony, 517
Sherman, Allan, 243, 267
Sherman, Bobby, 274, 313, 633
Sherman, Courtney, 620
Sherman, Harry (Harry R.), 930, 934, 938
Sherman, Hiram, 693
Sherman, Howard, 270
Sherman, Jenny, 178, 270
Sherman, Melissa, 198
Sherman, Ransom, 46, 239, 579
Sherrin, Ned, 701
Sherry, Bill, 411
Sherry, Diane, 95
Sherwood, Bobby, 82, 576, 666
Sherwood, Don, 151
Sherwood, Gale, 809, 810
Sherwood, Madeline, 249, 624
Sherwood, Robert, 571, 623

Shields, Arthur, 798
Shields, Fred, 457
Shields, Helen, 157
Shields, Robert, 427
Shields and Yarnell, 633, 654
Shimoda, Yuki, 372
Shindigger Dancers, 634
Shindogs, 633
Ship, Reuben, 407
Shipp, Mary, 491
Shire, Talia, 589
Shirley, Tom, 259, 419
Shoberg, Richard, 35
Shockley, Sallie, 613
Sholdar, Mickey, 238
Sholem, Lee, 680
Shor, Dan, 496
Shore, Dinah, 102, 147, 189, 190, 215, 216,
    806, 823, 824, 889, 890, 891, 892, 893,
    917, 924, 933
Shore, Roberta, 101, 464, 559, 751
Short, Martin, 64
Shortridge, Stephen, 765
Showalt, Max, 319
Shpetner, Stan (Stanley), 388, 579, 641
Shreve, Bob, 705
Shriner, Herb, 313, 741
Shriner, Kin, 270
Shriver, Sargent, 823
Shrock, Laura, 944
Shroyer, Sonny, 209
Shryer, Bret, 634
Shuker, Gregory, 822
Shull, Richard B., 186, 322
Shulman, Max, 193, 987
Shuman, Roy, 420, 619
Shuster, Frank, 319, 763
Shuster, Joe, 679
Shuster, Rosie, 498, 934, 936
Shutan, Jan, 654
Shutta, Ethel, 241
Sibbald, Laurie, 512
Sidaris, Andy, 907
Sidney, P. Jay, 791
Sidney, Robert, 546
Siebert, Charles, 21, 62, 333, 734
Siegel, Barbara, 610
Siegel, Janis, 438
Siegel, Jerry, 679
Siegel, Larry, 916, 920, 940
Siegel, Laura, 654
Siegman, Joe, 136
Siemanowski, Richard, 147
Sierra, Gregory, 17, 74, 611
Sierra, Margarita, 683
Sigman, Carl, 549
Signoret, Simone, 821, 901
Sikes, Cynthia, 91
Sikes, L. N., 700
Sikking, James, 270, 738

Silla, Felix, 22
Silliman, Maureen, 294
Silliphant, Sterling, 415
Sills, Beverly, 841, 926
Sills, Paul, 671
Silo, Susan, 304
Silver, Arthur, 69, 98, 114, 785
Silver, Borah, 388
Silver, Franelle, 940
Silver, Jeff, 140
Silver, Joe, 240, 420, 583
Silver, Ron, 179, 588
Silver, Roy, 906
Silvera, Frank, 316
Silverheels, Jay, 413
Silverman, Don, 777, 907
Silverman, Fred, 302
Silverman, Treva, 924, 925
Silvers, Phil, 57, 468, 508, 791, 816, 820, 889, 900
Sim, Alistair, 448
Simcox, Tom, 151, 270
Simeone, Harry, 381
Simmonds, Douglas, 314
Simmons, Ed, 383, 920, 925, 926, 929, 940
Simmons, Jean, 829
Simmons, Jim, 406
Simmons, Matty, 182
Simmons, Richard, 23, 337, 627
Simmons, Richard Alan, 188, 736
Simmons, Ronald, 337
Simms, Hal, 354
Simms, LuAnn, 58
Simms, Phillip, 123
Simon, Al, 474, 512
Simon, Danny, 468
Simon, Neil, 72, 468, 663, 797, 810, 836
Simon, Paul, 42, 933. See also Simon and Garfunkel
Simon, Peter, 620
Simon, Robert F., 40, 167, 501, 608
Simon, Scott, 630
Simon and Garfunkel, 828, 831
Simonson, Thol, 680
Simpson, Jim, 497
Simpson, O. J. 456, 682
Sims, Jerry, 906
Sinatra, Frank, 117, 214, 256, 257, 353, 571, 806, 807, 812, 816, 824, 826, 828, 830, 831, 842, 843, 844
Sinatra, Frank, Jr., 281
Sinatra, Richard, 476
Sinclair, Diane, 174
Sinclair, Madge, 287
Sing, Mai Tai, 324
Singer, Alexander, 915
Singer, Dulcy, 937, 942
Singer, Ray, 347
Singer, Raymond, 528
Singer, Stuffy, 86, 98

Singing Waiters, 565
Singleton, Doris, 48
Singleton, Penny, 98, 364
Sinutko, Shane, 14
Siodmy, Kanal, 351
Sipherd, Ray, 908, 911, 926
Sirgo, Lou, 499
Sirola, Joe, 111, 459, 481
Sisk, Robert F., 788
Sistrom, Joe, 441
Sivy, Michael, 621
Skala, Lilia, 620
Skelton, Red, 584, 887, 896
Skinner, Cornelia Otis, 770, 792, 809, 818
Skinner, Edith, 146
Skinner, Edna, 474, 733
Skinner, Thomas, 938
Skip-Jacks, 488
Skipper, Bill, 431
Skipper, Ross, 917
Skotch, Ed, 262, 488
Skulnik, Menasha, 281, 461
Skutch, Ira, 669
Skylarks, 190, 374
Slack, Ben, 241
Slack, Bill, 155
Slade, Bernie, 277, 283
Slade, Mark, 316, 608, 754
Slate, Henry, 24
Slate, Jeremy, 54, 433
Slate, Lane, 936
Slater, Bill, 113, 140, 246, 571, 739, 783
Slater, Gerald, 942
Slattery, Joe, 720
Slattery, Richard X., 123, 264
Slavin, Millie, 578, 673
Slesar, Henry, 217, 651, 925
Slevin, Thomas, 911
Slezak, Erica, 524
Slezak, Walter, 525, 677, 706, 743, 829
Sloan, Bonnie, 546
Sloan, Michael, 67
Sloan, P. F., 622
Sloan, Tina, 652
Sloane, Allan, 658, 916
Sloane, Everett, 260, 390, 517, 677, 813
Sloane, William, 91
Slocum, Charles, 267
Slout, Marte Boyle, 37
Sloyan, James, 768
Sly and the Family Stone, 636
Small, Karna, 352
Small, Mary, 558
Small, Millie, 822
Smallwood, Tucker, 621
Smart, Ralph, 345
Smight, Jack, 893
Smika, Gina Marie, 529
Smith and Dale, 468
Smith, Bernie, 697

Turner, Tierre, 160, 763
Turquand, Todd, 464
Turque, Mimi, 515
Turrene, Louis, 218
Turteltaub, Saul, 134, 286, 612, 701, 704, 733, 769, 988
Tutin, Dorothy, 640
Tuttle, Lurene, 239, 376, 407, 553
Tutty, Esther von Waggoner, 323
Twain, Mark, 14, 505
Twiggy, 375
Twohey, Ros, 308
Twomey, John, 363
Tygett, Bud, 781
Tyler, Beverly, 92
Tyler, Janet, 391
Tyler, Judy, 331
Tyler, Kim, 563
Tyler, Richard, 28, 300
Tynan, William, 786
Tyrrell, Ann, 49, 570
Tyson, Cicely, 456, 600, 834, 838, 843, 844, 923
Tyzack, Margaret, 254, 448

Uggams, Leslie, 69, 266, 401, 461, 600, 639, 688, 835
Ulene, Art, 719
Umeki, Miyoshi, 163
Underhill, Don, 464
Underwood, Ray, 397
Unger, Maurice, 592, 767
Unitas, Johnny, 925
Untermeyer, Louis, 770
U Nu, 626
Uppman, Theodor, 807
Upton, Gabrielle, 418
Urbisci, Rocco, 591
Urecal, Minerva, 553, 580, 737
Urich, Robert, 100, 607, 650, 688, 748
Uris, Leon, 838
Urquhart, Gordon, 144
Ustinov, Peter, 520, 833, 836, 845, 892, 903, 910
Utley, Garrick, 147, 245
Uttal, Fred, 575

Vaccaro, Brenda, 179, 289, 612, 923
Vacio, Natividad, 239
Vague, Vera, 250
Vainio, Aura, 265–266
Valdis, Sigrid, 318
Valens, Richie, 488
Valenta, Leonard, 141, 440, 781
Valente, Caterina, 224
Valente, Renee, 98
Valentine, Jack, 20
Valentine, Karen, 379, 599, 910
Valentino, Barry, 747, 750

Vallance, Louise, 601
Vallee, Rudy, 520, 729, 807, 813
Valli, June, 47, 670, 690, 796, 811
Van, Billy, 318, 332, 383, 581, 654
Van, Bobby, 23, 321, 431, 636
Van, Gloria, 411, 714, 781
Van, Jackie, 489
Van Ark, Joan, 14, 178, 697, 768, 987
Van Atta, Don, 305, 482, 556
Vance, Louis Joseph, 413
Vance, Vivian, 335, 424, 888
Van Cleef, Lee, 615
Vanda, Charles, 91
Vandeman, George, 347
Vanderbilt, Gloria, 551
Van der Pyl, Jean, 248, 773
Vanders, Warren, 223
Van Der Vlis, Diana, 606, 772
Van Deventer, Fred, 739
Van Devere, Trish, 524, 619
Van Doren, Charles, 379, 717, 739
Van Doren, Mamie, 580
Van Doren, Mark, 645
Van Druten, John, 434
Van Dyke, Barry, 305
Van Dyke, Dick, 30, 47, 119, 133, 189, 267, 398, 483, 484, 506, 714, 747, 791, 815, 899, 900, 901, 934
Van Dyke, Jerry, 19, 189, 309, 375, 492, 558, 704
van Eltz, Theodore, 526
Van Fleet, Jo, 823, 827
Van Fleet, Richard, 34
Van Horn, Arthur, 76
Van Horne, Courtney, 670
Van Horne, Randy, 502
Van Horne, Sonja, 670
Van Lawick, Hugo, 918
Van Moltke, Alexandra. See Moltke, Alexandra
Vanocur, Sander, 245
Vanoff, Nick, 200, 321, 376, 654, 724, 916
Van Patten, Dick, 220, 434, 506, 540, 772
Van Patten, Jimmy (James), 146, 985
Van Patten, Joyce, 62, 283, 445
Van Patten, Timothy, 774
Van Patten, Vincent, 53, 708
Van Scoyk, Robert, 578, 794
Van Voorhis, Westbrook, 166, 203, 439, 474, 512, 538
Van Wyk, Kenneth, 327
Varden, Norma, 308
Varney, Jim, 371, 528
Vasquez, Dennis, 566
Vaughan, Sarah, 836
Vaughn, Denny, 542
Vaughn, Heidi, 217
Vaughn, Hilda, 545

Wallechinsky, David, 769
Waller, Eddy, 668
Walley, Deborah, 485
Walling, Ernest, 440
Walmsley, Jon 759
Walpert, Dave, 192
Walsh, Bill, 192, 464
Walsh, Bob, 635
Walsh, Jimmy, 404
Walsh, Lory, 427
Walsh, M. Emmet, 611
Walston, Ray, 490
Walter, Jessica, 37, 45, 252, 420, 734, 829, 927
Walter, Rita McLaughlin. *See* McLaughlin, Rita
Walters, Barbara, 16, 484, 514, 717–719, 928
Walters, Cy, 709
Walters, Laurie, 220
Walters, Thorley, 448
Walther, Gretchen, 316, 421, 619
Walton, Kip, 325
Wambaugh, Joseph, 99, 563, 564
Wanamaker, Sam, 88
Wanderone, Rudolph, Jr. *See* Minnesota Fats
Wandrey, Donna, 63
Ward, Al C., 456
Ward, Burt, 75
Ward, Evelyn, 319
Ward, Janet, 51
Ward, Jay, 116, 166, 209, 272, 596
Ward, Larry, 111, 168
Ward, Richard, 78
Ward, Robin, 665, 832
Ward, Sean, 652
Ward, Simon, 97
Ward, Skip, 478
Warde, Harlan, 751
Warden, Jack, 63, 69, 476, 499, 557, 740, 754, 915
Ware, Midge, 295
Warfield, Don (Donald), 420, 421
Warfield, Marlene, 451
Warfield, Marsha, 591
Waring, Fred, 257
Warner, Eleanore, 489
Warner, Jackie, 631
Warner, Jody, 523
Warner, Lucy, 479, 671
Warner, Sandra, 477
Warnick, Clay, 101, 365
Warnoker, Si, 38
Warren, Ann, 190
Warren, Biff, 63, 384
Warren, Charles Marquis (Charles M.), 295, 580
Warren, Ed, 325, 563
Warren, Fran, 925

Warren, Jennifer, 648
Warren, Joe, 132, 245
Warren, Kenneth J., 162
Warren, Lesley (Lesley Ann), 472, 823
Warren, Mark, 737, 912
Warren, Mike (Michael), 178, 540, 763
Warren, Rod, 925, 934
Warrick, Lee, 271, 524
Warrick, Ruth, 34, 61, 239, 555
Warwick, Richard, 448
Washam, Ian Miller, 35
Washbrook, Johnny, 490
Washburn, Beverly, 508, 572
Washington, Jackie, 245
Washington, Kenneth, 318
Wass, Ted, 650
Wasson, Craig, 558, 989
Waterman, Dennis, 233
Waterman, Willard, 288
Waters, Ed, 73
Waters, Ethel, 86, 810
Waters, Reba, 546
Watkins, Jim, 429
Watling, Deborah, 345
Watson, Bobs, 364
Watson, David, 504, 580, 829
Watson, Debbie, 379, 692
Watson, Douglass, 51, 420, 479
Watson, Gary, 537
Watson, Justice, 319
Watson, Mills, 470
Watson, Vernée, 134
Watt, Billie Lou, 259, 620
Watt, Stan, 420
Wattis, Richard, 186, 405
Waxman, Al, 386
Wayland, Len, 259
Wayne, Carol, 126, 137, 439, 737
Wayne, David, 169, 222, 513, 815, 987
Wayne, Frank, 79, 514, 921
Wayne, John, 295, 323, 337, 602, 617, 816, 832, 834
Wayne, Johnny, 319, 763
Wayne, Nina, 126
Wayne, Patrick, 602, 634
Wayne, Paul, 193, 908
Wayne, Ronald, 357
Wayne, Ronnie, 200
Weatherwax, Ken, 22
Weatherwax, Rudd, 396
Weaver, Bobby, 989
Weaver, Buck, 115
Weaver, Charley. *See* Arquette, Cliff
Weaver, Dennis, 271, 296, 383, 453, 834, 893, 989
Weaver, Doodles, 203
Weaver, Fritz, 88, 818, 827
Weaver, Lee, 93
Weaver, Lois, 203
Weaver, Patty, 177

Williams, Tennessee, 498, 826
Williams, Tex, 579
Williams, Tom, 22
Williams, Van, 107, 290, 683, 741, 768
Williams, William B., 207, 609
Williams-Ellis, Clough, 570
Williamson, Fred, 376, 498
Williamson, Nicol, 828
Willingham, Noble, 989
Willis, Austin, 621
Willis, Chuck, 188
Willis, Curtiz, 160
Willis, Jack, 288, 911
Willis, John, 283, 670
Willis, Richard, 591
Willison, Walter, 454
Willock, Dave, 106, 173, 192, 440, 575
Willock, Margaret, 240
Willmore, Joe, 60
Wills, Anneke, 672
Wills, Chill, 602
Willson, Meredith, 461
Wilson, Anthony, 263, 539
Wilson, Brian, 105
Wilson, Cal, 363
Wilson, Dan (Daniel), 921, 941
Wilson, Dave, 933
Wilson, Demond, 68, 611, 612
Wilson, Dick, 454
Wilson, Don, 353
Wilson, Donald, 255
Wilson, Dooley, 86
Wilson, Doug, 907, 926, 930
Wilson, Earl, 661, 725
Wilson, Eileen, 796
Wilson, Elizabeth, 193, 212
Wilson, Flip, 142, 248, 315, 911, 913
Wilson, Greg, 429
Wilson, Harold, 822
Wilson, Hugh, 754
Wilson, "Iron Jaw," 585
Wilson, James, 907
Wilson, Jane, 595
Wilson, Joyce Vincent, 731
Wilson, Julie, 623
Wilson, Lanford, 326
Wilson, Lester, 610
Wilson, Lisle, 702
Wilson, Lois, 29
Wilson, Marie, 490, 773
Wilson, Mark, 428, 429
Wilson, Mary Louise, 522
Wilson, Mike, 429
Wilson, Nancy, 321, 648
Wilson, Robin, 326
Wilson, Slim, 246, 691
Wilson, Stuart, 449, 672
Wilson, Terry, 755
Wilson, Theodore (Teddy), 598, 612, 702
Wilson, Tony, 341

Wilson, Ward, 127
Wilson, "Whispering Joe," 107, 503
Winchell, Paul, 92, 134, 148, 210, 246, 283,
    545, 546, 566, 605, 811
Winchell, Walter, 336, 726, 745, 758
Windom, William, 83, 447, 494, 834, 909
Windsor, Frank, 355
Wines, Christopher, 35
Wines, William C., 703
Winfield, Paul, 376, 601, 843
Winfield, Rodney, 510
Winfrey, Carey, 922
Wingreen, Jason, 33, 414, 602
Winkelman, Michael, 582
Winkler, Harry, 889
Winkler, Henry, 259, 302, 841, 847
Winkworth, Mark, 676
Winn, Kitty, 78
Winn, May, 513
Winninger, Charles, 140
Winona, Kim, 109
Winsor, Roy, 418, 618, 622, 651
Winston, Hattie, 221
Winston, Helene, 386
Winston, Leslie, 760
Winter, Edward (Ed), 21, 573, 623, 652
Winter, Lynette, 276, 555
Winters, David, 332
Winters, Deborah, 829
Winters, Gloria, 407, 644
Winters, Jonathan, 46, 266, 284, 325, 354,
    373, 634, 754
Winters, Roland, 203, 458, 648
Winters, Shelley, 253, 899
Wintersole, William, 612
Wirth, Sandy, 678
Wisbar, Frank, 244
Wisdom, Norman, 828
Wise, Alfie, 744
Wise, Ernie, 558
Wise, Ray, 420
Wiseman, Frederick, 909
Wiseman, Joseph, 571
Wismer, Harry, 250, 514, 696
Wiss, Doris, 642
Wister, Owen, 751
Withers, Bernadette, 68, 379
Withers, Mark, 381
Witherspoon, John, 591
Witney, Michael, 734
Witt, Howard, 753
Witt, Kathryn, 249
Witt, Paul Younger, 82, 240, 423, 567, 913
Wittner, Meg, 651
Wixted, Michael-James, 645
Wohl, Jack, 630, 752, 931
Wolcott, Gregory, 220
Wolders, Robert, 395
Wolf, Herb, 547
Wolf, Jeanne, 361

York, Dick, 29, 87, 281, 629
York, Don, 630
York, Francine, 178, 644
York, Jeff, 28
York, Susannah, 833
Yorkin, Bud (Alan), 31, 134, 611 612, 650, 699, 704, 769, 813, 893, 894
Young, Agnes, 792
Young, Alan, 27, 474, 613
Young, Bob, 16
Young, Chic, 98
Young, Collier, 164, 472, 510, 526
Young, De De, 93
Young, Donna, Jean, 398, 748
Young, Gig, 275, 598, 761, 815, 816, 818
Young, Heather, 394
Young, Janice, 51
Young, Jeff, 197, 931
Young, Jim, 269
Young, Joe, 545
Young, John Sagret, 246
Young, John, W., 908
Young, Julie, 87
Young, Loretta, 415, 507, 533, 889, 890, 893
Young, Michael, 384
Young, Otis, 533
Young, Ralph, 389
Young, Ray, 93
Young, Robert, 15, 239, 411, 440, 780, 890, 892, 909
Young, Skip, 254, 535
Young, Stephen, 374, 621
Young, Tamer, 87
Young, Tony, 295
Young, Victoria, 410
Young, Wesley A., 48
Younger, Beverly, 675
Youngman, Henny, 312, 369

Youngquist, Arthur, 194
Youngstein, Max, 186
Yurka, Blanche, 390, 447
Yusen, Susan, 219
Yuskis, Antonette, 97

ZaBach, Florian, 249
Zacha, W. T., 151
Zachar, Glenn, 652
Zacharias, Ellis, M., 80
Zacharias, Steve, 763
Zachary, Beulah, 392
Zaharuk, William, 926
Zapata, Carmen, 750, 752, 987
Zaremba, John, 713
Zarit, Pam, 611
Zaslow, Michael, 294
Zeffirelli, Franco, 827, 845
Zeigler, Ted, 332, 633, 654
Zelinka, Sidney, 892
Zellman, David, 568
Zeman, Jackie, 271, 525
Zenk, Colleen, 63
Zenon, Michael, 254
Zenor, Suzanne, 178
Zerbe, Anthony, 304, 932
Zielinski, Bruno ("Junior"), 351
Zimbalist, Efrem, Jr., 157, 550, 629
Zimmer, Norma, 152, 400
Zimmerman, Ed, 293
Zinsser, William K., 677
Zmed, Adrian, 247, 987
Zobel, Myron, 279
Zousmer, Jesse, 551
Zovella, 428
Zuckert, Bill (William), 476, 754
Zulu, 306
Zurla, Martin, 421
Zweibel, Alan, 498, 934, 936